RULES OF DEBIT AND CREDIT

TEMPORARY ACCOUNTS

Withdrawals
(Sole Proprietorship/Partnership)

Debit	Credit
+	−
Increase	Decrease
Normal Balance	

Example: Linda Carter, Withdrawals

Revenue

Debit	Credit
−	+
Decrease	Increase
	Normal Balance

Examples: Fees Income
Sales

Contra Revenue

Debit	Credit
+	−
Increase	Decrease
Normal Balance	

Examples: Sales Discounts
Sales Returns and Allowances

Cost of Goods Sold

Debit	Credit
+	−
Increase	Decrease
Normal Balance	

Examples: Purchases
Freight In

Contra Cost of Goods Sold

Debit	Credit
−	+
Decrease	Increase
	Normal Balance

Example: Purchases Discounts
Purchases Returns and Allowances

Expenses

Debit	Credit
+	−
Increase	Decrease
Normal Balance	

Examples: Advertising Expense
Utilities Expense
Rent Expense

twelfth edition

College Accounting

Chapters 1–30

study on the go

THIS TEXT IS Media Integrated

It provides students with
portable educational content

Based on research and feedback, we realize the study habits of today's students are changing.

Students want the option to study when and where it's most convenient to them. They are asking for more than the traditional textbook to keep them motivated and to make course content more relevant. McGraw-Hill listened to these requests and is proud to bring you this **Media Integrated** textbook.

This **Media Integrated** edition adds new downloadable content for the Apple iPods® and most other MP3/MP4 devices. Throughout the text, students can refer to related audio and video presentations, quizzes and other related content that correlate to the text. iPod content can quickly be downloaded online from the text website.

This iPod content gives students a strong set of educational materials that will help them learn by listening to and/or watching them on their iPod.

Look for this iPod icon throughout the text.

Icons connect textbook content to your iPod or other MP3 device.

Images courtesy of Apple.

Don't have an iPod? Content can be viewed on any computer! Visit the text website for directions.

Want to see iPod in action?

Visit **www.mhhe.com/ipod** to view a demonstration of our iPod® content.

Website includes:

- Lecture presentations
    Audio and video
    Audio only
    Video only
- Demonstration problems[+]
- Interactive self quizzes
- Accounting videos[+]

+Available with some textbooks

McGraw-Hill's
HOMEWORK MANAGER PLUS™ HM online
THE COMPLETE SOLUTION

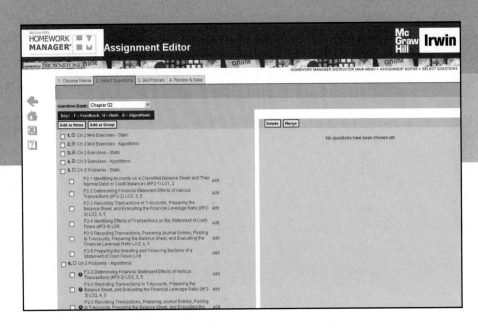

McGraw-Hill's
Homework Manager®

™ This online homework management solution contains this textbook's end-of-chapter material. Now you have the option to build assignments from static and algorithmic versions of the text problems and exercises or to build self-graded quizzes from the additional questions provided in the online test bank.

Features:

- Assigns book-specific problems/exercises to students
- Provides integrated test bank questions for quizzes and tests
- Automatically grades assignments and quizzes, storing results in one grade book
- Dispenses immediate feedback to students regarding their work

McGraw-Hill's HOMEWORK MANAGER PLUS™

THE COMPLETE SOLUTION

Price/Haddock/Farina
College Accounting, 12/e
978-0-07-336563-3

2 TERM

Interactive Online Version
of this Textbook

Online Learning Center

In addition to the textbook, students can rely on this online version of the text for a convenient way to study. The interactive content is fully *integrated* with McGraw-Hill's Homework Manager® system to give students quick access to relevant content as they work through problems, exercises, and practice quizzes.

Features:

- Online version of the text *integrated* with McGraw-Hill's Homework Manager system

- Students referred to appropriate sections of the online book as they complete an assignment or take a practice quiz

- Direct link to related material that corresponds with the learning objective within the text

McGraw-Hill's Homework Manager PLUS™ system combines the power of McGraw-Hill's Homework Manager® system with the latest interactive learning technology to create a comprehensive, fully integrated online study package. Students working on assignments in McGraw-Hill's Homework Manager system can click a simple hotlink and instantly review the appropriate material in the Interactive Online Textbook.

By including McGraw-Hill's Homework Manager PLUS system with your textbook adoption, you're giving your students a vital edge as they progress through the course and ensuring that the help they need is never more than a mouse click away. Contact your McGraw-Hill representative or visit the book's Website to learn how to add McGraw-Hill's Homework Manager PLUS system to your adoption.

McGraw-Hill's
HM PLUS™

Imagine being able to create and access your test anywhere, at any time without installing the testing software. Now with **McGraw-Hill's EZ Test Online**, instructors can select questions from multiple McGraw-Hill test banks, author their own and then either print the test for paper distribution or give it online.

Use our EZ Test Online to help your students prepare to succeed with Apple® iPod® iQuiz.

Using our EZ Test Online you can make test and quiz content available for a student's Apple iPod.

Students must purchase the iQuiz game application from Apple for 99¢ in order to use the iQuiz content. It works on fifth generation iPods and better.

Instructors only need EZ Test Online to produce iQuiz-ready content. Instructors take their existing tests and quizzes and export them to a file that can then be made available to the student to take as a self-quiz on their iPods. It's as simple as that.

twelfth edition

College Accounting

Chapters 1–30

JOHN ELLIS PRICE, Ph.D., CPA
Professor of Accounting and Vice Chancellor
University of North Texas–Dallas Campus
Dallas, Texas

M. DAVID HADDOCK, JR., Ed.D., CPA
Professor of Accounting Emeritus
Chattanooga State Technical Community College
Director of Training
Lattimore Black Morgan & Cain, PC
Brentwood, Tennessee

MICHAEL J. FARINA, MBA, CPA
Professor of Accounting
Cerritos College
Norwalk, California

Mc
Graw
Hill **McGraw-Hill**
Irwin

Boston   Burr Ridge, IL   Dubuque, IA   New York   San Francisco   St. Louis
Bangkok   Bogotá   Caracas   Kuala Lumpur   Lisbon   London   Madrid   Mexico City
Milan   Montreal   New Delhi   Santiago   Seoul   Singapore   Sydney   Taipei   Toronto

The McGraw·Hill Companies

COLLEGE ACCOUNTING

Chapter 1-30

1 2 3 4 5 6 7 8 9 0 DOW/DOW 0 9 8

ISBN: 978-0-07-340166-9 (chapters 1–30, student edition)
MHID: 0-07-340166-8 (chapters 1–30, student edition)
ISBN: 978-0-07-336560-2 (chapters 1–30, instructor's edition)
MHID: 0-07-336560-2 (chapters 1–30, instructor's edition)
ISBN: 978-0-07-336550-3 (chapters 1–24, student edition)
MHID: 0-07-336550-5 (chapters 1–24, student edition)
ISBN: 978-0-07-336549-7 (chapters 1–13, student edition)
MHID: 0-07-336549-1 (chapters 1–13, student edition)

Vice president and editor-in-chief: *Brent Gordon*
Editorial director: *Stewart Mattson*
Publisher: *Tim Vertovec*
Senior sponsoring editor: *Alice Harra*
Developmental editor: *Emily A. Hatteberg*
Marketing manager: *Scott S. Bishop*
Senior project manager: *Bruce Gin*
Lead production supervisor: *Michael R. McCormick*
Lead designer: *Matthew Baldwin*
Senior photo research coordinator: *Jeremy Cheshareck*
Photo researcher: *Robin Sand*
Lead media project manager: *Cathy L. Tepper*
Cover design: *Matthew Baldwin*
Cover image: *@ Getty Images*
Interior design: *Kay Lieberherr*
Typeface: *10.5/12 Times Roman*
Compositor: *Laserwords Private Limited*
Printer: *R. R. Donnelley*

Library of Congress Cataloging-in-Publication Data

Price, John Ellis.
    College accounting : chapters 1-30 / John Ellis Price, M. David Haddock, Jr.,
Michael J. Farina.—Twelfth ed.
        p. cm.
    Includes bibliographical references and index.
    ISBN-13: 978-0-07-340166-9 (chapters 1–30 student edition : alk. paper)
    ISBN-10: 0-07-340166-8 (chapters 1–30 student edition : alk. paper)
    ISBN-13: 978-0-07-336560-2 (chapters 1–30 instructors edition : alk. paper)
    ISBN-10: 0-07-336560-2 (chapters 1–30 instructors edition : alk. paper)
    [etc.]
    1. Accounting. I. Haddock, M. David. II. Farina, Michael J. III. Title.
HF5635.B8542 2009
657'.044—dc22
                                                    2008036017

www.mhhe.com

About the Authors

JOHN ELLIS PRICE is professor of accounting and vice chancellor of the University of North Texas (UNT) Dallas Campus. Dr. Price has previously held positions of professor and assistant professor, as well as chair and dean, at the University of North Texas, Jackson State University, and the University of Southern Mississippi. Dr. Price has also been active in the Internal Revenue Service as a member of the Commissioner's Advisory Group for two terms, and as an Internal Revenue agent.

Professor Price is a certified public accountant who has twice received the UNT College of Business Administration's Outstanding Teaching Award, and the university's President's Council Award. Majoring in accounting, he received his BBA and MS degrees from the University of Southern Mississippi, and his Ph.D. in accounting from the University of North Texas.

Dr. Price is a member of the Mississippi Society of Certified Public Accountants, the American Accounting Association, and the American Taxation Association (serving as past chair of the Subcommittee on Relations with the IRS and Treasury). Dr. Price has also served as chair of the American Institute of Certified Public Accountants Minority Initiatives Committee and as a member of the Foundation Trustees.

M. DAVID HADDOCK, JR., is currently director of training for Lattimore, Black, Morgan, and Cain, PC, one of the largest financial services firms in the Southeast. He is located in the Brentwood, Tennessee office. He recently retired from a 35-year career in higher education, having served in faculty and administrative roles at Auburn University at Montgomery, the University of Alabama in Birmingham, the University of West Georgia, and Chattanooga State Technical Community College. He retired as professor of accounting at Chattanooga State Technical Community College in Tennessee. In addition to his teaching, he maintained a sole proprietorship tax practice for 20 years prior to taking his current position.

He received his BS in accounting and MS in adult education from the University of Tennessee, and the DE degree in administration of higher education from Auburn University. He is a licensed CPA in Tennessee.

Professor Haddock was elected treasurer of the Tennessee Society of Certified Public Accountants in 2008 after serving on the board of directors and as the Chattanooga TSCPA chapter president. He is also active in the American Institute for Certified Public Accountants and the Tennessee Society of Accounting Educators. He is a frequent speaker for Continuing Professional Education programs.

MICHAEL J. FARINA is professor of accounting and finance at Cerritos College in California. Prior to joining Cerritos College, Professor Farina was a manager in the audit department at a large multinational firm of certified public accountants, and held management positions with other companies in private industry.

He received an AA in business administration from Cerritos College, a BA in business administration from California State University, Fullerton, and an MBA from the University of California, Irvine. Professor Farina is a member of Beta Gamma Sigma, an honorary fraternity for graduate business students. He is a licensed certified public accountant in California, and a member of the American Institute of Certified Public Accountants and the California Society of Certified Public Accountants.

Professor Farina is currently the cochair of the Accounting and Finance Department at Cerritos College. Professor Farina received an Outstanding Faculty award from Cerritos College in 2008.

Price/Haddock/Farina

For students just embarking on a college career, an accounting course can seem daunting, like a rushing river with no clear path to the other side. As the most trusted and readable text on the market, *College Accounting*, 12e, by Price, Haddock, and Farina presents material in a way that will help students understand the content better and more quickly. Through proven pedagogy, time-tested and accurate problem material, and a straightforward approach to the basics of accounting, Price/Haddock/Farina **bridges the rushing river,** offering first-time accounting students a path to understanding and mastery.

Whether a student is taking the course in preparation for a four-year degree or as the first step to a career in business, Price/Haddock/Farina guides them over the bridge to success. The authors represent the breadth of educational environments— a community college, a career school, and a four-year university—ensuring that the text is appropriate for all student populations. Throughout, they have adhered to a common philosophy about textbooks: they should be readable, contain many opportunities for practice, and be able to make accounting relevant for all.

Bridges College to Career

- **Encourages Reading** The authors' writing style and clear step-by-step examples make key concepts easy to grasp. *College Accounting*'s concise chapters are broken into manageable sections to avoid overwhelming students who might be seeing the material for the first time. Features like the Business Transaction Analysis Model make it easy for students to see how to analyze business transactions. The Important and Recall margin elements briefly highlight important concepts and remind students of key term definitions as the topics begin to build on each other.

- **Emphasizes Practice** Self reviews at the end of each section give students the opportunity to practice what they've just learned before moving on to the next topic. The author-created end-of-chapter material includes A and B problem sets, exercises, critical thinking problems, and Business Connection problems that utilize real-world companies and scenarios and address important topics like ethics. Mini-practice sets included within the text itself allow students to put theory into practice without paying additional money for a separate practice set. End-of-chapter content is tied to templates in **Excel, Quickbooks,** and **Peachtree,** allowing students to practice using software they are likely to encounter in the real world.

- **Answers the Question "Why Is Accounting Important?"** The "Why It's Important" explanation that accompanies each learning objective explains to students why the topics they're studying matter. Well-known companies like Google, Southwest, and Ikea are used in vignettes and examples throughout the text, making a clear bridge for students between the concepts they're learning and how those concepts are applied in the real world.

> Super book that presents a fresh outlook on accounting.
>
> —Anthony Newton
> Highland Community College

New to the Twelfth Edition

- **Examples** and **end-of-chapter material** have been **updated** throughout the text.
- All the **test bank questions have been tagged with AASCB-AICPA standards** and Bloom's Taxonomy, making it easier to tie assessment to your school's student learning outcomes.
- Chapter 26, **Internal Control and the Voucher System,** was eliminated as a stand-alone chapter. The **voucher content** has been **incorporated into Chapter 8.**
- **Internal control content has been integrated into the text** where appropriate and highlighted with an icon so students can immediately see the link between the concept of internal control and the topics they're studying.

- **Chapters 23 and 24 were combined** to present the financial ratios and statement analysis in one chapter.
- The **full text now has only 30 chapters,** making it a perfect fit for semester or quarter institutions.
- The **adjusting entries have been streamlined** in Chapter 12 to allow professors to better focus on those that are most relevant for students.
- **Chapter 14** now discusses the activities of the **Public Company Accounting Oversight Board.**
- **Break-even analysis coverage** has been added to Chapter 25.
- **International Insights and Accounting on the Job boxes** have been **moved to the Web site,** allowing professors and students to focus on the meat of the topics presented in each chapter.
- **Full media integration** with iPod icons throughout the text links content back to chapter-specific quizzes, audio and visual lecture presentations, and course-related videos available for download from the text's Web site. This gives students access to a portable, electronic learning option to support their classroom instruction.

- **The Quantum Tutors for the Accounting Cycle** help tutor students on the fundamental accounting concepts and problem-solving skills needed for principles, financial, and managerial accounting courses. Just like working with an excellent instructor, students can enter their own work into the software, ask questions, and receive step-by-step feedback at a detailed level not available with any other software or homework management system. The Quantum Tutors are ideal when the student needs immediate help and the instructor is not available to answer questions. Accessed over the Internet, students have unlimited, convenient access day or night and can study independently at their own pace.

> Price may be the ideal college accounting text.
>
> —Laverne Thomas–Vertrees
> St. Louis Community College

How Does Price/Haddock/Farina Bridge

College Accounting is designed to help students learn and master the material.

Chapter Opener

Brief features about **real-world companies**—like **Google**, **American Eagle Outfitters**, **Ikea, and McDonald's Corporation**—allow students to see how the chapter's information and insights apply to the world outside the classroom. Thinking Critically questions stimulate thought on the topics to be explored in the chapter.

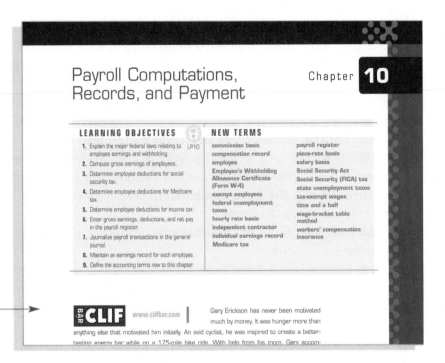

Payroll Computations, Records, and Payment — Chapter 10

LEARNING OBJECTIVES

1. Explain the major federal laws relating to employee earnings and withholding.
2. Compute gross earnings of employees.
3. Determine employee deductions for social security tax.
4. Determine employee deductions for Medicare tax.
5. Determine employee deductions for income tax.
6. Enter gross earnings, deductions, and net pay in the payroll register.
7. Journalize payroll transactions in the general journal.
8. Maintain an earnings record for each employee.
9. Define the accounting terms new to this chapter.

NEW TERMS

commission basis
compensation record
employee
Employee's Withholding Allowance Certificate (Form W-4)
exempt employees
federal unemployment taxes
hourly rate basis
independent contractor
individual earnings record
Medicare tax
payroll register
piece-rate basis
salary basis
Social Security Act
Social Security (FICA) tax
state unemployment taxes
tax-exempt wages
time and a half
wage-bracket table method
workers' compensation insurance

CLIF BAR www.clifbar.com

Gary Erickson has never been motivated much by money. It was hunger more than anything else that motivated him initially. An avid cyclist, he was inspired to create a better-tasting energy bar while on a 175-mile bike ride. With help from his mom, Gary accom-

---

> An excellent text.
>
> —David Laurel
> South Texas College

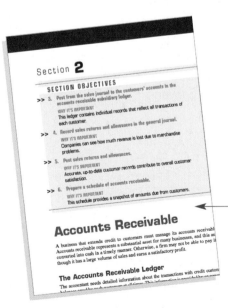

Section 2

SECTION OBJECTIVES

>> 3. Post from the sales journal to the customers' accounts in the accounts receivable subsidiary ledger.
WHY IT'S IMPORTANT
This ledger contains individual records that reflect all transactions of each customer.

>> 4. Record sales returns and allowances in the general journal.
WHY IT'S IMPORTANT
Companies can see how much revenue is lost due to merchandise problems.

>> 5. Post sales returns and allowances.
WHY IT'S IMPORTANT
Accurate, up-to-date customer records contribute to overall customer satisfaction.

>> 6. Prepare a schedule of accounts receivable.
WHY IT'S IMPORTANT
This schedule provides a snapshot of amounts due from customers.

Accounts Receivable

A business that extends credit to customers must manage its accounts receivable. Accounts receivable represents a substantial asset for many businesses, and this as converted into cash in a timely manner. Otherwise, a firm may not be able to pay it though it has a large volume of sales and earns a satisfactory profit.

The Accounts Receivable Ledger

The accountant needs detailed information about the transactions with credit custom

Learning Objectives

Appearing in the chapter opener and within the margins of the text, learning objectives alert students to what they should expect as they progress through the chapter. Many students question the relevance of what they're learning, which is why we explain **"Why It's Important."**

the Gap from Learning to Mastery?

Business Transaction Analysis Models

Instructors say mastering the ability to properly analyze transactions is critical to success in this course. Price's step-by-step transaction analysis illustrations show how to identify the appropriate general ledger accounts affected, determine debit or credit activity, present the transaction in T-account form, and record the entry in the general journal.

The Bottom Line

Appears in the margins alongside select transactions and concepts in the text. These visuals offer a summary of the effects of these transactions—the end result—on the financial statements of a business.

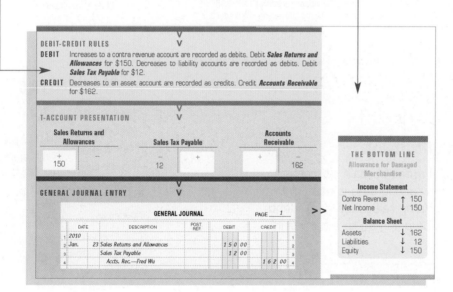

important!

General Journal and General Ledger

The general journal is the record of *original* entry. The general ledger is the record of *final* entry.

Recall and Important!

Recall is a series of brief reinforcements that serve as reminders of material covered in *previous* chapters that are relevant to the new information being presented. **Important!** draws students' attention to critical materials introduced in the *current* chapter.

> (The) business transaction models are excellent—I utilize them all the time.
>
> —Kathy Kircher
> Lansdale School of Business

Student learning outcomes (SLO) have become increasingly important for accreditation and assurance of learning. In recognition of this, Price/Haddock/Farina's test bank is now tied to AACSB-AICPA standards as well as Bloom's Taxonomy. Having each test bank item tagged to these standards makes it easier for instructors to choose quiz and exam questions that correspond to their school's student learning outcomes.

MANAGERIAL IMPLICATIONS <<

FINANCIAL INFORMATION

- Management needs timely and accurate financial information to control operations and make decisions.
- A well-designed and well-run accounting system provides reliable financial statements to management.
- Although management is not involved in day-to-day accounting procedures and end-of-period processes, the efficiency of the procedures affects the quality and promptness of the financial information that management receives.

THINKING CRITICALLY

If you owned or managed a business, how often would you want financial statements prepared? Why?

Managerial Implications

Puts your students in the role of managers and asks them to apply the concepts learned in the chapter.

ABOUT ACCOUNTING

IRS Electronic Filing

More than 19 million taxpayers have filed their tax returns electronically. Returns that are filed electronically are more accurate than paper returns. Electronic filing means refunds in half the time, especially if the taxpayer chooses direct deposit of the refund.

About Accounting

These marginal notes contain interesting examples of how accounting is used in the real world, providing relevance to students who might not be going on to a career in accounting.

Section 1 Self Review

QUESTIONS

1. Give two major reasons why the pronouncements of the Financial Accounting Standards Board have a major influence on accounting in this country.

2. Mayday is a corporation with only two shareholders (owners). Is the corporation required to file financial statements with the SEC?

3. Identify the governmental entity that has oversight of the development of accounting principles and explain its role in the development process.

4. What is the FASB's conceptual framework project? Why is an understanding of the conceptual framework important to those who make accounting and reporting rules?

EXERCISE

5. Four organizations that play important roles in the development of accounting

principles, standards, and reporting practices are the Securities and Exchange Commission (SEC), the Financial Accounting Standards Board (FASB), the Public Company Accounting Oversight Board (PCAOB), and the American Institute of Certified Public Accountants (AICPA). Indicate which organization is best described by each of the following statements.

a. This organization actually develops and issues most of the accounting standards today.

b. This organization has no legal role in the development of standards, but does exert influence because it points out to the other organizations areas in which reporting problems have developed and also through the fact that its members audit the records of most publicly held corporations.

c. This organization has legal responsibility for setting accounting requirements for publicly held corporations.

d. This organization has the power to limit nonaudit services by CPA firms to their audit clients.

ANALYSIS

6. The financial statements for Presto Services have an auditor's notation that the statements are "not prepared in conformity with GAAP." What does this mean to you as an investor?

(Answers to Section 1 Self Review are on page 512.)

Self Review

Each section concludes with a Self Review that includes questions, multiple-choice exercises, and an analysis assignment. A Comprehensive Self Review appears at the end of each chapter. Answers are provided at the end of the chapter.

How Can Price/Haddock/Farina Bridge the Gap from Learning to "Doing"?

Problem Sets A and B and Critical Thinking Problems conclude with an **Analyze** question asking the student to evaluate each problem critically.

Mini-Practice Sets

In addition to two full-length practice sets that are available to your students for purchase with the textbook, Price/Haddock/Farina offers a number of mini-practice sets right in the book. This means additional practice, but less cost, for your students.

Business Connections

Reinforces chapter materials from practical and real-world perspectives:

Managerial Focus: Applies accounting concepts to business situations.

Ethical Dilemma: Provides the opportunity for students to discuss ethics in the workplace, formulate a course of action for certain scenarios, and support their opinions.

Financial Statement Analysis:

A brief excerpt from a real-world annual report and questions that lead the student through an analysis of the statement, concluding with an Analyze Online activity where students research the company's most recent financial reports on the Internet.

Extending the Thought: Activities build on chapter concepts and present new issues and situations, asking students to recall and apply learned information.

Business Communication: These activities hone students' interpersonal skills through the preparation of a variety of business communication formats such as memos, oral presentations, outlines, and more.

TeamWork: Each chapter contains a collaborative learning activity to prepare students for team-oriented projects and work environments.

Internet Connection: These activities give students the opportunity to conduct online research about major companies, accounting trends, organizations, and government agencies.

> You have done an excellent job at introducing ethics, something which I haven't found in the other text we are using!! I always introduce ethics to my classes!!
>
> —Joanne Salas
> Olympic College

The Twelfth Edition brings accounting concepts to life with relevant real-world businesses.

American Eagle Outfitters	FedEx
Southwest Airlines	Circuit City Stores Inc.
Johnson & Johnson	The Coca-Cola Company
Adobe	ConocoPhillips
Wal-Mart	McDonald's Corporation
Boeing	3M
DuPont	UPS
Carnival Corporation	The Walt Disney Co.
CSX Corporation	Eastman Kodak Co.
Pier 1 Imports	Alcoa
Amazon.com	Avery Dennison Corp.
H&R Block	Harley-Davidson
Dell Inc.	Google
Ikea	Willamette Valley Farms
Safeway	Clif Bar
Mattel, Inc.	Toyota
Goodyear	

Quality was definitely an "A"!

—Jane Jones
Mt. Empire Community College

What Can McGraw-Hill Technology Offer You?

Online Learning Center

www.mhhe.com/price12e

More and more students are studying online. That's why we offer an Online Learning Center (OLC) that follows *College Accounting* chapter by chapter. It doesn't require any building or maintenance on the part of the instructor. It's ready to go the minute instructors or students log in. The Online Learning Center contains:

For the Instructor:
- Instructor's Manual
- PowerPoint® Slides
- Solutions Manual
- Excel Template Solutions
- Practice Set Answer Keys
- Peachtree and Quickbooks Templates Solutions

For the Student:
- Practice Quizzes
- Excel Templates
- PowerPoint® Slides
- International Insights
- Accounting on the Job Feature
- iPod Content

Carol Yacht's General Ledger and Peachtree Complete CD-ROM

Carol Yacht's General Ledger Software is McGraw-Hill/Irwin's custom-built general ledger package. Carol Yacht's General Ledger can help your students master every aspect of the general ledger, from inputting sales and cash receipts to calculating ratios for analysis or inventory valuations.

Also on Carol Yacht's General Ledger CD, students receive the educational version of Peachtree Complete, along with templates containing data for many of the text exercises and problems. Familiarity with Peachtree Complete will be essential for students entering the job market, and Carol Yacht's Peachtree templates that accompany College Accounting 12/e makes sure they get plenty of practice.

McGraw-Hill's Homework Manager™

McGraw-Hill's Homework Manager™ System is an online homework management solution that contains the textbook's end-of-chapter material as well as the test bank. Instructors have the option to build assignments from static and algorithmic versions of the end-of-chapter material or build self-graded quizzes from the test bank.

Features:
- Assigns book-specific problems/exercises to students.
- Provides integrated test bank questions for quizzes and tests.
- Automatically grades assignments and quizzes and stores results in one grade book.

Learn more about McGraw-Hill's Homework Manager system by referring to the opening pages of this text.

McGraw-Hill's Homework Manager Plus™

McGraw-Hill's Homework Manager PLUS™ system gathers all of *College Accounting*'s online student resources under one convenient access point, combining the power and flexibility of McGraw-Hill's Homework Manager system with the latest interactive learning technology to create a comprehensive, fully integrated online study package.

Students using McGraw-Hill's Homework Manager PLUS system can access not only McGraw-Hill's Homework Manager system itself, but the interactive online textbook as well, allowing students working on assignment to click a hotlink and instantly review the appropriate material in the textbook.

Students receive full access to McGraw-Hill's Homework Manager system when they purchase McGraw-Hill's Homework Manager PLUS system.

ALEKS

ALEKS for the Accounting Cycle provides a detailed, guided overview through every stage of the accounting cycle. ALEKS Math Prep for Accounting provides coverage of the basic math skills needed to succeed. ALEKS (Assessment and Learning in Knowledge Spaces) delivers precise, qualitative diagnostic assessments of students' knowledge, guides them in the selection of appropriate new study material, and records their progress toward mastery of curricular goals in a robust classroom management system.

ALEKS interacts with the student much as a skilled human tutor would, moving between explanation and practice as needed, correcting and analyzing errors, defining terms and changing topics on request. By sophisticated modeling of a student's knowledge state for a given subject, ALEKS can focus clearly on what the student is most ready to learn next. When students focus on exactly what they are ready to learn, they build confidence and a learning momentum that fuels success.

For more information, visit the ALEKS Web site at **www.business.aleks.com**.

Online Course Solutions

Use our online course tools to help launch your program.

• Enhance your current online curriculum with our assets.

• Use our courses in conjunction with the textbook of your choice.

• Customize our online content to meet your specific course needs.

McGraw-Hill Online Learning's range of online course solutions is designed to empower you to teach your online course the way you want to. The courses provide interactive digital content and activities aligned to learning objectives that work with most learning management systems and the instructor's text of choice. McGraw-Hill

Online Learning's innovative online courses combine cutting-edge technology and comprehensive instructional design for use in the higher education market.

Visit www.OnlineLearning.com or contact your local sales representative to learn more about how we can partner with you!

CourseSmart

CourseSmart is a new way to find and buy eTextbooks. At CourseSmart you can save up to 50 percent off the cost of a print textbook, reduce your impact on the environment, and gain access to powerful Web tools for learning. CourseSmart has the largest selection of eTextbooks available anywhere, offering thousands of the most commonly adopted textbooks from a wide variety of higher education publishers. CourseSmart eTextbooks are available in one standard online reader with full text search, notes and highlighting, and e-mail tools for sharing notes between classmates.

Apple iPod® iQuiz

Use our EZ Test Online to help your students prepare to succeed with Apple iPod® iQuiz.

Using our EZ Test Online you can make test and quiz content available for a student's Apple iPod®.

Students must purchase the iQuiz game application from Apple for 99¢ in order to use the iQuiz content. It works on the iPOD fifth-generation iPODs and better.

Instructors need only EZ Test Online to produce iQuiz ready content. Instructors take their existing tests and quizzes and export them to a file that can then be made available to the student to take as a self quiz on their iPods. It's as simple as that.

McGraw-Hill/Irwin CARES

At McGraw-Hill/Irwin, we understand that getting the most from new technology can be challenging. That's why our services don't stop after you purchase our book. You can e-mail our Product Specialists 24 hours a day, get product training online, or search our knowledge bank of Frequently Asked Questions on our support Website.

McGraw-Hill/Irwin Customer Care Contact Information

For all Customer Support call (800) 331-5094
Email be_support@mcgraw-hill.com
Or visit www.mhhe.com/support
One of our Technical Support Analysts will be able to assist you in a timely fashion.

Help your students master the accounting cycle with Quantum Tutors

Artificial intelligence tutoring software provides effective, step-by-step feedback and homework help for students in principles, financial and managerial accounting.

Topics include:

- Transaction Analysis
- Adjusting Entries
- Financial Statement Preparation

> "As the former Director of the Office of Educational Technology at the U.S. Department of Education, I have had the privilege of evaluating many new and evolving technologies. The cognitive learning approach of the Quantum Tutors is by far one of the most advanced and effective educational tools available for self-directed tutoring, homework help and test preparation."
>
> **Susan Patrick**
> President and CEO
> North American Council for Online Learning (NACOL)

Proven To Increase Test Scores

Students can improve test scores by at least a full letter grade and practice with more than 250 transactions for corporate accounting and sole proprietorship.

It's Just Like Working with a Human Tutor

Similar to working with an excellent tutor or instructor one-on-one, powerful artificial intelligence software interacts with students in a conversational manner so they spend time learning Accounting, not the software.

Step-by-Step Feedback on a Students Own Work

Students enter their own work and the Tutors interpret their responses and provide coaching and detailed feedback so students get the right answer for the right reason.

Immediate Answers to Students' Questions

Includes an evolving menu of questions that change based on students' unique responses. Their knowledge of the subject improves because they're learning to ask better questions.

Maximize Study Time - Day or Night

The online tutor is available to offer help and assistance when instructors can't be.

"There is no doubt that the future of education is in increasing personalization of the learning process, and assisting learners within the context in which they are learning. Volumes have been written about the importance of offering contextualized and personalized learning opportunities to students, but Quantum has made these theoretical concepts possible in education and has brought them to the classroom."

Farhad Saba, Ph.D.
CEO, Distance-Educator.com
Professor of Educational Technology
San Diego State University

Instructor Supplements

Assurance of Learning Ready

Many educational institutions today are focused on the notion of assurance of learning, an important element of some accreditation standards. *College Accounting*, 12e is designed specifically to support your assurance of learning initiatives with a simple, yet powerful, solution.

Each test bank question for *College Accounting*, 12e maps to a specific chapter learning outcome/objective listed in the text. You can use our test bank software, *EZ Test*, to easily query for learning outcomes/objectives that directly relate to the learning objectives for your course. You can then use the reporting features of *EZ Test* to aggregate student results in similar fashion, making the collection and presentation of assurance of learning data simple and easy. You can also use our Algorithmic-Diploma Test Bank to do this.

AACSB Statement

McGraw-Hill Companies is a proud corporate member of AACSB International. Recognizing the importance and value of AACSB accreditation, we have sought to recognize the curricula guidelines detailed in AACSB standards for business accreditation by connecting selected questions in *College Accounting*, 12e to the general knowledge and skill guidelines found in the AACSB standards.

The statements contained in *College Accounting*, 12e are provided only as a guide for the users of this text. The AACSB leaves content coverage and assessment clearly within the realm and control of individual schools, the mission of the school, and the faculty. The AACSB does also charge schools with the obligation of doing assessment against their own content and learning goals. While *College Accounting*, 12e and its teaching package make no claim of any specific AACSB qualification or evaluation, we have, within *College Accounting*, 12e, labeled selected questions according to the six general knowledge and skills areas. The labels or tags within *College Accounting*, 12e are as indicated. There are, of course, many more within the test bank, the text, and the teaching package which might be used as a "standard" for your course. However, the labeled questions are suggested for your consideration.

Instructor CD-ROM

ISBN: 9780073365619 (MHID: 0073365610)

This all-in-one resource incorporates the Test Bank, PowerPoint® Slides, Instructor's Manual, and Solutions Manual.

Instructor's Manual

ISBN: 9780073365589 (MHID: 0073365580)

This supplement contains extensive chapter-by-chapter lecture notes, along with useful suggestions for presenting key concepts and ideas, to help with classroom presentation. The lecture notes coordinate closely with the PowerPoint® Slides, making lesson planning even easier.

Instructor's Edition

Chapters 1–30—ISBN: 9780073365602 (MHID: 0073365602)

This special edition contains several types of marginal annotations to help you plan your lessons: Teaching Tips, Extending the Content, and Check Figures.

Solutions Manual

Chapters 1–13—ISBN: 9780073365749 (MHID: 0073365742)
Chapters 1–30—ISBN: 9780073365671 (MHID: 007336567X)

This supplement contains completed step-by-step calculations to all assignment and Study Guide material, as well as a general discussion of the Thinking Critically questions that appear throughout the text.

Test Bank (Print Version)

ISBN: 9780073365718 (MHID: 0073365718)

This comprehensive Test Bank includes more than 2,000 true/false, multiple-choice, and completion questions and problems.

Online Course Management

No matter what online course management system you use (WebCT, BlackBoard, or eCollege), we have a course cartridge available for Price 12e. Our cartridges are specifically designed to make it easy to navigate and access content online. They are easier than ever to install on the latest version of the course management system available today.

Don't forget that you can count on the highest level of service from McGraw-Hill. Our online course management specialists are ready to assist you with your online course needs. They provide training and will answer any questions you have throughout the life of your adoption. So try our course cartridge for Price 12e and make online course content delivery easy

Algorithmic-Diploma TestBank (from BrownStone)

ISBN: 9780073365534 (MHID: 007336553X)

This computerized test bank is an algorithmic problem generator enabling instructors to create similarly structured problems with different values, which allows every student to be assigned a unique quiz or test. The user-friendly interface gives faculty the ability to easily create different versions of the same test, change the answer order, edit or add questions, and even conduct online testing.

EZ Test

EZ Test is available on the Instructor's Resource CD-Rom.

McGraw-Hill's EZ Test is a flexible electronic testing program. The program allows instructors to create tests from book-specific items. It accommodates a wide range of question types, plus instructors may add their own questions and sort questions by format. EZ Test can also scramble questions and answers for multiple versions of the same test.

Student Supplements

Study Guide/Working Papers

Chapters 1–13—ISBN: 9780073365756 (MHID: 0073365750)
Chapters 14–24—ISBN: 9780073365701 (MHID: 007336570X)
Chapters 1–30—ISBN: 9780073365695 (MHID: 0073365696)

This study aid summarizes essential points in each chapter, tests students' knowledge using self test questions, and contains forms that help students organize their solutions to homework problems.

Action Video Practice Set

ISBN: 9780073365527 (MHID: 0073365521)

Completely revised for the twelfth edition, Action Video Productions is a sole proprietorship service business that uses source documents, a general journal, a general ledger, worksheets, and a filing system to provide students with a usable practice set. The strength of this set is the use of source documents in conjunction with the daily business activities. This set can be completed after Chapter 6 of *College Accounting*.

Home Team Advantage Practice Set

ISBN: 9780073365572 (MHID: 0073365572)

Home Team Advantage is a sole proprietorship merchandising business that uses source documents, special journals, a general ledger, a subsidiary ledger, a worksheet, accounting forms, and a filing system for student use. This very realistic retail business will give a student accounting practice where merchandise inventory and the cost of goods sold become an integral part of the income statement. This set can be completed after Chapter 13.

Microsoft Excel Templates

Available on the online learning center.

Prepared by Jack Terry of ComSource Associates, Inc., this spreadsheet-based software uses Excel to solve selected problems in the text, which are identified in the margins of the text with appropriate icons. The Student Excel Templates are available only on the text's Web site.

QuickBooks Pro Templates CD-ROM

ISBN: 9780073365664 (MHID: 0073365661)

Selected problems in the text are tied to templates created in QuickBooks Pro. Students can use the Student Guide for QuickBooks Pro to walk through the problems.

Carol Yacht's General Ledger and Peachtree Complete
ISBN: 9780073365541 (MHID: 0073365548)

Peachtree templates prepared by Carol Yacht

The CD-ROM includes fully functioning versions of McGraw-Hill's own General Ledger Application software as well as Peachtree Complete 2009. Problem templates and instructions are included that allow you to assign text problems for working in either Yacht's General Ledger or Peachtree 2009.

Student Guide for QuickBooks Pro
ISBN: 9780073365688 (MHID: 0073365688)

To better prepare students for accounting in the real world, end-of-chapter material in Price is tied to Quickbooks software. The accompanying study guide provides a step-by-step walkthrough for students on how to complete the problem in the software.

iPod Content
Available on the online learning center.

The online learning center contains course-related videos, chapter-specific quizzes, and audio and visual lecture presentations that tie directly to the text. Icons in the margins of the book direct students to the assets available on the Web site that can offer them additional help in understanding difficult topics.

Acknowledgments

The authors are deeply grateful to the following accounting educators for their input during development of *College Accounting,* 12e. The feedback of these knowledgeable instructors provided the authors with valuable assistance in meeting the changing needs of the college accounting classroom.

Reviewers and Event Participants

Diane Alejars,
ETI Technical College

Teresa Alenikov,
Cerritos College

Jack Aschkenazi,
American Intercontinental University Online

Linda Batiste,
Baton Rouge Community College

Antoinette Clegg,
Delta College

Janis Colehour,
Mclennan Community College

Andrew Cropsey,
Bob Jones University

Mark Fronke,
Cerritos College

Pradeep Ghimire,
Palo Alto College

Christina Hata,
Mira Costa College

Merrily Hoffman,
San Jacinto College–Central

Paul Hogan,
Northwest–Shoals Community College

Patricia Inkelaar,
Everest College

Jane Jones, *Mt. Empire Community College*

David Juriga,
St. Louis Community College

Dieter Kiefer,
American River College

Kathy Kircher,
Lansdale School of Business

Susan Koepke,
Illinois Valley Community College

Patty Kolarik,
Hutchinson Community College

David Laurel,
South Texas College

Dori Lombard,
DeVry University

Vanessa May,
Louisiana Technical College, Lafayette Campus

John Mayhorne,
Yorktowne Business Institute

Anita Morgan,
Colorado Tech University Online

Anthony Newton,
Highland Community College

Sandra O'Brien,
Kirkwood Community College

Barbara Parks,
American Intercontinental University Online

Stephen Ruggiero,
Briarwood College

Joanne Salas,
Olympic College

Karen Stanley,
Ozarks Technical College

Domenico Tavella,
Pittsburgh Technical Institute

Laverne Thomas-Vertrees,
St. Louis Community College

Connie Wedemeyer,
Mclennan Community College

Carol Wennagel,
San Jacinto College

Jack Wiehler,
San Joaquin Delta College

Survey Respondents

Robin Aliotti,
Los Medanos College

Cornelia Alsheimer,
Santa Barbara City College

Lashun Aron,
Brown Mackie College–Merrillville

Marjorie Ashton,
Truckee Meadows Community College

Allan Aspelund,
Century College

Don Babbitt,
St. Louis Community College, Florissant Valley

Steve Balassi,
Napa Valley College

Joyce Barnhart,
Lake Land College

John Bell,
Eagle Gate College

Angela Bogart,
University of Northwestern Ohio

Barry J. Bomboy,
J. Sargeant Reynolds Community College

Anna M. Boulware,
St. Charles Community College

Sharon Breeding,
Bluegrass Community and Technical College.

James Burke,
Cuyahoga Community College

Pat Burt,
Bevill State Community College Fayette Campus

Gerald Caton,
Yavapai College

Marilyn Ciolino,
Delgado Community College

Jay Cohen,
Oakton Community College

Don Curfman,
McHenry County College

Joann Dawe,
Front Range Community College

Elizabeth Drzewiecki,
Olympic College

John D. Durham,
University of Alaska Anchorage–Kodiak College

Steven L. Ernest,
Baton Rouge Community College

Katherine Falgout,
Louisiana Technical College–Lafourche South Campus

David Forester,
Haywood Community College

Don Foster,
Tacoma Community College

Ed Gehy,
Kirkwood Community College

Charles J. Gendusa,
Community College of Southern Nevada

Bea Gobeski,
Hawkeye Community College

Renee Goffinet,
Spokane Community College

Larena Grieshaber,
Flint Hills Technical College

Carmen Guerrero,
Oxnard College

Becky Hancock,
El Paso Community College

Kathy Hebert,
Louisiana Technical College

Lynne Heuber,
International Academy of Design and Technology

Melvyn Hutt,
ECPI College of Technology

Ray Ingram,
Southwest Georgia Technical College

Bradley Johnson,
Corinthian College, Inc.

Peg Johnson,
Metropolitan Community College

Kay Johnston,
Columbia Basin College

Dmitriy Kalyagin,
Chabot College

Rosemary Keasey,
*Butler County Community
College*

Nancy Kinchen,
Louisiana Technical College–Lafayette Campus

J. Knutson,
Gateway Technical College

Ken Kwok,
Pierce College–Puyallup

Marcus Lacher,
*Minnesota State Community and Technical
College–Detroit Lakes*

Lisa Leachman,
ECPI College of Technology

Terrell Mailhiot,
Tidewater Tech Online

Nelson Martin,
Wenatchee Valley College

Pablo Martinez,
Texas State Technical College

George Matthews,
ECPI College of Technology

Marie McCraw,
Brookstone College of Business

Donna McCullough,
*International Academy of Design and
Technology*

Suzanne McKee,
Jackson Community College

Noel McKeon,
*Florida Community College
at Jacksonville*

Catherine Merrikin,
Pearl River Community College

Mark Meuwissen,
Alexandria Technical College

John Miller,
Metropolitan Community College

Linda Miller,
Jefferson Davis Community College

Paul Muller,
Western Nevada College

Linda Napolitano,
F • E • G • S Trades & Business School

Jon Nitschke,
*Montana State University–Great Falls Campus,
College of Technology*

Jeanette Norwood,
Louisiana Technical College–Mansfield Campus

Tom O'Keefe,
St. Cloud Technical College

Carla Oster,
Prince William Sound Community College

David Ozag,
ECPI College of Technology

Susan L. Pallas,
Southest Community College

Kathy Rawson,
Bryan College

Gary Reynolds,
Ozarks Technical Community College

Reynaldo C. Robles,
Texas State Technical College

Rogelio A. Rodriguez,
Laredo Community College

L. Rourke,
Mohave Community College

Mark Rutter,
Community College of Allegheny County

Brian D. Schmoldt,
Madison Area Technical College

Maryann Sebelist,
*San Joaquin Valley Junior College–Rancho
Cucamonga*

Mona Sepulvado,
LTC–Sabine Valley Campus

William Shaver,
J. Sargeant Reynolds Community College

Sherril R. Shaw,
Portland Community College

William W. Shifflett,
Chattanooga State Technical Community College

Kim Silver,
Mesa Community College

Charles Smith,
Tri-State Business Institute

Jim Stanley,
Lower Columbia College

Louise Stein,
Hutchinson Community College

Regina Stinson,
Sarasota County Technical Institute

Jim Sumerel,
Johnston Community College

Richard Terrell,
Louisiana Technical College–Folkes Campus

Carolyn Terry,
Santa Barbara City College

Juanita Tookes,
Iverson Business School

William Vermie,
Bellevue Community College

Patricia Walczak,
Lansing Community College

Bea Wallace,
Great Basin College

Mark Wells,
Big Sandy Community and Technical College

Tim Whited,
National College

Linda Whitten,
Skyline College

Breck Withers,
Santa Rosa Junior College

Candace Witherspoon,
Bowling Green Community College

Thank You . . .

WE ARE GRATEFUL for the outstanding support from McGraw-Hill/Irwin. In particular, we would like to thank Stewart Mattson, Editorial Director; Alice Harra, Senior Sponsoring Editor; Emily Hatteberg, Developmental Editor; Scott Bishop, Marketing Manager; Bruce Gin, Senior Project Manager; Michael McCormick, Lead Production Supervisor; Matt Baldwin, Senior Designer; Jeremy Cheshareck, Photo Research Coordinator; and Cathy Tepper, Media Project Manager.

Finally, we would like to thank Beth Woods and Jocelyn Kauffunger for working so hard to ensure an error-free twelfth edition as well as Carolyn Terry and Joanne Butler for their contributions.

John Price • M. David Haddock • Michael Farina

To the Student

Welcome to *College Accounting.* This book and the accompanying study materials will help you bridge the gap from your first course in accounting to your next business course. . .and beyond, to your career.

Marginal Icons are used throughout the text to link content to support materials on the Web or via other media, or to highlight consistent elements throughout the text:

This icon indicates that the content being discussed is related to internal control.

Continuing problems build on one another from chapter to chapter, allowing you to use the concepts you've just been introduced to in a chapter to revisit and further reinforce material you've learned in previous chapters.

This icon means that you have the option of working the problem you see at the end of a chapter in Excel, a tool you will use often in the real world, even if you do not go on to be an accountant! The excel templates are available on the text's Web site.

Peachtree is an accounting tool you are likely to encounter if you decide to make accounting your career. This icon indicates that you can work the problem in Peachtree, gaining experience that will be invaluable once you graduate. The Peachtree templates are avaliable on a CD.

The Quickbooks software grew out of the success of the personal finance software Quicken. Problems are pulled into Quickbooks, just as they are into Excel and Peachtree, giving you yet another way to practice using software that you are likely to run into in the business world. There is also a Student Guide for Quickbooks Pro available to you as a printed supplement that will assist you in working with Quickbooks.

McGraw-Hill's Homework Manager system allows you to submit homework online if your professor chooses to utilize it in the classroom. Your professor will request that you obtain this software when you purchase your book if he/she plans to ask you to submit your homework online.

The media integrated icon means that there are videos, quizzes, and audio lectures available to you on the book's Web site that relates to the particular topic being covered in the text. All the additional materials can be downloaded onto your iPod®, Zune®, or other MP3 player so you can carry them with you and study on the go!

Self Reviews are a great way to double-check that you've understood what you've just read in your book or what your professor has just covered in lecture. There is a Self Review at the end of every section. Answers to the self reviews can be found at the end of each chapter so you can check your work and make sure you understand a topic before moving on to the next section.

Learning Objectives can be found at the beginning of each chapter as well as at the beginning of each section. The section opener objectives also contain a brief explanation for "Why It's Important" to study the concept presented.

Online Learning Center (www.mhhe.com/price12e) The Web site that accompanies Price/Haddock/Farina's *College Accounting,* 12e, is a great resource for you. Don't be afraid to use it! On the Online Learning Center (OLC), there are a lot of great materials that will help you not only get through your course, but also get a good grade and remember what you learned. You will find things like:

- Practice Quizzes
- PowerPoint® Slides
- International Insights
- Accounting on the Job Feature

To access the OLC, just go to the link above and look to the left. You'll see a link to the "Student Edition"—click on this and you will find a variety of Course-Wide Content in the top left corner, including accounting videos. Under this, you will see a drop-down menu from which you can choose whatever chapter you want and find additional resources. Finally, the OLC is where you will find the online version of Price/Haddock/Farina's *College Accounting,* 12e, if you've purchased McGraw-Hill's Homework Manager PLUS system.

Practice Sets *College Accounting,* 12e, comes with two different full-length practice sets (in addition to the Mini-Practice Sets included inside the textbook) that you can purchase to get additional practice applying the concepts you've learned in class. Both practice sets have been renewed and refreshed for this edition of the textbook. Your instructor can provide you with the answers so you can check your work.

Study Guide and Working Papers In addition to giving you a hard copy place to enter the answers to the questions, exercises, and problems your instructor assigns you in class, the Study Guide and Working Papers also include additional activities, exercises, true/false questions, and a demonstration problem that you can work—all of which give you more chances to practice what you're going to see on the test!

Our two main goals are to help you understand and apply accounting and prepare you for the future, whether that includes additional study or a new workplace. We hope the aids we've provided for you as listed above will help enhance your study and ultimately give you a greater understanding of accounting and how it applies in the real world.

Good luck with your studies. We think it will be well worth your efforts.

Brief Contents

Contents

Mini-Practice
Set 1 Service Business Accounting Cycle   **186**
Wells' Consulting Services

College Accounting

Accounting: The Language of Business

Chapter 1

LEARNING OBJECTIVES

1. Define accounting.   LP1
2. Identify and discuss career opportunities in accounting.
3. Identify the users of financial information.
4. Compare and contrast the three types of business entities.
5. Describe the process used to develop generally accepted accounting principles.
6. Define the accounting terms new to this chapter.

NEW TERMS

accounting
accounting system
auditing
auditor's report
certified public accountant (CPA)
corporation
creditor
discussion memorandum
economic entity
entity
exposure draft
financial statements
generally accepted accounting principles (GAAP)
governmental accounting
international accounting
management advisory services
managerial accounting
partnership
public accountants
separate entity assumption
social entity
sole proprietorship
Statements of Financial Accounting Standards
stock
stockholders
tax accounting

Google™ www.google.com

Can you imagine looking up stock quotes, getting directions, or checking the local weather without help from google.com? Before the development of the search engine that would revolutionize the Internet, finding such simple information quickly was nearly impossible. Thankfully, in 1995 Google's founders Larry Page and Sergey Brin developed a new approach to online search that took root in a Stanford University dorm room and quickly spread to information seekers around the globe.

As Google's features and performance evolved, it attracted new users at an astounding rate. By 2000, Google officially became the world's largest search engine with its introduction of a *billion-page index*—the first time so much of the Web's content had been made available in a searchable format. As a publicly owned global Internet communications, commerce, and media company, Google reports financial information to investors, owners, and managers every quarter. Revenues of $3.87 billion were reported for the quarter ending June 30, 2007, a 58 percent increase from the prior year's revenues.

thinking critically

If you were considering purchasing stock in Google Inc., how would a basic understanding of accounting assist you?

SECTION OBJECTIVES

>> 1. **Define accounting.**

WHY IT'S IMPORTANT

Business transactions affect many aspects of our lives.

>> 2. **Identify and discuss career opportunities in accounting.**

WHY IT'S IMPORTANT

There's something for everyone in the field of accounting. Accounting professionals are found in every workplace from public accounting firms to government agencies, from corporations to nonprofit organizations.

>> 3. **Identify the users of financial information.**

WHY IT'S IMPORTANT

A wide variety of individuals and businesses depend on financial information to make decisions.

TERMS TO LEARN

accounting

accounting system

auditing

certified public accountant (CPA)

financial statements

governmental accounting

management advisory services

managerial accounting

public accountants

tax accounting

What Is Accounting?

Accounting provides financial information about a business or a nonprofit organization. Owners, managers, investors, and other interested parties need financial information in order to make decisions. Because accounting is used to communicate financial information, it is often called the "language of business."

The Need for Financial Information

Suppose a relative leaves you a substantial sum of money and you decide to carry out your lifelong dream of opening a small sportswear shop. You rent space in a local shopping center, purchase fixtures and equipment, purchase goods to sell, hire salespeople, and open the store to customers. Before long you realize that, to run your business successfully, you need financial information about the business. You probably need information that provides answers to the following questions:

- How much cash does the business have?
- How much money do customers owe the business?
- What is the cost of the merchandise sold?
- What is the change in sales volume?
- How much money is owed to suppliers?
- What is the profit or loss?

As your business grows, you will need even more financial information to evaluate the firm's performance and make decisions about the future. An efficient accounting system allows owners and managers to quickly obtain a wide range of useful information. The need for timely information is one reason that businesses have an accounting system directed by a professional staff.

>>**1. OBJECTIVE**

Define accounting.

Accounting Defined

Accounting is the process by which financial information about a business is recorded, classified, summarized, interpreted, and communicated to owners, managers, and other interested parties. An **accounting system** is designed to accumulate data about a firm's financial affairs, classify the data in a meaningful way, and summarize it in periodic reports called **financial statements.** Owners and managers obtain a lot of information from financial statements. The accountant

- establishes the records and procedures that make up the accounting system,
- supervises the operations of the system,
- interprets the resulting financial information.

Most owners and managers rely heavily on the accountant's judgment and knowledge when making financial decisions.

LP1

Accounting Careers

Many jobs are available in the accounting profession, and they require varying amounts of education and experience. Bookkeepers and accountants are responsible for keeping records and providing financial information about the business. Generally, bookkeepers are responsible for recording business transactions. In large firms, bookkeepers may also supervise the work of accounting clerks. Accounting clerks are responsible for recordkeeping for a part of the accounting system—perhaps payroll, accounts receivable, or accounts payable. Accountants usually supervise bookkeepers and prepare the financial statements and reports of the business.

Newspapers and Web sites often have job listings for accounting clerks, bookkeepers, and accountants:

- Accounting clerk positions usually require one to two accounting courses and little or no experience.
- Bookkeeper positions usually require one to two years of accounting education plus experience as an accounting clerk.
- Accountant positions usually require a bachelor's degree but are sometimes filled by experienced bookkeepers or individuals with a two-year college degree. Most entry-level accountant positions do not have an experience requirement. Both the education and experience requirements for accountant positions vary according to the size of the firm.

Accountants usually choose to practice in one of three areas:

- public accounting
- managerial accounting
- governmental accounting

PUBLIC ACCOUNTING

Public accountants work for public accounting firms. Public accounting firms provide accounting services for other companies. Usually they offer three services:

- auditing
- tax accounting
- management advisory services

The largest public accounting firms in the United States are called the "Big Four." The "Big Four" are Deloitte & Touche, Ernst & Young, KPMG, and PricewaterhouseCoopers.

Many public accountants are **certified public accountants (CPAs).** To become a CPA, an individual must have a certain number of college credits in accounting courses, demonstrate good personal character, pass the Uniform CPA Examination, and fulfill the experience requirements of the state of practice. CPAs must follow the professional code of ethics.

Auditing is the review of financial statements to assess their fairness and adherence to generally accepted accounting principles. Accountants who are CPAs perform financial audits.

Tax accounting involves tax compliance and tax planning. *Tax compliance* deals with the preparation of tax returns and the audit of those returns. *Tax planning* involves giving advice to clients on how to structure their financial affairs in order to reduce their tax liability.

Management advisory services involve helping clients improve their information systems or their business performance.

>> 2. OBJECTIVE
Identify and discuss career opportunities in accounting.

LP1

ABOUT
ACCOUNTING

Accounting Services
The role of the CPA is expanding. In the past, accounting firms handled audits and taxes. Today accountants provide a wide range of services, including financial planning, investment advice, accounting and tax software advice, and profitability consulting. Accountants provide clients with information and advice on electronic business, health care performance measurement, risk assessment, business performance measurement, and information system reliability.

TAX AUTHORITIES

The Internal Revenue Service (IRS) and other state and local tax authorities are interested in financial information about your firm. This information is used to determine the tax base:

- Income taxes are based on taxable income.
- Sales taxes are based on sales income.
- Property taxes are based on the assessed value of buildings, equipment, and inventory (the goods available for sale).

The accounting process provides all of this information.

REGULATORY AGENCIES AND INVESTORS

If an industry is regulated by a governmental agency, businesses in that industry have to supply financial information to the regulating agency. For example, the Federal Communications Commission receives financial information from radio and television stations. The Securities and Exchange Commission (SEC) oversees the financial information provided by publicly owned corporations to their investors and potential investors. Publicly owned corporations trade their shares on stock exchanges and in over-the-counter markets. Congress passed the Securities Act of 1933 and the Securities Exchange Act of 1934 in order to protect those who invest in publicly owned corporations.

The SEC is responsible for reviewing the accounting methods used by publicly owned corporations. The SEC has delegated this review to the accounting profession but still has the final say on any financial accounting issue faced by publicly owned corporations. If the SEC does not agree with the reporting that results from an accounting method, the SEC can suspend trading of a company's shares on the stock exchanges.

> Major changes were made to the regulatory environment in the accounting profession with the passage of the Public Company Accounting Reform and Investor Protection Act of 2002 (also known as the Sarbanes-Oxley Act) that was signed into law by President Bush on August 2, 2002. The Act was the most far-reaching regulatory crackdown on corporate fraud and corruption since the creation of the Securities and Exchange Commission in 1934.

The Sarbanes-Oxley Act was passed in response to the wave of corporate accounting scandals starting with the demise of Enron Corporation in 2001, the arrest of top executives at WorldCom and Adelphia Communications Corporation, and ultimately the demise of Arthur Andersen, an international public accounting firm formerly a member of the "Big Five." Arthur Andersen was found guilty of an obstruction of justice charge after admitting that the firm destroyed thousands of documents and electronic files related to the Enron audit engagement. Although on May 31, 2005, the Supreme Court of the United States reversed the Andersen guilty verdict, Arthur Andersen has not returned as a viable business. As a result of the demise of Arthur Andersen, the "Big Five" are now the "Big Four."

The Act significantly tightens regulation of financial reporting by publicly held companies and their accountants and auditors. The Sarbanes-Oxley Act creates a five-member Public Company Accounting Oversight Board. The Board will have investigative and enforcement powers to oversee the accounting profession and to discipline corrupt accountants and auditors. The Securities and Exchange Commission will oversee the Board. Two members of the Board will be certified public accountants, to regulate the accountants who audit public companies, and the remaining three must not be and cannot have been CPAs. The chair of the Board may be held by one of the CPA members, provided that the individual has not been engaged as a practicing CPA for five years.

Major provisions of the bill include rules on consulting services, auditor rotation, criminal penalties, corporate governance, and securities regulation. The Act prohibits accountants from offering a broad range of consulting services to publicly traded companies that they audit and requires accounting firms to change the lead audit or coordinating partner and the reviewing partner for a company every five years. Additionally, it is a felony to "knowingly" destroy or create documents to "impede, obstruct or influence" any existing or contemplated federal investigation. Auditors are also required to maintain all audit or review work papers for seven years. Criminal penalties, up to 20 years in prison, are imposed for obstruction of justice and the Act raises the maximum sentence for defrauding pension funds to 10 years.

Chief executives and chief financial officers of publicly traded corporations are now required to certify their financial statements and these executives will face up to 20 years in prison if they "knowingly or willfully" allow materially misleading information into their financial statements. Companies must also disclose, as quickly as possible, material changes in their financial position. Wall Street investment firms are prohibited from retaliating against analysts who criticize investment-banking clients of the firm. The Act contains a provision with broad new protection for whistle blowers and lengthens the time that investors have to file lawsuits against corporations for securities fraud.

By narrowing the type of consulting services that accountants can provide to companies that they audit, requiring auditor rotation, and imposing stiff criminal penalties for violation of the Act, it appears that this new legislation will significantly help to restore public confidence in financial statements and markets and change the regulatory environment in which accountants operate.

CUSTOMERS

Customers pay special attention to financial information about the firms with which they do business. For example, before a business spends a lot of money on a new computer system, the business wants to know that the computer manufacturer will be around for the next several years in order to service the computer, replace parts, and provide additional components. The business analyzes the financial information about the computer manufacturer in order to determine its economic health and the likelihood that it will remain in business.

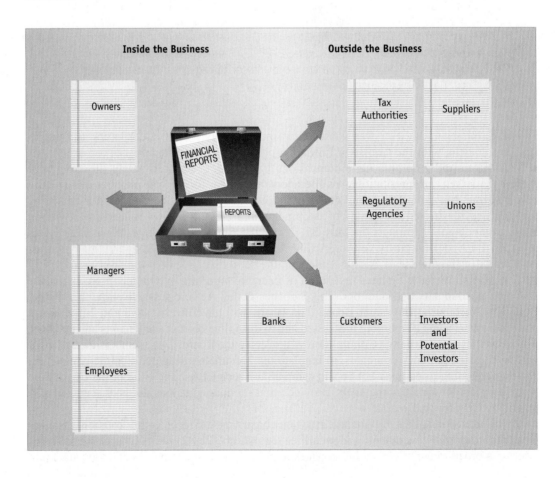

FIGURE 1.1

Users of Financial Information

EMPLOYEES AND UNIONS

Often employees are interested in the financial information of the business that employs them. Employees who are members of a profit-sharing plan pay close attention to the financial results because they affect employee income. Employees who are members of a labor union use financial information about the firm to negotiate wages and benefits.

Figure 1.1 illustrates different financial information users. As you learn about the accounting process, you will appreciate why financial information is so important to these individuals and organizations. You will learn how financial information meets users' needs.

Section 1 Self Review

QUESTIONS

1. What are the names of three accounting job positions?

2. Why is accounting called the "language of business"?

3. What are financial statements?

EXERCISES

4. One requirement for becoming a CPA is to pass the
   a. Final CPA Examination
   b. SEC Accounting Examination
   c. Uniform CPA Examination
   d. State Board Examination

5. Which organization has the final say on financial accounting issues faced by publicly owned corporations?
   a. Securities and Exchange Commission
   b. Federal Trade Commission
   c. U.S. Treasury Department
   d. Internal Revenue Service

ANALYSIS

6. The owner of the sporting goods store where you work has decided to expand the store. She has decided to apply for a loan. What type of information will she need to give to the bank?

(Answers to Section 1 Self Review are on page 19.)

SECTION OBJECTIVES

>> 4. **Compare and contrast the three types of business entities.**

WHY IT'S IMPORTANT

Each type of business entity requires unique legal and accounting considerations.

>> 5. **Describe the process used to develop generally accepted accounting principles.**

WHY IT'S IMPORTANT

Accounting professionals are required to use common standards and principles in order to produce reliable financial information.

TERMS TO LEARN

auditor's report

corporation

creditor

discussion memorandum

economic entity

entity

exposure draft

generally accepted accounting principles (GAAP)

international accounting

partnership

separate entity assumption

social entity

sole proprietorship

Statements of Financial Accounting Standards

stock

stockholders

Business and Accounting

The accounting process involves recording, classifying, summarizing, interpreting, and communicating financial information about an economic or social entity. An **entity** is recognized as having its own separate identity. An entity may be an individual, a town, a university, or a business. The term **economic entity** usually refers to a business or organization whose major purpose is to produce a profit for its owners. **Social entities** are nonprofit organizations, such as cities, public schools, and public hospitals. This book focuses on the accounting process for businesses, but keep in mind that nonprofit organizations also need financial information.

Types of Business Entities

The three major legal forms of business entity are the sole proprietorship, the partnership, and the corporation. In general, the accounting process is the same for all three forms of business. Later in the book you will study the different ways certain transactions are handled depending on the type of business entity. For now, however, you will learn about the different types of business entities.

SOLE PROPRIETORSHIPS

A **sole proprietorship** is a business entity owned by one person. The life of the business ends when the owner is no longer willing or able to keep the business going. Many small businesses are operated as sole proprietorships.

The owner of a sole proprietorship is legally responsible for the debts and taxes of the business. If the business is unable to pay its debts, the **creditors** (those people, companies, or government agencies to whom the business owes money) can turn to the owner for payment. The owner may have to pay the debts of the business from personal resources, including personal savings. When the time comes to pay income taxes, the owner's income and the income of the business are combined to compute the total tax responsibility of the owner.

It is important that the business transactions be kept separate from the owner's personal transactions. If the owner's personal transactions are mixed with those of the business, it will be difficult to measure the performance of the business. The term **separate entity assumption** describes the concept of keeping the firm's financial records separate from the owner's personal financial records.

PARTNERSHIPS

A **partnership** is a business entity owned by two or more people. The partnership structure is common in businesses that offer professional services, such as law firms, accounting firms, architectural firms, medical practices, and dental practices. At the beginning of the partnership, two or more individuals enter into a contract that details the rights, obligations, and limitations of each partner, including

- the amount each partner will contribute to the business,
- each partner's percentage of ownership,
- each partner's share of the profits,
- the duties each partner will perform,
- the responsibility each partner has for the amounts owed by the business to creditors and tax authorities.

The partners choose how to share the ownership and profits of the business. They may share equally or in any proportion agreed upon in the contract. When a partner leaves, the partnership is dissolved and a new partnership may be formed with the remaining partners.

Partners are individually, and as a group, responsible for the debts and taxes of the partnership. If the partnership is unable to pay its debts or taxes, the partners' personal property, including personal bank accounts, may be used to provide payment. It is important that partnership transactions be kept separate from the personal financial transactions of the partners.

>> 4. OBJECTIVE
Compare and contrast the three types of business entities.

important!

Separate Entity Assumption
For *accounting* purposes, all forms of business are considered separate entities from their owners. However, the corporation is the only form of business that is a separate *legal* entity.

> Under the Limited Liability Partnership Act of most states, a Limited Liability Partnership (LLP) may be formed. An LLP is a general partnership that provides some limited liability for all partners. LLP partners are responsible and have liability for their own actions and the actions of those under their control or supervision. They are not liable for the actions or malfeasance of another partner. Except for the limited liability aspect, LLPs generally have the same characteristics, advantages, and disadvantages as any other partnership.

CORPORATIONS

A **corporation** is a business entity that is separate from its owners. A corporation has a legal right to own property and do business in its own name. Corporations are very different from sole proprietorships and partnerships.

Stock, issued in the form of stock certificates, represents the ownership of the corporation. Corporations may be *privately* or *publicly* owned. Privately owned corporations are also called *closely held* corporations. The ownership of privately owned corporations is limited to specific individuals, usually family members. Stock of closely held corporations is not traded on an exchange. In contrast, stock of publicly owned corporations is bought and sold on stock exchanges and in over-the-counter markets. Most large corporations have issued (sold) thousands of shares of stock.

An owner's share of the corporation is determined by the number of shares of stock held by the owner compared to the total number of shares issued by the corporation. Assume that Hector Flores owns 600 shares of Sample Corporation. If Sample Corporation has issued 2,000 shares of stock, Flores owns 30 percent of the corporation (600 shares ÷ 2,000 shares = 0.30 or 30%). Some corporate decisions require a vote by the owners. For Sample Corporation, Flores has 600 votes, one for each share of stock that he owns. The other owners have 1,400 votes.

> Subchapter S Corporations, also known as S corporations, are entities formed as corporations which meet the requirements of Subchapter S of the Internal Revenue Code to be treated essentially as a partnership so the corporation pays no income tax. Instead, shareholders include their share of corporate profits, and any items that require special tax treatment, on their individual income tax returns. Otherwise, S corporations have all of the characteristics of regular corporations. The advantage of the S corporation is that the owners have limited liability and avoid double taxation.

One of the advantages of the corporate form of business is the indefinite life of the corporation. A sole proprietorship ends when the owner dies or discontinues the business. A partnership ends on the death or withdrawal of a partner. In contrast, a corporation does not end when ownership changes. Some corporations have new owners daily because their shares are actively traded (sold) on stock exchanges.

Corporate owners, called **stockholders** or *shareholders,* are not personally responsible for the debts or taxes of the corporation. If the corporation is unable to pay its bills, the most stockholders can lose is their investment in the corporation. In other words, the stockholders will not lose more than the cost of the shares of stock.

The accounting process for the corporate entity, like that of the sole proprietorship and the partnership, is separate from the financial affairs of its owners. Usually this separation is easy to maintain. Most stockholders do not participate in the day-to-day operations of the business.

Table 1.1 summarizes the business characteristics for sole proprietorships, partnerships, and corporations.

Generally Accepted Accounting Principles

The Securities and Exchange Commission has the final say on matters of financial reporting by publicly owned corporations. The SEC has delegated the job of determining proper accounting standards to the accounting profession. However, the SEC sometimes overrides decisions the accounting profession makes. To fulfill its responsibility, the accounting profession has developed, and continues to develop, **generally accepted accounting principles (GAAP).** Generally accepted accounting principles must be followed by publicly owned companies unless they can show that doing so would produce information which is misleading.

TABLE 1.1

Major Characteristics of Business Entities

Characteristic	Type of Business Entity		
	Sole Proprietorship	Partnership	Corporation
Ownership	One owner	Two or more owners	One or more owners, even thousands
Life of the business	Ends when the owner dies, is unable to carry on operations, or decides to close the firm	Ends when one or more partners withdraw, when a partner dies, or when the partners decide to close the firm	Can continue indefinitely; ends only when the business goes bankrupt or when the stockholders vote to liquidate
Responsibility for debts of the business	Owner is responsible for firm's debt when the firm is unable to pay	Partners are responsible individually and jointly for firm's debts when the firm is unable to pay	Stockholders are not responsible for firm's debts; they can lose only the amount they invested

THE DEVELOPMENT OF GENERALLY ACCEPTED ACCOUNTING PRINCIPLES

Generally accepted accounting principles are developed by the Financial Accounting Standards Board (FASB), which is composed of five full-time members. The FASB issues **Statements of Financial Accounting Standards.** The FASB develops these statements and, before issuing them, obtains feedback from interested people and organizations.

First, the FASB writes a **discussion memorandum** to explain the topic being considered. Then public hearings are held where interested parties can express their opinions, either orally or in writing. The groups that consistently express opinions about proposed FASB statements are the SEC, the American Institute of Certified Public Accountants (AICPA), public accounting firms, the American Accounting Association (AAA), and businesses with a direct interest in a particular statement.

The AICPA is a national association for certified public accountants. The AAA is a group of accounting educators. AAA members research possible effects of a proposed FASB statement and offer their opinions to the FASB.

After public hearings, the FASB releases an **exposure draft,** which describes the proposed statement. Then the FASB receives and evaluates public comments about the exposure draft. Finally, FASB members vote on the statement. If at least four members approve, the statement is issued. The process used to develop GAAP is shown in Figure 1.2 on page 14.

Accounting principles vary from country to country. **International accounting** is the study of the accounting principles used by different countries. In 1973, the International Accounting Standards Committee (IASC) was formed. Recently, the IASC's name was changed to the International Accounting Standards Board (IASB). The IASB deals with issues caused by the lack of uniform accounting principles. The IASB also makes recommendations to enhance comparability of reporting practices.

THE USE OF GENERALLY ACCEPTED ACCOUNTING PRINCIPLES

Every year publicly traded companies submit financial statements to the SEC. The financial statements are audited by independent certified public accountants (CPAs). The CPAs are called *independent* because they are not employees of the company being audited and they do not have a financial interest in the company. The financial statements include the auditor's report. The **auditor's report** contains the auditor's opinion about the fair presentation of the operating results and financial position of the business. The auditor's report also confirms that the financial information is prepared in conformity with generally accepted accounting principles. The financial statements and the auditor's report are made available to the public, including existing and potential stockholders.

---

important!

GAAP
The SEC requires all publicly owned companies to follow generally accepted accounting principles. As new standards are developed or refined, accountants interpret the standards and adapt accounting practices to the new standards.

>> 5. OBJECTIVE
Describe the process used to develop generally accepted accounting principles.

MANAGERIAL IMPLICATIONS   <<

FINANCIAL INFORMATION

- Managers of a business make sure that the firm's accounting system produces financial information that is timely, accurate, and fair.
- Financial statements should be based on generally accepted accounting principles.
- Each year a publicly traded company must submit financial statements, including an independent auditor's report, to the SEC.
- Internal reports for management need not follow generally accepted accounting principles but should provide

useful information that will aid in monitoring and controlling operations.

- Financial information can help managers to control present operations, make decisions, and plan for the future.
- The sound use of financial information is essential to good management.

THINKING CRITICALLY

If you were a manager, how would you use financial information to make decisions?

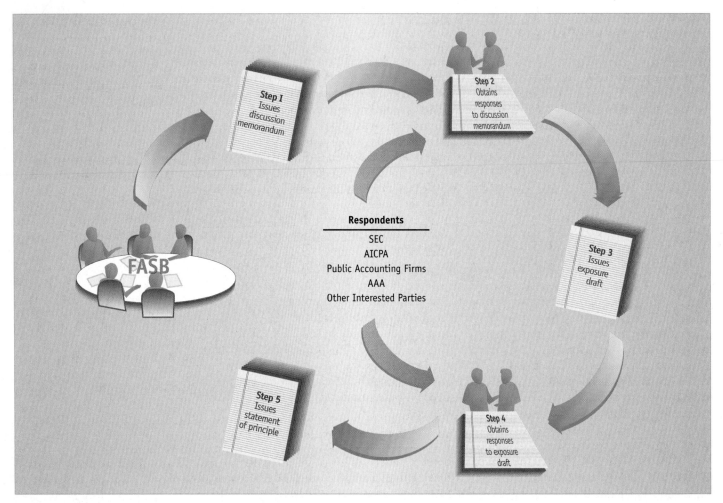

FIGURE 1.2

The Process Used by the FASB to Develop Generally Accepted Accounting Principles

Businesses and the environment in which they operate are constantly changing. The economy, technology, and laws change. Generally accepted accounting principles are changed and refined as accountants respond to the changing environment.

Section **2** Self Review

QUESTIONS

1. What are generally accepted accounting principles?

2. Why are generally accepted accounting principles needed?

3. How are generally accepted accounting principles developed?

EXERCISES

4. An organization that has two or more owners who are legally responsible for the debts and taxes of the business is a

a. social entity

b. partnership

c. sole proprietorship

d. corporation

5. A nonprofit organization such as a public school is a(n)

a. social unit

b. economic unit

c. social entity

d. economic entity

6. You plan to open a business with two of your friends. You would like to form a corporation, but your friends prefer the partnership form of business. What are some of the advantages of the corporate form of business?

(Answers to Section 2 Self Review are on page 20.)

REVIEW   Chapter Summary   Chapter 1

Accounting is often called the "language of business." The financial information about a business is communicated to interested parties in financial statements.

Learning Objectives

1   Define accounting.

Accounting is the process by which financial information about a business is recorded, classified, summarized, interpreted, and communicated to owners, managers, and other interested parties. Accurate accounting information is essential for making business decisions.

2   Identify and discuss career opportunities in accounting.

- There are many job opportunities in accounting.
- Accounting clerk positions, such as accounts receivable clerk, accounts payable clerk, and payroll clerk, require the least education and experience.
- Bookkeepers usually have experience as accounting clerks and a minimum of one to two years of accounting education.
- Most entry-level accounting positions require a college degree or significant experience as a bookkeeper.
- Accountants usually specialize in one of three major areas.
- Some accountants work for public accounting firms and perform auditing, tax accounting, or management advisory functions.
- Other accountants work in private industry where they set up and supervise accounting systems, prepare financial reports, prepare internal reports, or assist in determining the prices to charge for the firm's products.
- Still other accountants work for government agencies. They keep track of public funds and expenditures, or they audit the financial records of businesses and individuals to determine whether the records are in compliance with regulatory laws, tax laws, and other laws. The Securities and Exchange Commission, the Internal Revenue Service, the Federal Bureau of Investigation, and Homeland Security employ many accountants.

3   Identify the users of financial information.

All types of businesses need and use financial information. Users of financial information include owners and managers, employees, suppliers, banks, tax authorities, regulatory agencies, and investors. Nonprofit organizations need similar financial information.

4   Compare and contrast the three types of business entities.

- A sole proprietorship is owned by one person. The owner is legally responsible for the debts and taxes of the business.
- A partnership is owned by two or more people. The owners are legally responsible for the debts and taxes of the business.
- A corporation is a separate legal entity from its owners.
- Note that all three types of business entities are considered separate entities for accounting purposes.

5   Describe the process used to develop generally accepted accounting principles.

- The SEC has delegated the authority to develop generally accepted accounting principles to the accounting profession. The Financial Accounting Standards Board handles this task. A series of steps used by the FASB includes issuing a discussion memorandum, an exposure draft, and a statement of principle.
- The SEC oversees the Public Company Accounting Oversight Board that was created by the Sarbanes-Oxley Act. The Board regulates financial reporting by accountants and auditors of publicly held companies.
- Each year firms that sell stock on stock exchanges or in over-the-counter markets must publish audited financial reports that follow generally accepted accounting principles. They must submit their reports to the Securities and Exchange Commission. They must also make the reports available to stockholders.

6   Define the accounting terms new to this chapter.

Glossary

Accounting (p. 4) The process by which financial information about a business is recorded, classified, summarized, interpreted, and communicated to owners, managers, and other interested parties

Accounting system (p. 4) A process designed to accumulate, classify, and summarize financial data

Auditing (p. 5) The review of financial statements to assess their fairness and adherence to generally accepted accounting principles

Auditor's report (p. 13) An independent accountant's review of a firm's financial statements

Certified public accountant (CPA) (p. 5) An independent accountant who provides accounting services to the public for a fee

Corporation (p. 11) A publicly or privately owned business entity that is separate from its owners and has a legal right to own property and do business in its own name; stockholders are not responsible for the debts or taxes of the business

Creditor (p. 10) One to whom money is owed

Discussion memorandum (p. 13) An explanation of a topic under consideration by the Financial Accounting Standards Board

Economic entity (p. 10) A business or organization whose major purpose is to produce a profit for its owners

Entity (p. 10) Anything having its own separate identity, such as an individual, a town, a university, or a business

Exposure draft (p. 13) A proposed solution to a problem being considered by the Financial Accounting Standards Board

Financial statements (p. 5) Periodic reports of a firm's financial position or operating results

Generally accepted accounting principles (GAAP) (p. 12) Accounting standards developed and applied by professional accountants

Governmental accounting (p. 6) Accounting work performed for a federal, state, or local governmental unit

International accounting (p. 13) The study of accounting principles used by different countries

Management advisory services (p. 5) Services designed to help clients improve their information systems or their business performance

Managerial accounting (p. 6) Accounting work carried on by an accountant employed by a single business in industry

Partnership (p. 11) A business entity owned by two or more people who are legally responsible for the debts and taxes of the business

Public accountants (p. 5) Members of firms that perform accounting services for other companies

Separate entity assumption (p. 11) The concept of keeping a firm's financial records separate from the owner's personal financial records

Social entity (p. 10) A nonprofit organization, such as a city, public school, or public hospital

Sole proprietorship (p. 10) A business entity owned by one person who is legally responsible for the debts and taxes of the business

Statements of Financial Accounting Standards (p. 13) Accounting principles established by the Financial Accounting Standards Board

Stock (p. 11) Certificates that represent ownership of a corporation

Stockholders (p. 12) The owners of a corporation; also called shareholders

Tax accounting (p. 5) A service that involves tax compliance and tax planning

Comprehensive **Self Review**

1. What are the three types of business entities?
2. What does the accounting process involve?
3. How is the ownership of a corporation different from that of a sole proprietorship?
4. What is the purpose of accounting?
5. What is the purpose of the auditor's report?

(Answers to Comprehensive Self Review are on page 20.)

Discussion Questions

1. What is the purpose of the Public Company Accounting Oversight Board?
2. What led to the passage of the Public Company Accounting Reform and Investor Protection Act of 2002?
3. What are the major functions or activities performed by accountants in private industry?
4. What is tax planning?
5. What types of services do public accountants provide?
6. What are the three major areas of accounting?
7. What groups consistently offer opinions about proposed FASB statements?
8. What is the purpose of the Financial Accounting Standards Board?
9. Why is it important for business records to be separate from the records of the business's owner or owners? What is the term accountants use to describe this separation of personal and business records?
10. What are the three types of business entities, and how do they differ?
11. What is the function of the Securities and Exchange Commission?
12. What types of people or organizations are interested in financial information about a firm, and why are they interested in this information?

 Multiple choice questions are provided on the text Web site at www.mhhe.com/price12e

Quiz1

PROBLEM

Critical Thinking Problem

Which Type of Business Entity?

Since graduating from college five years ago, Ned Turner has worked for a national chain of men's clothing stores. Ned has held several positions with the company and is currently manager of a local branch store.

Over the past three years, Ned has observed a pattern in men who purchase suits. He believes that the majority of men's suit purchases are black, brown, blue, gray, and olive. He also notices that French cuff shirts are quite fashionable, but few stores carry a wide color selection. Since he has always wanted to be in business for himself, Ned's idea is to open a shop that sells suits that are black, brown, blue, gray, and olive and to carry a wide array of colors of French cuff shirts. The store will also sell fashionable ties and cuff links. Ned already has a name for his store, The Three B's and Go Suit Shop. Ned has discussed his plan with a number of people in the industry and they believe his idea is a viable one.

A new upscale shopping mall is opening nearby and Ned has decided that now is the time to take the plunge and go into business for himself. Ned plans to open the Three B's and Go Suit shop in the new mall.

One of the things Ned must decide in the process of transforming his idea to reality is the form of ownership for his new business. Should it be organized as a sole proprietorship, a partnership, or a corporation?

What advice would you give Ned? What advantages and disadvantages are there to each choice? The following diagram will help you organize your thoughts.

Business Entity	Advantages	Disadvantages
Sole Proprietorship		
Partnership		
Corporation		

BUSINESS CONNECTIONS

Know Accounting

1. Why is financial information important?

2. What is the role of the manager versus the accountant?

3. What would you tell a small business owner who says he does not see a need for an accounting system in his business because he closely supervises the day-to-day operations and knows exactly what is happening with the business?

4. As an owner or manager of a business, what questions would you ask to judge the firm's performance, control operations, make decisions, and plan for the future?

5. Besides earning a profit, what other objectives might a business have? Can financial information play an important role in these objectives?

6. What kind of problems can you foresee if a business owner and/or manager does not have a basic knowledge of accounting?

7. Why are international accounting standards important to management?

8. Does a business owner/manager need to worry about the separate entity assumption? Why or why not?

To Tell or Not to Tell

You are employed as an accountant for ABC Computers. Your company is in the process of signing a large contract with an electronics components supplier. You have a personal friend that works for the electronics components supplier, and you have personal knowledge that they have trouble paying their bills. Should you report this to your employer before the purchase?

Information

Refer to The Home Depot, Inc. *2006 Annual Report* in Appendix A.

1. Review the letter written by Francis S. Blake, Chairman and Chief Executive Officer. To what audiences is the letter directed? Describe the types of financial information presented in the letter. Why would this information be important to readers?

2. Information provided in a company's annual report can also include nonfinancial strategies for merchandising, customer service, or new ventures. Based on the letter presented from The Home Depot, Inc.'s chairman and CEO, describe two successful strategies that the company implemented in 2006.

Notes to Financial Statements

Within a company's annual report, a section called "Notes to Consolidated Financial Statements" offers general information about the company along with detailed notes related to its financial statements. An excerpt from American Eagle Outfitters, Inc.'s, "Notes to Consolidated Financial Statements," *2006 Annual Report,* is presented below.

> American Eagle Outfitters designs, markets and sells its own brand of laidback, current clothing targeting 15- to-25-year-olds, providing high-quality merchandise at affordable prices. The Company opened its first American Eagle Outfitters store in the United States in 1977 and expanded the brand into Canada in 2001. American Eagle also distributes merchandise via its e-commerce operation, ae.com, which offers additional sizes, colors and styles of favorite AE merchandise and ships to 41 countries around the world. AE's original collection includes standards like jeans and graphic Ts as well as essentials like accessories, outerwear, footwear, basics and swimwear under our American Eagle Outfitters, American Eagle and AE brand names. During Fiscal 2006, American Eagle launched its new intimates sub-brand, *airie* by American Eagle. The *aerie* collection of dorm wear and intimates includes bras, undies, camis, hoodies, robes, boxers and sweats for the AE girl.

Analyze:

1. Would American Eagle Outfitters, Inc., be considered an economic entity or a social entity? Why?

2. What types of merchandise does this company sell?

3. Who are the potential users of the information presented? Why would this information be helpful to these users?

Analyze Online: On the American Eagle Outfitters, Inc., Web site (www.ae.com), click on About AE located at the bottom of the page. Then click on AE Investment Info.

4. What age consumer does the company target?

5. What types of merchandise does the company offer? Has the merchandise selection changed from the merchandise described in the *2006 Annual Report?*

6. What information is offered to the shareholder on the Web site?

Independent Auditor

Why does a certified public accountant (CPA) need to be independent? What situations might affect a CPA's independence?

Extending | THE THOUGHT

Memo

As the manager of the accounting department, you have been asked by the human resources director to help prepare a job description for a job opening in your department. The company wishes to fill the position of bookkeeper. The heading of your memo should include the following:

Business | COMMUNICATION

Date:
To:
From:
Subject:

The body of your memo should include the job responsibilities and the training and experience necessary for the position.

Determining Information

Palfreyman Mattress Company is planning to expand into selling bedroom furniture. This expansion will require a loan from the bank. The bank has requested financial information. Discuss, in a group, the information the bank would require. What information, if any, would you not provide the bank?

TEAMWORK |

FASB—What is it?

Go to the FASB Web site at www.FASB.org. The FASB pronouncements are listed. How many FASB pronouncements are currently listed? How are they listed?

Internet | CONNECTION

Answers to **Self Reviews**

Answers to Section 1 Self Review

1. Clerk, bookkeeper, and accountant.

2. The results of the accounting process—financial statements—communicate essential information about a business to concerned individuals and organizations.

3. Periodic reports that summarize the financial affairs of a business.

4. **c.** Uniform CPA Examination

5. **a.** Securities and Exchange Commission

6. Current sales and expenses figures, anticipated sales and expenses, and the cost of the expansion.

Answers to Section 2 Self Review

1. Accounting standards that are changed and refined in response to changes in the environment in which businesses operate.
2. GAAP help to ensure that financial information fairly presents a firm's operating results and financial position.
3. The FASB develops proposed statements and solicits feedback from interested individuals, groups, and companies. The FASB evaluates the opinions received and votes on the statement.
4. **b.** partnership
5. **c.** social entity
6. The shareholders are not responsible for the debts and taxes of the corporation. Corporations can continue in existence indefinitely.

Answers to Comprehensive Self Review

1. Sole proprietorship, partnership, and corporation.
2. Recording, classifying, summarizing, interpreting, and communicating financial information about a business.
3. A sole proprietorship is a business entity owned by one person. A corporation is a separate legal entity that has a legal right to own property and do business in its own name.
4. To gather and communicate financial information about a business.
5. To obtain the objective opinion of a professional accountant from outside the company that the statements fairly present the operating results and financial position of the business and that the information was prepared according to GAAP.

Analyzing Business Transactions

LEARNING OBJECTIVES

1. Record in equation form the financial effects of a business transaction. LP2

2. Define, identify, and understand the relationship between asset, liability, and owner's equity accounts.

3. Analyze the effects of business transactions on a firm's assets, liabilities, and owner's equity and record these effects in accounting equation form.

4. Prepare an income statement.

5. Prepare a statement of owner's equity and a balance sheet.

6. Define the accounting terms new to this chapter.

NEW TERMS

accounts payable
accounts receivable
assets
balance sheet
break even
business transaction
capital
equity
expense
fair market value
fundamental accounting equation

income statement
liabilities
net income
net loss
on account
owner's equity
revenue
statement of owner's equity
withdrawals

www.southwest.com

Rollin King and Herb Kelleher had a simple notion when they got into the airline business: If you get your passengers to their destinations when they want to get there, on time, at the lowest possible fares, and make darn sure they have a good time doing it, people will fly your airline. What began as a small Texas airline has grown to become one of the largest airlines in America. Today, Southwest Airlines flies almost 100 million passengers a year to 63 cities all across the country.

In an economy where airlines struggle to stay out of bankruptcy, Southwest has flourished. Other airlines have tried to imitate its business strategy of operating high-frequency point-to-point service routes, but none have been as successful as Southwest, thanks to the company's unique culture. Consistently voted as one of the top places to work, Southwest has established a culture that encourages employees and customers to have fun. From chili cook-offs to paper airplane contests and dance competitions, you never know what might happen when you board a Southwest flight but you know you'll have a good time.

thinking critically

How can a company's corporate culture affect net profits and the company's bottom line?

SECTION OBJECTIVES

>> 1. **Record in equation form the financial effects of a business transaction.**

   WHY IT'S IMPORTANT
   Learning the fundamental accounting equation is a basis for understanding business transactions.

>> 2. **Define, identify, and understand the relationship between asset, liability, and owner's equity accounts.**

   WHY IT'S IMPORTANT
   The relationship between assets, liabilities, and owner's equity is the basis for the entire accounting system.

TERMS TO LEARN

accounts payable
assets
balance sheet
business transaction
capital
equity
liabilities
on account
owner's equity

Property and Financial Interest

The accounting process starts with the analysis of business transactions. A **business transaction** is any financial event that changes the resources of a firm. For example, purchases, sales, payments, and receipts of cash are all business transactions. The accountant analyzes each business transaction to decide what information to record and where to record it.

>> **1. OBJECTIVE**

Record in equation form the financial effects of a business transaction.

LP2

Beginning with Analysis

Let's analyze the transactions of Wells' Consulting Services, a firm that provides a wide range of accounting and consulting services. Carolyn Wells, CPA, has a master's degree in accounting. She is the sole proprietor of Wells' Consulting Services. Carlos Valdez, the office manager, has an associate's degree in business and has taken 12 semester hours of accounting. The firm is located in a large office complex.

Every month Wells' Consulting Services bills clients for the accounting and consulting services provided that month. Customers can also pay in cash when the services are rendered.

STARTING A BUSINESS

Let's start from the beginning. Carolyn Wells obtained the funds to start the business by withdrawing $100,000 from her personal savings account. The first transaction of the new business was opening a checking account in the name of Wells' Consulting Services. The separate bank account helps Wells keep her financial interest in the business separate from her personal funds.

When a business transaction occurs, it is analyzed to identify how it affects the equation *property equals financial interest*. This equation reflects the fact that in a free enterprise system, all property is owned by someone. In this case, Wells owns the business because she supplied the property (cash).

Use these steps to analyze the effect of a business transaction:

1. Describe the financial event.
   - Identify the property.
   - Identify who owns the property.
   - Determine the amount of increase or decrease.

2. Make sure the equation is in balance.

Property	=	Financial Interest

BUSINESS TRANSACTION

Carolyn Wells withdrew $100,000 from personal savings and deposited it in a new checking account in the name of Wells' Consulting Services.

ANALYSIS

a. The business received $100,000 of *property* in the form of cash.

b. Wells had a $100,000 *financial interest* in the business.

Note that the equation *property equals financial interest* remains in balance.

Property		=	Financial Interest
	Cash	=	Carolyn Wells, Capital
(a) Invested cash	+**$100,000**		
(b) Increased equity			+**$100,000**
New balances	$100,000	=	$100,000

An owner's financial interest in the business is called **equity,** or **capital.** Carolyn Wells has $100,000 equity in Wells' Consulting Services.

PURCHASING EQUIPMENT FOR CASH

The first priority for office manager Carlos Valdez was to get the business ready for opening day on December 1.

BUSINESS TRANSACTION

Wells' Consulting Services issued a $5,000 check to purchase a computer and other equipment.

ANALYSIS

c. The firm purchased new property (equipment) for $5,000.

d. The firm paid out $5,000 in cash.

The equation remains in balance.

Property			=	Financial Interest
	Cash	+ Equipment	=	Carolyn Wells, Capital
Previous balances	$100,000		=	$100,000
(c) Purchased equipment		+ $5,000		
(d) Paid cash	−5,000			
New balances	$95,000 +	$5,000	=	$100,000

Notice that there is a change in the composition of the firm's property. Now the firm has cash and equipment. The equation shows that the total value of the property remains the same, $100,000. Carolyn Wells' financial interest, or equity, is also unchanged. Note that property (Cash and Equipment) is equal to financial interest (Carolyn Wells, Capital).

These activities are recorded for the business entity Wells' Consulting Services. Carolyn Wells' personal assets, such as her personal bank account, house, furniture, and automobile, are kept separate from the property of the firm. Nonbusiness property is not included in the accounting records of the business entity.

PURCHASING EQUIPMENT ON CREDIT

Valdez purchased additional office equipment. Office Plus, the store selling the equipment, allows Wells' Consulting Services 60 days to pay the bill. This arrangement is called buying **on account.** The business has a *charge account,* or *open-account credit,* with its suppliers. Amounts that a business must pay in the future are known as **accounts payable.** The companies or individuals to whom the amounts are owed are called *creditors.*

BUSINESS TRANSACTION

Wells' Consulting Services purchased office equipment on account from Office Plus for $6,000.

ANALYSIS

e. The firm purchased new property (equipment) that cost $6,000.

f. The firm owes $6,000 to Office Plus.

The equation remains in balance.

	Property		=	Financial Interest		
	Cash	+ Equipment	=	Accounts Payable	+	Carolyn Wells, Capital
Previous balances	$95,000	+ $5,000	=			$100,000
(e) Purchased equip.		+ 6,000	=			
(f) Incurred debt				+$6,000		
New balances	$95,000	+ $11,000	=	$6,000	+	$100,000

Office Plus is willing to accept a claim against Wells' Consulting Services until the bill is paid. Now there are two different financial interests or claims against the firm's property—the creditor's claim (Accounts Payable) and the owner's claim (Carolyn Wells, Capital). Notice that the total property increases to $106,000. Cash is $95,000 and equipment is $11,000. Carolyn Wells, Capital stays the same; but the creditor's claim increases to $6,000. After this transaction is recorded, the left side of the equation still equals the right side.

When Ben Cohen and Jerry Greenfield founded Ben & Jerry's Homemade Ice Cream, Inc., in 1978, they invested $8,000 of their own funds and borrowed funds of $4,000. The equation *property equals financial interest* is expressed as

Property	=	**Financial Interest**
cash	=	creditors' claims
		+ owners' claims
$12,000	=	$ 4,000
		+ 8,000
		$12,000

PURCHASING SUPPLIES

Valdez purchased supplies so that Wells' Consulting Services could start operations. The company that sold the items requires cash payments from companies that have been in business less than six months.

BUSINESS TRANSACTION

Wells' Consulting Services issued a check for $1,500 to Office Delux, Inc., to purchase office supplies.

ANALYSIS

g. The firm purchased office supplies that cost $1,500.

h. The firm paid $1,500 in cash.

The equation remains in balance.

	Property					=	**Financial Interest**		
	Cash	+	**Supplies**	+	**Equipment**	=	**Accounts Payable**	+	**Carolyn Wells, Capital**
Previous balances	$95,000			+	$11,000	=	$6,000	+	$100,000
(g) Purchased supplies		+	$1,500						
(h) Paid cash	−$1,500								
New balances	$93,500	+	$1,500	+	$11,000	=	$6,000	+	$100,000

Notice that total property remains the same, even though the form of the property has changed. Also note that all of the property (left side) equals all of the financial interests (right side).

PAYING A CREDITOR

Valdez decided to reduce the firm's debt to Office Plus by $2,500.

BUSINESS TRANSACTION

Wells' Consulting Services issued a check for $2,500 to Office Plus.

ANALYSIS

i. The firm paid $2,500 in cash.

j. The claim of Office Plus against the firm decreased by $2,500.

The equation remains in balance.

	Property					=	Financial Interest		
	Cash	+	**Supplies**	+	**Equipment**	=	**Accounts Payable**	+	**Carolyn Wells, Capital**
Previous balances	$93,500	+	$1,500	+	$11,000	=	$6,000	+	$100,000
(i) Paid cash	**−$2,500**								
(j) Decreased debt							**−$2,500**		
New balances	$91,000	+	$1,500	+	$11,000	=	$3,500	+	$100,000

RENTING FACILITIES

In November, Valdez arranged to rent facilities for $4,000 per month, beginning in December. The landlord required that rent for the first two months—December and January—be paid in advance. The firm prepaid (paid in advance) the rent for two months. As a result, the firm obtained the right to occupy facilities for a two-month period. In accounting, this right is considered a form of property.

BUSINESS TRANSACTION

Wells' Consulting Services issued a check for $8,000 to pay for rent for the months of December and January.

ANALYSIS

k. The firm prepaid the rent for the next two months in the amount of $8,000.

l. The firm decreased its cash balance by $8,000.

The equation remains in balance.

	Property							=	Financial Interest		
	Cash	+	**Supplies**	+	**Prepaid Rent**	+	**Equipment**	=	**Accounts Payable**	+	**Carolyn Wells, Capital**
Previous balances	$91,000	+	$1,500			+	$11,000	=	$3,500	+	$100,000
(k) Paid cash	**−$8,000**										
(l) Prepaid rent					**+$8,000**						
New balances	$83,000	+	$1,500	+	$8,000	+	$11,000	=	$3,500	+	$100,000

Notice that when property values and financial interests increase or decrease, the total of the items on one side of the equation still equals the total on the other side.

Property		=	Financial Interest	
Cash	$ 83,000		Accounts Payable	$ 3,500
Supplies	1,500		Carolyn Wells, Capital	100,000
Prepaid Rent	8,000			
Equipment	11,000			
Total	$103,500		Total	$103,500

> The balance sheet is also called the *statement of financial position*. Caterpillar Inc. reported assets of $50.9 billion, liabilities of $44.0 billion, and owners' equity of $6.9 billion on its statement of financial position at December 31, 2006.

Assets, Liabilities, and Owner's Equity

Accountants use special accounting terms when they refer to property and financial interests. For example, they refer to the property that a business owns as **assets** and to the debts or obligations of the business as **liabilities.** The owner's financial interest is called **owner's equity.** (Sometimes owner's equity is called *proprietorship* or *net worth.* Owner's equity is the preferred term and is used throughout this book.) At regular intervals, Wells reviews the status of the firm's assets, liabilities, and owner's equity in a financial statement called a **balance sheet.** The balance sheet shows the firm's financial position on a given date. Figure 2.1 shows the firm's balance sheet on November 30, the day before the company opened for business.

The assets are listed on the left side of the balance sheet and the liabilities and owner's equity are on the right side. This arrangement is similar to the equation *property equals financial interest.* Property is shown on the left side of the equation, and financial interest appears on the right side.

The balance sheet in Figure 2.1 shows

- the amount and types of property the business owns,
- the amount owed to creditors,
- the owner's interest.

This statement gives Carolyn Wells a complete picture of the financial position of her business on November 30.

>> 2. OBJECTIVE
Define, identify, and understand the relationship between asset, liability, and owner's equity accounts.

LP2

FIGURE 2.1   Balance Sheet for Wells' Consulting Services

Wells' Consulting Services				
Balance Sheet				
November 30, 2010				
Assets		**Liabilities**		
Cash	83 0 0 0 00	Accounts Payable		3 5 0 0 00
Supplies	1 5 0 0 00			
Prepaid Rent	8 0 0 0 00	**Owner's Equity**		
Equipment	11 0 0 0 00	Carolyn Wells, Capital		100 0 0 0 00
Total Assets	103 5 0 0 00	Total Liabilities and Owner's Equity		103 5 0 0 00

Section **1** Self Review

QUESTIONS

1. Describe a transaction that increases an asset and the owner's equity.

2. What does the term "accounts payable" mean?

3. What is a business transaction?

EXERCISES

4. John Amos began a new business by depositing $75,000 in the business bank account. He wrote two checks from the business account: $12,000 for office furniture and $4,000 for office supplies. What is his financial interest in the company?

a. $61,000

b. $59,000

c. $63,000

d. $75,000

5. Teresa Wells purchased a computer for $3,250 on account for her business. What is the effect of this transaction?

a. Equipment increase of $3,250 and accounts payable increase of $3,250.

b. Equipment decrease of $3,250 and accounts payable increase of $3,250.

c. Equipment increase of $3,250 and cash increase of $3,250.

d. Cash decrease of $3,250 and owner's equity increase of $3,250.

ANALYSIS

6. Specialty Import Co. has no liabilities. The asset and owner's equity balances are as follows. What is the balance of "Supplies"?

Cash	$25,000
Office Equipment	$15,000
Supplies	????
Jason Odgen, Capital	$50,000

(Answers to Section 1 Self Review are on page 51.)

SECTION OBJECTIVES

>> 3. **Analyze the effects of business transactions on a firm's assets, liabilities, and owner's equity and record these effects in accounting equation form.**

WHY IT'S IMPORTANT

Property will always equal financial interest.

>> 4. **Prepare an income statement.**

WHY IT'S IMPORTANT

The income statement shows the results of operations.

>> 5. **Prepare a statement of owner's equity and a balance sheet.**

WHY IT'S IMPORTANT

These financial statements show the financial condition of a business.

TERMS TO LEARN

accounts receivable

break even

expense

fair market value

fundamental accounting equation

income statement

net income

net loss

revenue

statement of owner's equity

withdrawals

The Accounting Equation and Financial Statements

The word *balance* in the title "balance sheet" has a special meaning. It emphasizes that the total on the left side of the report must equal, or balance, the total on the right side.

The Fundamental Accounting Equation

In accounting terms, the firm's assets must equal the total of its liabilities and owner's equity. This equality can be expressed in equation form, as illustrated here. The amounts are for Wells' Consulting Services on November 30.

Assets	=	Liabilities	+	Owner's Equity
$103,500	=	$3,500	+	$100,000

The relationship between assets and liabilities plus owner's equity is called the **fundamental accounting equation.** The entire accounting process of analyzing, recording, and reporting business transactions is based on the fundamental accounting equation.

If any two parts of the equation are known, the third part can be determined. For example, consider the basic accounting equation for Wells' Consulting Services on November 30, with some information missing.

	Assets	=	Liabilities	+	Owner's Equity
1.	?	=	$3,500	+	$100,000
2.	$103,500	=	?	+	$100,000
3.	$103,000	=	$3,500	+	?

In the first case, we can solve for assets by adding liabilities to owner's equity ($3,500 + $100,000) to determine that assets are $103,500. In the second case, we can solve for liabilities by subtracting owner's equity from assets ($103,500 − $100,000) to determine that liabilities are $3,500. In the third case, we can solve for owner's equity by subtracting liabilities from assets ($103,500 − $3,500) to determine that owner's equity is $100,000.

>> **3. OBJECTIVE**

Analyze the effects of business transactions on a firm's assets, liabilities, and owner's equity and record these effects in accounting equation form.

LP2

important!

Revenues increase owner's equity.

Expenses decrease owner's equity.

EARNING REVENUE AND INCURRING EXPENSES

Wells' Consulting Services opened for business on December 1. Some of the other businesses in the office complex became the firm's first clients. Wells also used her contacts in the community to identify other clients. Providing services to clients started a stream of revenue for the business. **Revenue,** or *income,* is the inflow of money or other assets that results from the sales of goods or services or from the use of money or property. A sale on account does not increase money, but it does create a claim to money. When a sale occurs, the revenue increases assets and also increases owner's equity.

An **expense,** on the other hand, involves the outflow of money, the use of other assets, or the incurring of a liability. Expenses include the costs of any materials, labor, supplies, and services used to produce revenue. Expenses cause a decrease in owner's equity.

A firm's accounting records show increases and decreases in assets, liabilities, and owner's equity as well as details of all transactions involving revenue and expenses. Let's use the fundamental accounting equation to show how revenue and expenses affect the business.

SELLING SERVICES FOR CASH

During the month of December, Wells' Consulting Services earned a total of $36,000 in revenue from clients who paid cash for accounting and bookkeeping services. This involved several transactions throughout the month. The total effect of these transactions is analyzed below.

ANALYSIS

m. The firm received $36,000 in cash for services provided to clients.

n. Revenues increased by $36,000, which results in a $36,000 increase in owner's equity. The fundamental accounting equation remains in balance.

	Assets							=	Liabilities	+	Owner's Equity		
	Cash	+	Supplies	+	Prepaid Rent	+	Equipment	=	Accounts Payable	+	Carolyn Wells, Capital	+	Revenue
Previous balances	$ 83,000	+	$1,500	+	$8,000	+	$11,000	=	$3,500	+	$100,000		
(m) Received cash	+**$36,000**												
(n) Increased owner's equity by earning revenue												+	**$36,000**
New balances	$119,000	+	$1,500	+	$8,000	+	$11,000	=	$3,500	+	$100,000	+	$36,000
				$139,500							$139,500		

Notice that revenue amounts are recorded in a separate column under owner's equity. Keeping revenue separate from the owner's equity will help the firm compute total revenue more easily when the financial statements are prepared.

SELLING SERVICES ON CREDIT

Wells' Consulting Services has some charge account clients. These clients are allowed 30 days to pay. Amounts owed by these clients are known as **accounts receivable.** This is a new form of asset for the firm—claims for future collection from customers. During December, Wells' Consulting Services earned $11,000 of revenue from charge account clients. The effect of these transactions is analyzed on page 31.

ANALYSIS

o. The firm acquired a new asset, accounts receivable, of $11,000.

p. Revenues increased by $11,000, which results in an $11,000 increase in owner's equity.

The fundamental accounting equation remains in balance.

	Assets								=	Liab.	+	Owner's Equity		
	Cash	+	Accts. Rec.	+	Supp.	+	Prepaid Rent	+	Equip.	=	Accts. Pay.	+	Carolyn Wells, Capital	+	Rev.
Previous balances	$119,000			+	$1,500	+	$8,000	+	$11,000	=	$3,500	+	$100,000	+	$36,000
(o) Received new asset—accts. rec.		+$11,000													
(p) Increased owner's equity by earning revenue														+	$11,000
New balances	$119,000	+$11,000	+	$1,500	+	$8,000	+	$11,000	=	$3,500	+	$100,000	+	$47,000
		$150,500										$150,500			

COLLECTING RECEIVABLES

During December, Wells' Consulting Services received $6,000 on account from clients who owed money for services previously billed. The effect of these transactions is analyzed below.

ANALYSIS

q. The firm received $6,000 in cash.

r. Accounts receivable decreased by $6,000.

The fundamental accounting equation remains in balance.

	Assets								=	Liab.	+	Owner's Equity		
	Cash	+	Accts. Rec.	+	Supp.	+	Prepaid Rent	+	Equip.	=	Accts. Pay.	+	Carolyn Wells, Capital	+	Rev.
Previous balances	$119,000	+	$11,000	+	$1,500	+	$8,000	+	$11,000	=	$3,500	+	$100,000	+	$47,000
(q) Received cash	+$6,000														
(r) Decreased accounts receivable		−$6,000													
New balances	$125,000	+	$5,000	+	$1,500	+	$8,000	+	$11,000	=	$3,500	+	$100,000	+	$47,000
		$150,500										$150,500			

In this type of transaction, one asset is changed for another asset (accounts receivable for cash). Notice that revenue is not increased when cash is collected from charge account clients. The revenue was recorded when the sale on account took place (see entry (**p**)). Notice that the fundamental accounting equation, *assets equal liabilities plus owner's equity,* stays in balance regardless of the changes arising from individual transactions.

PAYING EMPLOYEES' SALARIES

So far Wells has done very well. Her equity has increased by the revenues earned. However, running a business costs money, and these expenses reduce owner's equity.

During the first month of operations, Wells' Consulting Services hired an accounting clerk. The salaries for the new accounting clerk and the office manager are considered an expense to the firm.

BUSINESS TRANSACTION

In December, Wells' Consulting Services paid $8,000 in salaries for the accounting clerk and Carlos Valdez.

ANALYSIS

s. The firm decreased its cash balance by $8,000.

t. The firm paid salaries expense in the amount of $8,000, which decreased owner's equity.

The fundamental accounting equation remains in balance.

	Assets					=	Liab. +		Owner's Equity		
	Cash +	Accts. Rec. +	Supp. +	Prepaid Rent +	Equip. =		Accts. Pay. +	Carolyn Wells, Capital	+	Rev. –	Exp.
Previous balances	$125,000 +	$5,000 +	$1,500 +	$8,000 +	$11,000 =		$3,500 +	$100,000	+	$47,000	
(s) Paid cash	−$8,000										
(t) Decreased owner's equity by incurring salaries exp.											+ $8,000
New balances	$117,000 +	$5,000 +	$1,500 +	$8,000 +	$11,000 =		$3,500 +	$100,000	+	$47,000 –	$8,000

$142,500 = $142,500

Notice that expenses are recorded in a separate column under owner's equity. The separate record of expenses is kept for the same reason that the separate record of revenue is kept—to analyze operations for the period.

PAYING UTILITIES EXPENSE

At the end of December, the firm received a $650 utilities bill.

BUSINESS TRANSACTION

Wells' Consulting Services issued a check for $650 to pay the utilities bill.

ANALYSIS

u. The firm decreased its cash balance by $650.

v. The firm paid utilities expense of $650, which decreased owner's equity.

The fundamental accounting equation remains in balance.

	Assets						=	Liab.	+	Owner's Equity			
	Cash	+	Accts. Rec.	+ Supp.	+	Prepaid Rent	+ Equip.	=	Accts. Pay.	+	C. Wells, Capital	+ Rev.	− Exp.
Previous balances	$117,000	+	$5,000	+ $1,500	+	$8,000	+ $11,000	=	$3,500	+	$100,000	+ $47,000	− $8,000
(u) Paid cash	**−$650**												
(v) Decreased owner's equity by utilities exp.													+ **$650**
New balances	$116,350	+	$5,000	+ $1,500	+	$8,000	+ $11,000	=	$3,500	+	$100,000	+ $47,000	− $8,650

$141,850 $141,850

EFFECT OF OWNER'S WITHDRAWALS

On December 30, Wells withdrew $5,000 in cash for personal expenses. **Withdrawals** are funds taken from the business by the owner for personal use. Withdrawals are not a business expense but a decrease in the owner's equity.

BUSINESS TRANSACTION

Carolyn Wells wrote a check to withdraw $5,000 cash for personal use.

ANALYSIS
w. The firm decreased its cash balance by $5,000.
x. Owner's equity decreased by $5,000.
The fundamental accounting equation remains in balance.

	Assets						=	Liab.	+	Owner's Equity			
	Cash	+	Accts. Rec.	+ Supp.	+	Prepaid Rent	+ Equip.	=	Accts. Pay.	+	Carolyn Wells, Capital	+ Rev.	− Exp.
Previous balances	$116,350	+	$5,000	+ $1,500	+	$8,000	+ $11,000	=	$3,500	+	$100,000	+ $47,000	− $8,650
(w) Withdrew cash	**−$5,000**												
(x) Decreased owner's equity											− **$5,000**		
New balances	$111,350	+	$5,000	+ $1,500	+	$8,000	+ $11,000	=	$3,500	+	$95,000	+ $47,000	− $8,650

$136,850 $136,850

SUMMARY OF TRANSACTIONS

Figure 2.2 on page 34 summarizes the transactions of Wells' Consulting Services through December 31. Notice that after each transaction, the fundamental accounting equation is in balance. Test your understanding by describing the nature of each transaction. Then check your results by referring to the discussion of each transaction.

		Assets					=	Liab.	+	Owner's Equity		
	Cash	+ Accts. Rec.	+ Supp.	+ Prepaid Rent	+ Equip.	=	Accts. Pay.	+	C. Wells, Capital	+ Rev.	− Exp.
(a) & (b)	+$100,000								+ $100,000		
Balances	100,000					=			100,000		
(c) & (d)	−5,000			+ $5,000							
Balances	95,000			+ 5,000		=			100,000		
(e) & (f)					+ 6,000		+ $6,000				
Balances	95,000				+ 11,000	=	6,000	+	100,000		
(g) & (h)	−1,500	+ $1,500									
Balances	93,500	+ 1,500			+ 11,000	=	6,000	+	100,000		
(i) & (j)	−2,500						−2,500				
Balances	91,000	+ 1,500			+ 11,000	=	3,500	+	100,000		
(k) & (l)	−8,000		+ $8,000								
Balances	83,000	+ 1,500	+ 8,000		+ 11,000	=	3,500	+	100,000		
(m) & (n)	+36,000									+ $36,000	
Balances	119,000	+ 1,500	+ 8,000		+ 11,000	=	3,500	+	100,000	+ 36,000	
(o) & (p)		+ $11,000								+ 11,000	
Balances	119,000	+ 11,000	+ 1,500		+ 8,000 + 11,000	=	3,500	+	100,000	+ 47,000	
(q) & (r)	+6,000	− 6,000									
Balances	125,000	+ 5,000	+ 1,500		+ 8,000 + 11,000	=	3,500	+	100,000	+ 47,000	
(s) & (t)	−8,000										+ $8,000
Balances	117,000	+ 5,000	+ 1,500		+ 8,000 + 11,000	=	3,500	+	100,000	+ 47,000	− 8,000
(u) & (v)	−650										+ 650
Balances	116,350	+ 5,000	+ 1,500		+ 8,000 + 11,000	=	3,500	+	100,000	+ 47,000	− 8,650
(w) & (x)	−5,000								− 5,000		
Balances	$111,350	+ $5,000	+ $1,500	+ $8,000	+ $11,000	=	$3,500	+	$95,000	+ $47,000	− $8,650

$136,850 = $136,850

FIGURE 2.2

Transactions of Wells' Consulting Services Through December 31, 2010

>> **4. OBJECTIVE**

Prepare an income statement.

recall

Financial Statements

Financial statements are reports that summarize a firm's financial affairs.

The Income Statement

To be meaningful to owners, managers, and other interested parties, financial statements should provide information about revenue and expenses, assets and claims on the assets, and owner's equity.

The **income statement** shows the results of business operations for a specific period of time such as a month, a quarter, or a year. The income statement shows the revenue earned and the expenses of doing business. (The income statement is sometimes called a *profit and loss statement* or a *statement of income and expenses.* The most common term, income statement, is used throughout this text.) Figure 2.3 shows the income statement for Wells' Consulting Services for its first month of operation.

The income statement shows the difference between income from services provided or goods sold and the amount spent to operate the business. **Net income** results when revenue is greater than the expenses for the period. When expenses are greater than revenue, the result is a **net loss.** In the rare case when revenue and expenses are equal, the firm is said to **break even.** The income statement in Figure 2.3 shows a net income; revenue is greater than expenses.

The three-line heading of the income statement shows *who, what,* and *when.*

- Who—the business name appears on the first line.

FIGURE 2.3

**Income Statement for Wells'
Consulting Services**

Wells' Consulting Services					
Income Statement					
Month Ended December 31, 2010					
Revenue					
Fees Income				47 000 00	
Expenses					
Salaries Expense	8 000 00				
Utilities Expense	6 50 00				
Total Expenses			8 650 00		
Net Income			38 350 00		

- What—the report title appears on the second line.
- When—the period covered appears on the third line.

The third line of the income statement heading in Figure 2.3 indicates that the report covers operations for the "Month Ended December 31, 2010." Review how other time periods are reported on the third line of the income statement heading.

Period Covered	Third Line of Heading
Jan., Feb., Mar.	Three-Month Period Ended March 31, 2010
Jan. to Dec.	Year Ended December 31, 2010
July 1 to June 30	Fiscal Year Ended June 30, 2010

Note the use of single and double rules in amount columns. A single line is used to show that the amounts above it are being added or subtracted. Double lines are used under the final amount in a column or section of a report to show that the amount is complete. Nothing is added to or subtracted from an amount with a double line.

> Some companies refer to the income statement as the *statement of operations.*
> American Eagle Outfitters, Inc., reported $2.8 billion in sales on consolidated
> statements of operations for the fiscal year ended January 2007. American
> Eagle Outfitters, Inc., was ranked as the sixteenth fastest-growing company in the
> United States by *Fortune* magazine in September 2000.

The income statement for Wells' Consulting Services does not have dollar signs because it was prepared on accounting paper with ruled columns. However, dollar signs are used on income statements that are prepared on plain paper, that is, not on a ruled form.

The Statement of Owner's Equity and the Balance Sheet

The **statement of owner's equity** reports the changes that occurred in the owner's financial interest during the reporting period. This statement is prepared before the balance sheet so that the amount of the ending capital balance is available for presentation on the balance sheet. Figure 2.4 on page 36 shows the statement of owner's equity for Wells' Consulting Services. Note that the statement of owner's equity has a three-line heading: *who, what,* and *when.*

- The first line of the statement of owner's equity is the capital balance at the beginning of the period.
- Net income is an increase to owner's equity; net loss is a decrease to owner's equity.
- Withdrawals by the owner are a decrease to owner's equity.

>> 5. OBJECTIVE

Prepare a statement of owner's equity and a balance sheet.

FIGURE 2.4

Statement of Owner's Equity for Wells' Consulting Services

Wells' Consulting Services			
Statement of Owner's Equity			
Month Ended December 31, 2010			
Carolyn Wells, Capital, December 1, 2010			1 0 0 0 0 0 00
Net Income for December	3 8 3 5 0 00		
Less Withdrawals for December	5 0 0 0 00		
Increase in Capital			3 3 3 5 0 00
Carolyn Wells, Capital, December 31, 2010			1 3 3 3 5 0 00

▪ Additional investments by the owners are an increase to owner's equity.

▪ The total of changes in equity is reported on the line "Increase in Capital" (or "Decrease in Capital").

▪ The last line of the statement of owner's equity is the capital balance at the end of the period.

If Carolyn Wells had made any additional investments during December, this would appear as a separate line on Figure 2.4. Additional investments can be cash or other assets such as equipment. If an investment is made in a form other than cash, the investment is recorded at its fair market value. **Fair market value** is the current worth of an asset or the price the asset would bring if sold on the open market.

The ending balances in the asset and liability accounts are used to prepare the balance sheet.

	Assets					=	Liab.	+	Owner's Equity			
	Cash	+ Accts. Rec.	+ Supp.	+ Prepaid Rent	+ Equip.	=	Accts. Pay.	+	C. Wells, Capital	+ Rev.	− Exp.	
New balances	$111,350	+ $5,000	+ $1,500	+ $8,000	+ $11,000	=	$3,500	+	$95,000	+ $47,000	− $8,650	
	$136,850						$136,850					

important!

Financial Statements

The balance sheet is a snapshot of the firm's financial position on a specific date. The income statement, like a movie or video, shows the results of business operations over a period of time.

The ending capital balance from the statement of owner's equity is also used to prepare the balance sheet. Figure 2.5 on page 37 shows the balance sheet for Wells' Consulting Services on December 31, 2010.

The balance sheet shows

▪ Assets—the types and amounts of property that the business owns,

▪ Liabilities—the amounts owed to creditors,

▪ Owner's Equity—the owner's equity on the reporting date.

In preparing a balance sheet, remember the following.

▪ The three-line heading gives the firm's name (who), the title of the report (what), and the date of the report (when).

▪ Balance sheets prepared using the account form (as in Figure 2.5) show total assets on the same horizontal line as the total liabilities and owner's equity.

▪ Dollar signs are omitted when financial statements are prepared on paper with ruled columns. Statements that are prepared on plain paper, not ruled forms, show dollar signs with the first amount in each column and with each total.

▪ A single line shows that the amounts above it are being added or subtracted. Double lines indicate that the amount is the final amount in a column or section of a report.

Figure 2.6 on page 37 shows the connections among the financial statements. Financial statements are prepared in a specific order:

▪ income statement

▪ statement of owner's equity

▪ balance sheet

Wells' Consulting Services
Balance Sheet
December 31, 2010

Assets				Liabilities			
Cash	1 1 1 3 5 0	00		Accounts Payable		3 5 0 0	00
Accounts Receivables	5 0 0 0	00					
Supplies	1 5 0 0	00					
Prepaid Rent	8 0 0 0	00		Owner's Equity			
Equipment	1 1 0 0 0	00		Carolyn Wells, Capital		1 3 3 3 5 0	00
Total Assets	1 3 6 8 5 0	00		Total Liabilities and Owner's Equity		1 3 6 8 5 0	00

FIGURE 2.5   **Balance Sheet for Wells' Consulting Services**

Step 1:   Prepare the Income Statement

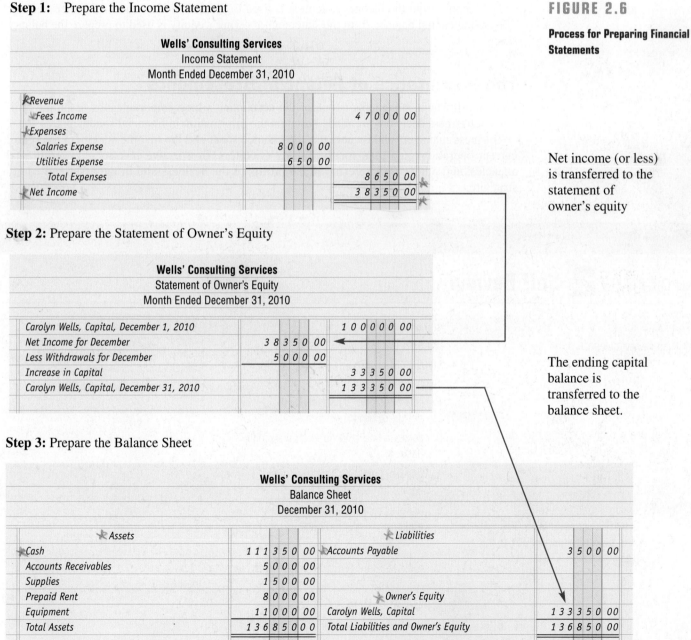

Wells' Consulting Services
Income Statement
Month Ended December 31, 2010

Revenue					
Fees Income				4 7 0 0 0	00
Expenses					
Salaries Expense	8 0 0 0	00			
Utilities Expense	6 5 0	00			
Total Expenses				8 6 5 0	00
Net Income				3 8 3 5 0	00

Step 2: Prepare the Statement of Owner's Equity

Wells' Consulting Services
Statement of Owner's Equity
Month Ended December 31, 2010

Carolyn Wells, Capital, December 1, 2010				1 0 0 0 0 0	00
Net Income for December	3 8 3 5 0	00			
Less Withdrawals for December	5 0 0 0	00			
Increase in Capital				3 3 3 5 0	00
Carolyn Wells, Capital, December 31, 2010				1 3 3 3 5 0	00

Step 3: Prepare the Balance Sheet

Wells' Consulting Services
Balance Sheet
December 31, 2010

Assets				Liabilities			
Cash	1 1 1 3 5 0	00		Accounts Payable		3 5 0 0	00
Accounts Receivables	5 0 0 0	00					
Supplies	1 5 0 0	00					
Prepaid Rent	8 0 0 0	00		Owner's Equity			
Equipment	1 1 0 0 0	00		Carolyn Wells, Capital		1 3 3 3 5 0	00
Total Assets	1 3 6 8 5 0 0 0			Total Liabilities and Owner's Equity		1 3 6 8 5 0	00

FIGURE 2.6

Process for Preparing Financial Statements

Net income (or less) is transferred to the statement of owner's equity

The ending capital balance is transferred to the balance sheet.

MANAGERIAL IMPLICATIONS

ACCOUNTING SYSTEMS

- Sound financial records and statements are necessary so that businesspeople can make good decisions.
- Financial statements show
  - the amount of profit or loss,
  - the assets on hand,
  - the amount owed to creditors,
  - the amount of owner's equity.

- Well-run and efficiently managed businesses have good accounting systems that provide timely and useful information.
- Transactions involving revenue and expenses are recorded separately from owner's equity in order to analyze operations for the period.

THINKING CRITICALLY

If you were buying a business, what would you look for in the company's financial statements?

Net income from the income statement is used to prepare the statement of owner's equity. The ending capital balance from the statement of owner's equity is used to prepare the balance sheet.

The Importance of Financial Statements

Preparing financial statements is one of the accountant's most important jobs. Each day millions of business decisions are made based on the information in financial statements.

Business managers and owners use the balance sheet and the income statement to control current operations and plan for the future. Creditors, prospective investors, governmental agencies, and others are interested in the profits of the business and in the asset and equity structure.

Section **2** Self Review

QUESTIONS

1. If an owner gives personal tools to the business, how is the transaction recorded?

2. What information is included in the financial statement headings?

3. What are withdrawals and how do they affect the basic accounting equation?

EXERCISES

4. Interior Designs has assets of $90,000 and liabilities of $35,000. What is the owner's equity?
   a. $25,000
   b. $15,000
   c. $80,000
   d. $55,000

5. What information is contained in the income statement?
   a. revenues and expenses for a period of time
   b. revenue and expenses on a specific date
   c. assets, liabilities, and owner's equity for a period of time
   d. assets, liabilities, and owner's equity on a specific date

ANALYSIS

6. Haden Hardware had revenues of $55,000 and expenses of $26,000. How does this affect owner's equity?

(Answers to Section 2 Self Review are on page 51.)

REVIEW   Chapter Summary

Accounting begins with the analysis of business transactions. Each transaction changes the financial position of a business. In this chapter, you have learned how to analyze business transactions and how they affect assets, liabilities, and owner's equity. After transactions are analyzed and recorded, financial statements reflect the summarized changes to and results of business operations.

Learning Objectives

1 **Record in equation form the financial effects of a business transaction.**

The equation *property equals financial interest* reflects the fact that in a free enterprise system all property is owned by someone. This equation remains in balance after each business transaction.

2 **Define, identify, and understand the relationship between asset, liability, and owner's equity accounts.**

The term *assets* refers to property. The terms *liabilities* and *owner's equity* refer to financial interest. The relationship between assets, liabilities, and owner's equity is shown in equation form.

Assets	=	Liabilities + Owner's Equity
Owner's Equity	=	Assets − Liabilities
Liabilities	=	Assets − Owner's Equity

3 **Analyze the effects of business transactions on a firm's assets, liabilities, and owner's equity and record these effects in accounting equation form.**

1. Describe the financial event.
   - Identify the property.
   - Identify who owns the property.
   - Determine the amount of the increase or decrease.
2. Make sure the equation is in balance.

4 **Prepare an income statement.**

The income statement summarizes changes in owner's equity that result from revenue and expenses. The difference between revenue and expenses is the net income or net loss of the business for the period.

An income statement has a three-line heading:
- who
- what
- when

For the income statement, "when" refers to a period of time.

5 **Prepare a statement of owner's equity and a balance sheet.**

Changes in owner's equity for the period are summarized on the statement of owner's equity.
- Net income increases owner's equity.
- Added investments increase owner's equity.
- A net loss for the period decreases owner's equity.
- Withdrawals by the owner decrease owner's equity.

A statement of owner's equity has a three-line heading:
- who
- what
- when

For the statement of owner's equity, "when" refers to a period of time.

The balance sheet shows the assets, liabilities, and owner's equity on a given date.

A balance sheet has a three-line heading:
- who
- what
- when

For the balance sheet, "when" refers to a single date.

The financial statements are prepared in the following order.
1. Income Statement
2. Statement of Owner's Equity
3. Balance Sheet

6 **Define the accounting terms new to this chapter.**

Glossary

Accounts payable (p. 24) Amounts a business must pay in the future

Accounts receivable (p. 30) Claims for future collection from customers

Assets (p. 27) Property owned by a business

Balance sheet (p. 27) A formal report of a business's financial condition on a certain date; reports the assets, liabilities, and owner's equity of the business

Break even (p. 34) A point at which revenue equals expenses

Business transaction (p. 22) A financial event that changes the resources of a firm

Capital (p. 23) Financial investment in a business; equity

Equity (p. 23) An owner's financial interest in a business

Expense (p. 30) An outflow of cash, use of other assets, or incurring of a liability

Fair market value (p. 36) The current worth of an asset or the price the asset would bring if sold on the open market

Fundamental accounting equation (p. 29) The relationship between assets and liabilities plus owner's equity

Income statement (p. 34) A formal report of business operations covering a specific period of time; also called a profit and loss statement or a statement of income and expenses

Liabilities (p. 27) Debts or obligations of a business

Net income (p. 34) The result of an excess of revenue over expenses

Net loss (p. 34) The result of an excess of expenses over revenue

On account (p. 24) An arrangement to allow payment at a later date; also called a charge account or open-account credit

Owner's equity (p. 27) The financial interest of the owner of a business; also called proprietorship or net worth

Revenue (p. 30) An inflow of money or other assets that results from the sales of goods or services or from the use of money or property; also called income

Statement of owner's equity (p. 35) A formal report of changes that occurred in the owner's financial interest during a reporting period

Withdrawals (p. 33) Funds taken from the business by the owner for personal use

Comprehensive Self Review

1. Describe a transaction that will cause Accounts Payable and Cash to decrease by $700.
2. In what order are the financial statements prepared? Why?
3. What effect do revenue and expenses have on owner's equity?
4. What is the difference between buying for cash and buying on account?
5. If one side of the fundamental accounting equation is decreased, what will happen to the other side? Why?

(Answers to Comprehensive Self Review are on page 51.)

Discussion Questions

1. What are expenses?
2. What is revenue?
3. What is the fundamental accounting equation?

4. What information does the balance sheet contain?

5. What are assets, liabilities, and owner's equity?

6. How does net income affect owner's equity?

7. What information does the statement of owner's equity contain?

8. Why does the third line of the headings differ on the balance sheet and the income statement?

9. What information is shown in the heading of a financial statement?

10. How is net income determined?

11. What information does the income statement contain?

12. Describe the effects of each of the following business transactions on assets, liabilities, and owner's equity.

   a. Sold services on credit.

   b. Bought furniture for cash.

   c. Paid cash to a creditor.

   d. Sold services for cash.

   e. Paid salaries to employees.

   f. Bought equipment on credit.

 Multiple choice questions are provided on the text Web site at www.mhhe.com/price12e

Quiz2

APPLICATIONS

Exercises

Completing the accounting equation.

The fundamental accounting equation for several businesses follows. Supply the missing amounts.

◀ **Exercise 2.1**
Objectives 1, 2

	Assets	=	Liabilities	+	Owner's Equity
1.	$24,250	=	$4,875	+	$?
2.	$19,700	=	$4,425	+	$?
3.	$12,450	=	$?	+	$ 9,950
4.	$?	=	$3,750	+	$31,500
5.	$31,300	=	$?	+	$22,950

Determining accounting equation amounts.

Just before Lewis Laboratories opened for business, Rosa Damon, the owner, had the following assets and liabilities. Determine the totals that would appear in the firm's fundamental accounting equation (Assets = Liabilities + Owner's Equity).

◀ **Exercise 2.2**
Objectives 1, 2

Cash	$36,200
Laboratory Equipment	81,000
Laboratory Supplies	5,500
Loan Payable	13,800
Accounts Payable	8,950

Exercise 2.3

Objectives 1, 2, 3

▶ **Determining balance sheet amounts.**

The following financial data are for the dental practice of Dr. Dennis Ortiz when he began operations in July. Determine the amounts that would appear in Dr. Ortiz's balance sheet.

1. Owes $19,000 to the Jones Equipment Company.
2. Has cash balance of $6,500.
3. Has dental supplies of $2,940.
4. Owes $3,350 to Ace Furniture Supply.
5. Has dental equipment of $25,800.
6. Has office furniture of $5,500.

Exercise 2.4

Objectives 1, 2, 3

▶ **Determining the effects of transactions on the accounting equation.**

Indicate the impact of each of the transactions below on the fundamental accounting equation (Assets = Liabilities + Owner's Equity) by placing a "+" to indicate an increase and a "−" to indicate a decrease. The first transaction is entered as an example.

	Assets	=	Liabilities	+	Owner's Equity
Transaction 1	+				+

TRANSACTIONS

1. Owner invested $60,000 in the business.
2. Purchased $24,000 supplies on account.
3. Purchased equipment for $19,000 cash.
4. Paid $3,000 for rent (in advance).
5. Performed services for $6,400 cash.
6. Paid $1,050 for utilities.
7. Performed services for $8,200 on account.
8. Received $3,300 from charge customers.
9. Paid salaries of $5,400 to employees.
10. Paid $4,000 to a creditor on account.

Exercise 2.5

Objectives 1, 2, 3

▶ **Determining the effects of transactions on the accounting equation.**

Quick Copy had the transactions listed below during the month of April. Show how each transaction would be recorded in the accounting equation. Compute the totals at the end of the month. The headings to be used in the equation follow.

Assets			=	Liabilities	+	Owner's Equity			
Cash +	Accounts Receivable +	Equipment =		Accounts Payable +		Amos Roberts, Capital +	Revenue −		Expenses

TRANSACTIONS

1. Amos Roberts started the business with a cash investment of $50,000.
2. Purchased equipment for $17,000 on credit.
3. Performed services for $2,100 in cash.

4. Purchased additional equipment for $3,600 in cash.

5. Performed services for $4,550 on credit.

6. Paid salaries of $3,950 to employees.

7. Received $2,200 cash from charge account customers.

8. Paid $9,000 to a creditor on account.

Computing net income or net loss.

◀ **Exercise 2.6**
Objective 4

Clark Computer Maintenance and Repair Shop had the following revenue and expenses during the month ended June 30. Did the firm earn a net income or incur a net loss for the period? What was the amount?

Fees for computer repairs	$39,600
Advertising expense	5,300
Salaries expense	18,100
Telephone expense	650
Fees for printer repairs	5,550
Utilities expense	1,100

Identifying transactions.

◀ **Exercise 2.7**
Objectives 1, 2, 3

The following equation shows the effects of a number of transactions that took place at Main Street Auto Repair Company during the month of August. Describe each transaction.

	Assets			=	Liabilities	+	Owner's Equity				
	Cash +	Accounts Receivable +	Equipment =		Accounts Payable +		Helen Rush, Capital +		Revenue	–	Expenses
Bal.	$80,000 +	$6,000 +	$64,000 =		$38,000 +		$112,000 +		0	–	0
1.	+10,000								+$10,000		
2.	–7,600		+7,600								
3.	–3,800				–3,800						
4.	–6,700										–$6,700
5.	+1,500	– 1,500									
6.		+12,000							+12,000		
7.	–4,100										–4,100

Computing net income or net loss.

◀ **Exercise 2.8**
Objective 4

On December 1, Doris Turner opened a speech and hearing clinic. During December, her firm had the following transactions involving revenue and expenses. Did the firm earn a net income or incur a net loss for the period? What was the amount?

Paid $2,600 for advertising.
✓Provided services for $2,300 in cash.
Paid $700 for telephone service.
Paid salaries of $2,100 to employees.
✓Provided services for $2,500 on credit.
Paid $350 for office cleaning service.

Preparing an income statement.

◀ **Exercise 2.9**
Objective 4

At the beginning of September, Alexander Parker started Parker Investment Services, a firm that offers advice about investing and managing money. On September 30, the accounting records of the business showed the following information. Prepare an income statement for the month of September 2010.

Cash	$32,100	Fees Income	$72,800
Accounts Receivable	3,000	Advertising Expense	5,500
Office Supplies	2,400	Salaries Expense	15,000
Office Equipment	36,500	Telephone Expense	700
Accounts Payable	4,700	Withdrawals	8,000
Alexander Parker, Capital, September 1, 2010	25,700		

Exercise 2.10 ▶

Objective 5

CONTINUING >>>
Problem

Preparing a statement of owner's equity and a balance sheet.

Using the information provided in Exercise 2.9, prepare a statement of owner's equity for the month of September and a balance sheet for Parker Investment Services as of September 30, 2010.

PROBLEMS

Problem Set A ▪▪

Problem 2.1A ▶

Objectives 1, 2, 3

Analyzing the effects of transactions on the accounting equation.

Andrew Wells is a painting contractor who specializes in painting commercial buildings. At the beginning of June, his firm's financial records showed the following assets, liabilities, and owner's equity.

Cash	$31,760	Accounts Payable	$8,200
Accounts Receivable	14,400	Andrew Wells, Capital	101,700
Office Furniture	33,800	Revenue	42,780
Auto	54,100	Expenses	18,620

INSTRUCTIONS

Set up an accounting equation using the balances given above. Record the effects of the following transactions in the equation. (Use plus, minus, and equals signs.) Record new balances after each transaction has been entered. Prove the equality of the two sides of the final equation on a separate sheet of paper.

TRANSACTIONS

1. Performed services for $5,350 on credit.
2. Paid $1,200 in cash for new office chairs.
3. Received $5,600 in cash from credit clients.
4. Paid $640 in cash for telephone service.
5. Sent a check for $1,500 in partial payment of the amount due creditors.
6. Paid salaries of $7,800 in cash.
7. Sent a check for $700 to pay electric bill.
8. Performed services for $9,700 in cash.
9. Paid $1,840 in cash for auto repairs.
10. Performed services for $8,900 on account.

Analyze: What is the amount of total assets after all transactions have been recorded?

Problem 2.2A ▶

Objectives 1, 2, 3

Analyzing the effects of transactions on the accounting equation.

On July 1, John Walker established Home Appraisal Services, a firm that provides expert residential appraisals and represents clients in home appraisal hearings.

INSTRUCTIONS

Analyze the following transactions. Record in equation form the changes that occur in assets, liabilities, and owner's equity. (Use plus, minus, and equals signs.)

TRANSACTIONS

1. The owner invested $92,000 in cash to begin the business.

2. Paid $18,750 in cash for the purchase of equipment.

3. Purchased additional equipment for $12,400 on credit.

4. Paid $10,800 in cash to creditors.

5. The owner made an additional investment of $25,000 in cash.

6. Performed services for $7,200 in cash.

7. Performed services for $4,300 on account.

8. Paid $3,000 for rent expense.

9. Received $2,500 in cash from credit clients.

10. Paid $5,460 in cash for office supplies.

11. The owner withdrew $8,000 in cash for personal expenses.

Analyze: What is the ending balance of cash after all transactions have been recorded?

Preparing an income statement, a statement of owner's equity, and a balance sheet.

◀ **Problem 2.3A**
Objectives 4, 5

eXcel

The following equation shows the transactions of West Cleaning Service during May. The business is owned by Carol West.

	Assets				=	Liab. +		Owner's Equity		
	Cash +	Accts. Rec. +	Supp. +	Equip. =		Accts. Pay. +	C. West, Capital +	Rev.	−	Exp.
Balances, May 1	14,000 +	2,000 +	4,800 +	32,800 =		6,000 +	47,600 +	0	−	0
Paid for utilities	−880									+880
New balances	13,120 +	2,000 +	4,800 +	32,800 =		6,000 +	47,600 +	0	−	880
Sold services for cash	+4,880							+4,880		
New balances	18,000 +	2,000 +	4,800 +	32,800 =		6,000 +	47,600 +	4,880	−	880
Paid a creditor	−1,600					−1,600				
New balances	16,400 +	2,000 +	4,800 +	32,800 =		4,400 +	47,600 +	4,880	−	880
Sold services on credit		+2,400						+2,400		
New balances	16,400 +	4,400 +	4,800 +	32,800 =		4,400 +	47,600 +	7,280	−	880
Paid salaries	−8,400									+8,400
New balances	8,000 +	4,400 +	4,800 +	32,800 =		4,400 +	47,600 +	7,280	−	9,280
Paid telephone bill	−304									+304
New balances	7,696 +	4,400 +	4,800 +	32,800 =		4,400 +	47,600 +	7,280	−	9,584
Withdrew cash for personal expenses	−2,000						−2,000			
New balances	5,696 +	4,400 +	4,800 +	32,800 =		4,400 +	45,600 +	7,280	−	9,584

INSTRUCTIONS

Analyze each transaction carefully. Prepare an income statement and a statement of owner's equity for the month. Prepare a balance sheet for May 31, 2010. List the expenses in detail on the income statement.

Analyze: In order to complete the balance sheet, which amount was transferred from the statement of owner's equity?

Preparing a balance sheet.

◀ **Problem 2.4A**
 Objective 5

Valdez Equipment Repair Service is owned by Francisco Valdez.

INSTRUCTIONS

Use the following figures to prepare a balance sheet dated February 28, 2010. (You will need to compute the owner's equity.)

Cash	$33,300	Equipment	$77,000
Supplies	5,380	Accounts Payable	23,000
Accounts Receivable	12,200		

Analyze: What is the net worth, or owner's equity, at February 28, 2010 for Valdez Equipment Repair Service?

Problem Set B

Problem 2.1B ▶

Objectives 1, 2, 3

Analyzing the effects of transactions on the accounting equation.

Rhonda Johnson owns Johnson's Consulting Service. At the beginning of September, her firm's financial records showed the following assets, liabilities, and owner's equity.

Cash	$19,000	Accounts Payable	$5,000
Accounts Receivable	6,000	Rhonda Johnson, Capital	24,900
Supplies	6,400	Revenue	26,000
Office Furniture	12,000	Expenses	12,500

INSTRUCTIONS

Set up an equation using the balances given above. Record the effects of the following transactions in the equation. (Use plus, minus, and equals signs.) Record new balances after each transaction has been entered. Prove the equality of the two sides of the final equation on a separate sheet of paper.

TRANSACTIONS

1. Performed services for $4,000 on credit.
2. Paid $1,440 in cash for utilities.
3. Performed services for $5,000 in cash.
4. Paid $800 in cash for office cleaning service.
5. Sent a check for $2,400 to a creditor.
6. Paid $960 in cash for the telephone bill.
7. Issued checks for $7,000 to pay salaries.
8. Performed services for $5,600 in cash.
9. Purchased additional supplies for $1,000 on credit.
10. Received $3,000 in cash from credit clients.

Analyze: What is the ending balance for owner's equity after all transactions have been recorded?

Problem 2.2B ▶

Objectives 1, 2, 3

Analyzing the effects of transactions on the accounting equation.

On September 1, Mireya Cortez opened Self Images Tutoring Service.

INSTRUCTIONS

Analyze the following transactions. Use the fundamental accounting equation form to record the changes in property, claims of creditors, and owner's equity. (Use plus, minus, and equals signs.)

TRANSACTIONS

1. The owner invested $18,000 in cash to begin the business.
2. Purchased equipment for $8,000 in cash.
3. Purchased $3,000 of additional equipment on credit.
4. Paid $1,500 in cash to creditors.
5. The owner made an additional investment of $3,000 in cash.
6. Performed services for $2,160 in cash.
7. Performed services for $1,560 on account.

8. Paid $1,300 for rent expense.
9. Received $1,100 in cash from credit clients.
10. Paid $1,550 in cash for office supplies.
11. The owner withdrew $2,000 in cash for personal expenses.

Analyze: Which transactions increased the company's debt? By what amount?

Preparing an income statement, a statement of owner's equity, and a balance sheet.

◀ **Problem 2.3B**
Objectives 4, 5

The equation below shows the transactions of Linda Carter, Attorney and Counselor of Law, during August. This law firm is owned by Linda Carter.

	Assets				=	Liab. +		Owner's Equity		
	Cash	+ Accts. Rec.	+ Supp.	+ Equip.	=	Accts. Pay.	+ L. Carter, Capital	+ Rev.	−	Exp.
Balances, Aug. 1	7,200	1,800	5,400	10,000	=	1,200	23,200	0	−	0
Paid for utilities	−600									+600
New balances	6,600	+ 1,800	+ 5,400	+ 10,000	=	1,200	+ 23,200	+ 0	−	600
Performed services for cash	+6,000							+6,000		
New balances	12,600	+ 1,800	+ 5,400	+ 10,000	=	1,200	+ 23,200	+ 6,000	−	600
Paid a creditor	−600					−600				
New balances	12,000	+ 1,800	+ 5,400	+ 10,000	=	600	+ 23,200	+ 6,000	−	600
Performed services on credit		+4,800						+4,800		
New balances	12,000	+ 6,600	+ 5,400	+ 10,000	=	600	+ 23,200	+ 10,800	−	600
Paid salaries	−5,400									+5,400
New balances	6,600	+ 6,600	+ 5,400	+ 10,000	=	600	+ 23,200	+ 10,800	−	6,000
Paid telephone bill	−600									+600
New balances	6,000	+ 6,600	+ 5,400	+ 10,000	=	600	+ 23,200	+ 10,800	−	6,600
Withdrew cash for personal expenses	−1,200						−1,200			
New balances	4,800	+ 6,600	+ 5,400	+ 10,000	=	600	+ 22,000	+ 10,800	−	6,600

INSTRUCTIONS

Analyze each transaction carefully. Prepare an income statement and a statement of owner's equity for the month. Prepare a balance sheet for August 31, 2010. List the expenses in detail on the income statement.

Analyze: In order to complete the statement of owner's equity, which amount was transferred from the income statement?

Preparing a balance sheet.

◀ **Problem 2.4B**
Objective 5

David Taylor is opening a tax preparation service on December 1, which will be called Taylor's Tax Service. David plans to open the business by depositing $24,000 cash into a business checking account. The following assets will also be owned by the business: furniture (fair market value of $8,000) and computers and printers (fair market value of $9,600). There are no outstanding debts of the business as it is formed.

INSTRUCTIONS

Prepare a balance sheet for December 1, 2010, for Taylor's Tax Service by entering the correct balances in the appropriate accounts. (You will need to use the accounting equation to compute owner's equity.)

Analyze: If Taylor's Tax Service had an outstanding debt of $8,000 when the business was formed, what amount should be reported on the balance sheet for owner's equity?

Critical Thinking Problem 2.1

Financial Statements

The following account balances are for Kawonza Carter, Certified Public Accountant, as of April 30, 2010.

Cash	$13,000
Accounts Receivable	5,600
Maintenance Expense	2,200
Advertising Expense	1,800
Fees Earned	19,000
Kawonza Carter, Capital, April 1	?
Salaries Expense	6,000
Equipment	17,000
Accounts Payable	6,400
Kawonza Carter, Drawing	2,400

INSTRUCTIONS

Using the accounting equation form, determine the balance for Kawonza Carter, Capital, April 1, 2010. Prepare an income statement for the month of April, a statement of owner's equity, and a balance sheet as of April 30, 2010. List the expenses on the income statement in alphabetical order.

Analyze: What net change in owner's equity occurred during the month of April?

Critical Thinking Problem 2.2

Accounting for a New Company

James Mitchell opened a gym and fitness studio called Body Builders Fitness Center at the beginning of November of the current year. It is now the end of December, and James is trying to determine whether he made a profit during his first two months of operations. You offer to help him and ask to see his accounting records. He shows you a shoe box and tells you that every piece of paper pertaining to the business is in that box.

As you go through the material in the shoe box, you discover the following:

a. A receipt from Clayton Properties for $8,000 for November's rent on the exercise studio.

b. Bank deposit slips totaling $7,360 for money collected from customers who attended exercise classes.

c. An invoice for $50,000 for exercise equipment. The first payment is not due until December 31.

d. A bill for $2,100 from the maintenance service that cleans the studio. James has not yet paid this bill.

e. A December 19 parking ticket for $200. James says he was in a hurry that morning to get to the Fitness Center on time and forgot to put money in the parking meter.

f. A handwritten list of customers and fees for the classes they have taken. As the customers attend the classes, James writes their names and the amount of each customer's fee on the list. As customers pay, James crosses their names off the list. Fees not crossed off the list amount to $2,400.

g. A credit card receipt for $800 for printing flyers advertising the grand opening of the studio. For convenience, James used his personal credit card.

h. A credit card receipt for $800 for four warm-up suits James bought to wear at the studio. He also put this purchase on his personal credit card.

Use the concepts you have learned in this chapter to help James.

1. Prepare an income statement for the first two months of operation of Body Builders Fitness Center.

2. How would you evaluate the results of the first two months of operation?

3. What advice would you give James concerning his system of accounting?

BUSINESS CONNECTIONS

Interpreting Results

1. How does an accounting system help managers control operations and make sound decisions?

2. Why should managers be concerned with changes in the amount of creditors' claims against the business?

3. Is it reasonable to expect that all new businesses will have a net income from the first month's operations? From the first year's operations?

4. After examining financial data for a monthly period, the owner of a small business expressed surprise that the firm's cash balance had decreased during the month even though there was substantial net income. Do you think this owner is right to expect cash to increase because of a substantial net income? Why or why not?

To Record or Not to Record

You are Sarineh, a new Accounts Receivable Clerk for Robinson Paper Supply. Toward the end of the month, Joseph Lee, a very personable sales associate, tells you that the previous A/R clerk always recorded a Sales Invoice when he got a verbal agreement from a customer to buy paper supplies. He has a verbal order from his favorite customer for $5,000 of paper and wants you to create a Sales Invoice today. You know that in order to create a Sales Invoice you need a purchase order from the customer. You also know that Mr. Lee receives a monthly bonus based on the monthly sales. If his sales are above $10,000, he gets a 10 percent bonus. Would you agree to record the sales of products before receiving the purchase order from the customer? What effect would it have on the customer, on the Sales Associate, on the company, and on the job?

Financial Information

Refer to The Home Depot, Inc. *2006 Annual Report* in Appendix A.

1. Locate the consolidated balance sheets. Based on this financial statement, what is the fundamental accounting equation for the year ended January 30, 2007? Note: Because this company is publicly traded, owners' equity is represented as stockholders' equity.

2. Locate the consolidated statements of earnings. The statement presents the results of operations for what periods of time? What result of operations is presented for the most recent operating period?

Income Statement

Review the following excerpt from the 2006 consolidated statement of income for Southwest Airlines Co. Answer the questions that follow.

Southwest Airlines Co. Consolidated Statement of Income Years Ended December 31, 2006			
	2006	*2005*	*2004*
Operating Revenues (in millions):			
Passenger	$8,750	$7,279	$6,280
Freight	134	133	117
Other	202	172	133
Total operating revenues	9,086	7,584	6,530
Net Income	$499	$484	$215

Analyze:

1. Although the format for the heading of an income statement can vary from company to company, the heading should contain the answers to who, what, and when. List the answers to each question for the statement presented above.

2. What three types of revenue are reflected on this statement?

3. The net income of $499,000,000 reflected on Southwest Airlines Co.'s consolidated statement of income for 2006 will be transferred to the next financial statement to be prepared. Net income is needed to complete which statement?

Analyze Online: Find the *Investor Relations* section of the Southwest Airlines Co. Web site (www.southwest.com) and answer the following questions.

4. What total operating revenues did Southwest Airlines Co. report for the most recent quarter?

5. Find the most recent press release posted on the Web site. Read the press release, and summarize the topic discussed. What effect, if any, do you think this will have on company earnings? Why?

Extending THE THOUGHT

Personal Financial Statements

The balance sheet for an individual is called a "statement of financial condition." What kinds of assets and liabilities would appear on a statement of financial condition?

Business COMMUNICATION

Creating an Outline

You are a senior accountant for a midsize apparel corporation. You have been asked to give a presentation on the basics of financial statements to the managers of the marketing, advertising, manufacturing, and sales departments. Each manager needs to understand what each financial statement presents and why each is important. Prepare an outline for your presentation. Be sure to cover the income statement, the statement of owner's equity, and the balance sheet.

Internet CONNECTION

Selling on Internet

Go to the Federated Corporation Web site at www.federated-fds.com. What companies are included in this corporation? Can you see a link to purchase items on line? What transaction, if any, would you record when an item is ordered from the Internet? Does the Web site include job offerings? What jobs would be available in Finance (go to Support operations, finance to find the requirements for a job)?

TEAMWORK

Working to Provide Accurate Data

Christy's Fabrics is a large fabric provider to the general public. The accounting office has three employees: accounts receivable clerk, accounts payable clerk, and full charge bookkeeper. The accounts receivable clerk creates the sales invoices and records the cash receipts, the accounts payable clerk creates and pays the purchase orders, and the full charge bookkeeper reconciles the checking account. Assign each group member one of the three jobs. Identify the accounts and describe the transactions that would be recorded by that assigned job. What effect would each trans-action have on each account? How would each member of the accounting department work together to present accurate information for the decision makers?

Answers to **Self Reviews**

Answers to Section 1 Self Review

1. An example is the initial investment of cash in a business by the owner.
2. Amounts that a company must pay to creditors in the future.
3. A financial event that changes the resources of the firm.
4. **d.** $75,000
5. **a.** Equipment is increased by $3,250 and accounts payable is increased by $3,250.
6. $10,000

Answers to Section 2 Self Review

1. As an additional investment by the owner recorded on the basis of fair market value.
2. The firm's name (who), the title of the statement (what), and the time period covered by the report (when).
3. Funds taken from the business to pay for personal expenses. They decrease the owner's equity in the business.
4. **d.** $55,000
5. **a.** revenue and expenses for a period of time
6. $29,000 increase

Answers to Comprehensive Self Review

1. The payment of $700 to a creditor on account.
2. The income statement is prepared first because the net income or loss is needed to complete the statement of owner's equity. The statement of owner's equity is prepared next to update the change in owner's equity. The balance sheet is prepared last.
3. Revenue increases owner's equity. Expenses decrease owner's equity.
4. Buying for cash results in an immediate decrease in cash; buying on account results in a liability recorded as accounts payable.
5. The opposite side of the accounting equation will decrease because a decrease in assets results in a corresponding decrease in either a liability or the owner's equity.

Analyzing Business Transactions Using T Accounts

Chapter 3

LEARNING OBJECTIVES

1. Set up T accounts for assets, liabilities, and owner's equity.   LP3
2. Analyze business transactions and enter them in the accounts.
3. Determine the balance of an account.
4. Set up T accounts for revenue and expenses.
5. Prepare a trial balance from T accounts.
6. Prepare an income statement, a statement of owner's equity, and a balance sheet.
7. Develop a chart of accounts.
8. Define the accounting terms new to this chapter.

NEW TERMS

account balance
accounts
chart of accounts
classification
credit
debit
double-entry system
drawing account

footing
normal balance
permanent account
slide
T account
temporary account
transposition
trial balance

Johnson & Johnson   www.jnj.com

In 1886, Robert Wood Johnson, James Wood, and Robert Mead Johnson recognized the need to improve antiseptic procedures in hospitals in order to reduce infection rates. The brothers purchased an old wallpaper factory, hired 14 employees, and designed a soft, absorbent dressing that could be mass produced and shipped in quantity to hospitals.

Over the past century the company has been in business, Johnson & Johnson has broadened its offerings through new-product development and diversification. Today, Johnson & Johnson is a worldwide family of 250 companies marketing health care products throughout the world. The company's 120,500 employees serve a broad segment of medical needs ranging from baby care, first aid, and hospital products to pharmaceuticals, diagnostics, and family planning. Worldwide sales in 2006 reached $53.3 billion.

thinking critically

How might accountants in 1886 have recorded Johnson & Johnson's first sales transaction? How did this transaction affect the fundamental accounting equation?

Transactions That Affect Assets, Liabilities, and Owner's Equity

In this chapter, you will learn how to record the changes caused by business transactions. This recordkeeping is a basic part of accounting systems.

Asset, Liability, and Owner's Equity Accounts

Video3.1

The accounting equation is one tool for analyzing the effects of business transactions. However, businesses do not record transactions in equation form. Instead, businesses establish separate records, called **accounts,** for assets, liabilities, and owner's equity. Use of accounts helps owners and staff analyze, record, classify, summarize, and report financial information. Accounts are recognized by their **classification** as assets, liabilities, or owner's equity. Asset accounts show the property a business owns. Liability accounts show the debts of the business. Owner's equity accounts show the owner's financial interest in the business. Each account has a name that describes the type of property, the debt, or the financial interest.

Accountants use T accounts to analyze transactions. A **T account** consists of a vertical line and a horizontal line that resemble the letter **T.** The name of the account is written on the horizontal (top) line. Increases and decreases in the account are entered on either side of the vertical line.

The following are T accounts for assets, liabilities, and owner's equity.

RECORDING A CASH INVESTMENT

Asset accounts show items of value owned by a business. Carolyn Wells invested $100,000 in the business. Carlos Valdez, the office manager for Wells' Consulting Services, set up a *Cash* account. Cash is an asset. Assets appear on the left side of the accounting equation. Cash increases appear on the left side of the *Cash* T account. Decreases are shown on the right side. Valdez entered the cash investment of $100,000 **(a)** on the left side of the *Cash* account.

T accounts normally do not have plus and minus signs. We show them to help you identify increases ($+$) and decreases ($-$) in accounts.

Carlos Valdez set up an account for owner's equity called *Carolyn Wells, Capital.* Owner's equity appears on the right side of the accounting equation (Assets = Liabilities + Owner's Equity). Increases in owner's equity appear on the right side of the T account. Decreases in owner's equity appear on the left side. Valdez entered the investment of $100,000 **(b)** on the right side of the *Carolyn Wells, Capital* account.

Use these steps to analyze the effects of the business transactions:

1. Analyze the financial event.
   - Identify the accounts affected.
   - Classify the accounts affected.
   - Determine the amount of increase or decrease for each account.
2. Apply the left-right rules for each account affected.
3. Make the entry in T-account form.

BUSINESS TRANSACTION

Carolyn Wells withdrew $100,000 from personal savings and deposited it in the new business checking account for Wells' Consulting Services.

ANALYSIS
a. The asset account, *Cash,* is increased by $100,000.
b. The owner's equity account, *Carolyn Wells, Capital,* is increased by $100,000.

LEFT-RIGHT RULES
LEFT   Increases to asset accounts are recorded on the left side of the T account. Record $100,000 on the left side of the *Cash* T account.
RIGHT   Increases to owner's equity accounts are recorded on the right side of the T account. Record $100,000 on the right side of the *Carolyn Wells, Capital* T account.

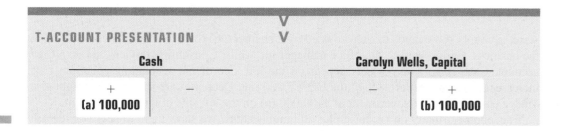

RECORDING A CASH PURCHASE OF EQUIPMENT

Carlos Valdez set up an asset account, *Equipment,* to record the purchase of a computer and other equipment.

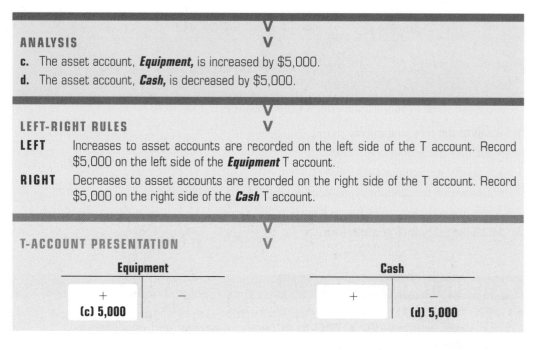

Let's look at the T accounts to review the effects of the transactions. Valdez entered $5,000 **(c)** on the left (increase) side of the *Equipment* account. He entered $5,000 **(d)** on the right (decrease) side of the *Cash* account. Notice that the *Cash* account shows the effects of two transactions.

	Equipment	
+		–
(c) 5,000		

	Cash	
+		–
(a) 100,000		(d) 5,000

RECORDING A CREDIT PURCHASE OF EQUIPMENT

Liabilities are amounts a business owes its creditors. Liabilities appear on the right side of the accounting equation (Assets = Liabilities + Owner's Equity). Increases in liabilities are on the right side of liability T accounts. Decreases in liabilities are on the left side of liability T accounts.

BUSINESS TRANSACTION

The firm bought office equipment for $6,000 on account from Office Plus.

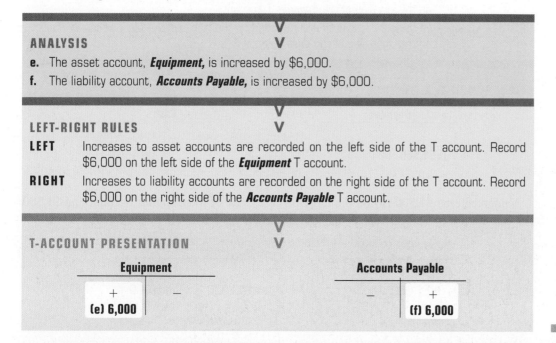

ANALYSIS

e. The asset account, *Equipment,* is increased by $6,000.

f. The liability account, *Accounts Payable,* is increased by $6,000.

LEFT-RIGHT RULES

LEFT   Increases to asset accounts are recorded on the left side of the T account. Record $6,000 on the left side of the *Equipment* T account.

RIGHT   Increases to liability accounts are recorded on the right side of the T account. Record $6,000 on the right side of the *Accounts Payable* T account.

T-ACCOUNT PRESENTATION

Equipment		
+	–	
(e) 6,000		

Accounts Payable		
–	+	
	(f) 6,000	

important!

For liability T accounts
- right side shows increases,
- left side shows decreases.

Let's look at the T accounts to review the effects of the transactions. Valdez entered $6,000 **(e)** on the left (increase) side of the *Equipment* account. It now shows two transactions. He entered $6,000 **(f)** on the right (increase) side of the *Accounts Payable* account.

Equipment	
+	–
(c) 5,000	
(e) 6,000	

Accounts Payable	
–	+
	(f) 6,000

The balance sheet of Avery Dennison Corporation at January 1, 2007, showed machinery and equipment balances of $1.3 billion.

RECORDING A CASH PURCHASE OF SUPPLIES

Carlos Valdez set up an asset account called *Supplies.*

BUSINESS TRANSACTION

Wells' Consulting Services issued a check for $1,500 to Office Delux Inc. to purchase office supplies.

ANALYSIS

g. The asset account, *Supplies,* is increased by $1,500.

h. The asset account, *Cash,* is decreased by $1,500.

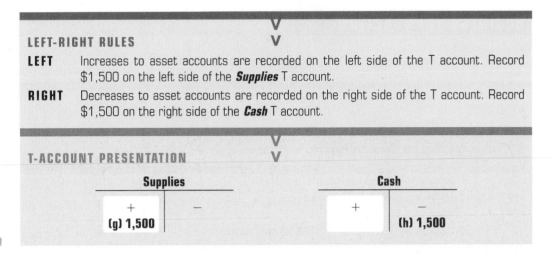

Valdez entered $1,500 **(g)** on the left (increase) side of the **Supplies** account and $1,500 **(h)** on the right (decrease) side of the **Cash** account.

Notice that the **Cash** account now shows three transactions: the initial investment by the owner (a), the cash purchase of equipment (d), and the cash purchase of supplies (h).

RECORDING A PAYMENT TO A CREDITOR

On November 30, the business paid $2,500 to Office Plus to apply against the debt of $6,000 shown in **Accounts Payable.**

BUSINESS TRANSACTION

Wells' Consulting Services issued a check in the amount of $2,500 to Office Plus.

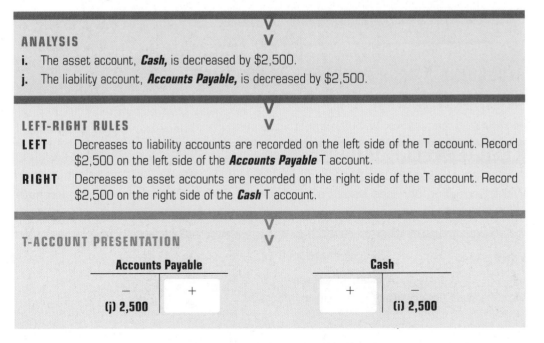

Let's look at the T accounts to review the effects of the transactions. Valdez entered $2,500 **(i)** on the right (decrease) side of the **Cash** account. He entered $2,500 **(j)** on the left (decrease) side of the **Accounts Payable** account. Notice that both accounts show the effects of several transactions.

Accounts Payable		Cash	
−	+	+	−
(j) 2,500	(f) 6,000	(a) 100,000	(d) 5,000
			(h) 1,500
			(i) 2,500

RECORDING PREPAID RENT

In November, Wells' Consulting Services was required to pay the December and January rent in advance. Valdez set up an asset account called **Prepaid Rent.**

BUSINESS TRANSACTION

Wells' Consulting Services issued a check for $8,000 to pay rent for the months of December and January.

ANALYSIS

k. The asset account, **Prepaid Rent,** is increased by $8,000.

l. The asset account, **Cash,** is decreased by $8,000.

LEFT-RIGHT RULES

LEFT   Increases to asset accounts are recorded on the left side of the T account. Record $8,000 on the left side of the **Prepaid Rent** T account.

RIGHT   Decreases to asset accounts are recorded on the right side of the T account. Record $8,000 on the right side of the **Cash** T account.

T-ACCOUNT PRESENTATION

Prepaid Rent		Cash	
+	−	+	−
(k) 8,000			(l) 8,000

Let's review the T accounts to see the effects of the transactions. Valdez entered $8,000 **(k)** on the left (increase) side of the **Prepaid Rent** account. He entered $8,000 **(l)** on the right (decrease) side of the **Cash** account.

Notice that the **Cash** account shows the effects of numerous transactions. It shows initial investment (a), equipment purchase (d), supplies purchase (h), payment on account (i), and advance rent payment (l).

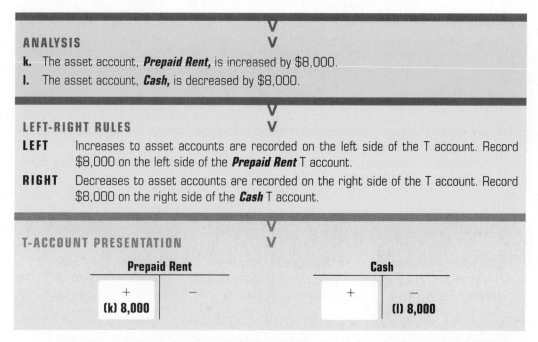

Prepaid Rent		Cash	
+	−	+	−
(k) 8,000		(a) 100,000	(d) 5,000
			(h) 1,500
			(i) 2,500
			(l) 8,000

>> 3. OBJECTIVE

Determine the balance of an account.

LP3

Account Balances

An **account balance** is the difference between the amounts on the two sides of the account. First add the figures on each side of the account. If the column has more than one figure, enter the total in small pencil figures called a **footing.** Then subtract the smaller total from the larger total. The result is the account balance.

- If the total on the right side is larger than the total on the left side, the balance is recorded on the right side.
- If the total on the left side is larger, the balance is recorded on the left side.
- If an account shows only one amount, that amount is the balance.
- If an account contains entries on only one side, the total of those entries is the account balance.

Let's look at the **Cash** account for Wells' Consulting Services. The left side shows $100,000. The total of the right side is $17,000. Subtract the footing of $17,000 from $100,000. The result is the account balance of $83,000. The account balance is shown on the left side of the account.

	Cash
+	−
(a) 100,000	(d) 5,000
	(h) 1,500
	(i) 2,500
	(l) 8,000
	17,000 ← Footing
Bal. 83,000	

Usually account balances appear on the increase side of the account. The increase side of the account is the **normal balance** of the account.

The following is a summary of the procedures to increase or decrease accounts and shows the normal balance of accounts.

ASSETS		=	LIABILITIES		+	OWNER'S EQUITY	
+	−		−	+		−	+
Increase (Normal Balance)	Decrease		Decrease	Increase (Normal Balance)		Decrease	Increase (Normal Balance)

Figure 3.1 shows a summary of the account balances for Wells' Consulting Services. Figure 3.2 shows a balance sheet prepared for November 30, 2010. In equation form, the firm's position after these transactions is:

Assets									=	Liabilities	+	Owner's Equity
Cash	+	Supp.	+	Prepaid Rent	+	Equip.			=	Accounts Payable	+	Carolyn Wells, Capital
$83,000	+	$1,500	+	$8,000	+	$11,000			=	$3,500	+	$100,000

FIGURE 3.1

T-Account Balances for Wells'
Consulting Services

ASSETS = LIABILITIES + OWNER'S EQUITY

Cash

+	–
(a) 100,000	(d) 5,000
	(h) 1,500
	(i) 2,500
	(l) 8,000
	17,000
Bal. 83,000	

Accounts Payable

–	+
(j) 2,500	(f) 6,000
	Bal. 3,500

Carolyn Wells, Capital

–	+
	(b) 100,000

Supplies

+	–
(g) 1,500	

Prepaid Rent

+	–
(k) 8,000	

Equipment

+	–
(c) 5,000	
(e) 6,000	
Bal. 11,000	

FIGURE 3.2 Balance Sheet for Wells' Consulting Services

Wells' Consulting Services
Balance Sheet
November 30, 2010

Assets						Liabilities					
Cash	8	3	0	0	0	00	Accounts Payable		3	5	0	0	00
Supplies		1	5	0	0	00						
Prepaid Rent		8	0	0	0	00	Owner's Equity					
Equipment		1	1	0	0	0	00	Carolyn Wells, Capital	100	0	0	0	00
Total Assets	1	0	3	5	0	0	00	Total Liabilities and Owner's Equity	103	5	0	0	00

Notice how the balance sheet reflects the fundamental accounting equation.

Section **1** Self Review

QUESTIONS

1. What is a footing?
2. What is meant by the "normal balance" of an account? What is the normal balance side for asset, liability, and owner's equity accounts? .
3. Increases are recorded on which side of asset, liability, and owner's equity accounts?

EXERCISES

4. The Wilson Company purchased new computers for $10,800 from Office Supplies, Inc., to be paid in 30 days. Which of the following is correct?

   a. *Equipment* is increased by $10,800. *Accounts Payable* is decreased by $10,800.
   b. *Equipment* is increased by $10,800. *Accounts Payable* is increased by $10,800.
   c. *Equipment* is decreased by $10,800. *Accounts Payable* is increased by $10,800.
   d. *Equipment* is increased by $10,800. *Cash* is decreased by $10,800.

5. Foot and find the balance of the *Cash* account.

   Cash

+	−
26,000	10,000
18,000	3,000
	2,500
	2,350

   a. 44,000
   b. 29,500
   c. 26,150
   d. 24,100

ANALYSIS

6. From the following accounts, show that the fundamental accounting equation is in balance. All accounts have normal balances.

   Cash—$15,400
   Accounts Payable—$10,000
   David Jenkins, Capital—$30,000
   Equipment—$20,000
   Supplies—$4,600

(Answers to Section 1 Self Review are on page 87.)

SECTION OBJECTIVES	TERMS TO LEARN
>> **4. Set up T accounts for revenue and expenses.** WHY IT'S IMPORTANT T accounts help you understand the effects of all business transactions. >> **5. Prepare a trial balance from T accounts.** WHY IT'S IMPORTANT The trial balance is an important check of accuracy at the end of the accounting period. >> **6. Prepare an income statement, a statement of owner's equity, and a balance sheet.** WHY IT'S IMPORTANT Financial statements summarize the financial activities and condition of the business. >> **7. Develop a chart of accounts.** WHY IT'S IMPORTANT Businesses require a system that allows accounts to be easily identified and located.	chart of accounts credit debit double-entry system drawing account permanent account slide temporary account transposition trial balance

Transactions That Affect Revenue, Expenses, and Withdrawals

Let's examine the revenue and expense transactions of Wells' Consulting Services for December to see how they are recorded.

Revenue and Expense Accounts

Some owner's equity accounts are classified as revenue or expense accounts. Separate accounts are used to record revenue and expense transactions.

RECORDING REVENUE FROM SERVICES SOLD FOR CASH

During December, the business earned $36,000 in revenue from clients who paid cash for bookkeeping, accounting, and consulting services. This involved several transactions. Carlos Valdez entered $36,000 **(m)** on the left (increase) side of the asset account *Cash*.

Cash	
+	−
Bal. 83,000	
(m) 36,000	

>> 4. OBJECTIVE

Set up T accounts for revenue
and expenses.

LP3

How is the increase in owner's equity recorded? One way would be to record the $36,000 on the right side of the **Carolyn Wells, Capital** account. However, the preferred way is to keep revenue separate from the owner's investment until the end of the accounting period. Therefore, Valdez opened a revenue account for **Fees Income.**

Valdez entered $36,000 (**n**) on the right side of the **Fees Income** account. Revenues increase owner's equity. Increases in owner's equity appear on the right side of the T account. Therefore, increases in revenue appear on the right side of revenue T accounts.

The right side of the revenue account shows increases and the left side shows decreases. Decreases in revenue accounts are rare but might occur because of corrections or transfers.

Let's review the effects of the transactions. Valdez entered $36,000 (**m**) on the left (increase) side of the **Cash** account and $36,000 (**n**) on the right (increase) side of the **Fees Income** account.

At this point, the firm needs just one revenue account. Most businesses have separate accounts for different types of revenue. For example, sales of goods such as clothes are recorded in the revenue account **Sales.**

RECORDING REVENUE FROM SERVICES SOLD ON CREDIT

In December, Wells' Consulting Services earned $11,000 from various charge account clients. Valdez set up an asset account, **Accounts Receivable.**

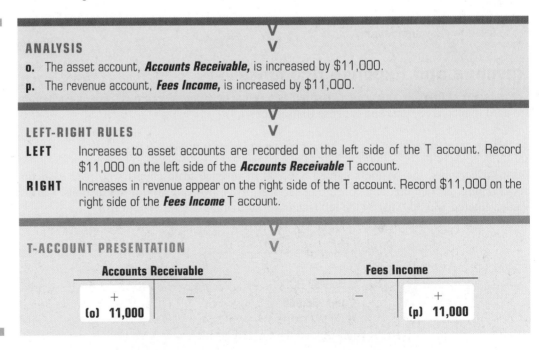

ANALYSIS

o. The asset account, **Accounts Receivable,** is increased by $11,000.

p. The revenue account, **Fees Income,** is increased by $11,000.

LEFT-RIGHT RULES

LEFT   Increases to asset accounts are recorded on the left side of the T account. Record $11,000 on the left side of the **Accounts Receivable** T account.

RIGHT Increases in revenue appear on the right side of the T account. Record $11,000 on the right side of the **Fees Income** T account.

T-ACCOUNT PRESENTATION

Let's review the effects of the transactions. Valdez entered $11,000 **(o)** on the left (increase) side of the **Accounts Receivable** account and $11,000 **(p)** on the right (increase) side of the **Fees Income** account.

Accounts Receivable			Fees Income	
+	−		−	+
(o) 11,000				(n) 36,000
				(p) 11,000

RECORDING COLLECTIONS FROM ACCOUNTS RECEIVABLE

Charge account clients paid $6,000, reducing the amount owed to Wells' Consulting Services.

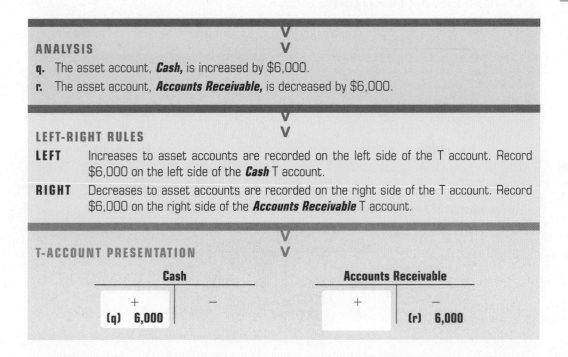

ANALYSIS

q. The asset account, **Cash,** is increased by $6,000.

r. The asset account, **Accounts Receivable,** is decreased by $6,000.

LEFT-RIGHT RULES

LEFT Increases to asset accounts are recorded on the left side of the T account. Record $6,000 on the left side of the **Cash** T account.

RIGHT Decreases to asset accounts are recorded on the right side of the T account. Record $6,000 on the right side of the **Accounts Receivable** T account.

T-ACCOUNT PRESENTATION

Cash			Accounts Receivable	
+	−		+	−
(q) 6,000				(r) 6,000

Let's review the effects of the transactions. Valdez entered $6,000 **(q)** on the left (increase) side of the **Cash** account and $6,000 **(r)** on the right (decrease) side of the **Accounts Receivable** account. Notice that revenue is not recorded when cash is collected from charge account clients. The revenue was recorded when the sales on credit were recorded **(p)**.

Cash			Accounts Receivable	
+	−		+	−
Bal. 83,000			(o) 11,000	(r) 6,000
(m) 36,000				
(q) 6,000				

RECORDING AN EXPENSE FOR SALARIES

Expenses decrease owner's equity. Decreases in owner's equity appear on the left side of the T account. Therefore, increases in expenses (which are decreases in owner's equity) are recorded on the left side of expense T accounts. Decreases in expenses are recorded on the right side of the T accounts. Decreases in expenses are rare but may result from corrections or transfers.

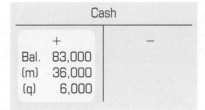

recall

Expense

An expense is an outflow of cash, the use of other assets, or the incurring of a liability.

BUSINESS TRANSACTION

In December, Wells' Consulting Services paid $8,000 in salaries.

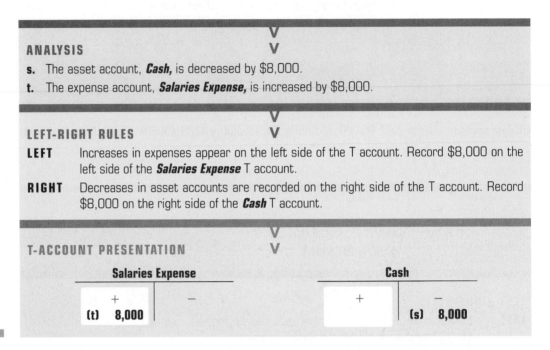

ANALYSIS
- **s.** The asset account, **Cash**, is decreased by $8,000.
- **t.** The expense account, **Salaries Expense**, is increased by $8,000.

LEFT-RIGHT RULES

LEFT Increases in expenses appear on the left side of the T account. Record $8,000 on the left side of the **Salaries Expense** T account.

RIGHT Decreases in asset accounts are recorded on the right side of the T account. Record $8,000 on the right side of the **Cash** T account.

T-ACCOUNT PRESENTATION

Salaries Expense			Cash	
+	–		+	–
(t) 8,000				(s) 8,000

Valdez entered $8,000 **(s)** on the right (decrease) side of the **Cash** T account.

Cash		
+	–	
Bal. 83,000	(s) 8,000	
(m) 36,000		
(q) 6,000		

How is the decrease in owner's equity recorded? One way would be to record the $8,000 on the left side of the **Carolyn Wells, Capital** account. However, the preferred way is to keep expenses separate from owner's investment. Therefore, Valdez set up a **Salaries Expense** account.

To record the salary expense, Valdez entered $8,000 **(t)** on the left (increase) side of the **Salaries Expense** account. Notice that the plus and minus signs in the **Salaries Expense** account show the effect on the expense account, not on owner's equity.

Salaries Expense	
+	–
(t) 8,000	

Most companies have numerous expense accounts. The various expense accounts appear in the Expenses section of the income statement.

RECORDING AN EXPENSE FOR UTILITIES

At the end of December, Wells' Consulting Services received a $650 bill for utilities. Valdez set up an account for **Utilities Expense.**

BUSINESS TRANSACTION

Wells' Consulting Services issued a check for $650 to pay the utilities bill.

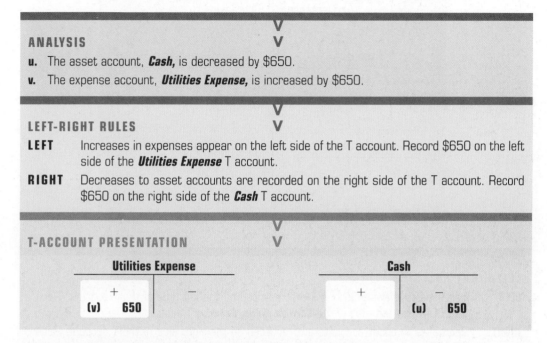

ANALYSIS
u. The asset account, *Cash,* is decreased by $650.
v. The expense account, *Utilities Expense,* is increased by $650.

LEFT-RIGHT RULES
LEFT Increases in expenses appear on the left side of the T account. Record $650 on the left side of the *Utilities Expense* T account.
RIGHT Decreases to asset accounts are recorded on the right side of the T account. Record $650 on the right side of the *Cash* T account.

T-ACCOUNT PRESENTATION

Utilities Expense		Cash	
+	−	+	−
(v) 650			(u) 650

Let's review the effects of the transactions.

Utilities Expense		Cash	
+	−	+	−
(v) 650		Bal. 83,000	(s) 8,000
		(m) 36,000	(u) 650
		(q) 6,000	

The Drawing Account

In sole proprietorships and partnerships, the owners generally do not pay themselves salaries. To obtain funds for personal living expenses, owners make withdrawals of cash. The withdrawals are against previously earned profits that have become part of capital or against profits that are expected in the future.

Since withdrawals decrease owner's equity, withdrawals could be recorded on the left side of the capital account. However, the preferred way is to keep withdrawals separate from the owner's capital account until the end of the accounting period. An owner's equity account called a **drawing account** is set up to record withdrawals. Increases in the drawing account (which are decreases in owner's equity) are recorded on the left side of the drawing T accounts.

BUSINESS TRANSACTION

Carolyn Wells wrote a check to withdraw $5,000 cash for personal use.

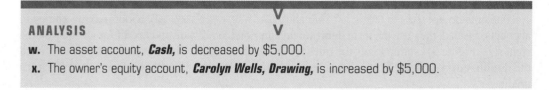

ANALYSIS
w. The asset account, *Cash,* is decreased by $5,000.
x. The owner's equity account, *Carolyn Wells, Drawing,* is increased by $5,000.

FIGURE 3.3

The Relationship Between
Owner's Equity and Revenue,
Expenses, and Withdrawals

important!

Normal Balances
Debit: Credit:
Asset   Liability
Expense Revenue
Drawing Capital

Let's review the transactions. Valdez entered $5,000 (**w**) on the right (decrease) side of the asset account, **Cash,** and $5,000 (**x**) on the left (increase) side of **Carolyn Wells, Drawing.** Note that the plus and minus signs show the effect on the drawing account, not on owner's equity.

Figure 3.3 shows a summary of the relationship between the capital account and the revenue, expense, and drawing accounts.

The Rules of Debit and Credit

Video3.1

Accountants do not use the terms *left side* and *right side* when they talk about making entries in accounts. Instead, they use the term **debit** for an entry on the left side and **credit** for an entry on the right side. Figure 3.4 summarizes the rules for debits and credits. The accounting system is called the **double-entry system.** This is because each transaction has at least two entries—a debit and a credit.

ASSET ACCOUNTS	
Debit +	Credit −
Increase Side (Normal Bal.)	Decrease Side

LIABILITY ACCOUNTS	
Debit −	Credit +
Decrease Side	Increase Side (Normal Bal.)

OWNER'S CAPITAL ACCOUNT	
Debit −	Credit +
Decrease Side	Increase Side (Normal Bal.)

OWNER'S DRAWING ACCOUNT	
Debit +	Credit −
Increase Side (Normal Bal.)	Decrease Side

REVENUE ACCOUNTS	
Debit −	Credit +
Decrease Side	Increase Side (Normal Bal.)

EXPENSE ACCOUNTS	
Debit +	Credit −
Increase Side (Normal Bal.)	Decrease Side

After the December transactions for Wells' Consulting Services are recorded, the account balances are calculated. Figure 3.5 below shows the account balances at the end of December. Notice that the fundamental accounting equation remains in balance (Assets = Liabilities + Owner's Equity).

FIGURE 3.4

Rules for Debits and Credits

The Trial Balance

Once the account balances are computed, a trial balance is prepared. The **trial balance** is a statement that tests the accuracy of total debits and credits after transactions have been

FIGURE 3.5

End-of-December 2010 Account Balances

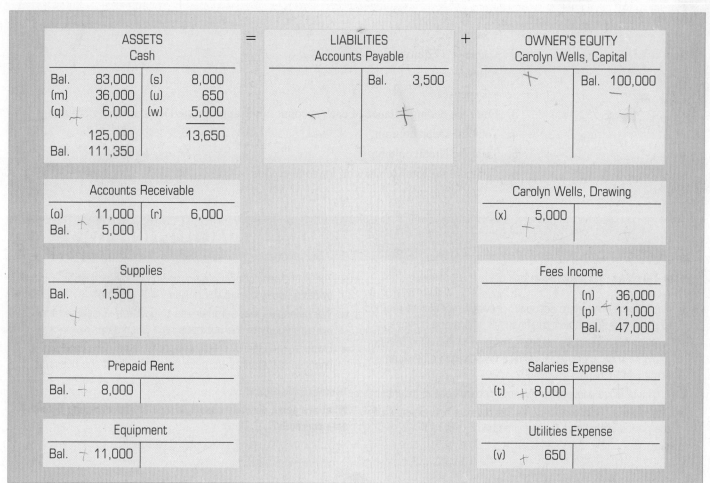

ASSETS				=	LIABILITIES		+	OWNER'S EQUITY	
Cash					**Accounts Payable**			**Carolyn Wells, Capital**	
Bal.	83,000	(s)	8,000			Bal. 3,500			Bal. 100,000
(m)	36,000	(u)	650						
(q)	6,000	(w)	5,000						
	125,000		13,650						
Bal.	111,350								

Accounts Receivable					**Carolyn Wells, Drawing**	
(o)	11,000	(r)	6,000		(x) 5,000	
Bal.	5,000					

Supplies	
Bal. 1,500	

Fees Income	
	(n) 36,000
	(p) 11,000
	Bal. 47,000

Prepaid Rent	
Bal. 8,000	

Salaries Expense	
(t) 8,000	

Equipment	
Bal. 11,000	

Utilities Expense	
(v) 650	

FIGURE 3.6

Trial Balance

recall

Financial Statement Headings

The financial statement headings answer three questions:

Who—the company name

What—the report title

When—the date of, or the period covered by, the report

Wells' Consulting Services			
Trial Balance			
December 31, 2010			
ACCOUNT NAME	DEBIT	CREDIT	
Cash	111 3 5 0 00		
Accounts Receivable	5 0 0 0 00		
Supplies	1 5 0 0 00		
Prepaid Rent	8 0 0 0 00		
Equipment	11 0 0 0 00		
Accounts Payable		3 5 0 0 00	
Carolyn Wells, Capital		100 0 0 0 00	
Carolyn Wells, Drawing	5 0 0 0 00		
Fees Income		47 0 0 0 00	
Salaries Expense	8 0 0 0 00		
Utilities Expense	6 5 0 00		
Totals	150 5 0 0 00	150 5 0 0 00	

recorded. If total debits do not equal total credits, there is an error. Figure 3.6 above shows the trial balance for Wells' Consulting Services. To prepare a trial balance, perform the following steps:

1. Enter the trial balance heading showing the company name, report title, and closing date for the accounting period.

2. List the account names in the same order as they appear on the financial statements.
   - Assets
   - Liabilities
   - Owner's Equity
   - Revenue
   - Expenses

3. Enter the ending balance of each account in the appropriate Debit or Credit column.

4. Total the Debit column.

5. Total the Credit column.

6. Compare the total debits with the total credits.

MANAGERIAL IMPLICATIONS   **<<**

FINANCIAL STATEMENTS

- Recording entries into accounts provides an efficient method of gathering data about the financial affairs of a business.
- A chart of accounts is usually similar from company to company; balance sheet accounts are first, followed by income statement accounts.
- A trial balance proves the financial records are in balance.
- The income statement reports the revenue and expenses for the period and shows the net income or loss.

- The statement of owner's equity shows the change in owner's equity during the period.
- The balance sheet summarizes the assets, liabilities, and owner's equity of the business on a given date.
- Owners, managers, creditors, banks, and many others use financial statements to make decisions about the business.

THINKING CRITICALLY

What are some possible consequences of not recording financial data correctly?

UNDERSTANDING TRIAL BALANCE ERRORS

If the totals of the Debit and Credit columns are equal, the financial records are in balance. If the totals of the Debit and Credit columns are not equal, there is an error. The error may be in the trial balance, or it may be in the financial records. Some common errors are

- adding trial balance columns incorrectly;
- recording only half a transaction—for example, recording a debit but not recording a credit, or vice versa;
- recording both halves of a transaction as debits or credits rather than recording one debit and one credit;
- recording an amount incorrectly from a transaction;
- recording a debit for one amount and a credit for a different amount;
- making an error when calculating the account balances.

FINDING TRIAL BALANCE ERRORS

If the trial balance does not balance, try the following procedures.

1. Check the arithmetic. If the columns were originally added from top to bottom, verify the total by adding from bottom to top.
2. Check that the correct account balances were transferred to the correct trial balance columns.
3. Check the arithmetic used to compute the account balances.
4. Check that each transaction was recorded correctly in the accounts by tracing the amounts to the analysis of the transaction.

Sometimes you can determine the type of the error by the amount of the difference. Compute the difference between the debit total and the credit total. If the difference is divisible by 2, a debit might be recorded as a credit, or a credit recorded as a debit.

If the difference is divisible by 9, there might be a transposition. A **transposition** occurs when the digits of a number are switched (357 for 375). The test for a transposition is

$$
\begin{array}{r}
375 \\
-357 \\
\hline
18
\end{array}
\qquad 18/9 = 2
$$

Also check for slides. A **slide** occurs when the decimal point is misplaced (375 for 37.50). We can test for a slide in the following manner.

$$
\begin{array}{r}
375.00 \\
-35.50 \\
\hline
337.50
\end{array}
\qquad 337.50/9 = 37.50
$$

Financial Statements

After the trial balance is prepared, the financial statements are prepared. Figure 3.7 shows the financial statements for Wells' Consulting Services. The amounts are taken from the trial balance. As you study the financial statements, note that net income from the income statement is used on the statement of owner's equity. Also note that the ending balance of the *Carolyn Wells, Capital* account, computed on the statement of owner's equity, is used on the balance sheet.

Chart of Accounts

A **chart of accounts** is a list of all the accounts used by a business. Figure 3.8 shows the chart of accounts for Wells' Consulting Services. Each account has a number and a name. The balance sheet accounts are listed first, followed by the income statement accounts. The account number is assigned based on the type of account.

>>**5. OBJECTIVE**

Prepare a trial balance from T accounts.

LP3

>>**6. OBJECTIVE**

Prepare an income statement, a statement of owner's equity, and a balance sheet.

>>**7. OBJECTIVE**

Develop a chart of accounts.

FIGURE 3.7

Financial Statements for Wells'
Consulting Services

Wells' Consulting Services
Income Statement
Month Ended December 31, 2010

Revenue			
Fees Income			47 000 00
Expenses			
Salaries Expense	8 000 00		
Utilities Expense	6 50 00		
Total Expenses		8 650 00	
Net Income		38 350 00	

Wells' Consulting Services
Statement of Owner's Equity
Month Ended December 31, 2010

Carolyn Wells, Capital, December 1, 2010		100 000 00
Net Income for December	38 350 00	
Less Withdrawals for December	5 000 00	
Increase in Capital		33 350 00
Carolyn Wells, Capital, December 31, 2010		133 350 00

Wells' Consulting Services
Balance Sheet
December 31, 2010

Assets		Liabilities	
Cash	111 350 00	Accounts Payable	3 500 00
Accounts Receivable	5 000 00		
Supplies	1 500 00		
Prepaid Rent	8 000 00	Owner's Equity	
Equipment	11 000 00	Carolyn Wells, Capital	133 350 00
Total Assets	136 850 00	Total Liabilities and Owner's Equity	136 850 00

Asset Accounts	100–199	Revenue Accounts	400–499
Liability Accounts	200–299	Expense Accounts	500–599
Owner's Equity Accounts	300–399		

Notice that the accounts are not numbered consecutively. For example, asset account numbers jump from 101 to 111 and then to 121, 137, and 141. In each block of numbers, gaps are left so that additional accounts can be added when needed.

Permanent and Temporary Accounts

The asset, liability, and owner's equity accounts appear on the balance sheet at the end of an accounting period. The balances of these accounts are then carried forward to start the new period. Because they continue from one accounting period to the next, these accounts are called **permanent accounts** or *real accounts*.

Revenue and expense accounts appear on the income statement. The drawing account appears on the statement of owner's equity. These accounts classify and summarize changes in owner's equity during the period. They are called **temporary accounts** or *nominal accounts* because the balances in these accounts are transferred to the capital account at the end of the accounting period. In the next period, these accounts start with zero balances.

Wells' Consulting Services
Chart of Accounts

Account Number	Account Name
Balance Sheet Accounts	
100–199	**ASSETS**
101	Cash
111	Accounts Receivable
121	Supplies
137	Prepaid Rent
141	Equipment
200–299	**LIABILITIES**
202	Accounts Payable
300–399	**OWNER'S EQUITY**
301	Carolyn Wells, Capital
Statement of Owner's Equity Account	
302	Carolyn Wells, Drawing (WITH I)
Income Statement Accounts	
400–499	**REVENUE**
401	Fees Income
500–599	**EXPENSES**
511	Salaries Expense
514	Utilities Expense

FIGURE 3.8

Chart of Accounts

important!

Balance Sheet Accounts
The amounts on the balance sheet are carried forward to the next accounting period.

important!

Income Statement Accounts
The amounts on the income statement are transferred to the capital account at the end of the accounting period.

Section 2 Self Review

QUESTIONS

1. What is a trial balance and what is its purpose?

2. What is a transposition? A slide?

3. What is the increase side for *Cash; Accounts Payable;* and *Carolyn Wells, Capital?*

EXERCISES

4. Which account has a normal debit balance?

 a. Accounts Payable

 b. L. T., Capital

 c. L. T., Drawing

 d. Fees Income

5. The company owner took $4,000 cash for personal use. What is the entry for this transaction?

a. Debit *Cash* and credit *Jason Taylor, Drawing.*

b. Debit *Jason Taylor, Drawing* and credit *Cash.*

c. Debit *Jason Taylor, Capital* and credit *Cash.*

d. Debit *Cash* and credit *Jason Taylor, Capital.*

ANALYSIS

6. Describe the errors in the Tuttle Interiors trial balance.

Tuttle Interiors
Trial Balance
December 31, 2010

	DEBIT	CREDIT
Cash	30 0 0 0 00	
Accts. Rec.	20 0 0 0 00	
Equip.	14 0 0 0 00	
Accts. Pay.		30 0 0 0 00
S. Tuttle, Capital		44 0 0 0 00
S. Tuttle, Drawing		20 0 0 0 00
Fees Income	28 0 0 0 00	
Rent Exp.	4 0 0 0 00	
Supplies Exp.	4 0 0 0 00	
Telephone Exp.	10 0 0 0 00	
Totals	110 0 0 0 00	94 0 0 0 00

(Answers to Section 2 Self Review are on pages 87–88.)

3 Chapter **REVIEW**   **Chapter Summary**

In this chapter, you have learned how to use T accounts to help analyze and record business transactions. A chart of accounts can be developed to easily identify all the accounts used by a business. After determining the balance for all accounts, the trial balance is prepared to ensure that all transactions have been recorded accurately.

Learning Objectives

1 Set up T accounts for assets, liabilities, and owner's equity.

T accounts consist of two lines, one vertical and one horizontal, that resemble the letter T. The account name is written on the top line. Increases and decreases to the account are entered on either the left side or the right side of the vertical line.

2 Analyze business transactions and enter them in the accounts.

Each business transaction is analyzed for its effects on the fundamental accounting equation, Assets = Liabilities + Owner's Equity. Then these effects are recorded in the proper accounts. Accounts are classified as assets, liabilities, or owner's equity.

- Increases in an asset account appear on the debit, or left, side because assets are on the left side of the accounting equation. The credit, or right, side records decreases.
- An increase in a liability account is recorded on the credit, or right, side. The left, or debit, side of a liability account is used for recording decreases.
- Increases in owner's equity are shown on the credit (right) side of an account. Decreases appear on the debit (left) side.
- The drawing account is used to record the withdrawal of cash from the business by the owner. The drawing account decreases owner's equity.

3 Determine the balance of an account.

The difference between the amounts recorded on the two sides of an account is known as the balance of the account.

4 Set up T accounts for revenue and expenses.

- Revenue accounts increase owner's equity; therefore, increases are recorded on the credit side of revenue accounts.
- Expenses are recorded on the debit side of the expense accounts because expenses decrease owner's equity.

5 Prepare a trial balance from T accounts.

The trial balance is a statement to test the accuracy of the financial records. Total debits should equal total credits.

6 Prepare an income statement, a statement of owner's equity, and a balance sheet.

The income statement is prepared to report the revenue and expenses for the period. The statement of owner's equity is prepared to analyze the change in owner's equity during the period. Then the balance sheet is prepared to summarize the assets, liabilities, and owner's equity of the business at a given point in time.

7 Develop a chart of accounts.

A firm's list of accounts is called its chart of accounts. Accounts are arranged in a predetermined order and are numbered for handy reference and quick identification. Typically, accounts are numbered in the order in which they appear on the financial statements. Balance sheet accounts come first, followed by income statement accounts.

8 Define the accounting terms new to this chapter.

Glossary

Account balance (p. 60) The difference between the amounts recorded on the two sides of an account

Accounts (p. 54) Written records of the assets, liabilities, and owner's equity of a business

Chart of accounts (p. 71) A list of the accounts used by a business to record its financial transactions

Classification (p. 54) A means of identifying each account as an asset, liability, or owner's equity

Credit (p. 68) An entry on the right side of an account

Debit (p. 68) An entry on the left side of an account

Double-entry system (p. 68) An accounting system that involves recording the effects of each transaction as debits and credits

Drawing account (p. 67) A special type of owner's equity account set up to record the owner's withdrawal of cash from the business

Footing (p. 60) A small pencil figure written at the base of an amount column showing the sum of the entries in the column

Normal balance (p. 60) The increase side of an account

Permanent account (p. 72) An account that is kept open from one accounting period to the next

Slide (p. 71) An accounting error involving a misplaced decimal point

T account (p. 54) A type of account, resembling a T, used to analyze the effects of a business transaction

Temporary account (p. 72) An account whose balance is transferred to another account at the end of an accounting period

Transposition (p. 71) An accounting error involving misplaced digits in a number

Trial balance (p. 69) A statement to test the accuracy of total debits and credits after transactions have been recorded

Comprehensive **Self Review**

1. What is a chart of accounts?
2. What are withdrawals and how are they recorded?
3. What type of accounts are found on the balance sheet?
4. On which side of asset, liability, and owner's equity accounts are decreases recorded?
5. Your friend has prepared financial statements for her business. She has asked you to review the statements for accuracy. The trial balance debit column totals $71,000 and the credit column totals $84,000. What steps would you take to find the error?

(Answers to Comprehensive Self Review are on page 88.)

 Multiple choice questions are provided on the text Web site at www.mhhe.com/price12e Quiz3

Discussion Questions

1. The terms *debit* and *credit* are often used in describing the effects of transactions on different accounts. What do these terms mean?
2. Why is the modern system of accounting usually called the double-entry system?
3. Why is *Prepaid Rent* considered an asset account?
4. Accounts are classified as permanent or temporary accounts. What do these classifications mean?
5. When a chart of accounts is created, number gaps are left within groups of accounts. Why are these number gaps necessary?
6. In what order do accounts appear in the chart of accounts?
7. What is the purpose of a chart of accounts?
8. How is the balance of an account determined?
9. What are accounts?
10. Indicate whether each of the following types of accounts would normally have a debit balance or a credit balance.
    a. An asset account
    b. A liability account

    c. The owner's capital account

    d. A revenue account

    e. An expense account

11. Are the following accounts permanent or temporary accounts?

    a. Fees Income

    b. Johnny Jones, Drawing

    c. Accounts Payable

    d. Accounts Receivable

    e. Johnny Jones, Capital

    f. Prepaid Rent

    g. Cash

    h. Advertising Expense

    i. Utilities Expense

    j. Equipment

    k. Salaries Expense

    l. Prepaid Insurance

APPLICATIONS

Exercises

Exercise 3.1
Objective 1

▶ **Setting up T accounts.**

Thompson Watch and Jewelry Repair Service has the following account balances on December 31, 2010. Set up a T account for each account and enter the balance on the proper side of the account.

Cash	$16,000	Accounts Payable	$12,000
Equipment	$32,000	Fred Thompson, Capital	$36,000

Exercise 3.2
Objective 2

▶ **Using T accounts to analyze transactions.**

Lisa Morgan decided to start a dental practice. The first five transactions for the business follow. For each transaction, (1) determine which two accounts are affected, (2) set up T accounts for the affected accounts, and (3) enter the debit and credit amounts in the T accounts.

1. Lisa invested $40,000 cash in the business.

2. Paid $10,000 in cash for equipment.

3. Performed services for cash amounting to $4,000.

4. Paid $1,400 in cash for advertising expense.

5. Paid $1,000 in cash for supplies.

Exercise 3.3
Objective 3

▶ **Determining debit and credit balances.**

Indicate whether each of the following accounts normally has a debit balance or a credit balance.

1. Mary Amos, Capital

2. Cash

3. Fees Income
4. Accounts Payable
5. Supplies
6. Salaries Expense
7. Accounts Receivable
8. Equipment

Identifying debits and credits.

In each of the following sentences, fill in the blanks with the word *debit* or *credit*.

1. The owner's capital account normally has a ___?___ balance. This account increases on the ___?___ side and decreases on the ___?___ side.

2. Liability accounts normally have ___?___ balances. These accounts increase on the ___?___ side and decrease on the ___?___ side.

3. Expense accounts normally have ___?___ balances. These accounts increase on the ___?___ side and decrease on the ___?___ side.

4. Asset accounts normally have ___?___ balances. These accounts increase on the ___?___ side and decrease on the ___?___ side.

5. Revenue accounts normally have ___?___ balances. These accounts increase on the ___?___ side and decrease on the ___?___ side.

◄ **Exercise 3.4**
Objective 3

Determining account balances.

The following T accounts show transactions that were recorded by Timeless Restorations, a firm that specializes in restoring antique furniture. The entries for the first transaction are labeled with the letter (a), the entries for the second transaction with the letter (b), and so on. Determine the balance of each account.

◄ **Exercise 3.5**
Objective 3

+ Cash −			
(a)	160,000	(b)	40,000
(d)	20,000	(e)	600
(g)	2,000	(h)	10,000
		(i)	4,000
	182,000		54,600

+ Equipment ~	
(c)	60,000

+ Accounts Receivable −			
(f)	8,000	(g)	2,000

~ Accounts Payable +			
		(c)	60,000

+ Supplies ~	
(b)	40,000

~ Susan Willis, Capital +			
		(a)	160,000

~ Fees Income +			
		(d)	20,000
		(f)	8,000

+ Telephone Expense −	
(e)	600

+ Susan Willis, Drawing −	
(i)	4,000

+ Salaries Expense ~	
(h)	10,000

Preparing a trial balance and an income statement.

Using the account balances from Exercise 3.5, prepare a trial balance and an income statement for Timeless Restorations. The trial balance is for December 31, 2010, and the income statement is for the month ended December 31, 2010.

◄ **Exercise 3.6**
Objectives 5, 6
CONTINUING >>>
Problem

Exercise 3.7

Objective 6

CONTINUING >>>
Problem

▶ **Preparing a statement of owner's equity and a balance sheet.**

From the trial balance and the net income or net loss determined in Exercise 3.6, prepare a statement of owner's equity and a balance sheet for Timeless Restorations as of December 31, 2010.

Exercise 3.8

Objective 7

▶ **Preparing a chart of accounts.**

The accounts that will be used by Zant Moving Company follow. Prepare a chart of accounts for the firm. Classify the accounts by type, arrange them in an appropriate order, and assign suitable account numbers.

Sue Zant, Capital	Salaries Expense
Office Supplies	Prepaid Rent
Accounts Payable	Fees Income
Cash	Accounts Receivable
Utilities Expense	Telephone Expense
Office Equipment	Sue Zant, Drawing

PROBLEMS

Problem Set A

Problem 3.1A

Objectives 1, 2

e**X**cel

▶ **Using T accounts to record transactions involving assets, liabilities, and owner's equity.**

The following transactions took place at Professional Counseling Services business established by Greta Davis.

INSTRUCTIONS

For each transaction, set up T accounts from this list: *Cash; Office Furniture; Office Equipment; Automobile; Accounts Payable; Greta Davis, Capital;* and *Greta Davis, Drawing.* Analyze each transaction. Record the amounts in the T accounts affected by that transaction. Use plus and minus signs to show increases and decreases in each account.

TRANSACTIONS

1. Greta Davis invested $60,000 cash in the business.
2. Purchased office furniture for $16,000 in cash.
3. Bought a fax machine for $950; payment is due in 30 days.
4. Purchased a used car for the firm for $16,000 in cash.
5. Davis invested an additional $10,000 cash in the business.
6. Bought a new computer for $3,000; payment is due in 60 days.
7. Paid $950 to settle the amount owed on the fax machine.
8. Davis withdrew $4,000 in cash for personal expenses.

Analyze: Which transactions affected asset accounts?

Using T accounts to record transactions involving assets, liabilities, and owner's equity.

◀ **Problem 3.2A**
Objective 1

The following transactions occurred at several different businesses and are not related.

INSTRUCTIONS

Analyze each of the transactions. For each, decide what accounts are affected and set up T accounts. Record the effects of the transaction in the T accounts. Use plus and minus signs before the amounts to show the increases and decreases.

TRANSACTIONS

1. James Mitchell, an owner, made an additional investment of $8,000 in cash.
2. A firm purchased equipment for $7,000 in cash.
3. A firm sold some surplus office furniture for $600 in cash.
4. A firm purchased a computer for $1,350, to be paid in 60 days.
5. A firm purchased office equipment for $5,100 on credit. The amount is due in 60 days.
6. Mesia Davis, owner of Davis Travel Agency, withdrew $2,000 of her original cash investment.
7. A firm bought a delivery truck for $18,000 on credit; payment is due in 90 days.
8. A firm issued a check for $1,100 to a supplier in partial payment of an open account balance.

Analyze: List the transactions that directly affected an owner's equity account.

Using T accounts to record transactions involving revenues and expenses.

◀ **Problem 3.3A**
Objectives 2, 4

The following occurred during June at Carter's Professional Counseling.

INSTRUCTIONS

Analyze each transaction. Use T accounts to record these transactions and be sure to put the name of the account on the top of each account. Record the effects of the transaction in the T accounts. Use plus and minus signs before the amounts to show the increases and decreases.

TRANSACTIONS

1. Purchased office supplies for $2,000.
2. Delivered monthly statements, collected fee income of $21,000.
3. Paid the current month's office rent of $4,000.
4. Completed professional counseling, billed client for $3,000.
5. Client paid fee of $1,000 for weekly counseling, previously billed.
6. Paid office salary of $3,600.
7. Paid telephone bill of $480.
8. Billed client for $2,000 fee for preparing a counseling memorandum.
9. Purchased office supplies of $1,000 on account.

10. Paid office salary of $3,600.

11. Collected $2,000 from client who was billed.

12. Clients paid a total of $8,100 cash in fees.

Analyze: How much cash did the business spend during the month of June?

Problem 3.4A ▶

Objectives 1, 2, 4

Using T accounts to record all business transactions.

The following accounts and transactions are for John Wilson, Landscape Consultant.

INSTRUCTIONS

Analyze the transactions. Record each in the appropriate T accounts. Use plus and minus signs in front of the amounts to show the increases and decreases. Identify each entry in the T accounts by writing the letter of the transaction next to the entry.

ASSETS
Cash
Accounts Receivable
Office Furniture
Office Equipment

LIABILITIES
Accounts Payable

OWNER'S EQUITY
John Wilson, Capital
John Wilson, Drawing

REVENUE
Fees Income

EXPENSES
Rent Expense
Utilities Expense
Salaries Expense
Telephone Expense
Miscellaneous Expense

TRANSACTIONS

a. Wilson invested $150,000 in cash to start the business.

b. Paid $5,000 for the current month's rent.

c. Bought office furniture for $15,720 in cash.

d. Performed services for $7,200 in cash.

e. Paid $1,150 for the monthly telephone bill.

f. Performed services for $13,000 on credit.

g. Purchased a computer and copier for $36,000, paid $12,000 in cash immediately with the balance due in 30 days.

h. Received $6,500 from credit clients.

i. Paid $3,000 in cash for office cleaning services for the month.

j. Purchased additional office chairs for $4,800; received credit terms of 30 days.

k. Purchased office equipment for $30,000 and paid half of this amount in cash immediately; the balance is due in 30 days.

l. Issued a check for $8,400 to pay salaries.

m. Performed services for $13,500 in cash.

n. Performed services for $15,000 on credit.

o. Collected $7,000 on accounts receivable from charge customers.

p. Issued a check for $2,400 in partial payment of the amount owed for office chairs.

q. Paid $600 to a duplicating company for photocopy work performed during the month.

r. Paid $1,120 for the monthly electric bill.

s. Wilson withdrew $8,000 in cash for personal expenses.

Analyze: What liabilities does the business have after all transactions have been recorded?

Preparing financial statements from T accounts.

The accountant for the firm owned by John Wilson prepares financial statements at the end of each month.

◄ **Problem 3.5A** ✳
Objectives 3, 5, 6
e**X**cel
CONTINUING >>>
          Problem

INSTRUCTIONS

Use the figures in the T accounts for Problem 3.4A to prepare a trial balance, an income statement, a statement of owner's equity, and a balance sheet. (The first line of the statement headings should read "John Wilson, Landscape Consultant.") Assume that the transactions took place during the month ended June 30, 2010. Determine the account balances before you start work on the financial statements.

Analyze: What is the change in owner's equity for the month of June?

Problem Set B

Using T accounts to record transactions involving assets, liabilities, and owner's equity.

The following transactions took place at Windmill Equipment Service.

◄ **Problem 3.1B**
Objectives 1, 2

INSTRUCTIONS

For each transaction, set up T accounts from the following list: *Cash*; *Shop Equipment; Store Equipment; Truck; Accounts Payable; Joseph Tejan, Capital;* and *Joseph Tejan, Drawing*. Analyze each transaction. Record the effects of the transactions in the T accounts. Use plus and minus signs before the amounts to show the increases and decreases.

TRANSACTIONS

1. Joseph Tejan invested $20,000 cash in the business.

2. Purchased shop equipment for $1,800 in cash.

3. Bought store fixtures for $1,200; payment is due in 30 days.

4. Purchased a used truck for $10,000 in cash.

5. Tejan gave the firm his personal tools that have a fair market value of $3,000.

6. Bought a used cash register for $2,500; payment is due in 30 days.

7. Paid $400 in cash to apply to the amount owed for store fixtures.

8. Tejan withdrew $1,600 in cash for personal expenses.

Analyze: Which transactions affect the *Cash* account?

Using T accounts to record transactions involving assets, liabilities, and owner's equity.

The following transactions occurred at several different businesses and are not related.

◄ **Problem 3.2B**
Objectives 1, 2

INSTRUCTIONS

Analyze each of the transactions. For each transaction, set up T accounts. Record the effects of the transaction in the T accounts. Use plus and minus signs to show the increases and decreases.

TRANSACTIONS

1. A firm purchased equipment for $16,000 in cash.
2. The owner Angie Carvajal withdrew $4,000 cash.
3. A firm sold a piece of surplus equipment for $3,000 in cash.
4. A firm purchased a used delivery truck for $12,000 in cash.
5. A firm paid $3,600 in cash to apply against an account owed.
6. A firm purchased office equipment for $5,000. The amount is to be paid in 60 days.
7. Chuck Vinson, owner of the company, made an additional investment of $20,000 in cash.
8. A firm paid $1,500 by check for office equipment that it had previously purchased on credit.

Analyze: Which transactions affect liability accounts?

Problem 3.3B
Objectives 2, 4

▶ ## Using T accounts to record transactions involving revenue and expenses.

The following transactions took place at Express Service Cleaning Company.

INSTRUCTIONS

Analyze each of the transactions. For each transaction, decide what accounts are affected and set up T accounts. Record the effects of the transaction in the T accounts. Use plus and minus signs before the amounts to show the increases and decreases.

TRANSACTIONS

1. Paid $3,200 for the current month's rent.
2. Performed services for $4,000 in cash.
3. Paid salaries of $4,800.
4. Performed additional services for $7,200 on credit.
5. Paid $600 for the monthly telephone bill.
6. Collected $2,000 from accounts receivable.
7. Received a $120 refund for an overcharge on the telephone bill.

8. Performed services for $4,800 on credit.

9. Paid $400 in cash for the monthly electric bill.

10. Paid $880 in cash for gasoline purchased for the firm's van during the month.

11. Received $3,600 from charge account customers.

12. Performed services for $7,200 in cash.

Analyze: What total cash was collected for accounts receivable during the month?

Using T accounts to record all business transactions.

The accounts and transactions of Kathryn Price, Counselor and Attorney at Law, follow.

◀ **Problem 3.4B**
Objectives 1, 2, 4

INSTRUCTIONS

Analyze the transactions. Record each in the appropriate T accounts. Use plus and minus signs in front of the amounts to show the increases and decreases. Identify each entry in the T accounts by writing the letter of the transaction next to the entry.

ASSETS
Cash
Accounts Receivable
Office Furniture
Office Equipment
Automobile

LIABILITIES
Accounts Payable

OWNER'S EQUITY
Kathryn Price, Capital
Kathryn Price, Drawing

REVENUE
Fees Income

EXPENSES
Automobile Expense
Rent Expense
Utilities Expense
Salaries Expense
Telephone Expense

TRANSACTIONS

a. Kathryn Price invested $120,000 in cash to start the business.

b. Paid $6,400 for the current month's rent.

c. Bought a used automobile for the firm for $36,000 in cash.

d. Performed services for $8,000 in cash.

e. Paid $1,600 for automobile repairs.

f. Performed services for $9,150 on credit.

g. Purchased office chairs for $5,600 on credit.

h. Received $4,500 from credit clients.

i. Paid $3,600 to reduce the amount owed for the office chairs.

j. Issued a check for $1,300 to pay the monthly utility bill.

k. Purchased office equipment for $19,600 and paid half of this amount in cash immediately; the balance is due in 30 days.

l. Issued a check for $13,700 to pay salaries.

m. Performed services for $4,750 in cash.

n. Performed services for $5,500 on credit.

o. Paid $796 for the monthly telephone bill.

p. Collected $3,800 on accounts receivable from charge customers.

q. Purchased additional office equipment and received a bill for $5,440 due in 30 days.

r. Paid $800 in cash for gasoline purchased for the automobile during the month.

s. Kathryn Price withdrew $6,000 in cash for personal expenses.

Analyze: What outstanding amount is owed to the company from its credit customers?

Problem 3.5B

Objectives 3, 5, 6

CONTINUING >>>
        Problem

▶ **Preparing financial statements from T accounts.**

The accountant for the firm owned by Kathryn Price prepares financial statements at the end of each month.

INSTRUCTIONS

Use the figures in the T accounts for Problem 3.4B to prepare a trial balance, an income statement, a statement of owner's equity, and a balance sheet. (The first line of the statement headings should read "Kathryn Price, Counselor and Attorney at Law.") Assume that the transactions took place during the month ended April 30, 2010. Determine the account balances before you start work on the financial statements.

Analyze: What net change in owner's equity occurred during the month of April?

Critical Thinking Problem 3.1

Sole Proprietorship

Helen Franz is an architect who operates her own business. The accounts and transactions for the business follow.

INSTRUCTIONS

(1) Analyze the transactions for January 2010. Record each in the appropriate T accounts. Use plus and minus signs in front of the amounts to show the increases and decreases. Identify each entry in the T account by writing the letter of the transaction next to the entry.

(2) Determine the account balances. Prepare a trial balance, an income statement, a statement of owner's equity, and a balance sheet.

ASSETS
Cash
Accounts Receivable
Office Furniture
Office Equipment

LIABILITIES
Accounts Payable

OWNER'S EQUITY
Helen Franz, Capital
Helen Franz, Drawing

REVENUE
Fees Income

EXPENSES
Advertising Expense
Utilities Expense
Salaries Expense
Telephone Expense
Miscellaneous Expense

TRANSACTIONS

a. Helen Franz invested $15,000 in cash to start the business.

b. Paid $1,000 for advertisements in a design magazine.

c. Purchased office furniture for $2,000 in cash.

d. Performed services for $2,100 in cash.

e. Paid $187.50 for the monthly telephone bill.

f. Performed services for $1,305 on credit.

g. Purchased a fax machine for $287.50; paid $87.50 in cash with the balance due in 30 days.

h. Paid a bill for $325 from the office cleaning service.

i. Received $1,080 from clients on account.

j. Purchased additional office chairs for $540; received credit terms of 30 days.

k. Paid $2,000 for salaries.

l. Issued a check for $270 in partial payment of the amount owed for office chairs.

m. Received $1,400 in cash for services performed.

n. Issued a check for $280 for utilities expense.

o. Performed services for $2,100 on credit.

p. Collected $600 from clients on account.

q. Helen Franz withdrew $1,750 in cash for personal expenses.

r. Paid $300 to Quick Copy Service for photocopy work performed during the month.

Analyze: Using the basic accounting equation, what is the financial condition of Helen Franz's business at month-end?

Critical Thinking Problem 3.2

Financial Condition

At the beginning of the summer, Ted Coe was looking for a way to earn money to pay for his college tuition in the fall. He decided to start a lawn service business in his neighborhood. To get the business started, Ted used $3,000 from his savings account to open a checking account for his new business, Elegant Lawn Care. He purchased two used power mowers and various lawn care tools for $1,000, and paid $1,800 for a second-hand truck to transport the mowers.

Several of his neighbors hired him to cut their grass on a weekly basis. He sent these customers monthly bills. By the end of the summer, they had paid him $600 in cash and owed him another $1,150. Ted also cut grass on an as-needed basis for other neighbors who paid him $500.

During the summer, Ted spent $200 for gasoline for the truck and mowers. He paid $500 to a friend who helped him on several occasions. An advertisement in the local paper cost $100. Now, at the end of the summer, Ted is concerned because he has only $500 left in his checking account. He says, "I worked hard all summer and have only $500 to show for it. It would have been better to leave the money in the bank."

Prepare an income statement, a statement of owner's equity, and a balance sheet for Elegant Lawn Care. Explain to Ted whether or not he is "better off" than he was at the beginning of the summer. (Hint: T accounts might be helpful in organizing the data.)

BUSINESS CONNECTIONS

Informed Decisions

1. How do the income statement and the balance sheet help management make sound decisions?

2. How can management find out, at any time, whether a firm can pay its bills as they become due?

Managerial | FOCUS

3. If a firm's expenses equal or exceed its revenue, what actions might management take?

4. In discussing a firm's latest financial statements, a manager says that it is the "results on the bottom line" that really count. What does the manager mean?

To Open or Not to Open

As the full charge bookkeeper, you are responsible for keeping the chart of accounts up to date. At the end of each year, you analyze the accounts to verify that each account should be active for accumulation of costs, revenues, and expenses. In July, the accounts payable clerk has asked you to open an account named New Expenses. You know that an account name should be specific and well defined. You feel that the A/P clerk might want to charge some expenses to that account that would not be appropriate. Why do you think the A/P clerk needs this New Expenses account? Who needs to know this information and what action should you consider?

Account Categories

Refer to the *2006 Annual Report* for The Home Depot, Inc., in Appendix A.

1. To prepare financial statements, The Home Depot, Inc., summarizes general ledger account balances into summary categories for presentation on statements. List five "permanent" summarized account categories reflected in these statements. List five "temporary" summarized account categories found in the statements.

2. Locate the consolidated balance sheet for The Home Depot, Inc. If The Home Depot, Inc., purchased new store fixtures on account for $25,000, describe the effect on the company's balance sheet categories.

Management Letter

Annual reports released by publicly held companies include a letter to the stockholders written by the chief executive officer, chairman of the board, or president. Excerpts from the Adobe Systems Incorporated *Annual Report* "2004 Letter to Stockholders" are presented below. The appearance of ellipses (. . .) indicates that some of the text of the letter has been deleted to save space.

> In fiscal year 2006, Adobe reached a major milestone, surpassing two billion dollars in revenue. This was achieved by delivering double-digit growth for the fourth consecutive year. Annual revenue grew to a record $2,575.3 billion in fiscal 2006, a 31% increase from fiscal 2005 revenue. . . . Creative Solutions . . . revenue was $1,424.9 billion, making it our largest business segment. . . . Knowledge Worker Solutions . . . achieved revenue of $671.0 million. . . . Enterprise and Developer Solutions . . . achieved revenue of $189.2 million and represents one of our largest growth opportunities. . . . Mobile and Device Solutions . . . achieved revenue of $37.8 million. Our Other segment comprises three categories . . . , Revenue for this segment was $252.5 million. 2006 was another hugely successful year for Adobe. We continue to have a healthy balance sheet, with a cash and cash equivalent position of approximately $2.3 billion at the end of fiscal year 2006, and no long-term debt. Results from our operations once again generated strong cash flow, which we use to invest for Adobe's future as well as to repurchase shares of our stock.

Analyze:

1. Based on the excerpts above, what types of information can a company's management deliver using the letter to stockholders?

2. What annual revenue did Adobe Systems Incorporated report for fiscal 2006?

3. Which of Adobe's revenue lines showed the highest percentage growth from fiscal 2005 to 2006?

Analyze Online: Locate the Adobe Systems Incorporated Web site (www.adobe.com). Within *Investor Relations* in the *About Adobe* link, find the annual report for the current year. Read the letter to the stockholders within the annual report.

4. Are the financial results presented in the current year more or less favorable than those presented for fiscal 2006?

5. What new products were introduced in the current year and mentioned in the stockholders' letter?

Systems

A company's chart of accounts is an organization system. Discuss similar organization systems in subject areas other than accounting.

Extending THE THOUGHT

Memo

The junior accountant in your department does not agree that a trial balance should be prepared before the financial statements are completed. As the senior accountant, write a memo to your co-worker explaining your position on the topic. Express possible ramifications that you foresee if the trial balance is not prepared.

Business COMMUNICATION

Specific Chart of Accounts

A chart of accounts varies with each type of business as well as each company. In a group, compare and contrast the accounts that would appear in Jones Real Estate Office, Christy's Clothing Emporium, Lee's Grocery Store, and Sarkis' Plumbing Service. What accounts would appear in all companies? What accounts would be specific to each business?

TEAMWORK

10K Reports

Financial statements can reveal a great deal about a company. Corporations are required to produce a 10K report that includes the income statement and balance sheet. Go to the companies' Web sites listed below, select investor relations, annual report, and 10K report. From the income statement, decide the most profitable company. From the balance sheet, decide the company with the largest amount of cash available and the one with the most assets. (www.federated-fds.com) (www.jcpenny.com) (www.honeywell.com)

Internet CONNECTION

Answers to **Self Reviews**

Answers to Section 1 Self Review

1. The sum of several entries on either side of an account that is entered in small pencil figures.

2. The increase side of an account. The normal balance of an asset account is on the left side. The normal balance of liability and owner's equity accounts is on the right side.

3. Increases in asset accounts are recorded on the left side. Increases in liability and owner's equity accounts are recorded on the right side.

4. **b.** *Equipment* is increased by $10,800. *Accounts Payable* is increased by $10,800.

5. **c.** 26,150

6.

Cash	+	Equipment	+	Supplies	=	Accounts Payable	+	David Jenkins
$15,400	+	$20,000	+	$4,600	=	$10,000	+	$30,000
				$40,000	=	$40,000		

Answers to Section 2 Self Review

1. The trial balance is a list of all the accounts and their balances. Its purpose is to prove the equality of the total debits and credits.

2. A transposition is an error in which the digits of a number are switched, for example, when 517 is recorded as 571. A slide is an error in which the decimal point is misplaced, for example, when 317 is written as 3.17.

3. The increase side of *Cash* is the left, or debit, side. The increase side of *Accounts Payable* is the right, or credit, side. The increase side of *Carolyn Wells, Capital* is the right, or credit, side.

4. **c.** *L. T., Drawing*

5. **b.** *Jason Taylor, Drawing* would be debited and *Cash* would be credited.

6. *S. Tuttle, Drawing*—20,000 should be in the Debit column.

   Fees Income—28,000 should be in the Credit column.

   The new column totals will be 102,000.

Answers to Comprehensive Self Review

1. A list of the numbers and names of the accounts of a business. It provides a system by which the accounts of the business can be easily identified and located.

2. Cash taken from the business by the owner to obtain funds for personal living expenses. Withdrawals are recorded in a special type of owner's equity account called a drawing account.

3. The asset, liability, and owner's equity accounts.

4. Decreases in asset accounts are recorded on the credit side. Decreases in liability and owner's equity accounts are recorded on the debit side.

5. ▪ Check the math by adding the columns again.

   ▪ Determine whether the account balances are in the correct columns.

   ▪ Check the accounts to see whether the balances in the accounts were computed correctly.

   ▪ Check the accuracy of transactions recorded during the period.

The General Journal and the General Ledger

LEARNING OBJECTIVES

1. Record transactions in the general journal. LP4
2. Prepare compound journal entries.
3. Post journal entries to general ledger accounts.
4. Correct errors made in the journal or ledger.
5. Define the accounting terms new to this chapter.

NEW TERMS

accounting cycle
audit trail
balance ledger form
chronological order
compound entry
correcting entry

general journal
general ledger
journal
journalizing
ledger
posting

www.willamettevalleyvineyards.com

The Willamette Valley is the heart of Oregon's agriculture country. The valley is one of Oregon's major wine-growing regions and boasts over 200 wineries that produce a variety of vintages. Willamette Valley Vineyards is regarded as one of Oregon's top wineries. Started in 1983 with a small 50-acre vineyard, the company has carefully nurtured its growth producing top-quality wines that have been served at the White House and consistently earn high marks from *Wine Spectator* and *Wine Enthusiast*.

The company pays alcohol excise taxes based on product sales to both the Oregon Liquor Control Commission and to the U.S. Department of the Treasury, Alcohol and Tobacco Tax and Trade Bureau. Though the winery paid more than $600,000 in excise taxes from 2004 through 2006, an audit by the Alcohol and Tobacco Tax Trade Board claimed the company had underpaid these taxes. Willamette Valley is contesting these claims. Jim Bernau, the president of Willamette Valley Vineyards, said the dispute is about "really esoteric accounting and recordkeeping issues." Even if the company is unsuccessful in overturning the tax claim, tax credits would reduce the excise tax owed, company officials said.

thinking critically

Careful recordkeeping is critical to all businesses, large and small. How might Willamette Valley Vineyards' recordkeeping impact the outcome of the dispute described above?

SECTION OBJECTIVES

>> 1. **Record transactions in the general journal.**

WHY IT'S IMPORTANT

Written records for all business transactions are necessary. The general journal acts as the "diary" of the business.

>> 2. **Prepare compound journal entries.**

WHY IT'S IMPORTANT

Compound entries contain several debits or credits for a single business transaction, creating efficiencies in journalizing.

TERMS TO LEARN

accounting cycle
audit trail
chronological order
compound entry
general journal
journal
journalizing

The General Journal

The **accounting cycle** is a series of steps performed during each accounting period to classify, record, and summarize data for a business and to produce needed financial information. The first step in the accounting cycle is to analyze business transactions. You learned this skill in Chapter 3. The second step in the accounting cycle is to prepare a record of business transactions.

Journals

Video4.1

Business transactions are recorded in a **journal,** which is a diary of business activities. The journal lists transactions in **chronological order,** that is, in the order in which they occur. The journal is sometimes called the *record of original entry* because it is where transactions are first entered in the accounting records. There are different types of journals. This chapter will examine the general journal. You will become familiar with other journals in later chapters.

> Most corporations use accounting software to record business transactions. Industry-specific software is available for accounting firms, oil and gas companies, construction firms, medical firms, and any other industry-specific business enterprise.

>>1. OBJECTIVE

Record transactions in the general journal.

important!

The Diary of a Business
The general journal is similar to a diary. The general journal details, in chronological order, the economic events of the business.

The General Journal

The **general journal** is a financial record for entering all types of business transactions. **Journalizing** is the process of recording transactions in the general journal.

Figure 4.1 shows the general journal for Wells' Consulting Services. Notice that the general journal has a page number. To record a transaction, enter the year at the top of the Date column. In the Date column, write the month and day on the first line of the first entry. After the first entry, enter the year and month only when a new page is started or when the year or the month changes. In the Date column, write the day of each transaction on the first line of each transaction.

In the Description column, enter the account to be debited. Write the account name close to the left margin of the Description column, and enter the amount on the same line in the Debit column.

Enter the account to be credited on the line beneath the debit. Indent the account name about one-half inch from the left margin. Enter the amount on the same line in the Credit column.

Then enter a complete but concise description of the transaction in the Description column. Begin the description on the line following the credit. The description is indented about one inch from the left margin.

Write account names exactly as they appear in the chart of accounts. This will minimize errors when amounts are transferred from the general journal to the accounts.

FIGURE 4.1

General Journal Entry

GENERAL JOURNAL   PAGE ___1___

	DATE	DESCRIPTION	POST. REF.	DEBIT	CREDIT	
1	2010					1
2	Nov. 6	Cash		100 000 00		2
3		Carolyn Wells, Capital			100 000 00	3
4		Investment by owner				4
5						5

Record the year first, then the month and day.
Record the debit first.
Indent about one-half inch and record the credit.
Indent again and write the description.

Leave a blank line between general journal entries. Some accountants use this blank line to number each general journal entry.

When possible, the journal entry description should refer to the source of the information. For example, the journal entry to record a payment should include the check number in the description. Document numbers are part of the audit trail. The **audit trail** is a chain of references that makes it possible to trace information, locate errors, and prevent fraud. The audit trail provides a means of checking the journal entry against the original data on the documents.

RECORDING NOVEMBER TRANSACTIONS IN THE GENERAL JOURNAL

In Chapters 2 and 3, you learned a step-by-step method for analyzing business transactions. In this chapter, you will learn how to complete the journal entry for a business transaction in the same manner. Review the following steps before you continue.

1. Analyze the financial event.
   - Identify the accounts affected.
   - Classify the accounts affected.
   - Determine the amount of increase or decrease for each account affected.
2. Apply the rules of debit and credit.
   a. Which account is debited? For what amount?
   b. Which account is credited? For what amount?
3. Make the entry in T-account form.
4. Record the complete entry in general journal form.

important!

Audit Trail

To maintain the audit trail, descriptions should refer to document numbers whenever possible.

BUSINESS TRANSACTION

On November 6, Carolyn Wells withdrew $100,000 from personal savings and deposited it in a new business checking account for Wells' Consulting Services.

MEMORANDUM 01

WELLS' CONSULTING SERVICES

TO: Carlos Valdez
FROM: Carolyn Wells
DATE: November 6, 2010
SUBJECT: Contributed personal funds to the business

I contributed $100,000 from my personal savings to Wells' Consulting Services.

ANALYSIS

a. The asset account, *Cash,* is increased by $100,000.

b. The owner's equity account, *Carolyn Wells, Capital,* is increased by $100,000.

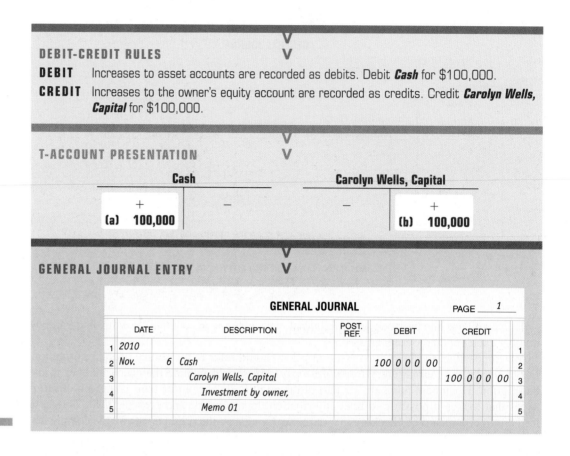

DEBIT-CREDIT RULES

DEBIT Increases to asset accounts are recorded as debits. Debit *Cash* for $100,000.

CREDIT Increases to the owner's equity account are recorded as credits. Credit *Carolyn Wells, Capital* for $100,000.

T-ACCOUNT PRESENTATION

Cash			
+		−	
(a) 100,000			

Carolyn Wells, Capital			
−		+	
		(b) 100,000	

GENERAL JOURNAL ENTRY

GENERAL JOURNAL   PAGE _____1_____

	DATE		DESCRIPTION	POST. REF.	DEBIT	CREDIT	
1	2010						1
2	Nov.	6	Cash		100 0 0 0 00		2
3			Carolyn Wells, Capital			100 0 0 0 00	3
4			Investment by owner,				4
5			Memo 01				5

BUSINESS TRANSACTION

On November 7, Wells' Consulting Services issued Check 1001 for $5,000 to purchase a computer and other equipment.

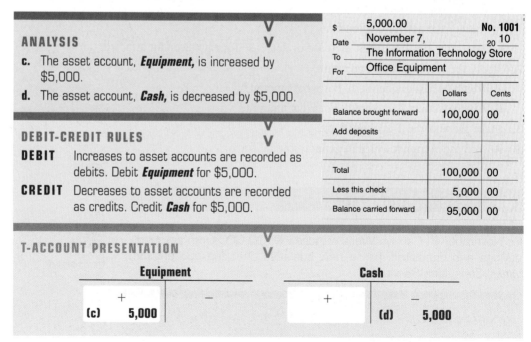

ANALYSIS

c. The asset account, *Equipment,* is increased by $5,000.

d. The asset account, *Cash,* is decreased by $5,000.

DEBIT-CREDIT RULES

DEBIT Increases to asset accounts are recorded as debits. Debit *Equipment* for $5,000.

CREDIT Decreases to asset accounts are recorded as credits. Credit *Cash* for $5,000.

$ 5,000.00		No. 1001
Date November 7,		20 10
To The Information Technology Store		
For Office Equipment		

	Dollars	Cents
Balance brought forward	100,000	00
Add deposits		
Total	100,000	00
Less this check	5,000	00
Balance carried forward	95,000	00

T-ACCOUNT PRESENTATION

Equipment			
+		−	
(c) 5,000			

Cash			
+		−	
		(d) 5,000	

GENERAL JOURNAL ENTRY

	DATE		DESCRIPTION	POST. REF.	DEBIT	CREDIT	
6	Nov.	7	Equipment		5 0 0 0 00		6
7			Cash			5 0 0 0 00	7
8			Purchased equip., Check 1001				8

GENERAL JOURNAL   PAGE ____1____

The check number appears in the description and forms part of the audit trail for the transaction.

BUSINESS TRANSACTION

On November 10, Wells' Consulting Services purchased office equipment on account for $6,000.

ANALYSIS

e. The asset account, **Equipment,** is increased by $6,000.

f. The liability account, **Accounts Payable,** is increased by $6,000.

DEBIT-CREDIT RULES

DEBIT   Increases to asset accounts are recorded as debits. Debit **Equipment** for $6,000.

CREDIT   Increases to liability accounts are recorded as credits. Credit **Accounts Payable** for $6,000.

T-ACCOUNT PRESENTATION

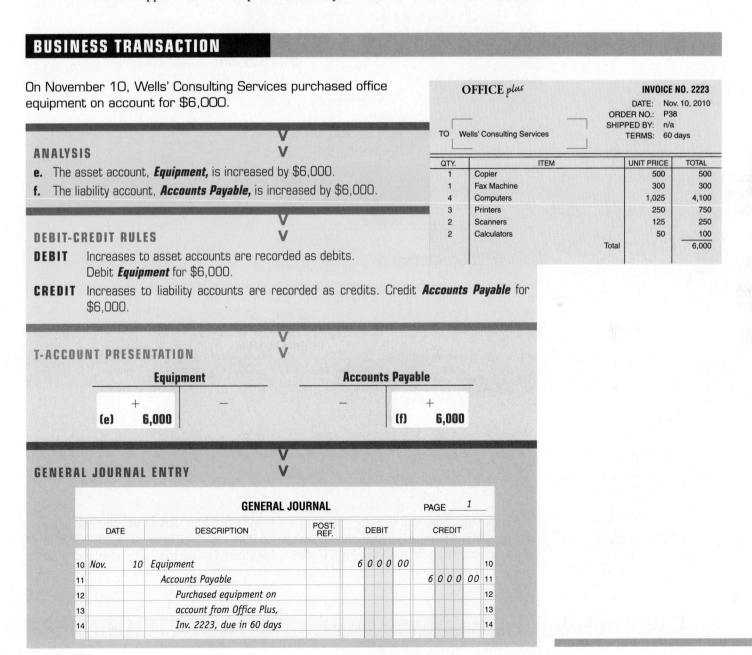

OFFICE *plus*				INVOICE NO. 2223

	DATE:	Nov. 10, 2010
	ORDER NO.:	P38
TO Wells' Consulting Services	SHIPPED BY:	n/a
	TERMS:	60 days

QTY.	ITEM	UNIT PRICE	TOTAL
1	Copier	500	500
1	Fax Machine	300	300
4	Computers	1,025	4,100
3	Printers	250	750
2	Scanners	125	250
2	Calculators	50	100
	Total		6,000

Equipment

+	−
(e) 6,000	

Accounts Payable

−	+
	(f) 6,000

GENERAL JOURNAL ENTRY

GENERAL JOURNAL   PAGE ____1____

	DATE		DESCRIPTION	POST. REF.	DEBIT	CREDIT	
10	Nov.	10	Equipment		6 0 0 0 00		10
11			Accounts Payable			6 0 0 0 00	11
12			Purchased equipment on				12
13			account from Office Plus,				13
14			Inv. 2223, due in 60 days				14

The supplier's name (Office Plus) and invoice number (2223) appear in the journal entry description and form part of the audit trail for the transaction. The journal entry can be checked against the data on the original document, Invoice 2223.

BUSINESS TRANSACTION

On November 28, Wells' Consulting Services purchased supplies for $1,500, Check 1002.

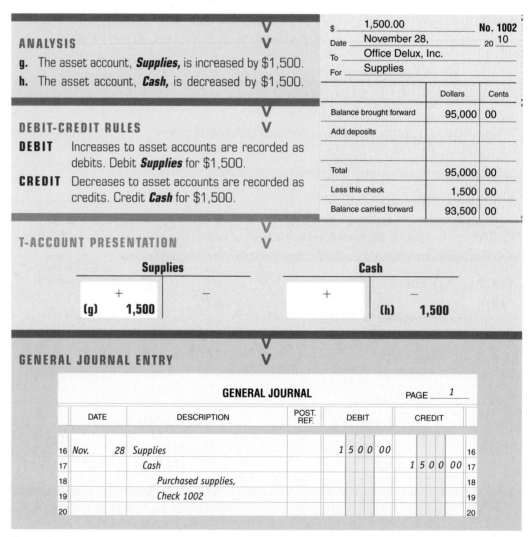

ANALYSIS

g. The asset account, **Supplies,** is increased by $1,500.

h. The asset account, **Cash,** is decreased by $1,500.

DEBIT-CREDIT RULES

DEBIT Increases to asset accounts are recorded as debits. Debit **Supplies** for $1,500.

CREDIT Decreases to asset accounts are recorded as credits. Credit **Cash** for $1,500.

	$ 1,500.00	No. 1002
Date	November 28,	20 10
To	Office Delux, Inc.	
For	Supplies	

	Dollars	Cents
Balance brought forward	95,000	00
Add deposits		
Total	95,000	00
Less this check	1,500	00
Balance carried forward	93,500	00

T-ACCOUNT PRESENTATION

Supplies	
+	−
(g) 1,500	

Cash	
+	−
	(h) 1,500

GENERAL JOURNAL ENTRY

GENERAL JOURNAL PAGE 1

	DATE		DESCRIPTION	POST. REF.	DEBIT	CREDIT	
16	Nov.	28	Supplies		1 5 0 0 00		16
17			Cash			1 5 0 0 00	17
18			Purchased supplies,				18
19			Check 1002				19
20							20

Carlos Valdez decided to reduce the firm's debt to Office Plus. Recall that the firm had purchased equipment on account in the amount of $6,000. On November 30, Wells' Consulting Services issued a check to Office Plus. Carlos Valdez analyzed the transaction and recorded the journal entry as follows.

BUSINESS TRANSACTION

On November 30, Wells' Consulting Services paid Office Plus $2,500 in partial payment of Invoice 2223, Check 1003.

ANALYSIS

i. The asset account, *Cash,* is decreased by $2,500.

j. The liability account, *Accounts Payable,* is decreased by $2,500.

DEBIT-CREDIT RULES

DEBIT Decreases to liability accounts are recorded as debits. Debit *Accounts Payable* for $2,500.

CREDIT Decreases to asset accounts are recorded as credits. Credit *Cash* for $2,500.

T-ACCOUNT PRESENTATION

Accounts Payable		Cash	
+	−	+	−
(j) 2,500			(i) 2,500

GENERAL JOURNAL ENTRY

	$	2,500.00		No. 1003
Date	November 30,		20	10
To	Office Plus			
For	Payment on Account			

	Dollars	Cents
Balance brought forward	93,500	00
Add deposits		
Total	93,500	00
Less this check	2,500	00
Balance carried forward	91,000	00

GENERAL JOURNAL   PAGE ___1___

	DATE		DESCRIPTION	POST. REF.	DEBIT	CREDIT	
21	Nov.	30	Accounts Payable		2 5 0 0 00		21
22			Cash			2 5 0 0 00	22
23			Paid on account, Office Plus,				23
24			Invoice 2223, Check 1003				24

Notice that the general journal Description column includes three important items for the audit trail:

- the supplier name,
- the invoice number,
- the check number.

In the general journal, always enter debits before credits. This is the case even if the credit item is considered first when mentally analyzing the transaction.

Wells' Consulting Services issued a check in November to pay December and January rent in advance. Recall that the right to occupy facilities is considered a form of property. Carlos Valdez analyzed the transaction and recorded the journal entry as follows.

BUSINESS TRANSACTION

On November 30, Wells' Consulting Services wrote Check 1004 for $8,000 to prepay rent for December and January.

	$	8,000.00		No. 1004
Date	November 30,		20	10
To	Davidson Properties			
For	Prepaid Rent			

	Dollars	Cents
Balance brought forward	91,000	00
Add deposits		
Total	91,000	00
Less this check	8,000	00
Balance carried forward	83,000	00

ANALYSIS

k. The asset account, *Prepaid Rent,* is increased by $8,000.

l. The asset account, *Cash,* is decreased by $8,000.

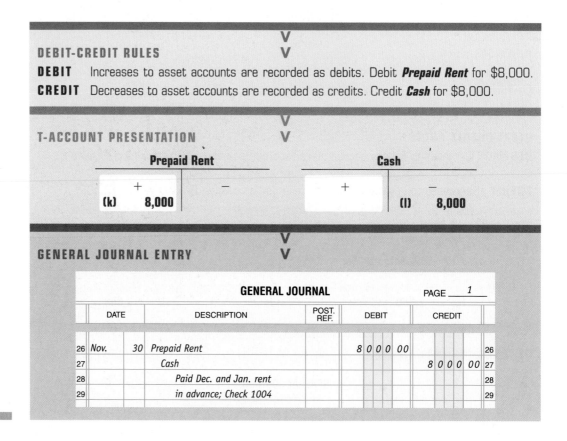

RECORDING DECEMBER TRANSACTIONS IN THE GENERAL JOURNAL

Wells' Consulting Services opened for business on December 1. Let's review the transactions that occurred in December. Refer to items **m** through **x** in Chapter 3 for the analysis of each transaction.

1. Performed services for $36,000 in cash.
2. Performed services for $11,000 on credit.
3. Received $6,000 in cash from credit clients on their accounts.
4. Paid $8,000 for salaries.
5. Paid $650 for a utility bill.
6. The owner withdrew $5,000 for personal expenses.

Figure 4.2 shows the entries in the general journal. In an actual business, transactions involving fees income and accounts receivable occur throughout the month and are recorded when they take place. For the sake of simplicity, these transactions are summarized and recorded as of December 31 for Wells' Consulting Services.

>> **2. OBJECTIVE**

Prepare compound journal entries.

LP4

PREPARING COMPOUND ENTRIES

So far, each journal entry consists of one debit and one credit. Some transactions require a **compound entry** —a journal entry that contains more than one debit or credit. In a compound entry, record all debits first followed by the credits.

> When Allstate purchased an insurance division of CNA Financial Corporation, Allstate paid cash and issued a 10-year note payable (a promise to pay). Detailed accounting records are not available to the public, but a compound journal entry was probably used to record this transaction.

FIGURE 4.2

General Journal Entries for December

	DATE		DESCRIPTION	POST. REF.	DEBIT	CREDIT	
1	2010						1
2	Dec.	31	Cash		36 000 00		2
3			Fees Income			36 000 00	3
4			Performed services for cash				4
5							5
6		31	Accounts Receivable		11 000 00		6
7			Fees Income			11 000 00	7
8			Performed services on credit				8
9							9
10		31	Cash		6 000 00		10
11			Accounts Receivable			6 000 00	11
12			Received cash from credit				12
13			clients on account				13
14							14
15		31	Salaries Expense		8 000 00		15
16			Cash			8 000 00	16
17			Paid monthly salaries to				17
18			employees, Checks				18
19			1005–1006				19
20							20
21		31	Utilities Expense		6 50 00		21
22			Cash			6 50 00	22
23			Paid monthly bill for utilities,				23
24			Check 1007				24
25							25
26		31	Carolyn Wells, Drawing		5 000 00		26
27			Cash			5 000 00	27
28			Owner withdrew cash for				28
29			personal expenses,				29
30			Check 1008				30
31							31
32							32
33							33
34							34
35							35

GENERAL JOURNAL   PAGE ___2___

Suppose that on November 7, when Wells' Consulting Services purchased the equipment for $5,000, Carolyn Wells paid $2,500 in cash and agreed to pay the balance in 30 days. This transaction is analyzed below and on page 98.

BUSINESS TRANSACTION

On November 7, the firm purchased equipment for $5,000, issued Check 1001 for $2,500, and agreed to pay the balance in 30 days.

ANALYSIS

The asset account, *Equipment*, is increased by $5,000. The asset account, *Cash*, is decreased by $2,500.
The liability account, *Accounts Payable*, is increased by $2,500.

DEBIT-CREDIT RULES

DEBIT Increases to assets are recorded as debits. Debit *Equipment* for $5,000.

CREDIT Decreases to assets are credits. Credit *Cash* for $2,500. Increases to liabilities are credits. Credit *Accounts Payable* for $2,500.

T-ACCOUNT PRESENTATION

Equipment		Cash		Accounts Payable	
+	–	+	–	–	+
5,000			2,500		2,500

recall

Debits = Credits

No matter how many accounts are affected by a transaction, total debits must equal total credits.

GENERAL JOURNAL ENTRY

	GENERAL JOURNAL				PAGE ___1___	
	DATE	DESCRIPTION	POST. REF.	DEBIT	CREDIT	
6	Nov. 7	Equipment		5 0 0 0 00		6
7		Cash			2 5 0 0 00	7
8		Accounts Payable			2 5 0 0 00	8
9		Bought equip. from The				9
10		Information Technology Store,				10
11		Inv. 11, issued Ck. 1001 for				11
12		$2,500, bal. due in 30 days				12

Section 1 Self Review

EXERCISES

1. A general journal is like a(n)
   a. address book.
   b. appointment calendar.
   c. diary.
   d. to-do list.
2. The part of the journal entry to be recorded first is the
   a. asset.
   b. credit.
   c. debit.
   d. liability.

QUESTIONS

3. In a compound journal entry, if two accounts are debited, must two accounts be credited?
4. Why are check and invoice numbers included in the journal entry description?
5. Why is the journal referred to as the "record of original entry"?

ANALYSIS

6. The accountant for Quality Lawncare never includes descriptions when making journal entries. What effect will this have on the accounting system?

(Answers to Section 1 Self Review are on page 120.)

SECTION OBJECTIVES	TERMS TO LEARN

>> 3. **Post journal entries to general ledger accounts.**

   WHY IT'S IMPORTANT

   The general ledger provides a permanent, classified record for a company's accounts.

>> 4. **Correct errors made in the journal or ledger.**

   WHY IT'S IMPORTANT

   Errors must be corrected to ensure a proper audit trail and to provide good information.

TERMS TO LEARN

balance ledger form
correcting entry
general ledger
ledger
posting

The General Ledger

You learned that a journal contains a chronological (day-by-day) record of a firm's transactions. Each journal entry shows the accounts and the amounts involved. Using the journal as a guide, you can enter transaction data in the accounts.

Ledgers

T accounts are used to analyze transactions quickly but are not used to maintain financial records. Instead, businesses keep account records on a special form that makes it possible to record all data efficiently. There is a separate form for each account. The account forms are kept in a book or binder called a **ledger.** The ledger is called the *record of final entry* because the ledger is the last place that accounting transactions are recorded.

The process of transferring data from the journal to the ledger is known as **posting.** Posting takes place after transactions are journalized. Posting is the third step of the accounting cycle.

THE GENERAL LEDGER

Every business has a general ledger. The **general ledger** is the master reference file for the accounting system. It provides a permanent, classified record of all accounts used in a firm's operations.

LEDGER ACCOUNT FORMS

There are different types of general ledger account forms. Carlos Valdez decided to use a balance ledger form. A **balance ledger form** shows the balance of the account after each entry is posted. Look at Figure 4.3 on page 100. It shows the first general journal entry, the investment by the owner. It also shows the general ledger forms for *Cash* and *Carolyn Wells, Capital.* On the ledger form, notice the

- account name and number;
- columns for date, description, and posting reference (post. ref.);
- columns for debit, credit, balance debit, and balance credit.

important!

General Journal and General Ledger

The general journal is the record of *original* entry. The general ledger is the record of *final* entry.

>> 3. OBJECTIVE

Post journal entries to general ledger accounts.

POSTING TO THE GENERAL LEDGER

Examine Figure 4.4 on page 101. On November 7, Carlos Valdez made a general journal entry to record the purchase of equipment. To post the data from the journal to the general ledger, Valdez entered the debit amount in the Debit column in the ***Equipment*** account and the credit amount in the Credit column in the ***Cash*** account.

In the general journal, identify the first account listed. In Figure 4.4, ***Equipment*** is the first account. In the general ledger, find the ledger form for the first account listed. In Figure 4.4, this is the ***Equipment*** ledger form.

The steps to post from the general journal to the general ledger follow.

1. On the ledger form, enter the date of the transaction. Enter a description of the entry, if necessary. Usually routine entries do not require descriptions.
2. On the ledger form, enter the general journal page in the Posting Reference column. On the ***Equipment*** ledger form, the **J1** in the Posting Reference column indicates that the journal entry is recorded on page 1 of the general journal. The letter **J** refers to the general journal.
3. On the ledger form, enter the debit amount in the Debit column or the credit amount in the Credit column. In Figure 4.4 on the ***Equipment*** ledger form, $5,000 is entered in the Debit column.
4. On the ledger form, compute the balance and enter it in the Debit Balance column or the Credit Balance column. In Figure 4.4, the balance in the ***Equipment*** account is a $5,000 debit.
5. On the general journal, enter the ledger account number in the Posting Reference column. In Figure 4.4, the account number 141 is entered in the Posting Reference column next to "Equipment."

Repeat the process for the next account in the general journal. In Figure 4.4, Valdez posted the credit amount from the general journal to the ***Cash*** ledger account. Notice on the ***Cash*** ledger form that he entered the credit of $5,000 and then computed the account balance. After the transaction is posted, the balance of the ***Cash*** account is $95,000.

Be sure to enter the numbers in the Posting Reference columns. This indicates that the entry was posted and ensures against posting the same entry twice. Posting references are part of the audit trail. They allow a transaction to be traced from the ledger to the journal entry, and then to the source document.

FIGURE 4.4   Posting to the General Ledger

Figure 4.5 on pages 101–103 shows the general ledger after all the entries for November and December are posted.

Each ledger account provides a complete record of the increases and decreases to that account. The balance ledger form also shows the current balance for the account.

In the general ledger accounts, the balance sheet accounts appear first and are followed by the income statement accounts. The order is:

- assets
- liabilities
- owner's equity
- revenue
- expenses

This arrangement speeds the preparation of the trial balance and the financial statements.

FIGURE 4.5

Posted General Ledger Accounts

ACCOUNT _Cash_   ACCOUNT NO. _101_

DATE		DESCRIPTION	POST. REF.	DEBIT	CREDIT	BALANCE DEBIT	BALANCE CREDIT
2010							
Nov.	6		J1	100 000 00		100 000 00	
	7		J1		5 000 00	95 000 00	
	28		J1		1 500 00	93 500 00	
	30		J1		2 500 00	91 000 00	
	30		J1		8 000 00	83 000 00	
Dec.	31		J2	36 000 00		119 000 00	
	31		J2	6 000 00		125 000 00	
	31		J2		8 000 00	117 000 00	
	31		J2		650 00	116 350 00	
	31		J2		5 000 00	111 350 00	

(continued)

FIGURE 4.5 (continued)

ACCOUNT _Accounts Receivable_   ACCOUNT NO. _111_

DATE		DESCRIPTION	POST. REF.	DEBIT	CREDIT	BALANCE	
						DEBIT	CREDIT
2010							
Dec.	31		J2	11 000 00		11 000 00	
	31		J2		6 000 00	5 000 00	

ACCOUNT _Supplies_   ACCOUNT NO. _121_

DATE		DESCRIPTION	POST. REF.	DEBIT	CREDIT	BALANCE	
						DEBIT	CREDIT
2010							
Nov.	28		J1	1 500 00		1 500 00	

ACCOUNT _Prepaid Rent_   ACCOUNT NO. _137_

DATE		DESCRIPTION	POST. REF.	DEBIT	CREDIT	BALANCE	
						DEBIT	CREDIT
2010							
Nov.	30		J1	8 000 00		8 000 00	

ACCOUNT _Equipment_   ACCOUNT NO. _141_

DATE		DESCRIPTION	POST. REF.	DEBIT	CREDIT	BALANCE	
						DEBIT	CREDIT
2010							
Nov.	7		J1	5 000 00		5 000 00	
	10		J1	6 000 00		11 000 00	

ACCOUNT _Accounts Payable_   ACCOUNT NO. _202_

DATE		DESCRIPTION	POST. REF.	DEBIT	CREDIT	BALANCE	
						DEBIT	CREDIT
2010							
Nov.	10		J1		6 000 00		6 000 00
	30		J1	2 500 00			3 500 00

ACCOUNT _Carolyn Wells, Capital_   ACCOUNT NO. _301_

DATE		DESCRIPTION	POST. REF.	DEBIT	CREDIT	BALANCE	
						DEBIT	CREDIT
2010							
Nov.	6		J1		100 000 00		100 000 00

ACCOUNT _Carolyn Wells, Drawing_   ACCOUNT NO. _302_

DATE		DESCRIPTION	POST. REF.	DEBIT	CREDIT	BALANCE	
						DEBIT	CREDIT
2010							
Dec.	31		J2	5 000 00		5 000 00	

FIGURE 4.5 (continued)

ACCOUNT _Fees Income_   ACCOUNT NO. _401_

DATE		DESCRIPTION	POST. REF.	DEBIT	CREDIT	BALANCE DEBIT	BALANCE CREDIT
2010							
Dec.	31		J2		36 000 00		36 000 00
	31		J2		11 000 00		47 000 00

ACCOUNT _Salaries Expense_   ACCOUNT NO. _511_

DATE		DESCRIPTION	POST. REF.	DEBIT	CREDIT	BALANCE DEBIT	BALANCE CREDIT
2010							
Dec.	31		J2	8 000 00		8 000 00	

ACCOUNT _Utilities Expense_   ACCOUNT NO. _514_

DATE		DESCRIPTION	POST. REF.	DEBIT	CREDIT	BALANCE DEBIT	BALANCE CREDIT
2010							
Dec.	31		J2	6 50 00		6 50 00	

Correcting Journal and Ledger Errors

Sometimes errors are made when recording transactions in the journal. For example, a journal entry may show the wrong account name or amount. The method used to correct an error depends on whether or not the journal entry has been posted to the ledger:

- If the error is discovered *before* the entry is posted, neatly cross out the incorrect item and write the correct data above it. Do not erase the error. To ensure honesty and provide a clear audit trail, erasures are not made in the journal.

- If the error is discovered *after* posting, a **correcting entry** —a journal entry made to correct the erroneous entry—is journalized and posted. Do not erase or change the journal entry or the postings in the ledger accounts.

Note that erasures are never permitted in the journal or ledger.

>>4. OBJECTIVE

Correct errors made in the journal or ledger.

recall

Order of Accounts

The general ledger lists accounts in the same order as they appear on the trial balance: assets, liabilities, owner's equity, revenue, and expenses.

MANAGERIAL IMPLICATIONS   <<

ACCOUNTING SYSTEMS

- Business managers should be sure that their firms have efficient procedures for recording transactions.
- A well-designed accounting system allows timely and accurate posting of data to the ledger accounts.
- The information that appears in the financial statements is taken from the general ledger.
- Since management uses financial information for decision making, it is essential that the financial statements be prepared quickly at the end of each period and that they contain the correct amounts.

- The promptness and accuracy of the statements depend on the efficiency of the recording process.
- A well-designed accounting system has a strong audit trail.
- Every business should be able to trace amounts through the accounting records and back to the documents where the transactions were first recorded.

THINKING CRITICALLY

What are the consequences of not having a good audit trait?

Let's look at an example. On September 1, an automobile repair shop purchased some shop equipment for $18,000 in cash. By mistake, the journal entry debited the **Office Equipment** account rather than the **Shop Equipment** account, as follows.

GENERAL JOURNAL   PAGE __16__

	DATE		DESCRIPTION	POST. REF.	DEBIT	CREDIT	
1	2010						1
2	Sept.	1	Office Equipment	141	18 000 00		2
3			Cash	101		18 000 00	3
4			Purchased equipment,				4
5			Check 1104				5
6							6
7							7

The error was discovered after the entry was posted to the ledger. To correct the error, a correcting journal entry was prepared and posted. The correcting entry debits **Shop Equipment** and credits **Office Equipment** for $18,000. This entry transfers $18,000 out of the **Office Equipment** account and into the **Shop Equipment** account.

GENERAL JOURNAL   PAGE __28__

	DATE		DESCRIPTION	POST. REF.	DEBIT	CREDIT	
1	2010						1
2	Oct.	1	Shop Equipment	151	18 000 00		2
3			Office Equipment	141		18 000 00	3
4			To correct error made on				4
5			Sept. 1 when a purchase				5
6			of shop equipment was				6
7			recorded as office				7
8			equipment				8
9							9

Suppose that the error was discovered before the journal entry was posted to the ledger. In that case, the accountant would neatly cross out "Office Equipment" and write "Shop Equipment" above it. The correct account (**Shop Equipment**) would be posted to the ledger in the usual manner.

Section 2 Self Review

QUESTIONS

1. Why are posting references made in ledger accounts and in the journal?

2. Are the following statements true or false? Why?

a. "If a journal entry that contains an error has been posted, erase the entry and change the posting in the ledger accounts."

b. "Once an incorrect journal entry has been posted, the incorrect amounts remain in the general ledger accounts."

3. What is entered in the Posting Reference column of the general journal?

EXERCISES

4. The general ledger organizes accounting information in

a. account order.

b. alphabetical order.

c. date order.

5. The general journal organizes accounting information in

a. account order.

b. alphabetical order.

c. date order.

ANALYSIS

6. Draw a diagram of the first three steps of the accounting cycle.

(Answers to Section 2 Self Review are on pages 120–121.)

REVIEW   Chapter Summary

Chapter 4

In this chapter, you have studied the method for journalizing business transactions in the records of a company. The details of each transaction are then posted to the general ledger. A well-designed accounting system provides for prompt and accurate journalizing and posting of all transactions.

Learning Objectives

1 Record transactions in the general journal.

- Recording transactions in a journal is called journalizing, the second step in the accounting cycle.
  - A journal is a daily record of transactions.
  - A written analysis of each transaction is contained in a journal.
- The general journal is widely used in business. It can accommodate all kinds of business transactions. Use the following steps to record a transaction in the general journal:
  - Number each page in the general journal. The page number will be used as a posting reference.
  - Enter the year at the top of the Date column. After that, enter the year only when a new page is started or when the year changes.
  - Enter the month and day in the Date column of the first line of the first entry. After that, enter the month only when a new page is started or when the month changes. Always enter the day on the first line of a new entry.
  - Enter the name of the account to be debited in the Description column.
  - Enter the amount to be debited in the Debit column.
  - Enter the name of the account to be credited on the next line. Indent the account name about one-half inch.
  - Enter the amount to be credited in the Credit column.
  - Enter a complete but concise description on the next line. Indent the description about one inch.
- Note that the debit portion is always recorded first.
- If possible, include source document numbers in descriptions in order to create an audit trail.

2 Prepare compound journal entries.

A transaction might require a journal entry that contains several debits or credits. All debits are recorded first, followed by the credits.

3 Post journal entries to general ledger accounts.

- Posting to the general ledger is the third step in the accounting cycle. Posting is the transfer of data from journal entries to ledger accounts.
- The individual accounts together form a ledger. All the accounts needed to prepare financial statements are found in the general ledger.
- Use the following steps to post a transaction.
  - On the ledger form:
    1. Enter the date of the transaction. Enter the description, if necessary.
    2. Enter the posting reference in the Posting Reference column. When posting from the general journal, use the letter **J** followed by the general journal page number.
    3. Enter the amount in either the Debit column or the Credit column.
    4. Compute the new balance and enter it in either the Debit Balance column or the Credit Balance column.
  - On the general journal:
    5. Enter the ledger account number in the Posting Reference column.
- To summarize the steps of the accounting cycle discussed so far:
  1. Analyze transactions.
  2. Journalize transactions.
  3. Post transactions.

4 Correct errors made in the journal or ledger.

To ensure honesty and to provide a clear audit trail, erasures are not permitted in a journal. A correcting entry is journalized and posted to correct a previous mistake. Posting references in the journal and the ledger accounts cross reference the entries and form another part of the audit trail. They make it possible to trace or recheck any transaction.

5 Define the accounting terms new to this chapter.

Glossary

Accounting cycle (p. 90) A series of steps performed during each accounting period to classify, record, and summarize data for a business and to produce needed financial information

Audit trail (p. 91) A chain of references that makes it possible to trace information, locate errors, and prevent fraud

Balance ledger form (p. 99) A ledger account form that shows the balance of the account after each entry is posted

Chronological order (p. 90) Organized in the order in which the events occur

Compound entry (p. 96) A journal entry with more than one debit or credit

Correcting entry (p. 103) A journal entry made to correct an erroneous entry

General journal (p. 90) A financial record for entering all types of business transactions; a record of original entry

General ledger (p. 99) A permanent, classified record of all accounts used in a firm's operation; a record of final entry

Journal (p. 90) The record of original entry

Journalizing (p. 90) Recording transactions in a journal

Ledger (p. 99) The record of final entry

Posting (p. 99) Transferring data from a journal to a ledger

Comprehensive Self Review

1. Give examples of items that might appear in an audit trail.
2. Why is the ledger called the "record of final entry"?
3. Which of the following shows both the debits and credits of the entire transaction?
   a. An entry in the general journal
   b. A posting to a general ledger account
4. What is recorded in the Posting Reference column of a general journal?
5. How do you correct a journal entry that has not been posted?

(Answers to Comprehensive Self Review are on page 121.)

 Multiple choice questions are provided on the text Web site at www.mhhe.com/price12e

Quiz4

Discussion Questions

1. What is posting?
2. In what order are accounts arranged in the general ledger? Why?
3. What are posting references? Why are they used?
4. What is an audit trail? Why is it desirable to have an audit trail?
5. How should corrections be made in the general journal?
6. What is the accounting cycle?
7. What is the purpose of a journal?
8. What procedure is used to record an entry in the general journal?
9. What is the value of having a description for each general journal entry?
10. What is a compound journal entry?
11. What is a ledger?

APPLICATIONS

Exercises ⊞™

Recording transactions in the general journal.

Selected accounts from the general ledger of Contemporary Creations Company follow. Record the general journal entries that would be made to record the following transactions. Be sure to include dates and descriptions in these entries.

◄ **Exercise 4.1**
Objective 1

101 Cash
111 Accounts Receivable
121 Supplies
131 Equipment
141 Automobile
202 Accounts Payable
301 Tina Turner, Capital
302 Tina Turner, Drawing
401 Fees Income
511 Rent Expense
514 Salaries Expense
517 Telephone Expense

DATE	TRANSACTIONS
2010	
Sept. 1	Tina Turner invested $31,000 in cash to start the firm.
4	Purchased office equipment for $4,250 on credit from Zen, Inc.; received Invoice 9823, payable in 30 days.
16	Purchased an automobile that will be used to visit clients; issued Check 1001 for $11,250 in full payment.
20	Purchased supplies for $210; paid immediately with Check 1002.
23	Returned damaged supplies for a cash refund of $60.
30	Issued Check 1003 for $2,800 to Zen, Inc., as payment on account for Invoice 9823.
30	Withdrew $1,000 in cash for personal expenses.
30	Issued Check 1004 for $600 to pay the rent for October.
30	Performed services for $850 in cash.
30	Paid $110 for monthly telephone bill, Check 1005.

Analyzing transactions.

Selected accounts from the general ledger of the Express Courier Service follow. Analyze the following transactions and indicate by number what accounts should be debited and credited for each transaction.

◄ **Exercise 4.2**
Objective 1

101 Cash
111 Accounts Receivable
121 Supplies
131 Equipment
202 Accounts Payable
301 Sam Taylor, Capital
401 Fees Income

511 Rent Expense

514 Salaries Expense

517 Utilities Expense

TRANSACTIONS

1. Gave a cash refund of $720 to a customer because of a lost package. (The customer had previously paid in cash.)

2. Sent a check for $1,500 to the utility company to pay the monthly bill.

3. Provided services for $13,000 on credit.

4. Purchased new equipment for $8,400 and paid for it immediately by check.

5. Issued a check for $6,000 to pay a creditor on account.

6. Performed services for $9,300 in cash.

7. Collected $11,200 from credit customers.

8. The owner made an additional investment of $40,000 in cash.

9. Purchased supplies for $4,000 on credit.

10. Issued a check for $3,700 to pay the monthly rent.

Exercise 4.3 ▶

Objectives 1, 3

Posting to the general ledger.

Post the journal entries that you prepared for Exercise 4.1 to the general ledger. Use the account names shown in Exercise 4.1.

Exercise 4.4 ▶

Objective 2

Compound journal entries.

The following transactions took place at the Cortez's Leading Ladies during November 2010. Record the general journal entries that would be made for these transactions. Use a compound entry for each transaction.

DATE	TRANSACTIONS
Nov. 5	Performed services for Talent Search, Inc., for $16,000; received $8,000 in cash and the client promised to pay the balance in 60 days.
18	Purchased a graphing calculator for $150 and some supplies for $250 from Office Supply; issued Check 1008 for the total.
23	Received Invoice 1602 for $540 from Automotive Technicians Repair for repairs to the firm's automobile; issued Check 1009 for half the amount and arranged to pay the other half in 30 days.

Exercise 4.5 ▶

Objective 4

Recording a correcting entry.

On July 9, 2010, an employee of Capital Corporation mistakenly debited *Utilities Expense* rather than *Telephone Expense* when recording a bill of $450 for the May telephone service. The error was discovered on July 30. Prepare a general journal entry to correct the error.

Exercise 4.6 ▶

Objective 4

Recording a correcting entry.

On September 16, 2010, an employee of Carmel Company mistakenly debited the *Truck* account rather than the *Repair Expense* account when recording a bill of $375 for repairs. The error was discovered on October 1. Prepare a general journal entry to correct the error.

PROBLEMS

Problem Set A HM

Recording transactions in the general journal.

The transactions that follow took place at Leisure Times Recreation Center during September 2010. This firm has indoor courts where customers can play tennis for a fee. It also rents equipment and offers tennis lessons.

◀ **Problem 4.1A**
Objective 1

eXcel

INSTRUCTIONS

Record each transaction in the general journal, using the following chart of accounts. Be sure to number the journal page 1 and to write the year at the top of the Date column. Include a description for each entry.

ASSETS
101 Cash
111 Accounts Receivable
121 Supplies
141 Equipment

LIABILITIES
202 Accounts Payable

OWNER'S EQUITY
301 Patrice Rebello, Capital
302 Patrice Rebello, Drawing

REVENUE
401 Fees Income

EXPENSES
511 Equipment Repair Expense
512 Rent Expense
513 Salaries Expense
514 Telephone Expense
517 Utilities Expense

DATE	TRANSACTIONS
Sept. 1	Issued Check 1169 for $700 to pay the September rent.
5	Performed services for $1,250 in cash.
6	Performed services for $1,088 on credit.
10	Paid $300 for monthly telephone bill; issued Check 1170.
11	Paid for equipment repairs of $420 with Check 1171.
12	Received $1,600 on account from credit clients.
15	Issued Checks 1172–1177 for $2,100 for salaries.
18	Issued Check 1178 for $1,000 to purchase supplies.
19	Purchased new tennis rackets for $1,125 on credit from The Tennis Supply Shop; received Invoice 3108, payable in 30 days.
20	Issued Check 1179 for $1,380 to purchase new nets. (Equip.)
21	Received $425 on account from credit clients.
21	Returned a damaged net and received a cash refund of $424.
22	Performed services for $1,630 in cash.
23	Performed services for $2,405 on credit.
26	Issued Check 1180 for $230 to purchase supplies.
28	Paid the monthly electric bill of $1,150 with Check 1181.
30	Issued Checks 1182–1187 for $2,100 for salaries.
30	Issued Check 1188 for $2,000 cash to Patrice Rebello for personal expenses.

Analyze: If the company paid a bill for supplies on October 1, what check number would be included in the journal entry description?

Problem 4.2A
Objectives 1, 2, 3

Journalizing and posting transactions.

On October 1, 2010, Connie Hernandez opened an advertising agency. She plans to use the chart of accounts listed below.

INSTRUCTIONS

1. Journalize the transactions. Number the journal page 1, write the year at the top of the Date column, and include a description for each entry.
2. Post to the ledger accounts. Before you start the posting process, open accounts by entering account names and numbers in the headings. Follow the order of the accounts in the chart of accounts.

ASSETS
101 Cash
111 Accounts Receivable
121 Supplies
141 Office Equipment
151 Art Equipment

LIABILITIES
202 Accounts Payable

OWNER'S EQUITY
301 Connie Hernandez, Capital
302 Connie Hernandez, Drawing

REVENUE
401 Fees Income

EXPENSES
511 Office Cleaning Expense
514 Rent Expense
517 Salaries Expense
520 Telephone Expense
523 Utilities Expense

DATE	TRANSACTIONS
Oct. 1	Connie Hernandez invested $35,000 cash in the business.
2	Paid October office rent of $1,125; issued Check 1001.
5	Purchased desks and other office furniture for $7,000 from Office Furniture Mart, Inc.; received Invoice 6704 payable in 60 days.
6	Issued Check 1002 for $2,175 to purchase art equipment.
7	Purchased supplies for $535; paid with Check 1003.
10	Issued Check 1004 for $250 for office cleaning service.
12	Performed services for $1,600 in cash and $1,400 on credit. (Use a compound entry.)
15	Returned damaged supplies for a cash refund of $150.
18	Purchased a computer for $1,025 from Office Furniture Mart, Inc., Invoice 7108; issued Check 1005 for a $525 down payment, with the balance payable in 30 days. (Use one compound entry.)
20	Issued Check 1006 for $3,500 to Office Furniture Mart, Inc., as payment on account for Invoice 6704.
26	Performed services for $1,950 on credit.
27	Paid $125 for monthly telephone bill; issued Check 1007.
30	Received $1,600 in cash from credit customers.
30	Mailed Check 1008 to pay the monthly utility bill of $296.
30	Issued Checks 1009–1011 for $3,775 for salaries.

Analyze: What is the balance of account 202 in the general ledger?

Recording correcting entries.

◄   **Problem 4.3A**
Objective 4

The following journal entries were prepared by an employee of Jupiter Company who does not have an adequate knowledge of accounting.

INSTRUCTIONS

Examine the journal entries carefully to locate the errors. Provide a brief written description of each error. Assume that *Office Equipment* and *Office Supplies* were recorded at the correct values.

			GENERAL JOURNAL		PAGE	3		
	DATE		DESCRIPTION	POST. REF.	DEBIT	CREDIT		
1	2010							1
2	April	1	Accounts Payable		12 4 0 0 00			2
3			Fees Income			12 4 0 0 00		3
4			Performed services on credit					4
5								5
6		2	Cash		5 0 0 00			6
7			Telephone Expense			5 0 0 00		7
8			Paid for March telephone					8
9			service, Check 1917					9
10								10
11		3	Office Equipment		7 2 0 0 00			11
12			Office Supplies		8 0 0 00			12
13			Cash			8 4 0 0 00		13
14			Purchased file cabinet and					14
15			office supplies, Check 1918					15
16								16
17								17
18								18
19								19
20								20

Analyze: After the correcting journal entries have been posted, what effect do the corrections have on the company's reported assets?

Problem 4.4A ▶

Objectives 1, 2, 3

Journalizing and posting transactions

Four transactions for Farm Supply & Repair that took place in November 2010 appear below, along with the general ledger accounts used by the company.

INSTRUCTIONS

Record the transactions in the general journal and post them to the appropriate ledger accounts. Be sure to number the journal page 1 and to write the year at the top of the Date column.

Cash	101	Equipment	151
Accounts Receivable	111	Accounts Payable	202
Office Supplies	121	Erwin Tobias, Capital	301
Tools	131	Fees Income	401
Machinery	141		

DATE		TRANSACTIONS
Nov.	1	Erwin Tobias invested $45,000 in cash plus tools with a fair market value of $1,000 to start the business.
	2	Purchased equipment for $1,950 and supplies for $450 from Office Depot, Invoice 501; issued Check 100 for $600 as a down payment with the balance due in 30 days.
	10	Performed services for James Wilson for $1,900, who paid $500 in cash with the balance due in 30 days.
	20	Purchased machinery for $3,000 from Cottle Machinery, Inc., Invoice 709; issued Check 101 for $1,000 in cash as a down payment with the balance due in 30 days.

Analyze: What liabilities does the business owe as of November 30?

Problem Set B

◄ **Problem 4.1B**
Objective 1

Recording transactions in the general journal.

The transactions listed below took place at Cardenas Building Cleaning Service during September 2010. This firm cleans commercial buildings for a fee.

INSTRUCTIONS

Analyze and record each transaction in the general journal. Choose the account names from the chart of accounts shown below. Be sure to number the journal page 1 and to write the year at the top of the Date column.

ASSETS
101 Cash
111 Accounts Receivable
141 Equipment

LIABILITIES
202 Accounts Payable

OWNER'S EQUITY
301 Gladys Cardenas, Capital
302 Gladys Cardenas, Drawing

REVENUE
401 Fees Income

EXPENSES
501 Cleaning Supplies Expense
502 Equipment Repair Expense
503 Office Supplies Expense
511 Rent Expense
514 Salaries Expense
521 Telephone Expense
524 Utilities Expense

DATE		TRANSACTIONS
Sept.	1	Gladys Cardenas invested $12,500 in cash to start the business.
	5	Performed services for $1,400 in cash.
	6	Issued Check 1000 for $900 to pay the September rent.
	7	Performed services for $1,800 on credit.
	9	Paid $200 for monthly telephone bill; issued Check 1001.
	10	Issued Check 1002 for $115 for equipment repairs.
	12	Received $488 from credit clients.
	14	Issued Checks 1003–1004 for $4,500 to pay salaries.
	18	Issued Check 1005 for $350 for cleaning supplies.
	19	Issued Check 1006 for $300 for office supplies.
	20	Purchased equipment for $3,000 from Reese Equipment, Inc., Invoice 1012; issued Check 1007 for $1,000 with the balance due in 30 days.
	22	Performed services for $2,475 in cash.
	24	Issued Check 1008 for $215 for the monthly electric bill.
	26	Performed services for $1,800 on account.
	30	Issued Checks 1009–1010 for $4,500 to pay salaries.
	30	Issued Check 1011 for $1,500 to Gladys Cardenas to pay for personal expenses.

Analyze: How many transactions affected expense accounts?

Problem 4.2B ▶
Objectives 1, 2, 3

Journalizing and posting transactions.

In June 2010, Wallace King opened a photography studio that provides services to public and private schools. His firm's financial activities for the first month of operations and the chart of accounts appear below.

INSTRUCTIONS

1. Journalize the transactions. Number the journal page 1 and write the year at the top of the Date column. Describe each entry.
2. Post to the ledger accounts. Before you start the posting process, open the accounts by entering the names and numbers in the headings. Follow the order of the accounts in the chart of accounts.

ASSETS
101 Cash
111 Accounts Receivable
121 Supplies
141 Office Equipment
151 Photographic Equipment

LIABILITIES
202 Accounts Payable

OWNER'S EQUITY
301 Wallace King, Capital
302 Wallace King, Drawing

REVENUE
401 Fees Income

EXPENSES
511 Office Cleaning Expense
514 Rent Expense
517 Salaries Expense
520 Telephone Expense
523 Utilities Expense

DATE		TRANSACTIONS
June	1	Wallace King invested $16,000 cash in the business.
	2	Issued Check 1001 for $900 to pay the June rent.
	5	Purchased desks and other office furniture for $3,750 from Brown, Inc., received Invoice 5312, payable in 60 days.
	6	Issued Check 1002 for $950 to purchase photographic equipment.
	7	Purchased supplies for $238; paid with Check 1003.
	10	Issued Check 1004 for $200 for office cleaning service.
	12	Performed services for $650 in cash and $650 on credit. (Use one compound entry.)
	15	Returned damaged supplies; received a $75 cash refund.
	18	Purchased a computer for $1,025 from Craft Office Supply, Invoice 304; issued Check 1005 for a $500 down payment. The balance is payable in 30 days. (Use one compound entry.)
	20	Issued Check 1006 for $2,100 to Brown, Inc., as payment on account for office furniture, Invoice 5312.
	26	Performed services for $1,000 on credit.
	27	Paid $290 for monthly telephone bill; issued Check 1007.
	30	Received $1,050 in cash from credit clients on account.
	30	Issued Check 1008 to pay the monthly utility bill of $275.
	30	Issued Checks 1009–1011 for $2,800 for salaries.

Analyze: What was the *Cash* account balance after the transaction of June 27 was recorded?

Recording correcting entries.

◄   Problem 4.3B
Objective 4

All the journal entries shown below contain errors. The entries were prepared by an employee of Texas Corporation who does not have an adequate knowledge of accounting.

INSTRUCTIONS

Examine the journal entries carefully to locate the errors. Provide a brief written description of each error. Assume that *Office Equipment* and *Office Supplies* were recorded at the correct values.

	GENERAL JOURNAL				PAGE ____1____	
DATE	DESCRIPTION	POST. REF.	DEBIT	CREDIT		
2010						1
Jan. 1	Accounts Payable		4 5 0 00			2
	Fees Income			4 5 0 00		3
	Performed services on credit					4
						5
2	Cash		6 2 50			6
	Telephone Expense			6 2 50		7
	Paid for January telephone					8
	service, Check 1601					9
						10
3	Office Equipment		3 7 5 00			11
	Office Supplies		9 5 00			12
	Cash			4 5 0 00		13
	Purchased file cabinet and					14
	office supplies, Check 1602					15
						16

Analyze: After the correcting journal entries have been posted, what effect do the corrections have on the reported assets of the company?

Journalizing and posting transactions.

Several transactions that occurred during December 2010, the first month of operation for Boley's Accounting Services, follow. The company uses the general ledger accounts listed below.

INSTRUCTIONS

Record the transactions in the general journal (page 1) and post to the appropriate accounts.

Cash	101	Furniture & Fixtures	151
Accounts Receivable	111	Accounts Payable	202
Office Supplies	121	Richard Boley, Capital	301
Computers	131	Fees Income	401
Office Equipment	141		

DATE	TRANSACTIONS
Dec. 3	Richard Boley began business by depositing $15,000 cash into a business checking account.
4	Purchased a computer for $1,200 cash.
5	Purchased furniture and fixtures on account for $4,000.
6	Purchased office equipment for $1,095 cash.
10	Rendered services to client and sent bill for $1,300.
11	Purchased office supplies for $450.
15	Received invoice for furniture purchased on December 5 and paid it.

Analyze: Describe the activity for account 202 during the month.

Critical Thinking Problem 4.1

Start-Up Business

On June 1, 2010, Wade Wilson opened the California Talent Agency. He plans to use the chart of accounts given below.

INSTRUCTIONS

1. Journalize the transactions. Be sure to number the journal pages and write the year at the top of the Date column. Include a description for each entry.

2. Post to the ledger accounts. Before you start the posting process, open the accounts by entering the account names and numbers in the headings. Using the list of accounts below, assign appropriate account numbers and place them in the correct order in the ledger.

3. Prepare a trial balance.

4. Prepare the income statement.

5. Prepare a statement of owner's equity.

6. Prepare the balance sheet.

ACCOUNTS

Accounts Payable	Wade Wilson, Drawing
Office Furniture	Recording Equipment
Accounts Receivable	Rent Expense
Advertising Expense	Salaries Expense
Cash	Supplies
Fees Income	Telephone Expense
Wade Wilson, Capital	Utilities Expense

DATE		TRANSACTIONS
June	1	Wade Wilson invested $15,000 cash to start the business.
	2	Issued Check 201 for $900 to pay the June rent for the office.
	3	Purchased desk and other office furniture for $6,000 from Davis Office Supply, Invoice 5103; issued Check 202 for a $2,000 down payment with the balance due in 30 days.
	4	Issued Check 203 for $800 for supplies.
	6	Performed services for $3,000 in cash.
	7	Issued Check 204 for $1,000 to pay for advertising expense.
	8	Purchased recording equipment for $7,500 from Rhythms & Moves, Inc., Invoice 2122; issued Check 205 for a down payment of $2,500 with the balance due in 30 days.
	10	Performed services for $2,450 on account.
	11	Issued Check 206 for $1,500 to Davis Office Supply as payment on account.
	12	Performed services for $4,500 in cash.
	15	Issued Check 207 for $2,500 to pay an employee's salary.
	18	Received payments of $2,000 from credit clients on account.
	20	Issued Check 208 for $3,000 to Rhythms & Moves, Inc. as payment on account.
	25	Issued Check 209 in the amount of $175 for the monthly telephone bill.
	27	Issued Check 210 in the amount of $400 for the monthly electric bill.
	28	Issued Check 211 to Wade Wilson for $2,000 for personal living expenses.
	30	Issued Check 212 for $2,500 to pay salary of an employee.

Analyze: How many postings were made to the **Cash** account?

Critical Thinking Problem 4.2

Financial Statements

Angela Evans is a new staff accountant for Denton Chemical Supply. She has asked you to review the financial statements prepared for April to find and correct any errors. Review the income statement and balance sheet that follow and identify the errors Evans made (she did not prepare a statement of owner's equity). Prepare a corrected income statement and balance sheet as well as a statement of owner's equity, for Denton Chemical Supply.

Denton Chemical Supply
Income Statement
April 30, 2010

Revenue		
Fees Income		9 1 5 0 00
Expenses		
Salaries Expense	2 2 5 0 00	
Rent Expense	4 5 0 00	
Repair Expense	7 5 00	
Utilities Expense	4 2 5 00	
Drawing	1 0 0 0 00	
Total Expenses		4 4 2 5 00
Net Income		5 3 5 0 00

Denton Chemical Supply
Balance Sheet
Month Ended April 30, 2010

Assets		Liabilities	
Land	3 0 0 0 00	Accounts Receivable	1 7 5 0 00
Building	10 0 0 0 00		
Cash	3 7 5 0 00	Owner's Equity	
Accounts Payable	1 2 5 0 00	Ann Denton, Capital, April 1, 2010	12 3 0 0 00
Total Assets	14 0 5 0 00	Total Liabilities and Owner's Equity	14 0 5 0 00

BUSINESS CONNECTIONS

Business Records

Managerial FOCUS

1. The owner of a new business recently questioned the accountant about the value of having both a journal and a ledger. The owner believes that it is a waste of effort to enter data about transactions in two different records. How would you explain the value of having both records?

2. Why should management insist that a firm's accounting system have a strong audit trail?

3. Why should management be concerned about the efficiency of a firm's procedures for journalizing and posting transactions?

4. How might a poor set of recording procedures affect the flow of information to management?

Correcting Entries

Ethical DILEMMA

As the full charge bookkeeper, your job is to make any corrections to the general ledger accounts. Each correction needs the reason for the change and the effect on each account, whether it is an increase or decrease.

Louisa has come to you for help. For the third time this month, she has recorded a cash receipt twice. She wants you to record a correcting entry that will reverse her mistakes. The correcting entry she wants you to make will record a credit to the Cash account and a debit to Sales. What should you investigate before making a decision about the correcting entry? What is happening to the cash account? Is this a continual problem for Louisa? Would you accept a dinner offer from Louisa if you fix her mistake?

General Ledger Accounts

STREETWISE:
Questions from the
REAL WORLD

Refer to The Home Depot, Inc., *2006 Annual Report* in Appendix A.

1. Review the report called *Executive Summary and Selected Consolidated Statements of Earnings Data.* How many sales transactions were reported for 2006? For sales on account transactions, which accounts would be affected when the transactions are recorded?

2. Based on the financial statements, which account categories would be affected by the following transactions?

   a. Paid $5,000 cash for store rent.

   b. Paid $2,000 cash for store utility bill.

   c. Received $1,000 from a customer in payment of their account.

Balance Sheet

Financial Statement
ANALYSIS

Review the following excerpt taken from the Wal-Mart Stores, Inc., consolidated balance sheet as of January 31, 2007.

Analyze:

(Amounts in millions) January 31, 2007	
Property, Plant and Equipment at cost:	
Land	$18,612
Building and improvements	64,052
Fixtures and equipment	25,168
Transportation equipment	1,966

1. When the accountant for Wal-Mart Stores, Inc., records a purchase of transportation equipment, what type of account is debited? If Wal-Mart purchases transportation equipment on credit, what account might be credited?

2. What type of source document might be reflected in the journal entry to record the purchase of equipment?

3. If the accounting manager reviewed the *Transportation Equipment* account in the general ledger, what types of information might be listed there? What ending balance would be reflected at January 31, 2007?

Analyze Online: Locate the Web site for the Wal-Mart Stores, Inc. (www.walmartstores.com), which provides an online store for consumers as well as corporate information. Within the Web site, locate the consolidated balance sheet for the current year.

4. What kinds of property, plant, and equipment are listed on the balance sheet?

5. What is the balance reported for transportation equipment?

Getting Organized

Extending THE THOUGHT

Business transactions are recorded in a financial record called a journal. List and discuss other organizational records and devices used in everyday life. Why are these records and devices used? What similarities do these records share with the journal used in accounting?

Training Manual

Business COMMUNICATION

You have been asked to teach a new accounting clerk how to journalize business transactions. Create a written step-by-step guide to give to the new accounting clerk on his first day at work. Use a sample business transaction of your choice to illustrate the process.

Audit Trail

TEAMWORK

An audit trail allows an individual to track a transaction from the journal entry to the general ledger through to the financial statements. The audit trail can also find all the transactions that comprise the dollar amount for each account listed on the income statement and balance sheet. Your team has been assigned the duty to diagram the audit trail for your company. In your diagram, show several transactions and how they would be tracked from the journal entry to the financial statement and back to the journal entry.

Accounting Careers

Internet CONNECTION

Enter "Accounting Careers" in a search tool like Google. Select a site that will provide the skills and talents required for an accountant. Also find the salaries for accountants in your local area. Note the amount of experience and education needed to receive the salary you want to be earning in the next five years.

Answers to **Self Reviews**

Answers to Section 1 Self Review

1. **c.** diary.
2. **c.** debit.
3. No. The only requirement is that the total debits must equal the total credits.
4. To provide an audit trail to trace information through the accounting system.
5. It is the first accounting record where transactions are entered.
6. The audit trail will be very difficult to follow.

Answers to Section 2 Self Review

1. They indicate that the entry has been posted and ensure against posting the same entry twice.
2. Both statements are false. If an incorrect journal entry was posted, a correcting entry should be journalized and posted. To ensure honesty and provide a clear audit trail, erasures are not permitted in the journal.
3. The ledger account number.

4. **a.** account order.

5. **c.** date order.

6.

Answers to Comprehensive Self Review

1. Check number

   Invoice number for goods purchased on credit from a vendor

   Invoice number for services billed to a charge account customer

   Memorandum number

2. It is the last accounting record in which a transaction is recorded.

3. **a.** An entry in the general journal

4. The general ledger account number.

5. Neatly cross out the incorrect item and write the correct data above it.

Adjustments and the Worksheet

Chapter 5

LEARNING OBJECTIVES

1. Complete a trial balance on a worksheet. **LP5**
2. Prepare adjustments for unrecorded business transactions.
3. Complete the worksheet.
4. Prepare an income statement, statement of owner's equity, and balance sheet from the completed worksheet.
5. Journalize and post the adjusting entries.
6. Define the accounting terms new to this chapter.

NEW TERMS

account form balance sheet
adjusting entries
adjustments
book value
contra account
contra asset account

depreciation
prepaid expenses
report form balance sheet
salvage value
straight-line depreciation
worksheet

---

 www.boeing.com

The International Space Station (ISS) is a global project, involving the scientific and technological resources of 16 countries and the efforts of more than 100,000 people throughout the world. As the prime contractor, Boeing has been responsible for design, development, construction, and integration of the ISS as well as assisting NASA with the operation of this orbital outpost.

The ISS is the largest, most complex international scientific project ever attempted in space. When completed, the ISS will be comprised of more than 100 major components that were launched into space during 88 assembly flights. The success of the ISS has validated Boeing's position as a leader in the aerospace and defense industry and has contributed to the company's overall revenue growth.

thinking critically
How do you think Boeing accounts for the wear and tear on its equipment?

The Worksheet

Financial statements are completed as soon as possible in order to be useful. One way to speed the preparation of financial statements is to use a worksheet. A **worksheet** is a form used to gather all data needed at the end of an accounting period to prepare the financial statements. Preparation of the worksheet is the fourth step in the accounting cycle.

Figure 5.1 shows a common type of worksheet. The heading shows the company name, report title, and period covered. In addition to the Account Name column, this worksheet contains five sections: Trial Balance, Adjustments, Adjusted Trial Balance, Income Statement, and Balance Sheet. Each section includes a Debit column and a Credit column. The worksheet has 10 columns in which to enter dollar amounts.

LP5

>>**1. OBJECTIVE**

Complete a trial balance on a worksheet.

recall

Trial Balance

If total debits do not equal total credits, there is an error in the financial records. The error must be found and corrected.

FIGURE 5.1

Ten-Column Worksheet

The Trial Balance Section

Refer to Figure 5.2 on page 125 as you read about how to prepare the Trial Balance section of the worksheet.

1. Enter the general ledger account names.
2. Transfer the general ledger account balances to the Debit and Credit columns of the Trial Balance section.
3. Total the Debit and Credit columns to prove that the trial balance is in balance.
4. Place a double rule under each Trial Balance column to show that the work in that column is complete.

		TRIAL BALANCE		ADJUSTMENTS	
	ACCOUNT NAME	DEBIT	CREDIT	DEBIT	CREDIT
1					
2					
3					
4					
5					

Wells' Consulting Services
Worksheet
Month Ended December 31, 2010

Wells' Consulting Services
Worksheet
Month Ended December 31, 2010

	ACCOUNT NAME	TRIAL BALANCE DEBIT	TRIAL BALANCE CREDIT	ADJUSTMENTS DEBIT	ADJUSTMENTS CREDIT
1	Cash	111 3 5 0 00			
2	Accounts Receivable	5 0 0 0 00			
3	Supplies	1 5 0 0 00			(a) 5 0 0 00
4	Prepaid Rent	8 0 0 0 00			(b) 4 0 0 0 00
5	Equipment	11 0 0 0 00			
6	Accumulated Depreciation—Equipment				(c) 1 8 3 00
7	Accounts Payable		3 5 0 0 00		
8	Carolyn Wells, Capital		100 0 0 0 00		
9	Carolyn Wells, Drawing	5 0 0 0 00			
10	Fees Income		47 0 0 0 00		
11	Salaries Expense	8 0 0 0 00			
12	Utilities Expense	6 5 0 00			
13	Supplies Expense			(a) 5 0 0 00	
14	Rent Expense			(b) 4 0 0 0 00	
15	Depreciation Expense—Equipment			(c) 1 8 3 00	
16	Totals	150 5 0 0 00	150 5 0 0 00	4 6 8 3 00	4 6 8 3 00
17					
18					
19					

FIGURE 5.2

A Partial Worksheet

Notice that the trial balance has four new accounts: ***Accumulated Depreciation—Equipment, Supplies Expense, Rent Expense,*** and ***Depreciation Expense—Equipment.*** These accounts have zero balances now, but they will be needed later as the worksheet is completed.

The Adjustments Section

Usually account balances change because of transactions with other businesses or individuals. For Wells' Consulting Services, the account changes recorded in Chapter 4 were caused by transactions with the firm's suppliers, customers, the landlord, and employees. It is easy to recognize, journalize, and post these transactions as they occur.

Some changes are not caused by transactions with other businesses or individuals. They arise from the internal operations of the firm during the accounting period. Journal entries made to update accounts for previously unrecorded items are called **adjustments** or **adjusting entries.** These changes are first entered on the worksheet at the end of each accounting period. The worksheet provides a convenient form for gathering the information and determining the effects of the changes. Let's look at the adjustments made by Wells' Consulting Services on December 31, 2010.

>>2. OBJECTIVE

Prepare adjustments for unrecorded business transactions.

LP5

	ADJUSTED TRIAL BALANCE DEBIT	ADJUSTED TRIAL BALANCE CREDIT	INCOME STATEMENT DEBIT	INCOME STATEMENT CREDIT	BALANCE SHEET DEBIT	BALANCE SHEET CREDIT	
							1
							2
							3
							4
							5

ADJUSTING FOR SUPPLIES USED

On November 28, 2010, Wells' Consulting Services purchased $1,500 of supplies. On December 31, the trial balance shows a $1,500 balance in the *Supplies* account. This amount is too high because some of the supplies were used during December.

An adjustment must be made for the supplies used. Otherwise, the asset account, *Supplies,* is overstated because fewer supplies are actually on hand. The expense account, *Supplies Expense,* is understated. The cost of the supplies used represents an operating expense that has not been recorded.

On December 31, Carlos Valdez counted the supplies. Remaining supplies totaled $1,000. This meant that supplies amounting to $500 were used during December ($1,500 − $1,000 = $500). At the end of December, an adjustment must be made to reflect the supplies used. The adjustment reduces the *Supplies* account to $1,000, the amount of supplies remaining. It increases the *Supplies Expense* account by $500 for the amount of supplies used. Notice that the adjustment for supplies is based on actual usage.

Refer to Figure 5.2 on page 125 to review the adjustment on the worksheet: a debit of $500 to *Supplies Expense* and a credit of $500 to *Supplies.* Both the debit and credit are labeled **(a)** to identify the two parts of the adjustment.

Supplies is a type of prepaid expense. **Prepaid expenses** are items that are acquired and paid for in advance of their use. Other common prepaid expenses are prepaid rent, prepaid insurance, and prepaid advertising. When cash is paid for these items, amounts are debited to *Prepaid Rent, Prepaid Insurance,* and *Prepaid Advertising;* all are asset accounts. As prepaid expenses are used, an adjustment is made to reduce the asset accounts and to increase the related expense accounts.

ADJUSTMENT

Record the adjustment for supplies.

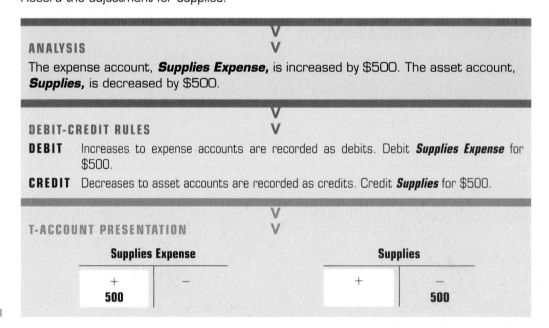

ANALYSIS

The expense account, *Supplies Expense,* is increased by $500. The asset account, *Supplies,* is decreased by $500.

DEBIT-CREDIT RULES

DEBIT   Increases to expense accounts are recorded as debits. Debit *Supplies Expense* for $500.

CREDIT   Decreases to asset accounts are recorded as credits. Credit *Supplies* for $500.

T-ACCOUNT PRESENTATION

Supplies Expense		Supplies	
+	−	+	−
500			500

Let's review the effect of the adjustment on the asset account, *Supplies.* Recall that the *Supplies* account already had a balance of $1,500. If no adjustment is made, the balance would remain at $1,500, even though only $1,000 of supplies are left.

Supplies

	+		–	
Bal.	1,500	Adj.	500	
Bal.	1,000			

ADJUSTING FOR EXPIRED RENT

On November 30, 2010, Wells' Consulting Services paid $8,000 rent for December and January. The right to occupy facilities for the specified period is an asset. The $8,000 was debited to *Prepaid Rent,* an asset account. On December 31, 2010, the *Prepaid Rent* balance is $8,000. This is too high because one month of rent has been used. The expired rent is $4,000 ($8,000 ÷ 2 months). At the end of December, an adjustment is made to reflect the expired rent.

ADJUSTMENT

Record the adjustment for expired rent.

ANALYSIS
The expense account, *Rent Expense,* is increased by $4,000. The asset account, *Prepaid Rent,* is decreased by $4,000.

DEBIT-CREDIT RULES
DEBIT   Increases to expense accounts are recorded as debits. Debit *Rent Expense* for $4,000.
CREDIT   Decreases to asset accounts are recorded as credits. Credit *Prepaid Rent* for $4,000.

T-ACCOUNT PRESENTATION

Rent Expense			Prepaid Rent	
+	–		+	–
4,000				4,000

Let's review the effect of the adjustment on the asset account, *Prepaid Rent.* The beginning balance of $8,000 represents prepaid rent for the months of December and January. By December 31, the prepaid rent for the month of December is "used up." The adjustment reducing *Prepaid Rent* recognizes the expense of occupying the facilities in December. The $4,000 ending balance represents prepaid rent for the month of January.

Prepaid Rent

	+		–	
Bal.	8,000	Adj.	4000	
Bal.				

important!

Prepaid Expense
Prepaid rent is recorded as an asset at the time it is paid. As time elapses, the asset is used up. An adjustment is made to reduce the asset and to recognize rent expense.

Refer again to Figure 5.2 to review the adjustment on the worksheet: a debit of $4,000 to *Rent Expense* and a credit of $4,000 to *Prepaid Rent.* Both parts of the adjustment are labeled (**b**).

ADJUSTING FOR DEPRECIATION

There is one more adjustment to make at the end of December. It involves the equipment purchased in November. The cost of long-term assets such as equipment is not recorded as an expense when purchased. Instead, the cost is recorded as an asset and spread over the time the assets are used for the business. **Depreciation** is the process of allocating the cost of long-term assets over their expected useful lives. There are many ways to calculate depreciation. Wells' Consulting Services uses the **straight-line depreciation** method. This method results in an equal amount of depreciation being charged to each accounting period during the asset's useful life. The formula for straight-line depreciation is

$$\text{Depreciation} = \frac{\text{Cost} - \text{Salvage value}}{\text{Estimated useful life}}$$

Salvage value is an estimate of the amount that may be received by selling or disposing of an asset at the end of its useful life.

Wells' Consulting Services purchased $11,000 worth of equipment. The equipment has an estimated useful life of five years and no salvage value. The depreciation for December, the first month of operations, is $183 (rounded).

$$\frac{\$11,000 - \$0}{60 \text{ months}} = \$183 \text{ (rounded)}$$

1. Convert the asset's useful life from years to months: 5 years $\times$ 12 months = 60 months.
2. Divide the total depreciation to be taken by the total number of months:
   $11,000 $\div$ 60 = $183 (rounded).
3. Record depreciation expense of $183 each month for the next 60 months.

> Conoco Inc. depreciates property such as refinery equipment, pipelines, and deepwater drill ships on a straight-line basis over the estimated life of each asset, ranging from 15 to 25 years.

important!

Contra Accounts

The normal balance for a contra account is the opposite of the related account.

Accumulated Depreciation is a contra asset account. The normal balance of an asset account is a *debit.* The normal balance of a contra asset account is a *credit.*

As the cost of the equipment is gradually transferred to expense, its recorded value as an asset must be reduced. This procedure cannot be carried out by directly decreasing the balance in the asset account. Generally accepted accounting principles require that the original cost of a long-term asset continue to appear in the asset account until the firm has used up or disposed of the asset.

The adjustment for depreciation is recorded in a contra account entitled *Accumulated Depreciation—Equipment.* A **contra account** has a normal balance that is opposite that of a related account. For example, the *Equipment* account is an asset and has a normal debit balance. *Accumulated Depreciation—Equipment* is a **contra asset account** with a normal credit balance, which is opposite the normal balance of an asset account. The adjustment to reflect depreciation for December is a $183 debit to *Depreciation Expense—Equipment* and a $183 credit to *Accumulated Depreciation—Equipment.*

The *Accumulated Depreciation—Equipment* account is a record of all depreciation taken on the equipment. The financial records show the original cost of the equipment (*Equipment,*

$11,000) and all depreciation taken (***Accumulated Depreciation—Equipment,*** $183). The difference between the two accounts is called book value. **Book value** is that portion of an asset's original cost that has not yet been depreciated. Three amounts are reported on the financial statements for equipment:

Equipment	$11,000
Less accumulated depreciation	– 183
Equipment at book value	$10,817

ADJUSTMENT

Record the adjustment for depreciation.

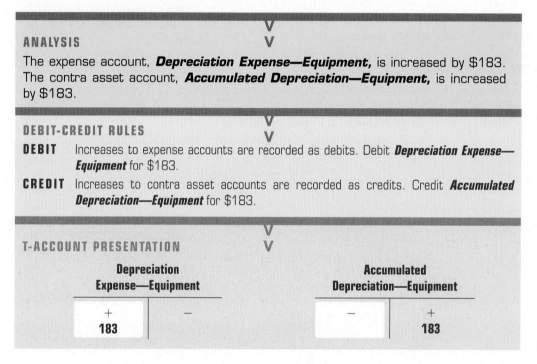

ANALYSIS

The expense account, ***Depreciation Expense—Equipment,*** is increased by $183. The contra asset account, ***Accumulated Depreciation—Equipment,*** is increased by $183.

DEBIT-CREDIT RULES

DEBIT   Increases to expense accounts are recorded as debits. Debit ***Depreciation Expense— Equipment*** for $183.

CREDIT   Increases to contra asset accounts are recorded as credits. Credit ***Accumulated Depreciation—Equipment*** for $183.

T-ACCOUNT PRESENTATION

Depreciation Expense—Equipment		Accumulated Depreciation—Equipment	
+	–	–	+
183			183

Refer to Figure 5.2 on page 125 to review the depreciation adjustment on the worksheet. The two parts of the adjustment are labeled **(c)**.

If Wells' Consulting Services had other kinds of long-term tangible assets, an adjustment for depreciation would be made for each one. Long-term tangible assets include land, buildings, equipment, trucks, automobiles, furniture, and fixtures. Depreciation is calculated on all long-term tangible assets except land. Land is not depreciated.

Notice that each adjustment involved a balance sheet account (an asset or a contra asset) and an income statement account (an expense). When all adjustments have been entered, total and rule the Adjustments columns. Be sure that the totals of the Debit and Credit columns are equal. If they are not, locate and correct the error or errors before continuing. Figure 5.2 shows the completed Adjustments section.

Section 1 Self Review

QUESTIONS

1. Why is the worksheet prepared?

2. Why are prepaid expenses adjusted at the end of an accounting period?

3. What are adjustments?

EXERCISES

4. A firm paid $1,200 for supplies during the accounting period. At the end of the accounting period, the firm had $300 of supplies on hand. What adjustment is entered on the worksheet?

   a. *Supplies Expense* is debited for $900 and *Supplies* is credited for $900.

   b. *Supplies* is debited for $300 and *Supplies Expense* is credited for $300.

   c. *Supplies Expense* is debited for $300 and *Supplies* is credited for $300.

   d. *Supplies* is debited for $900 and *Supplies Expense* is credited for $900.

5. On January 1, a firm paid $21,600 for six months' rent, January through June. What is the adjustment for rent expense at the end of January?

   a. *Rent Expense* is debited for $21,600 and *Prepaid Rent* is credited for $21,600.

   b. *Rent Expense* is debited for $3,600 and *Prepaid Rent* is credited for $3,600.

   c. *Prepaid Rent* is debited for $3,600 and *Rent Expense* is credited for $3,600.

   d. No adjustment is made until the end of June.

ANALYSIS

6. Three years ago HB Delivery bought a delivery truck for $70,000. The truck has no salvage value and a five-year useful life. What is the book value of the truck at the end of three years?

(Answers to Section 1 Self Review are on page 153.)

SECTION OBJECTIVES	TERMS TO LEARN
>> 3. Complete the worksheet. WHY IT'S IMPORTANT The worksheet summarizes both internal and external financial events of a period.	account form balance sheet report form balance sheet
>> 4. Prepare an income statement, statement of owner's equity, and balance sheet from the completed worksheet. WHY IT'S IMPORTANT Using a worksheet saves time in preparing the financial statements.	
>> 5. Journalize and post the adjusting entries. WHY IT'S IMPORTANT Adjusting entries update the financial records of the business.	

Financial Statements

The worksheet is used to prepare the financial statements. Preparing financial statements is the fifth step in the accounting cycle.

The Adjusted Trial Balance Section

The next task is to prepare the Adjusted Trial Balance section.

1. Combine the figures from the Trial Balance section and the Adjustments section of the worksheet. Record the computed results in the Adjusted Trial Balance columns.
2. Total the Debit and Credit columns in the Adjusted Trial Balance section. Confirm that debits equal credits.

>>3. OBJECTIVE
Complete the worksheet.

LP5

Figure 5.3 on pages 132–133 shows the completed Adjusted Trial Balance section of the worksheet. The accounts that do not have adjustments are simply extended from the Trial Balance section to the Adjusted Trial Balance section. For example, the *Cash* account balance of $111,350 is recorded in the Debit column of the Adjusted Trial Balance section without change.

The balances of accounts that are affected by adjustments are recomputed. Look at the *Supplies* account. It has a $1,500 debit balance in the Trial Balance section and shows a $500 credit in the Adjustments section. The new balance is $1,000 ($1,500 − $500). It is recorded in the Debit column of the Adjusted Trial Balance section.

Use the following guidelines to compute the amounts for the Adjusted Trial Balance section.

- If the account has a debit balance in the Trial Balance section and a debit entry in the Adjustments section, add the two amounts.

If the Trial Balance section has a:	AND if the entry in the Adjustments section is a:	Then:
Debit balance	Debit	Add the amounts.
Debit balance	Credit	Subtract the credit amount.
Credit balance	Credit	Add the amounts.
Credit balance	Debit	Subtract the debit amount.

Wells' Consulting Services
Worksheet
Month Ended December 31, 2010

	ACCOUNT NAME	TRIAL BALANCE DEBIT	TRIAL BALANCE CREDIT	ADJUSTMENTS DEBIT	ADJUSTMENTS CREDIT
1	Cash	111 350 00			
2	Accounts Receivable	5 000 00			
3	Supplies	1 500 00			(a) 500 00
4	Prepaid Rent	8 000 00			(b) 4 000 00
5	Equipment	11 000 00			
6	Accumulated Depreciation—Equipment				(c) 183 00
7	Accounts Payable		3 500 00		
8	Carolyn Wells, Capital		100 000 00		
9	Carolyn Wells, Drawing	5 000 00			
10	Fees Income		47 000 00		
11	Salaries Expense	8 000 00			
12	Utilities Expense	650 00			
13	Supplies Expense			(a) 500 00	
14	Rent Expense			(b) 4 000 00	
15	Depreciation Expense—Equipment			(c) 183 00	
16	Totals	150 500 00	150 500 00	4 683 00	4 683 00
17	Net Income				

FIGURE 5.3

A Partial Worksheet

- If the account has a debit balance in the Trial Balance section and a credit entry in the Adjustments section, subtract the credit amount.

- If the account has a credit balance in the Trial Balance section and a credit entry in the Adjustments section, add the two amounts.

- If the account has a credit balance in the Trial Balance section and a debit entry in the Adjustments section, subtract the debit amount.

Prepaid Rent has a Trial Balance debit of $8,000 and an Adjustments credit of $4,000. Enter $4,000 ($8,000 − $4,000) in the Adjusted Trial Balance Debit column.

Four accounts that started with zero balances in the Trial Balance section are affected by adjustments. They are **Accumulated Depreciation—Equipment, Supplies Expense, Rent Expense,** and **Depreciation Expense—Equipment.** The figures in the Adjustments section are simply extended to the Adjusted Trial Balance section. For example, **Accumulated Depreciation—Equipment** has a zero balance in the Trial Balance section and a $183 credit in the Adjustments section. Extend the $183 to the Adjusted Trial Balance Credit column.

Once all account balances are recorded in the Adjusted Trial Balance section, total and rule the Debit and Credit columns. Be sure that total debits equal total credits. If they are not equal, find and correct the error or errors.

The Income Statement and Balance Sheet Sections

The Income Statement and Balance Sheet sections of the worksheet are used to separate the amounts needed for the balance sheet and the income statement. For example, to prepare an income statement, all revenue and expense account balances must be in one place.

Starting at the top of the Adjusted Trial Balance section, examine each general ledger account. For accounts that appear on the balance sheet, enter the amount in the appropriate column of the Balance Sheet section. For accounts that appear on the income statement, enter the amount in the appropriate column of the Income Statement section. Take care to enter debit amounts in the Debit column and credit amounts in the Credit column.

ADJUSTED TRIAL BALANCE		INCOME STATEMENT		BALANCE SHEET		
DEBIT	CREDIT	DEBIT	CREDIT	DEBIT	CREDIT	
111 3 5 0 00						1
5 0 0 0 00						2
1 0 0 0 00						3
4 0 0 0 00						4
11 0 0 0 00						5
	1 8 3 00					6
	3 5 0 0 00					7
	100 0 0 0 00					8
5 0 0 0 00						9
	47 0 0 0 00					10
8 0 0 0 00						11
6 5 0 00						12
5 0 0 00						13
4 0 0 0 00						14
1 8 3 00						15
150 6 8 3 00	150 6 8 3 00					16
						17

PREPARING THE BALANCE SHEET SECTION

Refer to Figure 5.4 on pages 134–135 as you learn how to complete the worksheet. Asset, liability, and owner's equity accounts appear on the balance sheet. The first five accounts that appear on the worksheet are assets. Extend the asset accounts to the Debit column of the Balance Sheet section. The next account, ***Accumulated Depreciation—Equipment,*** is a contra asset account. Extend it to the Credit column of the Balance Sheet section. Extend ***Accounts Payable*** and ***Carolyn Wells, Capital*** to the Credit column of the Balance Sheet section. Extend ***Carolyn Wells, Drawing*** to the Debit column of the Balance Sheet section.

PREPARING THE INCOME STATEMENT SECTION

Revenue and expense accounts appear on the income statement. Extend the ***Fees Income*** account to the Credit column of the Income Statement section. The last five accounts on the worksheet are expense accounts. Extend these accounts to the Debit column of the Income Statement section.

After all account balances are transferred from the Adjusted Trial Balance section of the worksheet to the financial statement sections, total the Debit and Credit columns in the Income Statement section. For Wells' Consulting Services, the debits (expenses) total $13,333 and the credits (revenue) total $47,000.

Next total the columns in the Balance Sheet section. For Wells' Consulting Services, the debits (assets and drawing account) total $137,350 and the credits (contra asset, liabilities, and owner's equity) total $103,683.

Return to the Income Statement section. The totals of these columns are used to determine the net income or net loss. Subtract the smaller column total from the larger one. Enter the difference on the line below the smaller total. In the Account Name column, enter "Net Income" or "Net Loss."

In this case, the total of the Credit column, $47,000, exceeds the total of the Debit column, $13,333. The Credit column total represents revenue. The Debit column total represents expenses. The difference between the two amounts is a net income of $33,667. Enter $33,667 in the Debit column of the Income Statement section.

recall

Locating Errors

If total debits do not equal total credits, find the difference between total debits and total credits. If the difference is divisible by 9, there could be a transposition error. If the difference is divisible by 2, an amount could be entered in the wrong (Debit or Credit) column.

Wells' Consulting Services
Worksheet
Month Ended December 31, 2010

	ACCOUNT NAME	TRIAL BALANCE		ADJUSTMENTS	
		DEBIT	CREDIT	DEBIT	CREDIT
1	Cash	111 350 00			
2	Accounts Receivable	5 000 00			
3	Supplies	1 500 00			(a) 500 00
4	Prepaid Rent	8 000 00			(b) 4 000 00
5	Equipment	11 000 00			
6	Accumulated Depreciation—Equipment				(c) 183 00
7	Accounts Payable		3 500 00		
8	Carolyn Wells, Capital		100 000 00		
9	Carolyn Wells, Drawing	5 000 00			
10	Fees Income		47 000 00		
11	Salaries Expense	8 000 00			
12	Utilities Expense	650 00			
13	Supplies Expense			(a) 500 00	
14	Rent Expense			(b) 4 000 00	
15	Depreciation Expense—Equipment			(c) 183 00	
16	Totals	150 500 00	150 500 00	4 683 00	4 683 00
17	Net Income				
18					

FIGURE 5.4

A Completed Worksheet

>>4. OBJECTIVE

Prepare an income statement, statement of owner's equity, and balance sheet from the completed worksheet.

Net income causes a net increase in owner's equity. As a check on accuracy, the amount in the Balance Sheet Debit column is subtracted from the amount in the Credit column and compared to net income. In the Balance Sheet section, subtract the smaller column total from the larger one. The difference should equal the net income or net loss computed in the Income Statement section. Enter the difference on the line below the smaller total. For Wells' Consulting Services, enter $33,667 in the Credit column of the Balance Sheet section.

Total the Income Statement and Balance Sheet columns. Make sure that total debits equal total credits for each section.

Wells' Consulting Services had a net income. If it had a loss, the loss would be entered in the Credit column of the Income Statement section and the Debit column of the Balance Sheet section. "Net Loss" would be entered in the Account Name column on the worksheet.

Preparing Financial Statements

When the worksheet is complete, the next step is to prepare the financial statements, starting with the income statement. Preparation of the financial statements is the fifth step in the accounting cycle.

PREPARING THE INCOME STATEMENT

Use the Income Statement section of the worksheet to prepare the income statement. Figure 5.5 on page 136 shows the income statement for Wells' Consulting Services. Compare it to the worksheet in Figure 5.4.

If the firm had incurred a net loss, the final amount on the income statement would be labeled "Net Loss for the Month."

ADJUSTED TRIAL BALANCE		INCOME STATEMENT		BALANCE SHEET		
DEBIT	CREDIT	DEBIT	CREDIT	DEBIT	CREDIT	
111 350 00				111 350 00		1
5 000 00				5 000 00		2
1 000 00				1 000 00		3
4 000 00				4 000 00		4
11 000 00				11 000 00		5
	1 83 00				1 83 00	6
	3 500 00				3 500 00	7
	100 000 00				100 000 00	8
5 000 00				5 000 00		9
	47 000 00		47 000 00			10
8 000 00		8 000 00				11
650 00		650 00				12
500 00		500 00				13
4 000 00		4 000 00				14
1 83 00		1 83 00				15
150 683 00	150 683 00	13 333 00	47 000 00	137 350 00	103 683 00	16
		33 667 00			33 667 00	17
		47 000 00	47 000 00	137 350 00	137 350 00	18

PREPARING THE STATEMENT OF OWNER'S EQUITY

The statement of owner's equity reports the changes that have occurred in the owner's financial interest during the reporting period. Use the data in the Balance Sheet section of the worksheet, as well as the net income or net loss figure, to prepare the statement of owner's equity.

- From the Balance Sheet section of the worksheet, use the amounts for owner's capital; owner's withdrawals, if any; and owner's investments, if any.
- From the Income Statement section of the worksheet, use the amount calculated for net income or net loss.

The statement of owner's equity is prepared before the balance sheet because the ending capital balance is needed to prepare the balance sheet. The statement of owner's equity reports the change in owner's capital during the period ($28,667) as well as the ending capital ($128,667). Figure 5.6 on page 136 shows the statement of owner's equity for Wells' Consulting Services.

PREPARING THE BALANCE SHEET

The accounts listed on the balance sheet are taken directly from the Balance Sheet section of the worksheet. Figure 5.7 on page 136 shows the balance sheet for Wells' Consulting Services.

Note that the equipment's book value is reported on the balance sheet ($10,817). Do not confuse book value with market value. Book value is the portion of the original cost that has not been depreciated. *Market value* is what a willing buyer will pay a willing seller for the asset. Market value may be higher or lower than book value.

Notice that the amount for **Carolyn Wells, Capital,** $128,667, comes from the statement of owner's equity.

The balance sheet in Figure 5.7 is prepared using the report form. The **report form balance sheet** lists the asset accounts first, followed by liabilities and owner's equity. Chapters 2 and 3 illustrated the **account form balance sheet,** with assets on the left and liabilities and

(continued on page 137)

FIGURE 5.5

Income Statement

Wells' Consulting Services						
Income Statement						
Month Ended December 31, 2010						
Revenue						
Fees Income					47 0 0 0	00
Expenses						
Salaries Expense	8 0 0 0	00				
Utilities Expense	6 5 0	00				
Supplies Expense	5 0 0	00				
Rent Expense	4 0 0 0	00				
Depreciation Expense—Equipment	1 8 3	00				
Total Expenses					13 3 3 3	00
Net Income for the Month					33 6 6 7	00

FIGURE 5.6

Statement of Owner's Equity

Wells' Consulting Services						
Statement of Owner's Equity						
Month Ended December 31, 2010						
Carolyn Wells, Capital, December 1, 2010					100 0 0 0	00
Net Income for December	33 6 6 7	00				
Less Withdrawals for December	5 0 0 0	00				
Increase in Capital					28 6 6 7	00
Carolyn Wells, Capital, December 31, 2010					128 6 6 7	00

FIGURE 5.7

Balance Sheet

Wells' Consulting Services						
Balance Sheet						
December 31, 2010						
Assets						
Cash					111 3 5 0	00
Accounts Receivable					5 0 0 0	00
Supplies					1 0 0 0	00
Prepaid Rent					4 0 0 0	00
Equipment	11 0 0 0	00				
Less Accumulated Depreciation	1 8 3	00			10 8 1 7	00
Total Assets					132 1 6 7	00
Liabilities and Owner's Equity						
Liabilities						
Accounts Payable					3 5 0 0	00
Owner's Equity						
Carolyn Wells, Capital					128 6 6 7	00
Total Liabilities and Owner's Equity					132 1 6 7	00

FIGURE 5.8A Worksheet Summary

The worksheet is used to gather all the data needed at the end of an accounting period to prepare the financial statements. The worksheet heading contains the name of the company (WHO), in the title of the statement being prepared (WHAT), and the period covered (WHEN). The worksheet contains 10 money columns that are arranged in five sections labeled Trial Balance, Adjustments, Adjusted Trial Balance, Income Statement, and Balance Sheet. Each section includes a Debit column and a Credit column.

   The information reflected in the worksheet below is for Wells' Consulting Services for the period ending December 31, 2010. The illustrations that follow will highlight the preparation of each part of the worksheet.

WHO	Wells' Consulting Services									
WHAT	Worksheet									
WHEN	Month Ended December 31, 2010									

ACCOUNT NAME	TRIAL BALANCE		ADJUSTMENTS		ADJUSTED TRIAL BALANCE		INCOME STATEMENT		BALANCE SHEET	
	DEBIT	CREDIT	DEBIT	CREDIT	DEBIT	CREDIT	DEBIT	CREDIT	DEBIT	CREDIT

1 Record each general ledger account name.

2 Record account balances.

3 Record each adjustment.

4 Calculate new balances and extend amounts from the Trial Balance and Adjustments columns.

5 Extend income and expense account balances.

6 Extend asset, liability, and owner's equity account balances.

FIGURE 5.8B   The Trial Balance Columns

The first step in preparing the worksheet for Wells' Consulting Services is to list the general ledger accounts and their balances in the Account Name and Trial Balance sections of the worksheet. The equality of total debits and credits is proved by totaling the Debit and Credit columns.

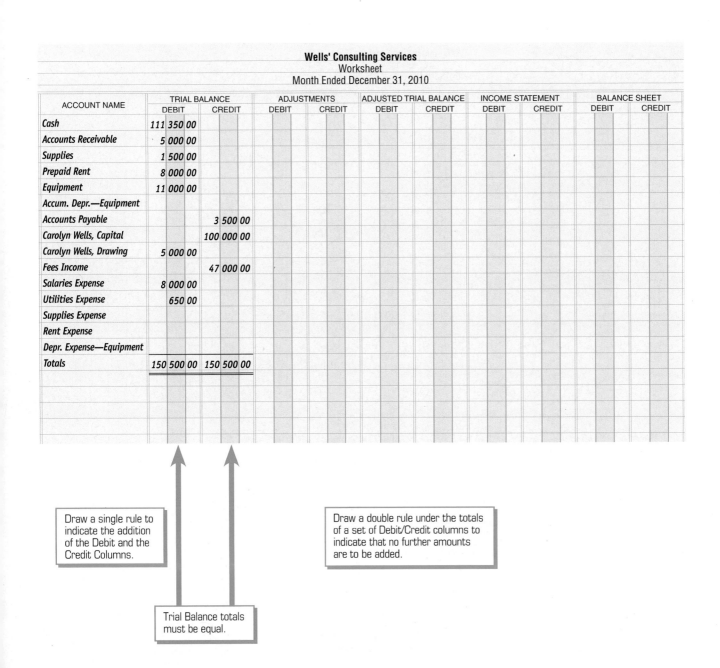

Wells' Consulting Services
Worksheet
Month Ended December 31, 2010

ACCOUNT NAME	TRIAL BALANCE		ADJUSTMENTS		ADJUSTED TRIAL BALANCE		INCOME STATEMENT		BALANCE SHEET	
	DEBIT	CREDIT	DEBIT	CREDIT	DEBIT	CREDIT	DEBIT	CREDIT	DEBIT	CREDIT
Cash	111 350 00									
Accounts Receivable	5 000 00									
Supplies	1 500 00									
Prepaid Rent	8 000 00									
Equipment	11 000 00									
Accum. Depr.—Equipment										
Accounts Payable		3 500 00								
Carolyn Wells, Capital		100 000 00								
Carolyn Wells, Drawing	5 000 00									
Fees Income		47 000 00								
Salaries Expense	8 000 00									
Utilities Expense	650 00									
Supplies Expense										
Rent Expense										
Depr. Expense—Equipment										
Totals	150 500 00	150 500 00								

Draw a single rule to indicate the addition of the Debit and the Credit Columns.

Draw a double rule under the totals of a set of Debit/Credit columns to indicate that no further amounts are to be added.

Trial Balance totals must be equal.

FIGURE 5.8G   Preparing the Financial Statements

The information needed to prepare the financial statements is obtained from the worksheet.

Wells' Consulting Services
Income Statement
Month Ended December 31, 2010

Revenue		
Fees Income		47 0 0 0 00
Expenses		
Salaries Expense	8 0 0 0 00	
Utilities Expense	6 5 0 00	
Supplies Expense	5 0 0 00	
Rent Expense	4 0 0 0 00	
Depreciation Expense—Equipment	1 8 3 00	
Total Expenses		13 3 3 3 00
Net Income for the Month		33 6 6 7 00

> When expenses for the period are less than revenue, a net income results. The net income is transferred to the statement of owner's equity.

Wells' Consulting Services
Statement of Owner's Equity
Month Ended December 31, 2010

Carolyn Wells, Capital, December 1, 2010		100 0 0 0 00
Net Income for December	33 6 6 7 00	
Less Withdrawals for December	5 0 0 0 00	
Increase in Capital		28 6 6 7 00
Carolyn Wells, Capital, December 31, 2010		128 6 6 7 00

> The withdrawals are subtracted from the net income for the period to determine the change in owner's equity.

Wells' Consulting Services
Balance Sheet
December 31, 2010

Assets		
Cash		111 3 5 0 00
Accounts Receivable		5 0 0 0 00
Supplies		1 0 0 0 00
Prepaid Rent		4 0 0 0 00
Equipment	11 0 0 0 00	
Less Accumulated Depreciation	1 8 3 00	10 8 1 7 00
Total Assets		132 1 6 7 00
Liabilities and Owner's Equity		
Liabilities		
Accounts Payable		3 5 0 0 00
Owner's Equity		
Carolyn Wells, Capital		128 6 6 7 00
Total Liabilities and Owner's Equity		132 1 6 7 00

> The ending capital balance is transferred from the statement of owner's equity to the balance sheet.

SUMMARY OF FINANCIAL STATEMENTS

THE INCOME STATEMENT

The income statement is prepared directly from the data in the Income Statement section of the worksheet. The heading of the income statement contains the name of the firm (WHO), the name of the statement (WHAT), and the period covered by the statement (WHEN). The revenue section of the statement is prepared first. The revenue account name is obtained from the Account Name column of the worksheet. The balance of the revenue account is obtained from the Credit column of the Income Statement section of the worksheet. The expenses section of the income statement is prepared next. The expense account titles are obtained from the Account Name column of the worksheet. The balance of each expense account is obtained from the Debit column of the Income Statement section of the worksheet.

Determining the net income or net loss for the period is the last step in preparing the income statement. If the firm has more revenue than expenses, a net income is reported for the period. If the firm has more expenses than revenue, a net loss is reported. The net income or net loss reported must agree with the amount calculated on the worksheet.

THE STATEMENT OF OWNER'S EQUITY

The statement of owner's equity is prepared from the data in the Balance Sheet section of the worksheet and the general ledger capital account. The statement of owner's equity is prepared before the balance sheet so that the amount of the ending capital balance is available for presentation on the balance sheet. The heading of the statement contains the name of the firm (WHO), the name of the statement (WHAT), and the date of the statement (WHEN).

The statement begins with the capital account balance at the beginning of the period. Next, the increase or decrease in the owner's capital account is determined. The increase or decrease is computed by adding the net income (or net loss) for the period to any additional investments made by the owner during the period and subtracting withdrawals for the period. The increase or decrease is added to the beginning capital balance to obtain the ending capital balance.

THE BALANCE SHEET

The balance sheet is prepared from the data in the Balance Sheet section of the worksheet and the statement of owner's equity. The balance sheet reflects the assets, liabilities, and owner's equity of the firm on the balance sheet date. The heading of the statement contains the name of the firm (WHO), the name of the statement (WHAT), and the date of the statement (WHEN).

The assets section of the statement is prepared first. The asset account titles are obtained from the Account Name column of the worksheet. The balance of each asset account is obtained from the Debit column of the Balance Sheet section of the worksheet. The liability and owner's equity section is prepared next. The liability and owner's equity account titles are obtained from the Account Name column of the worksheet. The balance of each liability account is obtained from the Credit column of the Balance Sheet section of the worksheet. The ending balance for the owner's capital account is obtained from the statement of owner's equity. Total liabilities and owner's equity must equal total assets.

(continued from page 135)

owner's equity on the right. The report form is widely used because it provides more space for entering account names and its format is easier to prepare.

> Some companies show long-term assets at a net amount. "Net" means that accumulated depreciation has been subtracted from the original cost. For example, The Boeing Company's consolidated statement of financial position as of December 31, 2006, states:
>   Property, plant, and equipment, net: $7,675 million
> The accumulated depreciation amount does not appear on the balance sheet.

Figure 5.8A through 5.8G on the preceding pages provides a step-by-step demonstration of how to complete the worksheet and financial statements for Wells' Consulting Services.

Journalizing and Posting Adjusting Entries

The worksheet is a tool. It is used to determine the effects of adjustments on account balances. It is also used to prepare the financial statements. However, the worksheet is not part of the permanent accounting record.

After the financial statements are prepared, the adjustments shown on the worksheet must become part of the permanent accounting record. Each adjustment is journalized and posted to the general ledger accounts. Journalizing and posting adjusting entries is the sixth step in the accounting cycle.

For Wells' Consulting Services, three adjustments are needed to provide a complete picture of the firm's operating results and its financial position. Adjustments are needed for supplies expense, rent expense, and depreciation expense.

Refer to Figure 5.4 on pages 134–135 for data needed to record the adjustments. Enter the words "Adjusting Entries" in the Description column of the general journal. Some accountants prefer to start a new page when they record the adjusting entries. Then journalize the adjustments in the order in which they appear on the worksheet.

After journalizing the adjusting entries, post them to the general ledger accounts. Figure 5.9 on page 138 shows how the adjusting entries for Wells' Consulting Services on December 31, 2010 were journalized and posted. Account numbers appear in the general journal Posting Reference column because all entries have been posted. In each general ledger account, the word "Adjusting" appears in the Description column.

Remember that the worksheet is not part of the accounting records. Adjustments that are on the worksheet must be recorded in the general journal and posted to the general ledger in order to become part of the permanent accounting records.

>>5. OBJECTIVE
Journalize and post the adjusting entries.

FIGURE 5.9

Journalized and Posted Adjusting Entries

GENERAL JOURNAL   PAGE ___3___

	DATE		DESCRIPTION	POST. REF.	DEBIT	CREDIT	
1	2010		Adjusting Entries				1
2	Dec.	31	Supplies Expense	517	5 0 0 00		2
3			Supplies	121		5 0 0 00	3
4							4
5		31	Rent Expense	520	4 0 0 0 00		5
6			Prepaid Rent	137		4 0 0 0 00	6
7							7
8		31	Depr. Expense—Equipment	523	1 8 3 00		8
9			Accum. Depr.—Equipment	142		1 8 3 00	9
10							10
11							

ACCOUNT Supplies   **ACCOUNT NO.** _121_

DATE		DESCRIPTION	POST. REF.	DEBIT	CREDIT	BALANCE DEBIT	BALANCE CREDIT
2010							
Nov.	28		J1	1 5 0 0 00		1 5 0 0 00	
Dec.	31	Adjusting	J3		5 0 0 00	1 0 0 0 00	

ACCOUNT Prepaid Rent   **ACCOUNT NO.** _137_

DATE		DESCRIPTION	POST. REF.	DEBIT	CREDIT	BALANCE DEBIT	BALANCE CREDIT
2010							
Nov.	30		J2	8 0 0 0 00		8 0 0 0 00	
Dec.	31	Adjusting	J3		4 0 0 0 00	4 0 0 0 00	

ACCOUNT Accumulated Depreciation—Equipment   **ACCOUNT NO.** _142_

DATE		DESCRIPTION	POST. REF.	DEBIT	CREDIT	BALANCE DEBIT	BALANCE CREDIT
2010							
Dec.	31	Adjusting	J3		1 8 3 00		1 8 3 00

ACCOUNT Supplies Expense   **ACCOUNT NO.** _517_

DATE		DESCRIPTION	POST. REF.	DEBIT	CREDIT	BALANCE DEBIT	BALANCE CREDIT
2010							
Dec.	31	Adjusting	J3	5 0 0 00		5 0 0 00	

ACCOUNT Rent Expense   **ACCOUNT NO.** _520_

DATE		DESCRIPTION	POST. REF.	DEBIT	CREDIT	BALANCE DEBIT	BALANCE CREDIT
2010							
Dec.	31	Adjusting	J3	4 0 0 0 00		4 0 0 0 00	

ACCOUNT Depreciation Expense—Equipment   **ACCOUNT NO.** _523_

DATE		DESCRIPTION	POST. REF.	DEBIT	CREDIT	BALANCE DEBIT	BALANCE CREDIT
2010							
Dec.	31	Adjusting	J3	1 8 3 00		1 8 3 00	

MANAGERIAL IMPLICATIONS

WORKSHEETS

- The worksheet permits quick preparation of the financial statements. Quick preparation of financial statements allows management to obtain timely information.
- Timely information allows management to
  - evaluate the results of operations,
  - evaluate the financial position of the business,
  - make decisions.
- The worksheet provides a convenient form for gathering information and determining the effects of internal changes such as
  - recording an expense for the use of a long-term asset like equipment,
  - recording the actual use of prepaid items.
- The more accounts that a firm has in its general ledger, the more useful the worksheet is in speeding the preparation of the financial statements.
- It is important to management that the appropriate adjustments are recorded in order to present a complete and accurate picture of the firm's financial affairs.

THINKING CRITICALLY

Why is it necessary to record an adjustment for depreciation?

Section **2** Self Review

QUESTIONS

1. What amounts appear on the statement of owner's equity?

2. What is the difference between a report form balance sheet and an account form balance sheet?

3. Why is it necessary to journalize and post adjusting entries even though the data are already recorded on the worksheet?

EXERCISES

4. On a worksheet, the adjusted balance of the **Supplies** account is extended to the

   a. Income Statement Debit column.
   b. Balance Sheet Debit column.
   c. Income Statement Credit column.
   d. Balance Sheet Credit column.

5. **Accumulated Depreciation—Equipment** is a(n)

   a. asset account.
   b. contra asset account.
   c. liability account.
   d. contra liability account.

ANALYSIS

6. Willis Repair Shop purchased equipment for $28,000. **Depreciation Expense** for the month is $500. What is the balance of the **Equipment** account after posting the depreciation entry? Why?

(Answers to Section 2 Self Review are on page 154.)

5 Chapter **REVIEW** Chapter Summary

At the end of the operating period, adjustments for internal events are recorded to update the accounting records. In this chapter, you have learned how the accountant uses the worksheet and adjusting entries to accomplish this task.

Learning Objectives

1 Complete a trial balance on a worksheet.

A worksheet is normally used to save time in preparing the financial statements. Preparation of the worksheet is the fourth step in the accounting cycle. The trial balance is the first section of the worksheet to be prepared.

2 Prepare adjustments for unrecorded business transactions.

Some changes arise from the internal operations of the firm itself. Adjusting entries are made to record these changes. Any adjustments to account balances should be entered in the Adjustments section of the worksheet.

■ Prepaid expenses are expense items that are acquired and paid for in advance of their use. At the time of their acquisition, these items represent assets and are recorded in asset accounts. As they are used, their cost is transferred to expense by means of adjusting entries at the end of each accounting period.

Examples of general ledger asset accounts and the related expense accounts follow:

Asset Accounts	Expense Accounts
Supplies	Supplies Expense
Prepaid Rent	Rent Expense
Prepaid Insurance	Insurance Expense

■ Depreciation is the process of allocating the cost of a long-term tangible asset to operations over its expected useful life. Part of the asset's cost is charged off as an expense at the end of each accounting period during the asset's useful life. The straight-line method of depreciation is widely used. The formula for straight-line depreciation is:

$$\text{Depreciation} = \frac{\text{Cost} - \text{Salvage value}}{\text{Estimated useful life}}$$

3 Complete the worksheet.

An adjusted trial balance is prepared to prove the equality of the debits and credits after adjustments have been entered on the worksheet. Once the Debit and Credit columns have been totaled and ruled, the Income Statement and Balance Sheet columns of the worksheet are completed. The net income or net loss for the period is determined, and the worksheet is completed.

4 Prepare an income statement, statement of owner's equity, and balance sheet from the completed worksheet.

All figures needed to prepare the financial statements are properly reflected on the completed worksheet. The accounts are arranged in the order in which they must appear on the income statement and balance sheet. Preparation of the financial statements is the fifth step of the accounting cycle.

5 Journalize and post the adjusting entries.

After the financial statements have been prepared, the accountant must make permanent entries in the accounting records for the adjustments shown on the worksheet. The adjusting entries are then posted to the general ledger. Journalizing and posting the adjusting entries is the sixth step in the accounting cycle.

To summarize the steps of the accounting cycle discussed so far:

1. Analyze transactions.
2. Journalize transactions.
3. Post the journal entries.
4. Prepare a worksheet.
5. Prepare financial statements.
6. Record adjusting entries.

6 Define the accounting terms new to this chapter.

Glossary

Account form balance sheet (p. 135) A balance sheet that lists assets on the left and liabilities and owner's equity on the right (see Report form balance sheet)

Adjusting entries (p. 125) Journal entries made to update accounts for items that were not recorded during the accounting period

Adjustments (p. 125) See Adjusting entries

Book value (p. 129) That portion of an asset's original cost that has not yet been depreciated

Contra account (p. 128) An account with a normal balance that is opposite that of a related account

Contra asset account (p. 128) An asset account with a credit balance, which is contrary to the normal balance of an asset account

Depreciation (p. 128) Allocation of the cost of a long-term asset to operations during its expected useful life

Prepaid expenses (p. 126) Expense items acquired, recorded, and paid for in advance of their use

Report form balance sheet (p. 135) A balance sheet that lists the asset accounts first, followed by liabilities and owner's equity

Salvage value (p. 128) An estimate of the amount that could be received by selling or disposing of an asset at the end of its useful life

Straight-line depreciation (p. 128) Allocation of an asset's cost in equal amounts to each accounting period of the asset's useful life

Worksheet (p. 124) A form used to gather all data needed at the end of an accounting period to prepare financial statements

Comprehensive Self Review

1. Why are assets depreciated?
2. Why is the net income for a period recorded in the Balance Sheet section of the worksheet as well as the Income Statement section?
3. The *Supplies* account has a debit balance of $6,000 in the Trial Balance column. The Credit column in the Adjustments section is $1,750. What is the new balance? The new balance will be extended to which column of the worksheet?
4. Is the normal balance for *Accumulated Depreciation* a debit or credit balance?
5. The *Drawing* account is extended to which column of the worksheet?

(Answers to Comprehensive Self Review are on page 154.)

 Multiple choice questions are provided on the text Web site at www.mhhe.com/price12e

Quiz5

Discussion Questions

1. Give three examples of assets that are subject to depreciation.
2. How does the straight-line method of depreciation work?
3. Why is an accumulated depreciation account used in making the adjustment for depreciation?
4. What is book value?
5. How does a contra asset account differ from a regular asset account?

6. What three amounts are reported on the balance sheet for a long-term asset such as equipment?

7. Why is it necessary to journalize and post adjusting entries?

8. What effect does each of the following items have on net income?

   a. The owner withdrew cash from the business.

   b. Credit customers paid $1,000 on outstanding balances that were past due.

   c. The business bought equipment on account that cost $10,000.

   d. The business journalized and posted an adjustment for depreciation of equipment.

9. What effect does each item in Question 8 have on owner's equity?

10. Are the following assets depreciated? Why or why not?

    a. Prepaid Insurance

    b. Delivery Truck

    c. Land

    d. Manufacturing Equipment

    e. Prepaid Rent

    f. Furniture

    g. Store Equipment

    h. Prepaid Advertising

    i. Computers

11. Why is it necessary to make an adjustment for supplies used?

12. What are prepaid expenses? Give four examples.

13. What adjustment would be recorded for expired insurance?

14. A firm purchases machinery, which has an estimated useful life of 10 years and no salvage value, for $30,000 at the beginning of the accounting period. What is the adjusting entry for depreciation at the end of one month if the firm uses the straight-line method of depreciation?

APPLICATIONS

Exercises

Exercise 5.1

Objective 2

▶ **Calculating adjustments.**

Determine the necessary end-of-June adjustments for Evenson Company.

1. On June 1, 2010, Evenson Company, a new firm, paid $4,500 rent in advance for a six-month period. The $4,500 was debited to the **Prepaid Rent** account.

2. On June 1, 2010, the firm bought supplies for $4,750. The $4,750 was debited to the **Supplies** account. An inventory of supplies at the end of June showed that items costing $1,800 were on hand.

3. On June 1, 2010, the firm bought equipment costing $54,000. The equipment has an expected useful life of 10 years and no salvage value. The firm will use the straight-line method of depreciation.

Exercise 5.2

Objective 2

▶ **Calculating adjustments.**

For each of the following situations, determine the necessary adjustments.

1. A firm purchased a two-year insurance policy for $3,000 on July 1, 2010. The $3,000 was debited to the **Prepaid Insurance** account. What adjustment should be made to record expired insurance on the firm's July 31, 2010, worksheet?

2. On December 1, 2010, a firm signed a contract with a local radio station for advertising that will extend over a one-year period. The firm paid $10,800 in advance and debited the amount to *Prepaid Advertising.* What adjustment should be made to record expired advertising on the firm's December 31, 2010, worksheet?

Worksheet through Adjusted Trial Balance.

◀ **Exercise 5.3**
Objectives 1, 2

On January 31, 2010, the general ledger of Nixon Company showed the following account balances. Prepare the worksheet through the Adjusted Trial Balance section. Assume that every account has the normal debit or credit balance. The worksheet covers the month of January.

ACCOUNTS	
Cash	124,000
Accounts Receivable	43,000
Supplies	16,000
Prepaid Insurance	14,400
Equipment	181,000
Accum. Depr.—Equip.	0
Accounts Payable	31,400
Robert Nixon, Capital	161,900
Fees Income	224,000
Depreciation Exp.—Equip.	0
Insurance Expense	0
Rent Expense	19,200
Salaries Expense	19,700
Supplies Expense	0

Additional information:

a. Supplies used during January totaled $10,400.

b. Expired insurance totaled $3,600.

c. Depreciation expense for the month was $3,150.

Correcting net income.

◀ **Exercise 5.4**
Objectives 2, 3

Assume that a firm reports net income of $80,000 prior to making adjusting entries for the following items: expired rent, $6,000; depreciation expense, $7,200; and supplies used, $2,600.
Assume that the required adjusting entries have not been made. What effect do these errors have on the reported net income?

Journalizing and posting adjustments.

◀ **Exercise 5.5**
Objective 5

Ross Company must make three adjusting entries on December 31, 2010.

a. Supplies used, $5,000; (supplies totaling $8,000 were purchased on December 1, 2010, and debited to the *Supplies* account).

b. Expired insurance, $3,600 on December 1, 2010; the firm paid $21,600 for six months' insurance coverage in advance and debited *Prepaid Insurance* for this amount.

c. Depreciation expense for equipment, $2,400.

Make the journal entries for these adjustments and post the entries to the general ledger accounts. Use page 3 of the general journal for the adjusting entries. Use the following accounts and numbers.

Supplies	121
Prepaid Insurance	131
Accum. Depr.—Equip.	142
Depreciation Exp.—Equip.	517
Insurance Expense	521
Supplies Expense	523

PROBLEMS

Problem Set A

Problem 5.1A ▶ **Completing the worksheet.**

Objectives 1, 2, 3

The trial balance of Dennis Company as of January 31, 2010, after the company completed the first month of operations, is shown in the partial worksheet below.

INSTRUCTIONS

1. Record the trial balance in the Trial Balance section of the worksheet.
2. Complete the worksheet by making the following adjustments: supplies on hand at the end of the month, $3,200; expired insurance, $5,000; depreciation expense for the period, $1,100.

Analyze: How does the insurance adjustment affect *Prepaid Insurance?*

		TRIAL BALANCE		ADJUSTMENTS	
	ACCOUNT NAME	DEBIT	CREDIT	DEBIT	CREDIT
1	Cash	52 0 0 0 00			
2	Accounts Receivable	10 4 0 0 00			
3	Supplies	19 2 0 0 00			
4	Prepaid Insurance	30 0 0 0 00			
5	Equipment	54 0 0 0 00			
6	Accumulated Depreciation—Equipment				
7	Accounts Payable		12 4 0 0 00		
8	Charles Dennis, Capital		126 0 0 0 00		
9	Charles Dennis, Drawing	7 2 0 0 00			
10	Fees Income		51 6 0 0 00		
11	Depreciation Expense—Equipment				
12	Insurance Expense				
13	Salaries Expense	15 6 0 0 00			
14	Supplies Expense				
15	Utilities Expense	1 6 0 0 00			
16	Totals	190 0 0 0 00	190 0 0 0 00		

Dennis Company
Worksheet (Partial)
Month Ended January 31, 2010

Problem 5.2A ▶ **Reconstructing a partial worksheet.**

Objectives 1, 2, 3

The adjusted trial balance of University Book Store as of November 30, 2010, after the firm's first month of operations, appears on page 145.
Appropriate adjustments have been made for the following items.

a. Supplies used during the month, $4,800.

b. Expired rent for the month, $6,000.

c. Depreciation expense for the month, $1,400.

INSTRUCTIONS

1. Record the Adjusted Trial Balance in the Adjusted Trial Balance columns of the worksheet.
2. Prepare the adjusting entries in the Adjustments columns.
3. Complete the Trial Balance columns of the worksheet prior to making the adjusting entries.

Analyze: What was the balance of *Prepaid Rent* prior to the adjusting entry for expired rent?

University Book Store
Adjusted Trial Balance
November 30, 2010

Account Name	Debit	Credit
Cash	45,150	
Accounts Receivable	6,624	
Supplies	7,200	
Prepaid Rent	36,000	
Equipment	54,000	
Accumulated Depreciation—Equipment		1,400
Accounts Payable		16,000
Julie Acker, Capital		81,674
Julie Acker, Drawing	6,000	
Fees Income		84,000
Depreciation Expense—Equipment	1,400	
Rent Expense	6,000	
Salaries Expense	15,000	
Supplies Expense	4,800	
Utilities Expense	900	
Totals	183,074	183,074

Preparing financial statements from the worksheet.

◄ **Problem 5.3A**
Objective 4

The completed worksheet for Orange Corporation as of December 31, 2010, after the company had completed the first month of operation, appears across the tops of pages 146–147.

INSTRUCTIONS

1. Prepare an income statement.
2. Prepare a statement of owner's equity. The owner made no additional investments during the month.
3. Prepare a balance sheet (use the report form).

Analyze: If the adjustment to *Prepaid Advertising* had been $4,800 instead of $2,400, what net income would have resulted?

Preparing a worksheet and financial statements, journalizing adjusting entries, and posting to ledger accounts.

◄ **Problem 5.4A**
Objectives
1, 2, 3, 4, 5

Sadie Palmer owns Palmer Creative Designs. The trial balance of the firm for January 31, 2010, the first month of operations, is shown on the bottom of page 146.

INSTRUCTIONS

1. Complete the worksheet for the month.
2. Prepare an income statement, statement of owner's equity, and balance sheet. No additional investments were made by the owner during the month.
3. Journalize and post the adjusting entries. Use 3 for the journal page number. Use the following account numbers: Supplies, 121; Prepaid Advertising, 130; Prepaid Rent, 131; Accumulated Depreciation—Equipment, 142; Supplies Expense, 517; Advertising Expense, 519; Rent Expense, 520; Depreciation Expense, 523.

End-of-the-month adjustments must account for the following items:

a. Supplies were purchased on January 1, 2010; inventory of supplies on January 31, 2010, is $1,100.
b. The prepaid advertising contract was signed on January 1, 2010, and covers a four-month period.

Orange Corporation
Worksheet
Month Ended December 31, 2010

ACCOUNT NAME	TRIAL BALANCE DEBIT	TRIAL BALANCE CREDIT	ADJUSTMENTS DEBIT	ADJUSTMENTS CREDIT
1 Cash	77 2 0 0 00			
2 Accounts Receivable	12 0 0 0 00			
3 Supplies	10 1 0 0 00			(a) 6 0 0 0 00
4 Prepaid Advertising	14 4 0 0 00			(b) 2 4 0 0 00
5 Equipment	60 0 0 0 00			
6 Accumulated Depreciation—Equipment				(c) 1 2 0 0 00
7 Accounts Payable		12 0 0 0 00		
8 Ted Coe, Capital		108 0 0 0 00		
9 Ted Coe, Drawing	7 2 0 0 00			
10 Fees Income		79 5 0 0 00		
11 Advertising Expense			(b) 2 4 0 0 00	
12 Depreciation Expense—Equipment			(c) 1 2 0 0 00	
13 Salaries Expense	16 8 0 0 00			
14 Supplies Expense			(a) 6 0 0 0 00	
15 Utilities Expense	1 8 0 0 00			
16 Totals	199 5 0 0 00	199 5 0 0 00	9 6 0 0 00	9 6 0 0 00
17 Net Income				
18				
19				

c. Rent of $1,600 expired during the month.

d. Depreciation is computed using the straight-line method. The equipment has an estimated useful life of 10 years with no salvage value.

Analyze: If the adjusting entries had not been made for the month, would net income be overstated or understated?

Palmer Creative Designs
Worksheet (Partial)
Month Ended January 31, 2010

ACCOUNT NAME	TRIAL BALANCE DEBIT	TRIAL BALANCE CREDIT
1 Cash	35 5 0 0 00	
2 Accounts Receivable	12 6 0 0 00	
3 Supplies	7 7 5 0 00	
4 Prepaid Advertising	8 4 0 0 00	
5 Prepaid Rent	19 2 0 0 00	
6 Equipment	21 6 0 0 00	
7 Accumulated Depreciation—Equipment		
8 Accounts Payable		15 5 5 0 00
9 Sadie Palmer, Capital		60 0 0 0 00
10 Sadie Palmer, Drawing	7 0 0 0 00	
11 Fees Income		47 6 0 0 00
12 Advertising Expense		
13 Depreciation Expense—Equipment		
14 Rent Expense		
15 Salaries Expense	9 7 0 0 00	
16 Supplies Expense		
17 Utilities Expense	1 4 0 0 00	
18 Totals	123 1 5 0 00	123 1 5 0 00
19		

	ADJUSTED TRIAL BALANCE		INCOME STATEMENT		BALANCE SHEET		
	DEBIT	CREDIT	DEBIT	CREDIT	DEBIT	CREDIT	
	77 2 0 0 00				77 2 0 0 00		1
	12 0 0 0 00				12 0 0 0 00		2
	4 1 0 0 00				4 1 0 0 00		3
	12 0 0 0 00				12 0 0 0 00		4
	60 0 0 0 00				60 0 0 0 00		5
		1 2 0 0 00				1 2 0 0 00	6
		12 0 0 0 00				12 0 0 0 00	7
		108 0 0 0 00				108 0 0 0 00	8
	7 2 0 0 00				7 2 0 0 00		9
		79 5 0 0 00		79 5 0 0 00			10
	2 4 0 0 00		2 4 0 0 00				11
	1 2 0 0 00		1 2 0 0 00				12
	16 8 0 0 00		16 8 0 0 00				13
	6 0 0 0 00		6 0 0 0 00				14
	1 8 0 0 00		1 8 0 0 00				15
	200 7 0 0 00	200 7 0 0 00	28 2 0 0 00	79 5 0 0 00	172 5 0 0 00	121 2 0 0 00	16
			51 3 0 0 00			51 3 0 0 00	17
			79 5 0 0 00	79 5 0 0 00	172 5 0 0 00	172 5 0 0 00	18
							19

Problem Set B

Completing the worksheet.

The trial balance of Torres Company as of February 28, 2010, appears below.

◄   **Problem 5.1B**
Objectives 1, 2, 3

Torres Company
Worksheet (Partial)
Month Ended February 28, 2010

	ACCOUNT NAME	TRIAL BALANCE		ADJUSTMENTS	
		DEBIT	CREDIT	DEBIT	CREDIT
1	Cash	36 5 0 0 00			
2	Accounts Receivable	3 2 0 0 00			
3	Supplies	2 1 0 0 00			
4	Prepaid Rent	12 0 0 0 00			
5	Equipment	23 0 0 0 00			
6	Accumulated Depreciation—Equipment				
7	Accounts Payable		6 0 0 0 00		
8	Paul Torres, Capital		49 2 5 0 00		
9	Paul Torres, Drawing	1 5 0 0 00			
10	Fees Income		27 0 0 0 00		
11	Depreciation Expense—Equipment				
12	Rent Expense				
13	Salaries Expense	3 1 5 0 00			
14	Supplies Expense				
15	Utilities Expense	8 0 0 00			
16	Totals	82 2 5 0 00	82 2 5 0 00		
17					

INSTRUCTIONS

1. Record the trial balance in the Trial Balance section of the worksheet.

2. Complete the worksheet by making the following adjustments: supplies on hand at the end of the month, $1,100; expired rent, $1,000; depreciation expense for the period, $500.

Analyze: Why do you think the account *Accumulated Depreciation—Equipment* has a zero balance on the trial balance shown?

Problem 5.2B
Objectives 1, 2, 3

▶ **Reconstructing a partial worksheet.**

The adjusted trial balance of Dennis Ortiz, Attorney-at-Law, as of November 30, 2010, after the company had completed the first month of operations, appears below.
Appropriate adjustments have been made for the following items.

a. Supplies used during the month, $3,600.

b. Expired rent for the month, $3,400.

c. Depreciation expense for the month, $550.

Dennis Ortiz, Attorney-at-Law Adjusted Trial Balance Month Ended November 30, 2010		
Account Name	Debit	Credit
Cash	35,050	
Accounts Receivable	8,500	
Supplies	6,800	
Prepaid Rent	40,800	
Equipment	66,000	
Accumulated Depreciation—Equipment		500
Accounts Payable		17,000
Dennis Ortiz, Capital		80,000
Dennis Ortiz, Drawing	6,000	
Fees Income		85,700
Depreciation Expense—Equipment	550	
Rent Expense	3,400	
Salaries Expense	10,800	
Supplies Expense	3,600	
Utilities Expense	1,750	
Totals	183,250	183,250

INSTRUCTIONS

1. Record the adjusted trial balance in the Adjusted Trial Balance columns of the worksheet.

2. Prepare the adjusting entries in the Adjustments columns.

3. Complete the Trial Balance columns of the worksheet prior to making the adjusting entries.

Analyze: Which contra asset account is on the adjusted trial balance?

Problem 5.3B
Objective 4

▶ **Preparing financial statements from the worksheet.**

The completed worksheet for JT's Accounting Services for the month ended December 31, 2010, appears on pages 150–151.

INSTRUCTIONS

1. Prepare an income statement.

2. Prepare a statement of owner's equity. The owner made no additional investments during the month.

3. Prepare a balance sheet.

Analyze: By what total amount did the value of assets reported on the balance sheet decrease due to the adjusting entries?

Preparing a worksheet and financial statements, journalizing adjusting entries, and posting to ledger accounts.

◄ Problem 5.4B
Objectives
1, 2, 3, 4, 5

Raul Rojas owns Rojas Estate Planning and Investments. The trial balance of the firm for June 30, 2010, the first month of operations, is shown below.

Rojas Estate Planning and Investments
Worksheet (Partial)
Month Ended June 30, 2010

	ACCOUNT NAME	TRIAL BALANCE		ADJUSTMENTS	
		DEBIT	CREDIT	DEBIT	CREDIT
1	Cash	19 7 0 0 00			
2	Accounts Receivable	6 1 0 0 00			
3	Supplies	7 6 0 0 00			
4	Prepaid Advertising	14 4 0 0 00			
5	Prepaid Rent	36 0 0 0 00			
6	Equipment	48 0 0 0 00			
7	Accumulated Depreciation—Equipment				
8	Accounts Payable		10 8 0 0 00		
9	Paul Rojas, Capital		60 1 0 0 00		
10	Paul Rojas, Drawing	4 0 0 0 00			
11	Fees Income		73 8 0 0 00		
12	Advertising Expense				
13	Depreciation Expense—Equipment				
14	Rent Expense				
15	Salaries Expense	7 6 0 0 00			
16	Supplies Expense				
17	Utilities Expense	1 3 0 0 00			
18	Totals	144 7 0 0 00	144 7 0 0 00		
19					

INSTRUCTIONS

1. Complete the worksheet for the month.

2. Prepare an income statement, statement of owner's equity, and balance sheet. No additional investments were made by the owner during the month.

3. Journalize and post the adjusting entries. Use 3 for the journal page number. Use the account numbers provided in Problem 5.4A.

End-of-month adjustments must account for the following.

a. The supplies were purchased on June 1, 2010; inventory of supplies on June 30, 2010, showed a value of $3,000.

b. The prepaid advertising contract was signed on June 1, 2010, and covers a four-month period.

c. Rent of $3,000 expired during the month.

d. Depreciation is computed using the straight-line method. The equipment has an estimated useful life of five years with no salvage value.

Analyze: Why are the costs that reduce the value of equipment not directly posted to the asset account Equipment?

		TRIAL BALANCE		ADJUSTMENTS			
ACCOUNT NAME		DEBIT	CREDIT	DEBIT		CREDIT	
1	Cash	33 9 0 0 00					
2	Accounts Receivable	4 4 0 0 00					
3	Supplies	3 0 0 0 00				(a)	1 2 0 0 00
4	Prepaid Advertising	8 0 0 0 00				(b)	1 6 0 0 00
5	Fixtures	36 0 0 0 00					
6	Accumulated Depreciation—Fixtures					(c)	6 0 0 00
7	Accounts Payable		15 0 0 0 00				
8	Jason Taylor, Capital		60 0 0 0 00				
9	Jason Taylor, Drawing	6 0 0 0 00					
10	Fees Income		62 6 6 0 00				
11	Advertising Expense			(b)	1 6 0 0 00		
12	Depreciation Expense—Fixtures			(c)	6 0 0 00		
13	Rent Expense	7 0 0 0 00					
14	Salaries Expense	37 2 0 0 00					
15	Supplies Expense			(a)	1 2 0 0 00		
16	Utilities Expense	2 1 6 0 00					
17	Totals	137 6 6 0 00	137 6 6 0 00	3 4 0 0 00		3 4 0 0 00	
18	Net Income						
19							
20							

JT's Accounting Services
Worksheet
Month Ended December 31, 2010

Critical Thinking Problem 5.1

Worksheet and Financial Statements

The account balances for the Thatcher International Company on January 31, 2010, follow. The balances shown are after the first month of operations.

101	Cash	$36,950	401	Fees Income	$61,850
111	Accounts Receivable	6,800	511	Advertising Expense	3,000
121	Supplies	4,300	514	Depr. Expense—Equip.	0
131	Prepaid Insurance	30,000	517	Insurance Expense	0
141	Equipment	48,000	518	Rent Expense	5,000
142	Accum. Depr.—Equip.	0	519	Salaries Expense	13,400
202	Accounts Payable	12,000	520	Supplies Expense	0
301	Maggie Thatcher, Capital	80,000	523	Telephone Expense	700
302	Maggie Thatcher, Drawing	4,000	524	Utilities Expense	1,700

INSTRUCTIONS

1. Prepare the Trial Balance section of the worksheet.
2. Record the following adjustments in the Adjustments section of the worksheet.

   a. Supplies used during the month amounted to $2,100.

   b. The amount in the *Prepaid Insurance* account represents a payment made on January 1, 2010, for six months of insurance coverage.

   c. The equipment, purchased on January 1, 2010, has an estimated useful life of 10 years with no salvage value. The firm uses the straight-line method of depreciation.

3. Complete the worksheet.

| ADJUSTED TRIAL BALANCE | | INCOME STATEMENT | | BALANCE SHEET | | |
DEBIT	CREDIT	DEBIT	CREDIT	DEBIT	CREDIT	
33 9 0 0 00				33 9 0 0 00		1
4 4 0 0 00				4 4 0 0 00		2
1 8 0 0 00				1 8 0 0 00		3
6 4 0 0 00				6 4 0 0 00		4
36 0 0 0 00				36 0 0 0 00		5
	6 0 0 00				6 0 0 00	6
	15 0 0 0 00				15 0 0 0 00	7
	60 0 0 0 00				60 0 0 0 00	8
6 0 0 0 00				6 0 0 0 00		9
	62 6 6 0 00		62 6 6 0 00			10
1 6 0 0 00		1 6 0 0 00				11
6 0 0 00		6 0 0 00				12
7 0 0 0 00		7 0 0 0 00				13
37 2 0 0 00		37 2 0 0 00				14
1 2 0 0 00		1 2 0 0 00				15
2 1 6 0 00		2 1 6 0 00				16
138 2 6 0 00	138 2 6 0 00	49 7 6 0 00	62 6 6 0 00	88 5 0 0 00	75 6 0 0 00	17
		12 9 0 0 00			12 9 0 0 00	18
		62 6 6 0 00	62 6 6 0 00	88 5 0 0 00	88 5 0 0 00	19
						20

4. Prepare an income statement, statement of owner's equity, and balance sheet (use the report form).

5. Record the balances in the general ledger accounts, then journalize and post the adjusting entries. Use 3 for the journal page number.

Analyze: If the useful life of the equipment had been 12 years instead of 10 years, how would net income have been affected?

Critical Thinking Problem 5.2

The Effect of Adjustments

Assume you are the accountant for Hatten Industries. Billy Hatten, the owner of the company, is in a hurry to receive the financial statements for the year ended December 31, 2010, and asks you how soon they will be ready. You tell him you have just completed the trial balance and are getting ready to prepare the adjusting entries. Mr. Hatten tells you not to waste time preparing adjusting entries but to complete the worksheet without them and prepare the financial statements based on the data in the trial balance. According to him, the adjusting entries will not make that much difference. The trial balance shows the following account balances:

Prepaid Rent	$ 21,000
Supplies	9,000
Building	210,000
Accumulated Depreciation—Building	16,800

If the income statement were prepared using trial balance amounts, the net income would be $82,500.

A review of the company's records reveals the following information:

1. Rent of $21,000 was paid on July 1, 2010, for 12 months.

2. Purchases of supplies during the year totaled $9,000. An inventory of supplies taken at year-end showed supplies on hand of $1,750.

3. The building was purchased three years ago and has an estimated life of 25 years.

4. No adjustments have been made to any of the accounts during the year.

Write a memo to Mr. Hatten explaining the effect on the financial statements of omitting the adjustments. Indicate the change to net income that results from the adjusting entries.

BUSINESS CONNECTIONS

Understanding Adjustments

Managerial FOCUS

1. A building owned by Amos Company was recently valued at $425,000 by a real estate expert. The president of the company is questioning the accuracy of the firm's latest balance sheet because it shows a book value of $275,000 for the building. How would you explain this situation to the president?

2. At the beginning of the year, Wilson Company purchased a new building and some expensive new machinery. An officer of the firm has asked you whether this purchase will affect the firm's year-end income statement. What answer would you give?

3. Suppose the president of a company where you work as an accountant questions whether it is worthwhile for you to spend time making adjustments at the end of each accounting period. How would you explain the value of the adjustments?

4. How does the worksheet help provide vital information to management?

Adjustments

Ethical DILEMMA

The supplies adjustment records the supplies used for the month from a cupboard that is filled at various times of the month. Sally asks you to record a larger supplies adjustment than is indicated from the ending balance in the supplies cupboard. Sally wants to use these supplies at the nonprofit organization she attends. Would you record a higher supplies expense so Sally could take these extra supplies to her charitable organization?

Internal Changes

STREETWISE: Questions from the REAL WORLD

Refer to The Home Depot, Inc., *2006 Annual Report* in Appendix A.

1. Based on the account categories listed on the consolidated statements of earnings and the consolidated balance sheets, what types of adjustments do you think the company makes each fiscal year? List three types of adjustments you believe would be necessary for this company. Describe your reasons for the adjustments you have listed.

2. By what amount has the account category "accumulated depreciation and amortization" increased from fiscal year 2005 to fiscal year 2006? Explain why you think this account has increased from 2005 to 2006.

Depreciation

Financial Statement ANALYSIS

DUPONT

DuPont reported depreciation expense of $1,157 million on its consolidated financial statements for the period ended December 31, 2006. The following excerpt is taken from the company's consolidated balance sheet for the same year.

Analyze:

1. What percentage of the original cost of property, plant, and equipment was depreciated *during* 2006?

2. What percentage of property, plant, and equipment cost was depreciated *as of* December 31, 2006?

(Dollars in millions, except per share) December 31, 2006

Property, Plant and Equipment	$25,719
Less: Accumulated depreciation	15,221
Net property, plant, and equipment	10,498

3. If the company continued to record depreciation expense at this level each year, how many years remain until all assets would be fully depreciated? (Assume no salvage values.)

Analyze Online: Connect to the DuPont Web Site (www.dupont.com). Click on the *Investor Center* link to find information on quarterly earnings.

4. What is the most recent quarterly earnings statement presented? What period does the statement cover?

5. For the most recent quarter, what depreciation expense was reported?

Adjusting Entries

Adjusting entries update accounts at the end of an accounting period. Items that belong to the period and were not previously recorded are recorded using an adjusting entry. Suppose a customer owes money to your business, but you are informed that the customer plans to file bankruptcy. You believe the customer will never pay the amount owed. Do you think an entry should be made for this event? Why or why not?

Extending THE THOUGHT

Prepare for a Telephone Meeting

The owner of a sparkling water bottling business believes that it is sufficient to record depreciation only at year-end, yet financial statements are prepared at the end of every month. As the accountant for the business, you believe adjusting entries should be made to update equipment depreciation expense on a monthly basis. You plan to call the owner to discuss the issue. How will you begin the conversation? How would you suggest that the situation be handled? Prepare notes on what you plan to say before you make the call to the owner.

Business COMMUNICATION

Matching Expenses with Revenues

Mike Mincks is a building contractor. He and his customer have agreed that he will submit a bill to them when he is 25 percent complete, 50 percent complete, 75 percent complete, and 100 percent complete. For example, he has a $100,000 room addition. When he has completed 25 percent, he will bill his customer $25,000. The problem occurs when he is 40 percent complete, has incurred expenses but cannot yet bill his customer. How can his revenue and expenses match? Discuss in a group several ways that Mike's accountant could solve this problem. What accounts would be used?

TEAMWORK

Prepaid Insurance

Prepaid insurance is the most common adjusting entry for a company. Use google.com to do a search of the various insurance companies that provide a variety of insurances to business. Try business insurance companies. Which type of insurances do they offer a business?

Internet CONNECTION

Answers to **Self Reviews**

Answers to Section 1 Self Review

1. So that the financial statements can be prepared more efficiently.

2. To properly reflect the remaining cost to be used by the business (asset) and the amount already used by the business (expense).

3. Entries made to update accounts at the end of an accounting period to include previously unrecorded items that belong to the period.

4. a. *Supplies Expense* is debited for $900. *Supplies* is credited for $900.

5. b. *Rent Expense* is debited for $3,600. *Prepaid Rent* is credited for $3,600.

6. $28,000

Answers to Section 2 Self Review

1. (a) Beginning owner's equity
   (b) Net income or net loss for the period
   (c) Additional investments by the owner for the period
   (d) Withdrawals by the owner for the period
   (e) Ending balance of owner's equity

2. On a report form balance sheet, the liabilities and owner's equity are listed under the assets. On the account form, they are listed to the right of the assets.

3. The worksheet is only a tool that aids in the preparation of financial statements. Any changes in account balances recorded on the worksheet are not shown in the general journal and the general ledger until the adjusting entries have been journalized and posted.

4. **b.** Balance Sheet Debit column.

5. **b.** contra asset account.

6. $28,000. The adjustment for equipment depreciation is a debit to *Depreciation Expense* and a credit to *Accumulated Depreciation—Equipment.* The *Equipment* account is not changed.

Answers to Comprehensive Self Review

1. To allocate the cost of the asset to operations during its expected useful life.
2. Net income causes a net increase in owner's equity.
3. $4,250. Debit column of the Balance Sheet section.
4. Credit balance.
5. Debit column of the Balance Sheet section.

Closing Entries and the Postclosing Trial Balance

LEARNING OBJECTIVES

1. Journalize and post closing entries.
2. Prepare a postclosing trial balance.
3. Interpret financial statements.
4. Review the steps in the accounting cycle.
5. Define the accounting terms new to this chapter.

LP6

NEW TERMS

closing entries
income summary account

interpret
postclosing trial balance

)Carnival. www.carnival.com
The Fun Ships.

The folks at Carnival Corporation have made it their business to help people enjoy their leisure time. For over 30 years, Carnival has made luxurious ocean cruising a reasonable vacation option for many individuals. For under $500 per person (less than the cost 25 years ago), passengers can enjoy a seven-day Caribbean cruise on a ship with soaring atriums, expansive spas, children's facilities, and double promenades offering a myriad of entertainment venues.

Since the TSS *Mardi Gras* made its first voyage in 1972, Carnival Corporation has grown to become the largest and most successful vacation company in the world, attracting 7 million guests annually. Headquartered in Miami, Florida, and London, England, Carnival operates a fleet of 82 ships, with another 17 ships scheduled for delivery between now and spring 2011. The company generated over $11 billion in revenues in 2006 and realized a total net income of over $2.2 billion.

thinking critically

How do Carnival Corporation's managers use financial statements to evaluate performance? How might these evaluations affect business policies or strategies?

SECTION OBJECTIVE

>> 1. **Journalize and post closing entries.**

WHY IT'S IMPORTANT

A business ends its accounting cycle at a given point in time. The closing process prepares the accounting records for the beginning of a new accounting cycle.

TERMS TO LEARN

closing entries
Income Summary account

Closing Entries

In Chapter 5, we discussed the worksheet and the adjusting entries. In this chapter, you will learn about closing entries.

Video6.1

The Closing Process

The seventh step in the accounting cycle is to journalize and post closing entries. **Closing entries** are journal entries that

- transfer the results of operations (net income or net loss) to owner's equity,
- reduce revenue, expense, and drawing account balances to zero.

THE INCOME SUMMARY ACCOUNT

The **Income Summary account** is a special owner's equity account that is used only in the closing process to summarize results of operations. *Income Summary* has a zero balance after the closing process, and it remains with a zero balance until after the closing procedure for the next period.

FIGURE 6.1   **Worksheet for Wells' Consulting Services**

										Wells' Consulting Services						
										Worksheet						
										Month Ended December 31, 2010						

	ACCOUNT NAME	TRIAL BALANCE		ADJUSTMENTS	
		DEBIT	CREDIT	DEBIT	CREDIT
1	Cash	111 3 5 0 00			
2	Accounts Receivable	5 0 0 0 00			
3	Supplies	1 5 0 0 00			(a) 5 0 0 00
4	Prepaid Rent	8 0 0 0 00			(b) 4 0 0 0 00
5	Equipment	11 0 0 0 00			
6	Accum. Dep.—Equipment				(c) 1 8 3 00
7	Accounts Payable		3 5 0 0 00		
8	Carolyn Wells, Capital		100 0 0 0 00		
9	Carolyn Wells, Drawing	5 0 0 0 00			
10	Fees Income		47 0 0 0 00		
11	Salaries Expense	8 0 0 0 00			
12	Utilities Expense	6 5 0 00			
13	Supplies Expense			(a) 5 0 0 00	
14	Rent Expense			(b) 4 0 0 0 00	
15	Dep. Expense—Equipment			(c) 1 8 3 00	
16					
17	Totals	150 5 0 0 00	150 5 0 0 00	4 6 8 3 00	4 6 8 3 00
18	Net Income				
19					

Income Summary is classified as a temporary owner's equity account. Other names for this account are *Revenue and Expense Summary* and *Income and Expense Summary*.

STEPS IN THE CLOSING PROCESS

There are four steps in the closing process:

1. Transfer the balance of the revenue account to the *Income Summary* account.
2. Transfer the expense account balances to the *Income Summary* account.
3. Transfer the balance of the *Income Summary* account to the owner's capital account.
4. Transfer the balance of the drawing account to the owner's capital account.

The worksheet contains the data necessary to make the closing entries. Refer to Figure 6.1 as you study each closing entry.

STEP 1: TRANSFER REVENUE ACCOUNT BALANCES

On December 31, the worksheet for Wells' Consulting Services shows one revenue account, *Fees Income.* It has a credit balance of $47,000. To *close* an account means to reduce its balance to zero. In the general journal, enter a debit of $47,000 to close the *Fees Income* account. To balance the journal entry, enter a credit of $47,000 to the *Income Summary* account. This closing entry transfers the total revenue for the period to the *Income Summary* account and reduces the balance of the revenue account to zero.

The analysis of this closing entry is shown on page 158. In this chapter, the visual analyses will show the beginning balances in all T accounts in order to illustrate closing entries.

>>**1. OBJECTIVE**
Journalize and post closing entries.

Video6.1

| ADJUSTED TRIAL BALANCE | | INCOME STATEMENT | | BALANCE SHEET | | |
DEBIT	CREDIT	DEBIT	CREDIT	DEBIT	CREDIT	
111 3 5 0 00				111 3 5 0 00		1
5 0 0 0 00				5 0 0 0 00		2
1 0 0 0 00				1 0 0 0 00		3
4 0 0 0 00				4 0 0 0 00		4
11 0 0 0 00				11 0 0 0 00		5
	1 8 3 00				1 8 3 00	6
	3 5 0 0 00				3 5 0 0 00	7
	100 0 0 0 00				100 0 0 0 00	8
5 0 0 0 00				5 0 0 0 00		9
	47 0 0 0 00		47 0 0 0 00			10
8 0 0 0 00		8 0 0 0 00				11
6 5 0 00		6 5 0 00				12
5 0 0 00		5 0 0 00				13
4 0 0 0 00		4 0 0 0 00				14
1 8 3 00		1 8 3 00				15
						16
150 6 8 3 00	150 6 8 3 00	13 3 3 3 00	47 0 0 0 00	137 3 5 0 00	103 6 8 3 00	17
		33 6 6 7 00			33 6 6 7 00	18
		47 0 0 0 00	47 0 0 0 00	137 3 5 0 00	137 3 5 0 00	19

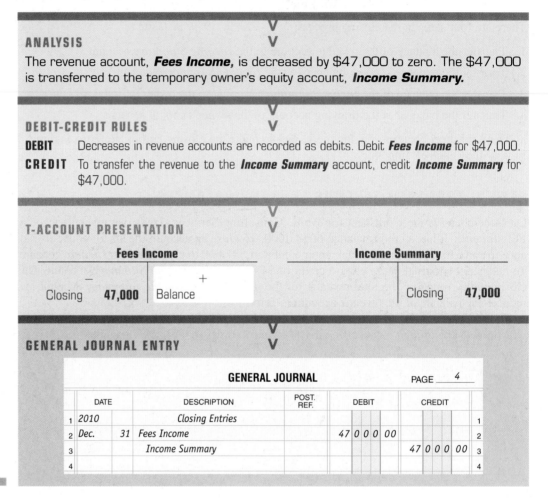

important!

Income Summary Account
The *Income Summary* account does not have an increase or decrease side and no normal balance side.

First Closing Entry—Close Revenue to Income Summary

ANALYSIS

The revenue account, *Fees Income,* is decreased by $47,000 to zero. The $47,000 is transferred to the temporary owner's equity account, *Income Summary.*

DEBIT-CREDIT RULES

DEBIT   Decreases in revenue accounts are recorded as debits. Debit *Fees Income* for $47,000.

CREDIT   To transfer the revenue to the *Income Summary* account, credit *Income Summary* for $47,000.

T-ACCOUNT PRESENTATION

Fees Income		Income Summary	
−	+		
Closing **47,000**	Balance		Closing **47,000**

GENERAL JOURNAL ENTRY

GENERAL JOURNAL   PAGE ____4____

	DATE		DESCRIPTION	POST. REF.	DEBIT	CREDIT	
1	2010		Closing Entries				1
2	Dec.	31	Fees Income		47 0 0 0 00		2
3			Income Summary			47 0 0 0 00	3
4							4

Write "Closing Entries" in the Description column of the general journal on the line above the first closing entry.

Safeway Inc. reported sales of $35.5 billion for the fiscal year ended December 31, 2003. To close the revenue, the company would debit the *Sales* account and credit the *Income Summary* account.

Video6.1

STEP 2: TRANSFER EXPENSE ACCOUNT BALANCES

The Income Statement section of the worksheet for Wells' Consulting Services lists five expense accounts. Since expense accounts have debit balances, enter a credit in each account to reduce its balance to zero. Debit the total of the expenses, $13,333, to the *Income Summary* account. This closing entry transfers total expenses to the *Income Summary* account and reduces the balances of the expense accounts to zero. This is a compound journal entry; it has more than one credit.

CLOSING ENTRY

Second Closing Entry—Close Expenses to Income Summary

ANALYSIS

The five expense account balances are reduced to zero. The total, $13,333, is transferred to the temporary owner's equity account, **Income Summary.**

DEBIT-CREDIT RULES

DEBIT   To transfer the expenses to the **Income Summary** account, debit **Income Summary** for $13,333.

CREDIT   Decreases to expense accounts are recorded as credits. Credit **Salaries Expense** for $8,000, **Utilities Expense** for $650, **Supplies Expense** for $500, **Rent Expense** for $4,000, and **Depreciation Expense—Equipment** for $183.

T-ACCOUNT PRESENTATION

Income Summary			
Closing	13,333	Balance	47,000

Salaries Expense			
+		–	
Balance	8,000	Closing	8,000

Utilities Expense			
+		–	
Balance	650	Closing	650

Supplies Expense			
+		–	
Balance	500	Closing	500

Rent Expense			
+		–	
Balance	4,000	Closing	4,000

Depreciation Expense—Equip			
+		–	
Balance	183	Closing	183

GENERAL JOURNAL ENTRY

GENERAL JOURNAL   PAGE ___4___

	DATE		DESCRIPTION	POST. REF.	DEBIT	CREDIT	
4	Dec.	31	Income Summary		13 3 3 3 00		4
5			Salaries Expense			8 0 0 0 00	5
6			Utilities Expense			6 5 0 00	6
7			Supplies Expense			5 0 0 00	7
8			Rent Expense			4 0 0 0 00	8
9			Depreciation Expense—Equip.			1 8 3 00	9
10							10

recall

Revenue
Revenue increases owner's equity.

recall

Expenses
Expenses decrease owner's equity.

After the second closing entry, the **Income Summary** account reflects all of the entries in the Income Statement columns of the worksheet.

	Income Summary		
Dr.		Cr.	
Closing	13,333	Closing	47,000
		Balance	33,667

For the year ended December 31, 2003, operating expenses for Amazon.com totaled $969.2 million. At the end of the year, accountants for Amazon.com transferred the balances of all expense accounts to the **Income Summary** account.

Video6.1

STEP 3: TRANSFER NET INCOME OR NET LOSS TO OWNER'S EQUITY

The next step in the closing process is to transfer the balance of **Income Summary** to the owner's capital account. After the revenue and expense accounts are closed, the **Income Summary** account has a credit balance of $33,667, which is net income for the month. The journal entry to transfer net income to owner's equity is a debit to **Income Summary** and a credit to **Carolyn Wells, Capital** for $33,667. When this entry is posted, the balance of the **Income Summary** account is reduced to zero and the owner's capital account is increased by the amount of net income.

CLOSING ENTRY

Third Closing Entry—Close Income Summary to Capital

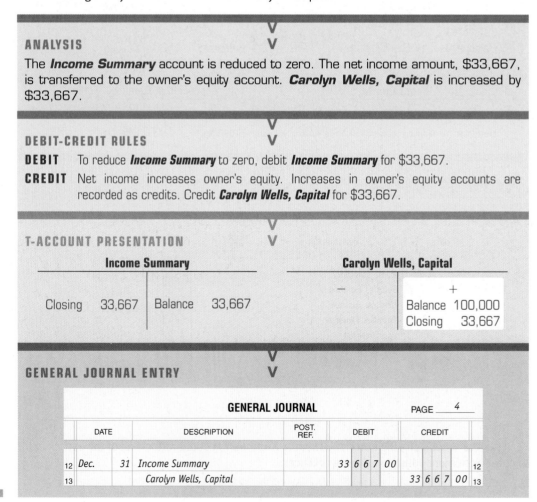

ANALYSIS

The **Income Summary** account is reduced to zero. The net income amount, $33,667, is transferred to the owner's equity account. **Carolyn Wells, Capital** is increased by $33,667.

DEBIT-CREDIT RULES

DEBIT   To reduce **Income Summary** to zero, debit **Income Summary** for $33,667.

CREDIT   Net income increases owner's equity. Increases in owner's equity accounts are recorded as credits. Credit **Carolyn Wells, Capital** for $33,667.

T-ACCOUNT PRESENTATION

Income Summary				Carolyn Wells, Capital		
				−	+	
Closing	33,667	Balance	33,667		Balance	100,000
					Closing	33,667

GENERAL JOURNAL ENTRY

		GENERAL JOURNAL			PAGE 4	
	DATE	DESCRIPTION	POST. REF.	DEBIT	CREDIT	
12	Dec. 31	Income Summary		33 6 6 7 00		12
13		Carolyn Wells, Capital			33 6 6 7 00	13

After the third closing entry, the ***Income Summary*** account has a zero balance. The summarized expenses ($13,333) and revenue ($47,000) have been transferred to the owner's equity account ($33,667 net income).

Income Summary	
Dr.	**Cr.**
Expenses 13,333	Revenue 47,000
Closing 33,667	
Balance 0	

Carolyn Wells, Capital	
Dr.	**Cr.**
−	+
	Balance 100,000
	Net Inc. 33,667
	Balance 133,667

STEP 4: TRANSFER THE DRAWING ACCOUNT BALANCE TO CAPITAL

You will recall that withdrawals are funds taken from the business by the owner for personal use. Withdrawals are recorded in the drawing account. Withdrawals are not expenses of the business. They do not affect net income or net loss.

Withdrawals appear in the statement of owner's equity as a deduction from capital. Therefore, the drawing account is closed directly to the capital account.

When this entry is posted, the balance of the drawing account is reduced to zero and the owner's capital account is decreased by the amount of the withdrawals.

Video6.1

recall

Withdrawals
Withdrawals decrease owner's equity.

CLOSING ENTRY

Fourth Closing Entry—Close Withdrawals to Capital

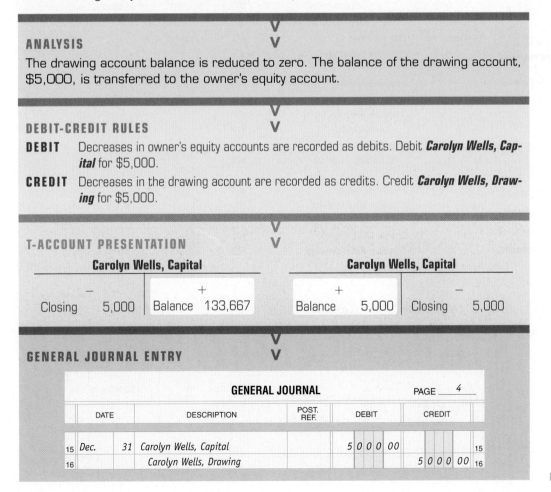

ANALYSIS
The drawing account balance is reduced to zero. The balance of the drawing account, $5,000, is transferred to the owner's equity account.

DEBIT-CREDIT RULES
DEBIT   Decreases in owner's equity accounts are recorded as debits. Debit *Carolyn Wells, Capital* for $5,000.
CREDIT   Decreases in the drawing account are recorded as credits. Credit *Carolyn Wells, Drawing* for $5,000.

T-ACCOUNT PRESENTATION

Carolyn Wells, Capital	
−	+
Closing 5,000	Balance 133,667

Carolyn Wells, Capital	
+	−
Balance 5,000	Closing 5,000

GENERAL JOURNAL ENTRY

	GENERAL JOURNAL			PAGE 4	
DATE	DESCRIPTION	POST. REF.	DEBIT	CREDIT	
15 Dec. 31	Carolyn Wells, Capital		5 0 0 0 00		15
16	Carolyn Wells, Drawing			5 0 0 0 00	16

The new balance of the **Carolyn Wells, Capital** account agrees with the amount listed in the Owner's Equity section of the balance sheet.

Carolyn Wells, Capital				Carolyn Wells, Capital			
Dr.		Cr.		Dr.		Cr.	
+		–		–		+	
						Balance	100,000
Balance	5,000	Closing	5,000	Drawing	5,000	Net Inc.	33,667
Balance	0					Balance	128,667

Figure 6.2 shows the general journal and general ledger for Wells' Consulting Services after the closing entries are recorded and posted. Note that

- "Closing" is entered in the Description column of the ledger accounts;
- the balance of **Carolyn Wells, Capital** agrees with the amount shown on the balance sheet for December 31;
- the ending balances of the drawing, revenue, and expense accounts are zero.

This example shows the closing process at the end of one month. Usually businesses make closing entries at the end of the fiscal year only.

FIGURE 6.2

Closing Process Completed: General Journal and General Ledger

GENERAL JOURNAL   PAGE ____4____

	DATE		DESCRIPTION	POST. REF.	DEBIT	CREDIT	
1	2010		*Closing Entries*				1
2	*Dec.*	*31*	*Fees Income*	401	47 0 0 0 00		2
3			*Income Summary*	309		47 0 0 0 00	3
4							4
5		*31*	*Income Summary*	309	13 3 3 3 00		5
6			*Salaries Expense*	511		8 0 0 0 00	6
7			*Utilities Expense*	514		6 5 0 00	7
8			*Supplies Expense*	517		5 0 0 00	8
9			*Rent Expense*	520		4 0 0 0 00	9
10			*Depreciation Expense—Equip.*	523		1 8 3 00	10
11							11
12		*31*	*Income Summary*	309	33 6 6 7 00		12
13			*Carolyn Wells, Capital*	301		33 6 6 7 00	13
14							14
15		*31*	*Carolyn Wells, Capital*	301	5 0 0 0 00		15
16			*Carolyn Wells, Drawing*	302		5 0 0 0 00	16
17							17

Step 1 — Close revenue.

Step 2 — Close expense accounts.

Step 3 — Close Income Summary.

Step 4 — Close Drawing account.

ACCOUNT ___Carolyn Wells, Capital___   ACCOUNT NO. __301__

DATE		DESCRIPTION	POST. REF.	DEBIT	CREDIT	BALANCE DEBIT	BALANCE CREDIT
2010							
Nov.	*6*		J1		100 0 0 0 00		100 0 0 0 00
Dec.	*31*	*Closing*	J4		33 6 6 7 00		133 6 6 7 00
	31	*Closing*	J4	5 0 0 0 00			128 6 6 7 00

ACCOUNT Carolyn Wells, Drawing   ACCOUNT NO. 302

| DATE | | DESCRIPTION | POST. REF. | DEBIT | CREDIT | BALANCE | |
						DEBIT	CREDIT
2010							
Dec.	31		J2	5 0 0 0 00		5 0 0 0 00	
	31	Closing	J4		5 0 0 0 00	– 0 –	

ACCOUNT Income Summary   ACCOUNT NO. 309

| DATE | | DESCRIPTION | POST. REF. | DEBIT | CREDIT | BALANCE | |
						DEBIT	CREDIT
2010							
Dec.	31	Closing	J4		47 0 0 0 00		47 0 0 0 00
	31	Closing	J4	13 3 3 3 00			33 6 6 7 00
	31	Closing	J4	33 6 6 7 00			– 0 –

ACCOUNT Fees Income   ACCOUNT NO. 401

| DATE | | DESCRIPTION | POST. REF. | DEBIT | CREDIT | BALANCE | |
						DEBIT	CREDIT
2010							
Dec.	31		J2		36 0 0 0 00		36 0 0 0 00
	31		J2		11 0 0 0 00		47 0 0 0 00
	31	Closing	J4	47 0 0 0 00			– 0 –

ACCOUNT Salaries Expense   ACCOUNT NO. 511

| DATE | | DESCRIPTION | POST. REF. | DEBIT | CREDIT | BALANCE | |
						DEBIT	CREDIT
2010							
Dec.	31		J2	8 0 0 0 00		8 0 0 0 00	
	31	Closing	J4		8 0 0 0 00	– 0 –	

ACCOUNT Utilities Expense   ACCOUNT NO. 514

| DATE | | DESCRIPTION | POST. REF. | DEBIT | CREDIT | BALANCE | |
						DEBIT	CREDIT
2010							
Dec.	31		J2	6 5 0 00		6 5 0 00	
	31	Closing	J4		6 5 0 00	– 0 –	

ACCOUNT Supplies Expense   ACCOUNT NO. 517

| DATE | | DESCRIPTION | POST. REF. | DEBIT | CREDIT | BALANCE | |
						DEBIT	CREDIT
2010							
Dec.	31	Adjusting	J3	5 0 0 00		5 0 0 00	
	31	Closing	J4		5 0 0 00	– 0 –	

ACCOUNT Rent Expense   ACCOUNT NO. 520

DATE		DESCRIPTION	POST. REF.	DEBIT	CREDIT	BALANCE	
						DEBIT	CREDIT
2010							
Dec.	31	Adjusting	J3	4 0 0 0 00		4 0 0 0 00	
	31	Closing	J4		4 0 0 0 00	– 0 –	

ACCOUNT Depreciation Expense—Equipment   ACCOUNT NO. 523

DATE		DESCRIPTION	POST. REF.	DEBIT	CREDIT	BALANCE	
						DEBIT	CREDIT
2010							
Dec.	31	Adjusting	J3	1 8 3 00		1 8 3 00	
	31	Closing	J4		1 8 3 00	– 0 –	

You have now seen seven steps of the accounting cycle. The steps we have discussed are (1) analyze transactions, (2) journalize the transactions, (3) post the transactions, (4) prepare a worksheet, (5) prepare financial statements, (6) record adjusting entries, and (7) record closing entries. Two steps remain. They are (8) prepare a postclosing trial balance, and (9) interpret the financial information.

Section 1 Self Review

QUESTIONS

1. How is the **Income Summary** account classified?

2. What are the four steps in the closing process?

3.. What is the journal entry to close the drawing account?

EXERCISES

4. After closing, which accounts have zero balances?

   a. asset and liability accounts

   b. liability and capital accounts

   c. liability, drawing, and expense accounts

   d. revenue, drawing, and expense accounts

5. After the closing entries are posted, which account normally has a balance other than zero?

   a. *Capital*

   b. *Fees Income*

   c. *Income Summary*

   d. *Rent Expense*

ANALYSIS

6. The business owner removes supplies that are worth $450 from the company stockroom. She intends to take them home for personal use. What effect will this have on the company's net income?

(Answers to Section 1 Self Review are on page 185.)

SECTION OBJECTIVES	TERMS TO LEARN
>> 2. Prepare a postclosing trial balance. WHY IT'S IMPORTANT The postclosing trial balance helps the accountant identify any errors in the closing process. **>> 3. Interpret financial statements.** WHY IT'S IMPORTANT Financial statements contain information that can impact and drive operating decisions and plans for the future of the company. **>> 4. Review the steps in the accounting cycle.** WHY IT'S IMPORTANT Proper treatment of data as it flows through the accounting system ensures reliable financial reports.	interpret postclosing trial balance

Using Accounting Information

In this section, we will complete the accounting cycle for Wells' Consulting Services.

Preparing the Postclosing Trial Balance

Video6.1

The eighth step in the accounting cycle is to prepare the postclosing trial balance, or *after-closing trial balance*. The **postclosing trial balance** is a statement that is prepared to prove the equality of total debits and credits. It is the last step in the end-of-period routine. The postclosing trial balance verifies that

- total debits equal total credits;
- revenue, expense, and drawing accounts have zero balances.

On the postclosing trial balance, the only accounts with balances are the permanent accounts:

- assets
- liabilities
- owner's equity

Figure 6.3 shows the postclosing trial balance for Wells' Consulting Services.

FIGURE 6.3

Postclosing Trial Balance

Wells' Consulting Services
Postclosing Trial Balance
December 31, 2010

ACCOUNT NAME	DEBIT	CREDIT
Cash	111 3 5 0 00	
Accounts Receivable	5 0 0 0 00	
Supplies	1 0 0 0 00	
Prepaid Rent	4 0 0 0 00	
Equipment	11 0 0 0 00	
Accumulated Depreciation—Equipment		1 8 3 00
Accounts Payable		3 5 0 0 00
Carolyn Wells, Capital		128 6 6 7 00
Totals	132 3 5 0 00	132 3 5 0 00

>>**2. OBJECTIVE**

Prepare a postclosing trial balance.

>>**3. OBJECTIVE**

Interpret financial statements.

LP6

FINDING AND CORRECTING ERRORS

If the postclosing trial balance does not balance, there are errors in the accounting records. Find and correct the errors before continuing. Refer to Chapter 3 for tips on how to find common errors. Also use the audit trail to trace data through the accounting records to find errors.

Interpreting the Financial Statements

The ninth and last step in the accounting cycle is interpreting the financial statements. Management needs timely and accurate financial information to operate the business successfully. To **interpret** the financial statements means to understand and explain the meaning and importance of information in accounting reports. Information in the financial statements provides answers to many questions:

- What is the cash balance?
- How much do customers owe the business?
- How much does the business owe suppliers?
- What is the profit or loss?

> Managers of The Home Depot, Inc., use the corporation's financial statements to answer questions about the business. How much cash does our business have? What net earnings did our company report this year? For the fiscal year ended January 3, 2007, The Home Depot, Inc., reported an ending cash balance of $614 million and net earnings of $5.8 billion.

Figure 6.4 shows the financial statements for Wells' Consulting Services at the end of its first accounting period. By interpreting these statements, management learns that

- the cash balance is $111,350,
- customers owe $5,000 to the business,
- the business owes $3,500 to its suppliers,
- the profit was $33,667.

FIGURE 6.4

End-of-Month Financial Statements

Wells' Consulting Services
Income Statement
Month Ended December 31, 2010

Revenue			
Fees Income		47 0 0 0 00	
Expenses			
Salaries Expense	8 0 0 0 00		
Utilities Expense	6 5 0 00		
Supplies Expense	5 0 0 00		
Rent Expense	4 0 0 0 00		
Depreciation Expense—Equipment	1 8 3 00		
Total Expenses		13 3 3 3 00	
Net Income for the Month		33 6 6 7 00	

Wells' Consulting Services
Statement of Owner's Equity
Month Ended December 31, 2010

Carolyn Wells, Capital, December 1, 2010		100 0 0 0 00	
Net Income for December	33 6 6 7 00		
Less Withdrawals for December	5 0 0 0 00		
Increase in Capital		28 6 6 7 00	
Carolyn Wells, Capital, December 31, 2010		128 6 6 7 00	

Wells' Consulting Services
Balance Sheet
December 31, 2010

Assets			
Cash		111 3 5 0 00	
Accounts Receivable		5 0 0 0 00	
Supplies		1 0 0 0 00	
Prepaid Rent		4 0 0 0 00	
Equipment	11 0 0 0 00		
Less Accumulated Depreciation	1 8 3 00	10 8 1 7 00	
Total Assets		132 1 6 7 00	
Liabilities and Owner's Equity			
Liabilities			
Accounts Payable		3 5 0 0 00	
Owner's Equity			
Carolyn Wells, Capital		128 6 6 7 00	
Total Liabilities and Owner's Equity		132 1 6 7 00	

ABOUT
ACCOUNTING

Professional Consultants
Professionals in the consulting field, such as accountants and lawyers, need to understand accounting so they can bill for services performed. Because clients have different billing rates depending on the service performed, specialized software is used to manage the paperwork and keep track of the billings and payments.

>>4. OBJECTIVE

Review the steps in the accounting cycle.

Video6.1

The Accounting Cycle

You have learned about the entire accounting cycle as you studied the financial affairs of Wells' Consulting Services during its first month of operations. Figure 6.5 summarizes the steps in the accounting cycle.

Step 1.   **Analyze transactions.** Analyze source documents to determine their effects on the basic accounting equation. The data about transactions appears on a variety of source documents such as:

- sales slips,
- purchase invoices,
- credit memorandums,
- check stubs.

Step 2.   **Journalize the transactions.** Record the effects of the transactions in a journal.

Step 3.   **Post the journal entries.** Transfer data from the journal to the general ledger accounts.

Step 4.   **Prepare a worksheet.** At the end of each period, prepare a worksheet.

- Use the Trial Balance section to prove the equality of debits and credits in the general ledger.
- Use the Adjustments section to enter changes in account balances that are needed to present an accurate and complete picture of the financial affairs of the business.
- Use the Adjusted Trial Balance section to verify the equality of debits and credits after the adjustments. Extend the amounts from the Adjusted Trial Balance section to the Income Statement and Balance Sheet sections.
- Use the Income Statement and Balance Sheet sections to prepare the financial statements.

Step 5.   **Prepare financial statements.** Prepare financial statements to report information to owners, managers, and other interested parties.

- The income statement shows the results of operations for the period.
- The statement of owner's equity reports the changes in the owner's financial interest during the period.
- The balance sheet shows the financial position of the business at the end of the period.

recall

The Accounting Cycle

The accounting cycle is a series of steps performed during each period to classify, record, and summarize data to produce needed financial information.

FIGURE 6.5

The Accounting Cycle

MANAGERIAL IMPLICATIONS   <<

FINANCIAL INFORMATION

■ Management needs timely and accurate financial information to control operations and make decisions.

■ A well-designed and well-run accounting system provides reliable financial statements to management.

■ Although management is not involved in day-to-day accounting procedures and end-of-period processes, the efficiency of the procedures affects the quality and promptness of the financial information that management receives.

THINKING CRITICALLY

If you owned or managed a business, how often would you want financial statements prepared? Why?

Step 6.   Record adjusting entries. Use the worksheet to journalize and post adjusting entries. The adjusting entries are a permanent record of the changes in account balances shown on the worksheet.

Step 7.   Record closing entries. Journalize and post the closing entries to

- transfer net income or net loss to owner's equity;
- reduce the balances of the revenue, expense, and drawing accounts to zero.

Step 8.   Prepare a postclosing trial balance. The postclosing trial balance shows that the general ledger is in balance after the closing entries are posted. It is also used to verify that there are zero balances in revenue, expense, and drawing accounts.

Step 9.   Interpret the financial information. Use financial statements to understand and communicate financial information and to make decisions. Accountants, owners, managers, and other interested parties interpret financial statements by comparing such things as profit, revenue, and expenses from one accounting period to the next.

> In addition to financial statements, Adobe Systems Incorporated prepares a Financial Highlights report. This report lists total assets, revenue, net income, and number of worldwide employees for the past five years.

After studying the accounting cycle of Wells' Consulting Services, you have an understanding of how data flows through a simple accounting system for a small business:

■ Source documents are analyzed.

■ Transactions are recorded in the general journal.

■ Transactions are posted from the general journal to the general ledger.

■ Financial information is proved, adjusted, and summarized on the worksheet.

■ Financial information is reported on financial statements.

Figure 6.6 illustrates this data flow.

As you will learn in later chapters, some accounting systems have more complex records, procedures, and financial statements. However, the steps of the accounting cycle and the underlying accounting principles remain the same.

FIGURE 6.6

Flow of Data through a Simple Accounting System

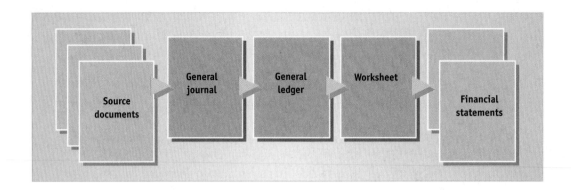

Section **2** Self Review

QUESTIONS

1. Why is a postclosing trial balance prepared?

2. What accounts appear on the postclosing trial balance?

3. What are the last three steps in the accounting cycle?

EXERCISES

4. Which of the following accounts will not appear on the postclosing trial balance?

   a. *J. T. Amos, Drawing*

   b. *Cash*

   c. *J. T. Amos, Capital*

   d. *Accounts Payable*

5. After the revenue and expense accounts are closed, *Income Summary* has a debit balance of $60,000. What does this figure represent?

   a. net profit of $60,000

   b. net loss of $60,000

   c. owner's withdrawals of $60,000

   d. increase in owner's equity of $60,000

ANALYSIS

6. On which financial statement would you find the answer to each question?

   • What were the total fees earned this month?

• How much money is owed to suppliers?

• Did the business make a profit?

• Is there enough cash to purchase new equipment?

• What were the expenses?

• Do customers owe money to the business?

(Answers to Section 2 Self Review are on page 185.)

REVIEW   Chapter Summary

Chapter **6**

After the worksheet and financial statements have been completed and adjusting entries have been journalized and posted, the closing entries are recorded and a postclosing trial balance is prepared.

Learning Objectives

1 Journalize and post closing entries.

Journalizing and posting the closing entries is the seventh step in the accounting cycle. Closing entries transfer the results of operations to owner's equity and reduce the balances of the revenue and expense accounts to zero. The worksheet provides the data necessary for the closing entries. A temporary owner's equity account, *Income Summary,* is used. There are four steps in the closing process:

1. The balance of the revenue account is transferred to the *Income Summary* account.

   Debit *Revenue*

   Credit *Income Summary*

2. The balances of the expense accounts are transferred to the *Income Summary* account.

   Debit *Income Summary*

   Credit *Expenses*

3. The balance of the *Income Summary* account— net income or net loss—is transferred to the owner's capital account.

   If *Income Summary* has a credit balance:

   Debit *Income Summary*

   Credit *Owner's Capital*

   If *Income Summary* has a debit balance:

   Debit *Owner's Capital*

   Credit *Income Summary*

4. The drawing account is closed to the owner's capital account.

   Debit *Owner's Capital*

   Credit *Drawing*

After the closing entries have been posted, the capital account reflects the results of operations for the period. The revenue and expense accounts, with zero balances, are ready to accumulate data for the next period.

2 Prepare a postclosing trial balance.

Preparing the postclosing trial balance is the eighth step in the accounting cycle. A postclosing trial balance is prepared to test the equality of total debit and credit balances in the general ledger after the adjusting and closing entries have been recorded. This report lists only permanent accounts open at the end of the period— asset, liability, and the owner's capital accounts. The temporary accounts—revenue, expenses, drawing, and *Income Summary*—apply only to one accounting period and do not appear on the postclosing trial balance.

3 Interpret financial statements.

The ninth step in the accounting cycle is interpreting the financial statements. Business decisions must be based on accurate and timely financial information.

4 Review the steps in the accounting cycle.

The accounting cycle consists of a series of steps that are repeated in each fiscal period. These steps are designed to classify, record, and summarize the data needed to produce financial information.

The steps of the accounting cycle are:

1. Analyze transactions.
2. Journalize the transactions.
3. Post the journal entries.
4. Prepare a worksheet.
5. Prepare financial statements.
6. Record adjusting entries.
7. Record closing entries.
8. Prepare a postclosing trial balance.
9. Interpret the financial information.

5 Define the accounting terms new to this chapter.

Glossary

Closing entries (p. 156) Journal entries that transfer the results of operations (net income or net loss) to owner's equity and reduce the revenue, expense, and drawing account balances to zero

Income Summary account (p. 156) A special owner's equity account that is used only in the closing process to summarize the results of operations

Interpret (p. 166) To understand and explain the meaning and importance of something (such as financial statements)

Postclosing trial balance (p. 165) A statement that is prepared to prove the equality of total debits and credits after the closing process is completed

Comprehensive **Self Review**

1. A firm has the following expenses: ***Rent Expense,*** $3,600; ***Salaries Expense,*** $7,000; ***Supplies Expense,*** $1,500. Give the entry to close the expense accounts.
2. A firm has $56,000 in revenue for the period. Give the entry to close the ***Fees Income*** account.
3. What three financial statements are prepared during the accounting cycle?
4. What is the last step in the accounting cycle?
5. Is the following statement true or false? Why? "All owner's equity accounts appear on the postclosing trial balance."

(Answers to Comprehensive Self Review are on page 185.)

 Multiple choice questions are provided on the text Web site at www.mhhe.com/price12e Quiz6

Discussion Questions

1. Why is a postclosing trial balance prepared?
2. What accounts appear on a postclosing trial balance?
3. What is the accounting cycle?
4. Name the steps of the accounting cycle.
5. Briefly describe the flow of data through a simple accounting system.
6. What three procedures are performed at the end of each accounting period before the financial information is interpreted?
7. Where does the accountant obtain the data needed for the adjusting entries?
8. Why does the accountant record closing entries at the end of a period?
9. How is the ***Income Summary*** account used in the closing procedure?
10. Where does the accountant obtain the data needed for the closing entries?

APPLICATIONS

Exercises

Exercise 6.1
Objective 1

▶ **Journalize closing entries.**

On December 31, the ledger of Anderson Company contained the following account balances:

Cash	$64,000	Hayward Anderson, Drawing	$25,000
Accounts Receivable	4,800	Fees Income	97,500
Supplies	3,200	Depreciation Expense	4,500
Equipment	50,000	Salaries Expense	32,000

Accumulated Depreciation	4,000	Supplies Expense	5,000
Accounts Payable	5,000	Telephone Expense	4,200
Hayward Anderson, Capital	94,500	Utilities Expense	8,300

All the accounts have normal balances. Journalize the closing entries. Use 4 as the general journal page number.

Postclosing trial balance.

From the following list, identify the accounts that will appear on the postclosing trial balance.

◄ **Exercise 6.2**
Objective 2

ACCOUNTS

1. Cash
2. Accounts Receivable
3. Supplies
4. Equipment
5. Accumulated Depreciation
6. Accounts Payable
7. Sally Harris, Capital
8. Sally Harris, Drawing
9. Fees Income
10. Depreciation Expense
11. Salaries Expense
12. Supplies Expense
13. Utilities Expense

Accounting cycle.

Following are the steps in the accounting cycle. Arrange the steps in the proper sequence.

◄ **Exercise 6.3**
Objective 4

1. Record closing entries.
2. Interpret the financial information.
3. Prepare a postclosing trial balance.
4. Prepare financial statements.
5. Prepare a worksheet.
6. Record adjusting entries.
7. Analyze transactions.
8. Journalize the transactions.
9. Post the journal entries.

Financial statements.

Managers often consult financial statements for specific types of information. Indicate whether each of the following items would appear on the income statement, statement of owner's equity, or the balance sheet. Use *I* for the income statement, *E* for the statement of owner's equity, and *B* for the balance sheet. If an item appears on more than one statement, use all letters that apply to that item.

◄ **Exercise 6.4**
Objective 3

1. Accumulated depreciation on the firm's equipment
2. Amount of depreciation charged off on the firm's equipment during the period
3. Original cost of the firm's equipment
4. Book value of the firm's equipment
5. Total expenses for the period
6. Accounts payable of the business
7. Owner's withdrawals for the period
8. Cash on hand

9. Revenue earned during the period
10. Total assets of the business
11. Net income for the period
12. Owner's capital at the end of the period
13. Supplies on hand
14. Cost of supplies used during the period
15. Accounts receivable of the business

Exercise 6.5
Objective 1

▶ **Closing entries.**

The *Income Summary* and *Paula King, Capital* accounts for King Production Company at the end of its accounting period follow.

ACCOUNT *Income Summary*   ACCOUNT NO. _399_

DATE		DESCRIPTION	POST. REF.	DEBIT	CREDIT	BALANCE DEBIT	BALANCE CREDIT
2010							
Dec.	31	Closing	J4		46 500 00		46 500 00
	31	Closing	J4	30 300 00			16 200 00
	31	Closing	J4	16 200 00			– 0 –

ACCOUNT *Paula King, Capital*   ACCOUNT NO. _301_

DATE		DESCRIPTION	POST. REF.	DEBIT	CREDIT	BALANCE DEBIT	BALANCE CREDIT
2010							
Dec.	1		J1		90 000 00		90 000 00
	31	Closing	J4		16 200 00		106 200 00
	31	Closing	J4	5 000 00			101 200 00

Complete the following statements.

1. Total revenue for the period is _____.
2. Total expenses for the period are _____.
3. Net income for the period is _____.
4. Owner's withdrawals for the period are _____.

Exercise 6.6
Objective 1

▶ **Closing entries.**

The ledger accounts of Easy Access Internet Company appear as follows on March 31, 2010.

ACCOUNT NO.	ACCOUNT	BALANCE
101	Cash	$69,000
111	Accounts Receivable	13,200
121	Supplies	8,100
131	Prepaid Insurance	20,880
141	Equipment	100,800
142	Accumulated Depreciation—Equipment	20,160
202	Accounts Payable	10,800
301	Elizabeth Chavez, Capital	117,600
302	Elizabeth Chavez, Drawing	6,000
401	Fees Income	276,000
510	Depreciation Expense—Equipment	10,080

511	Insurance Expense	9,600
514	Rent Expense	28,800
517	Salaries Expense	141,600
518	Supplies Expense	3,900
519	Telephone Expense	5,400
523	Utilities Expense	7,200

All accounts have normal balances. Journalize and post the closing entries. Use 4 as the page number for the general journal in journalizing the closing entries. Use account number 399 for the Income Summary Account.

Closing entries.

On December 31, the *Income Summary* account of Zamarripa Company has a debit balance of $54,000 after revenue of $58,000 and expenses of $112,000 were closed to the account. *Gladys Zamarripa, Drawing* has a debit balance of $6,000 and *Gladys Zamarripa, Capital* has a credit balance of $96,000. Record the journal entries necessary to complete closing the accounts. What is the new balance of *Gladys Zamarripa, Capital?*

◄ **Exercise 6.7**
Objective 1

Accounting cycle.

Complete a chart of the accounting cycle by writing the steps of the cycle in their proper sequence.

◄ **Exercise 6.8**
Objective 4

PROBLEMS

Problem Set A

Adjusting and closing entries.

The Sager Marketing Research Company, owned by Jeff Sager, is retained by large companies to test consumer reaction to new products. On January 31, 2010, the firm's worksheet showed the following adjustments data: (a) supplies used, $1,120; (b) expired rent, $6,000; and (c) depreciation on office equipment, $2,240. The balances of the revenue and expense accounts listed in the Income Statement section of the worksheet and the drawing account listed in the Balance Sheet section of the worksheet are given below.

◄ **Problem 6.1A**
Objective 1

REVENUE AND EXPENSE ACCOUNTS

401 Fees Income	$87,000 Cr.
511 Depr. Expense—Office Equipment	2,240 Dr.
514 Rent Expense	6,000 Dr.
517 Salaries Expense	46,200 Dr.
520 Supplies Expense	1,120 Dr.
523 Telephone Expense	985 Dr.
526 Travel Expense	9,280 Dr.
529 Utilities Expense	920 Dr.

DRAWING ACCOUNT

| 302 Jeff Sager, Drawing | 5,400 Dr. |

INSTRUCTIONS

1. Record the adjusting entries in the general journal, page 3.

2. Record the closing entries in the general journal, page 4.

Analyze: What closing entry is required to close a drawing account?

Problem 6.2A ▶
QB Objective 1, 2
eXcel

Journalizing and posting adjusting and closing entries and preparing a postclosing trial balance.

A completed worksheet for Bell Enterprises is shown on pages 176–177.

INSTRUCTIONS

1. Record balances as of December 31, 2010, in the ledger accounts.
2. Journalize (use 3 as the page number) and post the adjusting entries. Use account number 131 for Prepaid Advertising and the same account numbers for all other accounts shown on page 186 for Wells' Consulting Services chart of accounts.
3. Journalize (use 4 as the page number) and post the closing entries.
4. Prepare a postclosing trial balance.

Analyze: How many accounts are listed in the Adjusted Trial Balance section? How many accounts are listed on the postclosing trial balance?

Problem 6.3A ▶
Objective 1 **eXcel**

Journalizing and posting closing entries.

On December 31, after adjustments, Cavazos Company's ledger contains the following account balances.

101 Cash	$37,200 Dr.
111 Accounts Receivable	16,800 Dr.
121 Supplies	3,000 Dr.
131 Prepaid Rent	39,600 Dr.
141 Equipment	54,000 Dr.
142 Accumulated Depreciation—Equip.	1,500 Cr.
202 Accounts Payable	7,500 Cr.
301 Monica Cavazos, Capital (12/1/2010)	55,620 Cr.
302 Monica Cavazos, Drawing	7,200 Dr.

Bell Enterprises
Worksheet
Month Ended December 31, 2010

	ACCOUNT NAME	TRIAL BALANCE		ADJUSTMENTS		
		DEBIT	CREDIT	DEBIT	CREDIT	
1	Cash	46 2 0 0 00				
2	Accounts Receivable	6 0 0 0 00				
3	Supplies	3 0 0 0 00			(a) 1 2 0 0 00	
4	Prepaid Advertising	12 0 0 0 00			(b) 1 5 0 0 00	
5	Equipment	30 0 0 0 00				
6	Accumulated Depreciation—Equipment				(c) 1 2 0 0 00	
7	Accounts Payable		6 0 0 0 00			
8	Patonia Bell, Capital		66 0 0 0 00			
9	Patonia Bell, Drawing	4 2 0 0 00				
10	Fees Income		37 5 0 0 00			
11	Supplies Expense			(a) 1 2 0 0 00		
12	Advertising Expense			(b) 1 5 0 0 00		
13	Depreciation Expense—Equipment			(c) 1 2 0 0 00		
14	Salaries Expense	7 2 0 0 00				
15	Utilities Expense	9 0 0 00				
16	Totals	109 5 0 0 00	109 5 0 0 00	3 9 0 0 00	3 9 0 0 00	
17	Net Income					
18						
19						

401 Fees Income	138,000 Cr.
511 Advertising Expense	4,800 Dr.
514 Depreciation Expense—Equip.	900 Dr.
517 Rent Expense	3,600 Dr.
519 Salaries Expense	28,800 Dr.
523 Utilities Expense	6,720 Dr.

INSTRUCTIONS

1. Record the balances in the ledger accounts as of December 31.
2. Journalize the closing entries in the general journal, page 4. Use account number 399 for the Income Summary Account.
3. Post the closing entries to the general ledger accounts.

Analyze: What is the balance of the *Salaries Expense* account after closing entries are posted?

Worksheet, journalizing and posting adjusting and closing entries, and the postclosing trial balance.

◀ **Problem 6.4A**

Objective 1, 2

A partially completed worksheet for Nationwide Auto Detailing Service, a firm that details cars and vans, follows on page 178.

INSTRUCTIONS

1. Record balances as of December 31 in the ledger accounts.
2. Prepare the worksheet.
3. Journalize (use 3 as the journal page number) and post the adjusting entries. Use account number 131 for Prepaid Advertising and the same account numbers for all other accounts shown on page 186 for Wells' Consulting Services chart of accounts.
4. Journalize (use 4 as the journal page number) and post the closing entries.
5. Prepare a postclosing trial balance.

ADJUSTED TRIAL BALANCE		INCOME STATEMENT		BALANCE SHEET		
DEBIT	CREDIT	DEBIT	CREDIT	DEBIT	CREDIT	
46 2 0 0 00				46 2 0 0 00		1
6 0 0 0 00				6 0 0 0 00		2
1 8 0 0 00				1 8 0 0 00		3
10 5 0 0 00				10 5 0 0 00		4
30 0 0 0 00				30 0 0 0 00		5
	1 2 0 0 00				1 2 0 0 00	6
	6 0 0 0 00				6 0 0 0 00	7
	66 0 0 0 00				66 0 0 0 00	8
4 2 0 0 00				4 2 0 0 00		9
	37 5 0 0 00		37 5 0 0 00			10
1 2 0 0 00		1 2 0 0 00				11
1 5 0 0 00		1 5 0 0 00				12
1 2 0 0 00		1 2 0 0 00				13
7 2 0 0 00		7 2 0 0 00				14
9 0 0 00		9 0 0 00				15
110 7 0 0 00	110 7 0 0 00	12 0 0 0 00	37 5 0 0 00	98 7 0 0 00	73 2 0 0 00	16
		25 5 0 0 00			25 5 0 0 00	17
		37 5 0 0 00	37 5 0 0 00	98 7 0 0 00	98 7 0 0 00	18
						19

Nationwide Auto Detailing Service
Worksheet
Month Ended December 31, 2010

	ACCOUNT NAME	TRIAL BALANCE		ADJUSTMENTS	
		DEBIT	CREDIT	DEBIT	CREDIT
1	Cash	31 0 5 0 00			
2	Accounts Receivable	4 9 5 0 00			
3	Supplies	4 0 0 0 00			(a) 1 6 0 0 00
4	Prepaid Advertising	3 0 0 0 00			(b) 1 4 0 0 00
5	Equipment	20 0 0 0 00			
6	Accumulated Depreciation—Equipment				(c) 4 8 0 00
7	Accounts Payable		5 0 0 0 00		
8	Richard Harris, Capital		35 5 0 0 00		
9	Richard Harris, Drawing	2 0 0 0 00			
10	Fees Income		30 0 0 0 00		
11	Salaries Expense	4 8 0 0 00			
12	Utilities Expense	7 0 0 00			
13	Supplies Expense			(a) 1 6 0 0 00	
14	Advertising Expense			(b) 1 4 0 0 00	
15	Depreciation Expense—Equipment			(c) 4 8 0 00	
16	Totals	70 5 0 0 00	70 5 0 0 00	3 4 8 0 00	3 4 8 0 00
17					
18					
19					

Analyze: What total debits were posted to the general ledger to complete all closing entries for the month of December?

Problem Set B

Problem 6.1B ▶ **Adjusting and closing entries.**

Objective 1

Wilson Cleaning and Maintenance, owned by James Wilson, provides cleaning services to hotels, motels, and hospitals. On January 31, 2010, the firm's worksheet showed the following adjustment data. The balances of the revenue and expense accounts listed in the Income Statement section of the worksheet and the drawing account listed in the Balance Sheet section of the worksheet are also given.

ADJUSTMENTS

a. Supplies used, $2,860

b. Expired insurance, $1,480

c. Depreciation on machinery, $1,120

REVENUE AND EXPENSE ACCOUNTS

401 Fees Income	$32,800 Cr.
511 Depreciation Expense—Machinery	1,120 Dr.
514 Insurance Expense	1,480 Dr.
517 Rent Expense	3,000 Dr.
520 Salaries Expense	16,000 Dr.
523 Supplies Expense	2,860 Dr.
526 Telephone Expense	210 Dr.

529 Utilities Expense	640 Dr.	
DRAWING ACCOUNT		
302 James Wilson, Drawing	2,400 Dr.	

INSTRUCTIONS

1. Record the adjusting entries in the general journal, page 3.

2. Record the closing entries in the general journal, page 4. Use account numbers provided on page 186 for any account number not given.

Analyze: What effect did the adjusting entry for expired insurance have on the *Insurance Expense* account?

Journalizing and posting adjusting and closing entries and preparing a postclosing trial balance.

◀ **Problem 6.2B**
Objectives 1, 2

A completed worksheet for Big Valley Nursery and Landscape is shown on pages 180–181.

INSTRUCTIONS

1. Record the balances as of December 31 in the ledger accounts.

2. Journalize (use 3 as the page number) and post the adjusting entries. Use account number 131 for Prepaid Advertising and the same account numbers for all other accounts as shown on page 186 for Wells' Consulting Services chart of accounts.

3. Journalize (use 4 as the page number) and post the closing entries.

4. Prepare a postclosing trial balance.

Analyze: What total credits were posted to the general ledger to complete the closing entries?

Journalizing and posting closing entries.

◀ **Problem 6.3B**
Objective 1

On December 31, after adjustments, The Windmill Farm's ledger contains the following account balances.

101 Cash	$57,000 Dr.
111 Accounts Receivable	14,400 Dr.
121 Supplies	6,000 Dr.
131 Prepaid Rent	46,200 Dr.
141 Equipment	72,000 Dr.
142 Accumulated Depreciation—Equip.	1,800 Cr.
202 Accounts Payable	19,500 Cr.
301 Patty Slade, Capital (12/1/2010)	114,900 Cr.
302 Patty Slade, Drawing	7,200 Dr.
401 Fees Income	108,000 Cr.
511 Advertising Expense	6,600 Dr.
514 Depreciation Expense—Equip.	1,800 Dr.
517 Rent Expense	4,200 Dr.
519 Salaries Expense	21,600 Dr.
523 Utilities Expense	7,200 Dr.

INSTRUCTIONS

1. Record the balances in the ledger accounts as of December 31.

2. Journalize the closing entries in the general journal, page 4. Use account number 399 for the Income Summary Account

3. Post the closing entries to the general ledger accounts.

Analyze: List the accounts affected by closing entries for the month of December.

Big Valley Nursery and Landscape

Worksheet

Month Ended December 31, 2010

	ACCOUNT NAME	TRIAL BALANCE		ADJUSTMENTS		
		DEBIT	CREDIT	DEBIT		CREDIT
1	Cash	32 4 0 0 00				
2	Accounts Receivable	6 0 0 0 00				
3	Supplies	6 0 0 0 00			(a)	3 0 0 0 00
4	Prepaid Advertising	9 0 0 0 00			(b)	1 2 0 0 00
5	Equipment	60 0 0 0 00				
6	Accumulated Depreciation—Equipment				(c)	1 5 0 0 00
7	Accounts Payable		9 0 0 0 00			
8	James McDonald, Capital		82 2 0 0 00			
9	James McDonald, Drawing	8 4 0 0 00				
10	Fees Income		46 8 0 0 00			
11	Supplies Expense			(a) 3 0 0 0 00		
12	Advertising Expense			(b) 1 2 0 0 00		
13	Depreciation Expense—Equipment			(c) 1 5 0 0 00		
14	Salaries Expense	14 4 0 0 00				
15	Utilities Expense	1 8 0 0 00				
16	Totals	138 0 0 0 00	138 0 0 0 00	5 7 0 0 00		5 7 0 0 00
17	Net Income					
18						
19						
20						

Problem 6.4B ▶

Objectives 1, 2, 4

Worksheet, journalizing and posting adjusting and closing entries, and the postclosing trial balance.

A partially completed worksheet for Scott Wilson, CPA, for the month ending June 30, 2010, is shown below.

Scott Wilson, CPA

Worksheet

Month Ended June 30, 2010

	ACCOUNT NAME	TRIAL BALANCE		ADJUSTMENTS		
		DEBIT	CREDIT	DEBIT		CREDIT
1	Cash	31 9 5 0 00				
2	Accounts Receivable	11 3 4 0 00				
3	Supplies	15 7 5 0 00			(a)	2 7 0 0 00
4	Computers	28 8 0 0 00				
5	Accumulated Depreciation—Computers		2 8 8 0 00		(b)	2 4 0 00
6	Accounts Payable		12 6 0 0 00			
7	Scott Wilson, Capital		62 2 3 5 00			
8	Scott Wilson, Drawing	12 0 0 0 00				
9	Fees Income		67 9 5 0 00			
10	Salaries Expense	37 7 2 5 00				
11	Supplies Expense			(a) 2 7 0 0 00		
12	Depreciation Expense—Computers			(b) 2 4 0 00		
13	Travel Expense	5 4 0 0 00				
14	Utilities Expense	2 7 0 0 00				
15	Totals	145 6 6 5 00	145 6 6 5 00	2 9 4 0 00		2 9 4 0 00
16						
17						

ADJUSTED TRIAL BALANCE		INCOME STATEMENT		BALANCE SHEET		
DEBIT	CREDIT	DEBIT	CREDIT	DEBIT	CREDIT	
32 4 0 0 00				32 4 0 0 00		1
6 0 0 0 00				6 0 0 0 00		2
3 0 0 0 00				3 0 0 0 00		3
7 8 0 0 00				7 8 0 0 00		4
60 0 0 0 00				60 0 0 0 00		5
	1 5 0 0 00				1 5 0 0 00	6
	9 0 0 0 00				9 0 0 0 00	7
	82 2 0 0 00				82 2 0 0 00	8
8 4 0 0 00				8 4 0 0 00		9
	46 8 0 0 00		46 8 0 0 00			10
3 0 0 0 00		3 0 0 0 00				11
1 2 0 0 00		1 2 0 0 00				12
1 5 0 0 00		1 5 0 0 00				13
14 4 0 0 00		14 4 0 0 00				14
1 8 0 0 00		1 8 0 0 00				15
139 5 0 0 00	139 5 0 0 00	21 9 0 0 00	46 8 0 0 00	117 6 0 0 00	92 7 0 0 00	16
		24 9 0 0 00			24 9 0 0 00	17
		46 8 0 0 00	46 8 0 0 00	117 6 0 0 00	117 6 0 0 00	18
						19
						20

INSTRUCTIONS

1. Record the balances as of June 30 in the ledger accounts.

2. Prepare the worksheet.

3. Journalize (use 3 as the journal page number) and post the adjusting entries. Use account number 121 for Supplies; 131 for Computers; 142 for the Accumulated Depreciation account; 309 for Income Summary; 517 for Supplies Expense; 519 for Travel Expense; and 523 for Depreciation Expense.

4. Journalize (use 4 as the journal page number) and post the closing entries.

5. Prepare a postclosing trial balance.

Analyze: What is the reported net income for the month of June for Scott Wilson, CPA?

Critical Thinking Problem 6.1

The Closing Process

The Trial Balance section of the worksheet for The Style Shop for the period ended December 31, 2010, appears on the next page. Adjustments data are also given.

ADJUSTMENTS
a. Supplies used, $7,200
b. Expired insurance, $4,800
c. Depreciation expense for machinery, $2,400

INSTRUCTIONS

1. Complete the worksheet.

2. Prepare an income statement.

3. Prepare a statement of owner's equity.

The Style Shop
Worksheet
Month Ended December 31, 2010

	ACCOUNT NAME	TRIAL BALANCE		ADJUSTMENTS	
		DEBIT	CREDIT	DEBIT	CREDIT
1	Cash	81 6 0 0 00			
2	Accounts Receivable	18 0 0 0 00			
3	Supplies	14 4 0 0 00			(a) 7 2 0 0 00
4	Prepaid Insurance	21 6 0 0 00			(b) 4 8 0 0 00
5	Machinery	168 0 0 0 00			
6	Accumulated Depreciation—Machinery				(c) 2 4 0 0 00
7	Accounts Payable		27 0 0 0 00		
8	Sarah Palmer, Capital		149 1 6 0 00		
9	Sarah Palmer, Drawing	12 0 0 0 00			
10	Fees Income		165 0 0 0 00		
11	Supplies Expense			(a) 7 2 0 0 00	
12	Insurance Expense			(b) 4 8 0 0 00	
13	Salaries Expense	22 2 0 0 00			
14	Depreciation Expense—Machinery			(c) 2 4 0 0 00	
15	Utilities Expense	3 3 6 0 00			
16	Totals	341 1 6 0 00	341 1 6 0 00	14 4 0 0 00	14 4 0 0 00
17					
18					
19					

4. Prepare a balance sheet.

5. Journalize the adjusting entries in the general journal, page 3.

6. Journalize the closing entries in the general journal, page 4.

7. Prepare a postclosing trial balance.

Analyze: If the adjusting entry for expired insurance had been recorded in error as a credit to *Insurance Expense* and a debit to *Prepaid Insurance* for $4,800, what reported net income would have resulted?

Critical Thinking Problem 6.2

Owner's Equity

Wilson Reed, the bookkeeper for Home Interior Improvements and Designs Company, has just finished posting the closing entries for the year to the ledger. He is concerned about the following balances:

Capital account balance in the general ledger:	$48,550
Ending capital balance on the statement of owner's equity:	27,800

Wilson knows that these amounts should agree and asks for your assistance in reviewing his work.

Your review of the general ledger of Home Interior Improvements and Designs Company reveals a beginning capital balance of $25,000. You also review the general journal for the accounting period and find the closing entries shown on page 183.

1. What errors did Mr. Reed make in preparing the closing entries for the period?

2. Prepare a general journal entry to correct the errors made.

3. Explain why the balance of the capital account in the ledger after closing entries have been posted will be the same as the ending capital balance on the statement of owner's equity.

		GENERAL JOURNAL			PAGE 15	
	DATE	DESCRIPTION	POST. REF.	DEBIT	CREDIT	
1	2010	Closing Entries				1
2	Dec. 31	Fees Income		49 0 0 0 00		2
3		Accumulated Depreciation		4 2 5 0 00		3
4		Accounts Payable		16 5 0 0 00		4
5		Income Summary			69 7 5 0 00	5
6						6
7	31	Income Summary		46 2 0 0 00		7
8		Salaries Expense			39 0 0 0 00	8
9		Supplies Expense			2 5 0 0 00	9
10		Depreciation Expense			1 2 0 0 00	10
11		James Walker, Drawing			3 5 0 0 00	11
12						12
13						13
14						14

BUSINESS CONNECTIONS

Interpreting Financial Statements

Managerial FOCUS

1. An officer of Carson Company recently commented that when he receives the firm's financial statements, he looks at just the bottom line of the income statement—the line that shows the net income or net loss for the period. He said that he does not bother with the rest of the income statement because "it's only the bottom line that counts." He also does not read the balance sheet. Do you think this manager is correct in the way he uses the financial statements? Why or why not?

2. The president of Henderson Corporation is concerned about the firm's ability to pay its debts on time. What items on the balance sheet would help her to assess the firm's debt-paying ability?

3. Why is it important that a firm's financial records be kept up-to-date and that management receive the financial statements promptly after the end of each accounting period?

4. What kinds of operating and general policy decisions might be influenced by data on the financial statements?

Timing of a Check

Ethical DILEMMA

On the last day of the fiscal year, Gevok Means comes to you for a favor. He asks that you enter a check for $1,000 to GM Company for Miscellaneous Expense. You notice the invoice looks a little different from other invoices that are processed. Gevok needs the check immediately to get supplies today to complete the project for a favorite customer. You know that by preparing the closing entries tomorrow, Miscellaneous Expense will be set to zero for the beginning of the new year. Should you write this check and record the expense or find an excuse to write the check tomorrow? What would be the effect if the invoice to GM Company was erroneous and you had written the check?

Closing Process

STREETWISE: Questions from the REAL WORLD

Refer to The Home Depot, Inc., *2006 Annual Report* in Appendix A.

1. Locate the consolidated balance sheets and consolidated statements of earnings. List 10 permanent account categories and 5 temporary account categories found within these statements.

2. Based on the consolidated statements of earnings, what is the closing entry that should be made to zero out all operating expense categories?

Income Statement

In 2006, CSX Corporation, which operates under the name Surface Transportation, reported operating expenses of $7,440 million. A partial list of the company's operating expenses follows. CSX Corporation reported revenues from external customers to be $9,566 million for the year. These revenues are divided among two operations: intermodal and rail.

Revenue from External Customers

(Dollars in millions)

Intermodal	$1,412
Rail	8,154

Operating Expenses

(Dollars in millions)

Labor and Fringe Benefits	$2,922
Materials, Supplies, and Other	1,889
Conrail Fees, Rents, and Services	75
Gain on Insurance Recoveries	(168)
Inland Transportation	242
Depreciation	856
Fuel	1,112
Equipment and Other Rents	512

Analyze:

1. If the given categories represent the related general ledger accounts, what journal entry would be made to close the expense accounts at year-end?

2. What journal entry would be made to close the revenue accounts?

Analyze Online: Locate the Web site for CSX Corporation (www.csx.com). Click on *CSX Corporation* and then click on *Investor Relations*. Within the *Financial Information* link, find the most recent annual report.

3. On the consolidated statement of earnings, what was the amount reported for operating expenses?

4. What percentage increase or decrease does this figure represent from the operating expenses reported in 2006 of $7,440 million?

Worksheets

Suppose an accountant with many years' experience suggests that you skip preparation of the worksheet. The accountant claims that the financial statements can be prepared using only the general ledger account balances. What risks can you identify if the accountant uses this procedure? Do you agree or disagree with this approach? Why?

Training

As the general ledger accountant for a music supply store, you have just completed the trial balance, closing entries, and postclosing trial balance for the month. Next month, you will be on vacation during the closing process. Your boss has hired a temporary employee to perform these duties while you are away. Prepare a descriptive report for your replacement explaining the differences between a postclosing trial balance and a trial balance.

Accounting Cycle

Understanding the steps in the accounting cycle is important to get accurate information about the condition of your company. In teams, make strips of paper with the nine steps of the accounting cycle. Give two or three strips to each member of the group. Each team member needs to put his or her strips in the proper order of the nine steps.

Certified Bookkeeper

Certification in your field indicates you have a certain level of education and training. Go to the American Institute of Professional Bookkeepers Web site at www.aipb.com. From the certification program icon, determine the three requirements to become a certified bookkeeper.

Answers to **Self Reviews**

Answers to Section 1 Self Review

1. A temporary owner's equity account.
2. Close the revenue account to *Income Summary.*
   Close the expense accounts to *Income Summary.*
   Close the *Income Summary* account to the capital account.
   Close the drawing account to the capital account.
3. Debit *Capital* and credit *Drawing.*
4. **d.** revenue, drawing, and expense accounts
5. **a.** *Capital*
6. No effect on net income.

Answers to Section 2 Self Review

1. To make sure the general ledger is in balance after the adjusting and closing entries are posted.
2. Asset, liability, and the owner's capital accounts.
3. (7) Record closing entries, (8) prepare a postclosing trial balance, (9) interpret the financial statements.
4. **a.** *J. T. Amos, Drawing*
5. **b.** net loss of $60,000
6. The income statement will answer questions about fees earned, expenses incurred, and profit. The balance sheet will answer questions about the cash balance, the amount owed by customers, and the amount owed to suppliers.

Answers to Comprehensive Self Review

1. Income Summary	12,100	
Rent Expense		3,600
Salaries Expense		7,000
Supplies Expense		1,500
2. Fees Income	56,000	
Income Summary		56,000

3. Income statement, statement of owner's equity, and balance sheet.
4. Interpret the financial statements.
5. False. The *temporary* owner's equity accounts do not appear on the postclosing trial balance. The temporary owner's equity accounts are the drawing account and *Income Summary.*

Mini-Practice Set 1

Service Business Accounting Cycle

Wells' Consulting Services

This project will give you an opportunity to apply your knowledge of accounting principles and proce-dures by handling all the accounting work of Wells' Consulting Services for the month of January 2011.

INTRODUCTION

Assume that you are the chief accountant for Wells' Consulting Services. During January, the busi-ness will use the same types of records and procedures that you learned about in Chapters 1 through 6. The chart of accounts for Wells' Consulting Services has been expanded to include a few new accounts. Follow the instructions to complete the accounting records for the month of January.

Well's Consulting Services Chart of Accounts	
Assets	**Revenue**
101 Cash	401 Fees Income
111 Accounts Receivable	
121 Supplies	**Expenses**
134 Prepaid Insurance	511 Salaries Expense
~~137 Prepaid Rent~~	514 Utilities Expense
141 Equipment	517 Supplies Expense
142 Accumulated Depreciation—Equipment	~~520 Rent Expense~~
	523 Depreciation Expense—Equipment
Liabilities	526 Advertising Expense
202 Accounts Payable	529 Maintenance Expense
	532 Telephone Expense
Owner's Equity	535 Insurance Expense
301 Carolyn Wells, Capital	
302 Carolyn Wells, Drawing	
309 Income Summary	

INSTRUCTIONS

1. Open the general ledger accounts and enter the balances for January 1, 2011. Obtain the necessary figures from the postclosing trial balance prepared on December 31, 2010, which appears on pages ~~156-157~~. 166

2. Analyze each transaction and record it in the general journal. Use page 3 to begin January's transactions.

3. Post the transactions to the general ledger accounts.

4. Prepare the Trial Balance section of the worksheet.

5. Prepare the Adjustments section of the worksheet.

    a. Compute and record the adjustment for supplies used during the month. An inventory taken on January 31 showed supplies of $2,000 on hand.

    b. Compute and record the adjustment for expired insurance for the month.

    c. Record the adjustment for one month of expired rent of $4,000.

    d. Record the adjustment for depreciation of $183 on the old equipment for the month. The first adjustment for depreciation for the new equipment will be recorded in February.

6. Complete the worksheet.

7. Prepare an income statement for the month.

8. Prepare a statement of owner's equity.

9. Prepare a balance sheet using the report form.

10. Journalize and post the adjusting entries.

11. Journalize and post the closing entries.

12. Prepare a postclosing trial balance.

Analyze: Compare the January 31 balance sheet you prepared with the December 31 balance sheet shown on page 167.

a. What changes occurred in total assets, liabilities, and the owner's ending capital?

b. What changes occurred in *Cash* and *Accounts Receivable* accounts?

c. Has there been an improvement in the firm's financial position? Why or why not?

DATE	TRANSACTIONS
Jan. 2	Purchased supplies for $3,000; issued Check 1015.
2	Purchased a one-year insurance policy for $4,800; issued Check 1016.
7	Sold services for $15,000 in cash and $1,800 on credit during the first week of January.
12	Collected a total of $1,500 on account from credit customers during the first week of January.
12	Issued Check 1017 for $2,150 to pay for special promotional advertising to new businesses on the local radio station during the month.
13	Collected a total of $2,250 on account from credit customers during the second week of January.
14	Returned supplies that were damaged for a cash refund of $275.
15	Sold services for $18,250 in cash and $2,375 on credit during the second week of January.
20	Purchased supplies for $1,800 from White's, Inc.; received Invoice 2384 payable in 30 days.
20	Sold services for $9,050 in cash and $5,850 on credit during the third week of January.
20	Collected a total of $1,750 on account from credit customers during the third week of January.
21	Issued Check 1018 for $4,250 to pay for maintenance work on the office equipment.
22	Issued Check 1019 for $2,750 to pay for special promotional advertising to new businesses in the local newspaper.
23	Received the monthly telephone bill for $410 and paid it with Check 1020.
26	Collected a total of $4,570 on account from credit customers during the fourth week of January.
27	Issued Check 1021 for $2,000 to Office Plus, as payment on account for Invoice 2223.
28	Sent Check 1022 for $1,050 in payment of the monthly bill for utilities.
29	Sold services for $14,050 in cash and $2,250 on credit during the fourth week of January.
31	Issued Checks 1023–1027 for $15,500 to pay the monthly salaries of the regular employees and three part-time workers.
31	Issued Check 1028 for $6,000 for personal use.
31	Issued Check 1029 for $1,050 to pay for maintenance services for the month.
31	Purchased additional equipment for $10,500 from Contemporary Equipment Company; issued Check 1030 for $5,500 and bought the rest on credit. The equipment has a five-year life and no salvage value.
31	Sold services for $2,850 in cash and 1,450 on credit on January 31.

Accounting for Sales and Accounts Receivable

Chapter **7**

LEARNING OBJECTIVES

1. Record credit sales in a sales journal. **LP7**
2. Post from the sales journal to the general ledger accounts.
3. Post from the sales journal to the customers' accounts in the accounts receivable subsidiary ledger.
4. Record sales returns and allowances in the general journal.
5. Post sales returns and allowances.
6. Prepare a schedule of accounts receivable.
7. Compute trade discounts.
8. Record credit card sales in appropriate journals.
9. Prepare the state sales tax return.
10. Define the accounting terms new to this chapter.

NEW TERMS

accounts receivable ledger
charge-account sales
contra revenue account
control account
credit memorandum
invoice
list price
manufacturing business
merchandise inventory
merchandising business
net price
net sales

open-account credit
retail business
sales allowance
sales journal
sales return
schedule of accounts receivable
service business
special journal
subsidiary ledger
trade discount
wholesale business

Lands' End www.landsend.com

Lands' End is a direct merchant of clothing, soft luggage, and products for the home. As a direct merchant, Lands' End works directly with mills and manufacturers, eliminating wholesalers. Customers shop directly from home or office, by phone, mail, fax, or the Web.

Lands' End customers have learned to expect a high level of service. Lands' End offers one of the simplest guarantees in the industry—GUARANTEED. PERIOD.®—which allows customers to return items at any time, for any reason, for a full refund of the purchase price or a replacement. A few of the other unique services Lands' End offers follow:

- Hemming trousers is free of charge.
- Swatches of fabrics are available free of charge.
- Additional buttons, luggage parts, or repairs are all available free of charge.
- The company's Lost Mitten Club will replace any child's mitten lost in the same season as purchase at half the price of a pair, with free shipping.

thinking critically

What other factors besides customer service are important to the success of a company like Lands' End?

Section **1**

SECTION OBJECTIVES	TERMS TO LEARN

>> 1. Record credit sales in a sales journal.

WHY IT'S IMPORTANT

Credit sales are a major source of revenue for many businesses. The sales journal is an efficient option for recording large volumes of credit sales transactions.

>> 2. Post from the sales journal to the general ledger accounts.

WHY IT'S IMPORTANT

A well-designed accounting system prevents repetitive tasks.

TERMS TO LEARN

manufacturing business
merchandise inventory
merchandising business
retail business
sales journal
service business
special journal
subsidiary ledger

Merchandise Sales

When an accounting system is developed for a firm, one important consideration is the nature of the firm's operations. The three basic types of businesses are a **service business,** which sells services; a **merchandising business,** which sells goods that it purchases for resale; and a **manufacturing business,** which sells goods that it produces.

Wells' Consulting Services, the firm that was described in Chapters 2 through 6, is a service business. The firm that we will examine next, Maxx-Out Sporting Goods, is a merchandising business that sells the latest sporting goods and sportswear for men, women, and children. It is a **retail business,** which sells goods and services directly to individual consumers. Maxx-Out Sporting Goods is a sole proprietorship owned and operated by Max Ferraro, who was formerly a sales manager for a major retail clothing store.

Maxx-Out Sporting Goods must account for purchases and sales of goods, and for **merchandise inventory**—the stock of goods that is kept on hand. Refer to the chart of accounts for Maxx-Out Sporting Goods on page 191. You will learn about the accounts in this and following chapters.

To allow for efficient recording of financial data, the accounting systems of most merchandising businesses include special journals and subsidiary ledgers.

Special Journals and Subsidiary Ledgers

A **special journal** is a journal that is used to record only one type of transaction. A **subsidiary ledger** is a ledger that contains accounts of a single type. Table 7.1 lists the journals and ledgers that merchandising businesses generally use in their accounting systems. In this chapter, we will discuss the sales journal and the accounts receivable subsidiary ledger.

The Sales Journal

The **sales journal** is used to record only sales of merchandise on credit. To understand the need for a sales journal, consider how credit sales made at Maxx-Out Sporting Goods would be entered and posted using a general journal and general ledger. Refer to Figure 7.1 on pages 192–193.

Note the word "Balance" in the ledger accounts. To record beginning balances, enter the date in the Date column, the word "Balance" in the Description column, a check mark in the Posting Reference column, and the amount in the Debit or Credit Balance column.

Most state and many local governments impose a sales tax on retail sales of certain goods and services. Businesses are required to collect this tax from their customers and send it to the proper tax agency at regular intervals. When goods or services are sold on credit, the sales tax

important!

Business Classifications

The term *merchandising* refers to the type of business operation, not the type of legal entity. Maxx-Out Sporting Goods could have been a partnership or a corporation instead of a sole proprietorship.

is usually recorded at the time of the sale even though it will not be collected immediately. A liability account called *Sales Tax Payable* is credited for the sales tax charged.

JOURNALS	
Type of Journal	**Purpose**
Sales	To record sales of merchandise on credit
Purchases	To record purchases of merchandise on credit
Cash receipts	To record cash received from all sources
Cash payments	To record all disbursements of cash
General	To record all transactions that are not recorded in another special journal and all adjusting and closing entries

LEDGERS	
Type of Ledger	**Content**
General	Assets, liabilities, owner's equity, revenue, and expense accounts
Accounts receivable	Accounts for credit customers
Accounts payable	Accounts for creditors

TABLE 7.1

Journals and Ledgers Used by Merchandising Businesses

Maxx-Out Sporting Goods
Chart of Accounts

Assets

101 Cash
105 Petty Cash Fund
109 Notes Receivable
111 Accounts Receivable
112 Allowance for Doubtful Accounts
116 Interest Receivable
121 Merchandise Inventory
126 Prepaid Insurance
127 Prepaid Interest
129 Supplies
131 Store Equipment
132 Accumulated Depreciation—Store Equipment
141 Office Equipment
142 Accumulated Depreciation—Office Equipment

Liabilities

201 Notes Payable—Trade
202 Notes Payable—Bank
205 Accounts Payable
216 Interest Payable
221 Social Security Tax Payable
222 Medicare Tax Payable
223 Employee Income Tax Payable
225 Federal Unemployment Tax Payable
227 State Unemployment Tax Payable
229 Salaries Payable
231 Sales Tax Payable

Owner's Equity

301 Max Ferraro, Capital
302 Max Ferraro, Drawing
399 Income Summary

Revenue

401 Sales
451 Sales Returns and Allowances
491 Interest Income
493 Miscellaneous Income

Cost of Goods Sold

501 Purchases
502 Freight In
503 Purchases Returns and Allowances
504 Purchases Discounts

Expenses

611 Salaries Expense—Sales
612 Supplies Expense
614 Advertising Expense
617 Cash Short or Over
626 Depreciation Expense—Store Equipment
634 Rent Expense
637 Salaries Expense—Office
639 Insurance Expense
641 Payroll Taxes Expense
643 Utilities Expense
649 Telephone Expense
651 Uncollectible Accounts Expense
657 Bank Fees Expense
658 Delivery Expense
659 Depreciation Expense—Office Equipment
691 Interest Expense
693 Miscellaneous Expense

FIGURE 7.1

Journalizing and Posting Credit Sales

GENERAL JOURNAL   PAGE ___2___

	DATE		DESCRIPTION	POST. REF.	DEBIT	CREDIT	
1	2010						1
2	Jan.	3	Accounts Receivable	111	7 0 2 00		2
3			Sales Tax Payable	231		5 2 00	3
4			Sales	401		6 5 0 00	4
5			Sold merchandise on				5
6			credit to Ann Anh,				6
7			Sales Slip 1101				7
8							8
9		8	Accounts Receivable	111	6 4 8 00		9
10			Sales Tax Payable	231		4 8 00	10
11			Sales	401		6 0 0 00	11
12			Sold merchandise on				12
13			credit to Cathy Ball,				13
14			Sales Slip 1102				14
15							15
16		11	Accounts Receivable	111	7 5 6 00		16
17			Sales Tax Payable	231		5 6 00	17
18			Sales	401		7 0 0 00	18
19			Sold merchandise on				19
20			credit to Barbara Coe, Sales				20
21			Slip 1103				21
22							22
23		15	Accounts Receivable	111	3 2 4 00		23
24			Sales Tax Payable	231		2 4 00	24
25			Sales	401		3 0 0 00	25
26			Sold merchandise on				26
27			credit to Amalia Rodriguez,				27
28			Sales Slip 1104				28
29							29
30							30
31							31
32							32

ACCOUNT _Accounts Receivable_   ACCOUNT NO. __111__

DATE		DESCRIPTION	POST. REF.	DEBIT	CREDIT	BALANCE DEBIT	BALANCE CREDIT
2010							
Jan.	1	Balance	✓			3 2 4 0 00	
	3		J2	7 0 2 00		3 9 4 2 00	
	8		J2	6 4 8 00		4 5 9 0 00	
	11		J2	7 5 6 00		5 3 4 6 00	
	15		J2	3 2 4 00		5 6 7 0 00	

As you can see, a great amount of repetition is involved in both journalizing and posting these sales. The four credit sales made on January 3, 8, 11, and 15 required four separate entries in the general journal and involved four debits to **Accounts Receivable**, four credits to **Sales Tax Payable**, four credits to **Sales** (the firm's revenue account), and four descriptions. The posting of 12 items to the three general ledger accounts represents still further duplication of effort. This recording procedure is not efficient for a business that has a substantial number of credit sales each month.

ACCOUNT _Sales Tax Payable_   ACCOUNT NO. _231_

DATE		DESCRIPTION	POST. REF.	DEBIT	CREDIT	BALANCE DEBIT	BALANCE CREDIT
2010							
Jan.	1	Balance	✓				7 5 6 00
	3		J2		5 2 00		8 0 8 00
	8		J2		4 8 00		8 5 6 00
	11		J2		5 6 00		9 1 2 00
	15		J2		2 4 00		9 3 6 00

ACCOUNT _Sales_   ACCOUNT NO. _401_

DATE		DESCRIPTION	POST. REF.	DEBIT	CREDIT	BALANCE DEBIT	BALANCE CREDIT
2010							
Jan.	3		J2		6 5 0 00		6 5 0 00
	8		J2		6 0 0 00		1 2 5 0 00
	11		J2		7 0 0 00		1 9 5 0 00
	15		J2		3 0 0 00		2 2 5 0 00

RECORDING TRANSACTIONS IN A SALES JOURNAL

A special journal intended only for credit sales provides a more efficient method of recording these transactions. Figure 7.2 shows the January credit sales of Maxx-Out Sporting Goods recorded in a sales journal. Since Maxx-Out Sporting Goods is located in a state that has an 8 percent sales tax on retail transactions, its sales journal includes a Sales Tax Payable Credit column. For the sake of simplicity, the sales journal shown here includes a limited number of transactions. The firm actually has many more credit sales each month.

Notice that the headings and columns in the sales journal speed up the recording process. No general ledger account names are entered. Only one line is needed to record all information for each transaction—date, sales slip number, customer's name, debit to *Accounts Receivable,* credit to *Sales Tax Payable,* and credit to *Sales.* Since the sales journal is used for a single purpose, there is no need to enter any descriptions. Thus, a great deal of repetition is avoided.

Entries in the sales journal are usually made daily. In a retail business such as Maxx-Out Sporting Goods, the data needed for each entry is taken from a copy of the customer's sales slip, as shown in Figure 7.3.

>> 1. OBJECTIVE

Record credit sales in a sales journal.

LP7

recall

Journals

A journal is a day-to-day record of a firm's transactions.

FIGURE 7.2

A Sales Journal

	DATE		SALES SLIP NO.	CUSTOMER'S ACCOUNT DEBITED	POST. REF.	ACCOUNTS RECEIVABLE DEBIT	SALES TAX PAYABLE CREDIT	SALES CREDIT	
1	2010								1
2	Jan.	3	1101	Ann Anh		7 0 2 00	5 2 00	6 5 0 00	2
3		8	1102	Cathy Ball		6 4 8 00	4 8 00	6 0 0 00	3
4		11	1103	Barbara Coe		7 5 6 00	5 6 00	7 0 0 00	4
5		15	1104	Amalia Rodriguez		3 2 4 00	2 4 00	3 0 0 00	5
6		18	1105	Fred Wu		8 1 0 00	6 0 00	7 5 0 00	6
7		21	1106	Linda Carter		4 8 6 00	3 6 00	4 5 0 00	7
8		28	1107	Kim Ramirez		1 0 8 00	8 00	1 0 0 00	8
9		29	1108	Mesia Davis		1 0 8 0 00	8 0 00	1 0 0 0 00	9
10		31	1109	Alma Sanchez		9 7 2 00	7 2 00	9 0 0 00	10
11		31	1110	Ann Anh		2 7 0 00	2 0 00	2 5 0 00	11
12									12

SALES JOURNAL   PAGE _1_

Maxx-Out Sporting Goods

2007 Trendsetter Lane
Dallas, Texas 75268-0967

DATE	SALESPERSON	AUTH.
1/3/10	S.Harris	

Goods Taken [X]   To Be Delivered [ ]

S
e
n
d

t
o

Special Instructions:

I authorize this purchase to be charged
on my account.

Ann Anh
Signature

SALES SLIP 1101

Qty.	Description	Unit Price	Amount
1	Olympic weight set	350 00	350 00
1	Mountain Bike	300 00	300 00
	Sales Tax		52 00
	Amount		702 00

NAME: Ann Anh
ADDRESS: 8913 South Hampton Road
Dallas, TX 75232-6002

>> 2. OBJECTIVE

Post from the sales journal to the general ledger accounts.

LP7

Many small retail firms use a sales journal similar to the one shown in Figure 7.2. However, keep in mind that special journals vary in format according to the needs of individual businesses.

POSTING FROM A SALES JOURNAL

A sales journal not only simplifies the initial recording of credit sales, it also eliminates a great deal of repetition in posting these transactions. With a sales journal, it is not necessary to post each credit sale individually to general ledger accounts. Instead, summary postings are made at the end of the month after the amount columns of the sales journal are totaled. See Figure 7.4 on page 195 for an illustration of posting from the sales journal to the general ledger.

In actual practice, before any posting takes place, the equality of the debits and credits recorded in the sales journal is proved by comparing the column totals. The proof for the sales journal in Figure 7.4 is given below. All multicolumn special journals should be proved in a similar manner before their totals are posted.

Proof of Sales Journal	
	Debits
Accounts Receivable Debit column	$6,156.00
	Credits
Sales Tax Payable Credit column	$ 456.00
Sales Credit column	5,700.00
	$6,156.00

After the equality of the debits and credits has been verified, the sales journal is ruled and the column totals are posted to the general ledger accounts involved. To indicate that the postings have been made, the general ledger account numbers are entered in parentheses under the column totals in the sales journal. The abbreviation S1 is written in the Posting Reference column of the accounts, showing that the data was posted from page 1 of the sales journal.

The check marks in the sales journal in Figure 7.4 indicate that the amounts have been posted to the individual customer accounts. Posting from the sales journal to the customer accounts in the subsidiary ledger is illustrated later in this chapter.

FIGURE 7.4

End-of-Month Postings

SALES JOURNAL   PAGE ___1___

	DATE	SALES SLIP NO.	CUSTOMER'S ACCOUNT DEBITED	POST. REF.	ACCOUNTS RECEIVABLE DEBIT	SALES TAX PAYABLE CREDIT	SALES CREDIT	
1	2010							1
2	Jan. 3	1101	Ann Anh	✓	702 00	52 00	650 00	2
3	8	1102	Cathy Ball	✓	648 00	48 00	600 00	3
4	11	1103	Barbara Coe	✓	756 00	56 00	700 00	4
5	15	1104	Amalia Rodriguez	✓	324 00	24 00	300 00	5
6	18	1105	Fred Wu	✓	810 00	60 00	750 00	6
7	21	1106	Linda Carter	✓	486 00	36 00	450 00	7
8	28	1107	Kim Ramirez	✓	108 00	8 00	100 00	8
9	29	1108	Mesia Davis	✓	1080 00	80 00	1000 00	9
10	31	1109	Alma Sanchez	✓	972 00	72 00	900 00	10
11	31	1110	Ann Anh	✓	270 00	20 00	250 00	11
12	31		Totals		6156 00	456 00	5700 00	12
13					(111)	(231)	(401)	13
14								14

ACCOUNT _Accounts Receivable_   ACCOUNT NO. _111_

DATE	DESCRIPTION	POST. REF.	DEBIT	CREDIT	BALANCE DEBIT	BALANCE CREDIT
2010						
Jan. 1	Balance	✓			3240 00	
23		J2		162 00	3078 00	
25		J2		486 00	2592 00	
31		S1	6156 00		8748 00	

ACCOUNT _Sales Tax Payable_   ACCOUNT NO. _231_

DATE	DESCRIPTION	POST. REF.	DEBIT	CREDIT	BALANCE DEBIT	BALANCE CREDIT
2010						
Jan. 1	Balance	✓				756 00
11		CP1	756 00			—0—
23		J2	12 00		12 00	
25		J2	36 00		48 00	
31		S1		456 00		408 00

ACCOUNT _Sales_   ACCOUNT NO. _401_

DATE	DESCRIPTION	POST. REF.	DEBIT	CREDIT	BALANCE DEBIT	BALANCE CREDIT
2010						
Jan. 31	Balance	S1		5700 00		5700 00

ADVANTAGES OF A SALES JOURNAL

Using a special journal for credit sales saves time, effort, and recording space. Both the journalizing process and the posting process become more efficient, but the advantage in the posting process is especially significant. If a business used the general journal to record 300 credit sales a month, the firm would have to make 900 postings to the general ledger—300 to *Accounts Receivable,* 300 to *Sales Tax Payable,* and 300 to *Sales.* With a sales journal, the firm makes only three summary postings to the general ledger at the end of each month no matter how many credit sales were entered.

important!

Posting

When posting from the sales journal, post information moving from left to right across the ledger form.

The use of a sales journal and other special journals also allows division of work. In a business with a fairly large volume of transactions, it is essential that several employees be able to record transactions at the same time.

Finally, the sales journal improves the audit trail by bringing together all entries for credit sales in one place and listing them by source document number as well as by date. This procedure makes it easier to trace the details of such transactions.

Section 1 Self Review

QUESTIONS

1. What is a special journal? Give four examples of special journals.
2. What type of transaction is recorded in the sales journal?
3. What is a subsidiary ledger? Give two examples of subsidiary ledgers.

EXERCISES

4. Which of the following is not a reason to use a sales journal?
   a. increases efficiency
   b. allows division of work
   c. increases credit sales
   d. improves audit trail
5. Types of business operations are
   a. service, merchandising, corporation.
   b. sole proprietorship, merchandising, manufacturing.
   c. service, merchandising, manufacturing.

ANALYSIS

6. All sales recorded in this sales journal were made on account and are taxable at a rate of 8 percent. What errors have been made in the entries? Assume the Sales Credit column is correct.

(Answers to Section 1 Self Review are on page 233.)

SALES JOURNAL   PAGE ___1___

	DATE	SALES SLIP NO.	CUSTOMER'S ACCOUNT DEBITED	POST. REF.	ACCOUNTS RECEIVABLE DEBIT	SALES TAX PAYABLE CREDIT	SALES CREDIT	
12	Apr. 25	4100	Carolyn Harris		642 00	42 00	600 00	12
13	25	4101	Teresa Wells		872 00	72 00	900 00	13

Section 2

SECTION OBJECTIVES

>> 3. Post from the sales journal to the customers' accounts in the accounts receivable subsidiary ledger.

WHY IT'S IMPORTANT

This ledger contains individual records that reflect all transactions of each customer.

>> 4. Record sales returns and allowances in the general journal.

WHY IT'S IMPORTANT

Companies can see how much revenue is lost due to merchandise problems.

>> 5. Post sales returns and allowances.

WHY IT'S IMPORTANT

Accurate, up-to-date customer records contribute to overall customer satisfaction.

>> 6. Prepare a schedule of accounts receivable.

WHY IT'S IMPORTANT

This schedule provides a snapshot of amounts due from customers.

TERMS TO LEARN

accounts receivable ledger

contra revenue account

control account

credit memorandum

net sales

sales allowance

sales return

schedule of accounts receivable

Accounts Receivable

A business that extends credit to customers must manage its accounts receivable carefully. Accounts receivable represents a substantial asset for many businesses, and this asset must be converted into cash in a timely manner. Otherwise, a firm may not be able to pay its bills even though it has a large volume of sales and earns a satisfactory profit.

The Accounts Receivable Ledger

The accountant needs detailed information about the transactions with credit customers and the balances owed by such customers at all times. This information is provided by an **accounts receivable ledger** with individual accounts for all credit customers. The accounts receivable ledger is referred to as a subsidiary ledger because it is separate from and subordinate to the general ledger.

Using an accounts receivable ledger makes it possible to verify that customers are paying their balances on time and that they are within their credit limits. The accounts receivable ledger also provides a convenient way to answer questions from credit customers. Customers may ask about their current balances or about a possible billing error.

The accounts for credit customers are maintained in a balance ledger form with three money columns, as shown in Figure 7.5 on page 198. Notice that this form does not contain a column for indicating the type of account balance. The balances in the customer accounts are presumed to be debit balances since asset accounts normally have debit balances. However, occasionally there is a credit balance because a customer has overpaid an amount owed or has returned goods that were already paid for. One common procedure for dealing with this situation is to circle the balance in order to show that it is a credit amount.

For a small business such as Maxx-Out Sporting Goods, customer accounts are alphabetized in the accounts receivable ledger. Larger firms and firms that use computers assign an account number to each credit customer and arrange the customer accounts in numeric order. Postings to the accounts receivable ledger are usually made daily so that the customer accounts can be kept up to date at all times.

>> **3. OBJECTIVE**

Post from the sales journal to the customers' accounts in the accounts receivable subsidiary ledger.

LP7

POSTING A CREDIT SALE

Each credit sale recorded in the sales journal is posted to the appropriate customer's account in the accounts receivable ledger, as shown in Figure 7.5. The date, the sales slip number, and the amount that the customer owes as a result of the sale are transferred from the sales journal to the customer's account. The amount is taken from the Accounts Receivable Debit column of the journal and is entered in the Debit column of the account. Next, the new balance is determined and recorded.

To show that the posting has been completed, a check mark (✓) is entered in the sales journal and the abbreviation S1 is entered in the Posting Reference column of the customer's account. As noted before, this abbreviation identifies page 1 of the sales journal.

POSTING CASH RECEIVED ON ACCOUNT

When the transaction involves cash received on account from a credit customer, the cash collected is first recorded in a cash receipts journal. (The necessary entry in the cash receipts journal is discussed in Chapter 9.) The cash is then posted to the individual customer account in the accounts receivable ledger. Figure 7.6 shows a posting for cash received on January 7 from Ann Anh, a credit customer of Maxx-Out Sporting Goods.

>> **4. OBJECTIVE**

Record sales returns and allowances in the general journal.

LP7

Sales Returns and Allowances

A sale is entered in the accounting records when the goods are sold or the service is provided. If something is wrong with the goods or service, the firm may take back the goods, resulting in a **sales return,** or give the customer a reduction in price, resulting in a **sales allowance.**

When a return or allowance is related to a credit sale, the normal practice is to issue a document called a **credit memorandum** to the customer rather than giving a cash refund. The

FIGURE 7.5

Posting from the Sales Journal to the Accounts Receivable Ledger

FIGURE 7.6

Posting for Cash Received on Account

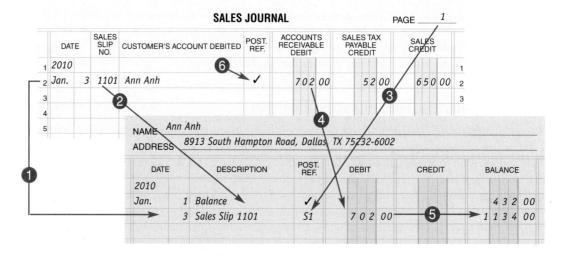

credit memorandum states that the customer's account is being reduced by the amount of the return or allowance plus any sales tax. A copy of the credit memorandum provides the data needed to enter the transaction in the firm's accounting records.

A debit to the *Sales Returns and Allowances* account is preferred to making a direct debit to *Sales.* This procedure gives a complete record of sales returns and allowances for each accounting period. Business managers use this record as a measure of operating efficiency. The *Sales Returns and Allowances* account is a **contra revenue account** because it has a debit balance, which is contrary, or opposite, to the normal balance for a revenue account.

BUSINESS TRANSACTION

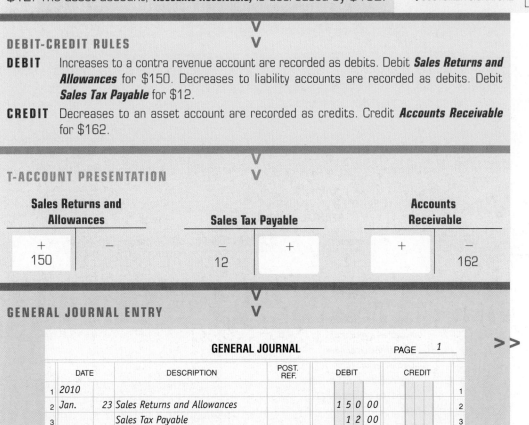

On January 23, Maxx-Out Sporting Goods issued Credit Memorandum 101 for a sales allowance to Fred Wu for merchandise purchased on account. The merchandise was damaged but still usable.

ANALYSIS

The contra revenue account, **Sales Returns and Allowances,** is increased by $150. The liability account, **Sales Tax Payable,** is decreased by $12. The asset account, **Accounts Receivable,** is decreased by $162.

DEBIT-CREDIT RULES

DEBIT Increases to a contra revenue account are recorded as debits. Debit *Sales Returns and Allowances* for $150. Decreases to liability accounts are recorded as debits. Debit *Sales Tax Payable* for $12.

CREDIT Decreases to an asset account are recorded as credits. Credit *Accounts Receivable* for $162.

T-ACCOUNT PRESENTATION

Sales Returns and Allowances		Sales Tax Payable		Accounts Receivable	
+	–	–	+	+	–
150		12			162

GENERAL JOURNAL ENTRY

GENERAL JOURNAL   PAGE 1

	DATE	DESCRIPTION	POST. REF.	DEBIT	CREDIT	
1	2010					1
2	Jan. 23	Sales Returns and Allowances		1 5 0 00		2
3		Sales Tax Payable		1 2 00		3
4		Accts. Rec.—Fred Wu			1 6 2 00	4

Maxx-Out Sporting Goods
2007 Trendsetter Lane, Dallas TX 75268-0967

CREDIT MEMORANDUM			NO. 101
ORIGINAL SALES DATE	ORIGINAL SALES SLIP	APPROVAL	X MDSE RET
Jan. 18, 2010	No. 1105	S.H.	

DATE: January 23, 2010

NAME: Fred Wu.
ADDRESS: 4640 Walnut Hill Lane
Dallas, TX 75267-6205

Fred Wu
CUSTOMER SIGNATURE

QTY	DESCRIPTION	AMOUNT
1	Athletic Suit	
		$150 00
REASON FOR RETURN	SUB	$150 00
damaged	TOTAL	
THE TOTAL SHOWN AT THE RIGHT WILL BE CREDITED TO YOUR ACCOUNT.	SALES TAX	12 00
	TOTAL	$162 00

THE BOTTOM LINE
Allowance for Damaged Merchandise

Income Statement

Contra Revenue	↑ 150
Net Income	↓ 150

Balance Sheet

Assets	↓ 162
Liabilities	↓ 12
Equity	↓ 150

What is the ultimate effect of this transaction on the financial statements? An increase in contra revenue causes a decrease in net income. Note that the $150 decrease in net income causes a $150 decrease in owner's equity. The asset *Accounts Receivable* is decreased, and the liability *Sales Tax Payable* is also decreased. The eventual effect of this transaction on the income statement and the balance sheet is summarized in the box titled *The Bottom Line.*

RECORDING SALES RETURNS AND ALLOWANCES

Depending on the volume of sales returns and allowances, a business may use a general journal to record these transactions, or it may use a special sales returns and allowances journal.

Using the General Journal for Sales Returns and Allowances A small firm that has a limited number of sales returns and allowances each month has no need to establish a special journal for such transactions. Instead, the required entries are made in the general journal.

Using a Sales Returns and Allowances Journal In a business having many sales returns and allowances, it is efficient to use a special journal for these transactions. An example of a *sales returns and allowances journal* is shown in Figure 7.7.

>> **5. OBJECTIVE**

Post sales returns and allowances.

LP7

POSTING A SALES RETURN OR ALLOWANCE

Whether sales returns and allowances are recorded in the general journal or in a special sales returns and allowances journal, each of these transactions must be posted from the general ledger to the appropriate customer's account in the accounts receivable ledger. Figure 7.8 below shows how a return of merchandise was posted from the general journal to the account of Linda Carter.

FIGURE 7.7

Sales Returns and Allowances Journal

SALES RETURNS AND ALLOWANCES JOURNAL PAGE __8__

	DATE	SALES SLIP NO.	CUSTOMER'S ACCOUNT CREDITED	POST. REF.	ACCOUNTS RECEIVABLE CREDIT	SALES TAX PAYABLE DEBIT	SALES RET. & ALLOW. DEBIT	
1	2010							1
2	Jan. 23	1105	Fred Wu	✓	1 62 00	12 00	1 50 00	2
3	25	1106	Linda Carter	✓	4 86 00	36 00	4 50 00	3
4								4
17	31		Totals		3 2 40 00	2 40 00	3 0 00 00	17
18					(111)	(231)	(451)	18
19								19

FIGURE 7.8

Posting a Sales Return to the Customer's Account

GENERAL JOURNAL PAGE __1__

	DATE	DESCRIPTION	POST. REF.	DEBIT	CREDIT	
1	2010					1
6	Jan. 25	Sales Returns and Allowances	451	4 5 0 00		6
7		Sales Tax Payable	231	3 6 00		7
8		Accounts Rec./Linda Carter	111 ✓		4 86 00	8
9		Accepted a return of				9
10		defective merchandise,				10
11		Credit Memorandum 102;				11
12		original sale made on Sales				12
13		Slip 1106 of January 21.				13
14						14
15						15

NAME _Linda Carter_
ADDRESS _1819 Belt Line Road, Dallas, Texas 75267-6318_

DATE		DESCRIPTION	POST. REF.	DEBIT	CREDIT	BALANCE
2010						
Jan.	1	Balance	✓			5 4 00
	21	Sales Slip 1106	S1	4 86 00		5 4 0 00
	25	CM 102	J1		4 86 00	5 4 00

Because the credit amount in the general journal entry for this transaction requires two postings, the account number 111 and a check mark are entered in the Posting Reference column of the journal. The 111 indicates that the amount was posted to the ***Accounts Receivable*** account in the general ledger, and the check mark indicates that the amount was posted to the customer's account in the accounts receivable ledger. Notice that a diagonal line was used to separate the two posting references.

Refer to Figure 7.7, which shows a special sales returns and allowances journal instead of a general journal. The account numbers at the bottom of each column are the posting references for the three general ledger accounts: ***Accounts Receivable, Sales Tax Payable,*** and ***Sales Returns and Allowances.*** The check marks in the Posting Reference column show that the credits were posted to individual customer accounts in the accounts receivable subsidiary ledger.

Remember that a business can use the general journal or special journals for transactions related to credit sales. A special journal is an efficient option for recording and posting large numbers of transactions.

Figure 7.9 on pages 201–203 shows the accounts receivable ledger after posting is completed.

REPORTING NET SALES

At the end of each accounting period, the balance of the ***Sales Returns and Allowances*** account is subtracted from the balance of the ***Sales*** account in the Revenue section of the income statement. The resulting figure is the **net sales** for the period.

For example, assume the ***Sales Returns and Allowances*** account contains a balance of $600 at the end of January. Also assume the ***Sales*** account has a balance of $25,700 at the end of January. The Revenue section of the firm's income statement will appear as follows.

Maxx-Out Sporting Goods Income Statement (Partial) Month Ended January 31, 2010	
Revenue	
Sales	$25,700
Less Sales Returns and Allowances	600
Net Sales	$25,100

FIGURE 7.9

Accounts Receivable Ledger

NAME __Ann Anh__
ADDRESS __8913 South Hampton Road, Dallas, Texas 75232-6002__

DATE		DESCRIPTION	POST. REF.	DEBIT	CREDIT	BALANCE
2010						
Jan.	1	Balance	✓			4 3 2 00
	3	Sales Slip 1101	S1	7 0 2 00		1 1 3 4 00
	7		CR1		4 3 2 00	7 0 2 00
	31	Sales Slip 1110	S1	2 7 0 00		9 7 2 00

NAME __Cathy Ball__
ADDRESS __7517 Woodrow Wilson Lane, Dallas, Texas 75267-6205__

DATE		DESCRIPTION	POST. REF.	DEBIT	CREDIT	BALANCE
2010						
Jan.	8	Sales Slip 1102	S1	6 4 8 00		6 4 8 00

(continued)

FIGURE 7.9

(continued)

NAME _Vickie Bowman_

ADDRESS _1712 Red Bird Lane, Dallas, Texas 75267-6502_

DATE		DESCRIPTION	POST. REF.	DEBIT	CREDIT	BALANCE
2010						
Jan.	1	Balance	✓			2 7 0 00
	11		CR1		2 7 0 00	—0—

NAME _Linda Carter_

ADDRESS _1819 Belt Line Road, Dallas, Texas 75267-6318_

DATE		DESCRIPTION	POST. REF.	DEBIT	CREDIT	BALANCE
2010						
Jan.	1	Balance	✓			5 4 00
	21	Sales Slip 1106	S1	4 8 6 00		5 4 0 00
	25	CM 102	J1		4 8 6 00	54 00

NAME _Barbara Coe_

ADDRESS _1864 Elm Street, Dallas, Texas 75267-6205_

DATE		DESCRIPTION	POST. REF.	DEBIT	CREDIT	BALANCE
2010						
Jan.	1	Balance	✓			1 0 8 0 00
	11	Sales Slip 1103	S1	7 5 6 00		1 8 3 6 00
	13		CR1		5 4 0 00	1 2 9 6 00

NAME _Mesia Davis_

ADDRESS _1008 University Boulevard, Dallas, Texas 75267-6318_

DATE		DESCRIPTION	POST. REF.	DEBIT	CREDIT	BALANCE
2010						
Jan.	1	Balance	✓			2 1 6 00
	29	Sales Slip 1108	S1	1 0 8 0 00		1 2 9 6 00
	31		CR1		2 7 5 00	1 0 2 1 00

NAME _Kim Ramirez_

ADDRESS _5787 Valley View Lane, Dallas, Texas 75267-6318_

DATE		DESCRIPTION	POST. REF.	DEBIT	CREDIT	BALANCE
2010						
Jan.	1	Balance	✓			2 1 6 00
	28	Sales Slip 1107	S1	1 0 8 00		3 2 4 00
	31		CR1		1 0 8 00	2 1 6 00

FIGURE 7.9

(concluded)

NAME   *Amalia Rodriguez*

ADDRESS   *8108 Sherman Drive, Dallas, Texas 75267-6205*

DATE		DESCRIPTION	POST. REF.	DEBIT	CREDIT	BALANCE
2010						
Jan.	1	Balance	✓			6 4 8 00
	15	Sales Slip 1104	S1	3 2 4 00		9 7 2 00

NAME   *Alma Sanchez*

ADDRESS   *1382 Clark Road, Dallas, Texas 75267-6205*

DATE		DESCRIPTION	POST. REF.	DEBIT	CREDIT	BALANCE
2010						
Jan.	1	Balance	✓			1 0 8 00
	16		CR1		1 0 8 00	—0—
	31	Sales Slip 1109	S1	9 7 2 00		9 7 2 00

NAME   *Fred Wu*

ADDRESS   *4640 Walnut Hill Lane, Dallas, Texas 75267-6205*

DATE		DESCRIPTION	POST. REF.	DEBIT	CREDIT	BALANCE
2010						
Jan.	1	Balance	✓			2 1 6 00
	18	Sales Slip 1105	S1	8 1 0 00		1 0 2 6 00
	22		CR1		4 0 0 00	6 2 6 00
	23	CM 101	J1		1 6 2 00	4 6 4 00

Schedule of Accounts Receivable

The use of an accounts receivable ledger does not eliminate the need for the *Accounts Receivable* account in the general ledger. This account remains in the general ledger and continues to appear on the balance sheet at the end of each fiscal period. However, the *Accounts Receivable* account is now considered a control account. A **control account** serves as a link between a subsidiary ledger and the general ledger. Its balance summarizes the balances of its related accounts in the subsidiary ledger.

At the end of each month, after all the postings have been made from the sales journal, the cash receipts journal, and the general journal to the accounts receivable ledger, the balances in the accounts receivable ledger must be proved against the balance of the *Accounts Receivable* general ledger account. First a **schedule of accounts receivable,** which lists the subsidiary ledger account balances, is prepared. The total of the schedule is compared with the balance of the *Accounts Receivable* account. If the two figures are not equal, errors must be located and corrected.

On January 31, the accounts receivable ledger at Maxx-Out Sporting Goods contains the accounts shown in Figure 7.9. To prepare a schedule of accounts receivable, the names of all customers with account balances are listed with the amount of their unpaid balances. Next the figures are added to find the total owed to the business by its credit customers.

>> 6. OBJECTIVE

Prepare a schedule of accounts receivable.

LP7

Best Buy Co., Inc., reported accounts receivable of $548 million at March 3, 2007.

FIGURE 7.10

Schedule of Accounts Receivable
and the Accounts Receivable
Account

Maxx-Out Sporting Goods
Schedule of Accounts Receivable
January 31, 2010

Ann Anh	9 7 2 00
Cathy Ball	6 4 8 00
Linda Carter	5 4 00
Barbara Coe	1 2 9 6 00
Mesia Davis	1 0 2 1 00
Kim Ramirez	2 1 6 00
Amalia Rodriguez	9 7 2 00
Alma Sanchez	9 7 2 00
Fred Wu	4 6 4 00
Total	6 6 1 5 00

ACCOUNT *Accounts Receivable*   ACCOUNT NO. *111*

DATE		DESCRIPTION	POST. REF.	DEBIT	CREDIT	BALANCE DEBIT	BALANCE CREDIT
2010							
Jan.	1	Balance	✓			3 2 4 0 00	
	23		J1		1 6 2 00	3 0 7 8 00	
	25		J1		4 8 6 00	2 5 9 2 00	
	31		S1	6 1 5 6 00		8 7 4 8 00	
	31		CR1		2 1 3 3 00	6 6 1 5 00	

A comparison of the total of the schedule of accounts receivable prepared at Maxx-Out Sporting Goods on January 31 and the balance of the ***Accounts Receivable*** account in the general ledger shows that the two figures are the same, as shown in Figure 7.10. The posting reference CR1 refers to the cash receipts journal, which is discussed in Chapter 9.

In addition to providing a proof of the subsidiary ledger, the schedule of accounts receivable serves another function. It reports information about the firm's accounts receivable at the end of the month. Management can review the schedule to see exactly how much each customer owes.

Section 2 Self Review

QUESTIONS

1. What are net sales?

2. What is a sales return? What is a sales allowance?

3. Which accounts are kept in the accounts receivable ledger?

EXERCISES

4. Which of the following general ledger accounts would appear in a sales returns and allowances journal?

   a. *Sales Returns and Allowances, Sales Tax Payable, Accounts Receivable*

   b. *Sales Returns and Allowances, Sales, Accounts Receivable*

   c. *Sales Returns, Sales Allowances, Sales*

5. Where would you report net sales?

   a. sales general ledger account

   b. general journal

   c. income statement

   d. sales journal

ANALYSIS

6. Draw a diagram showing the relationship between the accounts receivable ledger, the schedule of accounts receivable, and the general ledger.

(Answers to Section 2 Self Review are on page 233.)

SECTION OBJECTIVES

>> 7. **Compute trade discounts.**

WHY IT'S IMPORTANT

Trade discounts allow for flexible pricing structures.

>> 8. **Record credit card sales in appropriate journals.**

WHY IT'S IMPORTANT

Credit cards are widely used in merchandising transactions.

>> 9. **Prepare the state sales tax return.**

WHY IT'S IMPORTANT

Businesses are legally responsible for accurately reporting and remitting sales taxes.

TERMS TO LEARN

charge-account sales
invoice
list price
net price
open-account credit
trade discount
wholesale business

Special Topics in Merchandising

Merchandisers have many accounting concerns. These include pricing, credit, and sales taxes.

Credit Sales for a Wholesale Business

The operations of Maxx-Out Sporting Goods are typical of those of many retail businesses—businesses that sell goods and services directly to individual consumers. In contrast, a **wholesale business** is a manufacturer or distributor of goods that sells to retailers or large consumers such as hotels and hospitals. The basic procedures used by wholesalers to handle sales and accounts receivable are the same as those used by retailers. However, many wholesalers offer cash discounts and trade discounts, which are not commonly found in retail operations.

The procedures used in connection with cash discounts are examined in Chapter 9. The handling of trade discounts is described here.

COMPUTING TRADE DISCOUNTS

A wholesale business offers goods to trade customers at less than retail prices. This price adjustment is based on the volume purchased by trade customers and takes the form of a **trade discount,** which is a reduction from the **list price** —the established retail price. There may be a single trade discount or a series of discounts for each type of goods. The **net price** (list price less all trade discounts) is the amount the wholesaler records in its sales journal.

The same goods may be offered to different customers at different trade discounts, depending on the size of the order and the costs of selling to the various types of customers.

Single Trade Discount Suppose the list price of goods is $1,500 and the trade discount is 40 percent. The amount of the discount is $600, and the net price to be shown on the invoice and recorded in the sales journal is $900.

List price	$1,500
Less 40% discount ($1,500 × 0.40)	600
Invoice price	$ 900

>> **7. OBJECTIVE**

Compute trade discounts.

LP7

important!

Trade Discounts

The amount of sales revenue recorded is the list price minus the trade discount.

important!

Special Journal Format

Special journals such as the sales journal can vary in format from company to company.

Series of Trade Discounts If the list price of goods is $1,500 and the trade discount is quoted in a series such as 25 and 15 percent, a different net price will result.

List price	$1,500.00
Less first discount ($1,500 × 0.25)	375.00
Difference	$1,125.00
Less second discount ($1,125 × 0.15)	168.75
Invoice price	$ 956.25

USING A SALES JOURNAL FOR A WHOLESALE BUSINESS

Since sales taxes apply only to retail transactions, a wholesale business does not need to account for such taxes. Its sales journal may therefore be as simple as the one illustrated in Figure 7.11. This sales journal has a single amount column. The total of this column is posted to the general ledger at the end of the month as a debit to the *Accounts Receivable* account and a credit to the *Sales* account (Figure 7.12). During the month, the individual entries in the sales journal are posted to the customer accounts in the accounts receivable ledger.

Wholesale businesses issue invoices. An **invoice** is a customer billing for merchandise bought on credit. Copies of the invoices are used to enter the transactions in the sales journal.

The next merchandising topic, credit policies, applies to both wholesalers and retailers. The discussion in this textbook focuses on credit policies and accounting for retail firms.

FIGURE 7.11

Wholesaler's Sales Journal

FIGURE 7.12

General Ledger Accounts

Credit Policies

The use of credit is considered to be one of the most important factors in the rapid growth of modern economic systems. Sales on credit are made by large numbers of wholesalers and retailers of goods and by many professional people and service businesses. The assumption is that the volume of both sales and profits will increase if buyers are given a period of a month or more to pay for the goods or services they purchase.

However, the increase in profits a business expects when it grants credit will be realized only if each customer completes the transaction by paying for the goods or services purchased. If payment is not received, the expected profits become actual losses and the purpose for granting the credit is defeated. Business firms try to protect against the possibility of such losses by investigating a customer's credit record and ability to pay for purchases before allowing any credit to the customer.

Professional people such as doctors, lawyers, and architects, and owners of small businesses like Maxx-Out Sporting Goods usually make their own decisions about granting credit. Such decisions may be based on personal judgment or on reports available from credit bureaus, information supplied by other creditors, and credit ratings supplied by national firms such as Dun & Bradstreet.

> Equifax, a leader in providing consumer and commercial credit information, was founded in Atlanta in 1899. For the fiscal year ended December 2005, more than 100 years later, the company reported revenues of $1.44 billion.

Larger businesses maintain a credit department to determine the amounts and types of credit that should be granted to customers. In addition to using credit data supplied by institutions, the credit department may obtain financial statements and related reports from customers who have applied for credit. This information is analyzed to help determine the maximum amount of credit that may be granted and suitable credit terms for the customer. Financial statements that have been audited by certified public accountants are used extensively by credit departments.

Even though the credit investigation is thorough, some accounts receivable become uncollectible. Unexpected business developments, errors of judgment, incorrect financial data, and many other causes may lead to defaults in payments by customers. Experienced managers know that some uncollectible accounts are to be expected in normal business operations and that limited losses indicate that a firm's credit policies are sound. Provisions for such limited losses from uncollectible accounts are usually made in budgets and other financial projections.

Each business must develop credit policies that achieve maximum sales with minimum losses from uncollectible accounts:

- A credit policy that is too tight results in a low level of losses at the expense of increases in sales volume.
- A credit policy that is too lenient may result in increased sales volume accompanied by a high level of losses.

Good judgment based on knowledge and experience must be used to achieve a well-balanced credit policy.

Different types of credit have evolved with the growing economy and changing technology. The different types of credit require different accounting treatments.

ACCOUNTING FOR DIFFERENT TYPES OF CREDIT SALES

The most common types of credit sales are

- open-account credit,
- business credit cards,
- bank credit cards,
- cards issued by credit card companies.

Open-Account Credit The form of credit most commonly offered by professional people and small businesses permits the sale of services or goods to the customer with the understanding that the amount is to be paid at a later date. This type of arrangement is called **open-account credit.** It is usually granted on the basis of personal acquaintance or knowledge of the customer. However, formal credit checks may also be used. The amount involved in each transaction is usually small, and payment is expected within 30 days or on receipt of a monthly statement. Open-account sales are also referred to as **charge-account sales.**

Maxx-Out Sporting Goods uses the open-account credit arrangement. Sales transactions are recorded as debits to the *Accounts Receivable* account and credits to the *Sales* account. Collections on account are recorded as debits to the *Cash* account and credits to the *Accounts Receivable* account.

Business Credit Cards Many retail businesses, especially large ones such as department store chains and gasoline companies, provide their own credit cards (sometimes called charge cards) to customers who have established credit. Whenever a sale is completed using a business credit card, a sales slip is prepared in the usual manner. Then the sales slip and the credit card are placed in a mechanical device that prints the customer's name, account number, and other data on all copies of the sales slip. Some companies use computerized card readers and sales registers that print out a sales slip with the customer information and a line for the customer's signature. Many businesses require that the salesclerk contact the credit department by telephone or computer terminal to verify the customer's credit status before completing the transaction.

Business credit card sales are similar to open-account credit sales. A business credit card sale is recorded as

- a debit to *Accounts Receivable,*
- a credit to a revenue account such as *Sales.*

A customer payment is recorded as

- a debit to *Cash,*
- a credit to *Accounts Receivable.*

Bank Credit Cards Retailers can provide credit while minimizing or avoiding the risk of losses from uncollectible accounts by accepting bank credit cards. The most widely accepted bank credit cards are MasterCard and Visa. Many banks participate in one or both of these credit card programs, and other banks have their own credit cards. Bank credit cards are issued to consumers directly by banks.

A business may participate in these credit card programs by meeting the conditions set by the bank. When a sale is made to a cardholder, the business completes a special sales slip such as the one shown in Figure 7.13 on page 209. This form must be imprinted with data from the customer's bank credit card and then signed by the customer. Many businesses continue to complete their regular sales slips for internal control and other purposes.

When a business makes a sale on a bank credit card, it acquires an asset that can be converted into cash immediately without responsibility for later collection from the customer. Periodically (preferably each day) the completed sales slips from bank credit card sales are totaled. The number of sales slips and the total amount of the sales are recorded on a special deposit form, as shown in Figure 7.14.

The deposit form, along with the completed sales slips, is presented to the firm's bank in much the same manner as a cash deposit. Depending on the arrangements that have been made, either the bank will deduct a fee, called a *discount* (usually between 1 and 8 percent), and immediately credit the depositor's checking account with the net amount of the sales, or it will credit the depositor's checking account for the full amount of the sales and then deduct the discount at the end of the month. If the second procedure is used, the total discount for the month will appear on the bank statement.

The bank is responsible for collecting from the cardholder. If any amounts are uncollectible, the bank sustains the loss. For the retailer, bank credit card sales are like cash sales. The

FIGURE 7.13   **Sales Slip for a Bank Credit Card Transaction**

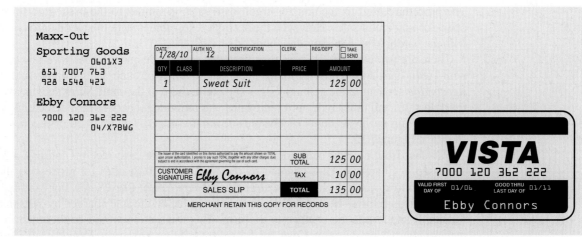

FIGURE 7.14

Deposit Form for Bank Credit Card Sales

accounting procedures for such sales are therefore quite similar to the accounting procedures for cash sales, which will be discussed in Chapter 9. If the business is billed once each month for the bank's discount, the total amount involved in the daily deposit of the credit card sales slips is debited to **Cash** and credited to **Sales.**

Credit Card Companies Credit cards such as American Express and Diners Club are issued by business firms or subsidiaries of business firms that are operated for the special purpose of handling credit card transactions. The potential cardholder must submit an application and pay an annual fee to the credit card company. If the credit references are satisfactory, the credit card is issued. It is normally reissued at one-year intervals so long as the company's credit experience with the cardholder remains satisfactory.

Hotels, restaurants, airline companies, many types of retail stores, and a wide variety of other businesses accept these credit cards. When making sales to cardholders, sellers usually prepare their own sales slip or bill and then complete a special sales slip required by the credit card company. As with the sales slips for bank credit cards, the forms must be imprinted with the identifying data on the customer's card and signed by the customer. Such sales slips are sometimes referred to as *sales invoices, sales drafts,* or *sales vouchers.* The term used varies from one credit card company to another.

The seller acquires an account receivable from the credit card company rather than from the customer. At approximately one-month intervals, the credit card company bills the cardholders for all sales slips it has acquired during the period. It is the responsibility of the credit card company to collect from the cardholders.

ACCOUNTING FOR CREDIT CARD SALES

The procedure used to account for credit card sales is similar to the procedure for recording open-account credit sales. However, the account receivable is with the credit card company, not with the cardholders who buy the goods or services.

There are two basic methods of recording these sales. Businesses that have few transactions with credit card companies normally debit the amounts of such sales to the usual **Accounts Receivable** account in the general ledger and credit them to the same **Sales** account that is used for cash sales and other types of credit sales. An individual account for each credit card company is set up in the accounts receivable subsidiary ledger. This method of recording sales is shown in Figure 7.15.

Payment from a credit card company is recorded in the cash receipts journal, a procedure discussed in Chapter 9. Fees charged by the credit card companies for processing these sales are debited to an account called **Discount Expense on Credit Card Sales.** For example, assume that American Express charges a 7 percent discount fee on the sale charged by Wilson Davis on January 3 and remits the balance to the firm. This transaction would be recorded in the cash receipts journal by debiting **Cash** for $502.20, debiting **Discount Expense on Credit Card Sales** for $37.80, and crediting **Accounts Receivable** for $540.00.

Firms that do a large volume of business with credit card companies may debit all such sales to a special **Accounts Receivable from Credit Card Companies** account in the general ledger, thus separating this type of receivable from the accounts receivable resulting from open-account credit sales. A special account called **Sales—Credit Card Companies** is credited for the revenue from these transactions. Figure 7.16 shows how the necessary entries are made in the sales journal.

FIGURE 7.15

Recording Credit Card Company Sales

SALES JOURNAL   PAGE ___17___

	DATE	SALES SLIP NO.	CUSTOMER'S ACCOUNT DEBITED	POST. REF.	ACCOUNTS RECEIVABLE DEBIT	SALES TAX PAYABLE CREDIT	SALES CREDIT	
1	2010							1
2	Jan. 3	533	American Express		540 00	40 00	500 00	2
3			(Wilson Davis)					3
26	11	651	Master Card		216 00	16 00	200 00	26
27			(Teresa Wells)					27
28								28

FIGURE 7.16   **Recording Sales for Accounts Receivable from Credit Card Companies**

SALES JOURNAL   PAGE ___7___

	DATE	SALES SLIP NO.	CUSTOMER'S ACCOUNT DEBITED	POST. REF.	ACCOUNTS RECEIVABLE DEBIT	ACCT. REC.— CREDIT CARD COMPANIES DEBIT	SALES TAX PAYABLE CREDIT	SALES CREDIT	SALES— CREDIT CARD COMPANIES CREDIT	
1	2010									1
2	Jan. 3		Summary of credit card sales/			9 720 00	720 00		9 000 00	2
3			American Express							3
5										5
16		11	Summary of credit card sales/			5 400 00	400 00		5 000 00	16
17			Master Card							17
29		31	Totals			48 600 00	3 600 00		45 000 00	29
30						(114)	(231)		(404)	30
31										31

Sales Taxes

Many cities and states impose a tax on retail sales. Sales taxes imposed by city and state governments vary. However, the procedures used to account for these taxes are similar.

A sales tax may be levied on all retail sales, but often certain items are exempt. In most cases, the amount of the sales tax is stated separately and then added to the retail price of the merchandise.

> The California State Board of Equalization collects approximately $44.3 billion annually from sales and use tax revenues. These revenues foot the bill for state and local programs, including hospitals, social welfare efforts, transportation, schools, and housing.

The retailer is required to collect sales tax from customers, make periodic (usually monthly) reports to the taxing authority, and pay the taxes due when the reports are filed. The government may allow the retailer to retain part of the tax as compensation for collecting it.

PREPARING THE STATE SALES TAX RETURN

At the end of each month, after the accounts have all been posted, Maxx-Out Sporting Goods prepares the sales tax return. The information required for the monthly return comes from the accounting data of the current month. Three accounts are involved: *Sales Tax Payable, Sales,* and *Sales Returns and Allowances.* In some states, the sales tax return is filed quarterly rather than monthly.

The procedures to file a sales tax return are similar to those used by Maxx-Out Sporting Goods on February 7 when it filed the monthly sales tax return for January with the state tax commissioner. The firm's sales are subject to an 8 percent state sales tax. To highlight the data needed, the January postings are shown in the ledger accounts in Figure 7.17.

>> **9. OBJECTIVE**

Prepare the state sales tax return.

LP7

FIGURE 7.17

Ledger Account Postings for Sales Tax

ACCOUNT __Sales Tax Payable__   ACCOUNT NO. __231__

DATE		DESCRIPTION	POST. REF.	DEBIT	CREDIT	BALANCE DEBIT	BALANCE CREDIT
2010							
Jan.	1	Balance	✓				7 5 6 00
	11		CP1	7 5 6 00			—0—
	23		J1	1 2 00		1 2 00	
	25		J1	3 6 00		4 8 00	
	31		S1		4 5 6 00		4 0 8 00
	31		CR1		1 8 0 0 00		2 2 0 8 00

ACCOUNT __Sales__   ACCOUNT NO. __401__

DATE		DESCRIPTION	POST. REF.	DEBIT	CREDIT	BALANCE DEBIT	BALANCE CREDIT
2010							
Jan.	31		S1		5 7 0 0 00		5 7 0 0 00
	31		CR1		22 5 0 0 00		28 2 0 0 00

ACCOUNT __Sales Returns and Allowances__   ACCOUNT NO. __451__

DATE		DESCRIPTION	POST. REF.	DEBIT	CREDIT	BALANCE DEBIT	BALANCE CREDIT
2010							
Jan.	23		J1	1 5 0 00		1 5 0 00	
	25		J1	4 5 0 00		6 0 0 00	

Using these figures as a basis, the amount of the firm's taxable gross sales for January is determined as follows:

Cash Sales	$22,500
Credit Sales	5,700
Total Sales	$28,200
Less Sales Returns and Allowances	600
Taxable Gross Sales for January	$27,600

<table>
<tr><td colspan="2">THE BOTTOM LINE</td></tr>
<tr><td colspan="2">Retail Sales</td></tr>
<tr><td colspan="2">Income Statement</td></tr>
<tr><td>Revenue</td><td>↑ 27,600</td></tr>
<tr><td>Net Income</td><td>↑ 27,600</td></tr>
<tr><td colspan="2">Balance Sheet</td></tr>
<tr><td>Assets</td><td>↑ 29,808.00</td></tr>
<tr><td>Liabilities</td><td>↑ 2,208.00</td></tr>
<tr><td>Equity</td><td>↑ 27,600.00</td></tr>
</table>

> > The 8 percent sales tax on the gross sales of $27,600 amounts to $2,208.00. Note that the firm's increase in assets (**Cash** and **Accounts Receivable**) is equal to sales revenue plus the sales tax liability on that revenue.

In the state where Maxx-Out Sporting Goods is located, a retailer who files the sales tax return (see Figure 7.18 on page 213) on time and who pays the tax when it is due is entitled to a discount. The discount is intended to compensate the retailer, at least in part, for acting as a collection agent for the government. The discount rate depends on the amount of tax to be paid. For amounts over $1,000, the rate is 1 percent of the total tax due. For Maxx-Out Sporting Goods, the discount for January is determined as follows:

Taxable Gross Sales for January	$27,600.00
8% Sales Tax Rate	× 0.08
Sales Tax Due	$ 2,208.00
1% Discount Rate	× 0.01
Discount	$22.08
Sales Tax Due	$ 2,208.00
Discount	(22.08)
Net Sales Tax Due	$ 2,185.92

The firm sends a check for the net sales tax due with the sales tax return. The accounting entry made to record this payment includes a debit to **Sales Tax Payable** and a credit to **Cash** (for $2,185.92 in this case). After the amount of the payment is posted, the balance in the **Sales Tax Payable** account should be equal to the discount, as shown in Figure 7.19. Slight differences can arise because the tax collected at the time of the sale is determined by a tax bracket method that can give results slightly more or less than the final computations on the tax return.

FIGURE 7.19

Effect of Paying Sales Tax

ACCOUNT _Sales Tax Payable_   ACCOUNT NO. _231_

DATE		DESCRIPTION	POST. REF.	DEBIT	CREDIT	BALANCE DEBIT	BALANCE CREDIT
2010							
Jan.	1	Balance	✓				7 5 6 00
	11		CP1	7 5 6 00			—0—
	23		J1	1 2 00		1 2 00	
	25		J1	3 6 00		4 8 00	
	31		S1		4 5 6 00		4 0 8 00
	31		CR1		1 8 0 0 00		2 2 0 8 00
Feb.	6		CP1	2 1 8 5 92			2 2 08

Tax payment ⟶   Amount of discount ⟶

FIGURE 7.18

State Sales Tax Return

SALES TAX RETURN

ALWAYS REFER TO THIS NUMBER WHEN WRITING THE DIVISION	LICENSE NUMBER
	217539

—IMPORTANT—
ANY CHANGE IN OWNERSHIP REQUIRES A NEW LICENSE: NOTIFY THIS DIVISION IMMEDIATELY.

This return DUE on the 1st day of month following period covered by the return, and becomes DELINQUENT on the 21st day.

37-9462315
FED. E.I. NO. OR S.S NO.

STATE TAX COMMISSION
SALES AND USE TAX DIVISION
DRAWER 20
CAPITAL CITY, STATE 78711
RETURN REQUESTED

January 31, 2010
—Sales for period ending—

MAKE ALL REMITTANCES
PAYABLE TO
STATE TAX COMMISSIOIN
DO NOT SEND CASH
STAMPS NOT ACCEPTED

OWNER'S NAME AND LOCATION

Maxx-Out Sporting Goods
2007 Trendsetter Lane
Dallas, Texas 75268-0967

COMPUTATION OF SALES TAX	For Taxpayer's Use	Do Not Use This Column
1. TOTAL Gross proceeds of sales or Gross Receipts (to include rentals)	27,600.00	
2. Add cost of personal property purchased on a RETAIL LICENSE FOR RESALE but USED BY YOU or YOUR EMPLOYEES, including GIFTS and PREMIUMS	–0–	
3. USE TAX—Add cost of personal property purchased outside of STATE for your use, storage, or consumption	–0–	
4. Total (Lines 1, 2, and 3)	27,600.00	
5. LESS ALLOWABLE DEDUCTIONS (Must be itemized on reverse side)	–0–	
6. Net taxable total (Line 4 minus Line 5)	27,600.00	
7. Sales and Use Tax Due (8% of Line 6)	2,208.00	
8. LESS TAXPAYER'S DISCOUNT—(Deductible only when amount of TAX due is not delinquent at time of payment)	22.08	
IF LINE 7 IS LESS THAN $100.00 —DEDUCT 3% / IF LINE 7 IS $100 BUT LESS THAN $1,000.00 —DEDUCT 2% / IF LINE 7 IS $1,000.00 OR MORE —DEDUCT 1%		
9. NET AMOUNT OF TAX PAYABLE (Line 7 minus Line 8)	2,185.92	
Add the following penalty and interest if return or remittance is late. 10. Specific Penalty: 25% of tax _ _ _ _ _ _ _ _ _ _ _ _ _ _ _ _ _ _ _ $ _____ 11. Interest: 1/2 of 1% per month from due date until paid. $ _____ TOTAL PENALTY AND INTEREST		
12. TOTAL TAX, PENALTY AND INTEREST	2,185.92	
13. Subtract credit memo No.		
14. TOTAL AMOUNT DUE (IF NO SALES MADE SO STATE)	2,185.92	

I certify that this return, including the accompanying schedules or statements, has been examined by me and to the best of my knowledge and belief, a true and complete return, made in good faith, for the period stated, pursuant to the provisions of the Code of Laws, 20–, and Acts Amendatory Thereto.

URGENT—SEE THAT LICENSE NUMBER IS ON RETURN

Max Ferraro
SIGNATURE

Owner	February 7, 2010
Owner, partner or title	Date

Return must be signed by owner or if corporation, authorized person.

Division Use Only

If there is a balance in the *Sales Tax Payable* account after the sales tax liability is satisfied, the balance is transferred to an account called *Miscellaneous Income* by a general journal entry. This entry consists of a debit to *Sales Tax Payable* and a credit to *Miscellaneous Income*.

RECORDING SALES TAX IN THE SALES ACCOUNT

In some states, retailers can credit the entire sales price plus tax to the *Sales* account. At the end of each month or quarter, they must remove from the *Sales* account the amount of tax included and transfer that amount to the *Sales Tax Payable* account. Assume that during January a retailer whose sales are all taxable sells merchandise for a total price of $20,250, which includes an 8 percent tax. The entry to record these sales is summarized in general journal form shown here.

GENERAL JOURNAL PAGE 4

	DATE		DESCRIPTION	POST. REF.	DEBIT	CREDIT	
1	2010						1
2	Jan.	31	Accounts Receivable	111	20 2 5 0 00		2
3			Sales	401		20 2 5 0 00	3
4			To record total sales and				4
5			sales tax collected during				5
6			the month				6
7							7

At the end of the month, the retailer must transfer the sales tax from the *Sales* account to the *Sales Tax Payable* account. The first step in the transfer process is to determine the amount of tax involved. The sales tax payable is computed as follows.

MANAGERIAL IMPLICATIONS

CREDIT SALES

■ Credit sales are a major source of revenue in many businesses, and accounts receivable represent a major asset.

■ Management needs up-to-date and correct information about both sales and accounts receivable in order to monitor the financial health of the firm.

■ Special journals save time and effort and reduce the cost of accounting work.

■ In a retail firm that must handle sales tax, the sales journal and the cash receipts journal provide a convenient method of recording the amounts owed for sales tax.

  ■ When the data is posted to the Sales Tax Payable account in the general ledger, the firm has a complete and systematic record that speeds the completion of the periodic sales tax return.

  ■ The firm has detailed proof of its sales tax figures in the case of a tax audit.

■ An accounts receivable subsidiary ledger provides management and the credit department with up-to-date information about the balances owed by all customers.

  ■ This information is useful in controlling credit and collections.

  ■ Detailed information helps in evaluating the effectiveness of credit policies.

  ■ Management must keep a close watch on the promptness of customer payments because much of the cash needed for day-to-day operations usually comes from payments on accounts receivable.

■ A well-balanced credit policy helps increase sales volume but also keeps losses from uncollectible accounts at an acceptable level.

■ Retailers are liable for any undercollection of sales taxes. This situation can be avoided with an efficient control system.

THINKING CRITICALLY

What are some possible consequences of out-of-date accounts receivable records?

Sales + tax	= $20,250
100% of sales + 8% of sales	= $20,250
108% of sales	= $20,250
Sales	= $20,250/1.08
Sales	= $18,750
Tax	= $18,750 × 0.08 = $1,500

The firm then makes the following entry to transfer the liability from the *Sales* account.

		GENERAL JOURNAL			PAGE ___4___	
	DATE	DESCRIPTION	POST. REF.	DEBIT	CREDIT	
1	2010					1
8	Jan. 31	Sales	401	1 5 0 0 00		8
9		Sales Tax Payable	231		1 5 0 0 00	9
10		To transfer sales tax				10
11		payable from the Sales				11
12		account to the liability				12
13		account				13
14						14
15						15

The retailer in this example originally recorded the entire sales price plus tax in the *Sales* account. The sales tax was transferred to the *Sales Tax Payable* account at the end of the month.

Section 3 Self Review

QUESTIONS

1. What account is used to record sales tax owed by a business to a city or state?

2. What is the difference between list price and net price?

3. What are four types of credit sales?

EXERCISES

4. A company that buys $4,000 of goods from a wholesaler offering trade discounts of 20 and 10 percent will pay what amount for the goods?

a. $1,760
b. $2,800
c. $2,880
d. $2,780

5. If a wholesale business offers a trade discount of 35 percent on a sale of $3,600, what is the amount of the discount?

a. $120
b. $126
c. $1,200
d. $1,260

ANALYSIS

6. What factors would you consider in deciding whether or not to extend credit to a customer?

(Answers to Section 3 Self Review are on page 234.)

7 Chapter REVIEW   Chapter Summary

The nature of the operations of a business, the volume of its transactions, and other factors influence the design of an accounting system. In this chapter, you have learned about the use of special journals and subsidiary ledgers suitable for a merchandising business. These additional journals and ledgers increase the efficiency of recording credit transactions and permit the division of labor.

Learning Objectives

1 Record credit sales in a sales journal.

The sales journal is used to record credit sales transactions, usually on a daily basis. For sales transactions that include sales tax, the sales tax liability is recorded at the time of the sale to ensure that company records reflect the appropriate amount of sales tax liability.

2 Post from the sales journal to the general ledger accounts.

At the end of each month, the sales journal is totaled, proved, and ruled. Column totals are then posted to the general ledger. Using a sales journal rather than a general journal to record sales saves the time and effort of posting individual entries to the general ledger during the month.

3 Post from the sales journal to the customers' accounts in the accounts receivable subsidiary ledger.

The accounts of individual credit customers are kept in a subsidiary ledger called the accounts receivable ledger. Daily postings are made to this ledger from the sales journal, the cash receipts journal, and the general journal or the sales returns and allowances journal. The current balance of a customer's account is computed after each posting so that the amount owed is known at all times.

4 Record sales returns and allowances in the general journal.

Sales returns and allowances are usually debited to a contra revenue account. A firm with relatively few sales returns and allowances could use the general journal to record these transactions.

5 Post sales returns and allowances.

Sales returns and allowances transactions must be posted to the general ledger and to the appropriate accounts receivable subsidiary ledgers. The balance of the *Sales Returns and Allowances* account is subtracted from the balance of the *Sales* account to show net sales on the income statement.

6 Prepare a schedule of accounts receivable.

Each month a schedule of accounts receivable is prepared. It is used to prove the subsidiary ledger against the *Accounts Receivable* account. It also reports the amounts due from credit customers.

7 Compute trade discounts.

Wholesale businesses often offer goods to trade customers at less than retail prices. Trade discounts are expressed as a percentage off the list price. Multiply the list price by the percentage trade discount offered to compute the dollar amount.

8 Record credit card sales in appropriate journals.

Credit sales are common, and different credit arrangements are used. Businesses that have few transactions with credit card companies normally record these transactions in the sales journal by debiting the usual *Accounts Receivable* account in the general ledger and crediting the same *Sales* account that is used for cash sales.

9 Prepare the state sales tax return.

In states and cities that have a sales tax, the retailer must prepare a sales tax return and send the total tax collected to the taxing authority.

10 Define the accounting terms new to this chapter.

Glossary

Accounts receivable ledger (p. 197) A subsidiary ledger that contains credit customer accounts

Charge-account sales (p. 208) Sales made through the use of open-account credit or one of various types of credit cards

Contra revenue account (p. 199) An account with a debit balance, which is contrary to the normal balance for a revenue account

Control account (p. 203) An account that links a subsidiary ledger and the general ledger since its balance summarizes the balances of the accounts in the subsidiary ledger

Credit memorandum (p. 198) A note verifying that a customer's account is being reduced by the amount of a sales return or sales allowance plus any sales tax that may have been involved

Invoice (p. 206) A customer billing for merchandise bought on credit

List price (p. 205) An established retail price

Manufacturing business (p. 190) A business that sells goods that it has produced

Merchandise inventory (p. 190) The stock of goods a merchandising business keeps on hand

Merchandising business (p. 190) A business that sells goods purchased for resale

Net price (p. 205) The list price less all trade discounts

Net sales (p. 201) The difference between the balance in the **Sales** account and the balance in the **Sales Returns and Allowances** account

Open-account credit (p. 208) A system that allows the sale of services or goods with the understanding that payment will be made at a later date

Retail business (p. 190) A business that sells directly to individual consumers

Sales allowance (p. 198) A reduction in the price originally charged to customers for goods or services

Sales journal (p. 190) A special journal used to record sales of merchandise on credit

Sales return (p. 198) A firm's acceptance of a return of goods from a customer

Schedule of accounts receivable (p. 203) A listing of all balances of the accounts in the accounts receivable subsidiary ledger

Service business (p. 190) A business that sells services

Special journal (p. 190) A journal used to record only one type of transaction

Subsidiary ledger (p. 190) A ledger dedicated to accounts of a single type and showing details to support a general ledger account

Trade discount (p. 205) A reduction from list price

Wholesale business (p. 205) A business that manufactures or distributes goods to retail businesses or large consumers such as hotels and hospitals

Comprehensive **Self Review**

1. Name the two different time periods usually covered in sales tax returns.
2. What is a control account?
3. Why does a small merchandising business usually need a more complex set of financial records and statements than a small service business?
4. Why is it useful for a firm to have an accounts receivable ledger?
5. Explain how service, merchandising, and manufacturing businesses differ from each other.

(Answers to Comprehensive Self Review are on page 234.)

Multiple choice questions are provided on the text Web site at www.mhhe.com/price12e

Quiz7

Discussion Questions

1. How do retail and wholesale businesses differ?
2. What purposes does the schedule of accounts receivable serve?
3. How are the net sales for an accounting period determined?

4. Why is a sales return or allowance usually recorded in a special *Sales Returns and Allowances* account rather than being debited to the *Sales* account?

5. What kind of account is *Sales Returns and Allowances?*

6. How is a multicolumn special journal proved at the end of each month?

7. The sales tax on a credit sale is not collected from the customer immediately. When is this tax usually entered in a firm's accounting records? What account is used to record this tax?

8. In a particular state, the sales tax rate is 5 percent of sales. The retailer is allowed to record both the selling price and the tax in the same account. Explain how to compute the sales tax due when this method is used.

9. What two methods are commonly used to record sales involving credit cards issued by credit card companies?

10. What procedure does a business use to collect amounts owed to it for sales on credit cards issued by credit card companies?

11. When a firm makes a sale involving a credit card issued by a credit card company, does the firm have an account receivable with the cardholder or with the credit card company?

12. What is the discount on credit card sales? What type of account is used to record this item?

13. Why are bank credit card sales similar to cash sales for a business?

14. What is open-account credit?

15. What is a trade discount? Why do some firms offer trade discounts to their customers?

APPLICATIONS

Exercises

Exercise 7.1
Objective 1

► **Identifying the journal to record transactions.**

The accounting system of Dave's Wildlife Resort includes the journals listed below. Indicate the specific journal in which each of the transactions listed below would be recorded.

JOURNALS

Cash receipts journal   Sales journal   Purchases journal
Cash payments journal   General journal

DATE	TRANSACTIONS
May 1	Sold merchandise on credit.
2	Accepted a return of merchandise from a credit customer.
3	Sold merchandise for cash.
4	Purchased merchandise on credit.
5	Gave a $400 allowance for damaged merchandise.
6	Collected sums on account from credit customers.
7	Received an additional cash investment from the owner.
8	Issued a check to pay a creditor on account.

Identifying the accounts used to record sales and related transactions.

◀ Exercise 7.2
Objective 1

The transactions below took place at Juan's Sporting Goods, a retail business that sells outdoor clothing and camping equipment. Indicate the numbers of the general ledger accounts that would be debited and credited to record each transaction.

GENERAL LEDGER ACCOUNTS

101	Cash	401	Sales
111	Accounts Receivable	451	Sales Returns and Allowances
231	Sales Tax Payable		

DATE	TRANSACTIONS
May 1	Sold merchandise on credit; the transaction involved sales tax.
2	Received checks from credit customers on account.
3	Accepted a return of merchandise from a credit customer; the original sale involved sales tax.
4	Sold merchandise for cash; the transaction involved sales tax.
5	Gave an allowance to a credit customer for damaged merchandise; the original sale involved sales tax.
6	Provided a cash refund to a customer who returned merchandise; the original sale was made for cash and involved sales tax.

Recording credit sales.

◀ Exercise 7.3
Objective 2
CONTINUING >>>
Problem

The following transactions took place at Juan's Sporting Goods, during May. Indicate how these transactions would be entered in a sales journal like the one shown in Figure 7.2.

DATE	TRANSACTIONS
May 1	Sold a tent and other items on credit to Roy Anderson; issued Sales Slip 1101 for $354 plus sales tax of $25.
2	Sold a backpack, an air mattress, and other items to John Amos; issued Sales Slip 1102 for $254 plus sales tax of $18.
3	Sold a lantern, cooking utensils, and other items to Teresa Wells; issued Sales Slip 1103 for $293 plus sales tax of $21.

Recording sales returns and allowances.

◀ Exercise 7.4
Objective 2

Record the general journal entries for the following transactions of The Mattress Center that occurred in June.

DATE	TRANSACTIONS
June 7	Accepted a return of damaged merchandise from Deborah Westgate, a credit customer; issued Credit Memorandum 301 for $324, which includes sales tax of $24; the original sale was made on Sales Slip 1610 of May 31.
22	Gave an allowance to Brian Barnett, a credit customer, for merchandise that was slightly damaged but usable; issued Credit Memorandum 121 for $486, which includes sales tax of $36; the original sale was made on Sales Slip 1663 of June 17.

Exercise 7.5

Objective 2

▶ **Posting from the sales journal.**

The sales journal for Carrington Company is shown below. Describe how the amounts would be posted to the general ledger accounts.

	DATE	SALES SLIP NO.	CUSTOMER'S ACCOUNT DEBITED	POST. REF.	ACCOUNTS RECEIVABLE DEBIT	SALES TAX PAYABLE CREDIT	SALES CREDIT	
1	2010							1
2	July 2	1101	Scott Cohen		540 00	40 00	500 00	2
3	7	1102	Julia Hoang		864 00	64 00	800 00	3
11	31	1110	Barbara Baxter		324 00	24 00	300 00	11
12	31		Totals		6 480 00	480 00	6 000 00	12
13					(111)	(231)	(401)	13
14								14

SALES JOURNAL   PAGE 1

Exercise 7.6

Objective 7

▶ **Computing a trade discount.**

The Wood Warehouse Wholesale Company made sales using the following list prices and trade discounts. What amount will be recorded for each sale in the sales journal?

1. List price of $500 and trade discount of 40 percent
2. List price of $790 and trade discount of 40 percent
3. List price of $130 and trade discount of 20 percent

Exercise 7.7

Objective 7

▶ **Computing a series of trade discounts.**

Patio Dudes, a wholesale firm, made sales using the following list prices and trade discounts. What amount will be recorded for each sale in the sales journal?

1. List price of $3,340 and trade discounts of 30 and 10 percent
2. List price of $4,720 and trade discounts of 30 and 10 percent
3. List price of $1,120 and trade discounts of 20 and 10 percent

Exercise 7.8

Objective 9

▶ **Computing the sales tax due and recording its payment.**

The balances of certain accounts of Carter Corporation on April 30, 2010, were as follows:

Sales	$228,000
Sales Returns and Allowances	$ 2,600

The firm's net sales are subject to a 5 percent sales tax. Prepare the general journal entry to record payment of the sales tax payable on April 30, 2010.

Exercise 7.9

Objective 6

▶ **Preparing a schedule of accounts receivable.**

The accounts receivable ledger for The Jean Barn follows on page 221.

1. Prepare a schedule of accounts receivable as of January 31, 2010.
2. What should the balance in the *Accounts Receivable* (control) account be?

Exercise 7.10

Objective 5

▶ **Posting sales returns and allowances.**

Post the journal entries below to the appropriate ledger accounts. Assume the following account balances as of March 1, 2010:

Accounts Receivable (control account)	$1,188
Accounts Receivable—Cara Fountain	540
Accounts Receivable—Sadie Palmer	648

NAME Cheryl Amos
ADDRESS 917 Broadway, New York, NY 10018

DATE		DESCRIPTION	POST. REF.	DEBIT	CREDIT	BALANCE
2010						
Jan.	1	Balance	✓			1 5 7 5 00
	2	Sales Slip 1801	S1	5 4 0 00		2 1 1 5 00

NAME Edward Cooke
ADDRESS 2022 5th Avenue, New York, NY 10018

DATE		DESCRIPTION	POST. REF.	DEBIT	CREDIT	BALANCE
2010						
Jan.	1	Balance	✓			3 7 8 00
	27	Sales Slip 1824	S1	1 8 9 00		5 6 7 00
	31		CR1		2 8 4 00	2 8 3 00

NAME Neal Fitzgerald
ADDRESS 98 Houston Street, New York, NY 10018

DATE		DESCRIPTION	POST. REF.	DEBIT	CREDIT	BALANCE
2010						
Jan.	1	Balance	✓			3 2 4 00
	15	Sales Slip 1812	CR1		3 2 4 00	—0—
	31		S1	7 5 6 00		7 5 6 00

NAME David Pifer
ADDRESS 5063 Park Avenue, New York, NY 10019

DATE		DESCRIPTION	POST. REF.	DEBIT	CREDIT	BALANCE
2010						
Jan.	1	Balance	✓			6 4 8 00
	20	Sales Slip 1819	S1	2 1 6 00		8 6 4 00
	21		CR1		4 5 0 00	4 1 4 00
	22	Sales Slip 1822	S1	8 1 0 00		1 2 2 4 00

NAME Lisa Stanton
ADDRESS 2111 West 32nd Street, New York, NY 10019

DATE		DESCRIPTION	POST. REF.	DEBIT	CREDIT	BALANCE
2010						
Jan.	1	Balance	✓			4 8 6 00
	31	Sales Slip 1840	S1	2 2 1 4 00		2 7 0 0 00

NAME Nikki Whitaker
ADDRESS 721 Lexington Avenue, New York, NY 10027

DATE		DESCRIPTION	POST. REF.	DEBIT	CREDIT	BALANCE
2010						
Jan.	1	Balance	✓			2 3 7 6 00
	12		CR1		1 1 8 8 00	1 1 8 8 00
	17	Sales Slip 1817	S1	8 6 4 00		2 0 5 2 00

		GENERAL JOURNAL				PAGE __42__		
	DATE	DESCRIPTION	POST. REF.	DEBIT		CREDIT		
1	2010							1
2	Mar. 14	Sales Returns and Allowances		3 0 0 00				2
3		Sales Tax Payable		2 4 00				3
4		Accounts Rec.—Cara Fountain				3 2 4 00		4
5		Accepted return on defective						5
6		merchandise, Credit Memo						6
7		101; original sale of Feb. 23,						7
8		Sales Slip 1101						8
9								9
10	22	Sales Returns and Allowances		1 0 0 00				10
11		Sales Tax Payable		8 00				11
12		Accounts Rec.—Sadie Palmer				1 0 8 00		12
13		Gave allowance for damaged						13
14		merchandise, Credit Memo						14
15		102; original sale Mar. 15,						15
16		Sales Slip 1150						16

PROBLEMS

Problem Set A

Problem 7.1A

Objectives 1, 2

► **Recording credit sales and posting from the sales journal.**

The Tri-County Appliance Emporium is a retail store that sells household appliances. The firm's credit sales for July are listed below, along with the general ledger accounts used to record these sales. The balance shown for *Accounts Receivable* is for the beginning of the month.

DATE	TRANSACTIONS
July 1	Sold a dishwasher to Bonnie Franklin; issued Sales Slip 501 for $850 plus sales tax of $68.
6	Sold a washer to Janet Judge; issued Sales Slip 502 for $2,625 plus sales tax of $210.
11	Sold a high-definition television set to Raymond Clay; issued Sales Slip 503 for $2,600 plus sales tax of $208.
17	Sold an electric dryer to Melissa Gray; issued Sales Slip 504 for $900 plus sales tax of $72.
23	Sold a trash compactor to Angela Nguyen; issued Sales Slip 505 for $500 plus sales tax of $40.
27	Sold a color television set to Clifton Wallace; issued Sales Slip 506 for $1,600 plus sales tax of $128.
29	Sold an electric range to Sally Wei; issued Sales Slip 507 for $1,300 plus sales tax of $104.
31	Sold a double oven to Ken Holt; issued Sales Slip 508 for $400 plus sales tax of $32.

INSTRUCTIONS

1. Open the general ledger accounts and enter the balance of *Accounts Receivable* for July 1, 2010.

2. Record the transactions in a sales journal like the one shown in Figure 7.4. Use 8 as the journal page number.

3. Total, prove, and rule the sales journal as of July 31.

4. Post the column totals from the sales journal to the proper general ledger accounts.

GENERAL LEDGER ACCOUNTS

111	Accounts Receivable, $31,400 Dr.
231	Sales Tax Payable
401	Sales

Analyze: What percentage of credit sales were for entertainment items?

Journalizing, posting, and reporting sales transactions.

◀ Problem 7.2A
Objectives 1, 2, 4

Spectra Furniture specializes in modern living room and dining room furniture. Merchandise sales are subject to an 8 percent sales tax. The firm's credit sales and sales returns and allowances for February 2010 are reflected below, along with the general ledger accounts used to record these transactions. The balances shown are for the beginning of the month.

DATE	TRANSACTIONS
Feb. 1	Sold a living room sofa to Julia Cheng; issued Sales Slip 1615 for $3,250 plus sales tax of $260.
5	Sold three recliners to Denise dela Hoya; issued Sales Slip 1616 for $2,100 plus sales tax of $168.
9	Sold a dining room set to Suzanne Tuttle; issued Sales Slip 1617 for $5,500 plus sales tax of $440.
11	Accepted a return of one damaged recliner from Denise dela Hoya that was originally sold on Sales Slip 1616 of February 5; issued Credit Memorandum 702 for $756.00, which includes sales tax of $56.00.
17	Sold living room tables and bookcases to Joan Clay; issued Sales Slip 1618 for $5,400 plus sales tax of $432.
23	Sold eight dining room chairs to Thomas Muir; issued Sales Slip 1619 for $3,400 plus sales tax of $272.
25	Gave Joan Clay an allowance for scratches on her bookcases; issued Credit Memorandum 703 for $432, which includes sales taxes of $32; the bookcases were originally sold on Sales Slip 1618 of February 17.
27	Sold a living room sofa and four chairs to Bernard Slaughter; issued Sales Slip 1620 for $3,975 plus sales tax of $318.
28	Sold a dining room table to Connie Taylor; issued Sales Slip 1621 for $1,800 plus sales tax of $144.
28	Sold a living room modular wall unit to James Walker; issued Sales Slip 1622 for $3,650 plus sales tax of $292.

INSTRUCTIONS

1. Open the general ledger accounts and enter the balances for February 1.

2. Record the transactions in a sales journal and in a general journal. Use 8 as the page number for the sales journal and 24 as the page number for the general journal.

3. Post the entries from the general journal to the general ledger.

4. Total, prove, and rule the sales journal as of February 28.

5. Post the column totals from the sales journal.

6. Prepare the heading and the Revenue section of the firm's income statement for the month ended February 28, 2010.

GENERAL LEDGER ACCOUNTS

111 Accounts Receivable, $15,636 Dr.
231 Sales Tax Payable, $7,170 Cr.
401 Sales
451 Sales Returns and Allowances

Analyze: Based on the beginning balance of the *Sales Tax Payable* account, what was the amount of net sales for January? (Hint: Sales tax returns are filed and paid to the state quarterly.)

Problem 7.3A
Objectives
1, 2, 3, 4, 6

▶ **Recording sales transactions, posting to the accounts receivable ledger, and preparing a schedule of accounts receivable.**

The Dining Elegance China Shop sells china, glassware, and other gift items that are subject to an 8 percent sales tax. The shop uses a general journal and a sales journal similar to those illustrated in this chapter.

DATE	TRANSACTIONS
Nov. 1	Sold china to Pauline Judge; issued Sales Slip 1001 for $1,500 plus $120 sales tax.
5	Sold a brass serving tray to Janet Hutchison; issued Sales Slip 1002 for $2,100 plus $168 sales tax.
6	Sold a vase to Charles Brown; issued Sales Slip 1003 for $700 plus $56 sales tax.
10	Sold a punch bowl and glasses to Lisa Morgan; issued Sales Slip 1004 for $1,700 plus $136 sales tax.
14	Sold a set of serving bowls to Dorothy Watts; issued Sales Slip 1005 for $550 plus $44 sales tax.
17	Gave Lisa Morgan an allowance because of a broken glass discovered when unpacking the punch bowl and glasses sold on November 10, Sales Slip 1004; issued Credit Memorandum 102 for $162.00, which includes sales tax of $12.
21	Sold a coffee table to Winnie Wu; issued Sales Slip 1006 for $3,200 plus $256 sales tax.
24	Sold sterling silver teaspoons to Henry Okafor; issued Sales Slip 1007 for $600 plus $48 sales tax.
25	Gave Winnie Wu an allowance for scratches on his coffee table sold on November 21, Sales Slip 1006; issued Credit Memorandum 103 for $378, which includes $28 in sales tax.
30	Sold a clock to Euline Brock; issued Sales Slip 1008 for $3,800 plus $304 sales tax.

INSTRUCTIONS

1. Record the transactions for November in the proper journal. Use 6 as the page number for the sales journal and 16 as the page number for the general journal.
2. Immediately after recording each transaction, post to the accounts receivable ledger.
3. Post the amounts from the general journal daily. Post the sales journal amount as a total at the end of the month.
4. Prepare a schedule of accounts receivable. Compare the balance of the *Accounts Receivable* control account with the total of the schedule.

Analyze: Which customer has the highest balance owed at November 30, 2010?

Recording sales transactions, posting to the accounts receivable ledger, and preparing a schedule of accounts receivable.

◀ **Problem 7.4A**

**Objectives
1, 2, 3, 4, 6**

Special Occasions Flower Shop is a wholesale shop that sells flowers, plants, and plant supplies. The transactions shown below took place during January.

DATE	TRANSACTIONS
Jan. 3	Sold a floral arrangement to Thomas Florist; issued Invoice 1081 for $500.
8	Sold potted plants to Carter Garden Supply; issued Invoice 1082 for $775.
9	Sold floral arrangements to Thomasville Flower Shop; issued Invoice 1083 for $462.
10	Sold corsages to Moore's Flower Shop; issued Invoice 1084 for $530.
15	Gave Thomasville Flower Shop an allowance because of withered blossoms discovered in one of the floral arrangements sold on Invoice 1083 on January 9; issued Credit Memorandum 101 for $50.
20	Sold table arrangements to Cedar Hill Floral Shop; issued Invoice 1085 for $480.
22	Sold plants to Applegate Nursery; issued Invoice 1086 for $680.
25	Sold roses to Moore's Flower Shop; issued Invoice 1087 for $427.
27	Sold several floral arrangements to Thomas Florist; issued Invoice 1088 for $925.
31	Gave Thomas Florist an allowance because of withered blossoms discovered in one of the floral arrangements sold on Invoice 1088 on January 27; issued Credit Memorandum 102 for $150.

INSTRUCTIONS

1. Record the transactions in the proper journal. Use 7 as the page number for the sales journal and 11 as the page number for the general journal.

2. Immediately after recording each transaction, post to the accounts receivable ledger.

3. Post the amounts from the general journal daily. Post the sales journal amount as a total at the end of the month.

4. Prepare a schedule of accounts receivable. Compare the balance of the *Accounts Receivable* control account with the total of the schedule.

Analyze: Damaged goods decreased the net sales by what dollar amount? By what percentage amount?

Problem Set B

Recording credit sales and posting from the sales journal.

◀ **Problem 7.1B**

Objectives 1, 2

Discount Appliance Center is a retail store that sells household appliances. The firm's credit sales for June are listed below, along with the general ledger accounts used to record these sales. The balance shown for Accounts Receivable is for the beginning of the month.

INSTRUCTIONS

1. Open the general ledger accounts and enter the balance of *Accounts Receivable* for June 1.

2. Record the transactions in a sales journal like the one shown in Figure 7.4. Use 8 as the journal page number.

3. Total, prove, and rule the sales journal as of June 30.

4. Post the column totals from the sales journal to the proper general ledger accounts.

DATE	TRANSACTIONS
June 1	Sold a dishwasher to Barbara Merino; issued Sales Slip 201 for $750 plus sales tax of $60.
6	Sold a washer to David Reed; issued Sales Slip 202 for $1,050 plus sales tax of $84.
11	Sold a high-definition television set to Brenda Davis; issued Sales Slip 203 for $2,600 plus sales tax of $208.
17	Sold an electric dryer to Beatrice Wilson; issued Sales Slip 204 for $900 plus sales tax of $72.
23	Sold a trash compactor to Doris Lazo; issued Sales Slip 205 for $500 plus sales tax of $40.
27	Sold a portable color television set to Carol West; issued Sales Slip 206 for $1,200 plus sales tax of $96.
29	Sold an electric range to Rickey Eddie; issued Sales Slip 207 for $1,500 plus sales tax of $120.
30	Sold a microwave oven to Bridgette Nelson; issued Sales Slip 208 for $600 plus sales tax of $48.

GENERAL LEDGER ACCOUNTS

111   Accounts Receivable, $72,800 Dr.

231   Sales Tax Payable

401   Sales

Analyze: What percentage of credit sales were for entertainment items?

Problem 7.2B ▶   **Journalizing, posting, and reporting sales transactions.**

**Objectives
1, 2, 4**

Super Furniture Mart is a retail store that specializes in modern living room and dining room furniture. Merchandise sales are subject to an 8 percent sales tax. The firm's credit sales and sales returns and allowances for June are reflected below, along with the general ledger accounts used to record these transactions. The balances shown are for the beginning of the month.

INSTRUCTIONS

1. Open the general ledger accounts and enter the balances for June 1.

2. Record the transactions in a sales journal and a general journal. Use 9 as the page number for the sales journal and 26 as the page number for the general journal.

3. Post the entries from the general journal to the general ledger.

4. Total, prove, and rule the sales journal as of June 30.

5. Post the column totals from the sales journal.

6. Prepare the heading and the Revenue section of the firm's income statement for the month ended June 30, 2010.

GENERAL LEDGER ACCOUNTS

111   Accounts Receivable, $22,576 Dr.

231   Sales Tax Payable, $4,515 Cr.

401   Sales

451   Sales Returns and Allowances

DATE	TRANSACTIONS
June 1	Sold a living room sofa to Christine Berry; issued Sales Slip 1601 for $2,050 plus sales tax of $164.
5	Sold three recliners to Paula Adams; issued Sales Slip 1602 for $1,300 plus sales tax of $104.
9	Sold a dining room set to Patrick Chen; issued Sales Slip 1603 for $7,000 plus sales tax of $560.
11	Accepted a return of a damaged chair from Paula Adams; the chair was originally sold on Sales Slip 1602 of June 5; issued Credit Memorandum 215 for $432, which includes sales tax of $32.
17	Sold living room tables and bookcases to Raul Alvarez; issued Sales Slip 1604 for $4,000 plus sales tax of $320.
23	Sold eight dining room chairs to Kenitra Brown; issued Sales Slip 1605 for $3,800 plus sales tax of $304.
25	Gave Raul Alvarez an allowance for scratches on his bookcases; issued Credit Memorandum 216 for $270, which includes sales taxes of $20; the bookcases were originally sold on Sales Slip 1604 of June 17.
27	Sold a living room sofa and four chairs to Charles Brown; issued Sales Slip 1606 for $3,600 plus sales tax of $288.
29	Sold a dining room table to Rosetta London; issued Sales Slip 1607 for $1,250 plus sales tax of $100.
30	Sold a living room modular wall unit to James Howard; issued Sales Slip 1608 for $3,100 plus sales tax of $248.

Analyze: Based on the beginning balance of the *Sales Tax Payable* account, what was the amount of total net sales for April and May? (Hint: Sales tax returns are filed and paid to the state quarterly.)

Recording sales transactions, posting to the accounts receivable ledger, and preparing a schedule of accounts receivable.

◀ Problem 7.3B
Objectives
1, 2, 3, 4, 6

Special Elegance Gift Shop sells cards, supplies, and various holiday gift items. All sales are subject to a sales tax of 8 percent. The shop uses a sales journal and general journal.

DATE	TRANSACTIONS
Feb. 3	Sold Ronald Brown a box of holiday greeting cards for $50 plus sales tax of $4 on Sales Slip 201.
4	Sold to Ken Hamlett a Valentine's Day party pack for $200 plus sales tax of $16 on Sales Slip 202.
5	Vickie Neal bought 10 boxes of Valentine's Day gift packs for her office. Sales Slip 203 was issued for $300 plus sales tax of $24.
8	Sold Amy Peloza a set of crystal glasses for $400 plus sales tax of $32 on Sales Slip 204.
9	Luther Evans purchased two statues for $400 plus $32 sales tax on Sales Slip 205.
9	Gave Vickie Neal an allowance because of incomplete items in two gift packs; issued Credit Memorandum 101 for $54, which includes sales tax of $4.
10	Sold Gordon Edwards a Valentine Birthday package for $150 plus $12 sales tax on Sales Slip 206.

DATE	7.3B (cont.) TRANSACTIONS
Feb. 13	Gave Amy Peloza an allowance of $50 because of two broken glasses in the set she purchased on February 8. Credit Memorandum 102 was issued for the allowance plus sales tax of $4.
14	Sold Ronald Brown 12 boxes of gift candy for $200 plus sales tax of $16 on Sales Slip 207.
15	Sold a punch serving set with glasses for $300 to Kerry Goree. Sales tax of $24 was included on Sales Slip 208.
20	Sold Ned Jones a box of holiday greeting cards for $100 plus sales tax of $8 on Sales Slip 209.
22	Sold Susan Anderson a set of crystal glasses for $500 plus sales tax of $40 on Sales Slip 210.
28	Melissa Thomas purchased three statues for $600 plus $48 sales tax on Sales Slip 211.

INSTRUCTIONS

1. Record the credit sale transactions for February in the proper journal. Use 6 as the page number for the sales journal and 16 as the page number for the general journal.

2. Immediately after recording each transaction, post to the accounts receivable ledger.

3. Post the entries to the appropriate accounts.

4. Prepare a schedule of accounts receivable and compare the balance due with the amount shown in the *Accounts Receivable* control account.

Analyze: How many postings were made to the general ledger?

Problem 7.4B
Objectives
1, 2, 3, 4, 6

▶ **Recording sales transactions, posting to the accounts receivable ledger, and preparing a schedule of accounts receivable.**

The Vintage Nursery is a wholesale shop that sells flowers, plants, and plant supplies. The transactions shown below took place during February.

DATE	TRANSACTIONS
Feb. 3	Sold a floral arrangement to Thompson Funeral Home; issued Invoice 2201 for $400.
8	Sold potted plants to Meadows Nursery; issued Invoice 2202 for $800.
9	Sold floral arrangements to DeSoto Flower Shop; issued Invoice 2203 for $1,050.
10	Sold corsages to Lovelace Nursery; issued Invoice 2204 for $700.
15	Gave DeSoto Flower Shop an allowance because of withered blossoms discovered in one of the floral arrangements sold on Invoice 2203 on February 9; issued Credit Memorandum 105 for $100.
20	Sold table arrangements to Lovelace Nursery; issued Invoice 2205 for $650.
22	Sold plants to Southwest Nursery; issued Invoice 2206 for $850.
25	Sold roses to Denton Flower Shop; issued Invoice 2207 for $450.
27	Sold several floral arrangements to Thompson Funeral Home; issued Invoice 2208 for $750.
28	Gave Thompson Funeral Home an allowance because of withered blossoms discovered in one of the floral arrangements sold on Invoice 2208 on February 27; issued Credit Memorandum 106 for $75.

INSTRUCTIONS

1. Record the transactions in the proper journal. Use 5 as the page number for the sales journal and 10 as the page number for the general journal.

2. Immediately after recording each transaction, post to the accounts receivable ledger.

3. Post the amounts from the general journal daily. Post the sales journal amount as a total at the end of the month.

4. Prepare a schedule of accounts receivable. Compare the balance of the *Accounts Receivable* control account with the total of the schedule.

Analyze: Damaged goods decreased the net sales by what dollar amount? By what percentage amount?

Critical Thinking Problem 7.1

Wholesaler Transactions

The Toy Shop Company sells toys and games to retail stores. The firm offers a trade discount of 40 percent on toys and 30 percent on games. Its credit sales and sales returns and allowances transactions for August are shown on page 230. The general ledger accounts used to record these transactions are listed below. The balance shown for *Accounts Receivable* is as of the beginning of August.

INSTRUCTIONS

1. Open the general ledger accounts and enter the balance of *Accounts Receivable* for August 1.

2. Set up an accounts receivable subsidiary ledger. Open an account for each of the credit customers listed below and enter the balances as of August 1.

Carter's Department Store	$28,900
Play Therapy Toy Stores	30,500
Delux Bookstores	
Pemberton Toy Center	
Metroplex Game Center	19,010
Hinton Game Store	

3. Record the transactions in a sales journal and in a general journal. Use 9 as the page number for the sales journal and 25 as the page number for the general journal. Be sure to enter each sale at its net price.

4. Post the individual entries from the sales journal and the general journal.

5. Total and rule the sales journal as of August 31.

6. Post the column total from the sales journal to the proper general ledger accounts.

7. Prepare the heading and the Revenue section of the firm's income statement for the month ended August 31.

8. Prepare a schedule of accounts receivable for August 31.

9. Check the total of the schedule of accounts receivable against the balance of the *Accounts Receivable* account in the general ledger. The two amounts should be equal.

GENERAL LEDGER ACCOUNTS

    111   Accounts Receivable, $78,410 Dr.
    401   Sales
    451   Sales Returns and Allowances

DATE	TRANSACTIONS
August 1	Sold toys to Carter's Department Store; issued Invoice 1001, which shows a list price of $18,500 and a trade discount of 40 percent.
5	Sold games to the Delux Bookstores; issued Invoice 1002, which shows a list price of $20,500 and a trade discount of 30 percent.
9	Sold games to the Metroplex Game Center; issued Invoice 1003, which shows a list price of $7,500 and a trade discount of 30 percent.
14	Sold toys to the Play Therapy Toy Stores; issued Invoice 1004, which shows a list price of $25,500 and a trade discount of 40 percent.
18	Accepted a return of all the games shipped to the Metroplex Game Center because they were damaged in transit; issued Credit Memo 151 for the original sale made on Invoice 1003 on August 9.
22	Sold toys to Hinton Game Store; issued Invoice 1005, which shows a list price of $18,400 and a trade discount of 40 percent.
26	Sold games to the Carter's Department Store; issued Invoice 1006, which shows a list price of $21,600 and a trade discount of 30 percent.
30	Sold toys to the Pemberton Toy Center; issued Invoice 1007, which shows a list price of $22,800 and a trade discount of 40 percent.

Analyze: What is the effect on net sales if the company offers a series of trade discounts on toys (25 percent, 15 percent) instead of a single 40 percent discount?

Critical Thinking Problem 7.2

Retail Store

Carlos Zayas is the owner of The Home Pantry, a housewares store that sells a wide variety of items for the kitchen, bathroom, and home. The Home Pantry offers a company credit card to customers.

The company has experienced an increase in sales since the credit card was introduced. Carlos is considering replacing his manual system of recording sales with electronic point-of-sale cash registers that are linked to a computer.

Cash sales are now rung up by the salesclerks on a cash register that generates a tape listing total cash sales at the end of the day. For credit sales, salesclerks prepare handwritten sales slips that are forwarded to the accountant for manual entry into the sales journal and accounts receivable ledger.

The electronic register system Carlos is considering would use an optical scanner to read coded labels attached to the merchandise. As the merchandise is passed over the scanner, the code is sent to the computer. The computer is programmed to read the code and identify the item being sold, record the amount of the sale, maintain a record of total sales, update the inventory record, and keep a record of cash received.

If the sale is a credit transaction, the customer's company credit card number is entered into the register. The computer updates the customer's account in the accounts receivable ledger stored in computer memory.

If this system is used, many of the accounting functions are done automatically as sales are entered into the register. At the end of the day, the computer prints a complete sales journal, along with up-to-date balances for the general ledger and the accounts receivable ledger accounts related to sales transactions.

Listed below are four situations that Carlos is eager to eliminate. Would use of an electronic point-of-sale system as described above reduce or prevent these problems? Why or why not?

1. The accountant did not post a sale to the customer's subsidiary ledger account.

2. The salesclerk did not charge a customer for an item.

3. The customer purchased merchandise using a stolen credit card.

4. The salesclerk was not aware that the item purchased was on sale and did not give the customer the sale price.

BUSINESS CONNECTIONS

Retail Sales

1. How does the *Sales Returns and Allowances* account provide management with a measure of operating efficiency? What problems might be indicated by a high level of returns and allowances?

2. Suppose you are the accountant for a small chain of clothing stores. Up to now the firm has offered open-account credit to qualified customers but has not allowed the used of bank credit cards. The president of the chain has asked your advice about changing the firm's credit policy. What advantages might there be in eliminating the open-account credit and accepting bank credit cards instead? Do you see any disadvantages?

3. During the past year, Cravens Company has had a substantial increase in its losses from uncollectible accounts. Assume that you are the newly hired controller of this firm and that you have been asked to find the reason for the increase. What policies and procedures would you investigate?

4. Suppose a manager in your company has suggested that the firm not hire an accountant to advise it on tax matters and to file tax returns. He states that tax matters are merely procedural in nature and that anyone who can read the tax form instructions can do the necessary work. Comment on this idea.

5. Why is it usually worthwhile for a business to sell on credit even though it will have some losses from uncollectible accounts?

6. How can a firm's credit policy affect its profitability?

7. Why should management insist that all sales on credit and other transactions affecting the firm's accounts receivable be journalized and posted promptly?

8. How can efficient accounting records help management maintain sound credit and collection policies?

Sales Return and Allowances

Credit memos are created when a product is returned. A debit to Sales Returns and Allowances and a credit to A/R is recorded when a credit memo is created. A credit memo will reduce A/R and write off the invoice. You have noticed Margarita has created an abnormally high number of credit memos. You notice the inventory does not reflect the additional inventory resulting from the Sales Returns and Allowances. What would you do and how would you document this decision?

Revenue Growth

Refer to the fiscal *2006 Annual Report* of The Home Depot, Inc., in Appendix A.

1. Locate Management's Discussion and Analysis of Results of Operations and Financial Condition. By what percentage did net sales increase from fiscal 2005 to fiscal 2006? What factors contributed to this growth?

2. Review the Consolidated Balance Sheets. By what percentage did net accounts receivable change from fiscal 2005 to fiscal 2006? Consider your answer to Question 1 above. Describe the relationship between your answer to Question 1 and the change in net accounts receivable.

**Financial Statement
ANALYSIS**

Income Statement

An excerpt from the Consolidated Statements of Income for Wal-Mart Stores, Inc., is presented below. Review the financial data and answer the following analysis questions:

(Amounts in millions except per share data) Fiscal Year Ended January 31,	2007	2006	2005
Revenues:			
Net Sales	$344,992	$308,945	$281,488
Membership and other income	3,658	3,156	2,822
Total Revenues	$348,650	$312,101	$284,310

Analyze:

1. Based on the financial statement presented above, what is Wal-Mart Stores, Inc.'s fiscal year period?

2. Wal-Mart Stores, Inc.'s statement reports one figure for net sales. Name one account whose balance may have been deducted from the *Sales* account balance to determine a net sales amount.

3. The data presented demonstrate a steady increase in net sales over the three-year period. By what percentage have net sales of 2007 increased over sales of 2005?

Analyze Online: Find the most recent consolidated statements of income on the Wal-Mart Stores, Inc., Web site (www.walmartstores.com). Click on *Investors* then *Financial Information* then *Annual Reports,* then select the link for the most recent annual report.

4. What dollar amount is reported for net sales for the most recent year?

5. What is the trend in net sales over the last three years?

6. What are some possible reasons for this trend?

Extending THE THOUGHT

e-Commerce

Some retailers operate only online and do not have "brick-and-mortar" physical locations where consumers can shop. What benefits and drawbacks do you see for retailers who operate entirely online?

Business COMMUNICATION

Memo

You and your partner own three children's bookstores. Your partner comments on the separate general ledger accounts used for *Sales, Sales Tax Payable,* and *Sales Returns and Allowances,* saying this seems like unnecessary "busy work." Write a memo to your partner in response to these concerns.

TEAMWORK

Customer to Vendor

Divide into groups of four individuals. Your company is named Cole's Cooking Supplies. Assign one person as Cole's sales associate; one as the company's A/R clerk; one as the customer, Louisa's Cooking School; and one as Louisa's A/P clerk. Record the transaction each individual would record from a sale of $50,000 for cooking supplies.

Internet CONNECTION

Accounting General Ledger Packages

Go to the QuickBooks and Peachtree Web sites at quickbooks.com and peachtree.com. Compare products at each site. What are some activities that each program can facilitate?

Answers to **Self Reviews**

Answers to Section 1 Self Review

1. A journal that is used to record only one type of transaction. Examples are the sales journal, the purchases journal, the cash receipts journal, and the cash payments journal.

2. Sales of merchandise on credit.

3. A ledger that contains accounts of a single type. Examples are the accounts receivable ledger and the accounts payable ledger.

4. **c.** increases credit sales

5. **c.** service, merchandising, manufacturing.

6. The sale to Harris was recorded at a taxable rate of 7 percent instead of 8 percent. Therefore, the Sales Tax Payable column should have an entry of $48, not $42. The Accounts Receivable Debit column should have an entry of $648, not $642.
   The sale to Wells should have an entry in the Accounts Receivable Debit column of $972, not $872.

Answers to Section 2 Self Review

1. Sales minus sales returns.

2. A sales return results when a customer returns goods and the firm takes them back. A sales allowance results when the firm gives a customer a reduction in the price of the good or service.

3. Individual accounts for all credit customers.

4. **a.** *Sales Returns and Allowances, Sales Tax Payable, Accounts Receivable*

5. **c.** income statement

6.

Answers to Section 3 Self Review

1. *Sales Tax Payable* is the account used to record the liability for sales taxes to be paid in the future.

2. List price is the established retail price of an item; net price is the amount left after all trade discounts are subtracted from the list price.

3. Four types of credit sales are open-account credit, business credit card sales, bank credit card sales, and credit card company sales.

4. **c.** $2,880

5. **d.** $1,260

6. Possible factors are payment history, amount of current debt, amount of potential debt (available credit cards), employment history, salary, references from other creditors.

Answers to Comprehensive Self Review

1. The month and the quarter.

2. A control account is an account that serves as a link between a subsidiary ledger and the general ledger because its balance summarizes the balances of the accounts in the subsidiary ledger.

3. A merchandising business must account for the purchase and sale of goods and for its merchandise inventory.

4. It contains detailed information about the transactions with credit customers and shows the balances owed by credit customers at all times.

5. A service business sells services; a merchandising business sells goods that it has purchased for resale; and a manufacturing business sells goods that it has produced.

Accounting for Purchases and Accounts Payable

LEARNING OBJECTIVES

1. Record purchases of merchandise on credit in a three-column purchases journal.
   LP8
2. Post from the three-column purchases journal to the general ledger accounts.
3. Post credit purchases from the purchases journal to the accounts payable subsidiary ledger.
4. Record purchases returns and allowances in the general journal and post them to the accounts payable subsidiary ledger.
5. Prepare a schedule of accounts payable.
6. Compute the net delivered cost of purchases.
7. Demonstrate a knowledge of the procedures for effective internal control of purchases.
8. Define the accounting terms new to this chapter.

NEW TERMS

accounts payable ledger
cash discount
cost of goods sold
Freight In account
purchase allowance
purchase invoice
purchase order
purchase requisition
purchase return

Purchases account
purchases discount
purchases journal
receiving report
sales discount
sales invoice
schedule of accounts payable
Transportation In account

Pier 1 imports®   www.pier1.com

In 1962, a small shop opened in San Mateo, California. Filled with incense, love beads, and beanbag chairs, Pier 1 was an immediate hit with the locals. Its reputation grew and so did its customer base. By 1966, there were 16 Pier 1 Stores and by 1970 when the firm went public there were over 100 stores nationwide. The firm now boasts 1,100 stores with sales of over $1.6 billion.

As the company has grown and evolved so has the merchandise it offers. Pier 1 has always prided itself on offering the most unique merchandise to its loyal customers and so is constantly updating its product line. As much as 75 percent of the merchandise in a Pier 1 store has been introduced within a single calendar year. All merchandise is carefully selected to offer customers exclusive one-of-a-kind pieces.

thinking critically

How do you think Pier 1's buyers determine the types of products that will appeal to its customers?

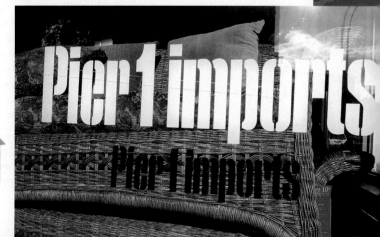

SECTION OBJECTIVES

>> 1. **Record purchases of merchandise on credit in a three-column purchases journal.**

   WHY IT'S IMPORTANT

   Most merchandisers purchase goods on credit, and the use of a special journal improves efficiency when recording these transactions.

>> 2. **Post from the three-column purchases journal to the general ledger accounts.**

   WHY IT'S IMPORTANT

   Summary postings from the purchases journal minimize repetitive tasks.

TERMS TO LEARN

cash discount
cost of goods sold
Freight In account
purchase invoice
purchase order
purchase requisition
Purchases account
purchases discount
purchases journal
receiving report
sales discount
sales invoice
Transportation In account

Merchandise Purchases

In this chapter, you will learn how Maxx-Out Sporting Goods manages its purchases of goods for resale and its accounts payable.

Accounting for Purchases

Most merchandising businesses purchase goods on credit under open-account arrangements. A large firm usually has a centralized purchasing department that is responsible for locating suppliers, obtaining price quotations, negotiating credit terms, and placing orders. In small firms, purchasing activities are handled by a single individual, usually the owner or manager.

PURCHASING PROCEDURES

When a sales department needs goods, it sends the purchasing department a purchase requisition (Figure 8.1 on page 237). A **purchase requisition** lists the items to be ordered. It is signed by someone with the authority to approve requests for merchandise, usually the manager of the sales department. The purchasing department selects a supplier who can furnish the goods at a competitive price and then issues a purchase order (Figure 8.2 on page 237). The **purchase order** specifies the exact items, quantity, price, and credit terms. It is signed by someone with authority to approve purchases, usually the purchasing agent.

When the goods arrive at the business, they are inspected. A **receiving report** is prepared to show the quantity and condition of the goods received. The purchasing department receives a copy of the receiving report and compares it to the purchase order. If defective goods or the wrong quantity of goods are received, the purchasing department contacts the supplier and settles the problem.

Figure 8.3 on page 237 shows the invoice, or *bill,* for items ordered and shipped. The customer, Maxx-Out Sporting Goods, calls it a **purchase invoice.** The supplier, International Sportsman, calls it a **sales invoice.** The customer's accounting department compares the invoice to copies of the purchase order and receiving report. The accounting department checks the quantities, prices, and math on the invoice and then records the purchase. It is important to record purchases in the accounting records as soon as the invoice is verified. Shortly before the due date of the invoice, the accounting department issues a check to the supplier and records the payment.

> The purchasing department for The Home Depot, Inc., purchases 35,000 to 45,000 different kinds of home improvement supplies, building materials, and lawn and garden products.

FIGURE 8.1

Purchase Requisition

Maxx-Out Sporting Goods
2007 Trendsetter Lane
Dallas, TX 75268-0967

PURCHASE REQUISITION

No. __325__

DEPARTMENT __Men's__   DATE OF REQUEST __January 2, 2010__

ADVISE ON DELIVERY __Max Ferraro__   DATE REQUIRED __January 25, 2010__

QUANTITY	DESCRIPTION
10	Assorted colors men's sweatsuits

APPROVED BY_____   REQUESTED BY _____

FOR PURCHASING DEPARTMENT USE ONLY

PURCHASE ORDER __9001__   ISSUED TO: __International Sportsman__
DATE __January 5, 2010__   __1718 Sherry Lane__
                                                __Dallas, TX 75267-6205__

FIGURE 8.2

Purchase Order

Maxx-Out Sporting Goods
2007 Trendsetter Lane
Dallas, TX 75268-0967

PURCHASE ORDER

To   __International Sportsman__   Date: __January 5, 2010__
     __1718 Sherry Lane__   Order No: __9001__
     __Dallas, TX 75267-6205__   Terms: __n/30__

QUANTITY	ITEM	UNIT PRICE	TOTAL
10	Assorted colors men's sweatsuits	55.00	550.00

APPROVED BY _____

FIGURE 8.3

Invoice

International Sportsman   **INVOICE NO. 7985**
1718 Sherry Lane
Dallas, TX 75267-6205

SOLD TO: Maxx-Out Sporting Goods   DATE: January 23, 2010
          2007 Trendsetter Lane   ORDER NO.: 9001
          Dallas, TX 75268-0967   SHIPPED BY: Metroplex Express
                                          TERMS: n/30

YOUR ORDER NO.	SALESPERSON		TERMS	
9001			n/30	
DATE SHIPPED	SHIPPED BY		FOB	
January 23, 2010	Metroplex Express		Dallas	
QUANTITY	DESCRIPTION	UNIT PRICE	TOTAL	
10	Assorted colors men's sweatsuits	55 00	550 00	
	Freight		50 00	
	Total		600 00	

Video8.1

THE PURCHASES ACCOUNT

The purchase of merchandise for resale is a cost of doing business. The purchase of merchandise is debited to the **Purchases account.** *Purchases* is a temporary account classified as a cost of goods sold account. The **cost of goods sold** is the actual cost to the business of the merchandise sold to customers.

Cost of goods sold accounts follow the debit and credit rules of expense accounts. The *Purchases* account is increased by debits and decreased by credits. Its normal balance is a debit. In the chart of accounts, the cost of goods sold accounts appear just before the expense accounts.

> Wal-Mart Stores, Inc., purchases private-label products from suppliers and markets these as Wal-Mart brands. Products such as Ol'Roy™ dog food, Spring Valley® vitamins, and EverStart® automotive batteries are purchased at lower costs than nationally known brands. Thus, Wal-Mart Stores, Inc., can sell these items at a lower price to its customers.

FREIGHT CHARGES FOR PURCHASES

Sometimes the buyer pays the freight charge—the cost of shipping the goods from the seller's warehouse to the buyer's location. There are two ways to handle the freight charges paid by the buyer:

- The buyer is billed directly by the transportation company for the freight charge. The buyer issues a check directly to the freight company.
- The seller pays the freight charge and includes it on the invoice. The invoice includes the price of the goods and the freight charge.

The freight charge is debited to the **Freight In** or **Transportation In account.** This is a cost of goods sold account showing transportation charges for merchandise purchased. The buyer enters three elements in the accounting records:

Price of goods (debit **Purchases**)	$550.00
Freight charge (debit **Freight In**)	50.00
Total invoice (credit **Accounts Payable**)	$600.00

Purchases			Freight In			Accounts Payable	
Dr.	Cr.		Dr.	Cr.		Dr.	Cr.
+	−		+	−		−	+
550			50				600

THE PURCHASES JOURNAL

For most merchandising businesses, it is not efficient to enter purchases of goods in the general journal. Instead, credit purchases of merchandise are recorded in a special journal called the **purchases journal.**

The following illustrates how credit purchases appear in a general journal. Each entry involves a debit to *Purchases* and *Freight In* and a credit to *Accounts Payable* plus a detailed explanation.

These 4 general journal entries require 12 separate postings to general ledger accounts: 4 to *Purchases,* 4 to *Freight In,* and 4 to *Accounts Payable.* As you can see from the ledger accounts that follow, it takes a great deal of time and effort to post these entries.

important!

Credit Purchases

The purchases journal is used to record *only credit purchases of merchandise for resale.* Credit purchases of other items used in the business are recorded in the general journal.

GENERAL JOURNAL   PAGE ___1___

	DATE		DESCRIPTION	POST. REF.	DEBIT	CREDIT	
1	2010						1
2	Jan.	3	Purchases	501	2 675 00		2
3			Freight In	502	190 00		3
4			Accounts Payable	205		2 865 00	4
5			Purchased merchandise from				5
6			Active Designs, Invoice 5879,				6
7			dated January 2, 2010,				7
8			terms 2/10, n/30				8
9							9
10		5	Purchases	501	3 880 00		10
11			Freight In	502	175 00		11
12			Accounts Payable	205		4 055 00	12
13			Purchased merchandise from				13
14			The Sports Warehouse, Invoice 633,				14
15			dated January 3, 2010,				15
16			terms n/30				16
17							17
18		6	Purchases	501	2 900 00		18
19			Freight In	502	240 00		19
20			Accounts Payable	205		3 140 00	20
21			Purchased merchandise from				21
22			The Modern Sportsman,				22
23			Invoice 8011, dated				23
24			January 4, 2010, terms n/30				24
25							25
26		7	Purchases	501	3 675 00		26
27			Freight In	502	260 00		27
28			Accounts Payable	205		3 935 00	28
29			Purchased merchandise from				29
30			World of Sports, Invoice 4321,				30
31			dated January 4, 2010,				31
			terms 2/10, n/30				

ACCOUNT _Accounts Payable_   ACCOUNT NO. _205_

DATE		DESCRIPTION	POST. REF.	DEBIT	CREDIT	BALANCE DEBIT	BALANCE CREDIT
2010							
Jan.	1	Balance	✓				10 800 00
	3		J1		2 865 00		13 665 00
	5		J1		4 055 00		17 720 00
	6		J1		3 140 00		20 860 00
	7		J1		3 935 00		24 795 00

ACCOUNT _Purchases_   ACCOUNT NO. _501_

DATE		DESCRIPTION	POST. REF.	DEBIT	CREDIT	BALANCE DEBIT	BALANCE CREDIT
2010							
Jan.	3		J1	2 675 00		2 675 00	
	5		J1	3 880 00		6 555 00	
	6		J1	2 900 00		9 455 00	
	7		J1	3 675 00		13 130 00	

>>**1. OBJECTIVE**

Record purchases of merchandise on credit in a three-column purchases journal.

LP8

ACCOUNT Freight In					ACCOUNT NO. 502	
DATE	DESCRIPTION	POST. REF.	DEBIT	CREDIT	BALANCE DEBIT	CREDIT
2010						
Jan. 3		J1	1 9 0 00		1 9 0 00	
5		J1	1 7 5 00		3 6 5 00	
6		J1	2 4 0 00		6 0 5 00	
7		J1	2 6 0 00		8 6 5 00	

Figure 8.4 shows the purchases journal for Maxx-Out Sporting Goods. Remember that the purchases journal is only for credit purchases of merchandise for resale to customers. Notice how the columns efficiently organize the data about the credit purchases. The purchases journal makes it possible to record each purchase on a single line. In addition, there is no need to enter account names and descriptions.

RECORDING TRANSACTIONS IN A PURCHASES JOURNAL

Use the information on the purchase invoice to make the entry in the purchases journal.

1. Enter the date, supplier name, invoice number, invoice date, and credit terms.
2. In the Accounts Payable Credit column, enter the total owed to the supplier.
3. In the Purchases Debit column, enter the price of the goods purchased.
4. In the Freight In Debit column, enter the freight amount.

The total of the Purchases Debit and Freight In Debit columns must equal the amount entered in the Accounts Payable Credit column.

The invoice date and credit terms determine when payment is due. The following credit terms often appear on invoices:

- *Net 30 days* or *n/30* means that payment in full is due 30 days after the date of the invoice.
- *Net 10 days EOM,* or *n/10 EOM,* means that payment in full is due 10 days after the end of the month in which the invoice was issued.
- *2% 10 days, net 30 days,* or *2/10, n/30* means that if payment is made within 10 days of the invoice date, the customer can take a 2 percent discount. Otherwise, payment in full is due in 30 days.

The 2 percent discount is a **cash discount;** it is a discount offered by suppliers to encourage quick payment by customers. To the customer it is known as a **purchases discount.** To the supplier it is known as a **sales discount.**

FIGURE 8.4 **Purchases Journal**

PURCHASES JOURNAL PAGE 1

DATE		CUSTOMER'S NAME	INVOICE NUMBER	INVOICE DATE	TERMS	POST. REF.	ACCOUNTS PAYABLE CREDIT	PURCHASES DEBIT	FREIGHT IN DEBIT
2010									
Jan.	3	Active Designs	5879	01/02/10	2/10, n/30		2 8 6 5 00	2 6 7 5 00	1 9 0 00
	5	The Sports Warehouse	633	01/03/10	n/30		4 0 5 5 00	3 8 8 0 00	1 7 5 00
	6	The Modern Sportsman	8011	01/04/10	n/30		3 1 4 0 00	2 9 0 0 00	2 4 0 00
	7	World of Sports	4321	01/04/10	2/10, n/30		3 9 3 5 00	3 6 7 5 00	2 6 0 00
	19	Athletic Equipment, Inc.	8997	01/15/10	2/10, n/30		4 2 0 0 00	3 8 6 0 00	3 4 0 00
	23	International Sportsman	7985	01/22/10	n/30		6 0 0 00	5 5 0 00	5 0 00
	31						18 7 9 5 00	17 5 4 0 00	1 2 5 5 00

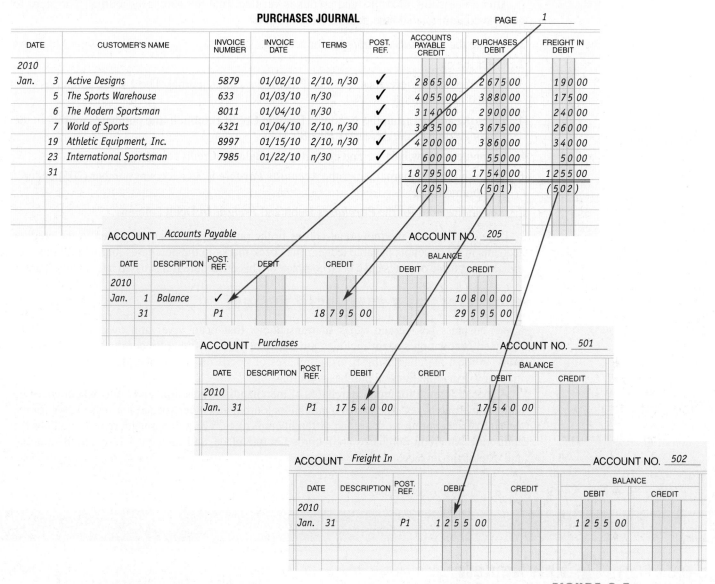

PURCHASES JOURNAL   PAGE ___1___

DATE		CUSTOMER'S NAME	INVOICE NUMBER	INVOICE DATE	TERMS	POST. REF.	ACCOUNTS PAYABLE CREDIT	PURCHASES DEBIT	FREIGHT IN DEBIT
2010									
Jan.	3	Active Designs	5879	01/02/10	2/10, n/30	✓	2 865 00	2 675 00	190 00
	5	The Sports Warehouse	633	01/03/10	n/30	✓	4 055 00	3 880 00	175 00
	6	The Modern Sportsman	8011	01/04/10	n/30	✓	3 140 00	2 900 00	240 00
	7	World of Sports	4321	01/04/10	2/10, n/30	✓	3 935 00	3 675 00	260 00
	19	Athletic Equipment, Inc.	8997	01/15/10	2/10, n/30	✓	4 200 00	3 860 00	340 00
	23	International Sportsman	7985	01/22/10	n/30	✓	600 00	550 00	50 00
	31						18 795 00	17 540 00	1 255 00
							(205)	(501)	(502)

ACCOUNT _Accounts Payable_   ACCOUNT NO. _205_

DATE		DESCRIPTION	POST. REF.	DEBIT	CREDIT	BALANCE DEBIT	BALANCE CREDIT
2010							
Jan.	1	Balance	✓				10 800 00
	31		P1		18 795 00		29 595 00

ACCOUNT _Purchases_   ACCOUNT NO. _501_

DATE		DESCRIPTION	POST. REF.	DEBIT	CREDIT	BALANCE DEBIT	BALANCE CREDIT
2010							
Jan.	31		P1	17 540 00		17 540 00	

ACCOUNT _Freight In_   ACCOUNT NO. _502_

DATE		DESCRIPTION	POST. REF.	DEBIT	CREDIT	BALANCE DEBIT	BALANCE CREDIT
2010							
Jan.	31		P1	1 255 00		1 255 00	

POSTING TO THE GENERAL LEDGER

The purchases journal simplifies the posting process. Summary amounts are posted at the end of the month. Refer to Figure 8.5 as you learn how to post from the purchases journal to the general ledger accounts.

Total the Accounts Payable Credit, the Purchases Debit, and the Freight In Debit columns. Before posting, prove the equality of the debits and credits recorded in the purchases journal.

Proof of Purchases Journal	
	Debits
Purchases Debit column	$17,540.00
Freight In Debit column	1,255.00
	$18,795.00
	Credits
Accounts Payable Credit column	$18,795.00

FIGURE 8.5

Posting to the General Ledger

>>2. OBJECTIVE
Post from the three-column purchases journal to the general ledger accounts.

LP8

important!

Cash Discounts
In the purchases journal, record the amount shown on the invoice. The cash discount is recorded when the payment is made.

After the equality of debits and credits is verified, rule the purchases journal. The steps to post the column totals to the general ledger follow.

1. Locate the *Accounts Payable* ledger account.

2. Enter the date.

3. Enter the posting reference, P1. The **P** is for purchases journal. The **1** is the purchases journal page number.

4. Enter the amount from the Accounts Payable Credit column in the purchases journal in the Credit column of the *Accounts Payable* ledger account.

5. Compute the new balance and enter it in the Balance Credit column.

6. In the purchases journal, enter the *Accounts Payable* ledger account number (205) under the column total.

7. Repeat the steps for the *Purchases* Debit and *Freight In* Debit columns.

During the month, the individual entries in the purchases journal are posted to the creditor accounts in the accounts payable ledger. The check marks in the purchases journal in Figure 8.5 indicate that these postings have been completed. This procedure is discussed later in this chapter.

ADVANTAGES OF A PURCHASES JOURNAL

Every business has certain types of transactions that occur over and over again. A well-designed accounting system includes journals that permit efficient recording of such transactions. In most merchandising firms, purchases of goods on credit take place often enough to make it worthwhile to use a purchases journal.

A special journal for credit purchases of merchandise saves time and effort when recording and posting purchases. The use of a purchases journal and other special journals allows for the division of accounting work among different employees. The purchases journal strengthens the audit trail. All credit purchases are recorded in one place, and each entry refers to the number and date of the invoice.

Section **1** Self Review

QUESTIONS

1. What activities does a purchasing department perform?

2. What type of transaction is recorded in the purchases journal?

3. What are the advantages of using a purchases journal?

EXERCISES

4. What form is sent to the supplier to order goods?

   a. Purchase invoice

   b. Purchase order

   c. Purchase requisition

   d. Sales invoice

5. When the sales department needs goods, what document is sent to the purchasing department?

   a. Purchase invoice

   b. Purchase order

   c. Purchase requisition

   d. Sales requisition

ANALYSIS

6. An invoice dated January 15 for $2,000 shows credit terms 2/10, n/30. What do the credit terms mean?

(Answers to Section 1 Self Review are on page 267.)

SECTION OBJECTIVES

>> **3. Post credit purchases from the purchases journal to the accounts payable subsidiary ledger.**

WHY IT'S IMPORTANT

Up-to-date records allow prompt payment of invoices.

>> **4. Record purchases returns and allowances in the general journal and post them to the accounts payable subsidiary ledger.**

WHY IT'S IMPORTANT

For unsatisfactory goods received, an allowance or return is reflected in the accounting records.

>> **5. Prepare a schedule of accounts payable.**

WHY IT'S IMPORTANT

This schedule provides a snapshot of amounts owed to suppliers.

>> **6. Compute the net delivered cost of purchases.**

WHY IT'S IMPORTANT

This is an important component in measuring operational results.

>> **7. Demonstrate a knowledge of the procedures for effective internal control of purchases.**

WHY IT'S IMPORTANT

Businesses try to prevent fraud, errors, and holding excess inventory.

TERMS TO LEARN

accounts payable ledger
purchase allowance
purchase return
schedule of accounts payable

Accounts Payable

Video8.2

Businesses that buy merchandise on credit can conduct more extensive operations and use financial resources more effectively than if they paid cash for all purchases. It is important to pay invoices on time so that the business maintains a good credit reputation with its suppliers.

The Accounts Payable Ledger

Businesses need detailed records in order to pay invoices promptly. The **accounts payable ledger** provides information about the individual accounts for all creditors. The accounts payable ledger is a subsidiary ledger; it is separate from and subordinate to the general ledger. The accounts payable ledger contains a separate account for each creditor. Each account shows purchases, payments, and returns and allowances. The balance of the account shows the amount owed to the creditor.

Figure 8.6 on page 244 shows the accounts payable ledger account for International Sportsman. Notice that the Balance column does not indicate whether the balance is a debit or a credit. The form assumes that the balance will be a credit because the normal balance of liability accounts is a credit. A debit balance may exist if more than the amount owed was paid to the creditor or if returned goods were already paid for. If the balance is a debit, circle the amount to show that the account does not have the normal balance.

Small businesses like Maxx-Out Sporting Goods arrange the accounts payable ledger in alphabetical order. Large businesses and businesses that use computerized accounting systems assign an account number to each creditor and arrange the accounts payable ledger in numeric order.

Post credit purchases from the purchases journal to the accounts payable subsidiary ledger.

LP8

POSTING A CREDIT PURCHASE

To keep the accounting records up to date, invoices are posted to the accounts payable subsidiary ledger every day. Refer to Figure 8.6 as you learn how to post to the accounts payable ledger.

1. Locate the accounts payable ledger account for the creditor International Sportsman.
2. Enter the date.
3. In the Description column, enter the invoice number and date.
4. In the Posting Reference column, enter the purchases journal page number.
5. Enter the amount from the *Accounts Payable* Credit column in the purchases journal in the Credit column of the accounts payable subsidiary ledger.
6. Compute and enter the new balance in the Balance column.
7. In the purchases journal (Figure 8.5 on page 241), enter a check mark (✓) in the Posting Reference column. This indicates that the transaction is posted in the accounts payable subsidiary ledger.

POSTING CASH PAID ON ACCOUNT

When the transaction involves cash paid on account to a supplier, the payment is first recorded in a cash payments journal. (The cash payments journal is discussed in Chapter 9.) The cash payment is then posted to the individual creditor's account in the accounts payable ledger. Figure 8.7 shows a posting for cash paid to a creditor on January 27.

Record purchases returns and allowances in the general journal and post them to the accounts payable subsidiary ledger.

LP8

recall

Subsidiary Ledger

The total of the accounts in the subsidiary ledger must equal the control account balance.

Purchases Returns and Allowances

When merchandise arrives, it is examined to confirm that it is satisfactory. Occasionally, the wrong goods are shipped, or items are damaged or defective. A **purchase return** is when the business returns the goods. A **purchase allowance** is when the purchaser keeps the goods but receives a reduction in the price of the goods. The supplier issues a credit memorandum for the return or allowance. The credit memorandum reduces the amount that the purchaser owes.

Purchases returns and allowances are entered in the *Purchases Returns and Allowances* account, not in the *Purchases* account. The *Purchases Returns and Allowances* account is a complete record of returns and allowances. Business managers analyze this account to identify problem suppliers.

Purchases Returns and Allowances is a contra cost of goods sold account. The normal balance of cost of goods sold accounts is a debit. The normal balance of *Purchases Returns and Allowances,* a contra cost of goods sold account, is a credit.

RECORDING PURCHASES RETURNS AND ALLOWANCES

Maxx-Out Sporting Goods received merchandise from International Sportsman on January 23. Some goods were damaged, and the supplier granted a $100 purchase allowance. Maxx-Out Sporting Goods recorded the full amount of the invoice, $600, in the purchases journal. The purchase allowance was recorded separately in the general journal.

FIGURE 8.6

Accounts Payable Ledger Account

NAME	International Sportsman				TERMS	n/30		
ADDRESS	1718 Sherry Lane, Dallas, Texas 75267-6205							

DATE		DESCRIPTION	POST. REF.	DEBIT	CREDIT	BALANCE
2010						
Jan.	1	Balance	✓			1 6 0 0 00
	23	Invoice 7985, 01/23/10	P1		6 0 0 00	2 2 0 0 00

NAME	International Sportsman			TERMS	n/30			
ADDRESS	1718 Sherry Lane, Dallas, Texas 75267-6205							

DATE		DESCRIPTION	POST. REF.	DEBIT	CREDIT	BALANCE
2010						
Jan.	1	Balance	✓			1 6 0 0 00
	23	Invoice 7985, 01/23/10	P1		6 0 0 00	2 2 0 0 00
	27		CP1	1 0 0 0 00		1 2 0 0 00

FIGURE 8.7

Posting a Payment Made on Account

BUSINESS TRANSACTION

On January 30, Maxx-Out Sporting Goods received a credit memorandum for $100 from International Sportsman as an allowance for damaged merchandise.

International Sportsman
1718 Sherry Lane
Dallas, TX 75267-6205

TO: Maxx-Out Sporting Goods
2007 Trendsetter Lane
Dallas, TX 75268-0967

CREDIT MEMORANDUM
NUMBER: 103
DATE: January 30, 2010

ORIGINAL INVOICE: 7985
INVOICE DATE: January 23, 2010
DESCRIPTION: Credit for damaged merchandise: $100.00

ANALYSIS

The liability account, **Accounts Payable**, is decreased by $100. The contra cost of goods sold account, **Purchases Returns and Allowances,** is increased by $100.

DEBIT-CREDIT RULES

DEBIT Decreases to liabilities are debits. Debit **Accounts Payable** for $100.

CREDIT Increases to contra cost of goods sold accounts are recorded as credits. Credit **Purchases Returns and Allowances** for $100.

T-ACCOUNT PRESENTATION

Accounts Payable		Purchases Returns and Allowances	
−	+	−	+
100			100

GENERAL JOURNAL ENTRY

	DATE		DESCRIPTION	POST. REF.	DEBIT	CREDIT	
15	Jan.	30	Accounts Payable/International Sportsman		1 0 0 00		15
16			Purchases Returns and Allowances			1 0 0 00	16
17			Received Credit Memo 103 for				17
18			damaged merchandise returned;				18
19			original Invoice 7985,				19
20			January 23, 2010				20

GENERAL JOURNAL   PAGE 1

THE BOTTOM LINE
Purchase Allowance

Income Statement

Contra Cost of Goods Sold	↑ 100
Net Income	↑ 100

Balance Sheet

Liabilities	↓ 100
Equity	↑ 100

FIGURE 8.8

Posting to a Creditor's Account

FIGURE 8.8

Posting to a Creditor's Account

recall

Contra Accounts
The *Purchases Returns and Allowances* account is a contra account. Contra accounts have normal balances that are the opposite of related accounts.

GENERAL JOURNAL   PAGE ____1____

	DATE	DESCRIPTION	POST. REF.	DEBIT	CREDIT	
1	2010					1
15	Jan. 30	Accounts Payable/International Sportsman	205 ✓	1 0 0 00		16
16		Purchases Returns and Allowances	503		1 0 0 00	17
17		Received Credit Memo 103 for				18
18		damaged merchandise				19
19		returned; original				20
20		Invoice 7985, January 23, 2010				21
21						22
22						

NAME ___International Sportsman___   TERMS __n/30__
ADDRESS ___1718 Sherry Lane, Dallas, Texas 75267-6205___

DATE		DESCRIPTION	POST. REF.	DEBIT	CREDIT	BALANCE
2010						
Jan.	1	Balance	✓			1 6 0 0 00
	23	Invoice 7985, 01/23/10	P1		6 0 0 00	2 2 0 0 00
	27		CP1	1 0 0 0 00		1 2 0 0 00
	30	CM 103	J1	1 0 0 00		1 1 0 0 00

Notice that this entry includes a debit to *Accounts Payable* and a credit to *Purchases Returns and Allowances.* In addition, there is a debit to the creditor's account in the accounts payable subsidiary ledger. Businesses that have few returns and allowances use the general journal to record these transactions. Businesses with many returns and allowances use a special journal for purchases returns and allowances.

POSTING A PURCHASES RETURN OR ALLOWANCE

Whether recorded in the general journal or in a special journal, it is important to promptly post returns and allowances to the creditor's account in the accounts payable ledger. Refer to Figure 8.8 to learn how to post purchases returns and allowances to the supplier's account.

1. Enter the date.
2. In the Description column, enter the credit memorandum number.
3. In the Posting Reference column, enter the general journal page number.
4. Enter the amount of the return or allowance in the Debit column.
5. Compute the new balance and enter it in the Balance column.
6. In the general journal, enter a check mark (✓) to show that the transaction was posted to the creditor's account in the accounts payable subsidiary ledger.

After the transaction is posted to the general ledger, enter the *Purchases Returns and Allowances* ledger account number in the Posting Reference column.

>>5. OBJECTIVE

Prepare a schedule of accounts payable.

LP8

Schedule of Accounts Payable

The total of the individual creditor accounts in the subsidiary ledger must equal the balance of the *Accounts Payable* control account. To prove that the control account and the subsidiary ledger are equal, businesses prepare a **schedule of accounts payable**—a list of all balances owed to creditors. Figure 8.9 on page 247 shows the accounts payable subsidiary ledger for Maxx-Out Sporting Goods on January 31.

Figure 8.10 on page 248 shows the schedule of accounts payable for Maxx-Out Sporting Goods. Notice that the accounts payable control account balance is $20,245. This equals the total on the schedule of accounts payable. If the amounts are not equal, it is essential to locate and correct the errors.

FIGURE 8.9

The Accounts Payable Ledger

NAME _Active Designs_   TERMS _2/10, n/30_

ADDRESS _2313 Belt Line Road, Dallas, Texas 75267-6205_

DATE		DESCRIPTION	POST. REF.	DEBIT	CREDIT	BALANCE
2010						
Jan.	1	Balance	✓			2 2 0 0 00
	3	Invoice 5879, 01/02/10	P1		2 8 6 5 00	5 0 6 5 00
	13		CP1	3 2 0 0 00		1 8 6 5 00
	30		CP1	8 0 0 00		1 0 6 5 00

NAME _Athletic Equipment, Inc._   TERMS _2/10, n/30_

ADDRESS _1027 St James Avenue, Dallas, Texas 75267-6205_

DATE		DESCRIPTION	POST. REF.	DEBIT	CREDIT	BALANCE
2010						
Jan.	19	Invoice 8997, 01/15/10	P1		4 2 0 0 00	4 2 0 0 00

NAME _International Sportsman_   TERMS _n/30_

ADDRESS _1718 Sherry Lane, Dallas, Texas 75267-6205_

DATE		DESCRIPTION	POST. REF.	DEBIT	CREDIT	BALANCE
2010						
Jan.	1	Balance	✓			1 6 0 0 00
	23	Invoice 7985, 01/23/10	P1		6 0 0 00	2 2 0 0 00
	27		CP1	1 0 0 0 00		1 2 0 0 00
	30	CM 103	J1	1 0 0 00		1 1 0 0 00

NAME _The Modern Sportsman_   TERMS _n/30_

ADDRESS _2860 Jackson Drive, Dallas, Texas 75267-6205_

DATE		DESCRIPTION	POST. REF.	DEBIT	CREDIT	BALANCE
2010						
Jan.	1	Balance	✓			1 6 0 0 00
	6	Invoice 8011, 01/04/10	P1		3 1 4 0 00	4 7 4 0 00

NAME _The Sports Warehouse_   TERMS _n/30_

ADDRESS _1313 Sunset Drive, Dallas, Texas 75267-6205_

DATE		DESCRIPTION	POST. REF.	DEBIT	CREDIT	BALANCE
2010						
Jan.	1	Balance	✓			2 4 0 0 00
	5	Invoice 633, 01/03/10	P1		4 0 5 5 00	6 4 5 5 00
	17		CP1	4 2 5 0 00		2 2 0 5 00

NAME _World of Sports_   TERMS _2/10, n/30_

ADDRESS _1729 Parker Road, Dallas, Texas 75267-6205_

DATE		DESCRIPTION	POST. REF.	DEBIT	CREDIT	BALANCE
2010						
Jan.	1	Balance	✓			3 0 0 0 00
	7	Invoice 4321, 01/04/10	P1		3 9 3 5 00	6 9 3 5 00

FIGURE 8.10

Schedule of Accounts Payable and the Accounts Payable Account

Maxx-Out Sporting Goods
Schedule of Accounts Payable
January 31, 2010

Active Designs	1 0 6 5 00
Athletic Equipment, Inc.	4 2 0 0 00
International Sportsman	1 1 0 0 00
The Modern Sportsman	4 7 4 0 00
The Sports Warehouse	2 2 0 5 00
World of Sports	6 9 3 5 00
Total	2 0 2 4 5 00

ACCOUNT Accounts Payable   ACCOUNT NO. 205

DATE		DESCRIPTION	POST. REF.	DEBIT	CREDIT	BALANCE DEBIT	BALANCE CREDIT
2010							
Jan.	1	Balance					10 8 0 0 00
	30		J1	1 0 0 00			10 7 0 0 00
	31		P1		18 7 9 5 00		29 4 9 5 00
	31		CP1	9 2 5 0 00			20 2 4 5 00

>>6. OBJECTIVE

Compute the net delivered cost of purchases.

LP8

Determining the Cost of Purchases

The *Purchases* account accumulates the cost of merchandise bought for resale. The income statement of a merchandising business contains a section showing the total cost of purchases. This section combines information about the cost of the purchases, freight in, and purchases returns and allowances for the period. Maxx-Out Sporting Goods has the following general ledger account balances at January 31:

Purchases	$17,540
Freight In	1,255
Purchases Returns and Allowances	100

The net delivered cost of purchases for Maxx-Out Sporting Goods for January is calculated as follows.

Purchases	$17,540
Freight In	1,255
Delivered Cost of Purchases	$18,795
Less Purchases Returns and Allowances	100
Net Delivered Cost of Purchases	$18,695

For firms that do not have freight charges, the amount of net purchases is calculated as follows.

Purchases	$17,540
Less Purchases Returns and Allowances	100
Net Purchases	$17,440

In Chapter 13, you will see how the complete income statement for a merchandising business is prepared. You will learn about the Cost of Goods Sold section and how the net delivered cost of purchases is used in calculating the results of operations.

Internal Control of Purchases

Because of the large amount of money spent to purchase goods, businesses should develop careful procedures to control purchases and payments. A business should ensure its control process includes sufficient safeguards to

- create written proof that purchases and payments are authorized;
- ensure that different people are involved in the process of buying goods, receiving goods, and making payments.

Separating duties among employees provides a system of check and balances. In a small business with just a few employees, it might be very difficult to separate duties. This means the owner must be involved in daily operations. Even a small business, however, should design a set of control procedures as effective as resources allow. Effective systems for small businesses should have the following controls in place.

1. All purchases should be made only after proper authorization has been given in writing.
2. Goods should be carefully checked when received. They should be then compared with the purchase order and with the invoice received from the supplier.
3. The purchase order, receiving report, and invoice should be checked to confirm that the information on the documents is in agreement.
4. The computations on the invoice should be checked for accuracy.
5. Authorization for payment should be made by someone other than the person who ordered the goods.
6. Another person should write the check for payment.
7. Prenumbered forms should be used for purchase requisitions, purchase orders, and checks. The numbers on the documents issued should be verified periodically to make sure all forms can be accounted for.

Medium- and large-sized businesses often use the voucher system. As a business grows, the owner finds it increasingly difficult to be involved in all the firm's transactions. The owner cannot personally approve or sign all checks. That's when the internal controls provided by the voucher system become increasingly important.

Controls built into a voucher system include the following:

- All liabilities are authorized. For example, a properly approved purchase order is required for each purchase of merchandise on account.
- All payments are made by check.
- All checks are issued based on a properly approved voucher.
- Vouchers are used to cover bills and invoices received from outside parties.
- All bills and invoices are verified before they are approved for payment.
- Only experienced and responsible employees are allowed to approve bills and invoices for payment.
- Invoices are attached to the vouchers to provide supporting documentation.
- Different employees approve the vouchers, record the vouchers and payments, and sign and mail the checks.
- All paid vouchers, including supporting documentation, are kept on file for a specified period of time.

>>7. OBJECTIVE

Demonstrate a knowledge of the procedures for effective internal control of purchases.

LP8

Employee Fraud
According to the U.S. Chamber of Commerce, businesses lose billions of dollars each year to employee fraud. The best defense against fraud is to use good internal controls: Have multiple employees in contact with suppliers and screen employees and vendors to reduce fraud opportunities.

MANAGERIAL IMPLICATIONS

ACCOUNTING FOR PURCHASES

- Management and the accounting staff need to work together to make sure that there are good internal controls over purchasing.

- A carefully designed system of checks and balances protects the business against fraud, errors, and excessive investment in merchandise.

- The accounting staff needs to record transactions efficiently so that up-to-date information about creditors is available.

- Using the purchases journal and the accounts payable subsidiary ledger improves efficiency.

- To maintain a good credit reputation with suppliers, it is important to have an accounting system that ensures prompt payment of invoices.

- A well-run accounting system provides management with information about cash: cash required to pay suppliers, short-term loans needed to cover temporary cash shortages, and cash available for short-term investments.

- Separate accounts for recording purchases, freight charges, and purchases returns and allowances make it easy to analyze the elements in the cost of purchases.

THINKING CRITICALLY
As a manager, what internal controls would you put in your accounting system?

Section 2 Self Review

QUESTIONS

1. What is the purpose of the schedule of accounts payable?

2. A firm has a debit balance of $60,550 in its **Purchases** account and a credit balance of $2,875 in its **Purchases Returns and Allowances** account. Calculate net purchases for the period.

3. A firm receives an invoice that reflects the price of goods as $1,275 and the freight charge as $82. How is this transaction recorded?

EXERCISES

4. In the accounts payable ledger, a supplier's account has a beginning balance of $4,800. A transaction of $1,600 is posted from the purchases journal. What is the balance of the supplier's account?

   a. $3,200 debit

   b. $3,200 credit

   c. $6,400 credit

   d. $6,400 debit

5. The net delivered cost of purchases for the period appears on the

   a. balance sheet.

   b. income statement.

   c. schedule of accounts payable.

   d. statement of owner's equity.

ANALYSIS

6. In the general ledger, the **Accounts Payable** account has a balance of $15,500. The schedule of accounts payable lists accounts totaling $20,500. What could cause this error?

(Answers to Section 2 Self Review are on page 267.)

REVIEW Chapter Summary

In this chapter, you have learned about the accounting journals and ledgers required for the efficient processing of purchases for a business. Businesses with strong internal controls establish and follow procedures for approving requests for new merchandise, choosing suppliers, placing orders with suppliers, checking goods after they arrive, identifying invoices, and approving payments.

Learning Objectives

1 Record purchases of merchandise on credit in a three-column purchases journal.

Purchases and payments on account must be entered in the firm's accounting records promptly and accurately. Most merchandising businesses normally purchase goods on credit. The most efficient system for recording purchases on credit is the use of a special purchases journal. With this type of journal, only one line is needed to enter all the data.

The purchases journal is used only to record the credit purchase of goods for resale. General business expenses are not recorded in the purchases journal.

2 Post from the three-column purchases journal to the general ledger accounts.

The use of the three-column purchases journal simplifies the posting process because nothing is posted to the general ledger until the month's end. Then, summary postings are made to the *Purchases, Freight In,* and *Accounts Payable* accounts.

3 Post credit purchases from the purchases journal to the accounts payable subsidiary ledger.

An accounts payable subsidiary ledger helps a firm keep track of the amounts it owes to creditors. Postings are made to this ledger on a daily basis.

- Each credit purchase is posted from the purchases journal to the accounts payable subsidiary ledger.

- Each payment on account is posted from the cash payments journal to the accounts payable subsidiary ledger.

4 Record purchases returns and allowances in the general journal and post them to the accounts payable subsidiary ledger.

Returns and allowances on purchases of goods are credited to an account called *Purchases Returns and Allowances.* These transactions may be recorded in the general journal or in a special purchases returns and allowances journal. Each return or allowance on a credit purchase is posted to the accounts payable subsidiary ledger.

5 Prepare a schedule of accounts payable.

At the month's end, a schedule of accounts payable is prepared. The schedule lists the balances owed to the firm's creditors and proves the accuracy of the subsidiary ledger. The total of the schedule of accounts payable is compared with the balance of the *Accounts Payable* account in the general ledger, which acts as a control account. The two amounts should be equal.

6 Compute the net delivered cost of purchases.

The net delivered cost of purchases is computed by adding the cost of purchases and freight in, then subtracting any purchases returns and allowances. Net delivered cost of purchases is reported in the Cost of Goods Sold section of the income statement.

7 Demonstrate a knowledge of the procedures for effective internal control of purchases.

Purchases and payments should be properly authorized and processed with appropriate documentation to provide a system of checks and balances. A division of responsibilities within the purchases process ensures strong internal controls.

8 Define the accounting terms new to this chapter.

Glossary

Accounts payable ledger (p. 243) A subsidiary ledger that contains a separate account for each creditor

Cash discount (p. 240) A discount offered by suppliers for payment received within a specified period of time

Cost of goods sold (p. 238) The actual cost to the business of the merchandise sold to customers

Freight In account (p. 238) An account showing transportation charges for items purchased

Purchase allowance (p. 244) A price reduction from the amount originally billed

Purchase invoice (p. 236) A bill received for goods purchased

Purchase order (p. 236) An order to the supplier of goods specifying items needed, quantity, price, and credit terms

Purchase requisition (p. 236) A list sent to the purchasing department showing the items to be ordered

Purchase return (p. 244) Return of unsatisfactory goods

Purchases account (p. 238) An account used to record cost of goods bought for resale during a period

Purchases discount (p. 240) A cash discount offered to the customer for payment within a specified period

Purchases journal (p. 238) A special journal used to record the purchase of goods on credit

Receiving report (p. 236) A form showing quantity and condition of goods received

Sales discount (p. 240) A cash discount offered by the supplier for payment within a specified period

Sales invoice (p. 236) A supplier's billing document

Schedule of accounts payable (p. 246) A list of all balances owed to creditors

Transportation In account (p. 238) See Freight In account

Comprehensive Self Review

1. What type of account is *Purchases Returns and Allowances?*
2. What is a cash discount and why is it offered?
3. What is the purpose of the *Freight In* account?
4. What is the purpose of a purchase requisition? A purchase order?
5. What is the difference between a receiving report and an invoice?

(Answers to Comprehensive Self Review are on page 267.)

Multiple choice questions are provided on the text Web site at www.mhhe.com/price12e

Quiz8

Discussion Questions

1. Why are the invoice date and terms recorded in the purchases journal?
2. What major safeguards should be built into a system of internal control for purchases of goods?
3. What is the purpose of a credit memorandum?
4. What is a purchase allowance?
5. What is a purchase return?
6. What is a schedule of accounts payable? Why is it prepared?
7. What is the relationship of the *Accounts Payable* account in the general ledger to the accounts payable subsidiary ledger?
8. What type of accounts are kept in the accounts payable ledger?
9. Why is it useful for a business to have an accounts payable ledger?
10. How is the net delivered cost of purchases computed?
11. What journals can be used to enter various merchandise purchase transactions?
12. What is the difference between a purchase invoice and a sales invoice?
13. What is the normal balance of the *Purchases* account?
14. On what financial statement do the accounts related to purchases of merchandise appear? In which section of this statement are they reported?

15. Why is the use of a *Purchases Returns and Allowances* account preferred to crediting these transactions to *Purchases?*

16. What do the following credit terms mean?

    a. n/30

    b. 2/10, n/30

    c. n/10 EOM

    d. n/20

    e. 1/10, n/20

    f. 3/5, n/30

    g. n/15 EOM

17. A business has purchased some new equipment for use in its operations, not for resale to customers. The terms of the invoice are n/30. Should this transaction be entered in the purchases journal? If not, where should it be recorded?

APPLICATIONS

Exercises

Identifying the journals used to record purchases and related transactions.

◄ **Exercise 8.1**
Objective 1

The accounting system of Shoe City includes the following journals. Indicate which journal is used to record each transaction.

JOURNALS

Cash receipts journal
Cash payments journal
Purchases journal
Sales journal
General journal

TRANSACTIONS

1. Purchased merchandise for $3,000; the terms are 2/10, n/30.

2. Returned damaged merchandise to a supplier and received a credit memorandum for $800.

3. Issued a check for $3,600 to a supplier as a payment on account.

4. Purchased merchandise for $2,000 plus a freight charge of $140; the supplier's invoice is payable in 30 days.

5. Received an allowance for merchandise that was damaged but can be sold at a reduced price; the supplier's credit memorandum is for $475.

6. Purchased merchandise for $3,500 in cash.

Identifying journals used to record purchases and related transactions.

◄ **Exercise 8.2**
Objective 1

The following transactions took place at Serene Trails Hike and Bike Shop. Indicate the general ledger account numbers that would be debited and credited to record each transaction.

GENERAL LEDGER ACCOUNTS

101   Cash
205   Accounts Payable

501 Purchases

502 Freight In

503 Purchases Returns and Allowances

TRANSACTIONS

1. Purchased merchandise for $1,500; the terms are 2/10, n/30.

2. Returned damaged merchandise to a supplier and received a credit memorandum for $300.

3. Issued a check for $800 to a supplier as a payment on account.

4. Purchased merchandise for $2,400 plus a freight charge of $260; the supplier's invoice is payable in 30 days.

5. Received an allowance for merchandise that was damaged but can be sold at a reduced price; the supplier's credit memorandum is for $400.

6. Purchased merchandise for $4,200 in cash.

Exercise 8.3 ▶
Objective 1

Recording credit purchases.

The following transactions took place at Anaheim Auto Parts and Custom Shop during the first week of July. Indicate how these transactions would be entered in a purchases journal like the one shown in this chapter.

DATE	TRANSACTIONS
July 1	Purchased batteries for $1,960 plus a freight charge of $122 from Auto Parts Corporation; received Invoice 6812, dated June 27, which has terms of n/30.
3	Purchased mufflers for $3,150 plus a freight charge of $79 from Aplex Company; received Invoice 441, dated June 30, which has terms of 1/10, n/60.
5	Purchased car radios for $2,370 plus freight of $117 from The Custom Sounds Shop, Inc.; received Invoice 5601, dated July 1, which has terms of 2/10, n/30.
10	Purchased truck tires for $4,170 from Specialty Tire Company; received Invoice 1102, dated July 8, which has terms of 2/10, n/30.

Exercise 8.4 ▶
Objective 4

Recording a purchase return.

On February 9, Modern Kitchens, a retail store, received Credit Memorandum 244 for $3,550 from Discount Appliance Corporation. The credit memorandum covered a return of damaged trash compactors originally purchased on Invoice 4101 dated January 3. Prepare the general journal entry that Modern Kitchens would make for this transaction.

Exercise 8.5 ▶
Objective 4

Recording a purchase allowance.

On March 17, The Wholesale Appliance Company was given an allowance of $1,030 by Town Appliance Mart, which issued Credit Memorandum 112. The allowance was for scratches on stoves that were originally purchased on Invoice 911 dated February 20. Prepare the general journal entry that The Wholesale Appliance Company would make for this transaction.

Exercise 8.6 ▶
Objective 4

Determining the cost of purchases.

On June 30 the general ledger of Trendsetters, a clothing store, showed a balance of $40,795 in the *Purchases* account, a balance of $2,226 in the *Freight In* account, and a balance of $4,860 in the *Purchases Returns and Allowances* account. What was the delivered cost of the purchases made during June? What was the net delivered cost of these purchases?

Errors in recording purchase transactions.

◀ **Exercise 8.7**
Objectives 1, 4

The following errors were made in recording transactions in posting from the purchases journal. How will these errors be detected?

a. A credit of $2,000 to Brock Furniture Company account in the accounts payable ledger was posted as $200.

b. The Accounts Payable column total of the purchases journal was understated by $200.

c. An invoice of $1,680 for merchandise from Jackson Company was recorded as having been received from Baxton Company, another supplier.

d. A $500 payment to Baxton Company was debited to Jackson Company.

Determining the cost of purchases.

◀ **Exercise 8.8**
Objective 4

Complete the following schedule by supplying the missing information.

Net Delivered Cost of Purchases	Case A	Case B
Purchases	(a)	96,970
Freight In	4,670	(c)
Delivered Cost of Purchases	98,090	(d)
Less Purchases Returns and Allowances	(b)	3,880
Net Delivered Cost of Purchases	94,840	96,770

PROBLEMS

Problem Set A

Journalizing credit purchases and purchases returns and allowances and posting to the general ledger.

◀ **Problem 8.1A**
Objectives 1, 2, 3

Photo Mart is a retail store that sells cameras and photography supplies. The firm's credit purchases and purchases returns and allowances transactions for June 2010 appear on page 256, along with the general ledger accounts used to record these transactions. The balance shown in *Accounts Payable* is for the beginning of June.

INSTRUCTIONS

1. Open the general ledger accounts and enter the balance of *Accounts Payable* for June 1, 2010.
2. Record the transactions in a three-column purchases journal and in a general journal. Use 14 as the page number for the purchases journal and 38 as the page number for the general journal.
3. Post entries from the general journal to the general ledger accounts.
4. Total and rule the purchases journal as of June 30.
5. Post the column totals from the purchases journal to the proper general ledger accounts.
6. Compute the net purchases of the firm for the month of June.

GENERAL LEDGER ACCOUNTS

205 Accounts Payable, $13,904 Cr.
501 Purchases
502 Freight In
503 Purchases Returns and Allowances

DATE	TRANSACTIONS
June 1	Purchased instant cameras for $1,995 plus a freight charge of $180 from Jones Company, Invoice 4241, dated May 27; the terms are 60 days net.
8	Purchased film for $1,390 from Camera & Films Products, Invoice 1102, dated June 3, net payable in 45 days.
12	Purchased lenses for $906 from The Optical Supply Store, Invoice 7282, dated June 9; the terms are 1/10, n/60.
18	Received Credit Memorandum 110 for $375 from Jones Company for defective cameras that were returned; they were originally purchased on Invoice 4241, dated May 27.
20	Purchased color film for $1,050 plus freight of $75 from Camera & Films Products, Invoice 1148, dated June 15, net payable in 45 days.
23	Purchased camera cases for $1,940 from Chicago Case Company, Invoice 3108, dated June 18, net due and payable in 45 days.
28	Purchased disk cameras for $2,470 plus freight of $120 from Zant Corporation, Invoice 5027, dated June 24; the terms are 2/10, n/30.
30	Received Credit Memorandum 1108 for $240 from Chicago Case Company; the amount is an allowance for damaged but usable goods purchased on Invoice 3108, dated June 18.

(**Note:** Save your working papers for use in Problem 8.2A.)

Analyze: What total purchases were posted to the *Purchases* general ledger account for June?

Problem 8.2A ▶

Objectives 4, 6

CONTINUING >>> Problem

Posting to the accounts payable ledger and preparing a schedule of accounts payable.

This problem is a continuation of Problem 8.1A.

INSTRUCTIONS

1. Set up an accounts payable subsidiary ledger for Photo Mart. Open an account for each of the creditors listed below and enter the balances as of June 1, 2010.

2. Post the individual entries from the purchases journal and the general journal prepared in Problem 8.1A.

3. Prepare a schedule of accounts payable for June 30.

4. Check the total of the schedule of accounts payable against the balance of the *Accounts Payable* account in the general ledger. The two amounts should be equal.

Creditors		
Name	**Terms**	**Balance**
Camera & Films Products	n/45	$10,480
Chicago Case Company	n/45	1,200
Jones Company	n/60	
The Optical Supply Store	1/10, n/60	2,224
Zant Corporation	2/10, n/30	

Analyze: What amount is owed to The Optical Supply Store on June 30?

Problem 8.3A ▶

QB **Objectives 1, 2, 3, 4, 5, 6**

Journalizing credit purchases and purchases returns and allowances, computing the net delivered cost of goods, posting to the general ledger, posting to the accounts payable ledger, and preparing a schedule of accounts payable.

The English Garden Shop is a retail store that sells garden equipment, furniture, and supplies. Its credit purchases and purchases returns and allowances for July are listed below. The general ledger accounts used to record these transactions are also provided. The balance shown is for the beginning of July 2010.

INSTRUCTIONS

PART I

1. Open the general ledger accounts and enter the balance of *Accounts Payable* for July 1.
2. Record the transactions in a three-column purchases journal and in a general journal. Use 8 as the page number for the purchases journal and 20 as the page number for the general journal.
3. Post the entries from the general journal to the proper general ledger accounts.
4. Total, prove, and rule the purchases journal as of July 31.
5. Post the column totals from the purchases journal to the proper general ledger accounts.
6. Compute the net delivered cost of the firm's purchases for the month of July.

GENERAL LEDGER ACCOUNTS

205	Accounts Payable, $35,880 Cr.	502	Freight In
501	Purchases	503	Purchases Returns and Allowances

DATE	TRANSACTIONS
July 1	Purchased lawn mowers for $9,210 plus a freight charge of $249 from Brown Corporation, Invoice 1011, dated June 26, net due and payable in 60 days.
5	Purchased outdoor chairs and tables for $4,370 plus a freight charge of $552 from Brooks Garden Furniture Company, Invoice 639, dated July 2, net due and payable in 45 days.
9	Purchased grass seed for $1,390 from Lawn and Gardens Supply, Invoice 8164, dated July 5; the terms are 30 days net.
16	Received Credit Memorandum 110 for $600 from Brooks Garden Furniture Company; the amount is an allowance for scratches on some of the chairs and tables originally purchased on Invoice 639, dated July 2.
19	Purchased fertilizer for $1,200 plus a freight charge of $256 from Lawn and Gardens Supply, Invoice 9050, dated July 15; the terms are 30 days net.
21	Purchased hoses from Cameron Rubber Company for $3,680 plus a freight charge of $224, Invoice 1785, dated July 17; terms are 1/15, n/60.
28	Received Credit Memorandum 223 for $430 from Cameron Rubber Company for damaged hoses that were returned; the goods were purchased on Invoice 1785, dated July 17.
31	Purchased lawn sprinkler systems for $10,310 plus a freight charge of $278 from Wilson Industrial Products, Invoice 8985, dated July 26; the terms are 2/10, n/30.

INSTRUCTIONS

PART II

1. Set up an accounts payable subsidiary ledger for The English Garden Shop. Open an account for each of the creditors listed below and enter the balances as of July 1.
2. Post the individual entries from the purchases journal and the general journal prepared in Part I.

3. Prepare a schedule of accounts payable for July 31, 2010.
4. Check the total of the schedule of accounts payable against the balance of the *Accounts Payable* account in the general ledger. The two amounts should be equal.

Creditors		
Name	**Terms**	**Balance**
Brooks Garden Furniture Company	n/45	$11,120
Brown Corporation	n/60	18,120
Cameron Rubber Company	1/15, n/60	
Lawn and Gardens Supply	n/30	6,640
Wilson Industrial Products	2/10, n/30	

Analyze: What total freight charges were posted to the general ledger for the month of July?

Problem 8.4A ▶

**Objectives
1, 2, 3, 4, 5, 6**

Journalizing credit purchases and purchases returns and allowances, posting to the general ledger, posting to the accounts payable ledger, and preparing a schedule of accounts payable.

Professional Office Products Center is a retail business that sells office equipment, furniture, and supplies. Its credit purchases and purchases returns and allowances for September are shown on page 259. The general ledger accounts and the creditors' accounts in the accounts payable subsidiary ledger used to record these transactions are also provided. All balances shown are for the beginning of September.

INSTRUCTIONS

1. Open the general ledger accounts and enter the balance of *Accounts Payable* for September 1, 2010.
2. Open the creditors' accounts in the accounts payable subsidiary ledger and enter the balances for September 1.
3. Record the transactions in a three-column purchases journal and in a general journal. Use 5 as the page number for the purchases journal and 14 as the page number for the general journal.
4. Post to the accounts payable subsidiary ledger daily.
5. Post the entries from the general journal to the proper general ledger accounts at the end of the month.
6. Total and rule the purchases journal as of September 30.
7. Post the column totals from the purchases journal to the proper general ledger accounts.
8. Prepare a schedule of accounts payable and compare the balance of the *Accounts Payable* control account with the schedule of accounts payable.

GENERAL LEDGER ACCOUNTS

205	Accounts Payable, $28,256 Cr.		502	Freight In
501	Purchases		503	Purchases Returns and Allowances

Creditors		
Name	**Terms**	**Balance**
Apex Office Machines, Inc.	n/60	$10,960
Brown Paper Company	1/10, n/30	2,120
Dalton Office Furniture Company	n/30	9,576
Davis Corporation	n/30	
Zenn Furniture, Inc.	2/10, n/30	5,600

DATE	TRANSACTIONS
Sept. 3	Purchased desks for $7,920 plus a freight charge of $212 from Dalton Office Furniture Company, Invoice 4213, dated August 29; the terms are 30 days net.
7	Purchased computers for $11,300 from Apex Office Machines, Inc., Invoice 9217, dated September 2, net due and payable in 60 days.
10	Received Credit Memorandum 511 for $600 from Dalton Office Furniture Company; the amount is an allowance for damaged but usable desks purchased on Invoice 4213, dated August 29.
16	Purchased file cabinets for $2,556 plus a freight charge of $124 from Davis Corporation, Invoice 8066, dated September 11; the terms are 30 days net.
20	Purchased electronic desk calculators for $1,000 from Apex Office Machines, Inc., Invoice 11011, dated September 15, net due and payable in 60 days.
23	Purchased bond paper and copy machine paper for $7,500 plus a freight charge of $100 from Brown Paper Company, Invoice 6498, dated September 18; the terms are 1/10, n/30.
28	Received Credit Memorandum 312 for $880 from Apex Office Machines, Inc., for defective calculators that were returned; the calculators were originally purchased on Invoice 11011, dated September 15.
30	Purchased office chairs for $3,840 plus a freight charge of $160 from Zenn Furniture, Inc., Invoice 696, dated September 25, the terms are 2/10, n/30.

Analyze: What total amount was recorded for purchases returns and allowances in the month of September? What percentage of total purchases does this represent?

Problem Set B

Journalizing credit purchases and purchases returns and allowances and posting to the general ledger.

◀ **Problem 8.1B**
Objectives 1, 2, 3

Denver Ski Shop is a retail store that sells ski equipment and clothing. The firm's credit purchases and purchases returns and allowances during May 2010 follow, along with the general ledger accounts used to record these transactions. The balance shown in *Accounts Payable* is for the beginning of May.

INSTRUCTIONS

1. Open the general ledger accounts and enter the balance of *Accounts Payable* for May 1, 2010.
2. Record the transactions in a three-column purchases journal and in a general journal. Use 15 as the page number for the purchases journal and 38 as the page number for the general journal.
3. Post the entries from the general journal to the proper general ledger accounts.
4. Total and rule the purchases journal as of May 30.
5. Post the column totals from the purchases journal to the proper general ledger accounts.
6. Compute the net purchases of the firm for the month of May.

GENERAL LEDGER ACCOUNTS

205   Accounts Payable, $21,608 Cr.
501   Purchases
502   Freight In
503   Purchases Returns and Allowances

DATE	TRANSACTIONS
May 1	Purchased ski boots for $6,600 plus a freight charge of $220 from Colorado Shop for Skiers, Invoice 6572, dated April 28; the terms are 45 days net.
8	Purchased skis for $11,100 from Alaska Supply Company, Invoice 4916, dated May 2; the terms are net payable in 30 days.
9	Received Credit Memorandum 155 for $1,600 from Colorado Shop for Skiers for damaged ski boots that were returned; the boots were originally purchased on Invoice 6572, dated April 28.
12	Purchased ski jackets for $5,000 from Barrons Winter Fashions, Inc., Invoice 986, dated May 11, net due and payable in 60 days.
16	Purchased ski poles for $3,160 from Alaska Supply Company, Invoice 5011, dated May 15; the terms are n/30.
22	Purchased ski pants for $2,240 from Cold Mountain Clothing Company, Invoice 4019, dated May 16; the terms are 1/10, n/60.
28	Received Credit Memorandum 38 for $420 from Alaska Supply Company for defective ski poles that were returned; the items were originally purchased on Invoice 5011, dated May 15.
31	Purchased sweaters for $3,300 plus a freight charge of $100 from Taylor Ski Goods, Invoice 8354, dated May 27; the terms are 2/10, n/30.

(**Note:** Save your working papers for use in Problem 8.2B.)

Analyze: What total accounts payable were posted from the purchases journal to the general ledger for the month?

Problem 8.2B ▶

Objectives 4, 6

CONTINUING >>>
Problem

Posting to the accounts payable ledger and preparing a schedule of accounts payable.

This problem is a continuation of Problem 8.1B.

INSTRUCTIONS

1. Set up an accounts payable subsidiary ledger for Denver Ski Shop. Open an account for each of the creditors listed and enter the balances as of May 1, 2010.

2. Post the individual entries from the purchases journal and the general journal prepared in Problem 8.1B.

3. Prepare a schedule of accounts payable for May 31.

4. Check the total of the schedule of accounts payable against the balance of the *Accounts Payable* account in the general ledger. The two amounts should be equal.

Creditors		
Name	**Terms**	**Balance**
Alaska Supply Company	n/30	$1,700
Barrons Winter Fashions, Inc.	n/60	8,720
Cold Mountain Clothing Company	1/10, n/60	5,000
Colorado Shop for Skiers	n/45	6,188
Taylor Ski Goods	2/10, n/30	

Analyze: What amount did Denver Ski Shop owe to its supplier, Colorado Shop for Skiers, on May 31?

Journalizing credit purchases and purchases returns and allowances, computing the net delivered cost of goods, posting to the general ledger, posting to the accounts payable ledger, and preparing a schedule of accounts payable.

◄ **Problem 8.3B**
Objectives
1, 2, 3, 4, 5, 6

The Landscape Supply Center is a retail store that sells garden equipment, furniture, and supplies. Its credit purchases and purchases returns and allowances for December are shown below. The general ledger accounts used to record these transactions are also provided. The balance shown is for the beginning of December 2010.

INSTRUCTIONS

PART I

1. Open the general ledger accounts and enter the balance of *Accounts Payable* for December 1.

2. Record the transactions in a three-column purchases journal and in a general journal. Use 8 as the page number for the purchases journal and 20 as the page number for the general journal.

3. Post the entries from the general journal to the proper general ledger accounts.

4. Total, prove, and rule the purchases journal as of December 31.

5. Post the column totals from the purchases journal to the proper general ledger accounts.

6. Compute the net delivered cost of the firm's purchases for the month of December.

GENERAL LEDGER ACCOUNTS

205   Accounts Payable, $13,490 Cr.
501   Purchases
502   Freight In
503   Purchases Returns and Allowances

DATE	TRANSACTIONS
Dec. 1	Purchased lawn mowers for $5,780 plus a freight charge of $156 from Selby Corporation, Invoice 2110, dated November 26, net due and payable in 45 days.
5	Purchased outdoor chairs and tables for $5,700 plus a freight charge of $100 from Patio Furniture Shop, Invoice 633, dated December 2; the terms are 1/15, n/60.
9	Purchased grass seed for $1,148 from Spring Lawn Center, Invoice 1127, dated December 4; the terms are 30 days net.
16	Received Credit Memorandum 101 for $400 from Patio Furniture Shop; the amount is an allowance for scratches on some of the chairs and tables originally purchased on Invoice 633, dated December 2.
19	Purchased fertilizer for $1,600 plus a freight charge of $156 from Spring Lawn Center, Invoice 1131, dated December 15; the terms are 30 days net.
21	Purchased garden hoses for $760 plus a freight charge of $76 from Delta Rubber Company, Invoice 8517, dated December 17; the terms are n/60.
28	Received Credit Memorandum 210 for $150 from Delta Rubber Company for damaged hoses that were returned; the goods were purchased on Invoice 8517, dated December 17.
31	Purchased lawn sprinkler systems for $3,700 plus a freight charge of $80 from Cason Industries, Invoice 8819, dated December 26; the terms are 2/10, n/30.

INSTRUCTIONS

PART II

1. Set up an accounts payable subsidiary ledger for The Landscape Supply Center. Open an account for each of the following creditors and enter the balances as of December 1.

2. Post the individual entries from the purchases journal and the general journal prepared in Part I.

3. Prepare a schedule of accounts payable for December 31.

4. Check the total of the schedule of accounts payable against the balance of the *Accounts Payable* account in the general ledger. The two amounts should be equal.

Creditors		
Name	Terms	Balance
Cason Industries	2/10, n/30	$2,150
Delta Rubber Company	n/60	3,850
Patio Furniture Shop	1/15, n/60	
Selby Corporation	n/45	4,842
Spring Lawn Center	n/30	2,648

Analyze: By what amount did Accounts Payable increase during the month of December?

Problem 8.4B ▶

Objectives
1, 2, 3, 4, 5, 6

Journalizing credit purchases and purchases returns and allowances, posting to the general ledger, posting to the accounts payable ledger, and preparing a schedule of accounts payable.

Simpson's Card and Novelty Shop is a retail card, novelty, and business supply store. Its credit purchases and purchases returns and allowances for February 2010 appear on page 263. The general ledger accounts and the creditors' accounts in the accounts payable subsidiary ledger used to record these transactions are also provided. The balance shown is for the beginning of February.

INSTRUCTIONS

1. Open the general ledger accounts and enter the balance of *Accounts Payable* for February.

2. Open the creditors' accounts in the accounts payable subsidiary ledger and enter the balances for February 1, 2010.

3. Record each transaction in the appropriate journal, purchases or general. Use page 4 in the purchases journal and page 12 in the general journal.

4. Post entries to the accounts payable subsidiary ledger daily.

5. Post entries in the general journal to the proper general ledger accounts at the end of the month.

6. Total and rule the purchases journal as of February 28.

7. Post the totals to the appropriate general ledger accounts.

8. Calculate the net delivered cost of purchases.

9. Prepare a schedule of accounts payable and compare the balance of the *Accounts Payable* control account with the schedule of accounts payable.

GENERAL LEDGER ACCOUNTS

203　Accounts Payable, $15,200 credit balance
501　Purchases
502　Freight In
503　Purchases Returns and Allowances

Creditors		
Name	**Terms**	**Balance**
Business Forms, Inc.	n/30	$8,000
Gifts and Holiday Cards	2/10, n/30	4,000
Packing and Mailing Supply Center	2/10, n/30	3,200
Specialty Business Cards	1/10, n/45	

DATE	TRANSACTIONS
Feb. 5	Purchased copy paper from Packing and Mailing Supply Center for $2,000 plus $100 shipping charges on Invoice 502, dated February 2.
8	Purchased assorted holiday cards from Gifts and Holiday Cards on Invoice 2808, $1,900, dated February 5.
12	Purchased five boxes of novelty items from Gifts and Holiday Cards for a total cost of $1,200, Invoice 2904, dated February 8.
13	Purchased tray of cards from Specialty Business Cards on Invoice 2013 for $1,100, dated February 9.
19	Purchased supply of forms from Business Forms, Inc., for $1,980 plus shipping charges of $60 on Invoice 2019, dated February 16.
20	One box of cards purchased on February 8 from Gifts and Holiday Cards was water damaged. Received Credit Memorandum 102 for $200.
21	Toner supplies are purchased from Specialty Business Cards for $3,600 plus shipping charges of $110, Invoice 1376, dated February 19.
27	Received Credit Memorandum 118 for $240 from Gifts and Holiday Cards as an allowance for damaged novelty items purchased on February 12.

Analyze: What total amount did Simpson's Card and Novelty Shop pay in freight charges during the month of February? What percentage of delivered cost of purchases does this represent?

Critical Thinking Problem 8.1

Merchandising: Sales and Purchases

World of Fashions is a retail clothing store. Sales of merchandise and purchases of goods on account for January 2010, the first month of operations, appear on page 264.

INSTRUCTIONS

1. Record the purchases of goods on account on page 6 of a three-column purchases journal.

2. Record the sales of merchandise on account on page 1 of a sales journal.

3. Post the entries from the purchases journal and the sales journal to the individual accounts in the accounts payable and accounts receivable subsidiary ledgers. Use the following account numbers:

   Accounts Receivable 111
   Accounts Payable 205
   Sales Tax Payable 231
   Sales 401
   Purchases 501
   Freight In 502

4. Total, prove, and rule the journals as of January 31.

5. Post the column totals from the special journals to the proper general ledger accounts.

6. Prepare a schedule of accounts payable for January 31.

7. Prepare a schedule of accounts receivable for January 31.

PURCHASES OF GOODS ON ACCOUNT
Jan. 3 — Purchased dresses for $5,000 plus a freight charge of $112 from Fashion Center, Invoice 101, dated December 26; the terms are net 30 days.
5 — Purchased handbags for $3,480 plus a freight charge of $89 from Handbag Depot, Invoice 223, dated December 28; the terms are 2/10, n/30.
7 — Purchased blouses for $3,900 plus a freight charge of $68 from House of Styles, Invoice 556, dated January 3; the terms are 2/10, n/30.
9 — Purchased casual pants for $2,360 from Modern Woman Pants and Suits Company, Invoice 110, dated January 5; terms are n/30.
12 — Purchased business suits for $5,400 plus a freight charge of $129 from International Executive, Invoice 104, dated January 9; the terms are 2/10, n/30.
18 — Purchased shoes for $3,120 plus freight of $80 from Mr. John's Shoes, Invoice 118, dated January 14; the terms are n/60.
25 — Purchased hosiery for $900 from Hosiery Warehouse, Invoice 1012, dated January 20; the terms are 2/10, n/30.
29 — Purchased scarves and gloves for $1,600 from Modern Woman Pants and Suits Company, Invoice 315, dated January 26; the terms are n/30.
31 — Purchased party dresses for $5,250 plus a freight charge of $225 from Special Occasion Wholesale Dress Shop, Invoice 1044, dated January 27; the terms are 2/10, n/30.

SALES OF MERCHANDISE ON ACCOUNT
Jan. 4 — Sold two dresses to Sarah Valdez; issued Sales Slip 101 for $800 plus $64 sales tax.
5 — Sold a handbag to Linda Carter; issued Sales Slip 102 for $400 plus $32 sales tax.
6 — Sold four blouses to Teresa Collins; issued Sales Slip 103 for $400 plus $32 sales tax.
10 — Sold casual pants and a blouse to Demetria Davis; issued Sales Slip 104 for $600 plus $48 sales tax.
14 — Sold a business suit to Jeraldine Wells; issued Sales Slip 105 for $500 plus $40 sales tax.
17 — Sold hosiery, shoes, and gloves to Amalia Rodriguez; issued Sales Slip 106 for $800 plus $64 sales tax.
21 — Sold dresses and scarves to Rosabla Vasquez; issued Sales Slip 107 for $2,000 plus $160 sales tax.
24 — Sold a business suit to Sherrye Samuels; issued Sales Slip 108 for $400 plus $32 sales tax.
25 — Sold shoes to Cecila Lin; issued Sales Slip 109 for $300 plus $24 sales tax.
29 — Sold a casual pants set to Tonya Ennis; issued Sales Slip 110 for $600 plus $48 sales tax.
31 — Sold a dress and handbag to Isabel James; issued Sales Slip 111 for $750 plus $60 sales tax.

Analyze: What is the net delivered cost of purchases for the month of January?

Critical Thinking Problem 8.2

Internal Control

Dora Alexander, owner of Passions Linen Shop, was preparing checks for payment of the current month's purchase invoices when she realized that there were two invoices from Sensuous Linen Company, each for the purchase of 100 red, heart-imprinted king size linen sets. Alexander thinks that Sensuous Linen Company must have billed Passions Linen Shop twice for the same shipment because she knows the shop would not have needed two orders for 100 red linen sets within a month.

1. How can Alexander determine whether Sensuous Linen Company billed Passions Linen Shop in error or whether Passions Linen Shop placed two identical orders for red, heart-imprinted linen sets?

2. If two orders were placed, how can Alexander prevent duplicate purchases from happening in the future?

BUSINESS CONNECTIONS

Cash Management

1. Why should management be concerned about the timely payment of invoices?

2. Why is it important for a firm to maintain a satisfactory credit rating?

3. Suppose you are the new controller of a small but growing company and you find that the firm has a policy of paying cash for all purchases of goods even though it could obtain credit. The president of the company does not like the idea of having debts, but the vice president thinks this is a poor business policy that will hurt the firm in the future. The president has asked your opinion. Would you agree with the president or the vice president? Why?

4. Why should management be concerned about the internal control of purchases?

5. How can good internal control of purchases protect a firm from fraud and errors and from excessive investment in merchandise?

6. In what way would excessive investment in merchandise harm a business?

Adding New Vendors

Anait Artununian is the accounts payable clerk for Jiffy Delivery Service. This company runs 10 branches in the San Diego area. The company pays for a variety of expenses. Anait writes the checks for each of the vendors and the controller signs the checks. Anait has decided she needs a raise and the controller has told her to wait for six months. Anait has devised a plan to get a raise on her own. She creates a new vendor for her friend's business with the name Gevok Car Detailing. She also creates two purchase orders for car detailing service from Gevok's for $75 and $70. She writes checks to Gevok Car Detailing to pay these invoices. She knows the controller will sign all checks only looking at the checks over $100. She delivers the checks to Gevok who will deposit the checks in his bank account. Gevok then writes a check to her for $145. Is this a good way for Anait to obtain a raise? Is it an ethical practice? Eventually what will be the effect of Anait's actions? What can the company do to prevent this type of behavior?

Accounts Payable and Cost of Merchandise

Refer to the *2006 Annual Report* for the Home Depot, Inc., in Appendix A.

1. Locate the consolidated balance sheets. What is the reported amount of accounts payable at January 30, 2007? Has this balance increased or decreased since the prior fiscal year-end? By what amount?

2. Review Management's Discussion and Analysis of Results of Operations and Financial Condition for The Home Depot, Inc. What factors contributed to the higher cost of merchandise for the operating period?

Managerial | FOCUS

Ethical | DILEMMA

STREETWISE:
Questions from the
REAL WORLD

Income Statement

The following financial statement excerpt is taken from the *2006 Annual Report* for Amazon.com, Inc.

Consolidated Statements of Operations		
December 31,	For the year ended December 31,	
	2006	2005
(In millions)		
Net Sales	$ 10,711	$ 8,490
Cost of Sales	8,255	6,451
Gross Profit	$ 2,456	$ 2,039

1. The Cost of Sales amount on Amazon.com, Inc., consolidated statements of operations represents the net cost of the goods that were sold for the period. For 2006, what percentage of net sales was the cost of sales? For fiscal 2005?

2. What factors might affect a merchandising company's cost of sales from one period to another?

Analyze Online: On the Amazon.com, Inc., Web site (www.amazon.com), locate the investor relation's section.

3. Review the consolidated statements of operations found in the current year's annual report.

4. What amount is reported for cost of sales?

5. What amount is reported for net sales?

Timing

A purchase order expresses an authorized intent to buy a particular item at a specific price from a supplier. Some companies record a debit to *Purchases* and a credit to *Accounts Payable* at the time the purchase order is issued. Other companies wait until the invoice for the merchandise arrives and then record the purchase. Which method do you think is better? Why?

Memo

You own a retail gourmet cooking supply store. As the owner of the business, you have noticed that your manager, bookkeeper, and sales clerk all place orders with suppliers, sometimes resulting in duplicate orders and confusion in processing invoices. You need to strengthen your internal controls in regard to the purchase of goods for resale. Prepare a memo to your staff that outlines proper procedures for placement of merchandise orders, receipt of goods, and payment of invoices.

Payment Terms

A company needs to develop an objective for paying bills. Do they want to stretch their cash flow as far as they can? Do they want to have a good reputation of always paying bills on time? Do they want to be sure to get paid by their customers before they pay their vendors? In a group, discuss what would be the best payment terms to use for each objective and its impact on the company.

Computer Check Format

Go to the QuickBooks and Peachtree Web sites at quickbooks.com and peachtree.com. Select product overview and more information. You want to be sure to see a copy of a check and purchase order. Compare and contrast the information contained on each check and purchase order. How many copies can you get of the check and purchase order? How is the form different? How is it the same? What information should be included on a company's check and purchase invoice?

Answers to **Self Reviews**

Answers to Section 1 Self Review

1. Locating suitable suppliers, obtaining price quotations and credit terms, and placing orders.
2. Merchandise purchased on credit for resale.
3. It saves time and effort, and it strengthens the audit trail.
4. **b.** Purchase order
5. **c.** Purchase requisition
6. The business will receive a 2 percent discount if the invoice is paid within 10 days. If the invoice is not paid within 10 days, the total amount is due within 30 days.

Answers to Section 2 Self Review

1. It lists all of the creditors to whom money is owed.
2. $57,675 ($60,550 – $2,875)
3. Purchases   1,275.00
   Freight In   82.00
      Accounts Payable   1,357.00
4. **c.** $6,400 credit ($4,800 + $1,600)
5. **b.** income statement.
6. A payment was made and recorded in the general ledger account, but was not recorded in the creditor's subsidiary ledger account.

Answers to Comprehensive Self Review

1. A contra cost of goods sold account.
2. A price reduction offered to encourage quick payment of invoices by customers.
3. To accumulate freight charges paid for purchases.
4. The purchase requisition is used by a sales department to notify the purchasing department of the items wanted. The purchase order is prepared by the purchasing department to order the necessary goods at an appropriate price from the selected supplier.
5. The receiving report shows the quantity of goods received and the condition of the goods. The invoice shows quantities and prices; it is the document from which checks are prepared in payment of purchases.

Cash Receipts, Cash Payments, and Banking Procedures

Chapter 9

LEARNING OBJECTIVES

1. Record cash receipts in a cash receipts journal. **LP9**
2. Account for cash short or over.
3. Post from the cash receipts journal to subsidiary and general ledgers.
4. Record cash payments in a cash payments journal.
5. Post from the cash payments journal to subsidiary and general ledgers.
6. Demonstrate a knowledge of procedures for a petty cash fund.
7. Demonstrate a knowledge of internal control procedures for cash.
8. Write a check, endorse checks, prepare a bank deposit slip, and maintain a checkbook balance.
9. Reconcile the monthly bank statement.
10. Record any adjusting entries required from the bank reconciliation.
11. Define the accounting terms new to this chapter.

NEW TERMS

bank reconciliation statement
blank endorsement
bonding
canceled check
cash
cash payments journal
cash receipts journal
cash register proof
Cash Short or Over account
check
credit memorandum
debit memorandum
deposit in transit
deposit slip

dishonored (NSF) check
drawee
drawer
endorsement
full endorsement
negotiable
outstanding checks
payee
petty cash analysis sheet
petty cash fund
petty cash voucher
postdated check
promissory note
restrictive endorsement
service charge
statement of account

H&R BLOCK®   www.hrblock.com

In the 1940s, Henry and Leon Bloch borrowed $5,000 from a relative and founded United Business Company, an accounting services firm. Business was good for the Bloch brothers and they were soon joined by their brother Richard. By the mid-1950s, they had 12 employees and were keeping books for various small local businesses in the Kansas City area. Things would change quickly, however. In 1954, on the basis of a recommendation from a client, the Blochs ran an ad for their tax preparation services and the small office was flooded with calls. It seems just as the IRS was phasing out its free tax preparation services and turning taxpayers away, the Bloch brothers were advertising their services.

United Business Company changed its name to H&R Block and shifted its focus from general accounting services to tax preparation. Within a year, business tripled and has kept growing ever since. The largest consumer tax services company in the U.S., in 2006, H&R Block earned $2.4 billion in revenues serving 21.9 million clients worldwide (19.4 million of those clients in the U.S.) with in-person and digital tax solutions.

thinking critically

What types of daily receipts and payments occur in a local H&R Block office?

Cash Receipts

Cash is the business asset that is most easily lost, mishandled, or even stolen. A well-managed business has careful procedures for controlling cash and recording cash transactions.

Cash Transactions

In accounting, the term **cash** is used for currency, coins, checks, money orders, and funds on deposit in a bank. Most cash transactions involve checks.

CASH RECEIPTS

The type of cash receipts depends on the nature of the business. Supermarkets receive checks as well as currency and coins. Department stores receive checks in the mail from charge account customers. Cash received by wholesalers is usually in the form of checks.

CASH PAYMENTS

For safety and convenience, most businesses make payments by check. Sometimes a limited number of transactions are paid with currency and coins. The **petty cash fund** is used to handle payments involving small amounts of money, such as postage stamps, delivery charges, and minor purchases of office supplies. Some businesses maintain a fund to provide cash for business-related travel and entertainment expenses.

The Cash Receipts Journal

To improve the recordkeeping of cash receipts, many businesses use a special **cash receipts journal.** The cash receipts journal simplifies the recording of transactions and eliminates repetition in posting.

>>1. OBJECTIVE

Record cash receipts in a cash receipts journal.

RECORDING TRANSACTIONS IN THE CASH RECEIPTS JOURNAL

The format of the cash receipts journal varies according to the needs of each business. Figure 9.1 on page 271 shows the cash receipts journal for Maxx-Out Sporting Goods, which

CASH RECEIPTS JOURNAL   PAGE ___1___

| DATE | | DESCRIPTION | POST. REF. | ACCOUNTS RECEIVABLE CREDIT | SALES TAX PAYABLE CREDIT | SALES CREDIT | OTHER ACCOUNTS CREDIT | | | CASH DEBIT |
							ACCOUNT NAME	POST. REF.	AMOUNT	
2010										
Jan.	7	Ann Anh		7 0 2 00						7 0 2 00
	8	Cash Sales			3 6 0 00	4 5 0 0 00				4 8 6 0 00
	11	Vickie Bowman		2 7 0 00						2 7 0 00
	12	Investment					M. Ferraro, Capital		1 5 0 0 0 00	1 5 0 0 0 00
	13	Barbara Coe		5 4 0 00						5 4 0 00
	15	Cash Sales			3 8 4 00	4 8 0 0 00	Cash Short/Over		⟨1 8 00⟩	5 1 6 6 00
	16	Alma Sanchez		1 0 8 00						1 0 8 00
	17	Cash Refund					Supplies		7 5 00	7 5 00
	22	Fred Wu		4 0 0 00						4 0 0 00
	22	Cash Sales			4 0 0 00	5 0 0 0 00				5 4 0 0 00
	29	Cash Sales			2 1 6 00	2 7 0 0 00	Cash Short/Over		1 6 00	2 9 3 2 00
	31	Kim Ramirez		1 0 8 00						1 0 8 00
	31	Mesia Davis		2 7 5 00						2 7 5 00
	31	Cash Sales			4 4 0 00	5 5 0 0 00				5 9 4 0 00
	31	Note Collection/					Notes Receivable		8 0 0 00	
		Stacee Fairley					Interest Income		3 6 00	8 3 6 00

FIGURE 9.1

Cash Receipts Journal

LP9

has two major sources of cash receipts: checks from credit customers who are making payments on account, and currency and coins from cash sales.

The cash receipts journal has separate columns for the accounts frequently used when recording cash receipts. There are columns for

- debits to **Cash,**
- credits to **Accounts Receivable** for payments received on account,
- credits to **Sales** and **Sales Tax Payable** for cash sales.

At the end of the month, the totals of these columns are posted to the general ledger.

Notice the Other Accounts Credit section, which is for entries that do not fit into one of the special columns. Entries in the Other Accounts Credit section are individually posted to the general ledger.

Cash Sales and Sales Taxes

Maxx-Out Sporting Goods uses a cash register to record cash sales and to store currency and coins. As each transaction is entered, the cash register prints a receipt for the customer. It also records the sale and the sales tax on an audit tape locked inside the machine. At the end of the day, when the machine is cleared, the cash register prints the transaction totals on the audit tape. The manager of the store removes the audit tape, and a cash register proof is prepared. The **cash register proof** is a verification that the amount in the cash register agrees with the amount shown on the audit tape. The cash register proof is used to record cash sales and sales tax in the cash receipts journal. The currency and coins are deposited in the firm's bank.

Refer to Figure 9.1, the cash receipts journal for Maxx-Out Sporting Goods. To keep it simple, it shows weekly, rather than daily, cash sales entries. Look at the January 8 entry. The steps to record the January 8 sales follow.

1. Enter the sales tax collected, $360.00, in the Sales Tax Payable Credit column.
2. Enter the sales, $4,500.00, in the Sales Credit column.
3. Enter the cash received, $4,860.00, in the Cash Debit column.
4. Confirm that total credits equal total debits ($360.00 + $4,500.00 = $4,860.00).

Cash Short or Over

Occasionally, errors occur when making change. When errors happen, the cash in the cash register is either more than or less than the cash listed on the audit tape. When cash in the register is more than the audit tape, cash is over. When cash in the register is

ABOUT
ACCOUNTING

Automated Teller Machines
The banking industry paved the way for the Internet's self-service applications (such as ordering products online) with ATMs.

>>2. OBJECTIVE
Account for cash short or over.

less than the audit tape, cash is *short*. Cash tends to be short more often than over because customers are more likely to notice and complain if they receive too little change.

Record short or over amounts in the **Cash Short or Over account.** If the account has a credit balance, there is an overage, which is treated as revenue. If the account has a debit balance, there is a shortage, which is treated as an expense.

Figure 9.1 shows how cash overages and shortages appear in the cash receipts journal. Look at the January 29 entry. Cash sales were $2,700. Sales tax collected was $216. The cash drawer was over $16. Overages are recorded as credits. Notice that the account name and the overage are entered in the Other Accounts Credit section.

Now look at the January 15 entry. This time the cash register was short. Shortages are recorded as debits. Debits are not the normal balance of the Other Accounts Credit column, so the debit entry is circled.

Businesses that have frequent entries for cash shortages and overages add a Cash Short or Over column to the cash receipts journal.

Cash Received on Account   Maxx-Out Sporting Goods makes sales on account and bills customers once a month. It sends a **statement of account** that shows the transactions during the month and the balance owed. Customers are asked to pay within 30 days of receiving the statement. Checks from credit customers are entered in the cash receipts journal, and then the checks are deposited in the bank.

Figure 9.1 shows how cash received on account is recorded. Look at the January 7 entry for Ann Anh. The check amount is entered in the Accounts Receivable Credit and the Cash Debit columns.

Cash Discounts on Sales   Maxx-Out Sporting Goods, like most retail businesses, does not offer cash discounts. However, many wholesale businesses offer cash discounts to customers who pay within a certain time period. For example, a wholesaler may offer a 1 percent discount if the customer pays within 10 days. To the wholesaler this is a *sales discount*. Sales discounts are recorded when the payment is received. Sales discounts are recorded in a contra revenue account, **Sales Discounts.** Businesses with many sales discounts add a Sales Discounts Debit column to the cash receipts journal.

Additional Investment by the Owner   Figure 9.1 shows that on January 12, the owner Max Ferraro invested an additional $15,000 in Maxx-Out Sporting Goods. He intends to use the money to expand the product line. The account name and amount are entered in the Other Accounts Credit section. The debit is entered in the Cash Debit column.

Receipt of a Cash Refund   Sometimes a business receives a cash refund for supplies, equipment, or other assets that are returned to the supplier. Figure 9.1 shows that on January 17, Maxx-Out Sporting Goods received a $75 cash refund for supplies that were returned to the seller. The account name and amount are entered in the Other Accounts Credit section. The debit is entered in the Cash Debit column.

Collection of a Promissory Note and Interest   A **promissory note** is a written promise to pay a specified amount of money on a certain date. Most notes require that interest is paid at a specified rate. Businesses use promissory notes to extend credit for some sales transactions.

$ 800.00   July 31, 2009

    Six Months   AFTER DATE   I   PROMISE TO PAY

    TO THE ORDER OF   Maxx-Out Sporting Goods

    Eight Hundred and no/100 ————————————— DOLLARS

    PAYABLE AT   First Texas Bank

    VALUE RECEIVED *with interest at 9%*

    NO. 30   DUE   January 31, 2010   Stacee Fairley

FIGURE 9.2

A Promissory Note

Sometimes promissory notes are used to replace an accounts receivable balance when the account is overdue. For example, on July 31 Maxx-Out Sporting Goods accepted a six-month promissory note from Stacee Fairley, who owed $800 on account (see Figure 9.2). Fairley had asked for more time to pay his balance. Maxx-Out Sporting Goods agreed to grant more time if Fairley signed a promissory note with 9 percent annual interest. The note provides more legal protection than an account receivable. The interest is compensation for the delay in receiving payment.

On the date of the transaction, July 31, Maxx-Out Sporting Goods recorded a general journal entry to increase notes receivable and to decrease accounts receivable for $800. The asset account, **Notes Receivable,** was debited and **Accounts Receivable** was credited.

GENERAL JOURNAL   PAGE _16_

	DATE		DESCRIPTION	POST. REF.	DEBIT	CREDIT	
1	2009						1
2	July	31	Notes Receivable	109	80000		2
3			Accounts Receivable/Stacee Fairley	111 ✓		80000	3
4			Received a 6-month, 9% note from				4
5			Stacee Fairley to replace open account				5

On January 31, the due date of the note, Maxx-Out Sporting Goods received a check for $836 from Fairley. This sum covered the amount of the note ($800) and the interest owed for the six-month period ($36). Figure 9.1 shows the entry in the cash receipts journal. The account names, **Notes Receivable** and **Interest Income,** and the amounts are entered on two lines in the Other Accounts Credit section. The debit is in the Cash Debit column.

POSTING FROM THE CASH RECEIPTS JOURNAL

During the month, the amounts recorded in the Accounts Receivable Credit column are posted to individual accounts in the accounts receivable subsidiary ledger. Similarly, the amounts that appear in the Other Accounts Credit column are posted individually to the general ledger accounts during the month. The "CR1" posting references in the **Cash Short or Over** general ledger account below show that the entries appear on the first page of the cash receipts journal.

ACCOUNT _Cash Short or Over_   ACCOUNT NO. _617_

DATE		DESCRIPTION	POST. REF.	DEBIT	CREDIT	BALANCE DEBIT	BALANCE CREDIT
2010							
Jan.	15		CR1	18 00		18 00	
	29		CR1		16 00	2 00	

Posting the Column Totals At the end of the month, the cash receipts journal is totaled and the equality of debits and credits is proved.

Proof of Cash Receipts Journal	
	Debits
Cash Debit column	$42,612.00
	Credits
Accounts Receivable Credit column	$ 2,403.00
Sales Tax Payable Credit column	1,800.00
Sales Credit column	22,500.00
Other Accounts Credit column	15,909.00
Total Credits	$42,612.00

>>**3. OBJECTIVE**

Post from the cash receipts journal to subsidiary and general ledgers.

LP9

CASH RECEIPTS JOURNAL   PAGE ___1___

DATE	DESCRIPTION	POST. REF.	ACCOUNTS RECEIVABLE CREDIT	SALES TAX PAYABLE CREDIT	SALES CREDIT	OTHER ACCOUNTS CREDIT			CASH DEBIT
						ACCOUNT NAME	POST. REF.	AMOUNT	
2010									
Jan. 7	Ann Anh	✓	702 00						702 00
8	Cash Sales			36 00	450 00				486 00
11	Vickie Bowman	✓	270 00						270 00
12	Investment					M. Ferraro, Capital	301	15000 00	15000 00
13	Barbara Coe	✓	540 00						540 00
15	Cash Sales			384 00	4800 00	Cash Short/Over	617	18 00	5166 00
16	Alma Sanchez	✓	108 00						108 00
17	Cash Refund					Supplies	129	75 00	75 00
22	Fred Wu	✓	400 00						400 00
22	Cash Sales			400 00	5000 00				5400 00
29	Cash Sales			216 00	2700 00	Cash Short/Over	617	16 00	2932 00
31	Kim Ramirez	✓	108 00						108 00
31	Mesia Davis	✓	275 00						275 00
31	Cash Sales			440 00	5500 00				5940 00
31	Note Collection/					Notes Receivable	109	800 00	
	Stacee Fairley					Interest Income	491	36 00	836 00
	Totals		2403 00	1800 00	22500 00			15909 00	42612 00
			(111)	(231)	(401)			(X)	(101)

FIGURE 9.3

Posted Cash Receipts Journal

Figure 9.3 shows the cash receipts journal after all posting is completed.

When the cash receipts journal has been proved, rule the columns and post the totals to the general ledger. Figure 9.4 on page 275 shows how to post from the cash receipts journal to the general ledger accounts.

To post a column total to a general ledger account, enter "CR1" in the Posting Reference column to show that the entry is from the first page of the cash receipts journal. Enter the column total in the general ledger account Debit or Credit column. Figure 9.4 shows the entries to **Accounts Receivable** (1), **Sales Tax Payable** (2), **Sales** (3), and **Cash** (4). Compute the new balance for each account and enter it in the Balance Debit or Balance Credit column.

Enter the general ledger account numbers under the column totals on the cash receipts journal. The (X) in the Other Accounts Credit Amount column indicates that the individual amounts were posted, not the total.

Posting to the Accounts Receivable Ledger To keep customer balances current, accountants post entries from the Accounts Receivable Credit column to the customers' accounts in the accounts receivable subsidiary ledger daily. For example, on January 7, $702 was posted to Ann Anh's account in the subsidiary ledger. The "CR1" in the Posting Reference column indicates that the transaction appears on page 1 of the cash receipts journal. The check mark (✓) in the Posting Reference column in the cash receipts journal (Figure 9.4 on page 275) shows that the amount was posted to Ann Anh's account in the accounts receivable subsidiary ledger.

NAME   Ann Anh

ADDRESS   8913 South Hampton Road, Dallas, Texas 75232-6002

DATE		DESCRIPTION	POST. REF.	DEBIT	CREDIT	BALANCE
2010						
Jan.	1	Balance	✓			432 00
	3	Sales Slip 1101	S1	702 00		1134 00
	7		CR1		702 00	432 00
	31	Sales Slip 1110	S1	267 50		699 50

FIGURE 9.4   Posting from the Cash Receipts Journal

ADVANTAGES OF THE CASH RECEIPTS JOURNAL

The cash receipts journal

- saves time and effort when recording and posting cash receipts,
- allows for the division of work among the accounting staff,
- strengthens the audit trail by recording all cash receipts transactions in one place.

Section **1** Self Review

QUESTIONS

1. How and when are the amounts in the Accounts Receivable Credit column posted?

2. What is a promissory note? In what situation would a business accept a promissory note?

3. What is a cash shortage? A cash overage? How are they recorded?

EXERCISES

4. Collection of a note receivable is recorded in the

   a. accounts receivable journal.

   b. cash receipts journal.

   c. general journal.

   d. promissory note journal.

5. Which items are considered cash?

   a. Currency

   b. Funds on deposit in the bank

   c. Money orders

   d. All of the above

ANALYSIS

6. You notice that the *Cash Short or Over* account has 15 entries during the month. The ending balance is a $10 shortage for the month. Is this a problem? Why or why not?

(Answers to Section 1 Self Review are on page 320.)

Section **2**

SECTION OBJECTIVES

>> 4. **Record cash payments in a cash payments journal.**

WHY IT'S IMPORTANT

The cash payments journal is an efficient option for recording payments by check.

>> 5. **Post from the cash payments journal to subsidiary and general ledgers.**

WHY IT'S IMPORTANT

The subsidiary and general ledgers must hold accurate, up-to-date information about cash transactions.

>> 6. **Demonstrate a knowledge of procedures for a petty cash fund.**

WHY IT'S IMPORTANT

Businesses use the petty cash fund to pay for small operating expenditures.

>> 7. **Demonstrate a knowledge of internal control procedures for cash.**

WHY IT'S IMPORTANT

Internal controls safeguard business assets.

TERMS TO LEARN

bonding
cash payments journal
petty cash analysis sheet
petty cash voucher

Cash Payments

A good system of internal control requires that payments be made by check. In a good internal control system, one employee approves payments, another employee prepares the checks, and another employee records the transactions.

The Cash Payments Journal

Unless a business has just a few cash payments each month, the process of recording these transactions in the general journal is time consuming. The **cash payments journal** is a special journal used to record transactions involving the payment of cash.

RECORDING TRANSACTIONS IN THE CASH PAYMENTS JOURNAL

Refer to Figure 9.5 on page 279 for Maxx-Out Sporting Goods' cash payments journal. Notice that there are separate columns for the accounts frequently used when recording cash payments—*Cash, Accounts Payable,* and *Purchases Discounts.* At the end of the month, the totals of these columns are posted to the general ledger.

The Other Accounts Debit section is for entries that do not fit into one of the special columns. Entries in the Other Accounts Debit section are individually posted to the general ledger.

Payments for Expenses Businesses write checks for a variety of expenses each month. In January, Maxx-Out Sporting Goods issued checks for rent, electricity, telephone service, advertising, and salaries. Refer to the January 3 entry for rent expense in Figure 9.5. Notice that the account name and amount are entered in the Other Accounts Debit section. The credit is in the Cash Credit column.

>>4. OBJECTIVE

Record cash payments in a cash payments journal.

LP9

> Most banks currently offer online banking (also called home and electronic banking) that allows a customer to access account information 24 hours a day, seven days a week. Online banking allows account viewing, bill payment for recurring and future transactions, and the ability to export account information to Quicken and other accounting software, and performs a variety of other transactions. To participate in online banking, bank customers must be accepted by the bank for the service, have a computer with Adobe Acrobat software, and have their own Internet access.

Payments on Account   Merchandising businesses usually make numerous payments on account for goods that were purchased on credit. If there is no cash discount, the entry in the cash payments journal is a debit to *Accounts Payable* and a credit to *Cash.* For an example of a payment without a discount, refer to the January 27 entry for International Sportsman in Figure 9.5.

recall

Discount Terms

The terms 2/10, n/30 mean that if payment is made within 10 days, the customer can take a 2 percent discount. Otherwise, payment in full is due in 30 days.

   Purchases Discounts is a contra cost of goods sold account that appears in the Cost of Goods Sold section of the income statement. Purchases discounts are subtracted from purchases to obtain net purchases.

   For an example of a payment with a discount, refer to the January 13 entry for Active Designs in Figure 9.5. Maxx-Out Sporting Goods takes a 2 percent discount for paying within the discount period ($2,865 \times 0.02 = 57.30). When there is a cash discount, three elements must be recorded.

- Debit *Accounts Payable* for the invoice amount, $2,865.
- Credit *Purchases Discounts* for the amount of the discount, $57.30.
- Credit *Cash* for the amount of cash paid, $2,807.70.

> Debit cards (also called check cards) look like credit cards or ATM (automated teller machine) cards, but operate like cash or a personal check. In this context, debit means "subtract" so when you use your debit card, you are subtracting your money from your bank account. Funds on deposit with a bank represent a liability to the bank. By debiting accounts when depositors use their debit cards, the bank reduces the depositors' account balances thus reducing the bank's liabilities to depositors. Debit cards are accepted almost everywhere including grocery stores, retail stores, gasoline stations, and restaurants. Debit cards are popular because they offer an alternative to carrying checks or cash. Transactions that are completed with the debit card will appear on your bank statement.

Cash Purchases of Equipment and Supplies   Businesses use cash to purchase equipment, supplies, and other assets. These transactions are recorded in the cash payments journal. In January, Maxx-Out Sporting Goods issued checks for store fixtures and store supplies. Refer to the entries on January 10 and 14 in Figure 9.5. Notice that the account names and amounts appear in the Other Accounts Debit section. The credits are recorded in the Cash Credit column.

Payment of Taxes   Retail businesses collect sales tax from their customers. Periodically the sales tax is remitted to the taxing authority. Refer to the entry on January 11 in Figure 9.5. Maxx-Out Sporting Goods issued a check for $756 to pay the December sales tax. Notice that the account name and amount appear in the Other Accounts Debit section. The credit is in the Cash Credit column.

Cash Purchases of Merchandise   Most merchandising businesses buy their goods on credit. Occasionally, purchases are made for cash. These purchases are recorded in the cash payments journal. Refer to the January 31 entry for the purchase of goods in Figure 9.5.

CASH PAYMENTS JOURNAL

PAGE ___1___

DATE	CK. NO.	DESCRIPTION	POST. REF.	ACCOUNTS PAYABLE DEBIT	OTHER ACCOUNTS DEBIT — ACCOUNT TITLE	POST. REF.	AMOUNT	PURCHASES DISCOUNTS CREDIT	CASH CREDIT
2010									
Jan. 3	111	January rent			Rent Expense		1 5 0 0 00		1 5 0 0 00
10	112	Store fixtures			Store Equipment		2 4 0 0 00		2 4 0 0 00
11	113	Tax remittance			Sales Tax Payable		7 5 6 00		7 5 6 00
11	114	World of Sports		3 9 3 5 00				7 8 70	3 8 5 6 30
13	115	Active Designs		2 8 6 5 00				5 7 30	2 8 0 7 70
14	116	Store Supplies			Supplies		9 0 0 00		9 0 0 00
15	117	Withdrawal			M. Ferraro, Drawing		3 0 0 0 00		3 0 0 0 00
17	118	Electric bill			Utilities Expense		3 1 8 00		3 1 8 00
17	119	The Sports Warehouse		4 2 5 0 00					4 2 5 0 00
21	120	Telephone bill			Telephone Expense		2 7 6 00		2 7 6 00
25	121	Newspaper ad			Advertising Expense		8 4 0 00		8 4 0 00
27	122	International Sportsman		1 0 0 0 00					1 0 0 0 00
30	123	Active Designs		1 1 3 5 00					1 1 3 5 00
31	124	World of Sports		5 6 5 00					5 6 5 00
31	125	January payroll			Salaries Expense		4 9 5 0 00		4 9 5 0 00
31	126	Purchase of goods			Purchases		3 2 0 0 00		3 2 0 0 00
31	127	Freight charge			Freight In		1 7 5 00		1 7 5 00
31	128	Cash refund			Sales Returns & Allow.		1 6 0 00		
					Sales Tax Payable		1 2 80		1 7 2 80
31	129	Note Paid to			Notes Payable		6 0 0 0 00		
		Metroplex Equip. Co.			Interest Expense		3 0 0 00		6 3 0 0 00
31	130	Establish Petty Cash fund			Petty Cash Fund		1 7 5 00		1 7 5 00
		TOTALS		1 3 7 5 0 00			2 4 9 6 2 80	1 3 6 00	3 8 5 7 6 80

FIGURE 9.5

Cash Payments Journal

Payment of Freight Charges Freight charges on purchases of goods are handled in two ways. In some cases, the seller pays the freight charge and then includes it on the invoice. This method was covered in Chapter 8. The other method is for the buyer to pay the transportation company when the goods arrive. The buyer issues a check for the freight charge and records it in the cash payments journal. Refer to the entry on January 31 in Figure 9.5. The account name and amount appear in the Other Accounts Debit section. The credit is in the Cash Credit column.

Payment of a Cash Refund When a customer purchases goods for cash and later returns them or receives an allowance, the customer is usually given a cash refund. Refer to the January 31 entry in Figure 9.5. Maxx-Out Sporting Goods issued a check for $172.80 to a customer who returned a defective item. When there is a cash refund, three elements are recorded.

- Debit *Sales Returns and Allowances* for the amount of the purchase, $160.00.
- Debit *Sales Tax Payable* for the sales tax, $12.80.
- Credit *Cash* for the amount of cash paid, $172.80.

Notice that the debits in the Other Accounts Debit section appear on two lines because two general ledger accounts are debited.

Payment of a Promissory Note and Interest A promissory note can be issued to settle an overdue account or to obtain goods, equipment, or other property. For example, on August 2 Maxx-Out Sporting Goods issued a six-month promissory note for $6,000 to purchase store fixtures from Metroplex Equipment Company. The note had an interest rate of 10 percent. Maxx-Out Sporting Goods recorded this transaction in the general journal by debiting *Store Equipment* and crediting *Notes Payable,* a liability account.

	GENERAL JOURNAL		PAGE	16		
DATE	DESCRIPTION	POST. REF.	DEBIT		CREDIT	
1	2009					1
2	Aug. 2 Store Equipment	131	6 0 0 0 00			2
3	Notes Payable	201			6 0 0 0 00	3
4	Issued a 6-month, 10% note to					4
5	Metroplex Equipment Company for					5
6	purchase of new store fixtures					6
7						7

On January 31, Maxx-Out Sporting Goods issued a check for $6,300 in payment of the note, $6,000, and the interest, $300. This transaction was recorded in the cash payments journal in Figure 9.5.

- Debit *Notes Payable,* $6,000.
- Debit *Interest Expense,* $300.
- Credit *Cash,* $6,300.

Notice that the debits in the Other Accounts Debit section appear on two lines.

>>**5. OBJECTIVE**

Post from the cash payments journal to subsidiary and general ledgers.

LP9

POSTING FROM THE CASH PAYMENTS JOURNAL

During the month, the amounts recorded in the Accounts Payable Debit column are posted to individual accounts in the accounts payable subsidiary ledger. The amounts in the Other Accounts Debit column are also posted individually to the general ledger accounts during the month. For example, the January 3 entry in the cash payments journal was posted to the *Rent Expense* account. The "CP1" indicates that the entry is recorded on page 1 of the cash payments journal.

ACCOUNT Rent Expense   ACCOUNT NO. 634

DATE	DESCRIPTION	POST. REF.	DEBIT	CREDIT	BALANCE DEBIT	BALANCE CREDIT
2010						
Jan. 3		CP1	1 5 0 0 00		1 5 0 0 00	

Posting the Column Totals   At the end of the month, the cash payments journal is totaled and proved. The total debits must equal total credits.

Proof of Cash Payments Journal	
	Debits
Accounts Payable Debit column	$13,750.00
Other Accounts Debit column	24,962.80
Total Debits	$38,712.80
	Credits
Purchases Discount Credit column	$ 136.00
Cash Credit column	38,576.80
Total Credits	$38,712.80

CASH PAYMENTS JOURNAL   PAGE ___1___

DATE	CK. NO.	DESCRIPTION	POST. REF.	ACCOUNTS PAYABLE DEBIT	ACCOUNT TITLE	POST. REF.	AMOUNT	PURCHASES DISCOUNTS CREDIT	CASH CREDIT
2010									
Jan. 3	111	January rent			Rent Expense	634	1 500 00		1 500 00
10	112	Store fixtures			Store Equipment	131	2 400 00		2 400 00
11	113	Tax remittance			Sales Tax Payable	231	756 00		756 00
11	114	World of Sports	✓	3 935 00				78 70	3 856 30
13	115	Active Designs	✓	2 865 00				57 30	2 807 70
14	116	Store Supplies			Supplies	129	900 00		900 00
15	117	Withdrawal			M. Ferraro, Drawing	302	3 000 00		3 000 00
17	118	Electric bill			Utilities Expense	643	318 00		318 00
17	119	The Sports Warehouse	✓	4 250 00					4 250 00
21	120	Telephone bill			Telephone Expense	649	276 00		276 00
25	121	Newspaper ad			Advertising Expense	614	840 00		840 00
27	122	International Sportsman	✓	1 000 00					1 000 00
30	123	Active Designs	✓	1 135 00					1 135 00
31	124	World of Sports	✓	565 00					565 00
31	125	January payroll			Salaries Expense	637	4 950 00		4 950 00
31	126	Purchase of goods			Purchases	501	3 200 00		3 200 00
31	127	Freight charge			Freight In	502	175 00		175 00
31	128	Cash refund			Sales Returns & Allow.	451	160 00		
					Sales Tax Payable	231	12 80		172 80
31	129	Note Paid to Metroplex			Notes Payable	201	6 000 00		
		Equipment Company			Interest Expense	691	300 00		6 300 00
31	130	Establish Petty Cash fund			Petty Cash Fund	105	175 00		175 00
31		Totals		13 750 00			24 962 80	136 00	38 576 80
				(205)			(X)	(504)	(101)

FIGURE 9.6

Posted Cash Payments Journal

Figure 9.6 shows the January cash payments journal after posting for Maxx-Out Sporting Goods. Notice that the account numbers appear in the Posting Reference column of the Other Accounts Debit section to show that the amounts were posted.

When the cash payments journal has been proved, rule the columns and post the totals to the general ledger. Figure 9.7 on page 282 shows how to post from the cash payments journal to the general ledger accounts.

To post a column total to a general ledger account, enter "CP1" in the Posting Reference column to show that the entry is from page 1 of the cash payments journal.

Enter the column total in the general ledger account Debit or Credit column. Figure 9.7 shows the entries to *Accounts Payable* (1), *Purchases Discounts* (2), and *Cash* (3). Compute the new balance and enter it in the Balance Debit or Balance Credit column.

Enter the general ledger account numbers under the column totals on the cash payments journal. The (X) in the Other Accounts Debit column indicates that the individual accounts were posted, not the total.

Posting to the Accounts Payable Ledger   To keep balances current, accountants post entries from the Accounts Payable Debit column of the cash payments journal to the vendor accounts in the accounts payable subsidiary ledger daily. For example, on January 13, $2,865 was posted to Active Designs account in the subsidiary ledger. The "CP1" in the Posting Reference column indicates that the entry is recorded on page 1 of the cash payments journal. The check mark (✓) in the Posting Reference column of the cash payments journal (Figure 9.7 on page 282) shows that the amount was posted to the supplier's account in the accounts payable subsidiary ledger.

NAME	*Active Designs*			TERMS	*2/10, n/30*	
ADDRESS	*2313 Belt Line Road, Dallas, Texas 75267-6205*					

DATE		DESCRIPTION	POST. REF.	DEBIT	CREDIT	BALANCE
2010						
Jan.	1	Balance	✓			2 2 0 0 00
	3	Invoice 5879, 01/02/10	P1		2 8 6 5 00	5 0 6 5 00
	13		CP1	2 8 6 5 00		2 2 0 0 00
	30		CP1	1 1 3 5 00		1 0 6 5 00

ADVANTAGES OF THE CASH PAYMENTS JOURNAL

The cash payments journal

- saves time and effort when recording and posting cash payments,
- allows for a division of labor among the accounting staff,
- improves the audit trail because all cash payments are recorded in one place and listed by check number.

FIGURE 9.7   **Posted General Ledger Accounts**

The Petty Cash Fund

In a well-managed business, most bills are paid by check. However, there are times when small expenditures are made with currency and coins. Most businesses use a petty cash fund to pay for small expenditures. Suppose that in the next two hours the office manager needs a $4 folder for a customer. It is not practical to obtain an approval and write a check for $4 in the time available. Instead, the office manager takes $4 from the petty cash fund to purchase the folder.

ESTABLISHING THE FUND

The amount of the petty cash fund depends on the needs of the business. Usually the office manager, cashier, or assistant is in charge of the petty cash fund. The cashier is responsible for petty cash. To set up the petty cash fund, Maxx-Out Sporting Goods wrote a $175 check to the cashier. She cashed the check and put the currency in a locked cash box.

The establishment of the petty cash fund should be recorded in the cash payments journal. Debit *Petty Cash Fund* in the Other Accounts Debit section of the journal, and enter the credit in the Cash Credit column.

MAKING PAYMENTS FROM THE FUND

Petty cash fund payments are limited to small amounts. A **petty cash voucher** is used to record the payments made from the petty cash fund. The petty cash voucher shows the voucher number, amount, purpose of the expenditure, and account to debit. The person receiving the funds signs the voucher, and the person who controls the petty cash fund initials the voucher. Figure 9.8 shows a petty cash voucher for $16.25 for office supplies.

THE PETTY CASH ANALYSIS SHEET

Most businesses use a **petty cash analysis sheet** to record transactions involving petty cash. The Receipts column shows cash put in the fund, and the Payments column shows the cash paid out. There are special columns for accounts that are used frequently, such as *Supplies,* *Freight In,* and *Miscellaneous Expense.* There is an Other Accounts Debit column for entries that do not fit in a special column. Figure 9.9 on page 284 shows the petty cash analysis sheet for Maxx-Out Sporting Goods for February.

Replenishing the Fund   The total vouchers plus the cash on hand should always equal the amount of the fund—$175 for Maxx-Out Sporting Goods. Replenish the petty cash fund at the end of each month or sooner if the fund is low. Refer to Figures 9.9 and 9.10 on page 284 as you learn how to replenish the petty cash fund.

1. Total the columns on the petty cash analysis sheet.
2. Prove the petty cash fund by adding cash on hand and total payments. This should equal the petty cash fund balance ($15.25 + $159.75 = $175.00).
3. Write a check to restore the petty cash fund to its original balance.
4. Record the check in the cash payments journal. Refer to the petty cash analysis sheet for the accounts and amounts to debit. Notice that the debits appear on four lines of the Other Accounts Debit section. The credit appears in the Cash Credit column.

>>6. OBJECTIVE
Demonstrate a knowledge of procedures for a petty cash fund.

LP9

important!

Petty Cash

Only one person controls the petty cash fund. That person keeps receipts for all expenditures.

PETTY CASH VOUCHER 1

NOTE: This form must be computer processed or filled out in black ink.

DESCRIPTION OF EXPENDITURE	ACCOUNTS TO BE CHARGED	AMOUNT	
Office supplies	Supplies 129	16	25
	Total	16	25

RECEIVED
THE SUM OF _Sixteen_ --- DOLLARS AND _25/100_ CENTS
SIGNED _L.T. Green_   DATE _2/3/10_   APPROVED BY _M.F._   DATE _2/3/10_
Metroplex Office Supply Co.

FIGURE 9.8

Petty Cash Voucher

FIGURE 9.9   **Petty Cash Analysis Sheet**

PETTY CASH ANALYSIS   PAGE 1

DATE	VOU. NO.	DESCRIPTION	RECEIPTS	PAYMENTS	SUPPLIES DEBIT	DELIVERY EXPENSE DEBIT	MISC. EXPENSE DEBIT	OTHER ACCOUNTS DEBIT ACCOUNT TITLE	AMOUNT
2010									
Feb. 1		Establish fund	175 00						
3	1	Office supplies		16 25	16 25				
6	2	Delivery service		24 00		24 00			
11	3	Withdrawal		25 00				M. Ferraro, Drawing	25 00
15	4	Postage stamps		37 00			37 00		
20	5	Delivery service		17 50		17 50			
26	6	Window washing		26 00			26 00		
28	7	Store supplies		14 00	14 00				
28		Totals	175 00	159 75	30 25	41 50	63 00		25 00
28		Balance on hand		15 25					
			175 00	175 00					
28		Balance on hand	15 25						
28		Replenish fund	159 75						
28		Carried forward	175 00						

CASH PAYMENTS JOURNAL   PAGE 1

DATE	CK. NO.	DESCRIPTION	POST. REF.	ACCOUNTS PAYABLE DEBIT	OTHER ACCOUNTS DEBIT ACCOUNT TITLE	POST. REF.	AMOUNT	PURCHASES DISCOUNTS CREDIT	CASH CREDIT
2010									
Feb. 28	191	Replenish Petty Cash fund			Supplies	129	30 25		
					M. Ferraro, Drawing	302	25 00		
					Delivery Expense	523	41 50		
					Miscellaneous Expense	593	63 00		159 75

FIGURE 9.10

Reimbursing the Petty Cash Fund

INTERNAL CONTROL OF THE PETTY CASH FUND

Whenever there is valuable property or cash to protect, appropriate safeguards must be established. Petty cash is no exception. The following internal control procedures apply to petty cash.

1. Use the petty cash fund only for small payments that cannot conveniently be made by check.

2. Limit the amount set aside for petty cash to the approximate amount needed to cover one month's payments from the fund.

3. Write petty cash fund checks to the person in charge of the fund, not to the order of "Cash."

4. Assign one person to control the petty cash fund. This person has sole control of the money and is the only one authorized to make payments from the fund.

5. Keep petty cash in a safe, a locked cash box, or a locked drawer.

6. Prepare a petty cash voucher for each payment. The voucher should be signed by the person who receives the money and should show the payment details. This provides an audit trail for the fund. Additionally, obtain a vendor's invoice or other receipt as documentation for each petty cash voucher.

Internal Control over Cash

In a well-managed business, there are internal control procedures for handling and recording cash receipts and cash payments. The internal control over cash should be tailored to the needs of the business. Accountants play a vital role in designing, establishing, and monitoring the cash control system. In developing internal control procedures for cash, certain basic principles must be followed.

CONTROL OF CASH RECEIPTS

As noted already, cash is the asset that is most easily stolen, lost, or mishandled. Yet cash is essential to carrying on business operations. It is important to protect all cash receipts to make sure that funds are available to pay expenses and take care of other business obligations. The following are essential cash receipt controls.

1. Have only designated employees receive and handle cash whether it consists of checks and money orders, or currency and coins. These employees should be carefully chosen for reliability and accuracy and should be carefully trained. In some businesses, employees who handle cash are bonded. **Bonding** is the process by which employees are investigated by an insurance company. Employees who pass the background check can be bonded; that is, the employer can purchase insurance on the employees. If the bonded employees steal or mishandle cash, the business is insured against the loss.
2. Keep cash receipts in a cash register, a locked cash drawer, or a safe while they are on the premises.
3. Make a record of all cash receipts as the funds come into the business. For checks, endorse each check when received. For currency and coins, this record is the audit tape in a cash register or duplicate copies of numbered sales slips. The use of a cash register provides an especially effective means of control because the machine automatically produces a tape showing the amounts entered. This tape is locked inside the cash register until it is removed by a supervisor.
4. Before a bank deposit is made, check the funds to be deposited against the record made when the cash was received. The employee who checks the deposit is someone other than the one who receives or records the cash.
5. Deposit cash receipts in the bank promptly—every day or several times a day. Deposit the funds intact—do not make payments directly from the cash receipts. The person who makes the bank deposit is someone other than the one who receives and records the funds.
6. Enter cash receipts transactions in the accounting records promptly. The person who records cash receipts is not the one who receives or deposits the funds.
7. Have the monthly bank statement sent to and reconciled by someone other than the employees who handle, record, and deposit the funds.

One of the advantages of efficient procedures for handling and recording cash receipts is that the funds reach the bank sooner. Cash receipts are not kept on the premises for more than a short time, which means that the funds are safer and are readily available for paying bills owed by the firm.

CONTROL OF CASH PAYMENTS

It is important to control cash payments so that the payments are made only for authorized business purposes. The following are essential cash payment controls.

1. Make all payments by check except for payments from special-purpose cash funds such as a petty cash fund or a travel and entertainment fund.
2. Issue checks only with an approved bill, invoice, or other document that describes the reason for the payment.

LP9

3. Have only designated personnel, who are experienced and reliable, approve bills and invoices.

4. Have checks prepared and recorded in the checkbook or check register by someone other than the person who approves the payments.

5. Have still another person sign and mail the checks to creditors. Consider requiring that two people sign all checks greater than a predesignated amount.

6. Use prenumbered check forms. Periodically the numbers of the checks that were issued and the numbers of the blank check forms remaining should be verified to make sure that all check numbers are accounted for.

7. During the bank reconciliation process, compare the canceled checks to the checkbook or check register. The person who does the bank reconciliation should be someone other than the person who prepares or records the checks.

8. Enter promptly in the accounting records all cash payment transactions. The person who records cash payments should not be the one who approves payments or the one who writes the checks.

Small businesses usually cannot achieve the division of responsibility recommended for cash receipts and cash payments. However, no matter what size the firm, efforts should be made to set up effective control procedures for cash.

Section 2 Self Review

QUESTIONS

1. How and when are amounts in the Other Accounts Debit column of the cash payments journal posted?

2. Why does a business use a petty cash fund?

3. What cash payments journal entry records a cash withdrawal by the owner of a sole proprietorship?

EXERCISES

4. To take the discount, what is the payment date for an invoice dated January 20 with terms 3/15, n/30?

    a. February 3
    b. February 4
    c. February 5
    d. February 6

5. Cash purchases of merchandise are recorded in the

    a. cash payments journal.
    b. general journal.
    c. merchandise journal.
    d. purchases journal.

ANALYSIS

6. Your employer keeps a $75 petty cash fund. She asked you to replenish the fund. She is missing a receipt for $7.40, which she says she spent on postage. How should you handle this?

(Answers to Section 2 Self Review are on page 320.)

SECTION OBJECTIVES

>> **8. Write a check, endorse checks, prepare a bank deposit slip, and maintain a checkbook balance.**

WHY IT'S IMPORTANT

Banking tasks are basic practices in every business.

>> **9. Reconcile the monthly bank statement.**

WHY IT'S IMPORTANT

Reconciliation of the bank statement provides a good control of cash.

>> **10. Record any adjusting entries required from the bank reconciliation.**

WHY IT'S IMPORTANT

Certain items are not recorded in the accounting records during the month.

TERMS TO LEARN

bank reconciliation statement
blank endorsement
canceled check
check
credit memorandum
debit memorandum
deposit in transit
deposit slip
dishonored (NSF) check
drawee
drawer
endorsement
full endorsement
negotiable
outstanding checks
payee
postdated check
restrictive endorsement
service charge

Banking Procedures

Businesses with good internal control systems safeguard cash. Many businesses make a daily bank deposit, and some make two or three deposits a day. Keeping excess cash is a dangerous practice. Also, frequent bank deposits provide a steady flow of funds for the payment of expenses.

Writing Checks

A **check** is a written order signed by an authorized person, the **drawer,** instructing a bank, the **drawee,** to pay a specific sum of money to a designated person or business, the **payee.** The checks in Figure 9.11 on page 288 are **negotiable,** which means that ownership of the checks can be transferred to another person or business.

Before writing the check, complete the check stub. In Figure 9.11, the check stub for Check 111 shows

- Balance brought forward: $12,025.50
- Check amount: $1,500.00
- Balance: $10,525.50
- Date: January 3, 2010
- Payee: Carter Real Estate Group
- Purpose: January rent

Once the stub has been completed, fill in the check. Carefully enter the date, the payee, and the amount in figures and words. Draw a line to fill any empty space after the payee's name and after the amount in words. To be valid, checks need an authorized signature. For Maxx-Out Sporting Goods only Max Ferraro, the owner, is authorized to sign checks.

Figure 9.11 shows the check stub for Check 112, a cash purchase from The Retail Equipment Center for $2,400. After Check 112, the account balance is $8,125.50 ($10,525.50 − $2,400.00).

Endorsing Checks

Each check needs an endorsement to be deposited. The **endorsement** is a written authorization that transfers ownership of a check. After the payee transfers ownership to the bank by an endorsement, the bank has a legal right to collect payment from the drawer, the person or business that issued the check. If the check cannot be collected, the payee guarantees payment to all subsequent holders.

Several forms of endorsement are shown in Figure 9.12, at the top of page 289. Endorsements are placed on the back of the check, on the left, near the perforated edge where the check was separated from the stub.

A **blank endorsement** is the signature of the payee that transfers ownership of the check without specifying to whom or for what purpose. Checks with a blank endorsement can be further endorsed by anyone who has the check, even if the check is lost or stolen.

A **full endorsement** is a signature transferring a check to a specific person, business, or bank. Only the person, business, or bank named in the full endorsement can transfer it to someone else.

The safest endorsement is the **restrictive endorsement.** A restrictive endorsement is a signature that transfers the check to a specific party for a specific purpose, usually for deposit to a bank account. Most businesses restrictively endorse the checks they receive using a rubber stamp.

FIGURE 9.11   Checks and Check Stubs

Full Endorsement

PAY TO THE ORDER OF
FIRST TEXAS NATIONAL BANK
Maxx-Out Sporting Goods
38-14-98867

Blank Endorsement

Max Ferraro
38-14-98867

Restrictive Endorsement

PAY TO THE ORDER OF
FIRST TEXAS NATIONAL BANK
FOR DEPOSIT ONLY
Maxx-Out Sporting Goods
38-14-98867

FIGURE 9.12

Types of Check Endorsement

CHECKING ACCOUNT DEPOSIT

DATE *January 8, 2010*

MAXX-OUT SPORTING GOODS
2007 Trendsetter Lane
Dallas, TX 75268-0967

FIRST TEXAS NATIONAL BANK
Dallas, TX 75267-6205

ENTER ADDITIONAL CHECKS ON OTHER SIDE

CURRENCY	DOLLARS	CENTS
	1810	00
COIN	219	80
1 11-2818	260	75
2 11-2818	290	18
3 11-1652	180	65
4 11-1652	598	32
5 11-5074	800	30
6 11-5074	700	00
7		
8		
9		
10		
11		
12		
TOTAL FROM OTHER SIDE OR ATTACHED LIST		
TOTAL	**4,860.00**	

Checks and other items are received for deposit subject to the terms and conditions of this bank's collection agreement.

⑆1210⑈8640⑆ ⑆38⑆ 149886 7⑈

FIGURE 9.13

Deposit Slip

Preparing the Deposit Slip

Businesses prepare a **deposit slip** to record each deposit of cash or checks to a bank account. Usually the bank provides deposit slips preprinted with the account name and number. Figure 9.13, above, shows the deposit slip for the January 8 deposit for Maxx-Out Sporting Goods.

Notice the printed numbers on the lower edge of the deposit slip. These are the same numbers on the bottom of the checks, Figure 9.11. The numbers are printed using a special *magnetic ink character recognition (MICR)* type that can be "read" by machine. Deposit slips and checks encoded with MICR are rapidly and efficiently processed by machine.

- The 12 indicates that the bank is in the 12th Federal Reserve District.
- The 10 is the routing number used in processing the document.
- The 8640 identifies First Texas National Bank.
- The 38 14 98867 is the account number.

The deposit slip for Maxx-Out Sporting Goods shows the date, January 8. *Currency* is the paper money, $1,810.00. *Coin* is the amount in coins, $219.80. The checks and money orders are individually listed. Some banks ask that the *American Bankers Association (ABA) transit number* for each check be entered on the deposit slip. The transit number appears on the top part of the fraction that appears in the upper right corner of the check. In Figure 9.11, the transit number is 11-8640.

>>8. OBJECTIVE

Write a check, endorse checks, prepare a bank deposit slip, and maintain a checkbook balance.

Handling Postdated Checks

Occasionally, a business will receive a postdated check. A **postdated check** is dated some time in the future. If the business receives a postdated check, it should not deposit it before the date on the check. Otherwise, the check could be refused by the drawer's bank. Postdated checks are written by drawers who do not have sufficient funds to cover the check. The drawer expects to have adequate funds in the bank by the date on the check. Issuing or accepting postdated checks is not a proper business practice.

Reconciling the Bank Statement

>>9. OBJECTIVE

Reconcile the monthly bank statement.

LP9

Once a month the bank sends a statement of the deposits received and the checks paid for each account. Figure 9.14 below shows the bank statement for Maxx-Out Sporting Goods. It shows a day-to-day listing of all transactions during the month. A code, explained at the bottom, identifies transactions that do not involve checks or deposits. For example, SC indicates a service charge. The last column of the bank statement shows the account balance at the beginning of the period, after each day's transactions, and at the end of the period.

Often the bank encloses canceled checks with the bank statement. **Canceled checks** are checks paid by the bank during the month. Canceled checks are proof of payment. They are filed after the bank reconciliation is complete.

Usually there is a difference between the ending balance shown on the bank statement and the balance shown in the checkbook. A bank reconciliation determines why the difference exists and brings the records into agreement.

FIRST TEXAS NATIONAL BANK

MAXX-OUT SPORTING GOODS
2007 Trendsetter Lane
Dallas, TX 75268-0967

Account Number: 38-14-98867

Period Ending   January, 31, 2010

CHECKS		DEPOSITS	DATE	BALANCE
Beginning Balance			December 31, 2009	$12,025.50
1,500.00-		702.00+	January 7	11,227.50
2,400.00-		4,860.00+	January 8	13,687.50
756.00-		270.00+	January 11	13,201.50
3,856.30-		15,000.00+	January 12	24,345.20
2,807.70-		540.00+	January 13	22,077.50
900.00-		5,166.00+	January 15	26,343.50
3,000.00-	318.00-	108.00+	January 17	23,133.50
276.00-	4,250.00-	75.00+	January 18	18,682.50
840.00-	1,000.00-	400.00+	January 22	17,242.50
1,600.00-		5,400.00+	January 22	21,042.50
525.00- DM		2,932.00+	January 29	23,449.50
25.00- SC		108.00+	January 31	23,532.50
1,135.00-		275.00+	January 31	22,672.50
		836.00+	January 31	23,508.50

LAST AMOUNT IN THIS
COLUMN IS YOUR BALANCE

Codes:	CC	Certified Check	EC	Error Correction
	CM	Credit Memorandum	OD	Overdrawn
	DM	Debit Memorandum	SC	Service Charge

PLEASE EXAMINE THIS STATEMENT UPON RECEIPT AND REPORT ANY ERRORS WITHIN TEN DAYS.

FIGURE 9.14

Bank Statement

CHANGES IN THE CHECKING ACCOUNT BALANCE

A **credit memorandum** explains any addition, other than a deposit, to the checking account. For example, when a note receivable is due, the bank may collect the note from the maker and place the proceeds in the checking account. The amount collected appears on the bank statement, and the credit memorandum showing the details of the transaction is enclosed with the bank statement.

A **debit memorandum** explains any deduction, other than a check, to the checking account. Service charges and dishonored checks appear as debit memorandums.

Bank **service charges** are fees charged by banks to cover the costs of maintaining accounts and providing services, such as the use of the night deposit box and the collection of promissory notes. The debit memorandum shows the type and amount of each service charge.

Figure 9.15 shows a debit memorandum for a $525.00 dishonored check. A **dishonored check** is one that is returned to the depositor unpaid. Normally, checks are dishonored because there are insufficient funds in the drawer's account to cover the check. The bank usually stamps the letters *NSF* for *Not Sufficient Funds* on the check. The business records a journal entry to debit Accounts Receivable and credit Cash for the amount of the dishonored check.

When a check is dishonored, the business contacts the drawer to arrange for collection. The drawer can ask the business to redeposit the check because the funds are now in the account. If so, the business records the check deposit again. Sometimes, the business requests a cash payment.

THE BANK RECONCILIATION PROCESS: AN ILLUSTRATION

When the bank statement is received, it is reconciled with the financial records of the business. On February 5, Maxx-Out Sporting Goods received the bank statement shown in Figure 9.14. The ending cash balance according to the bank is $23,508.50. On January 31, the *Cash* account, called the *book balance of cash,* is $16,060.70. The same amount appears on the check stub at the end of January.

Sometimes the difference between the bank balance and the book balance is due to errors. The bank might make an arithmetic error, give credit to the wrong depositor, or charge a check against the wrong account. Some banks require that errors in the bank statement be reported within a short period of time. The errors made by businesses include not recording a check or deposit, or recording a check or deposit for the wrong amount.

Other than errors, there are four reasons why the book balance of cash may not agree with the balance on the bank statement.

1. **Outstanding checks** are checks that are recorded in the cash payments journal but have not been paid by the bank.

2. **Deposit in transit** is a deposit that is recorded in the cash receipts journal but that reaches the bank too late to be shown on the monthly bank statement.

3. Service charges and other deductions are not recorded in the business records.

4. Deposits, such as the collection of promissory notes, are not recorded in the business records.

```
DEBIT:  MAXX-OUT SPORTING GOODS      FIRST TEXAS NATIONAL BANK
        2007 Trendsetter Lane
        Dallas, TX 75268-0967

        38-14-98867                  DATE:  January 31, 2010


        NSF Check - David Newhouse                        525  00




APPROVED: _____
```

FIGURE 9.15

Debit Memorandum

FIGURE 9.16

Bank Reconciliation Statement

Maxx-Out Sporting Goods Bank Reconciliation Statement January 31, 2010			
Balance on Bank Statement			23 5 0 8 50
Additions:			
Deposits of January 31 in transit	5 9 4 0 00		
Check incorrectly charged to account	1 6 0 0 00	7 5 4 0 00	
		31 0 4 8 50	
Deductions for outstanding checks:			
Check 124 of January 31	5 6 5 00		
Check 125 of January 31	4 9 5 0 00		
Check 126 of January 31	3 2 0 0 00		
Check 127 of January 31	1 7 5 00		
Check 128 of January 31	1 7 2 80		
Check 129 of January 31	6 3 0 0 00		
Check 130 of January 31	1 7 5 00		
Total Checks Outstanding		15 5 3 7 80	
Adjusted Bank Balance		15 5 1 0 70	
Balance in Books		16 0 6 0 70	
Deductions:			
NSF Check	5 2 5 00		
Bank Service Charge	2 5 00	5 5 0 00	
Adjusted Book Balance		15 5 1 0 70	

Figure 9.16 shows a **bank reconciliation statement** that accounts for the differences between the balance on the bank statement and the book balance of cash. The bank reconciliation statement format is:

First Section		**Second Section**	
	Bank statement balance		Book balance
+	deposits in transit	+	deposits not recorded
−	outstanding checks	−	deductions
+ **or** −	bank errors	+ **or** −	errors in the books
	Adjusted bank balance		Adjusted book balance

When the bank reconciliation statement is complete, the adjusted bank balance must equal the adjusted book balance.

Use the following steps to prepare the bank reconciliation statement:

First Section

1. Enter the balance on the bank statement, $23,508.50.

2. Compare the deposits in the checkbook with the deposits on the bank statement. Maxx-Out Sporting Goods had one deposit in transit. On January 31, receipts of $5,940.00 were placed in the bank's night deposit box. The bank recorded the deposit on February 1. The deposit will appear on the February bank statement.

3. List the outstanding checks.

   • Put the canceled checks in numeric order.

   • Compare the canceled checks to the check stubs, verifying the check numbers and amounts.

   • Examine the endorsements to make sure that they agree with the names of the payees.

- List the checks that have not cleared the bank.
- Maxx-Out Sporting Goods has seven outstanding checks totaling $15,537.80.

4. While reviewing the canceled checks for Maxx-Out Sporting Goods, Max Ferraro found a $1,600 check issued by The Dress Barn. The $1,600 was deducted from Maxx-Out Sporting Goods' account; it should have been deducted from the account for The Dress Barn. This is a bank error. Max Ferraro contacted the bank about the error. The correction will appear on the next bank statement. The bank error amount is added to the bank statement balance on the bank reconciliation statement.

5. The adjusted bank balance is $15,510.70.

Second Section

1. Enter the balance in books from the *Cash* account, $16,060.70.

2. Record any deposits made by the bank that have not been recorded in the accounting records. Maxx-Out Sporting Goods did not have any.

3. Record deductions made by the bank. There are two items:
   - the NSF check for $525,
   - the bank service charge for $25.

4. Record any errors in the accounting records that were discovered during the reconciliation process. Maxx-Out Sporting Goods did not have any errors in January.

5. The adjusted book balance is $15,510.70.

Notice that the adjusted bank balance and the adjusted book balance agree.

Adjusting the Financial Records

Items in the second section of the bank reconciliation statement include additions and deductions made by the bank that do not appear in the accounting records. Businesses prepare journal entries to record these items in the books.

For Maxx-Out Sporting Goods, two entries must be made. The first entry is for the NSF check from David Newhouse, a credit customer. The second entry is for the bank service charge. The effect of the two items is a decrease in the *Cash* account balance.

>>10. OBJECTIVE
Record any adjusting entries required from the bank reconciliation.

LP9

MANAGERIAL IMPLICATIONS   <<

CASH

- It is important to safeguard cash against loss and theft.
- Management and the accountant need to work together
  - to make sure that there are effective controls for cash receipts and cash payments,
  - to monitor the internal control system to make sure that it functions properly,
  - to develop procedures that ensure the quick and efficient recording of cash transactions.
- To make decisions, management needs up-to-date information about the cash position so that it can anticipate cash shortages and arrange loans or arrange for the temporary investment of excess funds.
- Management and the accountant need to establish controls over the banking activities—depositing funds, issuing checks, recording checking account transactions, and reconciling the monthly bank statement.

THINKING CRITICALLY

How would you determine how much cash to keep in the business checking account, as opposed to in a short-term investment?

BUSINESS TRANSACTION

The January bank reconciliation statement (Figure 9.16 on page 292) shows an NSF check of $525 and a bank service charge of $25.

ANALYSIS

The asset account, **Accounts Receivable,** is increased by $525 for the returned check. The expense account, **Bank Fees Expense,** is increased by $25 for the service charge. The asset account, **Cash,** is decreased by $550 ($525 + $25).

DEBIT-CREDIT RULES

DEBIT   Increases to assets are debits. Debit **Accounts Receivable** for $525. Increases to expenses are debits. Debit **Bank Fees Expense** for $25.

CREDIT   Decreases to assets are credits. Credit **Cash** for $550.

T-ACCOUNT PRESENTATION

Accounts Receivable		Bank Fees Expense		Cash	
+	−	+	−	+	−
525		25			550

GENERAL JOURNAL ENTRY

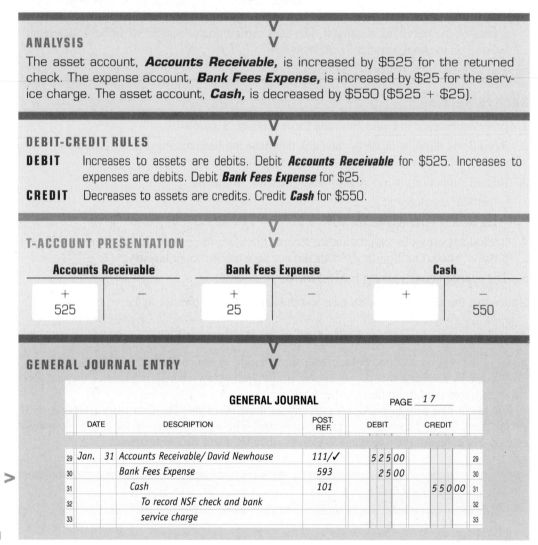

	GENERAL JOURNAL				PAGE _17_	
	DATE	DESCRIPTION	POST. REF.	DEBIT	CREDIT	
29	Jan. 31	Accounts Receivable/ David Newhouse	111/✓	525 00		29
30		Bank Fees Expense	593	25 00		30
31		Cash	101		550 00	31
32		To record NSF check and bank				32
33		service charge				33

THE BOTTOM LINE
Adjusting Entries

Income Statement

Expenses	↑ 25
Net Income	↓ 25

Balance Sheet

Assets	↓ 25
Equity	↓ 25

After posting, the **Cash** account appears as follows.

ACCOUNT _Cash_   ACCOUNT NO. _101_

DATE	DESCRIPTION	POST. REF.	DEBIT	CREDIT	BALANCE DEBIT	BALANCE CREDIT
2010						
Jan. 1	Balance	✓			12 025 50	
31		CR1	42 612 00		54 637 50	
31		CP1		38 576 80	16 060 70	
31		J17		550 00	15 510 70	

Notice that $15,510.70 is the adjusted bank balance, the adjusted book balance, and the general ledger **Cash** balance. A notation is made on the latest check stub to deduct the amounts ($525 and $25). The notation includes the reasons for the deductions.

Sometimes the bank reconciliation reveals an error in the firm's financial records. For example, the February bank reconciliation for Maxx-Out Sporting Goods found that Check 151 was written for $465. The amount on the bank statement is $465. However, the check was recorded in the accounting records as $445. The business made a $20 error when recording the check. Maxx-Out Sporting Goods prepared the following journal entry to correct the error. The $20 is also deducted on the check stub.

GENERAL JOURNAL   PAGE _18_

	DATE	DESCRIPTION	POST. REF.	DEBIT	CREDIT	
1	2010					1
2						2
29	Feb. 28	Advertising Expense	514	20 00		29
30		Cash	101		20 00	30
31		To correct error for check				31
32		151 of February 22				32

Internal Control of Banking Activities

Well-run businesses put the following internal controls in place.

1. Limit access to the checkbook to designated employees. When the checkbook is not in use, keep it in a locked drawer or cabinet.

2. Use prenumbered check forms. Periodically, verify and account for all checks. Examine checks before signing them. Match each check to an approved invoice or other payment authorization.

3. Separate duties.
   - The person who writes the check should not sign or mail the check.
   - The person who performs the bank reconciliation should not handle or deposit cash receipts or write, record, sign, or mail checks.

4. File all deposit receipts, canceled checks, voided checks, and bank statements for future reference. These documents provide a strong audit trail for the checking account.

internal CONTROL

Section 3 Self Review

9 Chapter REVIEW   Chapter Summary

In this chapter, you have learned the basic principles of accounting for cash payments and cash receipts.

Learning Objectives

1 Record cash receipts in a cash receipts journal.

Use of special journals leads to an efficient recording process for cash transactions. The cash receipts journal has separate columns for the accounts used most often for cash receipt transactions.

2 Account for cash short or over.

Errors can occur when making change. Cash register discrepancies should be recorded using the expense account **Cash Short or Over.**

3 Post from the cash receipts journal to subsidiary and general ledgers.

Individual accounts receivable amounts are posted to the subsidiary ledger daily. Figures in the Other Accounts Credit column are posted individually to the general ledger during the month. All other postings are done on a summary basis at month-end.

4 Record cash payments in a cash payments journal.

The cash payments journal has separate columns for the accounts used most often, eliminating the need to record the same account names repeatedly.

5 Post from the cash payments journal to subsidiary and general ledgers.

Individual accounts payable amounts are posted daily to the accounts payable subsidiary ledger. Amounts listed in the Other Accounts Debit column are posted individually to the general ledger during the month. All other postings are completed on a summary basis at the end of the month.

6 Demonstrate a knowledge of procedures for a petty cash fund.

Although most payments are made by check, small payments are often made through a petty cash fund. A petty cash voucher is prepared for each payment and signed by the person receiving the money. The person in charge of the fund records expenditures on a petty cash analysis sheet. The fund is replenished with a check for the sum spent.

An entry is made in the cash payments journal to debit the accounts involved.

7 Demonstrate a knowledge of internal control procedures for cash.

All businesses need a system of internal controls to protect cash from theft and mishandling and to ensure accurate records of cash transactions. A checking account is essential to store cash safely and to make cash payments efficiently. For maximum control over outgoing cash, all payments should be made by check except those from carefully controlled special-purpose cash funds such as a petty cash fund.

8 Write a check, endorse checks, prepare a bank deposit slip, and maintain a checkbook balance.

Check writing requires careful attention to details. If a standard checkbook is used, the stub should be completed before the check so that it will not be forgotten. The stub gives the data needed to journalize the payment.

9 Reconcile the monthly bank statement.

A bank statement should be immediately reconciled with the cash balance in the firm's financial records. Usually, differences are due to deposits in transit, outstanding checks, and bank service charges, but many factors can cause lack of agreement between the bank balance and the book balance.

10 Record any adjusting entries required from the bank reconciliation.

Some differences between the bank balance and the book balance may require that the firm's records be adjusted after the bank statement is reconciled. Journal entries are recorded and then posted to correct the *Cash* account balance and the checkbook balance.

11 Define the accounting terms new to this chapter.

Glossary

Bank reconciliation statement (p. 292) A statement that accounts for all differences between the balance on the bank statement and the book balance of cash

Blank endorsement (p. 288) A signature of the payee written on the back of the check that transfers ownership of the check without specifying to whom or for what purpose

Bonding (p. 285) The process by which employees are investigated by an insurance company that will insure the business against losses through employee theft or mishandling of funds

Canceled check (p. 290) A check paid by the bank on which it was drawn

Cash (p. 270) In accounting, currency, coins, checks, money orders, and funds on deposit in a bank

Cash payments journal (p. 277) A special journal used to record transactions involving the payment of cash

Cash receipts journal (p. 270) A special journal used to record and post transactions involving the receipt of cash

Cash register proof (p. 271) A verification that the amount of currency and coins in a cash register agrees with the amount shown on the cash register audit tape

Cash Short or Over account (p. 272) An account used to record any discrepancies between the amount of currency and coins in the cash register and the amount shown on the audit tape

Check (p. 287) A written order signed by an authorized person instructing a bank to pay a specific sum of money to a designated person or business

Credit memorandum (p. 291) A form that explains any addition, other than a deposit, to a checking account

Debit memorandum (p. 291) A form that explains any deduction, other than a check, from a checking account

Deposit in transit (p. 291) A deposit that is recorded in the cash receipts journal but that reaches the bank too late to be shown on the monthly bank statement

Deposit slip (p. 289) A form prepared to record the deposit of cash or checks to a bank account

Dishonored check (p. 291) A check returned to the depositor unpaid because of insufficient funds in the drawer's account; also called an NSF check

Drawee (p. 287) The bank on which a check is written

Drawer (p. 287) The person or firm issuing a check

Endorsement (p. 288) A written authorization that transfers ownership of a check

Full endorsement (p. 288) A signature transferring a check to a specific person, firm, or bank

Negotiable (p. 287) A financial instrument whose ownership can be transferred to another person or business

Outstanding checks (p. 291) Checks that have been recorded in the cash payments journal but have not yet been paid by the bank

Payee (p. 287) The person or firm to whom a check is payable

Petty cash analysis sheet (p. 283) A form used to record transactions involving petty cash

Petty cash fund (p. 270) A special-purpose fund used to handle payments involving small amounts of money

Petty cash voucher (p. 283) A form used to record the payments made from a petty cash fund

Postdated check (p. 290) A check dated some time in the future

Promissory note (p. 272) A written promise to pay a specified amount of money on a specific date

Restrictive endorsement (p. 288) A signature that transfers a check to a specific party for a stated purpose

Service charge (p. 291) A fee charged by a bank to cover the costs of maintaining accounts and providing services

Statement of account (p. 272) A form sent to a firm's customers showing transactions during the month and the balance owed

Comprehensive **Self Review**

1. Describe a full endorsement.
2. What is a petty cash voucher?
3. When is the petty cash fund replenished?
4. What are the advantages of using special journals for cash receipts and cash payments?
5. What does the term *cash* mean in business?

(Answers to Comprehensive Self Review are on page 321.)

 Multiple choice questions are provided on the text Web site at www.mhhe.com/price12e

Quiz9

Discussion Questions

1. What procedures are used to achieve internal control over banking activities?
2. Why are journal entries sometimes needed after the bank reconciliation statement is prepared?
3. Give some reasons why the bank balance and the book balance of cash might differ.
4. What is the book balance of cash?
5. Why is a bank reconciliation prepared?
6. What information is shown on the bank statement?
7. What type of information is entered on a check stub? Why should a check stub be prepared before the check is written?
8. What is a check?
9. Why are MICR numbers printed on deposit slips and checks?
10. Which type of endorsement is most appropriate for a business to use?
11. How are cash shortages and overages recorded?
12. Describe the major controls for petty cash.
13. When are petty cash expenditures entered in a firm's accounting records?
14. What type of account is **Purchases Discounts?** How is this account presented on the income statement?
15. How does a firm record a payment on account to a creditor when a cash discount is involved? Which journal is used?
16. How does a wholesale business record a check received on account from a customer when a cash discount is involved? Which journal is used?
17. Why do some wholesale businesses offer cash discounts to their customers?
18. What is a promissory note? What entry is made to record the collection of a promissory note and interest? Which journal is used?
19. Describe the major controls for cash payments.
20. Explain what *bonding* means. How does bonding relate to safeguarding cash?
21. Describe the major controls for cash receipts.
22. Explain the meaning of the following terms.
    a. Canceled check
    b. Outstanding check
    c. Deposit in transit
    d. Debit memorandum
    e. Credit memorandum
    f. Dishonored check

g. Blank endorsement

h. Deposit slip

i. Drawee

j. Restrictive endorsement

k. Payee

l. Drawer

m. Service charge

APPLICATIONS

Exercises

Recording cash receipts.

The following transactions took place at Sneaky Pete's Shoe Store during the first week of September 2010. Indicate how these transactions would be entered in a cash receipts journal.

◀ **Exercise 9.1**

Objective 1

DATE		TRANSACTIONS
Sept.	1	Had cash sales of $5,600 plus sales tax of $448; there was a cash overage of $16.
	2	Collected $720 on account from James Floyd, a credit customer.
	3	Had cash sales of $5,250 plus sales tax of $420.
	4	Susan Anderson, the owner, made an additional cash investment of $17,000.
	5	Had cash sales of $6,400 plus sales tax of $512; there was a cash shortage of $30.

Recording cash payments.

The following transactions took place at Sneaky Pete's Shoe Store during the first week of September 2010. Indicate how these transactions would be entered in a cash payments journal.

◀ **Exercise 9.2**

Objective 4

 >>>

Problem

DATE		TRANSACTIONS
Sept.	1	Issued Check 3850 for $2,400 to pay the monthly rent.
	1	Issued Check 3851 for $2,950 to Carter Company, a creditor, on account.
	2	Issued Check 3852 for $10,250 to purchase new equipment.
	2	Issued Check 3853 for $1,380 to remit sales tax to the state sales tax authority.
	3	Issued Check 3854 for $1,470 to Waller Company, a creditor, on account for invoice of $1,500 less cash discount of $30.
	4	Issued Check 3855 for $2,675 to purchase merchandise.
	5	Issued Check 3856 for $1,800 as a cash withdrawal for personal use by Susan Anderson, the owner.

Exercise 9.3

Objective 6

▶ **Recording the establishment of a petty cash fund.**

On January 2, Reddy Insurance Company issued Check 2108 for $180 to establish a petty cash fund. Indicate how this transaction would be recorded in a cash payments journal.

Exercise 9.4

Objective 6

▶ **Recording the replenishment of a petty cash fund.**

On January 31, Chloe Inc. issued Check 3144 to replenish its petty cash fund. An analysis of payments from the fund showed these totals: *Supplies,* $48; *Delivery Expense,* $39; and *Miscellaneous Expense,* $34. Indicate how this transaction would be recorded in a cash payments journal.

Exercise 9.5

Objectives 9, 10

▶ **Determining an adjusted bank balance.**

Chin Corporation received a bank statement showing a balance of $14,700 as of October 31, 2010. The firm's records showed a book balance of $14,262 on October 31. The difference between the two balances was caused by the following items. Prepare the adjusted bank balance section and the adjusted book balance section of the bank reconciliation statement. Also prepare the necessary journal entry.

1. A debit memorandum for an NSF check from James Dear for $424.
2. Three outstanding checks: Check 7017 for $124, Check 7098 for $55, and Check 7107 for $1,560.
3. A bank service charge of $20.
4. A deposit in transit of $857.

Exercise 9.6

Objective 9

▶ **Analyzing bank reconciliation items.**

At Thompson Delivery and Courier Service, the following items were found to cause a difference between the bank statement and the firm's records. Indicate whether each item will affect the bank balance or the book balance when the bank reconciliation statement is prepared. Also indicate which items will require an accounting entry after the bank reconciliation is completed.

1. A deposit in transit.
2. A debit memorandum for a dishonored check.
3. A credit memorandum for a promissory note that the bank collected for Thompson.
4. An error found in Thompson's records, which involves the amount of a check. The firm's checkbook and cash payments journal indicate $808 as the amount, but the canceled check itself and the listing on the bank statement show that $880 was the actual sum.
5. An outstanding check.
6. A bank service charge.
7. A check issued by another firm that was charged to Thompson's account by mistake.

Exercise 9.7

Objective 9

▶ **Preparing a bank reconciliation statement.**

Cantu Office Supply Company received a bank statement showing a balance of $68,005 as of March 31, 2010. The firm's records showed a book balance of $69,487 on March 31. The difference between the two balances was caused by the following items. Prepare a bank reconciliation statement for the firm as of March 31 and the necessary journal entries from the statement.

1. A debit memorandum for $50, which covers the bank's collection fee for the note.
2. A deposit in transit of $3,700.
3. A check for $248 issued by another firm that was mistakenly charged to Cantu's account.
4. A debit memorandum for an NSF check of $6,135 issued by Wilson Construction Company, a credit customer.
5. Outstanding checks: Check 3782 for $2,200; Check 3840 for $151.
6. A credit memorandum for a $6,300 noninterest-bearing note receivable that the bank collected for the firm.

PROBLEMS

Problem Set A

Journalizing cash receipts and posting to the general ledger.

Movie Courier Service is a retail store that rents movies and sells music CDs over the Internet. The firm's cash receipts for February are listed below. The general ledger accounts used to record these transactions appear below.

Problem 9.1A
Objectives 1, 2, 3

INSTRUCTIONS

1. Open the general ledger accounts and enter the balances as of February 1, 2010.
2. Record the transactions in a cash receipts journal. Use 4 as the page number.
3. Post the individual entries from the Other Accounts Credit section of the cash receipts journal to the proper general ledger accounts.
4. Total, prove, and rule the cash receipts journal as of February 28, 2010.
5. Post the column totals from the cash receipts journal to the proper general ledger accounts.

GENERAL LEDGER ACCOUNTS

101	Cash	$ 4,960 Dr.	401 Sales	
109	Notes Receivable	800 Dr.	491 Interest Income	
111	Accounts Receivable	4,075 Dr.	620 Cash Short or Over	
129	Supplies	610 Dr.		
231	Sales Tax Payable	295 Cr.		
301	Jason Wilson, Capital	34,000 Cr.		

DATE	TRANSACTIONS
Feb. 3	Received $500 from Danielle Pelzel, a credit customer, on account.
5	Received a cash refund of $120 for damaged supplies.
7	Had cash sales of $4,800 plus sales tax of $384 during the first week of February; there was a cash shortage of $60.
9	Jason Wilson, the owner, invested an additional $15,000 cash in the business.
12	Received $380 from Kyela Jones, a credit customer, in payment of her account.
14	Had cash sales of $4,050 plus sales tax of $324 during the second week of February; there was an overage of $28.
16	Received $450 from Sadie Nelson, a credit customer, to apply toward her account.
19	Received a check from Ketura Pittman to pay her $800 promissory note plus interest of $32.
21	Had cash sales of $4,550 plus sales tax of $364 during the third week of February.
25	Alfred Herron, a credit customer, sent a check for $580 to pay the balance he owes.
28	Had cash sales of $4,100 plus sales tax of $328 during the fourth week of February; there was a cash shortage of $36.

Analyze: What total accounts receivable were collected in February?

Problem 9.2A
Objectives 4, 5, 6

▶ **Journalizing cash payments, recording petty cash, and posting to the general ledger.**

The cash payments of Royalty Jewelry Store, a retail business, for June are listed below. The general ledger accounts used to record these transactions appear below.

INSTRUCTIONS

1. Open the general ledger accounts and enter the balances as of June 1.
2. Record all payments by check in a cash payments journal; use 8 as the page number.
3. Record all payments from the petty cash fund on a petty cash analysis sheet; use 8 as the sheet number.
4. Post the individual entries from the Other Accounts Debit section of the cash payments journal to the proper general ledger accounts.
5. Total, prove, and rule the petty cash analysis sheet as of June 30. Record the replenishment of the fund and the final balance on the sheet.
6. Total, prove, and rule the cash payments journal as of June 30.
7. Post the column totals from the cash payments journal to the proper general ledger accounts.

GENERAL LEDGER ACCOUNTS

101	Cash	$42,840 Dr.
105	Petty Cash Fund	
129	Supplies	1,060 Dr.
201	Notes Payable	3,200 Cr.
205	Accounts Payable	18,880 Cr.
231	Sales Tax Payable	4,200 Cr.
302	Larry Jennings, Drawing	
451	Sales Returns and Allowances	
504	Purchases Discounts	
611	Delivery Expense	
620	Rent Expense	
623	Salaries Expense	
626	Telephone Expense	
634	Interest Expense	
635	Miscellaneous Expense	

DATE		TRANSACTIONS
June	1	Issued Check 4121 for $2,500 to pay the monthly rent.
	2	Issued Check 4122 for $4,200 to remit the state sales tax.
	3	Issued Check 4123 for $2,780 to Perfect Timing Watch Company, a creditor, in payment of Invoice 6808, dated May 5.
	4	Issued Check 4124 for $200 to establish a petty cash fund. (After journalizing this transaction, be sure to enter it on the first line of the petty cash analysis sheet.)
	5	Paid $30 from the petty cash fund for office supplies, Petty Cash Voucher 1.
	7	Issued Check 4125 for $3,328 to Perry Corporation in payment of a $3,200 promissory note and interest of $128.
	8	Paid $20 from the petty cash fund for postage stamps, Petty Cash Voucher 2.
	10	Issued Check 4126 for $594 to a customer as a cash refund for a defective watch that was returned; the original sale was made for cash.

(continued)

DATE	9.2A (cont.) TRANSACTIONS
June 12	Issued Check 4127 for $276 to pay the telephone bill.
14	Issued Check 4128 for $5,880 to International Jewelry Company, a creditor, in payment of Invoice 8629, dated May 6 ($6,000), less a cash discount ($120).
15	Paid $18 from the petty cash fund for delivery service, Petty Cash Voucher 3.
17	Issued Check 4129 for $860 to purchase store supplies.
20	Issued Check 4130 for $3,430 to Nelson's Jewelry and Accessories, a creditor, in payment of Invoice 1513, dated June 12 ($3,500), less a cash discount ($70).
22	Paid $24 from the petty cash fund for a personal withdrawal by Larry Jennings, the owner, Petty Cash Voucher 4.
25	Paid $30 from the petty cash fund to have the store windows washed and repaired, Petty Cash Voucher 5.
27	Issued Check 4131 for $3,650 to Classy Creations, a creditor, in payment of Invoice 667, dated May 30.
30	Paid $24 from the petty cash fund for delivery service, Petty Cash Voucher 6.
30	Issued Check 4132 for $7,675 to pay the monthly salaries.
30	Issued Check 4133 for $5,000 to Larry Jennings, the owner, as a withdrawal for personal use.
30	Issued Check 4134 for $146 to replenish the petty cash fund. (Foot the columns of the petty cash analysis sheet in order to determine the accounts that should be debited and the amounts involved.)

Analyze: What total payments were made from the petty cash fund for the month?

Journalizing sales and cash receipts and posting to the general ledger.

◄ **Problem 9.3A**
   Objectives 1, 2, 3

Unlimited Sounds is a wholesale business that sells musical instruments. Transactions involving sales and cash receipts for the firm during April 2010 follow, along with the general ledger accounts used to record these transactions.

INSTRUCTIONS

1. Open the general ledger accounts and enter the balances as of April 1, 2010.
2. Record the transactions in a sales journal, a cash receipts journal, and a general journal. Use 7 as the page number for each of the special journals and 17 as the page number for the general journal.
3. Post the entries from the general journal to the general ledger.
4. Total, prove, and rule the special journals as of April 30, 2010.
5. Post the column totals from the special journals to the proper general ledger accounts.
6. Prepare the heading and the Revenue section of the firm's income statement for the month ended April 30.

GENERAL LEDGER ACCOUNTS

101	Cash	$16,400 Dr.
109	Notes Receivable	
111	Accounts Receivable	21,000 Dr.
401	Sales	
451	Sales Returns and Allowances	
452	Sales Discounts	

DATE	TRANSACTIONS
April 1	Sold merchandise for $3,900 to Soprano Music Center; issued Invoice 9312 with terms of 2/10, n/30.
3	Received a check for $1,470 from Music Supply Store in payment of Invoice 6718 of March 25 ($1,500), less a cash discount ($30.00).
5	Sold merchandise for $1,575 in cash to a new customer who has not yet established credit.
8	Sold merchandise for $4,500 to Music Warehouse, issued Invoice 9313 with terms of 2/10, n/30.
10	Soprano Music Center sent a check for $3,822 in payment of Invoice 9312 of April 1 ($3,900), less a cash discount ($78).
15	Accepted a return of damaged merchandise from Music Warehouse; issued Credit Memorandum 105 for $800; the original sale was made on Invoice 9313 of April 8.
19	Sold merchandise for $10,500 to Eagleton Music Center; issued Invoice 9314 with terms of 2/10, n/30.
23	Collected $2,975 from Sounds From Yesterday for Invoice 6725 of March 25.
26	Accepted a two-month promissory note for $5,500 from Country Music Store in settlement of its overdue account; the note has an interest rate of 12 percent.
28	Received a check for $10,290 from Eagleton Music Center in payment of Invoice 9314, dated April 19 ($10,500), less a cash discount ($210).
30	Sold merchandise for $9,800 to Contemporary Sounds, Inc.; issued Invoice 9315 with terms of 2/10, n/30.

Analyze: What total sales on account were made in the month of April prior to any returns or allowances?

Problem 9.4A
Objectives 4, 5

▶

Journalizing purchases, cash payments, and purchases discounts; posting to the general ledger.

The Hiker and Biker Outlet Center is a retail store. Transactions involving purchases and cash payments for the firm during June 2010 are listed on page 305. The general ledger accounts used to record these transactions appear on page 305.

INSTRUCTIONS

1. Open the general ledger accounts and enter the balances as of June 1, 2010.
2. Record the transactions in a purchases journal, a cash payments journal, and a general journal. Use 8 as the page number for each of the special journals and 20 as the page number for the general journal.
3. Post the entries from the general journal and from the Other Accounts Debit section of the cash payments journal to the proper general ledger accounts.
4. Total, prove, and rule the special journals as of June 30.
5. Post the column totals from the special journals to the general ledger.
6. Show how the firm's net cost of purchases would be reported on its income statement for the month ended June 30.

GENERAL LEDGER ACCOUNTS

101	Cash	$18,500 Dr.
131	Equipment	56,000 Dr.
201	Notes Payable	
205	Accounts Payable	4,880 Cr.
501	Purchases	
503	Purchases Ret. and Allow.	
504	Purchases Discounts	
611	Rent Expense	
614	Salaries Expense	
617	Telephone Expense	

DATE		TRANSACTIONS
June	1	Issued Check 1101 for $2,400 to pay the monthly rent.
	3	Purchased merchandise for $2,600 from Perfect Fit Shoe Shop, Invoice 746, dated May 30; the terms are 2/10, n/30.
	5	Purchased new store equipment for $4,500 from Middleton Company, Invoice 9067 dated June 4, net payable in 30 days.
	7	Issued Check 1102 for $1,470 to Leisure Wear Clothing Company, a creditor, in payment of Invoice 3342 of May 9.
	8	Issued Check 1103 for $2,548 to Perfect Fit Shoe Shop, a creditor, in payment of Invoice 746 dated May 30 ($2,600), less a cash discount ($52).
	12	Purchased merchandise for $2,050 from Juanda's Coat Shop, Invoice 9922, dated June 9, net due and payable in 30 days.
	15	Issued Check 1104 for $228 to pay the monthly telephone bill.
	18	Received Credit Memorandum 203 for $550 from Juanda's Coat Shop for defective goods that were returned; the original purchase was made on Invoice 9922 dated June 9.
	21	Purchased new store equipment for $9,500 from Warren Company; issued a three-month promissory note with interest at 12 percent.
	23	Purchased merchandise for $5,400 from The Motor Speedway, Invoice 1927, dated June 20; terms of 2/10, n/30.
	25	Issued Check 1105 for $1,250 to Juanda's Coat Shop, a creditor, in payment of Invoice 7416 dated May 28.
	28	Issued Check 1106 for $5,292 to The Motor Speedway, a creditor, in payment of Invoice 1927 of June 20 ($5,400), less a cash discount ($108).
	30	Purchased merchandise for $1,980 from Jogging Shoes Store, Invoice 4713, dated June 26; the terms are 1/10, n/30.
	30	Issued Check 1107 for $4,800 to pay the monthly salaries of the employees.

Analyze: Assuming that all relevant information is included in this problem, what total liabilities does the company have at month-end?

Preparing a bank reconciliation statement and journalizing entries to adjust the cash balance.

◄ **Problem 9.5A**
Objectives 9, 10

On May 2, 2010, Vacation Paradise received its April bank statement from First City Bank and Trust. Enclosed with the bank statement, which appears below, was a debit memorandum for $160

e**X**cel

that covered an NSF check issued by Doris Fisher, a credit customer. The firm's checkbook contained the following information about deposits made and checks issued during April. The balance of the *Cash* account and the checkbook on April 30, 2010, was $3,972.

DATE		TRANSACTIONS	
April	1	Balance	$6,089
	1	Check 1207	100
	3	Check 1208	300
	5	Deposit	350
	5	Check 1209	275
	10	Check 1210	2,000
	17	Check 1211	50
	19	Deposit	150
	22	Check 1212	9
	23	Deposit	150
	26	Check 1213	200
	28	Check 1214	18
	30	Check 1215	15
	30	Deposit	200

FIRST CITY BANK AND TRUST

Vacation Paradise　　　　　　　　　　Account Number: 23-11070-08
1718 Jade Lane
San Diego, CA 92111-4998　　　　　　　Period Ending April 30, 2010

CHECKS		DEPOSITS		DATE	BALANCE
				Beginning Balance	
				March 31	6,089.00
100.00-			350.00+	April 6	6,339.00
275.00-		300.00-		April 10	5,764.00
2,000.00-				April 13	3,764.00
6.00- SC				April 14	3,758.00
			150.00+	April 20	3,908.00
50.00-				April 22	3,858.00
			150.00+	April 25	4,008.00
				April 26	3,999.00
9.00-				April 29	3,639.00
200.00-		160.00- DM			

INSTRUCTIONS

1. Prepare a bank reconciliation statement for the firm as of April 30, 2010.
2. Record general journal entries for any items on the bank reconciliation statement that must be journalized. Date the entries April 30, 2010.

Analyze: What checks remain outstanding after the bank statement has been reconciled?

Problem 9.6A ▶ **Preparing a bank reconciliation statement and journalizing**
Objectives 9, 10   **entries to adjust the cash balance.**

eXcel　　On August 31, 2010, the balance in the checkbook and the *Cash* account of the Irvine Inn was $11,837. The balance shown on the bank statement on the same date was $13,097.

Notes

a. The firm's records indicate that a $1,200 deposit dated August 30 and a $745 deposit dated August 31 do not appear on the bank statement.

b. A service charge of $8 and a debit memorandum of $320 covering an NSF check have not yet been entered in the firm's records. (The check was issued by Neal Woodson, a credit customer.)

c. The following checks were issued but have not yet been paid by the bank.

> Check 712, $110
> Check 713, $25
> Check 716, $238
> Check 736, $577
> Check 739, $78
> Check 741, $150

d. A credit memorandum shows that the bank collected a $2,286 note receivable and interest of $69 for the firm. These amounts have not yet been entered in the firm's records.

INSTRUCTIONS

1. Prepare a bank reconciliation statement for the firm as of August 31.
2. Record general journal entries for items on the bank reconciliation statement that must be journalized. Date the entries August 31, 2010.

Analyze: What effect did the journal entries recorded as a result of the bank reconciliation have on the fundamental accounting equation?

Correcting errors revealed by a bank reconciliation.

◄ **Problem 9.7A**
Objectives 9, 10

e**X**cel

During the bank reconciliation process at Albert Company on May 2, 2010, the following two errors were discovered in the firm's records.

a. The checkbook and the cash payments journal indicated that Check 2104 dated April 15 was issued for $600 to make a cash purchase of supplies. However, examination of the canceled check and the listing on the bank statement showed that the actual amount of the check was $12.

b. The checkbook and the cash payments journal indicated that Check 2147 dated April 20 was issued for $190 to pay a utility bill. However, examination of the canceled check and the listing on the bank statement showed that the actual amount of the check was $239.

INSTRUCTIONS

1. Prepare the adjusted book balance section of the firm's bank reconciliation statement. The book balance as of April 30 was $20,275. The errors listed above are the only two items that affect the book balance.

2. Prepare general journal entries to correct the errors. Use page 11 and date the entries April 30, 2010. Check 2104 was correctly debited to *Supplies Expense* on April 15, and Check 2147 was debited to *Utilities Expense* on April 20.

Analyze: If the errors described had not been corrected, would net income for the period be overstated or understated? By what amount?

Problem Set B

Journalizing cash receipts and posting to the general ledger.

◄ **Problem 9.1B**
Objectives 1, 2, 3

The Avid Reader is a retail store that sells books, cards, business supplies, and novelties. The firm's cash receipts during June 2010 are shown below. The general ledger accounts used to record these transactions appear below.

INSTRUCTIONS

1. Open the general ledger accounts and enter the balances as of June 1.
2. Record the transactions in a cash receipts journal. (Use page 14.)
3. Post the individual entries from the Other Accounts Credit section of the cash receipts journal to the proper general ledger accounts.
4. Total, prove, and rule the cash receipts journal as of June 30.
5. From the cash receipts journal, post the totals to the general ledger.

GENERAL LEDGER ACCOUNTS

102	Cash	$1,200
111	Accounts Receivable	8,400
115	Notes Receivable	1,600
129	Office Supplies	1,000
231	Sales Tax Payable	$　400
302	Sergio Guzman, Capital	7,600
401	Sales	
791	Interest Income	

DATE	TRANSACTIONS
June　3	Received $400 from Clear Images Copy Center, a credit customer.
4	Received a check for $1,702 from Amanda Guttirez to pay her note receivable; the total included $102 of interest.
5	Received a $360 refund for damaged supplies purchased from Books-R-Us.
7	Recorded cash sales of $1,700 plus sales tax payable of $136.
10	Received $1,400 from Linda James, a credit customer.
13	Sergio Guzman, the owner, contributed additional capital of $10,000 to the business.
14	Recorded cash sales of $1,600 plus sales tax of $128.
18	Received $1,060 from Karen Carter, a credit customer.
19	Received $1,200 from Nelsy Marroquin, a credit customer.
21	Recorded cash sales of $1,800 plus sales tax of $144.
27	Received $800 from Alexander Neal, a credit customer.

Analyze: Assuming that all relevant information is included in this problem, what are total assets for The Avid Reader at June 30, 2010?

Problem 9.2B
Objectives 4, 5, 6

▶ ## Journalizing cash payments and recording petty cash; posting to the general ledger.

The cash payments of European Gift Shop, a retail business, for September are listed on page 309. The general ledger accounts used to record these transactions appear below and on page 309.

INSTRUCTIONS

1. Open the general ledger accounts and enter the balances as of September 1, 2010.
2. Record all payments by check in a cash payments journal. Use 12 as the page number.
3. Record all payments from the petty cash fund on a petty cash analysis sheet with special columns for *Delivery Expense* and *Miscellaneous Expense.* Use 12 as the sheet number.
4. Post the individual entries from the Other Accounts Debit section of the cash payments journal to the proper general ledger accounts.

5. Total, prove, and rule the petty cash analysis sheet as of September 30, then record the replenishment of the fund and the final balance on the sheet.

6. Total, prove, and rule the cash payments journal as of September 30.

7. Post the column totals from the cash payments journal to the proper general ledger accounts.

GENERAL LEDGER ACCOUNTS

101	Cash	$21,530 Dr.	504	Purchases Discounts
105	Petty Cash Fund		511	Delivery Expense
141	Equipment	43,000 Dr.	611	Interest Expense
201	Notes Payable	1,000 Cr.	614	Miscellaneous Expense
205	Accounts Payable	9,800 Cr.	620	Rent Expense
231	Sales Tax Payable	1,344 Cr.	623	Salaries Expense
302	Fred Lin, Drawing		626	Telephone Expense
451	Sales Ret. and Allow.			

DATE		TRANSACTIONS
Sept.	1	Issued Check 401 for $1,344 to remit sales tax to the state tax commission.
	2	Issued Check 402 for $1,700 to pay the monthly rent.
	4	Issued Check 403 for $100 to establish a petty cash fund. (After journalizing this transaction, be sure to enter it on the first line of the petty cash analysis sheet.)
	5	Issued Check 404 for $1,470 to Elegant Glassware, a creditor, in payment of Invoice 6793, dated August 28 ($1,500), less a cash discount ($30).
	6	Paid $12.00 from the petty cash fund for delivery service, Petty Cash Voucher 1.
	9	Purchased store equipment for $1,000; issued Check 405.
	11	Paid $16 from the petty cash fund for office supplies, Petty Cash Voucher 2 (charge to *Miscellaneous Expense*).
	13	Issued Check 406 for $970 to Taylor Company, a creditor, in payment of Invoice 7925, dated August 15.
	14	Issued Check 407 for $425 to a customer as a cash refund for a defective watch that was returned; the original sale was made for cash.
	16	Paid $10 from the petty cash fund for a personal withdrawal by Fred Lin, the owner, Petty Cash Voucher 3.
	18	Issued Check 408 for $187 to pay the monthly telephone bill.
	21	Issued Check 409 for $833 to African Imports, a creditor, in payment of Invoice 1822, dated September 13 ($850), less a cash discount ($17).
	23	Paid $13 from the petty cash fund for postage stamps, Petty Cash Voucher 4.
	24	Issued Check 410 for $1,040 to Zachary Corporation in payment of a $1,000 promissory note and interest of $40.
	26	Issued Check 411 for $1,240 to Atlantic Ceramics, a creditor, in payment of Invoice 3510, dated August 29.
	27	Paid $10 from the petty cash fund for delivery service, Petty Cash Voucher 5.
	28	Issued Check 412 for $1,500 to Fred Lin, the owner, as a withdrawal for personal use.
	30	Issued Check 413 for $2,500 to pay the monthly salaries of the employees.
	30	Issued Check 414 for $61 to replenish the petty cash fund. (Foot the columns of the petty cash analysis sheet in order to determine the accounts that should be debited and the amounts involved.)

Analyze: What was the amount of total debits to general ledger liability accounts during the month of September?

Problem 9.3B

Objectives 1, 2, 3

▶ **Journalizing sales and cash receipts and posting to the general ledger.**

Royal Construction Company is a wholesale business. The transactions involving sales and cash receipts for the firm during August 2010 are listed below. The general ledger accounts used to record these transactions are listed below.

INSTRUCTIONS

1. Open the general ledger accounts and enter the balances as of August 1, 2010.
2. Record the transactions in a sales journal, a cash receipts journal, and a general journal. Use 10 as the page number for each of the special journals and 24 as the page number for the general journal.
3. Post the entries from the general journal to the proper general ledger accounts.
4. Total, prove, and rule the special journals as of August 31, 2010.
5. Post the column totals from the special journals to the proper general ledger accounts.
6. Prepare the heading and the Revenue section of the firm's income statement for the month ended August 31, 2010.

GENERAL LEDGER ACCOUNTS

101	Cash	$15,070 Dr.	401	Sales
109	Notes Receivable		451	Sales Returns and Allowances
111	Accounts Receivable	22,507 Dr.	452	Sales Discounts

DATE		TRANSACTIONS
Aug.	1	Received a check for $6,468 from Construction Supply Company in payment of Invoice 8277 dated July 21 ($6,600), less a cash discount ($132).
	2	Sold merchandise for $19,450 to Jamison Builders; issued Invoice 2978 with terms of 2/10, n/30.
	4	Accepted a three-month promissory note for $12,000 from Davis Custom Homes to settle its overdue account; the note has an interest rate of 12 percent.
	7	Sold merchandise for $18,550 to Branch Construction Company; issued Invoice 2979 with terms of 2/10, n/30.
	11	Collected $19,061 from Jamison Builders for Invoice 2978 dated August 2 ($19,450), less a cash discount ($389.00).
	14	Sold merchandise for $7,050 in cash to a new customer who has not yet established credit.
	16	Branch Construction Company sent a check for $18,179 in payment of Invoice 2979 dated August 7 ($18,550), less a cash discount ($371.00).
	22	Sold merchandise for $6,850 to Contemporary Homes; issued Invoice 2980 with terms of 2/10, n/30.
	24	Received a check for $6,000 from Garcia Homes Center to pay Invoice 2877, dated July 23.
	26	Accepted a return of damaged merchandise from Contemporary Homes; issued Credit Memorandum 101 for $550; the original sale was made on Invoice 2980, dated August 22.
	31	Sold merchandise for $17,440 to Denton County Builders; issued Invoice 2981 with terms of 2/10, n/30.

Analyze: What total sales on account were made in August? Include sales returns and allowances in your computation.

Journalizing purchases, cash payments, and purchase discounts; posting to the general ledger.

◀ **Problem 9.4B**
Objectives 4, 5

Contemporary Appliance Center is a retail store that sells a variety of household appliances. Transactions involving purchases and cash payments for the firm during December 2010 are listed below and on page 312. The general ledger accounts used to record these transactions appear below.

INSTRUCTIONS

1. Open the general ledger accounts and enter the balances in these accounts as of December 1, 2010.

2. Record the transactions in a purchases journal, a cash payments journal, and a general journal. Use 12 as the page number for each of the special journals and 30 as the page number for the general journal.

3. Post the entries from the general journal and from the Other Accounts Debit section of the cash payments journal to the proper accounts in the general ledger.

4. Total, prove, and rule the special journals as of December 31, 2010.

5. Post the column totals from the special journals to the general ledger accounts.

6. Show how the firm's cost of purchases would be reported on its income statement for the month ended December 31, 2010.

GENERAL LEDGER ACCOUNTS

101	Cash	$60,700 Dr.
131	Equipment	68,000 Dr.
201	Notes Payable	
205	Accounts Payable	7,600 Cr.
501	Purchases	
503	Purchases Returns and Allowances	
504	Purchases Discounts	
611	Rent Expense	
614	Salaries Expense	
617	Telephone Expense	

DATE	TRANSACTIONS
Dec. 1	Purchased merchandise for $6,600 from Alexis Products for Homes, Invoice 6559, dated November 28; the terms are 2/10, n/30.
2	Issued Check 1801 for $3,000 to pay the monthly rent.
4	Purchased new store equipment for $14,000 from Kesterson Company; issued a two-month promissory note with interest at 10 percent.
6	Issued Check 1802 for $6,468 to Alexis Products for Homes, a creditor, in payment of Invoice 6559, dated November 28 ($6,600), less a cash discount ($132).
10	Purchased merchandise for $9,200 from the Baxter Corporation, Invoice 5119, dated December 7; terms of 2/10, n/30.
13	Issued Check 1803 for $265 to pay the monthly telephone bill.
15	Issued Check 1804 for $9,016 to Baxter Corporation, a creditor, in payment of Invoice 5119, dated December 7 ($9,200), less a cash discount ($184).
	(continued)

DATE	9.4B (cont.) TRANSACTIONS
Dec. 18	Purchased merchandise for $12,400 from Household Appliance Center, Invoice 7238, dated December 16; terms of 3/10, n/30.
20	Purchased new store equipment for $6,000 from Safety Security Systems Inc., Invoice 536, dated December 17, net payable in 45 days.
21	Issued Check 1805 for $4,200 to Chain Lighting and Appliances, a creditor, in payment of Invoice 7813, dated November 23.
22	Purchased merchandise for $5,800 from Zale Corporation, Invoice 3161, dated December 19, net due in 30 days.
24	Issued Check 1806 for $12,028 to Household Appliance Center, a creditor, in payment of Invoice 7238, dated December 16 ($12,400), less a cash discount ($372).
28	Received Credit Memorandum 201 for $1,050 from Zale Corporation for damaged goods that were returned; the original purchase was made on Invoice 3161, dated December 19.
31	Issued Check 1807 for $6,500 to pay the monthly salaries of the employees.

Analyze: List the dates for transactions in December that would be categorized as expenses of the business.

Problem 9.5B
Objectives 9, 10

▶ **Preparing a bank reconciliation statement and journalizing entries to adjust the cash balance.**

On October 7, 2010, Peter Chen, Attorney-at-Law, received his September bank statement from First Texas National Bank. Enclosed with the bank statement, which appears on page 313, was a debit memorandum for $118 that covered an NSF check issued by Annette Cole, a credit customer. The firm's checkbook contained the following information about deposits made and checks issued during September. The balance of the *Cash* account and the checkbook on September 30 was $8,134.

INSTRUCTIONS

1. Prepare a bank reconciliation statement for the firm as of September 30, 2010.
2. Record general journal entries for any items on the bank reconciliation statement that must be journalized. Date the entries September 30, 2010.

DATE	TRANSACTIONS	
Sept. 1	Balance	$6,500
1	Check 104	100
3	Check 105	10
3	Deposit	500
6	Check 106	225
10	Deposit	410
11	Check 107	200
15	Check 108	75
21	Check 109	60
22	Deposit	730
25	Check 110	16
25	Check 111	80
27	Check 112	140
28	Deposit	900

FIRST TEXAS NATIONAL BANK

Peter Chen, Attorney-at-Law
3510 North Central Expressway
Dallas, TX 75232-2709

Account Number: 22-8654-30

Period Ending September 30, 2010

CHECKS		DEPOSITS	DATE	BALANCE
Beginning Balance			August 31	6,500.00
		500.00+	September 3	7,000.00
100.00-			September 6	6,900.00
200.00-	10.00-	410.00+	September 11	7,100.00
225.00-			September 15	6,875.00
60.00-			September 19	6,815.00
		730.00+	September 23	7,545.00
80.00-	16.00-		September 25	7,449.00
7.50- SC	118.00- DM		September 28	7,323.50

Analyze: How many checks were paid (cleared the bank) according to the September 30 bank statement?

Preparing a bank reconciliation statement and journalizing entries to adjust the cash balance.

◄ **Problem 9.6B**
Objectives 9, 10

On June 30, 2010, the balance in Wells Builder's checkbook and *Cash* account was $6,418.59. The balance shown on the bank statement on the same date was $7,542.03.

Notes

a. The following checks were issued but have not yet been paid by the bank: Check 533 for $148.95, Check 535 for $97.50, and Check 537 for $425.40.

b. A credit memorandum shows that the bank has collected a $1,500 note receivable and interest of $30 for the firm. These amounts have not yet been entered in the firm's records.

c. The firm's records indicate that a deposit of $944.07 made on June 30 does not appear on the bank statement.

d. A service charge of $14.34 and a debit memorandum of $120 covering an NSF check have not yet been entered in the firm's records. (The check was issued by Robert Boley, a credit customer.)

INSTRUCTIONS

1. Prepare a bank reconciliation statement for the firm as of June 30, 2010.

2. Record general journal entries for any items on the bank reconciliation statement that must be journalized. Date the entries June 30, 2010.

Analyze: After all journal entries have been recorded and posted, what is the balance in the *Cash* account?

Correcting errors revealed by a bank reconciliation.

◄ **Problem 9.7B**
Objectives 9, 10

During the bank reconciliation process at Little Guy Movers Corporation on March 3, 2010, the following errors were discovered in the firm's records.

a. The checkbook and the cash payments journal indicated that Check 1201 dated February 8 was issued for $316 to pay for hauling expenses. However, examination of the canceled check and the listing on the bank statement showed that the actual amount of the check was $308.

b. The checkbook and the cash payments journal indicated that Check 1222 dated February 24 was issued for $404 to pay a telephone bill. However, examination of the canceled check and the listing on the bank statement showed that the actual amount of the check was $440.

INSTRUCTIONS

1. Prepare the adjusted book balance section of the firm's bank reconciliation statement. The book balance as of February 28, 2010, was $19,451. The errors listed are the only two items that affect the book balance.

2. Prepare general journal entries to correct the errors. Date the entries February 28, 2010. Check 1201 was debited to *Hauling Expense* on February 8, and Check 1222 was debited to *Telephone Expense* on February 24.

Analyze: What net change to the *Cash* account occurred as a result of the correcting journal entries?

Critical Thinking Problem 9.1

Special Journals

During September 2010, Interior Designs Specialty Shop, a retail store, had the transactions listed on pages 315–316. The general ledger accounts used to record these transactions are provided on page 315.

INSTRUCTIONS

1. Open the general ledger accounts and enter the balances as of September 1, 2010.

2. Record the transactions in a sales journal, a cash receipts journal, a purchases journal, a cash payments journal, and a general journal. Use page 12 as the page number for each of the special journals and page 32 as the page number for the general journal.

3. Post the entries from the general journal to the proper general ledger accounts.

4. Post the entries from the Other Accounts Credit section of the cash receipts journal to the proper general ledger accounts.

5. Post the entries from the Other Accounts Debit section of the cash payments journal to the proper general ledger accounts.

6. Total, prove, and rule the special journals as of September 30.

7. Post the column totals from the special journals to the proper general ledger accounts.

8. Set up an accounts receivable ledger for Interior Designs Specialty Shop. Open an account for each of the customers listed below, and enter the balances as of September 1. All of these customers have terms of n/30.

Credit Customers	
Name	**Balance 9/01/10**
Rachel Carter	
Mesia Davis	$1,260.00
Robert Kent	1,730.00
Pam Lawrence	
David Prater	1,050.00
Henry Tolliver	
Jason Williams	2,100.00

9. Post the individual entries from the sales journal, cash receipts journal, and the general journal to the accounts receivable subsidiary ledger.

10. Prepare a schedule of accounts receivable for September 30, 2010.

11. Check the total of the schedule of accounts receivable against the balance of the *Accounts Receivable* account in the general ledger. The two amounts should be the same.

Creditors		
Name	Balance 9/01/10	Terms
Booker, Inc.		n/45
McKnight Corporation	$5,500	1/10, n/30
Nelson Craft Products		2/10, n/30
Rocker Company		n/30
Reed Millings Company		2/10, n/30
Sadler Floor Coverings	1,940	n/30
Wells Products	2,120	n/30

12. Set up an accounts payable subsidiary ledger for Interior Designs Specialty Shop. Open an account for each of the creditors listed above, and enter the balances as of September 1, 2010.

13. Post the individual entries from the purchases journal, the cash payments journal, and the general journal to the accounts payable subsidiary ledger.

14. Prepare a schedule of accounts payable for September 1, 2010.

15. Check the total of the schedule of accounts payable against the balance of the *Accounts Payable* account in the general ledger. The two amounts should be the same.

GENERAL LEDGER ACCOUNTS

101	Cash	$18,945 Dr.	451	Sales Returns and Allowances	
109	Notes Receivable		501	Purchases	
111	Accounts Receivable	6,140 Dr.	502	Freight In	
121	Supplies	710 Dr.	503	Purchases Returns and Allowances	
131	Inventory	29,365 Dr.	504	Purchases Discounts	
201	Notes Payable		611	Cash Short or Over	
205	Accounts Payable	9,560 Cr.	614	Rent Expense	
231	Sales Tax Payable		617	Salaries Expense	
301	Sergio Cortez, Capital	45,600 Cr.	619	Utilities Expense	
401	Sales				

DATE	TRANSACTIONS
Sept. 1	Received a check for $1,050 from David Prater to pay his account.
1	Issued Check 1401 for $1,940 to Sadler Floor Coverings, a creditor, in payment of Invoice 6325 dated August 3.
2	Issued Check 1402 for $2,500 to pay the monthly rent.
3	Sold a table on credit for $650 plus sales tax of $52.00 to Pam Lawrence, Sales Slip 1850.
5	Sergio Cortez, the owner, invested an additional $15,000 cash in the business in order to expand operations.
6	Had cash sales of $3,900 plus sales tax of $312 during the period September 1–6; there was a cash shortage of $20.
6	Purchased carpeting for $4,450 from Reed Millings Company, Invoice 827, dated September 3; terms of 2/10, n/30.
	(continued)

DATE	SPECIAL JOURNALS (cont.) TRANSACTIONS
Sept 6	Issued Check 1403 for $158 to Tri-City Trucking Company to pay the freight charge on goods received from Reed Millings Company.
8	Purchased store supplies for $370 from Rocker Company, Invoice 4204, dated September 6, net amount due in 30 days.
8	Sold chairs on credit for $950 plus sales tax of $76.00 to Henry Tolliver, Sales Slip 1851.
11	Accepted a two-month promissory note for $2,100 from Jason Williams to settle his overdue account; the note has an interest rate of 10 percent.
11	Issued Check 1404 for $4,361 to Reed Millings Company, a creditor, in payment of Invoice 827 dated September 3 ($4,450) less a cash discount ($89).
13	Had cash sales of $3,850 plus sales tax of $308 during the period September 8–13.
14	Purchased carpeting for $3,700 plus a freight charge of $84 from Wells Products, Invoice 9453, dated September 11, net due and payable in 30 days.
15	Collected $1,260 on account from Mesia Davis.
17	Gave a two-month promissory note for $5,500 to McKnight Corporation, a creditor, to settle an overdue balance; the note bears interest at 12 percent.
19	Sold a lamp on credit to Rachel Carter for $250 plus sales tax of $20, Sales Slip 1852.
20	Had cash sales of $4,100 plus sales tax of $328 during the period September 15–20; there was a cash shortage of $9.00.
21	Purchased area rugs for $2,800 from Nelson Craft Products, Invoice 677, dated September 18; the terms are 2/10, n/30.
22	Issued Check 1405 for $306 to pay the monthly utility bill.
23	Granted an allowance to Rachel Carter for scratches on the lamp that she bought on Sales Slip 1852 of September 19; issued Credit Memorandum 151 for $54, which includes a price reduction of $50 and sales tax of $4.
24	Received Credit Memorandum 110 for $300 from Nelson Craft Products for a damaged rug that was returned; the original purchase was made on Invoice 677 dated September 18.
24	Robert Kent sent a check for $1,730 to pay the balance he owes.
25	Issued Check 1406 for $3,600 to make a cash purchase of merchandise.
26	Issued Check 1407 for $2,450 to Nelson Craft Products, a creditor, in payment of Invoice 677 of September 18 ($2,800), less a return ($300) and a cash discount ($50).
27	Purchased hooked rugs for $4,200 plus a freight charge of $128 from Booker, Inc., Invoice 1368, dated September 23, net payable in 45 days.
27	Had cash sales of $4,800 plus sales tax of $384 during the period September 22–27.
28	Issued Check 1408 for $2,120 to Wells Products, a creditor, in payment of Invoice 8984 dated August 30.
29	Sold a cabinet on credit to Mesia Davis for $1,200 plus sales tax of $96, Sales Slip 1853.
30	Had cash sales of $1,500 plus sales tax of $120 for September 29–30; there was a cash overage of $10.
30	Issued Check 1409 for $6,800 to pay the monthly salaries of the employees.

Analyze: What were the total cash payments for September?

Critical Thinking Problem 9.2

Cash Controls

Julius Wells is the owner of a successful small construction company. He spends most of his time out of the office supervising work at various construction sites, leaving the operation of the office to the company's cashier/bookkeeper, Gloria Harris. Gloria makes bank deposits, pays the company's bills, maintains the accounting records, and prepares monthly bank reconciliations.

Recently a friend told Julius that while he was at a party he overheard Gloria bragging that she paid for her new dress with money from the company's cash receipts. She said her boss would never know because he never checks the cash records.

Julius admits that he does not check on Gloria's work. He now wants to know if Gloria is stealing from him. He asks you to examine the company's cash records to determine whether Gloria has stolen cash from the business and, if so, how much.

Your examination of the company's cash records reveals the following information.

1. Gloria prepared the following August 31, 2010, bank reconciliation.

Balance in books, August 31, 2010		$18,786
Additions:		
Outstanding checks		
Check 1780	$ 792	
Check 1784	1,819	
Check 1806	384	2,695
		$21,481
Deductions:		
Deposit in transit, August 28, 2010	$4,882	
Bank service charge	10	4,892
Balance on bank statement, July 31, 2010		$16,589

2. An examination of the general ledger shows the *Cash* account with a balance of $18,786 on August 31, 2010.

3. The August 31 bank statement shows a balance of $16,589.

4. The August 28 deposit of $4,882 does not appear on the August 31 bank statement.

5. A comparison of canceled checks returned with the August 31 bank statement with the cash payments journal reveals the following checks as outstanding:

Check 1590	$ 263
Check 1680	1,218
Check 1724	486
Check 1780	792
Check 1784	1,819
Check 1806	384

Prepare a bank statement using the format presented in this chapter for the month of August. Assume there were no bank or bookkeeping errors in August. Did Gloria take cash from the company? If so, how much and how did she try to conceal the theft? What changes would you recommend to Julius to provide better internal control over cash?

BUSINESS CONNECTIONS

Cash Management

1. The new accountant for Asheville Hardware Center, a large retail store, found the following weaknesses in the firm's cash-handling procedures. How would you explain to management why each of these procedures should be changed?

   a. No cash register proof is prepared at the end of each day. The amount of money in the register is considered the amount of cash sales for the day.

   b. Small payments are sometimes made from the currency and coins in the cash register. (The store has no petty cash fund.)

   c. During busy periods for the firm, cash receipts are sometimes kept on the premises for several days before a bank deposit is made.

   d. When funds are removed from the cash register at the end of each day, they are placed in an unlocked office cabinet until they are deposited.

   e. The person who makes the bank deposits also records them in the checkbook, journalizes cash receipts, and reconciles the bank statement.

2. Why should management be concerned about having accurate information about the firm's cash position available at all times?

3. Many banks now offer a variety of computer services to clients. Why is it not advisable for a firm to pay its bank to complete the reconciliation procedure at the end of each month?

4. Assume that you are the newly hired controller at Norton Company and that you have observed the following banking procedures in use at the firm. Would you change any of these procedures? Why or why not?

   a. A blank endorsement is made on all checks to be deposited.

   b. The checkbook is kept on the top of a desk so that it will be handy.

   c. The same person prepares bank deposits, issues checks, and reconciles the bank statement.

   d. The reconciliation process usually takes place two or three weeks after the bank statement is received.

   e. The bank statement and the canceled checks are thrown away after the reconciliation process is completed.

   f. As a shortcut in the reconciliation process, there is no attempt to compare the endorsements on the back of the canceled checks with the names of the payees shown on the face of these checks.

5. Why should management be concerned about achieving effective internal control over cash receipts and cash payments?

6. How does management benefit when cash transactions are recorded quickly and efficiently?

7. Why do some companies require that all employees who handle cash be bonded?

8. Why is it a good practice for a business to make all payments by check except for minor payments from a petty cash fund?

Borrowing from Petty Cash

Daniel Garcia is in charge of the $100 petty cash for Garcia's Auto Repair Service. When an employee needs a special part that is not in inventory, Daniel takes money from petty cash to buy the part. One day Daniel was short of cash and needed some lunch money. He decides to borrow $10 that he will pay back on payday in three days. Daniel continues this practice for three days for a total of $30. He does not have enough to pay the petty cash back. When he reconciles the petty cash, he records this $30 as Cash short/over expense. This is the first time he has done it. Is this an ethical action? What should Daniel do to fix this problem if there is one?

Cash

Refer to the *2006 Annual Report* of The Home Depot, Inc., in Appendix A.

1. Review the consolidated balance sheet. Store operations provide the company with a significant source of cash. What amount is reported for "Cash and cash equivalents" for January 28, 2007? For January 29, 2006? What is the percentage change?

2. Locate the report named "Executive Summary and Selected Consolidated Statements of Earnings Data." How many sales transactions were reported for 2006? What was the amount of the average sale transaction?

Balance Sheet

Financial Statement **ANALYSIS**

Dell Inc. is a premier provider of computer products and services that enable customers to build their information-technology and Internet structures. In fiscal 2007, Dell's net sales totaled more than $57.4 billion. The following excerpt was taken from the company's *2007 Annual Report*.

Dell Inc. Consolidated Balance Sheets	As of	
Millions except for numbers of shares and per-share data	Jan. 26, 2007	Jan. 27, 2006
ASSETS		
Current Assets:		
Cash and cash equivalents*	$ 10,298	$ 9,070
Accounts receivable, net	4,622	4,082
Total current assets	$19,939	$17,794
* Cash and Cash Equivalents: Short-term investments that have maturities of three months or less when purchased are considered to be cash equivalents.		

Analyze:

1. What percentage of total current assets is made up of cash and cash equivalents for fiscal 2007?

2. Cash receipt and cash payment transactions affect the total value of a company's assets. By what amount did the category "Cash and cash equivalents" change from 2006 to 2007?

3. If accountants at Dell failed to record cash receipts of $125,000 on the final day of fiscal 2007, what impact would this error have on the balance sheet category "Cash and cash equivalents"?

e-Commerce

Extending THE THOUGHT

A small gift shop has just launched a new Web site where customers can purchase products. The Web site's e-commerce software systems automatically generate daily sales reports and forward the reports to the gift shop's accountant. The gift shop uses an online e-cash processing company, which deposits cash receipts to the gift shop's bank account automatically. What strategies should the gift shop implement to ensure proper accounting for cash receipts generated from online sales?

Agenda

Business COMMUNICATION

You have just been hired as the chief financial officer for a software development company. In an effort to familiarize yourself with the processes of the accounting office, you have requested a meeting with the accounting manager to discuss the company's internal control procedures. To prepare for the meeting, create a list of questions and topics that you would like to discuss. Your list should include questions to help you verify that the department is enforcing the appropriate controls over cash payments and cash receipts.

Internal Controls of Cash

TEAMWORK

You and four friends have decided to create a new service company called Unpacking for You. Your company unpacks for families once they have moved into a new house. Your business is primarily a cash business. Each family will pay you $100 for each room that is unpacked on the same day you finish the service. How will your business make sure that the payment from the customer is valid? How will you ensure that you will receive the cash when the customer pays the employee in cash?

Internet | CONNECTION

Bank Charges

Many times a negative cash flow is a potential problem in a business. Go to the Web site for the local banks in your community. Check the requirements for a line of credit or mortgage in case your company needs cash quickly to buy a product you know you will sell for a large profit. Some bank Web sites could be: www.bankofamerica.com   www.wellsfargo.com   www.chasebank.com

Answers to **Self Reviews**

Answers to Section 1 Self Review

1. Amounts from the Accounts Receivable Credit column are posted as credits to the individual customers' accounts in the accounts receivable subsidiary ledger daily. The total of the Accounts Receivable Credit column is posted as a credit to the *Accounts Receivable* control account in the general ledger at the end of the accounting period.

2. A written promise to pay a specified amount of money on a specified date. To grant credit in certain sales transactions or to replace open-account credit when a customer has an overdue balance.

3. A cash shortage occurs when cash in the register is less than the audit tape; an overage occurs when cash is more than the audit tape. Debit shortages and credit overages in the *Cash Short or Over* account.

4. **b.** cash receipts journal

5. **d.** all of the above

6. The frequency of cash discrepancies indicates that a problem may exist in the handling of the cash (depending on the size of the business and the number of registers, 15 entries may not be unusual).

Answers to Section 2 Self Review

1. Amounts in the Other Accounts Debit section are posted individually to the general ledger accounts daily. The total of the Other Accounts Debit column is not posted because the individual amounts were previously posted to the general ledger.

2. To make small expenditures that require currency and coins.

3. Record the name of the owner's drawing account and the amount in the Other Accounts Debit section of the cash payments journal, and record the amount in the Cash Credit column.

4. **b.** February 4

5. **a.** cash payments journal

6. You should explain to your employer that she must keep all receipts regardless of the amount. Ask your employer to complete a voucher for that amount, then record the entry in the proper account.

Answers to Section 3 Self Review

1. Items in the second section of the bank reconciliation statement require entries in the firm's financial records to correct the *Cash* account balance and make it equal to the checkbook balance. These may include bank fees, debit memorandums, NSF checks, and interest income.

2. Endorsement is the legal process by which the payee transfers ownership of the check to the bank.

3. A check that is dated in the future. It should not be deposited before its date because the drawer of the check may not have sufficient funds in the bank to cover the check at the current time.

4. **d.** Deposits in transit

5. **a.** canceled checks

6. Disagree. Good internal control requires separation of duties.

Answers to Comprehensive Self Review

1. A full endorsement contains the name of the payee plus the name of the firm or bank to whom the check is payable.

2. A record of when a payment is made from petty cash, the amount and purpose of the expenditure, and the account to be charged.

3. Petty cash can be replenished at any time if the fund runs low, but it should be replenished at the end of each month so that all expenses for the month are recorded.

4. They eliminate repetition in postings; the initial recording of transactions is faster.

5. Checks, money orders, and funds on deposit in a bank as well as currency and coins.

Chapter 10

Payroll Computations, Records, and Payment

LEARNING OBJECTIVES

1. Explain the major federal laws relating to employee earnings and withholding. **LP10**
2. Compute gross earnings of employees.
3. Determine employee deductions for social security tax.
4. Determine employee deductions for Medicare tax.
5. Determine employee deductions for income tax.
6. Enter gross earnings, deductions, and net pay in the payroll register.
7. Journalize payroll transactions in the general journal.
8. Maintain an earnings record for each employee.
9. Define the accounting terms new to this chapter.

NEW TERMS

commission basis
compensation record
employee
Employee's Withholding Allowance Certificate (Form W-4)
exempt employees
federal unemployment taxes
hourly rate basis
independent contractor
individual earnings record
Medicare tax
payroll register
piece-rate basis
salary basis
Social Security Act
social security (FICA) tax
state unemployment taxes
tax-exempt wages
time and a half
wage-bracket table method
workers' compensation insurance

www.clifbar.com

Gary Erickson has never been motivated much by money. It was hunger more than anything else that motivated him initially. An avid cyclist, he was inspired to create a better-tasting energy bar while on a 175-mile bike ride. With help from his mom, Gary accomplished his goal and the Clif Bar was introduced in 1992. The Luna Bar, the Builder's Bar, and the Mojo Bar have joined the original Clif Bar and Gary's idea for a better energy bar has evolved into a $150-million business. Though a financial success, Gary and his employees are proudest of their success as a "green" company. Shifting to organic ingredients, eliminating shrink-wrap, and supporting a wind farm to offset fossil fuel usage are all examples of the company's commitment to the health of the environment.

Clif Bar & Company is equally dedicated to the health and welfare of its employees. It is an unusual work environment filled with climbing walls, dogs, yoga classes, and employees running out to volunteer, but it works. Just ask the "Creative Implementation Expert" or the "Sports Marketing Dude," two of the many unique employees you'll find at Clif Bar & Company.

thinking critically

What types of benefits do you think are important to people working at a place like Clif Bar & Company? What would be important to you?

>> 1. **Explain the major federal laws relating to employee earnings and withholding.**

WHY IT'S IMPORTANT

Tax and labor laws protect the rights of both the employee and the employer. Income tax withholding laws ensure continued funding of certain federal and state programs.

TERMS TO LEARN

employee
federal unemployment taxes
independent contractor
Medicare tax
Social Security Act
social security (FICA) tax
state unemployment taxes
time and a half
workers' compensation insurance

Video10.1

Payroll Laws and Taxes

A large component of the activity of any business is concerned with payroll work. Payroll accounting is so important that it requires special consideration.

Who Is an Employee?

Payroll accounting relates only to earnings of those individuals classified as employees. An **employee** is hired by and works under the control and direction of the employer. Usually the employer provides the tools or equipment used by the employee, sets the employee's working hours, and determines how the employee completes the job. Examples of employees are the company president, the bookkeeper, the sales clerk, and the warehouse worker.

In contrast to an employee, an **independent contractor** is paid by the company to carry out a specific task or job, but is not under the direct supervision or control of the company. The independent contractor is told what needs to be done, but the means of doing the job are left to the independent contractor. Examples of independent contractors are the accountant who performs the independent audit, the outside attorney who renders legal advice, and the consultant who installs a new accounting system.

This text addresses issues related to employees but not to independent contractors. When dealing with independent contractors, businesses do not have to follow federal labor laws regulating minimum rates of pay and maximum hours of employment. The business is not required to withhold or match payroll taxes on amounts paid to independent contractors.

>> 1. OBJECTIVE

Explain the major federal laws relating to employee earnings and withholding.

LP10

Federal Employee Earnings and Withholding Laws

Since the 1930s many federal and state laws have affected the relationship between employers and employees. Some of these laws deal with working conditions, including hours and earnings. Others relate to income tax withholding. Some concern taxes that are levied against the employer to provide specific employee benefits.

THE FAIR LABOR STANDARDS ACT

The *Fair Labor Standards Act* of 1938, often referred to as the Wage and Hour Law, applies only to firms engaged directly or indirectly in interstate commerce. It sets a minimum hourly rate of pay and maximum hours of work per week to be performed at the regular rate of pay. When this book was printed, the minimum hourly rate of pay was $5.85, and the maximum number of hours at the regular pay rate was 40 hours per week. When an employee works more than 40 hours in a week, the employee earns at least one and one-half times the regular hourly rate of pay for the extra hours. This overtime rate is called **time and a half.** Even if the federal law does not apply to them, many employers pay time and a half for overtime because of union contracts or simply as good business practice.

SOCIAL SECURITY TAX

The *Federal Insurance Contributions Act (FICA)* is commonly referred to as the **Social Security Act.** The act, first passed in the 1930s, has been amended frequently. The Social Security Act provides the following benefits:

- Retirement benefits, or pension, when a worker reaches age 62.
- Benefits for the dependents of the retired worker.
- Benefits for the worker and the worker's dependents when the worker is disabled.

These retirement and disability benefits are paid by the **social security tax,** sometimes called the **FICA tax.** Both the employer and the employee pay an equal amount of social security tax. The employer is required to withhold social security tax from the employee's pay. Periodically the employer sends the social security tax withheld to the federal government.

The rate of the social security tax and the calendar year earnings base to which it applies are frequently changed by Congress. In recent years, the social security tax rate has remained constant at 6.2 percent. The earnings base to which the tax applies has increased yearly. In 2007, the social security tax rate was 6.2 percent of the first $97,500 of salary or wages paid to each employee. In examples and problems, this text uses a social security tax rate of 6.2 percent of the first $97,500 of salary or wages.

MEDICARE TAX

The Medicare tax is closely related to the social security tax. Prior to 1992 it was a part of the social security tax. The **Medicare tax** is a tax levied equally on employees and employers to provide medical care for the employee and the employee's spouse after each has reached age 65.

In recent years, the Medicare tax rate has remained constant at 1.45 percent. The Medicare tax applies to all salaries and wages paid during the year. The employer is required to withhold the Medicare tax from the employee's pay and periodically send it to the federal government.

Note that the social security tax has an earnings base limit. The Medicare tax does not have an earnings base limit. The Medicare tax applies to *all* earnings paid during the year.

FEDERAL INCOME TAX

Employers are required to withhold from employees' earnings an estimated amount of income tax that will be payable by the employee on the earnings. The amount depends on several factors. Later in this chapter you will learn how to determine the amount to withhold from an employee's paycheck.

State and Local Taxes

Most states, and many local governments, require employers to withhold income taxes from employees' earnings to prepay the employees' state and local income taxes. These rules are generally almost identical to those governing federal income tax withholding, but they require separate general ledger accounts in the firm's accounting system.

Employer's Payroll Taxes and Insurance Costs

Remember that employers withhold social security and Medicare taxes from employees' earnings. In addition, employers pay social security and Medicare taxes on their employees'

important!

Wage Base Limit
The social security tax has a wage base limit. There is no wage base limit for the Medicare tax. All salaries and wages are subject to the Medicare tax.

earnings. Employers are also required to pay federal and state taxes for unemployment benefits and to carry workers' compensation insurance.

SOCIAL SECURITY TAX

The employer's share of the social security tax is 6.2 percent up to the earnings base. (In this text, the social security tax is 6.2 percent of the first $97,500 of earnings.) Periodically the employer pays to the federal government the social security tax withheld plus the employer's share of the social security tax.

	FICA
Employee (withheld)	6.2%
Employer (match)	6.2
Total	12.4%

MEDICARE TAX

The employer's share of Medicare tax is 1.45 percent of earnings. Periodically the employer pays to the federal government the Medicare tax withheld plus the employer's share of the Medicare tax.

The Medicare taxes the employer remits to the federal government are shown below.

	Medicare
Employee (withheld)	1.45%
Employer (match)	1.45
Total	2.90%

FEDERAL UNEMPLOYMENT TAX

The *Federal Unemployment Tax Act (FUTA)* provides benefits for employees who become unemployed. Taxes levied by the federal government against employers to benefit unemployed workers are called **federal unemployment taxes (FUTA).** Employers pay the entire amount of these taxes. In this text, we assume that the taxable earnings base is $7,000. That is, the tax applies to the first $7,000 of each employee's earnings for the year. The FUTA tax rate is 6.2 percent, but can be reduced by the state unemployment tax rate. The FUTA tax rate is scheduled to decrease to 6 percent in 2008.

STATE UNEMPLOYMENT TAX

The federal and state unemployment programs work together to provide benefits for employees who become unemployed. Employers pay all of the **state unemployment taxes (SUTA).** Usually the earnings base for the federal and state unemployment taxes are the same, the first $7,000 of each employee's earnings for the year. For many states the SUTA tax rate is 5.4 percent.

The federal tax rate (6.2 percent) can be reduced by the rate charged by the state (5.4 percent in this example), so the FUTA rate can be as low as 0.8 percent (6.2% − 5.4%).

SUTA tax		5.4%
FUTA tax rate	6.2%	
Less SUTA tax	(5.4)	
Net FUTA tax		0.8
Total federal and state unemployment tax		6.2%

WORKERS' COMPENSATION INSURANCE

Workers' compensation insurance is not a tax, but insurance that protects employees against losses from job-related injuries or illnesses, or compensates their families if death occurs in the course of the employment. Workers' compensation requirements are defined by each state. Most states mandate workers' compensation insurance.

Employee Records Required by Law

> Many companies outsource payroll duties to professional payroll companies. ADP, Inc., is the world's largest provider of payroll services and employee information systems.

Federal laws require that certain payroll records be maintained. For each employee the employer must keep a record of

- the employee's name, address, social security number, and date of birth;
- hours worked each day and week, and wages paid at the regular and overtime rates (certain exceptions exist for employees who earn salaries);
- cumulative wages paid throughout the year;
- amount of income tax, social security tax, and Medicare tax withheld for each pay period;
- proof that the employee is a United States citizen or has a valid work permit.

Section **1** Self Review

QUESTIONS

1. How are social security benefits financed?

2. How are unemployment insurance benefits financed?

3. What is "time and a half"?

EXERCISES

4. The purpose of FUTA is to provide benefits for

  a. employees who become unemployed.

  b. employees who become injured while on the job.

  c. retired workers.

  d. disabled employees.

5. The earnings base limit for Medicare

  a. is the same as the earnings base limit for social security.

  b. is lower than the earnings base limit for social security.

  c. is higher than the earnings base limit for social security.

  d. does not exist.

ANALYSIS

6. Susan Kennedy was hired by Harvey Architects to create three oil paintings for the president's office. Is Kennedy an employee? Why or why not?

(Answers to Section 1 Self Review are on page 357.)

SECTION OBJECTIVES

>> 2. **Compute gross earnings of employees.**

WHY IT'S IMPORTANT

Payroll is a large part of business activity.

>> 3. **Determine employee deductions for social security tax.**

WHY IT'S IMPORTANT

Employers are legally responsible for collecting and remitting this tax.

>> 4. **Determine employee deductions for Medicare tax.**

WHY IT'S IMPORTANT

Employers have legal responsibility.

>> 5. **Determine employee deductions for income tax.**

WHY IT'S IMPORTANT

Employers are legally responsible.

>> 6. **Enter gross earnings, deductions, and net pay in the payroll register.**

WHY IT'S IMPORTANT

The payroll register provides information needed to prepare paychecks.

TERMS TO LEARN

commission basis

Employee's Withholding Allowance Certificate (Form W-4)

exempt employees

hourly rate basis

payroll register

piece-rate basis

salary basis

tax-exempt wages

wage-bracket table method

Calculating Earnings and Taxes

Sanchez Furniture Company is a sole proprietorship owned and managed by Sarah Sanchez. Sanchez Furniture Company imports furniture and novelty items to sell over the Internet. It has five employees. The three shipping clerks and the shipping supervisor are paid on an hourly basis. The office clerk is paid a weekly salary. Payday is each Monday; it covers the wages and salaries earned the previous week. The employees are subject to withholding of social security, Medicare, and federal income taxes. The business pays social security and Medicare taxes, and federal and state unemployment insurance taxes. The business is required by state law to carry workers' compensation insurance. Since it is involved in interstate commerce, Sanchez Furniture Company is subject to the Fair Labor Standards Act.

From time to time, Sarah Sanchez, the owner, makes cash withdrawals to cover her personal expenses. The withdrawals of the owner of a sole proprietorship are not treated as salaries or wages.

Computing Total Earnings of Employees

The first step in preparing payroll is to compute the gross wages or salary for each employee. There are several ways to compute earnings.

Hourly rate basis workers earn a stated rate per hour. Gross pay depends on the number of hours worked.

Salary basis workers earn an agreed-upon amount for each week, month, or other period.

Commission basis workers, usually salespeople, earn a percentage of net sales.

Piece-rate basis manufacturing workers are paid based on the number of units produced.

Wal-Mart Stores, Inc., has approximately 1,500,000 employees in its world-wide operations, which include Wal-Mart Discount Stores, SAM's Clubs, the distribution centers, and the home office. Nearly 75 percent of its stores are in the United States, but Wal-Mart is expanding internationally. It is the number 1 retailer in Canada and Mexico. It also has operations in Asia, Europe, and South America. The company reports that 65 percent of Wal-Mart managers, who are compensated on a salary basis, first entered the company as hourly employees.

Determining Pay for Hourly Employees

Two pieces of data are needed to compute gross pay for hourly rate basis employees: the number of hours worked during the payroll period, and the rate of pay.

HOURS WORKED

At Sanchez Furniture Company, the shipping supervisor keeps a weekly time sheet. Each day she enters the hours worked by each shipping clerk. At the end of the week, the office clerk uses the time sheet to compute the total hours worked and to prepare the payroll.

Many businesses use time clocks for hourly employees. Each employee has a time card and inserts it in the time clock to record the times of arrival and departure. The payroll clerk collects the cards at the end of the week, determines the hours worked by each employee, and multiplies the number of hours by the pay rate to compute the *gross pay*. Some time cards are machine readable. A computer determines the hours worked and makes the earnings calculations.

GROSS PAY

Alicia Martinez, Jorge Rodriguez, and George Dunlap are shipping clerks at Sanchez Furniture Company. They are hourly employees. Their gross pay for the week ended January 6 is determined as follows:

- Martinez worked 40 hours. She earns $10 an hour. Her gross pay is $400 (40 hours × $10).
- Rodriguez worked 40 hours. He earns $9.50 an hour. His gross pay is $380 (40 × $9.50).
- Dunlap earns $9 per hour. He worked 45 hours. He is paid 40 hours at regular pay and 5 hours at time and a half. There are two ways to compute Dunlap's gross pay:

1. The Wage and Hour Law method identifies the *overtime premium,* the amount the firm could have saved if all the hours were paid at the regular rate. The overtime premium rate is $4.50, one-half of the regular rate ($9 × 1/2 = $4.50).

Total hours × regular rate:	
45 hours × $9	$405.00
Overtime premium:	
5 hours × $4.50	22.50
Gross pay	$427.50

>>2. OBJECTIVE

Compute gross earnings of employees.

LP10

recall

Owner Withdrawals
Withdrawals by the owner of a sole proprietorship are debited to a temporary owner's equity account (in this case, **Sarah Sanchez, Drawing**). Withdrawals are not treated as salary or wages.

2. The second method identifies how much the employee earned by working overtime.

Regular earnings:	
40 hours × $9	$360.00
Overtime earnings:	
5 hours × $13.50 ($9 × 1 1/2)	67.50
Gross pay	$427.50

Cecilia Wu is the shipping supervisor at Sanchez Furniture Company. She is an hourly employee. She earns $14 an hour, and she worked 40 hours. Her gross pay is $560 (40 × $14).

WITHHOLDINGS FOR HOURLY EMPLOYEES REQUIRED BY LAW

Recall that three deductions from employees' gross pay are required by federal law. They are FICA (social security) tax, Medicare tax, and federal income tax withholding.

>>**3. OBJECTIVE**

Determine employee deductions for social security tax.

LP10

Social Security Tax The social security tax is levied on both the employer and the employee. This text calculates social security tax using a 6.2 percent tax rate on the first $97,500 of wages paid during the calendar year. **Tax-exempt wages** are earnings in excess of the base amount set by the Social Security Act ($97,500). Tax-exempt wages are not subject to FICA withholding.

If an employee works for more than one employer during the year, the FICA tax is deducted and matched by each employer. When the employee files a federal income tax return, any excess FICA tax withheld from the employee's earnings is refunded by the government or applied to payment of the employee's federal income taxes.

To determine the amount of social security tax to withhold from an employee's pay, multiply the taxable wages by the social security tax rate. Round the result to the nearest cent.

The following shows the social security tax deductions for Sanchez Furniture Company's hourly employees.

Employee	Gross Pay	Tax Rate	Tax
Alicia Martinez	$400.00	6.2%	$ 24.80
Jorge Rodriguez	380.00	6.2	23.56
George Dunlap	427.50	6.2	26.51
Cecilia Wu	560.00	6.2	34.72
Total social security tax			$109.59

>>**4. OBJECTIVE**

Determine employee deductions for Medicare tax.

LP10

Medicare Tax The Medicare tax is levied on both the employee and the employer. To compute the Medicare tax to withhold from the employee's paycheck, multiply the wages by the Medicare tax rate, 1.45 percent. The following shows the Medicare tax deduction for hourly employees.

Employee	Gross Pay	Tax Rate	Tax
Alicia Martinez	$400.00	1.45%	$ 5.80
Jorge Rodriguez	380.00	1.45	5.51
George Dunlap	427.50	1.45	6.20
Cecilia Wu	560.00	1.45	8.12
Total Medicare tax			$25.63

Federal Income Tax A substantial portion of the federal government's revenue comes from the income tax on individuals. Employers are required to withhold federal income tax from employees' pay. Periodically the employer pays the federal income tax withheld to the federal government. After the end of the year, the employee files an income tax return. If the amount of federal income tax withheld does not cover the amount of income tax due, the employee pays the balance. If too much federal income tax has been withheld, the employee receives a refund.

>> **5. OBJECTIVE**
Determine employee deductions for income tax.

LP10

> The federal income tax is a pay-as-you-go tax. There are two ways to pay. If you are an employee, your employer will withhold income tax from your pay based on your instructions in Form W-4. If you do not pay tax through withholdings, or do not pay enough taxes through withholdings because of income from other sources, you might have to pay estimated taxes. Individuals who are in business for themselves generally have to pay taxes through the estimated tax system. The Electronic Federal Tax Payment System (EFTPS) is a free service from the IRS through which taxpayers can use the Internet or telephone to pay their federal taxes, especially 1040 estimated taxes.

Withholding Allowances The amount of federal income tax to withhold from an employee's earnings depends on the

- earnings during the pay period,
- length of the pay period,
- marital status,
- number of withholding allowances.

Determining the number of withholding allowances for some taxpayers is complex. In the simplest circumstances, a taxpayer claims a withholding allowance for

- the taxpayer,
- a spouse who does not also claim an allowance,
- each dependent for whom the taxpayer provides more than half the support during the year.

As the number of withholding allowances increases, the amount of federal income tax withheld decreases. The goal is to claim the number of withholding allowances so that the federal income tax withheld is about the same as the employee's tax liability.

To claim withholding allowances, employees complete **Employee's Withholding Allowance Certificate, Form W-4.** The employee gives the completed Form W-4 to the employer. If the number of exemption allowances decreases, the employee must file a new Form W-4 within 10 days. If the number of exemption allowances increases, the employee may, but is not required to, file another Form W-4. If an employee does not file a Form W-4, the employer withholds federal income tax based on zero withholding allowances.

Figure 10.1 shows Form W-4 for Alicia Martinez. Notice that on Line 5, Martinez claims one withholding allowance.

Computing Federal Income Tax Withholding Although there are several ways to compute the federal income tax to withhold from an employee's earnings, the **wage-bracket table method** is almost universally used. The wage-bracket tables are in *Publication 15, Circular E.* This publication contains withholding tables for weekly, biweekly, semimonthly, monthly, and daily or miscellaneous payroll periods for single and married persons. Figure 10.2 on pages 333–334 shows partial tables for single and married persons who are paid weekly.

Use the following steps to determine the amount to withhold:

1. Choose the table for the pay period and the employee's marital status.
2. Find the row in the table that matches the wages earned. Find the column that matches the number of withholding allowances claimed on Form W-4. The income tax to withhold is the intersection of the row and the column.

important!

Pay-As-You-Go
Employee income tax withholding is designed to place employees on a pay-as-you-go basis in paying their federal income tax.

important!

Get It in Writing
Employers need a signed Form W-4 in order to change the employee's federal income tax withholding.

Employee	Gross Pay	Marital Status	Withholding Allowances	Income Tax Withholding
Alicia Martinez	$400.00	Married	1	$ 19.00
Jorge Rodriguez	380.00	Single	1	34.00
George Dunlap	427.50	Single	3	23.00
Cecilia Wu	560.00	Married	2	30.00
				$106.00

As an example, let's determine the amount to withhold from Cecilia Wu's gross pay. Wu is married, claims two withholding allowances, and earned $560 for the week.

1. Go to the table for married persons paid weekly, Figure 10.2b.

2. Find the line covering wages between $560 and $570. Find the column for two withholding allowances. The tax to withhold is $30; this is where the row and the column intersect.

Using the wage-bracket tables, can you find the federal income tax amounts to withhold for Martinez, Rodriguez, and Dunlap?

Other Deductions Required by Law   Most states and some local governments require employers to withhold state and local income taxes from earnings. In some states, employers are also required to withhold disability or other taxes. The procedures are similar to those for federal income tax withholding. Apply the tax rate to the earnings, or use withholding tables.

FIGURE 10.1   Form W-4 (Partial)

Cut here and give Form W-4 to your employer. Keep the top part for your records.

Form **W-4**

Employee's Withholding Allowance Certificate

OMB No. 1545-0010

2010

Department of the Treasury
Internal Revenue Service

► **Whether you are entitled to claim a certain number of allowances or exemption from withholding is subject to review by the IRS. Your employer may be required to send a copy of this form to the IRS.**

1 Type or print your first name and middle initial	Last name	2 Your social security number
Alicia	**Martinez**	123 : 45 : 6789

Home address (number and street or rural route)
1712 Windmill Hill Lane

3 ☐ Single ☑ Married ☐ Married, but withhold at higher Single rate.
Note. If married, but legally separated, or spouse is a nonresident alien, check the "Single" box.

City or town, state, and ZIP code
Dallas, TX   75232-6002

4   If your last name differs from that shown on your social security card, check here. You must call 1-800-772-1213 for a new card. ► ☐

5   Total number of allowances you are claiming (from line **H** above **or** from the applicable worksheet on page 2)   **5** | 1

6   Additional amount, if any, you want withheld from each paycheck . . . .   **6** $

7   I claim exemption from withholding for 2010, and I certify that I meet **both** of the following conditions for exemption.
   • Last year I had a right to a refund of **all** federal income tax withheld because I had **no** tax liability **and**
   • This year I expect a refund of **all** federal income tax withheld because I expect to have **no** tax liability.
   If you meet both conditions, write "Exempt" here . . . . ► **7**

Under penalties of perjury, I declare that I have examined this certificate and to the best of my knowledge and belief, it is true, correct, and complete.

Employee's signature
(Form is not valid
unless you sign it.) ►   *Alicia Martinez*

Date ► *November 5, 2010*

8   Employer's name and address (Employer: Complete lines 8 and 10 only if sending to the IRS.)
Sanchez Furniture Co. 5910 Lake June Road, Dallas, TX   75232-6017

9 Office code (optional)

10 Employer identification number (EIN)
75 : 1234567

For Privacy Act and Paperwork Reduction Act Notice, see page 2.

Cat. No.   220Q

Form **W-4** (2010)

SINGLE Persons—WEEKLY Payroll Period   (For Wages Paid Through December 2010)

If the wages are –		And the number of withholding allowances claimed is –										
At least	But less than	0	1	2	3	4	5	6	7	8	9	10
		The amount of income tax to be withheld is –										
$0	$55	$0	$0	$0	$0	$0	$0	$0	$0	$0	$0	$0
55	60	1	0	0	0	0	0	0	0	0	0	0
60	65	1	0	0	0	0	0	0	0	0	0	0
65	70	2	0	0	0	0	0	0	0	0	0	0
70	75	2	0	0	0	0	0	0	0	0	0	0
75	80	3	0	0	0	0	0	0	0	0	0	0
80	85	3	0	0	0	0	0	0	0	0	0	0
85	90	4	0	0	0	0	0	0	0	0	0	0
90	95	4	0	0	0	0	0	0	0	0	0	0
95	100	5	0	0	0	0	0	0	0	0	0	0
100	105	5	0	0	0	0	0	0	0	0	0	0
105	110	6	0	0	0	0	0	0	0	0	0	0
110	115	6	0	0	0	0	0	0	0	0	0	0
115	120	7	1	0	0	0	0	0	0	0	0	0
120	125	7	1	0	0	0	0	0	0	0	0	0
125	130	8	2	0	0	0	0	0	0	0	0	0
130	135	8	2	0	0	0	0	0	0	0	0	0
135	140	9	3	0	0	0	0	0	0	0	0	0
140	145	9	3	0	0	0	0	0	0	0	0	0
145	150	10	4	0	0	0	0	0	0	0	0	0
150	155	10	4	0	0	0	0	0	0	0	0	0
155	160	11	5	0	0	0	0	0	0	0	0	0
160	165	11	5	0	0	0	0	0	0	0	0	0
165	170	12	6	0	0	0	0	0	0	0	0	0
170	175	12	6	0	0	0	0	0	0	0	0	0
175	180	13	7	1	0	0	0	0	0	0	0	0
180	185	13	7	1	0	0	0	0	0	0	0	0
185	190	14	8	2	0	0	0	0	0	0	0	0
190	195	14	8	2	0	0	0	0	0	0	0	0
195	200	15	9	3	0	0	0	0	0	0	0	0
200	210	16	9	3	0	0	0	0	0	0	0	0
210	220	18	10	4	0	0	0	0	0	0	0	0
220	230	19	11	5	0	0	0	0	0	0	0	0
230	240	21	12	6	1	0	0	0	0	0	0	0
240	250	22	13	7	2	0	0	0	0	0	0	0
250	260	24	15	8	3	0	0	0	0	0	0	0
260	270	25	16	9	4	0	0	0	0	0	0	0
270	280	27	18	10	5	0	0	0	0	0	0	0
280	290	28	19	11	6	0	0	0	0	0	0	0
290	300	30	21	12	7	1	0	0	0	0	0	0
300	310	31	22	13	8	2	0	0	0	0	0	0
310	320	33	24	15	9	3	0	0	0	0	0	0
320	330	34	25	16	10	4	0	0	0	0	0	0
330	340	36	27	18	11	5	0	0	0	0	0	0
340	350	37	28	19	12	6	0	0	0	0	0	0
350	360	39	30	21	13	7	1	0	0	0	0	0
360	370	40	31	22	14	8	2	0	0	0	0	0
370	380	42	33	24	15	9	3	0	0	0	0	0
380	390	43	34	25	17	10	4	0	0	0	0	0
390	400	45	36	27	18	11	5	0	0	0	0	0
400	410	46	37	28	20	12	6	0	0	0	0	0
410	420	48	39	30	21	13	7	1	0	0	0	0
420	430	49	40	31	23	14	8	2	0	0	0	0
430	440	51	42	33	24	15	9	3	0	0	0	0
440	450	52	43	34	26	17	10	4	0	0	0	0
450	460	54	45	36	27	18	11	5	0	0	0	0
460	470	55	46	37	29	20	12	6	0	0	0	0
470	480	57	48	39	30	21	13	7	1	0	0	0
480	490	58	49	40	32	23	14	8	2	0	0	0
490	500	60	51	42	33	24	15	9	3	0	0	0
500	510	61	52	43	35	26	17	10	4	0	0	0
510	520	63	54	45	36	27	18	11	5	0	0	0
520	530	64	55	46	38	29	20	12	6	0	0	0
530	540	66	57	48	39	30	21	13	7	1	0	0
540	550	67	58	49	41	32	23	14	8	2	0	0
550	560	69	60	51	42	33	24	15	9	3	0	0
560	570	70	61	52	44	35	26	17	10	4	0	0
570	580	72	63	54	45	36	27	18	11	5	0	0
580	590	73	64	55	47	38	29	20	12	6	0	0
590	600	75	66	57	48	39	30	21	13	7	1	0

FIGURE 10.2A

Sample Federal Withholding Tax Tables (Partial) Single Persons— Weekly Payroll Period

This table does not contain actual withholding amounts for the year 2010, and should not be used to determine payroll withholdings for 2010.

FIGURE 10.2B

Sample Federal Withholding Tax
Tables (Partial) Married
Persons—Weekly Payroll Period

MARRIED Persons—**WEEKLY** Payroll Period   (For Wages Paid Through December 2010)

If the wages are —		And the number of withholding allowances claimed is —										
At least	But less than	0	1	2	3	4	5	6	7	8	9	10
		The amount of income tax to be withheld is —										
$0	$125	$0	$0	$0	$0	$0	$0	$0	$0	$0	$0	$0
125	130	0	0	0	0	0	0	0	0	0	0	0
130	135	0	0	0	0	0	0	0	0	0	0	0
135	140	0	0	0	0	0	0	0	0	0	0	0
140	145	0	0	0	0	0	0	0	0	0	0	0
145	150	0	0	0	0	0	0	0	0	0	0	0
150	155	0	0	0	0	0	0	0	0	0	0	0
155	160	0	0	0	0	0	0	0	0	0	0	0
160	165	1	0	0	0	0	0	0	0	0	0	0
165	170	1	0	0	0	0	0	0	0	0	0	0
170	175	2	0	0	0	0	0	0	0	0	0	0
175	180	2	0	0	0	0	0	0	0	0	0	0
180	185	3	0	0	0	0	0	0	0	0	0	0
185	190	3	0	0	0	0	0	0	0	0	0	0
190	195	4	0	0	0	0	0	0	0	0	0	0
195	200	4	0	0	0	0	0	0	0	0	0	0
200	210	5	0	0	0	0	0	0	0	0	0	0
210	220	6	0	0	0	0	0	0	0	0	0	0
220	230	7	1	0	0	0	0	0	0	0	0	0
230	240	8	2	0	0	0	0	0	0	0	0	0
240	250	9	3	0	0	0	0	0	0	0	0	0
250	260	10	4	0	0	0	0	0	0	0	0	0
260	270	11	5	0	0	0	0	0	0	0	0	0
270	280	12	6	0	0	0	0	0	0	0	0	0
280	290	13	7	1	0	0	0	0	0	0	0	0
290	300	14	8	2	0	0	0	0	0	0	0	0
300	310	15	9	3	0	0	0	0	0	0	0	0
310	320	16	10	4	0	0	0	0	0	0	0	0
320	330	17	11	5	0	0	0	0	0	0	0	0
330	340	18	12	6	0	0	0	0	0	0	0	0
340	350	19	13	7	1	0	0	0	0	0	0	0
350	360	20	14	8	2	0	0	0	0	0	0	0
360	370	21	15	9	3	0	0	0	0	0	0	0
370	380	22	16	10	4	0	0	0	0	0	0	0
380	390	23	17	11	5	0	0	0	0	0	0	0
390	400	24	18	12	6	0	0	0	0	0	0	0
400	410	25	19	13	7	1	0	0	0	0	0	0
410	420	26	20	14	8	2	0	0	0	0	0	0
420	430	27	21	15	9	3	0	0	0	0	0	0
430	440	28	22	16	10	4	0	0	0	0	0	0
440	450	30	23	17	11	5	0	0	0	0	0	0
450	460	31	24	18	12	6	0	0	0	0	0	0
460	470	33	25	19	13	7	1	0	0	0	0	0
470	480	34	26	20	14	8	2	0	0	0	0	0
480	490	36	27	21	15	9	3	0	0	0	0	0
490	500	37	28	22	16	10	4	0	0	0	0	0
500	510	39	30	23	17	11	5	0	0	0	0	0
510	520	40	31	24	18	12	6	0	0	0	0	0
520	530	42	33	25	19	13	7	1	0	0	0	0
530	540	43	34	26	20	14	8	2	0	0	0	0
540	550	45	36	27	21	15	9	3	0	0	0	0
550	560	46	37	29	22	16	10	4	0	0	0	0
560	570	48	39	30	23	17	11	5	0	0	0	0
570	580	49	40	32	24	18	12	6	0	0	0	0
580	590	51	42	33	25	19	13	7	1	0	0	0
590	600	52	43	35	26	20	14	8	2	0	0	0
600	610	54	45	36	27	21	15	9	3	0	0	0
610	620	55	46	38	29	22	16	10	4	0	0	0
620	630	57	48	39	30	23	17	11	5	0	0	0
630	640	58	49	41	32	24	18	12	6	0	0	0
640	650	60	51	42	33	25	19	13	7	1	0	0
650	660	61	52	44	35	26	20	14	8	2	0	0
660	670	63	54	45	36	27	21	15	9	3	0	0
670	680	64	55	47	38	29	22	16	10	4	0	0
680	690	66	57	48	39	30	23	17	11	5	0	0
690	700	67	58	50	41	32	24	18	12	6	0	0
700	710	69	60	51	42	33	25	19	13	7	1	0
710	720	70	61	53	44	35	26	20	14	8	2	0
720	730	72	63	54	45	36	27	21	15	9	3	0
730	740	73	64	56	47	38	29	22	16	10	4	0

This table does not contain actual withholding amounts for the year 2010, and should not be used to determine payroll withholdings for 2010.

WITHHOLDINGS NOT REQUIRED BY LAW

There are many payroll deductions not required by law but made by agreement between the employee and the employer. Some examples are

- group life insurance,
- group medical insurance,

- company retirement plans,
- bank or credit union savings plans or loan repayments,
- United States saving bonds purchase plans,
- stocks and other investment purchase plans,
- employer loan repayments,
- union dues.

These and other payroll deductions increase the payroll recordkeeping work but do not involve any new principles or procedures. They are handled in the same way as the deductions for social security, Medicare, and federal income taxes.

Sanchez Furniture Company pays all medical insurance premiums for each employee. If the employee chooses to have medical coverage for a spouse or dependent, Sanchez Furniture Company deducts $40 per week for coverage for the spouse and each dependent. Dunlap and Wu each have $40 per week deducted to obtain the medical coverage.

Determining Pay for Salaried Employees

A salaried employee earns a specific sum of money for each payroll period. The office clerk at Sanchez Furniture Company earns a weekly salary.

HOURS WORKED

Salaried workers who do not hold supervisory jobs are covered by the provisions of the Wage and Hour Law that deal with maximum hours and overtime premium pay. Employers keep time records for all nonsupervisory salaried workers to make sure that their hourly earnings meet the legal requirements.

Salaried employees who hold supervisory or managerial positions are called **exempt employees.** They are not subject to the maximum hour and overtime premium pay provisions of the Wage and Hour Law.

GROSS EARNINGS

Cynthia Booker is the office clerk at Sanchez Furniture Company. During the first week of January, she worked 40 hours, her regular schedule. There are no overtime earnings because she did not work more than 40 hours during the week. Her salary of $480 is her gross pay for the week.

WITHHOLDINGS FOR SALARIED EMPLOYEES REQUIRED BY LAW

The procedures for withholding taxes for salaried employees is the same as withholding for hourly rate employees. Apply the tax rate to the earnings, or use withholding tables.

Recording Payroll Information for Employees

A payroll register is prepared for each pay period. The **payroll register** shows all the payroll information for the pay period.

THE PAYROLL REGISTER

Figure 10.3 on pages 336–337 shows the payroll register for Sanchez Furniture Company for the week ended January 7. Note that all employees were paid for eight hours on January 1, a holiday. To learn how to complete the payroll register, refer to Figure 10.3 and follow these steps.

1. *Columns A, B, and E.* Enter the employee's name (Column A), number of withholding allowances and marital status (Column B), and rate of pay (Column E). In a computerized payroll system, this information is entered once and is automatically retrieved each time payroll is prepared.
2. *Column C.* The Cumulative Earnings column (Column C) shows the total earnings for the calendar year before the current pay period. This figure is needed to determine

>>**6. OBJECTIVE**
Enter gross earnings, deductions, and net pay in the payroll register.

LP10

PAYROLL REGISTER   **WEEK BEGINNING** *January 1, 2010*

NAME	NO. OF ALLOW.	MARITAL STATUS	CUMULATIVE EARNINGS	NO. OF HRS.	RATE/ SALARY	EARNINGS			CUMULATIVE EARNINGS
						REGULAR	OVERTIME	GROSS AMOUNT	
Martinez, Alicia	1	M		40	10.00	400 00		400 00	400 00
Rodriguez, Jorge	1	S		40	9.50	380 00		380 00	380 00
Dunlap, George	3	S		45	9.00	360 00	67 50	427 50	427 50
Wu, Cecilia	2	M		40	14.00	560 00		560 00	560 00
Booker, Cynthia	1	S		40	480.00	480 00		480 00	480 00
			0 00			2 180 00	67 50	2 247 50	2 247 50
(A)	(B)		(C)	(D)	(E)	(F)	(G)	(H)	(I)

FIGURE 10.3   Payroll Register

whether the employee has exceeded the earnings limit for the FICA and FUTA taxes. Since this is the first payroll period of the year, there are no cumulative earnings prior to the current pay period.

3. *Column D.* In Column D, enter the total number of hours worked in the current period. This data comes from the weekly time sheet.

4. *Columns F, G, and H.* Using the hours worked and the pay rate, calculate regular pay (Column F), the overtime earnings (Column G), and gross pay (Column H).

5. *Column I.* Calculate the cumulative earnings after this pay period (Column I) by adding the beginning cumulative earnings (Column C) and the current period's gross pay (Column H).

6. *Columns J, K, and L.* The Taxable Wages columns show the earnings subject to taxes for social security (Column J), Medicare (Column K), and FUTA (Column L). Only the earnings at or under the earnings limit are included in these columns.

7. *Columns M, N, O, and P.* The Deductions columns show the withholding for social security tax (Column M), Medicare tax (Column N), federal income tax (Column O), and medical insurance (Column P).

8. *Column Q.* Subtract the deductions (Columns M, N, O, and P) from the gross earnings (Column H). Enter the results in the Net Amount column (Column Q). This is the amount paid to each employee.

9. *Column R.* Enter the check number in Column R.

10. *Columns S and T.* The payroll register's last two columns classify employee earnings as office salaries (Column S) or shipping wages (Column T).

When the payroll data for all employees has been entered in the payroll register, total the columns. Check the balances of the following columns:

■ Total regular earnings plus total overtime earnings must equal the gross amount (Columns F + G = Column H).

■ The total gross amount less total deductions must equal the total net amount.

Gross amount		$2,247.50
Less deductions:		
Social security tax	$139.35	
Medicare tax	32.59	
Income tax	155.00	
Health insurance	80.00	
Total deductions		406.94
Net amount		$1,840.56

AND ENDING _January 6, 2010_   **PAID** _January 8, 2010_

TAXABLE WAGES			DEDUCTIONS				DISTRIBUTION			
SOCIAL SECURITY	MEDICARE	FUTA	SOCIAL SECURITY	MEDICARE	INCOME TAX	HEALTH INSURANCE	NET AMOUNT	CHECK NO.	OFFICE SALARIES	SHIPPING WAGES
400 00	400 00	400 00	24 80	5 80	19 00		350 40	1601		400 00
380 00	380 00	380 00	23 56	5 51	34 00		316 93	1602		380 00
427 50	427 50	427 50	26 51	6 20	23 00	40 00	331 79	1603		427 50
560 00	560 00	560 00	34 72	8 12	30 00	40 00	447 16	1604		560 00
480 00	480 00	480 00	29 76	6 96	49 00		394 28	1605	480 00	
2 247 50	2 247 50	2 247 50	139 35	32 59	155 00	80 00	1 840 56		480 00	1 767 50
(J)	(K)	(L)	(M)	(N)	(O)	(P)	(Q)	(R)	(S)	(T)

■ The office salaries and the shipping wages must equal gross earnings (Columns S + T = Column H).

The payroll register supplies all the information to make the journal entry to record the payroll. Journalizing the payroll is discussed in Section 3.

Section **2** Self Review

QUESTIONS

1. List four payroll deductions that are not required by law but can be made by agreement between the employee and the employer.

2. What factors determine the amount of federal income tax to be withheld from an employee's earnings?

3. What three payroll deductions does federal law require?

EXERCISES

4. Which of the following affects the amount of Medicare tax to be withheld from an hourly rate employee's pay?

   a. medical insurance premium

   b. marital status

   c. withholding allowances claimed on Form W-4

   d. hours worked

5. Stacy Amos worked 48 hours during the week ending November 17. Her regular rate is $9 per hour. Calculate her gross earnings for the week.

   a. $432

   b. $492

   c. $468

   d. $444

ANALYSIS

6. Rosie Perez left a voice mail asking you to withhold an additional $40 of federal income tax from her wages each pay period, starting June 1. When should you begin withholding the extra amount?

(Answers to Section 2 Self Review are on page 357.)

>> 7. **Journalize payroll transactions in the general journal.**

WHY IT'S IMPORTANT

Payroll cost is an operating expense.

>> 8. **Maintain an earnings record for each employee.**

WHY IT'S IMPORTANT

Federal law requires that employers maintain records.

Recording Payroll Information

In this section you will learn how to prepare paychecks and journalize and post payroll transactions by following the January payroll activity for Sanchez Furniture Company.

>>7. OBJECTIVE

Journalize payroll transactions in the general journal.

LP10

Recording Payroll

Recording payroll involves two separate entries: one to record the payroll expense and another to pay the employees. The general journal entry to record the payroll expense is based on the payroll register. The gross pay is debited to *Shipping Wages Expense* for the shipping clerks and supervisor and to *Office Salaries Expense* for the office clerk. Each type of deduction is credited to a separate liability account *(Social Security Tax Payable, Medicare Tax Payable, Employee Income Tax Payable, Health Insurance Premiums Payable)*. Net pay is credited to the liability account, *Salaries and Wages Payable.*

Refer to Figure 10.3 on pages 336–337 to see how the data on the payroll register is used to prepare the January 8 payroll journal entry for Sanchez Furniture Company. Following is an analysis of the entry.

BUSINESS TRANSACTION

The information in the payroll register (Figure 10.3) is used to record the payroll expense.

ANALYSIS

The expense account, **Office Salaries Expense,** is increased by $480.00. The expense account, **Shipping Wages Expense,** is increased by $1,767.50. The liability account for each deduction is increased: **Social Security Tax Payable,** $139.35; **Medicare Tax Payable,** $32.59; **Employee Income Tax Payable,** $155.00; **Health Insurance Premiums Payable,** $80.00. The liability account, **Salaries and Wages Payable,** is increased by the net amount of the payroll, $1,840.56.

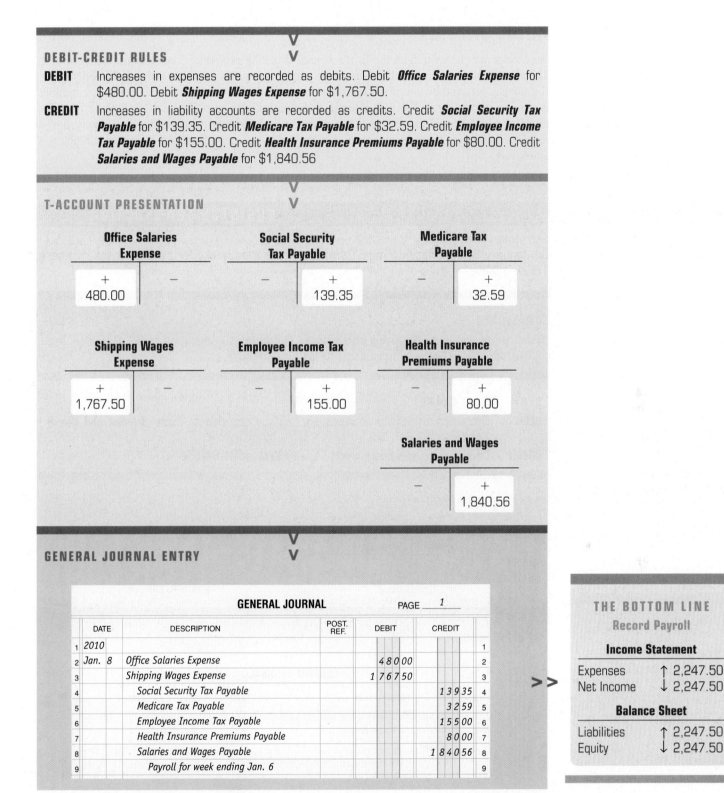

DEBIT-CREDIT RULES

DEBIT Increases in expenses are recorded as debits. Debit *Office Salaries Expense* for $480.00. Debit *Shipping Wages Expense* for $1,767.50.

CREDIT Increases in liability accounts are recorded as credits. Credit *Social Security Tax Payable* for $139.35. Credit *Medicare Tax Payable* for $32.59. Credit *Employee Income Tax Payable* for $155.00. Credit *Health Insurance Premiums Payable* for $80.00. Credit *Salaries and Wages Payable* for $1,840.56

T-ACCOUNT PRESENTATION

Office Salaries Expense		Social Security Tax Payable		Medicare Tax Payable	
+	–	–	+	–	+
480.00			139.35		32.59

Shipping Wages Expense		Employee Income Tax Payable		Health Insurance Premiums Payable	
+	–	–	+	–	+
1,767.50			155.00		80.00

Salaries and Wages Payable	
–	+
	1,840.56

GENERAL JOURNAL ENTRY

GENERAL JOURNAL   PAGE ___1___

	DATE	DESCRIPTION	POST. REF.	DEBIT	CREDIT	
1	2010					1
2	Jan. 8	Office Salaries Expense		480 00		2
3		Shipping Wages Expense		1 767 50		3
4		Social Security Tax Payable			139 35	4
5		Medicare Tax Payable			32 59	5
6		Employee Income Tax Payable			155 00	6
7		Health Insurance Premiums Payable			80 00	7
8		Salaries and Wages Payable			1 840 56	8
9		Payroll for week ending Jan. 6				9

>>

THE BOTTOM LINE
Record Payroll

Income Statement

Expenses	↑ 2,247.50
Net Income	↓ 2,247.50

Balance Sheet

Liabilities	↑ 2,247.50
Equity	↓ 2,247.50

Southwest Airlines Co. recorded salaries, wages, and benefits of more than $3.20 billion for the year ended December 31, 2007.

Paying Employees

Most businesses pay their employees by check or by direct deposit. By using these methods, the business avoids the inconvenience and risk involved in dealing with currency.

important!

Payroll Liabilities

Deductions from employee paychecks are liabilities for the employer.

PAYING BY CHECK

Paychecks may be written on the firm's regular checking account or on a payroll bank account. The check stub shows information about the employee's gross earnings, deductions, and net pay. Employees detach the stubs and keep them as a record of their payroll data. The check number is entered in the Check Number column of the payroll register (Figure 10.3, Column R). The canceled check provides a record of the payment, and the employee's endorsement serves as a receipt. Following is an analysis of the transaction to pay Sanchez Furniture Company's employees.

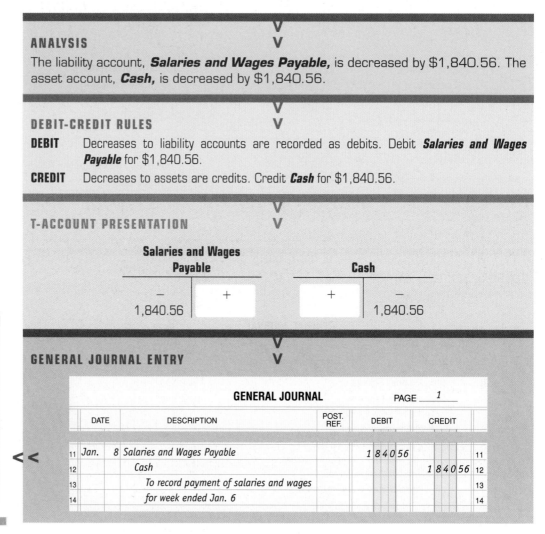

BUSINESS TRANSACTION

On January 8, Sanchez Furniture Company wrote five checks for payroll, check numbers 1601–1605.

ANALYSIS

The liability account, **Salaries and Wages Payable,** is decreased by $1,840.56. The asset account, **Cash,** is decreased by $1,840.56.

DEBIT-CREDIT RULES

DEBIT Decreases to liability accounts are recorded as debits. Debit **Salaries and Wages Payable** for $1,840.56.

CREDIT Decreases to assets are credits. Credit **Cash** for $1,840.56.

T-ACCOUNT PRESENTATION

Salaries and Wages Payable		Cash	
−	+	+	−
1,840.56			1,840.56

GENERAL JOURNAL ENTRY

		GENERAL JOURNAL			PAGE 1	
	DATE	DESCRIPTION	POST. REF.	DEBIT	CREDIT	
11	Jan. 8	Salaries and Wages Payable		1 840 56		11
12		Cash			1 840 56	12
13		To record payment of salaries and wages				13
14		for week ended Jan. 6				14

THE BOTTOM LINE

Issue Paychecks

Income Statement

No effect on net income

Balance Sheet

Assets	↓ 1,840.56
Liabilities	↓ 1,840.56

No effect on equity

Checks Written on Regular Checking Account The above entry is shown in general journal form for illustration purposes only. When paychecks are written on the regular checking account, the entries are recorded in the cash payments journal. Figure 10.4 on page 341 shows the January 8 entries to pay employees. Notice that there is a separate Salaries and Wages Payable Debit column.

FIGURE 10.4

Cash Payments Journal

CASH PAYMENTS JOURNAL   PAGE _____1_____

DATE		CK. NO.	DESCRIPTION	POST. REF.	ACCOUNTS PAYABLE DEBIT	SALARIES AND WAGES PAYABLE DEBIT	PURCHASES DISCOUNT CREDIT	CASH CREDIT
Jan.	2	1711	International Furniture Company		1 400 00		28 00	1 372 00
	8	1601	Alicia Martinez			350 40		350 40
	8	1602	Jorge Rodriguez			316 93		316 93
	8	1603	George Dunlap			331 79		331 79
	8	1604	Cecilia Wu			447 16		447 16
	8	1605	Cynthia Booker			394 28		394 28
	31		Totals		XX XXX XX	X XXX XX	XXX XX XX	XX XXX XX

important!

Separate Payroll Account
Using a separate payroll account facilitates the bank reconciliation and provides better internal control.

Checks Written on a Separate Payroll Account Many businesses write payroll checks from a separate payroll bank account. This is a two-step process.

1. A check is drawn on the regular bank account for the total amount of net pay and deposited in the payroll bank account.
2. Individual payroll checks are issued from the payroll bank account.

Using a separate payroll account simplifies the bank reconciliation of the regular checking account and makes it easier to identify outstanding payroll checks.

PAYING BY DIRECT DEPOSIT

A popular method of paying employees is the direct deposit method. The bank electronically transfers net pay from the employer's account to the personal account of the employee. On payday, the employee receives a statement showing gross earnings, deductions, and net pay.

Individual Earnings Records

An **individual earnings record,** also called a **compensation record,** is created for each employee. This record contains the employee's name, address, social security number, date of birth, number of withholding allowances claimed, rate of pay, and any other information needed to compute earnings and complete tax reports.

>>8. OBJECTIVE
Maintain an earnings record for each employee.

MANAGERIAL IMPLICATIONS   <<

LAWS AND CONTROLS

- It is management's responsibility to ensure that the payroll procedures and records comply with federal, state, and local laws.
- For most businesses, wages and salaries are a large part of operating expenses. Payroll records help management to keep track of and control expenses.
- Management should investigate large or frequent overtime expenditures.

- To prevent errors and fraud, management periodically should have the payroll records audited and payroll procedures evaluated.
- Two common payroll frauds are the overstatement of hours worked and the issuance of checks to nonexistent employees.

THINKING CRITICALLY

What controls would you put in place to prevent payroll fraud?

FIGURE 10.5   **An Individual Earnings Record**

EARNINGS RECORD FOR _2010_

NAME _Alicia Martinez_   RATE _$10 per hour_   SOCIAL SECURITY NO. _123-45-6789_
ADDRESS _1712 Windmill Hill Lane, Dallas, TX 75232-6002_   DATE OF BIRTH _November 23, 1979_
WITHHOLDING ALLOWANCES _1_   MARITAL STATUS _M_

PAYROLL NO.	DATE WK. END.	DATE PAID	HOURS RG	HOURS OT	EARNINGS REGULAR	EARNINGS OVERTIME	EARNINGS TOTAL	EARNINGS CUMULATIVE	DEDUCTIONS SOCIAL SECURITY	DEDUCTIONS MEDICARE	DEDUCTIONS INCOME TAX	DEDUCTIONS OTHER	NET PAY
1	1/06	1/08	40		4 0 0 00		4 0 0 00	4 0 0 00	2 4 80	5 80	1 9 00		3 5 0 40
2	1/13	1/15	40		4 0 0 00		4 0 0 00	8 0 0 00	2 4 80	5 80	1 9 00		3 5 0 40
3	1/20	1/22	40		4 0 0 00		4 0 0 00	1 2 0 0 00	2 4 80	5 80	1 9 00		3 5 0 40
4	1/27	1/29	40		4 0 0 00		4 0 0 00	1 6 0 0 00	2 4 80	5 80	1 9 00		3 5 0 40
	January				1 6 0 0 00		1 6 0 0 00		9 9 20	2 3 20	7 6 00		1 4 0 1 60

The payroll register provides the details that are entered on the employee's individual earnings record for each pay period. Figure 10.5 shows the earnings record for Alicia Martinez.

The earnings record shows the payroll period, the date paid, the regular and overtime hours, the regular and overtime earnings, the deductions, and the net pay. The cumulative earnings on the earnings record agrees with Column I of the payroll register (Figure 10.3). The earnings records are totaled monthly and at the end of each calendar quarter. This provides information needed to make tax payments and file tax returns.

Completing January Payrolls

Figure 10.6 on pages 342–343 shows the entire cycle of computing, paying, journalizing, and posting payroll data. In order to complete the January payroll for Sanchez Furniture Company, assume that all employees worked the same number of hours each week of the month as they did the first week. Thus they had the same earnings, deductions, and net pay each week.

FIGURE 10.6   **Journalizing and Posting Payroll Data**

AND ENDING _January 6, 2010_   PAID _January 8, 2010_

TAXABLE WAGES SOCIAL SECURITY	TAXABLE WAGES MEDICARE	TAXABLE WAGES FUTA	DEDUCTIONS SOCIAL SECURITY	DEDUCTIONS MEDICARE	DEDUCTIONS INCOME TAX	DEDUCTIONS HEALTH INSURANCE	DISTRIBUTION NET AMOUNT	DISTRIBUTION CHECK NO.	DISTRIBUTION OFFICE SALARIES	DISTRIBUTION SHIPPING WAGES
4 0 0 00	4 0 0 00	4 0 0 00	2 4 80	5 80	1 9 00		3 5 0 40	1601		4 0 0 00
3 8 0 00	3 8 0 00	3 8 0 00	2 3 56	5 51	3 4 00		3 1 6 93	1602		3 8 0 00
4 2 7 50	4 2 7 50	4 2 7 50	2 6 51	6 20	2 3 00	4 0 00	3 3 1 79	1603		4 2 7 50
5 6 0 00	5 6 0 00	5 6 0 00	3 4 72	8 12	3 0 00	4 0 00	4 4 7 16	1604		5 6 0 00
4 8 0 00	4 8 0 00	4 8 0 00	2 9 76	6 96	4 9 00		3 9 4 28	1605	4 8 0 00	
2 2 4 7 50	2 2 4 7 50	2 2 4 7 50	1 3 9 35	3 2 59	1 5 5 00	8 0 00	1 8 4 0 56		4 8 0 00	1 7 6 7 50
(J)	(K)	(L)	(M)	(N)	(O)	(P)	(Q)	(R)	(S)	(T)

1	2010							1
2	Jan.	8	Office Salaries Expense	541	4 8 0 00			2
3			Shipping Wages Expense	542	1 7 6 7 50			3
4			Social Security Tax Payable	221		1 3 9 35		4
5			Medicare Tax Payable	222		3 2 59		5
6			Employee Income Tax Payable	223		1 5 5 00		6
7			Health Insurance Premiums Payable	224		8 0 00		7
8			Salaries and Wages Payable	229		1 8 4 0 56		8
9			Payroll for week ending Jan. 6					9

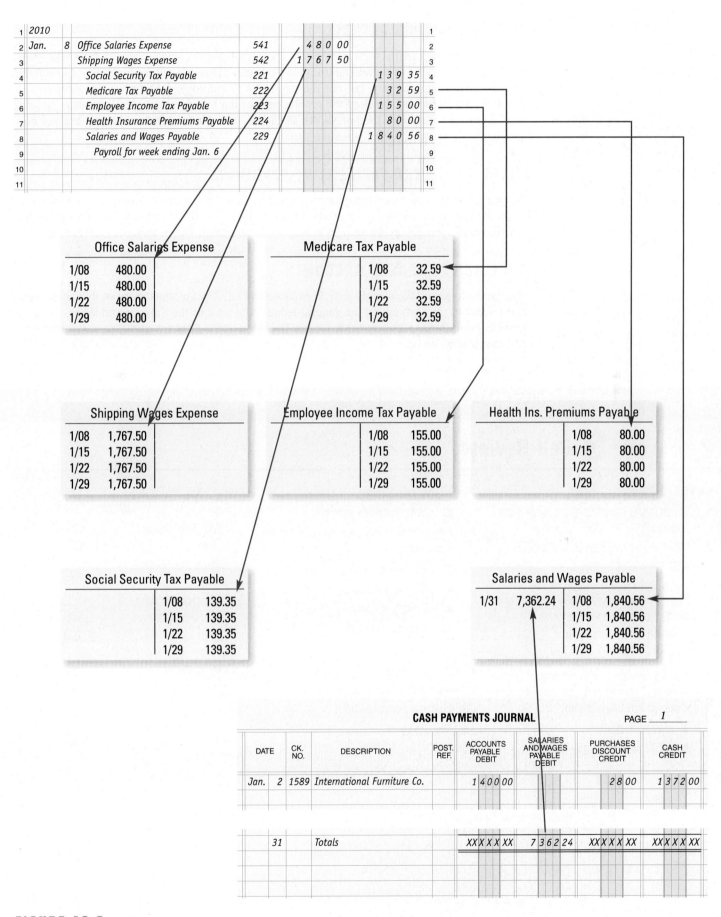

1	2010																	1
2	Jan.	8	Office Salaries Expense		541		4	8	0	00								2
3			Shipping Wages Expense		542	1	7	6	7	50								3
4			Social Security Tax Payable		221							1	3	9	35		4
5			Medicare Tax Payable		222								3	2	59		5
6			Employee Income Tax Payable		223							1	5	5	00		6
7			Health Insurance Premiums Payable		224								8	0	00		7
8			Salaries and Wages Payable		229						1	8	4	0	56		8
9			Payroll for week ending Jan. 6														9
10																	10
11																	11

Office Salaries Expense

1/08	480.00
1/15	480.00
1/22	480.00
1/29	480.00

Medicare Tax Payable

		1/08	32.59
		1/15	32.59
		1/22	32.59
		1/29	32.59

Shipping Wages Expense

1/08	1,767.50
1/15	1,767.50
1/22	1,767.50
1/29	1,767.50

Employee Income Tax Payable

		1/08	155.00
		1/15	155.00
		1/22	155.00
		1/29	155.00

Health Ins. Premiums Payable

		1/08	80.00
		1/15	80.00
		1/22	80.00
		1/29	80.00

Social Security Tax Payable

		1/08	139.35
		1/15	139.35
		1/22	139.35
		1/29	139.35

Salaries and Wages Payable

1/31	7,362.24	1/08	1,840.56
		1/15	1,840.56
		1/22	1,840.56
		1/29	1,840.56

CASH PAYMENTS JOURNAL   PAGE ___1___

DATE		CK. NO.	DESCRIPTION	POST. REF.	ACCOUNTS PAYABLE DEBIT	SALARIES AND WAGES PAYABLE DEBIT	PURCHASES DISCOUNT CREDIT	CASH CREDIT
Jan.	2	1589	International Furniture Co.		1 4 0 0 00		2 8 00	1 3 7 2 00
	31		Totals		XX X X X XX	7 3 6 2 24	XX X X X XX	XX X X X XX

FIGURE 10.6   (continued)

ENTRY TO RECORD PAYROLL

As illustrated earlier in this section, one general journal entry is made to record the weekly payroll for all employees of Sanchez Furniture Company. This general journal entry records the payroll expense and liability, but not the payments to employees. Since we are assuming an identical payroll for each week of the month, each of the four weekly payrolls requires general journal entries identical to the one shown in Figure 10.6. Notice how the payroll register column totals are recorded in the general journal.

ENTRY TO RECORD PAYMENT OF PAYROLL

The weekly entries in the cash payments journal to record payments to employees are the same as the January 8 entries in Figure 10.4 on page 341. At the end of January, the columns in the cash payments journal are totaled, including the Salaries and Wages Payable Debit column.

POSTINGS TO LEDGER ACCOUNTS

The entries to record the weekly payroll expense and liability amounts are posted from the general journal to the accounts in the general ledger. The total of the Salaries and Wages Payable Debit column in the cash payments journal is posted to the **Salaries and Wages Payable** general ledger account.

Section 3 Self Review

QUESTIONS

1. What is the purpose of a payroll bank account?

2. What appears on an individual earnings record?

3. What accounts are debited and credited when individual payroll checks are written on the regular checking account?

EXERCISES

4. Details related to all employees' gross earnings, deductions, and net pay for a period are found in the

   a. payroll register.

   b. individual earnings record.

   c. general journal.

   d. cash payments journal.

5. Payroll deductions are recorded in a separate

   a. asset account.

   b. expense account.

   c. liability account.

   d. revenue account.

ANALYSIS

6. This general journal entry was made to record the payroll liability.

   Ofc. Salaries Exp. 600.00

   Shipping Wages
   Exp.   2,586.00

   Health Ins. Prem.
   Exp.   40.00

   Soc. Sec. Taxes
   Exp.   197.41

   Medicare Taxes
   Pay.   48.17

   Employee Income
   Tax Payable   266.00

   Cash   2,634.42

   What corrections should be made to this journal entry?

(Answers to Section 3 Self Review are on page 358.)

REVIEW   Chapter Summary

Chapter **10**

The main goal of payroll work is to compute the gross wages or salaries earned by each employee, the amounts to be deducted for various taxes and other purposes, and the net amount payable.

Learning Objectives

1 Explain the major federal laws relating to employee earnings and withholding.

Several federal laws affect payroll.

- The federal Wage and Hour Law limits to 40 the number of hours per week an employee can work at the regular rate of pay. For more than 40 hours of work a week, an employer involved in interstate commerce must pay one and one-half times the regular rate.

- Federal laws require that the employer withhold at least three taxes from the employee's pay: the employee's share of social security tax, the employee's share of Medicare tax, and federal income tax. Instructions for computing these taxes are provided by the government.

- If required, state disability and other income taxes can also be deducted.

- Voluntary deductions can also be made.

2 Compute gross earnings of employees.

To compute gross earnings for an employee, it is necessary to know whether the employee is paid using an hourly rate basis, a salary basis, a commission basis, or a piece-rate basis.

3 Determine employee deductions for social security tax.

The social security tax is levied in an equal amount on both the employer and the employee. The tax is a percentage of the employee's gross wages during a calendar year up to a wage base limit.

4 Determine employee deductions for Medicare tax.

The Medicare tax is levied in an equal amount on both the employer and the employee. There is no wage base limit for Medicare taxes.

5 Determine employee deductions for income tax.

Income taxes are deducted from an employee's paycheck by the employer and then are paid to the government periodically. Although several methods can be used to compute the amount of federal income tax to be withheld from employee earnings, the wage-bracket table method is most often used. The wage-bracket tables are in *Publication 15, Circular E, Employer's Tax Guide.* Withholding tables for various pay periods for single and married persons are contained in *Circular E.*

6 Enter gross earnings, deductions, and net pay in the payroll register.

Daily records of the hours worked by each nonsupervisory employee are kept. Using these hourly time sheets, the payroll clerk computes the employees' earnings, deductions, and net pay for each payroll period and records the data in a payroll register.

7 Journalize payroll transactions in the general journal.

The payroll register is used to prepare a general journal entry to record payroll expense and liability amounts. A separate journal entry is made to record payments to employees.

8 Maintain an earnings record for each employee.

At the beginning of each year, the employer sets up an individual earnings record for each employee. The amounts in the payroll register are posted to the individual earnings records throughout the year so that the firm has detailed payroll information for each employee. At the end of the year, employers provide reports that show gross earnings and total deductions to each employee.

9 Define the accounting terms new to this chapter.

Glossary

Commission basis (p. 329) A method of paying employees according to a percentage of net sales

Compensation record (p. 341) See Individual earnings record

Employee (p. 324) A person who is hired by and works under the control and direction of the employer

Employee's Withholding Allowance Certificate, Form W-4 (p. 331) A form used to claim exemption (withholding) allowances

Exempt employees (p. 335) Salaried employees who hold supervisory or managerial positions who are not subject to the maximum hour and overtime pay provisions of the Wage and Hour Law

Federal unemployment taxes (FUTA) (p. 326) Taxes levied by the federal government against employers to benefit unemployed workers

Hourly rate basis (p. 328) A method of paying employees according to a stated rate per hour

Independent contractor (p. 324) One who is paid by a company to carry out a specific task or job but is not under the direct supervision or control of the company

Individual earnings record (p. 341) An employee record that contains information needed to compute earnings and complete tax reports

Medicare tax (p. 325) A tax levied on employees and employers to provide medical care for the employee and the employee's spouse after each has reached age 65

Payroll register (p. 335) A record of payroll information for each employee for the pay period

Piece-rate basis (p. 329) A method of paying employees according to the number of units produced

Salary basis (p. 329) A method of paying employees according to an agreed-upon amount for each week or month

Social Security Act (p. 325) A federal act providing certain benefits for employees and their families; officially the Federal Insurance Contributions Act

Social security (FICA) tax (p. 325) A tax imposed by the Federal Insurance Contributions Act and collected on employee earnings to provide retirement and disability benefits

State unemployment taxes (SUTA) (p. 326) Taxes levied by a state government against employers to benefit unemployed workers

Tax-exempt wages (p. 330) Earnings in excess of the base amount set by the Social Security Act

Time and a half (p. 325) Rate of pay for an employee's work in excess of 40 hours a week

Wage-bracket table method (p. 331) A simple method to determine the amount of federal income tax to be withheld using a table provided by the government

Workers' compensation insurance (p. 327) Insurance that protects employees against losses from job-related injuries or illnesses, or compensates their families if death occurs in the course of the employment

Comprehensive Self Review

1. How does an independent contractor differ from an employee?
2. What is the purpose of the payroll register?
3. From an accounting and internal control viewpoint, would it be preferable to pay employees by check or cash? Explain.
4. How is the amount of social security tax to be withheld from an employee's earnings determined?
5. What is the purpose of workers' compensation insurance?

(Answers to Comprehensive Self Review are on page 358.)

 Multiple choice questions are provided on the text Web site at www.mhhe.com/price12e

Quiz10

Discussion Questions

1. What factors affect how much federal income tax must be withheld from an employee's earnings?
2. How does the Fair Labor Standards Act affect the wages paid by many firms? What types of firms are regulated by the act?

3. What aspects of employment are regulated by the Fair Labor Standards Act? What is another commonly used name for this act?

4. Give two examples of common payroll fraud.

5. What is an exempt employee?

6. How are the federal and state unemployment taxes related?

7. Does the employee bear any part of the SUTA tax? Explain.

8. How are earnings determined when employees are paid on the hourly rate basis?

9. What is the purpose of the Medicare tax?

10. What is the purpose of the social security tax?

11. How does the direct deposit method of paying employees operate?

12. What are the four bases for determining employee gross earnings?

13. What is the simplest method for finding the amount of federal income tax to be deducted from an employee's gross pay?

14. What publication of the Internal Revenue Service provides information about the current federal income tax rates and the procedures that employers should use to withhold federal income tax from an employee's earnings?

15. How does the salary basis differ from the hourly rate basis of paying employees?

APPLICATIONS

Exercises

Computing gross earnings.

The hourly rates of four employees of Brown Enterprises follow, along with the hours that these employees worked during one week. Determine the gross earnings of each employee.

◀ **Exercise 10.1**
Objective 2

Employee No.	Hourly Rate	Hours Worked
1	$9.70	38
2	8.75	40
3	9.50	40
4	8.90	35

Computing regular earnings, overtime earnings, and gross pay.

During one week, four production employees of Mason Manufacturing Company worked the hours shown below. All these employees receive overtime pay at one and one-half times their regular hourly rate for any hours worked beyond 40 in a week. Determine the regular earnings, overtime earnings, and gross earnings for each employee.

◀ **Exercise 10.2**
Objective 2

Employee No.	Hourly Rate	Hours Worked
1	$9.75	45
2	9.71	46
3	9.55	39
4	8.52	50

Exercise 10.3

Objective 3

▶ **Determining social security withholding.**

The monthly salaries for December and the year-to-date earnings of the employees of Canarelli Consulting Company as of November 30 follow.

Employee No.	December Salary	Year-to-Date Earnings through November 30
1	$8,800	$87,900
2	8,900	83,450
3	9,900	97,600
4	6,200	67,500

Determine the amount of social security tax to be withheld from each employee's gross pay for December. Assume a 6.2 percent social security tax rate and an earnings base of $97,500 for the calendar year.

Exercise 10.4

Objective 4

CONTINUING >>>
Problem

▶ **Determining deduction for Medicare tax.**

Using the earnings data given in Exercise 10.3, determine the amount of Medicare tax to be withheld from each employee's gross pay for December. Assume a 1.45 percent Medicare tax rate and that all salaries and wages are subject to the tax.

Exercise 10.5

Objective 5

▶ **Determining federal income tax withholding.**

Data about the marital status, withholding allowances, and weekly salaries of the four office workers at Amos Publishing Company follow. Use the tax tables in Figure 10.2 on pages 333–334 to find the amount of federal income tax to be deducted from each employee's gross pay.

Employee No.	Marital Status	Withholding Allowances	Weekly Salary
1	M	1	$650
2	S	2	595
3	M	3	735
4	S	2	590

Exercise 10.6

Objective 7

▶ **Recording payroll transactions in the general journal.**

Imperial Corporation has two office employees. A summary of their earnings and the related taxes withheld from their pay for the week ending August 7, 2010, follows.

	Sandra Chin	David Matthews
Gross earnings	$1,310.00	$1,190.00
Social security deduction	(81.22)	(73.78)
Medicare deduction	(19.00)	(17.26)
Income tax withholding	(350.69)	(214.32)
Net pay for week	$ 859.09	$ 884.64

1. Prepare the general journal entry to record the company's payroll for the week. Use the account names given in this chapter.

2. Prepare the general journal entry to summarize the checks to pay the weekly payroll.

Journalizing payroll transactions.

◄ Exercise 10.7
Objective 7

On July 31, 2010, the payroll register of Harris Institutional Wholesale Company showed the following totals for the month: gross earnings, $38,600; social security tax, $2,393.20; Medicare tax, $559.70; income tax, $3,055.96; and net amount due, $32,591.14. Of the total earnings, $30,558.46 was for sales salaries and $8,041.54 was for office salaries. Prepare a general journal entry to record the monthly payroll of the firm on July 31, 2010.

PROBLEMS

Problem Set A HM™

Computing gross earnings, determining deductions, journalizing payroll transactions.

◄ Problem 10.1A
Objectives
eXcel 2, 3, 4, 5, 7

Cindy Brown works for Trinity Industries. Her pay rate is $12.70 per hour and she receives overtime pay at one and one-half times her regular hourly rate for any hours worked beyond 40 in a week. During the pay period that ended December 31, 2010, Cindy worked 48 hours. Cindy is married and claims three withholding allowances on her W-4 form. Cindy's cumulative earnings prior to this pay period total $28,000. Cindy's wages are subject to the following deductions:

1. Social Security tax at 6.2 percent

2. Medicare tax at 1.45 percent

3. Federal income tax (use the withholding table shown in Figure 10.2b on page 334)

4. Health and disability insurance premiums, $165

5. United Way contribution, $19

6. United States Savings Bond, $75

INSTRUCTIONS

1. Compute Cindy's regular, overtime, gross, and net pay.

2. Journalize the payment of her wages for the week ended December 31, 2010.

Analyze: Based on Cindy's cumulative earnings through December 31, how much overtime pay did she earn this year?

Computing gross earnings, determining deductions, preparing payroll register, journalizing payroll transactions.

◄ Problem 10.2A
Objectives 2, 3, 4, 5

City Place Movie Theaters has four employees and pays them on an hourly basis. During the week beginning June 24 and ending June 30, 2010, these employees worked the hours shown below. Information about hourly rates, marital status, withholding allowances, and cumulative earnings prior to the current pay period also appears below.

eXcel

Employee	Regular Hours Worked	Hourly Rate	Marital Status	Withholding Allowances	Cumulative Earnings
Nelda Anderson	48	$11.75	M	1	$17,540
Earl Benson	49	10.50	M	4	16,875
Frank Cortez	40	10.25	M	1	15,980
Winnie Wu	52	9.75	S	2	14,560

INSTRUCTIONS

1. Enter the basic payroll information for each employee in a payroll register. Record the employee's name, number of withholding allowances, marital status, total and overtime hours, and regular hourly rate. Consider any hours worked beyond 40 in the week as overtime hours.

2. Compute the regular, overtime, and gross earnings for each employee. Enter the figures in the payroll register.

3. Compute the amount of social security tax to be withheld from each employee's earnings. Assume a 6.2 percent social security rate on the first $97,500 earned by the employee during the year. Enter the figures in the payroll register.

4. Compute the amount of Medicare tax to be withheld from each employee's earnings. Assume a 1.45 percent Medicare tax rate on all salaries and wages earned by the employee during the year. Enter the figures in the payroll register.

5. Determine the amount of federal income tax to be withheld from each employee's total earnings. Use the tax tables in Figure 10.2 on pages 333–334. Enter the figures in the payroll register.

6. Compute the net pay of each employee and enter the figures in the payroll register.

7. Total and prove the payroll register.

8. Prepare a general journal entry to record the payroll for the week ended June 30, 2010.

9. Record the general journal entry to summarize payment of the payroll on July 3, 2010.

Analyze: What are Nelda Anderson's cumulative earnings on June 30, 2010?

Problem 10.3A
Objectives 2, 3, 4, 5

▶ **Computing gross earnings, determining deductions, preparing payroll register, journalizing payroll transactions.**

Alexander Wilson operates Metroplex Courier and Delivery Service. He has four employees who are paid on an hourly basis. During the work week beginning December 15 and ending December 21, 2010, his employees worked the number of hours shown below. Information about their hourly rates, marital status, and withholding allowances also appears below, along with their cumulative earnings for the year prior to the December 15–21 payroll period.

Employee	Hours Worked	Regular Hourly Rate	Marital Status	Withholding Allowances	Cumulative Earnings
Gloria Bahamon	46	$15.75	M	4	$32,760
Alex Garcia	42	27.50	S	1	57,200
Ron Price	48	25.90	M	3	53,872
Sara Russell	40	12.75	S	0	26,520

INSTRUCTIONS

1. Enter the basic payroll information for each employee in a payroll register. Record the employee's name, number of withholding allowances, marital status, total and overtime hours, and regular hourly rate. Consider any hours worked beyond 40 in the week as overtime hours.

2. Compute the regular, overtime, and gross earnings for each employee. Enter the figures in the payroll register.

3. Compute the amount of social security tax to be withheld from each employee's gross earnings. Assume a 6.2 percent social security rate on the first $97,500 earned by the employee during the year. Enter the figures in the payroll register.

4. Compute the amount of Medicare tax to be withheld from each employee's gross earnings. Assume a 1.45 percent Medicare tax rate on all salaries and wages earned by the employee during the year. Enter the figures in the payroll register.

5. Determine the amount of federal income tax to be withheld from each employee's total earnings. Use the tax tables in Figure 10.2 on pages 333–334 to determine the withholding for Russell. Withholdings for Bahamon is $103.00, $299.00 for Garcia, and $241 for Price. Enter the figures in the payroll register.

6. Compute the net amount due each employee and enter the figures in the payroll register.

7. Total and prove the payroll register. Bahamon and Russell are office workers. Garcia and Price are delivery workers.

8. Prepare a general journal entry to record the payroll for the week ended December 21, 2010.

9. Give the entry in general journal form on December 23 to summarize payment of wages for the week.

Analyze: What percentage of total taxable wages was delivery wages?

Computing gross earnings, determining deduction and net amount due, journalizing payroll transactions.

◀ **Problem 10.4A**
Objectives
2, 3, 4, 5, 6, 7
e**X**cel

Taylor-Wells Publishing Company pays its employees monthly. Payments made by the company on October 31, 2010, follow. Cumulative amounts paid to the persons named prior to October 31 are also given.

1. James Taylor, president, gross monthly salary of $19,000; gross earnings prior to October 31, $171,000.

2. Carolyn Wells, vice president, gross monthly salary of $17,000; gross earnings paid prior to October 31, $153,000.

3. Kawonza Carter, independent accountant who audits the company's accounts and performs consulting services, $16,500; gross amounts paid prior to October 31, $42,500.

4. Linda Taylor, treasurer, gross monthly salary of $6,000; gross earnings prior to October 31, $54,000.

5. Payment to Editorial Publishing Services for monthly services of Betty Jo Bradley, an editorial expert, $5,500; amount paid to Editorial Publishing Services prior to October 31, 2010, $32,500.

INSTRUCTIONS

1. Use an earnings ceiling of $97,500 for social security taxes and a tax rate of 6.2 percent and a tax rate of 1.45 percent on all earnings for Medicare taxes. Prepare a schedule showing the following information:

   a. Each employee's cumulative earnings prior to October 31.

   b. Each employee's gross earnings for October.

   c. The amounts to be withheld for each payroll tax from each employee's earnings; the employee's income tax withholdings are James Taylor, $5,088; Carolyn Wells, $4,388; Linda Taylor, $1,147.

   d. The net amount due each employee.

   e. The total gross earnings, the total of each payroll tax deduction, and the total net amount payable to employees.

2. Give the general journal entry to record the company's payroll on October 31. Use journal page 22. Omit explanations.

3. Give the general journal entry to record payments to employees on October 31.

Analyze: What distinguishes an employee from an independent contractor?

Problem Set B

Computing gross earnings, determining deductions, journalizing payroll transactions.

◀ **Problem 10.1B**
Objectives
2, 3, 4, 5, 7

Kris Stamos works for Green Valley Builders, Inc. Her pay rate is $12.84 per hour and she receives overtime pay at one and one-half times her regular hourly rate for any hours worked beyond 40 in a week. During the pay period ended December 31, 2010, Kris worked 48 hours. Kris is married and claims three withholding allowances on her W-4 form. Kris's cumulative earnings prior to this pay period total $27,900. Kris's wages are subject to the following deductions:

1. Social security tax at 6.2 percent
2. Medicare tax at 1.45 percent
3. Federal income tax (use the withholding table shown in Figure 10.2b on page 334)
4. Health insurance premiums, $179
5. American Cancer Society contribution, $27
6. Credit Union Savings, $75

INSTRUCTIONS

1. Compute Kris's regular, overtime, gross, and net pay.
2. Journalize the payment of her wages for the week ended December 31, 2010.

Analyze: Based on Kris's cumulative earnings through December 31, how much overtime pay did she earn this year?

Problem 10.2B ▶
Objectives 2, 3, 4, 5

Computing earnings, determining deductions and net amount due, preparing payroll register, journalizing payroll transactions.

The four employees for Cotton Cleaners are paid on an hourly basis. During the week of December 25–31, 2010, these employees worked the hours indicated. Information about their hourly rates, marital status, withholding allowances, and cumulative earnings prior to the current pay period also appears below.

Employee	Hours Worked	Regular Hourly Rate	Marital Status	Withholding Allowances	Cumulative Earnings
Barbara Brooks	47	$12.75	M	3	$ 44,179.00
Cynthia Carter	48	13.25	M	2	53,015.00
Mabel Easley	44	29.50	M	4	82,748.00
James Periot	28	37.25	S	2	104,486.00

INSTRUCTIONS

1. Enter the basic payroll information for each employee in a payroll register. Record the employee's name, number of withholding allowances, marital status, total hours, overtime hours, and regular hourly rate. Consider any hours worked beyond 40 in the week as overtime hours.
2. Compute the regular earnings, overtime premium, and gross earnings for each employee. Enter the figures in the payroll register.
3. Compute the amount of social security tax to be withheld from each employee's gross earnings. Assume a 6.2 percent social security tax rate on the first $97,500 earned by each employee during the year. Enter the figures in the payroll register.
4. Compute the amount of Medicare tax to be withheld from each employee's gross earnings. Assume a 1.45 percent Medicare tax rate on all earnings for each employee during the year. Enter the figure on the payroll register.
5. Determine the amount of federal income tax to be withheld from each employee's gross earnings. Income tax withholdings for Easley is $235 and $238 for Periot. Enter these figures in the payroll register.
6. Compute the net amount due each employee and enter the figures in the payroll register.
7. Complete the payroll register for the store employees.

8. Prepare a general journal entry to record the payroll for the week ended December 31, 2010. Use page 18 for the journal.

9. Record the general journal entry to summarize the payment on December 31, 2010, of the net amount due employees.

Analyze: What is the difference between the amount credited to the *Cash* account on December 31, 2010, for the payroll week ended December 31 and the amount debited to *Wages Expense* for the same payroll period? What causes the difference between the two figures?

◀ **Problem 10.3B**
Objectives 2, 3, 4, 5

Computing earnings, determining deductions and net amount due, preparing payroll register, journalizing payroll transactions.

Barbara Merino operates Merino Consulting Services. She has four employees and pays them on an hourly basis. During the week ended November 12, 2010, her employees worked the number of hours shown below. Information about their hourly rates, marital status, withholding allowances, and cumulative earnings for the year prior to the current pay period also appears below.

Employee	Hours Worked	Regular Hourly Rate	Marital Status	Withholding Allowances	Cumulative Earnings
Kathryn Allen	43	$10.50	M	3	$26,565
Calvin Cooke	36	10.25	S	2	25,933
Maria Vasquez	45	29.75	M	4	75,268
Hollie Visage	41	32.75	S	2	82,858

INSTRUCTIONS

1. Enter the basic payroll information for each employee in a payroll register. Record the employee's name, number of withholding allowances, marital status, total hours, overtime hours, and regular hourly rate. Consider any hours worked beyond 40 in the week as overtime hours.

2. Compute the regular earnings, overtime premium, and gross earnings for each employee. Enter the figures in the payroll register.

3. Compute the amount of social security tax to be withheld from each employee's gross earnings. Assume a 6.2 percent social security rate on the first $97,500 earned by the employee during the year. Enter the figures in the payroll register.

4. Compute the amount of Medicare tax to be withheld from each employee's gross earnings. Assume a 1.45 percent Medicare tax rate on all earning paid during the year. Enter the figures in the payroll register.

5. Use the tax tables in Figure 10.2 on pages 333–334 to determine the federal income tax to be withheld. Federal income tax to be withheld from Vasquez's pay is $192 and from Visage's pay is $267. Enter the figures in the payroll register.

6. Compute the net amount due each employee and enter the figures in the payroll register.

7. Complete the payroll register. Allen and Cooke are office workers. Earnings for Vasquez and Visage are charged to consulting wages.

8. Prepare a general journal entry to record the payroll for the week ended November 12, 2010. Use the account titles given in this chapter.

9. Prepare the general journal entry to summarize payment of amounts due employees on November 15, 2010.

Analyze: What total deductions were taken from employee paychecks for the pay period ended November 12?

◀ **Problem 10.4B**
Objectives 2, 3, 4, 5, 6, 7

Computing gross earnings, determining deduction and net amount due, journalizing payroll transactions.

Braxton Media and Public Relations pays its employees monthly. Payments made by the company on November 30, 2010, follow. Cumulative amounts paid to the persons named prior to November 30 are also given.

1. Troy Braxton, president, gross monthly salary of $18,500; gross earnings prior to November 30, $185,000.

2. Sherrye Braxton, vice president, gross monthly salary of $16,000; gross earnings paid prior to November 30, $160,000.

3. Brenda Cates, independent media buyer who purchases media contracts for companies and performs other public relations consulting services, $15,650; gross amounts paid prior to November 30, $52,850.

4. Henry Thomas, treasurer, gross monthly salary of $6,250; gross earnings prior to November 30, $62,500.

5. Payment to the King Marketing Group for monthly services of Johnny King, a marketing and public relations expert, $15,500; amount paid to the King Marketing Group prior to November 30, $46,500.

INSTRUCTIONS

1. Use an earnings ceiling of $97,500 and a tax rate of 6.2 percent for social security taxes and a tax rate of 1.45 percent on all earnings for Medicare taxes. Prepare a schedule showing the following information:

   a. Each employee's cumulative earnings prior to November 30.

   b. Each employee's gross earnings for November.

   c. The amounts to be withheld for each payroll tax from each employee's earnings; the employee's income tax withholdings are Troy Braxton, $5,110; Sherrye Braxton, $3,640; Henry Thomas, $1,190.

   d. The net amount due each employee.

   e. The total gross earnings, the total of each payroll tax deduction, and the total net amount payable to employees.

2. Give the general journal entry to record the company's payroll on November 30. Use journal page 24. Omit explanations.

3. Give the general journal entry to record payments to employees on November 30.

Analyze: What month in 2010 did Troy Braxton reach the withholding limit for social security?

Critical Thinking Problem 10.1

Payroll Accounting

Arizona Company pays salaries and wages on the last day of each month. Payments made on December 31, 2010, for amounts incurred during December are shown below. Cumulative amounts paid prior to December 31 to the persons named are also shown.

a. Cynthia Arnold, president, gross monthly salary $15,000; gross earnings paid prior to December 31, $165,000.

b. Richard Chen, vice president, gross monthly salary $13,000; gross earnings paid prior to December 31, $78,000.

c. Jean Keller, independent accountant who audits the company's accounts and performs certain consulting services, $13,000; gross amount paid prior to December 31, $39,000.

d. Viadimir Grebennikov, treasurer, gross monthly salary $6,000; gross earnings paid prior to December 31, $66,000.

e. Payment to Wright Security Services for Eddie Wright, a security guard who is on duty on Saturdays and Sundays, $1,050; amount paid to Wright Security Services prior to December 31, $11,550.

INSTRUCTIONS

1. Using the tax rates and earnings ceilings given in this chapter, prepare a schedule showing the following information:

   a. Each employee's cumulative earnings prior to December 31.

   b. Each employee's gross earnings for December.

c. The amounts to be withheld for each payroll tax from each employee's earnings (employee income tax withholdings for Arnold are $3,206; for Chen, $2,646; and for Grebennikov, $801).

d. The net amount due each employee.

e. The total gross earnings, the total of each payroll tax deduction, and the total net amount payable to employees.

2. Record the general journal entry for the company's payroll on December 31.

3. Record the general journal entry for payments to employees on December 31.

Analyze: What is the balance of the *Salaries Payable* account after all payroll entries have been posted for the month?

Critical Thinking Problem 10.2

Payroll Internal Controls

Several years ago, Paul Torres opened Taco Havana, a restaurant specializing in homemade tacos. The restaurant was so successful that Torres was able to expand, and his company now operates eight restaurants in the local area.

Torres tells you that when he first started, he handled all aspects of the business himself. Now that there are eight Taco Havanas, he depends on the managers of each restaurant to make decisions and oversee day-to-day operations. Paul oversees operations at the company's headquarters, which is located at the first Taco Havana.

Each manager interviews and hires new employees for a restaurant. The new employee is required to complete a W-4, which is sent by the manager to the headquarters office. Each restaurant has a time clock and employees are required to clock in as they arrive or depart. Blank time cards are kept in a box under the time clock. At the beginning of each week, employees complete the top of the card they will use during the week. The manager collects the cards at the end of the week and sends them to headquarters.

Paul hired his cousin Mireya to prepare the payroll instead of assigning this task to the accounting staff. Because she is a relative, Paul trusts her and has confidence that confidential payroll information will not be divulged to other employees.

When Mireya receives a W-4 for a new employee, she sets up an individual earnings record for the employee. Each week, using the time cards sent by each restaurant's manager, she computes the gross pay, deductions, and net pay for all the employees. She then posts details to the employees' earnings records and prepares and signs the payroll checks. The checks are sent to the managers, who distribute them to the employees.

As long as Mireya receives a time card for an employee, she prepares a paycheck. If she fails to get a time card for an employee, she checks with the manager to see if the employee was terminated or has quit. At the end of the month, Mireya reconciles the payroll bank account and prepares quarterly and annual payroll tax returns.

1. Identify any weaknesses in Taco Havana's payroll system.

2. Identify one way a manager could defraud Taco Havana under the present payroll system.

3. What internal control procedures would you recommend to Paul to protect against the fraud you identified above?

BUSINESS CONNECTIONS

Cash Management

Managerial FOCUS

1. Why should managers check the amount spent for overtime?

2. The new controller for Ellis Company, a manufacturing firm, has suggested to management that the business change from paying the factory employees in cash to paying them by check. What reasons would you offer to support this suggestion?

3. Why should management make sure that a firm has an adequate set of payroll records?

4. How can detailed payroll records help managers control expenses?

Salary vs. Hourly

Jeremy's Sweater Factory employs two managers for the factory. These managers work 12 hours per day at $15 per hour. After eight hours, they receive overtime pay. Management is trying to cut costs. They have decided to promote the managers to a salary position. The managers will be offered a daily salary of $200. Since they would be promoted to a salary position they will not receive overtime. The company has required they accept the promotion or find employment elsewhere. Is it ethical for the company to offer the managers a salary position? Is it ethical to require the employee to accept the promotion? Should the managers accept the promotion?

Human Resources

Refer to the *2006 Annual Report* of The Home Depot, Inc., in Appendix A.

1. Locate the section entitled "Our Associates." Describe the goals and company vision in regard to the employees of The Home Depot. Based on your knowledge of The Home Depot stores and the financial information presented in Appendix A, what types of positions do you think the company hires? Describe whether you think each job position listed is paid on hourly rate, commission, or salary basis.

2. Locate the financial discussion titled "Fiscal 2006 Compared to Fiscal 2005." Describe the financial data regarding payroll expenses. What factors contributed to increases or decreases in payroll expenses?

Income Statement

Southwest Airlines Co. reported the following data on its consolidated statement of income for the years ended December 31, 2006, 2005, and 2004.

Southwest Airlines Co. Consolidated Statement of Income			
(in millions except per share amounts)	Years Ended December 31		
	2006	*2005*	*2004*
Operating expenses:			
Salaries, wages, and benefits	*3,052*	*2,782*	*2,443*
Total operating expenses	*8,152*	*6,859*	*5,976*

Analyze:

1. The amounts reported for the line item "Salaries, wages, and benefits" include expenses for company retirement plans and profit-sharing plans. If Southwest Airlines Co. spent approximately $1,905 million on wages and salaries alone, compute the employer's Medicare tax expense for 2006. Use a rate of 1.45 percent.

2. What percentage of total operating expenses was spent on salaries, wages, and benefits in 2006?

3. By what amount did salaries, wages, and benefits increase from 2004 to 2006?

Analyze Online: Go to the company Web site for Southwest Airlines Co. (www.southwest.com). Locate the company fact sheet within the *About SWA* section of the site.

4. How many employees does Southwest Airlines Co. employee?

5. How many resumes were submitted to the company for consideration in the current year?

Exempt Employees

Salaried exempt employees generally work for a predetermined annual rate regardless of the actual number of hours they work. In many cases, supervisors and managers work considerably more than 40 hours per week. What do you think of this practice from the employee's perspective? From the employer's perspective?

Pie Chart

Employees should understand how take-home, or net, pay is computed. As the payroll manager, you have been asked to make a presentation to the employees of Broad Street Bakery on how their gross earnings are allocated to taxes and net pay. You decide that a visual representation of the allocation would be most effective. Create a pie chart for the following information.

Employee: Carol Blakley

Gross earnings:	$312.00
Social security tax:	19.34
Medicare tax:	4.52
Federal income tax:	35.00
State income tax:	6.71
Medical insurance:	4.10
Net pay:	242.33

Cycle to Pay Employee

There are many approvals needed to create a paycheck for an employee. Divide into groups of five to identify the jobs necessary to create a paycheck for an employee. Describe the function and, if necessary, the journal entry for each job.

Certified Payroll Professional

Log onto the Certified Payroll Professional (CPP) Web site at www.americanpayroll.org. Find the requirements to become a CPP. How many years of experience are required? What is the fee to take the exam? Describe the testing procedure.

Answers to **Self Reviews**

Answers to Section 1 Self Review

1. By a tax levied equally on both employers and employees. The tax amount is based on the earnings.
2. By state and federal taxes levied on the employer.
3. The federal requirement that covered employees be paid at a rate equal to one and one-half times their normal hourly rate for each hour worked in excess of 40 hours per week.
4. **a.** employees who become unemployed
5. **d.** does not exist
6. She is not an employee. She is an independent contractor because she has been hired to complete a specific job and is not under the control of the employer.

Answers to Section 2 Self Review

1. Health insurance premiums, life insurance premiums, union dues, retirement plans.
2. Amount of earnings, period covered by the payment, employee's marital status, and the number of withholding allowances.
3. Social security tax, Medicare tax, and federal income tax.
4. **d.** hours worked
5. **c.** $468
6. When you receive a signed Form W-4 for the change in withholding.

Answers to Section 3 Self Review

1. Using a separate payroll account simplifies the bank reconciliation procedure and makes it easier to identify outstanding payroll checks.

2. Employee's name, address, social security number, date of birth, number of withholding allowances claimed, marital status, rate of pay, and any other information needed to compute earnings and complete tax reports.

3. Debit *Salaries and Wages Payable* and credit *Cash.*

4. **a.** payroll register

5. **c.** liability account

6. *Health Insurance Premiums Expense* Dr. 40.00 should be *Health Insurance Premiums Payable* Cr. 40.00; *Social Security Taxes Expense* Cr. 197.41 should be *Social Security Tax Payable* Cr. 197.41; *Cash* Cr. 2,634.42 should be *Salaries and Wages Payable* Cr. 2,634.42

Answers to Comprehensive Self Review

1. An employee is one who is hired by the employer and who is under the control and direction of the employer. An independent contractor is paid by the company to carry out a specific task or job and is not under the direct supervision and control of the employer.

2. To record in one place all information about an employee's earnings and withholdings for the period.

3. By check because there is far less possibility of mistake, lost money, or fraud. The check serves as a receipt and permanent record of the transaction.

4. Social security taxes are determined by multiplying the amount of taxable earnings by the social security tax rate.

5. To compensate workers for losses suffered from job-related injuries or to compensate their families if the employee's death occurs in the course of employment.

Chapter 11

Payroll Taxes, Deposits, and Reports

LEARNING OBJECTIVES

1. Explain how and when payroll taxes are paid to the government.
2. Compute and record the employer's social security and Medicare taxes.
3. Record deposit of social security, Medicare, and employee income taxes.
4. Prepare an Employer's Quarterly Federal Tax Return, Form 941.
5. Prepare Wage and Tax Statement (Form W-2) and Annual Transmittal of Wage and Tax Statements (Form W-3).
6. Compute and record liability for federal and state unemployment taxes and record payment of the taxes.
7. Prepare an Employer's Federal Unemployment Tax Return, Form 940 or 940-EZ.
8. Compute and record workers' compensation insurance premiums.
9. Define the accounting terms new to this chapter.

LP11

NEW TERMS

Employer's Annual Federal Unemployment Tax Return, Form 940 or Form 940-EZ

Employer's Quarterly Federal Tax Return, Form 941

experience rating system

merit rating system

Transmittal of Wage and Tax Statements, Form W-3

unemployment insurance program

Wage and Tax Statement, Form W-2

withholding statement

  www.Ikea.com

Ingvar Kamprad was only 17 when he began his retail career. The young entrepreneur got his start selling pens, wallets, table runners, and jewelry. He eventually expanded his offerings to include furniture and opened the first IKEA showroom in 1953. Innovative designs, the development of flat packaging, and the consistent dedication to a vision of "a better everyday life" have all contributed to the huge success of IKEA—revenues exceeded $20 billion in 2005.

Pernille Spiers-Lopez, president, IKEA North America, attributes much of this success to IKEA's co-workers. "When people work in an environment in which they are supported and encouraged by their co-workers, they are more passionate and creative in their daily responsibilities, enabling them to perform at their highest potential. This approach has had a significant impact on our co-worker turnover rate, professional development, and long-term retention." This strategy has resulted in a turnover rate that is less than half the retail industry's standard rate.

thinking critically

How does a lower staff turnover rate affect IKEA's payroll accounting department?

Section 1

SECTION OBJECTIVES

>> 1. Explain how and when payroll taxes are paid to the government.

WHY IT'S IMPORTANT
Employers are required by law to deposit payroll taxes.

>> 2. Compute and record the employer's social security and Medicare taxes.

WHY IT'S IMPORTANT
Accounting records should reflect all liabilities.

>> 3. Record deposit of social security, Medicare, and employee income taxes.

WHY IT'S IMPORTANT
Payments decrease the payroll tax liability.

>> 4. Prepare an Employer's Quarterly Federal Tax Return, Form 941.

WHY IT'S IMPORTANT
Completing a federal tax return is part of the employer's legal obligation.

>> 5. Prepare Wage and Tax Statement (Form W-2) and Annual Transmittal of Wage and Tax Statements (Form W-3).

WHY IT'S IMPORTANT
Employers are legally required to provide end-of-year payroll information.

TERMS TO LEARN

Employer's Quarterly Federal Tax Return, Form 941

Transmittal of Wage and Tax Statements, Form W-3

Wage and Tax Statement, Form W-2

withholding statement

Social Security, Medicare, and Employee Income Tax

In Chapter 10, you learned that the law requires employers to act as collection agents for certain taxes due from employees. In this chapter, you will learn how to compute the employer's taxes, make tax payments, and file the required tax returns and reports.

>> **1. OBJECTIVE**

Explain how and when payroll taxes are paid to the government.

LP11

Payment of Payroll Taxes

The payroll register provides information about wages subject to payroll taxes. Figure 11.1 on page 361 shows a portion of the payroll register for Sanchez Furniture Company for the week ending January 6.

Employers make tax deposits for federal income tax withheld from employee earnings, the employees' share of social security and Medicare taxes withheld from earnings, and the employer's share of social security and Medicare taxes. The deposits are made in a Federal Reserve Bank or other authorized financial institution. Businesses usually make payroll tax deposits at their own bank. There are two ways to deposit payroll taxes: by electronic deposit or with a tax deposit coupon.

The *Electronic Federal Tax Payment System (EFTPS)* is a system for electronically depositing employment taxes using a telephone or a computer. Any employer can use EFTPS. An employer *must* use EFTPS if the annual federal tax deposits are more than $200,000. Employers who are required to make electronic deposits and do not do so can be subject to a 10 percent penalty.

Employers who are not required to use EFTPS may deposit payroll taxes using a *Federal Tax Deposit Coupon, Form 8109*. The employer's name, tax identification number, and address are preprinted on Form 8109. The employer enters the deposit amount on the form and makes the payment with a check, money order, or cash.

AND ENDING _January 7, 2010_   **PAID** _January 8, 2010_

TAXABLE WAGES			DEDUCTIONS				DISTRIBUTION			
SOCIAL SECURITY	MEDICARE	FUTA	SOCIAL SECURITY	MEDICARE	INCOME TAX	HEALTH INSURANCE	NET AMOUNT	CHECK NO.	OFFICE SALARIES	SHIPPING WAGES
400 00	400 00	400 00	24 80	5 80	19 00		350 40	1601		400 00
380 00	380 00	380 00	23 56	5 51	34 00		316 93	1602		380 00
427 50	427 50	427 50	26 51	6 20	23 00	40 00	331 79	1603		427 50
560 00	560 00	560 00	34 72	8 12	30 00	40 00	447 16	1604		560 00
480 00	480 00	480 00	29 76	6 96	49 00		394 28	1605	480 00	
2 247 50	2 247 50	2 247 50	139 35	32 59	155 00	80 00	1 840 56		480 00	1 767 50

FIGURE 11.1   Portion of a Payroll Register

In some cases, an employer may use Form 8109-B. *Form 8109-B* is a coupon that is *not* preprinted. Form 8109-B may be used if a new employer has been assigned an identification number but has not yet received a supply of Forms 8109, or an employer has not received a resupply of Forms 8109. Figure 11.2 shows the completed Form 8109-B for Sanchez Furniture Company.

The frequency of deposits depends on the amount of tax liability. The amount currently owed is compared to the tax liability threshold. For simplicity this textbook uses $2,500 as the tax liability threshold.

The deposit schedules are not related to how often employees are paid. The deposit schedules are based on the amount currently owed and the amount reported in the lookback period. The *lookback period* is a four-quarter period ending on June 30 of the preceding year.

1. If the amount owed is less than $2,500, payment is due quarterly with the payroll tax return (Form 941).

    Example. An employer's tax liability is as follows:

January	$580
February	640
March	620
	$1,840

FIGURE 11.2   Federal Tax Deposit Coupon, Form 8109-B

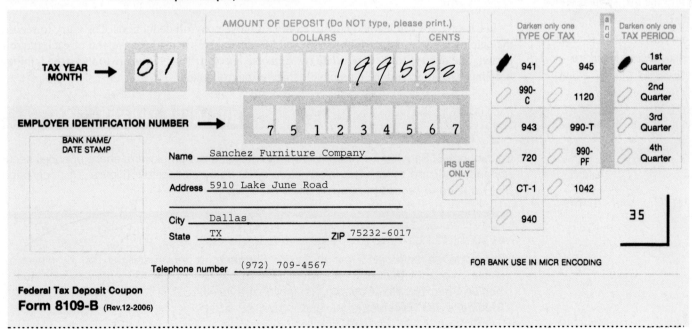

Since at no time during the quarter is the accumulated tax liability $2,500 or more, no deposit is required during the quarter. The employer may pay the amount with the payroll tax returns.

2. If the amount owed is $2,500 or more, the schedule is determined from the total taxes reported on Form 941 during the lookback period.

 a. If the amount reported in the lookback period was $50,000 or less, the employer is subject to the *Monthly Deposit Schedule Rule.* Monthly payments are due on the 15th day of the following month. For example, the January payment is due by February 15.

 b. If the amount reported in the lookback period was more than $50,000, the employer is subject to the *Semiweekly Deposit Schedule Rule.* "Semiweekly" refers to the fact that deposits are due on either Wednesdays or Fridays, depending on the employer's payday.

 • If payday is a Wednesday, Thursday, or Friday, the deposit is due on the following Wednesday.

 • If payday is a Saturday, Sunday, Monday, or Tuesday, the deposit is due on the following Friday.

 c. For new employers with no lookback period, if the amount owed is $2,500 or more, payments are due under the Monthly Deposit Schedule Rule.

3. If the total accumulated tax liability reaches $100,000 or more on any day, a deposit is due on the next banking day. This applies even if the employer is on a monthly or a semiweekly deposit schedule.

EMPLOYER'S SOCIAL SECURITY AND MEDICARE TAX EXPENSES

>>2. OBJECTIVE

Compute and record the employer's social security and Medicare taxes.

LP11

important!

Tax Liability

The employer's tax liability is the amount owed for

• employee withholdings (income tax, social security tax, Medicare tax);

• employer's share of social security and Medicare taxes.

Remember that both employers and employees pay social security and Medicare taxes. Figure 11.1 shows the *employee's* share of these payroll taxes. The *employer* pays the same amount of payroll taxes. At the assumed rate of 6.2 percent for social security and 1.45 percent for Medicare tax, the employer's tax liability is $343.88.

	Employee (Withheld)	Employer (Matched)
Social security	$139.35	$139.35
Medicare	32.59	32.59
	$171.94	$171.94
Total	$343.88	

In Chapter 10, you learned how to record employee payroll deductions. The entry to record the employer's share of social security and Medicare taxes is made at the end of each payroll period. The debit is to the **Payroll Taxes Expense** account. The credits are to the same liability accounts used to record the employee's share of payroll taxes.

BUSINESS TRANSACTION

On January 8, Sanchez Furniture Company recorded the employer's share of social security and Medicare taxes. The information on the payroll register (Figure 11.1 on page 361) is used to record the payroll taxes expense.

ANALYSIS

The expense account, **Payroll Taxes Expense,** is increased by the employer's share of social security and Medicare taxes, $171.94. The liability account, **Social Security Tax Payable,** is increased by $139.35. The liability account, **Medicare Tax Payable,** is increased by $32.59.

DEBIT-CREDIT RULES

DEBIT   Increases to expense accounts are recorded as debits. Debit **Payroll Taxes Expense** for $171.94.

CREDIT   Increases to liability accounts are recorded as credits. Credit **Social Security Tax Payable** for $139.35. Credit **Medicare Tax Payable** for $32.59.

T-ACCOUNT PRESENTATION

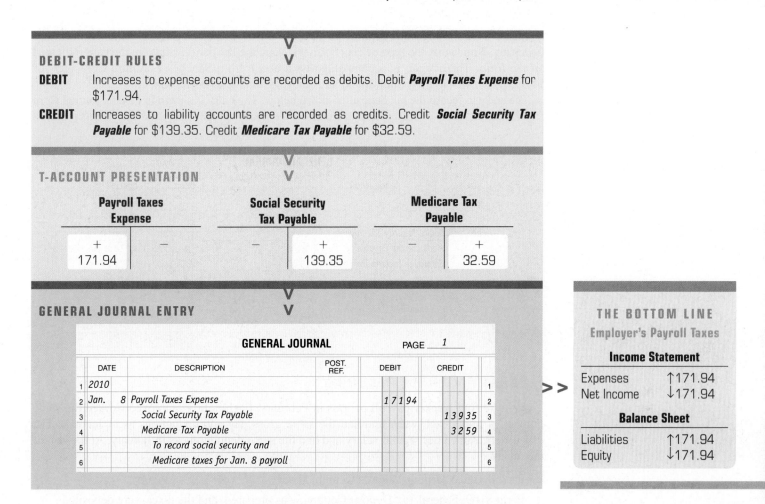

Payroll Taxes Expense		Social Security Tax Payable		Medicare Tax Payable	
+	−	−	+	−	+
171.94			139.35		32.59

GENERAL JOURNAL ENTRY

GENERAL JOURNAL   PAGE ___1___

	DATE		DESCRIPTION	POST. REF.	DEBIT	CREDIT	
1	2010						1
2	Jan.	8	Payroll Taxes Expense		171 94		2
3			Social Security Tax Payable			139 35	3
4			Medicare Tax Payable			32 59	4
5			To record social security and				5
6			Medicare taxes for Jan. 8 payroll				6

THE BOTTOM LINE

Employer's Payroll Taxes

Income Statement

Expenses	↑171.94
Net Income	↓171.94

Balance Sheet

Liabilities	↑171.94
Equity	↓171.94

According to the American Payroll Association, the Social Security Administration provides benefits to approximately 44 million men, women, and children. It is essential that earnings are correctly reported so that future benefits can be calculated accurately.

RECORDING THE PAYMENT OF TAXES WITHHELD

At the end of January, the accounting records for Sanchez Furniture Company contained the following information.

>>3. OBJECTIVE

Record deposit of social security, Medicare, and employee income taxes.

LP11

	Employee (Withheld)	Employer (Matched)	Total
Social security	$ 557.40	$557.40	$1,114.80
Medicare	130.36	130.36	260.72
Federal income tax	620.00	—	620.00
Total	$1,307.76	$687.76	$1,995.52

Sanchez Furniture Company is on a monthly payment schedule. The amount reported in the lookback period is less than $50,000. The payroll tax liability for the quarter ending March 31, 2010, is more than $2,500. (Recall that this textbook uses $2,500 as the tax liability threshold.) A tax payment is due on the 15th day of the following month, February 15.

Figure 11.2 on page 361 shows the Federal Tax Deposit Coupon for Sanchez Furniture Company. Notice that the type of tax (Form 941) and the tax period (first quarter) are indicated on the form. The coupon is accompanied by a check from Sanchez Furniture Company for $1,995.52 written to First State Bank, an authorized financial institution.

The entry to record the tax deposit is shown below. The entry is shown in general journal form for illustration purposes only. (Sanchez Furniture Company actually uses a cash payments journal.)

	DATE		DESCRIPTION	POST. REF.	DEBIT	CREDIT	
1	2010						1
21							21
22	Feb.	15	Social Security Tax Payable		1 1 1 4 80		22
23			Medicare Tax Payable		2 6 0 72		23
24			Employee Income Tax Payable		6 2 0 00		24
25			Cash			1 9 9 5 52	25
26			Deposit of payroll taxes withholding				26
27			at First State Bank				27
28							28

GENERAL JOURNAL   PAGE __2__

FEBRUARY PAYROLL RECORDS

There were four weekly payroll periods in February. Each hourly employee worked the same number of hours each week and had the same gross pay and deductions as in January. The office clerk earned her regular salary and had the same deductions as in January. At the end of the month

- the individual earnings records were updated;
- Form 8109, Federal Tax Deposit Coupon, was prepared, and the taxes were deposited before March 15;
- the tax deposit was recorded in the cash payments journal.

MARCH PAYROLL RECORDS

There were five weekly payroll periods in March. Assume that the payroll period ended on March 31, and the payday was on March 31. Also assume that the earnings and deductions of the employees were the same for each week as in January and February. At the end of the month, the individual earnings records were updated, the taxes were deposited, and the tax deposit was recorded in the cash payments journal.

QUARTERLY SUMMARY OF EARNINGS RECORDS

At the end of each quarter, the individual earnings records are totaled. This involves adding the columns in the Earnings, Deductions, and Net Pay sections. Figure 11.3 on page 365 shows the earnings record, posted and summarized, for Alicia Martinez for the first quarter.

Table 11.1 below shows the quarterly totals for each employee of Sanchez Furniture Company. This information is taken from the individual earnings records. Through the end of the first quarter, no employee has exceeded the social security earnings limit ($97,500) and the FUTA/SUTA limit ($7,000) has only been exceeded by Cecilia Wu.

>>**4. OBJECTIVE**

Prepare an Employer's Quarterly Federal Tax Return, Form 941.

LP11

EMPLOYER'S QUARTERLY FEDERAL TAX RETURN

Each quarter an employer files an **Employer's Quarterly Federal Tax Return, Form 941** with the Internal Revenue Service. Form 941 must be filed by all employers subject to federal income tax withholding, social security tax, or Medicare tax, with certain exceptions as specified in *Publication 15, Circular E*. This tax return provides information about employee earnings, the tax liability for each month in the quarter, and the deposits made.

EARNINGS RECORD FOR _2010_

NAME _Alicia Martinez_   RATE _$10 per hour_   SOCIAL SECURITY NO. _123-45-6789_
ADDRESS _1712 Windmill Hill Lane, Dallas TX 75232-6002_   DATE OF BIRTH _October 31, 1979_
WITHHOLDING ALLOWANCES _1_   MARITAL STATUS _M_

PAYROLL NO.	WK. END.	PAID	RG	OT	REGULAR	OVERTIME	TOTAL	CUMULATIVE	SOCIAL SECURITY	MEDICARE	INCOME TAX	OTHER	NET PAY
1	1/06	1/08	40		400 00		400 00	400 00	24 80	5 80	19 00		350 40
2	1/13	1/15	40		400 00		400 00	400 00	24 80	5 80	19 00		350 40
3	1/20	1/22	40		400 00		400 00	400 00	24 80	5 80	19 00		350 40
4	1/27	1/29	40		400 00		400 00	400 00	24 80	5 80	19 00		350 40
	January				1600 00		1600 00	1600 00	99 20	23 20	76 00		1401 60
1	2/03	2/05	40		400 00		400 00	400 00	24 80	5 80	19 00		350 40
2	2/10	2/12	40		400 00		400 00	400 00	24 80	5 80	19 00		350 40
3	2/17	2/19	40		400 00		400 00	400 00	24 80	5 80	19 00		350 40
4	2/24	2/25	40		400 00		400 00	400 00	24 80	5 80	19 00		350 40
	February				1600 00		1600 00	1600 00	99 20	23 20	76 00		1401 60
1	3/03	3/05	40		400 00		400 00	400 00	24 80	5 80	19 00		350 40
2	3/10	3/12	40		400 00		400 00	400 00	24 80	5 80	19 00		350 40
3	3/17	3/19	40		400 00		400 00	400 00	24 80	5 80	19 00		350 40
4	3/24	3/26	40		400 00		400 00	400 00	24 80	5 80	19 00		350 40
5	3/31	3/31	40		400 00		400 00	400 00	24 80	5 80	19 00		350 40
	March				2000 00		2000 00	2000 00	124 00	29 00	95 00		1752 00
					5200 00		5200 00	5200 00	322 40	75 40	247 00		4555 20
	First Quarter												

FIGURE 11.3 Individual Earnings Record

The Social Security Administration administers the Old Age and Survivors, Disability Insurance, and Supplemental Security Income Programs. These programs are funded by the social security taxes collected from employees and matched by employers. The system currently takes in more in revenue from the 12.4 percent payroll taxes than it pays out in benefits. The trust fund is expected to begin paying out more in benefits than it collects in 2018.

TABLE 11.1

Summary of Earnings, Quarter Ended March 31, 2010

Employee	Taxable Earnings				Deductions		
	Total Earnings	Social Security	Medicare	SUTA & FUTA	Social Security	Medicare Tax	Income Tax
Alicia Martinez	5,200.00	5,200.00	5,200.00	5,200.00	322.40	75.40	247.00
Jorge Rodriguez	4,940.00	4,940.00	4,940.00	4,940.00	306.28	71.63	442.00
George Dunlap	5,557.50	5,557.50	5,557.50	5,557.50	344.57	80.58	299.00
Cecilia Wu	7,280.00	7,280.00	7,280.00	7,000.00	451.36	105.56	390.00
Cynthia Booker	6,240.00	6,240.00	6,240.00	6,240.00	386.88	90.48	637.00
Totals	29,217.50	29,217.50	29,217.50	28,937.50	1,811.49	423.65	2,015.00

When to File Form 941 The due date for Form 941 is the last day of the month following the end of each calendar quarter. If the taxes for the quarter were deposited when due, the due date is extended by 10 days.

Completing Form 941 Figure 11.4 on pages 367 and 368 shows Form 941 for Sanchez Furniture Company. Form 941 is prepared using the data on the quarterly summary of earnings records, Table 11.1 on page 365. Let's examine Form 941.

- Use the preprinted form if it is available. Otherwise, enter the employer's name, address, and identification number at the top of Form 941. Check the applicable quarter.
- *Line 1* is completed for each quarter. Enter the number of employees for the pay periods indicated.
- *Line 2* shows total wages and tips subject to withholding. For Sanchez Furniture Company the total subject to withholdings is $29,217.50.
- *Line 3* shows the total employee income tax withheld during the quarter, $2,015.00.
- *Line 4* is checked if no wages or tips are subject to social security or Medicare tax.
- *Line 5a* shows the total amount of wages that are subject to social security taxes, $29,217.50. The amount is multiplied by the combined social security rate, 12.4 percent.

Social Security Tax:	
Employee's share	6.2%
Employer's share	6.2
Total	12.4%

  The amount of taxes is $3,622.97 ($29,217.50 × 12.4%).

- *Line 5b* is left blank since no employees at Sanchez Furniture Company had taxable social security tips.
- *Line 5c* shows the total amount of wages that are subject to Medicare taxes, $29,217.50. The amount is multiplied by the combined Medicare tax rate, 2.9 percent.

Medicare Tax:	
Employee's share	1.45%
Employer's share	1.45
Total	2.90%

  The amount of taxes is $847.31 ($29,217.50 × 2.90%).

- *Line 5d* shows the total social security and Medicare taxes, $4,470.28.
- *Line 6* shows the total tax liability for withheld income taxes, social security, and Medicare Taxes, $6,485.28.
- *Lines 7a* through *7h* are for adjustments. Sanchez Furniture Company had no adjustments this quarter. If there is a difference due to rounding that difference can be adjusted on line 7a.
- *Line 8* shows total taxes after adjustments, $6,485.28.
- *Line 9* is for deducting the amount of any advance earned income credit payments to employees. Sanchez Furniture Company had no advance payments for earned income credit payments to employees.
- *Line 10* shows total taxes after adjustments, $6,485.28.
- *Line 11* shows total deposits made during the quarter including overpayments applied from a prior quarter, $6,485.28.
- Any balance due is entered on *Line 12* or overpayment is entered on *Line 13*.
- The state where deposits were made is entered on *Line 14*.
- *Line 15* shows the monthly deposits made by Sanchez Furniture Company.

Form **941 for 2010:** **Employer's Quarterly Federal Tax Return**   9901
(Rev. January 2007)   Department of the Treasury — Internal Revenue Service
                                                                              OMB No. 1545-0029

Employer identification number   [7] [5] — [1] [2] [3] [4] [5] [6] [7]

Name *(not your trade name)*   Sarah Sanchez

Trade name *(if any)*   Sanchez Furniture Company

Address   5910 Lake June Road
             Number   Street   Suite or room number

             Dallas   TX   75232-6017
             City   State ZIP code

Report for this Quarter ...
(Check one.)

[✔] **1:** January, February, March

[ ] **2:** April, May, June

[ ] **3:** July, August, September

[ ] **4:** October, November, December

Read the separate instructions before you fill out this form. Please type or print within the boxes.

Part 1: Answer these questions for this quarter.

1 Number of employees who received wages, tips, or other compensation for the pay period
   including: *Mar. 12* (Quarter 1), *June 12* (Quarter 2), *Sept. 12* (Quarter 3), *Dec. 12* (Quarter 4)   **1** | 5 |

2 Wages, tips, and other compensation . . . .   **2** | 29,217 . 50 |

3 Total income tax withheld from wages, tips, and other compensation . . . .   **3** | 2,015 . 00 |

4 If no wages, tips, and other compensation are subject to social security or Medicare tax . . [ ] Check and go to line 6.

5 Taxable social security and Medicare wages and tips:

	Column 1		Column 2
5a Taxable social security wages	29,217 . 50	× .124 =	3,622 . 97
5b Taxable social security tips	.	× .124 =	.
5c Taxable Medicare wages & tips	29,217 . 50	× .029 =	847 . 31

5d Total social security and Medicare taxes (*Column 2*, lines 5a + 5b + 5c = line 5d) . . **5d** | 4,470 . 28 |

6 Total taxes before adjustments (lines 3 + 5d = line 6) . . . .   **6** | 6,485 . 28 |

7 Tax adjustments (If your answer is a negative number, write it in brackets.):

7a Current quarter's fractions of cents . . . . | . |

7b Current quarter's sick pay . . . . | . |

7c Current quarter's adjustments for tips and group-term life insurance | . |

7d Current year's income tax withholding (Attach Form 941c) . . . | . |

7e Prior quarters' social security and Medicare taxes (Attach Form 941c) | . |

7f Special additions to federal income tax (reserved use) . . . . . | . |

7g Special additions to social security and Medicare (reserved use) | . |

7h Total adjustments (Combine all amounts: lines 7a through 7g.) . . . .   **7h** | . |

8 Total taxes after adjustments (Combine lines 6 and 7h.) . . . .   **8** | 6,485 . 28 |

9 Advance earned income credit (EIC) payments made to employees . . . .   **9** | . |

10 Total taxes after adjustment for advance EIC (lines 8 – 9 = line 10) . . . .   **10** | 6,485 . 28 |

11 Total deposits for this quarter, including overpayment applied from a prior quarter . . .   **11** | 6,485 . 28 |

12 Balance due (lines 10 – 11 = line 12) Make checks payable to the *United States Treasury* . .   **12** | 0 . |

13 Overpayment (If line 11 is more than line 10, write the difference here.) | . | Check one [ ] Apply to next return.
                                                                                        [ ] Send a refund.

                                                                              Next ➡

For Privacy Act and Paperwork Reduction Act Notice, see the back of the Payment Voucher.   Cat. No. 17001Z   Form **941**

FIGURE 11.4   **Employer's Quarterly Federal Tax Return, Form 941**

9902

Name *(not your trade name)*	Employer identification number
Sarah Sanchez	75-1234567

Part 2: Tell us about your deposit schedule for this quarter.

If you are unsure about whether you are a monthly schedule depositor or a semiweekly schedule depositor, see *Pub. 15 (Circular E),* section 11.

14 [T][X]   Write the state abbreviation for the state where you made your deposits OR write "MU" if you made your deposits in *multiple* states.

15 Check one: ☐ Line 10 is less than $2,500. Go to Part 3.

☑ You were a monthly schedule depositor for the entire quarter. Fill out your tax liability for each month. Then go to Part 3.

Tax liability:	Month 1	1,995 . 52
	Month 2	1,995 . 52
	Month 3	2,494 . 24
	Total	6,485 . 28 Total must equal line 10.

☐ You were a semiweekly schedule depositor for any part of this quarter. Fill out *Schedule B (Form 941): Report of Tax Liability for Semiweekly Schedule Depositors,* and attach it to this form.

Part 3: Tell us about your business. If a question does NOT apply to your business, leave it blank.

16 If your business has closed and you do not have to file returns in the future . . . . ☐ Check here, and

enter the final date you paid wages [/ /] .

17 If you are a seasonal employer and you do not have to file a return for every quarter of the year . . ☐ Check here.

Part 4: May we contact your third-party designee?

Do you want to allow an employee, a paid tax preparer, or another person to discuss this return with the IRS? See the instructions for details.

☐ Yes. Designee's name [　　　　　　　　　　　]

Phone (   )   –   Personal Identification Number (PIN) ☐ ☐ ☐ ☐ ☐

☑ No.

Part 5: Sign here

Under penalties of perjury, I declare that I have examined this return, including accompanying schedules and statements, and to the best of my knowledge and belief, it is true, correct, and complete.

X

Sign your name here	
Print name and title	Sarah Sanchez, Owner
Date	04 / 30 / 10 Phone (972) 709 – 4567

Part 6: For paid preparers only *(optional)*

Preparer's signature			
Firm's name			
Address		EIN	
		ZIP code	
Date	/ / Phone ( ) –	SSN/PTIN	

☐ Check if you are self-employed.

FIGURE 11.4 (concluded)

Notice that on Line 15 if the amount of taxes is less than $2,500, the amount may be paid with the return or with a financial depositor. There is no need to complete the record of monthly deposits. Since the amount of taxes due for Sanchez Furniture Company is greater than $2,500, and Sanchez is a monthly depositor, the record of monthly tax deposits must be completed on Line 15. The total deposits shown on Line 15 must equal the taxes shown on Line 10.

If the employer did not make sufficient deposits, a check for the balance due is mailed to the Internal Revenue Service with Form 941. An employer may instead make a deposit at an authorized financial institution.

If the employer did not deduct enough taxes from an employee's earnings, the business pays the difference. The deficiency is debited to *Payroll Taxes Expense.*

Wage and Tax Statement, Form W-2

Employers provide a **Wage and Tax Statement, Form W-2,** to each employee by January 31 of the following year. Form W-2 is sometimes called a **withholding statement.** Form W-2 contains information about the employee's earnings and tax withholdings for the year. The information for Form W-2 comes from the employee's earnings record.

Employees who stop working for the business during the year may ask that a Form W-2 be issued early. The Form W-2 must be issued within 30 days after the request or after the final wage payment, whichever is later.

Figure 11.5 on page 370 shows Form W-2 for Alicia Martinez. This is the standard form provided by the Internal Revenue Service (IRS). Some employers use a "substitute" Form W-2 that is approved by the IRS. The substitute form permits the employer to list total deductions and to reconcile the gross earnings, the deductions, and the net pay. If the firm issues 250 or more Forms W-2, the returns must be filed electronically.

At least four copies of each of Form W-2 are prepared:

1. One copy for the employer to send to the Social Security Administration, which shares the information with the IRS.

2. One copy for the employee to attach to the federal income tax return.

3. One copy for the employee's records.

4. One copy for the employer's records.

If there is a state income tax, two more copies of Form W-2 are prepared:

5. One copy for the employer to send to the state tax department.

6. One copy for the employee to attach to the state income tax return.

Additional copies are prepared if there is a city or county income tax.

Annual Transmittal of Wage and Tax Statements, Form W-3

The **Transmittal of Wage and Tax Statements, Form W-3,** is submitted with Forms W-2 to the Social Security Administration. Form W-3 reports the total social security wages; total Medicare wages; total social security tax withheld; total Medicare tax withheld; total wages, tips, and other compensation; total federal income tax withheld; and other information.

A copy of Form W-2 for each employee is attached to Form W-3. Form W-3 is due by the last day of February following the end of the calendar year. The Social Security Administration shares the tax information on Forms W-2 with the Internal Revenue Service. Figure 11.6 on page 371 shows the completed Form W-3 for Sanchez Furniture Company.

>>5. OBJECTIVE

Prepare Wage and Tax Statement (Form W-2) and Annual Transmittal of Wage and Tax Statements (Form W-3).

important!

Form W-2
The employer must provide each employee with a Wage and Tax Statement, Form W-2, by January 31 of the following year.

ABOUT
ACCOUNTING

IRS Electronic Filing
More than 19 million taxpayers have filed their tax returns electronically. Returns that are filed electronically are more accurate than paper returns. Electronic filing means refunds in half the time, especially if the taxpayer chooses direct deposit of the refund.

a Control number	22222	Void ☐	For Official Use Only ▶ OMB No. 1545-0008		

b Employer identification number 75-1234567			1 Wages, tips, other compensation 20,800.00	2 Federal income tax withheld 988.00
c Employer's name, address, and ZIP code Sanchez Furniture Co. 5910 Lake June Road Dallas, TX 75232-6017			3 Social security wages 20,800.00	4 Social security tax withheld 1,289.60
			5 Medicare wages and tips 20,800.00	6 Medicare tax withheld 301.60
			7 Social security tips	8 Allocated tips
d Employee's social security number 123-45-6789			9 Advance EIC payment	10 Dependent care benefits
e Employee's first name and initial Alicia Last name Martinez 1712 Windmill Hill Lane Dallas, Texas 75232-6002			11 Nonqualified plans	12a See instructions for box 12
			13 Statutory employee ☐ Retirement plan ☐ Third-party sick pay ☐	12b
			14 Other	12c
				12d
f Employee's address and ZIP code				

15 State Employer's state I.D. no. TX 12-9876500	16 State wages, tips, etc. 20,800.00	17 State income tax	18 Local wages, tips, etc.	19 Local income tax	20 Locality name

Form **W-2** Wage and Tax Statement **2010**

Department of the Treasury—Internal Revenue Service

For Privacy Act and Paperwork Reduction Act Notice, see back of Copy D.

Copy A For Social Security Administration—Send this entire page with Form W-3 to the Social Security Administration; photocopies are **not** acceptable.

Cat. No. 10134D

Do NOT Cut, Fold, or Staple Forms on This Page—Do NOT Cut, Fold, or Staple Forms on This Page

FIGURE 11.5   Wage and Tax Statement, Form W-2

The amounts on Form W-3 must equal the sums of the amounts on the attached Forms W-2. For example, the amount entered in Box 1 of Form W-3 must equal the sum of the amounts entered in Box 1 of all the Forms W-2.

The amounts on Form W-3 also must equal the sums of the amounts reported on the Forms 941 during the year. For example, the social security wages reported on the Form W-3 must equal the sum of the social security wages reported on the four Forms 941.

The filing of Form W-3 marks the end of the routine procedures needed to account for payrolls and for payroll tax withholdings.

a	Control number	33333	For Official Use Only ▶ OMB No. 1545-0008			

| b | Kind of Payer ▶ | 941 ☒ Military ☐ 943 ☐
CT-1 ☐ Hshld. emp. ☐ Medicare govt. emp. ☐ Third-party sick pay ☐ | 1 Wages, tips, other compensation
116,870.00 | 2 Federal income tax withheld
8,060.00 |

		3 Social security wages 116,870.00	4 Social security tax withheld 7,246.20

| c | Total number of Forms W-2
5 | d Establishment number | 5 Medicare wages and tips
116,870.00 | 6 Medicare tax withheld
1,694.68 |

e	Employer identification number 75-1234567	7 Social security tips	8 Allocated tips

| f | Employer's name
Sanchez Furniture Co. | 9 Advance EIC payments | 10 Dependent care benefits |

| | 11 Nonqualified plans | 12 Deferred compensation |

5910 Lake June Road
Dallas, TX 75232-6017

13 For third-party sick pay use only

14 Income tax withheld by third-party sick pay

g	Employer's address and ZIP code
h	Other EIN used this year

15 State TX	Employer's state I.D. no. 12-9876500	16 State wages, tips, etc.	17 State income tax
		18 Local wages, tips, etc.	19 Local income tax

Contact person Sarah Sanchez	Telephone number (972) 709-4567	For Official Use Only
E-mail address Sanchez@aol.net	Fax number ( )	

Under penalties of perjury, I declare that I have examined this return and accompanying documents, and, to the best of my knowledge and belief, they are true, correct, and complete.

Signature ▶ *Sarah Sanchez*   Title ▶ *Owner*   Date ▶ *February 16, 2011*

Form **W-3** Transmittal of Wage and Tax Statements **2010**   Department of the Treasury
Internal Revenue Service

FIGURE 11.6   **Transmittal of Wage and Tax Statements, Form W-3**

Section 1 Self Review

QUESTIONS

1. What is the purpose of Form W-2?
2. Where does a business deposit federal payroll taxes?
3. What is the purpose of Form 941?

EXERCISES

4. Which tax is shared equally by the employee and employer?
   a. Federal income tax
   b. State income tax
   c. Social security tax
   d. Federal unemployment tax

5. Employers usually record social security taxes in the accounting records at the end of
   a. each payroll period.
   b. each month.
   c. each quarter.
   d. the year.

ANALYSIS

6. Your business currently owes $2,910 in payroll taxes. During the lookback period, your business paid $10,000 in payroll taxes. How often does your business need to make payroll tax deposits?

(Answers to Section 1 Self Review are on page 393.)

SECTION OBJECTIVES

>> 6. **Compute and record liability for federal and state unemployment taxes and record payment of the taxes.**

WHY IT'S IMPORTANT

Businesses need to record all payroll tax liabilities.

>> 7. **Prepare an Employer's Federal Unemployment Tax Return, Form 940 or 940-EZ.**

WHY IT'S IMPORTANT

The unemployment insurance programs provide support to individuals during temporary periods of unemployment.

>> 8. **Compute and record workers' compensation insurance premiums.**

WHY IT'S IMPORTANT

Businesses need insurance to cover workplace injury claims.

TERMS TO LEARN

Employer's Annual Federal Unemployment Tax Return, Form 940 or Form 940-EZ

experience rating system

merit rating system

unemployment insurance program

Unemployment Tax and Workers' Compensation

In Section 1, we discussed taxes that are withheld from employees' earnings and, in some cases, matched by the employer. In this section, we will discuss payroll related expenses that are paid solely by the employer.

Unemployment Compensation Insurance Taxes

The unemployment compensation tax program, often called the **unemployment insurance program,** provides unemployment compensation through a tax levied on employers.

COORDINATION OF FEDERAL AND STATE UNEMPLOYMENT RATES

The unemployment insurance program is a federal program that encourages states to provide unemployment insurance for employees working in the state. The federal government allows a credit—or reduction—in the federal unemployment tax for amounts charged by the state for unemployment taxes.

This text assumes that the federal unemployment tax rate is 6.2 percent less a state unemployment tax credit of 5.4 percent; thus the federal tax rate is reduced to 0.8 percent (6.2% − 5.4%). The earnings limits for the federal and the state unemployment tax are usually the same, $7,000.

A few states levy an unemployment tax on the employee. The tax is withheld from employee pay and remitted by the employer to the state.

For businesses that provide steady employment, the state unemployment tax rate may be lowered based on an **experience rating system,** or a **merit rating system.** Under the experience rating system, the state tax rate may be reduced to less than 1 percent for businesses that provide steady employment. In contrast, some states levy penalty rates as high as 10 percent for employers with poor records of providing steady employment.

The reduction of state unemployment taxes because of favorable experience ratings does not affect the credit allowable against the federal tax. An employer may take a credit against the federal unemployment tax as though it were paid at the normal state rate even though the employer actually pays the state a lower rate.

Because of its experience rating, Sanchez Furniture Company pays state unemployment tax of 4.0 percent, which is less than the standard rate of 5.4 percent. Note that the business may take the credit for the full amount of the state rate (5.4%) against the federal rate, even though the business actually pays a state rate of 4.0%.

COMPUTING AND RECORDING UNEMPLOYMENT TAXES

Sanchez Furniture Company records its state and federal unemployment tax expense at the end of each payroll period. The unemployment taxes for the payroll period ending January 6 are as follows.

Federal unemployment tax	($2,247.50 × 0.008)	=	$ 17.98
State unemployment tax	($2,247.50 × 0.040)	=	89.90
Total unemployment taxes		=	$107.88

The entry to record the employer's unemployment payroll taxes follows.

>>6. OBJECTIVE

Compute and record liability for federal and state unemployment taxes and record payment of the taxes.

LP11

GENERAL JOURNAL   PAGE __1__

	DATE		DESCRIPTION	POST. REF.	DEBIT	CREDIT	
1	2010						1
8	Jan.	8	Payroll Taxes Expense		1 0 7 88		8
9			Federal Unemployment Tax Payable			1 7 98	9
10			State Unemployment Tax Payable			8 9 90	10
11			Unemployment taxes on				11
12			weekly payroll				12

REPORTING AND PAYING STATE UNEMPLOYMENT TAXES

In most states, the due date for the unemployment tax return is the last day of the month following the end of the quarter. Generally the tax is paid with the return.

Employer's Quarterly Report Figure 11.7 on page 374 shows the Employer's Quarterly Report for the State of Texas filed by Sanchez Furniture Company in April for the first quarter. The report for Texas is similar to the tax forms of other states. The top of the form contains information about the company.

- *Block 4* at the top of the form shows the tax rate assigned by the state based on the experience rating. The tax rate for Sanchez Furniture Company is 4.0 percent.
- *Block 10* (3 boxes) shows the number of employees in the state on the 12th day of each month of the quarter.
- *Line 13* shows the total wages paid during the quarter to employees in the state, $29,217.50.
- *Line 14* shows the total *taxable* wages paid during the quarter, $28,937.50. Note that the limit on taxable wages is $7,000. Table 11.1 on page 365 shows that at the end of the first quarter, one employee, Cecilia Wu, earned more than $7,000. All other wages and salaries are taxable for state unemployment. Actually, the base in Texas is $9,000. We use a base of $7,000 for the sake of simplicity.
- *Line 15* shows the total tax for the quarter. Taxable wages are multiplied by the tax rate ($28,937.50 × 0.04 = $1,157.50).
- *Lines 16a* and *b* are a breakdown of the amount on Line 15. In Texas, part of the 4 percent tax is set aside for job training and other incentive programs. Box 4a contains the tax rate for the unemployment tax (3.9%). Box 4b contains the tax rate for training incentives or *Smart Jobs Assessment* (0.1%).
- *Lines 17* and *18* are blank. There are no penalties or interest because no taxes or reports are past due.
- *Line 19* is blank. There is no balance due from prior periods.
- *Line 20* shows the tax due.

TEXAS WORKFORCE COMMISSION
AUSTIN, TEXAS 78714-9037
(512)-463-2222

EMPLOYER'S QUARTERLY REPORT

11111

1. ACCOUNT NUMBER	2. COUNTY CODE	3. TAX AREA	4. TAX RATE	5. SIC CODE	6. FEDERAL I.D. NUMBER	7. QTR. YR.
12-9876500	121	2	4.0 %	59	75-1234567	1st/2010

8. EMPLOYER NAME AND ADDRESS (SEE ITEM 25 FOR CHANGES TO NAME, ADDRESS, ETC.)

9. TELEPHONE NUMBER

(972) 709-4567

Sarah Sanchez

Sanchez Furniture Company

5910 Lake June Road

Dallas, TX 75232-6017

4a. UI TAX RATE	4b. SMART JOBS ASSESSMENT
3.9 %	.1 %

☐☐☐ ALIGNMENT

9A. QUARTER ENDING

9B. PENALTIES WILL BE ASSESSED IF REPORT IS NOT POSTMARKED BY

1st Month	2nd Month	3rd Month
5	5	5

11. SHOW THE COUNTY CODE (see list on the back of this form) in which you had the greatest number of employees. **121**

12. IF you have employees in more than one county in TEXAS, how many are outside the county shown in Item 11?

10. Enter in the boxes above the number of employees both full-time and part-time, in pay periods that include 12th day of the calendar month. (ENTER NUMERALS ONLY)

	DOLLARS	CENTS
13. Total (Gross) Wages Paid During this Quarter to Texas Employees	29,217	50
14. Taxable Wages paid this quarter to each employee up to $7000, the annual maximum amount. (If none, enter "0")	28,937	50
15. Tax Due (Multiply Taxable Wages By Tax Rate, Item 4 Above)	1,157	50

You must FILE this return even though you had no payroll this quarter. If you had no payroll show '0' in item 13 and sign the declaration (Item 26) on this form.

14a. ☐ Mark box with an 'X' if reporting wages to another state during the year for employees listed in Item 22.

16a. UI TAX	1128	56
b. Smart Jobs Assessment	28	94
17. Interest, If Tax is Past Due		
18. Penalty, If Report Is Past Due		
19. Balance Due From Prior Periods (Subtract Credit Or Add Debit)		
20. Total Due - Make Remittance Payable To TEXAS WORKFORCE COMMISSION	1,157	50

FOR TWC USE ONLY

	MONTH	DAY	YEAR
POSTMARK DATE C3			
POSTMARK DATE $			
EX DATE C3			
EX DATE $			

☐ Est

DOLLARS	CENTS	INITIALS

AMOUNT RECEIVED

21. SOCIAL SECURITY NUMBER	1ST INIT	2ND INIT	22. EMPLOYEE NAME LAST NAME	23. TOTAL WAGES PAID THIS QUARTER	
1	587-XX-XXXX	C. Booker		6,240	00
2	427-XX-XXXX	G. Dunlap		5,557	50
3	687-XX-XXXX	A. Martinez		5,200	00
4	123-XX-XXXX	J. Rodriguez		4,940	00
5	587-XX-XXXX	C. Wu		7,280	00
6					
7					
8					
9					
10					

26. I DECLARE that the information herein is true and correct to the best of my knowledge and belief.

SIGNATURE *Sarah Sanchez*

TITLE *Owner* DATE *4/29/2010*

PREPARERS NAME *Sarah Sanchez*

PREPARERS PHONE NUMBER *(972) 709-4567*

For assistance in completing form call,

24. PAGE TOTAL	29,217	50

MAIL REPORT AND REMITTANCE TO:
CASHIER
TEXAS WORKFORCE COMMISSION
P.O. BOX 149037
AUSTIN, TEXAS 78714-9037

DO NOT STAPLE REPORT
(Write Account No. On Check)

FORM C - 3 (6/99)
SCANC3

25. MAKE CHANGES TO EMPLOYER INFORMATION USING C-3 **INSTRUCTION SHEET**. CHANGES NOTED ON THIS FORM MAY NOT BE CAPTURED DURING PROCESSING.

FIGURE 11.7 **Employer's Quarterly Report Form for State Unemployment Taxes**

Sanchez Furniture Company submits the report and issues a check payable to the state tax authority for the amount shown on Line 20. The entry is recorded in the cash payments journal. The transaction is shown here in general journal form for purposes of illustration.

GENERAL JOURNAL   PAGE _____

	DATE	DESCRIPTION	POST. REF.	DEBIT	CREDIT	
1	2010					1
2	Apr. 29	State Unemployment Tax Payable		1 1 5 7 50		2
3		Cash			1 1 5 7 50	3
4		Paid SUTA taxes for quarter				4
5		ending March 31				5
6						6

Earnings in Excess of Base Amount State unemployment tax is paid on the first $7,000 of annual earnings for each employee. Earnings over $7,000 are not subject to state unemployment tax.

For example, Cecilia Wu earns $560 every week of the year. Table 11.1 on page 365 shows that she earned $7,280 at the end of the first quarter. In the four weeks of January, February, and March she earned $2,240 ($560 × 4).

	Earnings	Cumulative Earnings
January	$2,240	$2,240
February	2,240	4,480
March	2,240	6,720
March, week 5	560	7,280

In the fifth week of March, Wu earned $560, but only $280 of it is subject to state unemployment tax ($7,000 earnings limit − $6,720 cumulative earnings = $280). For the rest of the calendar year, Wu's earnings are not subject to state unemployment tax.

REPORTING AND PAYING FEDERAL UNEMPLOYMENT TAXES

The rules for reporting and depositing federal unemployment taxes differ from those used for social security and Medicare taxes.

Depositing Federal Unemployment Taxes There are two ways to make federal unemployment tax deposits: with electronic deposits using EFTPS or with a Federal Tax Deposit Coupon, Form 8109, at an authorized financial institution. Deposits are made quarterly and are due on the last day of the month following the end of the quarter.

The federal unemployment tax is calculated at the end of each quarter. It is computed by multiplying the first $7,000 of each employee's wages by 0.008. A deposit is required when more than $100 of federal unemployment tax is owed. If $100 or less is owed, no deposit is due. The deposit requirement has changed to $500 for tax years after 2004. For simplicity, we use $100 in the text.

For example, suppose that a business calculates its federal unemployment tax to be $90 at the end of the first quarter. Since it is not more than $100, no deposit is due. At the end of the second quarter, it calculates its federal unemployment taxes on second quarter wages to be $70. The total undeposited unemployment tax now is more than $100, so a deposit is required.

First quarter undeposited tax	$ 90
Second quarter undeposited tax	70
Total deposit due	$160

In the case of Sanchez Furniture Company, the company owed $231.50 in federal unemployment tax at the end of March. Since this is more than $100, a deposit of $231.50 is due by April 30.

Month	Taxable Earnings Paid	Rate	Tax Due	Deposit Due Date
January	$ 8,990.00	0.008	$ 71.92	April 30
February	8,990.00	0.008	71.92	April 30
March	10,957.50	0.008	87.66	April 30
Total	$28,937.50		$231.50	

On April 30, Sanchez Furniture Company records the payment of federal unemployment tax in the cash payments journal. The transaction is shown here in general journal form for illustration purposes.

GENERAL JOURNAL PAGE _____

	DATE		DESCRIPTION	POST. REF.	DEBIT	CREDIT	
1	2010						1
8	Apr.	30	Federal Unemployment Tax Payable		2 3 1 50		8
9			Cash			2 3 1 50	9
10			Deposit FUTA due				10
11							11

>>7. OBJECTIVE

Prepare an Employer's Federal Unemployment Tax Return, Form 940 or 940-EZ.

LP11

Reporting Federal Unemployment Tax, Form 940 or 940-EZ Tax returns are not due quarterly for the federal unemployment tax. The employer submits an annual return. The **Employer's Annual Federal Unemployment Tax Return, Form 940 or 940-EZ,** is a preprinted government form used to report unemployment taxes for the calendar year. It is due by January 31 of the following year. The due date is extended to February 10 if all tax deposits were made on time. Instead of using Form 940, businesses can use Form 940-EZ if

- they paid unemployment tax to only one state,
- they paid all federal unemployment taxes by January 31 of the following year,
- all wages that were taxable for federal unemployment were also taxable for state unemployment.

Sanchez Furniture Company prepares Form 940-EZ. The information needed to complete Form 940-EZ comes from the annual summary of individual earnings records and from the state unemployment tax returns filed during the year.

Figure 11.8 on page 377 shows Form 940-EZ prepared for Sanchez Furniture Company. Refer to it as you learn how to complete Form 940-EZ.

- *Line A* shows the total state unemployment tax paid. All five employees of Sanchez Furniture Company reached the earnings limit during the year. Wages subject to state unemployment tax are $35,000 ($7,000 × 5 employees). The state rate is 4 percent. Sanchez Furniture Company paid state unemployment tax of $1,400 ($35,000 × 0.04).

Form **940-EZ**	Employer's Annual Federal Unemployment (FUTA) Tax Return	OMB No. 1545-1110
Department of the Treasury Internal Revenue Service	▶ See the separate Instructions for Form 940-EZ for information on completing this form.	20**10**

			T	
	Name (as distinguished from trade name)	Calendar year	FF	
You must complete this section. ▶	Sarah Sanchez	**2010**	FD	
	Trade name, if any	Employer identification number (EIN)	FP	
	Sanchez Furniture Company	**75-1234567**	I	
	Address (number and street)	City, state, and ZIP code	T	
	5910 Lake June Road	**Dallas, TX 75232-6017**		

Answer the questions under Who May Use Form 940-EZ on page 2. If you cannot use Form 940-EZ, you must use Form 940.

A   Enter the amount of contributions paid to your state unemployment fund (see the separate instructions) . . ▶ $ .... **1,400** | **00**

B   (1) Enter the name of the state where you have to pay contributions . . . . ▶ **TX**
        (2) Enter your state reporting number as shown on your state unemployment tax return ▶   **12-9876500**

If you will not have to file returns in the future, check here (see **Who Must File** in separate instructions) **and complete and sign the return.** ▶ ☐

If this is an Amended Return, check here (see **Amended Returns** in the separate instructions) . . . . ▶ ☐

Part I   Taxable Wages and FUTA Tax

1	Total payments (including payments shown on lines 2 and 3) during the calendar year for services of employees	**1**	**116,870**	**00**
2	Exempt payments. (Explain all exempt payments, attaching additional sheets if necessary.) ▶	**2**		
3	Payments of more than $7,000 for services. Enter only amounts over the first $7,000 paid to each employee **(see the separate instructions)**	**3** **81,870** **00**		
4	Add lines 2 and 3	**4**	**81,870**	**00**
5	**Total taxable wages** (subtract line 4 from line 1) . . . . ▶	**5**	**35,000**	**00**
6	**FUTA tax.** Multiply the wages on line 5 by .008 and enter here. **(If the result is over $100, also complete Part II.)**	**6**	**280**	**00**
7	Total FUTA tax deposited for the year, including any overpayment applied from a prior year	**7**	**280**	**00**
8	**Balance due** (subtract line 7 from line 6). Pay to the "United States Treasury." . . . . . . ▶	**8**	**0**	
	If you owe more than $100, see **Depositing FUTA tax** in the separate instructions.			
9	**Overpayment** (subtract line 6 from line 7). Check if it is to be: ☐ **Applied to next return** or ☐ **Refunded** ▶	**9**		

Part II   Record of Quarterly Federal Unemployment Tax Liability (Do not include state liability.) **Complete only if line 6 is over $100.**

Quarter	First (Jan. 1 – Mar. 31)	Second (Apr. 1 – June 30)	Third (July 1 – Sept. 30)	Fourth (Oct. 1 – Dec. 31)	Total for year
Liability for quarter	**231.50**	**48.50**			**280.00**

Third–Party Designee	Do you want to allow another person to discuss this return with the IRS (see the separate instructions)? ☐ **Yes.** Complete the following. ☑ **No**		
	Designee's name ▶	Phone no. ▶ ( )	Personal identification number (PIN) ▶

Under penalties of perjury, I declare that I have examined this return, including accompanying schedules and statements, and, to the best of my knowledge and belief, it is true, correct, and complete, and that no part of any payment made to a state unemployment fund claimed as a credit was, or is to be, deducted from the payments to employees.

Signature ▶ *Sarah Sanchez*   Title (Owner, etc.) ▶ **Owner**   Date ▶ *January 31, 2011*

For Privacy Act and Paperwork Reduction Act Notice, see the separate instructions. ▼ **DETACH HERE** ▼   Cat. No. 10983G   Form **940-EZ**

Form **940-V(EZ)**	**Payment Voucher**	OMB No. 1545-1110
Department of the Treasury Internal Revenue Service	**Use this voucher only when making a payment with your return.**	20**10**

Complete boxes 1, 2, and 3. Do not send cash, and do not staple your payment to this voucher. Make your check or money order payable to the "United States Treasury." Be sure to enter your employer identification number (EIN), "Form 940-EZ," and "2004" on your payment.

1 Enter your employer identification number (EIN).	2		Dollars	Cents
	Enter the amount of your payment. ▶			
	3 Enter your business name (individual name for sole proprietors).			
	Enter your address.			
	Enter your city, state, and ZIP code.			

FIGURE 11.8   Employer's Annual Federal Unemployment Tax Return, Form 940-EZ

PART I: Taxable Wages and FUTA Tax

- *Line 1* shows the total compensation paid to employees, $116,870.00.

- *Line 2* is blank because there were no exempt payments for Sanchez Furniture Company.

- *Line 3* shows the compensation that exceeds the $7,000 earnings limit, $81,870 ($116,870 − $35,000).

- *Line 4* shows the wages not subject to federal unemployment tax, $81,870.

- *Line 5* shows the taxable wages for the year, $35,000. This amount must agree with the total taxable FUTA wages shown on the individual employee earnings records for the year.

- *Line 6* shows the FUTA tax, $280 ($35,000 × 0.008).

- *Line 7* shows the FUTA tax deposited during the year, $280.

- *Line 8* shows the balance due. Sanchez Furniture Company deposited $280, so there is no balance due.

- *Line 9* is blank because there is no overpayment.

PART II: Record of Quarterly Federal Unemployment Tax Liability shows the FUTA tax due for each quarter. The total for the year must equal Line 6.

>>8. OBJECTIVE

Compute and record workers' compensation insurance premiums.

LP11

WORKERS' COMPENSATION INSURANCE

Workers' compensation provides benefits for employees who are injured on the job. The insurance premium, which is paid by the employer, depends on the risk involved with the work performed. It is important to classify earnings according to the type of work the employees perform and to summarize labor costs according to the insurance premium classifications.

There are two ways to handle workers' compensation insurance. The method a business uses depends on the number of its employees.

Estimated Annual Premium in Advance. Employers who have few employees pay an estimated premium in advance. At the end of the year, the employer calculates the actual premium. If the actual premium is more than the estimated premium paid, the employer pays the balance due. If the actual premium is less than the estimated premium paid, the employer receives a refund.

Sanchez Furniture Company has two work classifications: office work and shipping work. The workers' compensation premium rates are

Office workers	$0.45 per $100 of labor costs
Shipping workers	1.25 per $100 of labor costs

The insurance premium rates recognize that injuries are more likely to occur to shipping workers than to office workers. Based on employee earnings for the previous year, Sanchez Furniture Company paid an estimated premium of $1,000 for the new year. The payment was made on January 15.

			GENERAL JOURNAL				PAGE _____		
	DATE		DESCRIPTION	POST. REF.	DEBIT		CREDIT		
1	2010								1
14	Jan.	15	Workers' Compensation Insurance Expense		1 000 00				14
15			Cash				1 000 00		15
16			Estimated workers' compensation						16
17			insurance for 2007						17
18									18

At the end of the year, the actual premium was computed, $1,261.20. The actual premium was computed by applying the proper rates to the payroll data for the year:

- The office wages were $24,960.

  ($24,960 ÷ $100)   × $0.45   =

         249.60   × $0.45   = $ 112.32

- The shipping wages were $91,910.

  ($91,910 ÷ $100)   × $1.25   =

         919.1   × $1.25   = $1,148.88

- Total premium for year   = $1,261.20

Classification	Payroll	Rate	Premium
Office work	$24,960	$0.45 per $100	$ 112.32
Shipping work	91,910	1.25 per $100	1,148.88
Total premium for year			$1,261.20
Less estimated premium paid			1,000.00
Balance of premium due			$ 261.20

On December 31, the balance due to the insurance company is recorded as a liability by an adjusting entry. Sanchez Furniture Company owes $261.20 ($1,261.20 − $1,000.00) for the workers' compensation insurance.

GENERAL JOURNAL   PAGE _____

	DATE		DESCRIPTION	POST. REF.	DEBIT	CREDIT	
1	2010						1
2	Dec.	31	Workers' Compensation Insurance Expense		2 6 1 20		2
3			Workers' Compensation Insurance Payable			2 6 1 20	3
4							4

MANAGERIAL IMPLICATIONS

PAYROLL TAXES

- Management must ensure that payroll taxes are computed properly and paid on time.

- In order to avoid penalties, it is essential that a business prepares its payroll tax returns accurately and files the returns and required forms promptly.

- The payroll system should ensure that payroll reports are prepared in an efficient manner.

- Managers need to be familiar with all payroll taxes and how they impact operating expenses.

- Managers must be knowledgeable about unemployment tax regulations in their state because favorable experience ratings can reduce unemployment tax expense.

- Management is responsible for developing effective internal control procedures over payroll operations and ensuring that they are followed.

THINKING CRITICALLY

What accounting records are used to prepare Form 941?

Suppose that on January 15 Sanchez Furniture Company had paid an estimated premium of $1,400 instead of $1,000. The actual premium at the end of the year was $1,261.20. Sanchez Furniture Company would be due a refund from the insurance company for the amount overpaid, $138.80 ($1,400.00 − $1,261.20).

THE BOTTOM LINE

Workers' Compensation Refund Receivable

Income Statement

Expenses	↓ 138.80
Net Income	↑ 138.80

Balance Sheet

Assets	↑138.80
Equity	↑138.80

> > **Deposit and Monthly Premium Payments** Employers with many employees use a different method to handle workers' compensation insurance. At the beginning of the year, they make large deposits, often 25 percent of the estimated annual premium. From January through November, they pay the actual premium due based on an audit of the month's wages. The premium for the last month is deducted from the deposit. Any balance is refunded or applied toward the following year's deposit.

Internal Control over Payroll Operations

Now that we have examined the basic accounting procedures used for payrolls and payroll taxes, let's look at some internal control procedures that are recommended to protect payroll operations.

1. Assign only highly responsible, well-trained employees to work in payroll operations.
2. Keep payroll records in locked files. Train payroll employees to maintain confidentiality about pay rates and other information in the payroll records.
3. Add new employees to the payroll system and make all changes in employee pay rates only with proper written authorization from management.
4. Make changes to an employee's withholding allowances based only on a Form W-4 properly completed and signed by the employee.
5. Make voluntary deductions from employee earnings based only on a signed authorization from the employee.
6. Have the payroll checks examined by someone other than the person who prepares them. Compare each check to the entry for the employee in the payroll register.
7. Have payroll checks distributed to the employees by someone other than the person who prepares them.
8. Have the monthly payroll bank account statement received and reconciled by someone other than the person who prepares the payroll checks.
9. Use prenumbered forms for the payroll checks. Periodically the numbers of the checks issued and the numbers of the unused checks should be verified to make sure that all checks can be accounted for.
10. Maintain files of all authorization forms for adding new employees, changing pay rates, and making voluntary deductions. Also retain all Forms W-4.

Section 2 Self Review

QUESTIONS

1. Why is it important for workers' compensation wages to be classified according to the type of work performed?
2. Who pays the federal unemployment tax? The state unemployment tax?
3. How does a favorable experience rating affect the state unemployment tax rate?

EXERCISES

4. The federal unemployment taxes are reported on
   a. Form 941.
   b. Form 8109.
   c. Form W-3.
   d. Form 940.
5. State unemployment taxes are filed
   a. monthly.
   b. quarterly.
   c. yearly.
   d. at the end of each pay period.

ANALYSIS

6. At the end of the year, the business has a balance due for workers' compensation insurance. If no adjusting entry is made, will the amount of net income reported be correct? If not, how will it be wrong?

(Answers to Section 2 Self Review are on page 393.)

REVIEW   Chapter Summary

Chapter **11**

Employers must pay social security, SUTA, FUTA, and Medicare taxes. They must also collect federal and state taxes from their employees and then remit those taxes to the appropriate taxing authorities. In this chapter, you have learned how to compute the employer's taxes and how to file the required tax returns and reports.

Learning Objectives

1 Explain how and when payroll taxes are paid to the government.

Employers act as collection agents for social security, Medicare, and federal income taxes withheld from employee earnings. Employers must remit these sums, with their own share of social security and Medicare taxes, to the government. The taxes must be deposited in an authorized depository, usually a commercial bank. The methods and schedules for deposits vary according to the sums involved.

2 Compute and record the employer's social security and Medicare taxes.

Employers should multiply the social security and Medicare tax rates by taxable wages to compute the employer's portion of taxes due.

3 Record deposit of social security, Medicare, and employee income taxes.

As taxes are paid to the government, the accounting records should be updated to reflect the payment, thereby reducing tax liability accounts.

4 Prepare an Employer's Quarterly Federal Tax Return, Form 941.

The Form 941 reports wages paid, federal employee income tax withheld, and applicable social security and Medicare taxes.

5 Prepare Wage and Tax Statement (Form W-2) and Annual Transmittal of Wage and Tax Statements (Form W-3).

By the end of January, each employee must be given a Wage and Tax Statement, Form W-2, showing the previous year's earnings and withholdings for social security, Medicare, and employee income tax. The employer files a Transmittal of Wage and Tax Statements, Form W-3, with copies of employees' Forms W-2. Form W-3 is due by the last day of February following the end of the calendar year.

6 Compute and record liability for federal and state unemployment taxes and record payment of the taxes.

Unemployment insurance taxes are paid by the employer to both state and federal governments. State unemployment tax returns differ from state to state but usually require a list of employees, their social security numbers, and taxable wages paid. The rate of state unemployment tax depends on the employer's experience rating. The net federal unemployment tax rate can be as low as 0.8 percent.

7 Prepare an Employer's Federal Unemployment Tax Return, Form 940 or 940-EZ.

An Employer's Annual Federal Unemployment Tax Return, Form 940 or 940-EZ, must be filed in January for the preceding calendar year. The form shows the total wages paid, the amount of wages subject to unemployment tax, and the federal unemployment tax owed for the year. A credit is allowed against gross federal tax for unemployment tax charged under state plans, up to 5.4 percent of wages subject to the federal tax.

8 Compute and record workers' compensation insurance premiums.

By state law, employers might be required to carry workers' compensation insurance. For companies with a few employees, an estimated premium is paid at the start of the year. A final settlement is made with the insurance company on the basis of an audit of the payroll after the end of the year. Premiums vary according to the type of work performed by each employee. Other premium payment plans can be used for larger employers.

9 Define the accounting terms new to this chapter.

Glossary

Employer's Annual Federal Unemployment Tax Return, Form 940 (p. 376) Preprinted government form used by the employer to report unemployment taxes for the calendar year

Employer's Annual Federal Unemployment Tax Return, Form 940-EZ (p. 376) See Employer's Annual Federal Unemployment Tax Return, Form 940

Employer's Quarterly Federal Tax Return, Form 941 (p. 364) Preprinted government form used by the employer to report payroll tax information relating to social security, Medicare, and employee income tax withholding to the Internal Revenue Service

Experience rating system (p. 372) A system that rewards an employer for maintaining steady employment conditions by reducing the firm's state unemployment tax rate

Merit rating system (p. 372) See Experience rating system

Transmittal of Wage and Tax Statements, Form W-3 (p. 369) Preprinted government form submitted with Forms W-2 to the Social Security Administration

Unemployment insurance program (p. 372) A program that provides unemployment compensation through a tax levied on employers

Wage and Tax Statement, Form W-2 (p. 369) Preprinted government form that contains information about an employee's earnings and tax withholdings for the year

Withholding statement (p. 369) See Wage and Tax Statement, Form W-2

Comprehensive **Self Review**

1. What is Form W-3?

2. Is the ceiling on earnings subject to unemployment taxes larger than or smaller than the ceiling on earnings subject to the social security tax?

3. How do the FUTA and SUTA taxes relate to each other?

4. Under the monthly deposit schedule rule, when must deposits for employee income tax and other withheld taxes be made?

5. Which of the following factors determine the frequency of deposits of social security, Medicare, and income tax withholdings?

    a. Experience rating.

    b. Amount of taxes reported in the lookback period.

    c. Company's net income.

    d. Amount of taxes currently owed.

    e. How often employees are paid.

(Answers to Comprehensive Self Review are on page 394.)

 Multiple choice questions are provided on the text Web site at www.mhhe.com/price12e

Quiz11

Discussion Questions

1. Which of the following are withheld from employees' earnings?

    a. FUTA

    b. income tax

    c. Medicare

    d. social security

    e. SUTA

    f. workers' compensation

2. What does "monthly" refer to in the Monthly Deposit Schedule Rule?

3. What does "semiweekly" refer to in the Semiweekly Deposit Schedule Rule?

4. What is EFTPS? When is EFTPS required?

5. When is the use of Form 8109-B permitted?

6. What is a business tax identification number?

7. What are the four taxes levied on employers?

8. What is the lookback period?

9. What is the purpose of Form W-3? When must it be issued? To whom is it sent?

10. When must Form W-2 be issued? To whom is it sent?

11. What happens if the employer fails to deduct enough employee income tax or FICA tax from employee earnings?

12. What government form is prepared to accompany deposits of federal taxes?

13. How can an employer keep informed about changes in the rates and bases for the social security, Medicare, and FUTA taxes?

14. When is the premium for workers' compensation insurance usually paid?

15. Who pays for workers' compensation insurance?

16. What is Form 941? How often is the form filed?

17. Is the employer required to deposit the federal unemployment tax during the year? Explain.

18. A state charges a basic SUTA tax rate of 5.4 percent. Because of an excellent experience rating, an employer in the state has to pay only 1.0 percent of the taxable payroll as state tax. What is the percentage to be used in computing the credit against the federal unemployment tax?

19. What is the purpose of Form 940? How often is it filed?

20. What is the purpose of allowing a credit against the FUTA for state unemployment taxes?

21. Why was the unemployment insurance system established?

APPLICATIONS

Exercises HM™

Depositing payroll taxes.

◄ **Exercise 11.1**
Objective 1

The amounts of employee income tax withheld and social security and Medicare taxes (both employee and employer shares) shown below were owed by different businesses on the specified dates. In each case, decide whether the firm is required to deposit the sum in an authorized financial institution. If a deposit is necessary, give the date by which it should be made. The employers are monthly depositors.

1. Total taxes of $550 owed on July 31, 2010.

2. Total taxes of $1,650 owed on April 30, 2010.

3. Total taxes of $1,200 owed on March 31, 2010.

4. Total taxes of $8,750 owed on February 28, 2010.

Recording deposit of social security, Medicare, and income taxes.

◄ **Exercise 11.2**
Objective 3

After Hennessey Corporation paid its employees on July 15, 2010, and recorded the corporation's share of payroll taxes for the payroll paid that date, the firm's general ledger showed a balance of $20,160 in the *Social Security Tax Payable* account, a balance of $4,725 in the *Medicare Tax Payable* account, and a balance of $18,360 in the *Employee Income Tax Payable* account. On July 16, the business issued a check to deposit the taxes owed in the First Texas Bank. Record this transaction in general journal form.

Computing employer's payroll taxes.

◄ **Exercise 11.3**
Objectives 2, 6

At the end of the weekly payroll period on June 30, 2010, the payroll register of Seymore Professional Consultants Company showed employee earnings of $71,200. Determine the firm's payroll taxes for the period. Use a social security rate of 6.2 percent, Medicare rate of 1.45 percent, FUTA rate of 0.8 percent, and SUTA rate of 5.4 percent. Consider all earnings subject to social security tax and Medicare tax and $39,000 subject to FUTA and SUTA taxes.

Exercise 11.4 ▶ **Depositing federal unemployment tax.**

Objective 6

On March 31, 2010, the *Federal Unemployment Tax Payable* account in the general ledger of The Chapman Company showed a balance of $1,146. This represents the FUTA tax owed for the first quarter of the year. On April 30, 2010, the firm issued a check to deposit the amount owed in the First Security National Bank. Record this transaction in general journal form.

Exercise 11.5 ▶ **Computing SUTA tax.**

Objective 6

On April 30, 2010, Wang Furniture Company prepared its state unemployment tax return for the first quarter of the year. The firm had taxable wages of $100,600. Because of a favorable experience rating, Wang pays SUTA tax at a rate of 1.7 percent. How much SUTA tax did the firm owe for the quarter?

Exercise 11.6 ▶ **Paying SUTA tax.**

Objective 6

On June 30, 2010, the *State Unemployment Tax Payable* account in the general ledger of Allen Party Supplies showed a balance of $3,547. This represents the SUTA tax owed for the second quarter of the year. On July 31, 2010, the business issued a check to the state unemployment insurance fund for the amount due. Record this payment in general journal form.

Exercise 11.7 ▶ **Computing FUTA tax.**

Objective 6

On January 31, Girardi Accountancy Corp. prepared its Employer's Annual Federal Unemployment Tax Return, Form 940. During the previous year, the business paid total wages of $396,100 to its nineteen employees. Of this amount, $128,502 was subject to FUTA tax. Using a rate of 0.8 percent, determine the FUTA tax owed and the balance due on January 31, 2010, when Form 940 was filed. A deposit of $700 was made during the year.

Exercise 11.8 ▶ **Computing workers' compensation insurance premiums.**

Objective 8

Canzano Medical Supplies Company estimates that its office employees will earn $160,000 next year and its factory employees will earn $950,000. The firm pays the following rates for workers' compensation insurance: $0.37 per $100 of wages for the office employees and $8.71 per $100 of wages for the factory employees. Determine the estimated premium for each group of employees and the total estimated premium for next year.

PROBLEMS

Problem Set A

Problem 11.1A ▶ **Computing and recording employer's payroll tax expense.**

Objectives 2, 6

The payroll register of Quality Lawn Care showed total employee earnings of $2,800 for the payroll period ended June 14, 2010.

eXcel

INSTRUCTIONS

1. Compute the employer's payroll taxes for the period. Use rates of 6.2 percent for the employer's share of the social security tax, 1.45 percent for Medicare tax, 0.8 percent for FUTA tax, and 5.4 percent for SUTA tax. All earnings are taxable.

2. Prepare a general journal entry to record the employer's payroll taxes for the period.

Analyze: Which of the above taxes are paid by the employee and matched by the employer?

Problem 11.2A ▶ **Computing employer's social security tax, Medicare tax, and unemployment taxes.**

Objectives 2, 3

A payroll summary for Mike Turner, who owns and operates Turner Consulting Company, for the quarter ending June 30, 2010, appears on page 385. The firm prepared the required tax deposit forms and issued checks as follows.

a. Federal Tax Deposit Coupon, Form 8109, check for April taxes, paid on May 15.

b. Federal Tax Deposit Coupon, Form 8109, check for May taxes, paid on June 17.

Date Wages Paid	Total Earnings	Social Security Tax Deducted	Medicare Tax Deducted	Income Tax Withheld
April 8	$ 2,332.00	$ 144.58	$ 33.81	$ 231.00
15	2,420.00	150.04	35.09	238.00
22	2,332.00	144.58	33.81	231.00
29	2,376.00	147.31	34.45	235.00
	$ 9,460.00	$ 586.51	$137.16	$ 935.00
May 5	$ 2,288.00	$ 141.86	$ 33.18	227.00
12	2,332.00	144.58	33.81	231.00
19	2,332.00	144.58	33.81	231.00
26	2,376.00	147.31	34.45	235.00
	$ 9,328.00	$ 578.33	$135.25	$ 924.00
June 2	$ 2,420.00	$ 150.04	$ 35.09	$ 238.00
9	2,332.00	144.58	33.81	231.00
16	2,376.00	147.31	34.45	235.00
23	2,332.00	144.58	33.81	231.00
30	2,288.00	141.86	33.18	227.00
	$11,748.00	$ 728.37	$170.34	$1,162.00
Total	$30,536.00	$1,893.21	$442.75	$3,021.00

INSTRUCTIONS

1. Using the tax rates given below, and assuming that all earnings are taxable, make the general journal entry on April 8, 2010, to record the employer's payroll tax expense on the payroll ending that date.

Social security	6.2	percent
Medicare	1.45	
FUTA	0.8	
SUTA	5.4	

2. Prepare the entries in general journal form to record deposit of the employee income tax withheld and the social security and Medicare taxes (employee and employer shares) on May 15 for April taxes and on June 17 for May taxes.

Analyze: How were the amounts for *Income Tax Withheld* determined?

This is a continuation of Problem 11.2A for Turner Consulting Company; recording payment of taxes and preparing employer's quarterly federal tax return.

CONTINUING >>>
Problem
◀ Problem 11.3A
Objectives 4, 6

1. On July 15, the firm issued a check to deposit the federal income tax withheld and the FICA tax (both employee and employer shares for the third month [June]). Based on your computations in Problem 11.2A, record the issuance of the check in general journal form.

2. Complete Form 941 in accordance with the discussions in this chapter. Use a 12.4 percent social security rate and a 2.9 percent Medicare rate in computations. Use the following address for the company: 3750 Belt Line Parkway, Dallas, TX 76539-6205. Use 75-4444444 as the employer identification number. Date the return July 31, 2010. Mr. Turner's phone number is 972-709-3654.

Analyze: Based on the entries that you have recorded, what is the balance of the *Employee Income Tax Payable* account at July 15?

Problem 11.4A ▶
Objectives 6, 7

Computing and recording unemployment taxes; completing Form 940.

Certain transactions and procedures relating to federal and state unemployment taxes follow for The Style Shop, a retail store owned by Mary Amos. The firm's address is 2007 Trendsetter Lane, Dallas, TX 75268-0967. The employer's federal and state identification numbers are 75-9462315 and 37-9462315, respectively. Carry out the procedures as instructed in each of the following steps.

INSTRUCTIONS

1. Compute the state unemployment insurance tax owed on the employees' wages for the quarter ended March 31, 2010. This information will be shown on the employer's quarterly report to the state agency that collects SUTA tax. The employer has recorded the tax on each payroll date. Although the state charges a 5.4 percent unemployment tax rate, The Style Shop's rate is only 1.7 percent because of its experience rating. The employee earnings for the first quarter are shown below. All earnings are subject to SUTA tax.

Name of Employee	Total Earnings
Terri Wells	$ 5,810
Jelencia Guyton	3,775
Gloria Harris	4,098
Stacee Fairley	5,270
Anita Thomas	4,000
Jeraldine Wells	2,910
Total	$25,863

2. On April 30, 2010, the firm issued a check to the state employment commission for the amount computed above. In general journal form, record the issuance of the check.

Analyze: Why is the business experience rating important with regard to the state unemployment tax rate?

Problem 11.5A ▶
Objectives 6, 7

Problem

This is a continuation of Problem 11.4A for The Style Shop; computing and recording unemployment taxes; completing Form 940.

1. Complete Form 940-EZ, the Employer's Annual Federal Unemployment Tax Return. Assume that all wages have been paid and that all quarterly payments have been submitted to the state as required. The payroll information for 2010 appears below. The required federal tax deposit forms and checks were submitted as follows: a deposit of $206.90 on April 21, a deposit of $198.72 on July 22, and a deposit of $74.64 on October 21. Date the unemployment tax return January 28, 2011. A check for the balance due will be sent with Form 940.

Quarter Ended	Total Wages Paid	Wages Paid in Excess of $7,000	State Unemployment Tax Paid
Mar. 31	$ 25,863.00	–0–	$ 439.67
June 30	28,915.00	$ 4,075.00	422.28
Sept. 30	29,880.00	20,550.00	158.61
Dec. 31	31,350.00	28,910.00	41.48
Totals	$116,008.00	$53,535.00	$1,062.04

2. In general journal form, record issuance of a check on January 28, 2011, for the balance of FUTA tax due for 2010.

Analyze: What total debits were made to liability accounts for entries you recorded in Problem 11.4A and Problem 11.5A?

Computing and recording workers' compensation insurance premiums.

◀ **Problem 11.6A**
Objective 8

e**X**cel

The following information relates to Pondexter Manufacturing Company's workers' compensation insurance premiums for 2010. On January 15, 2011, the company estimated its premium for workers' compensation insurance for the year on the basis of that data.

Work Classification	Amount of Estimated Wages	Insurance Rates
Office work	$ 68,000	$0.40/$100
Shop work	315,000	$5.00/$100

INSTRUCTIONS

1. Compute the estimated premiums.
2. Record in general journal form payment of the estimated premium on January 15, 2010.
3. On January 4, 2011, an audit of the firm's payroll records showed that it had actually paid wages of $72,000 to its office employees and wages of $319,000 to its shop employees. Compute the actual premium for the year and the balance due the insurance company or the credit due the firm.
4. Prepare the general journal entry to adjust the *Workers' Compensation Insurance Expense* account as of the end of 2010. Date the entry December 31, 2010.

Analyze: If all wages were attributable to shop employees, what premium estimate would have been calculated and recorded on January 15, 2010?

Problem Set B

Computing and recording employer's payroll tax expense.

◀ **Problem 11.1B**
Objectives 2, 6

The payroll register of Clifton's Automotive and Detail Repair Shop showed total employee earnings of $2,890 for the week ended April 8, 2010.

INSTRUCTIONS

1. Compute the employer's payroll taxes for the period. The tax rates are as follows:

Social security	6.2 percent
Medicare	1.45
FUTA	0.8
SUTA	2.2

2. Prepare a general journal entry to record the employer's payroll taxes for the period.

Analyze: If the FUTA tax rate had been 1.2 percent, what total employer payroll taxes would have been recorded?

Computing employer's social security tax, Medicare tax, and unemployment taxes.

◀ **Problem 11.2B**
Objectives 2, 3

A payroll summary for Carolyn Wells, who owns and operates The Fashion Shop, for the quarter ending September 30, 2010, appears below. The business prepared the tax deposit forms and issued checks as follows during the quarter.

a. Federal Tax Deposit Coupon, Form 8109, check for July taxes, paid on August 15.
b. Federal Tax Deposit Coupon, Form 8109, check for August taxes, paid on September 15.

Date Wages Paid	Total Earnings	Social Security Tax Withheld	Medicare Tax Withheld	Income Tax Withheld
July 7	$ 1,980.00	$ 122.76	$ 28.71	$ 192.50
14	1,980.00	122.76	28.71	192.50
21	2,310.00	143.22	33.50	225.50
28	1,980.00	122.76	28.71	192.50
	$ 8,250.00	$ 511.50	$119.63	$ 803.00
Aug. 4	$ 2,310.00	$ 143.22	$ 33.50	225.50
11	2,970.00	184.14	43.07	291.50
18	2,970.00	184.14	43.07	291.50
25	2,640.00	163.68	38.28	258.50
	$10,890.00	$ 675.18	$157.92	$1,067.00
Sept. 2	$ 1,980.00	$ 122.76	$ 28.71	$ 192.50
9	2,310.00	143.22	33.50	225.50
16	2,310.00	143.22	33.50	225.50
23	2,310.00	143.22	33.50	225.50
30	1,980.00	122.76	28.71	192.50
	$10,890.00	$ 675.18	$157.92	$1,061.50
Total	$30,030.00	$1,861.86	$435.47	$2,931.50

INSTRUCTIONS

1. Prepare the general journal entry on July 7, 2010, to record the employer's payroll tax expense on the payroll ending that date. All earnings are subject to the following taxes:

Social security	6.2	percent
Medicare	1.45	
FUTA	0.8	
SUTA	2.2	

2. Make the entries in general journal form to record deposit of the employee income tax withheld and the social security and Medicare taxes (both employees' withholding and employer's matching portion) on August 15 for July taxes and on September 15 for the August taxes.

Analyze: How much would a SUTA rate of 1.5 reduce the tax for the payroll of July 7?

Problem 11.3B
Objectives 4, 6
CONTINUING >>>
Problem

This is a continuation of Problem 11.2B for The Fashion Shop; recording payment of taxes and preparing employer's quarterly federal tax return.

1. On October 15, the firm issued a check to deposit the federal income tax withheld and the FICA tax (both employees' withholding and employer's matching portion). Based on your computations in Problem 11.2B, record the issuance of the check in general journal form.

2. Complete Form 941 in accordance with the discussions in this chapter and the instructions on the form. Use a 12.4 percent social security rate and a 2.9 percent Medicare rate in computations. Use the following address for the company: 2008 Trendsetter Lane, Dallas, TX 75268-0967. Use 75-5555555 as the employer identification number. Date the return October 31, 2010.

Analyze: What total taxes were deposited with the IRS for the quarter ended September 30, 2010?

Computing and recording unemployment taxes; completing Form 940.

◀ **Problem 11.4B**
Objectives 6, 7

Certain transactions and procedures relating to federal and state unemployment taxes are given below for The Hobby Shop, a retail store owned by Helen Franz. The firm's address is 4560 LBJ Freeway, Dallas, TX 75232-6002. The employer's federal and state identification numbers are 75-9999999 and 37-6789015, respectively. Carry out the procedures as instructed in each step.

INSTRUCTIONS

1. Compute the state unemployment insurance tax owed for the quarter ended March 31, 2010. This information will be shown on the employer's quarterly report to the state agency that collects SUTA tax. The employer has recorded the tax expense and liability on each payroll date. Although the state charges a 5.4 percent unemployment tax rate, The Hobby Shop has received a favorable experience rating and therefore pays only a 2.3 percent state tax rate. The employee earnings for the first quarter are given below. All earnings are subject to SUTA tax.

Name of Employee	Total Earnings
Amy Booker	$ 3,880
Stanley Carpenter	3,650
Alicia Cantu	3,225
Robert Dragon	3,780
Patricia Ellis	2,890
John Williams	2,910
Total	$20,335

2. On April 30, 2010, the firm issued a check for the amount computed above. Record the transaction in general journal form.

Analyze: If all employees made the same amount for the quarter ended June 30, 2010, how much would be subject to the federal unemployment tax?

This is a continuation of Problem 11.4B for The Hobby Shop; computing and recording unemployment taxes; completing Form 940.

◀ **Problem 11.5B**
Objectives 6, 7

CONTINUING >>>
Problem

1. Complete Form 940-EZ, the Employer's Annual Federal Unemployment Tax Return. Assume that all wages have been paid and that all quarterly payments have been submitted to the state as required. The payroll information for 2010 appears below. The required federal tax deposit forms and checks were submitted as follows: a deposit of $162.68 on April 12, a deposit of $170.00 on July 14, and a deposit of $102.00 on October 12. Date the unemployment tax return January 27, 2011. A check for the balance due will be sent with Form 940.

Quarter Ended	Total Wages Paid	Wages Paid in Excess of $7,000	State Unemployment Tax Paid
Mar. 31	$20,335.00	–0–	$ 467.71
June 30	21,250.00	–0–	488.75
Sept. 30	22,050.00	$ 9,300.00	293.25
Dec. 31	24,800.00	20,250.00	104.65
Totals	$88,435.00	$29,550.00	$1,354.36

2. On January 27, 2011, the firm issued a check for the amount shown on line 8, Part I of form 940-EZ. In general journal form, record issuance of a check.

Analyze: What is the balance of the *Federal Unemployment Tax Payable* account on January 27, 2011?

Problem 11.6B ▶
Objectives 8

Computing and recording premiums on workers' compensation insurance.

The following information is for Union Express Delivery Service workers' compensation insurance premiums. On January 15, 2010, the company estimated its premium for workers' compensation insurance for the year on the basis of the following data.

Work Classification	Amount of Estimated Wages	Insurance Rates
Office work	$ 48,000	$0.40/$100
Delivery work	280,000	$5.00/$100

INSTRUCTIONS

1. Use the information to compute the estimated premium for the year.

2. A check was issued to pay the estimated premium on January 17, 2010. Record the transaction in general journal form.

3. On January 19, 2011, an audit of the firm's payroll records showed that it had actually paid wages of $55,450 to its office employees and wages of $286,220 to its delivery employees. Compute the actual premium for the year and the balance due the insurance company or the credit due the firm.

4. Give the general journal entry to adjust the *Workers' Compensation Insurance Expense* account. Date the entry December 31, 2010.

Analyze: What is the balance of the *Workers' Compensation Insurance Expense* account at December 31, 2010, after all journal entries have been posted?

Critical Thinking Problem 11.1

Determining Employee Status

In each of the following independent situations, decide whether the business organization should treat the person being paid as an employee and should withhold social security, Medicare, and employee income taxes from the payment made.

1. After working several years as an editor for a magazine publisher, Leora quit her job to stay at home with her two small children. Later the publisher asked her to work in her home performing editorial work as needed. Leora is paid an hourly fee for the work she performs. In some cases, she goes to the publishing company's offices to pick up or return a manuscript. In other cases the firm sends a manuscript to her, or she returns one by mail. During the current month, Leora's hourly earnings totaled $2,250.

2. Ken, a registered nurse, has retired from full-time work. However, because of his experience and special skills, on each Monday, Wednesday, and Thursday afternoon he assists Dr. Wilson Kent, a dermatologist. Ken is paid an hourly fee by Dr. Kent. During the current week, his hourly fees totaled $1,050.

3. Horace Jones owns and operates a crafts shop, using the sole proprietorship form of business. Each week a check for $2,000 is written on the crafts shop's bank account as a salary payment to Jones.

4. Guy Gagliardi is a public stenographer, or court reporter. He has an office at the Metroplex Court Reporting Center but pays no rent. The manager of the center receives requests from attorneys for public stenographers to take depositions at legal hearings. The manager then chooses a stenographer who best meets the needs of the client and contacts the stenographer chosen. The stenographer has the right to refuse to take on the job, and the stenographer

controls his or her working hours and days. Clients make payments to the center, which deducts a 30 percent fee for providing facilities and rendering services to support the stenographer. The balance is paid to the stenographer. During the current month, the center collected fees of $30,000 for Guy, deducted $7,500 for the center's fee, and remitted the proper amount to Guy.

5. Investor Corporation carries on very little business activity. It merely holds land and certain assets. The board of directors has concluded that they need no employees. They have decided instead to pay Sherry Peoples, one of the shareholders, a consulting fee of $15,000 per year to serve as president, secretary, and treasurer and to manage all the affairs of the company. Peoples spends an average of one hour per week on the corporation's business affairs. However, her fee is fixed regardless of how few or how many hours she works.

Analyze: What characteristics do the persons you identified as "employees" have in common?

Critical Thinking Problem 11.2

Comparing Employees and Independent Contractors

The *Town Record Chronicle* is a local newspaper that is published Monday through Friday. It sells 90,000 copies daily. The paper is currently in a profit squeeze, and the publisher, Brenda Davis, is looking for ways to reduce expenses.

A review of current distribution procedures reveals that the *Town Record Chronicle* employs 110 truck drivers to drop off bundles of newspapers to 1,300 teenagers who deliver papers to individual homes. The drivers are paid an hourly wage while the teenagers receive 4 cents for each paper they deliver.

Davis is considering an alternative method of distributing the papers, which she says has worked in other cities the size of Flower Mound (where the *Town Record Chronicle* is published). Under the new system, the newspaper would retain 30 truck drivers to transport papers to five distribution centers around the city. The distribution centers are operated by independent contractors who would be responsible for making their own arrangements to deliver papers to subscribers' homes. The 30 drivers retained by the *Town Record Chronicle* would receive the same hourly rate as they currently earn, and the independent contractors would receive 20 cents for each paper delivered.

1. What payroll information does Davis need in order to make a decision about adopting the alternative distribution method?

2. Assume the following information:

   a. The average driver earns $48,000 per year.

   b. Average employee income tax withholding is 18 percent.

   c. The social security tax is 6.2 percent of the first $97,500 of earnings.

   d. The Medicare tax is 1.45 percent of all earnings.

   e. The state unemployment tax is 5 percent, and the federal unemployment tax is 0.8 percent of the first $7,000 of earnings.

   f. Workers' compensation insurance is 70 cents per $100 of wages.

   g. The paper pays $310 per month for health insurance for each driver and contributes $250 per month to each driver's pension plan.

   h. The paper has liability insurance coverage for all teenage carriers that costs $110,000 per year.

   Prepare a schedule showing the costs of distributing the newspapers under the current system and the proposed new system. Based on your analysis, which system would you recommend to Davis?

3. What other factors, monetary and nonmonetary, might influence your decision?

BUSINESS CONNECTIONS

Managerial | FOCUS

Payroll

1. Davis Company recently discovered that a payroll clerk had issued checks to nonexistent employees for several years and cashed the checks himself. The firm does not have any internal control procedures for its payroll operations. What specific controls might have led to the discovery of this fraud more quickly or discouraged the payroll clerk from even attempting the fraud?

2. Johnson Company has 20 employees. Some employees work in the office, others in the warehouse, and still others in the retail store. In the company's records, all employees are simply referred to as "general employees." Explain to management why this is not an acceptable practice.

3. Why should management be concerned about the accuracy and promptness of payroll tax deposits and payroll tax returns?

4. What is the significance to management of the experience rating system used to determine the employer's tax under the state unemployment insurance laws?

Ethical | DILEMMA

Ghost Employee

Johan Jones owns a dress shop that has been very successful. He employs 3 sales associates who get paid $10 per hour for a 40-hour week. He decides to open up another dress shop on the other side of town. He hires three more sales associates with the same pay arrangements. After three months, Johan notices he is not making the same profit he did. His sales have doubled and his expenses are the same proportion except for wages. He knows that each sales associate should receive $1,720 each month yet his total wages expense for the month is $12,040. He worries that he is not paying close enough attention to the old store. What is his problem? Should he discuss this problem with all the sales associates?

STREETWISE:
Questions from the
REAL WORLD

Payroll and Promotions

Refer to The Home Depot, Inc., *2006 Annual Report* in Appendix A.

1. Locate the consolidated balance sheets. When The Home Depot, Inc., records payroll tax liabilities, which category reflected on the balance sheet most likely contains these obligations?

2. The Home Depot, Inc., employed 364,000 associates at the close of fiscal 2006. According to the company's employment strategies, store managers are rarely recruited externally. Most store managers are promoted from within the organization. Discuss why you think The Home Depot, Inc., employs this strategy. What advantages and disadvantages do you think the company experiences as a result of this procedure?

Financial Statement
ANALYSIS

Income Statement

The following excerpt was taken from Southwest Airlines, Inc.'s consolidated statement of earnings for the year ended December 31, 2006.

Southwest Airlines, Inc. Consolidated Statements of Earnings			
	Years Ended		
(in millions, except per share amounts)	*2006*	*2005*	*2004*
Expenses:			
Salaries, wages and benefits	$3,052	$2,782	$2,578
Fuel and oil	2,138	1,341	1,000
Maintenance materials and repairs	468	446	472
Aircraft rentals	158	163	179
Landing fees and other rentals	495	454	408
Depreciation and amortization	515	469	431
Other operation expenses	1,326	1,204	1,058
Total Operating Expenses	$8,152	$6,859	$6,126

Analyze:

1. What percentage of total operating expenses was spent on salaries, wages, and benefits in the year ended December 31, 2006?

2. Assume that FICA (social security) wages for the first quarter of 2006 were $434,728,000. What deposit did Southwest Airlines send to the federal government for FICA taxes for the quarter? (Assume FICA rate of 6.2%.)

3. By what percentage did salaries, wages, and benefits increase from the years ended December 31, 2004 to 2005 and 2005 to 2006?

Analyze Online: Find the Southwest Airlines Web site (www.southwest.com). Click Our Company, then Investors. Find the most recent annual report.

4. What percentage of total operating expenses was spent on salaries, wages, and benefits?

5. Which expense line had the highest percentage increase in the last two years?

Unemployment Insurance

Businesses must pay unemployment insurance taxes required by federal and state agencies. The program provides benefits to unemployed workers. Your business has never fired or laid off an employee, yet you are required to pay the minimum tax rate on gross salaries. Do you agree or disagree with this system? Why?

Extending THE THOUGHT

Memo—Payroll Forms

You have opened a new office supply store and plan to hire 10 employees to help with sales, inventory maintenance, and advertising. You would like your payroll clerk to set up his office to prepare for the year's payroll duties. Write a memo to your payroll clerk requesting that he gather all the necessary employee forms, payroll tax return forms, and accounting forms that will be needed for payroll. Include a detailed list of the items that should be gathered.

Business COMMUNICATION

Determining Information

Wages and payroll tax expense are the largest cost that a company incurs. At times, a company has a problem paying wages and cash deposits for payroll taxes. Your company has a cash flow problem. In a group of 4 employees, brainstorm ways to cut the costs of wages and payroll taxes.

TEAMWORK

Internal Revenue Service

Go to the Internal Revenue Web site at www.irs.gov. Does the Web site contain the necessary federal forms? Can you use these forms to submit your report? What reports must be obtained from the IRS in an original, not downloaded, form?

Internet CONNECTION

Answers to **Self Reviews**

Answers to Section 1 Self Review

1. Form W-2 provides information to enable the employees to complete their federal income tax return. Copies are given to the employee and to the federal government (and to other governmental units that levy an income tax).

2. Federal Reserve Bank or a commercial bank that is designated as a federal depository.

3. Form 941 shows income taxes withheld, social security and Medicare taxes due for the quarter, and tax deposits. The form is due on the last day of the month following the end of the quarter.

4. **c.** Social security tax

5. **a.** each payroll period

6. Monthly

Answers to Section 2 Self Review

1. The amount of the premium depends on the type of work the employee performs.

2. The employer pays FUTA. Usually the employer pays SUTA, although a few states also levy SUTA on employees.

3. It reduces the rate of SUTA tax that must actually be paid.

4. **d.** Form 940

5. **b.** quarterly

6. Expenses will be understated. Net income will be overstated.

Answers to Comprehensive Self Review

1. Form W-3 is sent to the Social Security Administration. It reports the total social security wages; total Medicare wages; total social security and Medicare taxes withheld; total wages, tips, and other compensation; total employee income tax withheld; and other information.

2. Smaller

3. A credit, with limits, is allowed against the federal tax for unemployment tax charged by the state.

4. By the 15th day of the following month.

5. **b.** Amount of taxes reported in the lookback period

   d. Amount of taxes currently owed

Accruals, Deferrals, and the Worksheet

AMERICAN EAGLE OUTFITTERS
ae.com

www.ae.com

Clothing from American Eagle Outfitters® is hip, fun, and youthful. American Eagle designs, markets, and sells its own brand of casual clothing focusing on wardrobe staples like jeans, khakis, and graphic Ts for 15- to 25-year-olds.

When store sales started to decline in the early 2000s, American Eagle undertook extensive market research to better understand their customers. Based on this market research American Eagle made adjustments to their merchandise assortment boosting sales and profitability. The company also recently introduced MARTIN + OSA™, a new sportswear concept targeting 25- to 40-year-olds.

thinking critically

What types of adjustments do you think American Eagle Outfitters recorded when sales were declining?

SECTION OBJECTIVES

>> 1. Determine the adjustment for merchandise inventory, and enter the adjustment on the worksheet.

WHY IT'S IMPORTANT

The change in merchandise inventory affects the financial statements.

>> 2. Compute adjustments for accrued and prepaid expense items, and enter the adjustments on the worksheet.

WHY IT'S IMPORTANT

Each expense item needs to be assigned to the accounting period in which it helped to earn revenue.

>> 3. Compute adjustments for accrued and deferred income items, and enter the adjustments on the worksheet.

WHY IT'S IMPORTANT

The accrual basis of accounting states that income is recognized in the period it is earned.

TERMS TO LEARN

accrual basis
accrued expenses
accrued income
deferred expenses
deferred income
inventory sheet
prepaid expenses
property, plant, and equipment
unearned income

Calculating and Recording Adjustments

In Chapter 5, you learned how to make adjustments so that all revenue and expenses that apply to a fiscal period appear on the income statement for that period. In this chapter, you will learn more about adjustments and how they affect Whiteside Antiques, a retail merchandising business owned by Bill Whiteside.

The Accrual Basis of Accounting

Financial statements usually are prepared using the **accrual basis** of accounting because it most nearly attains the goal of matching expenses and revenue in an accounting period.

■ *Revenue is recognized when earned, not necessarily when the cash is received.* Revenue is recognized when the sale is complete. A sale is complete when title to the goods passes to the customer or when the service is provided. For sales on account, revenue is recognized when the sale occurs even though the cash is not collected immediately.

■ *Expenses are recognized when incurred or used, not necessarily when cash is paid.* Each expense is assigned to the accounting period in which it helped to earn revenue for the business, even if cash is not paid at that time. This is often referred to as *matching revenues and expenses.*

Sometimes cash changes hands before the revenue or expense is recognized. For example, insurance premiums are normally paid in advance, and the coverage extends over several accounting periods. In other cases, cash changes hands after the revenue or expense has been recognized. For example, employees might work during December but be paid in January of the following year. Because of these timing differences, adjustments are made to ensure that revenue and expenses are recognized in the appropriate period.

Using the Worksheet to Record Adjustments

The worksheet is used to assemble data about adjustments and to organize the information for the financial statements. Figure 12.1 on pages 398–399 shows the first two sections of the worksheet for Whiteside Antiques. Let's review how to prepare the worksheet.

- Enter the trial balance in the Trial Balance section. Total the columns. Be sure that total debits equal total credits.

- Enter the adjustments in the Adjustments section. Use the same letter to identify the debit part and the credit part of each adjustment. Total the columns. Be sure that total debits equal total credits.

- For each account, combine the amounts in the Trial Balance section and the Adjustments section. Enter the results in the Adjusted Trial Balance section, total the columns, and make sure that total debits equal total credits.

- Extend account balances to the Income Statement and Balance Sheet sections and complete the worksheet.

ADJUSTMENT FOR MERCHANDISE INVENTORY

Merchandise inventory consists of the goods that a business has on hand for sale to customers. An asset account for merchandise inventory is maintained in the general ledger. During the accounting period, all purchases of merchandise are debited to the **Purchases** account. All sales of merchandise are credited to the revenue account **Sales.**

Notice that no entries are made directly to the **Merchandise Inventory** account during the accounting period. Consequently, when the trial balance is prepared at the end of the period, the **Merchandise Inventory** account still shows the *beginning* inventory for the period. At the end of each period, a business determines the *ending* balance of the **Merchandise Inventory** account. The first step in determining the ending inventory is to count the number of units of each type of item on hand. As the merchandise is counted, the quantity on hand is entered on an inventory sheet. The **inventory sheet** lists the quantity of each type of goods a firm has in stock. This process is called a physical inventory. For each item the quantity is multiplied by the unit cost to find the totals per item. The totals for all items are added to compute the total cost of merchandise inventory.

The trial balance for Whiteside Antiques shows **Merchandise Inventory** of $52,000. Based on a count taken on December 31, merchandise inventory at the end of the year actually totaled $47,000. Whiteside Antiques needs to adjust the **Merchandise Inventory** account to reflect the balance at the end of the year.

The adjustment is made in two steps, using the accounts **Merchandise Inventory** and **Income Summary.**

1. The beginning inventory ($52,000) is taken off the books by transferring the account balance to the **Income Summary** account. This entry is labeled **(a)** on the worksheet in Figure 12.1 and is illustrated in T-account form below.

2. The ending inventory ($47,000) is placed on the books by debiting **Merchandise Inventory** and crediting **Income Summary.** This entry is labeled **(b)** on the worksheet in Figure 12.1.

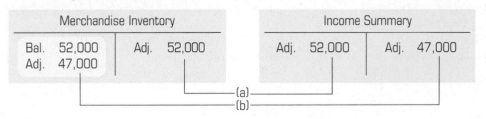

>>1. OBJECTIVE
Determine the adjustment for merchandise inventory, and enter the adjustment on the worksheet.

Video12.1

recall

Income Summary
The **Income Summary** account is a temporary owner's equity account used in the closing process.

FIGURE 12.1　10-Column Worksheet—Partial

Whiteside Antiques
Worksheet
Year Ended December 31, 2010

#	ACCOUNT NAME	TRIAL BALANCE DEBIT	TRIAL BALANCE CREDIT	ADJUSTMENTS DEBIT	ADJUSTMENTS CREDIT
1	Cash	13 136 00			
2	Petty Cash Fund	100 00			
3	Notes Receivable	1 200 00			
4	Accounts Receivable	32 000 00			
5	Allowance for Doubtful Accounts		250 00		(c) 800 00
6	Interest Receivable			(m) 30 00	
7	Merchandise Inventory	52 000 00		(b) 47 000 00	(a) 52 000 00
8	Prepaid Insurance	7 350 00			(k) 2 450 00
9	Prepaid Interest	225 00			(l) 150 00
10	Supplies	6 300 00			(j) 4 975 00
11	Store Equipment	30 000 00			
12	Accumulated Depreciation—Store Equipment				(d) 2 400 00
13	Office Equipment	5 000 00			
14	Accumulated Depreciation—Office Equipment				(e) 700 00
15	Notes Payable—Trade		2 000 00		
16	Notes Payable—Bank		9 000 00		
17	Accounts Payable		24 129 00		
18	Interest Payable				(i) 20 00
19	Social Security Tax Payable		1 084 00		(g) 74 40
20	Medicare Tax Payable		250 00		(g) 17 40
21	Employee Income Taxes Payable		990 00		
22	Federal Unemployment Tax Payable				(h) 9 60
23	State Unemployment Tax Payable				(h) 64 80
24	Salaries Payable				(f) 1 200 00
25	Sales Tax Payable		7 200 00		
26	Bill Whiteside, Capital		61 221 00		
27	Bill Whiteside, Drawing	27 600 00			
28	Income Summary			(a) 52 000 00	(b) 47 000 00
29	Sales		561 650 00		
30	Sales Returns and Allowances	12 500 00			
31	Interest Income		136 00		(m) 30 00
32	Miscellaneous Income		366 00		
33	Purchases	321 500 00			
34	Freight In	9 800 00			
35	Purchases Returns and Allowances		3 050 00		
36	Purchase Discounts		3 130 00		
37	Salaries Expense—Sales	78 490 00		(f) 1 200 00	
38	Advertising Expense	7 425 00			
39	Cash Short or Over	125 00			
40	Supplies Expense			(j) 4 975 00	

FIGURE 12.1   (concluded) 10-Column Worksheet—Partial

	ACCOUNT NAME	TRIAL BALANCE		ADJUSTMENTS	
		DEBIT	CREDIT	DEBIT	CREDIT
41	Depreciation Expense—Store Equipment			(d) 2 4 0 0 00	
42	Rent Expense	27 6 0 0 00			
43	Salaries Expense—Office	26 5 0 0 00			
44	Insurance Expense			(k) 2 4 5 0 00	
45	Payroll Taxes Expense	7 2 0 5 00		(g) 9 1 80	
46				(h) 7 4 40	
47	Telephone Expense	1 8 7 5 00			
48	Uncollectible Accounts Expense			(c) 8 0 0 00	
49	Utilities Expense	5 9 2 5 00			
50	Depreciation Expense—Office Equipment			(e) 7 0 0 00	
51	Interest Expense	6 0 0 00		(i) 2 0 00	
52				(l) 1 5 0 00	
53	Totals	674 4 5 6 00	674 4 5 6 00	111 8 9 1 20	111 8 9 1 20

The effect of this adjustment is to remove the beginning merchandise inventory balance and replace it with the ending merchandise inventory balance. Merchandise inventory is adjusted in two steps on the worksheet because both the beginning and the ending inventory figures appear on the income statement, which is prepared directly from the worksheet.

ADJUSTMENT FOR LOSS FROM UNCOLLECTIBLE ACCOUNTS

Credit sales are made with the expectation that the customers will pay the amount due later. Sometimes the account receivable is never collected. Losses from uncollectible accounts are classified as operating expenses.

Under accrual accounting, the expense for uncollectible accounts is recorded in the same period as the related sale. The expense is estimated because the actual amount of uncollectible accounts is not known until later periods. To match the expense for uncollectible accounts with the sales revenue for the same period, the estimated expense is debited to an account named ***Uncollectible Accounts Expense.***

Several methods exist for estimating the expense for uncollectible accounts. Whiteside Antiques uses the *percentage of net credit sales* method. The rate used is based on the company's past experience with uncollectible accounts and management's assessment of current business conditions. Whiteside Antiques estimates that four-fifths of 1 percent (0.80 percent) of net credit sales will be uncollectible. Net credit sales for the year were $100,000. The estimated expense for uncollectible accounts is $800 ($100,000 × 0.0080).

The entry to record the expense for uncollectible accounts includes a credit to a contra asset ◄◄ account, ***Allowance for Doubtful Accounts.*** This account appears on the balance sheet as follows.

Accounts Receivable	$32,000
Allowance for Doubtful Accounts ($800 + $250)	1,050
Net Accounts Receivable	$30,950

Adjustment **(c)** appears on the worksheet in Figure 12-1 for the expense for uncollectible accounts.

>>**2. OBJECTIVE**

Compute adjustments for accrued and prepaid expense items, and enter the adjustments on the worksheet.

LP12

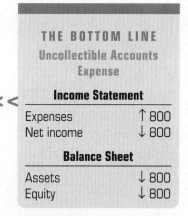

THE BOTTOM LINE
Uncollectible Accounts
Expense

Income Statement

Expenses	↑ 800
Net income	↓ 800

Balance Sheet

Assets	↓ 800
Equity	↓ 800

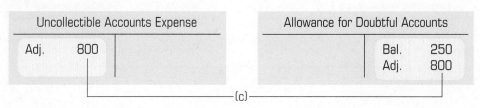

Uncollectible Accounts Expense		Allowance for Doubtful Accounts	
Adj. 800			Bal. 250
			Adj. 800

When a specific account becomes uncollectible, it is written off.

- The entry is a debit to *Allowance for Doubtful Accounts* and a credit to *Accounts Receivable.*
- The customer's account in the accounts receivable subsidiary ledger is also reduced.

Uncollectible Accounts Expense is not affected by the write-off of individual accounts identified as uncollectible. It is used only when the end-of-period adjustment is recorded.

Notice that net income is decreased at the end of the period when the adjustment for *estimated* expense for uncollectible accounts is made. When a specific customer account is written off, net income is *not* affected. The write-off of a specific account affects only the balance sheet accounts *Accounts Receivable* (asset) and *Allowance for Doubtful Accounts* (contra asset).

The balance of *Allowance for Doubtful Accounts* is reduced throughout the year as customer accounts are written off. Notice that *Allowance for Doubtful Accounts* already has a credit balance of $250 in the Trial Balance section of the worksheet. When the estimate of uncollectible accounts expense is based on sales, any remaining balance from previous periods is not considered when recording the adjustment.

ADJUSTMENTS FOR DEPRECIATION

Most businesses have long-term assets that are used in the operation of the business. These are often referred to as **property, plant, and equipment.** Property, plant, and equipment includes buildings, trucks, automobiles, machinery, furniture, fixtures, office equipment, and land.

Property, plant, and equipment costs are not charged to expense accounts when purchased. Instead, the cost of a long-term asset is allocated over the asset's expected useful life by depreciation. This process involves the gradual transfer of acquisition cost to expense. There is one exception. Land is not depreciated.

There are many ways to calculate depreciation. Whiteside Antiques uses the straight-line method, so an equal amount of depreciation is taken in each year of the asset's useful life. The formula for straight-line depreciation is

$$\frac{\text{Cost} - \text{Salvage value}}{\text{Estimated useful life}} = \text{Depreciation}$$

Salvage value is an estimate of the amount that could be obtained from the sale or disposition of an asset at the end of its useful life. Cost minus salvage value is called the *depreciable base.*

Depreciation of Store Equipment   The trial balance shows that Whiteside Antiques has $30,000 of store equipment. Estimated salvage value is $6,000. What is the amount of annual depreciation expense using the straight-line method?

Cost of store equipment	$30,000
Salvage value	(6,000)
Depreciable base	$24,000
Expected useful life	10 years

$$\frac{\$30,000 - \$6,000}{10 \text{ years}} = \$2,400 \text{ per year}$$

The annual depreciation expense is $2,400. Adjustment **(d)** appears on the worksheet in Figure 12.1 for the depreciation expense for store equipment.

important!

Depreciation

To calculate monthly straight-line depreciation, divide the depreciable base by the number of months in the useful life.

Depr. Expense—Store Equipment	Accum. Depr.—Store Equipment
Adj. 2,400	Adj. 2,400

(d)

Depreciation of Office Equipment Whiteside Antiques reports $5,000 of office equipment on the trial balance. What is the amount of annual depreciation expense using the straight-line method if estimated salvage value is $800 and estimated life is 6 years?

Cost of office equipment	$5,000
Salvage value	(800)
Depreciable base	$4,200
Expected useful life	6 years

$$\frac{\$5,000 - \$800}{6 \text{ Years}} = \$700 \text{ per year}$$

Annual depreciation expense is $700. Adjustment **(e)** appears on the worksheet in Figure 12.1 for depreciation expense for office equipment.

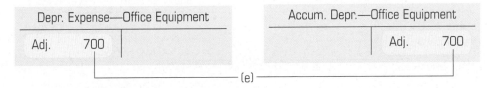

ADJUSTMENTS FOR ACCRUED EXPENSES

Many expense items are paid for, recorded, and used in the same accounting period. However, some expense items are paid for and recorded in one period but used in a later period. Other expense items are used in one period and paid for in a later period. In these situations, adjustments are made so that the financial statements show all expenses in the appropriate period.

Accrued expenses are expenses that relate to (are used in) the current period but have not yet been paid and do not yet appear in the accounting records. Whiteside Antiques makes adjustments for three types of accrued expenses:

- accrued salaries
- accrued payroll taxes
- accrued interest on notes payable

Because accrued expenses involve amounts that must be paid in the future, the adjustment for each item is a debit to an expense account and a credit to a liability account.

Accrued Salaries At Whiteside Antiques, all full-time sales and office employees are paid semimonthly—on the 15th and the last day of the month. The trial balance in Figure 12.1 shows the correct salaries expense for the full-time employees for the year. From December 28 to January 3, the firm hired several part-time sales clerks for the year-end sale. Through December 31, 2010, these employees earned $1,200. The part-time salaries expense has not yet been recorded because the employees will not be paid until January 3, 2011. An adjustment is made to record the amount owed, but not yet paid, as of the end of December.

Adjustment **(f)** appears on the worksheet in Figure 12.1 for accrued salaries.

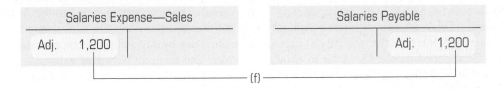

Accrued Payroll Taxes Payroll taxes are not legally owed until the salaries are paid. Businesses that want to match revenue and expenses in the appropriate period make adjustments to accrue the employer's payroll taxes even though the taxes are technically not yet due. Whiteside Antiques makes adjustments for accrued employer's payroll taxes.

The payroll taxes related to the full-time employees of Whiteside Antiques have been recorded and appear on the trial balance. However, the payroll taxes for the part-time sales clerks have not been recorded. None of the part-time clerks have reached the social security wage base limit. The entire $1,200 of accrued salaries is subject to the employer's share of social security and Medicare taxes. The accrued employer's payroll taxes are

Social security tax	$1,200	×	0.0620	=	$74.40
Medicare tax	$1,200	×	0.0145	=	17.40
Total accrued payroll taxes					$91.80

Adjustment **(g)** appears on the worksheet in Figure 12.1 for accrued payroll taxes.

The entire $1,200 of accrued salaries is also subject to unemployment taxes. The unemployment tax rates for Whiteside Antiques are 0.8 percent for federal and 5.4 percent for state.

Federal unemployment tax	$1,200	×	0.008	=	$ 9.60
State unemployment tax	$1,200	×	0.054	=	64.80
Total accrued taxes					$74.40

Adjustment **(h)** appears on the worksheet in Figure 12.1 for accrued unemployment taxes.

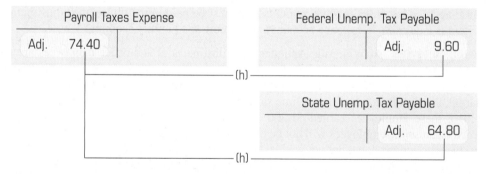

Accrued Interest on Notes Payable On December 1, 2010, Whiteside Antiques issued a two-month note for $2,000, with annual interest of 12 percent. The note was recorded in the *Notes Payable—Trade* account. Whiteside Antiques will pay the interest when the note matures on February 1, 2011. However, the interest expense is incurred day by day and should be allocated to each fiscal period involved in order to obtain a complete and accurate picture of expenses. The accrued interest amount is determined by using the interest formula Principal × Rate × Time.

Principal	×	**Rate**	×	**Time**		
$2,000	×	0.12	×	1/12	=	$20

The fraction ½ represents one month, which is 1/12 of a year.

Adjustment **(i)** appears on the worksheet in Figure 12.1 for the accrued interest expense.

Interest Expense			Interest Payable		
Adj.	20			Adj.	20

———— (i) ————

Other Accrued Expenses Most businesses pay property taxes to state and local governments. They accrue these taxes at the end of the accounting period. Adjustments might also be necessary for commissions, professional services, and many other accrued expenses.

ADJUSTMENTS FOR PREPAID EXPENSES

Prepaid expenses, or **deferred expenses,** are expenses that are paid for and recorded before they are used. Often a portion of a prepaid item remains unused at the end of the period; it is applicable to future periods. When paid for, these items are recorded as assets. At the end of the period, an adjustment is made to recognize as an expense the portion used during the period. Whiteside Antiques makes adjustments for three types of prepaid expenses:

- prepaid supplies
- prepaid insurance
- prepaid interest on notes payable

> In its balance sheet for February 3, 2007, American Eagle Outfitters reported total current liabilities of $460.5 million. Included in that total were these items (all expressed in millions of dollars): Accounts Payable, $171.2; Current Portion of Deferred Lease Credits, $12.8; Accrued Compensation and Payroll Taxes, $58.4; Accrued Rent, $57.5; Accrued Income and Other Taxes, $87.8; Unredeemed Stored Value Cards and Gift Certificates, $54.6; Other Liabilities and Accrued Expenses, $18.2.

Supplies Used When supplies are purchased, they are debited to the asset account **Supplies.** On the trial balance in Figure 12.1, **Supplies** has a balance of $6,300. A physical count on December 31 showed $1,325 of supplies on hand. This means that $4,975 ($6,300 − $1,325) of supplies were used during the year. An adjustment is made to charge the cost of supplies used to the current year's operations and to reflect the value of the supplies on hand.

Adjustment **(j)** appears on the worksheet in Figure 12.1 for supplies expense.

Supplies Expense			Supplies		
Adj.	4,975		Bal. 6,300	Adj.	4,975

———— (j) ————

Expired Insurance On January 2, 2010, Whiteside Antiques wrote a check for $7,350 for a three-year insurance policy. The asset account **Prepaid Insurance** was debited for $7,350. On December 31, 2010, one year of insurance had expired. An adjustment for $2,450 ($7,350 × 1/3) was made to charge the cost of the expired insurance to operations and to decrease **Prepaid Insurance** to reflect the prepaid insurance premium that remains.

Adjustment **(k)** appears on the worksheet in Figure 12.1 for the insurance.

Insurance Expense			Prepaid Insurance		
Adj.	2,450		Bal. 7,350	Adj.	2,450

———— (k) ————

Prepaid Interest on Notes Payable On November 1, 2010, Whiteside Antiques borrowed $9,000 from its bank and signed a three-month note at an annual interest rate of 10 percent. The bank deducted the entire amount of interest in advance. The interest for three months is $225.

Principal	×	Rate	×	Time		
$9,000	×	0.10	×	3/12	=	$225

Whiteside Antiques received $8,775 ($9,000 − $225). The transaction was recorded as a debit to *Cash* for $8,775, a debit to *Prepaid Interest* for $225, and a credit to *Notes Payable—Bank* for $9,000.

On December 31, two months of prepaid interest ($225 × 2/3 = $150) had been incurred and needed to be recorded as an expense. The adjustment consists of a debit to *Interest Expense* and a credit to *Prepaid Interest.*

Adjustment (l) appears on the worksheet in Figure 12.1 for the interest expense.

Interest Expense				Prepaid Interest	
Adj.	150		Bal.	225	Adj.	150

———————————— (l) ————————————

important!

Some assets and liabilities always require adjustments
Although prepaid expenses are usually charged to an asset account when they are paid, some businesses charge most prepayments to expense. In either case, at the time financial statements are prepared the accounts must be adjusted to show the correct expense and prepayment.

Other Prepaid Expenses Other common prepaid expenses are prepaid rent, prepaid advertising, and prepaid taxes. When paid, the amounts are debited to the asset accounts *Prepaid Rent, Prepaid Advertising,* and *Prepaid Taxes.* At the end of each period, an adjustment is made to transfer the portion used from the asset account to an expense account. For example, the adjustment for expired rent would be a debit to *Rent Expense* and a credit to *Prepaid Rent.*

Alternative Method Some businesses use a different method for prepaid expenses. At the time cash is paid, they debit an expense account (not an asset account). At the end of each period, they make an adjustment to transfer the portion that is not used from the expense account to an asset account.

Suppose that Whiteside used this alternative method when purchasing the two-year insurance policy. On January 1, 2010, the transaction would have been recorded as a debit to *Insurance Expense* for $7,350 and a credit to *Cash* for $7,350. On December 31, 2010, after the insurance coverage for one year had expired, coverage for two years remained. The adjustment would be recorded as a debit to *Prepaid Insurance* for $4,900 ($7,350 × 2/3) and a credit to *Insurance Expense* for $4,900.

Identical amounts appear on the financial statements at the end of each fiscal period, no matter which method is used to handle prepaid expenses.

>>3. OBJECTIVE
Compute adjustments for accrued and deferred income items, and enter the adjustments on the worksheet.

LP12

ADJUSTMENTS FOR ACCRUED INCOME

Accrued income is income that has been earned but not yet received and recorded. On December 31, 2010, Whiteside Antiques had accrued interest on notes receivable.

Accrued Interest on Notes Receivable Interest-bearing notes receivable are recorded at face value and are carried in the accounting records at this value until they are collected. The interest income is recorded when it is received, which is normally when the note matures. However, interest income is earned day by day. At the end of the period, an adjustment is made to recognize interest income earned but not yet received or recorded.

On November 1, 2010, Whiteside Antiques accepted from a customer a four-month, 15 percent note for $1,200. The note and interest are due on March 1, 2011. As of December 31, 2010, two months (November and December) of interest income was earned but not received. The amount of earned interest income is $30.

Principal	$\times$	Rate	$\times$	Time		
$1,200	$\times$	0.15	$\times$	2/12	=	$30

Adjustment (**m**) appears on the worksheet in Figure 12.1 for the interest income. To record the interest income of $30 earned, but not yet received, an adjustment debiting the asset account *Interest Receivable* and crediting a revenue account called *Interest Income* is made.

Interest Receivable		Interest Income	
Adj. 30			Bal. 136
			Adj. 30

————————————(m)————————————

ADJUSTMENTS FOR UNEARNED INCOME

Unearned income, or **deferred income,** exists when cash is received before income is earned. Under the accrual basis of accounting, only income that has been earned appears on the income statement. Whiteside Antiques has no unearned income. The following is an example of unearned income for another business.

Unearned Subscription Income for a Publisher Magazine publishers receive cash in advance for subscriptions. When the publisher receives the cash, it is unearned income and is a liability. It is a liability because the publisher has an obligation to provide magazines during the subscription period. As the magazines are sent to the subscribers, income is earned and the liability decreases.

Tech Publishing Corporation publishes *Consumer Technology Today.* When subscriptions are received, *Cash* is debited and *Unearned Subscription Income,* a liability account, is credited. At the end of the year, *Unearned Subscription Income* had a balance of $450,000. During the year, $184,000 of magazines were delivered; income was earned in the amount of $184,000. The adjustment to recognize income is a debit to *Unearned Subscription Income* for $184,000 and a credit to *Subscription Income* for $184,000.

After the adjustment, the *Unearned Subscription Income* account has a balance of $266,000, which represents subscriptions for future periods.

Unearned Subscription Income		
12/31 Adj. 184,000	12/31 Bal.	450,000
	12/31 Bal.	266,000

Other Unearned Income Items Other types of unearned income include management fees, rental income, legal fees, architectural fees, construction fees, and advertising income. The cash received in advance is recorded as unearned income. As the income is earned, the amount is transferred from the liability account to a revenue account.

Alternative Method Some businesses use a different method to handle unearned income. At the time the cash is received, a credit is made to a revenue account (not a liability account). At the end of each period, the adjustment transfers the portion that is not earned to a liability account. For example, suppose Tech Publishing Corporation uses this method. When cash for subscriptions is received, it is credited to *Subscription Income.* At the end of the period, an adjustment is made to transfer the unearned income to a liability account. The entry is a debit to *Subscription Income* and a credit to *Unearned Subscription Income.*

Identical amounts appear on the financial statements at the end of each fiscal period no matter which method is used to handle unearned income.

recall

Two Ways to Record Transactions

Earlier in this chapter you learned that prepaid expenses are usually charged to an asset account when paid, but may be charged to an expense account at that time. Likewise, unearned income is usually credited to a liability account when received, but may be credited to an income account. Be sure to understand how the transaction was originally entered before you begin making the adjusting entry.

Section 1 Self Review

QUESTIONS

1. Why is a 10-column worksheet used as part of the procedures for adjusting and closing accounts and preparing financial statements?

2. Why are there two amounts (a debit and a credit) in the adjustments column on the line for Merchandise Inventory in the 10-column worksheet?

3. Why are adjusting entries necessary?

EXERCISES

4. Samek Company adjusts and closes its accounts and prepares financial statements each month. In the December 31 Trial Balance column for debit balances, a balance of $6,000 is found in the Prepaid Rent account. A payment of $12,000 for prepayment of six months' rent was made on September 1.

   a. What is the amount of the adjusting entry for this item?

   b. What account would be debited and what account would be credited in the December 31 adjustments?

5. In Samek's December 31 trial balance, a credit balance of $14,000 appears in Unearned Fee Income. This amount represents a part of $21,000 received from a customer on November 1 covering work to be performed by Samek in November through January. What account will be debited and what account will be credited in the adjusting entry on December 31? What is the amount of the adjustment?

ANALYSIS

6. Your company prepares financial statements each month, using a 10-column worksheet to assemble data. What is the primary difference between the adjustments made on a monthly basis and those made on an annual basis?

(Answers to Section 1 Self Review are on page 430.)

SECTION OBJECTIVES

>> 4. **Complete a 10-column worksheet.**

   WHY IT'S IMPORTANT
   Using the worksheet is a convenient way to gather the information
   needed for the financial statements.

TERMS TO LEARN

net income line
updated account balances

Completing the Worksheet

After all adjustments have been entered on the worksheet, total the Adjustments Debit and
Credit columns and verify that debits and credits are equal. The next step in the process is to
prepare the Adjusted Trial Balance section.

Preparing the Adjusted Trial Balance Section

Figure 12.2 on pages 408–411 shows the completed worksheet for Whiteside Antiques. The
Adjusted Trial Balance section of the worksheet is completed as follows.

1. Combine the amount in the Trial Balance section and the Adjustments section for each
    account.
2. Enter the results in the Adjusted Trial Balance section. The accounts that do not have
    adjustments are simply extended from the Trial Balance section to the Adjusted Trial
    Balance section. For example, the balance of the *Cash* account is recorded in the Debit
    column of the Adjusted Trial Balance section without change.
3. The accounts that are affected by adjustments are recomputed. Follow these rules to com-
    bine amounts on the worksheet.

>> **4. OBJECTIVE**
Complete a 10-column
worksheet.

LP12

Trial Balance Section	Adjustments Section	Action
Debit	Debit	Add
Debit	Credit	Subtract
Credit	Credit	Add
Credit	Debit	Subtract

- If the account has a debit balance in the Trial Balance section and a debit entry in the
  Adjustments section, add the two amounts. Look at the *Salaries Expense—Sales*
  account. It has a $78,490 debit balance in the Trial Balance section and a $1,200 debit
  entry in the Adjustments section. The new balance is $79,690 ($78,490 + $1,200). It is
  entered in the Debit column of the Adjusted Trial Balance section.

- If the account has a debit balance in the Trial Balance section and a credit entry in the
  Adjustments section, subtract the credit amount. Look at the *Supplies* account. It has a
  $6,300 debit balance in the Trial Balance section and a $4,975 credit entry in the
  Adjustments section. The new balance is $1,325 ($6,300 − $4,975). It is entered in the
  Debit column of the Adjusted Trial Balance section.

Whiteside Antiques

Worksheet

Year Ended December 31, 2010

	ACCOUNT NAME	TRIAL BALANCE DEBIT	TRIAL BALANCE CREDIT	ADJUSTMENTS DEBIT	ADJUSTMENTS CREDIT
1	Cash	13 1 3 6 00			
2	Petty Cash Fund	1 0 0 00			
3	Notes Receivable	1 2 0 0 00			
4	Accounts Receivable	32 0 0 0 00			
5	Allowance for Doubtful Accounts		2 5 0 00		(c) 8 0 0 00
6	Interest Receivable			(m) 3 0 00	
7	Merchandise Inventory	52 0 0 0 00		(b) 47 0 0 0 00	(a) 52 0 0 0 00
8	Prepaid Insurance	7 3 5 0 00			(k) 2 4 5 0 00
9	Prepaid Interest	2 2 5 00			(l) 1 5 0 00
10	Supplies	6 3 0 0 00			(j) 4 9 7 5 00
11	Store Equipment	30 0 0 0 00			
12	Accumulated Depreciation—Store Equipment				(d) 2 4 0 0 00
13	Office Equipment	5 0 0 0 00			
14	Accumulated Depreciation—Office Equipment				(e) 7 0 0 00
15	Notes Payable—Trade		2 0 0 0 00		
16	Notes Payable—Bank		9 0 0 0 00		
17	Accounts Payable		24 1 2 9 00		
18	Interest Payable				(i) 2 0 00
19	Social Security Tax Payable		1 0 8 4 00		(g) 7 4 40
20	Medicare Tax Payable		2 5 0 00		(g) 1 7 40
21	Employee Income Taxes Payable		9 9 0 00		
22	Federal Unemployment Tax Payable				(h) 9 60
23	State Unemployment Tax Payable				(h) 6 4 80
24	Salaries Payable				(f) 1 2 0 0 00
25	Sales Tax Payable		7 2 0 0 00		
26	Bill Whiteside, Capital		61 2 2 1 00		
27	Bill Whiteside, Drawing	27 6 0 0 00			
28	Income Summary			(a) 52 0 0 0 00	(b) 47 0 0 0 00
29	Sales		561 6 5 0 00		
30	Sales Returns and Allowances	12 5 0 0 00			
31	Interest Income		1 3 6 00		(m) 3 0 00
32	Miscellaneous Income		3 6 6 00		
33	Purchases	321 5 0 0 00			
34	Freight In	9 8 0 0 00			
35	Purchases Returns and Allowances		3 0 5 0 00		
36	Purchase Discounts		3 1 3 0 00		
37	Salaries Expense—Sales	78 4 9 0 00		(f) 1 2 0 0 00	
38	Advertising Expense	7 4 2 5 00			
39	Cash Short or Over	1 2 5 00			
40	Supplies Expense			(j) 4 9 7 5 00	

FIGURE 12.2   Ten-Column Worksheet—Complete

ADJUSTED TRIAL BALANCE		INCOME STATEMENT		BALANCE SHEET		
DEBIT	CREDIT	DEBIT	CREDIT	DEBIT	CREDIT	
13 1 3 6 00				13 1 3 6 00		1
1 0 0 00				1 0 0 00		2
1 2 0 0 00				1 2 0 0 00		3
32 0 0 0 00				32 0 0 0 00		4
	1 0 5 0 00				1 0 5 0 00	5
3 0 00				3 0 00		6
47 0 0 0 00				47 0 0 0 00		7
4 9 0 0 00				4 9 0 0 00		8
7 5 00				7 5 00		9
1 3 2 5 00				1 3 2 5 00		10
30 0 0 0 00				30 0 0 0 00		11
	2 4 0 0 00				2 4 0 0 00	12
5 0 0 0 00				5 0 0 0 00		13
	7 0 0 00				7 0 0 00	14
	2 0 0 0 00				2 0 0 0 00	15
	9 0 0 0 00				9 0 0 0 00	16
	24 1 2 9 00				24 1 2 9 00	17
	2 00				2 00	18
	1 1 5 8 40				1 1 5 8 40	19
	2 6 7 40				2 6 7 40	20
	9 9 0 00				9 9 0 00	21
	9 60				9 60	22
	6 4 80				6 4 80	23
	1 2 0 0 00				1 2 0 0 00	24
	7 2 0 0 00				7 2 0 0 00	25
	61 2 2 1 00				61 2 2 1 00	26
27 6 0 0 00				27 6 0 0 00		27
52 0 0 0 00	47 0 0 0 00	52 0 0 0 00	47 0 0 0 00			28
	561 6 5 0 00		561 6 5 0 00			29
12 5 0 0 00		12 5 0 0 00				30
	1 6 6 00		1 6 6 00			31
	3 6 6 00		3 6 6 00			32
321 5 0 0 00		321 5 0 0 00				33
9 8 0 0 00		9 8 0 0 00				34
	3 0 5 0 00		3 0 5 0 00			35
	3 1 3 0 00		3 1 3 0 00			36
79 6 9 0 00		79 6 9 0 00				37
7 4 2 5 00		7 4 2 5 00				38
1 2 5 00		1 2 5 00				39
4 9 7 5 00		4 9 7 5 00				40

(continued)

FIGURE 12.2   (continued) Ten-Column Worksheet—Complete

	ACCOUNT NAME	TRIAL BALANCE		ADJUSTMENTS	
		DEBIT	CREDIT	DEBIT	CREDIT
41	Depreciation Expense—Store Equipment			(d) 2 4 0 0 00	
42	Rent Expense	27 6 0 0 00			
43	Salaries Expense—Office	26 5 0 0 00			
44	Insurance Expense			(k) 2 4 5 0 00	
45	Payroll Taxes Expense	7 2 0 5 00		(g) 9 1 80	
46				(h) 7 4 40	
47	Telephone Expense	1 8 7 5 00			
48	Uncollectible Accounts Expense			(c) 8 0 0 00	
49	Utilities Expense	5 9 2 5 00			
50	Depreciation Expense—Office Equipment			(e) 7 0 0 00	
51	Interest Expense	6 0 0 00		(i) 2 0 00	
52				(l) 1 5 0 00	
53	Totals	674 4 5 6 00	674 4 5 6 00	111 8 9 1 20	111 8 9 1 20
54	Net Income				

FIGURE 12.2 (continued) Ten-Column Worksheet—Complete

- If the account has a credit balance in the Trial Balance section and a credit entry in the Adjustments section, add the two amounts. Look at *Allowance for Doubtful Accounts.* It has a $250 credit balance in the Trial Balance section and an $800 credit entry in the Adjustments section. The new balance is $1,050 ($250 + $800). It is entered in the Credit column of the Adjusted Trial Balance section.

- If the account has a credit balance in the Trial Balance section and a debit entry in the Adjustments section, subtract the debit amount. Whiteside Antiques had no such adjustments.

The Adjusted Trial Balance section now contains the **updated account balances** that will be used in preparing the financial statements.

Look at the *Income Summary* account. Recall that the debit entry in this account removed the *beginning* balance from *Merchandise Inventory* and the credit entry added the *ending* balance to *Merchandise Inventory.* Notice that the debit and credit amounts in *Income Summary* are not combined in the Adjusted Trial Balance section.

Once all the updated account balances have been entered in the Adjusted Trial Balance section, total and rule the columns. Confirm that total debits equal total credits.

Preparing the Balance Sheet and Income Statement Sections

To complete the Income Statement and Balance Sheet sections of the worksheet, identify the accounts that appear on the balance sheet. On Figure 12.2, the accounts from *Cash* through *Bill Whiteside, Drawing* appear on the balance sheet. For each account enter the amount in the appropriate Debit or Credit column of the Balance Sheet section of the worksheet.

For accounts that appear on the income statement, *Sales* through *Interest Expense,* enter the amounts in the appropriate Debit or Credit column of the Income Statement section. The *Income Summary* debit and credit amounts are also entered in the Income Statement section of the worksheet. Notice that the debit and credit amounts in *Income Summary* are not combined in the Income Statement section.

Calculating Net Income or Net Loss

Once all account balances have been entered in the financial statement sections of the worksheet, the net income or net loss for the period is determined.

	ADJUSTED TRIAL BALANCE		INCOME STATEMENT		BALANCE SHEET		
	DEBIT	CREDIT	DEBIT	CREDIT	DEBIT	CREDIT	
	2 400 00		2 400 00				41
	27 600 00		27 600 00				42
	26 500 00		26 500 00				43
	2 450 00		2 450 00				44
	7 371 20		7 371 20				45
							46
	1 875 00		1 875 00				47
	800 00		800 00				48
	5 925 00		5 925 00				49
	700 00		700 00				50
	770 00		770 00				51
							52
	726 772 20	726 772 20	564 406 20	615 362 00	162 366 00	111 410 20	53
			50 955 80			50 955 80	54
			615 362 00	615 362 00	162 366 00	162 366 00	55
							56

FIGURE 12.2   (concluded) Ten-Column Worksheet—Complete

1. Total the Debit and Credit columns in the Income Statement section. For Whiteside Antiques, the debits total $564,406.20 and the credits total $615,362.00. Since the credits exceed the debits, the difference represents net income of $50,955.80.

2. To balance the Debit and the Credit columns in the Income Statement section, enter $50,955.80 in the Debit column of the Income Statement section. Total each column again and record the final total of each column ($615,362.00) on the worksheet.

3. Total the columns in the Balance Sheet section. Total debits are $162,366.00 and total credits are $111,410.20. The difference must equal the net income for the year, $50,955.80.

MANAGERIAL IMPLICATIONS   <<

EFFECT OF ADJUSTMENTS ON FINANCIAL STATEMENTS

If managers are to know the true revenue, expenses, and net income or net loss for a period, the matching process is necessary.

If accounts are not adjusted, the financial statements will be incomplete, misleading, and of little help in evaluating operations.

Managers need to be familiar with the procedures and underlying assumptions used by the accountant to make adjustments because adjustments increase or decrease net income.

Managers need information about uncollectible accounts expense in order to review the firm's credit policy. If losses are too high, management might tighten the requirements

for obtaining credit. If losses are very low, management might investigate whether easing credit requirements would increase net income.

The worksheet is a useful device for gathering data about adjustments and for preparing the financial statements.

Managers are keenly interested in receiving timely financial statements, especially the income statement, which shows the results of operations.

Managers are also interested in the prompt preparation of the balance sheet because it shows the financial position of the business at the end of the period.

THINKING CRITICALLY

What are some possible consequences of not making adjusting entries?

4. Enter $50,955.80 in the Credit column of the Balance Sheet section. Total each column again and record the final total in each column ($162,366.00).

5. Rule the Debit and Credit columns in all sections to show that the worksheet is complete.

Notice that the net income is recorded in two places on the **net income line** of the worksheet. It is recorded in the Credit column of the Balance Sheet section because net income *increases* owner's equity. It is recorded in the Debit column of the Income Statement section to balance the two columns in that section.

Section 2 Self Review

QUESTIONS

1. In the adjusting entry for depreciation, is the *Depreciation Expense* account increased or decreased? Is the book value of the asset being depreciated increased or is it decreased?

2. In its December 31, 2010, financial reports, St. Claire Company's accountant made two errors: (1) failed to record interest of $300 accrued on a note payable and (2) failed to record interest of $800 accrued on a note receivable. What is the net effect of these two errors on assets, on liabilities, on expenses, on income, and on owner's equity?

3. The trial balance in the first two columns of the worksheet balances and the adjustments in the next two columns balance. However, the adjusted trial balance does not balance. What is likely the source of the trouble?

EXERCISES

4. The amount of net income appears on the worksheet in the
   a. Credit column of the balance sheet section.
   b. Debit column of the balance sheet section.
   c. Credit column of the income statement section.
   d. Debit column of the income statement section.

5. What account is debited and what account is credited to accrue interest on notes payable?

ANALYZE

6. Explain why an error in the amount of an adjusting entry usually affects at least two accounting periods.

(Answers to Section 2 Self Review are on page 430.)

REVIEW   Chapter Summary

Accrual basis accounting requires that all revenue and expenses for a fiscal period be matched and reported on the income statement to determine net income or net loss for the period. In this chapter, you have learned the techniques used to adjust accounts so that they accurately reflect the operations of the period.

Learning Objectives

1 **Determine the adjustment for merchandise inventory, and enter the adjustment on the worksheet.**

Merchandise inventory consists of goods that a business has on hand for sale to customers. When the trial balance is prepared at the end of the period, the *Merchandise Inventory* account still reflects the beginning inventory. Before the financial statements can be prepared, *Merchandise Inventory* must be updated to reflect the ending inventory for the period. The actual quantity of the goods on hand at the end of the period must be counted. Then the adjustment is completed in two steps:

1. Remove the beginning inventory balance from the *Merchandise Inventory* account. Debit *Income Summary;* credit *Merchandise Inventory.*

2. Add the ending inventory to the *Merchandise Inventory* account. Debit *Merchandise Inventory;* credit *Income Summary.*

2 **Compute adjustments for accrued and prepaid expense items, and enter the adjustments on the worksheet.**

Expense accounts are adjusted at the end of the period so that they correctly reflect the current period. Examples of adjustments include provision for uncollectible accounts and depreciation. Other typical adjustments of expense accounts involve accrued expenses and prepaid expenses.

- Accrued expenses are expense items that have been incurred or used but not yet paid or recorded. They include salaries, payroll taxes, interest on notes payable, and property taxes.

- Prepaid expenses are expense items that a business pays for and records before it actually uses the

items. Rent, insurance, and advertising paid in advance are examples.

3 **Compute adjustments for accrued and deferred income items, and enter the adjustments on the worksheet.**

Revenue accounts are adjusted at the end of the period so that they correctly reflect the current period.

- Adjustments can affect either accrued income or deferred income.

- Accrued income is income that has been earned but not yet received and recorded.

- Deferred, or unearned, income is income that has not yet been earned but has been received.

4 **Complete a 10-column worksheet.**

When all adjustments have been entered on the worksheet, the worksheet is completed so that the financial statements can be prepared easily.

1. Figures in the Trial Balance section are combined with the adjustments to obtain an adjusted trial balance.

2. Each item in the Adjusted Trial Balance section is extended to the Income Statement and Balance Sheet sections of the worksheet.

3. The Income Statement columns are totaled and the net income or net loss is determined and entered in the net income line.

4. The amount of net income or net loss is entered in the net income line in the Balance Sheet section. After net income or net loss is added, the total debits must equal the total credits in the Balance Sheet section columns.

5 **Define the accounting terms new to this chapter.**

Glossary

Accrual basis (p. 396) A system of accounting by which all revenues and expenses are matched and reported on financial statements for the applicable period, regardless of when the cash related to the transaction is received or paid

Accrued expenses (p. 401) Expense items that relate to the current period but have not yet been paid and do not yet appear in the accounting records

Accrued income (p. 404) Income that has been earned but not yet received and recorded

Deferred expenses (p. 403) See Prepaid expenses

Deferred income (p. 405) See Unearned income

Inventory sheet (p. 397) A form used to list the volume and type of goods a firm has in stock

Net income line (p. 412) The worksheet line immediately following the column totals on which net income (or net loss) is recorded in two places: the Income Statement section and the Balance Sheet section

Prepaid expenses (p. 403) Expenses that are paid for and recorded before they are used, such as rent or insurance

Property, plant, and equipment (p. 400) Long-term assets that are used in the operation of a business and that are subject to depreciation (except for land, which is not depreciated)

Unearned income (p. 405) Income received before it is earned

Updated account balances (p. 410 The amounts entered in the Adjusted Trial Balance section of the worksheet

---

Comprehensive **Self Review**

1. Why is the accrual basis of accounting favored?

2. What is meant by the term "accrued income"?

3. How, if at all, does "accrued income" differ from "unearned income"?

4. On July 1, 2010, a landlord received $24,000 cash from a tenant, covering rent from that date through June 30, 2011. The payment was credited to *Rent Income.* Assuming no entry has been made in the income account since receipt of the payment, what would be the adjusting entry on December 31, 2010?

5. A completed worksheet for Holiday Company on December 31, 2010, showed a total of $930,000 in the debit column of the Income Statement section and a total credit of $905,000 in the credit column. Does this represent a profit or a loss for the year? How much?

(Answers to Comprehensive Self Review are on page 431.)

 Multiple choice questions are provided on the text Web site at www.mhhe.com/price12e

Quiz12

Discussion Questions

1. When a specific account receivable is deemed uncollectible it is written off by debiting _____ and crediting _____.

2. Income Summary amounts are extended to which statement columns on the worksheet?

3. What adjustment is made to record the estimated expense for uncollectible accounts?

4. Why is depreciation recorded?

5. What types of assets are subject to depreciation? Give three examples of such assets.

6. Explain the meaning of the following terms that relate to depreciation.

   a. Salvage value

   b. Depreciable base

   c. Useful life

   d. Straight-line method

7. What adjustment is made for depreciation on office equipment?

8. What is an accrued expense? Give three examples of items that often become accrued expenses.

9. What adjustment is made to record accrued salaries?

10. What is a prepaid expense? Give three examples of prepaid expense items.

11. How is the cost of an insurance policy recorded when the policy is purchased?

12. What adjustment is made to record expired insurance?

13. What is the alternative method of handling prepaid expenses?

14. What is accrued income? Give an example of an item that might produce accrued income.

15. What adjustment is made for accrued interest on a note receivable?

16. What is unearned income? Give two examples of items that would be classified as unearned income.

17. How is unearned income recorded when it is received?

18. What adjustment is made to record income earned during a period?

19. What is the alternative method of handling unearned income?

20. How does the worksheet help the accountant to prepare financial statements more efficiently?

21. *Unearned Fees Income* is classified as which type of account?

APPLICATIONS

Exercises

Determining the adjustments for inventory.

The beginning inventory of a merchandising business was $118,000, and the ending inventory is $100,519. What entries are needed at the end of the fiscal period to adjust *Merchandise Inventory?*

◀ **Exercise 12.1**
Objective 1

Determining the adjustments for inventory.

The Income Statement section of the worksheet of Smith Company for the year ended December 31, has $169,000 recorded in the Debit column and $193,434 in the Credit column on the line for the *Income Summary* account. What were the beginning and ending balances for *Merchandise Inventory?*

◀ **Exercise 12.2**
Objective 1

Computing adjustments for accrued and prepaid expense items.

For each of the following independent situations, indicate the adjusting entry that must be made on the December 31, 2010, worksheet. Omit descriptions.

◀ **Exercise 12.3**
Objective 2

a. During the year 2010, Sam & Sons Company had net credit sales of $941,000. Past experience shows that 0.6 percent of the firm's net credit sales result in uncollectible accounts.

b. Equipment purchased by One Stop Shops for $29,355 on January 2, 2010, has an estimated useful life of nine years and an estimated salvage value of $1,743. What adjustment for depreciation should be recorded on the firm's worksheet for the year ended December 31, 2010?

c. On December 31, 2010, Parrish Plumbing Supply owed wages of $6,546 to its factory employees, who are paid weekly.

d. On December 31, 2010, Parrish Plumbing Supply owed the employer's social security (6.2%) and Medicare (1.45%) taxes on the entire $6,546 of accrued wages for its factory employees.

e. On December 31, 2010, Parrish Plumbing Supply owed federal (0.8%) and state (5.4%) unemployment taxes on the entire $6,546 of accrued wages for its factory employees.

Computing adjustments for accrued and prepaid expense items.

For each of the following independent situations, indicate the adjusting entry that must be made on the December 31, 2010, worksheet. Omit descriptions.

◀ **Exercise 12.4**
Objective 2

a. On December 31, 2010, the *Notes Payable* account at King Manufacturing Company had a balance of $14,000. This balance represented a three-month, 9 percent note issued on November 1.

b. On January 2, 2010, Wayland's Word Processing Service purchased flash drives, paper, and other supplies for $5,950 in cash. On December 31, 2010, an inventory of supplies showed that items costing $1,517 were on hand. The *Supplies* account has a balance of $5,950.

c. On August 1, 2010, North Texas Manufacturing paid a premium of $12,324 in cash for a one-year insurance policy. On December 31, 2010, an examination of the insurance records showed that coverage for a period of five months had expired.

d. On April 1, 2010, Connie Crafts signed a one-year advertising contract with a local radio station and issued a check for $12,960 to pay the total amount owed. On December 31, 2010, the *Prepaid Advertising* account has a balance of $12,960.

Exercise 12.5
Objective 2

▶ **Recording adjustments for accrued and prepaid expense items.**

On December 1, 2010, Joe's Java Joint borrowed $31,000 from its bank in order to expand its operations. The firm issued a four-month, 11 percent note for $31,000 to the bank and received $29,864 in cash because the bank deducted the interest for the entire period in advance. In general journal form, show the entry that would be made to record this transaction and the adjustment for prepaid interest that should be recorded on the firm's worksheet for the year ended December 31, 2010. Omit descriptions. Round your answers to the nearest dollar.

Exercise 12.6
Objective 2

▶ **Recording adjustments for accrued and prepaid expense items.**

On December 31, 2010, the *Notes Payable* account at Beth's Boutique Shop had a balance of $42,000. This amount represented funds borrowed on a six-month, 10 percent note from the firm's bank on December 1. Record the journal entry for interest expense on this note that should be recorded on the firm's worksheet for the year ended December 31, 2010. Omit descriptions.

Exercise 12.7
Objective 3

▶ **Recording adjustments for accrued and deferred income items.**

For each of the following independent situations, indicate the adjusting entry that must be made on the December 31, 2010, worksheet. Omit descriptions.

a. On December 31, 2010, the *Notes Receivable* account at Montague Materials had a balance of $15,600, which represented a six-month, 13 percent note received from a customer on July 1.

b. During the week ended January 7, 2010, Taylor Magazine Publishing received $30,000 from customers for subscriptions to its magazine *Modern Business*. On December 31, 2010, an analysis of the *Unearned Subscription Revenue* account showed that $13,500 of the subscriptions were earned in 2010.

c. On October 1, 2010, Peacock Realty Company rented a commercial building to a new tenant and received $49,000 in advance to cover the rent for seven months. Upon receipt, the $49,000 was recorded in the Unearned Rent account.

d. On November 1, 2010, the Mighty Bucks Hockey Club sold season tickets for 40 home games, receiving $32,000,000. Upon receipt, the $32,000,000 was recorded in the Unearned Admissions account. At December 31, 2010, the mighty Bucks Hockey Club had played 10 home games.

PROBLEMS

Problem Set A

Problem 12.1A
Objectives 2, 3, 6

▶ **Recording adjustments for accrued and prepaid expense items and unearned income.**

On July 1, 2010, Shawn Smith established his own accounting practice. Selected transactions for the first few days of July follow.

INSTRUCTIONS

1. Record the transactions on page 1 of the general journal. Omit descriptions. Assume that the firm initially records prepaid expenses as assets and unearned income as a liability.

2. Record the adjusting journal entries that must be made on July 31, 2010, on page 2 of the general journal. Omit descriptions.

DATE		TRANSACTIONS
July	1	Signed a lease for an office and issued Check 101 for $13,200 to pay the rent in advance for six months.
	1	Borrowed money from First National Bank by issuing a four-month, 12 percent note for $24,000; received $23,040 because the bank deducted the interest in advance.
	1	Signed an agreement with Young Corp. to provide accounting and tax services for one year at $6,000 per month; received the entire fee of $72,000 in advance.
	1	Purchased office equipment for $17,000 from Office Outfitters; issued a two-month, 12 percent note in payment. The equipment is estimated to have a useful life of six years and a $1,160 salvage value. The equipment will be depreciated using the straight-line method.
	1	Purchased a one-year insurance policy and issued Check 102 for $1,620 to pay the entire premium.
	3	Purchased office furniture for $16,600 from Office Warehouse; issued Check 103 for $8,400 and agreed to pay the balance in 60 days. The equipment has an estimated useful life of five years and a $1,000 salvage value. The office furniture will be depreciated using the straight-line method.
	5	Purchased office supplies for $1,810 with Check 104. Assume $800 of supplies are on hand July 31, 2010.

Analyze: What balance should be reflected in *Unearned Accounting Fees* at July 31, 2010?

Recording adjustments for accrued and prepaid expense items and earned income.

◄ **Problem 12.2A**

Objectives 2, 3

e**X**cel

On July 31, 2010, after one month of operation, the general ledger of Sarah Webb, Consultant, contained the accounts and balances given below.

INSTRUCTIONS

1. Prepare a partial worksheet with the following sections: Trial Balance, Adjustments, and Adjusted Trial Balance. Use the data about the firm's accounts and balances to complete the Trial Balance section.

2. Enter the adjustments described below in the Adjustments section. Identify each adjustment with the appropriate letter.

3. Complete the Adjusted Trial Balance section.

ACCOUNTS AND BALANCES

Cash	$22,010	Dr.
Accounts Receivable	1,300	Dr.
Supplies	860	Dr.
Prepaid Rent	9,000	Dr.
Prepaid Insurance	1,620	Dr.
Prepaid Interest	400	Dr.
Furniture	12,050	Dr.
Accumulated Depreciation—Furniture		

ACCOUNTS AND BALANCES (CONT.)

Equipment	6,400	Dr.
Accumulated Depreciation—Equipment		
Notes Payable	17,900	Cr.
Accounts Payable	4,500	Cr.
Interest Payable		
Unearned Consulting Fees	3,600	Cr.
Sarah Webb, Capital	25,220	Cr.
Sarah Webb, Drawing	2,000	Dr.
Consulting Fees	8,000	Cr.
Salaries Expense	3,200	Dr.
Utilities Expense	220	Dr.
Telephone Expense	160	Dr.
Supplies Expense		
Rent Expense		
Insurance Expense		
Depreciation Expense—Furniture		
Depreciation Expense—Equipment		
Interest Expense		

ADJUSTMENTS

a. On July 31, an inventory of the supplies showed that items costing $680 were on hand.

b. On July 1, the firm paid $9,000 in advance for six months of rent.

c. On July 1, the firm purchased a one-year insurance policy for $1,620.

d. On July 1, the firm paid $400 interest in advance on a four-month note that it issued to the bank.

e. On July 1, the firm purchased office furniture for $12,050. The furniture is expected to have a useful life of seven years and a salvage value of $1,550.

f. On July 1, the firm purchased office equipment for $6,400. The equipment is expected to have a useful life of five years and a salvage value of $1,600.

g. On July 1, the firm issued a three-month, 12 percent note for $7,250.

h. On July 1, the firm received a consulting fee of $3,600 in advance for a one-year period.

Analyze: By what total amount were the expense accounts of the business adjusted?

Problem 12.3A ▶
Objectives 1, 2, 3, 4
e**X**cel

Recording adjustments and completing the worksheet.

The Green Thumb Gallery is a retail store that sells plants, soil, and decorative pots. On December 31, 2010, the firm's general ledger contained the accounts and balances that appear below.

INSTRUCTIONS

1. Prepare the Trial Balance section of a 10-column worksheet. The worksheet covers the year ended December 31, 2010.

2. Enter the adjustments below in the Adjustments section of the worksheet. Identify each adjustment with the appropriate letter.

3. Complete the worksheet.

ACCOUNTS AND BALANCES

Cash	$ 5,700	Dr.
Accounts Receivable	2,600	Dr.
Allowance for Doubtful Accounts	52	Cr.
Merchandise Inventory	11,300	Dr.
Supplies	1,200	Dr.

ACCOUNTS AND BALANCES (CONT.)

Prepaid Advertising	960	Dr.
Store Equipment	8,100	Dr.
Accumulated Depreciation—Store Equipment	1,500	Cr.
Office Equipment	1,600	Dr.
Accumulated Depreciation—Office Equipment	280	Cr.
Accounts Payable	2,625	Cr.
Social Security Tax Payable	430	Cr.
Medicare Tax Payable	98	Cr.
Federal Unemployment Tax Payable		
State Unemployment Tax Payable		
Salaries Payable		
Beth Argo, Capital	25,457	Cr.
Beth Argo, Drawing	20,000	Dr.
Sales	90,048	Cr.
Sales Returns and Allowances	1,100	Dr.
Purchases	46,400	Dr.
Purchases Returns and Allowances	430	Cr.
Rent Expense	6,000	Dr.
Telephone Expense	590	Dr.
Salaries Expense	14,100	Dr.
Payroll Taxes Expense	1,270	Dr.
Income Summary		
Supplies Expense		
Advertising Expense		
Depreciation Expense—Store Equipment		
Depreciation Expense—Office Equipment		
Uncollectible Accounts Expense		

ADJUSTMENTS

a.–b. Merchandise inventory on December 31, 2010, is $12,321.

c. During 2010, the firm had net credit sales of $35,000; the firm estimates that 0.6 percent of these sales will result in uncollectible accounts.

d. On December 31, 2010, an inventory of the supplies showed that items costing $275 were on hand.

e. On October 1, 2010, the firm signed a six-month advertising contract for $960 with a local newspaper and paid the full amount in advance.

f. On January 2, 2009, the firm purchased store equipment for $8,100. At that time, the equipment was estimated to have a useful life of five years and a salvage value of $600.

g. On January 2, 2009, the firm purchased office equipment for $1,600. At that time, the equipment was estimated to have a useful life of five years and a salvage value of $200.

h. On December 31, 2010, the firm owed salaries of $1,830 that will not be paid until 2011.

i. On December 31, 2010, the firm owed the employer's social security tax (assume 6.2 percent) and Medicare tax (assume 1.45 percent) on the entire $1,830 of accrued wages.

j. On December 31, 2010, the firm owed federal unemployment tax (assume 0.8 percent) and state unemployment tax (assume 5.4 percent) on the entire $1,830 of accrued wages.

Analyze: By what total amount were the net assets of the business affected by adjustments?

Recording adjustments and completing the worksheet.

Healthy Habits Foods Company is a distributor of nutritious snack foods such as granola bars. On December 31, 2010, the firm's general ledger contained the accounts and balances that follow.

◄ **Problem 12.4A**

Objectives 1, 2, 3, 4

CONTINUING >>>
Problem

INSTRUCTIONS

1. Prepare the Trial Balance section of a 10-column worksheet. The worksheet covers the year ended December 31, 2010.

2. Enter the adjustments in the Adjustments section of the worksheet. Identify each adjustment with the appropriate letter.

3. Complete the worksheet.

Note: This problem will be required to complete Problem 13.3A in Chapter 13.

ACCOUNTS AND BALANCES

Cash	$ 30,100	Dr.
Accounts Receivable	35,200	Dr.
Allowance for Doubtful Accounts	420	Cr.
Merchandise Inventory	86,000	Dr.
Supplies	10,400	Dr.
Prepaid Insurance	5,400	Dr.
Office Equipment	8,300	Dr.
Accum. Depreciation—Office Equipment	2,650	Cr.
Warehouse Equipment	28,000	Dr.
Accum. Depreciation—Warehouse Equipment	9,600	Cr.
Notes Payable—Bank	32,000	Cr.
Accounts Payable	12,200	Cr.
Interest Payable		
Social Security Tax Payable	1,680	Cr.
Medicare Tax Payable	388	Cr.
Federal Unemployment Tax Payable		
State Unemployment Tax Payable		
Salaries Payable		
Phillip Tucker, Capital	108,684	Cr.
Phillip Tucker, Drawing	56,000	Dr.
Sales	653,778	Cr.
Sales Returns and Allowances	10,000	Dr.
Purchases	350,000	Dr.
Purchases Returns and Allowances	9,200	Cr.
Income Summary		
Rent Expense	36,000	Dr.
Telephone Expense	2,200	Dr.
Salaries Expense	160,000	Dr.
Payroll Taxes Expense	13,000	Dr.
Supplies Expense		
Insurance Expense		
Depreciation Expense—Office Equip.		
Depreciation Expense—Warehouse Equip.		
Uncollectible Accounts Expense		
Interest Expense		

ADJUSTMENTS

a.–b. Merchandise inventory on December 31, 2010, is $78,000.

c. During 2010, the firm had net credit sales of $560,000; past experience indicates that 0.5 percent of these sales should result in uncollectible accounts.

d. On December 31, 2010, an inventory of supplies showed that items costing $1,180 were on hand.

e. On May 1, 2010, the firm purchased a one-year insurance policy for $5,400.

f. On January 2, 2008, the firm purchased office equipment for $8,300. At that time, the equipment was estimated to have a useful life of six years and a salvage value of $350.

g. On January 2, 2008, the firm purchased warehouse equipment for $28,000. At that time, the equipment was estimated to have a useful life of five years and a salvage value of $4,000.

h. On November 1, 2010, the firm issued a four-month, 12 percent note for $32,000.

i. On December 31, 2010, the firm owed salaries of $5,000 that will not be paid until 2011.

j. On December 31, 2010, the firm owed the employer's social security tax (assume 6.2 percent) and Medicare tax (assume 1.45 percent) on the entire $5,000 of accrued wages.

k. On December 31, 2010, the firm owed the federal unemployment tax (assume 0.8 percent) and the state unemployment tax (assume 5.4 percent) on the entire $5,000 of accrued wages.

Analyze: When the financial statements for Healthy Habits Foods Company are prepared, what net income will be reported for the period ended December 31, 2010?

Problem Set B

Recording adjustments for accrued and prepaid expense items and unearned income.

◀ **Problem 12.1B**
Objectives 2, 3

On June 1, 2010, Penelope Bermudez established her own advertising firm. Selected transactions for the first few days of June follow.

1. Record the transactions on page 1 of the general journal. Omit descriptions. Assume that the firm initially records prepaid expenses as assets and unearned income as a liability.

2. Record the adjusting journal entries that must be made on June 30, 2010, on page 2 of the general journal. Omit descriptions.

DATE	TRANSACTIONS
2010	
June 1	Signed a lease for an office and issued Check 101 for $18,000 to pay the rent in advance for six months.
1	Borrowed money from National Trust Bank by issuing a three-month, 10 percent note for $18,000; received $17,550 because the bank deducted interest in advance.
1	Signed an agreement with Glass Decorations, Inc. to provide advertising consulting for one year at $4,550 per month; received the entire fee of $54,600 in advance.
1	Purchased office equipment for $15,400 from The Equipment Depot; issued a three-month, 12 percent note in payment. The equipment is estimated to have a useful life of five years and a $1,000 salvage value and will be depreciated using the straight-line method.
1	Purchased a one-year insurance policy and issued Check 102 for $1,944 to pay the entire premium.
3	Purchased office furniture for $17,400 from Office Gallery; issued Check 103 for $8,400 and agreed to pay the balance in 60 days. The equipment is estimated to have a useful life of five years and a $1,200 salvage value and will be depreciated using the straight-line method.
5	Purchased office supplies for $2,810 with Check 104; assume $1,150 of supplies are on hand June 30, 2010.

Analyze: At the end of the year, 2010, how much of the rent paid on June 1 will have been charged to expense?

Problem 12.2B ▶
Objectives 2, 3

Recording adjustments for accrued and prepaid expense items and unearned income.

On September 30, 2010, after one month of operation, the general ledger of Cross Timbers Company contained the accounts and balances shown below.

INSTRUCTIONS

1. Prepare a partial worksheet with the following sections: Trial Balance, Adjustments, and Adjusted Trial Balance. Use the data about the firm's accounts and balances to complete the Trial Balance section.

2. Enter the adjustments described below in the Adjustments section. Identify each adjustment with the appropriate letter. (Some items may not require adjustments.)

3. Complete the Adjusted Trial Balance section.

ACCOUNTS AND BALANCES

Cash	$26,460	Dr.
Supplies	740	Dr.
Prepaid Rent	4,200	Dr.
Prepaid Advertising	3,750	Dr.
Prepaid Interest	450	Dr.
Furniture	4,840	Dr.
Accumulated Depreciation—Furniture		
Equipment	9,000	Dr.
Accumulated Depreciation—Equipment		
Notes Payable	20,250	Cr.
Accounts Payable	4,400	Cr.
Interest Payable		
Unearned Course Fees	22,000	Cr.
Scott Nelson, Capital	6,730	Cr.
Scott Nelson, Drawing	2,000	Dr.
Course Fees		
Salaries Expense	1,600	Dr.
Telephone Expense	120	Dr.
Entertainment Expense	220	Dr.
Supplies Expense		
Rent Expense		
Advertising Expense		
Depreciation Expense—Furniture		
Depreciation Expense—Equipment		
Interest Expense		

ADJUSTMENTS

a. On September 30, an inventory of the supplies showed that items costing $705 were on hand.

b. On September 1, the firm paid $4,200 in advance for six months of rent.

c. On September 1, the firm signed a six-month advertising contract for $3,750 and paid the full amount in advance.

d. On September 1, the firm paid $450 interest in advance on a three-month note that it issued to the bank.

e. On September 1, the firm purchased office furniture for $4,840. The furniture is expected to have a useful life of five years and a salvage value of $340.

f. On September 3, the firm purchased equipment for $9,000. The equipment is expected to have a useful life of five years and a salvage value of $1,200.

g. On September 1, the firm issued a two-month, 8 percent note for $5,250.

h. During September, the firm received $22,000 fees in advance. An analysis of the firm's records shows that $7,000 applies to services provided in September and the rest pertains to future months.

Analyze: What was the net dollar effect on income of the adjustments to the accounting records of the business?

Recording adjustments and completing the worksheet.

◀ **Problem 12.3B**
Objectives 1, 2, 3, 4

Fun Depot is a retail store that sells toys, games, and bicycles. On December 31, 2010, the firm's general ledger contained the following accounts and balances.

INSTRUCTIONS

1. Prepare the Trial Balance section of a 10-column worksheet. The worksheet covers the year ended December 31, 2010.
2. Enter the adjustments below in the Adjustments section of the worksheet. Identify each adjustment with the appropriate letter.
3. Complete the worksheet.

ACCOUNTS AND BALANCES

Cash	$ 26,400	Dr.
Accounts Receivable	22,700	Dr.
Allowance for Doubtful Accounts	320	Cr.
Merchandise Inventory	138,000	Dr.
Supplies	11,600	Dr.
Prepaid Advertising	5,280	Dr.
Store Equipment	32,500	Dr.
Accumulated Depreciation—Store Equipment	$ 5,760	Cr.
Office Equipment	8,400	Dr.
Accumulated Depreciation—Office Equipment	1,440	Cr.
Accounts Payable	8,600	Cr.
Social Security Tax Payable	5,920	Cr.
Medicare Tax Payable	1,368	Cr.
Federal Unemployment Tax Payable		
State Unemployment Tax Payable		
Salaries Payable		
Janie Fielder, Capital	112,250	Cr.
Janie Fielder, Drawing	100,000	Dr.
Sales	1,043,662	Cr.
Sales Returns and Allowances	17,200	Dr.
Purchases	507,600	Dr.
Purchases Returns and Allowances	5,040	Cr.
Rent Expense	125,000	Dr.
Telephone Expense	4,280	Dr.

ACCOUNTS AND BALANCES (CONT.)

Salaries Expense	164,200	Dr.
Payroll Taxes Expense	15,200	Dr.
Income Summary		
Supplies Expense		
Advertising Expense	6,000	Dr.
Depreciation Expense—Store Equipment		
Depreciation Expense—Office Equipment		
Uncollectible Accounts Expense		

ADJUSTMENTS

a.–b.   Merchandise inventory on December 31, 2010, is $148,000.

c. During 2010, the firm had net credit sales of $440,000. The firm estimates that 0.7 percent of these sales will result in uncollectible accounts.

d. On December 31, 2010, an inventory of the supplies showed that items costing $2,960 were on hand.

e. On September 1, 2010, the firm signed a six-month advertising contract for $5,280 with a local newspaper and paid the full amount in advance.

f. On January 2, 2009, the firm purchased store equipment for $32,500. At that time, the equipment was estimated to have a useful life of five years and a salvage value of $3,700.

g. On January 2, 2009, the firm purchased office equipment for $8,400. At that time, the equipment was estimated to have a useful life of five years and a salvage value of $1,200.

h. On December 31, 2010, the firm owed salaries of $8,000 that will not be paid until 2011.

i. On December 31, 2010, the firm owed the employer's social security tax (assume 6.2 percent) and Medicare tax (assume 1.45 percent) on the entire $8,000 of accrued wages.

j. On December 31, 2010, the firm owed federal unemployment tax (assume 0.8 percent) and state unemployment tax (assume 5.4 percent) on the entire $8,000 of accrued wages.

Analyze: If the adjustment for advertising had not been recorded, what would the reported net income have been?

Problem 12.4B ▶

Objectives 1, 2, 3, 4

Problem

Recording adjustments and completing the worksheet.

Whatnots is a retail seller of cards, novelty items, and business products. On December 31, 2010, the firm's general ledger contained the following accounts and balances.

INSTRUCTIONS

1. Prepare the Trial Balance section of a 10-column worksheet. The worksheet covers the year ended December 31, 2010.

2. Enter the adjustments in the Adjustments section of the worksheet. Identify each adjustment with the appropriate letter.

3. Complete the worksheet.

Note: This problem will be required to complete Problem 13.3B in Chapter 13.

ACCOUNTS AND BALANCES

Cash	$ 3,235	Dr.
Accounts Receivable	6,910	Dr.
Allowance for Doubtful Accounts	600	Cr.
Merchandise Inventory	16,985	Dr.

ACCOUNTS AND BALANCES (CONT.)

Supplies	750	Dr.
Prepaid Insurance	2,400	Dr.
Store Equipment	6,000	Dr.
Accumulated Depreciation—Store Equip.	2,000	Cr.
Store Fixtures	15,760	Dr.
Accumulated Depreciation—Store Fixtures	4,100	Cr.
Notes Payable	4,000	Cr.
Accounts Payable	600	Cr.
Interest Payable		
Social Security Tax Payable		
Medicare Tax Payable		
Federal Unemployment Tax Payable		
State Unemployment Tax Payable		
Salaries Payable		
Preston Allen, Capital	39,780	Cr.
Preston Allen, Drawing	8,000	Dr.
Sales	236,560	Cr.
Sales Returns and Allowances	6,000	Dr.
Purchases	160,000	Dr.
Purchases Returns and Allowances	2,000	Cr.
Income Summary		
Rent Expense	18,000	Dr.
Telephone Expense	2,400	Dr.
Salaries Expense	40,000	Dr.
Payroll Tax Expense	3,200	Dr.
Supplies Expense		
Insurance Expense		
Depreciation Expense—Store Equipment		
Depreciation Expense—Store Fixtures		
Uncollectible Accounts Expense		
Interest Expense		

ADJUSTMENTS

a.–b. Merchandise inventory on hand on December 31, 2010, is $15,840.

c. During 2010, the firm had net credit sales of $160,000. Past experience indicates that 0.8 percent of these sales should result in uncollectible accounts.

d. On December 31, 2010, an inventory of supplies showed that items costing $245 were on hand.

e. On July 1, 2010, the firm purchased a one-year insurance policy for $2,400.

f. On January 2, 2008, the firm purchased store equipment for $6,000. The equipment was estimated to have a five-year useful life and a salvage value of $1,000.

g. On January 4, 2008, the firm purchased store fixtures for $15,760. At the time of the purchase, the fixtures were assumed to have a useful life of seven years and a salvage value of $1,410.

h. On October 1, 2010, the firm issued a six-month, $4,000 note payable at 9 percent interest with a local bank.

i. At year-end (December 31, 2010), the firm owed salaries of $1,450 that will not be paid until January 2011.

j. On December 31, 2010, the firm owed the employer's social security tax (assume 6.2 percent) and Medicare tax (assume 1.45 percent) on the entire $1,450 of accrued wages.

k. On December 31, 2010, the firm owed federal unemployment tax (assume 1.0 percent) and state unemployment tax (assume 5.0 percent) on the entire $1,450 of accrued wages.

Analyze: After all adjustments have been recorded, what is the net book value of the company's assets?

Critical Thinking Problem 12.1

Completing the Worksheet

The unadjusted trial balance of Jerry's Jewelers on December 31, 2010, the end of its fiscal year, appears on page 427.

INSTRUCTIONS

1. Copy the unadjusted trial balance onto a worksheet and complete the worksheet using the following information.

   a.–b. Ending merchandise inventory, $98,700.

   c. Uncollectible accounts expense, $1,000.

   d. Store supplies on hand December 31, 2010, $625.

   e. Office supplies on hand December 31, 2010, $305.

   f. Depreciation on store equipment, $11,360.

   g. Depreciation on office equipment, $3,300.

   h. Accrued sales salaries, $4,000, and accrued office salaries, $1,000.

   i. Social security tax on accrued salaries, $326; Medicare tax on accrued salaries, $76. (Assumes that tax rates have increased.)

   j. Federal unemployment tax on accrued salaries, $56; state unemployment tax on accrued salaries, $270.

2. Journalize the adjusting entries on page 30 of the general journal. Omit descriptions.

3. Journalize the closing entries on page 32 of the general journal. Omit descriptions.

4. Compute the following:

   a. net sales

   b. net delivered cost of purchases

   c. cost of goods sold

   d. net income or net loss

   e. balance of *Jerry Whatley, Capital* on December 31, 2010.

Analyze: What change(s) to *Jerry Whatley, Capital* will be reported on the statement of owner's equity?

JERRY'S JEWELERS Trial Balance December 31, 2010		
Cash	$ 13,050	Dr.
Accounts Receivable	49,900	Dr.
Allowance for Doubtful Accounts	2,000	Cr.
Merchandise Inventory	105,900	Dr.
Store Supplies	4,230	Dr.
Office Supplies	2,950	Dr.
Store Equipment	113,590	Dr.
Accumulated Depreciation—Store Equipment	13,010	Cr.
Office Equipment	27,640	Dr.
Accumulated Depreciation—Office Equipment	4,930	Cr.
Accounts Payable	4,390	Cr.
Salaries Payable		
Social Security Tax Payable		
Medicare Tax Payable		
Federal Unemployment Tax Payable		
State Unemployment Tax Payable		
Jerry Whatley, Capital	166,310	Cr.
Jerry Whatley, Drawing	30,000	Dr.
Income Summary		
Sales	862,230	Cr.
Sales Returns and Allowances	7,580	Dr.
Purchases	504,810	Dr.
Purchases Returns and Allowances	4,240	Cr.
Purchases Discounts	10,770	Cr.
Freight In	7,000	Dr.
Salaries Expense—Sales	75,950	Dr.
Rent Expense	35,500	Dr.
Advertising Expense	12,300	Dr.
Store Supplies Expense		
Depreciation Expense—Store Equipment		
Salaries Expense—Office	77,480	Dr.
Payroll Taxes Expense		
Uncollectible Accounts Expense		
Office Supplies Expense		
Depreciation Expense—Office Equipment		

Critical Thinking Problem 12.2

Net Profit

When Waylon Skagg's father died suddenly, Waylon had just completed the semester in college, so he stepped in to run the family business, Skagg's Delivery Service, until it could be sold. Under his father's direction, the company was a successful operation and provided ample money to meet the family's needs.

Waylon was majoring in music in college and knew little about business or accounting, but he was eager to do a good job of running the business so it would command a good selling price. Since all of the services performed were paid in cash, Waylon figured that he would do all right as long as the *Cash* account increased. Thus he was delighted to watch the cash balance increase from $24,800 at the beginning of the first month to $63,028 at the end of the second month—an increase of $38,228 during the two months he had been in charge. When he was presented an income statement for the two months by the company's bookkeeper, he could not understand why it did not show that amount as income but instead reported only $21,100 as net income.

Knowing that you are taking an accounting class, Waylon brings the income statement, shown below, to you and asks if you can help him understand the difference.

SKAGG'S DELIVERY SERVICE		
Income Statement		
Months of June and July, 2010		
Operating Revenues		
Delivery Fees		$205,018
Operating Expenses		
Salaries and Related Taxes	$128,224	
Gasoline and Oil	31,000	
Repairs Expense	6,570	
Supplies Expense	2,268	
Insurance Expense	2,856	
Depreciation Expense	13,000	
Total Operating Expense		183,918
Net Income		$ 21,100

In addition, Waylon permits you to examine the accounting records, which show that the balance of *Salaries Payable* was $2,680 at the beginning of the first month but had increased to $4,240 at the end of the second month. Most of the balance in the *Insurance Expense* account reflects monthly insurance payments covering only one month each. However, the *Prepaid Insurance* account had decreased $300 during the two months, and all supplies had been purchased before Waylon took over. The balances of the company's other asset and liability accounts showed no changes.

1. Explain the cause of the difference between the increase in the *Cash* account balance and the net income for the two months.

2. Prepare a schedule that accounts for this difference.

BUSINESS CONNECTIONS

Out of Balance

Ethical DILEMMA

The president of Murray Stainless Steel Corporation has told you to go out to the factory and count merchandise inventory. He said the stockholders were coming for a meeting and he wanted to put on a good show. He asked you to make the inventory a bit heavy by counting one row twice. The higher ending inventory will show a higher net income. What should you do?

Balance Sheet Accounts

STREETWISE:
Questions from the
REAL WORLD

Refer to the 2006 *Annual Report* for The Home Depot, Inc., found in Appendix A.

1. Review the balance sheet. Based only on the asset account categories shown, list two types of adjusting entries you think are required each fiscal period. Which accounts are affected?

2. Based on the account categories found in the Liabilities section, describe two types of adjusting entries that may be recorded by The Home Depot, Inc., in an effort to match revenues with expenses.

Balance Sheet

The following financial data was reported in the DuPont 2006 *Annual Report*.

Consolidated Balance Sheet As of December 31		
(Dollars in millions, except per share)	**2006**	**2005**
Assets		
Current Assets		
Cash and Cash Equivalents	$ 1,814	$ 1,736
Marketable Securities	79	115
Accounts and Notes Receivable	5,198	4,801
Inventories	4,941	4,743
Prepaid Expenses	182	199
Deferred Income Taxes	656	828
Total Current Assets	12,870	12,422
Property, Plant and Equipment	25,719	24,963
Less: Accumulated Depreciation	15,221	14,654
Net Property, Plant and Equipment	10,498	10,309

Analyze:

1. Based on the information presented above, which categories do you think might require adjustments at the end of an operating period?

2. List the potential adjusting entries that would be necessary. Do not worry about the dollar amounts.

3. By what percentage did DuPont's inventories increase from 2005 to 2006?

Analyze Online: Log on to the DuPont Web site (www.dupont.com). Review the current annual report and answer the following questions.

4. What method is used to depreciate property, plant, and equipment at DuPont?

5. What is the company's policy for revenue recognition?

Catalog Sales

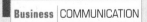

Extending THE THOUGHT

JC Penney Company, Inc., records sales for in-store purchases, catalog, and Internet transactions. For catalog orders, sales are not recorded in the accounting records until customers pick up the merchandise they have ordered. Other retailers record catalog or Internet sales at the point that an order is placed and credit card information has been submitted. Do you agree or disagree with the method that JC Penney, Inc., uses to record catalog sales? Prepare a statement supporting your opinion.

Memo

Business COMMUNICATION

You are the owner of a raw furniture company that sells products via two channels of distribution: the Internet and catalogs. Your accounting clerk has prepared a ten-column worksheet for the month ended September 30, 2010. As you review the worksheet, you notice the following errors.

1. The balances of the **Depreciation Expense** account and the **Insurance Expense** account were carried over into the Balance Sheet Debit columns in error.

2. There were no adjustments recorded for **Merchandise Inventory.**

Prepare a memo to the accounting clerk outlining the errors you have noticed. Explain the impact of the errors on the financial statements. Be sure to explain the importance of the adjustment to the **Merchandise Inventory** account.

Both Sellers and Servers Adjust

Accruals and deferrals can vary for each company. The adjusting entries for a service company will differ from those of a merchandising company. Brainstorm the adjusting entries similarities and differences for a service company and a merchandising company.

There Is Help for Preparing a Trial Balance

The trial balance worksheet is an organizational tool to view the accruals and deferrals on one piece of paper. Use your search engine to search for *Trial Balance Worksheet Templates*. Download several different forms of worksheets and notice the number of helpful excel templates available to download.

Answers to **Self Reviews**

Answers to Section 1 Self Review

1. The worksheet facilitates the end-of-period activities by assembling in one document all data needed. The worksheet provides a place for the trial balance, for entering the necessary adjusting entries, an adjusted trial balance to greatly reduce the chance for mathematical errors, and all the information necessary for closing entries and preparing the income statement and balance sheet.

2. Both the beginning and ending inventory are presented in the income statement, so both should ultimately appear in the Income Statement columns. In the adjusting entries, in effect the beginning balance is closed and transferred to the Income Summary. The ending inventory is entered in the Inventory account by a debit in the Adjustments column and a credit to Income Summary because it reduces the cost of goods sold.

3. Adjusting entries are necessary because the amounts shown for many accounts in the trial balance reflect old data that ignore the fact that assets shown have been partially consumed, that expenses and incomes have not been entered in the accounts even though they have been incurred or earned, and that some liabilities and assets are not reflected in the accounts.

4. **a.** The amount of adjustments is $2,000 ($12,000 ÷ 6).

   b. *Rent Expense* will be debited and *Prepaid Rent* will be credited.

5. *Unearned Fee Income* will be debited for $7,000 and *Fee Income* will be credited for that amount.

6. There is no difference except that the amounts will be different because in one case they reflect only one month's activities and in the other case they reflect 12 months' activities.

Answers to Section 2 Self Review

1. The *Depreciation Expense* account is increased. The book value of the asset is decreased.

2. The net effects are:

   a. Assets are understated by $800.

   b. Liabilities are understated by $300.

   c. Income is understated by $800.

   d. Expenses are understated by $300.

   e. Owner's equity is understated by $500.

3. It appears that there is an error in adding the adjustment amount, or subtracting that amount from, some trial balance amount(s).

4. **a.** "credit" balance sheet column

   d. "debit" income statement column

5. *Interest Expense* is debited and *Interest Payable* is credited.

6. Adjusting entries almost invariably involve the assignment of revenues or expenses to a specific accounting period. If the revenue or expense is not assigned to the correct period, it is assigned to an incorrect period. Thus, both periods are incorrectly stated.

Answers to Comprehensive Self Review

1. The accrual method properly matches expenses with revenues in each accounting period so that statement users can rely on the financial statements prepared for each period.

2. Accrued income is income that has been earned but which has not yet been received in cash or other assets.

3. Accrued income is income earned but not yet received. Unearned income is the reverse of accrued income: It is an amount that has been received, but which has not yet been earned.

4. *Rent Income* will be debited for $12,000 and *Unearned Rent Income* will be credited for that amount.

5. This represents a loss because expenses are greater than income. The loss is $25,000.

Chapter 13

Financial Statements and Closing Procedures

LEARNING OBJECTIVES

1. Prepare a classified income statement from the worksheet.   LP13
2. Prepare a statement of owner's equity from the worksheet.
3. Prepare a classified balance sheet from the worksheet.
4. Journalize and post the adjusting entries.
5. Journalize and post the closing entries.
6. Prepare a postclosing trial balance.
7. Journalize and post reversing entries.
8. Define the accounting terms new to this chapter.

NEW TERMS

classified financial statement
current assets
current liabilities
current ratio
gross profit
gross profit percentage
inventory turnover
liquidity

long-term liabilities
multiple-step income statement
plant and equipment
reversing entries
single-step income statement
working capital

Whole Foods   www.wholefoodsmarket.com

Founded in 1980 in Austin, Texas, Whole Foods Market® is the world's leading retailer of natural and organic foods. In 2007, the company reported sales of $6.6 billion, a 15% increase from the previous year sales. The company operates approximately 275 stores in the United States, Canada, and the United Kingdom.

In early 2007, Whole Foods Market entered into a merger agreement with Wild Oats, a competing organic food retailer. As a result of the merger, Whole Foods Market will gain immediate entry into a significant number of new markets. Whole Foods Market expects to make significant investments in upgrading and improving Wild Oats stores.

The recent merger, combined with the solid historical sales growth of Whole Foods and its significant store development plans for the next couple of years, puts the company on solid financial footing. The company has set some aggressive goals for growth, hoping to reach over $10 billion in sales by 2010.

thinking critically

If you owned stock in Whole Foods Market, what types of financial information would be most important to you?

SECTION OBJECTIVES

>> 1. **Prepare a classified income statement from the worksheet.**

WHY IT'S IMPORTANT

To help decision makers, financial information needs to be presented in a meaningful and easy-to-use way.

>> 2. **Prepare a statement of owner's equity from the worksheet.**

WHY IT'S IMPORTANT

The statement of owner's equity reports changes to and balances of the owner's equity account.

>> 3. **Prepare a classified balance sheet from the worksheet.**

WHY IT'S IMPORTANT

Grouping accounts helps financial statement users to identify total assets, equity, and financial obligations of the business.

TERMS TO LEARN

classified financial statement
current assets
current liabilities
gross profit
liquidity
long-term liabilities
multiple-step income statement
plant and equipment
single-step income statement

Preparing the Financial Statements

The information needed to prepare the financial statements is on the worksheet in the Income Statement and Balance Sheet sections. At the end of the period, Whiteside Antiques prepares three financial statements: income statement, statement of owner's equity, and balance sheet, based on the worksheet you studied in Chapter 12. The income statement and the balance sheet are arranged in a classified format. On **classified financial statements,** revenues, expenses, assets, and liabilities are divided into groups of similar accounts and a subtotal is given for each group. This makes the financial statements more useful to the readers.

Video 13.1

> The annual report of the Coca-Cola Company includes Consolidated Balance Sheets, Consolidated Statements of Income, and Consolidated Statements of Share-Owners' Equity. The annual report also contains a table of Selected Financial Data that reports five consecutive years of summarized financial information.

The Classified Income Statement

A classified income statement is sometimes called a **multiple-step income statement** because several subtotals are computed before net income is calculated. The simpler income statement you learned about in previous chapters is called a **single-step income statement.** It lists all revenues in one section and all expenses in another section. Only one computation is necessary to determine the net income (Total Revenue − Total Expenses = Net Income).

Figure 13.1 on page 435 shows the classified income statement for Whiteside Antiques. Refer to it as you learn how to prepare a multiple-step income statement.

>>**1. OBJECTIVE**

Prepare a classified income statement from the worksheet.

OPERATING REVENUE

The first section of the classified income statement contains the revenue from operations. This is the revenue earned from normal business activities. Other income is presented separately near the bottom of the statement. For Whiteside Antiques, all operating revenue comes from sales of merchandise.

Whiteside Antiques
Income Statement
Year Ended December 31, 2010

Operating Revenue					
Sales					561 650 00
Less Sales Returns and Allowances					12 500 00
Net Sales					549 150 00
Cost of Goods Sold					
Merchandise Inventory, Jan. 1, 2010				52 000 00	
Purchases			321 500 00		
Freight In			9 800 00		
Delivered Cost of Purchases			331 300 00		
Less Purchases Returns and Allowances	3 050 00				
Purchases Discounts	3 130 00		6 180 00		
Net Delivered Cost of Purchases				325 120 00	
Total Merchandise Available for Sale				377 120 00	
Less Merchandise Inventory, Dec. 31, 2010				47 000 00	
Cost of Goods Sold					330 120 00
Gross Profit on Sales					219 030 00
Operating Expenses					
Selling Expenses					
Salaries Expense—Sales			79 690 00		
Advertising Expense			7 425 00		
Cash Short or Over			125 00		
Supplies Expense			4 975 00		
Depreciation Expense—Store Equipment			2 400 00		
Total Selling Expenses				94 615 00	
General and Administrative Expenses					
Rent Expense			27 600 00		
Salaries Expense—Office			26 500 00		
Insurance Expense			2 450 00		
Payroll Taxes Expense			7 371 20		
Telephone Expense			1 875 00		
Uncollectible Accounts Expense			800 00		
Utilities Expense			5 925 00		
Depreciation Expense—Office Equipment			700 00		
Total General and Administrative Expenses				73 221 20	
Total Operating Expenses					167 836 20
Net Income from Operations					51 193 80
Other Income					
Interest Income			166 00		
Miscellaneous Income			366 00		
Total Other Income				532 00	
Other Expenses					
Interest Expense				770 00	
Net Nonoperating Expense					238 00
Net Income for Year					50 955 80

FIGURE 13.1   Classified Income Statement

Because Whiteside Antiques is a retail firm, it does not offer sales discounts to its customers. If it did, the sales discounts would be deducted from total sales in order to compute net sales. The net sales amount is computed as follows.

```
Sales
(Sales Returns and Allowances)
(Sales Discounts)
_____
Net Sales
```

The parentheses indicate that the amount is subtracted. Net sales for Whiteside Antiques are $549,150 for 2010.

COST OF GOODS SOLD

The Cost of Goods Sold section contains information about the cost of the merchandise that was sold during the period. Three elements are needed to compute the cost of goods sold: beginning inventory, net delivered cost of purchases, and ending inventory. The format is

```
      Purchases
  +   Freight In
      (Purchases Returns and Allowances)
      (Purchases Discounts)
      _____
      Net Delivered Cost of Purchases
      Beginning Merchandise Inventory
  +   Net Delivered Cost of Purchases
      _____
      Total Merchandise Available for Sale
      (Ending Merchandise Inventory)
      _____
      Cost of Goods Sold
```

For Whiteside Antiques, the net delivered cost of purchases is $325,120 and the cost of goods sold is $330,120. *Merchandise Inventory* is the one account that appears on both the income statement and the balance sheet. Beginning and ending merchandise inventory balances appear on the income statement. Ending merchandise inventory also appears on the balance sheet in the Assets section.

GROSS PROFIT ON SALES

The **gross profit** on sales is the difference between the net sales and the cost of goods sold. For Whiteside, net sales is the revenue earned from selling antique items. Cost of goods sold is what Whiteside paid for the antiques that were sold during the fiscal period. Gross profit is what is left to cover operating expenses and provide a profit. The format is

```
Net Sales
(Cost of Goods Sold)
_____
Gross Profit on Sales
```

The gross profit on sales is $219,030.

OPERATING EXPENSES

Operating expenses are expenses that arise from normal business activities. Whiteside Antiques separates operating expenses into two categories: *Selling Expenses* and *General and Administrative Expenses*. The selling expenses relate directly to the sale and delivery of goods. The general and administrative expenses are necessary for business operations but are not directly connected with the sales function. Rent, utilities, and salaries for office employees are examples of general and administrative expenses.

FIGURE 13.2

Statement of Owner's Equity

Whiteside Antiques								
Statement of Owner's Equity								
Year Ended December 31, 2010								
Bill Whiteside, Capital, January 1, 2010					61	2 2 1	00	
Net Income for Year	50	9 5 5	80					
Less Withdrawals for the Year	27	6 0 0	00					
Increase in Capital					23	3 5 5	80	
Bill Whiteside, Capital, December 31, 2010					84	5 7 6	80	

NET INCOME OR NET LOSS FROM OPERATIONS

Keeping operating and nonoperating income separate helps financial statement users learn about the operating efficiency of the firm. The format for determining net income (or net loss) from operations is

> Gross Profit on Sales
> (Total Operating Expenses)
> _____
> Net Income (or Net Loss) from Operations

For Whiteside Antiques, net income from operations is $51,193.80.

OTHER INCOME AND OTHER EXPENSES

Income that is earned from sources other than normal business activities appears in the Other Income section. For Whiteside Antiques, other income includes interest on notes receivable and one miscellaneous income item.

Expenses that are not directly connected with business operations appear in the Other Expenses section. The only other expense for Whiteside Antiques is interest expense.

NET INCOME OR NET LOSS

Net income is all the revenue minus all the expenses. For Whiteside Antiques, net income is $50,955.80. If there is a net loss, it appears in parentheses. Net income or net loss is used to prepare the statement of owner's equity.

LP13

The Statement of Owner's Equity

>>2. OBJECTIVE
Prepare a statement of owner's equity from the worksheet.

The statement of owner's equity reports the changes that occurred in the owner's financial interest during the period. Figure 13.2 shows the statement of owner's equity for Whiteside Antiques. The ending capital balance for Bill Whiteside, $84,576.80, is used to prepare the balance sheet.

The Classified Balance Sheet

>>3. OBJECTIVE
Prepare a classified balance sheet from the worksheet.

The classified balance sheet divides the various assets and liabilities into groups. Figure 13.3 on page 438 shows the balance sheet for Whiteside Antiques. Refer to it as you learn how to prepare a classified balance sheet.

Video13.1

CURRENT ASSETS

Current assets consist of cash, items that will normally be converted into cash within one year, and items that will be used up within one year. Current assets are usually listed in order of liquidity. **Liquidity** is the ease with which an item can be converted into cash. Current assets

Whiteside Antiques					
Balance Sheet					
December 31, 2010					
Assets					
Current Assets					
Cash				13 1 3 6 00	
Petty Cash Fund				1 0 0 00	
Notes Receivable				1 2 0 0 00	
Accounts Receivable		32 0 0 0 00			
Less Allowance for Doubtful Accounts		1 0 5 0 00	30 9 5 0 00		
Interest Receivable			3 0 00		
Merchandise Inventory			47 0 0 0 00		
Prepaid Expenses					
Supplies		1 3 2 5 00			
Prepaid Insurance		4 9 0 0 00			
Prepaid Interest		7 5 00	6 3 0 0 00		
Total Current Assets			98 7 1 6 00		
Plant and Equipment					
Store Equipment	30 0 0 0 00				
Less Accumulated Depreciation	2 4 0 0 00	27 6 0 0 00			
Office Equipment	5 0 0 0 00				
Less Accumulated Depreciation	7 0 0 00	4 3 0 0 00			
Total Plant and Equipment			31 9 0 0 00		
Total Assets			130 6 1 6 00		
Liabilities and Owner's Equity					
Current Liabilities					
Notes Payable—Trade		2 0 0 0 00			
Notes Payable—Bank		9 0 0 0 00			
Accounts Payable		24 1 2 9 00			
Interest Payable		2 0 00			
Social Security Tax Payable		1 1 5 8 40			
Medicare Tax Payable		2 6 7 40			
Employee Income Tax Payable		9 9 0 00			
Federal Unemployment Tax Payable		9 60			
State Unemployment Tax Payable		6 4 80			
Salaries Payable		1 2 0 0 00			
Sales Tax Payable		7 2 0 0 00			
Total Current Liabilities			46 0 3 9 20		
Owner's Equity					
Bill Whiteside, Capital			84 5 7 6 80		
Total Liabilities and Owner's Equity			130 6 1 6 00		

recall

Book Value

Book value is the portion of the original cost that has not been depreciated. Usually, book value bears no relation to the market value of the asset.

are vital to the survival of a business because they provide the funds needed to pay bills and meet expenses. The current assets for Whiteside Antiques total $98,716.

PLANT AND EQUIPMENT

Noncurrent assets are called *long-term assets*. An important category of long-term assets is plant and equipment. **Plant and equipment** consists of property that will be used in the business for longer than one year. For many businesses, plant and equipment represents a sizable investment. The balance sheet shows three amounts for each category of plant and equipment:

Asset

(Accumulated depreciation)

Book value

For Whiteside Antiques, total plant and equipment is $31,900.

CURRENT LIABILITIES

Current liabilities are the debts that must be paid within one year. They are usually listed in order of priority of payment. Management must ensure that funds are available to pay current liabilities when they become due in order to maintain the firm's good credit reputation. For Whiteside Antiques, total current liabilities are $46,039.20.

LONG-TERM LIABILITIES

Long-term liabilities are debts of the business that are due more than one year in the future. Although repayment of long-term liabilities might not be due for several years, management must make sure that periodic interest is paid promptly. Long-term liabilities include mortgages, notes payable, and loans payable. Whiteside Antiques had no long-term liabilities on December 31, 2010.

OWNER'S EQUITY

Whiteside Antiques prepares a separate statement of owner's equity that reports all information about changes that occurred in Bill Whiteside's financial interest during the period. The ending balance from that statement is transferred to the Owner's Equity section of the balance sheet.

Section 1 Self Review

QUESTIONS

1. Why are financial statements prepared in classified form?

2. What is the distinction between current liabilities and long-term liabilities?

3. What is gross profit on sales?

EXERCISES

4. Which of the following is not a current asset?

   a. Merchandise inventory

   b. A note receivable due in 13 months

   c. Prepaid insurance covering the next eight months

   d. A note receivable due in eight months

5. How should purchases returns and allowances be shown on the income statement?

   a. As Other Income

   b. As a deduction from the delivered cost of purchases

   c. As an addition to Sales

   d. As Other Expenses

ANALYSIS

6. Assume that a business listed the *Freight In* account in the Operating Expense section of the income statement. What is the effect on net purchases? On total operating expenses? On net income from operations?

(Answers to Section 1 Self Review are on page 473.)

SECTION OBJECTIVES	TERMS TO LEARN

SECTION OBJECTIVES

>> **4. Journalize and post the adjusting entries.**

WHY IT'S IMPORTANT
Adjusting entries match revenue and expenses to the proper periods.

>> **5. Journalize and post the closing entries.**

WHY IT'S IMPORTANT
The temporary accounts are closed in order to prepare for the next accounting period.

>> **6. Prepare a postclosing trial balance.**

WHY IT'S IMPORTANT
The general ledger must remain in balance.

>> **7. Journalize and post reversing entries.**

WHY IT'S IMPORTANT
Reversing entries are made so that transactions can be recorded in the usual way in the next accounting period.

TERMS TO LEARN

current ratio
gross profit percentage
inventory turnover
reversing entries
working capital

Completing the Accounting Cycle

The complete accounting cycle was presented in Chapter 6 (pages 168–169). In this section, we will complete the accounting cycle for Whiteside Antiques.

>>**4. OBJECTIVE**

Journalize and post the adjusting entries.

Journalizing and Posting the Adjusting Entries

All adjustments are shown on the worksheet. After the financial statements have been prepared, the adjustments are made a permanent part of the accounting records. They are recorded in the general journal as adjusting journal entries and are posted to the general ledger.

JOURNALIZING THE ADJUSTING ENTRIES

Figure 13.4 on pages 441–443 shows the adjusting journal entries for Whiteside Antiques. Each adjusting entry shows how the adjustment was calculated. Supervisors and auditors need to understand, without additional explanation, why the adjustment was made.

Let's review the types of adjusting entries made by Whiteside Antiques:

Type of Adjustment	Worksheet Reference	Purpose
Inventory	(a–b)	Removes beginning inventory and adds ending inventory to the accounting records.
Expense	(c–e)	Matches expense to revenue for the period; the credit is to a contra asset account.
Accrued Expense	(f–i)	Matches expense to revenue for the period; the credit is to a liability account.
Prepaid Expense	(j–l)	Matches expense to revenue for the period; the credit is to an asset account.
Accrued Income	(m–n)	Recognizes income earned in the period. The debit is to an asset account *(Interest Receivable)*.

GENERAL JOURNAL   PAGE ___25___

	DATE		DESCRIPTION	POST. REF.	DEBIT	CREDIT	
1			*Adjusting Entries*				1
2	2010		(Adjustment a)				2
3	Dec.	31	Income Summary	399	52 000 00		3
4			Merchandise Inventory	121		52 000 00	4
5			To transfer beginning inventory				5
6			to Income Summary				6
7							7
8			(Adjustment b)				8
9		31	Merchandise Inventory	121	47 000 00		9
10			Income Summary	399		47 000 00	10
11			To record ending inventory				11
12							12
13			(Adjustment c)				13
14		31	Uncollectible Accounts Expense	685	800 00		14
15			Allowance For Doubtful Accounts	112		800 00	15
16			To record estimated loss				16
17			from uncollectible accounts				17
18			based on 0.80% of net				18
19			credit sales of $100,000				19
20							20
21			(Adjustment d)				21
22		31	Depreciation Expense—Store Equip.	620	2 400 00		22
23			Accum. Depreciation—Store Equip.	132		2 400 00	23
24			To record depreciation				24
25			for 2010 as shown by				25
26			schedule on file				26
27							27
28			(Adjustment e)				28
29		31	Depreciation Expense—Office Equip.	689	700 00		29
30			Accum. Depreciation—Office Equip.	142		700 00	30
31			To record depreciation				31
32			for 2010 as shown by				32
33			schedule on file				33
34							34
35			(Adjustment f)				35
36		31	Salaries Expense—Sales	602	1 200 00		36
37			Salaries Payable	229		1 200 00	37
38			To record accrued salaries				38
39			of part-time sales clerks				39
40			for Dec. 28–31				40

(continued)

FIGURE 13.4

Adjusting Entries in the General Journal

FIGURE 13.4

(continued) Adjusting Entries in
the General Journal

GENERAL JOURNAL   PAGE ___26___

	DATE		DESCRIPTION	POST. REF.	DEBIT	CREDIT	
1			*Adjusting Entries*				1
2	2010		(Adjustment g)				2
3	Dec.	31	Payroll Taxes Expense	665	9 1 80		3
4			Social Security Tax Payable	221		7 4 40	4
5			Medicare Tax Payable	223		1 7 40	5
6			To record accrued payroll				6
7			taxes on accrued salaries				7
8			for Dec. 28–31				8
9							9
10			(Adjustment h)				10
11		31	Payroll Taxes Expense	665	7 4 40		11
12			Fed. Unemployment Tax Payable	225		9 60	12
13			State Unemployment Tax Payable	227		6 4 80	13
14			To record accrued payroll				14
15			taxes on accrued salaries				15
16			for Dec. 28–31				16
17							17
18			(Adjustment i)				18
19		31	Interest Expense	695	2 0 00		19
20			Interest Payable	216		2 0 00	20
21			To record interest on a				21
22			2-month, $2,000, 12%				22
23			note payable dated				23
24			Dec. 1, 2010				24
25							25
26			(Adjustment j)				26
27		31	Supplies Expense	615	4 9 7 5 00		27
28			Supplies	129		4 9 7 5 00	28
29			To record supplies used				29
30							30
31			(Adjustment k)				31
32		31	Insurance Expense	660	2 4 5 0 00		32
33			Prepaid Insurance	126		2 4 5 0 00	33
34			To record expired				34
35			insurance on 3-year				35
36			policy purchased for				36
37			$7,350 on Jan. 2, 2010				37
38							38
39							39
40							40

GENERAL JOURNAL   PAGE ___27___

	DATE		DESCRIPTION	POST. REF.	DEBIT	CREDIT	
1	2010		(Adjustment l)				1
2	Dec.	31	Interest Expense	695	1 5 0 00		2
3			Prepaid Interest	127		1 5 0 00	3
4			To record transfer of 2/3				4
5			of prepaid interest of				5
6			$225 for a 3-month,				6
7			10% note payable issued				7
8			to bank on Nov. 1, 2010				8
9							9
10			(Adjustment m)				10
11		31	Interest Receivable	116	3 0 00		11
12			Interest Income	491		3 0 00	12
13			To record accrued interest				13
14			earned on a 4-month,				14
15			15% note receivable				15
16			dated Nov. 1, 2010				16
17			($1,200 x 0.15 x 2/12)				17
18							18

FIGURE 13.4

(concluded) Adjusting Entries in the General Journal

POSTING THE ADJUSTING ENTRIES

After the adjustments have been recorded in the general journal, they are promptly posted to the general ledger. The word *Adjusting* is entered in the Description column of the general ledger account. This distinguishes it from entries for transactions that occurred during that period. After the adjusting entries have been posted, the general ledger account balances match the amounts shown in the Adjusted Trial Balance section of the worksheet in Figure 12.2.

Video13.2

Journalizing and Posting the Closing Entries

At the end of the period, the temporary accounts are closed. The temporary accounts are the revenue, cost of goods sold, expense, and drawing accounts.

JOURNALIZING THE CLOSING ENTRIES

The Income Statement section of the worksheet in Figure 12.2 on pages 408–410 provides the data needed to prepare closing entries. There are four steps in the closing process.

1. Close revenue accounts and cost of goods sold accounts with credit balances to *Income Summary.*
2. Close expense accounts and cost of goods sold accounts with debit balances to *Income Summary.*
3. Close *Income Summary,* which now reflects the net income or loss for the period, to owner's capital.
4. Close the drawing account to owner's capital.

Step 1: Closing the Revenue Accounts and the Cost of Goods Sold Accounts with Credit Balances. The first entry closes the revenue accounts and other temporary income statement accounts with credit balances. Look at the Income Statement

>>5. OBJECTIVE

Journalize and post the closing entries.

LP13

section of the worksheet in Figure 12.2. There are five items listed in the Credit column, not including *Income Summary.* Debit each account, except *Income Summary,* for its balance. Credit *Income Summary* for the total, $568,362.

GENERAL JOURNAL   PAGE ___28___

	DATE	DESCRIPTION	POST. REF.	DEBIT	CREDIT	
1	2010	*Closing Entries*				1
2	Dec. 31	Sales	401	561 650 00		2
3		Interest Income	491	166 00		3
4		Miscellaneous Income	493	366 00		4
5		Purchases Returns and Allowances	503	3 050 00		5
6		Purchases Discounts	504	3 130 00		6
7		Income Summary			568 362 00	7

Step 2: **Closing the Expense Accounts and the Cost of Goods Sold Accounts with Debit Balances.** The Debit column of the Income Statement section of the worksheet in Figure 12.2 shows the expense accounts and the cost of goods sold accounts with debit balances. Credit each account, *except Income Summary,* for its balance. Debit *Income Summary* for the total, $512,406.20.

GENERAL JOURNAL   PAGE ___28___

	DATE	DESCRIPTION	POST. REF.	DEBIT	CREDIT	
1	2010					1
9	Dec. 31	Income Summary	399	512 406 20		9
10		Sales Returns and Allowances	451		12 500 00	10
11		Purchases	501		321 500 00	11
12		Freight In	502		9 800 00	12
13		Salaries Expense—Sales	602		79 690 00	13
14		Advertising Expense	605		7 425 00	14
15		Cash Short or Over	610		125 00	15
16		Supplies Expense	615		4 975 00	16
17		Depreciation Expense—Store Equip.	620		2 400 00	17
18		Rent Expense	640		27 600 00	18
19		Salaries Expense—Office	645		26 500 00	19
20		Insurance Expense	660		2 450 00	20
21		Payroll Taxes Expense	665		7 371 20	21
22		Telephone Expense	680		1 875 00	22
23		Uncollectible Accounts Expense	685		800 00	23
24		Utilities Expense	687		5 925 00	24
25		Depreciation Expense—Office Equip.	689		700 00	25
26		Interest Expense	695		770 00	26

Step 3: **Closing the Income Summary Account.** After the first two closing entries have been posted, the balance of the *Income Summary* account is equal to the net income or net loss for the period. The third closing entry transfers the *Income Summary* balance to the owner's capital account. *Income Summary* after the second closing entry has a balance of $50,955.80.

Income Summary			
12/31	52,000.00	12/31	47,000.00
12/31	512,406.20	12/31	568,362.00
	564,406.20		615,362.00
		Bal.	50,955.80

Adjusting Entries (a–b)
Closing Entries

For Whiteside Antiques, the third closing entry is as follows. This closes the *Income Summary* account, which remains closed until it is used in the end-of-period process for the next year.

GENERAL JOURNAL   PAGE ___28___

	DATE		DESCRIPTION	POST. REF.	DEBIT	CREDIT	
28	Dec.	31	Income Summary	399	50 955 80		28
29			Bill Whiteside, Capital	301		50 955 80	29

Step 4: Closing the Drawing Account. This entry closes the drawing account and updates the capital account so that its balance agrees with the ending capital reported on the statement of owner's equity and on the balance sheet.

GENERAL JOURNAL   PAGE ___28___

	DATE		DESCRIPTION	POST. REF.	DEBIT	CREDIT	
31	Dec.	31	Bill Whiteside, Capital	301	27 600 00		31
32			Bill Whiteside, Drawing	302		27 600 00	32

POSTING THE CLOSING ENTRIES

The closing entries are posted from the general journal to the general ledger. The word *Closing* is entered in the Description column of each account that is closed. After the closing entry is posted, each temporary account balance is zero.

Preparing a Postclosing Trial Balance

After the closing entries have been posted, prepare a postclosing trial balance to confirm that the general ledger is in balance. Only the accounts that have balances—the asset, liability and owner's capital accounts—appear on the postclosing trial balance. The postclosing trial balance matches the amounts reported on the balance sheet. To verify this, compare the postclosing trial balance, Figure 13.5 on page 446, with the balance sheet, Figure 13.3 on page 438.

If the postclosing trial balance shows that the general ledger is out of balance, find and correct the error or errors immediately. Any necessary correcting entries must be journalized and posted so that the general ledger is in balance before any transactions can be recorded for the new period.

>>6. OBJECTIVE

Prepare a postclosing trial balance.

LP13

FIGURE 13.5

Postclosing Trial Balance

		Whiteside Antiques					
		Postclosing Trial Balance					
		December 31, 2010					
ACCOUNT NAME				DEBIT			CREDIT	
Cash			13	1 3 6	00		
Petty Cash Fund				1 0 0	00		
Notes Receivable			1	2 0 0	00		
Accounts Receivable			32	0 0 0	00		
Allowance for Doubtful Accounts						1 0 5 0	00
Interest Receivable				3 0	00		
Merchandise Inventory			47	0 0 0	00		
Supplies			1	3 2 5	00		
Prepaid Insurance			4	9 0 0	00		
Prepaid Interest				7 5	00		
Store Equipment			30	0 0 0	00		
Accumulated Depreciation—Store Equipment						2 4 0 0	00
Office Equipment			5	0 0 0	00		
Accumulated Depreciation—Office Equipment						7 0 0	00
Notes Payable—Trade						2 0 0 0	00
Notes Payable—Bank						9 0 0 0	00
Accounts Payable						24 1 2 9	00
Interest Payable						2 0	00
Social Security Tax Payable						1 1 5 8	40
Medicare Tax Payable						2 6 7	40
Employee Income Taxes Payable						9 9 0	00
Federal Unemployment Tax Payable						9	60
State Unemployment Tax Payable						6 4	80
Salaries Payable						1 2 0 0	00
Sales Tax Payable						7 2 0 0	00
Bill Whiteside, Capital						84 5 7 6	80
Totals			134	7 6 6	00	134 7 6 6	00

Interpreting the Financial Statements

Interested parties analyze the financial statements to evaluate the results of operations and to make decisions. Interpreting financial statements requires an understanding of the business and the environment in which it operates as well as the nature and limitations of accounting information. Ratios and other measurements are used to analyze and interpret financial statements. Four such measurements are used by Whiteside Antiques.

The **gross profit percentage** reveals the amount of gross profit from each sales dollar. The gross profit percentage is calculated by dividing gross profit by net sales. For Whiteside, for every dollar of net sales, gross profit was almost 40 cents.

important!

Current Ratio

Banks and other lenders look closely at the current ratio of each loan applicant.

$$\frac{\text{Gross profit}}{\text{Net sales}} = \frac{\$219,030}{\$549,150} = 0.3988 = 39.9\%$$

Working capital is the difference between total current assets and total current liabilities. It is a measure of the firm's ability to pay its current obligations. Whiteside Antiques' working capital is $52,676.80, calculated as follows:

Current assets − Current liabilities = $98,716.00 − 46,039.20 = $52,676.80

The **current ratio** is a relationship between current assets and current liabilities that provides a measure of a firm's ability to pay its current debts. Whiteside has $2.14 in current assets for every dollar of current liabilities. The current ratio may also be compared to other firms in the same business. The current ratio is calculated in the following manner.

$$\frac{\text{Current assets}}{\text{Current liabilities}} = \frac{\$98,716.00}{\$46,039.20} = 2.14 \text{ to } 1$$

Caterpillar Inc. reported current assets of $23.1 billion and current liabilities of $19.3 billion on December 31, 2006. The current ratio shows that the business has $1.20 of current assets for each dollar of current liabilities.

Inventory turnover shows the number of times inventory is replaced during the accounting period. Inventory turnover is calculated in the following manner.

$$\text{Inventory turnover} = \frac{\text{Cost of goods sold}}{\text{Average inventory}}$$

$$\text{Average inventory} = \frac{\text{Beginning inventory + Ending inventory}}{2}$$

$$\text{Average inventory} = \frac{\$52,000 + \$47,000}{2} = \$49,500$$

$$\text{Inventory turnover} = \frac{\$330,120}{\$49,500} = 6.67 \text{ times}$$

For Whiteside Antiques, the average inventory for the year was $49,500. The inventory turnover was 6.67; that is, inventory was replaced about seven times during the year.

Journalizing and Posting Reversing Entries

Some adjustments made at the end of one period can cause problems in the next period. **Reversing entries** are made to reverse the effect of certain adjustments. This helps prevent errors in recording payments or cash receipts in the new accounting period.

Let's use adjustment **(f)** as an illustration of how reversing entries are helpful. On December 31, Whiteside Antiques owed $1,200 of salaries to its part-time sales clerks. The salaries will be paid in January. To recognize the salaries expense in December, adjustment **(f)** was made to debit *Salaries Expense—Sales* for $1,200 and credit *Salaries Payable* for $1,200. The adjustment was recorded and posted in the accounting records.

By payday on January 3, the part-time sales clerks have earned $1,700:

$1,200   earned in December
$ 500   earned in January

The entry to record the January 3 payment of the salaries is a debit to *Salaries Expense—Sales* for $500, a debit to *Salaries Payable* for $1,200, and a credit to *Cash* for $1,700. This entry recognizes the salary expense for January and reduces the *Salaries Payable* account to zero.

Salaries Expense—Sales				Cash			
1/3	500			12/31	13,136	1/3	1,700
				Bal.	11,436		

Salaries Expense—Sales			
1/3	1,200	12/31	1,200
		Bal.	0

To record this transaction, the accountant had to review the adjustment in the end-of-period records and divide the amount paid between the expense and liability accounts. This review is time consuming, can cause errors, and is sometimes forgotten.

>>**7. OBJECTIVE**
Journalize and post reversing entries.

LP13

recall

Accrual Basis
Revenues are recognized when earned, and expenses are recognized when incurred or used, regardless of when cash is received or paid.

Reversing entries provide a way to guard against oversights, eliminate the review of accounting records, and simplify the entry made in the new period. As an example of a reversing entry, we will analyze the same transaction (January 3 payroll of $1,700) if reversing entries are made.

First, record the adjustment on December 31. Then record the reversing entry on January 1. Note that the reversing entry is the exact opposite (the reverse) of the adjustment. After the reversing entry is posted, the **Salaries Payable** account shows a zero balance and the **Salaries Expense—Sales** account has a credit balance. This is unusual because the normal balance of an expense account is a debit.

GENERAL JOURNAL   PAGE ___25___

	DATE		DESCRIPTION	POST. REF.	DEBIT	CREDIT	
1	2010		Adjusting Entries				1
35			(Adjustment f)				35
36	Dec.	31	Salaries Expense—Sales	602	1 2 0 0 00		36
37			Salaries Payable	229		1 2 0 0 00	37

GENERAL JOURNAL   PAGE ___29___

	DATE		DESCRIPTION	POST. REF.	DEBIT	CREDIT	
1	2011		Reversing Entries				1
2	Jan.	1	Salaries Payable	229	1 2 0 0 00		2
3			Salaries Expense—Sales	602		1 2 0 0 00	3

ACCOUNT _Salaries Payable_   ACCOUNT NO. _229_

DATE		DESCRIPTION	POST. REF.	DEBIT	CREDIT	BALANCE DEBIT	BALANCE CREDIT
2010							
Dec.	31	Adjusting	J25		1 2 0 0 00		1 2 0 0 00
2011							
Jan.	1	Reversing	J29	1 2 0 0 00			—0—

ACCOUNT _Salaries Expense—Sales_   ACCOUNT NO. _602_

DATE		DESCRIPTION	POST. REF.	DEBIT	CREDIT	BALANCE DEBIT	BALANCE CREDIT
2010							
Dec.	31	Balance				78 4 9 0 00	
	31	Adjusting	J25	1 2 0 0 00		79 6 9 0 00	
	31	Closing	J28		79 6 9 0 00	—0—	
2011							
Jan.	1	Reversing	J29		1 2 0 0 00		1 2 0 0 00

On January 3, the payment of $1,700 of salaries is recorded in the normal manner. Notice that this entry reduces cash and increases the expense account for the entire $1,700. It does not allocate the $1,700 between the expense and liability accounts.

GENERAL JOURNAL   PAGE ___30___

	DATE		DESCRIPTION	POST. REF.	DEBIT	CREDIT	
1	2011						1
2	Jan.	3	Salaries Expense—Sales	602	1 7 0 0 00		2
3			Cash	101		1 7 0 0 00	3

After this entry is posted, the expenses are properly divided between the two periods: $1,200 in December and $500 in January. The **Salaries Payable** account has a zero balance. The accountant did not have to review the previous records or allocate the payment between two accounts when the salaries were paid.

ACCOUNT _Salaries Expense—Sales_   ACCOUNT NO. _602_

DATE		DESCRIPTION	POST. REF.	DEBIT	CREDIT	BALANCE DEBIT	BALANCE CREDIT
2010							
Dec.	31	Balance				78 4 9 0 00	
	31	Adjusting	J25	1 2 0 0 00		79 6 9 0 00	
	31	Closing	J28		79 6 9 0 00	—0—	
2011							
Jan.	1	Reversing	J29		1 2 0 0 00		1 2 0 0 00
	3		J30	1 7 0 0 00		5 0 0 00	

IDENTIFYING ITEMS FOR REVERSAL

Not all adjustments need to be reversed. Normally, reversing entries are made for accrued items that involve future payments or receipts of cash. Reversing entries are not made for uncollectible accounts, depreciation, and prepaid expenses—if they are initially recorded as assets. However, when prepaid expenses are initially recorded as expenses (the alternative method), the end-of-period adjustment needs to be reversed.

Whiteside Antiques makes reversing entries for:

- accrued salaries—adjustment (**f**),
- accrued payroll taxes—adjustments (**g**) and (**h**),
- interest payable—adjustment (**i**),
- interest receivable—adjustment (**m**).

JOURNALIZING REVERSING ENTRIES

We just analyzed the reversing entry for accrued salaries, adjustment (**f**). The next two reversing entries are for accrued payroll taxes. Making these reversing entries means that the accountant does not have to review the year-end adjustments before recording the payment of payroll taxes in the next year.

GENERAL JOURNAL   PAGE _29_

	DATE		DESCRIPTION	POST. REF.	DEBIT	CREDIT	
1	2011						1
6	Jan.	1	Social Security Tax Payable	221	7 4 40		6
7			Medicare Tax Payable	223	1 7 40		7
8			Payroll Taxes Expense	665		9 1 80	8
9			To reverse adjusting entry				9
10			(g) made Dec. 31, 2010				10
11							11
12		1	Federal Unemployment Tax Payable	225	9 60		12
13			State Unemployment Tax Payable	227	6 4 80		13
14			Payroll Taxes Expense	665		7 4 40	14
15			To reverse adjusting entry				15
16			(h) made Dec. 31, 2010				16

The next reversing entry is for accrued interest expense. The reversing entry that follows prevents recording difficulties when the note is paid on February 1.

GENERAL JOURNAL PAGE 29

	DATE	DESCRIPTION	POST. REF.	DEBIT	CREDIT	
18	Jan. 1	Interest Payable	216	2 0 00		18
19		Interest Expense	695		2 0 00	19
20		To reverse adjusting entry				20
21		(i) made Dec. 31, 2010				21

In addition to adjustments for accrued expenses, Whiteside Antiques made two adjustments for accrued income items. The next reversing entry is for accrued interest income on the note receivable. Whiteside will receive cash for the note and the interest on March 1. The reversing entry eliminates any difficulties in recording the interest income when the note is paid on March 1.

GENERAL JOURNAL PAGE 29

	DATE	DESCRIPTION	POST. REF.	DEBIT	CREDIT	
23	Jan. 1	Interest Income	491	3 0 00		23
24		Interest Receivable	116		3 0 00	24
25		To reverse adjusting entry				25
26		(m) made Dec. 31, 2010				26

After the reversing entry has been posted, the **Interest Receivable** account has a zero balance and the **Interest Income** account has a debit balance of $30. This is unusual because the normal balance of **Interest Income** is a credit.

On March 1, Whiteside Antiques received a check for $1,260 in payment of the note ($1,200) and the interest ($60). The transaction is recorded in the normal manner as a debit to **Cash** for $1,260, a credit to **Notes Receivable** for $1,200, and a credit to **Interest Income** for $60.

Refer to the **Interest Income** general ledger account below. After this entry has been posted, interest income is properly divided between the two periods, $30 in the previous year and $30 in the current year. The balance of **Interest Receivable** is zero. The accountant does not have to review the year-end adjustments before recording the receipt of the principal and interest relating to the note receivable on March 1.

ACCOUNT Interest Receivable   ACCOUNT NO. 116

DATE		DESCRIPTION	POST. REF.	DEBIT	CREDIT	BALANCE DEBIT	BALANCE CREDIT
2010							
Dec.	31	Adjusting	J27	3 0 00		3 0 00	
2011							
Jan.	1	Reversing	J29		3 0 00	–0–	

ACCOUNT Interest Income   ACCOUNT NO. 491

DATE		DESCRIPTION	POST. REF.	DEBIT	CREDIT	BALANCE DEBIT	BALANCE CREDIT
2010							
Dec.	31	Balance					1 3 6 00
	31	Adjusting	J27		3 0 00		1 6 6 00
	31	Closing	J28	1 6 6 00			–0–
2011							
Jan.	1	Reversing	J29	3 0 00		3 0 00	
Mar.	1		CR3		6 0 00		3 0 00

Review of the Accounting Cycle

In Chapters 7, 8, and 9, Maxx-Out Sporting Goods was used to introduce accounting procedures, records, and statements for merchandising businesses. In Chapters 12 and 13, Whiteside Antiques was used to illustrate the end-of-period activities for merchandising businesses. Underlying the various procedures described were the steps in the accounting cycle. Let's review the accounting cycle.

1. *Analyze transactions.* Transaction data comes into an accounting system from a variety of source documents—sales slips, purchase invoices, credit memorandums, check stubs, and so on. Each document is analyzed to determine the accounts and amounts affected.

2. *Journalize the data about transactions.* Each transaction is recorded in either a special journal or the general journal.

3. *Post the data about transactions.* Each transaction is transferred from the journal to the ledger accounts. Merchandising businesses typically maintain several subsidiary ledgers in addition to the general ledger.

4. *Prepare a worksheet.* At the end of each period, a worksheet is prepared. The Trial Balance section of the worksheet is used to prove the equality of the debits and credits in the general ledger. Adjustments are entered in the Adjustments section so that the financial statements will be prepared using the accrual basis of accounting. The Adjusted Trial Balance section is used to prove the equality of the debit and credits of the updated account balances. The Income Statement and Balance Sheet sections are used to arrange data in an orderly manner.

5. *Prepare financial statements.* A formal set of financial statements is prepared to report information to interested parties.

6. *Journalize and post adjusting entries.* Adjusting entries are journalized and posted in the accounting records. This creates a permanent record of the changes shown on the worksheet.

7. *Journalize and post closing entries.* Closing entries are journalized and posted in order to transfer the results of operations to owner's equity and to prepare the temporary accounts for the next period. The closing entries reduce the temporary account balances to zero.

8. *Prepare a postclosing trial balance.* The postclosing trial balance confirms that the general ledger is still in balance and that the temporary accounts have zero balances.

9. *Interpret the financial information.* The accountant, owners, managers, and other interested parties interpret the information shown in the financial statements and other less formal financial reports that might be prepared. This information is used to evaluate the results of operations and the financial position of the business and to make decisions.

In addition to the nine steps listed here, some firms record reversing entries. Reversing entries simplify the recording of cash payments for accrued expenses and cash receipts for accrued income.

Figure 13.6 on page 452 shows the flow of data through an accounting system that uses special journals and subsidiary ledgers. The system is composed of subsystems that perform specialized functions.

The accounts receivable area records transactions involving sales and cash receipts and maintains the individual accounts for credit customers. This area also handles billing for credit customers.

The accounts payable area records transactions involving purchases and cash payments and maintains the individual accounts for creditors.

The general ledger and financial reporting area records transactions in the general journal, maintains the general ledger accounts, performs the end-of-period procedures, and prepares financial statements. This area is the focal point for the accounting system because all transactions eventually flow into the general ledger. In turn, the general ledger provides the data that appear in the financial statements.

Video 13.2

ABOUT ACCOUNTING

Professional Conduct
In September 1998, the Securities and Exchange (SEC) defined improper professional conduct by accountants. The new rule allowed the SEC to censure, suspend, or bar accountants who violate it. The American Institute of Certified Public Accountants (AICPA) supported the rule. The rule led to the dissolution of one of the nation's "big five" accounting firms (Arthur Andersen) in 2003 following the imposition of severe sanctions of the firm in the "Enron Affair," in which Arthur Andersen was the auditor for Enron. The Sarbanes-Oxley Act has further strengthened the SEC's power over professional conduct by accountants.

MANAGERIAL IMPLICATIONS `<<`

FINANCIAL STATEMENTS

■ Managers carefully study the financial statements to evaluate the operating efficiency and financial strength of the business.

■ A common analysis technique is to compare the data on current statements with the data from previous statements. This can reveal developing trends.

■ In large businesses, financial statements are compared with the published financial reports of other companies in the same industry.

■ In order to evaluate information on classified financial statements, managers need to understand the nature and significance of the groupings.

■ Management ensures that closing entries are promptly made so that transactions for the new period can be recorded. Any significant delay means that valuable information, such as the firm's cash position, will not be available or up to date.

■ The efficiency and effectiveness of the adjusting and closing procedures can have a positive effect on the annual independent audit. For example, detailed descriptions in the general journal make it easy for the auditor to understand the adjusting entries.

THINKING CRITICALLY

How can managers use the financial statements to learn about a company's operating efficiency?

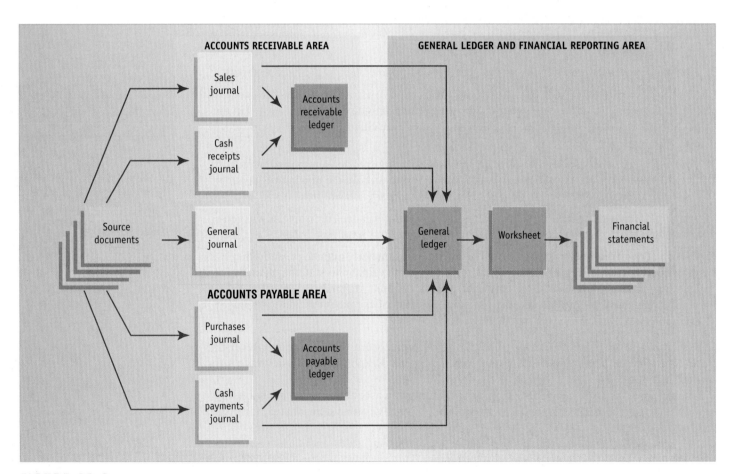

FIGURE 13.6   **Flow of Financial Data through an Accounting System**

Section 2 Self Review

QUESTIONS

1. Which adjusting entries should be reversed?

2. Why do adjusting entries need detailed explanations in the general journal?

3. What do the four steps in the closing process accomplish?

EXERCISES

4. A reversing entry is made for an end-of-period adjustment that recorded

   a. estimated bad debts for the period.

   b. an accrued expense that involves future cash payments.

   c. a transfer of an amount from a prepaid expense account to an expense account.

   d. the change in merchandise inventory.

5. The current ratio is

   a. current liabilities divided by current assets,

   b. the sum of Cash, Accounts Receivable and Notes Receivable, divided by Current Liabilities.

   c. current assets divided by total liabilities.

   d. current assets divided by current liabilities.

ANALYSIS

6. At the end of the previous accounting period, an adjusting entry to record accrued employer's payroll taxes was made. Reversing entries were not made for the current accounting period. What effect will this have on the current period's financial statements?

(Answers to Section 2 Self Review are on page 473.)

13 Chapter REVIEW   Chapter Summary

In this chapter, you have learned how to prepare classified financial statements from the worksheet and how to close the accounting records for the period.

Learning Objectives

1 Prepare a classified income statement from the worksheet.

- A classified income statement for a merchandising business usually includes these sections: Operating Revenue, Cost of Goods Sold, Gross Profit on Sales, Operating Expenses, and Net Income.
- To make the income statement even more useful, operating expenses may be broken down into categories, such as selling expenses and general and administrative expenses.

2 Prepare a statement of owner's equity from the worksheet.

A statement of owner's equity is prepared to provide detailed information about the changes in the owner's financial interest during the period. The ending owner's capital balance is used to prepare the balance sheet.

3 Prepare a classified balance sheet from the worksheet.

- Assets are usually presented in two groups—current assets, and plant and equipment. Current assets consist of cash, items to be converted into cash within one year, and items to be used up within one year. Plant and equipment consists of property that will be used for a long time in the operations of the business.
- Liabilities are also divided into two groups—current liabilities and long-term liabilities. Current liabilities will normally be paid within one year. Long-term liabilities are due in more than one year.

4 Journalize and post the adjusting entries.

When the year-end worksheet and financial statements have been completed, adjusting entries are recorded in the general journal and posted to the general ledger. The data comes from the worksheet Adjustments section.

5 Journalize and post the closing entries.

After the adjusting entries have been journalized and posted, the closing entries should be recorded in the records of the business. The data in the Income Statement section of the worksheet can be used to journalize the closing entries.

6 Prepare a postclosing trial balance.

To confirm that the general ledger is still in balance after the adjusting and closing entries have been posted, a postclosing trial balance is prepared.

7 Journalize and post reversing entries.

At the start of each new period, most firms follow the practice of reversing certain adjustments that were made in the previous period.

- This is done to avoid recording problems with transactions that will occur in the new period.
- Usually, only adjusting entries for accrued expenses and accrued income need be considered for reversing. Of these, usually only accrued expense and income items involving future payments and receipts of cash can cause difficulties later and should therefore be reversed.
- The use of reversing entries is optional. Reversing entries save time, promote efficiency, and help to achieve a proper matching of revenue and expenses in each period.
- With reversing entries, there is no need to examine each transaction to see whether a portion applies to the past period and then divide the amount of the transaction between the two periods.

8 Define the accounting terms new to this chapter.

Glossary

Classified financial statement (p. 434) A format by which revenues and expenses on the income statement, and assets and liabilities on the balance sheet, are divided into groups of similar accounts and a subtotal is given for each group

Current assets (p. 437) Assets consisting of cash, items that normally will be converted into cash within one year, or items that will be used up within one year

Current liabilities (p. 439) Debts that must be paid within one year

Current ratio (p. 446) A relationship between current assets and current liabilities that provides a measure of a firm's ability to pay its current debts (current ratio = current assets ÷ current liabilities)

Gross profit (p. 436) The difference between net sales and the cost of goods sold (gross profit = net sales − cost of goods sold)

Gross profit percentage (p. 446) The amount of gross profit from each dollar of sales (gross profit percentage = gross profit ÷ net sales)

Inventory turnover (p. 447) The number of times inventory is purchased and sold during the accounting period (inventory turnover = cost of goods sold ÷ average inventory)

Liquidity (p. 437) The ease with which an item can be converted into cash

Long-term liabilities (p. 439) Debts of a business that are due more than one year in the future

Multiple-step income statement (p. 434) A type of income statement on which several subtotals are computed before the net income is calculated

Plant and equipment (p. 438) Property that will be used in the business for longer than one year

Reversing entries (p. 447) Journal entries made to reverse the effect of certain adjusting entries involving accrued income or accrued expenses to avoid problems in recording future payments or receipts of cash in a new accounting period

Single-step income statement (p. 434) A type of income statement where only one computation is needed to determine the net income (total revenue − total expenses = net income)

Working capital (p. 446) The difference between current assets and current liabilities. It is a measure of the firm's ability to pay current obligations.

Comprehensive **Self Review**

1. Explain the difference between a single-step income statement and a multiple-step income statement. Which is normally favored?

2. What journal entry(ies) is (are) made in the adjustment column for beginning and ending inventories?

3. Why would a fax machine used in the office not be considered a current asset?

4. Immediately after closing entries are posted, which of the following types of accounts will have zero balances?

    a. asset accounts
    b. expense accounts
    c. liability accounts
    d. owner's drawing account
    e. *Income Summary* account
    f. owner's capital account
    g. revenue accounts

5. Give the sequence in which the following journal entries are posted to the accounts.

    a. adjusting entries
    b. entries to close expense accounts
    c. entries to close revenue accounts
    d. reversing entries

6. Describe the entry that would be made to close the *Income Summary* account in each of the following cases. The owner of the firm is Dorothy Hitt.

    a. There is net income of $38,000.
    b. There is a net loss of $18,000.

7. Which of the following accounts should have debit balances in the adjusted trial balance?

    a. *Sales Returns and Allowances*
    b. *Purchases Discounts*
    c. *Salaries Payable*
    d. *Unearned Rental Income*

(Answers to Comprehensive Self Review are on page 473.)

Multiple choice questions are provided on the text Web site at www.mhhe.com/price12e

Quiz13

Discussion Questions

1. What is the difference, if any, between the classification Other Revenue and Expense and the classification Extraordinary Gains and Losses?

2. What are operating expenses?

3. Which section of the income statement contains information about the purchases made during the period and the beginning and ending inventories?

4. What is the purpose of the balance sheet?

5. What are current assets that usually are classified as Current Assets on the balance sheet?

6. How do current liabilities and long-term liabilities differ?

7. What information is provided by the statement of owner's equity?

8. What account balances or other amount are included on two different financial statements for the period? Which statements are involved?

9. What is the purpose of the postclosing trial balance?

10. What accounts appear on the postclosing trial balance?

11. If the totals of the adjusted trial balance Debit and Credit columns are equal, but the postclosing trial balance does not balance, what is the likely cause of the problem?

12. What types of adjustments are reversed?

13. On December 31, Klien Company made an adjusting entry debiting *Interest Receivable* and crediting *Interest Income* for $300 of accrued interest. What reversing entry, if any, should be recorded for this item on January 1?

14. Various adjustments made at Acres Company are listed below. Which of the adjustments would normally be reversed?
    a. Adjustment for accrued payroll taxes expense
    b. Adjustment for supplies used
    c. Adjustment for depreciation on the building
    d. Adjustment for estimated uncollectible accounts
    e. Adjustment for accrued interest income
    f. Adjustment for beginning inventory
    g. Adjustment for estimated uncollectible accounts
    h. Adjustment to record portion of insurance premiums that have expired

15. What are the steps in the accounting cycle?

16. If the owner invests additional capital in the business during the month, how would that new investment be shown in the financial statements?

APPLICATIONS

Exercises

Exercise 13.1   ▶   **Classifying income statement items.**

Objective 1

The following accounts appear on the worksheet of Odds and Ends Craft Store. Indicate the section of the classified income statement in which each account will be reported.

SECTIONS OF CLASSIFIED INCOME STATEMENT

a. Operating Revenue

b. Cost of Goods Sold

c. Operating Expenses

d. Other Income

e. Other Expenses

ACCOUNTS

1. Rent Expense
2. Depreciation Expense—Store Equipment
3. Sales
4. Interest Expense
5. Merchandise Inventory
6. Interest Income
7. Purchases
8. Sales Returns and Allowances
9. Utilities Expense
10. Purchases Returns and Allowances

Classifying balance sheet items.

◀ **Exercise 13.2**
Objective 3

The following accounts appear on the worksheet of Odds and Ends Craft Store. Indicate the section of the classified balance sheet in which each account will be reported.

SECTIONS OF CLASSIFIED BALANCE SHEET

a. Current Assets

b. Plant and Equipment

c. Current Liabilities

d. Long-Term Liabilities

e. Owner's Equity

ACCOUNTS

1. Rent Payable
2. Cash
3. Raja Julia, Capital
4. Merchandise Inventory
5. Accounts Payable
6. Store Supplies
7. Sales Tax Payable
8. Prepaid Insurance
9. Delivery Van
10. Accounts Receivable

Preparing a classified income statement.

◀ **Exercise 13.3**
Objective 1

The worksheet of Alec's Office Supplies contains the following revenue, cost, and expense accounts. Prepare a classified income statement for this firm for the year ended December 31, 2010. The merchandise inventory amounted to $58,775 on January 1, 2010, and $51,725 on December 31, 2010. The expense accounts numbered 611 through 617 represent selling expenses, and those numbered 631 through 646 represent general and administrative expenses.

ACCOUNTS

401	Sales	$245,600	Cr.
451	Sales Returns and Allowances	4,250	Dr.
491	Miscellaneous Income	300	Cr.
501	Purchases	102,600	Dr.

ACCOUNTS (CONT.)

502	Freight In	1,875	Dr.
503	Purchases Returns and Allowances	3,500	Cr.
504	Purchases Discounts	1,700	Cr.
611	Salaries Expense—Sales	44,300	Dr.
614	Store Supplies Expense	2,210	Dr.
617	Depreciation Expense—Store Equipment	1,410	Dr.
631	Rent Expense	12,500	Dr.
634	Utilities Expense	2,900	Dr.
637	Salaries Expense—Office	20,100	Dr.
640	Payroll Taxes Expense	5,000	Dr.
643	Depreciation Expense—Office Equipment	470	Dr.
646	Uncollectible Accounts Expense	620	Dr.
691	Interest Expense	540	Dr.

Exercise 13.4
Objective 2

▶ **Preparing a statement of owner's equity.**

The worksheet of Alec's Office Supplies contains the following owner's equity accounts. Use this data and the net income determined in Exercise 13.3 to prepare a statement of owner's equity for the year ended December 31, 2010. No additional investments were made during the period.

ACCOUNTS

301	Alec Patel, Capital	$62,760	Cr.
302	Alec Patel, Drawing	40,200	Dr.

Exercise 13.5
Objective 3

▶ **Preparing a classified balance sheet.**

The worksheet of Alec's Office Supplies contains the following asset and liability accounts. The balance of the *Notes Payable* account consists of notes that are due within a year. Prepare a balance sheet dated December 31, 2010. Obtain the ending capital for the period from the statement of owner's equity completed in Exercise 13.4.

ACCOUNTS

101	Cash	$9,780	Dr.
107	Change Fund	400	Dr.
111	Accounts Receivable	5,040	Dr.
112	Allowance for Doubtful Accounts	760	Cr.
121	Merchandise Inventory	51,250	Dr.
131	Store Supplies	1,000	Dr.
133	Prepaid Interest	80	Dr.
141	Store Equipment	10,200	Dr.
142	Accum. Depreciation—Store Equipment	1,080	Cr.
151	Office Equipment	3,200	Dr.
152	Accum. Depreciation—Office Equipment	400	Cr.
201	Notes Payable	5,400	Cr.
203	Accounts Payable	3,625	Cr.
216	Interest Payable	60	Cr.
231	Sales Tax Payable	1,790	Cr.

Exercise 13.6
Objective 5

▶ **Recording closing entries.**

On December 31, 2010, the Income Statement section of the worksheet for Thomason Company contained the following information. Give the entries that should be made in the general journal to close the revenue, cost of goods sold, expense, and other temporary accounts.

INCOME STATEMENT SECTION

	Debit	Credit
Income Summary	$ 38,600	$ 41,900
Sales		254,500
Sales Returns and Allowances	3,900	
Sales Discounts	2,900	
Interest Income		170
Purchases	134,400	
Freight In	2,200	
Purchases Returns and Allowances		2,000
Purchases Discounts		1,530
Rent Expense	8,500	
Utilities Expense	2,930	
Telephone Expense	1,540	
Salaries Expense	66,100	
Payroll Taxes Expense	5,270	
Supplies Expense	1,700	
Depreciation Expense	2,500	
Interest Expense	340	
Totals	$270,880	$300,100

Assume further that the owner of the firm is Bobby Thomason and that the **Bobby Thomason, Drawing** account had a balance of $26,200 on December 31, 2010.

Journalizing reversing entries.

◀ **Exercise 13.7**
Objective 7

Examine the following adjusting entries and determine which ones should be reversed. Show the reversing entries that should be recorded in the general journal as of January 1, 2011. Include appropriate descriptions.

2010	(Adjustment a)		
Dec. 31	Uncollectible Accounts Expense	3,625.00	
	Allowance for Doubtful Accounts		3,625.00
	To record estimated loss from uncollectible accounts based on 0.5% of net credit sales, $725,000		
	(Adjustment b)		
Dec. 31	Supplies Expense	4,700.00	
	Supplies		4,700.00
	To record supplies used during the year		
	(Adjustment c)		
31	Insurance Expense	1,350.00	
	Prepaid Insurance		1,350.00
	To record expired insurance on 1-year $5,400 policy purchased on Oct. 1		
	(Adjustment d)		
31	Depreciation. Exp.—Store Equipment	14,300.00	
	Accum. Depreciation—Store Equip.		14,300.00
	To record depreciation		
	(Adjustment e)		
31	Salaries Expense—Office	2,800.00	
	Salaries Payable		2,800.00
	To record accrued salaries for Dec. 29–31		

	(Adjustment f)			
31	Payroll Tax Expense		214.20	
	Social Security Tax Payable			173.60
	Medicare Tax Payable			40.60

To record accrued payroll taxes on accrued
salaries: social security, 6.2% × 2,800 =
$173.60; Medicare, 1.45% × 2,800 = $40.60

(Adjustment g)

31	Interest Expense	200.00	
	Interest Payable		200.00

To record accrued interest on a 4-month,
6% trade note payable dated Nov. 1:
$20,000 × 0.06 × $^2/_{12}$ = $200

(Adjustment h)

31	Interest Receivable	215.00	
	Interest Income		215.00

To record interest earned on 6-month,
10% note receivable dated Oct. 1:
$8,600 × 0.10 × $^3/_{12}$ = $215

Exercise 13.8
Objective 6

▶ **Preparing a postclosing trial balance.**

The Adjusted Trial Balance section of the worksheet for Harmon Farm Supply follows. The owner made no additional investments during the year. Prepare a postclosing trial balance for the firm on December 31, 2010.

ACCOUNTS

	Debit	Credit
Cash	$ 18,600	
Accounts Receivable	59,800	
Allowance for Doubtful Accounts		$ 120
Merchandise Inventory	186,200	
Supplies	7,140	
Prepaid Insurance	3,060	
Equipment	51,000	
Accumulated Depreciation—Equipment		17,800
Notes Payable		9,500
Accounts Payable		8,700
Social Security Tax Payable		1,392
Medicare Tax Payable		324
Ken Harmon, Capital		267,964
Ken Harmon, Drawing	74,000	
Income Summary	180,000	186,200
Sales		773,000
Sales Returns and Allowances	14,400	
Purchases	486,900	
Freight In	5,400	
Purchases Returns and Allowances		8,500
Purchases Discounts		5,300
Rent Expense	33,800	
Telephone Expense	6,246	

ACCOUNTS (CONT.)

	Debit	Credit
Salaries Expense	123,140	
Payroll Taxes Expense	11,734	
Supplies Expense	6,600	
Insurance Expense	1,560	
Depreciation Expense—Equipment	8,100	
Uncollectible Accounts Expense	1,120	
Totals	$1,278,800	$1,278,800

◀ **Exercise 13.9**
Objective 6

Calculating ratios.

The following selected accounts were taken from the financial records of Bermudez Wholesalers at December 31, 2010. All accounts have normal balances.

Cash	$ 22,500
Accounts receivable	46,700
Note receivable, due 2011	8,500
Merchandise inventory	34,700
Prepaid insurance	2,250
Supplies	1,310
Equipment	42,500
Accumulated depreciation, equipment	22,500
Note payable to bank, due 2011	25,000
Accounts payable	18,500
Interest payable	250
Sales	525,000
Sales discounts	2,200
Cost of goods sold	365,960

Merchandise inventory at December 31, 2009 was $56,790. Based on the account balances above, calculate the following:

a. The gross profit percentage
b. Working capital
c. The current ratio
d. The inventory turnover

PROBLEMS

Problem Set A

Preparing classified financial statements.

Exotic Woods Company distributes hardwood products to small furniture manufacturers. The adjusted trial balance data given below is from the firm's worksheet for the year ended December 31, 2010.

◀ **Problem 13.1A**
Objectives 1, 2, 3

INSTRUCTIONS

1. Prepare a classified income statement for the year ended December 31, 2010. The expense accounts represent warehouse expenses, selling expenses, and general and administrative expenses.

2. Prepare a statement of owner's equity for the year ended December 31, 2010. No additional investments were made during the period.

3. Prepare a classified balance sheet as of December 31, 2010. The mortgage and the loans extend for more than a year.

ACCOUNTS

	Debit	Credit
Cash	$ 34,100	
Petty Cash Fund	400	
Notes Receivable	10,800	
Accounts Receivable	57,299	
Allowance for Doubtful Accounts		$ 5,000
Merchandise Inventory	224,000	
Warehouse Supplies	2,760	
Office Supplies	1,320	
Prepaid Insurance	7,200	
Land	36,000	
Building	168,000	
Accumulated Depreciation—Building		48,000
Warehouse Equipment	32,000	
Accumulated Depreciation—Warehouse Equipment		14,400
Delivery Equipment	46,000	
Accumulated Depreciation—Delivery Equipment		17,600
Office Equipment	20,000	
Accumulated Depreciation—Office Equipment		9,000
Notes Payable		19,200
Accounts Payable		49,000
Interest Payable		480
Mortgage Payable		56,000
Loans Payable, Long-term		12,000
Joan Park, Capital (Jan. 1)		397,640
Joan Park, Drawing	126,000	
Income Summary	234,000	224,000
Sales		1,665,949
Sales Returns and Allowances	17,200	
Interest Income		1,480
Purchases	759,000	
Freight In	12,800	
Purchases Returns and Allowances		7,440
Purchases Discounts		10,160
Warehouse Wages Expense	189,600	
Warehouse Supplies Expense	6,100	
Depreciation Expense—Warehouse Equipment	4,800	
Salaries Expense—Sales	259,200	
Travel and Entertainment Expense	20,500	
Delivery Wages Expense	85,060	
Depreciation Expense—Delivery Equipment	8,800	
Salaries Expense—Office	69,600	
Office Supplies Expense	3,000	
Insurance Expense	5,200	

ACCOUNTS (CONT.)

	Debit	Credit
Utilities Expense	9,490	
Telephone Expense	5,520	
Payroll Taxes Expense	54,000	
Property Taxes Expense	4,600	
Uncollectible Accounts Expense	4,800	
Depreciation Expense—Building	8,000	
Depreciation Expense—Office Equipment	3,000	
Interest Expense	7,200	
Totals	$2,537,349	$2,537,349

Analyze: What is the current ratio for this business?

Preparing classified financial statements.

Good to Go Auto Products distributes automobile parts to service stations and repair shops. The adjusted trial balance data that follows is from the firm's worksheet for the year ended December 31, 2010.

◀ **Problem 13.2A**
Objectives 1, 2, 3
e**X**cel

INSTRUCTIONS

1. Prepare a classified income statement for the year ended December 31, 2010. The expense accounts represent warehouse expenses, selling expenses, and general and administrative expenses.

2. Prepare a statement of owner's equity for the year ended December 31, 2010. No additional investments were made during the period.

3. Prepare a classified balance sheet as of December 31, 2010. The mortgage and the long-term notes extend for more than one year.

ACCOUNTS

	Debit	Credit
Cash	$ 98,000	
Petty Cash Fund	500	
Notes Receivable	10,000	
Accounts Receivable	139,200	
Allowance for Doubtful Accounts		$ 2,800
Interest Receivable	100	
Merchandise Inventory	127,500	
Warehouse Supplies	2,300	
Office Supplies	600	
Prepaid Insurance	3,640	
Land	15,000	
Building	102,000	
Accumulated Depreciation—Building		16,200
Warehouse Equipment	18,800	
Accumulated Depreciation—Warehouse Equipment		9,000
Office Equipment	8,400	
Accumulated Depreciation—Office Equipment		3,400
Notes Payable—Short-Term		14,000
Accounts Payable		55,900
Interest Payable		300
Notes Payable—Long-Term		12,000
Mortgage Payable		15,000

ACCOUNTS (CONT.)

	Debit	Credit
Colin O'Brien, Capital (Jan. 1)		317,020
Colin O'Brien, Drawing	69,650	
Income Summary	130,400	127,500
Sales		1,090,300
Sales Returns and Allowances	7,400	
Interest Income		480
Purchases	453,000	
Freight In	8,800	
Purchases Returns and Allowances		12,650
Purchases Discounts		8,240
Warehouse Wages Expense	107,600	
Warehouse Supplies Expense	4,800	
Depreciation Expense—Warehouse Equipment	2,400	
Salaries Expense—Sales	150,700	
Travel Expense	23,000	
Delivery Expense	36,425	
Salaries Expense—Office	84,000	
Office Supplies Expense	1,120	
Insurance Expense	8,875	
Utilities Expense	7,000	
Telephone Expense	3,180	
Payroll Taxes Expense	30,600	
Building Repairs Expense	2,700	
Property Taxes Expense	15,400	
Uncollectible Accounts Expense	2,580	
Depreciation Expense—Building	4,600	
Depreciation Expense—Office Equipment	1,520	
Interest Expense	3,000	
Totals	$1,684,790	$1,684,790

Analyze: What percentage of total operating expenses is attributable to warehouse expenses?

Problem 13.3A ▶

Objectives 4, 5, 7

CONTINUING >>>
Problem

Journalizing adjusting, closing, and reversing entries.

Obtain all data that is necessary from the worksheet prepared for Healthy Habits Foods Company in Problem 12.4A at the end of chapter 12. Then follow the instructions to complete this problem.

INSTRUCTIONS

1. Record adjusting entries in the general journal as of December 31, 2010. Use 25 as the first journal page number. Include descriptions for the entries.

2. Record closing entries in the general journal as of December 31, 2010. Include descriptions.

3. Record reversing entries in the general journal as of January 1, 2011. Include descriptions.

Analyze: Assuming that the firm did not record a reversing entry for salaries payable, what entry is required when salaries of $5,000 are paid in January?

Problem 13.4A ▶

Objectives 4, 7

Journalizing adjusting and reversing entries.

The data below concerns adjustments to be made at Vaughn Company.

INSTRUCTIONS

1. Record the adjusting entries in the general journal as of December 31, 2010. Use 25 as the first journal page number. Include descriptions.

2. Record reversing entries in the general journal as of January 1, 2011. Include descriptions.

ADJUSTMENTS

a. On October 1, 2010, the firm signed a lease for a warehouse and paid rent of $17,700 in advance for a six-month period.

b. On December 31, 2010, an inventory of supplies showed that items costing $1,840 were on hand. The balance of the *Supplies* account was $11,120.

c. A depreciation schedule for the firm's equipment shows that a total of $8,200 should be charged off as depreciation for 2010.

d. On December 31, 2010, the firm owed salaries of $4,400 that will not be paid until January 2011.

e. On December 31, 2010, the firm owed the employer's social security (6.2 percent) and Medicare (1.45 percent) taxes on all accrued salaries.

f. On September 1, 2010, the firm received a five-month, 8 percent note for $4,500 from a customer with an overdue balance.

Analyze: After the adjusting entries have been posted, what is the balance of the *Prepaid Rent* account on January 1, 2011?

Problem Set B

Preparing classified financial statements.

◀ **Problem 13.1B**
Objectives 1, 2, 3

Flash Electronics Store is a retail store that sells computers and computer supplies. The adjusted trial balance data given below is from the firm's worksheet for the year ended December 31, 2010.

INSTRUCTIONS

1. Prepare a classified income statement for the year ended December 31, 2010. The expense accounts represent warehouse expenses, selling expenses, and general and administrative expenses.

2. Prepare a statement of owner's equity for the year ended December 31, 2010. No additional investments were made during the period.

3. Prepare a classified balance sheet as of December 31, 2010. The mortgage and the loans extend for more than one year.

ACCOUNTS

	Debit	Credit
Cash	$ 9,842	
Petty Cash Fund	100	
Notes Receivable	3,200	
Accounts Receivable	16,326	
Allowance for Doubtful Accounts		$ 2,250
Merchandise Inventory	35,400	
Warehouse Supplies	775	
Office Supplies	780	
Prepaid Insurance	2,200	
Land	7,642	
Building	48,500	
Accum. Depr.—Building		13,000

ACCOUNTS (CONT.)

	Debit	Credit
Warehouse Equipment	8,000	
Accumulated Depreciation—Warehouse Equipment		2,300
Delivery Equipment	16,400	
Accumulated Depreciation—Delivery Equipment		3,600
Office Equipment	6,000	
Accumulated Depreciation—Office Equipment		2,500
Notes Payable		5,000
Accounts Payable		11,700
Interest Payable		240
Mortgage Payable		15,950
Loans Payable		4,000
Franz Ulrich, Capital (Jan. 1)		60,940
Franz Ulrich, Drawing	24,000	
Income Summary	33,125	35,400
Sales		431,100
Sales Returns and Allowances	3,150	
Interest Income		462
Purchases	186,600	
Freight In	2,200	
Purchases Returns and Allowances		2,520
Purchases Discounts		2,350
Warehouse Wages Expense	38,900	
Warehouse Supplies Expense	1,790	
Depreciation Expense—Warehouse Equipment	1,400	
Salaries Expense—Sales	67,200	
Travel and Entertainment Expense	6,300	
Delivery Wages Expense	24,642	
Depreciation Expense—Delivery Equipment	2,440	
Salaries Expense—Office	15,900	
Office Supplies Expense	1,150	
Insurance Expense	1,500	
Utilities Expense	2,800	
Telephone Expense	1,380	
Payroll Taxes Expense	15,250	
Property Taxes Expense	1,750	
Uncollectible Accounts Expense	1,050	
Depreciation Expense—Building	3,000	
Depreciation Expense—Office Equipment	1,020	
Interest Expense	1,600	
Totals	$593,312	$593,312

Analyze: What is the gross profit percentage for the period ended December 31, 2010?

Problem 13.2B ▶ **Preparing classified financial statements.**

Objectives 1, 2, 3

Hog Wild is a retail firm that sells motorcycles, parts, and accessories. The adjusted trial balance data given below is from the firm's worksheet for the year ended December 31, 2010.

INSTRUCTIONS

1. Prepare a classified income statement for the year ended December 31, 2010. The expense accounts represent warehouse expenses, selling expenses, and general and administrative expenses.

2. Prepare a statement of owner's equity for the year ended December 31, 2010. No additional investments were made during the period.

3. Prepare a classified balance sheet as of December 31, 2010. The mortgage and the long-term notes extend for more than one year.

ACCOUNTS

	Debit	Credit
Cash	$ 14,350	
Petty Cash Fund	200	
Notes Receivable	6,000	
Accounts Receivable	54,600	
Allowance for Doubtful Accounts		$ 5,000
Interest Receivable	200	
Merchandise Inventory	87,915	
Warehouse Supplies	3,700	
Office Supplies	1,800	
Prepaid Insurance	6,900	
Land	20,400	
Building	53,100	
Accumulated Depreciation—Building		8,400
Warehouse Equipment	24,000	
Accumulated Depreciation—Warehouse Equipment		4,000
Office Equipment	12,800	
Accumulated Depreciation—Office Equipment		1,800
Notes Payable—Short-Term		8,000
Accounts Payable		32,500
Interest Payable		1,800
Notes Payable—Long-Term		6,000
Mortgage Payable		35,875
Nick Henry, Capital (Jan. 1)		198,710
Nick Henry, Drawing	56,000	
Income Summary	88,980	87,915
Sales		608,417
Sales Returns and Allowances	9,400	
Interest Income		720
Purchases	230,050	
Freight In	9,600	
Purchases Returns and Allowances		6,420
Purchases Discounts		5,760
Warehouse Wages Expense	64,300	
Warehouse Supplies Expense	4,300	
Depreciation Expense—Warehouse Equipment	2,400	
Salaries Expense—Sales	78,900	

ACCOUNTS (CONT.)

	Debit	Credit
Travel Expense—Sales	21,000	
Delivery Expense	35,400	
Salaries Expense—Office	57,500	
Office Supplies Expense	1,360	
Insurance Expense	9,500	
Utilities Expense	6,912	
Telephone Expense	4,370	
Payroll Taxes Expense	19,200	
Building Repairs Expense	3,100	
Property Taxes Expense	11,700	
Uncollectible Accounts Expense	2,900	
Depreciation Expense—Building	3,200	
Depreciation Expense—Office Equipment	1,680	
Interest Expense	3,600	
Totals	$1,011,317	$1,011,317

Analyze: What is the inventory turnover for Hog Wild?

Problem 13.3B ▶

Objectives 4, 5, 7

CONTINUING >>>
Problem

Journalizing adjusting, closing, and reversing entries.

Obtain all data that is necessary from the worksheet prepared for Whatnots in Problem 12.4B at the end of chapter 12. Then follow the instructions to complete this problem.

INSTRUCTIONS

1. Record adjusting entries in the general journal as of December 31, 2010. Use 29 as the first journal page number. Include descriptions for the entries.
2. Record closing entries in the general journal as of December 31, 2010. Include descriptions.
3. Record reversing entries in the general journal as of January 1, 2011. Include descriptions.

Analyze: Assuming that the company did not record a reversing entry for salaries payable, what entry is required when salaries of $2,600 are paid in January? (Ignore payroll taxes withheld.)

Problem 13.4B ▶

Objectives 4, 7

Journalizing adjusting and reversing entries.

The data below concerns adjustments to be made at Ramos Company.

INSTRUCTIONS

1. Record the adjusting entries in the general journal as of December 31, 2010. Use 25 as the first journal page number. Include descriptions.
2. Record reversing entries in the general journal as of January 1, 2011. Include descriptions.

ADJUSTMENTS

a. On August 1, 2010, the firm signed a one-year advertising contract with a trade magazine and paid the entire amount, $17,700, in advance. *Prepaid Advertising* had a balance of $17,700 on December 31, 2010.

b. On December 31, 2010, an inventory of supplies showed that items costing $1,840 were on hand. The balance of the *Supplies* account was $11,120.

c. A depreciation schedule for the firm's store equipment shows that a total of $8,200 should be charged off as depreciation for 2010.

d. On December 31, 2010, the firm owed salaries of $4,400 that will not be paid until January 2011.

e. On December 31, 2010, the firm owed the employer's social security (6.2 percent) and Medicare (1.45 percent) taxes on all accrued salaries.

f. On September 1, 2010, the firm received a five-month, 8 percent note for $4,500 from a customer with an overdue balance.

Analyze: After the adjusting entries have been posted, what is the balance of the Prepaid Advertising account on December 31?

Critical Thinking Problem 13.1

Year-End Processing

Programs Plus is a retail firm that sells computer programs for home and business use. On December 31, 2010, its general ledger contained the accounts and balances shown below.

ACCOUNTS	BALANCES	
Cash	$ 15,280	Dr.
Accounts Receivable	26,600	Dr.
Allowance for Doubtful Accounts	95	Cr.
Merchandise Inventory	62,375	Dr.
Supplies	6,740	Dr.
Prepaid Insurance	2,380	Dr.
Equipment	34,000	Dr.
Accumulated Depreciation—Equipment	10,100	Cr.
Notes Payable	7,264	Cr.
Accounts Payable	6,500	Cr.
Social Security Tax Payable	560	Cr.
Medicare Tax Payable	130	Cr.
Yasser Tousson, Capital	93,620	Cr.
Yasser Tousson, Drawing	50,000	Dr.
Sales	514,980	Cr.
Sales Returns and Allowances	9,600	Dr.
Purchases	319,430	Dr.
Freight In	3,600	Dr.
Purchases Returns and Allowances	7,145	Cr.
Purchases Discounts	5,760	Cr.
Rent Expense	14,500	Dr.
Telephone Expense	2,164	Dr.
Salaries Expense	92,000	Dr.
Payroll Taxes Expense	7,300	Dr.
Interest Expense	185	Dr.

The following accounts had zero balances:

  Interest Payable
  Salaries Payable
  Income Summary
  Supplies Expense
  Insurance Expense
  Depreciation Expense—Equipment
  Uncollectible Accounts Expense

The data needed for the adjustments on December 31 are as follows:

a.–b. Ending merchandise inventory, $67,850.

c. Uncollectible accounts, 0.5 percent of net credit sales of $245,000.

d. Supplies on hand December 31, $1,020.

e. Expired insurance, $1,190.

    f. *Depreciation Expense—Equipment,* $5,600.

    g. Accrued interest expense on notes payable, $325.

    h. Accrued salaries, $2,100.

    i. *Social Security Tax Payable* (6.2 percent) and *Medicare Tax Payable* (1.45 percent) of accrued salaries.

INSTRUCTIONS

1. Prepare a worksheet for the year ended December 31, 2010.
2. Prepare a classified income statement. The firm does not divide its operating expenses into selling and administrative expenses.
3. Prepare a statement of owner's equity. No additional investments were made during the period.
4. Prepare a classified balance sheet. All notes payable are due within one year.
5. Journalize the adjusting entries.
6. Journalize the closing entries.
7. Journalize the reversing entries.

Analyze: By what percentage did the owner's capital account change in the period from January 1, 2010, to December 31, 2010?

Critical Thinking Problem 13.2

Classified Balance Sheet

Lea Simone is the owner of Sweaters Galore, a store specializing in women's and children's sweaters. During the past year, in response to increased demand, Lea doubled her selling space by expanding into the vacant building space next door to her store. This expansion has been expensive because of the need to increase inventory and to purchase new store fixtures and equipment, including carpeting and state-of-the-art built-in fixtures. Lea notes that the company's cash position has gone down and she is worried about future demands on cash to finance the growth.

    Lea presents you with a statement showing the assets, liabilities, and her equity for year-end 2009 and 2010, and asks your opinion on the company's ability to pay for the recent expansion. She did not have income and expense data available at the time. She commented that she had not made any new investment in the business in the past two years and was not financially able to do so presently. The information presented is shown below.

	December 31, 2009		December 31, 2010
Assets			
Cash	$150,000		$ 30,000
Accounts Receivable	45,000		91,500
Inventory	105,000		234,000
Prepaid Expenses	6,000		9,000
Store Fixtures and Equipment	180,000		390,000
Total Assets		$486,000	$754,500
Liabilities and Owner's Equity			
Liabilities			
Notes Payable (due in 4 years)	$ 90,000		$240,000
Accounts Payable	132,000		171,000
Salaries Payable	18,000		19,500
Total Liabilities		$240,000	$430,500
Owner's Equity			
Lea Simone, Capital		246,000	324,000
Total Liabilities and Owner's Equity		$486,000	$754,500

INSTRUCTIONS

1. Prepare classified balance sheets for Sweaters Galore for December 31, 2009, and December 31, 2010. (Ignore depreciation.)

2. Based on the information presented in the classified balance sheets, what is your opinion of Sweaters Galore's ability to pay its current bills in a timely manner?

3. What is the advantage of a classified balance sheet over a balance sheet that is not classified?

BUSINESS CONNECTIONS

Understanding Financial Statements

| Managerial | FOCUS |

1. Why should management be concerned about the efficiency of the end-of-period procedures?

2. Spector Company had an increase in sales and net income during its last fiscal year, but cash decreased and the firm was having difficulty paying its bills by the end of the year. What factors might cause a shortage of cash even though a firm is profitable?

3. For the last three years, the balance sheet of Desai Hardware Center, a large retail store, has shown a substantial increase in merchandise inventory. Why might management be concerned about this development?

4. Why is it important to compare the financial statements of the current year with those of prior years?

5. Should a manager be concerned if the balance sheet shows a large increase in current liabilities and a large decrease in current assets? Explain your answer.

6. The latest income statement prepared at Wilkes Company shows that net sales increased by 10 percent over the previous year and selling expenses increased by 25 percent. Do you think that management should investigate the reasons for the increase in selling expenses? Why or why not?

7. Why is it useful for management to compare a firm's financial statements with financial information from other companies in the same industry?

Helping Your Boss May Be Wrong

| Ethical | DILEMMA |

It is standard accounting procedures, or GAAP, to make an adjusting entry to remove the current year's principle from the long-term liabilities. This entry reduces the long-term liabilities and increases the current liabilities. You are the bookkeeper for Biker's Business. Biker's Business has a bank loan that requires a current ratio of 1.5 times. The owner has asked that you do not make the adjusting entry to take the current portion from the long-term liabilities. You know if you make the adjusting entry Biker's Business' loan will need to be repaid immediately (or the loan called). What should you do?

Financial Performance

STREETWISE:
Questions from the
REAL WORLD

Refer to The Home Depot, Inc., 2006 *Annual Report* in Appendix A.

1. Locate the consolidated statements of earnings. What gross profit was reported for the year ended January 28, 2007? For January 29, 2006? If the company had targeted a 20 percent increase in gross profit between the fiscal years ended January 29, 2006, and January 28, 2007, respectively, was the goal achieved?

2. Using the financial statements, calculate the following measurements of financial performance and condition for The Home Depot, Inc. as of January 28, 2007.

   a. Gross profit percentage

   b. Current ratio

Balance Sheet

Financial Statement
ANALYSIS

The following excerpts were taken from the Mattel, Inc., 2006 *Annual Report.*

Consolidated Balance Sheets		
	December 31	
(in thousands)	2006	2005
Assets		
Current Assets		
Cash and short-term investments	$ 1,205,552	$ 997,734
Accounts receivable, less allowances of		
$19.4 million at December 31, 2006,		
and $24.6 million at December 31, 2005	943,813	760,643
Inventories	383,149	376,897
Prepaid expenses and other current assets	317,624	277,226
Total current assets	2,850,138	2,412,500
Liabilities and Stockholders' Equity		
Current Liabilities		
Short-term borrowings	—	$ 117,994
Current portion of long-term liabilities	64,286	100,000
Accounts payable	375,882	265,936
Accrued liabilities	980,435	796,473
Income taxes payable	161,917	182,782
Total current liabilities	1,582,520	1,463,185

Analyze:

1. What is the current ratio for 2006? For 2005?
2. Has the current ratio improved from 2005 to 2006?
3. The company reported net sales of $5,650,156 and gross profit of $2,611,793 for the period ended December 31, 2006. What is the gross profit percentage for this period?

Analyze Online: On the Mattel, Inc. Web site (www.mattel.com), find the investor relations section. Locate the consolidated statements of operations and the consolidated balance sheets within the most recent annual report. Answer the following questions.

4. What is the current ratio?
5. What is the gross profit percentage?
6. Compare these calculations with your calculations for 2004. Based on these two measurements, do you think the company is in a better financial position than it was in 2004? Why or why not?

Extending THE THOUGHT

Annual Report

Once the year-end financial statements have been prepared, companies often publish an annual report, containing both financial and nonfinancial information about the company's operation over the past fiscal year.

In addition to the financial statements for the period, the report frequently includes

- a letter to its shareholders,
- management's discussion and analysis of the company's performance,
- notes that accompany the financial statements.

Although there is no comprehensive list of items that should be disclosed in an annual report, the accountants of the business must use their best professional judgment when deciding what information to include. What types of information do you think should be included in a company's annual report? Why?

Business COMMUNICATION

Memo

You have been placed in charge of the closing process for Magnolia Tree Services for the period ending December 31. Time is short, and you must delegate the closing tasks to three accountants in your department: Brenda Calhoun, Sean Miele, and Cassandra Wilson. Write an e-mail to your co-workers, assigning each of them specific tasks to complete by the end of the week. In the e-mail, list the required closing tasks and identify which employee is responsible for each task. Make sure that your co-workers understand the order of the tasks that they are to perform.

Analyzing Home Depot

Ratios are an important part of financial analysis. Divide into groups of two or three. Each person should choose one year from the Home Depot *Annual Report* in Appendix A. Calculate the current ratio, gross profit percentage, and inventory turnover. Is Home Depot doing better or worse than the previous year? What account is causing this change?

TEAMWORK

Using Financial Statements from the Internet

Choose the Web site of a corporation. You can find most corporate Web sites by typing the corporation's name after www., then .com. Find the 10K or annual report. Locate the Income Statement, Balance Sheet, and Cash Flow statements for the corporation. Notice the current assets and current liabilities. Calculate the current ratio, gross profit percentage, and inventory turnover.

Internet | CONNECTION

Answers to **Self Reviews**

Answers to Section 1 Self Review

1. Classified statements permit users to better interpret the statements and analyze operations and financial conditions.
2. Current liabilities are those that fall due within one year. Long-term liabilities are those that will be due in more than one year.
3. Gross profit is the difference between net sales and the cost of goods sold.
4. **b.** A note receivable due in 13 months
5. **b.** As a deduction from the delivered cost of purchases
6. Net delivered cost of purchases is understated. Operating expenses are overstated. The net income from operations is unchanged.

Answers to Section 2 Self Review

1. Adjustments that include entries in asset and liability accounts that have not been used during the period.
2. So that anyone who needs to examine the entries at a later date will understand how and why the adjustments were made.
3. They provide a systematic and uniform method for closing all accounts that affect profit or loss for the period and transferring that profit or loss, adjusted for owner's withdrawals, to the owner's capital account.
4. **b.** an accrued expense that involves future cash payments.
5. **d.** current assets divided by current liabilities.
6. If the accountant correctly allocates the entire future payment to the payroll taxes expense account and the accrued liability account, there will be no effects on the proper allocation of expense between periods. If the accountant debits the payment in the subsequent month to the payroll taxes expense account, payroll tax expense will be correctly stated in the earlier period and overstated in the current period. *Payroll Taxes Payable* will be overstated during the later period.

Answers to Comprehensive Self Review

1. Single-step: all revenues listed in one section and all related costs and expenses in another section. Multiple-step: various sections in which subtotals and totals are computed in arriving at net income. Multi-step statements are generally preferred.
2. An entry in the debit column on the *Income Summary* line and a credit to *Merchandise Inventory* for the amount of beginning inventory closes the beginning inventory. A debit on the

Merchandise Inventory line and a credit to *Income Summary* for the amount of ending inventory sets up the ending inventory.

3. It generally has a life of more than one year and is used in carrying on the business.

4. **b.** expense accounts   **e.** *Income Summary* account

   d. owner's drawing account   **g.** revenue accounts

5. **a.** adjusting entries; **c.** entries to close revenue accounts; **b.** entries to close expense accounts; **d.** reversing entries

6. **a.** Debit *Income Summary* and credit *Dorothy Hitt, Capital* for $38,000.

   b. Debit **Dorothy Hitt, Capital** for $18,000 and credit **Income Summary** for $18,000.

7. **a.** *Sales Returns and Allowances*

Mini-Practice Set 2

Merchandising Business Accounting Cycle

The Fashion Rack

The Fashion Rack is a retail merchandising business that sells brand-name clothing at discount prices. The firm is owned and managed by Teresa Lojay, who started the business on May 1, 2010. This project will give you an opportunity to put your knowledge of accounting into practice as you handle the accounting work of The Fashion Rack during the month of October 2010.

INTRODUCTION

The Fashion Rack has a monthly accounting period. The firm's chart of accounts is shown below and on the next page. The journals used to record transactions are the sales journal, purchases journal, cash receipts journal, cash payments journal, and general journal. Postings are made from the journals to the accounts receivable ledger, accounts payable ledger, and general ledger. The employees are paid at the end of the month. A computerized payroll service prepares all payroll records and checks.

INSTRUCTIONS

1. Open the general ledger accounts and enter the balances for October 1, 2010. Obtain the necessary figures from the postclosing trial balance prepared on September 30, 2010, which is shown on page 478. (If you are using the *Study Guide & Working Papers,* you will find that the general ledger accounts are already open.)

2. Open the subsidiary ledger accounts and enter the balances for October 1, 2010. Obtain the necessary figures from the schedule of accounts payable and schedule of accounts receivable prepared on September 30, 2010, which appear on page 479. (If you are using the *Study Guide & Working Papers,* you will find that the subsidiary ledger accounts are already open.)

3. Analyze the transactions for October and record each transaction in the proper journal. (Use 10 as the number for the first page of each special journal and 16 as the number for the first page of the general journal.)

4. Post the individual entries that involve customer and creditor accounts from the journals to the subsidiary ledgers on a daily basis. Post the individual entries that appear in the general journal and in the Other Accounts sections of the cash receipts and cash payments journals to the general ledger on a daily basis.

5. Total, prove, and rule the special journals as of October 31, 2010.

6. Post the column totals from the special journals to the general ledger accounts.

The Fashion Rack		
Chart of Accounts		
Assets		**Liabilities**
101 Cash		203 Accounts Payable
111 Accounts Receivable		221 Social Security Tax Payable
112 Allowance for Doubtful Accounts		222 Medicare Tax Payable
121 Merchandise Inventory		223 Employee Income Tax Payable
131 Supplies		225 Federal Unemployment Tax Payable
133 Prepaid Insurance		227 State Unemployment Tax Payable
135 Prepaid Advertising		229 Salaries Payable
141 Equipment		231 Sales Tax Payable
142 Accumulated Depreciation—Equipment		

The Fashion Rack
Chart of Accounts (continued)

Owner's Equity

301   Teresa Lojay, Capital

302   Teresa Lojay, Drawing

399   Income Summary

Revenues

401   Sales

402   Sales Returns and Allowances

Cost of Goods Sold

501   Purchases

502   Freight In

503   Purchases Returns and Allowances

504   Purchases Discounts

Expenses

611   Advertising Expense

614   Depreciation Expense—Equipment

617   Insurance Expense

620   Uncollectible Accounts Expense

623   Janitorial Services Expense

626   Payroll Taxes Expense

629   Rent Expense

632   Salaries Expense

635   Supplies Expense

638   Telephone Expense

644   Utilities Expense

7. Check the accuracy of the subsidiary ledgers by preparing a schedule of accounts receivable and a schedule of accounts payable as of October 31, 2010. Compare the totals with the balances of the *Accounts Receivable* account and the *Accounts Payable* account in the general ledger.

8. Check the accuracy of the general ledger by preparing a trial balance in the first two columns of a 10-column worksheet. Make sure that the total debits and the total credits are equal.

9. Complete the Adjustments section of the worksheet. Use the following data. Identify each adjustment with the appropriate letter.

   a. During October, the firm had net credit sales of $9,410. From experience with similar businesses, the previous accountant had estimated that 0.9 percent of the firm's net credit sales would result in uncollectible accounts. Record an adjustment for the expected loss from uncollectible accounts for the month of October.

   b. On October 31, an inventory of the supplies showed that items costing $2,640 were on hand. Record an adjustment for the supplies used in October.

   c. On September 30, 2010, the firm purchased a one-year insurance policy for $8,400. Record an adjustment for the expired insurance for October.

   d. On October 1, the firm signed a four-month advertising contract for $3,200 with a local cable television station and paid the full amount in advance. Record an adjustment for the expired advertising for October.

   e. On May 1, 2010, the firm purchased equipment for $83,000. The equipment was estimated to have a useful life of five years and a salvage value of $12,500. Record an adjustment for depreciation on the equipment for October.

   f.–g. Based on a physical count, ending merchandise inventory was determined to be $79,400.

10. Complete the Adjusted Trial Balance section of the worksheet.

11. Determine the net income or net loss for October and complete the worksheet.

12. Prepare a classified income statement for the month ended October 31, 2010. (The firm does not divide its operating expenses into selling and administrative expenses.)

13. Prepare a statement of owner's equity for the month ended October 31, 2010.

14. Prepare a classified balance sheet as of October 31, 2010.

15. Journalize and post the adjusting entries using general journal page 17.

16. Prepare and post the closing entries using general journal page 18.

17. Prepare a postclosing trial balance.

DATE	TRANSACTIONS
Oct. 1	Issued Check 601 for $4,000 to pay City Properties the monthly rent.
1	Signed a four-month radio advertising contract with Cable Station KOTU for $3,200; issued Check 602 to pay the full amount in advance.
2	Received $520 from Megan Greening, a credit customer, in payment of her account.
2	Issued Check 603 for $17,820 to remit the sales tax owed for July through September to the State Tax Commission.
2	Issued Check 604 for $7,673.40 to Fashion Statement, a creditor, in payment of Invoice 9387 ($7,830), less a cash discount ($156.60).
3	Sold merchandise on credit for $2,480 plus sales tax of $124 to Emile Sahliveh, Sales Slip 241.
4	Issued Check 605 for $1,050 to BMX Supply Co. for supplies.
4	Issued Check 606 for $8,594.60 to Today's Woman, a creditor, in payment of Invoice 5671 ($8,770), less a cash discount ($175.40).
5	Collected $1,700.00 on account from Emily Tran, a credit customer.
5	Accepted a return of merchandise from Emile Sahliveh. The merchandise was originally sold on Sales Slip 241, dated October 3; issued Credit Memorandum 18 for $630, which includes sales tax of $30.
5	Issued Check 607 for $1,666 to Classy Threads, a creditor, in payment of Invoice 3292 ($1,700), less a cash discount ($34).
6	Had cash sales of $17,500 plus sales tax of $875 during October 1–6.
8	Received a check from James Maldonado, a credit customer, for $832 to pay the balance he owes.
8	Issued Check 608 for $1,884 to deposit social security tax ($702), Medicare tax ($162), and federal income tax withholding ($1,020) from the September payroll.
9	Sold merchandise on credit for $2,050 plus sales tax of $102.50 to Emma Helmer, Sales Slip 242.
10	Issued Check 609 for $2,100 to pay *The City Daily* for a newspaper advertisement that appeared in October.
11	Purchased merchandise for $4,820 from Fashion Statement, Invoice 9422, dated October 8; the terms are 2/10, n/30.
12	Issued Check 610 for $300 to pay freight charges to Ace Freight Company, the trucking company that delivered merchandise from Fashion Statement on September 27 and October 11.
13	Had cash sales of $11,990 plus sales tax of $599.50 during October 8–13.
15	Sold merchandise on credit for $1,840 plus sales tax of $92 to James Maldonado, Sales Slip 243.
16	Purchased discontinued merchandise from Acme Jobbers; paid for it immediately with Check 611 for $4,800.
16	Received $510 on account from Emile Sahliveh, a credit customer.
16	Issued Check 612 for $4,723.60 to Fashion Statement, a creditor, in payment of Invoice 9422 ($4,820.00), less cash discount ($96.40).
18	Issued Check 613 for $6,250 to Teresa Lojay as a withdrawal for personal use.
20	Had cash sales of $12,800 plus sales tax of $640 during October 15–20.
22	Issued Check 614 to City Utilities for $831 to pay the monthly electric bill.
24	Sold merchandise on credit for $820 plus sales tax of $41 to Megan Greening, Sales Slip 244.

(continued)

DATE	TRANSACTIONS (CONTD.)
Oct. 25	Purchased merchandise for $3,380 from Classy Threads, Invoice 3418, dated October 23; the terms are 2/10, n/30.
26	Issued Check 615 to Regional Telephone for $480 to pay the monthly telephone bill.
27	Had cash sales of $12,240 plus sales tax of $612 during October 22–27.
29	Received Credit Memorandum 175 for $430 from Classy Threads Inc. for defective goods that were returned. The original purchase was made on Invoice 3418, dated October 23.
29	Sold merchandise on credit for $2,820 plus sales tax of $141 to Emily Tran, Sales Slip 245.
29	Recorded the October payroll. The records prepared by the payroll service show the following totals: earnings, $10,800; social security, $702.00; Medicare, $162.00; income tax, $1,020; and net pay, $8,916. The excess withholdings corrected an error made in withholdings in September.
29	Recorded the employer's payroll taxes, which were calculated by the payroll service: social security, $702; Medicare, $162; federal unemployment tax, $118; and state unemployment tax, $584. This, too, reflects an understatement of taxes recorded in September and corrected in this month.
30	Purchased merchandise for $2,440 from Today's Woman, Invoice 5821, dated October 26; the terms are 1/10, n/30.
31	Issued Checks 616 through 619, totaling $8,916.00, to employees to pay October payroll. For the sake of simplicity, enter the total of the checks on single line.
31	Issued Check 620 for $250 to Handy Janitors for October janitorial services.
31	Had cash sales of $1,600 plus sales tax of $80 for October 29–31.

The Fashion Rack

Postclosing Trial Balance

September 30, 2010

ACCOUNT NAME	DEBIT	CREDIT
Cash	59 8 0 0 00	
Accounts Receivable	6 2 1 0 00	
Allowance for Doubtful Accounts		4 2 0 00
Merchandise Inventory	88 9 9 6 00	
Supplies	4 1 0 0 00	
Prepaid Insurance	8 4 0 0 00	
Equipment	83 0 0 0 00	
Accumulated Depreciation—Equipment		7 0 5 0 00
Accounts Payable		18 3 0 0 00
Social Security Tax Payable		7 0 2 00
Medicare Tax Payable		1 6 2 00
Employee Income Tax Payable		1 0 2 0 00
Federal Unemployment Tax Payable		5 1 2 00
State Unemployment Tax Payable		1 2 6 8 00
Sales Tax Payable		17 8 2 0 00
Teresa Lojay, Capital		203 2 5 2 00
Totals	250 5 0 6 00	250 5 0 6 00

The Fashion Rack
Schedule of Accounts Payable
September 30, 2010

Fashion Statement	7 8 3 0 00
Classy Threads	1 7 0 0 00
Today's Woman	8 7 7 0 00
Total	18 3 0 0 00

The Fashion Rack
Schedule of Accounts Receivable
September 30, 2010

Jennifer Brown	7 9 5 00
Megan Greening	5 2 0 00
James Maldonado	8 3 2 00
Emma Helmer	2 3 2 00
John Flanagan	1 6 2 1 00
Emile Sahliveh	5 1 0 00
Emily Tran	1 7 0 0 00
Total	6 2 1 0 00

Accounting Principles and Reporting Standards

LEARNING OBJECTIVES

1. Understand the process used to develop generally accepted accounting principles. LP14
2. Identify the major accounting standards-setting bodies and their roles in the standards-setting process.
3. Describe the users and uses of financial reports.
4. Identify and explain the qualitative characteristics of accounting information.
5. Describe and explain the basic assumptions about accounting reports.
6. Explain and apply the basic principles of accounting.
7. Describe and apply the modifying constraints on accounting principles.
8. Define the accounting terms new to this chapter.

NEW TERMS

accrual basis
conceptual framework
conservatism
cost-benefit test
full disclosure principle
going concern assumption
historical cost basis principle
industry practice constraint
matching principle
materiality constraint
monetary unit assumption

neutrality concept
periodicity of income assumption
private sector
public sector
qualitative characteristic
realization
revenue recognition principle
separate economic entity assumption
transparency

 www.goodyear.com

The Goodyear Tire & Rubber Company is one of the world's largest tire companies, with operations in most regions of the world. Goodyear primarily manufactures and markets tires. In addition, Goodyear operates more than 1,800 tire and auto service centers.

In early 2007, Goodyear released its 2006 Annual Report containing financial statements, a letter to stockholders, operating highlights and goals, management's discussion of financial condition, and notes on standard accounting practices and procedures. The financial notes included a description of the accounting policies used to prepare the financial statements. Topics like revenue recognition, inventory, income taxes, and property and plant costing were covered to help financial report readers understand how the statements were prepared. A couple of examples of financial notes include the fact that Goodyear recognizes revenue when finished products are shipped to unaffiliated customers and that expenses for transportation of products are recorded as a component of cost of goods sold.

thinking critically

If Goodyear were to change its revenue recognition policy, why would it be important to report this change in the financial notes of the company's annual report?

Generally Accepted Accounting Principles

In previous chapters, you learned how to record business transactions and summarize them in financial statements. Financial statements are prepared using generally accepted accounting principles and rules. In the first section of this chapter, you will learn how these principles and rules are developed. In the second section, you will learn about the conceptual framework of accounting underlying all financial reporting for business enterprises.

The Need for Generally Accepted Accounting Principles

In order to ensure that they are meaningful and useful, financial statements are prepared using generally accepting accounting principles (GAAP). GAAP is used whether the business is a sole proprietorship managed by the owner or is a large company such as Wal-Mart. GAAP allows the financial statements of different companies to be compared and meaningful conclusions drawn from the comparison. It also allows a company to compare its own statements from period to period.

>>**1. OBJECTIVE**

Understand the process used to develop generally accepted accounting principles.

The Development of Generally Accepted Accounting Principles

Accepted accounting principles are developed in several ways in the United States. In the past, unique accounting procedures and practices became widely used over time by specific industries or in accounting for specific transactions. These industry practices have sometimes become accepted as GAAP even though they may not be entirely consistent with the general requirements. In some cases, accounting rules result from a decision by the authoritative rule-making organization to permit more than one method because of industry practice. This is true, for example, in the oil and gas industries in which two methods of accounting for certain activities are allowed by the Securities and Exchange Commission (SEC). The use of two methods may yield widely differing results.

For the past half-century, however, accounting principles in the United States have been developed through a cooperative effort between the **private sector** (business) and the **public sector** (government). The Securities and Exchange Commission is the legal rule-making body from the public sector and the Financial Accounting Standards Board (FASB) is the primary representative of the private sector. Most official pronouncements of accounting principles and rules today represent a joint effort of these two organizations.

THE SECURITIES AND EXCHANGE COMMISSION

In 1934, the Congress of the United States established the Securities and Exchange Commission (SEC) to administer the Securities Act of 1933 and the Securities Exchange Act of 1934. Among its powers, the SEC has authority to define accounting terms and to prescribe accounting principles for companies under its jurisdiction. The SEC also determines the form and content of accounting reports that are required to be filed with the SEC. The SEC regulates the financial reporting of publicly held corporations (basically, companies whose stocks are traded in the securities exchanges and over-the-counter markets). The SEC is a dominant force in accounting because its rules must be followed by publicly held companies. Historically, however, the SEC has used its powers sparingly, preferring to let the accounting profession develop accounting principles and financial reporting standards, which are then usually adopted by the SEC as official rules. Since its inception in 1973, the Financial Accounting Standards Board (FASB) has been recognized by the SEC as the authoritative setter of accounting principles and standards in the private sector. The Sarbanes-Oxley Act, passed by the U.S. Congress in 2002 in reaction to the "accounting scandals" of public companies in the early 2000s, reaffirms the SEC's role as the authoritative accounting rule-making body. The Act goes further to permit the SEC to accept the accounting and reporting rules developed by "a private-sector organization," provided certain requirements are met. Sec. 108 of the Act states: ". . . the Commission may recognize as 'generally accepted' for purposes of the securities laws, any accounting principles established by a standard setting body" (meeting certain tests). In April 2003, the SEC officially recognized the FASB as the accounting standard setter under Sarbanes-Oxley. (Other aspects of Sec. 108 of Sarbanes-Oxley will be discussed throughout this section.)

PUBLIC COMPANY ACCOUNTING OVERSIGHT BOARD

The Sarbanes-Oxley Act also created the Public Company Accounting Oversight Board (PCAOB). The PCAOB is a private-sector, nonprofit corporation whose purpose is to oversee the CPA firms auditing publicly held companies. The PCAOB has five members, who are appointed by the SEC. Two members of the PCAOB (and only two) must be CPAs.

The PCAOB has the power to, among other things, set auditing, quality control, ethics, independence, and other standards for CPA firms engaged in auditing publicly held companies. This includes regulating the nonaudit services CPA firms provide to their audit clients, such as tax and consulting services. This authority was given to the PCAOB as a reaction to audit failures at several publicly held companies including WorldCom and Enron. Many people felt the auditors' independence from their clients had been impaired because of the large amount of fees they earned from consulting and tax services.

THE FINANCIAL ACCOUNTING STANDARDS BOARD

The authoritative pronouncements of the FASB are known as *Statements of Financial Accounting Standards,* or simply Standards. Since its formation in 1973, the FASB has issued more than 160 such standards. A Standard is frequently referred to with the abbreviation FAS and the sequential number of the Standard, for example "FAS 130." Some statements are broad in nature and apply to all types of businesses and transactions, for example, FAS 130—*Comprehensive*

>>2. OBJECTIVE

Identify the major accounting standards-setting bodies and their roles in the standards-setting process.

LP14

ABOUT
ACCOUNTING

Authority of the SEC
The SEC is given statutory power to establish accounting and reporting rules for publicly held companies. Thus, it has the "final voice" in accounting principles for those companies.

Income. Others apply to a single industry, for example, FAS 19—*Financial Accounting and Reporting by Oil and Gas Producing Companies.* Still others deal with specialized transactions or contracts, for example, FAS 45—*Accounting for Franchise Fee Revenue.* Several of the statements, for example, FAS 119—*Disclosure About Derivative Financial Instruments and Fair Value of Financial Instruments,* are concerned with disclosure issues. The pronouncements of the FASB almost automatically become generally accepted accounting principles, often called "accounting rules," because they are accepted by the SEC. This practice will continue under the Sarbanes-Oxley Act.

The FASB's *Statements of Financial Accounting Standards* are based on a fundamental framework of accounting, developed under its **conceptual framework** project. The goal of the project is to provide a cohesive set of closely related objectives and concepts to be used in developing accounting and reporting standards. The FASB has issued seven *Statements of Financial Accounting Concepts* which provide the guidelines on which the official *Statements of Financial Accounting Standards* are to be based. The process used by the FASB in developing the conceptual framework statements reflects deductive reasoning and involves essentially the following steps.

1. Define the goals and objectives of accounting.
2. Identify users of financial reports and the uses made of the reports.
3. Examine the qualitative characteristics that make accounting information useful.
4. Identify and define the financial elements such as assets, liabilities, revenues, and expenses, whose inclusion and classification make financial statements meaningful and useful.
5. Establish the form and content of financial statements.
6. Set forth fundamental recognition criteria.
7. Develop measurement standards for financial elements that appear in the financial statements.

Sec. 108 of the 2002 Sarbanes-Oxley Act requires the SEC to "conduct a study on the adoption by the United States financial reporting system of a principles-based accounting system." The FASB itself conducted a study and issued a report in October 2002. In July 2003, the SEC completed its study and made its report to Congress. The result is an intention for the FASB to issue "objectives-oriented standards" and to "address deficiencies in the conceptual framework." The goal is to arrive at an "internally consistent" and "complete" framework.

THE AMERICAN INSTITUTE OF CERTIFIED PUBLIC ACCOUNTANTS

The American Institute of Certified Public Accountants (AICPA) is the national organization of certified public accountants. Prior to formation of the FASB, the AICPA's Accounting Principles Board was recognized by the SEC as the preeminent private-sector group in developing accounting rules. Although the AICPA has much less authority and a less active role in the development of accounting standards than it held before its APB was superseded by the FASB in 1973, it continues to play an important role through its Accounting Standards Executive Committee (AcSEC). AcSEC issues three important types of documents:

1. **Accounting and auditing guides.** These releases provide guidance on accounting matters not addressed directly by the FASB and summarize the accounting and auditing practices in specific industries—for example casinos, airlines, insurance companies, and oil- and gas-producing companies.
2. **Statements of position (SOP).** SOPs provide guidance on a financial accounting question that has been raised until the FASB issues an official pronouncement on the topic.
3. **Practice bulletins.** Practice bulletins express the AICPA's position on narrow accounting issues that have not been considered by the FASB or SEC.

In addition to its work through AcSEC, the AICPA regulates auditing practices and takes the lead role in developing and enforcing ethical standards for auditors. In this role, the AICPA gives the statements of the FASB additional support by requiring that AICPA members make sure the companies being audited follow the accounting and reporting standards specified in the FASB Statements.

Until the Sarbanes-Oxley Act of 2002, the various pronouncements by the AICPA were generally viewed as a second-tier (below the FASB's pronouncements) set of GAAP and the SEC generally recognized them if there were no clear areas of variance from GAAP. The Sarbanes-Oxley Act seems to make it clear that there is only one private-sector organization designated as a standards setter. It remains to be seen what status the various AICPA pronouncements will possess in the future.

FEDERAL AND STATE AGENCIES OTHER THAN THE SEC

Historically, many other federal and state agencies have strongly influenced accounting and reporting standards. Regulatory agencies have had the power to prescribe detailed systems of accounting for public utilities, including the railroad and electric power industries. These agencies are concerned with regulation of price and competition more than with the development of accounting principles. As a result, the accounting and reporting requirements imposed on regulated industries frequently have not reflected GAAP.

Similarly, federal income tax requirements have had an impact on financial accounting. Businesses are not required to use the same financial accounting and tax accounting practices. However, some taxpayers adopt tax accounting rules where possible to avoid keeping two sets of records. This is possible if the tax requirements do not conflict with authoritative financial accounting principles. There almost inevitably are differences between required tax treatment and required GAAP. These differences often give rise to a unique accounting problem—the requirement that the current financial income statement should reflect the tax expense applicable to the income reported in the financial statements even though the actual tax paid is different because it is not levied on the income reported in the financial statement.

OTHER ORGANIZATIONS IN THE UNITED STATES

Other organizations and groups have over several decades been instrumental in the development and evolution of accounting principles and rules. The American Accounting Association (AAA) is one such organization. About half its members teach accounting. Many of them have written textbooks and articles dealing with accounting principles and concepts and often are involved in other accounting organizations, including the FASB. In a variety of ways, the AAA has been able to stimulate acceptance of the principles it has helped develop and perfect over the years.

As early as 1930, the New York Stock Exchange (NYSE) required corporations whose securities were traded on a public stock exchange to publish annual reports. Later, quarterly reports were required. In 1933, the NYSE insisted upon independent audits for all corporations that applied to have their securities (stocks and bonds) listed on the exchange, a policy that remains in effect today.

THE INTERNATIONAL ACCOUNTING STANDARDS BOARD

Accounting principles vary from country to country. Although the variations have been narrowed in recent years, there remain wide variations from country to country. The International Accounting Standards Board (IASB) was formed to develop accounting standards that can be adopted throughout the world. The organization has issued about 50 "International Accounting Standards" that are structured in much the same way as the FASB's Standards. Some IASB Standards deal with basic principles, while others cover more complicated areas of accounting and deal with specific industries. Every year the number of countries adopting IASB Standards increases. In an important move, in 2002 the European Union voted to require companies whose securities are traded on exchanges in member countries to prepare financial reports on the basis of IASB Standards.

Accounting rule-making bodies in the United States historically have been reluctant to recognize as "authoritative" the standards issued by the IASB or its predecessor, the International Accounting Standards Committee (IASC). Presently, however, the SEC, the FASB, the International Accounting Standards Board, and accounting rule-making bodies from many countries are working toward the "congruence" of the standards issued by each organization. In other words, the organizations are attempting to make the standards issued by one body consistent with those issued by other bodies. Because of this, new rules developed by the FASB and by the IASB have become more consistent with one another. The two organizations and accounting rule-setting bodies from other countries have worked closely in developing almost identical standards on new issues.

Section 108 of the Sarbanes-Oxley Act, in describing the attributes of a private-sector organization that might be accepted as the accounting standards setter, included: ". . . considers, in adopting accounting principles, . . . the extent to which international convergence on high quality accounting standards is necessary or appropriate in the public interest and for the protection of investors."

It can be reasonably expected that the gap between accounting statements in countries around the world will decrease dramatically in the next decade. This means that students of accounting can look forward to learning more about international accounting standards.

>>**3. OBJECTIVE**

Describe the users and uses of financial reports.

LP14

ABOUT
ACCOUNTING

Accounting Is Designed for Users

In order to develop accounting principles and reporting standards, it is necessary to know for whom reports are being prepared and to what uses they are put.

Users and Uses of Financial Reports

In its conceptual framework, the FASB concluded that financial reporting rules should concentrate on providing information that is helpful to current and potential investors and creditors in making investment and credit decisions. The focus is not on providing information to management, tax authorities, or regulatory agencies, because they have access to specific information from the firm's records not available to the public and often the information they need is not the same as that needed by investors and creditors.

In its conceptual framework project, the FASB also concluded that the information needed by investors and creditors should help them assess the likelihood of receiving a future cash flow, the amount of such a cash flow, and the time when the cash flow may be received. This conclusion is based on the idea that investors and creditors expect to receive a cash flow directly or indirectly from the business entity:

- *directly* from the distribution of the company's earnings, or
- *indirectly* through the disposition of their interests for cash.

Thus, financial report users need information about

- profits
- economic resources (assets)
- claims against the assets (liabilities and owner's equity)
- changes in assets and in the claims against the assets

Information about profits appears in the income statement. Information about assets, liabilities, and owner's equity is provided primarily in the balance sheet.

The statement of cash flows provides information about the cash received from major sources during the period and the uses made of that cash. The statement of cash flows is discussed in Chapter 24.

Certain analyses of the financial statements also supply meaningful information about the results of operations and the financial condition of a business. The analysis of financial statements is discussed in Chapter 23.

It is clear from the actions of the SEC and the FASB that they interpret the Sarbanes-Oxley Act to require a stronger conceptual framework of accounting. It is equally clear that the two organizations also agree that accounting standards must be based on the conceptual framework. The SEC's 2003 report to the Congress on "principles-based" accounting observed that the first characteristic of objectives-based standards, dictated by the Sarbanes-Oxley Act, is that any standard must "be based on an improved and consistently applied framework." It is essential that accounting students understand the framework.

Section 1 Self Review

QUESTIONS

1. Give two major reasons why the pronouncements of the Financial Accounting Standards Board have a major influence on accounting in this country.

2. Mayday is a corporation with only two shareholders (owners). Is the corporation required to file financial statements with the SEC?

3. Identify the governmental entity that has oversight of the development of accounting principles and explain its role in the development process.

4. What is the FASB's conceptual framework project? Why is an understanding of the conceptual framework important to those who make accounting and reporting rules?

EXERCISE

5. Four organizations that play important roles in the development of accounting principles, standards, and reporting practices are the Securities and Exchange Commission (SEC), the Financial Accounting Standards Board (FASB), the Public Company Accounting Oversight Board (PCAOB), and the American Institute of Certified Public Accountants (AICPA). Indicate which organization is best described by each of the following statements.

a. This organization actually develops and issues most of the accounting standards today.

b. This organization has no legal role in the development of standards, but does exert influence because it points out to the other organizations areas in which reporting problems have developed and also through the fact that its members audit the records of most publicly held corporations.

c. This organization has legal responsibility for setting accounting requirements for publicly held corporations.

d. This organization has the power to limit nonaudit services by CPA firms to their audit clients.

ANALYSIS

6. The financial statements for Presto Services have an auditor's notation that the statements are "not prepared in conformity with GAAP." What does this mean to you as an investor?

(Answers to Section 1 Self Review are on page 512.)

SECTION OBJECTIVES

>> **4.** Identify and explain the qualitative characteristics of accounting information.

WHY IT'S IMPORTANT

The qualitative characteristics provide the users a basis for relying on the statements.

>> **5.** Describe and explain the basic assumptions about accounting reports.

WHY IT'S IMPORTANT

The accountant bases financial reports on standard assumptions, so understanding of these assumptions is essential to understanding reports.

>> **6.** Explain and apply the basic principles of accounting.

WHY IT'S IMPORTANT

All accounting reports rest on the basic principles. Knowledge of the principles is essential to prepare statements and to understand statements.

>> **7.** Describe and apply the modifying constraints on accounting principles.

WHY IT'S IMPORTANT

Modifying conventions may justify or require the modification of basic accounting principles.

TERMS TO LEARN

accrual basis
conservatism
cost-benefit test
full disclosure principle
going concern assumption
historical cost basis principle
industry practice constraint
matching principle
materiality constraint
monetary unit assumption
neutrality concept
periodicity of income assumption
qualitative characteristics
realization
revenue recognition principle
separate economic entity assumption
transparency

The FASB's Conceptual Framework of Accounting

The rules of accounting that you are learning in this textbook are all based on the FASB's conceptual framework, so it is important that you understand the basic elements of the framework. The conceptual framework of the FASB is focused on four levels of concepts: (1) qualitative characteristics of financial reports, (2) basic assumptions underlying financial reports, (3) basic accounting principles, and (4) modifying constraints. An understanding of these elements will be of great benefit in this course as you learn how to account for and report various transactions affecting the financial statements.

Qualitative Characteristics of Financial Reports

The **qualitative characteristics** are the qualities that make accounting information useful for decision making by investors, creditors, and other users. The meanings of most of these characteristics are self-evident from their names.

Qualitative Characteristics	
Usefulness and	Reliability
Understandability	Verifiability
Relevance	Representational Faithfulness
Predictive Value	Neutrality
Feedback Value	Comparability
Timeliness	Consistency

USEFULNESS AND UNDERSTANDABILITY

These two qualitative characteristics are closely related and interdependent. First, the information should be useful to decision makers. Further, the information should be presented in a clear and understandable manner. However, the framework assumes that financial statement users will have a basic knowledge of business and economics and they will devote an appropriate amount of time to studying and analyzing the statements. Published financial reports are not designed for individuals who do not possess such knowledge.

>>4. OBJECTIVE

Identify and explain the qualitative characteristics of accounting information.

LP14

RELEVANCE

Relevance means that accounting information is capable of making a difference in a decision by the report user. Conversely, if information is not capable of being useful to the user in making a decision, it is not relevant.

Predictive Value If information is relevant, it will help statement users in making predictions about the meaning and ultimate outcome of events giving rise to the information.

Feedback Value Information that helps the statement user confirm fulfillment or nonfulfillment of prior expectations or decisions is said to have feedback value. For example, a quarterly income statement may provide evidence that prior expectations have been met. In this context, feedback value deals with verifying past expectations. However, information providing feedback value also may be useful in predicting future results.

Timeliness Timeliness is a simple concept. Information is timely only if it is presented soon enough after events are reported to be useful in decision making. For example, an income statement prepared eight months after the close of the year for which statements are prepared would not likely satisfy the timeliness criterion.

RELIABILITY

Reliability means simply that the information should be dependable. Reliable information is verifiable, is a faithful representation of the company's financial affairs, and is reasonably free of error and bias.

Verifiability Verifiability is indicated when independent measurers obtain similar results. If persons outside the entity arrive at different conclusions about measurements, then the statements cannot be said to be verifiable.

Representational Faithfulness Representational faithfulness is the concept that data shown in the financial reports reflect what really happened. If an enterprise reports sales of $544,000, that figure should reflect the true sales for the period.

NEUTRALITY

Neutrality, often referred to as "objectivity," is the idea that the financial statements are not prepared in a way to favor one group of users (management, owners, creditors, employees, etc.) over other groups. The information should be prepared in such a way that it is helpful to all groups.

COMPARABILITY

Comparability means that the financial data is presented in such a manner that it can be meaningfully compared with the same data for other companies. Another aspect of comparability is that a company's financial reports for one period may be meaningfully compared with its own statements for another period. Uniform and consistent accounting principles provide support for achieving this goal.

CONSISTENCY

Consistency means that an entity uses the same accounting treatment for similar events and data from period to period. Consistency permits meaningful comparison of statements for one year with those of another year. Companies may switch from one method of accounting to another more generally accepted method. However, changes should be very infrequent, and the change and its financial impact must be disclosed.

>>5. OBJECTIVE

Describe and explain the basic assumptions about accounting reports.

LP14

Underlying Assumptions

The FASB's conceptual framework lists four assumptions financial statement users should be able to assume that preparers of the statements have made in preparing the statements.

Underlying Assumptions
Separate Economic Entity
Going Concern
Monetary Unit
Periodicity of Income

ABOUT
ACCOUNTING

The Business and Its Owners as Separate Entities

If the business entity is a sole proprietorship, it may be difficult to think in terms of the owner and the business as separate entities.

SEPARATE ECONOMIC ENTITY ASSUMPTION

Accounting records are kept for a specific business or activity. The **separate economic entity assumption** assumes that the business is separate from its owners. Transactions in the records of a business and the resulting financial statements reflect the affairs of the business—not the affairs of the owners.

It is easy to understand the separate assumption for a corporation such as Microsoft because Microsoft is legally separate from its owners. However, the separate entity concept applies equally to sole proprietorships and partnerships, even though the owners may be legally liable for all debts of the business and for actions carried out on behalf of the business.

GOING CONCERN ASSUMPTION

When transactions are recorded and financial statements are prepared, it is assumed that the business is a **going concern**—that is, it will continue to operate indefinitely. This assumption permits businesses to record property and equipment as assets at their cost without having to be concerned about what they are worth in case of liquidation in the near future.

MONETARY UNIT ASSUMPTION

There are two aspects to the **monetary unit assumption.** First is the idea that expressing financial facts and events is meaningful only when they can be expressed in monetary terms. The entity may possess many assets, usually intangible—such as goodwill it has created among customers—that cannot be specifically identified and their values determined. If these assets cannot be expressed in meaningful monetary amounts, an attempt to include them in the financial statements would result in the violation of one or more of the qualitative characteristics or basic assumptions. Similarly, there may be potential liabilities, such as a lawsuit which appears to have little validity, that has been filed against the entity. However, it may be appropriate or even necessary to discuss such potential assets or liabilities in disclosures accompanying the statements in order to give a full presentation, even though they do not possess the characteristics necessary to assign a monetary value to them.

The second aspect of the monetary unit assumption is that the value of money is stable. The assumption that the value of the monetary unit is stable allows the cost of assets purchased many years ago to be added to the costs of recently purchased assets of the same kind and the total dollar amount reported on the financial statements. This means that it is deemed to be unnecessary for accountants to convert dollars spent in different years, when the purchasing power might be quite different, to a common unit of purchasing power. This assumption has been criticized because the value of money does not, in fact, remain stable. Its purchasing power changes substantially over the years. In the late 1970s and early 1980s, the purchasing power of the dollar decreased between 4 percent and 8 percent during each year. As a result, there was a great deal of complaint that the stable monetary unit assumption was no longer appropriate. Proposals have been made for abandoning the stable monetary concept, but the practical problems involved and the objectivity and reliability of historical cost figures have prevailed to this time.

PERIODICITY OF INCOME ASSUMPTION

The income statement covers a certain time period and the balance sheet is prepared as of the end of that time period. It is assumed that the activities of the business can be separated into time periods with revenues and expenses being assigned on a logical basis to those periods. This assumption is called the **periodicity of income assumption.** In reality, the final results of a business are known only when the business ceases to exist. When all assets are sold and all liabilities paid, the owners can determine the amount of the overall profit or loss. However, owners, creditors, and other interested parties cannot wait until a business is dissolved to make decisions. Operating and financing decisions must be made constantly throughout the life of the business. Many of these decisions are based on profit or loss for a specified period of time. Others are based on assets and liabilities as of the end of the period. Accountants have developed techniques, including the accrual basis of accounting, to prepare financial statements at regular intervals to meet the goals implied by this assumption. Many, if not most, of the concepts you learn in accounting result from the periodicity assumption.

Although the fiscal year is generally perceived as the standard accounting period, the SEC and FASB require that the same accounting rules be applied in measuring income for each quarter. Many businesses assume that the periodicity assumption can be extended even further to monthly financial statements. Obviously the assumption of periodicity has more validity for some type of business. For example, a merchandising business can measure assets, liabilities, revenues, and expenses easily each quarter, or even each month. However, an enterprise growing timber may find it much more difficult to get an accurate measure of financial results each quarter.

General Principles

Four basic principles to serve as guides to preparing financial statements are presented in the FASB's basic concepts.

Basic Principles
Historical Cost Basis
Revenue Recognition
Matching
Full Disclosure

HISTORICAL COST BASIS PRINCIPLE

Business transactions are, with few exceptions, recorded on a **historical cost basis,** which is the amount of consideration, expressed in monetary terms, involved in a transaction through dealings in the market between the business and outsiders. Assets are generally carried at historical cost, adjusted for depreciation, until they are removed from use and disposed of. Historical cost is the cost when an asset is acquired. Historical cost is preferred to some possible

>>6. OBJECTIVE
Explain and apply the basic principles of accounting.

LP14

recall

Recording Assets and Depreciation
Property, plant, and equipment assets are recorded at historical, or original, cost. Depreciation is recorded in a separate accumulated depreciation account.

important!

Criteria for Revenue Recognition

Two tests must be met before revenue can be recognized: (1) the revenue must have been earned and (2) the revenue must have been realized.

important!

When Is Revenue Earned?

Revenue is earned when the entity has done all that it has to do to be entitled to all benefits to be received from the sale or service.

important!

When Is Revenue Realized?

Revenue is realized when cash, financial claims, or other assets have been received as a result of the income-earning activity.

alternatives to cost because cost, when determined in an "arm's length" transaction with independent outsiders, is an objective, verifiable measure of initial economic value. The alternatives to using cost involve some measure or estimate of value, which is generally neither an objective nor verifiable quantity. As a result of this principle, generally an asset is recorded and remains in the account at its original cost even though its value may increase to an amount materially in excess of cost.

There are, however, important exceptions to the general rule that historical cost remains the basic carrying amount in the financial reports. For example, certain current assets—those that will be converted into cash within the next year—are carried at "the lower of cost or market" because market value is a reasonable measure of the amount that can be expected to be received for the asset within the next 12 months. Investments in securities that are expected to be sold within the next year would be shown at their market value rather than cost. ***Accounts Receivable*** is usually shown at the amount expected to be collected from customers, through the use of an ***Allowance for Doubtful Accounts.*** In addition, an asset included in plant and equipment is shown at its "impaired value" (a complex calculation) if it is apparent that future net cash flows from its future use will be less than its present book value. Nevertheless, the cost principle remains a fundamental concept in financial reporting.

REVENUE RECOGNITION PRINCIPLE

One of the greatest challenges an accountant faces is determining the period in which to record revenue and report it on the income statement. Revenue represents the inflow of new assets resulting from the sale of goods or services to an outsider. Under the **revenue recognition principle,** revenue is recognized when it is both earned and realized. The earning process is completed when the product or service has been delivered and related costs have been incurred. Usually **realization** is deemed to occur at the point at which a sale is made or a service is rendered to an outsider and delivery has been made. This is the point at which new assets are created in the form of money or in claims against others (usually taking the form of accounts receivable). The realization principle requires objective, verifiable evidence of both the earning and realization of revenue in order for income to be recorded.

However, the realization principle is the subject of much criticism. For example, if a company owns stock in another publicly traded corporation, some accountants believe that an increase in the market value of the stock should be recognized as income. This practice would, in most cases, violate the realization principle, which suggests that gain should not be recognized until the stock is sold. Accountants who support the realization principle are concerned that the "gain" might be eliminated by a decrease in stock price before the stock is sold.

There are some exceptions to the realization principle for reporting revenue. For example, contractors who build long-term projects often report income on a "percentage-of-completion" basis. If a bridge takes three years to complete, a portion of the estimated profit can be recognized by the contractor each year under the percentage-of-completion method.

In contrast, some businesses, especially service providers such as physicians, architects, and accountants, frequently recognize income only when cash is received, not when it is earned, because the rate of losses from uncollectible accounts is very high in these businesses.

> The revenue recognition principle has been the subject of many SEC complaints and legal actions against registrants in recent years. Frequently these actions result in large penalties and fines against registrants. On October 15, 2007, the Securities and Exchange Commission filed civil fraud charges against Nortel Networks Corporation. The SEC alleged that Nortel engaged in accounting fraud from 2000 through 2003 to close gaps between its true performance, its internal targets, and Wall Street expectations. Nortel is a Canadian manufacturer of telecommunications equipment.
>
> According to the commission's complaint, from late 2000 through January 2001, Nortel made changes to its revenue recognition policies that did not comply with U.S. GAAP.

The SEC also alleged that Nortel fraudulently manipulated accounting reserves and revenue entries on its books during the years 2000 through 2003 so that publicly announced revenue targets could be met.

Without admitting or denying the SEC's charges, Nortel agreed to be permanently enjoined from violating the antifraud, reporting, books and records, and internal control provisions of the federal securities laws. Nortel also paid a $35 million civil penalty. Nortel also agreed to report periodically to the SEC staff on its progress in implementing remedial measures and resolving an outstanding material weakness over its revenue recognition procedures.

MATCHING PRINCIPLE

To properly measure income, revenue must be matched against expired costs incurred in earning the revenue. This concept is called the **matching principle.** Many of the controversial questions in accounting involve determining when a cost should be charged as an expense. Accountants seek systematic, rational approaches for determining when to recognize revenue and when costs should be charged against revenue.

There are numerous ways to match revenue and expenses. Here are some examples:

- Manufacturing costs are identified with specific products and are charged to cost of goods sold when the products are sold.
- The cost of a building is recorded as an asset. Depreciation expense is recognized over the periods in which the asset is expected to help earn revenues for the business.
- Insurance premiums cover specific periods and are charged to expense over those periods.
- General office salaries do not clearly benefit future periods and are charged to expense when they are incurred.

The matching principle has given rise to a process referred to as the accrual basis of accounting, which you learned about in Chapter 12. The **accrual basis** calls for recognizing revenues or expenses in the period to which they apply, rather than in some later period when the cash is received or paid. The adjustments for prepaid rent, expired insurance, unearned income, and salaries payable that you learned in Chapter 12 were made under the accrual method of accounting to conform to the matching principle.

FULL DISCLOSURE PRINCIPLE

The **full disclosure principle** requires that all information that might affect the user's interpretation of the profitability and financial position of a business must be disclosed in the financial statements or in notes to the statements.

The accountant and company management are constantly faced with the question: "How much information is enough and how much is too much?" In recent years, there have been numerous lawsuits charging that the financial statements did not disclose facts that would have influenced investor or creditor decisions. As a result, accountants must be careful to include sufficient information so that an informed reader can obtain a complete understanding of the financial position of the business.

A primary emphasis of the SEC in financial reporting is "full disclosure." The SEC's full-disclosure policy is essentially that any information that would be likely, if disclosed, to change the user's interpretation of the statement should be disclosed. As a result, the basic financial statements may occupy only two or three pages in a corporation's annual report, but the "notes to the financial statements" explaining the items in the statements may occupy 10 or 12 pages. Because of federal regulatory legislation enacted in recent years, there is even more pressure to increase disclosures in order to help statement users better understand and evaluate the company's financial affairs.

In recent years, much attention has been given in the news media to the idea of **transparency** in financial reporting. Both the SEC and FASB have focused recently on the

recall

Why Adjustments Are Made
End-of-period adjustments are made to record income and expenses in the appropriate accounting period. The goal of adjustments is to match revenues and expenses.

important!

Importance of Notes in Statements
The notes to the financial statements explain or give details of items shown in the financial statements. These notes are considered an integral part of the statements and are audited by the independent auditor.

important!

When Supplemental Information Should Be Provided

Supplemental information is information that is helpful to understanding the statements. However, it may be low in reliability or not essential to an understanding of the statements. It may be required by the FASB or SEC, or it may be voluntarily provided.

>>7. OBJECTIVE

Describe and apply the modifying constraints on accounting principles.

important!

What Is a Material Item?

It is difficult to develop firm rules or guides to be followed in determining whether an item is material or is immaterial. A rule-of-thumb sometimes followed is that if an individual item, or the total of all items, being considered is less than 5 percent of net income, the items are not material. However, other factors must be considered, and this rule-of-thumb is by no means a standard.

ABOUT
ACCOUNTING

The Cost-Benefit Test

In many cases, the cost-benefit relationship is very difficult to determine. Both costs and, especially, benefits are hard to measure. Benefits are often difficult to quantify and verify.

topic of transparency in their public comments and in their authoritative pronouncements. Essentially, this notion is that the financial statements and the related disclosures taken together should permit interested users to receive a clear and concise understanding of the activities of the enterprise and its financial affairs.

Modifying Constraints

The accounting principles and their underlying assumptions provide a framework for analyzing business transactions in determining the accounting treatment they should be given in the financial reports. However, a number of practical considerations are recognized as constraining or modifying the application of the general principles. Here are the most important of these constraints.

Constraints
Materiality
Cost-Benefit Test
Conservatism
Industry Practice

MATERIALITY

 Materiality refers to the significance of an item of financial data in relation to other financial data. The rigid application of the recommended accounting treatment of an item may depend on whether or not the item is considered material in light of other items in the financial reports. Suppose that during the year a small business purchases small items of equipment, each costing $200, but with a total cost of $1,800. If the company's usual net income is only $15,000, the $1,800 cost would likely be considered material. As a result, the concept of matching would require that the assets be capitalized and depreciated. However, if Microsoft Corp. purchased items of equipment costing only $1,800, the amount would be insignificant and the company likely would simply charge the costs to expense when purchased. The difference in either net income or in total assets as a result of deciding to charge the cost to expense instead of capitalizing it would be insignificant. This example suggests that the materiality constraint goes hand-in-hand with the cost-benefit test.

COST-BENEFIT TEST

Sometimes it is difficult and expensive to gather information to fully comply with an accounting principle or rule that should theoretically be applied in preparing financial statements. As a result, the conceptual framework suggests that it may be necessary to use the **cost-benefit test** to determine whether the increased cost of complying with an accounting principle or standard is justified by the benefit (increased usefulness of the statements) which would result if the preferred treatment is followed.

For example, a large business may purchase thousands of inexpensive small tools with useful lives ranging from six months to two years. In theory, those tools lasting more than one year should be capitalized and their costs depreciated. However, the entity might have to incur large costs to simply keep records and identify the individual tools. The difference that might result in annual income from using the theoretically correct accounting treatment, compared to that resulting from simply charging the tools to expense when they are purchased, may be very small. As a result the tools would likely be charged to expense when purchased.

As suggested earlier, the cost-benefit constraint goes hand-in-hand with the materiality constraint. In some instances, an improvement in financial reporting resulting from applying a theoretically superior treatment to a transaction may be so small when compared to income that

MANAGERIAL IMPLICATIONS   <<

FINANCIAL STATEMENTS

- Management relies on the information in financial statements to make decisions.
- Management needs to understand the underlying principles used to prepare financial statements.
- Managers of large businesses compare their financial statements with those of their competitors. The universal application of accounting assumptions, principles, and modifying conventions allows financial statements to be compared.

- Proper accounting using generally accepted accounting principles can help prevent lawsuits by financial statement users.
- Full disclosure of pertinent information in financial statements and accompanying footnotes can reduce the possibility of lawsuits.

THINKING CRITICALLY

What are some income statement and balance sheet items that could mislead investors?

---

almost any cost of implementing the theoretically correct approach might warrant ignoring the conceptual rule. Conversely, even though an item might appear to be immaterial, that is no justification for applying the materiality constraint and arbitrarily applying a treatment that does not correspond with GAAP without applying the cost-benefit test.

CONSERVATISM

Accountants have long followed a doctrine of conservatism. **Conservatism** in accounting is the idea that "when in doubt, take the conservative action." Thus, if there is no clear evidence of how a transaction or situation should be accounted for or if there are two or more equally acceptable treatments of the transaction, the accountant should choose the conservative approach. The conservative approach is the one that would result in the least possible reported income or largest reported loss. In accounting, the conservatism notion comes into play when there is little evidence, or there is conflicting evidence, about the facts or their interpretation.

For example, Seligmann Company purchased a new machine designed specifically to produce a single product and with a useful physical life of 10 years. However, there is a strong likelihood that the product will be replaced in about five years by newer products and that the machine will be of no further use to the company when that occurs. In this circumstance, conservatism dictates that the machine be depreciated over five years.

On the other hand, if there is no reason to think that the machine will not be used to manufacture the product for 10 years, but the owner feels that "you just can't ever be sure how long it might last, so we should be conservative and depreciate it over five years," it would be inappropriate to use the five-year life for depreciation. The conservatism constraint does not override other accounting concepts and principles that are clearly appropriate in the circumstances. Conservatism is not a constraint to be applied without considering other factors.

INDUSTRY PRACTICE

It was pointed out in the first section of this chapter that existing accounting practices have sometimes become acceptable as GAAP. Typically this situation exists in an industry where there are unusual tax laws or regulatory requirements, an industry which has unusually high risks, or one which has activities or transactions to which it is difficult to apply GAAP. One example where GAAP has evolved to conform to **industry practice** is the public utility industry. For many decades, public utilities treated interest incurred on money borrowed to build a power plant as a cost of the plant, just like the cost of cement or steel. Public utility regulatory agencies required or permitted interest to be included in the cost of the plant, rather than charged to an interest expense account. This accounting practice has come to be required under GAAP for all construction projects, regardless of the industry.

ABOUT
ACCOUNTING

What "Conservatism" Does Not Mean in Accounting
In the past, accountants have been accused of being overly conservative, to the point that they were encouraged to understate assets. This is not a proper understanding of the constraint of conservatism.

ABOUT
ACCOUNTING

Special Accounting Rules for Specific Industries
Most of the accounting practices related to specific industries have been adjusted to fit into the conceptual framework. In cases where they have not (e.g., the oil industry), it is because of unusual operating activities or high risks involved.

The Impact of Generally Accepted Accounting Principles

This book contains many references to accounting principles, assumptions, and modifying constraints. Being familiar with these concepts will help you understand how individual transactions are accounted for and why they are handled in a specific way. Often businesses encounter new or unusual transactions that give rise to accounting questions that do not appear to have simple solutions. Almost invariably, the solutions to these questions will fall back on the concepts discussed in this chapter. Thus, an understanding of these concepts is essential to your understanding of complex accounting issues.

Section **2** Self Review

QUESTIONS

1. Why is historical cost used to initially record transactions?

2. How are the qualitative characteristics of consistency and comparability similar? How are they different?

3. What are the four basic assumptions underlying financial accounting?

4. How is the constraint of materiality applied in accounting? List some factors that might be considered in deciding whether an item is material.

EXERCISE

5. Which of the four underlying assumptions (separate entity, materiality, stable monetary unit, and periodicity of income) is most important in each situation below?

   a. Owens Company prepares financial statements for each quarter of the year.

   b. Mentor Company immediately charges to expense any asset costing less than $50.

   c. Morton Company issues each month a check to Stan Morton, the sole proprietor, for $8,000 because he deems this a reasonable payment for the time he spends in the business. The amount paid is not charged to Salary Expense but to his Drawing account.

   d. Bob LaMarque purchased a building for his business in 1983 for $300,000. In 2010, the building is still being used and has a remaining expected life of 25 years. LaMarque points out that cumulative inflation has been about 100 percent since 1980, so he proposes changing the asset account from $300,000 to $600,000.

ANALYSIS

6. One week ago, James Sternface was appointed manager of the company for which you work. He has looked at the draft of the annual report for last year, scheduled to be issued in a few days. He states that the company needs to "take no chances" and should be conservative in its reporting. He has asked that two things be done.

   a. The company is engaged in several lawsuits, some of which are very material. The company's lawyer and its former manager think the suits are almost certain to be decided in favor of your employer and therefore they plan to ignore them in the financial reports. The new manager wants to either show a potential loss as an expense or to disclose the lawsuits in footnotes to the statements.

   b. Because losses from bad debts have been running at a fairly high rate (4 percent of net sales), he proposes that revenue should not be recognized from credit sales until the money is actually collected from customers.

   Give your recommendations on his suggestions, stating the conceptual bases for your conclusions.

(Answers to Section 2 Self Review are on page 513.)

REVIEW   Chapter Summary

The increasing interest of a large and diverse group—government, owners, analysts, creditors, and economists—in financial reports ensures continuing progress in the search for accounting principles that will make the reports more meaning, useful, and reliable. In this chapter, you have learned how accounting principles are developed and the roles of various organizations and groups in that development. In addition, you have learned fundamental facts about the Financial Accounting Standards Board's conceptual framework underlying modern-day financial reports. The importance of underlying qualitative characteristics, underlying assumptions, and basic principles in this framework has been stressed.

Learning Objectives

1 Understand the process used to develop generally accepted accounting principles.

In the United States, GAAP are developed cooperatively by the public and private sectors. Although the SEC has power to establish accounting rules for publicly held companies, it usually delegates the job to the private sector through the FASB.

2 Identify the major accounting standards-setting bodies and explain their roles in the standards-setting process.

The SEC has legislative responsibility for developing accounting and reporting rules for publicly held companies, but has authority to accept standards set by the FASB. The AICPA, the AAA, and governmental regulatory bodies also have played a role in developing GAAP. The PCAOB regulates CPA firms that audit publicly traded companies.

3 Describe the users and uses of financial reports.

The users of statements are the present and potential investors and creditors who use the statements in making credit and investment decisions. The focus is on information to help users assess future cash flows.

4 Identify and explain the qualitative characteristics of accounting information.

The basic characteristics are:
- Usefulness
- Timeliness
- Understandability
- Neutrality
- Relevance
- Reliability
- Consistency
- Comparability

5 Describe and explain the basic assumptions about accounting reports.

Major assumptions that preparers of financial reports should generally make:

- The business is an economic entity separate and apart from its owner(s).
- The entity will remain a going concern.
- Monetary terms is the significant feature of economic data.
- The statements are objective and not biased to benefit any involved party.
- Income is periodic, so that income can be meaningfully measured for each period and compared with other periods.

6 Explain and apply the basic principles of accounting.

- Transactions are recorded on a cost basis.
- Revenues are recognized when earned and realized.
- Revenues and costs should be matched in the financial reports for appropriate periods.
- Full disclosure means that all information that might affect the reader's interpretation of the statements should be disclosed.

7 Describe and apply the modifying constraints on accounting principles.

The modifying constraints are factors that may in some cases overrule the necessity to apply GAAP.

These constraints are:
- Materiality
- Cost-benefits test
- Conservatism
- Industry practice

8 Define the accounting terms new to this chapter.

Glossary

Accrual basis (p. 493) A system of accounting by which all revenues and expenses are matched and reported on financial statements for the applicable period, regardless of when the cash related to the transaction is received or paid.

Conceptual framework (p. 484) A basic framework developed by the FASB to provide conceptual guidelines for financial accounting and statements. The most important topics are explanations of qualitative features of financial statements, basic assumptions underlying statements, basic accounting principles, and modifying constraints.

Conservatism (p. 495) If alternative treatments of items are of equal validity, the conservatism constraint suggests that the alternative resulting in lowest profit should be used.

Cost-benefit test (p. 494) If accounting concepts suggest a particular accounting treatment for an item but it appears that the theoretically correct treatment would require an unreasonable amount of work, the accountant may analyze the benefits and costs of the preferred treatment to see if the benefit gained from its adoption is justified by the cost.

Full disclosure principle (p. 493) All information that might affect the user's interpretation of the profitability and financial condition of a business should be disclosed.

Going concern assumption (p. 490) The assumption that a business will continue to operate indefinitely.

Historical cost basis principle (p. 491) The principle that requires assets and services to be recorded at their cost at the time they are acquired and that, generally, long-term assets remain at historical costs in the asset accounts.

Industry practice constraint (p. 495) In a few limited cases, the unusual operating characteristics of an industry, usually based on risk, special accounting principles, and procedures, have been developed. These may not conform completely with GAAP for other industries.

Matching principle (p. 493) The concept that revenues and the costs incurred in earning those revenues should be matched in the appropriate accounting periods.

Materiality constraint (p. 494). In some cases where an accounting item is deemed too small to affect a user's decisions, the "required" accounting may be ignored.

Monetary unit assumption (p. 490) It is assumed that only those items and events that can be measured in monetary terms are included in the financial statements. An inherent part of this assumption is that the monetary unit is stable. Thus, assets purchased one year may be combined in the accounts with those purchased in other years even though the dollars used in each year actually may have different purchasing power.

Neutrality concept (p. 489) Neutrality is the concept that information in financial statements cannot be selected or presented in a way to favor one set of interested parties over another.

Periodicity of income assumption (p. 491) Periodicity is the idea that economic activities of an entity can be divided logically and identified with specific time periods, such as the year or quarter.

Private sector (p. 483) This is the nongovernmental sector of society. In an accounting context, it is the business sector, represented in the accounting rule-making process by the Financial Accounting Standards Board.

Public sector (p. 483) This is the governmental sector, represented in the accounting rule-making process by the Securities and Exchange Commission.

Qualitative characteristics (p. 488) These are necessary characteristics that must be present in financial statements if they are to be credible.

Realization (p. 492) Realization of revenue takes place only when cash, a financial claim, or other consideration is received for the sale of goods or services.

Revenue recognition principle (p. 492) Revenue is recognized when it has been earned and realized.

Separate economic entity assumption (p. 490) This is the concept that a business is separate from its owner or owners and the financial statements reflect the affairs of the business, not those of the owner.

Transparency (p. 493) The transparency notion is that information provided in the financial statements and the notes accompanying them should provide a clear and accurate picture of the financial affairs of the company. The key to this idea is that of disclosure.

Comprehensive **Self Review**

1. In what circumstances is industry practice likely to be a factor in "generally accepted accounting principles"?
2. How does the AICPA still have an influence on the development of accounting principles and standards?
3. What is the full disclosure principle? How are disclosures made in financial reports?
4. Explain the matching principle. What impact does this principle have on end-of-period adjustments?
5. If the "stable monetary assumption" were not made, what impact would this likely have on record keeping and financial statements?
6. Name one alternative to the cost basis. Why is it not widely used?

(Answers to Comprehensive Self Review are on p. 513.)

 Multiple choice questions are provided on the text Web site at www.mhhe.com/price12e

Quiz14

Discussion Questions

1. What are the two most important bodies or organizations involved in developing generally accepted accounting principles in the United States?
2. Why is it desirable to have a set of fundamental concepts to be used in developing accounting standards and rules?
3. Explain how the concept of relevance is related to the users of accounting data.
4. What is meant by the concept of neutrality in accounting?
5. Explain the qualitative characteristic of comparability.
6. How is the matching concept related to the accrual basis of accounting?
7. It can be argued that the cost principle is dependent on the going concern assumption. Why?
8. How does the materiality convention affect day-to-day accounting?
9. How are the concepts of materiality and cost-benefit related?
10. What is the periodicity of income concept?
11. In recent years, there have been many charges, some of them substantiated, that large companies have manipulated business transactions and accounting records to move income from one year to another in order to change the income reported in different years. Suggest three concepts, assumptions, principles, or conventions that such manipulation would violate.
12. Many current assets are not shown at historic cost in the financial statements. For example, investments in stocks and bonds that are being held as investments for only a short period are shown at "the lower of cost or market." Inventories also are usually shown at the "lower of cost or market." What concepts or conventions warrant this practice?
13. What is meant by full disclosure?
14. Why is a conceptual framework necessary in developing accounting standards and rules?
15. What two tests must be met in order for revenues to be recognized?

APPLICATIONS

Exercises HM™

Exercise 14.1

Objectives 5, 6

▶ **Applying accounting principles and concepts.**

For each of the following cases, respond to the question and indicate the accounting principle or concept that applies.

1. O'Hara Company paid insurance premiums of $9,360 on December 1, 2010. These premiums covered a two-year period beginning on that date. What amount should the corporation show as insurance expense for the year 2010? What accounting principles, conventions, or assumptions support your answer?

2. KBGS Building Company signed a contract with a customer on October 1, 2010. The contract called for construction of a building to begin by December 31, 2010, and to be completed by December 31, 2012. The contract price was $6.0 million. KBGS estimated that the building would cost $4.5 million. On November 7, 2010, the customer was required to make an advance payment of $500,000. No work was done on the project until January 2011. How much income from the project should KBGS report in 2010? Why?

3. Tom Harpool buys and sells real estate. On December 31, 2010, his inventory of property included a tract of undeveloped land for which he had paid $900,000. The fair market value of the land was $1,000,000 at that date. How much income should Harpool report for 2010 in connection with this land? Why?

Exercise 14.2

Objectives 5, 6, 7

▶ **Applying accounting principles and concepts.**

For each of the following cases, respond to the question asked and indicate the accounting principle or concept that applies.

1. Rigsby Company purchased many small tools during 2010 at a total cost of $9,500. Some tools were expected to last for a few weeks, some for several months, and some for several years. Rigsby's income for 2010 will be about $5.2 million. How should Rigsby account for the small tools in order to be theoretically correct? As a practical matter, how should Rigsby account for these tools? Why?

2. Bill Evanston is the sole proprietor of Fast Serve Mini Market. Evanston's accountant insists that he keep a detailed record of money and merchandise that he takes out of the business for his personal use. Why?

3. At the end of each fiscal period, the accountant for Eastern Company requires that a careful inventory be made of the office supplies and that the amount on hand be reported as an asset and the amount used during the period be reported as an expense. Why?

Exercise 14.3

Objectives 5, 6

▶ **Applying accounting principles and concepts.**

For each of the following cases, respond to the question asked and indicate the accounting principle or concept that applies.

1. Three years ago Hyun Company purchased a machine for $575,000. The machine is expected to have no salvage value. Nevertheless, Hyun continues to keep the asset's cost in its accounting records and to depreciate the asset over its 10-year useful life. Is this correct or incorrect accounting? Why?

2. On January 20 of last year, Coto Company purchased land for $220,000, on which it planned to construct an office building. At the end of the year, the land had increased in value to $240,000. Nevertheless, Coto recognized no income as a result of the increase in value. Is this correct or incorrect accounting? Why?

3. Norwalk Company has decided to charge off as a loss the portion of its accounts receivable that it estimates will be uncollectible. The accounts involved resulted from the current year's sales. Is this correct or incorrect accounting? Why?

Applying accounting principles and concepts.

◀ **Exercise 14.4**
Objectives 6, 7

For each of the following cases, respond to the question asked and indicate the accounting principle or concept that applies.

1. Dry Creek Company charges off the cost of all Internet advertising in the year it is incurred even though the advertising probably results in some sales in later years. Why?

2. Jackson Company's net income is about $4.0 million a year. Jackson charges to expense all property insurance premiums when paid. Last year approximately $4,500 of these premiums represented amounts applicable to future years. Is this proper? Why or why not?

3. Dewey Corporation charges all of its research and development costs to expense when incurred. Why?

Applying accounting principles and concepts.

◀ **Exercise 14.5**
Objective 6

Baxter Company sells computer equipment. It grants all customers a 12-month warranty, agreeing to make necessary repairs within the following 12-month after-sale period free of charge. At the end of each year, the company estimates the total cost to be incurred during the next period under the warranties for equipment sold during the current period and charges that amount to expense, crediting a liability account. Is this appropriate accounting? Why or why not?

Applying accounting principles and concepts.

◀ **Exercise 14.6**
Objective 6

O'Toole Jewelers has never borrowed money. Because of rapid growth, on July 25, 2010, Jenny O'Toole, the owner, applied for a loan of $125,000 from her bank. The banker asked O'Toole for copies of financial reports of O'Toole Jewelers for 2009 and quarterly statements for 2010. O'Toole had never prepared formal financial statements for the business. She and the company's bookkeeper obtained some information from her 2009 income tax return and estimated other items for which information was not readily available. O'Toole took the statements to the banker on August 2. The banker expressed his concern over the statements. What are the most important fundamental financial reporting concepts that seem to have been violated?

PROBLEMS

Problem Set A **H·M**™

Understanding how and why accounting and auditing principles and standards are developed.

◀ **Problem 14.1A**
Objectives 1, 2, 3

Read each of the following statements carefully and indicate whether each is true or false.

1. The FASB is a part of the Internal Revenue Service.

2. Many nonpublic companies are not legally required to follow GAAP.

3. The American Institute of CPAs has in the past had a strong influence on the development of accounting principles.

4. The Sarbanes-Oxley Act places great emphasis on internal controls and fraud prevention.

5. Accounting principles and standards are based on the assumption that the statements will be read by individuals who have little understanding of accounting and financial reporting.

6. The SEC has authority to accept or reject financial accounting principles and standards developed by the FASB.

7. The FASB Standards are designed primarily for the use of regulatory agencies.

8. Because of the Sarbanes-Oxley Act, it is probable that the FASB's conceptual framework will become less important in developing accounting principles and standards.

9. It is unlikely that in the future there will be a convergence of U.S. financial reporting standards and those of the International Accounting Standards Board.

10. The PCAOB regulates CPA firms that audit nonpublic companies.

Problem 14.2A ▶
Objectives 4, 5, 6

Applying accounting principles and concepts.

The accounting treatment or statement presentation of various items is discussed below. The items pertain to unrelated businesses.

INSTRUCTIONS

Indicate in each case whether the item has been handled in accordance with generally accepted accounting principles. If so, indicate the key basic concept that has been followed. If not, indicate which concept has been violated and tell how the item should have been recorded or presented.

1. At the beginning of 2010, MPO Company bought a building for $3,000,000. At the end of 2010, the building's value was appraised at $3,300,000. Since there was an increase in value, the company did not record depreciation on the building and also did not increase the $3,000,000 recorded in the building account at time of purchase.

2. The equipment of Ace Plastics Company has a book value (cost less accumulated depreciation) of $180,000. However, the equipment could not be sold for more than $40,000 today. The company's owner thinks that the machinery should nevertheless be reported on the balance sheet at $180,000 and depreciated over its useful life, because the equipment is being used regularly in the business and it is expected to be used profitably for the next five years—the remaining useful life that is being used for depreciation purposes.

3. On December 31, 2010, an account receivable of $1,800 due from Joe Johnson, who is in the county jail on charges of passing bad checks, is not included in the balance sheet. The owner of the business has written off the amount because he feels certain that the debt will not be paid, even though Johnson insists that he will pay after he gets out of jail and finds a job.

4. Sele Company manufactured machinery for its own use at a cost of $600,000. The lowest bid from an outsider was $650,000. Nevertheless, the company recorded the machinery at $600,000.

5. On December 31, 2010, the balance sheet of DVD Depot reported prepaid insurance at $1,000. The prepaid insurance reflects the refund value of a three-year fire insurance policy that originally cost $6,000 on January 1, 2009.

6. The assets listed in the accounting records of Cobb's Pharmacy include a money market account of Jason Cobb, owner of the business. Cobb has established the savings account so that if he needs to invest more cash in the pharmacy, it will be readily available.

Analyze: If MPO Company uses the accounting treatment described in Item 1, is net income overstated or understated for 2010?

Problem 14.3A ▶
Objectives 5, 6

Reconstructing an income statement to reflect proper accounting principles.

The income statement shown on page 503 was sent by Steve Cortez, owner of Cortez Video Center, to several of his creditors who had asked for financial statements. The business is a sole proprietorship that sells audio and other electronic equipment. One of the creditors looked over the income statement and reported that it did not conform to generally accepted accounting principles.

INSTRUCTIONS

Prepare an income statement in accordance with generally accepted accounting principles.

Cortez Video Center
Income Statement
December 31, 2010

Cash Collected from Customers		$689,000
Cost of Goods Sold		
Merchandise Inventory, Jan. 1	$ 72,000	
Payments to Suppliers	435,000	
	507,000	
Less Merchandise Inventory, Dec. 31	82,000	
Cost of Goods Sold		425,000
Gross Profit on Sales		264,000
Operating Expenses		
Salaries of Employees	$ 80,500	
Salary of Owner	25,200	
Office Expense	31,000	
Depreciation Expense	21,120	
Income Tax of Owner	8,000	
Payroll Taxes Expense	9,000	
Advertising and Other Selling Expenses	22,900	
Repairs Expense	12,000	
Insurance Expense	4,400	
Interest Expense	12,000	
Utility and Telephone Expense	18,500	
Legal and Audit Expense	3,500	
Miscellaneous Expense	28,500	
Total Expenses		276,620
Net Loss from Operations		(12,620)
Increase in Appraised Value of Land during Year		15,000
Net Income		$ 2,380

The following additional information was made available by Cortez.

a. On January 1, 2010, accounts receivable from customers totaled $26,700. On December 31, 2010, the receivables totaled $33,000.

b. No effort has been made to charge off worthless accounts. An analysis shows that $1,300 of the accounts receivable on December 31, 2010, will never be collected.

c. The beginning and ending merchandise inventories were valued at their estimated selling price. The cost of the ending inventory is determined to be $48,500, and the cost of the beginning inventory is determined at $44,800.

d. On January 1, 2010, suppliers of merchandise were owed $39,200, while on December 31, 2010, these debts were $45,425.

e. The owner paid himself a salary of $2,100 per month from the funds of the business and charged this amount to an account called *Salary of Owner.*

f. The owner also withdrew cash from the firm's bank account to pay himself $4,400 interest on his capital investment. This amount was charged to *Interest Expense.*

g. A check for $8,000 to cover the owner's personal income tax for the previous year was issued from the firm's bank account. This was charged to *Income Tax of Owner.*

h. Depreciation on assets was computed at 8 percent of the gross profit. An analysis of assets showed that the original cost of the equipment and fixtures was $64,500. Their estimated useful life is 12 years with no salvage value. The building cost $150,330. Its useful life is expected to be 25 years with no salvage value.

i. Included in *Repairs Expense* was $6,100 paid on December 22 for a new parking lot completed that day.

j. The increase in land value was based on an appraisal by a qualified real estate appraiser.

Analyze: What is the gross profit percentage based on the income statement you prepared?

Problem 14.4A ▶
Objectives 5, 6

e**X**cel

Reconstructing a balance sheet to reflect proper accounting principles.

Arthur Martin owns The Art Haven, a small arts supply store. He recently approached the local bank for a loan to finance a planned expansion of his store. Martin prepared the balance sheet shown below and submitted it to one of the bank's loan officers in support of his loan application.

INSTRUCTIONS

1. Identify any errors in the balance sheet, and explain why they should be considered errors.
2. Prepare a corrected balance sheet in accordance with generally accepted accounting principles.

The Art Haven
Balance Sheet
December 31, 2010

Assets	
Cash	$ 13,400
Accounts Receivable	16,000
Inventory	40,000
Equipment (cost)	30,000
Personal Residence	198,000
Supplies	2,060
Family Auto	30,000
Total Assets	$329,460
Liabilities and Owner's Equity	
Accounts Payable	$16,450
Note Payable on Family Car	12,000
Mortgage on House	102,000
Arthur Martin, Capital	199,010
Total Liabilities and Owner's Equity	$329,460

The following additional information was made available by Martin.

a. The inventory has an original cost of $31,900. It is listed on the balance sheet at the estimated selling price.

b. The cash listed on the balance sheet includes $3,200 in Arthur Martin's personal account. The remainder of the cash is in the store's account.

c. The store recently purchased a delivery truck for $34,000, financed through a bank loan. The bank has legal title to the truck. To date, the store has paid $10,000 on the loan. Of the remaining $24,000 liability, $9,600 is current and the remainder long-term. Martin did not include the truck or the liability on the balance sheet because neither he nor the business owns it.

d. Depreciation allowable to date is $6,000 on the equipment and $4,000 on the truck.

Analyze: If Martin knew that $800 of accounts receivable was not collectible, what should be done to reflect this fact on the records of the business? On the balance sheet?

Applying accounting principles and concepts.

◄ **Problem 14.5A**
Objectives 5, 6, 7

For each of the unrelated situations below, identify the accounting principle or concept violated (if a violation exists) and explain the nature of the violation. If you believe that the treatment is in accordance with GAAP, state the major principle or concept in support.

1. Marketing Opportunities Company sells such items as discontinued products and merchandise purchased from bankrupt companies. Freight costs on goods purchased are quite high. The company adds the freight costs to the purchase price and treats the total as cost of inventory.

2. Chu Technics Company uses a large quantity of small tools. The annual purchases of the tools, which have a life of about two years, are approximately 2 percent of the company's net income for the year. Chu has followed the practice of capitalizing the cost of the tools and depreciating the cost over two years. The owner asks why the accountant spends so much time on "bookkeeping" and tells her to simply charge the tools to expense when they are purchased.

3. Harry Smith owns a travel tour service. Customers must make a deposit of one-half the tour price at the time they book reservations. The balance is due 60 days prior to departure. Partial refunds are provided, depending on the date of cancellation. At the time deposits are received, Smith records them as revenue. Refunds are treated as expenses at the time they are made.

4. Each year Web Support Company has a large number of uncollectible accounts. Web charges uncollectible accounts to expense when they are written off. On the average, this is about 18 months after the due date of the account.

5. Martin Company manufactures paving equipment. It pays its salespeople a commission of 15 percent of the sales price as their remuneration. During 2010, its sales were $20,000,000 and commissions were $3,000,000. In the income statement, sales are shown as $17,000,000.

Analyze: What is the effect on sales of the procedure used by Martin Company in question 5, above?

Problem Set B

Understanding how and why accounting and auditing principles and standards are developed.

◄ **Problem 14.1B**
Objectives 1, 2, 3

Read each of the following statements carefully and indicate whether each is true or false.

1. The income statement is the statement user's primary source of information about cash flows in a business.

2. The FASB has placed little emphasis on cash flows in its conceptual framework.

3. Because tax rules and financial accounting are so different, federal income tax requirements have had little impact on financial accounting in the United States.

4. The Sarbanes-Oxley Act suggests a problem-by-problem approach to establishing accounting standards rather than developing standards founded on basic principles.

5. The requirements of state and federal regulatory bodies, such as commissions regulating public utilities, have had little impact on accounting standards in this country.

6. Providing useful information to management is one of the major considerations of the FASB in developing financial reporting standards.

7. The SEC is the private sector's voice in the accounting rule-making process.

8. FASB *Statements of Financial Accounting Standards* are normally accepted by the SEC as GAAP.

9. Although accounting rule-making organizations in the United States have been reluctant to embrace international accounting standards, there is now a move toward developing congruence between U.S. and international standards.

10. The PCAOB has the power to set independence standards for CPA firms that audit publicly traded companies.

Problem 14.2B ▶ **Applying accounting principles and concepts.**

Objectives 5, 6

The accounting treatment or statement presentation of various items is discussed below. The items pertain to unrelated businesses.

INSTRUCTIONS

Indicate in each case whether the item has been handled in accordance with generally accepted accounting principles. If so, indicate which of the basic concepts has been followed. If not, indicate which concept has been violated and tell how the item should have been recorded or presented.

1. Kamp Manufacturing Company makes air cleaning units. The cost of manufacturing a particular unit is $320. However, when the inventory amounts are computed for the balance sheet, the amount used for this unit is $450, the normal selling price.

2. Included on the balance sheet of Mary's Massage Center is the personal automobile of Mary Smith, the owner.

3. On October 1, 2010, Delite Manufacturing Company purchased some highly specialized, custom-made equipment for $936,000. Since the equipment is of no use to anyone else and has no salvage value, it was recorded in the asset account at $1. The equipment is projected to be used regularly in the business until the equipment wears out, approximately six years from the date of its purchase.

4. In 2010, Perfect Bakeries had sales of $22 million, all on credit. Statistics of the company for prior years show that losses from uncollectible accounts are equal to about 1.5 percent of sales each year. However, Perfect Bakeries charges off a loss from uncollectible accounts only when a specific account is found to be uncollectible.

5. Each year Cuna Company values its investments in land at the current market price.

6. On December 31, 2009, Morrisson Corporation valued its inventory according to an acceptable accounting method. On December 31, 2010, the inventory was valued by a different but also acceptable method, and on December 31, 2011, the inventory was valued by the method that was used in 2009.

Analyze: If the equipment described in item 3 is depreciated using the straight-line method and has no salvage value, what amount should be charged to expense for the year ended December 31, 2010?

Problem 14.3B ▶ **Reconstructing an income statement to reflect proper accounting principles.**

Objectives 4, 5, 6

The income statement shown below was prepared by Vanessa Moreno, owner of Vanessa's Beauty Supplies. The business is a sole proprietorship that sells skin and hair care products. An accountant who looked at the income statement told Moreno that the statement does not conform to generally accepted accounting principles.

INSTRUCTIONS

Prepare an income statement for Vanessa's Beauty Supplies in accordance with generally accepted accounting principles.

Vanessa's Beauty Supplies
Income Statement
Year Ended December 31, 2010

Cash Receipts from Customers		$407,000
Cost of Goods Sold		
Merchandise Inventory, Jan. 1	$ 36,000	
Payments to Creditors	300,000	
	336,000	
Less Merchandise Inventory, Dec. 31	45,000	
Cost of Goods Sold		291,000
Gross Profit on Sales		116,000
Expenses		
Salaries Expense	$ 62,000	
Insurance Expense	2,800	
Payroll Taxes Expense	5,060	
Repairs Expense	3,500	
Supplies and Other Office Expenses	7,000	
Advertising and Other Selling Expenses	12,000	
Utilities Expense	5,600	
Interest Expense	6,500	
Total Expenses		104,460
Net Income from Operations		11,540
Increase in Market Value of Store Equipment		6,400
Net Income for Year		$ 17,940

The following additional information was made available by Moreno.

a. On January 1, 2010, accounts receivable from customers totaled $30,000. On December 31, 2010, receivables totaled $25,250.

b. On December 31, 2010, accounts receivable amounting to $1,800 were expected to be uncollectible.

c. On January 1, 2010, accounts payable owed to merchandise suppliers were $18,000. On December 31, 2010, the outstanding accounts payable were $32,250.

d. Included in *Salaries Expense* is $16,000 that Moreno was "paid" for her personal work in the business.

e. Included in *Interest Expense* is $3,200 that Moreno withdrew as interest on her capital investment.

f. Miscellaneous repairs of $1,000 were charged to *Store Equipment* during the year. No new equipment was purchased.

g. Moreno explains that since the estimated value of her store equipment has increased by $6,400 during the year, no depreciation expense was recorded. The store equipment cost $52,000 and had an estimated useful life of 10 years with estimated salvage value of $4,000.

Analyze: The entries required to correct situations a.–g. would affect several permanent accounts for Vanessa's Beauty Supplies. List the permanent accounts affected.

Problem 14.4B

Objectives 4, 5, 6

▶ **Reconstructing a balance sheet to reflect proper accounting principles.**

City Kitchen–Country Cooks is a retail shop owned by Ann Barnett. She wants to expand her business and has submitted the following balance sheet to her bank as part of the business loan application.

INSTRUCTIONS

1. Identify any errors in the balance sheet and explain why they should be considered errors.
2. Prepare a corrected balance sheet in accordance with generally accepted accounting principles.

City Kitchen–Country Cooks Balance Sheet December 31, 2010	
Assets	
Cash	$ 18,000
Accounts Receivable	7,200
Inventory	38,550
Store Fixtures	28,000
Store Equipment	16,000
Personal Residence	340,000
Personal Automobile	33,250
Total Assets	$481,000
Liabilities and Owner's Equity	
Accounts Payable	$ 26,000
Note Payable on Personal Automobile	16,280
Mortgage Payable on Personal Residence	108,750
Ann Barnett, Capital	329,970
Total Liabilities and Owner's Equity	$481,000

The following additional information is provided by Barnett.

a. The inventory has an original cost of $35,000. Barnett has valued it on the balance sheet at what it would cost today.

b. Barnett has counted $7,000 in her personal savings account in the business cash account.

c. The store fixtures, shown at original cost, were purchased two years ago. No depreciation has been taken on them. Depreciation for the two years, based on their estimated life of 10 years, would be $5,600.

d. The store equipment cost $19,200. No depreciation has been computed on the equipment, but it has been written down to its estimated replacement cost by a charge to expense. Depreciation on the equipment's original cost for the 24 months since its purchase would be $3,800.

e. Both the personal residence and personal automobile are only occasionally used for business purposes.

Analyze: Based on the new balance sheet that you have prepared, what are the total current assets for City Kitchen–Country Cooks?

Applying accounting principles and concepts.

◀ **Problem 14.5B**
Objectives 5, 6, 7

For each of the unrelated situations below, identify the accounting principle or concept violated (if a violation exists) and explain the nature of the violation. If you believe that the treatment is in accordance with GAAP, state this as your position and defend it.

1. A building repair company opened for business in late 2010. On December 31 the Services Revenue account contained a balance of $248,000. Of that amount, $63,420 represents deposits received on contracts for services to be performed in January and February 2011.

2. In recent years, Painting.com has enjoyed rapid growth in profits because of customer loyalty and its reputation of putting the needs of customers first. The company recently debited an account called *Goodwill,* in the amount of $100,000. The owner says this reflects the company's success in the business and the true worth of the business. The offsetting credit was to the owner's equity account.

3. Curtain Company sold for $800,000 land that was purchased 20 years ago for $420,000. Even though the general price level had doubled during this period, Curtain reported a profit of $380,000 on the sale.

4. Larramie Company manufactures a product requiring several parts. The company manufactures the parts, even though almost all competitors purchase the parts from outside sources, because Larramie can manufacture the parts for about 15 percent less than it would have to pay for the parts. Larramie thinks that comparability is very important in financial reporting, so when the parts are manufactured they are recorded at what the purchase price would have been. At the same time, income is recorded equal to the difference between actual cost and the hypothetical purchase price. The Inventory of Parts account reflects this outside purchase price and the Finished Products Inventory also reflects the hypothetical purchase price of the part used in manufacturing the products.

5. R. L. Mason owns Mason Computer Services. His annual net income is $1,000,000 and his owner's equity is $2,200,000. In December of 2010 an irate customer sued Mason for $3,500,000, alleging that an error made by Mason had resulted in damages of that amount. Mason's attorney thinks there may be substantial liability. Mason does not disclose the suit in the financial statements sent to the firm's banker and to providers of equipment and services.

Analyze: Refer to question 2, above. Assume that in item 2, Martin Company bought all of the assets of Painting.com, paying an amount equal to book value for all assets, including $100,000 for goodwill. Assume, too that the actual values of all the other assets purchased were equal to the purchase price. Do you think that it would be appropriate for Martin Company to record the purchase price of the goodwill at the $100,000 paid for it?

Critical Thinking Problem 14.1

Applying GAAP

Assume that you are an independent CPA performing audits of financial statements. In the course of your work, you encounter the following independent situations. Review each of the situations. If you consider the treatment to be in conformity with generally accepted accounting principles and concepts, explain why. If you do not, explain which principle or concept has been violated and how the situation should have been reported.

1. Jacksboro Oil and Gas Company produces oil and gas from the ground. It drills wells to attempt to find the oil and gas and to produce any minerals found. On average, about one out of four wells that the company drills produces oil and gas. Drilling costs range from $600,000 to $2,500,000 for each well. The company has adopted a rule that if the well results in finding oil and gas that can be produced profitably, the drilling costs will be recorded as an asset. If a dry hole results, the drilling costs are charged to expense.

2. Vacation City Resort recognizes room rental revenue on the date that a reservation is made. For the summer season, many guests make reservations as far as a year in advance of their intended visit.

3. The Discount Palace spends a large sum on advertising for various sales promotions during the year. The advertising includes "institutional" ads designed to bring in customers in future years. The owner is sure that the advertising will generate revenue in future periods, but she has no idea of how much revenue will be produced or over what period of time it will be earned. In the current year, $600,000 was paid for advertising, and all of this amount was charged as an expense in the current period.

4. Equitex Supply Company has constructed special-purpose equipment designed to manufacture other equipment that will be sold to computer chip manufacturers. Due to the special nature of this equipment, it has virtually no resale value to any other company. Therefore, Equitex Supply has charged the entire cost to construct the equipment, $80 million, to expense in the current period.

5. Ponder Company prepares financial statements four times each year. For convenience, these statements are prepared when business is slow and the accounting staff is less busy with other matters. Last year "quarterly" financial statements were prepared for the 5-month period ended May 31, the 2-month period ended July 31, the 3-month period ended October 31, and the 2-month period ended December 31.

6. In its regional office, Midwestern Stores purchases at least 120 storage bins each year. These baskets cost approximately $18 each and have useful lives ranging from 2 to 6 years. They are depreciated over a period of 4 years, the estimated average life. One of the company's accountants has suggested that the costs of the baskets should be charged to expense at the time they are purchased.

Analyze: If item 2 were recorded as described, what possible implications would this have for stockholders in the company?

Critical Thinking Problem 14.2

Judgment Call

Monroe Distribution Center receives a number of different products in its warehouse. Monroe distributes these products by truck to customers within a radius of 80 miles. The company is located near the Madison Regional Airport, which is owned and operated by the city of Madison. Most of the products are received by rail or truck, but some are received by air.

The city and the local Chamber of Commerce have announced a joint undertaking to build a new divided highway to connect the airport with the interstate highway approximately three miles away. The Chamber of Commerce is attempting to raise $2,000,000 as its contribution to the new highway's cost. The Chamber has asked the 10 largest enterprises in the city to make substantial contributions. Monroe has been asked to contribute $400,000 of the total amount.

At a meeting of Monroe's board of directors, the request was considered. It was pointed out that although Monroe is not located on the route of the proposed new road, the road's construction would speed up access of trucks to the warehouse and should substantially increase the value of Monroe's property. It is difficult to measure the benefits of either of these factors. The company's president suggested that a major reason for making the contribution was to get good publicity and to improve the company's image in the community. "It is good advertising," he said.

The company's controller is asked how the contribution would be accounted for in the company's accounts. A major question is whether the $400,000 should be

- charged to expense when the contribution is made (thus reducing income of that period),
- capitalized as part of the cost of the land owned by the company in the area (increasing assets and not affecting income),
- recorded as an asset and charged to expense over a period of five years (thus increasing assets in the short run and spreading out the effects of the contribution on income).

What answer would you give if you were the controller? In your answer, consider the principles, assumptions, and concepts that you have studied in this chapter.

BUSINESS CONNECTIONS

Judgment and Objectivity

Managerial | FOCUS

1. How can the element of personal judgment, which is involved in such matters as estimates of salvage value and useful life, be minimized to preserve the objectivity of an accounting system?

2. What arguments can be given that the historical cost framework should be abandoned?

3. In what situations would the going concern assumption *not* be useful to management?

4. A new manager of a retail company suggests that the company should prepare its income statement on the basis of cash receipts and cash expenditures (except for the acquisition of fixed assets, such as plant and equipment). He argues that managers, investors, creditors, and others are more interested in cash receipts and disbursements than in accrual-based accounting. Do you think he is correct? Explain.

Going Concern

Ethical | DILEMMA

Gevok Industries has just started business as a computer-based gaming company. Knowing that small computer businesses rarely remain in business longer than 5 years, Gevok depreciates all his assets for 5 years. The assets include a building, integrated circuit shaper, and vehicles. Is this ethical? What impact will this action have on net income? What if any is the correct action?

Accounting Principles

STREETWISE:
Questions from the
REAL WORLD

Refer to the 2006 *Annual Report* for The Home Depot, Inc., in Appendix A.

1. Discuss the qualitative characteristics of comparability and understandability in relation to the financial statements presented. In your opinion, do the statements satisfy these two criteria required by the FASB for financial reporting?

2. "Notes to Consolidated Financial Statements" are published along with the financial statements of a fiscal period, offering detailed information on significant accounting policies and financial data. Review the consolidated balance sheets and excerpts from "Notes to Consolidated Financial Statements." Are the company's "Commitments and Contingencies" represented on the balance sheet? Describe the discussion found in Note 10 and the principle addressed by it.

Notes to Financial Statements

Financial Statement
ANALYSIS

The following excerpts were taken from the Avery Dennison 2006 *Annual Report*. The Notes to Consolidated Financial Statements contain the following details regarding significant accounting policies.

> **Use of Estimates** The preparation of financial statements in conformity with accounting principles generally accepted in the United States of America requires management to make estimates and assumptions for the reporting period and as of the financial statement date. These estimates and assumptions affect the reported amounts of assets and liabilities, the disclosure of contingent liabilities and the reported amounts of revenue and expense. Actual results could differ from these estimates.
>
> **Revenue Recognition** Sales are recognized when persuasive evidence of an arrangement exists, pricing is determinable, and collection is reasonably assured. Furthermore, sales, provisions for estimated returns, and the cost of products sold are recorded at the time title transfers to customers and when the customers assume the risks and rewards of ownership. Sales terms are generally f.o.b. (free on board) shipping point or f.o.b. destination, depending upon local business customs. For most regions in which we operate, f.o.b. shipping point terms are utilized and sales are recorded at the time of shipment, because this is when title and risk of loss are transferred. In certain regions, notably in Europe, f.o.b. destination terms are generally utilized and sales are recorded when the products are delivered to the customer's delivery site, because this is when

title and risk of loss are transferred. Actual product returns are charged against estimated sales return allowances. Volume, promotional, price, cash and other discounts and customer incentives are accounted for as a reduction to gross sales.

Analyze:

1. Name one type of estimate that might affect the company's assets. What type of estimate might affect the company's liabilities?

2. What accounting principle does the *Revenue Recognition* text above address?

Analyze Online: At Avery Dennison's Web site (www.averydennison.com), review the most recent annual report found within the *Investor Relations* section.

3. The Notes to Consolidated Financial Statements contain summaries of significant accounting policies. What categories or topics are presented?

4. Has the company's revenue recognition policy changed since 2004? If so, describe the change.

The Big Four

Extending THE THOUGHT

The Big Four accounting firms perform many functions for their clients. In 2000, the Chairman of the Securities and Exchange Commission became concerned that a conflict of interest existed between the accountants' role as auditor and the role they sometimes play as consultant to the same business. Do you agree or disagree? Explain. What underlying accounting assumption could be compromised by this practice? If accountants perform inadequately as auditors, what implications exist for the investor?

Memo

Business COMMUNICATION

You are an accountant for a privately owned company. The owner believes that only publicly traded companies need to be audited and follow GAAP. The previous accountant kept the company's books according to income tax requirements. Write a one-page memo to the owner containing benefits of following GAAP.

Accounting Conventions

TEAMWORK

Every business manager should know and implement the accounting conventions. Put the accounting conventions on 3x5 cards. Divide into groups of three to five students. Each student in the group will pick a 3x5 card and give an example of a violation of and compliance with the convention listed on the card.

AICPA and IMA

Internet CONNECTION

Certified Public Accountant (CPA) and Certified Management Accountant (CMA) are two major certifications recognized by the accounting industry. Go to the aicpa.org Web site and find the requirements to become a CPA. Go to the imanet.org Web site and find the requirements to become a CMA. The American Accounting Association serves accounting professors. Go to the AAA Web site at aaahq.org, and select "Placement." Determine the requirements to teach at a university.

Answers to **Self Reviews**

Answers to Section 1 Self Review

1. **a.** The SEC relies on the FASB as the provider of accounting standards.

   b. The AICPA requires its members to follow the FASB standards.

2. No. It would not be a publicly held corporation.

3. The SEC has oversight. It has the authority to develop accounting and reporting standards, but has stated that it will accept the standards of the FASB if the SEC is satisfied that those standards meet the SEC's requirements.

4. The conceptual framework project is designed to develop basic concepts, assumptions, and principles to be followed in developing accounting rules. It is necessary for rule makers to use a framework of concepts so that standards and rules are consistent with one another.

5. a. FASB

   b. AICPA

   c. SEC

   d. PCAOB

6. If statements are not prepared in conformity with GAAP, they may be unreliable and they do not present financial affairs in accordance with established accounting principles.

Answers to Section 2 Self Review

1. Historical costs are objective and verifiable.

2. Both contain an element of comparability. Consistency means using the same principles and applications each accounting period (comparability from period to period). Comparability refers to the ability to compare one company's statements with another company's statements.

3. a. Separate entity

   b. Going concern

   c. Monetary unit of measure

   d. Periodicity of income.

4. Materiality is whether the omission of an item or not following GAAP for an item is likely to change the user's interpretations of statements. Factors that might be considered in determining materiality are total assets, net income, total liabilities, and owner's equity.

5. a. Periodicity of income

   b. Materiality

   c. Separate entity

   d. Stable monetary unit

6. a. Since the lawsuits involve material amounts and are uncertain, it would be appropriate to disclose their existence in a footnote. Given the conclusion of the attorney and former manager, along with the uncertainty about any amount of loss, it would probably not be appropriate to record a loss.

   b. Reporting revenues only when credit sales are collected would violate the matching principle (matching revenues with costs incurred). However, management should make certain that the allowance for uncollectible accounts is adequate.

Answers to Comprehensive Self Review

1. Industry practice is likely to be an important consideration where there are unique operating circumstances or unique contracts involved in that industry and there is no clearly preferable application of the conceptual framework.

2. The AICPA influence is primarily through its committees that examine current issues arising in practice for which there is no clear guidance from the FASB. Under the Sarbanes-Oxley Act giving express power to the SEC to accept rules developed by (one) private-sector organization, it is possible that the direct impact of AICPA pronouncements will be limited in the future.

3. The full disclosure principle is that all events and factors that are likely to impact the interpretation of the statements should be disclosed. Disclosures can be made in parenthetical notes to the statements or by "notes to the statements" (deemed to be an integral part of the statements). In addition, "supplemental notes" which may be not directly related to amounts shown in the statements may be included.

4. Applicable costs should be matched with revenues in the income statement the same year—generally in the year of sale. This requires adjustments for prepaid and accrued expenses and for unearned and accrued income items, as well as such items as depreciation and uncollectible accounts.

5. The result would be that record keeping would be much more complicated, probably involving separate accounts for transactions (such as machinery purchases) made in each year. Another approach might be to attempt to keep all records in terms of "value" at the statement date.

6. One alternative would be to make "price-level adjustments" to convert all amounts in the accounts to a dollar with a common purchasing power. Another alternative might be to value all assets and liabilities at "present values." Both price-level adjustments and "present value" computations are difficult and costly. In addition, present value determinations may be very imprecise and subjective.

Accounts Receivable and Uncollectible Accounts

Chapter **15**

LEARNING OBJECTIVES

1. Record the estimated expense from uncollectible accounts receivable using the allowance method. **LP15**
2. Charge off uncollectible accounts using the allowance method.
3. Record the collection of accounts previously written off using the allowance method.
4. Record losses from uncollectible accounts using the direct charge-off method.
5. Record the collection of accounts previously written off using the direct charge-off method.
6. Recognize common internal controls for accounts receivable.
7. Define the accounting terms new to this chapter.

NEW TERMS

aging the accounts receivable
allowance method
direct charge-off method
valuation account

  www.fedex.com

Making a sale does not always mean collecting cash. Companies that extend credit to their customers understand the benefits and drawbacks of lines of credit. While credit allows customers to purchase goods and services more efficiently, every day a company does not receive payment for a delivered product is a day that company loses opportunities to invest that money and grow its business.

FedEx® offers transportation, e-commerce, and business solutions to its loyal customers. Converting accounts receivable into cash is critical for a service-based organization like FedEx. Most companies realize that they will never collect 100 percent of their receivables. An allowance, or estimate, for uncollectibles is established. In 2007, FedEx accountants deducted estimated uncollected accounts of approximately $106 million from the amount of total accounts receivable.

thinking critically
How do you think accountants at FedEx estimated the company's uncollected accounts?

FedEx services marks used by permission.

SECTION OBJECTIVES

>> 1. **Record the estimated expense from uncollectible accounts receivable using the allowance method.**

   WHY IT'S IMPORTANT

   Assets should not be overstated. In accordance with the matching principle, bad debt losses are matched with the related sales revenue.

   2. **Charge off uncollectible accounts using the allowance method.**

>> **WHY IT'S IMPORTANT**

   When an account is uncollectible, it should be charged off. The accounts receivable ledger should contain complete and accurate information so that future credit decisions are sound.

   3. **Record the collection of accounts previously written off using the allowance method.**

>> **WHY IT'S IMPORTANT**

   Customers' accounts should reflect actual payment histories.

TERMS TO LEARN

aging the accounts receivable
allowance method
direct charge-off method
valuation account

Video 15.1

The Allowance Method of Accounting for Uncollectible Accounts

important!

The Credit Manager

The credit manager plays a very important role in improving profitability of the business.

Most businesses extend credit to their customers because it increases sales revenues. Manufacturing enterprises, wholesale distributors, and organizations providing services to other businesses typically sell an overwhelming portion of their goods and services on credit. Service businesses such as medical providers, attorneys, auto repair garages, and others offering services to individuals also frequently extend credit. Almost invariably, when a business extends credit some customers will not pay their bills. A firm's credit department and its management try to reduce the losses from uncollectible accounts. Typically a customer seeking credit privileges must complete a credit application form. The applicant must provide financial information requested. In most cases, the applicant's credit record is checked through a credit report obtained from a credit agency. A credit report shows the payment record of a customer and some reports include historical or other information concerning the business or person about whom inquiry is being made.

No matter what tools are used, however, it is almost impossible to forecast with certainty whether a specific customer will prove to be a good risk. If a company has no credit losses, the business may be losing substantial sales by having an ultrastrict credit policy. Management must constantly balance the risk of higher credit losses resulting from giving credit to more applicants or from setting higher limits on the amount of credit extended individual customers (both of which may lead to increased losses) against the possibility of losing sales volume as a result of giving credit to fewer customers or setting lower limits on each customer. However, losses resulting from failure of customers to pay the amounts owed, called "uncollectible accounts expense," "losses from uncollectible accounts," or sometimes referred to as "bad debts expense," are a normal cost of doing business.

A basic question faced in accounting for uncollectible accounts is determining when they should be charged to expense. A corollary question is how to determine the amount to be charged to expense during each accounting period. Related issues for the accountant are how to make the resulting accounting entries and how to show the information in the financial statements.

Methods of Accounting for Uncollectible Accounts

Two methods are used to account for uncollectible accounts. These are the "allowance method" and the "direct charge-off method." The latter is sometimes called the "specific charge-off method."

THE ALLOWANCE METHOD

Under the **allowance method,** an estimate is made and recorded each year of the bad debt losses applicable to sales of that year, even though it may be a year or more before it is known which specific accounts are uncollectible. At the end of the accounting period, the estimated loss for the period is debited to *Uncollectible Accounts Expense* and credited to *Allowance for Doubtful Accounts.* This approach matches the estimated expense from uncollectible accounts to the revenue in the period the revenue is recognized. *Allowance for Doubtful Accounts* is subtracted from *Accounts Receivable* on the balance sheet. The net accounts receivable reflects the amount that the business thinks will be collected. For this reason, the allowance account is called a **valuation account.** The allowance method meets two of the basic concepts in the FASB's Conceptual Framework. The principle of matching revenues and related costs is applied. In addition, current assets that will be converted into cash should not be shown at more than the amount expected to be realized when they are converted. Because of these characteristics, the allowance method is required under generally accepted accounting principles.

THE DIRECT CHARGE-OFF METHOD

Under the **direct charge-off method** losses from uncollectible accounts are recorded only when specific customers' accounts become uncollectible. When that occurs, the balance due is removed from *Accounts Receivable* and the customer's account in the subsidiary ledger and is charged to *Uncollectible Accounts Expense.* The direct charge-off method is used primarily by small businesses, many of whom do not have external audits. It may also be used by large businesses that have relatively insignificant accounts receivable, in keeping with the concept of materiality. The direct charge-off method does not reflect generally accepted accounting principles because a loss from sales on account in one year frequently will not be charged to expense until a subsequent year (a violation of the matching principle) if the direct charge-off method is followed. In addition, the accounts receivable are shown at an amount greater than will ultimately be realized in cash from them. Federal income tax laws now require that the direct charge-off method be used in preparing the federal tax return. The allowance method is not acceptable for tax purposes. Using the direct charge-off method for financial reporting as well as income tax purposes, reduces the amount of time spent in accounting for uncollectible accounts. As a result, the tax requirement leads some businesses to also use the direct charge-off method for financial reporting purposes.

Because the allowance method is the generally accepted procedure and is therefore much more widely used, details of that method are discussed before the direct charge-off method is examined in detail.

Applying the Allowance Method

You will learn how to use the allowance method to account for losses from uncollectible accounts by studying Kathy's Kitchens, a retail store selling kitchen appliances, gadgets, and kitchen remodeling services. Kathy's Kitchens is owned by Kathy Kaymark, and has been in business several years. The store offers charge accounts to customers who meet its credit

---

important!

When Uncollectible Accounts Expense Is Recorded Under the Allowance Method
Under the allowance method, uncollectible accounts expense is recorded at the end of the period as an adjusting entry.

important!

Matching Uncollectible Accounts with Sales
The allowance method matches the uncollectible accounts expense with sales in the period the sales are recorded.

important!

Recording Uncollectible Accounts Expense Under the Direct Charge-Off Method
Under the direct charge-off method, bad debt expense is recorded when a customer's account becomes uncollectible.

important!

Uncollectible Accounts
Only the direct charge-off method is allowed for federal income tax purposes. The use of the allowance method is required under generally accepted accounting principles.

standards. Kathy sends customers statements of their accounts on the last day of each month, and the balance owed is due to be paid by the 20th day of the following month. Kathy understands that the allowance method is preferred to the direct charge-off method, so she has adopted the allowance method.

>>1. OBJECTIVE

Record the estimated expense from uncollectible accounts receivable using the allowance method.

LP15

RECORDING THE ESTIMATED EXPENSE FROM UNCOLLECTIBLE ACCOUNTS WHEN THE ALLOWANCE METHOD IS USED

At the end of 2009, Kathy analyzed the bad debts record in prior years and also the amounts owed currently by each customer. On the basis of this analysis, along with information from her trade association about typical bad debt losses in that type business and from talks with other merchants in similar businesses in the community, Kathy estimated the provision for uncollectible accounts necessary at year-end 2009 to be $1,900. (Do not be concerned with the details of how this amount was determined. Three methods, to be examined later in this chapter, are commonly used as a basis for the estimate. At this point, we are interested only in the basic concepts of the recording procedure.)

When adjusting entries were made at the end of the year 2009, the estimated loss ($1,900) was recorded as a debit to the expense account, *Uncollectible Accounts Expense,* sometimes called *Bad Debts Expense* or *Losses from Uncollectible Accounts.* This account is shown in the income statement as a general expense or as a selling expense, depending on which department in the business has responsibility for making credit decisions. Good internal controls generally suggest that the credit function should not be in the sales department, a department very interested in increasing sales. As a result, *Uncollectible Accounts Expense* is usually shown under General Expenses.

The credit part of the adjusting entry was to *Allowance for Doubtful Accounts.* Sometimes the allowance account is called *Allowance for Bad Debts* or *Allowance for Uncollectible Accounts.* Here is the journal entry made at the end of 2009 in the records of Kathy's Kitchens.

important!

Uncollectible Accounts Expense on the Income Statement
Usually, *Uncollectible Accounts Expense* is shown as a general expense.

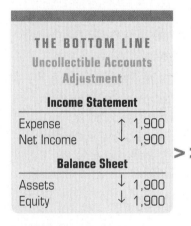

	THE BOTTOM LINE	
	Uncollectible Accounts Adjustment	
Income Statement		
Expense	↑	1,900
Net Income	↓	1,900
Balance Sheet		
Assets	↓	1,900
Equity	↓	1,900

GENERAL JOURNAL   PAGE ___1___

DATE		DESCRIPTION	POST. REF.	DEBIT	CREDIT
		Adjusting Entries			
2009					
Dec.	31	Uncollectible Accounts Expense		1 90 0 00	
		Allowance for Doubtful Accounts			1 90 0 00

>> Remember that *Allowance for Doubtful Accounts,* which reflects the estimate of losses to be incurred on sales already made, is shown on the balance sheet as a deduction from *Accounts Receivable.* Assuming that there was a zero balance in *Allowance for Doubtful Accounts* prior to the adjusting entry, that account will have a credit balance of $1,900 on December 31, 2009, after the above adjusting entry. The allowance account is a *contra* account because it is subtracted from an asset account (*Accounts Receivable*) in the balance sheet. It reduces the carrying value of the asset and is referred to a valuation account. Here is how the accounts receivable information appeared on the balance sheet for Kathy's Kitchens on December 31, 2009.

recall

Contra Asset Account
Allowance for Doubtful Accounts is a contra asset account. Its normal balance is a credit. It is reported in the balance sheet as a deduction from *Accounts Receivable* to provide an estimate of collectible receivables. For this reason, it is called a valuation account.

Kathy's Kitchens Balance Sheet (partial) December 31, 2009		
Current Assets		
Cash		$ 9,320
Accounts Receivable	$46,400	
Less Allowance for Doubtful Accounts	1,900	44,500

Alternatively, the balance sheet may show only the net amount of **Accounts Receivable**, after subtracting out the allowance, with the amount of the allowance shown in a parenthetical note.

> For its fiscal year (52 weeks) ending on May 2, 2007, H. J. Heinz Company and Subsidiaries reported **Receivables, Net of Allowances** of $996.9 million. A parenthetical note indicated that the allowances totaled $14.7 million.

Note again that under the allowance method the financial statements reflect the matching principle. The estimated expense for losses on sales made in 2009 is deducted in the 2009 income statement—the same year that the related revenues from sales were reported. Also, the net **Accounts Receivable** on the balance sheet reflects the amount expected to be received in cash from the debtors.

FACTORS USED TO COMPUTE THE YEAR-END PROVISION FOR UNCOLLECTIBLE ACCOUNTS

In the discussion of Kathy's Kitchens provision for uncollectible accounts at the end of 2009, you were not told how the $1,900 provision was determined. The end-of-year estimate of the amount to be charged to **Uncollectible Accounts Expense** and credited to the **Allowance for Doubtful Accounts** is usually based on one of three factors:

- net credit sales for the year
- total accounts receivable on December 31
- aging of accounts receivable on December 31

When the amount of net credit sales for the year is the basis for the provision, it is often said that the preparer is using the "income statement approach." Using sales as the estimation base emphasizes the importance of matching uncollectible accounts expense with the net credit sales generated in the same year. In this approach, the key factor is the matching principle. When the provision is based on total accounts receivable or the aging of accounts receivable, the emphasis is on the balance sheet, so it is often called the "balance sheet approach." It emphasizes the appropriate valuation of receivables—not showing the net receivables at an amount greater than the cash expected to be received from their collection.

The calculations of the uncollectible accounts adjustment for Kathy's Kitchens on December 31, 2010, under each of these three approaches illustrate how they are determined. During 2010, Kathy's Kitchens had net credit sales of $600,000. Accounts receivable at the end of the year totaled $49,000. There was a credit balance of $1,900 in the allowance account on January 1, 2010. Assume that accounts totaling $1,792 were charged off in 2010, so that there is a credit balance of $108 in **Allowance for Doubtful Accounts** prior to adjusting entries on December 31. Here is how the three approaches would be applied by Kathy's Kitchens.

PERCENTAGE OF NET CREDIT SALES

One way to estimate to uncollectible accounts expense is to multiply the net credit sales by a percentage. The percentage is based on the company's previous experience with losses from uncollectible accounts. New businesses often base the percentage on the experience of other businesses in the same industry. The percentage is calculated as follows:

$$\frac{\text{Losses from uncollectible accounts}}{\text{Net credit sales}}$$

Net credit sales is calculated as total credit sales minus the sales return and allowances on credit sales.

Kathy's Kitchens estimates that three-quarters of 1 percent (0.0075) of the net credit sales will be uncollectible. If net credit sales in 2010 are $600,000, the estimated loss from uncollectible accounts is $4,500 (0.0075 × $600,000). This is the amount to be charged to **Uncollectible Accounts Expense** and credited to **Allowance for Doubtful Accounts** in the

important!
Reporting Uncollectible Accounts Under GAAP
The allowance method meets the conservatism constraint.

important!
Effects of Different Estimation Bases on Entries
The accounts used to record the provision are the same for all three estimation bases. The difference is in how the amount of adjustment is computed.

important!
Matching Costs and Revenues
Although basing the uncollectible account estimate on receivables is not tied directly to sales for the year, generally the accounts receivable balance will reflect sales made in the current year. For this reason, accountants say that this approach is "matching revenues and costs."

important!
Using Total Sales as the Base
Some companies do not have separate data for sales on account and cash sales. In that case, the percentage may be applied to total sales. If the ratio between cash sales and credit sales changes from year to year, this is not a satisfactory approach.

adjusting entry. It is entered on the worksheet and is later recorded in the general journal, along with other adjusting entries.

		GENERAL JOURNAL		PAGE ___1___			
	DATE	DESCRIPTION	POST. REF.	DEBIT	CREDIT		
1	2010	*Adjusting Entries*					1
22	Dec. 31	Uncollectible Accounts Expense	561	4 5 0 0 00			22
23		Allowance for Doubtful Accounts	112		4 5 0 0 00		23
24		To record estimated bad debt losses					24
25		for the year, based on 0.75 percent of					25
26		net credit sales of $600,000					26

Note again that the expense charge is the focal point when sales is used as the basis for the estimate. The balance in the allowance account before the adjustment is ignored in determining how much will be charged to expense and credited to the allowance account. This is why the method is referred to as an "income statement approach."

PERCENTAGE OF TOTAL ACCOUNTS RECEIVABLE

Some accountants think that it is more important to focus on the balance in the allowance account than on the amount charged to expense. Under their approach, it is necessary to first determine the amount in the accounts estimated to be uncollectible and to adjust the *Allowance for Doubtful Accounts* to that amount. The offsetting debit to expense is the result of focusing on the balance sheet accounts.

A simple approach to determining the appropriate balance for *Allowance for Doubtful Accounts* is to apply a single percentage to the balance of the *Accounts Receivable* account. This percentage is typically based on the experience of the company during the last three or four years. The average of accounts that became uncollectible during each year of the base period is calculated. Similarly the average of accounts receivable at the end of each base period year is determined. Then the ratio of the average uncollectible accounts to the average ending balance of accounts receivable is computed. The ratio is applied to the *Accounts Receivable* balance at the date of the computation to arrive at the estimated worthless accounts. Kathy's Kitchens decides to use the ratio of average uncollectible accounts for the last three years to the ending balance in *Accounts Receivable* for the three years. The records of Kathy's Kitchens show the following.

Date	Accounts Receivable	Uncollectible Accounts
12/31/07	$ 39,600	$2,083
12/31/08	44,360	2,145
12/31/09	46,400	2,240
Total	$130,360	$6,468
Average	$ 43,453	$2,156

The average loss over the three-year period is 4.962 percent of accounts receivable.

$$\frac{\text{Average Uncollectible Accounts}}{\text{Average Accounts Receivable}} = \frac{\$2,156}{\$43,453} = 0.04962$$

It is customary to round the percentage of loss to the nearest one-tenth of one percent. Under this convention, Kathy's rate would be rounded to 5.0 percent.

If the balance of *Accounts Receivable* on December 31, 2010, is $49,000, estimated uncollectible accounts will be $2,450 (0.05 × $49,000). Under the balance sheet approach, *Allowance for Uncollectible Accounts* is adjusted to the amount estimated to be *uncollectible*.

Assuming that the *Allowance for Doubtful Accounts* has a credit balance of $108 on December 31, before the adjusting entry has been made, it will be necessary to add $2,342 to the account to bring it to the desired balance ($2,450 − $108 = $2,342). Here is the necessary entry.

GENERAL JOURNAL   PAGE __12__

	DATE		DESCRIPTION	POST. REF.	DEBIT	CREDIT	
1	2010						1
2	Dec.	31	Uncollectible Accounts Expense		2 3 4 2 00		2
3			Allowance for Doubtful Accounts			2 3 4 2 00	3

After the entry has been posted, the *Allowance for Doubtful Accounts* has a credit balance of $2,450. If *Allowance for Uncollectible Accounts* had a *debit* balance of $240 prior to the adjusting entry, it would be necessary to credit the allowance account for $2,690 ($2,450 + $240 = $2,690) to arrive at the required balance of $2,450.

AGING THE ACCOUNTS RECEIVABLE

Another way to estimate uncollectible accounts is a procedure called **aging the accounts receivable.** This procedure involves classifying receivables according to how long they have been outstanding. The first step is to prepare an aging schedule. Figure 15.1 shows the aging schedule for Kathy's Kitchens. Each account is listed by name and balance. Each invoice is classified as current (within the credit period), 1–30 days past due, 31–60 days past due, or over 60 days past due. Notice that Robert Brown owes $400. Of this amount, $80 is over 60 days past due and $320 is between 31 and 60 days past due.

The longer an account is past due, the less likely it is to be collected. Following are estimated uncollectible percentages for each age group shown in the analysis of Kathy's receivables.

important!

Collect Accounts as Quickly as Possible
Experience has shown that the older an account receivable becomes, the less likely it is to be collected.

Category	Percentage Uncollectible
Current Accounts	0.5%
1–30 days past due	6.0%
31–60 days past due	20.0%
Over 60 days past due	60.0%

Kathy's Kitchens
Schedule of Accounts Receivable by Age
December 31, 2010

Customer	Balance	Current	1–30	31–60	Over 60
Anderson, Nick	820		820		
Anh, Susie	1,200	1,200			
Benson, Samuel	257	37		200	20
Brown, Robert	400			320	80
All other accounts	46,323	36,763	6,180	1,080	2,300
Totals	49,000	38,000	7,000	1,600	2,400

FIGURE 15.1

Kathy's Kitchens Aged Accounts Receivable Schedule

important!

Aging the Accounts Receivable
The aged accounts receivable schedule serves several purposes.
- It proves that the accounts receivable subsidiary ledger balances with the accounts receivable control account.
- It identifies slow-paying customers.
- It is used to estimate the amount of accounts that will become uncollectible.

Based on these percentages, the estimated uncollectible accounts on December 31 total $2,370.

Current	0.005	×	$38,000	=	$ 190
1–30 days past due	0.06	×	$ 7,000	=	$ 420
31–60 days past due	0.20	×	$ 1,600	=	$ 320
Over 60 days past due	0.60	×	$ 2,400	=	$1,440
Totals			$49,000		$2,370

Allowance for Doubtful Accounts should then be adjusted so that its ending balance is a $2,370 credit. On December 31, before adjustments have been made, ***Allowance for Doubtful Accounts*** has a credit balance of $108. A credit adjustment of $2,262 ($2,370 − $108) will bring the account balance to the desired amount.

Allowance for Doubtful Accounts	
−	+
	Bal. 108.00
	Adj. 2,262.00
	Bal. 2,370.00

The adjustment is recorded in the general journal as follows.

GENERAL JOURNAL   PAGE ___1___

1	2010		*Adjusting Entries*			1
22	Dec.	31	Uncollectible Accounts Expense	561	2 26 2 00	22
23			Allowance for Doubtful Accounts	112	2 26 2 00	23
24			*To adjust allowance account to $2,370,*			24
25			*based on aging of accounts receivable*			25

>>2. OBJECTIVE
Charge off uncollectible accounts using the allowance method.

Video15.1

important!

Removing a Charged-Off Account
When the allowance method is used, ***Accounts Receivable*** (and the customer's account) is always credited when an account is determined to be uncollectible.

WRITING OFF A CUSTOMER'S ACCOUNT DETERMINED TO BE UNCOLLECTIBLE WHEN THE ALLOWANCE METHOD IS USED

A basic rule is that the longer past due an account becomes, the less likely it is to be collectible. When it is concluded that a specific account is not collectible, it should be "charged off" or "written off." For example, on January 24, 2010, Kathy's Kitchens concluded that the account of James McDonald should be charged off. Kathy's had sent him numerous letters, made several telephone calls, and sent a number of e-mails. The account had a balance of $224, resulting from a sale on August 22, 2009.

The general journal entry required to charge off a customer's account when the allowance method is used is a simple one. ***Accounts Receivable*** and McDonald's account in the subsidiary ledger are credited to remove the amount due. The debit is to ***Allowance for Doubtful Accounts.*** When the allowance was credited previously by an adjusting entry, it was not known which specific accounts would be uncollectible. It is now assumed that the provision included McDonald's account, so there is no longer a need to include in ***Allowance for Uncollectible Accounts*** an amount to cover a future loss from McDonald's failure to pay this debt. Here is the journal entry to write off McDonald's account.

GENERAL JOURNAL   PAGE ___12___

DATE		DESCRIPTION	POST. REF.	DEBIT	CREDIT
2010					
Jan.	24	Allowance for Doubtful Accounts		2 24 00	
		Accounts Receivable/James McDonald			2 24 00

The debit to *Allowance for Doubtful Accounts* reduces the credit balance in that account. The total amount of accounts receivable charged off in 2010 may be more than, or less than, the balance in *Allowance for Uncollectible Accounts* at the start of the year. What happens if the amount debited to *Allowance for Doubtful Accounts* exceeds the beginning amount in the account? For example, what happens if during 2010 Kathy's Kitchens removes from *Accounts Receivable* and charges to *Allowance for Doubtful Accounts* a total of $2,018? Remember that the balance in the allowance account was only $1,900 at the start of the year. Thus, at the end of 2010 *Allowance for Doubtful Accounts* would contain a debit balance of $118 ($2,018 debit − $1,900 credit = $118 debit). On the other hand, if the amount of uncollectible accounts charged off in 2010 is only $1,700, there would have been a credit balance of $200 ($1,900 credit − $1,700 debit = $200 credit) in the allowance account before adjustments at the end of 2010. The existence of a debit balance or a credit balance in the allowance account before adjustments at the end of the year is not generally a cause for concern. When the adjusting entries have been made, that situation will be corrected. We will see later how this situation is handled in the adjustments at the end of 2010. Obviously, management will need to keep close watch every year to make sure that the estimation process being used is reasonable and the allowance balance is adequate, but not excessive.

It is important to remember that the charge-off of a specific account receivable has no impact on total assets if the allowance method is used. The credit to the asset account *Accounts Receivable* is exactly the same amount as the debit to the contra account, *Allowance for Doubtful Accounts,* so there is no change in the net amount of *Accounts Receivable.*

At its fiscal year ending June 30, 2007, Microsoft Corporation's balance sheet showed "Accounts Receivable, Net" of $11.34 billion. A note to the financial statements states:

The allowance for doubtful accounts reflects our best estimate of probable losses inherent in the accounts receivable balance. We determine the allowance based on known troubled accounts, historical experience, and other currently available evidence.

The note goes further to analyze the allowance for doubtful accounts for 2007, which includes the following information.

Beginning balance (July 1, 2006)	$142,000,000
Charges to costs and expenses	+ 64,000,000
Write-offs and other	− 89,000,000
Balance at end of period (June 30, 2007)	+ $117,000,000

COLLECTING AN ACCOUNT THAT HAS BEEN PREVIOUSLY WRITTEN OFF

Occasionally, an account that was written off is later collected, in whole or in part. When a firm uses the allowance method to provide for losses, the recovery of an account previously charged off as uncollectible requires two entries to record the transaction. The first entry reinstates the account receivable, and the second entry records the receipt of cash. For example, the recovery on February 9, 2011, of the $160 account of Richard Strong, charged off on July 13, 2010, is recorded in the general journal as follows.

>>3. OBJECTIVE
Record the collection of accounts previously written off using the allowance method.

GENERAL JOURNAL   PAGE _____

	DATE		DESCRIPTION	POST. REF.	DEBIT	CREDIT	
1	2011						1
20	Feb.	09	Accounts Receivable/Richard Strong	111/✓	160 00		20
21			Allowance for Doubtful Accounts	112		160 00	21
22			To reverse entry dated July 13, 2010,				22
23			writing off this account, collected in				23
24			full today.				24

An entry in the cash receipts journal is then made in the usual way to record the collection—by a debit to *Cash* and a credit to *Accounts Receivable.*

If the amount recovered is only part of the balance written off, an entry is made to restore *only the amount actually collected* unless the firm is almost certain that the remainder will be paid. For example, if Richard Strong pays only $60 that is the amount that will be reinstated unless Kathy's is reasonably sure the additional $100 Strong owes will be paid. After the proper reinstatement is made, an entry in the cash receipts journal is then made in the usual way to record the collection of the account receivable.

Section 1 Self Review

QUESTIONS

1. What major accounting principle supports the allowance method for reporting uncollectible accounts?

2. Martin Company determines its allowance for uncollectible accounts by applying an expected loss percentage of 1.5 percent to the total of accounts receivable, $1,000,000. Prior to the adjusting entry the allowance account has a debit balance of $800. How much will be charged to expense in the adjusting entry?

3. Adolph Industries determines its provision for uncollectible accounts by applying an estimated loss percentage of 1 percent to net credit sales. In 2010, net credit sales were $5,200,000. Prior to the adjusting entry, **Allowance for Uncollectible**

Accounts contained a credit balance of $2,500. How much will be charged to **Uncollectible Accounts Expense** in 2010?

EXERCISES

4. Cooper Company uses the allowance method to record uncollectible accounts. In January 2010, it charged off the $300 account balance of Barrington as uncollectible. In June 2010, Barrington paid the entire amount charged off. What journal entries are made at the time of receipt of payment? (Give accounts and amounts.)

5. Assume the same facts as in 4, above, except that Barrington made the repayment in 2011. What journal entries would be made on receipt of payment?

ANALYSIS

6. The credit manager at Lock's Office Supply has learned that a former customer who did not pay his debt, and whose account Lock had charged off as uncollectible, has just won the state lottery and the customer may now pay the debt. Should the customer's account be reinstated?

7. Ace Company bases its provision for uncollectible accounts on sales. At the end of each of the past four years, the ratio of **Allowance for Uncollectible Accounts** to **Accounts Receivable** at the end of the year has been greater than it was for the prior year. What does this suggest? Explain.

(Answers to Section 1 Self Review are on page 541.)

SECTION OBJECTIVES

>> 4. **Record losses from uncollectible accounts using the direct charge-off method.**

   WHY IT'S IMPORTANT

   Some small businesses and larger businesses with immaterial amounts of accounts receivable use this method, even though it does not comply with GAAP. Also, the direct charge-off method is required for federal income tax reporting.

>> 5. **Record the collection of accounts previously written off using the direct charge-off method.**

   WHY IT'S IMPORTANT

   Customers' accounts should reflect actual payment histories.

>> 6. **Recognize common internal controls for accounts receivable.**

   WHY IT'S IMPORTANT

   There are many activities involving accounts receivable and uncollectible accounts that provide opportunities for mishandling of funds. The accountant should be aware of steps to be taken to provide protection.

Applying the Direct Charge-Off Method: Internal Control of Accounts Receivable

Video15.1

The direct charge-off method for recording uncollectible account expense is simple to apply, but does not comply with generally accepted accounting principles. As discussed earlier in this chapter, however, the method is often used by small businesses and by some larger enterprises when the impact on financial statements would be immaterial. In addition, because it is required for federal income tax purposes, an understanding of the system is essential.

Recording Uncollectible Accounts When the Direct Charge-Off Method Is Used

Earlier in this chapter it was pointed out that the direct charge-off method records uncollectible accounts expense at the time a specific customer's account is deemed to be uncollectible. Certain transactions of Romano's Auto Repair Shop will be used to demonstrate the accounting entries made when the direct charge-off method is used.

On December 22, 2009, Romano made repairs to Mike Miller's RV, charging $520 to *Accounts Receivable* and to Miller's account in the accounts receivable subsidiary ledger. On July 10, 2010, after several weeks of trying to collect the account, Romano discovered that Miller had left his job and moved to another state. Romano concludes that the account must be written off. The loss is debited to *Uncollectible Accounts Expense.* The credit is to *Accounts Receivable* and to Miller's account in the accounts receivable subsidiary ledger.

>> **4. OBJECTIVE**
Record losses from uncollectible accounts using the direct charge-off method.

LP15

GENERAL JOURNAL   PAGE _____

DATE		DESCRIPTION	POST. REF.	DEBIT	CREDIT
2010					
July	10	Uncollectible Account Expense		5 2 0 00	
		Accounts Receivable/Mike Miller			5 2 0 00
		To write off uncollectible account			

There are several important points to remember about the direct charge-off method.

■ It does not always match revenue and expenses. Revenue for the work done on Miller's vehicle was recognized in 2009. The bad debt expense, however, is recorded in 2010.

■ It can overstate accounts receivable. Under this method, the *Accounts Receivable* balance reflects all outstanding unpaid accounts that have not been written off. No estimate is made for the accounts that might be uncollectible in the future.

■ It is the only method acceptable for federal income tax purposes.

Collecting an Account Previously Written Off When the Direct Charge-Off Method Is Used

>>5. OBJECTIVE
Record the collection of accounts previously written off using the direct charge-off method.

Under the direct charge-off method, the appropriate entries to record the collection of an account after it has been charged off depends on whether the collection is made in the same accounting period that the account was written off or occurs in a subsequent period.

PAYMENT RECEIVED IN PERIOD IN WHICH ACCOUNT IS CHARGED OFF

THE BOTTOM LINE

Reinstating an Account Using the Direct Charge-Off Method

Income Statement

Expense	↓	520
Net Income	↑	520

Balance Sheet

Assets	↑	520
Equity	↑	520

>>

In the above example, Miller's account of $520 was written off on July 10, 2010, under the direct charge-off method. The entry was a debit to *Uncollectible Accounts Expense* and a credit to *Accounts Receivable.* Suppose that on October 29, 2010, Romano's Auto Repair Shop received $520 from Miller in full payment of his account. It takes two entries to record the transaction. The first entry is to reinstate in *Accounts Receivable* the amount being paid. This entry, which simply reverses the entry made to charge off the account as uncollectible, is made so that the customer's account will show the full history of the customer's payment record. The credit is made to *Uncollectible Accounts Expense* so that the expense account for the period will not be overstated. To the extent that there is payment in the same year, there was no net expense for the year.

GENERAL JOURNAL   PAGE _____

DATE		DESCRIPTION	POST. REF.	DEBIT	CREDIT
2010					
Oct.	2 9	Accounts Receivable/Mike Miller		5 2 0 00	
		Uncollectible Account Expense			5 2 0 00
		To reinstate Miller's account receivable			
		that was written off on July 10 and			
		collected in full today.			

The second entry records the customer's payment in the cash receipts journal in the usual way, as a debit to *Cash* and a credit to *Accounts Receivable* (and to Miller's account).

PAYMENT RECEIVED IN PERIOD SUBSEQUENT TO THAT IN WHICH ACCOUNT WAS CHARGED OFF

Suppose that the collection of Miller's account is made in January 2011, a period subsequent to that of the charge-off. In that event, the entry to reinstate the account is a debit to *Accounts Receivable* and a credit to *Uncollectible Accounts Recovered.*

	DATE		DESCRIPTION	POST. REF.	DEBIT	CREDIT
	2010					
	Jan.	0 9	Accounts Receivable/Mike Miller		5 2 0 00	
			Uncollectible Accounts Recovered			5 2 0 00
			To reinstate Miller's account receivable			
			that was written off on July 10, 2010,			
			and collected in full today.			

GENERAL JOURNAL — PAGE _____

(2011 handwritten in margin)

If the amount recovered in a period subsequent to the write-off is credited to *Uncollectible Accounts Expense,* the expense for the period of recovery will be understated.

The balance in *Uncollectible Accounts Recovered* is shown on the income statement as Other Income.

Accounting for Other Receivables and Bad Debt Losses

As with accounts receivable, notes receivable and other receivables can prove uncollectible. Losses from uncollectible notes receivable and other receivables can be handled by the direct charge-off method or the allowance method. *Uncollectible Accounts Expense* and *Allowance for Doubtful Accounts* can be used for losses from all types of receivables.

MANAGERIAL IMPLICATIONS   <<

MANAGING CREDIT

- It is essential that managers establish formal procedures for granting credit to customers, for tracking accounts receivable, for ensuring that customers are paying promptly, and for collecting past-due accounts.
- Management needs to be informed about the losses from uncollectible accounts so they can
  - establish effective credit policies,
  - weigh the cost of uncollectible account losses against the reduced sales volume caused by tight credit policies.
- Managers should use the allowance method for uncollectible accounts in order to match revenue and expenses.
- Managers are responsible for developing procedures to handle payments from customers whose accounts have been written off.

THINKING CRITICALLY

What reports would provide information to managers about how well the accounts receivable function is being managed?

>>6. OBJECTIVE

Recognize common internal controls for accounts receivable.

int rnal **CONTROL**

Video15.1

Internal Control of Accounts Receivable

Internal control of the accounts receivable process is very important because accounts receivable represents one of the largest assets on the balance sheet for many companies. Common internal controls for accounts receivable include the following:

- Authorizing all credit sales.
- Developing procedures that ensure that all credit sales are recorded and customers' accounts are debited.
- Separating the following duties:
  - authorizing credit sales,
  - recording the accounts receivable transactions,
  - preparing bills or statements for customers,
  - mailing the bills or statements,
  - processing payments received from customers.
- Sending invoices and monthly statements.
- Authorizing charge-off of accounts.
- Aging the accounts receivable to allow management to identify and monitor slow-paying accounts.
- Investigating and taking appropriate action on past due accounts.
- Approving the write-off of accounts by authorized individuals only, and making the approvals in writing.
- Trying to collect past due accounts even if they have been written off.

Section 2 Self Review

QUESTIONS

1. Under the direct charge-off method, when a specific account receivable is written off, what account is debited? What is the effect of the write-off on net income and on assets?

2. What basic accounting assumptions, principles, or constraints may be used as the basis for criticizing the direct charge-off method for recording uncollectible accounts?

3. If an account receivable of $800 charged off in 2010 under the direct charge-off method is recovered in 2011, in what way does accounting for the recovery differ from that used if the recovery had been made in 2010?

EXERCISES

4. March 31, 2010, Baker Company wrote off the $500 account of Herman

Barrington as uncollectible. The company uses the direct charge-off method. What account is debited and what account is credited to record the write-off?

5. Assume the same facts as in Exercise 4, except that Baker Company uses the allowance method. What account is debited and what account is credited to record the write-off?

ANALYSIS

6. Howard Kline started business in March 2010. His sales for the year were $875,000 and his credit sales were $130,000. His accounts receivable on December 31 total $10,500. Kline plans to charge off uncollectible accounts only when specific accounts are deemed to be uncollectible. His accountant argues that in order to

match the uncollectible accounts that may result in the future against the sales revenue in the year of sale, Kline should estimate future losses and record them in 2010. What arguments can Kline make to justify his own position?

7. The sales manager in your company insists that the sales department should have the authority to make final decisions in all questions that arise about credit and accounts receivable. What is your opinion? What are the reasons for your answer?

(Answers to Section 2 Self Review are on page 542.)

REVIEW Chapter Summary

Chapter **15**

When credit is extended, uncollectible accounts inevitably occur. Before receivables can be accurately presented in the balance sheet and net income can be properly measured, the accounts must be studied for possible adjustment to reflect such losses. In this chapter, you have learned how to adjust the value of receivables to account for uncollectible accounts.

Learning Objectives

1 Record the estimated expense from uncollectible accounts receivable using the allowance method.

The allowance method matches bad debt losses for a period against revenue received in the same period. It is consistent with generally accepted accounting principles and is the preferred method for recognizing uncollectible accounts.

- The estimate of losses from uncollectible accounts can be based on a percentage (determined by experience) of credit sales. The estimated amount is debited to *Uncollectible Accounts Expense* and credited to *Allowance for Doubtful Accounts*.

- The estimate can be based on a single rate of expected noncollectibility of all accounts receivable. On the basis of past experience, the rate is applied to the balance of *Accounts Receivable* to determine the anticipated losses from the accounts. The balance in *Allowance for Doubtful Accounts* is adjusted to this estimated loss amount.

- The estimate of uncollectible accounts can also be based on the age of accounts receivable. A different percentage for credit losses is applied to each age group, and the resulting amounts are added together. Then *Allowance for Doubtful Accounts* is adjusted to the proper balance and the same amount is charged to *Allowance for Doubtful Accounts*.

2 Charge off uncollectible accounts using the allowance method.

Under the allowance method, an account that proves uncollectible is written off by a debit to *Allowance for Uncollectible Accounts* and a credit to both *Accounts Receivable* and the customer's account in the subsidiary ledger.

3 Record the collection of accounts previously written off using the allowance method.

Under the allowance method, if all or part of an account previously written off as uncollectible is subsequently paid, the amount being paid is reinstated by a debit to *Accounts Receivable* and a credit to *Allowance for Doubtful Accounts* and to the customer's account in the subsidiary ledger. Any cash

paid at that time is recorded by debiting Cash and crediting *Accounts Receivable* and the customer's account in the subsidiary ledger.

4 Record losses from uncollectible accounts using the direct charge-off method.

Under the direct charge-off method of recording uncollectible accounts, *Uncollectible Accounts Expense* is debited at the time specific accounts receivable are deemed to be uncollectible. Because the expense resulting from uncollectible accounts may not be matched in the same accounting period with the revenue that gave rise to the receivable, this method is not generally acceptable. It does not conform to the matching principle. However, many small businesses, and even some larger ones with relatively small amounts of receivables, use the method. It is required to be used for federal income tax purposes.

5 Record the collection of accounts previously written off using the direct charge-off method.

Under the direct charge-off method, if an account previously charged off as uncollectible is subsequently collected in the same accounting period, the original entry to charge off the account (to the extent it is collected) is reversed. The reversing entry is a debit to *Accounts Receivable* and the customer's account in the subsidiary ledger, and a credit to *Uncollectible Accounts Expense.* At the same time, an entry is made in the cash receipts journal debiting *Cash* and crediting *Accounts Receivable* and the customer's subsidiary ledger account. If the collection is made in a year subsequent to the year in which the write-off was recorded, the entry to record the reinstatement is a debit to *Accounts Receivable* and the customer's subsidiary account and a credit to *Uncollectible Accounts Recovered.*

6 Recognize common internal controls for accounts receivable.

It is very important that management establish formal procedures for approving and granting credit, for keeping close watch on customers' accounts to assure they are paid promptly, and for properly assigning duties related to accounts receivable. A key element in internal control is to avoid giving any one person responsibility for a large number of the functions related to receivables. These functions include granting credit, recording accounts receivable transactions, preparing bills for customers, mailing the bills and statements, processing payments from customers, approving write-offs, and trying to collect past-due accounts.

7 **Define the accounting terms new to this chapter.**

Glossary

Aging the accounts receivable (p. 521) Classifying accounts receivable balances according to how long they have been outstanding

Allowance method (p. 517) A method of recording uncollectible accounts that estimates losses from uncollectible accounts and charges them to expense in the period when the sales are recorded

Direct charge-off method (p. 517) A method of recording uncollectible account losses as they occur

Valuation account (p. 517) An account, such as *Allowance for Doubtful Accounts,* whose balance is revalued or reappraised in light of reasonable expectations

Comprehensive Self Review

1. If the allowance method is used, what account is debited when an account is determined uncollectible?

2. Which method of accounting for uncollectible accounts, the direct charge-off method or the allowance method, is considered generally acceptable?

3. Which method of accounting for uncollectible accounts, the direct charge-off or the allowance method, must be used for tax purposes?

4. A business using the direct charge-off method charged off the account of Samuel Adams in 2010. Adams made full payment in 2011. What account is credited when the account is reinstated?

5. In Blevins Company, the accounts receivable clerk prepares and mails statements to customers, opens mail, and makes a list of receipts, then deposits the cash and approves the write-off of delinquent accounts. Comment on this arrangement of duties.

6. When a specific account is written off under the allowance method, does the net accounts receivable balance increase or decrease? Why?

(Answers to Comprehensive Self Review are on page 542.)

 Multiple choice questions are provided on the text Web site at www.mhhe.com/price12e

Quiz15

Discussion Questions

1. Explain the purpose of the allowance method of accounting for losses from uncollectible accounts.

2. Name three approaches to estimating losses from uncollectible accounts when the allowance method is used.

3. If a company is interested primarily in matching expenses and revenues each period, would it base its estimate of uncollectible accounts on sales or on accounts receivable? Explain.

4. Suppose that the estimate of uncollectible accounts is based on credit sales and that *Allowance for Doubtful Accounts* has a debit balance before the adjustment is made. Explain how this situation is handled.

5. What is meant by aging the accounts receivable?

6. Under the allowance method, what account is credited in the adjusting entry to record estimated uncollectible accounts?

7. Under the allowance method, what entry is made when a specific customer's account is deemed to be uncollectible?

8. What basic accounting concepts, assumptions, principles, or constraints support the allowance method?

9. Explain how to record the collection of an account receivable in the same year in which it was previously written off if the allowance method of recording estimated doubtful accounts is used.

10. Suppose that the estimate of uncollectible accounts is based on the aging of accounts receivable and that the *Allowance for Uncollectible Accounts* has a credit balance before the adjustment is made. Explain how this situation is handled.

11. How is *Allowance for Uncollectible Accounts* shown in the balance sheet?

12. How is *Uncollectible Accounts Expense* shown on the income statement?

13. Explain the direct charge-off method for recording uncollectible accounts expense.

14. What are the major weaknesses of the direct charge-off method?

15. Under what conditions would the direct charge-off method be appropriate?

16. What entry is made to record an uncollectible account under the direct charge-off method?

17. Under the direct charge-off method, what entry is made when a firm collects an account that was charged off in a prior year?

18. List some common internal controls for accounts receivable.

19. List some duties that should routinely be separated as part of the internal control procedures for accounts receivable.

APPLICATIONS

Exercises ▆▆

Estimating and recording uncollectible accounts on the basis of net credit sales.

◀ Exercise 15.1
Objective 1

On December 31, 2010, certain account balances at Gaetano Company were as follows before year-end adjustments.

Accounts Receivable	$ 1,863,000
Allowance for Uncollectible Accounts (credit)	3,621
Sales	18,311,000
Sales Returns and Allowances	76,300

A further examination of the records showed that the "Sales" included $1,907,400 million of cash sales during the year. Of the sales returns and allowances, $61,600 came from credit sales. Assume that Gaetano Company estimates its losses from uncollectible accounts to be 0.3 percent of net credit sales. Compute the estimated amount of *Uncollectible Accounts Expense* for 2010 and prepare the journal entry to record the provision for uncollectible accounts.

Exercise 15.2
Objective 1

▶ **Estimating and recording uncollectible accounts on the basis of accounts receivable when there is a credit balance in Allowance for Doubtful Accounts.**

Assume that Gaetano Company (Exercise 15.1) makes its estimate of uncollectible accounts on December 31 as 3.3 percent of total accounts receivable. Compute the estimated amount of uncollectible accounts and give the general journal entry to record the provision for uncollectible accounts. (Obtain any information you need from Exercise 15.1.)

Exercise 15.3
Objective 1

▶ **Estimating and recording uncollectible accounts on the basis of accounts receivable when there is a debit balance in Allowance for Doubtful Accounts.**

On December 31, 2010, before adjusting entries, the balances of selected accounts of the Lakeside Equipment Company were as follows:

Accounts Receivable	860,000
Allowance for Uncollectible Accounts (debit balance)	1,500 dr.

The company has determined that historically about 2.5 percent of accounts receivable are never collected and uses this basis to determine its bad debts provision. Give the journal entry to record the company's estimated loss from uncollectible accounts on December 31.

Exercise 15.4
Objective 2

▶ **Recording actual uncollectible amounts under the allowance method.**

On April 30, 2010, The Handyman Company, which uses the allowance method, decided that the $3,200 account of Michele Wilson was worthless and should be written off. Give the general journal entry to record the write-off.

Exercise 15.5
Objective 3

▶ **Recording the collection of an account written off in the same year under the allowance method.**

On December 8, 2010, after a threatened lawsuit by The Handyman Company, Wilson paid the $3,200 account charged off on April 30, 2010 (Exercise 15.4). Give the entries in general journal form to reinstate Wilson's account and to record the receipt of her check.

Exercise 15.6
Objective 3

▶ **Recording the collection of an account written off in a prior year under the allowance method.**

Assume the same facts as in Exercise 15.5, except that the recovery of the $3,200 from Wilson was received on February 28, 2011. Give the entry in general journal form to record the reinstatement of Wilson's account and to record the receipt of her check.

Exercise 15.7
Objective 4

▶ **Recording uncollectible accounts using the direct charge-off method.**

Zenith Electric Services Company uses the direct charge-off method to record uncollectible accounts. On September 10, 2010, the company learned that Chris Freyer, a customer who owed $840, had moved and left no forwarding address. Zenith concluded that no part of the debt was collectible. Prepare the general journal entry to write off the account.

Exercise 15.8
Objective 5

▶ **Recording collection of an account previously written off using the direct charge-off method.**

On December 8, 2010, Zenith Electric Services Company received a check for $420 from Chris Freyer, whose $840 account was written off on September 10 (Exercise 15.7). In the accompanying letter, Freyer apologized and said he probably would be unable to pay any of the remaining balance. Give the general journal entry necessary (the entry in the cash receipts journal has been made).

Recording collection of an account written off in a prior period under the direct charge-off method.

◀ **Exercise 15.9**
Objective 5

Use the information given in Exercise 15.8, except assume that Zenith received the check for $420 on January 28, 2011 (instead of on December 8, 2010). Give the general journal entry necessary. The cash receipt has already been entered in the cash receipts journal.

PROBLEMS

Problem Set A

Estimating and recording uncollectible accounts transactions on the basis of sales.

◀ **Problem 15.1A**
Objectives 1, 2, 3, 4

e**X**cel **QB**

Ultra Leather Products sells leather clothing at both wholesale and retail. The company has found that there is a higher rate of uncollectible accounts from retail credit sales than from wholesale credit sales. Ultra computes its estimated loss from uncollectible accounts at the end of each year. The amount is based on the rates of loss that the firm has developed from experience for each division. A separate computation is made for each of the two types of sales. The firm uses the percentage of net credit sales method.

As of December 31, 2010, *Accounts Receivable* has a balance of $392,000, and *Allowance for Doubtful Accounts* has a debit balance of $326.80. The following table provides a breakdown of the credit sales for the year 2010 and the estimated rates of loss.

Category	Amount	Estimated Rate of Loss
Wholesale	$2,040,000	0.5%
Retail	548,600	1.2%

INSTRUCTIONS

1. Compute the estimated amount of uncollectible accounts expense for each of the two categories of net credit sales for the year.

2. Prepare an adjusting entry in general journal form to provide for the estimated uncollectible accounts on December 31, 2010. Use *Uncollectible Accounts Expense.*

3. Show how *Accounts Receivable* and *Allowance for Doubtful Accounts* should appear on the balance sheet of Ultra Leather Products as of December 31, 2010.

4. On January 20, 2011, the account receivable of Delphi Clothiers, amounting to $830, is determined to be uncollectible and is to be written off. Record this transaction in the general journal.

5. On November 26, 2011, the attorneys for Ultra turned over a check for $830 that they obtained from Delphi Clothiers in settlement of its account, which had been written off on January 20. The money has already been recorded in the cash receipts journal. Give the general journal entry to reverse the original write-off.

Analyze: When the financial statements are prepared for the year ended December 31, 2010, what net accounts receivable should be reported?

Estimating and recording uncollectible account transactions on the basis of accounts receivable.

◀ **Problem 15.2A**
Objectives 1, 2, 3

e**X**cel

The schedule of accounts receivable by age shown below was prepared for the Barranca Company at the end of the firm's fiscal year on December 31, 2010.

BARRANCA COMPANY
Schedule of Accounts Receivable by Age
December 31, 2011

Account	Balance	Current	Past Due—Days 1–30	Past Due—Days 31–60	Past Due—Days Over 60
Adson, Paul	750.00	750.00			
Allen, Alfred	800.00		600.00	200.00	
Ash, John	416.00				416.00
Bae, John	160.00	160.00			
Barker, Kelsie	124.00	84.00	40.00		
Bentley, Maggie	450.00	170.00	200.00	80.00	
Blair, Herman	96.00			64.00	32.00
(All other accts.)	43,792.00	36,684.00	4,400.00	1,624.00	1,084.00
Totals	46,588.00	37,848.00	5,240.00	1,968.00	1,532.00

INSTRUCTIONS

1. Compute the estimated uncollectible accounts at the end of the year using the following rates.

Current	1%
1–30 days past due	3%
31–60 days past due	9%
Over 60 days past due	25%

2. As of December 31, 2010, there is a credit balance of $208.20 in *Allowance for Doubtful Accounts.* Compute the amount of the adjustment for uncollectible accounts expense that must be made as part of the adjusting entries.

3. In general journal form, record the adjustment for the estimated losses. Use *Uncollectible Accounts Expense* and *Allowance for Doubtful Accounts.*

4. On May 10, 2011, the $416 account receivable of John Ash was recognized as uncollectible. Record this entry.

5. On June 12, 2011, a check for $200 was received from Zeke Martin to apply to his account, which had been written off on November 8, 2010, as uncollectible. Record the reversal of the previous write-off in the general journal. The cash obtained has already been entered in the cash receipts journal.

6. Suppose that instead of aging the accounts receivable, the company estimated the uncollectible accounts to be 2.5 percent of the total accounts receivable on December 31, 2010. Give the general journal entry to record the adjustment for estimated losses from uncollectible accounts. Assume that *Allowance for Doubtful Accounts* has a credit balance of $208.20 before the adjusting entry.

Analyze: What impact would the change in estimation method described in Instruction 6 have on the net income for fiscal 2010?

Problem 15.3A ▶ **Using different methods to estimate uncollectible accounts.**

Objective 1

The balances of selected accounts of the June Company on December 31, 2010, are given below.

Accounts Receivable	$ 830,000
Allowance for Doubtful Accounts (credit)	2,000
Total Sales	8,950,000
Sales Returns and Allowances (total)	190,000

   (Credit sales were $7,500,000. Returns and allowances on these sales were $150,000.)

INSTRUCTIONS

1. Compute the amount to be charged to *Uncollectible Accounts Expense* under each of the following different assumptions.

    a. Uncollectible accounts are estimated to be 0.25 percent of net credit sales.

    b. Experience has shown that about 3.3 percent of the accounts receivable will prove worthless.

2. Suppose *Allowance for Doubtful Accounts* has a debit balance of $2,000 instead of a credit balance of $2,000, but all other account balances remain the same. Compute the amount to be charged to *Uncollectible Accounts Expense* under each assumption in item 1.

Analyze: If you were the owner of June Company and wished to maximize profits reported for 2010, which method would you prefer to use?

Recording uncollectible account transactions under the direct charge-off method.

◀ **Problem 15.4A**

Objectives 1, 2, 3

eXcel   QB

Rainier Company records uncollectible accounts expense as they occur. Selected transactions for 2010 and 2011 are described below. The accounts involved in these transactions are *Notes Receivable, Accounts Receivable,* and *Uncollectible Accounts Expense.* Record each transaction in general journal form.

DATE	TRANSACTIONS
2010	
Feb. 7	The $600 account receivable of Anne Baker is determined to be uncollectible and is to be written off.
May 16	Because of the death of Martha Falls, her account receivable of $1,000 is considered uncollectible and is to be written off.
July 2	Received $300 from Anne Baker in partial payment of her account, which had been written off on February 7. The cash obtained has already been recorded in the cash receipts journal. There is doubt that the balance of Baker's account will be collected.
July 29	Received $300 from Anne Baker to complete payment of her account, which had been written off on February 7. The cash obtained has already been recorded in the cash receipts journal.
Aug. 18	The $324 account receivable of David Nye is determined to be uncollectible and is to be written off.
2011	
Sept. 28	Received $500 from the estate of Martha Falls as part of the settlement of affairs. This amount is applicable to the account receivable written off on May 16, 2010. The cash obtained has already been recorded in the cash receipts journal.

Analyze: Based on these transactions, what net uncollectible accounts expense was recorded for the year 2010?

Problem Set B

Estimating and recording uncollectible account transactions on the basis of sales.

◀ **Problem 15.1B**

Objectives 1, 2, 3

The Ideal Plumbing Company provides plumbing installation for both business and individual customers. The company records sales for the two types of customers in separate *Sales* accounts. The company's experience has been that each type of sales has a different rate of losses from uncollectible accounts. Thus, the total that the company charges off for these losses at the end of each accounting period is based on two computations (one computation for each sales account). The firm uses the percentage of net credit sales method.

As of December 31, 2010, **Accounts Receivable** has a balance of $281,500, and **Allowance for Doubtful Accounts** has a credit balance of $600. The following table provides a breakdown of the credit sales by division for the year 2010 and the estimated rates of loss.

Division	Amount	Rate of Loss
Business	$1,800,000	0.4%
Individual	1,200,000	0.9%

INSTRUCTIONS

1. Compute the estimated amount of losses in uncollectible accounts expense for each of the two types of sales for the year.

2. Prepare an adjusting entry in general journal form to provide for the estimated losses from uncollectible accounts. Use **Uncollectible Accounts Expense** and **Allowance for Doubtful Accounts.**

3. Show how **Accounts Receivable** and **Allowance for Doubtful Accounts** should appear on the balance sheet of Ideal Plumbing Company as of December 31, 2010.

4. On January 28, 2011, the account receivable of Fain Enterprises, amounting to $788, is determined to be uncollectible and is to be written off. Record the transaction in general journal form.

5. On June 15, 2011, the attorneys for Ideal Plumbing Company turned over a check for $400 that they obtained from Fain Enterprises in settlement of their account, which had been written off on January 28, 2011. The money has already been entered in the cash receipts journal. Record the general journal entry to reinstate the proper amount of Fain's account.

Analyze: Assume that Ideal Plumbing Company uses a predetermined 7.0 percent rate on total accounts receivable to compute the estimated amount of uncollectible accounts receivable. What would be the amount charged to **Uncollectible Accounts Expense** on December 31, 2010?

Problem 15.2B
Objectives 1, 2, 3

▶ **Estimating and recording uncollectible account transactions on the basis of accounts receivable.**

The schedule of accounts receivable by age shown below was prepared for the Custom Windows Shop at the end of the firm's fiscal year on July 31, 2010.

CUSTOM WINDOWS SHOP Schedule of Accounts Receivable by Age July 31, 2010					
			Past Due—Days		
Account	Balance	Current	1–30	31–60	Over 60
Alvarado, Steve	300.00	175.00	125.00		
Brass, Dennis	608.00	120.00	400.00	88.00	
Chang, Charles	196.00	196.00			
Cook, Elaine	38.00	38.00			
Edwards, Brad	632.00			416.00	216.00
Kieffer, Carl	264.00		264.00		
(All other accts.)	14,610.00	8,286.00	3,600.00	1,894.00	830.00
Totals	16,648.00	8,815.00	4,389.00	2,398.00	1,046.00

INSTRUCTIONS

1. Compute the estimated uncollectible accounts at the end of the year using these rates.

Current	1%
1–30 days past due	4%
31–60 days past due	14%
Over 60 days past due	40%

2. As of July 31, 2010, there is a debit balance of $310.00 in *Allowance for Doubtful Accounts.* Compute the amount of the adjustment for uncollectible accounts expense that must be made as part of the adjusting entries.

3. In general journal form, record the adjustment for the estimated losses. Use *Uncollectible Accounts Expense* and *Allowance for Doubtful Accounts.*

4. On August 28, 2010, the account receivable of Jorge Urbina, amounting to $182, was recognized as uncollectible. Record this write-off in the general journal.

5. On September 21, 2010, a check for $250 was received from Barry King to apply on his $250 account, which had been written off as uncollectible on December 19, 2009. Record the reversal of the previous write-off in the general journal. The cash obtained has already been entered in the cash receipts journal.

6. Suppose that instead of aging the accounts receivable, the company estimated the uncollectible accounts to be 8 percent of the total accounts receivable on July 31. Assume also that *Allowance for Doubtful Accounts* has a credit balance of $125.00 before the adjusting entry. Give the general journal entry to record the adjustment for estimated losses from uncollectible accounts.

Analyze: Based on the percentages presented in Item 1, what is the average uncollectible rate for all accounts receivable?

Using different methods to estimate uncollectible accounts.

◀ **Problem 15.3B**
Objective 1, 2, 3

The balances of selected accounts of National Sportswear Company on December 31, 2010, are given below. Credit sales totaled $39,100,000. The returns and allowances on these sales were $230,000.

Accounts Receivable	$ 3,910,000
Allowance for Doubtful Accounts	6,500 (credit)
Total Sales	42,200,000
Total Sales Returns and Allowances	290,000

INSTRUCTIONS

1. Compute the amount to be charged to *Uncollectible Accounts Expense* under each of the following different sets of assumptions. Round computations to nearest dollar.

   a. Bad debt losses are estimated to be 0.34 percent of net credit sales.

   b. Experience has shown that about 2.8 percent of the accounts receivable are uncollectible.

2. Suppose that *Allowance for Doubtful Accounts* has a *debit* balance of $6,500 instead of a credit balance of that amount before adjustments, but all other account balances remain the same. Compute the amount to be charged to *Uncollectible Accounts Expense* under each of the assumptions listed in the first instruction.

Analyze: Which method results in the highest uncollectible expense for the period?

Recording transactions related to uncollectible accounts using the direct charge-off method.

◀ **Problem 15.4B**
Objectives 4, 5

Premium Software uses the direct charge-off method to account for uncollectible accounts expenses as they occur. Selected transactions for 2010 and 2011 follow. The accounts involved are *Accounts*

Receivable, Notes Receivable, and *Uncollectible Accounts Expense.* Record each transaction in general journal form.

DATE	TRANSACTIONS
2010	
March 15	Tony Sanchez, a credit customer, dies owing the firm $4,000. The account is written off.
April 22	Jared Greenberg, a credit customer who owes the firm $2,000, declares bankruptcy. The amount is considered uncollectible and written off.
June 16	The executor of the estate of Tony Sanchez sends the firm $1,000 in partial settlement of the account written off on March 15. The cash obtained has already been recorded in the cash receipts journal.
July 13	The bankruptcy court sends the firm $1,200 in settlement of the account receivable of Jared Greenberg, which was written off on April 22. The cash obtained has already been recorded in the cash receipts journal.
Oct. 8	The account owed by a customer, Laticia Holmes, in the amount of $1,200 is determined worthless and is written off.
2011	
Feb. 12	Jared Greenberg pays the remainder of the account that had previously been written off. (See transactions of April 22 and July 13). The cash obtained has already been recorded in the cash receipts journal.

Analyze: When the worksheet is prepared at the end of 2010, what balance should be listed for *Uncollectible Accounts Expense?* Assume that the transactions given are the only transactions that affected the account.

Critical Thinking Problem 15.1

Managing Uncollectible Accounts

The Dream Kitchen is a small chain of kitchen remodeling stores. The company's year-end trial balance on December 31, 2010, included the information shown below.

Accounts Receivable	$940,440
Allowance for Doubtful Accounts (credit)	21,200

Net credit sales for 2010, were $8,600,000. *Allowance for Doubtful Accounts* has not yet been adjusted.

INSTRUCTIONS

1. At the end of 2010, the following additional accounts receivable are deemed uncollectible:

James Allen	$ 9,800
Suzanne Barnes	1,180
Jeremy O'Toole	3,200
Omar Torrez	4,230
Casey Wells	2,100
Total	$20,510

Prepare the December 31, 2010, journal entry to write off the above accounts. Of the accounts to be charged off, $17,200 are more than 60 days past due, and $3,310 are from 31 to 60 days past due. Post this transaction to the skeleton T-accounts for **Accounts Receivable** and **Allowance for Doubtful Accounts.**

2. Assume that the company uses the percentage of sales method to estimate uncollectible accounts expense. After analyzing the prior year's activities, management determined that losses from uncollectible accounts for 2010 should be 0.32 percent of net credit sales. Prepare the necessary adjusting journal entry. Round calculation to nearest dollar.

3. Assume that the company uses the aging of accounts receivable method. The following information was furnished by the credit manager for use in calculating the estimated loss from uncollectible accounts. The balances of accounts were computed prior to the charge-offs in Instruction 1.

Receivable Category	Estimated Loss Rate	Balances of Accounts (before charge-offs)
Current	1%	$760,000
1–30 days past due	4%	90,000
31–60 days past due	9%	49,400
Over 60 days past due	40%	41,040
Total		$940,440

Compute the estimated uncollectible accounts as of December 31, 2010, rounded to the nearest dollar.

4. Prepare the necessary adjusting journal entry to record the estimated uncollectible accounts expense on December 31, using the aging method.

Analyze: If a company has used three different methods for estimating uncollectible accounts for the past three years, which basic accounting principle may have been violated? Why?

Critical Thinking Problem 15.2

Credit Decisions and Consequences

Bette Springer is president of Springer Company, a manufacturer of decorative art objects. For the past 10 years, the company has sold its product both to wholesale and to retail dealers of art objects in the northeast United States. Over the years the company has come to know its customers well. While all sales are made on credit, few credit losses have occurred. The company's experience has shown that an annual provision for uncollectible accounts of 0.3 of 1 percent of sales is adequate.

Early in 2010, Springer Company decided to expand and develop a new sales base in the southeastern United States. Springer was pleased when credit sales of $200,000 were achieved in the new territory during the year. To achieve this level of sales and get a foothold in the new territory, though, credit was granted to some customers with lower credit ratings than had been granted in the past. Springer estimated that during the initial period of development, losses from uncollectible accounts would be 3 percent of sales in the new territory.

The credit losses connected with sales in the southeast became apparent by the end of 2010. The following losses from new territory customers had been identified before year-end.

1. On September 30, it was determined that nothing could be collected from Craine Toy Outlets which owed Springer $22,200. The account was written off.

2. On December 10, another new customer, Youth Fun Shops, which owed Springer $50,000, entered receivership. On that date Springer was offered, and accepted, a check for $25,000 in final settlement of the debt. The balance was charged off.

3. On December 18, Toys on the Square went out of business and no collection of the $6,800 owed Springer is anticipated. The account was charged off.

The following additional information about the old territory became available on December 31.

- Sales in the old territory totaled $6,280,000 in 2010.
- Accounts receivable of $22,600 attributed to customers in the old sales territory were determined to be uncollectible and were written off.

INSTRUCTIONS

1. Record in general journal entries the transactions described above for Springer Company. All sales are on account. Use date of December 31 to make the entry to summarize sales for the year and to record uncollectible accounts in the old territory.

2. Give the entry on December 31 to record uncollectible accounts expense for 2010, for both territories. Make the calculation using the percentages developed by Springer.

3. Assume that the *Allowance for Uncollectible Accounts* had a credit balance of $6,200 on September 30 before any of the above entries were made. Calculate the balance in the allowance account after all of the above entries have been posted.

Analyze: Was Springer's provision for losses from uncollectible accounts adequate? Explain.

BUSINESS CONNECTIONS

Managerial | FOCUS

Uncollectible Accounts

1. Why would managers use the allowance method for recording uncollectible accounts instead of the direct charge-off method?

2. Should the sales department be given final authority for approving credit applications? Why?

3. Why is an account receivable that was written off as uncollectible reinstated if it is later collected?

4. Why does management separate the authority to charge off uncollectible accounts from the authority to receive customers' cash?

Ethical | DILEMMA

Percent Uncollectible

Historical data should be used to determine the percentage for uncollectible account expense. The higher the percentage, the lower the net income and the lower the income tax. Jitters Corporation, a coffee distributor, has historical data that indicate 5 percent of its sales will become uncollectible. This has been a great year for Jitters. It is feared that the income tax will be very high this year. Jitters has decided to increase the percentage for uncollectibles to 9 percent because of the high sales volume. This will increase the uncollectible account expense and thus reduce the income tax to be paid. Is this ethical? If not, what would be a preferred action?

STREETWISE:
Questions from the REAL WORLD

Accounts Receivable

Refer to The Home Depot, Inc., *2006 Annual Report* in Appendix A.

1. Find the consolidated balance sheets. What amount is reported for "Receivables, net" as of January 30, 2007? What deduction do you think was made to arrive at this figure?

2. What percentage of total current assets is net accounts receivable as of January 30, 2007?

Financial Statement ANALYSIS

Pier 1 imports

Balance Sheet

The following excerpts were taken from the Pier 1 Imports, Inc., *2007 Annual Report.*

Consolidated Balance Sheets		
(in thousands except per share data)	**2007**	**2006**
ASSETS		
Current Assets		
Accounts receivable, net of allowance for doubtful accounts of $566 and $1,119, respectively	$ 21,437	$ 13,916
Total Assets	$916,470	$1,169,861

Analyze:

1. Compute the total accounts receivable for Pier 1 Imports in 2007 prior to allowance for doubtful accounts. What percentage of total accounts receivable was estimated to be uncollectible?

2. By what percentage did net accounts receivable increase from 2006 to 2007?

3. What percentage of total assets are made up of net accounts receivable in 2006? In 2007?

Analyze Online: On the Pier 1 Imports Web site (www.pier1.com), click on the *Pier 1 Credit Card* link.

4. What credit options are available to customers of Pier 1 Imports?

5. What fees or limits are applicable to each credit option?

Cash Flow

The chief financial officers of many companies believe they should wait as long as possible to pay their debts. Since cash flow is considered the lifeblood of a company, payments of trade accounts are delayed in order to maximize their float. As a supplier to these companies, this practice translates to outstanding receivables and additional costs related to collection. What do you think the phrase "maximizing float" means? How do you think this practice of delaying payment affects the business economy as a whole?

Extending THE THOUGHT

Memo

You are the senior accountant for Big Reef Dive Shops. The peak season for the chain of stores is June through August. In November and December, the shops do very little business. You prepare financial statements on a quarterly basis and have chosen to estimate uncollectible accounts using a percentage of net credit sales. The firm's previous accountant used the direct charge-off method. In a memo to the owner, describe your reasons for using an allowance method. Explain the implications this has for the quarterly income statements.

Business COMMUNICATION

Life of an Invoice

In small groups, create a scenario for the life of an invoice. How does a sale become an uncollectible? Start at the sale of a product, when it became uncollectible, and then finally paid. Present each account receivable scenario to the class. Be sure to include all the journal entries.

TEAMWORK

Commercial Credit

The ability to buy products and services for your business on credit is important to its cash flow. Go to the Dun and Bradstreet Web site at www.dnb.com. Select *My Business Credit*, then *Basics of Business Credit*. Find out the importance of commercial credit.

Internet CONNECTION

Answers to **Self Reviews**

Answers to Section 1 Self Review

1. Matching principle

2. $15,800

3. $52,000

4. (a) Debit *Accounts Receivable* and Barrington's account in the *Accounts Receivable* ledger, $300; credit *Allowance for Doubtful Accounts,* $300. (b) Debit *Cash* and credit *Accounts Receivable* (and Barrington's account in the subsidiary ledger), $300.

5. Same as in answer 4.

6. No. Nothing has happened to validate such an entry. However, every effort should be made to collect the account. The customer has the money and should be able to pay.

7. The increasing ratio of allowance to accounts receivable suggests that the rate being used is greater than needed and should be reduced.

Answers to Section 2 Self Review

1. *Uncollectible Accounts Expense* is debited. The write-off decreases net income and assets.

2. The method does not match revenues and expenses. It does not provide a realistic valuation of receivables and it does not comply with GAAP.

3. Under the direct method, reinstatement of a charge-off in the same year as the charge-off is credited to *Uncollectible Accounts Expense.* If recovery is in later years, *Uncollectible Accounts Recovered* is credited.

4. *Uncollectible Accounts Expense* is debited for $500. *Accounts Receivable* and Barrington's subsidiary ledger account are credited for $500.

5. *Allowance for Doubtful Accounts* is debited and *Accounts Receivable* and Barrington's subsidiary ledger account are credited.

6. It appears that the uncollectible accounts are not material. The present method is much simpler and less time-consuming, especially since it is required for federal income tax purposes.

7. Generally, the sales department should not have final authority on granting credit because there is a conflict of interest. In order to increase sales, the sales department may be inclined to grant credit to less qualified applicants.

Answers to Comprehensive Self Review

1. *Allowance for Doubtful Accounts*

2. Allowance method is generally accepted.

3. The direct charge-off method

4. *Uncollectible Accounts Recovered*

5. This is an unsatisfactory arrangement because it places in the hands of one person the opportunity to misappropriate funds and cover it up in the accounting records without detection by others.

6. Remains the same. The debit to *Allowance for Doubtful Accounts* offsets the credit to *Accounts Receivable.*

Notes Payable and Notes Receivable

Chapter 16

Bank of America   www.bankofamerica.com

Bank of America is one of the world's largest financial institutions, serving more than 55 million consumer and small business relationships with retail banking offices, ATMs, and online banking. Bank of America is the largest overall Small Business Administration (SBA) lender in the United States. The corporation provides a diversified range of banking and nonbanking financial services and products domestically and internationally through three business segments: Global Consumer & Small Business Banking, Global Corporate & Investment Banking, and Global Wealth & Investment Management.

The mortgage business is one of Bank of America's clearest growth opportunities. In 2006, only 9.7 percent of deposit customers of Bank of America were mortgage customers. By expanding products and eligibility, eliminating fees, and simplifying the mortgage process, Bank of America is educating its millions of customers that there are clear advantages to getting a mortgage with Bank of America.

thinking critically

How has Bank of America's strong financial position paved the way for growth of the company?

Accounting for Notes Payable

In this chapter, you will learn about negotiable instruments, in particular, promissory notes.

>>**1. OBJECTIVE**

Determine whether an instrument meets all the requirements for negotiability.

LP16

Negotiable Instruments

The law covering negotiable instruments is a part of the Uniform Commercial Code (UCC). The UCC has been adopted by all of the states. A **negotiable instrument** is a financial document, containing a promise or order to pay, that meets all the requirements of the UCC in order to be transferable to another party. The UCC requirements specify that to be negotiable an instrument must

- be in writing and must be signed by the maker or drawer,
- contain an unconditional promise or order to pay a definite amount of money,
- be payable either on demand or at a future time that is fixed or that can be determined,
- be payable to the order of a specific person or to the bearer,
- clearly name or identify the drawee if addressed to a drawee.

Checks are negotiable instruments. Another important negotiable instrument is the promissory note. Promissory notes may be either notes payable or notes receivable.

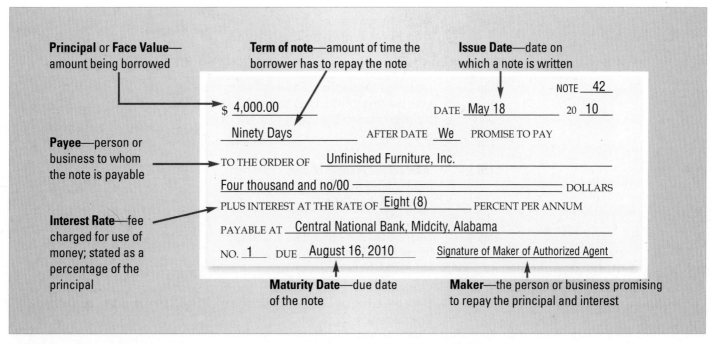

FIGURE 16.1   Promissory Note

Notes Payable

On May 18, 2010, Kathy's Kitchens purchased store equipment for $4,000 from Unfinished Furniture, Inc. The supplier agreed to accept payment in 90 days if Kathy Kaymark, the owner, signed the promissory note shown in Figure 16.1. A **promissory note** is a written promise to pay a certain amount of money at a specific future time. For Unfinished Furniture, Inc., the promissory note provides more legal protection than an account payable.

The promissory note is a negotiable instrument. It is in writing and signed by Kathy Kaymark, owner of Kathy's Kitchens. It is an unconditional promise to pay a definite sum, $4,000. It is payable on a date that can be determined exactly, 90 days after May 18. It is payable to a specific party, Unfinished Furniture, Inc. Although not necessary for negotiability, the note specifies a rate of interest, 8 percent. The maturity value of this note is $4,080.

CALCULATING THE INTEREST ON A NOTE

Interest is the fee charged for the use of money. Interest is calculated using the following formula:

$$\text{Interest} = \text{Principal} \times \text{Rate} \times \text{Time}$$

The time period is indicated in fractions of a year. A 360-day period, called a **banker's year,** is used for simplicity to calculate interest on a note. Interest on the note in Figure 16.1 is $80 ($4,000 × 0.08 × 90/360).

The note in Figure 16.1 shows a $4,000 amount, called the **principal, face value,** or *face amount.* The **maturity value** is the total amount (principal plus interest) that must be paid when a note comes due. For the note in Figure 16.1, the maturity value is $4,080 ($4,000 + $80).

CALCULATING THE MATURITY DATE OF A NOTE

A note's maturity date is the number of days from the date of issue until it is due. The issue date itself is not counted. For example, a 30-day note issued on January 1 matures on January 31, 30 days after January 1. Let's find the maturity date for the note in Figure 16.1.

>>**2. OBJECTIVE**
Calculate the interest on a note.

LP16

>>**3. OBJECTIVE**
Determine the maturity date of a note.

Step 1.	Determine the number of days remaining in the month in which the note is issued. Do not count the issue date.	31 days in May −18 days issue date 13 days
Step 2.	Determine the number of days remaining after the first month. To do this, subtract the days calculated in Step 1 from the term of the note.	90 days term of note −13 days May days 77 days remaining
Step 3.	Subtract the number of days in the next month (June) from the number of days remaining after Step 2.	77 days −30 days in June 47 days remaining
Step 4.	Subtract the number of days in the next month (July) from the days remaining after Step 3.	47 days −31 days in July 16 days remaining
Step 5.	Since there are only 16 days remaining, the due date is 16 days into the next month (August).	The due date is August 16.
Step 6.	Prove the calculation. Add the days together to see if they equal the period of the note.	Proof: May 13 days June 30 days July 31 days August 16 days Total 90 days

Sometimes the term of a note is described in months instead of days. In this case, the maturity date is determined by counting ahead to the same date of the following month or months. For example, a three-month note issued on May 18 is due on August 18, regardless of the number of days in the period. If a note is issued at the end of a month, and there is no corresponding date in the month due, then the note is due on the first day of the following month. For example, a six-month note issued on August 30 should mature on February 30. Since there is no February 30, the note matures on March 1.

LP16

>>**4. OBJECTIVE**

Record routine notes payable transactions.

RECORDING THE ISSUANCE OF A NOTE PAYABLE

A **note payable** is a liability that represents a written promise by the maker of the note (the debtor) to pay another party (the creditor) a specified amount at a specified future date. The following shows how Kathy's Kitchens records the May 18 transaction to issue a 90-day, $4,000 note payable at 8 percent annual interest to purchase store equipment.

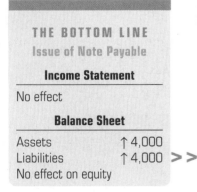

THE BOTTOM LINE

Issue of Note Payable

Income Statement

No effect

Balance Sheet

Assets ↑ 4,000
Liabilities ↑ 4,000 >>
No effect on equity

GENERAL JOURNAL   PAGE ___3___

	DATE		DESCRIPTION	POST. REF.	DEBIT	CREDIT	
1	2010						1
6	May	18	Store Equipment		4 0 0 0 00		6
7			Notes Payable—Trade			4 0 0 0 00	7
8			Issued note payable to Unfinished				8
9			Furniture, Inc., for purchase of store				9
10			equipment				10

RECORDING PAYMENT OF A NOTE AND INTEREST

On the maturity date, August 16, Kathy's Kitchens pays the $4,000 principal plus the $80 in interest. This transaction is recorded as follows.

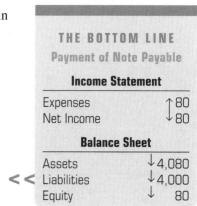

GENERAL JOURNAL   PAGE ___6___

	DATE		DESCRIPTION	POST. REF.	DEBIT	CREDIT	
1	2010						1
11	Aug	16	Notes Payable—Trade		4 0 0 0 00		11
12			Interest Expense		8 0 00		12
13			Cash			4 0 8 0 00	13
14			Payment of May 18 note to				14
15			Unfinished Furniture, Inc.,				15

THE BOTTOM LINE
Payment of Note Payable

Income Statement

Expenses	↑↓ 80
Net Income	↓ 80

Balance Sheet

Assets	↓ 4,080
Liabilities	↓ 4,000
Equity	↓ 80

RENEWING OR MAKING A PARTIAL PAYMENT ON A NOTE

If the issuer of a note asks and receives an extension to the maturity date, no additional accounting entries are required. On the extended maturity date, an entry is made to record payment of the note and interest for the entire period of the debt.

Sometimes at the maturity date only part of the note is paid. The partial payment is shown on the existing note, or the existing note is canceled and a new note is issued for the balance.

RECORDING THE ISSUANCE OF A DISCOUNTED NOTE PAYABLE

Businesses often borrow money from banks and sign notes payable as evidence of the debts. Banks always charge interest on loans. For some promissory notes, such as the one to Unfinished Furniture, Inc. in Figure 16.1, interest is paid on the maturity date. The interest on a bank loan is usually paid at maturity. Often, however, the bank deducts the interest in advance, and the borrower receives only the difference between the face amount of the note and the interest on it to maturity. This practice of deducting the interest in advance from the principal on a note payable is called **discounting.**

On June 1, Kathy's Kitchens signed a $10,000, 6 percent, 60-day note payable with the bank. The note was issued at a discount. The interest is $100.

$$\text{Interest} = \text{Principal} \times \text{Rate} \times \text{Time}$$
$$\$100 = \$10,000 \times 0.06 \times (60/360)$$

The bank deducted the $100 interest from the face amount of the note, and Kathy's Kitchens received $9,900 ($10,000 − $100).

Kathy's Kitchens uses two note payable accounts—one for notes to vendors and the other for notes to the bank. The transaction is recorded as follows.

>>5. OBJECTIVE

Record discounted notes payable transactions.

LP16

GENERAL JOURNAL   PAGE ___5___

	DATE		DESCRIPTION	POST. REF.	DEBIT	CREDIT	
1	2010						1
2	June	1	Cash		9 9 0 0 00		2
3			Interest Expense		1 0 0 00		3
4			Notes Payable—Bank			1 0 0 0 0 00	4
5			To record note payable issued at				5
6			a discount				6
7							7

THE BOTTOM LINE
Issue of Discounted Note Payable

Income Statement

Expenses	↑ 100
Net Income	↓ 100

Balance Sheet

Assets	↑ 9,900
Liabilities	↑ 10,000
Equity	↓ 100

RECORDING THE PAYMENT OF A DISCOUNTED NOTE PAYABLE

At maturity, July 31, Kathy's Kitchens prepares a check for $10,000 to pay the note. There is no entry for interest expense because interest was paid and recorded when the note was issued. The entry is recorded as follows.

GENERAL JOURNAL PAGE ___6___

	DATE	DESCRIPTION	POST. REF.	DEBIT	CREDIT	
1	2010					1
33	July 31	Notes Payable—Bank		10 000 00		33
34		Cash			10 000 00	34
35		Record payment of note				35
36						36

USING A NOTES PAYABLE REGISTER

If a business issues many notes payable, it is convenient to maintain a notes payable register. The notes payable register shows the important information about each note payable on a single line.

At the end of each accounting period, a schedule of notes payable is prepared from the information in the notes payable register. The schedule of notes payable must agree with the *Notes Payable* account in the general ledger.

For each note payable, the notes payable register shows the following information:

- the issue date,
- the payee,
- where the note is payable,
- the term of the note,
- the maturity date,
- the face amount,
- the interest rate, if any,
- the interest amount, if any.

REPORTING NOTES PAYABLE AND INTEREST EXPENSE

Notes payable represent financial obligations of the business. They appear on the balance sheet as liabilities.

- Notes due within one year are classified as current liabilities.
- Notes due in more than one year are classified as long-term liabilities.

The notes presented in this chapter are current liabilities. Long-term liabilities are discussed in Chapter 22.

Interest expense appears on the income statement as a nonoperating expense. It is listed in the Other Income and Expenses section and is deducted from Income from Operations as follows.

Sales	$550,000
Cost of Goods Sold	(320,000)
Gross Profit on Sales	230,000
Operating Expenses	(164,000)
Income from Operations	66,000
Other Income and Expenses	
Interest Expense	(1,800)
Net Income	$ 64,200

Section 1 Self Review

QUESTIONS

1. What is the maturity date of a 120-day note issued on April 10?

2. What is the interest due on a note for $24,000 at 8 percent for 75 days?

3. How much cash will the borrower receive for a $24,000, 75 day, noninterest-bearing note discounted at 8 percent?

EXERCISES

4. Which of the following is not required for an instrument to be negotiable?

   a. It must be payable on demand or at a fixed or determinable date.

   b. It must contain an unconditional promise or order to pay a definite amount.

   c. It must be in writing.

   d. All of the above are required.

5. The total to be received when a note receivable is due is known as the

   a. principal

   b. maturity value

   c. interest

   d. face value

ANALYSIS

6. Refer to Questions 2 and 3, above. Is the effective interest rate in each of these two situations identical? Explain.

(Answers to Section 1 Self Review are on page 567.)

Video16.1

SECTION OBJECTIVES

>> **6. Record routine notes receivable transactions.**

WHY IT'S IMPORTANT

Many businesses accept notes receivable from customers to purchase goods or to replace existing accounts receivable.

>> **7. Compute the proceeds from a discounted note receivable, and record transactions related to discounting of notes receivable.**

WHY IT'S IMPORTANT

Businesses can raise cash by discounting notes receivable at the bank.

>> **8. Understand how to use bank drafts and trade acceptances and how to record transactions related to those instruments.**

WHY IT'S IMPORTANT

Various financial instruments are used because they provide flexibility in cash management.

TERMS TO LEARN

bank draft
bill of lading
cashier's check
commercial draft
contingent liability
draft
note receivable
sight draft
time draft
trade acceptance

Accounting for Notes Receivable

Section 1 discussed promissory notes from the debtor's perspective. This section considers the creditor's perspective.

Notes Receivable

Some businesses allow customers to issue a promissory note to finance the purchase of goods. Sometimes a business requires a customer with an overdue account to sign a promissory note for the account balance. In these cases, the promissory note is classified as a **note receivable,** which is an asset that represents a creditor's written promise to pay a specified amount at a specified future date. There are many similarities between notes payable and notes receivable. Of course, the journal entries are different.

NONINTEREST-BEARING NOTES RECEIVABLE

Customer Isabel Huang owes $1,500 to Kathy's Kitchens. The account is overdue, and Huang needs more time to pay. On September 18, Huang signs a 30-day, noninterest-bearing note for $1,500. In the event legal action becomes necessary, the note provides additional protection to Kathy's Kitchens.

1	2010				1
2	Sept. 18	Notes Receivable	1 500 00		2
3		Accounts Receivable/Isabel Huang		1 500 00	3
4		To record 30-day note receivable to			4
5		replace an overdue account receivable			5

The maturity date of the note is October 18.

Days note is issued in September (30 − 18)	12 days
Days in October`	18 days
Duration of note (proof)	30 days

At maturity when Huang pays the note, the entry in the cash receipts journal is a debit to **Cash** and a credit to **Notes Receivable.** Huang's note is marked "Paid" and returned to her.

> Cat Financial, a division of Caterpillar Inc., extends long-term credit to its customers to purchase Caterpillar equipment. At December 31, 2006, Cat Financial's total notes receivable (installment contracts) of $7.53 billion, before deducting unearned income, were listed on the balance sheet of Caterpillar Inc. Amounts of $3.0 billion, $2.2 billion, $1.4 billion, $679 million, $220 million, and $31 million are due in 2007, 2008, 2009, 2010, 2011, and thereafter, respectively.

INTEREST-BEARING NOTES RECEIVABLE

>>6. OBJECTIVE

Record routine notes receivable transactions.

LP16

Customers who do not pay their bills when due are expected to pay interest. Normally, promissory notes issued to replace overdue accounts are interest bearing. Interest on notes is generally paid at the maturity date. On June 12, Kathy's Kitchens accepted a 60-day, 10 percent note for $1,200 from John Woods to replace his past-due account. The transaction is recorded as follows.

1	2010					1
2	June	12	Notes Receivable	1 2 0 0 00		2
3			Accounts Receivable/John Woods		1 2 0 0 00	3
4			To record 60-day note receivable to			4
5			replace an overdue account receivable			5

The maturity date of the note is August 11.

Days note is issued in June (30 − 12)	18 days
Days in July	31 days
Total days to the end of July	49 days
Days in August to maturity (60 − 49 = 11)	11 days
Duration of note (proof)	60 days

The interest on $1,200 for 60 days at 10 percent is $20 ($1,200 × 0.10 × 60/360). Woods's payment of the note on the maturity date will include the $1,200 face amount of the note plus $20 interest. The payment would be recorded as follows.

1	2010					1
2	Aug.	11	Cash	1 2 2 0 00		2
3			Notes Receivable		1 2 0 0 00	3
4			Interest Income		2 0 00	4
5			Collection of John Woods's note			5
6			receivable			6

NOTES RECEIVABLE—SPECIAL SITUATIONS

Accountants must know how to record notes receivable for special situations.

Accounting for Partial Collection of a Note On August 11, Kathy's Kitchens learned that John Woods could pay only half the $1,200 note receivable. Kathy's Kitchens agreed to extend the due date for another 30 days for half the principal, $600. Kathy's Kitchens accepted payment of $20 interest and $600 principal. Partial payments are applied first to interest and then to principal. The journal entry to record the transaction is as follows.

1	2010					1
2	Aug.	11	Cash	6 2 0 00		2
3			Notes Receivable		6 0 0 00	3
4			Interest Income		2 0 00	4
5			Collection of interest and one-half			5
6			of John Woods's note; balance renewed			6
7			for 30 days			7

The original note can be endorsed to reflect the partial payment and the new maturity date, or Kathy's Kitchens can cancel the original note and ask John Woods to sign a new interest-bearing note for $600.

Note Receivable Not Collected at Maturity If a note is not paid at maturity and there are no arrangements for renewal, the note is said to be "dishonored." Dishonored notes do not belong in the *Notes Receivable* account. If John Woods dishonored the original $1,200 note, the entry to transfer the balance out of *Notes Receivable* and back to *Accounts Receivable* would be as follows.

1	2010					1
2	Aug.	11	Accounts Receivable/John Woods	1 2 2 0 00		2
3			Notes Receivable		1 2 0 0 00	3
4			Interest Income		2 0 00	4
5			To charge back Woods's dishonored			5
6			note plus interest to maturity			6

Note that Woods now owes the original balance of $1,200 plus $20 interest on the note. After a note is dishonored, interest continues to accrue on the note. The interest rate is usually specified by law. In most cases, it is higher than the rate shown on the note, although the parties may agree on a rate different from the statutory rate. Promissory notes usually require the maker to pay attorney's fees and all other costs incurred by the holder for efforts to collect the note.

Notes Received at the Time of a Sale Sometimes Kathy's Kitchens asks a customer to sign a promissory note at the time of sale. The transaction is recorded in the general journal as follows.

1	2010					1
2	Aug.	15	Notes Receivable	3 0 0 00		2
3			Sales		3 0 0 00	3
4			Received 60-day, 9% note from			4
5			Sylvia Montes on sale of goods			5

If a business routinely receives notes from customers at the time of sale, the transactions are recorded in a special Notes Receivable column of the sales journal.

DISCOUNTING A NOTE RECEIVABLE

A note receivable is an asset. At maturity date, the holder will receive cash for the note receivable. If the holder wants cash before the maturity date, the note can be discounted (sold) at the bank. The bank pays the holder the maturity value (principal plus any interest) minus the discount charge.

Noninterest-Bearing Note Receivable Discounted On September 18, Kathy's Kitchens needed cash to pay some bills. Kathy Kaymark decided to discount a 90-day, noninterest-bearing note receivable for $3,000 that the business received from John Nguyen on July 20. The maturity date of the note is October 18.

Days note is issued in July (31 − 20)	11 days
Days in August	31 days
Days in September	30 days
Total days to the end of September	72 days
Days in October to maturity (90 − 72)	18 days
Duration of note (proof)	90 days

On September 18, Kathy's Kitchens discounts the note at Central National Bank. The bank's discount rate is 10 percent.

Calculating the Discount and the Proceeds The steps to determine the discount and the proceeds on notes receivable follow.

>>7. OBJECTIVE
Compute the proceeds from a discounted note receivable, and record transactions related to discounting of notes receivable.

LP16

Step 1. *Determine the maturity value of the note.* Since the note from Nguyen is noninterest-bearing, its maturity value and face amount are the same, $3,000.

Step 2. *Calculate the number of days in the discount period.* The discount period is the number of days from the discount date to the maturity date. The discount period is 30 days.

Days note is discounted in September (30 − 18)	12 days
Days in October until maturity	18 days
Total days in discount period	30 days

Step 3. *Compute the discount charged by the bank.* The discount formula is similar to the interest formula. The time is the number of days in the discount period. The discount is $20.

Discount = Maturity Value × Discount Rate × Discount Period
$25 = $3,000 × 0.10 × (30/360)

Step 4. *Calculate the proceeds,* the amount received from the bank. This is the maturity value of the note less the discount, $2,975 ($3,000 − $25).

Kathy's Kitchens received cash for the note 30 days before the note matured in exchange for a discount fee of $25.

The discount is debited to ***Interest Expense.*** The credit is to ***Notes Receivable—Discounted,*** a contra asset account. The following is the journal entry to record the discounting of the note receivable.

1	2010				1
2	Sept. 18	Cash	2 9 7 5 00		2
3		Interest Expense	2 5 00		3
4		Notes Receivable—Discounted		3 0 0 0 00	4
5		To record discounting of			5
6		John Nguyen note			6

Contingent Liability for a Discounted Note When a note receivable is discounted, the party discounting the note endorses it. If the maker (Nguyen) does not pay the note at maturity, the bank can obtain payment from the endorser (Kathy's Kitchens). Hence Kathy's Kitchens has a contingent liability of $3,000. A **contingent liability** can become a liability if certain things happen. Contingent liabilities are shown on the financial statements so that the users are aware that the business might have a liability in the future. The contingent liability for discounted notes receivable appears on the balance sheet as follows.

Notes Receivable	$7,400
Notes Receivable—Discounted	(3,000)
Net Notes Receivable	$4,400

Another common way to show contingent liabilities is to present the net notes receivable on the balance sheet and to include a footnote with the information about the discounted notes receivable.

Discounted Noninterest-Bearing Note Receivable at Maturity If on October 18, the maturity date, Nguyen pays the note, Kathy's Kitchens is no longer contingently liable for the note. The following journal entry removes the asset and the contingent liability.

1	2010					1
2	Oct.	18	Notes Receivable—Discounted	3 000 00		2
3			Notes Receivable		3 000 00	3
4			Record payment of discounted note			4
5			of John Nguyen			5

Suppose on October 18 Nguyen dishonored the note by not paying it. The bank filed a formal protest. Kathy's Kitchens became liable to the bank for the maturity value of the note plus a protest fee. Central National Bank deducted the note ($3,000) and the protest fee ($30) from the checking account for Kathy's Kitchens. The bank sent a debit memorandum with the dishonored note and the protest form to Kathy's Kitchens. The journal entries to record this transaction are as follows:

- Record the amount owed by Nguyen including the protest fee. Debit *Accounts Receivable/ John Nguyen* for $3,030 and credit *Cash* for $3,030.
- Debit *Notes Receivable—Discounted* for $3,000 and credit *Notes Receivable* for $3,000.

Kathy's Kitchens contacted Nguyen and asked for payment of the note. Payment was not received, so Kathy's Kitchens turned the note over to an attorney for collection.

Interest-Bearing Note Receivable Discounted Kathy Kaymark discounted another note receivable in order to meet cash needs. The $1,800, 90-day, 6 percent note was received from Kim Myers on September 29. The maturity date of the note is December 28.

Calculating the Discount and the Proceeds On November 28, Kathy's Kitchens discounted Myers's note at the bank at 10 percent. The steps to compute the discount and the proceeds on the note receivable follow.

Step 1. *Determine the maturity value of the note.* The interest is $27 ($1,800 × 0.06 × 90/360). The maturity value is the principal and interest, $1,827 ($1,800 + $27).

Step 2. *Calculate the number of days in the discount period.* The discount period is 30 days.

Days note is discounted in November (30 − 28)	2 days
Days in December until maturity	28 days
Total days in discount period	30 days

Step 3. *Compute the discount charged by the bank.* The bank charges $15.23, 10 percent of the maturity value for the discount period ($1,827 × 0.10 × 30/360).

Step 4. *Calculate the proceeds.* The proceeds are $1,811.77, the maturity value minus the discount ($1,827.00 − $15.23).

Interest income of $11.77 will be recorded. This represents the total interest used to compute the maturity value, minus the discount charged by the bank ($27.00 − $15.23 = $11.77). It also reflects the amount by which the proceeds from discounting the note exceeds the principal of the note ($1,811.77 − $1,800.00 = $11.77).

GENERAL JOURNAL   PAGE ___10___

	DATE		DESCRIPTION	POST. REF.	DEBIT	CREDIT	
1	2010						1
32	Nov.	28	Cash		1 811 77		32
33			Notes Receivable—Discounted			1 800 00	33
34			Interest Income			11 77	34
35			To record discounting of Kim				35
36			Myers's note				36

The amount received from discounting an interest-bearing note may be less than the face value of the note. In that event, ***Interest Expense*** would be debited for the difference. For example, if the discount rate charged by the bank when the Myers note, above, was discounted on November 28 is 20 percent, the discount would be \$30.45 (\$1,827 × .20 × 30/360), and the proceeds would have been \$1,796.55 (\$1,827.00 − \$30.45). Here is the necessary entry.

1	2010						1
2	Nov.	28	Cash		1 796 55		2
3			Interest Expense		3 45		3
4			Notes Receivable—Discounted			1 800 00	4
5			To record discounting of Myers's note				5
6							6

Maturity of Discounted Interest-Bearing Note Receivable If the maker of a note receivable that has been discounted pays the holder of the note at maturity, the contingent liability of the endorser is ended. The endorser completely removes the note from the accounts. For example, if on the maturity date, December 28, Myers pays the Central National Bank, the entry below would be made.

1	2010						1
2	Dec.	28	Notes Receivable—Discounted		1 800 00		2
3			Notes Receivable			1 800 00	3
4			To record payment by Myers of discounted				4
5			note receivable				5

If Myers dishonors the discounted note on December 28, the bank will deduct from Kathy's account the maturity value of the note, plus a small service fee—\$25 in this example. Kathy's Kitchens would again remove the note from the accounts by debiting ***Notes Receivable— Discounted*** and crediting ***Notes Receivable.*** In addition, the entire amount that the bank deducted from Kathy's account would be charged back to ***Accounts Receivable*** and to Myers's account (\$1,827 maturity value + \$25 fee).

1	2010						1
2	Dec.	28	Notes Receivable—Discounted		1 800 00		2
3			Accounts Receivable/Kim Myers		1 852 00		3
4			Notes Receivable			1 800 00	4
5			Cash			1 852 00	5
6			To record dishonor of note by Myers				6

THE NOTES RECEIVABLE REGISTER

If a firm has many notes receivable, it is convenient to maintain a notes receivable register. For each note, the notes receivable register shows the date of the note, the maker, where the note is payable, the duration, the maturity date, the face amount, the rate of interest, and the amount of interest. For each discounted note, the register also shows the discount date and the bank holding the note.

REPORTING NOTES RECEIVABLE AND INTEREST INCOME

Notes receivable appear on the balance sheet as assets.

- Notes that mature within one year are classified as current assets.
- Notes that mature in more than one year are classified as long-term assets.

The contra asset account *Notes Receivable—Discounted* appears as a deduction from *Notes Receivable.*

> Presentation of information in the balance sheet about notes payable and other liabilities varies widely from company to company. For example, a balance sheet prepared for SEC filing by Caterpillar, Inc., for June 30, 2006, showed total current liabilities of $19.3 billion. This number included $5.2 billion of "Short-Term Borrowings." Presumably this number includes notes payable and other forms of short-term obligations.

Interest income is classified as nonoperating income. It is listed in the Other Income and Expenses section of the income statement and is added to income from operations. The discount charged for discounting notes is shown as interest expense in the Other Income and Expenses section and is deducted from Income from Operations. The income statement for a business that received and paid interest follows.

Sales		$550,000
Cost of Goods Sold		(320,000)
Gross Profit on Sales		230,000
Operating Expenses		(164,000)
Income from Operations		66,000
Other Income and Expenses		
Interest Income	$1,800	
Interest Expense	(2,350)	(550)
Net Income		65,450

Drafts and Acceptances

Negotiable instruments include drafts and acceptances.

DRAFTS

A **draft** is a written order that requires one party (a person or business) to pay a stated sum of money to another party. A check is one type of draft. Other types are bank drafts and commercial drafts.

Bank Drafts A **bank draft** is a check written by a bank that orders another bank to pay the stated amount to a specific party. A bank draft is more readily accepted than a personal or business check. Bank drafts are used to pay debts to suppliers with whom credit has not been established.

A **cashier's check** is a draft on the issuing bank's own funds. Cashier's checks are sometimes used to pay bills. For the creditor, a cashier's check offers more protection than a business or personal check.

The business pays for the bank draft or cashier's check by issuing a business check to cover the amount of the draft or cashier's check plus the service charge.

NEGOTIABLE INSTRUMENTS

■ Because notes payable and notes receivable are negotiable instruments, they fall under the rules and regulations of the Uniform Commercial Code. Management needs to understand the rights, responsibilities, and obligations of the business for negotiable instruments.

■ Management should carefully control and limit borrowing to minimize the interest charged for the use of funds.

■ In a well-run business, managers ensure the prompt payment of debts to minimize interest expense and to maintain the company's credit rating.

■ Management authorizes specific individuals to approve the use of debt.

■ When cash is needed for current operations, managers need to know that notes receivable can be discounted.

■ Good managers ensure that past due accounts receivable are converted into notes receivable because notes provide more legal protection and are more likely to be collected.

■ Because notes and drafts are negotiable, management ensures that internal control procedures are in place.

THINKING CRITICALLY

Why might managers use outside sources of funds for their business operations? How do they acquire these funds?

On May 18, Kathy's Kitchens purchased a $1,412 bank draft and sent it to Home Supplies, Inc., to pay an overdue account payable to that company. The service charge for the bank draft was $12. The journal entry to record the transaction is as follows.

1	2010					1
2	May	18	Accounts Payable/Home Supplies, Inc.	1 4 0 0 00		2
3			Miscellaneous Bank Expense	1 2 00		3
4			Cash		1 4 1 2 00	4
5			To record payment of past-due			5
6			account and bank charge with draft			6

Commercial Drafts A **commercial draft** is a note issued by one party that orders another party to pay a specified amount on a specified date. Commercial drafts are used for special shipment and collection situations. Commercial drafts may be either sight drafts or time drafts.

A **sight draft** is a commercial draft that is payable on presentation. When a sight draft is issued, no journal entry is made. When a sight draft is honored, the transaction is recorded as a cash receipt.

Sight drafts are used to collect past-due accounts receivable. Customers are more likely to honor a sight draft than a collection letter. The sight draft is sent to the customer's bank. If the customer does not honor the draft, the customer's credit reputation at the bank can be damaged.

Sight drafts are also used to obtain cash on delivery when shipments are made to customers with poor credit or to new customers with no credit established. The sight draft is attached to a **bill of lading,** which is a business document that lists the goods accepted for transportation by a carrier. The bill of lading is sent to a bank near the customer. The customer pays the draft in order to get the bill of lading. The customer needs the bill of lading in order to obtain the goods. The collecting bank sends the money, less a collection fee, to the business issuing the draft. When the funds arrive, the business records the transaction as a cash sale and debits an expense account for the collection fee.

A **time draft** is a commercial draft that is payable during a period of time. The time period may be a specific date, or a specific number of days either after the date of the draft or after acceptance of the draft.

No journal entry is made when a time draft is issued. If the business honors (pays) the draft, the word "Accepted" is written on the draft and it is signed and dated. The business records the acceptance of a draft as a note payable. It is returned to the drawer, who records it as a note receivable.

TRADE ACCEPTANCES

A **trade acceptance** is a form of commercial time draft used in transactions involving the sale of goods. The original transaction is recorded as a sale on credit. When the draft is accepted, it is accounted for as a promissory note. Merchants have fewer credit losses on trade acceptances than on accounts receivable. Trade acceptances can be discounted.

 internal CONTROL

Internal Control of Notes Payable, Notes Receivable, and Drafts

The following are internal controls for notes payable, notes receivable, and drafts:

- Limit the number of people who can sign notes for the firm.
- Record all notes payable immediately.
- Identify a specific person or department to be responsible for prompt payment of interest and principal for notes payable.
- When paid, mark the note payable "Canceled" or "Paid" and file the note.
- Handle drafts as carefully as checks.
- Authorize certain persons only to accept notes.
- Record all notes receivable in the accounting records.
- Store notes receivable securely in a safe or fireproof vault to which access is limited.
- Verify and compare the actual notes receivable to the notes receivable register.
- Near the maturity date, inform the issuer of the approaching due date and the amount owed.
- If payment is not received on the due date, contact the issuer immediately.
- Review all past-due notes promptly and take necessary steps, including legal action, to ensure payment.

Section **2** Self Review

QUESTIONS

1. Why do businesses sometimes accept notes receivable from customers?

2. What does it mean to dishonor a note?

3. A note receivable with a maturity value of $3,100 is discounted at 10 percent with 90 days remaining until the maturity date. What are the proceeds from discounting the note?

EXERCISES

4. A company that discounts an interest-bearing note receivable:

   a. always recognizes interest income when the note is discounted.

   b. never recognizes interest income when the note is discounted.

   c. recognizes interest income only if the proceeds from discounting exceed the maturity value of the note discounted.

   d. recognizes interest income if the proceeds exceed the face value of the note discounted.

5. The **Notes Receivable—Discounted** account

   a. contains a debit balance.

   b. reflects the amounts due on dishonored notes receivable.

   c. is shown as a liability on the balance sheet.

   d. is deducted from **Notes Receivable** on the balance sheet.

ANALYSIS

6. When an interest-bearing note receivable is accepted, instead of cash at the time of sale, does the interest on the note increase the amount reported as Sales? Explain.

(Answers to Section 2 Self Review are on page 567.)

REVIEW   Chapter Summary

In this chapter, you have learned how businesses use promissory notes, drafts, or trade acceptances to pay large amounts over a period of time. You have learned about negotiable instruments and how to record common notes payable and notes receivable.

Learning Objectives

1 Determine whether an instrument meets all the requirements of negotiability.

A negotiable instrument is a financial document that

- contains an order or promise to pay,
- meets all the requirements of the Uniform Commercial Code (UCC) to be transferable to another party.

The UCC requirements are as follows.

- It must be in writing.
- It must be signed by the maker.
- It must define the amount due and payment terms.
- It must list the payee.
- If addressed to a drawee, it must clearly name the person.

2 Calculate the interest on a note.

The borrower who signs a note payable usually pays interest on the amount borrowed. To determine the interest amount for any time period, use the formula Interest = Principal × Interest Rate × Time (years).

3 Determine the maturity date of a note.

The note's maturity date is determined at the time the note is issued, excluding the issue date itself.

4 Record routine notes payable transactions.

When purchasing an asset with a note, debit the asset account and credit *Notes Payable.* When paying the note payable, debit *Notes Payable* for the face of the note, debit *Interest Expense* for the interest, and credit *Cash* for the total paid (principal plus interest). *Interest Expense* appears on the income statement below Net Income from Operations in Other Income/Other Expense.

5 Record discounted notes payable transactions.

When money is borrowed on a note payable, the bank can deduct its interest charge immediately, called *discounting.* The borrower discounting a note payable receives the difference between the discount and the principal.

6 Record routine notes receivable transactions.

Notes receivable can be noninterest- or interest-bearing. Most firms charge interest.

- If the note receivable is issued at the time of a sale, record the transaction by debiting *Notes Receivable* and crediting *Sales.*
- If the note receivable results from a customer's failure to pay an accounts receivable, debit *Notes Receivable,* and credit *Accounts Receivable.*
- The recipient credits *Interest Income* for interest received when the note is paid.

7 Compute the proceeds from a discounted note receivable, and record transactions related to discounting of notes receivable.

A firm with an immediate need for cash can discount a note receivable. Debit *Cash* for the proceeds, credit *Notes Receivable—Discounted* for the face value, and either debit *Interest Expense* (if the proceeds are less than the principal) or credit *Interest Income* (if the proceeds exceed the principal). *Notes Receivable—Discounted* represent a contingent liability. If the note's maker fails to pay at maturity, the business must pay the bank.

8 Understand how to use bank drafts and trade acceptances and how to record transactions related to those instruments.

Bank drafts, commercial drafts, and trade acceptances are negotiable instruments used in business.

- Bank drafts are checks written by a bank ordering another bank in which it has funds to pay the indicated amount to a specific person or business.
- Businesses issue commercial drafts to order a person or firm to pay a sum of money at a specific time.
- Trade acceptances arise from the sale of goods. The original transaction is recorded in the same way as a sale on credit. When the draft has been accepted, it is accounted for as a promissory note.

9 Define the accounting terms new to this chapter.

Glossary

Bank draft (p. 556) A check written by a bank that orders another bank to pay the stated amount to a specific party

Banker's year (p. 545) A 360-day period used to calculate interest on a note

Bill of lading (p. 557) A business document that lists goods accepted for transportation

Cashier's check (p. 556) A draft on the issuing bank's own funds

Commercial draft (p. 557) A note issued by one party that orders another party to pay a specified sum on a specified date

Contingent liability (p. 553) An item that can become a liability if certain things happen

Discounting (p.547) Deducting the interest from the principal on a note payable or receivable in advance

Draft (p. 556) A written order that requires one party (a person or business) to pay a stated sum of money to another party

Face value (p. 545) An amount of money indicated to be paid, exclusive of interest or discounts

Interest (p. 545) The fee charged for the use of money

Maturity value (p. 545) The total amount (principal plus interest) payable when a note comes due

Negotiable instrument (p. 544) A financial document containing a promise or order to pay that meets all requirements of the Uniform Commercial Code in order to be transferable to another party

Note payable (p. 546) A liability representing a written promise by the maker of the note (the debtor) to pay another party (the creditor) a specified amount at a specified future date

Note receivable (p. 550) An asset representing a written promise by another party (the debtor) to pay the note holder (the creditor) a specified amount at a specified future date

Principal (p. 545) The amount shown on the face of a note

Promissory note (p. 545) A written promise to pay a certain amount of money at a specific future time

Sight draft (p. 557) A commercial draft that is payable on presentation

Time draft (p. 557) A commercial draft that is payable during a specified period of time

Trade acceptance (p. 558) A form of commercial time draft used in transactions involving the sale of goods

Comprehensive **Self Review**

1. How is maturity value of a note computed?

2. When is *Interest Expense* debited if an interest-bearing note payable is issued? If a note payable is discounted?

3. List the elements of a negotiable instrument.

4. What type of account is *Notes Receivable—Discounted?* How should the *Notes Receivable—Discounted* account be shown on the balance sheet?

5. Which account(s) will be debited and which will be credited when an interest-bearing note receivable that has been discounted is dishonored at the time of maturity?

(Answers to Comprehensive Self Review are on page 568.)

 Multiple choice questions are provided on the text Web site at www.mhhe.com/price12e Quiz16

Discussion Questions

1. What are the requirements that must be met in order for a document to be negotiable?
2. What is the face amount of a note? The maturity value?
3. If a note dated February 28 has a three-month term, on what date must the note be paid?
4. What is the maturity value of an $8,000 note, bearing interest at 9 percent, and due 105 days after date of issue of the note?
5. What is meant by "discounting a note payable"?
6. How are notes payable maturing less than one year from the balance sheet date shown on the balance sheet?
7. Are notes payable likely to be given in borrowing money? The purchase of merchandise? The purchase of equipment? Why?
8. Explain why records must be kept of the due dates of all notes payable.
9. How does a note receivable differ from an account receivable?
10. How, if at all, does computation of the maturity value of an interest-bearing note receivable differ from that for an interest-bearing note payable?
11. What is a dishonored note receivable?
12. What is meant by "discounting a note receivable"?
13. Explain how to compute the proceeds from discounting a note receivable.
14. When is a discounted note receivable considered a contingent liability?
15. Explain a cashier's check.
16. Explain a sight draft.

APPLICATIONS

Exercises

Determining the due dates of notes.

Find the due date of each of the following notes.

1. A note dated April 10, 2010, due six months from that date.
2. A note dated June 12, 2010, due in 120 days.
3. A note dated November 1, 2010, due two years from that date.

◄ **Exercise 16.1**
Objective 3

Determining the maturity value of notes.

Compute the maturity value for each of the following notes.

1. A note payable with a face amount of $4,000, dated May 5, 2010, due in 60 days, bearing interest at 9 percent.
2. A note payable with a face amount of $7,000, dated June 15, 2010, due in three months, bearing interest at 6 percent.

◄ **Exercise 16.2**
Objectives 2, 3

Computing the maturity value of notes payable.

Find the maturity value of each of the following notes payable.

1. A 90-day note, dated February 15, 2010, with a face value of $12,000, bearing interest at 8 percent.
2. A six-month note, dated March 10, 2010, with a face value of $6,600, bearing interest at 10 percent.

◄ **Exercise 16.3**
Objective 3

Exercise 16.4
Objectives 4, 5

▶ **Recording the issuance of notes payable to borrow money.**

During 2010, Martin Company borrowed money at Western Bank on two occasions. On May 8, the company borrowed $18,000, giving a 90-day, 7 percent note, and on August 8, the company discounted at 7 percent an $18,000, 90-day note payable.

1. Give entries in general journal form to record issuance of each of these notes.
2. Record in general journal form issuance of a check to pay each note.

Exercise 16.5
Objective 4

▶ **Recording a note given for a purchase of equipment.**

On August 1, 2010, the Olvera Company purchased a truck (delivery equipment) for $36,200, signing a 90-day, 8 percent note for the entire purchase price. Give the entry in general journal form to record this transaction.

Exercise 16.6
Objective 7

▶ **Recording receipt of a note receivable and subsequent discounting of the note.**

On June 3, 2010, Statewide Company received a $2,400, 60-day, 10 percent note from Ron Cosby, a customer whose account was past due.

1. Record in the general journal receipt of the note.
2. Give the entry in general journal form to record the discounting of this note receivable on June 18 at the First State Bank. The bank charged a discount rate of 12 percent.

Exercise 16.7
Objective 7

▶ **Recording payment of a discounted note receivable.**

In general journal form, give the entry required by Statewide when Cosby paid the note discounted in Exercise 16.6 on the maturity date.

Exercise 16.8
Objective 7

▶ **Recording a dishonored note receivable.**

Give the entries in general journal form that Statewide Company would make if Ron Cosby dishonored the note receivable discounted by Statewide in Exercise 16.6, assuming the bank deducted the maturity value of the dishonored note plus a $25 service charge from Statewide's bank account on the due date of the note.

PROBLEMS

Problem Set A **HM**

Problem 16.1A
Objective 2 **eXcel**

▶ **Computing interest on notes payable.**

Bonney Company issued the following notes during 2010. Find the interest due on each of the notes, using the interest formula method. Show all calculations.

1. A $10,000 note at 8 percent for 180 days, issued February 15.
2. A $3,000 note at 12 percent for three months. issued October 3.
3. A $50,000 note at 9 percent for 120 days, issued October 18.

Analyze: What is the balance in *Notes Payable* on December 31, 2010, assuming that all notes were paid when due?

Problem 16.2A
Objectives 2, 3, 4, 5
QB

▶ **Recording transactions involving notes payable.**

Give the general journal entry to record each of the following transactions for Iowa Company.

1. Issued a 6-month, 8 percent note for $50,000 to purchase two forklifts on May 14, 2010 (debit Warehouse Equipment).
2. Discounted its own 180-day, noninterest-bearing note with a principal amount of $14,500 at the Mart National Bank on May 28, 2010. The bank charged a discount rate of 9 percent.

3. Paid the May 14 note on its due date.

4. Paid the note discounted on May 28 on its due date.

Analyze: What is the total interest expense for the year as a result of these transactions?

Computing interest and maturity value.

The following notes were received by Evans Company during 2010.

◀ **Problem 16.3A**

e**X**cel **Objectives 2, 3**

Note No.	Date	Face Amount	Period	Interest Rate
21	Jan. 5	$20,000	3 months	10%
22	June 3	6,000	90 days	9%
23	Sept. 28	3,000	3 months	8%

Compute the maturity value of each note.

Analyze: What is the total interest expense on these notes for the year?

Computing the proceeds from discounted notes receivable.

The notes receivable held by the NAFTA Company on August 3, 2010, are summarized below. On August 4, 2010, NAFTA discounted all of these notes at Community Bank at a discount rate of 10 percent. Compute the net proceeds received from discounting each note.

◀ **Problem 16.4A**

e**X**cel **Objectives 3, 7**

Note No.	Date	Face Amount	Period	Interest Rate
31	Apr. 4, 2010	$20,000	6 months	8%
32	June 11, 2010	6,000	120 days	6%
33	July 31, 2010	4,000	60 days	10%

Analyze: What is the net interest income or expense to be reported from these transactions assuming all notes are paid when due?

Recording the receipt, discounting, and payment of notes receivable.

On May 16, 2010, Morton Company received a 90-day, 8 percent, $6,600 interest-bearing note from Ivers Company in settlement of Ivers's past-due account. On June 30, Morton discounted this note at Southern Bank. The bank charged a discount rate of 13 percent. On August 15, Morton received a notice that Ivers had paid the note and the interest on the due date. Give entries in general journal form to record these transactions.

◀ **Problem 16.5A**

Objectives 3, 4, 6 7

Analyze: If the company prepared a balance sheet on July 31, 2010, how should *Notes Receivable—Discounted* be presented on the statement?

Problem Set B

Computing interest on notes payable.

The notes listed below were issued by Bonaparte Company during 2010.

◀ **Problem 16.1B**

Objective 2

1. A $4,400 note at 10 percent for 90 days, issued on June 15.

2. A $9,000 note at 6 percent for 30 days, issued on August 21.

3. A $10,000 note at 7.5 percent for 6 months, issued on September 28.

Compute the interest due on each of the notes at maturity, using the interest formula method. Show all calculations.

Analyze: What would be the accrued interest payable on December 31 as a result of these transactions?

Recording transactions involving notes payable.

Give the general journal entry to record each of the following transactions.

◀ **Problem 16.2B**

Objectives 2, 3, 4, 5

1. On June 3, 2010, Queen Company issued a 120-day, 9 percent note for $31,000 to purchase new office equipment.

2. Queen Company paid the June 3 note when it became due.

3. On September 18, 2010, Queen Company borrowed money from the Aliso Viego National Bank by discounting its own 90-day noninterest-bearing $12,000 note payable at a discount rate of 10 percent.

4. Queen Company paid the September 18 note when it became due.

Analyze: If Queen had borrowed $12,000 from the bank on September 18, signing a 90-day note, bearing interest of 10 percent, would these be more favorable or less favorable terms for Queen than discounting the $12,000 note at 10 percent? Why?

Problem 16.3B
Objectives 2, 3

▶ **Computing interest and maturity value.**

Zang Company received the notes listed below in 2010. Compute the interest to be paid and the maturity value of each note. Show all computations.

Note No.	Date	Face Amount	Period	Interest Rate
30	May 4	$6,000	60 days	10.5%
31	July 8	4,000	90 days	8.5%
32	Aug. 20	8,400	4 months	9.0%

Analyze: Assuming all notes are paid when due, what would be the balance in *Notes Receivable* on July 31?

Problem 16.4B
Objective 7

▶ **Computing the proceeds from discounted notes receivable.**

The following notes receivable are held by the Rowen Company on January 1, 2010. On January 2, 2010, Rowen discounted all of these notes at First Commerce Bank at a discount rate of 10 percent. Compute the net proceeds the firm received from discounting each note (2010 was not a leap year).

Note No.	Date	Face Amount	Period	Interest Rate
20	Sept. 20, 2009	$16,000	120 days	8%
21	Sept. 10, 2009	6,000	6 months	9%
22	Dec. 1, 2009	4,000	120 days	12%

Analyze: How would *Notes Receivable* be shown on a balance sheet prepared on January 2, 2010, after the transactions above have been entered?

Problem 16.5B
Objectives 2, 3, 4, 6, 7

▶ **Recording the receipt, discounting, and payment of notes receivable.**

On April 2, 2010, Chu Company received a 6-month, 8 percent interest-bearing note from Matt Jones in settlement of a past-due account receivable of $8,200. On April 28, Chu discounted this note at Mercantile State Bank. The bank charged a discount rate of 10 percent. On October 2, Chu received word that the note and interest had been paid in full.

1. Give all entries, in general journal form, to record these events.

2. Assume that Jones had failed to pay the note and that the bank charged Chu's account with the note and a $50 protest fee. Give the journal entry(ies) necessary to record these facts.

Analyze: What amount of interest income or interest expense will Chu report in 2010 as a result of these transactions assuming Jones paid the note when due?

Critical Thinking Problem 16.1

Notes Payable and Notes Receivable

Henry Hays owns Hays' Boat Sales. He periodically borrows money from Meridian State Bank. He permits some customers to sign short-term notes for their purchases. He usually discounts these notes at the bank. Following are selected transactions that occurred in March 2010. (2010 is not a leap year.)

INSTRUCTIONS

1. Record each of the March transactions in the general journal. (Omit explanations.)
2. Record the additional data related to these notes for months other than March in the general journal using the appropriate dates.

DATE	TRANSACTIONS
2010	
Mar. 4	Mr. Hays borrows $8,000 from the bank on a note payable for the business. Terms of the note are 8 percent interest for 45 days.
11	A 90-day $9,000 note payable to the bank is discounted at a rate of 10 percent.
22	Sold a boat to Brian Fields for $4,200 on a 75-day note receivable, bearing interest at 10 percent.
23	Discounted the Fields note with the bank. The bank charges a discount rate of 12 percent.
25	Sold a boat for $4,000 to Jeff Towne. Towne paid $2,000 cash and signed a 30-day note, bearing interest at 10 percent, for the balance.
28	Jason Cobb's account receivable is overdue. Hays requires him to sign a 12 percent, 30-day note for the balance of $4,500.

Additional Data

a. Hays pays all the company's notes payable on time.
b. Brian Fields defaults on his $4,200 note and the bank charges the company's checking account for the maturity value of the note and a service fee of $30.
c. Jeff Towne pays his note on time.
d. Jason Cobb pays his note on time.

Analyze: What is the *Notes Payable* account balance on March 25?

Critical Thinking Problem 16.2

Notes Receivable Discounted

Casual Living, a wholesale distributor of modern casual furniture, frequently accepts promissory notes from its customers at the time of sale. Since Casual Furniture regularly needs cash to meet its own obligations, it frequently discounts these notes at the bank.

Casual Living's accountant tells you that she does not bother to credit discounted notes to a *Notes Receivable—Discounted* account. Instead, she makes an entry debiting *Cash* and *Interest Expense* and crediting *Notes Receivable* (and *Interest Income* when appropriate). She says that using a *Notes Receivable—Discounted* account "just makes extra work, and, anyway, once the note is discounted, it becomes the bank's problem."

What is your reaction to the bookkeeper's comments?

BUSINESS CONNECTIONS

Cash Management

Managerial | FOCUS

1. How can management use notes receivable as a way to acquire cash?
2. You are a member of Signal Company's internal audit staff. A review of office practices indicates that an accounting assistant routinely makes arrangements with the bank for short-term notes payable and signs the notes. Evaluate this practice. Would you recommend any changes?

3. As a manager, why would you insist that dishonored notes receivable be charged back to the *Accounts Receivable* control account and the maker's subsidiary ledger account?

4. Under what circumstances would management insist on having a notes receivable register and/or a notes payable register?

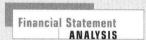

Contingent Liability

Mills Corporation has a practice of discounting the notes receivable to the bank to increase its cash flow. Since the maker of the notes receivable has always paid the bank, Mills Corporation does not list the notes receivable as a contingent liability. Is this an ethical practice? What would be compromised if the liability did not appear in the notes of the annual report?

STREETWISE:
Questions from the
REAL WORLD

Long-Term Debt

Refer to the *2006 Annual Report* for The Home Depot, Inc., in Appendix A.

1. The Notes to Consolidated Financial Statements offer details about the company's financial condition. Describe the types of outstanding long-term debt listed in Note 4 for the period ending January 30, 2007.

2. Based on the information presented in Note 4, what portion of long-term debt is considered a current liability as of January 30, 2007?

Financial Statement
ANALYSIS

Balance Sheet

The following excerpt was taken from the McCormick Company *2006 Annual Report*. The Notes to Consolidated Financial Statements contained the following details on the company's long-term debt.

Note 7—Financing Arrangements

Long-term debt consisted of the following amounts:

(in millions)	2006	2005
Notes payable with interest rate soft		
5.78%–7.77% medium-term notes due 2004 to 2006	—	$ 47.0
6.40%–6.80% medium-term notes due 2006 to 2008	$149.8	298.6
3.35% medium-term notes due 2009	48.6	47.8
5.80% medium-term notes due 2011	100.0	—
5.20% medium-term notes due 2015	201.0	—
7.63%–8.12% medium-term notes due 2024	55.0	55.0
Other	15.8	16.2
	570.2	464.6
Less current portion	0.6	0.7
	569.6	463.9

Analyze:

1. What percentage of total debt is represented by the current portion in 2006? In 2005?

2. Which category of notes was newly issued in 2006?

3. If interest payments totaled $36 million in 2006, what average interest rate was paid on total debt?

Analyze Online: Find the McCormick Company Web site (www.mccormick.com). Recent financial reports are found within the *Investors* link.

4. What is the fiscal period for the most recent annual report presented?

5. What long-term debt amount is reported on the balance sheet?

6. What amount of long-term debt matured in this fiscal period?

Lenders

Extending THE THOUGHT

Firms sometimes negotiate a note payable to fund expansion or to purchase equipment. If a company does not have sufficient funds to execute expansion plans or to buy equipment, why would a lending institution extend a loan? What are the risks for the borrower and for the lender? What agreements between the lender and borrower can increase the lender's confidence in the borrower?

Memo

Business COMMUNICATION

The owner of Kinder Space wants to expand the parking lot. As the firm's accountant, you have been asked to compare interest-bearing notes available from two banks. The owner believes $18,000 will be needed. He assumes that the note carrying a lower interest rate is the preferred note. One note is for 90 days, 12 percent interest, and the other is for 120 days, 10% interest. Determine which note results in lower total interest payments. Then prepare a memo to the owner, recommending which note requires lower total interest payments. Explain your reasoning and include any computations you make.

Negotiating Terms

TEAMWORK

A business manager should know how one company's transaction will affect another company. In teams of two students, assign one student to be the notes receivable clerk of Passion Industries and another to be Super Scents, the borrowing company's notes payable clerk. Super Scents cannot make the payment on a $30,000 invoice. Negotiate the necessary arrangements between the two parties.

Uniform Commercial Code

Internet CONNECTION

Each state develops a Uniform Commercial Code that regulates commercial transactions. Select the secretary of state for your state and locate your state's commercial code on the Web site. Define the Uniform Commercial Code and its purpose.

Answers to Self Reviews

Answers to Section 1 Self Review

1. August 8
2. Interest = $24,000 \times .08 \times 75/360 = $400
3. Proceeds = Face amount − Discount

   Discount = $24,000 \times .08 \times 75/360 = $400

   Proceeds = $24,000 − $400 = $23,600
4. **d.** All of the above are required.
5. **b.** maturity value
6. No. The effective rate for a discounted note is higher. In both cases, the interest paid was $400. However, in Question 2, the borrower would have the use of $24,000 for 75 days, whereas in Question 3 the borrower would have the use of only $23,600 for 75 days.

Answers to Section 2 Self Review

1. If a customer is unable to pay a currently due account receivable, it is wise to have a note receivable signed. The note receivable provides greater legal protection to its holder than does an account receivable claim.
2. Dishonor of a note means that the maker of the note does not pay it when it is due.
3. Proceeds = Maturity value − Discount

   Discount = $3,100 \times .10 \times 90/360 = $77.50

   Proceeds = $3,100 − $77.50 = $3,022.50
4. **d.** recognizes interest income if the proceeds exceed the face value of the note discounted.
5. **d.** is deducted from *Notes Receivable* on the balance sheet.

6. No. Sales are recorded at the principal amount of the note. The interest is reported as *Interest Income.*

Answers to Comprehensive Self Review

1. Maturity value of the note is the sum of (a) the principal amount of the note and (b) interest on the principal amount at the rate specified, computed from the date the note is dated until the maturity date.

2. For an interest-bearing note issued, *Interest Expense* is debited when the note matures. The interest on a note payable discounted is recorded at the date of the discounting.

3. (a) must be in writing and signed by the maker, (b) contains an unconditional promise or order to pay a definite amount of money, (c) is payable on demand or at a time that can be determined, (d) is payable to the order of the bearer, and (e) if addressed to a drawee, the drawee must be clearly identified.

4. *Notes Receivable—Discounted* is a contra asset account. This means that it is deducted from *Notes Receivable* on the balance sheet.

5. Accounts debited and credited: *Notes Receivable—Discounted* will be debited and *Notes Receivable* will be credited. Also, *Accounts Receivable* and the customer's account in the subsidiary ledger will be debited and *Cash* will be credited.

Merchandise Inventory

www.circuitcity.com

It is hard to imagine a world without computers, much less a world without televisions. But 60 years ago the highest-tech appliance in most homes was the radio. In 1949, Samuel Wurtzel introduced the television to his local community when he opened Richmond, Virginia's first television store. Since then, his local shop has grown into over 600 stores under the Circuit City name. The products have changed too, evolving from tiny black-and-white TVs to computers, DVD players, and giant plasma screen TVs.

Circuit City has made it a priority to help customers find the products they want when they want them. The company's Web site, www.circuitcity.com, allows customers to check inventories in warehouses and stores in real time. Products can be purchased online and shipped or reserved for in-store pickup. Not only do customers get superior service, Circuit City can measure product demand in real time and most effectively manage inventory levels. Sales originating from the store's Web site have grown strongly since its introduction in 1999. The results reflect the tight integration between the online and the "brick and mortar" Circuit City stores.

thinking critically

What operational benefits do you think Circuit City has gained by allowing customers to order products online for in-store pickup?

SECTION OBJECTIVES

>> 1. **Compute inventory cost by applying four commonly used costing methods.**

   WHY IT'S IMPORTANT

   Factors such as industry practices, merchandise types, and business operations affect how a business assigns costs to inventories.

>> 2. **Compare the effects of different methods of inventory costing.**

   WHY IT'S IMPORTANT

   Inventory valuation affects the net income or net loss of a business.

TERMS TO LEARN

average cost method

first in, first out (FIFO) method

last in, first out (LIFO) method

periodic inventory

perpetual inventory

physical inventory

specific identification method

weighted average method

Video17.1

Inventory Costing Methods

Businesses report information about merchandise inventory on the financial statements. This section covers four methods used to compute the value of merchandise inventory based on original cost.

Importance of Inventory Valuation

Assigning an appropriate value to merchandise inventory is important because the **Merchandise Inventory** account appears on both the balance sheet and the income statement. Often inventory represents the largest current asset on the balance sheet. Inventory valuation also affects the net income or net loss reported on the income statement.

A higher ending inventory value results in a lower cost of goods sold, which results in higher income from operations. On the other hand, a lower ending inventory value results in a higher cost of goods sold, which results in a lower income from operations.

> On its consolidated balance sheet for fiscal year 2007, ending on February 1, 2007, The Home Depot reported inventories of $12.822 billion. Inventory represents about 24.5 percent of the company's total assets of $52.26 billion.

We learned in Chapter 12 that many firms value merchandise inventory at the original cost of the items on hand. Merchandise inventory is counted at the end of the accounting period. The inventory value is calculated by multiplying the number of units on hand by the cost per item. Taking an actual count of the number of units of each type of good on hand is known as taking a **physical inventory.** An inventory system in which the amount of goods on hand is determined by periodic counts is called a **periodic inventory** system. It is the method that we use in this chapter.

Some businesses need to know the number of units and the unit cost for the inventory on hand at all times. These businesses use a **perpetual inventory** system, in which inventory is based on a running total number of units. Electronic equipment, such as point-of-sale cash registers and scanners, helps track all of the items as they are purchased and sold. Perpetual inventory records are discussed in a later chapter.

Assigning Costs to Inventory

The cost of sold merchandise is transferred from the balance sheet (current assets) to the income statement (cost of goods sold). The amount of cost that is transferred depends on the method used to value inventory. Four methods are commonly used to value inventory. Accountants choose the method that works best for the industry and the company.

SPECIFIC IDENTIFICATION METHOD

The **specific identification method** of inventory valuation is based on the actual cost of each item of merchandise. Cost of goods sold is the exact cost of the specific merchandise sold, and the ending inventory balance is the exact cost of the specific inventory items on hand. Businesses that sell high-priced or one-of-a-kind items, such as art and automobile dealers, use the specific identification method. However, this method is not practical for a business where hundreds of similar items of relatively small unit value are carried in inventory.

AVERAGE COST METHOD

The **average cost method** uses the average cost of units of an item available for sale during the period to arrive at the value of ending inventory. It is advantageous to use the average cost method when a company's inventory is composed of many similar items that are not subject to significant price and style changes. Table 17.1, which provides an example of the average cost method, contains the following information:

- There were 200 units in beginning inventory valued at $18 each.
- There were three purchases during the year, at different costs.
- The beginning inventory and purchases are added together to determine that during the year 1,000 units were available for sale at a total cost of $20,600.
- The average cost per unit is $20.60 ($20,600 ÷ 1,000).
- A physical inventory count showed 206 units on hand on December 31.
- During the year, 794 units were sold (1,000 − 206).
- Under the average cost method, the total cost of units available for sale ($20,600) is divided between the financial statements as follows:
  - Balance sheet—ending inventory is $4,243.60 (206 units × $20.60).
  - Income statement—cost of goods sold is $16,356.40 (794 units × $20.60).

>>1. OBJECTIVE

Compute inventory cost by applying four commonly used costing methods.

Video17.1

important!

Physical Inventory
Whether a perpetual or periodic inventory system is used, a physical inventory should be taken at least once a year.

recall

Cost of Goods Sold
The formula for cost of goods sold is
  Beginning inventory
+ Purchases
− Ending inventory
= Cost of goods sold

TABLE 17.1

Average Cost Method of Inventory Valuation

Explanation	Number of Units	Unit Cost	Total Cost
Beginning inventory, January 1, 2010	200	$18.00	$ 3,600.00
Purchases:			
February 19	400	20.00	8,000.00
May 12	300	22.00	6,600.00
October 3	100	24.00	2,400.00
Total merchandise available for sale	1,000		$20,600.00
Average cost ($20,600 ÷ 1,000 = $20.60)			
Ending inventory, December 31, 2010	206	20.60	$ 4,243.60
Cost of goods sold ($20,600 − $4,243.60)	794	20.60	$16,356.40

This method is sometimes referred to as the **weighted average method** because it considers the number of units in each purchase and the unit purchase price to compute a "weighted average" cost per unit.

The average cost method of inventory valuation is relatively simple to use, but it reflects the limitations of any procedure that involves average figures. The average unit cost is not related to any specific unit, and it does not clearly reveal price changes. In highly competitive businesses that are subject to considerable model or style upgrades and price fluctuations, it is desirable to have a more specific and revealing method of cost determination.

> The Coca-Cola Company's inventories are shown in the company's *2006 Annual Report* as $1.641 billion, which is approximately 19.4 percent of its current assets. A note to the financial statements comments: "We determine cost on the basis of average cost or first-in, first-out methods."

recall

Disclosure

The method of inventory valuation must be disclosed in the financial reports.

FIRST IN, FIRST OUT METHOD

For most businesses, the physical flow of inventory is "the first item purchased is the first item sold." This certainly makes sense for perishable items. Some businesses assign inventory costs using this flow. The **first in, first out method** of inventory valuation, usually referred to as **FIFO,** assumes that the oldest merchandise is sold first.

Let's calculate ending inventory under FIFO using the information in Table 17.1. During the period, 794 units were sold. Under FIFO the "first cost in is the first cost transferred out" to cost of goods sold. This matches the earliest costs with the revenue from the units sold. So the cost of the ending inventory is computed by using the cost of the most recent purchases.

Table 17.2 shows that the cost assigned to the 206 units in ending inventory is $4,732.00: 100 units purchased in October at $24 and 106 units purchased in May at $22, for a total of 206 units. During the period, there was $20,600.00 of inventory available for sale. Under the FIFO method, the cost is divided between the financial statements as follows:

- Balance sheet—ending inventory is $4,732.00.
- Income statement—cost of goods sold is $15,868 ($20,600 − $4,732.00).

TABLE 17.2

FIFO Method of Inventory Costing

Explanation	Number of Units	Unit Cost	Total Cost
From purchase of October 3, 2010	100	$24.00	$2,400.00
From purchase of May 12, 2010	106	22.00	2,332.00
Ending inventory	206		$4,732.00

> A company can use several inventory valuation methods. Most inventory costs for Dole Food Company, Inc., are determined principally on a first in, first out basis. However, specific identification and average cost methods are used for certain packing material and operating inventories.

important!

Inventory Costing and Net Income

Gross profit on sales and net income are affected by the inventory costing method.

LAST IN, FIRST OUT METHOD

The **last in, first out (LIFO) method** assumes that the most recently purchased merchandise is sold first, and thus assigns the most recent costs to cost of goods sold. The "last cost in is the first cost transferred out" to cost of goods sold. Thus, the cost of ending inventory is computed using the cost of the oldest merchandise on hand during the period.

Using the figures from Table 17.1 but applying the LIFO method, Table 17.3 shows that the cost assigned to the 206 units in ending inventory is 200 at $18 from the beginning inventory and 6 at $20 from the February 19 purchases. During the period, there was $20,600 of inventory available for sale. Under the LIFO method, the cost is divided between the financial statements as follows:

- Balance sheet—ending inventory is $3,720.00.
- Income statement—cost of goods sold is $16,880 ($20,600 − $3,720).

Under the LIFO method, the balance sheet reflects the earliest costs. The cost of goods sold reflects the costs applicable to the most recent purchases.

Explanation	Number of Units	Unit Cost	Total Cost
Beginning inventory, Jan. 1, 2010	200	$18.00	$3,600.00
From purchase of February 19	6	20.00	120.00
Ending inventory, Dec. 31, 2010	206		$3,720.00

TABLE 17.3

LIFO Method of Inventory Valuation

Comparing Results of Inventory Costing Methods

Table 17.4 shows the results obtained for the average cost, FIFO, and LIFO inventory methods. The ending inventory is highest under FIFO and lowest under LIFO. The cost of goods sold is highest under LIFO and lowest under FIFO. This is true because costs have risen during the year.

>>2. OBJECTIVE
Compare the effects of different methods of inventory costing.

Explanation	Units	Unit Cost	Total Cost	Ending Inventory Valuation	Cost of Goods Sold
Beginning inventory, January 1, 2010	200	$18.00	$3,600.00		
Purchases:					
February 19	400	20.00	8,000.00		
May 12	300	22.00	6,600.00		
October 3	100	24.00	2,400.00		
Total merchandise available for sale	1,000		$20,600.00		
1. Average cost method	206	$20.60		$4,243.60	$16,356.40
2. FIFO	100	24.00	$2,400.00		
	106	22.00	2,332.00		
	206		$4,732.00	$4,732.00	$15,868.00
3. LIFO	200	18.00	$3,600.00	$3,720.00	$16,880.00
	6	20.00	120.00		
	206		3,720.00		

TABLE 17.4

Comparison of Results of Inventory Costing Methods

Remember the following important points about inventory valuation methods:

- Except for specific identification, the physical flow of inventory and the costs assigned to inventory are not specifically matched. Average, FIFO, and LIFO cost methods *assign* costs to inventory but do not track the cost to the specific inventory item.
- Businesses can use separate inventory valuation methods for different classes of inventory.

LP17

- Following the consistency principle, once a business adopts an inventory valuation method, it uses that method consistently from one period to the next. A business cannot change its inventory valuation method at will, although a one-time change is acceptable.
- A business can use one inventory costing method for financial accounting purposes and another for federal income tax, with the exception of LIFO costing. A taxpayer who adopts LIFO for federal tax purposes must also adopt it for financial accounting purposes.
- FIFO focuses on the balance sheet. The most current costs are in ending inventory.
- LIFO focuses on the income statement and the matching principle. The most recent costs are matched with revenue. LIFO is considered the most conservative costing method in a period of rising prices.

A major argument supporting the LIFO method is that when sales are made the goods sold must be replaced at current costs. It is logical that current costs incurred for replaced goods should be charged against the revenue leading to the replacement.

Since price trends represent a vital element in any inventory valuation, remember these basic rules:

- When prices are rising, cost of goods sold is highest and net income is lowest under LIFO. Therefore, in periods of inflation, LIFO results in the lowest income tax expense.
- When prices are falling, cost of goods sold is lower and net income is higher under LIFO.
- Whatever direction prices take, the average cost method almost always results in net income between the amounts obtained with FIFO and LIFO.

LIFO Use Internationally

Most of the major industrialized countries use the methods of accounting for inventories discussed in this chapter. In some countries, however, LIFO is not generally accepted.

Section **1** Self Review

QUESTIONS

1. Is it possible to apply the LIFO inventory method if items in the inventory cannot be identified as having been received as parts of specific purchases? Explain.

2. In a period of rising prices, which inventory method (LIFO, FIFO, average cost) results in the lowest reported net income?

3. Is a company permitted to change its inventory valuation method each year?

What accounting principle is involved in your answer?

EXERCISES

4. Under FIFO costing, which costs are assigned to the goods sold during the period?

5. What does LIFO mean, and what is the LIFO cost flow method?

ANALYSIS

6. Before recommending an inventory valuation method, what questions would you ask the manager about the business and its inventory?

(Answers to Section 1 Self Review are on page 593.)

SECTION OBJECTIVES	TERMS TO LEARN

>> 3. Compute inventory value under the lower of cost or market rule.

WHY IT'S IMPORTANT

The conservatism convention is important when determining the cost of inventory.

>> 4. Estimate inventory cost using the gross profit method.

WHY IT'S IMPORTANT

Often businesses need to determine the cost of inventory without taking a physical count.

>> 5. Estimate inventory cost using the retail method.

WHY IT'S IMPORTANT

The retail method provides an easy and quick estimation of the cost of the inventory.

gross profit method
lower of cost or market rule
markdown
market price
markon
markup
replacement cost
retail method

Inventory Valuation and Control

Video17.1

According to the historical cost principle, assets are reported on the balance sheet at their historical cost. The conservatism convention, however, states that assets should not be overstated. This section discusses how to report the value of inventory when the cost is above the market price.

Lower of Cost or Market Rule

Market price or **replacement cost** is the price the business would have to pay to buy an item of inventory through usual channels in usual quantities. To determine market price, businesses contact their suppliers, read trade publications, or review recent purchases. If the current market price is lower than the original cost, the business uses the **lower of cost or market rule.** That is, inventory is reported at its original cost or its replacement cost, whichever is lower. There are three ways to apply the lower of cost or market rule: by item, in total, or by group.

LOWER OF COST OR MARKET RULE BY ITEM

Table 17.5 illustrates the lower of cost or market rule by item. Inventory consists of two groups of two stock items each. The report shows the quantity, cost, and market price of each item. Cost is determined using one of the acceptable methods—specific identification, average cost, FIFO, or LIFO. Each item's valuation basis (cost or market, whichever is lower) is determined; for item 2810, it is cost, $1.80, and for item 2870 it is market, $2.05. The quantity is multiplied by valuation basis and the amounts are totaled. The inventory balance reported on the balance sheet is $1,461.25.

>>3. OBJECTIVE

Compute inventory value under the lower of cost or market rule.

LP17

TABLE 17.5

Establishing Lower of Cost or Market Valuation by Item

Description	Quantity	Unit Price Cost	Unit Price Market	Lower of Cost or Market Valuation Basis	Lower of Cost or Market Amount
Group 1					
Stock 2810	150	1.80	1.95	Cost	$ 270.00
Stock 2870	225	2.10	2.05	Market	461.25
Total, Group 1					$ 731.25
Group 2					
Stock 4625	100	3.10	3.05	Market	$ 305.00
Stock 4633	250	1.70	1.80	Cost	425.00
Total, Group 2					$ 730.00
Inventory valuation (lower of cost or market by item)					$1,461.25

LOWER OF TOTAL COST OR TOTAL MARKET

Table 17.6 illustrates the lower of cost or market rule applied to total inventory, not to individual items. The cost of inventory is computed using both cost and market and then the results are compared. Inventory is valued in the balance sheet at the lower amount, $1,477.50.

> The inventories of Pier 1 Imports, Inc., are stated at the lower of average cost or market. Cost is determined using the weighted average method.

LOWER OF COST OR MARKET RULE BY GROUPS

Another way to apply the lower of cost or market rule is by groups. The lower figure (cost or market) for each group is added to the lower figures for the other groups to obtain the total

Description	Quantity	Unit Price Unit Cost	Unit Price Unit Market	Total Cost	Total Market
Group 1					
Stock 2810	150	1.80	1.95	$ 270.00	$ 292.50
Stock 2870	225	2.10	2.05	472.50	461.25
Total, Group 1				$ 742.50	$ 753.75
Group 2					
Stock 4625	100	3.10	3.05	$ 310.00	$ 305.00
Stock 4633	250	1.70	1.80	425.00	450.00
Total, Group 2				$ 735.00	$ 755.00
Total Inventory				$1,477.50	$1,508.75
Inventory valuation (lower of total cost or total market)					$1,477.50

TABLE 17.6

Establishing Lower of Total Cost or Total Market Valuation

TABLE 17.7

Establishing the Lower of Total
Cost or Total Market by Groups

Lower of cost or market valuation by group (as shown in Table 17.6)	
Group 1 Cost	$ 742.50
Group 2 Cost	735.00
Total inventory valuation	$1,477.50

TABLE 17.7

**Establishing the Lower of Total
Cost or Total Market by Groups**

inventory valuation. As shown in Table 17.7, the valuation basis of both Group 1 and Group 2 is cost. Inventory is valued on the balance sheet at $1,477.50

Depending on the method used, inventory could appear on the balance sheet as one of the following amounts.

Lower of Cost or Market	
By Item	$1,461.25
By Total	1,477.50
By Group	1,477.50

Accountants select the method based on the size and variety of inventory, the margin of profit, industry practices, and plans for expansion.

- Some accountants believe that the total method should be used. They think that the lower of cost or market rule should apply to the total inventory, not item by item. If market value of the inventory as a whole has not declined below cost, they believe inventory should be presented at historical cost.

- Other accountants prefer the group method because it does not reflect individual fluctuations as does the item method, and it does not lump together all types of items as does the total method.

- Some accountants choose the item method because it is the most conservative method. Almost without exception the item method results in the lowest inventory amount.

Inventory Estimation Procedures

Occasionally, managers need to know the inventory cost and cannot or do not want to take a physical count. For example, after a fire the business cannot count the items destroyed. However, for insurance and income tax purposes, the business must determine the cost of the goods destroyed. Two common techniques to estimate the cost of inventory are the gross profit method and the retail method.

GROSS PROFIT METHOD OF INVENTORY VALUATION

The **gross profit method** assumes that the rate of gross profit on sales and the ratio of cost of goods sold to net sales are relatively constant from period to period. Applying these ratios to information that may be gleaned from the records on any date of the year permits an estimate to be made of the cost of inventory at the end of a period ending on that date. This process is illustrated for the Posey Corporation, whose inventory was destroyed by fire on June 30, 2010. However, accounting records were not destroyed.

The averages of sales and data related to cost of goods sold in the years 2008 and 2009 for Posey Corporation, along with the computation of the gross profit and the cost of goods sold ratios, are determined:

Net sales	$850,000	
Cost of goods sold	493,000	
Gross profit on sales	$357,000	
Gross profit rate		$357,000/$850,000 = 42%
Cost of goods sold to net sales ratio		$493,000/$850,000 = 58%

These rates have been typical of those in prior years for the business. The accounting records for the period January 1 through June 30, date of the fire, show:

Inventory (at cost), January 1	$210,000
Net purchases, January 1 through June 30	315,000
Net sales, January 1 through June 30	450,000

The following steps are used to estimate the cost of inventory on hand at the time of the fire.

Step 1: *Estimate the cost of goods sold.* Sales were $450,000 for January 1 through June 30. Using the 58 percent ratio for cost of goods sold to net sales, based on averages for the prior two years, the estimated cost of goods sold is $261,000 ($450,000 × 0.58).

Step 2: *Determine the cost of goods available for sale.* Include in the computation freight-in charges and purchases returns.

Beginning inventory	$210,000
Net purchases	315,000
Cost of goods available for sale	$525,000

Step 3: *Compute the ending (destroyed) inventory.* Subtract the estimated cost of goods sold from the cost of goods available for sale.

Cost of goods available for sale (Step 2)	$525,000
Estimated cost of goods sold (Step 1)	(261,000)
Estimated cost of ending inventory	$264,000

The cost of inventory destroyed in the fire is estimated to be $264,000.

>>5. OBJECTIVE

Estimate inventory cost using the retail method.

LP17

RETAIL METHOD OF INVENTORY VALUATION

The **retail method** estimates inventory cost by applying the ratio of cost to selling price in the current accounting period to the retail price of the inventory. This widely used method permits businesses to determine the approximate cost of ending inventory from the financial records. It makes it possible for the business to prepare financial statements easily and often without taking a physical inventory count.

Using the retail method, inventory is classified into groups of items that have about the same rate of markon. **Markon** is the difference between the cost and the initial retail price of merchandise. The following steps use assumed figures to estimate the cost of inventory using the retail method.

MANAGERIAL IMPLICATIONS

INVENTORY

- Good managers carefully control inventory because it may represent a large part of the assets of the business.
- Management should help select an inventory costing method that is practical, reliable, and as simple as possible to apply.
- Management needs to understand how the inventory valuation method affects net income and income taxes.
- Based on the gross profit method of estimating inventory, managers can prepare budgets and financial statements

when a physical inventory count is not practical or possible.

- Retail managers use the retail method of inventory valuation to estimate the cost of goods on hand. Department managers, who are not permitted to exceed their inventory budgets, use this method as often as every week.

THINKING CRITICALLY

Should the gross profit method or the retail method of calculating inventory replace the physical count of inventory?

Step 1: List the beginning inventory at both cost ($95,400) and retail ($138,700).

Step 2: When merchandise is purchased, record it at cost ($526,800 including $2,400 freight) and determine its retail value ($819,500).

Step 3: Compute merchandise available for sale at cost ($622,200) and at retail ($958,200).

Step 4: Determine net sales at retail ($815,300).

Step 5: Subtract retail sales from the retail merchandise available for sale. The difference is the ending inventory at retail ($958,200 − $815,300 = $142,900).

Step 6: Compute the cost ratio.

$$\frac{\text{Merchandise Available for Sale at Cost}}{\text{Merchandise Available for Sale at Retail}} = \frac{\$622,200}{\$958,200} = 65 \text{ percent}$$

Step 7: Multiply the ending inventory at retail by the cost ratio. The result is an estimate of the ending inventory cost, $92,885 ($142,900 × 0.65).

Step 8: Estimate the cost of goods sold by subtracting the ending inventory at cost from the merchandise available for sale at cost, $529,315 ($622,200 − $92,885).

The calculations for each step are shown below.

	Cost	Retail
Step 1: Beginning inventory	$ 95,400	$138,700
Step 2: Purchases	526,800	819,500
Step 3: Total merchandise available for sale	$622,200	$958,200
Step 4: Less sales		815,300
Step 5: Ending inventory priced at retail		$142,900

Step 6: Cost ratio = ($622,200 ÷ $958,200) = 65%

Step 7: Conversion to approximate cost:

Ending inventory at retail × Cost ratio = $142,900 × 0.65

Ending inventory at cost = $92,885

Step 8: Cost of goods sold = $622,200 − $92,885 = $529,315

The benefit of the retail method is that without counting inventory the business is able to estimate the ending inventory balance at cost.

The retail method is not as simple as this example suggests. Adjustments must be made for **markups,** price increases above the original markons, and markup cancellations. Adjustments are also made for **markdowns,** price reductions below the original markon, and for markdown cancellations. These details are not covered in this text.

A more accurate application of the retail method involves taking a physical inventory, which is facilitated by using scanning devices to capture the sales price marked on the merchandise. The physical inventory at retail is converted to cost by applying the cost ratio. For example, if the physical inventory count shows retail cost of $60,000 and the cost ratio is 66.67 percent, the cost of the inventory is estimated to be $40,000 ($60,000 × 0.667).

The retail method for determining cost is used by many large retailers. For example, in notes to its financial statements for the fiscal year ending February 1, 2007, The Home Depot, Inc., states:

> The majority of the Company's Merchandise Inventories are stated at the lower of cost (first-in first-out) or market, as determined by the retail inventory method.

Internal Control of Inventories

The internal controls over inventory depend on the nature of the inventory. For example, controls for expensive jewelry are more elaborate than controls over lumber. Typical inventory controls are as follows:

- Limit access to inventory of small valuable items.

- Require documents, such as approved shipping orders, before allowing items to leave the warehouse.

- Take a physical inventory count at least annually to verify that the goods on hand match the amounts in the accounting records. Use spot checks to verify the counting techniques and the item costs. Have an independent auditor observe the count.

The notes to the financial statements in The Home Depot's *2007 Annual Report* stress the importance of periodic inventories when a perpetual inventory system is used.

> Independent physical inventory counts are taken on a regular basis in each store to ensure that amounts reflected in the accompanying Consolidated Financial Statements for Merchandise Inventories are properly stated. During the period between physical inventory counts, the Company accrues for estimated losses related to shrink on a store-by-store basis based on historical shrink results and current trends in the business. Shrink is the difference between the recorded amount of inventory and the physical inventory. Shrink (or in the case of excess inventory, "swell") may occur due to theft, loss, improper records for the receipt of inventory or deterioration of goods, among other things.

New Technology in Inventory Control

One of the problems with the use of "bar scanners" in checking inventories is that the methodology requires "line of sight" contact between the scanner and the bar code on the merchandise. This often requires physical movement of goods in the warehouse in order to obtain the line of sight. This is true not only at time of inventory taking, but in searching for goods that have been "recalled" by the manufacturer and in finding goods to move from the warehouse to the salesroom. This may be labor intensive and slow.

In the summer of 2003, Wal-Mart Stores launched an RFID (radio frequency identification) initiative. It asked its largest 100 suppliers to apply a "passive" electronic tag to all pallets and cases of merchandise shipped to three of its distribution centers. The system will enable a company to determine quickly whether merchandise is on hand in the warehouse or has been moved to the floor of the store. It is obvious that the technique could be very valuable, especially in the control of warehouse stocks.

The U.S. Department of Defense has announced a similar program using RFID, which means that two of the world's largest purchasers of goods plan to install the program. Other major retailers, such as Best Buy, Target, and The Home Depot, Inc., are also considering installing the technology. The system also promises to aid suppliers of merchandise in planning and controlling inventory sales to buyers using the program.

Up-to-date information about RFID can be obtained by accessing the Web site of the American Production and Inventory Control Society (www.apics.org).

Section **2** Self Review

QUESTIONS

1. Which accounting principles, concepts, or modifying conventions underlie the valuation of inventories at the lower of cost or market?

2. What does "the lower of cost or market" mean?

3. Name three ways by which the lower of cost or market rule might be applied. Which will give the lowest ending inventory valuation?

EXERCISES

4. Which of these inventory costing procedures does not require a physical count of the inventory items?
   a. Retail method
   b. Specific identification method
   c. Lower of cost or market method
   d. Average cost method

5. Under what circumstances would the gross profit method of estimating inventory be used?

ANALYSIS

6. When would a business use the gross profit method instead of the retail method to estimate the cost of ending inventory?

(Answers to Section 2 Self Review are on page 593.)

17 Chapter   REVIEW   Chapter Summary

It is important to account for merchandise inventory because the information appears on both the balance sheet and the income statement. Industry practices, merchandise unit costs, and merchandise price fluctuations affect how costs are assigned to inventory.

Chapter 17

Learning Objectives

1 Compute inventory cost by applying four commonly used costing methods.

There are four common inventory cost flow assumptions.

- The specific identification method uses the actual purchase price of the specific items in inventory.
- The average cost method averages the cost of all like items for sale during the period to value the ending inventory unit cost.
- The FIFO method develops the cost of the ending inventory from the cost of latest purchases.
- The LIFO method develops the cost of the ending inventory from the cost of beginning inventory and earlier purchases.

2 Compare the effects of different methods of inventory costing.

The method used affects the net income reported.

- With rising prices, LIFO gives a lower reported net income than FIFO, as well as lower income taxes payable.
- With falling prices, LIFO gives a higher reported net income than FIFO.
- The average cost method almost always gives a result between these.

3 Compute inventory value under the lower of cost or market rule.

- Assets are reported on financial statements at their historical cost. However, assets should not be overstated.
- If the replacement cost of an inventory item is below its original purchase cost, it is necessary to value the inventory at the lower current value in the firm's financial records.

- Consequently, inventory is valued at either its original cost, or its replacement cost, whichever is lower. This is called the lower of cost or market.
- Cost refers to the historical cost.
- Market refers to the replacement cost.
- The lower of cost or market can be applied to individual items in the inventory, to groups of items, or to the inventory as a whole.

4 Estimate inventory cost using the gross profit method.

The gross profit method of estimating inventory assumes that the rate of gross profit on sales and the ratio of cost of goods sold to net sales are relatively constant from period to period. Ending inventory can be estimated using three steps:

1) Estimate the cost of goods sold by multiplying net sales by the normal ratio of cost of goods sold to net sales.
2) Determine goods available for sale by adding beginning inventory and net purchases.
3) Compute ending inventory by subtracting the estimated cost of goods sold (in step 1) from goods available for sale (in step 2).

5 Estimate inventory cost using the retail method.

The retail method uses the retail selling price of items remaining. The retail value is multiplied by the cost ratio of the current period to determine the approximate cost. This method entails a full consideration of markups, markup cancellations, markdowns, and markdown cancellations.

6 Define the accounting terms new to this chapter.

Glossary

Average cost method (p. 571) A method of inventory costing using the average cost of units of an item available for sale during the period to arrive at cost of the ending inventory

First in, first out (FIFO) method (p. 572) A method of inventory costing that assumes the oldest merchandise is sold first

Gross profit method (p. 577) A method of estimating inventory cost based on the assumption that the rate of gross profit on sales and the ratio of cost of goods sold to net sales are relatively constant from period to period

Last in, first out (LIFO) method (p. 572) A method of inventory costing that assumes that the most recently purchased merchandise is sold first

Lower of cost or market rule (p. 575) The principle by which inventory is reported at either its original cost or its replacement cost, whichever is lower

Markdown (p. 579) Price reduction below the original markon

Market price (p. 575) The price the business would pay to buy an item of inventory through usual channels in usual quantities

Markon (p. 578) The difference between the cost and the initial retail price of merchandise

Markup (p. 579) A price increase above the original markon

Periodic inventory (p. 570) Inventory based on a periodic count of goods on hand

Perpetual inventory (p. 570) Inventory based on a running total of number of units

Physical inventory (p. 570) An actual count of the number of units of each type of good on hand

Replacement cost (p. 575) See Market price

Retail method (p. 578) A method of estimating inventory cost by applying the ratio of cost to selling price in the current accounting period to the retail price of the inventory

Specific identification method (p.571) A method of inventory costing based on the actual cost of each item of merchandise

Weighted average method (p. 572) See Average cost method

Comprehensive **Self Review**

1. Suggest two situations in which it might be desirable (or necessary) to estimate inventories without a physical count.
2. How do the gross profit method and the retail method used to estimate inventory differ, if at all?
3. What is the formula for the cost ratio used in the retail method of estimating inventory?
4. How often should a physical inventory be taken?
5. Under what circumstances would it be logical to use specific identification in determining the ending inventory?
6. Name four commonly used methods or assumptions for determining the cost of an inventory.

(Answers to Comprehensive Self Review are on page 593.)

 Multiple choice questions are provided on the text Web site at www.mhhe.com/price12e

Quiz17

Discussion Questions

1. What accounting principle or constraint underlies the lower of cost or market rule for inventory valuation?
2. Suggest some specific controls that management must provide over inventory in a business that sells diamonds.
3. Suggest two situations where it may be necessary or desirable to estimate the inventory without a physical count.
4. Explain the retail method of inventory estimation.
5. A company uses the *LIFO* inventory method to determine cost. One of the managers complains that this is improper. He states: "We always sell our oldest products first. So we should be using *first in, first out* inventory costing." What would you say in response to his comment?

6. In a period of rising prices, is the *LIFO* method or the *FIFO* method likely to yield the larger inventory cost?

7. Is the value of inventory likely to be lower if the cost or market rule is applied on an item-by-item basis, on a group basis, or to the inventory as a whole?

8. Explain how the lower of cost or market method is applied on a group basis.

9. What is meant by the term *market* as it is used in the lower of cost or market rule?

10. What is meant by the *first in, first out* assumption?

11. Explain briefly the average cost method.

12. Under what circumstances is the specific identification method for determining cost of inventory items logical?

13. Why is a perpetual inventory easier to maintain today than it would have been 50 years ago?

14. Does the maintenance of a perpetual inventory eliminate the need for taking physical inventory? Explain.

15. What impact does the ending inventory have on net income for the period covered by the financial statements?

APPLICATIONS

Exercises

Exercise 17.1

Objective 1

▶ **Using the various costing methods of inventory valuation.**

Information about Carter Company's inventory of one item follows. Compute the cost of the ending inventory under (1) the average cost method (round unit cost to nearest cent), (2) the FIFO method, and (3) the LIFO method.

Explanation	Number of Units	Unit Cost
Beginning inventory, January 1	90	$315
Purchases:		
April	110	320
August	120	325
October	95	327
Ending inventory, December 31	90	

Exercise 17.2

Objective 3

▶ **Using the lower of cost or market method.**

The following information concerns four items that Chris Cobb Clothiers has in its ending inventory on December 31. Two of these items are in the accessories department, and two are in the men's jackets department.

	Quantity	Unit Cost	Market Value
Accessories			
Item 620	120	$19	$22
Item 621	75	45	42
Men's jackets			
Item 726	50	85	92
Item 727	65	36	35

1. What is the valuation of ending inventory if the firm uses the lower of cost or market method and applies it on an item-by-item basis?

2. If the company applies the lower of cost or market method on the basis of total cost or total market, what is the value of ending inventory?

3. If the company elects to apply the lower of cost or market method to inventory groups, what is the value of the ending inventory?

Determining the effect on income of different costing assumptions.

◀ **Exercise 17.3**
  Objective 2

Given the choice between average cost, FIFO, and LIFO, which method will give the lowest net income and which will give the highest net income in a period of rising prices?

Estimating inventory cost under the gross profit method.

◀ **Exercise 17.4**
  Objective 4

Use the following data to compute the estimated inventory cost for Zebco Company under the gross profit method.

Average gross profit rate: 35% of sales

Inventory on January 1 (at cost): $110,000

Purchases from January 1 to date of inventory estimate: $720,000

Net sales for period: $1,000,000

Estimating inventory cost under the retail method.

◀ **Exercise 17.5**
  Objective 5

Based on the following data, compute the estimated cost of the ending inventory at Gray Goose Company. Use the retail method.

	Cost	Retail
Beginning inventory	$105,000	$171,500
Purchases	160,000	253,500
Freight in	3,000	
Sales		251,000

PROBLEMS

Problem Set A

Computing inventory costs under different valuation methods.

◀ **Problem 17.1A**
  Objective 1

The following data concerns inventory and purchases at New Horizons Company.

Inventory, January 1	90 units at $102
Purchases:	
January 6	60 units at $101
January 15	45 units at $101
January 22	35 units at $95
Inventory, January 31	88 units

INSTRUCTIONS

Determine the cost of the ending inventory on July 31 under each of the following methods: (a) average cost method; (b) first in, first out (FIFO) method; and (c) last in, first out (LIFO) method. When using the average cost method, compute the unit cost to two decimal places.

Analyze: Which inventory valuation method resulted in the highest dollar amount for ending inventory?

Problem 17.2A ▶
Objectives 1, 3
eXcel

Computing inventory costs under different valuation methods and applying the lower of cost or market rule.

The following data pertains to Smart Investment Accounting software packages in the inventory of Computer Program Smart Outlets.

Inventory, January 1	170 units at $106
Purchases:	
May 10	110 units at $104
August 18	180 units at $103.50
October 1	170 units at $104.25
Inventory, December 31	175 units

INSTRUCTIONS

1. Determine the cost of the inventory on December 31 and the cost of goods sold for the year ending on that date under each of the following valuation methods: (a) FIFO, (b) LIFO, and (c) average cost. When using the average cost method, compute the unit cost to the nearest cent.

2. Assume that the replacement cost of each unit on December 31 is $105.25. Using the lower of cost or market rule, find the inventory amount under each of the methods given in instruction 1.

Analyze: What is the difference between the cost and market value of the inventory using the LIFO method?

Problem 17.3A ▶
Objective 3
eXcel

Applying the lower of cost or market rule by different methods.

This data is for selected inventory items at Contemporary Electronics Supply.

	Quantity	Unit Cost	Market Value
Printer Cartridges			
Item 119	50	$ 15.00	$ 15.50
Item 120	60	18.20	17.90
Item 121	90	22.00	22.50
Fax Machines			
Item 210	15	85.00	88.00
Item 211	10	190.00	185.00
Item 212	9	220.00	215.00

INSTRUCTIONS

Determine the amount to be reported as the inventory valuation at cost or market, whichever is lower, under each of these methods.

1. Lower of cost or market for each item separately.

2. Lower of total cost or total market.

3. Lower of total cost or total market by group.

Analyze: Which valuation method will yield the highest net income?

Estimating inventory by the gross profit method.

◀ **Problem 17.4A**
Objective 4

Over the past several years, Mountain Springs Company has had an average gross profit of 30 percent. At the end of 2010, the income statement of the company included the following information.

Sales		$2,225,000
Cost of Goods		
Inventory, January 1, 2010	$ 156,000	
Purchases	1,560,680	
Total Merchandise Available for Sale	1,716,680	
Less Inventory, December 31, 2010	182,500	
Cost of Goods Sold		1,534,180
Gross Profit on Sales		$ 690,820

Investigation revealed that employees of the company had not taken an actual physical count of the inventory on December 31. Instead, they had merely estimated the inventory.

INSTRUCTIONS

Using the gross profit method of inventory estimation, verify the reasonableness (or lack of reasonableness) of the ending inventory shown on the income statement.

Analyze: If a physical inventory count on December 31, 2010, revealed an ending inventory of $180,750, calculate the gross profit percentage to the nearest one-tenth of 1 percent.

Estimating inventory by the retail method.

◀ **Problem 17.5A**
Objective 5

The August 1 inventory of Hazlenut Company had a cost of $80,000 and a retail value of $115,000. During August, merchandise was purchased for $95,000 and marked to sell for $142,000. August sales totaled $126,000.

INSTRUCTIONS

1. Compute the retail value of the ending inventory as of August 31.
2. Compute the approximate cost of the ending inventory.
3. Compute the cost of goods sold during August.

Analyze: What is the amount of estimated gross profit on sales for the month ending August 31?

Applying the correct method of evaluating inventory.

◀ **Problem 17.6A**
Objectives 1, 2
e**X**cel

Anderson Sailing Company sells boats as a supplement to its boat storage operations. Data for its boat sales for August 2010 are given below. The beginning inventory on August 1 was composed of the following items:

	Cost	Retail
28′ Starfish	$35,000	$47,000
30′ Perch	55,000	75,000
24′ Sea King	21,000	25,000
30′ Holiday	41,000	50,000
20′ Lake King	23,000	29,500

INSTRUCTIONS

Sales during the month were the 30′ Holiday and the 20′ Lake King, sold at the retail values shown on August 1.

1. What is the best method of valuing the ending inventory?

2. Determine the value of Anderson Sailing Company's ending inventory of items that were brought over from the beginning inventory using this method. Assume that the company's retail values had not changed.

3. Determine the cost of goods sold during August.

Analyze: What is the estimated gross profit on sales for August?

Problem Set B

Problem 17.1B

Objective 1

▶ **Computing inventory costs under different valuation methods.**

The following data relates to the inventory and purchases of item 125 for City Wholesale Company during May.

Inventory, May 1	250 units at $20.10
Purchases:	
May 10	180 units at $20.08
May 19	130 units at $20.09
May 25	150 units at $20.05
Inventory, May 31	222 units

INSTRUCTIONS

Determine the cost of the ending inventory on May 31 under each of the following methods: (a) average cost method; (b) first in, first out (FIFO) method; and, (c) last in, first out (LIFO) method. When using the average cost method, compute the unit cost to two decimal places.

Analyze: Which inventory amount will result in the highest income for the period?

Problem 17.2B

Objectives 1, 3

▶ **Computing inventory costs under different valuation methods and applying the lower of cost or market rule.**

The following data pertain to Model M two-wheeled trailers in the inventory of Travelers Equipment Company during the year 2010.

Inventory, January 1	20 units at $2,600
Purchases:	
February 27	18 units at $2,450
August 16	22 units at $2,425
November 19	16 units at $2,395
Inventory, December 31	16 units

INSTRUCTIONS

1. Determine the cost of the inventory on December 31 and the cost of goods sold for the year ending on that date under each of the following valuation methods: (a) FIFO, (b) LIFO, and (c) average cost. When using the average cost method, compute the unit cost to the nearest cent.

2. Assume that the replacement cost of each unit on December 31 is $2,410. Using the lower of cost or market rule, find the inventory amount under each of the methods given in instruction 1.

Analyze: Using the lower of cost or market rule, which inventory amount will result in the highest net income for the period?

Applying the lower of cost or market rule by different methods.

The following data concerns inventory at Leisure Products, Inc.

◀ Problem 17.3B
Objective 3

	Quantity	Unit Cost	Market Value
Motor Bike Department			
Model 705	14	$ 9,600	$ 9,550
Model 766	20	10,500	11,400
Model 815	10	12,500	12,750
Boat Department			
Model BX12	6	5,180	5,416
Model BX14	8	7,200	6,950
Model BX16	6	5,075	5,350

INSTRUCTIONS

Determine the amount that the company should report as the inventory valuation at cost or market, whichever is lower. Use each of the following three valuation methods:

1. Lower of cost or market for each item separately.
2. Lower of total cost or total market.
3. Lower of total cost or total market by group.

Analyze: Which valuation method will yield the highest net income?

Estimating inventory by the gross profit method.

Over the last two years, McGowan Company has averaged 35 percent gross profit. At the end of 2010, the auditor found the following data in the records of the company.

◀ Problem 17.4B
Objective 4

Sales		$6,100,000
Cost of goods sold:		
Inventory, January 1, 2010	$ 410,000	
Purchases	4,160,000	
Total merchandise available for sale	4,570,000	
Less inventory, December 31, 2010	596,000	
Cost of goods sold		3,974,000
Gross profit on sales		$2,126,000

Inquiry by the auditor revealed that employees of McGowan Company had estimated the inventory on December 31, 2010, instead of taking a complete physical count.

INSTRUCTIONS

Using the gross profit method of inventory estimation, verify the reasonableness (or lack of reasonableness) of the inventory estimate made by the company's employees.

Analyze: If a physical inventory count on December 31, 2010, revealed an ending inventory of $510,000, calculate the gross profit percentage.

Estimating inventory by the retail method.

The April 1 inventory of Alexis Stores had a cost of $918,000 and a retail value of $1,340,000. During April, merchandise was purchased for $1,069,000 and marked to sell for $1,676,000. Freight In was $18,000. April sales totaled $2,150,000.

◀ Problem 17.5B
Objective 5

INSTRUCTIONS

1. Compute the retail value of the ending inventory as of April 30.
2. Compute the approximate cost of the ending inventory.
3. Compute the cost of goods sold during April.

Analyze: What is the gross profit on sales for the period ending April 30?

Problem 17.6B ▶ **Using the correct inventory valuation method.**

Objectives 1, 2   Buxton Realty Group had two completed unsold buildings on hand on January 1, 2010.

> Unit 06-92: Cost, $790,000; retail price, $964,000
> Unit 06-94: Cost, $873,000; retail price, $1,008,000

During the period January 1 through March 31, the company completed the following construction jobs.

	Cost	Sales Price
Unit 06-95	$1,900,000	$2,290,000
Unit 07-01	919,000	1,178,000
Unit 07-03	836,000	1,115,000
Unit 07-05	1,120,000	1,450,500

All the units except 06-92 and 07-05 were sold in the quarter ending March 31.

INSTRUCTIONS

1. Determine the appropriate costing method for inventory in this construction business.
2. What value should be reported in the balance sheet for the company for the unsold units on March 31? Assume that it is firmly believed that the two houses will be sold for the retail price shown.
3. Determine the cost of goods sold in the first quarter, assuming that all houses sold were sold for the retail prices listed.

Analyze: What is gross profit on sales for the quarter ending March 31?

Critical Thinking Problem 17.1

Inventory Estimation

One of Powell Company's retail outlets was destroyed by fire on March 18. All merchandise was burned. The company has fire insurance on its merchandise inventory. It will therefore file a claim for recovery of cost of the lost inventory. Clearly, a physical inventory cannot be taken because the inventory has been destroyed. The branch's records were kept by the home office, and you have been asked to examine the records to determine an estimate of the cost of the lost merchandise. As of March 18, the firm's records disclosed the following data about the beginning inventory for the year, the merchandise purchases made during the period, and total sales during the period.

	Actual Cost	Retail Sales Price
Beginning inventory, January 1	$ 75,000	$108,000
Merchandise purchases, January 1–March 18	230,000	319,000
Freight on purchases	7,800	
Total sales, January 1–March 18		330,000

INSTRUCTIONS

Determine the approximate cost of the inventory destroyed on March 18.

Analyze: Based on the cost you have computed for merchandise inventory, calculate the cost of goods sold for the period.

Critical Thinking Problem 17.2

Inventory Estimation

Nelson Computer Supply Company has just been destroyed by fire. Fortunately, however, the computerized accounting records had been "backed up" and were in a remote computer location so that the records were not destroyed. The company does not use the retail method of accounting, so although beginning inventory at cost, purchases at cost, purchases returns and allowances, freight in, sales, sales returns and allowances, and other accounting information is available, the retail method of estimating inventory destroyed cannot be used.

What suggestion can you give for determining the estimated cost of the inventory destroyed? What information is needed, and where would this information be found?

BUSINESS CONNECTIONS

Inventory Methods

Managerial FOCUS

1. What are two specific managerial reasons for using the LIFO method of inventory valuation during a period of rising prices?

2. In order to achieve better control over its investment in inventory, the management of a retail store wishes to get an estimate of the cost of inventory at the close of business each week. Outline a procedure to obtain this estimate without actually taking a physical count.

3. Explain briefly how computers and other electronic devices, such as scanners, have made perpetual inventories more practical.

4. The purchasing manager of a retail store has suggested that the company should maintain a perpetual inventory. The controller opposes this suggestion. In your opinion, on what basis does the controller probably oppose the idea?

5. In what special situations are inventory estimation procedures extremely useful?

6. The manager of a retail store has become concerned about the time taken to count the merchandise on hand each quarter. She argues that too much time is spent on this activity with a resulting high cost of labor. She suggests that the company need not take a physical inventory at all but could rely on the retail inventory estimation procedure to arrive at the cost of the inventory. Respond to this argument.

Missing Inventory

Ethical DILEMMA

Shelia has a baby clothing shop called Good to Grow. Shelia has worked in her shop for several months. Her sales have doubled each month. Shelia has decided to hire Nancy, a sales associate, since she needs to be away from the shop on a regular basis. After several months, Shelia noticed that her purchases increased but sales did not go up in the same proportion and inventory is low. She is finding her net income is lower than previous months. State the cause of her decreased income and determine the actions that should be taken.

Inventory Costs

STREETWISE:
Questions from the
REAL WORLD

Refer to the *2006 Annual Report* of The Home Depot, Inc., in Appendix A.

1. In the Notes to Consolidated Financial Statements, review Note 1, Summary of Significant Accounting Policies. What method is used to value the majority of the company's merchandise inventories?

2. Find the Consolidated Balance Sheets for The Home Depot, Inc., in Appendix A. What is the value of merchandise inventories at January 28, 2007? At January 29, 2006? By what percentage has this figure increased?

Balance Sheet

The following excerpt was taken from the American Eagle Outfitters, Inc., *2006 Annual Report.*

Consolidated Balance Sheets

(Dollars in thousands)	Feb. 3, 2007	Jan. 28, 2006
Assets		
Current Assets:		
Cash and cash equivalents	$ 59,737	$ 130,529
Short-term investments	767,376	620,989
Merchandise inventory	263,644	210,739
Other current assets	107,497	114,524
Total Current Assets	$1,198,254	$1,076,781

Analyze:

1. By what amount has merchandise inventory increased from January 28, 2006, to February 3, 2007?
2. What percentage of current assets is attributable to inventories at February 3, 2007?

Analyze Online: Locate the American Eagle Outfitters, Inc., Web site (www.ae.com), and click on the *About AE* link, then click on *AE Investment Info.*

3. Find the most recent annual report. What method is used to assign cost to the merchandise inventory? (Hint: See the Notes to Consolidated Financial Statements.)
4. What is the stated value of the most recent year's merchandise inventory?

Inventory Levels

Extending THE THOUGHT

Tykes 'N Toys, a retail toy store, records peak sales in December. The store operates on a fiscal period ending December 31. As the fourth quarter begins, the store manager is worried that the store is carrying too much merchandise. Discuss the implications that a business faces if inventories are carried at excess levels. What inventory-related costs might the company face? What effects might this have on net profits for the business year?

List of Questions

Business COMMUNICATION

You are considering purchasing a retail pet supply store. The inventory is valued at $225,000. Since the inventory makes up 40 percent of the cost of the business, you want to verify that the merchandise is valued properly. Make a list of questions that you plan to ask the current accountant of the pet store about the methods used for inventory valuation. What inventory records would you review?

Inventory Controls

TEAMWORK

Inventory control measures vary depending on the type of product to be sold. As a team, choose a type of product to be sold. Develop inventory control measures for your particular product. Determine control measures that would be the same for each business and one that would be unique for the chosen product.

Inventory Costing Methods

Internet CONNECTION

A corporation must disclose in the annual report how inventory is valued and costed. Go to the Balance Sheet of five retail stores, e.g., Home Depot, American Outfitter (ae.com), Krugers, or others. Make a comparison chart showing the inventory dollars listed in the balance sheet for the current and previous years. Go to the notes included in the annual report. The notes are listed in the same order as the accounts in the balance sheet. Find the note about inventory. List the valuation and costing method for each corporation. Is the inventory the same for each type of corporation? Has the inventory decreased, remained the same, or increased? Is there a dollar difference between the LIFO and FIFO methods?

Answers to **Self Reviews**

Answers to Section 1 Self Review

1. LIFO (or FIFO) may be used regardless of actual physical flow of merchandise.

2. LIFO pricing will produce the highest cost of goods sold and the lowest net income in a period of rising prices.

3. The principle of consistency requires that the same method of pricing inventory should be used each year.

4. FIFO assumes that merchandise is sold in the order it is received. In this way, the oldest costs identified with merchandise are charged to cost of goods sold.

5. LIFO stands for last in, first out. This method computes the cost of the inventory on hand as though the last merchandise received is the first to be sold. This is done so that the most current costs are matched with revenue.

6. You will want to know current and future economic outlook for the industry—how the cost of merchandise and the demands for products are likely to change.

Answers to Section 2 Self Review

1. The conservatism constraint is the primary underlying concept that supports the lower of cost or market rule.

2. This means the lower amount of (a) the net cost of merchandise, including freight in, or (b) the amount that it would cost to replace the merchandise today if it were bought in normal quantities and under normal operating conditions.

3. It may be applied: (a) item by item, (b) by groups of items, or (c) by total cost and total market for the entire inventory. Application on an item-by-item basis will yield the lowest inventory value.

4. **a.** The retail method does not require a physical count of inventory items.

5. The gross profit method would be used if the inventory has been destroyed by fire, theft, or other means. It may also be used to quickly estimate the cost of inventory on hand without taking a physical inventory when cost estimates are needed for managerial or operational purposes.

6. The retail method assumes that perpetual records are kept of the sales price of inventory items. The gross profit method does not require that the selling price of items on hand be known.

Answers to Comprehensive Self Review

1. The most obvious cases are when a fire or theft has occurred. Any other situation where the inventory has been physically removed or when a quick estimate is needed may call for an estimate.

2. The retail method assumes that records have been kept of all inventory transactions at sales price (including price adjustments of merchandise), as well as cost, so that the inventory value at sales price of the merchandise is always known and readily convertible to a cost basis. The gross profit method is used when retail price of inventory is unknown and has to be computed.

3. Cost ratio = Cost of merchandise available for sale/Retail sales price of merchandise available for sale.

4. Generally, inventory is taken once a year. If there is a history of thefts, breakage, overstocking or understocking, or other operational problems, it may be necessary to make physical counts more often.

5. When there are relatively few items and each has a high cost.

6. Specific identification, average costing, FIFO, and LIFO.

Property, Plant, and Equipment

Chapter 18

LEARNING OBJECTIVES

1. Determine the amount to record as an asset's cost.   LP18
2. Compute and record depreciation of property, plant, and equipment by commonly used methods.
3. Apply the Modified Accelerated Cost Recovery System (MACRS) for federal income tax purposes.
4. Record sales of plant and equipment.
5. Record asset trade-ins using financial accounting rules and income tax requirements.
6. Compute and record depletion of natural resources.
7. Recognize asset impairment and understand the general concepts of accounting for impairment.
8. Compute and record amortization and impairment of intangible assets.
9. Define the accounting terms new to this chapter.

NEW TERMS

accelerated method of depreciation
amortization
brand name
capitalized costs
computer software
copyright
declining-balance method
depletion
double-declining-balance method
franchise
gain
goodwill
impairment
income tax method
intangible assets

loss
net book value
net salvage value
patent
real property
recoverability test
residual value
scrap value
sum-of-the-years'-digits method
tangible personal property
trade name
trademark
units-of-output method
units-of-production method

 www.cocacola.com

In the early 1800s, if you wanted an icy, cold Coke you had to head to your local soda fountain and sit at the counter and drink your Coke. It wasn't until 1899 that two attorneys from Tennessee paid The Coca-Cola Company $1 for the exclusive rights to bottle and sell Coca-Cola across the United States. By the late 1920s, there were 2,000 bottling plants in operation and bottle sales had exceeded sales at the soda fountain.

Coca-Cola operations now span the globe. Around the world, in more than 200 countries, Coca-Cola beverages are produced by local people with local resources. The company recently spent $500 million to acquire leading Russian juice maker Multon, further diversifying the product line and expanding distribution channels.

thinking critically

Why would The Coca-Cola Company invest such a substantial amount of money in a new market?

Acquisition and Depreciation

Setting up and maintaining a business often requires a large investment in property, plant, and equipment—assets often referred to as *fixed assets* or *capital assets.* In this section, two aspects of accounting for property, plant, and equipment are discussed:

- The costs of acquiring the assets.
- The transfer of the costs of these assets to expense through depreciation.

>>**1. OBJECTIVE**

Determine the amount to record as an asset's cost.

Video18.1

Property, Plant, and Equipment Classifications

As discussed in Chapter 12, *property, plant, and equipment* includes real property and tangible personal property purchased for use in the business and having a life of more than one year. **Real property** consists of land, land improvements (such as sidewalks and parking lots), buildings, and other structures attached to the land. **Tangible personal property** includes machinery, equipment, furniture, and fixtures that can be removed and used elsewhere.

   The property, plant, and equipment classification does not include assets purchased for investment reasons. For example, land purchased for investment purposes is classified as other assets or investments.

Acquisition of Property, Plant, and Equipment

An important issue in accounting for property, plant, and equipment is determining which costs should be capitalized. **Capitalized costs** are all costs recorded as part of the asset's cost.

COSTS OF EQUIPMENT AND OTHER TANGIBLE PERSONAL PROPERTY

The total cost of an asset can consist of several elements. Each element is debited to the account for that asset. The acquisition cost of an asset includes

- gross purchase price less discounts, including cash discounts for prompt payment;
- transportation costs;

- installation costs;
- costs of adjustments or modifications needed to prepare the asset for use.

On January 2, 2010, Hazlenut Company purchased store equipment for $18,000 and paid state and local sales taxes of $1,400. Transportation costs were $680. When the equipment arrived, extra features were installed at a cost of $800. The *Store Equipment* account is debited for $10,440.

Purchase price	$18,000
Sales taxes	1,400
Transportation costs	680
Modification and installation costs	800
Total acquisition cost of machine	$20,880

COST OF LAND AND BUILDING

The cost of land includes its purchase price, legal costs in connection with the acquisition, abstracts, title insurance, recording fees, and any other costs paid by the purchaser that are related to the acquisition.

The acquisition cost of land purchased for a building site should include the net costs (less salvage) of removing unwanted buildings and grading and draining the land. Remember that land is not depreciated.

Land improvements include the cost of installing permanent walks or roadways, curbing, gutters, and drainage facilities. These costs are debited to the asset account *Land Improvements.* Land improvements are depreciated.

If land and a building are purchased together for a single price, the purchase price is allocated between the *Land* and *Building* accounts. The amount allocated to the building is depreciated. The amount allocated to land is not depreciated.

ASSETS CONSTRUCTED BY OR FOR THE BUSINESS

When a building or other property, plant, and equipment is constructed and used by the business, the capitalized costs include all costs of labor, materials, permits and fees, insurance, measurable direct overhead, and other reasonable and necessary costs of construction. Interest costs incurred on borrowed funds during the construction period are capitalized as part of the asset.

Depreciation of Property, Plant, and Equipment

Buildings, machinery, equipment, furniture, and fixtures are depreciated because they have a limited life and will get used up or deteriorate over time. Depreciation is the allocation of the cost of the asset over the asset's useful life. Depreciation does not refer to a decrease in the market value of the asset.

RECORDING DEPRECIATION

Assets that are used for more than one year are capitalized. Asset account names are descriptive, for example, *Office Equipment, Store Equipment, Vehicles,* or *Buildings.* At the end of each accounting period, depreciation for the period is debited to *Depreciation Expense* and credited to a contra asset account, *Accumulated Depreciation. Accumulated Depreciation* shows all depreciation that has been taken during the asset's life.

For example, a business purchased a building for $500,000 on January 2, 2010. At the end of the first year, annual depreciation expense of $12,500 was entered on the worksheet as an adjustment. It was recorded as an adjusting entry in the general journal as follows.

important!

Tangible Personal Property
The term "personal" means that the property has a physical substance and is something other than real estate. Personal property is owned by the business, not by the individual owners.

ABOUT
ACCOUNTING

Fixed Assets
According to Asset Advisors, a Florida consulting firm, fixed assets represent 35 to 50 percent of the typical Fortune 500 company's assets.

recall

Land
Land is not depreciated. Land has an indefinite life. Land does not deteriorate or get used up.

>>2. OBJECTIVE
Compute and record depreciation of property, plant, and equipment by commonly used methods.

	Dec.	31	Depreciation Expense—Buildings		12 50 0 00		
11					12 50 0 00		11
12			Accumulated Depreciation—Buildings			12 50 0 00	12
13			To record depreciation for the year				13

LP18

The balance sheet shows a long-term asset's cost minus its accumulated depreciation. The difference is its book value, also known as its **net book value.** Book value is rarely the same as fair market value, which is the asset's price on the open market. After two years of depreciation, the balance sheet presentation for the building is as follows:

Property, Plant, and Equipment

Building	$500,000.00
Less Accumulated Depreciation	25,000.00
	$475,000.00

> In fiscal 2006, Coca-Cola recorded *Depreciation and Amortization Expense* of $938 million. On December 31, 2006, the cost of its property, plant, and equipment was shown in the balance sheet at a net book value of $6.903 billion.

Depreciation information shown on the financial statements or in notes accompanying the financial statements includes

- depreciation expense for the period;
- balances in the depreciable asset accounts, classified according to their nature or their function;
- accumulated depreciation;
- description of the method(s) used to compute depreciation.

DEPRECIATION METHODS

Several methods are used to compute depreciation. Some of them use salvage value in the calculation. Under these methods, assets are not depreciated below salvage value. *Salvage value,* **residual value,** or **scrap value** is an estimate of the amount that could be obtained from an asset's sale or disposition at the end of its useful life. The **net salvage value** is the salvage value of the asset less any costs to remove or sell it.

Straight-Line Method The straight-line method introduced in Chapter 5 is the most widely used method of computing depreciation expense for financial statement purposes. Under the straight-line method, an equal amount of depreciation is recorded for each period over the useful life of the asset. Figure 18.1 shows straight-line depreciation of $432 per year.

Determining Annual Depreciation

The asset cost, the estimated salvage value, and the estimated useful life are needed in order to determine the annual depreciation.

FIGURE 18.1

Straight-Line Depreciation

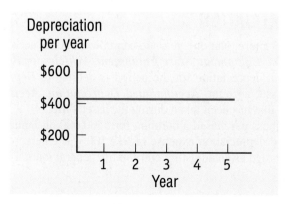

The formula for straight-line depreciation is as follows:

$$\text{Depreciation} = \frac{\text{Cost} - \text{Salvage Value}}{\text{Estimated Useful Life}}$$

On January 2, 2010, Hazlenut Company purchased office equipment for $2,400. The equipment has an estimated useful life of five years, with a net salvage value of $240. Using the straight-line method, the annual depreciation is $432 [($2,400 − $240)/5]. **Depreciation Expense—Office Equipment** will be debited for $432 and **Accumulated Depreciation— Office Equipment** will be credited for $432 each year.

When an asset is acquired during the year, depreciation is typically calculated to the nearest month. If the asset is acquired during the first 15 days of the month, depreciation is taken for the full month. If the asset is acquired after the 15th, depreciation starts in the following month. Suppose that Hazlenut Company purchased the office equipment on September 5. The monthly depreciation is $36 ($432 ÷ 12). Depreciation for the first year is $144 (4 months × $36). The journal entry is as follows:

11	Dec.	31	Depreciation Expense—Office Equip.	1 4 4 00		11
12			Accumulated Depreciation—Office Equip.		1 4 4 00	12
13			To record depreciation for four			13
14			months on equipment acquired			14
15			September 5			15

Declining-Balance Method Under the **declining-balance method** of depreciation, the book value of an asset at the beginning of the year is multiplied by a percentage to determine depreciation for the year. The declining-balance method is an **accelerated method of depreciation,** which allocates greater amounts of depreciation to an asset's early years of useful life. The declining-balance computation ignores salvage value until the year in which the book value is reduced to estimated salvage value. Figure 18.2 illustrates the declining-balance method in graphical form.

Another method often used is the **double-declining-balance method (DDB).** DDB uses a rate equal to twice the straight-line rate and applies that rate to the book value of the asset at the beginning of the year. Follow these steps to calculate double-declining-balance depreciation on the office equipment for which straight-line depreciation was illustrated above.

Step 1. *Calculate the straight-line rate.*

$$\frac{100 \text{ Percent}}{\text{Useful Life}} = \frac{100 \text{ Percent}}{5 \text{ Years}} = 20 \text{ Percent}$$

Step 2. *Calculate the double-declining rate.* The double-declining rate is the straight-line rate multiplied by 2, or 40 percent (20 percent × 2).

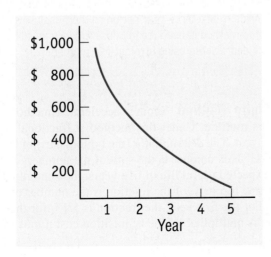

FIGURE 18.2

Declining-Balance Depreciation

TABLE 18.1

Depreciation Under Double-Declining-Balance Method

Year	Beginning Book Value	Rate, %	Depreciation for Year	Depreciation to Date
1	$2,400.00	40	$960.00	$ 960.00
2	1,440.00	40	576.00	1,536.00
3	864.00	40	345.60	1,881.60
4	518.40	40	207.36	2,088.96
5	311.04	Limited	71.04	2,160.00

Book value at the end of five years = $240.00 ($2,400.00 − $2,160.00)

Step 3. *Compute depreciation for the period by multiplying the book value by the double-declining rate.* Repeat this step each year during the asset's useful life until the year in which the net book value would be less than salvage value.

Step 4. In the final year of depreciation, take only the amount of depreciation that will reduce the asset's net book value to its salvage value.

Here is how the double-declining-balance method would be applied to the asset purchased by Hazlenut Company.

▪ In the first year, the depreciation is $960 ($2,400 × 40%). *Note that salvage value is ignored in this computation.*

▪ At the start of the second year, the book value is $1,440 ($2,400 − $960). Depreciation for the second year is $576 ($1,440 × 40%). Note that the salvage value is again ignored in the computation.

▪ Similar computations are made in the third and fourth years and result in depreciation of $345.60 and $207.36 for the two years, respectively, as shown in Table 18.1. That table shows that the cumulative depreciation at the end of four years is $2,088.96. As a result, at the start of the fifth year, the asset's net book value is $311.04 ($2,400 cost − $2,088.96 depreciation taken = $311.04) This is only $71.04 greater than the estimated salvage ($311.04 − $240.00 = $71.04).

▪ *Remember that an asset should not be depreciated to a point that the net book value is less than the salvage value.* As a result, the depreciation for the fifth year is limited to $71.04 (unless there has been a change in the salvage value). Table 18.1 therefore shows depreciation for the fifth year is only $71.04. As a result, at the end of the fifth year the accumulated depreciation will be $2,160 and the net book value at the end of the fifth year will be $240 ($2,400 cost − $2,160 accumulated depreciation), an amount equal to estimated salvage value.

> Hasbro, the maker of games, toys, and entertainment products, depreciates tools, dies, and molds over a three-year period or their useful lives, whichever is less. An accelerated method is used. Land improvements, buildings, equipment, and machinery are depreciated using straight-line methods.

Sum-of-the-Years'-Digits Method Another accelerated method of depreciation is the **sum-of-the-years'-digits method.** Under this method, a fractional part of the asset cost is charged to expense each year. The denominator (the bottom part) of the fraction is always the "sum of the years' digits." This number is the sum of the numbers in the asset's useful life. For a machine with an expected useful life of five years, the denominator is 15 (1 + 2 + 3 + 4 + 5). The numerator (the top part) of the fraction is the number of years remaining in the useful life of the asset. For the first year, the fraction is 5/15, for the second year it is 4/15, and so on. This fraction is multiplied by the acquisition cost minus the net salvage value of the asset.

TABLE 18.2

Comparison of Depreciation Methods

	Sum-of-the-Years'-Digits Method			Other Methods	
Year	Fraction	Cost Minus Salvage	Depreciation for Year	Declining-Balance	Straight-Line
1	5/15	$2,160.00	$ 720.00	$ 960.00	$ 432.00
2	4/15	2,160.00	576.00	576.00	432.00
3	3/15	2,160.00	432.00	345.60	432.00
4	2/15	2,160.00	288.00	207.36	432.00
5	1/15	2,160.00	144.00	71.04	432.00
Total depreciation, 5 years			$2,160.00	$2,160.00	$2,160.00

The first four columns of Table 18.2 show the sum-of-the-years'-digits method for the office equipment purchased by Hazlenut Company. Depreciation for the first year of the asset's life is $720 ($2,160 × 5/15) and for the second year of life depreciation is $576 ($2,160 × 4/15). Table 18.2 compares this method with the other two commonly used methods.

Suppose that the equipment was purchased on September 5, 2010. Depreciation for the four months in 2010 would be a proportionate part of the depreciation for the first year of the asset's life, or $240 ($2,160 × 5/15 × 4/12).

For 2011, depreciation consists of the total of two parts: the depreciation for the remaining eight months of the first year (12 months) of life and depreciation for four months of the second year of life.

$2,160 × 8/12 (8 months) × 5/15 (1st year fraction)	$480
$2,160 × 4/12 (4 months) × 4/15 (2nd year fraction)	192
Depreciation for 2011	$672

Comparison of Depreciation Methods When choosing a depreciation method, much consideration is given to the matching principle. The goal is to match the cost of the asset to the periods when the asset provides benefits to the business. Review Table 18.2, which compares the three widely used methods. Notice that during the early years, the sum-of-the-years'-digits and declining-balance methods result in a larger depreciation expense than the straight-line method.

Accountants who favor the straight-line method believe that the asset provides equal benefits over its useful life. Many, however, suggest that accelerated depreciation is more logical than straight-line depreciation. They argue that typically assets are more productive in the early years of their lives so greater benefit is gained from their use in those years. Additionally, repair costs and other maintenance costs are almost invariably higher when an asset gets older. The facts may suggest that straight-line depreciation results in a lower total cost per unit in the early years than in later years. Under the double-declining-balance and the sum-of-years'-digits methods, the higher depreciation costs in early years are partially offset by lower operating costs, so that there is a more nearly uniform total cost per unit of use.

Units-of-Output Method Under the straight-line and accelerated methods, depreciation is computed as a function of time. For some assets, depreciation is more directly related to the units of work produced. The **units-of-output method,** also known as the **units-of-production method,** calculates depreciation at the same rate for each unit produced. The unit of production may be measured in terms of the

- physical quantities of production,
- number of hours the asset is used,
- other measures.

This method is often used to depreciate the cost of cars, trucks, and other motor vehicles, using miles as a measure of production.

Suppose that a business purchased a delivery truck for $64,000 in February 2010. It is expected to be driven for 112,000 miles before being traded in and its expected salvage value at that time is $8,000. During 2010, the truck was driven 17,400 miles.

Follow these steps to calculate depreciation under the units-of-production method.

Step 1. *Determine the depreciation per unit (per mile).* Divide the depreciable cost (the cost, minus estimated net salvage value) by the total miles expected to be driven during the truck's life.

$$\frac{\$64,000 - \$8,000}{112,000 \text{ miles}} = 50 \text{ cents for each mile driven}$$

Step 2. *Compute depreciation.* Multiply the number of units produced (miles driven) by the rate for each unit.

$$17,400 \text{ miles} \times \$.50 \text{ per mile} = \$8,700$$

In its first year of operation, the truck would have depreciation expense of $8,700.

>>3. OBJECTIVE

Apply the Modified Accelerated Cost Recovery System (MACRS) for federal income tax purposes.

LP18

Federal Income Tax Requirements for "Cost Recovery" (Depreciation) of Property, Plant, and Equipment

The beginning accounting course focuses on financial accounting and reporting, so generally accepted accounting principles (GAAP) are of paramount importance. However, accountants commonly are involved in maintaining tax records and in preparing federal and state income tax returns. The treatments of many items of revenue and expense for income tax purposes differ greatly from those required under generally accepted accounting principles. It is therefore important that the accountant have a basic understanding of some of the major income tax rules that differ from financial accounting.

In addition, some small businesses that do not have audits by certified public accountants may adopt some tax requirements as part of their financial accounting in order to avoid confusion and duplication of work. One of those important differences is in the area of depreciation.

Federal income tax rules basically replace the depreciation rules of generally accepted accounting principles with the Modified Accelerated Cost Recovery System (MACRS), which applies to all assets purchased after December 31, 1986. (If appropriate, however, the taxpayer can use the units-of-production depreciation method instead of MACRS.)

MACRS was designed to encourage taxpayers to invest in business property and to simplify depreciation computations. Under MACRS, the portion of asset costs charged to expense is higher in the early years of an asset's life and lower in the later years. In that sense, it is akin to accelerated depreciation methods. This results in lower taxable income and tax savings in the early years with higher taxable income and taxes in later years.

Under MACRS, property is separated into defined classes. For tangible personal property, there are six classes of property. However, almost all personal property falls in three of those classes. Those three are

- 5-year class—automobiles, lightweight trucks, computers, and certain special-purpose property.
- 7-year class—office furniture and fixtures and most manufacturing equipment.
- 10-year class—special purpose property, such as equipment used in the manufacture of food and tobacco products.

Under MACRS, the recovery periods for real property are:

- residential rental buildings—27.5 years,
- nonresidential buildings (office buildings) placed in service after May 12, 1993—39 years,
- nonresidential buildings placed in service on or before May 12, 1993—31.5 years.

Each MACRS class has a table of percentages. To determine the cost recovery (depreciation) under MACRS, multiply the asset's cost by the MACRS percentage. Salvage value is ignored. The following table shows the MACRS cost recovery for a $20,000 five-year asset, using the percentages required each year. Almost all businesses have assets in this rate class.

Year	Percent	Original Cost	Cost Recovery
1	20.00%	$20,000	$ 4,000
2	32.00	20,000	6,400
3	19.20	20,000	3,840
4	11.52	20,000	2,304
5	11.52	20,000	2,304
6	5.76	20,000	1,152
Totals	100.00%		$20,000

Note that it takes six years to recover the entire cost of five-year properties. That is because MACRS uses the *half-year convention*. Regardless of purchase date, MACRS calculates depreciation for six months in the first year of the asset's life. The remaining six months of cost recovery is taken in the year after the end of the class life (in the sixth year for five-year property). (There are complex exceptions to the half-year convention.)

It is important that you know the basic concept of MACRS as demonstrated in the above example. It is also important to keep in mind that MACRS is not acceptable under GAAP.

important!

Different Depreciation Methods Used

Most businesses use straight-line depreciation when preparing financial statements and MACRS when preparing tax returns.

Section **1** Self Review

QUESTIONS

1. Name two methods of accelerated depreciation.

2. What account is debited and what account is credited in the journal entry to record depreciation for the year?

3. What is depreciation?

EXERCISES

4. Assuming a five-year life, a cost of $18,000, and an estimated net salvage value of $2,000, what would be the depreciation for the second year of the life of an asset if the double-declining-balance method is used?

5. An asset acquired on May 22, 2010, cost $24,000, has an estimated useful life of five years, and a net salvage value of $4,000. What is the amount of depreciation expense for 2010 if the straight-line method is used?

6. What is the numerator and what is the denominator to be used in computing depreciation for the third year of use of an asset with a life of seven years if the sum-of-years'-digits method is used?

ANALYSIS

7. Which method of depreciation, straight-line, or double-declining balance, will result in a higher net income during the first year the asset is in use? Why?

(Answers to Section 1 Self Review are on page 636.)

SECTION OBJECTIVES	TERMS TO LEARN
>> **4.** **Record sales of plant and equipment.** **WHY IT'S IMPORTANT** Businesses routinely sell or dispose of plant assets that are no longer useful to the business. >> **5.** **Record asset trade-ins using financial accounting rules and income tax requirements.** **WHY IT'S IMPORTANT** Both methods are important to businesses.	gain income tax method loss

Disposition of Assets

The disposition of assets involves removing the asset's cost and its accumulated depreciation from the firm's accounting records. This section discusses the accounting treatment for three asset disposal methods: scrapping, sale, and trade-in.

Method of Disposition

Most business assets are eventually disposed of. They are either scrapped because they are worn out and have no value, sold because they are no longer needed by the business, or traded in on the purchase of new assets.

When assets are disposed of, the business often incurs a gain or a loss. A **gain** is the disposition of an asset for more than its book value. A **loss** is the disposition of an asset for less than its book value. The formula is

Proceeds — Book value = Gain or loss

There is a gain when proceeds are higher than book value. There is a loss when proceeds are lower than book value.

A gain results from a peripheral activity of the business. In contrast, revenue involves the routine activities of the business such as selling goods and rendering services. A loss also results from a peripheral activity of the business. In contrast, expenses involve the day-to-day activities of the business.

The rules of debit and credit for gain accounts are the same as for revenue accounts. Similarly, expense accounts and loss accounts follow the same rules of debit and credit.

Loss		Gain	
+	−	−	+
Increase	Decrease	Decrease	Increase

DISPOSAL BY SCRAPPING OR DISCARDING

When an asset is worn out, often it is simply discarded. For example, the computer used by Sam's Discount Stores cost $5,250 and is fully depreciated. On June 30, the computer crashed and could not be repaired for a reasonable fee. It was worthless and was discarded. There were no proceeds from the disposal and no costs were incurred in the disposal. There is no gain or loss from the disposition.

	Proceeds		$0					
	(Book value)		(0)					
	Gain or loss		$0					

The following journal entry records the asset's disposal.

11	June	30	Accum. Depreciation—Office Equipment		5 2 5 0 00			11
12			Office Equipment			5 2 5 0 00		12
13			Discarded computer					13

If the discarded asset is not fully depreciated, depreciation is recorded up to the date of disposal. Suppose that the computer used by Sam's Discount Stores cost $5,250. Accumulated depreciation through December 31, 2009, was $4,200. On June 30, 2010, the computer crashed. The depreciation for the period January 1 through June 30 is $525. The depreciation is recorded through June 30 as follows: debit **Depreciation Expense** for $525 and credit **Accumulated Depreciation** for $525. After this entry, **Accumulated Depreciation** account balance is $4,725 ($4,200 + 525). The book value of the computer is $525 ($5,250 − 4,725). There are no proceeds and no costs incurred for the disposal. There is a loss of $525 on the disposition.

Proceeds		$0
(Book value)		(525)
Gain or loss		$(525)

The entry to record the disposal of the computer removes the cost of the asset and its accumulated depreciation from the accounting records. The difference, book value, is recorded as a loss.

June	30	Accum. Depreciation—Office Equipment		4 7 2 5 00			
		Loss on Disposal of Fixed Assets		5 2 5 00			
		Office Equipment			5 2 5 0 00		
		Discarded computer					

DISPOSAL BY SALE

Sometimes useful assets are sold so the company can purchase better assets or because the assets are no longer needed. When an asset is sold, follow these steps to record the transaction.

Step 1. *Record depreciation to the date of disposition.*

Step 2. *Remove the cost of the asset.*

Step 3. *Remove the accumulated depreciation.*

Step 4. *Record the proceeds.*

Step 5. *Determine and record the gain or loss, if any.*

Several years ago, Hunter Laboratories purchased laboratory equipment for $12,000. The balance in **Accumulated Depreciation** was $6,480 on July 1, 2010, the date the equipment is sold. This balance reflects depreciation through December 31 of the prior year. The first step is to record the depreciation expense since depreciation was last recorded. Annual depreciation is $1,080. Depreciation for the period January 1 through June 30 is therefore $540 ($1,080 ÷ 2). The entry is a debit to **Depreciation Expense—Laboratory Equipment** and a credit to **Accumulated Depreciation—Laboratory Equipment** for $540. After this entry, the accumulated depreciation account has a balance of $7,020 ($6,480 + 540) and the book value of the laboratory equipment is $4,980 ($12,000 − 7,020).

Sale for an Amount Equal to Book Value Suppose that the equipment was sold on account for book value, $4,980. Step 1, record depreciation to the date of disposition, has been illustrated. Steps 2–5 are as follows:

Step 2. *Remove the cost of the asset.* Credit **Laboratory Equipment** for $12,000.

Step 3. *Remove the accumulated depreciation.* Debit **Accumulated Depreciation—Laboratory Equipment** for $7,020.

>>4. OBJECTIVE

Record sales of plant and equipment.

LP18

Step 4. *Record the proceeds.* Debit ***Accounts Receivable*** for $4,980.

Step 5. *Determine and record the gain or loss, if any.*

Proceeds	$4,980
(Book value)	(4,980)
Gain or loss	$0

>>

GENERAL JOURNAL   PAGE ___7___

	DATE		DESCRIPTION	POST. REF.	DEBIT	CREDIT	
1	2010						1
22	July	1	Accounts Receivable		4 9 8 0 00		22
23			Accum. Depreciation—Laboratory Equipment		7 0 2 0 00		23
24			Laboratory Equipment			12 0 0 0 00	24
25			Sold Laboratory equipment at				25
26			book value				26

Sale for More Than Book Value Suppose the equipment was sold on account for $5,520. The equipment was sold at a gain of $540.

Proceeds	$5,520
(Book value)	(4,980)
Gain	$540

The gain is recorded in the ***Gain on Sale of Equipment*** account. The gain is shown on the income statement in the Other Income section.

>>

GENERAL JOURNAL   PAGE ___7___

	DATE		DESCRIPTION	POST. REF.	DEBIT	CREDIT	
1	2010						1
22	July	1	Accounts Receivable		5 5 2 0 00		22
23			Accum. Depreciation—Laboratory Equipment		7 0 2 0 00		23
24			Laboratory Equipment			12 0 0 0 00	24
25			Gain on Sale of Equipment			5 4 0 00	25
26			Sale of Laboratory equipment				26
27			at a gain				27

Sale for Less Than Book Value Suppose the equipment was sold on account for $4,520. The equipment was sold at a loss of $460.

Proceeds	$4,520
(Book value)	(4,980)
Loss	$460

The loss is recorded in the ***Loss on Sale of Equipment*** account. The loss appears on the income statement in the Other Expenses section.

	DATE		DESCRIPTION	POST. REF.	DEBIT	CREDIT	
GENERAL JOURNAL					**PAGE** 7		
1	2010						1
22	July	1	Accounts Receivable		4 5 2 0 00		22
23			Accum. Depreciation—Laboratory Equipment		7 0 2 0 00		23
24			Loss on Sale of Equipment		4 6 0 00		24
25			Laboratory Equipment			1 2 0 0 0 00	25
26			Sale of Laboratory equipment				26
27			at a loss				27

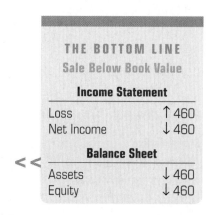

THE BOTTOM LINE

Sale Below Book Value

Income Statement

Loss	↑ 460
Net Income	↓ 460

Balance Sheet

Assets	↓ 460
Equity	↓ 460

Some companies use a single account to record both gains and losses on sales of assets. The account is called **Gains and Losses on Sales of Assets.** It appears on the income statement in the Other Income section (if net gain) or Other Expenses section (if net loss).

DISPOSAL BY TRADE-IN

Businesses often trade in old equipment when they purchase new equipment. Trade-in transactions are recorded in two steps.

Step 1. *Record the depreciation up to the date of trade-in.*

Step 2. *Record the trade-in of the old asset and the purchase of the new asset.*

Step 1 presents no new problem. Bringing the depreciation up to date involves precisely the same calculations that would be made if an asset were sold. Depreciation is recorded for the period beginning when the date of depreciation was last recorded and ending at the end of the month nearest the date of the trade-in.

Step 2 is somewhat more complicated.

a. *Under financial accounting rules, losses on trade-ins are recorded, but gains on trade-ins are not recorded.*

b. *For federal income tax purposes, neither gains nor losses are recognized on trade-ins.*

To illustrate the financial accounting rules and the income tax rules, we will examine a typical situation. Assume that on October 1, 2010, Howard Company traded in an old truck acquired several years ago for $40,000, on a new truck. After bringing depreciation up to date, the total accumulated depreciation was $33,000, so that the book value was $7,000. The difference between the trade-in allowed and the agreed-on price of the truck is to be paid in cash

APPLYING THE FINANCIAL ACCOUNTING RULES FOR TRADE-INS

Actual gain or loss is the difference between the amount of allowance received on the trade-in and the book value of the old asset. The allowance is the difference between the fair value of the new asset and the amount of cash paid. For example, if Howard received a trade-in allowance of $7,800 on the old asset with a book value of $7,000, there is an implicit gain of $800. On the other hand, if the trade-in allowance is only $6,700 on an asset with a book value of $7,000, there is an implicit loss of $300.

Financial Accounting for Trade-In if Gain Is Realized on the Transaction Suppose that the new truck Howard acquired has an agreed-on price of $42,000, which is also its fair value. The dealer granted Howard a trade-in allowance of $7,800 and Howard paid cash of $34,200. As a result, Howard is deemed to have received $7,800 for the old truck. The implicit gain on the trade-in is $800 ($7,800 trade-in allowance, minus $7,000 book value of the old truck.) However, gains on trade-ins are *not* recognized for financial accounting purposes. This

>>5. OBJECTIVE

Record asset trade-ins using financial accounting rules and income tax requirements.

rule is based on the conservatism concept and the realization principle, which hold that gains should not be recognized until cash or other types of liquid assets have been received in return.

In this situation, the cost of the new asset is deemed to be the sum of the book value of the old asset and the amount of cash paid.

Book value of old truck	$ 7,000
Cash payment	34,200
Cost of new asset	$41,200

Here are the steps to record the trade-in if there is a gain on the transaction.

Step 1. *Remove the cost of the old asset ($40,000).*

Step 2. *Remove the accumulated depreciation for the old asset ($33,000).*

Step 3. *Record the payment ($34,200).*

Step 4. *Record the new asset as the sum of the cash paid and the book value of the old asset ($41,200).*

The journal entry to record the transaction would be:

GENERAL JOURNAL   PAGE ___7___

	DATE		DESCRIPTION	POST. REF.	DEBIT	CREDIT	
1	2010						1
2	Oct.	1	Truck (new)		41 200 00		2
3			Accum. Depreciation (old truck)		33 000 00		3
4			Truck (old)			40 000 00	4
5			Cash			34 200 00	5
6			Trade in of truck				6

Financial Accounting for Trade-In if Loss Is Realized on Transaction Although gains on trade-ins are not recognized under financial accounting rules, as illustrated in the above example, *losses are recognized*. This treatment is based on the conservatism concept.

Suppose the amount allowed Howard as a trade-in value of the old asset had been $6,700, instead of $7,800 and Howard paid cash of $35,300 ($42,000 − $6,700). As a result, there would be a realized loss of $300 on the trade-in ($7,000 book value, minus $6,700 received as trade-in allowance). Remember that for financial accounting purposes, losses *are* recognized. To record a trade-in under the financial accounting rules when there is a loss on the transaction, follow these steps:

Step 1. *Remove the cost of the old asset ($40,000).*

Step 2. *Remove the accumulated depreciation for the old asset ($33,000).*

Step 3. *Record the payment ($35,300).*

Step 4. *Record the new asset at its fair market value ($42,000).*

Step 5. *Determine and record the loss ($300).*

Here is the entry required to record the trade in of the truck by Howard.

GENERAL JOURNAL   PAGE ___7___

	DATE		DESCRIPTION	POST. REF.	DEBIT	CREDIT	
1	2010						1
2	Oct.	1	Truck (new)		42 000 00		2
3			Accum. Depreciation (old truck)		33 000 00		3
4			Loss on Trade-in of Truck		300 00		4
5			Truck (old)			40 000 00	5
6			Cash			35 300 00	6
7			Trade in of truck at a loss				7

---

recall

Conservatism

According to the modifying convention of conservatism, accountants record transactions using the alternative that is least likely to overstate income.

THE BOTTOM LINE

Trade-In of an Asset
(Loss)

Income Statement

Loss	↑ 300
Net Income	↓ 300

Balance Sheet

Assets	↓ 300
Equity	↓ 300

Some smaller businesses follow the income tax rules discussed below in recording trade-in transactions because it may eliminate keeping two sets of records for the same transaction. It should be noted, however, that this is not always feasible because the cost and depreciation amounts may differ for financial accounting and tax purposes.

APPLYING THE INCOME TAX RULES FOR TRADE-INS

The federal **income tax method** for trade-in transactions are easier than those for financial accounting because neither gain nor loss is recognized for tax purposes. The steps in applying the tax rules are:

Step 1. *Remove the cost of the old asset.*

Step 2. *Remove the accumulated depreciation for the old asset.*

Step 3. *Record the cash payment.*

Step 4. *Record the new asset at the sum of the book value of the old asset and the cash paid.*

Applying this basic rule to the two situations discussed above: (1) cash of $34,200 was paid on the trade-in and (2) cash of $35,300 was paid on the trade-in, no gain or loss would be recorded in either case for tax purposes. Assuming the same book value for both tax and financial reporting purposes (which is not the normal case because of the differences between depreciation calculations and MACRS cost recovery), in the first situation, the new truck would be recorded at $41,200 ($34,200 cash plus $7,000 book value of the old truck). In the second situation, the new truck would be recorded at $42,300 ($35,300 cash plus $7,000 book value of the old truck).

Section 2 Self Review

QUESTIONS

1. If an item of equipment is retired and scrapped or sold, how should the retirement be accounted for?

2. Explain the difference, if any, between federal income tax rules and financial accounting principles in recognizing gain or loss on the trade-in of plant and equipment assets.

3. For financial reporting purposes, in what circumstances is a loss on the sale of a long-term asset recognized?

EXERCISES

4. An asset that cost $40,000 and on which depreciation of $30,000 has been recorded is traded in on a new replacement asset. The sales price, also the fair value, of the new asset is $54,000. The owner of the old asset was given an allowance of $14,000 for the old asset and paid $40,000 in cash. The amount of gain or loss recorded is

   a. a gain of $4,000.

   b. no gain or loss.

   c. a loss of $4,000.

   d. a gain of $14,000.

5. An asset that cost $48,000 was retired and sold for $30,000 cash. Accumulated depreciation on the asset was $26,000. The entry to record this retirement and sale calls for recognizing

   a. no gain or loss.

   b. a gain of $8,000.

   c. a loss of $18,000.

   d. a gain of $4,000.

ANALYSIS

6. If a company's fully depreciated asset was scrapped but not removed from the accounting records, what would be the effect on the company's financial statements? Assume the asset has no net salvage value.

(Answers to Section 2 Self Review are on page 636.)

SECTION OBJECTIVES	TERMS TO LEARN

>> **6. Compute and record depletion of natural resources.**

WHY IT'S IMPORTANT

Depletion matches an asset's costs with the benefits derived from its use.

>> **7. Recognize asset impairment and understand the general concepts of accounting for impairment.**

WHY IT'S IMPORTANT

Sometimes assets do not retain their ability to generate expected revenues. In these cases, the asset cost is adjusted in the accounting records.

>> **8. Compute and record amortization and impairment of intangible assets.**

WHY IT'S IMPORTANT

An intangible asset's cost is charged to expense over its assumed life.

TERMS TO LEARN

amortization
brand names
computer software
copyright
depletion
franchises
goodwill
impairment
intangible assets
patent
recoverability test
trade names
trademarks

Special Topics in Long-Term Assets

In the first two sections of this chapter, you have learned how to account for costs incurred in connection with the acquisition, operation, and disposition of property, plant, and equipment. These are very common transactions arising in almost every business. In the final section of the chapter, you will learn how to handle three less commonly encountered transactions related to assets of this type:

1. Depletion of costs of natural resources.
2. Impairment of property, plant, and equipment.
3. Costs incurred to acquire intangible assets.

In addition, you will learn some of the basic internal controls used to safeguard property, plant, and equipment—the asset category representing the largest investment of funds for most types of business.

Depletion

Natural resources, such as iron ore, oil, gold, and coal are physically removed from the land in the production process. Businesses must know how to allocate the cost of natural resources as they are taken from their source. As the resources are extracted, part of their cost is charged to expense. **Depletion** is the term used to describe allocating the cost of the natural resource to expense over the period in which the resource produces revenue.

DEPLETION FOR FINANCIAL STATEMENT PURPOSES

Depletion of the cost of natural resources for financial statement preparation is called *cost depletion*. It is similar to the units-of-output method of depreciation. The formula is

$$\frac{\text{Cost of natural resource}}{\text{Estimated units of the resource}} = \text{Depletion per unit}$$

A business purchased a clay pit for $80,000. The clay pit is estimated to contain 500,000 tons of extractable clay suitable for making bricks. The depletion cost for each ton of clay is $0.16 ($80,000 ÷ 500,000 tons). During the first year, the business extracted 30,000 tons of clay. The depletion is $4,800 (30,000 × $0.16). The adjusting entry to record depletion follows.

11	Dec.	31	Depletion Expense	4 80 0 00		11
12			Accumulated Depletion		4 80 0 00	12
13			To record the extraction of			13
14			30,000 tons of clay			14

After the first year, the natural resource appears on the balance sheet as follows. The net book value of the natural resource is $75,200.

Property, Plant, and Equipment

Clay Deposits	$80,000
Less Accumulated Depletion	4,800
Net Clay Deposits	$75,200

Oil and gas production and mining operations use long-lived assets such as oil pumps and mining equipment. These assets are depreciated, usually using the units-of-output method.

DEPLETION FOR FEDERAL INCOME TAX PURPOSES

Depletion for federal income tax purposes is the larger of cost depletion or percentage depletion. Cost depletion for tax purposes is computed in the same way as it is for financial statement preparation. However, the amount of cost depletion may be different because the cost (the numerator) for financial purposes may be different than the cost for tax purposes. If percentage depletion is taken on the tax return, the amount taken in any year will reduce the cost on which cost depletion is based in future years.

Percentage depletion for a property is calculated by multiplying the gross income from the sale of the natural resource by a percentage. The percentage depends on the specific natural resource.

In 2010, a mining company has sales of $1,800,000 for ore produced from a mine. For tax purposes, the book value (capitalized costs, less depletion taken in prior years) of the minerals at the beginning of the year was $16,000. The allowable percentage depletion rate for the minerals produced is 15 percent. The company will deduct $270,000 on its federal income tax return ($1,800,000 × 0.15 = $270,000). In future years, there will be no allowable *cost depletion,* but *percentage depletion* may continue to be taken even though the book value for tax purposes is zero.

>>6. OBJECTIVE
Compute and record depletion of natural resources.

Impairment of Property, Plant, and Equipment

Relying on the historical cost concept and the going concern assumption, many accountants have assumed that if a long-term asset continues to be used in income production the asset will generate future cash revenues and the value of those revenues will exceed the book value of the asset. However, in the late 1980s and early 1990s, many businesses recorded "write-offs" of assets when their values declined substantially.

Because of concern over situations in which doubt exists as to whether the asset's use will generate adequate cash flows to recover the book value of assets, the Financial Accounting Standards Board, issued *Financial Accounting Statement 121,* "Accounting for Impairment of Long-Lived Assets." This Statement lays out guidelines for recording impairment of property, plant, and equipment when it appears that the carrying amount of the assets may not be recoverable. Stated simply, **impairment** exists when book value exceeds the "fair value" of the asset.

The procedures and measurement techniques for recording impairment are quite complex and are beyond the scope of this textbook, but a brief summary of measuring and recording

>>7. OBJECTIVE
Recognize asset impairment and understand the general concepts of accounting for impairment.

LP18

impairment will provide you with a basic understanding when you encounter circumstances suggesting that impairment may exist.

Three steps in the process of determining an impairment loss are suggested in FASB *Statement 121.*

Step 1. *Review circumstances that suggest impairment may have occurred.* FASB Statement 121 gives examples of events and changes in circumstance that suggest impairment *may have* occurred.

    a. A significant decrease in the market value of an asset,

    b. A significant change in the extent of use or way in which the asset is used.

    c. A significant adverse change in the legal environment or in the manner in which an asset is used.

    d. A forecast suggesting continuing losses associated with the asset. There are, however, many other economic and technical factors that may suggest assets should be analyzed for possible impairment, for example, increased competition, new technical developments, a forecast of decreased demand for the products, and so forth.

Turner Disposal Company has operated a facility to separate liquids and gaseous products from a stream of crude oil crude from wells. Present book value of the facility is $792,000. Revenues from the facility have decreased by approximately 14 percent during each of the last two years. *This suggests that impairment may have occurred.*

Step 2. *Apply the recoverability test.* If circumstances suggest that impairment may have occurred, the **recoverability test** should be applied to determine whether impairment does exist. The recoverability test is a comparison of the asset's carrying value (net book value) with the estimated net cash flows from future use of the asset, including eventual disposition of the asset. If the estimated net future cash flows are less than the asset's book value, impairment has occurred.

Obviously, in most cases it is not possible to estimate future net cash flows that are expected to be generated by a single item of equipment, such as a computer used in the office, a display rack used in a retail store, or a piece of machinery in a factory. FASB *Statement 121* states that in making impairment calculations, the unit of measurement is not a single asset, but the smallest unit of the business for which net cash flows can be determined from the assets used.

Turner made a projection of future cash inflows from services and cash outflows from expenses over the expected remaining life of the facilities and estimates that future net cash

MANAGERIAL IMPLICATIONS

PROPERTY, PLANT, AND EQUIPMENT

- Property, plant, and equipment often represent the largest cash investment by the owners of a business.

- Managers are responsible for establishing strong internal controls over property, plant, and equipment.

- Managers should understand the different depreciation methods and how they impact the financial statements and income tax returns of the business.

- Management should ensure that procedures are in place to monitor repairs, power consumed, and other operating costs to make sure that assets are functioning efficiently.

- Managers must understand the methods used to record asset sales and trade-ins because the different methods have different results that impact the financial statements of the business.

THINKING CRITICALLY

How does the choice of depreciation method impact the financial statements?

flows from its operations will total $690,000. These future cash flows are less than the asset's $792,000 book value, so impairment does exist.

Step 3. *Compute the amount of the impairment.* The amount of impairment is the amount by which the asset's book value exceeds its market value. There may be instances in which the market value of an asset can be determined by quoted prices in the markets. However, these quotations may be scarce for many assets, so market value must be determined by other means. The usual methodology is to compute the "discounted value" (present value) of the stream of future net cash flows from use of the assets, calculated in step 2. Essentially, the present value of the estimated future cash flows is the amount that it would be necessary to invest today in order to earn a specific rate of return on the investment, considering the cash flows expected to be received each year during the future life of the asset. If the market value, or present value, is less than the net book value of the asset, impairment exists and should be recorded in the amount of the excess of book value over market value.

In step 2, above, Turner estimated that future cash flows were only $690,000 from an asset with a book value of $792,000. Turner then applied to the future cash stream a discount factor based on its expected rate of return on an asset of this type. In applying the discount rate, Turner estimated that the company would be willing to pay $540,000 for the asset today. That is its market value to the firm. Turner records impairment by debiting *Loss from Impairment of Separation Equipment* for $252,000 and crediting *Separation Equipment* for that amount.

> Once an impairment write-down of an asset has been made, the amount charged off is not reinstated even if the market value subsequently increases—the conservatism constraint and the realization principle in effect.

In the year following Turner's write-down of the separation equipment in the preceding example, the price of oil and gas increased dramatically, and as a result the value of the processing facility increased to $858,000. However, this increase in value is not recognized in the accounts.

Intangible Assets

In addition to property, plant, and equipment, many businesses have intangible assets. **Intangible assets** are assets that lack a physical substance. The major types of intangible assets are patents, copyrights, franchises, trademarks, brand names, organizational costs, computer software, and goodwill. With the exception of computer software, intangible assets usually do not have any physical attributes.

Video18.1

CLASSIFYING INTANGIBLE ASSETS

A **patent** is an exclusive right given by the U.S. Patent Office to manufacture and sell an invention for a period of 17 years from the date the patent is granted. A patent may not be renewed; however, a new patent may be obtained if significant improvements in the original idea can be demonstrated. The right to the patent may be sold, assigned, or otherwise controlled by the owner.

A **copyright** is the exclusive right granted by the federal government to produce, publish, and sell a literary or artistic work for a period equal to the creator's life plus 70 years.

There are two types of **franchises.** The first type is a right granted by a governmental unit for the business to provide a service to the governmental unit (such as cable television). The second type is an exclusive dealership or an exclusive arrangement between a manufacturer and a dealer or distributor.

Trademarks, trade names, and **brand names** are used to build consumer confidence and loyalty. They can be registered with the U.S. Patent Office. They can be sold, traded, or otherwise controlled by the owner.

Organizational costs are the costs incurred when organizing a business. Organizational costs include attorneys' fees, accountants' fees, legal filing fees, and other costs of beginning a business.

Computer software consists of written programs that instruct a computer's hardware to do certain tasks. Software can be developed by the company's employees or purchased outside the company. For some firms, computer software is the most important (and most costly) asset owned.

Goodwill represents the value of a business in excess of the value of its identifiable assets. Goodwill is recorded only at the time of the purchase of a business. It usually occurs when a business being purchased has extraordinary earnings or earnings potential.

> For many companies, intangible assets are a very important part of the total assets. For example, in its balance sheet at the end of 2006, Johnson & Johnson reported total assets of $70.556 billion. This total included *Goodwill,* $13.340 billion and other intangibles of $15.348 billion.

ACQUIRING INTANGIBLE ASSETS

There are two ways to acquire intangible assets: (1) produce or develop them or (2) purchase them. The general rule is that an intangible asset is recorded in the books of the firm only if it is purchased from another party. Costs to develop intangible assets internally are expensed in the year incurred to the *Research and Development Expense* account. Similarly, costs related to software development by a company are expensed in the year incurred. However, there are special rules if the software is to be sold, leased, or otherwise marketed:

1. Costs are expensed as incurred when creating the software product until technological feasibility is established for the product. *Technological feasibility* is deemed to occur when a detailed program design or a working model of the product has been developed.

2. Costs are capitalized to an asset account once a product is deemed to be technologically feasible.

>>8. OBJECTIVE

Compute and record amortization and impairment of intangible assets.

LP18

DISPOSITION OF CAPITALIZED ACQUISITION COSTS OF INTANGIBLE ASSETS

For accounting purposes, costs of intangibles that have been acquired for a cost and are identified as being appropriately capitalized are classified into two groups.

1. Those that are determined to have lives that are definite or can be reasonably estimated. The most common of these are patents, copyrights, most franchises, and purchased computer software.

2. Those that do not have definite or reasonably estimable useful lives. These include organization costs, purchased goodwill, trademarks, brand names, and trade names.

Amortization of Cost of Intangibles with Estimable Useful Lives The accounting treatment of costs of intangibles in this category is very similar to depreciation of property, plant, and equipment. The periodic transfer of intangible's cost to expense is known as **amortization.** The costs are typically amortized on a straight-line basis or on a units-of-production basis.

In January 2010, Marcus Company purchased for $200,000 a patent which had a remaining life of 10 years. Based on straight-line amortization, Marcus recorded the following entry for amortization at the end of 2010.

11	Dec.	31	Amortization of Patent	20 000 00	11
12			Patent	20 000 00	12
13			To record annual amortization		13
14			of patent		14

An identical entry will be made at the end of 2011 so that the balance remaining in the *Patent* account on January 1, 2012, will be $160,000. Suppose in 2012 it is estimated that the patent will be of benefit only through the year 2015. Based on this estimate, the patent amortization for each year 2012 to 2015 will be $40,000 ($160,000 ÷ 4 years).

Impairment of Cost of Intangibles with Indefinite Useful Lives

When intangibles that do not have estimable lives have been purchased, an assessment must be made each year to estimate the value of the intangible. If the estimate is less than the existing book value, impairment must be recorded in the same way that impairment of property, plant, and equipment is recorded. Here, the concept of conservatism comes into play.

In 1998, Marcus Company purchased from another business a "brand name" for $400,000 and charged it to the intangible asset account *Brand Names.* Because of declining sales of the products covered by the brand and the decrease in profits on sales of the products, Marcus concluded in 2010 that the brand name was no longer worth $400,000 and that a conservative estimate of its value was $100,000. Based on that, the following entry was made by Marcus.

11	Dec.	31	Loss from Impairment of Brand Name	300 00 0 00	11
12			Brand Names		300 00 0 00	12
13			To record impairment of brand name		13
14					14

A similar assessment should be made each year to see if further impairment should be recorded. However, if the value of the intangible asset increases in years subsequent to recording impairment, the carrying value of the asset *is not increased.*

> The annual report for Coca-Cola Company and Subsidiaries for 2006 contained the following as part of its note explaining its accounting for "Goodwill, Trademarks and Other Intangible Assets."
>
> **Goodwill, Trademarks, and Other Intangible Assets**
>
> In accordance with SFAS No. 142, "Goodwill and Other Intangible Assets," we classify intangible assets into three categories: (1) intangible assets with definite lives subject to amortization, (2) intangible assets with indefinite lives not subject to amortization, and (3) goodwill. We test intangible assets with definite lives for impairment if conditions exist that indicate the carrying value may not be recoverable. Such conditions may include an economic downturn in a geographic market or a change in the assessment of future operations. We record an impairment charge when the carrying value of the definite lived intangible asset is not recoverable by the cash flows generated from the use of the asset.
>
> Intangible assets with indefinite lives and goodwill are not amortized. We test these intangible assets and goodwill for impairment at least annually or more frequently if events or circumstances indicate that such intangible assets or goodwill might be impaired. Such tests for impairment are also required for intangible assets with indefinite lives and/or goodwill recorded by our equity method investees. All goodwill is assigned to reporting units, which are one level below our operating segments. Goodwill is assigned to the reporting unit that benefits from the synergies arising from each business combination. We perform our impairment tests of goodwill at our reporting unit level. Such impairment tests for goodwill include comparing the fair value of the respective reporting unit with its carrying value, including goodwill. We use a variety of methodologies in conducting these impairment tests, including discounted cash flow analyses with a number of scenarios, where applicable, that are weighted based on the probability of different outcomes. When appropriate, we consider the assumptions that
>
> *(continued)*

(concluded)

we believe hypothetical marketplace participants would use in estimating future cash flows. In addition, where applicable, an appropriate discount rate is used, based on the Company's cost of capital rate or location-specific economic factors. When the fair value is less than the carrying value of the intangible assets or the reporting unit, we record an impairment charge to reduce the carrying value of the assets to fair value. These impairment charges are generally recorded in the line item other operating charges or, to the extent they relate to equity method investees, as a reduction of equity income—net, in the consolidated statements of income.

Our Company determines the useful lives of our identifiable intangible assets after considering the specific facts and circumstances related to each intangible asset. Factors we consider when determining useful lives include the contractual term of any agreement, the history of the asset, the Company's long-term strategy for the use of the asset, any laws or other local regulations which could impact the useful life of the asset, and other economic factors, including competition and specific market conditions. Intangible assets that are deemed to have definite lives are amortized, generally on a straight-line basis, over their useful lives, ranging from 1 to 45 years. Intangible assets with definite lives have estimated remaining useful lives ranging from 1 to 35 years.

Internal Control of Property, Plant, and Equipment

The internal control of property, plant, and equipment involves physical safeguards to prevent theft or misuse. The following are standard internal control procedures for fixed assets:

- Authorize and justify the purchase of all long-lived assets.
- Assign and, if possible, engrave an identification number on each asset.
- Maintain an asset register listing all capital assets, their costs, acquisition dates, location, and any other useful information.
- Assign responsibility for safekeeping, maintaining, and operating each asset to a specific person.
- Take a physical inventory periodically. Compare the physical inventory with the asset register and investigate any differences.
- Establish procedures to authorize asset retirement, sale, or other disposition.

The internal control of intangible assets consists primarily of the safe storage of documents and protection of the storage location. Businesses need to be alert to copyright and trademark infringements. Legal action is required when an infringement of an intangible asset occurs.

Section 3 Self Review

QUESTIONS

1. If it is determined that an asset is impaired, how is the amount of impairment to be charged to expense computed?

2. Daytime Company spent $80 million in 2010 on research and development costs (R&D). Some work was general research seeking basic knowledge about products. Other work was getting several projects started to look into ways to develop and improve a line of drugs manufactured by the company. Other costs were incurred in the final stages of perfecting new products. How should these costs be accounted for by Daytime?

3. Explain the test used to determine whether an asset is impaired.

EXERCISES

4. Over a period of 50 years, Good Taste Company developed a great reputation for its soft drinks. In 2010, Happy Times Company purchased Good Taste for $400 million. The purchase price included about $300 million as the actual value of identifiable assets and $100 million for the ownership of the trade name "Good Taste." Should the cost assigned to Good Taste be depreciated (or amortized)? If so, on what basis?

5. An oil company paid a landowner $20,000 for the mineral rights underlying his property. The well was drilled and equipped at a cost of $800,000. It is estimated that 300,000 barrels of oil will be produced from the property. Describe the method that should be used to measure and record depletion of the cost of the mineral rights as the oil is produced. How should depreciation of the costs of drilling and equipping the well be measured and recorded?

6. (Refer to Exercise 4.) Suppose that in 2012, two years after Happy Times acquired Good Taste, the sales of Good Taste soft drinks decreased drastically. Assume that Happy Times had not recorded any amortization of the $100 million assigned to the trade name. What course of action should the management of Happy Times take?

ANALYSIS

7. How are depreciation, depletion and amortization different? How are they similar?

(Answers to Section 3 Self Review are on page 637.)

18 Chapter REVIEW Chapter Summary

Property, plant, and equipment are those tangible assets used in carrying out the company's business operations. In this chapter, you have learned how to record transactions for the purchase, use, and disposition of these assets. You have also studied the accounting methods required to record the acquisition of intangible assets such as copyrights and patents, as well as the costs of amortization.

Learning Objectives

1 Determine the amount to record as an asset's cost.

The cost of an asset is its net purchase price, plus costs of transportation, installation, and all other costs necessary to put the asset into normal operation.

2 Compute and record depreciation of property, plant, and equipment by commonly used methods.

Costs of a tangible asset should be charged to expense over its useful life through systematic depreciation charges. Depreciation is recorded by a debit to *Depreciation Expense* and a credit to *Accumulated Depreciation*. Four widely used methods of computing depreciation for financial accounting purposes are the

- straight-line method,
- declining-balance method,
- sum-of-the-years'-digits method,
- units-of-production method.

3 Apply the Modified Accelerated Cost Recovery System (MACRS) for federal income tax purposes.

Under the federal income tax laws, new assets must be depreciated under the Modified Accelerated Cost Recovery System (MACRS), with minor exceptions. Under MACRS, each type of asset is assigned to a MACRS class. Each class is assigned a different depreciable life.

4 Record sales of plant and equipment.

Property, plant, and equipment are disposed of in various ways; most commonly, they are sold or scrapped. At an asset's sale, its depreciation is brought up to date. Gain or loss at the time of disposal is computed by comparing the asset's net book value with the proceeds, if any, received on its disposal. For financial accounting purposes, a gain or loss may be recorded from the sale, retirement, or scrapping of an asset.

5 Record asset trade-ins using financial accounting rules and income tax requirements.

If a business trades old equipment when purchasing new equipment, two transactions must be recorded. The depreciation on the used equipment must be brought up to date. Then, the trade and purchase are recorded. Using the financial accounting rules, a gain is not recognized, but a loss is recognized. Using the income tax method, no gain or loss is recorded on the trade-in of an asset on a new similar asset.

6 Compute and record depletion of natural resources.

The costs of natural resources such as mineral deposits are charged to expense on a per-unit-of-production basis for financial accounting and reporting purposes. Special rules apply for income tax purposes.

7 Recognize asset impairment and understand the general concepts of accounting for impairment.

If an asset's expected future net cash flows are less than the asset's book value, impairment may need to be recognized. The amount of impairment is the amount by which the book value exceeds the asset's fair value—usually defined as the discounted value of the future net cash flows from its use.

8 Compute and record amortization and impairment of intangible assets.

Except for software, intangibles have no physical characteristics. If they are bought from outside parties, intangibles are recorded at cost. Costs incurred by firms who produce their own intangible assets are not capitalized but are charged to *Research and Development Expense* in the year incurred. Costs of intangibles with identifiable lives are amortized. Costs of those with indefinite lives are charged to expense through impairment tests.

9 Define the accounting terms new to this chapter.

Glossary

Accelerated method of depreciation (p. 599) A method of depreciating asset cost that allocates greater amounts of depreciation to an asset's early years of useful life

Amortization (p. 614) The process of periodically transferring the acquisition cost of intangible assets with estimated useful lives to an expense account

Brand name (p. 613) See Trade name

Capitalized costs (p. 596) All costs recorded as part of an asset's costs

Computer software (p. 614) An intangible asset; written programs that instruct a computer's hardware to do certain tasks

Copyright (p. 613) An intangible asset; an exclusive right granted by the federal government to produce, publish, and sell a literary or artistic work for a period equal to the creator's life plus 70 years

Declining-balance method (p. 599) An accelerated method of depreciation in which an asset's book value at the beginning of a year is multiplied by a constant percentage (usually equal to double the straight-line rate) to determine depreciation for the year

Depletion (p. 610) Allocating the cost of a natural resource to expense over the period in which the resource produces revenue

Double-declining-balance method (p. 599) A method of depreciation that uses a rate equal to twice the straight-line rate and applies that rate to the book value of the asset at the beginning of the year

Franchise (p. 613) An intangible asset; a right to exclusive dealership granted by a governmental unit or a business entity

Gain (p. 604) The disposition of an asset for more than its book value

Goodwill (p. 614) An intangible asset; the value of a business in excess of the net value of its identifiable assets

Impairment (p. 611) A situation that occurs when the asset is determined to have a market value or a value in use less than its book value

Income tax method (p. 609) A method of recording the trade-in of an asset for income tax purposes. It does not permit a gain or loss to be recognized on the transaction

Intangible assets (p. 613) Assets that lack a physical substance, such as goodwill, patents, copyrights, and computer software, although software has, in a sense, a physical attribute

Loss (p. 604) The disposition of an asset for less than its book value

Net book value (p. 598) The cost of an asset minus its accumulated depreciation, depletion, or amortization, also known as book value

Net salvage value (p. 598) The salvage value of an asset less any costs to remove or sell the asset

Patent (p. 613) An intangible asset; an exclusive right given by the U.S. Patent Office to manufacture and sell an invention for a period of 17 years from the date the patent is granted

Real property (p. 596) Assets such as land, land improvements, buildings, and other structures attached to the land

Recoverability test (p. 612) Test for possible impairment that compares the asset's net book value with the estimated net cash flows from future use of the asset

Residual value (p. 598) The estimate of the amount that could be obtained from the sale or disposition of an asset at the end of its useful life; also called salvage or scrap value

Scrap value (p. 598) See Residual value

Sum-of-the-years'-digits method (p. 600) A method of depreciating asset costs by allocating as expense each year a fractional part of the asset's depreciable cost, based on the sum of the digits of the number of years in the asset's useful life

Tangible personal property (p. 596) Assets such as machinery, equipment, furniture, and fixtures that can be removed and used elsewhere

Trade name (p. 613) An intangible asset; an exclusive business name registered with the U.S. Patent Office; also called brand name

Trademark (p. 613) An intangible asset; an exclusive business symbol registered with the U.S. Patent Office

Units-of-output method (p. 601) See Units-of-production method

Units-of-production method (p. 601) A method of depreciating asset cost at the same rate for each unit produced during each period

Comprehensive **Self Review**

1. An asset with a cost of $28,000 and accumulated depreciation of $25,400 is retired and sold as junk for $600. How much gain or loss is recorded on the retirement?

2. Distinguish between the legal life and the economic life of an intangible asset. Which is used in computing amortization if amortization is appropriate?

3. How does real property differ from personal property?

4. What is the denominator of the fraction used in the calculation of annual depreciation using the sum-of-years'-digits method of depreciation for an asset with a useful life of ten years?

5. What generally accepted accounting principle or convention supports the writing down of impaired assets to their fair market values?

6. Under what circumstances would the unit-of-production depreciation method be the logical choice from the different methods available?

(Answers to Comprehensive Self Review are on page 637.)

 Multiple choice questions are provided on the text Web site at www.mhhe.com/price12e

Quiz18

Discussion Questions

1. Which, if any, of the depreciation methods discussed in this chapter ignore salvage value?

2. Name two accelerated depreciation methods.

3. What is meant by the term "personal property"?

4. Explain how straight-line depreciation is computed.

5. A company purchased some land on which an old building is located. The building has to be torn down to enable construction of a new building. Which if any of the following costs related to the old building should be capitalized as part of the land cost?

   a. Purchase price of the property.

   b. Permit fee for tearing down the old building

   c. Cost of tearing down the building in excess of salvage proceeds

   d. Costs of hauling off debris of old building

6. What is meant by "capitalized costs"?

7. Which of these, if any, is not "real property"?

   a. Land

   b. A building

   c. A motor home being used as an office

   d. Pavement for a parking lot

8. Name three or more events, developments, or situations that indicate impairment of property, plant, and equipment may exist.

9. What information related to the company's property, plant, and equipment must be presented in the financial statements and in the notes to the financial statements?

10. Under what circumstances is the units-of-production method of depreciation especially desirable?

11. Which method will give you a higher amount of depreciation expense in the later years of an asset's life, straight-line or declining-balance? Explain.

12. Is MACRS used for federal income tax rules acceptable under GAAP?

13. Explain how the sum-of-years'-digits method would be applied to an asset with a life of six years.

14. What account is debited and what account is credited to record depreciation on trucks?

15. Explain how double-declining-balance depreciation is computed on an asset with a life of six years.

16. What are the two categories of intangible assets for the purposes of disposing of their capitalized costs?

17. What are the rules for determining the amount of cost in each category of intangibles in question 16 to be removed from the asset account during each accounting period?

18. What accounting treatment is given to most research costs?

19. Are gains and losses on trade-in transactions recognized and recorded under GAAP?

20. What are the requirements for recording an intangible asset such as goodwill?

21. Explain how to measure the gain or loss when an old asset is traded in on a new one.

22. What is name given the process by which costs of a natural resource deposit are removed from the asset account as the resources are produced?

23. How is the amount of impairment to be recorded determined?

24. What is the basic test for determining whether impairment does, in fact, exist?

APPLICATIONS

Exercises HM™

Determining the elements that make up the cost of an asset.   ◀   **Exercise 18.1**
Objective 1

The following costs were incurred by City Auto Parts in connection with the construction of a retail store building.

Cost of land, including $16,000 of legal costs	$200,000
Cost to demolish old building	12,500
Costs of grading land for building site	7,000
Costs related to building construction	800,000
Legal costs relating to building permits	6,000
Costs of paving parking lot	82,000

1. What is the capitalized cost of the land?
2. What is the capitalized cost of the new building?

Determining the elements that make up the cost of an asset.   ◀   **Exercise 18.2**
Objective 1

Inwood Development Company incurred the costs below related to a new packing machine.

Invoice price of packing machine	$160,000
Cash discount for prompt payment	3,200
Transportation costs	3,400
Installation costs	1,050

What is the capitalized cost of the new packing machine?

Exercise 18.3
Objective 2

▶ **Recording depreciation.**

For the year ending December 31, 2010, Johnson Manufacturing Company had depreciation totaling $38,000 on its office equipment. Give the general journal entry to record the adjusting entry.

Exercise 18.4
Objective 2

▶ **Computing depreciation under various methods.**

Nelson Company acquired an asset on January 2, 2010, at a cost of $440,000. The asset's useful life is five years and its salvage value is $40,000. Compute the depreciation expense for each of the first two years, using the straight-line method, the double-declining-balance method, and the sum-of-the-years'-digits method.

Exercise 18.5
Objective 2

▶ **Computing depreciation under the units-of-production method.**

On January 10, 2010, Iowa Company purchased a machine to mold components for one of its products. Total cost of the machine was $320,000. It is expected to produce 400,000 units and to have a salvage value of $20,000. The company used the units-of-production method of depreciation.

a. In 2009, it produced 40,000 units. Compute the depreciation expense for 2010.

b. During 2011, 55,000 units were produced. Compute the depreciation expense for 2011.

Exercise 18.6
Objective 3

▶ **Applying Modified Accelerated Cost Recovery (MACRS) under federal income tax rules.**

On January 20, 2011, Wilner Home Maintenance Company purchased a new lightweight truck for $20,000.

1. Into which MACRS "class" is this asset classified?

2. What would be the amount of cost recovery on the truck in 2011 and in 2012?

Exercise 18.7
Objective 4

▶ **Recording the sale of plant and equipment.**

Estrada Company owns a truck that cost $82,000. Depreciation totaling $50,000 had been taken on the truck up to January 8, 2011, when it was sold for $28,500.

1. Give the journal entry to record the sale.

2. Assume, instead, that the truck is sold for $34,000. Give the journal entry to record the sale.

Exercise 18.8
Objective 5

▶ **Recording asset trade-ins using financial accounting rules.**

On January 5, 2006, Mountbatten Company purchased construction equipment for $800,000, with a useful life of eight years and estimated salvage value of $80,000. The company uses the straight-line method of depreciation. On July 3, 2010, this equipment was traded for new similar construction equipment that has a value of $900,000. The company paid $490,000 cash and was given a trade-in allowance of $410,000 for the old equipment.

1. Give the general journal entry needed on July 3, 2010, to record the trade-in. (Assume that entry to bring depreciation up to date has been made.)

2. Assume the same facts as stated above, except that Mountbatten paid cash of $525,000 on the trade-in and was given an allowance of $375,000 for the old equipment. Give the journal entry to record the trade-in.

Exercise 18.9
Objective 5

▶ **Reporting asset trade-ins using federal income tax requirements.**

(Refer to the truck purchased by Wilner Home Maintenance, Exercise 18.6.)

In 2010, it became obvious that the truck purchased the year before was too small to handle many of Wilner's jobs. On January 4, 2011, Wilner traded in the old truck on a new, larger lightweight truck. Its sale price (and fair market value) was $29,000. The dealer gave Wilner a trade-in allowance of $7,200 for the old truck and Wilner paid the balance ($21,800) in cash.

1. For tax purposes, how much gain or loss is recognized on the trade-in?

2. For tax purposes, what is the basis (the cost) to be recorded for the new truck?

Computing depletion of mineral property cost.   ◀ **Exercise 18.10**
                                                              Objective 6

Mountain Mining Company acquired a mine in 2010. Capitalized costs of the minerals were $2,400,000. The company mined 100,000 tons of ore in 2010 and on December 31, 2010, it is estimated that 1,400,000 tons of ore remained in the ground.

Compute the amount of depletion expense for 2010.

Recognize asset impairment and understand the general   ◀ **Exercise 18.11**
concepts of accounting for impairment.   **Objective 7**

a. Martin Farm Company operates, on a contract basis, equipment that grinds and mixes grains used as animal feed. In September 2010, the book value of the equipment was $124,000. Because of declining processing fees, the company's chief financial officer became concerned that the asset might be impaired. An analysis of expected future cash flows from use of the asset resulted in an estimate of $123,000 of future cash flows. Further study led to the company's finding several almost identical processors that ranged in price from $89,000 to $91,000. The CFO decided that the asset was impaired and should be "written down" to $89,000. Do you agree?

b. What account would be debited and what account would be credited to record impairment? What would be the amount of the impairment recorded?

Computing and recording amortization and impairment of   ◀ **Exercise 18.12**
intangible assets.   **Objective 8**

On December 31, 2010, Jason Company's *Intangible Assets* account reflects two assets:

1. *Goodwill*, $125,000. This amount was recorded in December 2009 as part of the cost of acquiring an existing business. It represents the excess of the total purchase price, over the value of net identifiable assets. Jason has studied carefully the operations and concluded that the fair value of goodwill on December 31, 2010, is $100,000 and that benefits should exist for at least another 10 years.

2. *Patent*, $234,000. The patent was purchased on January 2009 for $252,000, when it had a remaining legal life of 14 years. On December 31, 2009, $18,000 of cost was amortized. On December 31, 2010, Jason estimates that the patent will be useful for only another 9 years (through December 31, 2019). However, it is estimated that the patent still has a value to the company of over $240,000.

For each of the intangibles—goodwill and patent—explain what entry, if any, is necessary at the end of 2010 to adjust the accounts.

PROBLEMS

Problem Set A

Determining the cost to be capitalized for acquisition of assets.   ◀ **Problem 18.1A**
                                                                                  Objective 1

On January 6, 2010, Fairley Company purchased a site for a new manufacturing plant for $1,800,000. At a cost of $8,000, it razed an existing facility (fair market value $150,000) and received $10,000 from its salvage. The company also paid $3,200 in attorney fees, $910 in inspection fees, and $525 for a permit to raze the facility. After the facility was torn down, the following costs were incurred: $25,200 for fill dirt for the site, $16,000 for leveling the site, $97,000 for paving sidewalks and curbs, and $3,600,000 for building costs of the new facility. The parking area was paved at a cost of $98,900.

INSTRUCTIONS

Compute the capitalized costs of (1) the manufacturing plant, (2) the land, and (3) the land improvements.

Analyze: Unfortunately, Fairley's new building was not completed on schedule, but the company had to vacate the old building. As a result the business was shut down for two months. During this period, the company reported a net loss of $223,800. The president suggests that the loss should be capitalized as part of the cost of the new building. What is your recommendation?

Problem 18.2A ▶
Objective 2 e**X**cel

Using different depreciation methods and comparing the results.

On January 4, 2010, Illinois Company purchased new equipment for $225,000 that had a useful life of four years and a salvage value of $25,000.

INSTRUCTIONS

Prepare a schedule showing the annual depreciation and end-of-year accumulated depreciation for the first three years of the asset's life under (1) the straight-line method, (2) the sum-of-the-years'-digits method, and (3) the double-declining-balance method.

Analyze: If the sum-of-years'-digits method is used to compute depreciation, what would be the book value of the asset at the end of 2011?

Problem 18.3A ▶
Objective 2 e**X**cel

Using the straight-line and units-of-output methods of depreciation.

On January 5, 2010, Hall Company purchased equipment for $280,000, having an estimated useful life of five years or 100,000 units of product. The estimated salvage value was $10,000. Actual production data for the first three years were: 2010—20,000 units; 2011—28,000 units; and 2012—23,000 units.

INSTRUCTIONS

Compute each year's depreciation and the end-of-year accumulated depreciation under (1) the straight-line method and (2) the units-of-output method.

Analyze: Would the total depreciation taken over the five-year life depend on which of the two methods is used? Why?

Problem 18.4A ▶
Objectives 2, 3

Computing depreciation and MACRS on assets.

On January 12, 2010, Maryland Company purchased a computer (cost, $4,100; expected life four years; estimated salvage value, $500) and a lightweight van for delivery purposes (cost, $32,500; estimated life, eight years; estimated salvage value, $2,500). For financial accounting purposes, the company uses straight-line depreciation on all assets.

INSTRUCTIONS

1. Compute depreciation of the computer cost for financial accounting purposes for 2010 and 2011.

2. Compute cost recovery of the computer cost for income tax purposes for 2010 and 2011.

3. Compute depreciation of the van cost for financial accounting purposes for 2010 and 2011.

4. Compute cost recovery of the van cost for income tax purposes for 2010 and 2011.

Analyze: What objectives or principles account for the differences between the financial accounting depreciation rules and the income tax cost recovery rules?

Problem 18.5A ▶
Objectives 2, 4, 5

Recording asset trade-ins and sales.

The transactions listed below occurred at Winspear Company during 2010.

DATE	TRANSACTIONS
Mar. 25	Exchanged a printer (Office Equipment) that had an original cost of $6,800 when purchased on January 4, 2008. The useful life of the old asset was originally estimated at six years and the salvage value at $200. The new printer had a price and market value of $9,600. Winspear gave up the old machine and paid $4,800 cash. The new printer is estimated to have a useful life of five years and a salvage value of $600.
July 19	Exchanged a truck (Vehicles) for a new one that had a sales price, and fair value, of $42,800. Received a trade-in allowance of $10,500 on the old truck and paid cash of $32,300. The old truck had been purchased for $34,000 on May 27, 2007, three years earlier. The life of the old truck was originally estimated at four years and the salvage value at $5,800. The life of the new truck is estimated to be five years and it is estimated to have a salvage value of $8,800.
Aug. 18	Sold a truck that was purchased on January 5, 2008, for $39,000. It had an estimated life of four years and an estimated salvage value of $7,000. Sales price is as indicated in Instructions, below.

INSTRUCTIONS

Note: In following these instructions, assume that straight-line depreciation is used and that depreciation was last recorded on December 31, 2009. Compute depreciation to the nearest whole dollar.

1. Give the entries in general journal form to record the two exchange transactions.

2. Give the entries in general journal form to record the sale of the truck, assuming

    a. The sales price was $19,000.

    b. The sales price was $16,000.

Analyze: What was the book value of the truck sold on August 18?

Recording asset sales and trade-ins.

◀ **Problem 18.6A**
Objectives 4, 5

Thames Company purchased four identical machines on January 10, 2010, paying $3,000 for each. The useful life of each machine is expected to be six years, with a salvage value of $600 each. The company uses the straight-line method of depreciation. Selected transactions involving the machines follow. The accounts for recording these transactions are also given.

INSTRUCTIONS

1. Record the transactions in general journal form. Round all calculations to the nearest whole dollar.

ACCOUNTS

101	Cash
141	Machinery
142	Accumulated Depreciation—Machinery
495	Gain on Sale of Machinery
541	Depreciation Expense—Machinery
595	Loss on Sale of Machinery
597	Loss on Stolen Machinery

DATE	TRANSACTIONS FOR 2010
Jan. 10	Paid $3,000, in cash, for each of four machines.
Dec. 31	Recorded depreciation for the year on the four machines.

DATE	TRANSACTIONS FOR 2011
Apr. 3	Machine 1 was stolen; no insurance was carried.
Dec. 31	Recorded depreciation for the year for the three remaining machines.

DATE	TRANSACTIONS FOR 2012
Sept. 18	Sold machine 2 for $2,200 cash.
Dec. 31	Recorded depreciation for the year on the two remaining machines.

DATE	TRANSACTIONS FOR 2013
June 4	Machine 3 was traded in for a similar machine (no. 5) with a $3,900 list price and fair market value. A trade-in allowance of $1,900 was received. The balance was paid in cash. The new machine has an estimated life of six years and salvage value of $600.
Aug. 29	Machine 4 was traded in for a similar machine (no. 6) with a $4,000 list price and fair market value. A trade-in allowance of $1,050 was received. The balance was paid in cash. The new machine has an estimated life of six years, with salvage value of $600.
Dec. 31	Record depreciation on the two new machines.

Analyze: What is the balance of the *Accumulated Depreciation* account on December 31, 2013?

Problem 18.7A
Objective 6

Compute and record depletion of natural resources.

Mayfair Mining Company had total depletable capitalized costs of $656,000 for a mine acquired in early 2010. It was estimated that the mine contained 820,000 tons of recoverable ore when production began. During 2010, 20,500 tons were mined, and 41,000 tons were mined in 2011.

INSTRUCTIONS

1. Compute the depletion expense in 2010 and 2011 for financial accounting purposes. What accounts will be debited and credited to record the depletion?
2. **a.** In 2010, 20,500 tons of ore were sold for $2,050,000. For tax purposes, operating expenses of the mine were $500,000. The taxpayer may deduct either cost depletion or percentage depletion, which for the type ore produced is 8 percent of production sold from the mine. (Assume, however, that percentage depletion is limited to the amount of net income from the property.) What would be the amount of percentage depletion allowable in 2010?
   b. What would be the amount of cost depletion allowable for tax purposes in 2010, assuming that capitalized mineral costs are the same for tax purposes as for financial accounting purposes?

c. What will be the amount of depletion based on cost that the company could deduct on its tax return in 2011 if it deducts percentage depletion in 2010?

d. Suppose that in the first three years of the mine's life, the company took percentage depletion totaling $654,000. In the fifth year of the mine's life, production proceeds were $4,300,000. How much percentage depletion could the company deduct in the fifth year?

Analyze: What explanation do you think might be given for the deviation of income tax rules from basic accounting principles in the determination of depletion of costs of minerals?

Recording impairment of property, plant, and equipment.

◀ **Problem 18.8A**
Objective 7

Herron Realty Company owns a number of large office buildings in several cities in the United States. One of the buildings is 16 years old and has had a large number of vacant office suites for several years. The building's book value is $13 million. The company has examined carefully its future cash flows and has determined that it is highly unlikely that the company can recover the building's book value from future cash flows. Further study in November 2010 has resulted in three estimates of the market value of the building. All of the estimates of value are approximately $8.2 million.

INSTRUCTIONS

1. Should Herron record impairment of the building? Why?

2. If impairment should be recorded, what is the amount of impairment?

3. What accounting entry would be necessary based on the above facts?

4. If impairment is recorded in 2010 and subsequently the value of the building increases in 2011 so that the market value exceeds the book value, should the book value of the building be increased at that time?

Analyze: How could the company use its estimates of cash flows to arrive at a "market value" of the building?

Recording intangible asset acquisition, amortization, and impairment.

◀ **Problem 18.9A**
Objective 8

Selected accounts of the Zelma Company are listed below. On January 1, 2010, the only intangible asset in the company's account was *Goodwill*. This was recorded in 2003 when the company acquired another company and paid $200,000 more than the fair market value of the net identifiable tangible assets acquired. For two years, the company amortized the costs on the basis of a 40-year life, charging a total of $20,000 to an account called *Amortization Expense—Goodwill*. However, no amortization of goodwill has been recorded since 2004. Transactions and events that took place at the company during 2010 are given below.

INSTRUCTIONS

1. Record the transactions for 2010 in general journal form.

2. Record amortization of the intangible assets, where appropriate, for the year ended December 31, 2010.

3. Record impairment of assets where appropriate on December 31, 2010.

ACCOUNTS

Cash
Computer Software
Patents
Product Formulas
Goodwill
Amortization Expense—Patents
Amortization Expense—Computer Software
Amortization Expense—Product Formulas
Impairment of Intangibles

TRANSACTIONS AND OTHER INFORMATION

1. On May 10, 2010, the company paid $192,000 to purchase a product formula. The formula is expected to have a useful life of eight years.

2. On July 5, the company paid $640,000 for a patent having a useful life of 10 years.

3. On September 22, the company purchased a unique computer program for $240,000. This program has an estimated useful life of five years.

4. During the year, the company recorded various cash expenditures of $210,000 for labor and supplies used in its research department. (Date entry December 31.)

5. At the end of 2010, the company reviewed the goodwill shown in the accounts. Based on the profitability of activities acquired in purchasing the other business, the owners of the business think the goodwill has a value of $150,000 and should be of benefit for many more years.

Analyze: Based on the transactions above, what is the total net book value of Zelma Company's intangible assets on December 31, 2010?

Problem Set B

Problem 18.1B
Objective 1

▶ **Determining the costs to be capitalized for acquisition of an asset.**

On July 5, 2010, the Hilton Company purchased a site for its new headquarters for $250,000. At a cost of $25,000, it razed two existing houses, with a total appraised value of $80,000, and received $15,000 from salvage. The firm also paid $4,500 in attorney's fees, $500 in inspection fees, and $250 for a permit to raze the houses. After the houses were razed, the firm incurred these costs:

$20,000 for fill dirt for the site
$10,000 for leveling the site
$70,000 for paving sidewalks and curbs
$98,500 for paving a parking lot
$3,225,000 for construction costs of new building

INSTRUCTIONS

Compute the capitalized costs of (1) the land, (2) the building, and (3) the land improvements.

Analyze: What net effect did these transactions have on the total owner's equity?

Problem 18.2B
Objective 2

▶ **Using different depreciation methods and comparing the results.**

On January 5, 2010, Mandy Company purchased a new $560,000 machine with five-year useful life and an estimated salvage value of $30,000.

INSTRUCTIONS

Prepare a schedule showing the annual depreciation and accumulated depreciation for each of the first three years of the asset's life under (1) the straight-line method, (2) the sum-of-the-years'-digits method, and (3) the double-declining-balance method.

Analyze: If the double-declining-balance method is used, what would be the book value of the machine at the end of 2011?

Problem 18.3B
Objective 2

▶ **Using various methods to compute depreciation.**

Kirk Company purchased a carton fabrication unit for $440,000 on January 8, 2010. The machine's useful life is estimated as 1,600,000 units of product or eight years and its salvage value is estimated at $40,000. The number of cartons fabricated in each year, 2010 to 2012, is as follows:

Year	Cartons Fabricated
2010	160,000
2011	168,400
2012	236,000

INSTRUCTIONS

Compute the depreciation expense and accumulated depreciation at year end for each of the three years under (1) the straight-line method and (2) the units-of-production method.

Analyze: If the units-of-output method were used, what would be the book value of the machine at the end of 2011?

Computing depreciation and MACRS on assets.

On January 6, 2010, Webb Company purchased a computer (cost, $16,400; expected life, four years; estimated salvage value, $2,000) and an eight-passenger van (cost, $34,000; estimated life, seven years; estimated salvage value, $6,000). For financial accounting purposes, the company has always used straight-line depreciation on all assets.

◄ **Problem 18.4B**
Objectives 2, 3

INSTRUCTIONS

1. Compute depreciation of the computer's cost for financial accounting purposes for 2010 and 2011.
2. Compute MACRS cost recovery of the computer's cost for income tax purposes for 2010 and 2011.
3. Compute depreciation of the van's cost for financial accounting purpose for 2010 and 2011.
4. Compute MACRS cost recovery of the van's cost for income tax purposes for 2010 and 2011.

Analyze: The owner suggests that to avoid duplication of work, the company should use the amount of cost recovery taken on the tax return for each asset as the amount to be used for depreciation in financial statements. Do you agree? Why?

Recording asset trade-ins and sales.

The following transactions occurred at Anderson Company during 2010.

◄ **Problem 18.5B**
Objectives 2, 4, 5

DATE	TRANSACTIONS
Apr. 2	Traded in a copy machine (Office Equipment) that had been purchased for $5,200 on December 29, 2007. Straight-line depreciation of the old copier has been based on an estimated useful life of five years, with salvage value of $800. The new copier had a purchase price and value of $12,000. Anderson received a trade-in allowance of $3,500 on the old machine and paid cash of $8,500. The new copier has a useful life of five years and an estimated salvage value of $600.
July 8	Exchanged a delivery truck (Vehicles) for a new one with a list price of $44,000, estimated useful life of five years and salvage value of $8,400. A trade-in allowance of $10,000 was received on the old truck, which had been purchased on July 1, 2007, for $33,000. Depreciation on the old truck has been based on an estimated $5,000 salvage value and a five-year life.
Sept. 23	Sold a refrigeration unit (Store Equipment) for cash (see Instruction 2). The unit was purchased on January 3, 2007, for $32,000 and was depreciated on the straight-line basis, using an estimated life of six years and a salvage value of $2,000.

INSTRUCTIONS

Note: In each case, assume that straight-line depreciation is used and that depreciation was last recorded on December 31, 2009. Compute depreciation to the nearest whole dollar.

1. Record in general journal form the two trade-in transactions on April 2 and July 8.
2. Record the sale of the refrigeration unit, assuming
   a. the sales price was $13,500
   b. the sales price was $10,200

Analyze: What accounting concepts underlie the accounting treatments for the transactions of April 2 and July 8?

Problem 18.6B ▶ **Recording asset sales and trade-ins.**

Objectives 2, 4, 5

Freedom Company purchased four identical machines on January 4, 2010, paying $9,000 for each machine. The useful life of each machine is expected to be five years, with no salvage value expected. The company uses the straight-line method of depreciation. Selected transactions involving the machines are listed below. The necessary accounts for recording these transactions are also given.

INSTRUCTIONS

Record the transactions in general journal form. Use the following accounts, as necessary.

ACCOUNTS

101	Cash	541	Depreciation Expense—Machinery
141	Machinery	595	Loss on Sale of Machinery
142	Accumulated Depreciation—Machinery	596	Loss on Trade-In of Machinery
495	Gain on Sale of Machinery	597	Fire Loss on Machinery

DATE	TRANSACTIONS FOR 2010
Jan. 4	Paid $9,000 each for four machines.
Dec. 31	Recorded depreciation for the year on the four machines.

DATE	TRANSACTIONS FOR 2011
Mar. 31	Machine 1 was destroyed by fire; no insurance was carried.
Dec. 31	Recorded depreciation for the year for the three remaining machines.

DATE	TRANSACTIONS FOR 2012
Oct. 2	Sold machine 2 for $4,400 cash.
Dec. 31	Recorded depreciation for the year on the two remaining machines.

DATE	TRANSACTIONS FOR 2013
May 28	Traded machine 3 for a similar machine (no. 5) with an $8,800 price and fair market value. A trade-in allowance of $2,800 was received. The balance of $6,000 was paid in cash.
Sept. 3	Traded in machine 4 for a similar machine (no. 6) with a $9,200 list price and fair value. A trade-in allowance of $2,000 was received. The balance was paid in cash.
Sept. 3	Assume that the company somehow has adopted a policy of recording trade-in transactions using the rules required for federal income tax purposes—even though the cost of assets and the depreciation are determined under financial accounting rules as you have computed them previously in this problem. Give the entry that would be recorded on September 3 to record the trade-in of machine 4 on machine 6, using the facts given.

Analyze: What is the difference between the financial accounting entries and tax entries for the trade-in of machine 4?

Compute and record depletion of natural resources.

◀ **Problem 18.7B**
Objective 6

Vinzant Company acquired a mineral property and drilled an oil well in 2010. Capitalized costs subject to depletion totaled $900,000. When the well began producing in late 2010, it was estimated that one million barrels of oil could ultimately be produced from the property. In 2010, 4,000 barrels were produced and sold for $160,000. Operating costs for the property were $159,200. Sixty thousand barrels were produced and sold for $2,500,000 in 2011 and operating costs that year were $320,000.

INSTRUCTIONS

1. Compute the depletion expense in 2010 and 2011 for financial accounting purposes. What accounts will be debited and credited to record the depletion?

2. Assume that capitalized costs and operating expenses were the same for financial accounting and tax purposes. The taxpayer may deduct either cost depletion or percentage depletion. The percentage depletion for oil and gas production is 15 percent of gross income from the property, but limited to 100 percent of net income from the property. Assume that all of the oil produced is eligible for percentage depletion.

   a. What would be the amount of cost depletion allowable for tax purposes in 2010?

   b. What will be the amount of depletion that the company could deduct on its tax return in 2010?

   c. What amount of cost depletion could the company deduct on its tax return in 2011?

   d. What would be the amount, if any, of percentage depletion deductible in 2011?

   e. Suppose that in the first four years of the property's life, the company deducted depletion totaling $798,800 on the tax returns. No additional depletable costs were capitalized. In the fifth year of the property's life, proceeds of $4,800,000 were received from the oil produced, and operating expenses of $900,000 were incurred. What amount, if any, of percentage depletion may be deducted on the company's tax return in that year?

Analyze: Would the company be entitled to percentage depletion in the sixth and future years in which there was gross income that exceeded the operating expenses?

Recognize and record impairment of property, plant, and equipment.

◀ **Problem 18.8B**
Objective 7

South Coast Airlines is a small commercial airline operating in the United States. Because of poor economic conditions in the airline industry in 2010, South Coast has eliminated some routes and reduced the frequency of flights on all other routes. As a result, the airline has indefinitely stored 8 of its 20 aircraft. The company continues to lose money and sees no time in the foreseeable future that the parked aircraft will be operated again. The company's public accountant has told the airline officials that it must assess whether the parked planes (and perhaps some of those flying routes) should be assessed for impairment. The parked planes have a combined book value of $46 million.

Company officials have researched the problem and found that there is an abundance of identical or similar planes that could be purchased for approximately $4 million each. Several of these similar planes have been recently sold and the $4 million value for each has been accepted by company officials as being a good estimate of the going sales price and of their fair value. It has been impossible for company officials to estimate future cash flows, or if there will be any future cash flows from those planes.

INSTRUCTIONS

Answer the following questions.

1. Should South Coast Airlines record impairment of the parked planes? Why or why not?

2. If impairment should be recorded, what is the amount of impairment?

3. What accounting entry would be necessary based on the above facts?

4. If impairment is recorded in 2010 and subsequently the value of the planes increases before they are sold, with the result that market value exceeds the book value, should the value of the planes be increased at that time?

Analyze: What steps can you suggest the company take in considering whether the planes that are still flying also may be impaired?

Problem 18.9B ▶ **Recording intangible asset acquisition, amortization, and impairment.**

Objective 8

Selected accounts of the Howard Medical Labs are listed below. Also given are some transactions and events that took place at the company during 2010.

INSTRUCTIONS

1. Record in general journal form the transactions for 2010 described.

2. Record amortization of the intangible assets for the year ended December 31, 2010.

3. Indicate what steps should be taken, if any, to properly account for the balance of $1,200,000 in the *Goodwill* account on December 31. The following accounts related to intangible assets are found in Howard's general ledger.

ACCOUNTS

Cash	Research and Development Expense
Patents	Amortization of Patents
Computer Software	Amortization of Computer Software
Goodwill	Impairment of Intangibles

DATE	TRANSACTIONS AND INFORMATION
April 10	Purchased for cash of $400,000 a patent related to a chemical compound. It has a legal life of 12 years remaining, but is expected to be used for only 8 years because of new patents for similar products being developed.
Sept. 1	Purchased a computer software program for $32,000 in cash from a computer software supply firm. The software program is to be used in the company's inventory control system and has an estimated useful life of seven years.
Dec. 31	(Date of journal entry, reflecting summary for year.) During year, made cash expenditures of $3,000,000 for research and development costs related to a new electronic medical procedure being developed. Researchers have worked on the project for 10 months of the year and think the project will result in a valuable patent.
Dec. 31	The company examined the balance of $1,800,000 in the *Goodwill* account. This balance arose from purchase of another business two years earlier and represents the amount paid for the acquired business in excess of the value of the net identifiable assets acquired. The examination concluded that the activities acquired have continued to be very profitable and that there is no reason to record impairment on the $1,800,000 balance.

Analyze: Suppose that the examination of goodwill had revealed that the benefits (future profits) resulting from the acquisition two years ago are decreasing. Based on the estimated value of the excess of the future profits over the value of the net assets acquired, the value of goodwill is estimated to be currently only $1,200,000. What accounting entry, if any, should be made to record this fact?

Critical Thinking Problem 18.1

Cost Capitalization, Depreciation, MACRS, Impairment

Beatrice Company operates a real estate abstract, title, and insurance company. Below are selected transactions and events that occurred during the years 2010 to 2013. Using those transactions and events, follow the instructions given.

INSTRUCTIONS

1. Give the adjusting entries on December 31, 2011, to record depreciation expense for the year on all assets.

2. **a.** Compute the amount of MACRS cost recovery for tax purposes on the furniture and fixtures in (1) 2011 and (2) 2012.

   b. What is the MACRS recovery period for the building?

3. Should Beatrice's management be concerned with the possibility of asset impairment at the end of 2013? Explain.

4. Do you agree with the company's financial manager that depreciation should be reduced in 2013 because of the decline in business? Explain your answer.

TRANSACTIONS AND EVENTS 2010 AND 2011

The company purchased a building site for $400,000 on August 2, 2010. Preparation for construction began in October. Costs, other than land costs, incurred in 2010 and 2011 were

a. grading and preparing the site, $30,000

b. paving the sidewalks and parking lot, $65,000 (estimated life 25 years, no salvage value; straight-line depreciation to be used)

c. fencing back of the property, $15,000, erected in same week building was completed (estimated life, 15 years; no salvage value; straight-line depreciation to be used)

d. building construction contract costs $520,000, completed June 25, 2011 (estimated life, 35 years; salvage value, $25,000; straight-line depreciation to be used)

e. telephone system installed in the last week of June 2011, $18,000 (estimated life, six years; estimated salvage value $1,800; sum-of-years' digits depreciation method to be used)

f. furniture and fixtures purchased in late June 2011, $64,000 (estimated life, 10 years; estimated salvage value, $4,000; double-declining-balance method to be used)

The company opened for business in the new building on July 5, 2011. During the remainder of 2011, the business grew at about the pace anticipated by the company's management when the project was planned.

2012 AND 2013

1. The business continued to grow at the anticipated pace in 2012.

2. In June 2013, a rumor was circulated that a hazardous waste deposit existed on the company's property, but no evidence was presented to support the allegation. In November 2013, an investigative team from local, state, and federal health services arrived on the scene to conduct a detailed investigation of the property. In the third week of December, they reported having found what had once been a dump site. The investigators took many samples and sent these to laboratories, then left, stating they would return in the second week of January. They hope to have tentative laboratory reports at the time of their return. The company's attorneys are concerned about the investigation because the company's insurance does not cover losses from this problem and the state law places responsibility on the current owner to clean up the property. Because of the rumors, customers were reluctant to come to the building and business declined dramatically in November and December 2013.

3. In late December, the company's executive manager suggested that because of the decline in business the company should reduce its current depreciation charge, resulting in lower depreciation in the next few years, with greater depreciation in subsequent years. The manager thinks his plan is akin to units-of-production depreciation and he expects future business to be greater, resulting in higher depreciation at that time.

Critical Thinking Problem 18.2

Depreciation Expense Company Practices

In a review of the annual reports of P&E Wholesale Company and Pierce Distributors, you note that P&E Wholesale uses straight-line depreciation and Pierce Distributors uses the declining-balance method.

1. Are these companies violating the generally accepted accounting principle of consistency by using different depreciation methods?

2. If you examined the federal income tax returns of these companies, would you expect the deductions, similar to depreciation taken on their income tax returns, to be the same as the depreciation expenses shown on their financial statements? Why or why not?

3. Assume that these companies are similar in all respects except for their difference in computing depreciation. Which company would you expect to report the lower net income for the year?

4. Who is responsible for determining the depreciation method used by the company for financial accounting purposes?

BUSINESS CONNECTIONS

Plant Asset Procedures

Managerial FOCUS

1. Suggest three key procedures involving internal control of property, plant, and equipment that relate to accounting records.

2. Suggest three key procedures involving internal control of property, plant, and equipment that do not relate specifically to accounting records.

3. Assume that you are the accountant at a fabricating plant. One of the vice presidents has asked you why one of the pieces of equipment used in the plant is shown at its original cost in the asset accounts. Respond to the question.

4. Suppose you are on the controller's staff at a large company. You have suggested assigning responsibility for the company's equipment to specific individuals. One supervisor has objected, saying it is a waste of time. Defend your suggestion to the controller and to the supervisor.

5. Generally accepted accounting principles require that all research and development costs be expensed in the year they are incurred. An officer of the company wants to amortize these costs. What can you say to explain why this accounting requirement exists?

Goodwill

Ethical DILEMMA

Lin's Auto Repair Service has been in business for five years. He has developed a great reputation of doing a good job at reasonable prices. His reputation has given him a large, loyal clientele. During those years, Mr. Lin has purchased net assets of $150,000 on which he owes $50,000. Lin has decided to sell his business and open another one 10 miles away. Hector Lopez has agreed to purchase the business for $200,000. Is it ethical for Mr. Lin to accept a larger amount for this business than its value? If so, how would Mr. Lopez record this transaction? Is it ethical for Mr. Lin to open a new business so close to the old business?

Depreciation Amounts and Method

Refer to the *2006 Annual Report* for The Home Depot, Inc., in Appendix A.

1. Locate the Notes to Consolidated Financial Statements. Review Note 1, Summary of Significant Accounting Policies. What method is used to depreciate the company's furniture, fixtures and equipment? What estimated useful life is assigned to buildings?

2. Find the Consolidated Balance Sheets. What amount was charged to accumulated depreciation and amortization for the year ended January 28, 2007? What net value is reported for Property and Equipment?

Annual Report

The following excerpts were taken from the Pier 1 Imports, Inc., *2007 Annual Report*.

NOTES TO CONSOLIDATED FINANCIAL STATEMENTS

Properties, maintenance, and repairs—Buildings, equipment, furniture, and fixtures, and leasehold improvements are carried at cost less accumulated depreciation. Depreciation is computed using the straight-line method over estimated remaining useful lives of the assets, generally 30 years for buildings and 3 to 10 years for equipment, furniture, and fixtures. Depreciation of improvements to leased properties is based upon the shorter of the remaining primary lease term or the estimated useful lives of such assets. Depreciation related to the Company's distribution centers is included in cost of sales. All other depreciation costs are included in depreciation and amortization. Depreciation costs were $46,984,000, $54,870,000 and $54,404,000 in fiscal 2007, 2006, and 2005, respectively.

STREETWISE:
Questions from the
REAL WORLD

Financial Statement
ANALYSIS

Pier 1 imports

Note 4—Properties		
Properties are summarized as follows at March 3, 2007, and February 25, 2006 (in thousands):		
	2007	**2006**
Land	$ 18,315	$ 18,778
Buildings	94,444	95,056
Equipment, furniture, and fixtures	259,458	271,702
Leasehold improvements	199,879	217,795
Computer software	72,027	60,208
Projects in progress	1,557	5,673
. . . .	645,680	669,212
Less accumulated depreciation and amortization	406,132	370,290
Properties, net	$239,548	$298,922

Analyze:

1. Based on the information presented above, what is the historical cost of the assets reflected on the consolidated balance sheet for Pier 1 Imports, Inc., for fiscal 2007?

2. What journal entry would be necessary to record a repair to equipment that did not materially extend the useful life of the equipment? Assume Pier 1 paid $250 for the repair with check 13389 on March 28, 2006.

3. What percentage of total property costs has been depreciated on March 3, 2007?

Analyze Online: Locate the Pier 1 Imports Web site (www.pier1.com). Review the most recent annual report provided on the site by clicking *Investor Relations,* then answer the following questions.

4. What net book value of "Properties" is reflected on the consolidated balance sheets?

5. What percentage of total property costs has been depreciated at the fiscal year-end?

Extending THE THOUGHT

Employees as Assets

A company's employees are often referred to as valuable assets of the company, yet the balance sheet makes no reference to employees. Do you agree with this? Why or why not?

Business COMMUNICATION

Short Speech

You have owned and operated Gailery's Automotive Repair Shop for 20 years. As a business owner and accountant, you have been invited to speak at the next Small Business Administration luncheon for new business owners. "Accounting for Plant Assets" is the topic. Prepare a five-minute speech on plant assets and depreciation. It might be helpful to use note cards containing three or four major points that you plan to discuss. Remember that you will be speaking to new business owners who need to understand how assets should be recorded in their accounting records and why depreciation of those assets is important.

TEAMWORK

Asset's Salvage Value

Property, plant, and equipment can be depreciated in various methods. As a team, select an asset to acquire and depreciate; for example, a large stamping machine. Determine the asset's cost, salvage value, life, depreciation method, and annual depreciation. Double the salvage value of the asset and explain the effect it would have on depreciation expense. Is it favorable or unfavorable and why? Present your finding to the class.

Internet CONNECTION

MACRS

Depreciation is calculated differently for financial records than depreciation (cost recovery) for income tax reporting. The Internal Revenue Service recognizes only the MACRS method. *Publication 17, Your Federal Income Tax,* is an important reference for income tax preparation. Go to the www.irs.gov Web site and *Publication 17.* From the *Publication 17*'s Table of Contents, select MACRS under GDS (General Depreciation System). Find the MACRS Table of Percentages. How does it compare to the table listed in the textbook? Go back to search and enter Topic 704. What are the five tests that must be met for an asset to be depreciable?

Answers to **Self Reviews**

Answers to Section 1 Self Review

1. Sum-of-years'-digits and double-declining methods.
2. Debit *Depreciation Expense,* credit *Accumulated Depreciation.*
3. Depreciation is the allocation of the cost of a long-term asset to expense during its useful life.
4. $4,320.
5. $2,333.33.
6. Numerator = 5; denominator = 28.
7. Under double-declining-balance depreciation, salvage is initially ignored and the rate is twice the straight-line rate. Straight-line depreciation yields higher income in early years and lower income in later years.

Answers to Section 2 Self Review

1. The asset account and accumulated depreciation account are removed, the sales proceeds are recorded. The difference between the proceeds and net book value (cost minus accumulated depreciation) is recorded as gain or loss.

2. Under tax rules, neither gain nor loss is recorded on the trade-in of an asset on a like-kind asset. Under financial accounting rules, gain is not recognized, but a loss must be recognized.

3. When the net book due exceeds the sales price.

4. **b.** no gain or loss.

5. **b.** a gain of $8,000.

6. The asset account and the accumulated depreciation would be overstated by the same amount. There would be no effect on net asset book value.

Answers to Section 3 Self Review

1. By comparing its fair value to its book value. There may be no ready indication, such as a ready market price, of an asset's fair value. A common approach is to estimate the future cash flows from the asset's use on a year-by-year basis and to discount these future cash flows to their current value.

2. GAAP requires that "research and development costs" must be charged to expense when incurred. There are a few specified exceptions to this rule, but the costs incurred by Daytime do not fall within these exceptions.

3. If the expected future cash flows from the asset are less than its book value, the asset is impaired.

4. The trade name is an intangible asset that does not have a legal or other definable life, so its cost is not amortized. Therefore, its cost would be subject to the impairment rules in the same way as the cost of goodwill.

5. All of these costs should be transferred to expense (depletion for the mineral rights and depreciation for drilling equipment) on the unit-of-production basis as the oil is produced.

6. The company should assess operations to determine that profits are adequately above what they would be without the trade name in order to assure that its carrying value is not impaired.

7. Depreciation is the allocation of cost of personal and real tangible property to expense over the property's useful life. Depletion is the allocation of cost of mineral rights. Amortization is the allocation costs of intangibles with estimated useful lives. All refer to the charging of the costs of assets to expense over their useful lives, but apply to different types of long-term assets.

Answers to Comprehensive Self Review

1. $2,000 loss ($2,600 book value − $600 sales price)

2. Legal life is the time period that the business or individual has legal rights to utilize whatever rights can be derived from the intangible asset. Intangibles such as copyrights, patents, and most franchises may be used exclusively only for a limited period. The economic life is the period that the intangible will provide economic benefits to the holder of the right. For example, a patent owned by a business may provide exclusive right to produce a product for another 15 years. This is the legal life. However, new processes being developed may make the existing patent obsolete within three years. Three years is the economic life.

3. Real property comprises land and other assets that are affixed permanently to the land. It includes land, land improvements, buildings, and other structures attached to the land. Personal property comprises those assets that are not affixed to the land and are relatively moveable—such as furniture, equipment, and vehicles.

4. 55 (10 + 9 + 8 + 7 + 6 + 5 + 4 + 3 + 2 + 1).

5. The matching principle of matching costs with revenues. The constraint of conservatism plays an important role in applying the matching principle.

6. When the life of the asset is limited to an estimable number of units of production.

Accounting for Partnerships Chapter 19

 www.hvpros.com

Healthcare Venture Professionals, LLC (HVP) is a full-service management company that provides professional leadership and consultative resources to hospitals and physicians. The company has been successful working with their clients to develop joint-ventured outpatient centers. Some of the services HVP provides include:

- Comprehensive marketing feasibility analysis to determine the viability of new medical facilities.
- Regulatory review to determine the types of certification, licenses, and accreditation that will be required to run a facility.
- Facility design and equipment planning.
- Ongoing management and consulting to ensure the successful operation of a new facility.

The founders of HVP chose to personally fund the company toeliminate undue influences from outside investors so the company isfree to act in the best interest of its clients. All senior-level employeesenjoy a degree of ownership and share in the success of HVP.

thinking critically

If you were one of the partners of HVP, what responsibilities or liabilities might you carry?

Section 1

SECTION OBJECTIVES

>> 1. Explain the major advantages and disadvantages of a partnership.

WHY IT'S IMPORTANT

Selecting the most advantageous form of business organization contributes to the overall success of a company.

>> 2. State the important provisions that should be included in every partnership agreement.

WHY IT'S IMPORTANT

A partnership agreement is a legal document that dictates the operating structure and terms of the business entity.

>> 3. Account for the formation of a partnership.

WHY IT'S IMPORTANT

Assets, liabilities, and owners' capital must all be correctly stated from the partnership's start.

TERMS TO LEARN

articles of partnership
general partner
limited partner
limited partnership
memorandum entry
mutual agency
partnership
partnership agreement
unlimited liability

Forming a Partnership

Accounting procedures for a sole proprietorship have been covered in previous chapters. This chapter discusses accounting for partnerships.

The Characteristics of a Partnership

The *Uniform Partnership Act,* adopted by all 50 states, defines a **partnership** as "an association of two or more persons who carry on, as co-owners, a business for profit." The partnership form of organization is widely used in small service, merchandising, and manufacturing businesses. Historically, professionals such as accountants, lawyers, and physicians have formed partnerships to pool their talents and abilities.

> Woolpert LLP began operations in 1911. Charlton Putnam, a surveyor and landscape engineer, joined forces with Edward Deeds and Charles Kettering, inventors of the self-starting automobile ignition system. In 1916, Ralph L. Woolpert, a civil engineer, joined the company as a partner. Throughout the years, the company extended partner status to others who contributed their expertise.

>>**1. OBJECTIVE**

Explain the major advantages and disadvantages of a partnership.

LP19

ADVANTAGES OF THE PARTNERSHIP

A partnership has three important advantages. It pools the skills, abilities, and financial resources of two or more individuals. It is easy and inexpensive to form, especially when compared with a corporation. A partnership does not pay income tax. The partners report their shares of the partnership's income or loss on their individual income tax returns.

DISADVANTAGES OF THE PARTNERSHIP

Certain characteristics of partnerships are clearly disadvantages. Each partner has **unlimited liability** for the partnership's debts. Thus, a partner's personal assets as well as the partnership's assets can be required in payment of the firm's debts. This characteristic enhances the credit standing of the business, but it can be a danger to the individual partners.

In most states, it is possible for some partners to have limited liability. A **limited partnership** is a partnership with one or more limited partners. **Limited partners** are liable only for their investment in the partnership. State laws generally require that limited partnerships have at least one **general partner,** a partner who has unlimited liability. Limited partners are prohibited from taking an active management role and from having their names in the partnership's name.

The partnership is a **mutual agency;** each partner is empowered to act as an agent for the partnership, binding the firm by those acts so long as they are within the normal scope of the partnership's activities.

A partnership lacks continuity; it has a limited life. When a partner dies or is incapacitated, the partnership is dissolved.

Partnership interest is not freely transferable; other partners must approve the sale of a partner's interest to a new partner. Upon a transfer of interest, the existing partnership is dissolved and a new partnership must be formed.

PARTNERSHIP AGREEMENTS

It is easy to form a partnership. Two or more partners agree to form the business entity by entering into an oral or written contract. A partnership may be deemed to have been formed without an explicit agreement if the behavior of the parties implies that a partnership exists. An oral agreement is binding on the partners, but a written contract is preferred. To avoid any future misunderstandings, an attorney prepares a legal contract forming a partnership and specifying certain details of the operation, called a **partnership agreement.** This is legally known as the **articles of partnership.** The partnership agreement can be simple, or complex and detailed. Every partnership agreement should contain the

- names of the partners;
- name, location, and nature of the business;
- starting date of the agreement;
- life of the partnership;
- rights and duties of each partner;
- amount of capital to be contributed by each partner;
- drawings by the partners;
- fiscal year and accounting method;
- method of allocating income or loss to the partners;
- procedures to be followed if the partnership is dissolved or the business is liquidated.

Partnerships dissolve upon a partner's death, incapacity, or withdrawal.

>>**2. OBJECTIVE**
State the important provisions that should be included in every partnership agreement.

LP19

Accounting for the Formation of a Partnership

Partnerships and sole proprietorships use the same types of journals and ledgers as well as asset, liability, revenue, and expense accounts. The only difference is that in a partnership, each partner has a capital account and a drawing account.

There are many ways to form a partnership. Partnerships are often formed when a sole proprietorship "takes in" a partner or partners to continue an existing business. Usually the new partners invest cash, and the sole proprietor contributes noncash assets and liabilities of the existing business. Sometimes two sole proprietors combine their operations into a partnership. Often partners start a completely new business with initial investments of cash.

>>**3. OBJECTIVE**
Account for the formation of a partnership.

LP19

When noncash assets are transferred to a partnership, they are recorded at their fair market value, as agreed to by the partners, on the transfer date. Liabilities are stated at their correct balances on the transfer date.

> Sometimes two existing companies form a partnership with a new objective or mission in mind. In February 2005, America Online, Inc., and Time Warner Cable established a partnership designed to connect computer users to the Internet. The two companies joined together to provide high-speed Internet service in New York and other areas. The cable company furnishes physical connections to the Internet, while AOL provides e-mail services and other online content.

Let's look at a partnership formed by Ellen Barret and Jerry Reed. Barret operates Old Army, a small clothing store that sells T-shirts, jeans, and other casual clothing. Reed works in another store selling athletic shoes. To get additional capital and to obtain Reed's talents, Barret offered to make Reed a partner in the business. Barret agreed to transfer the assets (except cash) and the liabilities of Old Army to the new partnership. Reed agreed to invest cash of $28,000 in the business. Figure 19.1 below shows the balance sheet of Old Army on December 31, 2009.

After examining Old Army's assets, Barret and Reed agreed that

- Net accounts receivable is $19,300.

Accounts receivable on balance sheet	$22,300
Definitely uncollectible	(1,800)
Accounts receivable, adjusted	$20,500
Likely to be uncollectible	(1,200)
Net accounts receivable	$19,300

- The value of merchandise inventory is $105,200.
- The store equipment's value is $3,000 based on an appraisal.

recall

Allowance Method

Under the allowance method for uncollectible accounts, an estimate is made before actual losses occur.

Old Army
Balance Sheet
December 31, 2009

Assets				
Cash			2 6 0 0	00
Accounts Receivable	22 3 0 0	00		
Less Allowance for Doubtful Accounts	7 5 0	00	21 5 5 0	00
Merchandise Inventory			115 0 0 0	00
Store Equipment	10 4 5 0	00		
Less Accumulated Depreciation	8 0 0 0	00	2 4 5 0	00
Total Assets			141 6 0 0	00
Liabilities and Owner's Equity				
Liabilities				
Notes Payable—Bank	39 1 0 0	00		
Accounts Payable	36 0 0 0	00		
Total Liabilities			75 1 0 0	00
Owner's Equity				
Ellen Barret			66 5 0 0	00
Total Liabilities and Owner's Equity			141 6 0 0	00

FIGURE 19.1

Balance Sheet for a Sole Proprietor

- Accrued interest payable on the note payable is $500. This liability was not recorded as of December 31.
- Accounts payable total is $34,700 as the result of settling a dispute with a creditor after the balance sheet was prepared.

Thus, Barret and Reed have agreed that the net assets Barret transferred are $53,200:

Accounts receivable	$ 19,300
Merchandise inventory	105,200
Store equipment	3,000
Notes payable	(39,100)
Interest payable	(500)
Accounts payable	(34,700)
Total	$ 53,200

MEMORANDUM ENTRY TO RECORD FORMATION OF PARTNERSHIP

The first entry in the general journal of the new partnership is a **memorandum entry,** which is an informational entry. It indicates the name of the business, the partners' names, and other pertinent information. Note that the memorandum entry references the partnership agreement, which provides information about the capital contributed by each partner and the division of income.

2010			
Jan.	1	On this date, a partnership was formed	
		between Ellen Barret and Jerry Reed to	
		carry on a retail clothing business under	
		the name of Old Army, according to the	
		terms of the partnership agreement effective	
		this date.	

INVESTMENT OF ASSETS AND LIABILITIES BY SOLE PROPRIETOR

The first journal entry records the transfer of Barret's assets and liabilities to the partnership.

Jan.	1	Account	No.	Debit	Credit
		Accounts Receivable	111	20 500 00	
		Merchandise Inventory	121	105 200 00	
		Store Equipment	131	3 000 00	
		Allowance for Doubtful Accounts	112		1 200 00
		Notes Payable—Bank	201		39 100 00
		Accounts Payable	205		34 700 00
		Interest Payable	215		500 00
		Ellen Barret, Capital	301		53 200 00
		Investment of Barret			

Note that the entry includes *Accounts Receivable* of $20,500 and *Allowance for Doubtful Accounts* of $1,200. All individual customers' balances, except for those that were definitely uncollectible, were transferred to the partnership. Consequently, the *Accounts Receivable* control account agrees with the total of the accounts receivable subsidiary ledger. Note that *Store Equipment* is transferred at fair market value. No accumulated depreciation is transferred. Depreciation on plant and equipment that was recorded by the previous owner is irrelevant. Depreciation will be recorded by the partnership based on the asset's value at the date of transfer.

INVESTMENT OF CASH BY PARTNER

The next journal entry records the investment of cash by Reed.

19	Jan.	1	Cash	101	28 00 0 00		19
20			Jerry Reed, Capital	311		28 00 0 00	20
21			Investment of cash by Reed				21
22							22

SUBSEQUENT INVESTMENTS AND PERMANENT WITHDRAWALS

During the life of the partnership, additional investments are recorded in the same manner as the initial investments. When partners make cash withdrawals that are intended to be permanent reductions of capital, the withdrawals are recorded as debits to the partners' capital accounts.

DRAWING ACCOUNTS

Partners need funds with which to pay their living expenses. Partners can obtain funds by making withdrawals against anticipated income. Each partner has a drawing account to record withdrawals.

The partnership agreement of Old Army specifies that Barret can withdraw up to $2,500 each month and that Reed can withdraw up to $1,900 each month. The withdrawals are recorded in the cash payments journal. The entry is a debit to the partners' drawing accounts and a credit to cash. At the end of 12 months, on December 31, Barret's drawing account has a debit balance of $30,000 ($2,500 $\times$ 12), and Reed's drawing account has a debit balance of $22,800 ($1,900 $\times$ 12).

Partners sometimes pay their personal bills with partnership funds. This practice is not sound because it leads to confusion between business and personal transactions. If the business pays a partner's personal expense, however, the debit in the cash payments journal is to the partner's drawing account, not an expense account.

It is common for partners to take merchandise from the business for their personal use. The cost of merchandise is debited to the partner's drawing account. The credit is to the ***Purchases*** account if the periodic inventory method is used and to the ***Merchandise Inventory*** account if the perpetual inventory method is used. Note that the inventory account is not involved—beginning inventory in the current period's cost of goods sold should agree with ending inventory of the prior period. Barret withdrew merchandise that cost $180 and had a retail sales price of $230. The transaction is recorded as follows.

1	2010						1
2	June	14	Ellen Barret, Drawing	302	1 8 0 00		2
3			Purchases	501		1 8 0 00	3
4			Cost of merchandise withdrawn				4
5			by Barret				5
6							6
7							7
8							8

recall

Separate Entity

The separate entity assumption states that the business is separate from its owners. This explains why personal expenses paid by the business are charged to the partner's drawing account rather than to a business expense account.

Section 1 Self Review

QUESTIONS

1. A business owner has agreed to transfer the assets and liabilities of her business to a new partnership. The new partner will invest cash in the new business in return for one-half interest. At what values should assets and liabilities of the old business be recorded in the accounts of the partnership?

2. Mason and Peters, partners in the MP Grocery Group, frequently withdraw merchandise for personal use. How should these merchandise withdrawals be recorded in the records of the partnership?

3. What are the major disadvantages of the partnership form of business?

EXERCISES

4. If the periodic inventory method is used, a withdrawal of merchandise from the business by one of the partners should be recorded as

a. a debit to the partner's drawing account and a credit to **Merchandise Inventory** for the sales price of the merchandise.

b. a debit to the partner's drawing account and a credit to **Merchandise Inventory** for the cost of the merchandise.

c. a debit to the partner's drawing account and a credit to **Purchases** for the cost of the merchandise.

d. Some other entry.

5. An investment of cash in the partnership by James Smith, a partner in Smith-Keyes Web Services, should be recorded by

a. a debit to **Cash** and a credit to **Smith-Keyes, Capital**.

b. a debit to **Smith-Keyes, Capital** and a credit to **Cash**.

c. a debit to **Cash** and a credit to **James Smith, Capital**.

d. a debit to **James Smith, Capital** and a credit to **Cash**.

ANALYSIS

6. James Mitchell and Rudy Hernandez are combining their businesses to form a new partnership. Mitchell invests merchandise inventory valued at $52,200, store equipment with a book value of $600 but appraised at $3,500, and accounts receivable of $10,000, of which $720 is assumed to be uncollectible. In addition, he is transferring liabilities of $5,000 owed to creditors. After the entry to record his investment is posted, what is the balance in Mitchell's partnership capital account?

(Answers to Section 1 Self Review are on page 680.)

>> **4.** **Compute and record the division of net income or net loss between partners in accordance with the partnership agreement.**

WHY IT'S IMPORTANT

The records must reflect the partnership agreement's allocation of profit and loss.

>> **5.** **Prepare a statement of partners' equities.**

WHY IT'S IMPORTANT

The statement of partners' equities summarizes the changes that have occurred in each partner's equity account. The ending balance appears on the balance sheet.

Allocating Income or Loss

Recall that a partnership does not pay income tax. The net income or net loss "flows through" to the partners, who report their share of the partnership income on their individual tax returns.

Allocating Partnership Income or Loss

At the end of a period, the closing procedures for a partnership are similar to those used for a sole proprietorship.

Step 1: *Close revenue to **Income Summary**.*

Step 2: *Close expenses to **Income Summary**.*

Step 3: *Close **Income Summary** to the partners' capital accounts.*

Step 4: *Close each partner's drawing account to the partner's capital account.*

In step 3, the business needs to determine the **distributive share,** which is the amount of net income or net loss allocated to each partner. Distributive share refers solely to the division of net income or net loss among partners, not to cash distributions.

Partners may agree to divide or allocate the income in any manner they desire. Typical considerations for each partner include the

- amount of time spent in the business,
- skills, expertise, and experience,
- amount of capital invested.

The partnership agreement should clearly and carefully spell out the basis for allocation so that there will be no misunderstanding among the partners. *In the absence of an agreement to the contrary, partners share income and losses equally.* Typical allocations are based on a fixed ratio or on capital account balances. Some agreements call for salary allowances and interest allowances.

Let's examine the end-of-year procedures for the partnership of Barret and Reed. The following T accounts show the capital and drawing accounts for Barret and Reed at the end of the first year of business before the accounts have been closed for the year. Note that the capital accounts reflect the amounts of original investment at this point.

important!

Distribution of Income

Income allocation or division is frequently referred to as the distribution of income. This does not mean that cash is distributed to the partners.

important!

Income Allocation

Unless the partnership agreement provides otherwise, net income or net loss is allocated equally to the partners.

To illustrate the most common allocation methods, the allocation of income or loss is shown under four different arrangements.

AGREED UPON RATIO

Assume that Barret and Reed agreed that net income will be split in the ratio of 3:2 (3 to 2) to Barret and Reed, respectively. Follow these steps to convert the ratios to decimals.

Step 1: *Add the figures given in the ratio.*

Barret	3
Reed	2
Total	5

Step 2: *Express each figure as a fraction of the total.*

Barret's share	3/5
Reed's share	2/5

Step 3: *Convert each fraction into a percentage by dividing the numerator by the denominator.*

Barret's share	3/5 = 0.60 or 60 percent
Reed's share	2/5 = 0.40 or 40 percent

Allocating Net Income Assume that *Income Summary* has a credit balance of $100,000 (net income) after closing the revenue and expense accounts. Net income is allocated as follows.

Barret	$100,000 × 0.60 = $60,000
Reed	$100,000 × 0.40 = $40,000

Step 3 of the closing process is to close *Income Summary* to the partners' capital accounts as follows.

1	2010				1
2	Dec. 31	Income Summary	399	100 000 00	2
3		Ellen Barret, Capital	301		60 000 00	3
4		Jerry Reed, Capital	311		40 000 00	4
5		To record allocation of net income in			5
6		ratio of 3:2			6

The partners' drawing accounts are then closed to their capital accounts.

1	2010				1
8	Dec. 31	Ellen Barret, Capital	301	30 000 00	8
9		Ellen Barret, Drawing	302		30 000 00	9
10					10
11		31 Jerry Reed, Capital	311	22 800 00	11
12		Jerry Reed, Drawing	312		22 800 00	12

>>4. OBJECTIVE

Compute and record the division of net income or net loss between partners in accordance with the partnership agreement.

LP19

After posting the closing entries, the T accounts appear as follows.

Income Summary	399
Dec. 31	Dec. 31
Clos. 100,000	Net Inc. 100,000
	Bal. 0

Ellen Barret, Capital	301
Dec. 31	Dec. 31
Draw. 30,000	Bal. 53,200
	Dec. 31
	Net Inc. 60,000
	Bal. 83,200

Jerry Reed, Capital	311
Dec. 31	Dec. 31
Draw. 22,800	Bal. 28,000
	Dec. 31
	Net Inc. 40,000
	Bal. 45,200

Ellen Barret, Drawing	302
Dec. 31	Dec. 31
Bal. 30,000	Clos. 30,000
Bal. 0	

Jerry Reed, Drawing	312
Dec. 31	Dec. 31
Bal. 22,800	Clos. 22,800
Bal. 0	

Allocating Net Loss   Assume that *Income Summary* has a debit balance of $30,000 (net loss) after closing revenue and expense accounts. This represents a net loss for the year. The loss is allocated as follows, using their allocation ratio of 3:2.

Barret $30,000 × 0.60 = $18,000

Reed $30,000 × 0.40 = $12,000

Steps 3 and 4 of the closing process are recorded as follows.

1	2010						1
14	Dec.	31	Ellen Barret, Capital	301	18 00 0 00		14
15			Jerry Reed, Capital	311	12 00 0 00		15
16			Income Summary	399		30 00 0 00	16
17							17
18		31	Ellen Barret, Capital	301	30 00 0 00		18
19			Ellen Barret, Drawing	302		30 00 0 00	19
20							20
21		31	Jerry Reed, Capital	311	22 80 0 00		21
22			Jerry Reed, Drawing	312		22 80 0 00	22

CAPITAL ACCOUNT BALANCES

Allocating net income or net loss on the basis of capital account balances is quite logical when capital is extremely important in the income-earning process. For example, partnerships that own and rent real estate often allocate income or loss based on capital account balances.

Barret and Reed agreed that net income or net loss will be allocated based on the ratio of capital account balances at the beginning of the year. The beginning balances for Barret and

Reed were $53,200 and $28,000, respectively. Follow the steps below to convert the capital account ratio to decimals.

Step 1: *Add the capital account balances.*

Barret	$53,200
Reed	28,000
Total	$81,200

Step 2: *Express each balance as a fraction and convert it to a decimal.*

Barret $53,200/$81,200 = 0.65517 or 65.517 percent

Reed $28,000/$81,200 = 0.34483 or 34.483 percent

Using these percentages, net income of $100,000 would be allocated as follows.

Barret $100,000 × 0.65517 = $65,517

Reed $100,000 × 0.34483 = $34,483

Assuming a profit of $100,000 and withdrawals of $30,000 for Barret and $22,800 for Reed, the steps 3 and 4 closing entries are as follows.

2010					
Dec.	31	Income Summary	399	100 000 00	
		Ellen Barret, Capital	301		65 517 00
		Jerry Reed, Capital	311		34 483 00
	31	Ellen Barret, Capital	301	30 000 00	
		Ellen Barret, Drawing	302		30 000 00
	31	Jerry Reed, Capital	311	22 800 00	
		Jerry Reed, Drawing	312		22 800 00

A net loss would be allocated in the same ratio as net income. ***Income Summary*** would be credited to close the debit balance to the capital accounts.

SALARY ALLOWANCES

Salary allowances are intended to reward the partners for the time they spend in the business and for the expertise and talents they bring to it. Barret and Reed agreed that each would work full-time in the business. Both partners recognize Barret's long experience in retail trade, her superior skill and ability, and her good reputation and established clientele.

Barret and Reed agreed that each will receive a salary allowance equal to the monthly withdrawals permitted in the partnership agreement. After considering the salary allowance, the balance of net income or net loss will be divided between Barret and Reed in the ratio of 3:2.

Salary allowances are allocations of income. Salary allowances paid in cash to partners are withdrawals. They do not represent salary expense. They do not appear in the expense section of the income statement. Salary allowances are not subject to payroll taxes or withholdings.

When salary allowances are included in the income or loss distribution formula, step 3 of the closing process has two parts:

a. *Record the salary allowances; debit **Income Summary** and credit the partners' capital accounts.*

b. *Close **Income Summary** to the partners' capital accounts based on the partnership agreement.*

important!

Salary Withdrawals
A salary withdrawal is a cash payment to a partner and is debited to the partner's drawing account. It does not represent an expense of the partnership.

Allocating Net Income Assume that the net income of Old Army was $112,800.

Step 3a: Record the salary allowances of $30,000 to Barret and $22,800 to Reed as follows.

1	2010					1
2	Dec.	31 Income Summary	399	52 80 0 00		2
3		Ellen Barret, Capital	301		30 00 0 00	3
4		Jerry Reed, Capital	311		22 80 0 00	4

After recording the salary allowances, ***Income Summary*** has a credit balance of $60,000.

Income Summary	399
Dec. 31	Dec. 31
Sal. All. 52,800	Net Inc. 112,800
	Bal. 60,000

The balance of ***Income Summary*** is allocated as follows.

Barret $60,000 × 0.60 = $36,000

Reed $60,000 × 0.40 = $24,000

Step 3b: Record the entry to close the credit balance of ***Income Summary*** as follows.

1	2010					1
6	Dec.	31 Income Summary	399	60 00 0 00		6
7		Ellen Barret, Capital	301		36 00 0 00	7
8		Jerry Reed, Capital	311		24 00 0 00	8

The partners' drawing accounts are closed to the capital accounts in the usual manner. Remember that the fact that a partner has or has not withdrawn cash as a salary allowance does not affect the profit or loss allocation.

Allocating Net Loss Assume net loss for Old Army is $30,000. Entries to record the loss distribution follow.

Step 3a: Record the salary allowances of $30,000 to Barret and $22,800 to Reed:

1	2010					1
2	Dec.	31 Income Summary	399	52 80 0 00		2
3		Ellen Barret, Capital	301		30 00 0 00	3
4		Jerry Reed, Capital	311		22 80 0 00	4

After this entry is posted, ***Income Summary*** has a debit balance of $82,800.

Income Summary	399
Dec. 31	
Net Loss 30,000	
Dec. 31	
Sal. All. 52,800	
Bal. 82,800	

The balance of *Income Summary* is allocated as follows.

Barret $82,800 × 0.60 = $49,680
Reed $82,800 × 0.40 = $33,120

Step 3b: Record the entry to close *Income Summary* as follows.

1	2010						1
6	Dec.	31 Ellen Barret, Capital	301	49 680 00			6
7		Jerry Reed, Capital	311	33 120 00			7
8		Income Summary	399		82 800 00		8

The partners' drawing accounts are closed to the capital accounts in the usual way.

1	2010						1
10	Dec.	31 Ellen Barret, Capital	301	30 000 00			10
11		Ellen Barret, Drawing	302		30 000 00		11
12							12
13		31 Jerry Reed, Capital	311	22 800 00			13
14		Jerry Reed, Drawing	312		22 800 00		14

After the closing entries are posted, the T accounts appear as follows.

Income Summary   399

Dec. 31		Dec. 31	
Net Loss	30,000	Clos.	82,800
Dec. 31			
Sal. All.	52,800		
	82,800		
		Bal.	0

Ellen Barret, Capital   301

Dec. 31		Dec. 31	
Net Loss	49,680	Bal.	53,200
Dec. 31		Dec. 31	
Draw.	30,000	Sal. All.	30,000
	79,680		83,200
		Bal.	3,520

Jerry Reed, Capital   311

Dec. 31		Dec. 31	
Net Loss	33,120	Bal.	28,000
Dec. 31		Dec. 31	
Draw.	22,800	Sal. All.	22,800
	55,920		50,800
Bal.	5,120		

Ellen Barret, Drawing   302

Dec. 31		Dec. 31	
Bal.	30,000	Clos.	30,000
Bal.	0		

Jerry Reed, Drawing   312

Dec. 31		Dec. 31	
Bal.	22,800	Clos.	22,800
Bal.	0		

SALARY AND INTEREST ALLOWANCES

Assume that Barret and Reed want to reward themselves for their time and skills through salary allowances of $30,000 to Barret and $22,800 to Reed. They also wish to recognize their capital investments by allowing each partner 8 percent interest on his or her capital balance at the start of the period.

The partnership agreement does not specify how the remaining income or loss is to be allocated. Remember that if the partnership agreement is silent on this matter, the remaining net income or net loss is divided equally.

Step 3 of the closing process has three parts:

a. Record the salary allowances.

b. Record the interest allowances. Credit each partner's capital account for the interest allowed, and debit *Income Summary* for the total interest.

c. Close *Income Summary* to the partners' capital accounts. Again, remember that the fact that cash has or has not been paid to the partner for this allowance does not affect these entries.

Allocation When Net Income Is Adequate to Cover Allowances   Assume net income of $100,000.

Step 3a: Record the salary allowances of $30,000 to Barret and $22,800 to Reed as follows.

1	2010				1
2	Dec.	31 Income Summary	399	52 800 00	2
3		Ellen Barret, Capital	301	30 000 00	3
4		Jerry Reed, Capital	311	22 800 00	4

Step 3b: Record the interest allowances. The interest allowed is 8 percent of the beginning capital balance.

Barret $53,200 × 0.08 × 1 year = $4,256

Reed $28,000 × 0.08 × 1 year = $2,240

The journal entry to record the interest allowances is as follows.

1	2010				1
6	Dec.	31 Income Summary	399	6 496 00	6
7		Ellen Barret, Capital	301	4 256 00	7
8		Jerry Reed, Capital	311	2 240 00	8
9		To record 8% interest allowance on			9
10		beginning investments			10

After recording the salary and interest allowances, *Income Summary* has a credit balance of $40,704.

Income Summary	399
Dec. 31	Dec. 31
Sal. All. 52,800	Net Inc. 100,000
Dec. 31	
Int. All. 6,496	
59,296	
	Bal. 40,704

Step 3c: Close *Income Summary* to the partners' capital accounts. The balance is divided equally between Barret and Reed. The entry to close the credit balance of *Income Summary* is as follows.

1	2010						1
11	Dec.	31	Income Summary	399	40 70 4 00		11
12			Ellen Barret, Capital	301		20 35 2 00	12
13			Jerry Reed, Capital	311		20 35 2 00	13

Allocation of Net Loss   Assume that Old Army had a $40,000 net loss for the year.

Step 3a: Record the salary allowances of $30,000 to Barret and $22,800 to Reed.

Step 3b: Record the interest allowances of $4,256 to Barret and $2,240 to Reed.

After these steps, *Income Summary* has a debit balance of $99,296.

```
            Income Summary        399
  _____
  Net Loss  40,000  |
                    |
  Dec. 31           |
  Sal. All.  52,800 |
                    |
  Dec. 31           |
  Int. All.   6,496 |
  Bal.       99,296 |
```

The debit balance of $99,296 is divided equally between Barret and Reed.

Step 3c: Record the entry to close *Income Summary*. Debit each partner's capital account $49,648; credit *Income Summary; $99,296.

After the closing entries are posted, the T accounts appear as follows.

```
            Income Summary        399
  _____
  Net Loss  40,000  |  Dec. 31
                    |  Closing   99,296
  Dec. 31           |
  Sal. All.  52,800 |
                    |
  Dec. 31           |
  Int. All.   6,496 |
            99,296  |
                    |  Bal.            0
```

```
        Ellen Barret, Capital   301                    Jerry Reed, Capital    311
  _____      _____
                 |  Bal.      53,200                     |  Bal.      28,000
  Dec. 31        |  Dec. 31                  Dec. 31      |  Dec. 31
  Net Loss 49,648|  Sal. All.  30,000        Net Loss 49,648|  Sal. All.  22,800
                 |  Dec. 31                               |  Dec. 31
                 |  Int. All.   4,256                     |  Int. All.   2,240
                 |            87,456                       |            53,040
                 |  Bal.      37,808                       |  Bal.       3,392
```

The partners' drawing accounts are closed to the capital accounts in the usual manner.

Income Less Than Difference Between Partners' Allocations Assume that Old Army had net income of $3,400.

Step 3a: Record the salary allowances of $30,000 to Barret and $22,800 to Reed.

Step 3b: Record the interest allowances of $4,256 to Barret and $2,240 to Reed.

After recording the salary and interest allowances, *Income Summary* has a debit balance of $55,896. The balance of *Income Summary* is divided equally between Barret and Reed.

Step 3c: Record the entry to close *Income Summary.*

After the closing entries are posted, the T accounts appear as follows.

Income Summary		399	
Dec. 31		Dec. 31	
Sal. All.	52,800	Net Inc.	3,400
Dec. 31		Dec. 31	
Int. All.	6,496	Closing	55,896
	59,296		59,296
		Bal.	0

Ellen Barret, Capital		301	
Dec. 31		Dec. 31	
Loss	27,948	Bal.	53,200
		Dec. 31	
		Sal. All.	30,000
		Dec. 31	
		Int. All.	4,256
			87,456
		Bal.	59,508

Jerry Reed, Capital		311	
Dec. 31		Dec. 31	
Loss	27,948	Bal.	28,000
		Dec. 31	
		Sal. All.	22,800
		Dec. 31	
		Int. All.	2,240
			53,040
		Bal.	25,092

Notice that at this point, prior to closing the drawing accounts, the capital account balance for Barret increased by $6,308 and for Reed decreased by $2,908. This is due to the relationships between the income-sharing agreements and the amount of net income reported.

	Barret	Reed
Beginning capital balance	$53,200	$28,000
Ending capital balance	59,508	25,092
Difference	$ 6,308	($2,908)

Partnership Financial Statements

Once the net income or net loss distribution is complete, the financial statements are prepared.

INCOME STATEMENT PRESENTATION

With one exception, the income statements for a partnership and a sole proprietorship are identical. On a partnership's income statement, it is customary to show on the bottom of the statement the division of net income or net loss among partners. The salary allowances, interest allowances, and other allocation factors are shown.

Old Army's income statement for the most recent example follows. Revenue and expense details are omitted.

Net Income for Year			$ 3,400
Allocation of Net Income	Barret	Reed	Total
Salary Allowance	$30,000	$22,800	$52,800
Interest Allowance	4,256	2,240	6,496
Balance Equally	(27,948)	(27,948)	(55,896)
Totals	$ 6,308	($ 2,908)	$ 3,400

BALANCE SHEET PRESENTATION

The balance sheet of a partnership is identical to that of a sole proprietorship, except that the partnership's balance sheet shows the balance of each partner's capital account. The capital account partnership balance sheet appears in the Partners' Equity section.

The **statement of partners' equities** summarizes the changes in the partners' capital accounts during an accounting period. It includes the following:

- beginning capital,
- additional investments,
- share of net income or net loss,
- withdrawals,
- ending capital.

Figure 19.2 shows the statement of partners' equities for Old Army.

>>**5. OBJECTIVE**

Prepare a statement of partners' equities.

LP19

Old Army Statement of Partners' Equities Year Ended December 31, 2010			
	Barret *Capital*	*Reed* *Capital*	*Total* *Capital*
Capital Balances, Jan. 1, 2010	0 00	0 00	0 00
Investment During Year	53 2 0 0 00	28 0 0 0 00	81 2 0 0 00
Net Income (Loss) for Year	6 3 0 8 00	(2 9 0 8 00)	3 4 0 0 00
Totals	59 5 0 8 00	25 0 9 2 00	84 6 0 0 00
Less Withdrawals During Year	30 0 0 0 00	22 8 0 0 00	52 8 0 0 00
Capital Balances, Dec. 31, 2010	29 5 0 8 00	2 2 9 2 00	31 8 0 0 00

FIGURE 19.2

Statement of Partners' Equities

Section 2 Self Review

QUESTIONS

1. What two allowances are commonly used in allocating net income or net loss to partners?

2. If both salary and interest allowances are made to the partners, what are the three steps in closing the *Income Summary* account to the partners' capital accounts?

3. In the absence of an agreement to the contrary, how are partnership income and losses allocated among the partners?

EXERCISES

4. The entry to record the equal distribution of net income between two partners consists of a

   a. debit to *Income Summary* and a credit to each partner's capital account.

   b. debit to each partner's capital account and a credit to *Cash.*

   c. debit to *Income Summary* and a credit to each partner's drawing account.

   d. debit to *Income Summary* and a credit to *Cash.*

5. The amount that each partner withdraws from a partnership

   a. should be specified in the partnership agreement.

   b. is the base on which federal income taxes are levied on the partnership income.

   c. cannot exceed the net income reported by the partnership.

   d. is always divided evenly among the partners.

ANALYSIS

6. Alan Hanks and Peter Olson formed a partnership. Hanks invested $40,000. Olson invested $60,000. Net income for the year is $48,000. If net income is allocated based on the capital account balances at the beginning of the year, what is the income allocation for Hanks and Olson?

(Answers to Section 2 Self Review are on page 680.)

Section 3

SECTION OBJECTIVES

>> 6. **Account for the revaluation of assets and liabilities prior to the dissolution of a partnership.**

WHY IT'S IMPORTANT

The gains or losses must be properly allocated to the partners.

>> 7. **Account for the sale of a partnership interest.**

WHY IT'S IMPORTANT

The capital account of the new partner must be properly stated.

>> 8. **Account for the investment of a new partner in an existing partnership.**

WHY IT'S IMPORTANT

The capital account of the new partner must reflect the interest to be received by the new partner.

>> 9. **Account for the withdrawal of a partner from a partnership.**

WHY IT'S IMPORTANT

The withdrawal of a partner from a business changes the equity ratios and the valuation of the partnership.

Partnership Changes

The partners in an existing business can change. Former partners might withdraw, sell their interests, or die. New partners may be admitted.

Changes in Partners

A partnership has a limited life. Whenever a partner dies or withdraws, or when a new partner is admitted, a dissolution of the old partnership occurs. If the surviving partners continue the business, a new partnership legally exists. **Dissolution** is the legal term for termination of a partnership. It has little impact on the business activities of the partnership. On the other hand, when the business is completely terminated, it is called a **liquidation.** The business ceases to exist, and the partnership agreement is void.

When a partnership is dissolved, two steps are taken.

Step 1: *The accounting records are closed and the net income or net loss on the date of dissolution is recorded and transferred to the partners' capital accounts.*

Step 2: *Assets and liabilities are revalued at fair market value. The partners, including any newly admitted partners, agree on the amounts.*

RECORDING REVALUATION OF ASSETS

>>6. OBJECTIVE

Account for the revaluation of assets and liabilities prior to the dissolution of a partnership.

The partnership agreement usually provides that when a partnership is dissolved and the business is to be continued as a new partnership, the assets and liabilities are revalued. The revaluation may require the services of a professional appraiser. The revaluation is made because the difference between the fair market value and the book value is a gain or loss resulting from events that occurred during the old partnership. The new partner does not share the gain or loss.

LP19

Based on the revaluation, the assets and liabilities are written up or down, and the difference between the book and fair market values is allocated to the original partners' capital accounts. The allocation of gains and losses is made in accordance with the formula used for sharing net income or net loss.

The partners of Key Notes Music Store agreed to admit a new partner, effective April 1. The assets and liabilities will be revalued following the close of business on March 31. Figure 19.3 shows the balance sheet of Key Notes after the closing entries are made on March 31 and net income or net loss is transferred to the partners' capital accounts.

The partners agree that

- *Allowance for Doubtful Accounts* should be increased to $4,300,
- *Value of Merchandise Inventory* is $79,000,
- *Land* is worth $22,000 according to an appraisal,
- Liabilities are properly stated.

The result is a $6,700 net increase in assets:

Merchandise inventory	$9,000
Accounts receivable/Allowance for doubtful accounts	(2,300)
Net increase in assets	$6,700

Assume that the partners share income and losses as follows.

Lee	40 percent
Wilner	40 percent
Flores	20 percent

important!

Asset Revaluation

When transferred from one partnership to another, assets are revalued to their fair market value. The new value will not necessarily agree with the book value carried by the old firm.

Key Notes Music Store
Balance Sheet
March 31, 2010

Assets			
Cash			60 000 00
Accounts Receivable	40 000 00		
Less Allowance for Doubtful Accounts	2 000 00	38 000 00	
Merchandise Inventory		70 000 00	
Land		22 000 00	
Total Assets		190 000 00	
Liabilities and Partners' Equity			
Liabilities			
Notes Payable—Bank	19 000 00		
Accounts Payable	23 200 00		
Total Liabilities		42 200 00	
Partners' Equity			
Tom Lee, Capital	38 300 00		
Joan Wilner, Capital	58 500 00		
Nau Flores, Capital	51 000 00		
Total Partners' Equity		147 800 00	
Total Liabilities and Partners' Equity		190 000 00	

FIGURE 19.3
Partnership Balance Sheet

The gain on revaluation of the assets is allocated as follows.

Lee	$6,700 × 0.40 = $2,680
Wilner	$6,700 × 0.40 = $2,680
Flores	$6,700 × 0.20 = $1,340

Revaluation of the assets is recorded as follows.

GENERAL JOURNAL PAGE ___4___

	DATE		DESCRIPTION	POST. REF.	DEBIT	CREDIT	
1	2010						1
2	April	1	Merchandise Inventory	121	9 000 00		2
3			Allowance for Doubtful Accounts	112		2 300 00	3
4			Tom Lee, Capital	301		2 680 00	4
5			Joan Wilner, Capital	311		2 680 00	5
6			Nau Flores, Capital	321		1 340 00	6
7			To record revaluation of assets and				7
8			allocations of gain to partners.				8
9							9

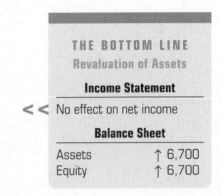

THE BOTTOM LINE

Revaluation of Assets

Income Statement

<< No effect on net income

Balance Sheet

Assets	↑ 6,700
Equity	↑ 6,700

After the entry is posted, the capital accounts contain the following balances.

Lee	($38,300 + $2,680)	$ 40,980
Wilner	($58,500 + $2,680)	61,180
Flores	($51,000 + $1,340)	52,340
Total		$154,500

ADMISSION OF A NEW PARTNER

There are two ways to admit a new partner.

1. The new partner may purchase all or part of the interest of an existing partner, making payment directly to the selling partner. In this case, no cash or other asset is transferred to the partnership.

2. The new partner may invest cash or other assets directly in the existing partnership.

Purchase of an Interest One way to join an existing partnership is to buy a portion of a partner's share of capital. The prospective partner must have the approval of the existing partners. The money or other consideration passes directly from the new partner to the selling partner and does not appear in the accounting records of the partnership.

Suppose Key Notes' books are closed and the assets revalued as described. Lee sells half his interest in the business to Beth Rivera for $32,000. Rivera pays $32,000 directly to Lee. The partnership's records do not reflect this cash transaction. In the partnership's accounting records, the transfer is recorded by a debit to **Tom Lee, Capital** for $20,490 and a credit to **Beth Rivera, Capital** for $20,490. The $20,490 is one-half of Lee's capital account balance after revaluation (0.50 × $40,980). (The other partners would have to agree to this transfer of interest to Rivera.)

Frequently the amount paid by the new partner is not the same as the amount credited to the new partner's capital account. The value of the partner's interest is a matter for bargaining between the two parties. Rivera paid $32,000 in order to obtain a capital account of $20,490. The difference between the two amounts does not affect the partnership's accounting records.

With the admission of the new partner, the current partnership comes to an end and a new partnership is established. The partners should draw up a new partnership agreement.

>>7. OBJECTIVE

Account for the sale of a partnership interest.

LP19

>>8. OBJECTIVE

Account for the investment of a new partner in an existing partnership.

LP19

Investment of Assets by a New Partner A new partner may invest money or other property to obtain admission to the partnership while the existing partners remain as partners in the business. The new partner's investment, share of ownership in capital, and share of the net income or net loss are agreed upon among the partners and specified in the partnership agreement for the new partnership. The new partner may receive credit for the amount invested or for a higher or lower amount.

New Partner Given Credit for Amount Invested Suppose the four parties involved in Key Notes Music agree that Rivera will receive a one-fourth interest in the capital of the business for cash equal to one-fourth of the total capital in the new partnership. After revaluation, the capital accounts of the three existing partners total $154,500. The investment for Rivera to own one-fourth of the capital of the new partnership is $51,500.

- The three existing partners, whose capital accounts total $154,500 after the revaluation, will own three-fourths of the business. The $154,500 is three-fourths (or 75 percent) of the new partnership capital. Each quarter interest is therefore $51,500.
- The new partnership capital is $206,000 ($51,500 × 4).
- Rivera is purchasing one-fourth (or 25 percent) of the new partnership capital, $51,500.

The entry to record Rivera's investment is as follows.

1	2010					1
10	April	1	Cash	101	51 50 00	10
11			Beth Rivera, Capital	331	51 50 00	11
12			To record investment of Rivera for			12
13			one-fourth interest in partnership			13

New Partner Given Credit for More Than Amount Invested The new partner can be given credit for more capital than the amount invested. This is often done if the new partner brings to the business skills that the existing partners are eager to have. Suppose Rivera agreed to invest $45,500 for a one-fourth interest in the partnership. It takes two steps to record the investment: record the cash investment and adjust the capital account balances.

The cash investment is recorded as a debit to **Cash** for $45,500 and a credit to **Beth Rivera, Capital** for $45,500. After this entry is posted, the capital account balances are $200,000.

Lee	$ 40,980
Wilner	61,180
Flores	52,340
Rivera	45,500
Total	$200,000

According to the capital account balances, Rivera owns 22.75 percent of the partnership ($45,500/$200,000). However, Rivera paid $45,500 to purchase a one-fourth interest in the partnership. Rivera's capital account balance should be $50,000 ($200,000 × 1/4). The $4,500 ($50,000 − $45,500) increase necessary to bring Rivera's account to $50,000 is referred to as a "bonus to the new partner." The $4,500 is credited to Rivera's capital account. The debit is deducted from the original partners' capital accounts on the basis of the former partnership income and loss ratio. The amounts deducted from the original partners' accounts are as follows.

Lee	$4,500 × 0.40 = $1,800
Wilner	$4,500 × 0.40 = $1,800
Flores	$4,500 × 0.20 = $900

The general journal entry to record the bonus is as follows.

	2010								
1	2010								1
10	April	1	Tom Lee, Capital	301	1 8 0 0 00				10
11			Joan Wilner, Capital	311	1 8 0 0 00				11
12			Nau Flores, Capital	321	9 0 0 00				12
13			Beth Rivera, Capital	331			4 5 0 0 00		13
14			To record bonus allowed new partner						14

The partners' capital accounts after posting the entry for the bonus appear as follows.

Tom Lee, Capital	301		
April 1		April 1	
Rivera bonus 1,800		Bal. 40,980	
		Bal. 39,180	

Joan Wilner, Capital	311		
April 1		April 1	
Rivera bonus 1,800		Bal. 61,180	
		Bal. 59,380	

Nau Flores, Capital	321		
April 1		April 1	
Rivera bonus 900		Bal. 52,340	
		Bal. 51,440	

Beth Rivera, Capital	331		
		April 1	
		Invest. 45,500	
		April 1	
		Bonus 4,500	
		Bal. 50,000	

New Partner Given Credit for Less Than Amount Invested Suppose that Rivera agreed to invest $45,500 for a one-fifth interest in the capital of the partnership. The $45,500 investment is recorded as a debit to **Cash** for $45,500 and a credit to **Beth Rivera, Capital** for $45,500.

After this entry is posted, the capital account balances are $200,000.

Lee	$ 40,980
Wilner	61,180
Flores	52,340
Rivera	45,500
Total	$200,000

According to the capital account balances at this point, Rivera owns 22.75 percent of the partnership ($45,500/$200,000). However, she paid $45,500 for a one-fifth (or 20 percent) interest in the partnership. Rivera's capital account balance should be $40,000 ($200,000 × 0.20). The $5,500 ($40,000 − $45,500) decrease necessary to bring Rivera's capital account to $40,000 is referred to as "bonus allowed the original partners." The $5,500 is debited to Rivera's capital account and credited to the original partners' capital accounts on the basis of the former partnership income and loss ratio. The amounts credited to the original partners' capital accounts are as follows.

Lee	$5,500 × 0.40 = $2,200
Wilner	$5,500 × 0.40 = $2,200
Flores	$5,500 × 0.20 = $1,100

	2010							1
10	April	1 Beth Rivera, Capital	331	5 5 0 0 00				10
11		Tom Lee, Capital	301			2 2 0 0 00		11
12		Joan Wilner, Capital	311			2 2 0 0 00		12
13		Nau Flores, Capital	321			1 1 0 0 00		13
14		To record bonus to original partners						14
15								15

After this entry is posted, Rivera's capital account balance will be $40,000, or one-fifth of the total partnership capital of $200,000.

>>9. OBJECTIVE

Account for the withdrawal of a partner from a partnership.

LP19

WITHDRAWAL OF A PARTNER

The partnership agreement should contain provisions specifying the procedures to be followed for the withdrawal of a partner. The partnership agreement for Key Notes provides that, upon withdrawal of a partner, the assets are to be revalued and the retiring partner is to be paid an amount equal to that partner's capital account after revaluation. Suppose that the partners of Key Notes agree that Nau Flores is to withdraw from the partnership after the close of business on March 31. He is to receive cash in an amount equal to the balance of his capital account after revaluation of the assets.

The revalued assets result in the following capital account balances.

Lee	$ 40,980
Wilner	61,180
Flores	52,340
Total	$154,500

The entry to record the withdrawal of Flores from the partnership is as follows.

	2010							1
2	Mar.	31 Nau Flores, Capital	321	52 3 4 0 00				2
3		Cash	101			52 3 4 0 00		3
4		To record cash payment made to Flores						4
5		on withdrawal from partnership						5
6								6
7								7

MANAGERIAL IMPLICATIONS

PARTNERSHIP CONSIDERATIONS

- Management and owners need to understand the advantages the partnership form of business offers to sole proprietors who need more capital, managerial assistance, or technical help.
- The partnership does not pay taxes. The partnership's taxable income "flows through" to the individual partners.
- It is essential that individuals who enter into a partnership have a clear understanding of the duties, obligations, rights, and responsibilities of each partner.

- There should be a written partnership agreement drafted by a lawyer and reviewed by the partners' accountants.
- The partnership agreement should be very specific about the income and loss allocation formula.
- Upon dissolution, the partnership assets and liabilities should be revalued.

THINKING CRITICALLY

What are the essential elements of a partnership agreement?

The parties might agree that the withdrawing partner is to receive either more or less than the balance of that partner's capital account at the time of withdrawal. In this event, the withdrawing partner's capital account is debited for the balance of the account.

- If the amount paid is higher than the withdrawing partner's capital account balance, the excess is debited to the capital accounts of the remaining partners according to their income and loss ratio.

- If the amount paid is less than the withdrawing partner's capital account balance, the difference is credited to the remaining partners' capital accounts based on their income and loss ratio.

After the assets of Key Notes are revalued, Flores's capital account balance is $52,340. Flores wishes to withdraw, and the partners agree to pay him $61,340 from partnership funds. The $9,000 ($61,340 – $52,340) bonus paid to the withdrawing partner is divided between the remaining partners according to their income and loss ratio of 40:40 (equally). The general journal entry to record the withdrawal of Flores is as follows.

1	2010					1
2	Mar.	31	Nau Flores, Capital	321	52 340 00	2
3			Tom Lee, Capital	301	4 500 00	3
4			Joan Wilner, Capital	311	4 500 00	4
5			Cash	101	61 340 00	5
6			To record cash payment made to Flores			6
7			on withdrawal from partnership			7
8						8
9						9

Section 3 Self Review

QUESTIONS

1. If a withdrawing partner is paid less than his capital account balance, how is the excess accounted for?

2. An existing partner sells one-half of his capital interest to a new partner. What is the accounting entry to record this transaction?

3. A new partner invests cash greater than the fractional share of the total capital being purchased. What are the accounting entries to record this transaction?

EXERCISES

4. The profit sharing percentages of partners Hayes, Harris, and Hickman are 40 percent, 40 percent, and 20 percent, respectively. Their capital account balances are $40,000, $30,000, and $20,000, respectively. Hayes withdraws from the partnership and receives $38,000 from the partnership

in settlement of his withdrawal. As a result of this transaction:

a. the capital account of Harris is not affected.

b. the capital account of Harris is credited for $1,000.

c. the capital account of Harris is debited for $1,000.

d. the capital account of Harris is credited for $1,333.

5. When a partner withdraws from the partnership and receives cash in excess of the balance in his capital account, the excess is

a. debited to the capital accounts of the remaining partners, allocated to those partners on the basis of the ratio of their capital account balances.

b. credited to the capital accounts of the remaining partners, allocated

to those partners in proportion to their profit and loss percentages.

c. debited to the capital accounts of the remaining partners, allocated to those partners in proportion to their profit and loss percentages.

d. debited to the capital accounts of the remaining partners, allocated equally to those partners.

ANALYSIS

6. James Miller paid $28,000 to Pete Mason for one-half of his interest in the partnership of Lane and Mason. Mason's capital account balance prior to the purchase was $50,000. What is the entry required in the partnership's accounts to record this transaction?

(Answers to Section 3 Self Review are on page 680.)

19 Chapter **REVIEW**   **Chapter Summary**

A partnership is the joining together of two or more persons under a written or oral contract as co-owners of a business. You have learned about the advantages and disadvantages of the partnership form of business. In addition, you have studied the accounting methods and procedures unique to partnerships.

Learning Objectives

1 Explain the major advantages and disadvantages of a partnership.

There are advantages to a partnership:

- It is relatively easy and inexpensive to form.
- It permits pooling of skills and resources.
- No income tax is paid on its profits, although partners report their share of income or loss on their tax returns.

There are disadvantages to a partnership:

- Partners have unlimited liability.
- Any partner can bind the other partners.
- The business lacks continuity.
- Ownership rights are not freely transferable.

2 State the important provisions that should be included in every partnership agreement.

A written agreement should detail the partnership specifics: amount of initial investment, partners' duties, fiscal year, accounting method, division of gains or losses (including any allowances for salaries and interest), policy for withdrawals, and length of partnership life.

3 Account for the formation of a partnership.

Assets and liabilities may be exchanged for a partnership interest.

- Assets are appraised and recorded at the agreed-upon fair market value at the transfer date.
- Each partner's capital account is credited for the amount of the investment.

4 Compute and record the division of net income or net loss between partners in accordance with the partnership agreement.

Division of partnership income and losses can be made in any manner. If no agreement has been made, income and losses are divided equally.

5 Prepare a statement of partners' equities.

A statement of partners' equities summarizes the changes in the capital accounts during the period.

6 Account for the revaluation of assets and liabilities prior to the dissolution of a partnership.

Before a partnership is dissolved, the business assets are revalued and the income or loss allocated according to the original agreement.

7 Account for the sale of a partnership interest.

A new partner may purchase a partnership interest from a current partner. The portion of ownership sold is transferred from the existing partner's capital account to the new partner's capital account.

8 Account for the investment of a new partner in an existing partnership.

A new partner may invest more or less than the proportionate part of total capital that the new partner will own after the investment.

- If more is invested, a bonus is recorded to the current partners (the new partner's capital account is debited and the current partners' capital accounts are credited).
- If less is invested, a bonus is recorded to the new partner (the new partner's capital account is credited and the current partners' capital accounts are debited).

9 Account for the withdrawal of a partner from a partnership.

When a partner withdraws, the assets and liabilities are revalued and the income or loss allocated according to the original agreement. If the amount the retiring partner is paid is different from the capital account balance, the difference is allocated to the remaining partners in accordance with their profit and loss ratios.

10 Define the accounting terms new to this chapter.

Glossary

Articles of partnership (p. 641) See Partnership agreement

Dissolution (p. 657) The legal term for termination of a partnership

Distributive share (p. 646) The amount of net income or net loss allocated to each partner

General partner (p. 641) A member of a partnership who has unlimited liability

Limited partner (p. 641) A member of a partnership whose liability is limited to his or her investment in the partnership

Limited partnership (p. 641) A partnership having one or more limited partners

Liquidation (p. 657) Termination of a business by distributing all assets and discontinuing the business

Memorandum entry (p. 643) An informational entry in the general journal

Mutual agency (p. 641) The characteristic of a partnership by which each partner is empowered to act as an agent for the partnership, binding the firm by his or her acts

Partnership (p. 640) An association of two or more persons who carry on, as co-owners, a business for profit

Partnership agreement (p. 641) A legal contract forming a partnership and specifying certain details of operation

Statement of partners' equities (p. 655) A financial statement prepared to summarize the changes in partners' capital accounts during an accounting period

Unlimited liability (p. 641) The implication that a creditor can look to all partners' personal assets as well as the assets of the partnership for payment of the firm's debts

Comprehensive **Self Review**

1. Why are the assets and liabilities revalued prior to a dissolution?
2. Explain the difference between the accounting treatment of "salary withdrawals" and "salary allowances" in allocating income or loss.
3. Explain how one partner might receive a profit allocation even though the partnership has a loss for the period.
4. What are the major disadvantages of the partnership form of business enterprise?
5. What nonfinancial information should be considered in forming a partnership?

(Answers to Comprehensive Self Review are on page 681.)

 Multiple choice questions are provided on the text Web site at www.mhhe.com/price12e

Quiz19

Discussion Questions

1. List the major advantages of the partnership form of business over a corporation.
2. What are the major disadvantages of the partnership form of business entity?
3. Does a partnership continue to exist after the death of a partner? Explain.
4. Does a partnership pay federal income tax? Explain.
5. Why are assets of an existing proprietorship revalued when they are transferred to a partnership?
6. Is *Allowance for Doubtful Accounts* brought forward from the general ledger of a sole proprietorship when the firm's assets and liabilities are being transferred to the partnership? Why?
7. How does the balance sheet of a partnership differ from that of a sole proprietorship?

8. What is the advantage of a limited partnership?

9. Are partners' salaries considered to be expenses of the partnership? Explain.

10. Explain how the net income of a partnership is allocated if it is less than the salary and interest allowances.

11. Explain what the term "mutual agency" means in regard to a partnership.

12. Why should the assets and liabilities of an existing partnership be revalued when a new partner is to be admitted by the investment of cash in the organization?

13. Explain the use of a drawing account in a partnership.

14. List the steps required to dissolve a partnership.

15. What are typical considerations that affect the way income is allocated among partners?

16. What is the difference between a dissolution and liquidation?

17. Explain how the partnership accounts for the sale by a partner of a portion of his partnership interest to another individual.

18. The two partners in a business often pay personal bills by writing checks on the business bank account. Is this a good business practice? Explain. How should such payments be recorded?

19. What information appears on a statement of partners' equities?

APPLICATIONS

Exercises

Exercise 19.1

Objective 3

▶ **Recording cash investment in a partnership.**

Rosa Valdez invests cash of $170,000 in a newly formed partnership that will operate The Tennis Shop. In return, Valdez receives a one-third interest in the capital of the partnership. In general journal form, record Valdez's investment in the partnership.

Exercise 19.2

Objective 3

▶ **Recording investment of assets and liabilities in a partnership.**

Pamela Oliver operates a sole proprietorship business that sells golf equipment. Oliver has agreed to transfer her assets and liabilities to a partnership that will operate The Golf Shop. Oliver will own a two-thirds interest in the capital of the partnership. The agreed upon values of assets and liabilities to be transferred follow.

> Total Accounts receivable of $60,000 will be transferred and approximately $2,000 of these accounts may be uncollectible
>
> Merchandise inventory, $90,500
>
> Furniture and fixtures, $35,000
>
> Accounts payable, $13,500

Record the receipt of the assets and liabilities by the partnership in the general journal.

Exercise 19.3

Objective 3

▶ **Preparing a balance sheet for a partnership.**

On May 1, 2010, James Dear and Joan Clay formed The Leisure Room. The two partners invested cash and other assets and liabilities with the following agreed upon values.

James: Cash, $6,000; Merchandise inventory, $12,000; Equipment, $38,000;
           Accounts payable, $5,000.
Joan: Furniture, $12,000; Cash, $18,000.

James is to own two-thirds of the capital, and Joan is to own one-third of the capital, but they will split profits and losses equally. Prepare a balance sheet for the partnership just after the assets and liabilities have been transferred to it.

Computing and recording allocation of net income with salaries and interest allowed.

◀ **Exercise 19.4**

Objective 4

Jackie Chanda and Janet Jones are partners who share profits and losses in the following manner. Chanda receives a salary of $48,000, and Jones receives a salary of $70,000. These amounts were paid to the partners and charged to their drawing accounts. Both partners also receive 10 percent interest on their capital balances at the beginning of the year. The balance of any remaining profits or losses is divided equally. The beginning capital accounts for 2010 were Chanda, $204,000, and Jones, $254,000. At the end of the year, the partnership had a net income of $144,000.

Compute the amount of net income or loss to be allocated to each partner.

Computing and recording allocation of net income with interest allowed.

◀ **Exercise 19.5**

Objective 4

Reagan and Carter are partners. Their partnership agreement provides that, in dividing profits, each is to be allocated interest at 10 percent of her beginning capital balance. The balance of net income or loss after the interest allowances is to be split in the ratio of 60:40 to Reagan and Carter, respectively. The beginning capital balances were Reagan, $60,000 and Carter, $12,000. Net income for the year was $120,000. Compute the amount of net income to be allocated to each partner.

Computing and recording division of net income, with salaries allowed.

◀ **Exercise 19.6**

Objective 4

Raymond Zeidan and Abe Foras are partners who share profits and losses in the ratio of 60 and 40 percent, respectively. Their partnership agreement provides that each will be paid a yearly salary of $42,000. The salaries were paid to the partners during 2010 and were charged to the partners' drawing accounts. The *Income Summary* account has a credit balance of $165,400 after revenue and expense accounts are closed at the end of the year. What amount of net income or net loss will be allocated to each?

Computing and recording division of net loss, with no partnership agreement on method of allocation.

◀ **Exercise 19.7**

Objective 4

After revenue and expense accounts of The Quick Stop were closed on December 31, 2010, *Income Summary* contained a credit balance of $48,000. The drawing accounts of the two partners, Gabe Monte and Bob Ferguson, showed debit balances of $35,000 and $87,000, respectively. Profits and losses are to be shared equally. Record the general journal entries to close the *Income Summary* account and the partners' drawing accounts.

Computing and recording division of net income based on fixed ratio.

◀ **Exercise 19.8**

Objective 4

The net income for the new partnership known as The Super Store for the year ended December 31, 2010, was $12,000. The partners, Dan Chase and Chris Torres, share profits in the ratio of 60 and 40 percent, respectively. Record the general journal entry (or entries) to close the *Income Summary* account.

Exercise 19.9

Objective 4

▶ **Computing the division of net income of a partnership.**

The partnership agreement of Mary Ayers and Neil Stewart does not indicate how the profits and losses will be shared. Before dividing the net income, Ayers's capital account balance was $160,000, and Stewart's capital balance was $40,000. The net income of their firm for the year that just ended was $94,000. How much income will be allocated to Ayers and how much to Stewart?

Exercise 19.10

Objective 6

▶ **Recording revaluation of assets prior to dissolution of a partnership.**

Howard Johnson and Neil Wilner are partners who share profits and losses in the ratio of 60:40, respectively. On December 31, 2010, they decide that Wilner will sell one-half of his interest to Ben Reed. At that time, the balances of the capital accounts are $125,000 for Johnson and $175,000 for Wilner. The partners agree that before the new partner is admitted, certain assets should be revalued. These assets include merchandise inventory carried at $102,800 revalued at $100,900, and a building with a book value of $65,000 revalued at $112,500.

1. Record the revaluations in the general journal.
2. What will the capital balances of the two existing partners be after the revaluation is made?

Exercise 19.11

Objective 7

▶ **Recording sale of a part interest.**

James Walker and Phillip Turner are partners who share profits and losses in the ratio of 60 and 40 percent, respectively. The balances of their capital accounts on December 31, 2009, are Walker, $100,000 and Turner, $110,000. With Turner's agreement, Walker sells one-half of his interest in the partnership to Gloria Cox for $75,000 on January 1, 2010. What will the capital account balances for each of the three partners be after this sale?

Exercise 19.12

Objective 9

▶ **Recording withdrawal of a partner.**

Wells, Harris, and Masten are partners, sharing profits and losses in the ratio of 30, 40, and 30 percent, respectively. Their partnership agreement provides that if one of them withdraws from the partnership, the assets and liabilities are to be revalued, the gain or loss allocated to the partners, and the retiring partner paid the balance of his account. Masten withdraws from the partnership on December 31, 2010. The capital account balances before recording revaluation are Wells, $57,500; Harris, $62,500; and Masten, $55,000. The effect of the revaluation is to increase *Merchandise Inventory* by $10,500 and the *Building* account balance by $5,000. How much cash will be paid to Masten?

PROBLEMS

Problem Set A [HM]

Problem 19.1A

Objective 3

eXcel

▶ **Accounting for formation of a partnership.**

Will Clark operates a store that sells computer software. Clark has agreed to enter into a partnership with Alexander Pettit, effective January 1, 2010. The new firm will be called Contemporary Computing. Clark is to transfer all assets and liabilities of his firm to the partnership at the values agreed on. Pettit will invest cash that is equal to 80 percent of Clark's investment after revaluation. The accounts shown on Clark's books and the agreed-on value of assets and liabilities are shown below.

INSTRUCTIONS

1. Prepare the general journal entries to record the following transactions in the books of the partnership on January 1, 2010.

	Balances Shown in Clark's Records	Value Agreed to by Partners
Assets Transferred		
Cash		$ 20,000	$ 20,000
Accounts Receivable	$ 58,000		
Allowance for Doubtful Accounts	2,000	56,000	53,600
Merchandise Inventory		334,000	346,000
Furniture and Equipment	112,000		71,600
Accumulated Depreciation	46,000	66,000	
Total Assets		$476,000	$491,200
Liabilities and Owner's Equity Transferred		
Accounts Payable		44,000	44,000
Will Clark, Capital		$432,000	$447,200

Note: the table above shows three monetary columns (Clark's records detail, Balances Shown in Clark's Records, Value Agreed to by Partners).

a. Receipt of Clark's investment of assets and liabilities.

b. Receipt of Pettit's investment of cash.

2. Prepare a balance sheet for the partnership as of the beginning of its operations on January 1, 2010.

Analyze: Based on the balance sheet you have prepared, what percentage (to the nearest 1/10 of 1%) of total equity is owned by Will Clark?

Accounting for formation of a partnership.

◄ **Problem 19.2A**

Objective 3

Brittany O'Grady operates a small shop that sells fishing equipment. Her postclosing trial balance on December 31, 2010, is shown below.

O'Grady plans to enter into a partnership with Inez Loche, effective January 1, 2011. Profits and losses will be shared equally. O'Grady is to transfer all assets and liabilities of her store to the partnership after revaluation as agreed. Loche will invest cash equal to O'Grady's investment after revaluation. The agreed values are *Accounts Receivable* (net) $13,500; *Merchandise Inventory,* $48,900; and *Furniture and Equipment,* $11,300. The partnership will operate as O'Grady and Loche Angler's Outpost.

O'Grady's Tackle Center
Postclosing Trial Balance
December 31, 2010

ACCOUNT NAME	DEBIT	CREDIT
Cash	3 7 5 0 00	
Accounts Receivable	14 9 0 0 00	
Allowance for Doubtful Accounts		1 5 0 0 00
Merchandise Inventory	44 0 0 0 00	
Furniture and Equipment	28 1 0 0 00	
Accumulated Depreciation		22 0 0 0 00
Accounts Payable		3 0 0 0 00
Capital		64 2 5 0 00
Totals	90 7 5 0 00	90 7 5 0 00

INSTRUCTIONS

1. In general journal form, prepare the entries to record
   a. The receipt of O'Grady's investment of assets and liabilities by the partnership.
   b. The receipt of Loche's investment of cash.
2. Prepare a balance sheet for O'Grady and Loche Angler's Outpost just after the investments.

Analyze: By what net amount were the net assets of O'Grady's Tackle Center adjusted before they were transferred to the partnership?

Problem 19.3A ▶

Objective 4

Computing and recording the division of net income or loss between partners.

Samantha Gaddis and Patty Lane own The Blossom Flower Shop. The partnership agreement provides that Gaddis can withdraw $3,000 a month and Lane $3,800 a month in anticipation of profits. The withdrawals, which are not considered to be salaries, were made each month. Net income and net losses are to be allocated 60 percent to Gaddis and 40 percent to Lane. For the year ended December 31, 2010, the partnership earned a net income of $70,000.

INSTRUCTIONS

1. Prepare general journal entries to
   a. Close the *Income Summary* account.
   b. Close the partners' drawing accounts.
2. Assume that there was a net loss of $20,000 for the year instead of a profit of $70,000. Give the general journal entries to
   a. Close the *Income Summary* account.
   b. Close the partners' drawing accounts.

Analyze: Assume the business earned net income of $70,000. If 2010 was the first year of operation for The Blossom Flower Shop, what balance should be reflected for the *Samantha Gaddis, Capital* account at the end of the year if Gaddis's beginning capital was $50,000?

Problem 19.4A ▶

Objectives 4, 5

QB   **eXcel**

Computing and recording the division of net income or loss between partners; preparing a statement of partners' equities.

French Taylor and Larry Willis own Taylor Antiques. Their partnership agreement provides for annual salary allowances of $88,000 for Taylor and $72,000 for Willis, and interest of 10 percent on each partner's invested capital at the beginning of the year. The remainder of the net income or loss is to be distributed 40 percent to Taylor and 60 percent to Willis. The partners withdraw their salary allowances monthly. On January 1, 2010, the capital account balances were Taylor, $340,000, and Willis, $420,000. On December 15, 2010, Willis made a permanent withdrawal of $80,000. The net income for 2010 was $288,000.

INSTRUCTIONS

1. Prepare the general journal entry on December 15, 2010, to record the permanent withdrawal by Willis.
2. Prepare the general journal entries on December 31, 2010, to
   a. Record the salary allowances for the year.
   b. Record the interest allowances for the year.
   c. Record the division of the balance of net income.
   d. Close the drawing accounts into the capital accounts, assuming that Taylor and Willis have withdrawn their full salary allowances.

3. Prepare a schedule showing the division of net income to the partners as it would appear on the income statement for 2010.

4. Prepare a statement of partners' equities showing the changes that took place in the partners' capital accounts during 2010.

Analyze: By what percentage did Taylor's capital account increase in the fiscal year 2010?

Accounting for revaluation of assets and liabilities of a partnership, investment of a new partner, and withdrawal of a partner.

◀ **Problem 19.5A**

Objectives 6, 8, 9

QB

The balance sheet of Thomas Pharmacy after the revenue, expense, and partners' drawing accounts have been closed on December 31, 2010, follows:

Thomas Pharmacy			
Balance Sheet			
December 31, 2010			
Assets			
Cash			82 400 00
Accounts Receivable			16 000 00
Merchandise Inventory			420 000 00
Equipment	164 000 00		
Allowance for Depreciation—Equipment	96 000 00		68 000 00
Building	400 000 00		
Allowance for Depreciation—Building	320 000 00		80 000 00
Land			40 000 00
Total Assets			706 400 00
Liabilities and Partners' Equity			
Liabilities			
Accounts Payable			404 200 00
Taxes Payable			22 200 00
Total Liabilities			426 400 00
Partners' Equity			
Larry Thomas, Capital	160 000 00		
Hazel Thomas, Capital	60 000 00		
Isiah Thomas, Capital	60 000 00		
Total Partners' Equity			280 000 00
Total Liabilities and Partners' Equity			706 400 00

On that date, Larry Thomas, Hazel Thomas, and Isiah Thomas agree to admit Kathryn Thomas to the partnership. The partnership agreement provides that, in case of dissolution of the partnership, all assets and liabilities should be revalued. Profits and losses are shared in the ratio of 50:25:25, to Larry, Hazel, and Isiah, respectively. The agreed upon values of the assets are as follows:

Accounts receivable	$ 14,800	Building	$124,000
Merchandise inventory	398,400	Land	88,000
Equipment	68,000		

All liabilities are properly recorded.

INSTRUCTIONS

1. Prepare the general journal entries to record revaluation of the assets.

2. Prepare the general journal entry (or entries) to record Kathryn Thomas's investment of $120,000, assuming that she is to receive capital equal to the amount invested.

3. Prepare the general journal entry (or entries) to record Kathryn Thomas's investment of $120,000, assuming that she is to receive one-fifth of the capital of the partnership.

4. Prepare the general journal entry (or entries) to record Kathryn Thomas's investment of $120,000, assuming that she is to receive one-third of the capital of the partnership.

5. Assume that after the revaluation had been recorded, the existing partners and Kathryn Thomas decided that their previous agreement should be canceled and that Kathryn Thomas should not become a partner. Instead, the partners agreed that Hazel Thomas would withdraw from the partnership and be paid cash by the partnership.

   a. Prepare the general journal entry to record the payment to Hazel Thomas if she is paid an amount equal to her capital account balance after the revaluation.

   b. Prepare the general journal entry to record the payment to Hazel Thomas if she is paid an amount equal to $12,000 less than her capital account balance after revaluation.

   c. Prepare the general journal entry to record the payment to Hazel Thomas if she is paid an amount equal to $9,600 more than her capital account balance after revaluation.

Analyze: Assume that only items 1 and 3 have been recorded in the records of the partnership. What is the balance of Isiah Thomas's capital account at January 1, 2011?

Problem 19.6A
Objectives 7, 8
▶ **Accounting for sale of a partnership interest and investment of a new partner.**

David Masters and Luis Anton, attorneys, operate a law practice. They would like to expand the expertise of their firm. In anticipation of this, they have agreed to admit June Cho to the partnership on January 1, 2010. The capital account balances on January 1, 2010, after revaluation of assets, are Masters, $180,000, and Anton, $140,000. Net income or net loss is shared equally.

INSTRUCTIONS

Prepare the entries in general journal form to record the admission of Cho to the partnership on January 1, 2010, under each of the following independent conditions.

1. Masters sells one-half of his interest in the partnership to Cho for $128,000 cash.

2. Masters sells one-half of his interest in the partnership to Cho for $84,000 cash.

3. Cho invests $120,000 in the business for a 25 percent interest in the partnership.

4. Cho invests $124,000 in the business for a 30 percent interest in the partnership.

Analyze: Based only on item 3, what percentage of total equity does each partner own?

Problem Set B

Problem 19.1B
Objective 3
▶ **Accounting for the formation of a partnership.**

Ted Nursy operates the Turner Broadcast Company. His postclosing trial balance on December 31, 2010, is as follows:

Turner Broadcast Company
Postclosing Trial Balance
December 31, 2010

ACCOUNT NAME	DEBIT	CREDIT
Cash	6 2 0 0 00	
Accounts Receivable	6 0 0 0 00	
Allowance for Doubtful Accounts		1 2 0 0 00
Merchandise Inventory	45 0 0 0 00	
Fixtures and Store Equipment	60 0 0 0 00	
Accumulated Depreciation		40 0 0 0 00
Accounts Payable		2 0 0 0 00
Ted Nursy, Capital		74 0 0 0 00
Totals	117 2 0 0 00	117 2 0 0 00

Nursy agrees to enter into a partnership with Annie McGowan, effective January 1, 2011. Profits and losses will be shared equally. Nursy is to transfer the assets and liabilities of his store to the partnership after revaluation as agreed. McGowan will invest cash equal to one-half of Nursy's investment after revaluation. The agreed upon values are *Accounts Receivable* (net), $2,400; *Merchandise Inventory,* $46,000; and *Fixtures and Store Equipment* (net), $44,000. The partnership will operate as the Turner-McGowan Broadcast Company.

INSTRUCTIONS

1. In general journal form, prepare the entries to record the following on the books of the partnership:

   a. The receipt of Nursy's investment of assets and liabilities in the partnership.

   b. The receipt of McGowan's investment of cash.

2. Prepare a balance sheet for Turner-McGowan Broadcast Company for January 1, 2011.

Analyze: By what net amount was Nursy's equity adjusted before the partnership was formed?

Accounting for formation of a partnership.

◀ **Problem 19.2B**
Objective 3

Homer Litton operates a store that sells paintings and portraits by local artists. Litton has agreed to enter into a partnership with Deborah Simpson, effective January 1, 2010. The new firm will be called The Artist's Supply. Litton is to transfer the assets and liabilities of his business to the partnership at the values agreed on. Simpson will invest cash that is equal to Litton's investment after revaluation. The accounts shown on Litton's books and the agreed-on value of assets and liabilities follow.

		Balances Shown in Litton's Records	Value Agreed to by Partners
Assets Transferred			
Cash		$ 9,000	$ 9,000
Accounts Receivable	$ 9,000		
Allowance for Doubtful Accounts	1,000	8,000	6,800
Merchandise Inventory		96,000	86,000
Furniture and Equipment	54,000		23,800
Accumulated Depreciation	41,000	13,000	
Total Assets		$126,000	$125,600
Liabilities and Owner's Equity Transferred			
Accounts Payable		0	8,000
Homer Litton, Capital		$126,000	$117,200

INSTRUCTIONS

1. Prepare the general journal entries to record the following transactions on the books of the partnership on January 1, 2010.

   a. Receipt of Litton's investment of assets and liabilities.

   b. Receipt of Simpson's investment of cash.

2. Prepare a balance sheet for the partnership as of the beginning of its operations on January 1, 2010.

Analyze: If Deborah Simpson agreed to a cash investment equal to 80 percent of the value of Homer Litton's investment, what would the balance of Deborah Simpson's capital account be after the formation of the partnership?

Problem 19.3B ▶
Objective 4

Computing and recording the division of net income or loss between partners.

David Kesterson and Alan Mayper operate a retail furniture store. Under the terms of the partnership agreement, Kesterson is authorized to withdraw $6,800 a month and Mayper $4,600 a month. The withdrawals, which are not considered to be salaries, were made each month and charged to the drawing accounts. The partners have agreed that net income or loss is to be allocated 35 percent to Kesterson and 65 percent to Mayper. For the year ended December 31, 2010, the partnership earned a net income of $196,000.

INSTRUCTIONS

1. Prepare general journal entries to

   a. Close the *Income Summary* account.

   b. Close the partners' drawing accounts.

2. Assume that there had been a net loss of $73,000 instead of net income of $196,000. Prepare the general journal entries to

   a. Close the *Income Summary* account.

   b. Close the partners' drawing accounts.

Analyze: Alan Mayper's capital account on January 1, 2010, was $120,000. What is the balance in that account as the end of 2010, assuming the profit for the year was $196,000?

Problem 19.4B ▶
Objectives 4, 5

Computing and recording the division of net income or loss between partners; preparing a statement of partners' equities.

Alika Myers and Cliff Hanson operate Downtown Apartments. Their partnership agreement provides for salaries of $60,000 a year for Myers and $48,000 for Hanson and for an interest allowance of 10 percent on each partner's invested capital at the beginning of the year. The remainder of the net income or loss is to be distributed equally to the two partners. On January 1, 2010, the capital account balances were $104,000 for Myers and $224,000 for Hanson. On July 15, 2010, Hanson made a permanent withdrawal of capital of $80,000 for a down payment on a yacht. The net income for 2010 was $192,800.

INSTRUCTIONS

1. Prepare the general journal entry on July 15, 2010, to record the permanent withdrawal by Hanson.

2. Prepare the general journal entries on December 31, 2010, to

   a. Record the salary allowances for the year.

   b. Record the interest allowances for the year.

   c. Record the division of the balance of net income.

   d. Close the drawing accounts into the capital accounts, assuming that the partners had withdrawn only the full amount of their salary allowances.

3. Prepare a schedule showing the division of net income to the partners as it would appear on the income statement for 2010.

4. Prepare a statement of partners' equities showing the changes that took place in the partners' capital accounts during the year 2010.

Analyze: Do the facts stated in the problem suggest changes that probably should be made in the provision for interest in allocating income? Explain.

Accounting for revaluation of assets and liabilities of a partnership, investment of a new partner, and withdrawal of a partner.

The balance sheet of The Office Supply Shop after the revenue, expense, and partners' drawing accounts have been closed on December 31, 2010, is provided below.

On that date, Rush, Hatten, and Booker agree to admit Rosie Hinojosa to the partnership. The partnership agreement among Rush, Hatten, and Booker provides that in case of dissolution of the partnership, all assets and liabilities should be revalued. Profits and losses are shared in the ratio of 50:20:30 to Rush, Hatten, and Booker, respectively. The agreed upon values of the assets are given below.

Accounts receivable	$ 7,020
Merchandise inventory	199,960
Equipment	34,000
Building	57,000
Land	44,320

All liabilities are properly recorded.

The Office Supply Shop
Balance Sheet
December 31, 2010

Assets		
Cash		44 000 00
Accounts Receivable		10 000 00
Merchandise Inventory		208 000 00
Equipment	84 000 00	
Allowance for Depreciation—Equipment	48 000 00	36 000 00
Building	200 000 00	
Allowance for Depreciation—Building	154 000 00	46 000 00
Land		20 000 00
Total Assets		364 000 00
Liabilities and Partners' Equity		
Liabilities		
Accounts Payable		210 000 00
Taxes Payable		14 000 00
Total Liabilities		224 000 00
Partners' Equity		
Helen Rush, Capital	70 000 00	
Billy Hatten, Capital	28 000 00	
Quinton Booker, Capital	42 000 00	
Total Partners' Equity		140 000 00
Total Liabilities and Partners' Equity		364 000 00

INSTRUCTIONS

1. Prepare the general journal entries to record revaluation of the partnership's assets.

2. Prepare the general journal entry (or entries) to record Hinojosa's investment of $66,000, assuming that she is to receive credit for the amount invested.

3. Prepare the general journal entry (or entries) to record Hinojosa's investment of $66,000, assuming that she is to receive one-fifth of the capital of the entity.

4. Prepare the general journal entry (or entries) to record Hinojosa's investment of $66,000, assuming that she is to receive 45 percent of the capital of the entity.

5. Assume that after the revaluation had been recorded, the existing partners and Hinojosa decided that their previous agreement should be canceled and that Hinojosa should not become a partner. Instead, the partners agreed that Booker would withdraw from the partnership.

a. Prepare the general journal entry to record the payment to Booker if he is paid an amount equal to his capital account balance after the revaluation.

b. Prepare the general journal entry to record the payment to Booker if he is paid an amount equal to $5,600 less than his capital account balance after the revaluation.

c. Prepare the general journal entry to record the payment to Booker if he is paid an amount equal to $8,400 more than his capital account balance after the revaluation.

Analyze: Assume only items 1 and 5(b) occurred. What is the balance of the *Billy Hatten, Capital* account at December 31, 2010?

Problem 19.6B
Objectives 7, 8

▶ **Accounting for sale of partnership interest and investment of a new partner.**

Haywood Nelson and Fred Kenamond are partners in Technology Applications. The balances of their capital accounts on January 2, 2010, after revaluation of assets were Nelson, $240,000, and Kenamond, $320,000. Profits and losses are shared in the ratio of 55:45 between Nelson and Kenamond. The partners agree to admit Stanley Carpenter to the partnership, effective January 3, 2010.

INSTRUCTIONS

Give the entries in general journal form to record the admission of Carpenter under each of the following independent conditions.

1. Nelson sells one-half of his interest in the partnership to Carpenter for $176,000 in cash.

2. Kenamond sells one-half of his interest in the partnership to Carpenter for $128,000 in cash.

3. Carpenter invests $240,000 in the business for a one-fourth interest in the partnership.

4. Carpenter invests $240,000 in the business for a 35 percent interest in the partnership.

Analyze: What percentage of partnership equity is owned by Nelson and by Kenamond after transaction 4?

Critical Thinking Problem 19.1

From Sole Proprietor to Partner

For several years, Richard Harris had operated Management Consulting Company as its sole proprietor. On January 1, 2010, he formed a partnership with John Amos to operate the company under the name Amos-Harris Professional Management Consultants. Pertinent terms of the partnership agreement are as follows.

1. Harris was to transfer to the partnership the accounts receivable, merchandise inventory, furniture and equipment, and all liabilities of the sole proprietorship in return for a partnership interest of 60 percent of the partnership capital. Assets were appraised and transferred to the partnership at the appraised values.

   Balances in the relevant accounts of Harris's sole proprietorship at the close of business on December 31, 2009, are shown below.

Accounts Receivable	$126,000 Dr.
Allowance for Doubtful Accounts	8,000 Cr.
Merchandise Inventory	174,400 Dr.
Furniture and Equipment	119,600 Dr.
Allowance for Depreciation—Furniture & Equipment	76,000 Cr.
Accounts Payable	26,000 Cr.

The two parties agreed to the following:

■ There were unrecorded accounts payable of $2,000.

■ Accounts receivable of $3,000 were definitely uncollectible and should not be transferred to the partnership.

■ The value of *Allowance for Doubtful Accounts* should be $7,200.

■ The appraised value of *Merchandise Inventory* was $162,200.

■ The appraised value of *Furniture and Equipment* was $32,000.

2. In return for a 40 percent interest in partnership capital, Amos invested cash in an amount equal to two-thirds of Harris's net investment in the business.

3. Each partner was allowed a salary payable on the 15th day of each month. Harris's salary was to be $8,400 per month, and Amos's salary was to be $6,000 per month.

4. The partners were to be allowed interest of 7 percent of their beginning capital balances.

5. No provision was made for profit division except for the salaries and interest previously discussed.

6. The partnership's revenues for the year 2011 were $1,750,000, and expenses were $1,590,000. Payments for salary allowances were charged to the partners' drawing accounts.

INSTRUCTIONS

1. Record the following information in general journal form in the partnership's records.

   a. Receipt of assets and liabilities from Harris.

   b. Investment of cash by Amos.

   c. Summary of cash withdrawals for salaries by the two partners during the year.

   d. Profit or loss division including salary and interest allowances and the closing balance of the *Income Summary* account determined on an appropriate basis.

2. Record the journal entry to close the partners' drawing accounts into the capital accounts. No other cash was withdrawn.

3. Open general ledger accounts for the partners' capital accounts. The account numbers are: *Richard Harris, Capital* 301, and *John Amos, Capital* 311. Post the journal entries from instructions 1 and 2 to the capital accounts.

4. Prepare a schedule showing the division of net income to the partners as it would appear on the income statement for 2011.

5. Prepare a statement of partners' equities for the year.

6. On January 1, 2011, the partners agreed to admit Mary Wells as a partner. Wells is to invest cash of $120,000 for a one-fourth interest in the capital of the partnership. The three parties agree that the book value of assets and liabilities properly reflects their values. Give the general journal entry to record Wells' investment.

Analyze: What percentage of the total partnership capital after the admission of Wells on January 1, 2011, is owned by Harris?

Critical Thinking Problem 19.2

New Partnership

Andrew Wilson has operated a successful motorcycle repair business for the past several years. Wilson thinks his business is almost too successful because he has very little time for himself. Wilson and Beatrice Kelly, who is also a motorcycle enthusiast, have had a number of discussions about her joining him in the business. Finally, they agree to form a partnership that will operate under the name WK Motorcycle Repair Shop. They have asked you to provide assistance, particularly with help in establishing terms for dividing partnership profits and losses.

The partners give you the following information about their plans for the business:

a. Wilson plans to contribute to the partnership the assets of his sole proprietorship. They have been appraised to have a fair market value of $352,000.

b. Kelly will invest $480,000 in cash.

c. Wilson will work full-time in the business while Kelly will work part-time and continue to attend the class she is taking in pursuit of a college degree.

Assume that WK Motorcycle Repair earned a net income of $221,560 during its first year of operation.

INSTRUCTIONS

1. What division of profits and losses would you suggest for Wilson and Kelly?

2. Using your proposed plan of profit sharing, prepare a schedule showing the distribution of the first year's net income to the partners.

BUSINESS CONNECTIONS

Managerial | FOCUS

Forming a Partnership

1. The owner of an accounting practice is considering establishing a partnership with two other persons to carry on the business. What are the major disadvantages of the partnership form of organization that she should consider in making her decision?

2. Your employer is planning to form a partnership with one of his close friends. He explains to you that because he is well acquainted with the prospective partner, there is no need to have a written partnership agreement. He asks your advice. Give him your recommendation and the reasons for it.

3. Your employer is considering investing $25,000 in a partnership. In discussing the advantages and disadvantages of the arrangement, the employer informs you that a friend has told him that his potential loss is limited to the amount invested, $25,000. Is his information regarding this arrangement correct?

4. Two individuals who are forming a partnership ask you how they should divide the income and losses of the business. What factors should you consider in making a recommendation?

5. You work for a partnership. The partnership agreement between the two partners specifies that one partner is allowed a monthly draw of $1,500 and the other a monthly draw of $1,000. The agreement does not mention salary allowances for the partners. At the end of the year, one partner maintains that a drawing is the same as a salary allowance. They ask your opinion. What do you tell them?

6. One of the partners in a partnership that employs you is retiring from the business. Her capital account has a balance of $128,000. She tells you that she expects to receive a check for $128,000 from the partnership. Explain to her the proper procedure for determining the amount she will be paid.

Ethical | DILEMMA

Know Thy Partner

Donald Wilson has a great deal of experience with respiratory therapy. James Smith has the business connection and knowledge. They have decided to start a partnership that sells respiratory equipment, employing several sales representatives. They have decided to share equally in the net income and net losses. After two years, the business is thriving having sold more than 1,000 units this year. One day, Donald receives a call from the Internal Revenue Service (IRS). Unknown to Donald, James has not paid the payroll taxes for last year and is behind on the payroll taxes in the current quarter. Donald learns that James has a gambling problem and there is insufficient money to pay the IRS. James has no personal assets that can be confiscated. What are Donald's options for the resolution of the IRS problem? What is Donald's liability? What actions should Donald have taken prior to the partnership agreement?

STREETWISE:
Questions from the
                 REAL WORLD

Consolidated Financial Statements

Refer to The Home Depot, Inc., *2006 Annual Report* in Appendix A.

1. In a partnership, two or more persons contract as co-owners of a business. For a corporation such as The Home Depot, Inc., many stockholders jointly participate as its owners. Review the consolidated balance sheets. How many shares of common stock were issued and outstanding at January 28, 2007?

2. The financial statements of a corporation often reflect consolidated, or combined, financial data from various holdings of the company. Locate Note 1 and review the "Business,

Consolidation and Presentation" section. How many segments are included in the consolidated statements of The Home Depot, Inc.?

Partners' Equity

The following excerpts were taken from the 10-K Annual Report filed by Kinder Morgan Energy Partners, L.P., for the year ended December 31, 2006.

Balance Sheets

December 31 (in thousands)	2006	2005
Partners' equity:		
General partner	$ 109,667	$ 119,898
Limited partners and other	3,911,986	3,493,842
Total partners' equity	$4,021,653	$3,613,740

Consolidated Statements of Income

Year Ended December 31 (Unaudited)	2006	2005
Net income	$972,143	$812,227
Net income attributable to general partner	$512,967	$477,300
Net income attributable to limited partners	$459,176	$334,927

Analyze:

1. On December 31, 2006, what percentage of total equity belongs to the general partner of Kinder Morgan Energy Partners, L.P.?

2. By what amount has the equity of the limited partners increased from December 31, 2005, to December 31, 2006?

3. Based on the net earnings allocation reflected on the 2006 income statement, what percentage of earnings is allocated to the general partner? To the limited partners?

Analyze Online: Locate Kinder Morgan's Web site (www.kindermorgan.com). Click on *investors*, then *KMP*, and find the most recent 10-K SEC filing for Kinder Morgan Energy Partners, L.P.

4. What is the year covered by the 10-K filing?

5. What partners' equity is reported for the general partner?

6. What was the earnings allocation to the general partner? To the limited partners?

Limited Liability Companies

Between 1997 and 2000, approximately 1.9 million businesses organized as a limited liability company or LLC. Considered a hybrid form of organization, the LLC offers the flexibility and tax advantages of a partnership while maintaining the limited liability benefits of a corporation. Partners in an LLC are not personally liable for any debts or obligations that the business incurs. Based on these provisions, members of an LLC may execute contracts or make operating decisions that they are not personally liable for. Do you agree or disagree with this practice? Why?

Pitching a Partnership Idea

You possess more than 10 years' experience in corporate accounting, and a professional colleague of yours has practiced law in the community for 7 years. Your city has become a hotbed for Internet start-ups, and there is a strong demand for consulting services. You would like to

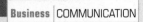

propose a partnership with your friend to provide consultation services for financial and legal matters. Draft a letter to your colleague containing tentative provisions of the partnership. Use the new terms introduced in this chapter in your letter. Be sure to include your proposed name for the new partnership.

Partnership Agreements

Each partner brings certain personal skills and assets into a partnership. One partner could have the technical knowledge while the other partner has the business knowledge. This partnership agreement would easily be 50/50. However, when there are multiple partners and one brings in time, one talent, and the other physical assets, the partnership agreement becomes complicated.

In groups of three or four, decide on a partnership business. Determine what the partnership business will provide, how the partnership will allocate income and loss, and any salary arrangements. Decide when and how the partnership is dissolved should it become necessary.

Small Business Administration

The Small Business Administration (SBA) Web site at www.sba.gov provides information for potential businesses. Find out what the SBA considers the advantages and disadvantages of partnerships. What other information does this Web site contain about partnerships?

Answers to **Self Reviews**

Answers to Section 1 Self Review

1. At their current values as of the date of the partnership formation.
2. As debits to their drawing accounts and credits to *Purchases.*
3. Unlimited liability of partners for partnership debts, binding obligation of partnerships for most acts of partners in business, lack of continuity, partnership equity not freely transferable.
4. **c.** a debit to the partner's drawing account and a credit to *Purchases* for the cost of the merchandise withdrawn.
5. **c.** a debit to *Cash* and a credit to *James Smith, Capital.*
6. $59,980.

Answers to Section 2 Self Review

1. Salary and interest.
2. (a) Record salary allowances.
   (b) Record interest allowances.
   (c) Close balance to *Income Summary.*
   [**Note:** Steps (a) and (b) may be reversed.]
3. Equally between the partners.
4. **a.** debit to *Income Summary* and a credit to each partner's capital account.
5. **a.** Should be specified in the partnership agreement.
6. Hanks: $19,200 [($40,000 ÷ $100,000) × $48,000].
   Olson: $28,800 [($60,000 ÷ $100,000) × $48,000].

Answers to Section 3 Self Review

1. The excess is debited to the retiring partner's capital account and credited to the capital accounts of the remaining partners. It is allocated to them in proportion to their old relative profit and loss allocation percentages.
2. Debit the old partner's capital account for one-half of the balance of that account and credit the new partner's capital account for the same amount.

3. The first entry is to debit *Cash* and credit the new partner's capital account for the amount invested. The second entry is to debit the new partner's capital account for an amount that will reduce the new owner's capital account balance to the new owner's fractional interest multiplied by the total capital after recording the cash invested by the new owner. The reduction in the new partner's capital account is credited to the accounts of old partners in proportion to the income or loss distribution ratio of the old partners.

4. **d.** the capital account of Harris is credited for $1,333.

5. **c.** debited to the capital accounts of the remaining partners, allocated to those partners in proportion to their profit and loss percentages.

6. Debit *Pete Mason, Capital* for $25,000 and credit *James Miller, Capital* for $25,000.

Answers to Comprehensive Self Review

1. The value changes represent income or loss that should be shared by the existing partners, not by the new partner.

2. Salary withdrawals are cash payments to be charged to the partners' drawing accounts. Salary allowances are part of the income or loss allocation and are charged to *Income Summary* and credited to the partners' capital accounts.

3. One partner may receive an interest and/or salary allowance considerably larger than the other partner receives. Allowances must be recorded, even if there is a loss.

4. The disadvantages of a partnership stem from its inherent characteristics; that is, it brings unlimited liability, mutual agency, lack of continuity, and lack of transferability.

5. Answers may vary but could include:
    - Future plans for the partnership.
    - Potential personality conflicts.
    - Differences in ethical codes of conduct.

Corporations: Formation and Capital Stock Transactions

LEARNING OBJECTIVES

1. Explain the characteristics of a corporation. LP20
2. Describe special "hybrid" organizations that have some characteristics of partnerships and some characteristics of corporations.
3. Describe the different types of stock.
4. Compute the number of shares of common stock to be issued on the conversion of convertible preferred stock.
5. Compute dividends payable on stock.
6. Record the issuance of capital stock at par value.
7. Prepare a balance sheet for a corporation.
8. Record organization costs.
9. Record stock issued at a premium and stock with no par value.
10. Record transactions for stock subscriptions.
11. Describe the capital stock records for a corporation.
12. Define the accounting terms new to this chapter.

NEW TERMS

authorized capital stock
bylaws
callable preferred stock
capital stock ledger
capital stock transfer journal
common stock
convertible preferred stock
corporate charter
cumulative preferred stock
dividends
limited liability company (LLC)
limited liability partnership (LLP)
liquidation value
market value
minute book
noncumulative preferred stock
nonparticipating preferred stock
no-par-value stock
organization costs
par value
participating preferred stock
preemptive right
preference dividend
preferred stock
registrar
shareholder
stated value
stock certificate
stockholders' equity
stockholders' ledger
subchapter S corporation (S Corporation)
subscribers' ledger
subscription book
transfer agent

ConAgra Foods   www.conagra.com

ConAgra Foods is a leading food company that is organized into three business operations—Consumer Foods, International Foods, and Commercial Products. Its brands and products fill the pantries of 95 percent of America's households. Healthy Choice, Chef Boyardee, Hebrew National, PAM, Egg Beaters, Orville Redenbacher's, and Hunt's are just a few of the brands in the ConAgra family that contributed to the over $12 billion in sales in 2007.

The ConAgra story is a complex one. Throughout the early 1900s, numerous food companies got into the business of providing ready-made food to hungry Americans. In 1919, four Nebraska flour mills consolidated and formed the Nebraska Consolidated Mills, and eventually ConAgra.

Through strategic mergers and acquisitions, ConAgra expanded beyond simple flour to become the market leader it is today.

thinking critically

What issues do you think ConAgra stockholders have the right to vote on?

ConAgra Foods
WORLD HEADQUARTERS

SECTION OBJECTIVES

>> 1. **Explain the characteristics of a corporation.**

   WHY IT'S IMPORTANT

   The corporate form of business is widely used in the national and international marketplace.

>> 2. **Describe special "hybrid" organizations that have some characteristics of partnerships and some characteristics of corporations.**

   WHY IT'S IMPORTANT

   "Hybrid" organizations are becoming increasingly popular for the tax advantages and limited liability features they offer.

TERMS TO LEARN

bylaws

corporate charter

limited liability company (LLC)

limited liability partnership (LLP)

shareholder

stockholders' equity

subchapter S corporation (S corporation)

Forming a Corporation

Previous chapters focused on sole proprietorships and partnerships. Now we consider the third form of business organization, the corporation.

Characteristics of a Corporation

Corporate enterprises account for a majority of business transactions, even though there are more sole proprietorships and partnerships than corporations. Most large national and international businesses use the corporate business form.

In 1818, Chief Justice John Marshall of the U.S. Supreme Court defined the *corporation* as "an artificial being, invisible, intangible, and existing only in contemplation of the law." The corporation is a legal entity, completely separate and apart from its owners. It is created by a **corporate charter** issued by a state government. Since it is a legal entity, a corporation can enter into contracts, can own property, and has almost all of the rights and privileges of a sole proprietorship or a partnership.

Corporations can have few or many owners. A *privately held* corporation is one that is owned by one or more persons and whose stock is not traded on an organized stock exchange. A *publicly held* corporation has many owners and its stock is traded on an organized stock exchange.

A **shareholder** or *stockholder* is a person who owns shares of stock in a corporation and is thus one of the owners of the corporation.

>> **1. OBJECTIVE**

Explain the characteristics of a corporation.

LP20

ADVANTAGES OF THE CORPORATE FORM

The corporate form offers some major advantages:

- *Limited Liability.* Sole proprietors and general partners have unlimited liability; they are personally liable for all debts of the business. Shareholders have no personal liability for the corporation's debts. The corporation's creditors must look to the assets of the business to satisfy their claims, not to the owners' personal property, even in the event of liquidation. It is not unusual, however, for major shareholders of small corporations to give personal guarantees to repay its loans.

- *Restricted Agency.* A shareholder has no right to act on behalf of the business. Instead, the board of directors controls the corporation, and the corporate officers are in direct charge of operations. For example, a person who owns 10,000 shares of Microsoft Corporation has no greater power to act on behalf of Microsoft than a person who has no ownership interest at all.

- *Continuous Existence.* The death, disability, or withdrawal of a shareholder has no effect on the life of a corporation.
- *Transferability of Ownership Rights.* Generally, shareholders can sell their stock without consulting or obtaining the consent of the other owners. Shareholders are free to shift their investments at any time, provided they can find buyers for their stock. Organized stock markets, such as the New York Stock Exchange, make it easy to sell or buy interests in corporations whose stocks are traded.

  Small companies often sell shares of stock with a contract that gives the corporation or the existing shareholders "the right of first refusal" to repurchase the shares when the shareholder wishes to sell them.
- *Ease of Raising Capital.* A corporation can have an unlimited number of shareholders. Some corporations have more than a million shareholders, making available a vast pool of capital.

DISADVANTAGES OF THE CORPORATE FORM

Although the advantages are impressive, the corporate form of operation also has certain disadvantages:

- *Corporate Income Tax.* Corporate profits are subject to federal income tax. Profits distributed to shareholders in the form of dividends are taxed a second time as part of the personal income of the stockholder. The taxation of profits at the corporate level and at the shareholder level is known as *double taxation.*

  State and local governments can also levy income taxes on corporations. In addition, most states require corporations to pay an annual franchise tax for the privilege of carrying on business in the state. In some states, especially those that have no corporate income tax, the franchise tax can be quite burdensome.
- *Governmental Regulation.* Corporations are subject to laws and regulations imposed by the state. In general, the state regulatory bodies exercise closer supervision and control over corporations than they do over sole proprietorships or partnerships. State laws may prohibit corporations from entering into particular types of transactions or from owning specific types of property. Special reports are frequently required of corporations.

ENTITIES HAVING ATTRIBUTES OF BOTH PARTNERSHIPS AND CORPORATIONS

Some business entities have characteristics of partnerships and of corporations. Three of these special entities are Subchapter S corporations, limited liability partnerships, and limited liability companies.

Subchapter S Corporations **Subchapter S corporations,** also known as *S corporations,* are entities formed as corporations which meet the requirements of Subchapter S of the Internal Revenue Code to be treated essentially as a partnership so the corporation pays no income tax. Instead, shareholders include their share of corporate profits, and any items that require special tax treatment, on their individual income tax returns. Otherwise, S corporations have all the characteristics of regular corporations. The advantage of S corporations is that the owners have limited liability and avoid double taxation.

Limited Liability Partnerships The **limited liability partnership (LLP)** is a general partnership that provides some limited liability for all partners. LLP partners are responsible and have liability for their own actions and the actions of those under their control or supervision. They are not liable for the actions or malfeasance of another partner. LLPs must have more than one owner, so a sole proprietorship cannot be treated as one. In some states, LLPs are for the service professions only, such as law, accounting, medicine, and engineering.

Except for the limited liability aspect, LLPs generally have the same characteristics, advantages, and disadvantages as any other partnership.

Limited Liability Companies **Limited liability companies (LLCs)** provide limited liability to the owners, who can elect to have the profits taxed at the LLC level or on their individual

>>2. OBJECTIVE
Describe special "hybrid" organizations that have some characteristics of partnerships and some characteristics of corporations.

LP20

income tax returns. The profits and losses can be allocated to the owners other than in proportion to the ownership interests. In most states, one individual can form an LLC. Its ownership interests are not freely transferable; other owners must approve a transfer of ownership interest. When transferring ownership, the existing LLC is terminated and a new one formed. Unlike the limited partners discussed in Chapter 19, LLC owners can take part in policy and operating decisions.

Formation of a Corporation

To understand why and how a corporation is formed, place yourself in the shoes of Jerome Tarvin. Tarvin is the sole proprietor of Tarvin's Camping Supply Store, a retail business selling camping equipment. Tarvin wants to expand the variety of equipment he sells and add guidebooks.

To expand his operations, Tarvin needs more money to remodel the store and buy new fixtures, to acquire more inventory, and to extend more credit to customers. Several of Tarvin's friends are willing to invest as partners in his business, but he has some doubts about this. Although he needs the extra funds, he does not want to share operating control with people who know nothing about the business. Also, he does not wish to go further in debt.

Tarvin's prospective backers have some doubts, too. They do not mind risking the money they invest, but they do not want to be responsible for the debts of the business. Although they do not mind letting Tarvin run the business, they do want to have some voice in general policy. They would also like to be assured of a reasonable and regular return on their money.

Tarvin and his friends consulted an attorney who specializes in business law and taxation. The lawyer suggested that a corporation offers the best solution to their needs. She explained the necessary steps to form a corporation. Requirements differ from state to state, but typically the process is as follows.

One or more persons, the "organizers" or "promoters," apply to a state officer, usually the secretary of state, for a charter permitting the proposed corporation to do business. The state charges a fee for the charter.

When issued, the charter specifies the exact name, length of life (usually unlimited), rights and duties, and scope of operations of the corporation. Most corporate charters grant the corporation a broad sphere of operation. The charter also sets forth the classes of stock and number of shares in each class that can be issued in exchange for money, property, or services.

Shortly after the charter is issued, the organizers meet to elect an acting board of directors. The corporation proceeds to issue shares of stock to individuals who have paid the full purchase price of the stock. The shareholders then elect permanent directors, usually the same individuals as the acting directors. The directors or shareholders approve the corporation's **bylaws,** which are the guidelines for conducting the corporation's business affairs. The board then selects officers, who hire employees and begin operating the business.

The amount received for the capital stock issued by the corporation appears on the balance sheet. The corporate equivalent of owner's equity is called **stockholders' equity** or shareholders' equity.

Structure of a Corporation

Stockholders can participate in stockholders' meetings, elect a board of directors, and vote on basic corporate policy.

The board of directors formulates general operating policies and is responsible for seeing that the corporation's activities are conducted. The board selects officers and other top management personnel to direct everyday operations. The officers hire managers who hire other employees. Officers and managers make the day-to-day decisions necessary to operate the business.

A corporation's officers include the president, one or more vice presidents, a corporate secretary, and a treasurer. The top accounting official is called the *controller* or *chief financial officer.* Large firms might have several layers of management, including division managers, department heads, and supervisors. The levels depend on the nature and complexity of the operations.

Table 20.1 shows the flow of authority and responsibility in a corporate entity.

Stockholders	• Elect directors
Directors	• Make policies
	• Appoint officers
Officers	• Carry out policies
	• Hire managers
Managers	• Oversee and supervise operations
Other employees	• Perform assigned tasks

TABLE 20.1

Flow of Corporate Authority and Responsibility

Section 1 Self Review

QUESTIONS

1. What are the primary advantages of the corporate form of business?

2. Which level of government is responsible for issuing charters for most corporations?

3. What is the role of stockholders in running the business of a corporation?

EXERCISES

In each exercise, choose the correct option(s).

4. In a corporate organization, the stockholders

   a. must pay federal income tax on their proportional shares of profits reported by the corporation.

   b. have the right to surrender preferred stock to the corporation at any time for a payment equal to the par value of the stock.

   c. elect the directors of the corporation.

   d. are entitled to a proportionate share of dividends declared on their classes of stock.

5. The stockholders of a corporation

   a. have power to act for the business unless specifically prohibited by the corporate charter.

   b. are generally liable for the debts of the corporation.

   c. can sell their shares of stock without permission from other stockholders.

   d. are forbidden to be employees of the corporation.

ANALYSIS

6. Lucia Urbina and her husband, Jorje, are sole shareholders in a corporation they formed to operate their existing chain of five restaurants. Their corporation earned net income of approximately $100,000 in their first year of operations. One of Lucia's friends suggested to her that she and Jorje had made a mistake in incorporating and should operate as a sole proprietorship or partnership. What reasons may Lucia use to support their decision to incorporate?

(Answers to Section 1 Self Review are on page 721.)

TERMS TO LEARN

authorized capital stock
callable preferred stock
common stock
convertible preferred stock
cumulative preferred stock
dividends
liquidation value
market value
noncumulative preferred stock
nonparticipating preferred stock
par value
participating preferred stock
preemptive right
preference dividend
preferred stock
stated value

Types of Capital Stock

Decisions about the classes of stock to be offered and the number of shares of each class must be made before the charter application is filed.

Capital Stock

The **authorized capital stock** is the number of shares authorized for issue by the corporate charter. Usually the authorized stock is more than the number of shares the corporation plans to issue in the foreseeable future. This gives the corporation flexibility to issue stock in the future without having to amend the corporate charter.

When a corporation *issues* stock, the stock is sold (transferred to stockholders). *Outstanding* stock is stock that has been issued and is still in circulation, meaning it is still in the hands of stockholders.

CAPITAL STOCK VALUES

There are three terms commonly used to describe stock values.

Par Value. **Par value** is an amount assigned by the corporate charter to each share of stock for accounting purposes. It is usually $100 or less; it can be $25, $5, or even less than $1 per share. Stock can be issued for more than par value. State laws prohibit the issuance of par-value stock for less than the par value.

Stated Value. State laws permit stock to be issued without par value. This type of stock is called *no-par-value stock.* The value that can be assigned to no-par-value stock by a board of directors for accounting purposes is called the **stated value.**

Market Value. **Market value** is the price per share at which stock is bought and sold. After the corporation issues stock, it can be resold for any price that can be agreed on between the shareholder and purchaser. Usually a stock's market value has little relation to its par or stated value.

CLASSES OF CAPITAL STOCK

Each type, or class, of stock has different rights and privileges.

Common Stock If there is only one class of stock, the stock is called **common stock.** Each share of common stock conveys to the owner the same rights and privileges as every other share including the right to

- attend stockholders' meetings,
- vote in the election of directors and on other matters (each share entitles the owner to one vote),
- receive dividends as declared by the board of directors,
- purchase a proportionate amount of any new stock issued at a later date, referred to as the **preemptive right.**

If a corporation has two or more classes of stock, one class is common. The other class or classes of stock have certain preferences over the common shares.

> Some corporations have more than one class of preferred stock issued. Typically these shares are issued to help finance specific activities and bear different dividend rates reflecting the differences in economic factors, interest rates prevailing, and relative risks at the time of issuance. For example, Citigroup Corporation has at least seven classes of preferred stock traded on the New York Stock Exchange.

Preferred Stock **Preferred stock** has special claims on the corporate profits or, in case of liquidation, on corporate assets. In receiving special preferences, the owners of preferred stock might lose some of their general rights, such as the right to vote. Unless the charter specifies otherwise, however, preferred stock has voting rights.

Liquidation Preferences on Preferred Stock In case of liquidation, preferred stockholders have a claim on assets before that of common stockholders. A **liquidation value** (usually par value or an amount higher than par value) is assigned to the preferred stock. After the creditors are paid, the preferred stockholders are paid the liquidation value for each share of preferred stock before any assets are distributed to common stockholders. The liquidation value of preferred stock includes any cumulative dividends that have not been paid. (Cumulative dividends are explained later in this chapter.) The liquidation preference on preferred stock is disclosed in the Stockholders' Equity section of the balance sheet.

Assume that a corporation is going out of business. It has paid all of its liabilities. There remains $1,700,000 to distribute to the shareholders. The company has outstanding 25,000 shares of $50 preferred stock, with a liquidation value of $52 per share, and 50,000 shares of $20 par-value common stock. The preferred stockholders will receive $1,300,000 (25,000 shares × $52 per share). The common stockholders will receive what's left, $400,000 ($1,700,000 − $1,300,000).

Convertible Preferred Stock **Convertible preferred stock** is preferred stock that conveys the right to convert that stock to common stock after a specified date or during a period of time. The conversion ratio is the number of shares of common stock that will be issued for each share of preferred stock surrendered. The conversion ratio is indicated on the preferred stock certificate.

Some investors are reluctant to purchase preferred stock because its market price does not increase significantly even if the corporation is quite profitable. The ability to convert preferred stock to common stock can make the preferred stock more attractive to investors. The decision to convert the preferred stock to common stock depends on the market prices, the relative dividends paid on the common and the preferred stock, and the degree of risk involved.

Assume that a corporation has outstanding 100,000 shares of 12 percent, $25 par-value preferred stock that can be converted into common stock. (The term "12 percent" refers to

>>3. OBJECTIVE

Describe the different types of stock.

LP20

>>4. OBJECTIVE

Compute the number of shares of common stock to be issued on the conversion of convertible preferred stock.

LP20

the dividend rate and is discussed below.) The conversion ratio is two shares of common stock for each share of preferred stock surrendered. The conversion privilege is exercisable on or after January 1, 2010. A stockholder can convert 400 shares of preferred stock into 800 (400 × 2) shares of common stock.

Callable Preferred Stock   Callable preferred stock gives the issuing corporation the right to repurchase the preferred shares from the stockholders at a specific price. The call price is usually substantially greater than the original issue price. The rights are effective after some specified date. Callable stock gives the corporation flexibility in controlling its capital structure.

The following example illustrates the call feature. Assume a corporation issued 50,000 shares of 10 percent, $40 par-value preferred stock at $40 per share. The corporation has the right to call any part of the preferred stock any time after December 31, 2010, for $53 per share. If the corporation has funds available, or if money can be borrowed at substantially less than 10 percent, the corporation may call the preferred stock and retire it.

>>5. OBJECTIVE

Compute dividends payable on stock.

Video20.1

Dividends on Stock

Dividends are distributions of the profits of a corporation to its shareholders. The right to receive a dividend is one of the major incentives for buying stock. The board of directors declares dividends. The board of directors has complete discretion, subject to certain legal restrictions or contractual restrictions, in deciding whether to declare a dividend and the amount of the dividend. The amount of the dividend depends on the corporation's earnings and on the need to keep profits for use in the business. Dividends are usually paid on a quarterly basis.

DIVIDENDS ON PREFERRED STOCK

Preferred stock has a priority with respect to dividends. The priority is specified in the corporate charter. Preferred stock bears a basic or stated dividend rate, called the **preference dividend,** that must be paid before dividends can be paid on common stock. The *dividend rate* is expressed in dollars-per-share per year or as a percentage. When the dividend is expressed as a percentage, the dividend amount is par value of the stock multiplied by the percentage. For example, the annual dividend on 8 percent preferred stock with a par value of $50 is $4 per share ($50 × 0.08).

Special dividend rights can improve the market demand for preferred shares of stock.

- **Cumulative preferred stock** conveys to its owners the right to receive the preference dividend for the current year and any prior years in which the preference dividend was not paid before common stockholders receive any dividends.

- **Noncumulative preferred stock** conveys to its owners the stated preference dividend for the current year, but stockholders have no rights to dividends for years in which none were declared.

- **Nonparticipating preferred stock** conveys to its owners the right to only the preference dividend amount specified on the stock certificate.

- **Participating preferred stock** conveys the right not only to the preference dividend amount but also to a share of other dividends paid.

DIVIDENDS ON COMMON STOCK

Common stock dividends are paid only after preferred dividend requirements have been met. The fewer the dividend privileges enjoyed by preferred stockholders, the higher the dividends that common stockholders can receive, especially in prosperous years.

The amount of dividends paid each year reflects such factors as the company's trend of profits and cash flows, tax laws, availability of cash, plans for future expansion, and so on. Typically, a company avoids decreases in dividend payouts because a decrease often leads to loss of investor confidence and reduced prices for the stock.

Many companies reduced dividend distributions in the years 2000–2003 because of lower profits and cash flows. Hasbro's cash dividends declared per share of common stock for the years 2000–2006 reflect this pattern.

Dividends Declared per Share on Common Stock
Years 2000 Through 2006

Year	Cash Dividends per Share (In Cents)
2000	21
2001	12
2002	12
2003	12
2004	24
2005	36
2006	48

COMPARISON OF DIVIDEND PROVISIONS

Let's analyze several dividend plans.

Only Common Stock Issued Suppose that a corporation has only one class of stock—common stock. Assume that 15,000 shares of $50 par-value common stock are authorized, issued, and outstanding.

- *Situation 1.* The board of directors declared a 5 percent dividend for the year. Total dividends are $37,500 (15,000 shares × $50 par × 0.05). (The dividend is usually announced as $2.50 per share.)
- *Situation 2.* The board of directors decides to *pass* the dividend (not declare or pay it).

There is no guarantee that the corporation will pay dividends. The uncertainty of dividends is a risk of owning common stock.

Common and Noncumulative Nonparticipating Preferred Stock Issued Preferred stock reduces the uncertainty of dividends. Assume that a corporation has issued preferred stock and common stock as follows.

Preferred stock, 10% noncumulative, nonparticipating, ($50 par value, 1,000 shares)	$ 50,000
Common stock ($20 par value, 10,000 shares)	200,000
Total capital stock	$250,000

- *Situation 1.* The board of directors declares dividends of $20,000. The preferred stockholders get first consideration. They receive the preference dividend of $5,000 (1,000 shares × $50 par × 0.10). There is $15,000 ($20,000 − $5,000) to distribute to the common stockholders. The dividend per share for common stock is $1.50 ($15,000 ÷ 10,000 shares).
- *Situation 2.* The board of directors declares dividends of $10,000. The preferred stockholders receive the preference dividend of $5,000. There is $5,000 ($10,000 − $5,000) to distribute to the common stockholders. The dividend per share of common stock is $0.50 ($5,000 ÷ 10,000 shares).
- *Situation 3.* The board of directors declares dividends of $4,000. The preferred stockholders receive all of it. The portion of the preference dividend not paid this year ($1,000) will never be paid since the stock is noncumulative. The common stockholders receive no dividends.

Common and Cumulative Nonparticipating Preferred Stock Issued When business conditions are poor, preferred stockholders have a better chance of receiving a dividend than do common stockholders. In turn, cumulative preferred stockholders have a better chance of receiving a dividend than do noncumulative preferred stockholders. The dividends not paid on cumulative preferred stock are carried forward as a continuing claim into future periods.

Cumulative preferred dividends not previously paid are shown on the balance sheet or in the footnotes to the financial statements.

When dividends are paid, they are paid in the following order.

1. To holders of cumulative preferred stock for prior year dividends not paid.
2. To preferred stockholders for the preference dividend for the current year.
3. To common stockholders.

Assume that a corporation has issued preferred and common stock as follows.

Preferred stock, 10% cumulative, nonparticipating, ($50 par value, 1,000 shares)	$ 50,000
Common stock ($20 par value, 10,000 shares)	200,000
Total capital stock	$250,000

■ *Situation 1.* Last year, $2,000 of preferred dividends were not paid. This year the board of directors declared dividends of $9,000. The dividends are distributed as follows.

1. To cumulative preferred stockholders for prior year dividends — $2,000
2. To preferred stockholders for this year's preference dividend (1,000 shares × $50 par value × 0.10) — $5,000
3. To common stockholders ($9,000 − $2,000 − $5,000) — $2,000

■ *Situation 2.* The board of directors declares dividends of $45,000. In previous years, all preferred dividends were paid. The cumulative preferred stockholders will receive the preference dividend of $5,000. There is $40,000 ($45,000 − $5,000) to distribute to common shareholders. The dividend per share of common stock is $4 ($40,000 ÷ 10,000 shares).

Common and Cumulative Participating Preferred Stock Issued When cumulative participating preferred stock is issued, dividend distributions are allocated to preferred and common stock as follows.

1. Preferred stockholders receive any prior year dividends not paid plus the preference dividend for the current year.
2. A specific rate of dividend is paid to common stockholders, equal to the same percentage rate paid to preferred.
3. The dividends that remain are shared between preferred and common stockholders. The participation terms determine how the dividends are shared. Typically, equal rates are paid on common stock and preferred stock.

Since almost all preferred stock is nonparticipating, this textbook provides examples of nonparticipating preferred stock only.

Table 20.2 on page 693 summarizes the dividend rights of the different classes of stock.

CAPITAL STOCK ON THE BALANCE SHEET

Owner's equity for a corporation is known as stockholders' equity. The Stockholders' Equity section of the balance sheet includes the following information for each class of stock: the number of shares authorized and issued, the par value, and any special privileges carried by the stock. The following illustrates a typical balance sheet presentation for a corporation.

Stockholders' Equity

Preferred Stock (10% noncumulative, $50 par value, 5,000 shares authorized)	$ 50,000
At Par Value (1,000 shares issued)	
Common Stock ($20 par value, 15,000 shares authorized)	
At Par Value (10,000 shares issued)	200,000
Total Stockholders' Equity	$250,000

Type of Stock	Dividend Rights
Noncumulative, nonparticipating preferred stock	• Has right to receive preference dividend each year before any dividend can be paid on common stock • If dividend is passed (not paid) in one year, the amount not paid is not cumulative and does not affect dividend payments in future years
Cumulative preferred stock	• Has right to receive preference dividend each year before any dividend can be paid on common stock • If dividend is passed in one year, the amount not paid carries over and must be paid in subsequent year before any dividend can be paid on common stock
Participating preferred stock	• Has right to receive preference dividend each year before any dividend can be paid on common stock • After preference dividend is paid, any additional dividend up to specified rate or amount is paid to common stockholders • After common shareholders have received the specified dividend, preferred and common stock share in remaining dividends
Common stock	• Receives dividends after preferred stock dividends are paid in accordance with contractual obligation

TABLE 20.2

Dividend Rights of Different Classes of Stock

Section 2 Self Review

QUESTIONS

1. In what ways, if any, may common stock be preferable to preferred stock?

2. How does "participating" preferred stock differ from "cumulative" preferred stock?

3. Why is preferred stock called "preferred"?

EXERCISES

4. If the preferred shareholders are entitled to receive the preference rate, and in addition to share in any further dividends declared in a year, the stock is known as

   a. cumulative.

   b. participating.

   c. nonparticipating.

   d. quasi-common.

5. Karen Company has outstanding 10,000 shares of 10 percent, $50 par-value, cumulative, nonparticipating preferred stock and 25,000 shares of $20 par-value common stock. No dividends were declared in 2010. In 2011, the directors voted to distribute dividends of $48,000.

   a. What amount of dividends, if any, will be distributed to holders of preferred stock?

   b. What amount, if any, will be distributed to holders of common stock?

ANALYSIS

6. Roseberry Company has outstanding 10,000 shares of 8 percent, $50 par-value, cumulative, participating preferred stock and 20,000 shares of $25 par-value common stock. There are no dividends in arrears on the preferred stock. In 2010, the corporation distributed dividends of $100,000. How much will be distributed to common stockholders and to preferred stockholders?

(Answers to Section 2 Self Review are on page 721.)

Section 3

TERMS TO LEARN

capital stock ledger
capital stock transfer journal
minute book
no-par-value stock
organization costs
registrar
stock certificate
stockholders' ledger
subscribers' ledger
subscription book
transfer agent

Video20.1

Recording Capital Stock Transactions

In this section, you will learn about the entries necessary to record the issuance of capital stock and the records needed to manage capital stock.

>>**6. OBJECTIVE**

Record the issuance of capital stock at par value.

LP20

Recording the Issuance of Stock

Stock is issued after the purchaser has paid for it in full with one of the following:

- cash
- noncash assets
- services rendered

STOCK ISSUED AT PAR VALUE

Assume that Jerome Tarvin and his associates determine that their new corporation, Camping Supply Center, Inc., will ultimately have capital requirements of $1,800,000. The incorporators decide to issue two classes of stock, preferred and common.

Preferred stock (10%, $100 par value, noncumulative and nonparticipating, 8,000 shares)	$ 800,000
Common stock ($25 par value, 40,000 shares)	1,000,000
Total capital stock	$1,800,000

Tarvin transferred the noncash assets and the liabilities of his existing business to the new corporation at the close of business on December 31, 2010. Tarvin also invested cash for shares of common stock in the new corporation. Tarvin's friends invested cash for common and preferred stock.

When the corporate charter was received, the accounting records were established. The following memorandum entry provides the details of the authorized capital stock.

1	2010					1
2	Dec.	31	Camping Supply Center, Inc., was formed to			2
3			sell camping equipment and supplies and to			3
4			carry on all necessary and related activities.			4
5			It is authorized to issue 40,000 shares of			5
6			$25 par-value common stock and 8,000			6
7			shares of $100 par-value, 10% preferred			7
8			stock that is noncumulative			8
9			and nonparticipating.			9

Data relating to each class of stock are entered on ledger sheets.

ACCOUNT Common Stock ($25 Par Value; 40,000 Shares Authorized) ACCOUNT NO. 301

		POST.			BALANCE	
DATE	DESCRIPTION	REF.	DEBIT	CREDIT	DEBIT	CREDIT

ACCOUNT Preferred Stock (10% Noncumulative, Nonparticipating; $100 Par Value; 8,000 Shares Authorized) ACCOUNT NO. 311

		POST.			BALANCE	
DATE	DESCRIPTION	REF.	DEBIT	CREDIT	DEBIT	CREDIT

Stock Issued at Par Value for Cash When stock is issued for cash equal to the par value of the shares, cash proceeds are credited to the capital stock account. Tarvin and his colleagues purchased the following number of shares at par value for cash.

	Common Stock Shares	Preferred Stock Shares
Jerome Tarvin	528	
Karen Wilcox	600	400
Wibb Kamp	400	400
Jill Carrell	200	
Ramon Hill	700	

The receipt of cash was recorded in the cash receipts journal. To simplify the illustration, the entry is shown for Karen Wilcox only in general journal form. Similar entries would be made for other cash purchases of stock.

1	2010					1
11	Dec.	31	Cash ($15,000 + $40,000)	55 00 00		11
12			Common Stock (600 x $25)		15 00 00	12
13			Preferred Stock (400 x $100)		40 00 00	13
14			Issuance of stock to Karen Wilcox:			14
15			600 shares of common at par ($25 per			15
16			share) and 400 shares of preferred at			16
17			par ($100 per share)			17

important!

Capital Stock Account
The amount credited to the capital stock account is the par value of the stock issued.

Stock Issued at Par Value for Noncash Assets The following are the assets and liabilities transferred by Tarvin to the corporation.

Assets

Accounts receivable	$ 22,500
Allowance for doubtful accounts	(1,500)
Merchandise inventory	40,000
Land	30,000
Building	72,000
Equipment and fixtures	8,000
Total assets	$171,000

Liabilities

Accounts payable	19,200
Net value of assets transferred	$151,800

Tarvin and the other shareholders agreed that Tarvin would be issued 800 shares of the $100 par value preferred stock, to be recorded at par value ($80,000). In addition, shares of the $25 par-value common stock are to be issued to Tarvin for the difference between the net value of the noncash assets received by the corporation and the par value of the 800 shares of preferred stock. Thus, 2,872 shares of common stock are also issued.

Net value of assets transferred	$151,800
Par value of preferred stock issued (800 shares × $100/share)	80,000
Par value of common stock to be issued	$ 71,800

Number of common shares to be issued:
     $71,800 ÷ $25 per share = 2,872 shares

The transaction is recorded as follows.

1	2010				1
18	Dec.	31	Accounts Receivable	22 500 00	18
19			Merchandise Inventory	40 000 00	19
20			Land	30 000 00	20
21			Building	72 000 00	21
22			Equipment and Fixtures	8 000 00	22
23			Allowance for Doubtful Accounts		1 500 00	23
24			Accounts Payable		19 200 00	24
25			Common Stock (2,872 x $25)		71 800 00	25
26			Preferred Stock (800 x $100)		80 000 00	26
27			Issuance of stock in payment for net			27
28			noncash assets of Camping Supply			28
29			Store, 2,872 shares of $25 par			29
30			common stock at $25 per share and			30
31			800 shares of $100 par preferred			31
32			stock at $100 per share			32

recall

Owner's Investment

Common and preferred stock are owners' (stockholders') equity accounts. Increases to owners' equity accounts are recorded as credits.

The assets and liability are recorded at fair market value. ***Accounts Receivable*** and ***Allowance for Doubtful Accounts*** are recorded separately. The $22,500 balance in the ***Accounts Receivable*** control account agrees with the total of the accounts receivable subsidiary ledger.

>>7. OBJECTIVE

Prepare a balance sheet for a corporation.

Preparing a Balance Sheet for a Corporation Figure 20.1 on page 697 shows the balance sheet for Camping Supply Center, Inc., immediately following the organization of the corporation. The balance sheet reflects the acquisition of the assets and liabilities of Tarvin's Camping Supply Store by the issuance of stock and the issuance of stock for cash.

Camping Supply Center, Inc.
Balance Sheet
December 31, 2010

Assets				
Current Assets				
Cash			140 7 0 0 00	
Accounts Receivable	22 5 0 0 00			
Less Allowance for Doubtful Accounts	1 5 0 0 00		21 0 0 0 00	
Merchandise Inventory			40 0 0 0 00	
Total Current Assets			201 7 0 0 00	
Property, Plant, and Equipment				
Land	30 0 0 0 00			
Building	72 0 0 0 00			
Equipment and Fixtures	8 0 0 0 00			
Total Property, Plant, and Equipment			110 0 0 0 00	
Total Assets			311 7 0 0 00	
Liabilities and Stockholders' Equity				
Current Liabilities				
Accounts Payable			19 2 0 0 00	
Stockholders' Equity				
Preferred Stock (10%, $100 par value,				
8,000 shares authorized)				
At Par Value (1,600 shares issued)	160 0 0 0 00			
Common Stock ($25 par value, 40,000				
shares authorized)				
At Par Value (5,300 shares issued)	132 5 0 0 00			
Total Stockholders' Equity			292 5 0 0 00	
Total Liabilities and Stockholders' Equity			311 7 0 0 00	

FIGURE 20.1

**Corporate Balance Sheet
Prepared After Organization**

Recording Organization Costs A variety of costs are incurred when a business is incorporated, including legal fees, attorneys' fees, charter fees paid to the state, and the cost of the organizational meeting of the directors.

Organization costs are incurred to provide benefit over the entire life of the corporation because they are necessary in order for the entity to exist and carry on business. For this reason, organization costs in the past have been capitalized and amortized over an arbitrary period. A common amortization period was five years. That practice resulted from federal income tax requirements that the costs be capitalized and subsequently amortized over a period of not less than 60 months. Some corporations, however, simply recorded the costs as an intangible asset and did not amortize the costs for financial accounting purposes.

In Chapter 18, the accounting requirements for intangible assets that do not have an identifiable economic or legal life were discussed. You will recall that intangibles such as purchased "goodwill," which has an indefinite life, must be examined each year to see whether there have been developments suggesting impairment. If such developments have occurred, further tests must be made to see if there is impairment and, if so, how much. Since organization costs have no fixed legal life, these costs would, if capitalized be an intangible that would have to be tested for impairment. But it is even more difficult to estimate the value of organization

>>8. OBJECTIVE

Record organization costs.

LP20

costs than to estimate the value of goodwill. Because of this fact, and the additional fact that the amount spent for organization costs is typically immaterial, the usual practice today is to charge organization costs to expense during the first financial reporting period after the corporation begins activities.

Some smaller companies whose shares are not publicly traded and who do not have audits by CPAs attesting that the corporation follows generally accepted accounting principles continue to capitalize organization costs and typically amortize the costs over the same period used for income tax purposes.

On January 18, Camping Supply Center, Inc., paid $2,000 of organization costs to its attorney. The amount includes legal fees, reimbursement for the charter fee, and the cost of drafting and printing the stock certificates. This reimbursement is recorded by a debit to *Organization Expense* and a credit to *Cash.*

>>**9. OBJECTIVE**

Record stock issued at a premium and stock with no par value.

LP20

STOCK ISSUED AT A PREMIUM

If the corporation has the potential for earning very attractive profits, investors are willing to pay more than par value to become stockholders. Likewise, if the preferred stock dividend is more attractive than other investments with similar risk, investors are willing to pay more than par value. The amount received by a corporation that is in excess of the par value is called a *premium.* A premium on preferred stock is credited to an account called *Paid-in Capital in Excess of Par Value—Preferred Stock.*

Suppose that Mai Nguyen, a new shareholder, agreed to pay $105 per share for 400 shares of preferred stock of Camping Supply Center, Inc. She paid a premium of $5 per share ($105 price−$100 par). The general journal entry for this transaction is below.

THE BOTTOM LINE

Purchase of Preferred Stock at a Premium

Income Statement

No effect on net income

Balance Sheet

Assets	↑ 42,000
Equity	↑ 42,000

---

important!

In Excess of Par

The amount credited to the *Paid-In Capital in Excess of Par Value* account is the price paid by the stockholder minus the par value of the stock multiplied by the number of shares issued.

>>

	2011					1
2	Mar.	2	Cash	42 00 00		2
3			Preferred Stock		40 00 00	3
4			Paid-in Capital in Excess of Par			4
5			Value—Preferred Stock		2 00 00	5
6			Issuance of 400 shares for $105			6
7			per share			7

In the Stockholders' Equity section of the balance sheet shown below, the amount of the new account, *Paid-in Capital in Excess of Par Value—Preferred Stock,* is added to the par value of the shares issued to show the total paid in by that class of stockholder. (The account title might also be *Premium on Preferred Stock* or a similar name.)

Stockholders' Equity

Preferred Stock (10%, $100 par value, 8,000 shares authorized)

At Par Value (2,000 shares issued)	$200,000
Paid-in Capital in Excess of Par Value	2,000
	$202,000

> At the end of its fiscal year ending January 31, 2006, Wal-Mart had authorized 100 million shares of preferred stock with 10 cents par value, of which none had been issued. The company's authorized common stock was 11 billion shares, with par value of $0.10. The company had issued 4.17 billion shares of common stock. As a result, its Common Stock account had a balance of $417 million. At the same time, the balance sheet reflected "Capital In Excess of Par Value" of $2.596 billion and Retained Earnings of $49.105 billion.

ISSUANCE OF NO-PAR-VALUE STOCK

No-par-value stock is not assigned a par value in the corporate charter. No-par-value stock has theoretical advantages over par-value stock.

- No-par-value stock can be issued at any price. Par-value stock cannot be issued for less than its par value.

- If there is no par value, investors cannot confuse par value and market value.

No-Par-Value Stock Without Stated Value   Some states require no-par-value stock to be assigned a stated value. Even if it is not required, the board of directors can assign a stated value. If no-par-value stock does not have a stated value, the proceeds from the issue of shares are credited to the **Common Stock** account. For example, suppose that Nature's Best Snacks Corporation is authorized to issue no-par-value common stock. A stated value has not been assigned the shares. On March 4, the corporation issued 1,000 shares for $20 per share, and on March 15, it issued 600 shares for $22 per share. The two stock issues are recorded as follows.

1	2010					1
2	Mar.	4	Cash	20 00 0 00		2
3			Common Stock		20 00 0 00	3
4			Issue of 1,000 shares of no-par-value			4
5			common stock at $20 per share			5
6						6
7		15	Cash	13 20 0 00		7
8			Common Stock		13 20 0 00	8
9			Issue of 600 shares of no-par-value			9
10			common stock at $22 per share			10

No-Par-Value Stock with Stated Value   Most no-par-value stock is assigned a stated value by the board of directors. The stated value is treated like par value. If no-par-value common stock with a stated value is issued at a price higher than the stated value, the stated value is credited to the **Common Stock** account. Any excess received over stated value is treated as a premium and credited to **Paid-in Capital in Excess of Stated Value.**

For example, Midland Music Corporation is authorized to issue no-par-value common stock. The board of directors assigned $25 as the stated value of the stock. On April 1, the corporation issued 2,400 shares at $26 per share. The stock issuance is recorded as shown.

1	2010					1
2	Apr.	1	Cash	62 40 0 00		2
3			Common Stock		60 00 0 00	3
4			Paid-in Capital in Excess of Stated			4
5			Value		2 40 0 00	5
6			Issue of 2,400 shares of common			6
7			stock at $26 per share			7

The credit to the **Paid-in Capital in Excess of Stated Value** account is $2,400 [($26 price − $25 stated value) × 2,400 shares]. On the balance sheet, the premium is shown as an addition to the stated value to show the total paid by common stockholders.

SUMMARY OF RECORDING RULES FOR PAR-VALUE AND NO-PAR-VALUE STOCK

Table 20.3 on page 700 summarizes the effects on the capital accounts of issuing stock with and without a par value.

MANAGERIAL IMPLICATIONS

CORPORATION CONSIDERATIONS

- New business owners should have a clear idea of the nature of a corporation, its rights and limitations, and how the corporation differs from other forms of business organization.
- Management and stockholders need to realize that the corporation is a separate legal entity apart from its owners and that regardless of changes in ownership, the corporation continues to exist.
- New business owners need to understand the disadvantages of the corporate form of business including double taxation and government regulation.
- In order to select the most beneficial capital structure, management needs to be familiar with the various classes of stock. Management is responsible for ensuring the following:
  - Assets acquired through the issue of stock are recorded at fair market value so that the corporation's profitability can be properly computed and evaluated.
  - Capital stock issues are properly recorded and tracked.
  - Stock subscriptions are in conformity with state laws and the accounting records fully reflect all information relating to stock subscriptions.
  - The corporation has adequate records to comply with legal requirements and to track stockholder transactions.
  - Officers act within the limitations set by the board of directors and the shareholders.
  - The bylaws and charter provisions of the corporation are carefully followed, and minutes are kept of all meetings of directors and stockholders.
- Management needs to be aware that state laws prohibit the issuance of stock at less than par value.
- Management must be aware that actions of the board of directors, as reported in the corporate minutes, often have accounting effects.

THINKING CRITICALLY

Why must the management and directors of a corporation be fully informed about laws and regulations affecting corporations? How can they find out what they need to know?

TABLE 20.3

Comparison of Rules for Par-Value and No-Par-Value Stock

Par-Value Stock	No-Par-Value Stock	
	Stated Value	**No Stated Value**
Par value is specified in corporate charter.	Stated value is assigned by directors. Corporate charter indicates that stock is no-par-value stock.	Corporate charter indicates that stock is no-par-value stock.
Stock certificate indicates par value.	Stock certificate generally does not show stated value.	Stock certificate shows that stock is no-par-value stock.
Change in par value requires revision of charter.	Stated value can be changed by directors.	
On issue of stock, par value is credited to capital stock account.	On issue of stock, stated value is credited to capital stock account.	On issue of stock, entire proceeds are credited to capital stock account.

Subscriptions for Capital Stock

Some prospective stockholders want to buy stock and pay for it later. They sign a subscription contract that states the stock price and describes the payment plan. They receive the stock when payment is made. A stock subscription is recorded as a receivable from the subscriber. The corporation must have stock available to issue when the subscription is paid in full.

RECEIPT OF SUBSCRIPTIONS

On May 1, Camping Supply Center, Inc., received a subscription from Tyrone Coles to purchase 400 shares of common stock at $25 per share. Coles is to pay for the stock in full on June 1. The corporation also received a subscription from Remu Patel to purchase 400 shares of preferred stock at $105 per share. Patel is to pay for the stock in two equal installments, on June 1 and July 1. These subscriptions are recorded as follows.

>>10. OBJECTIVE

Record transactions for stock subscriptions.

LP20

1	2010					1
2	May	1	Subscriptions Receivable—Common	10 000 00		2
3			Common Stock Subscribed		10 000 00	3
4			Subscription from Tyrone Coles to buy			4
5			400 shares of common stock at par			5
6			value of $25 per share			6
7						7
8		1	Subscriptions Receivable—Preferred	42 000 00		8
9			Preferred Stock Subscribed		40 000 00	9
10			Paid-in Capital in Excess of Par Value—			10
11			Preferred Stock		2 000 00	11
12			Subscription from Remu Patel to buy			12
13			400 shares of $100 par preferred stock			13
14			at $105 per share			14

A separate *Subscriptions Receivable* account is used for each class of stock. There are also separate *Stock Subscribed* accounts. When the subscriptions are paid in full, the stock is issued. Until then, the *Stock Subscribed* accounts appear in the Stockholders' Equity section of the balance sheet as additions to the class of stock issued.

For example, immediately after the receipt of Patel's stock subscription, the preferred stock in the Stockholders' Equity section of the balance sheet appears as follows.

Stockholders' Equity

Preferred Stock (10%, $100 par value, 8,000 shares authorized)

At Par Value (2,000 shares issued)	$200,000
Subscribed (400 shares)	40,000
Paid-in Capital in Excess of Par Value	4,000
	$244,000

COLLECTION OF SUBSCRIPTIONS AND ISSUANCE OF STOCK

When Coles pays his $10,000 subscription in full on June 1, the corporation issues 400 shares of common stock to him. The $10,000 is recorded in the cash receipts journal. To simplify the illustration, the transaction is shown in general journal form, followed by an entry to record the issuance of the stock.

1	2010					1
2	June	1	Cash	10 000 00		2
3			Subscriptions Receivable—Common		10 000 00	3
4			Received Tyrone Coles's subscription			4
5			in full			5
6						6
7		1	Common Stock Subscribed	10 000 00		7
8			Common Stock		10 000 00	8
9			Issued 400 shares of common stock to			9
10			Tyrone Coles			10

When these entries are posted, the **Subscriptions Receivable—Common** and **Common Stock Subscribed** accounts are closed. Both **Cash** and **Common Stock** are increased by $10,000.

Subscriptions Receivable—Common	
May 1 10,000	June 1 10,000

Cash	
June 1 10,000	

Common Stock Subscribed	
June 1 10,000	May 1 10,000

Common Stock	
	June 1 10,000

Patel paid his preferred stock subscription in two monthly installments of $21,000 each. The company debits each payment to **Cash** and credits **Subscriptions Receivable—Preferred.**

After Patel makes the second payment, the corporation issues the stock to him. The collection of the final installment and the issuance of the stock are recorded in the general journal as shown.

1	2010					1
2	July	1	Cash	21 000 00		2
3			Subscriptions Receivable—Preferred		21 000 00	3
4			Receipt of final installment from			4
5			Remu Patel on his stock subscription			5
6						6
7		1	Preferred Stock Subscribed	40 000 00		7
8			Preferred Stock		40 000 00	8
9			Issuance of 400 shares of preferred			9
10			stock to Remu Patel			10

This stock subscription transaction resulted in a $42,000 increase in **Cash,** a $40,000 increase in **Preferred Stock,** and a $2,000 increase in **Paid-in Capital in Excess of Par Value—Preferred Stock.**

Cash	
June 1 21,000	
July 1 21,000	

Subscriptions Receivable—Preferred	
May 1 42,000	June 1 21,000
	July 1 21,000

Preferred Stock Subscribed	
July 1 40,000	May 1 40,000

Preferred Stock	
	July 1 40,000

Paid-In Capital in Excess of Par Value—Preferred Stock	
	May 1 2,000

Special Corporation Records and Agents

Corporations keep detailed records of stockholders' equity. They maintain special corporate records such as

- minutes of meetings of stockholders and directors,
- corporate bylaws,
- stock certificate books,
- stock ledgers,
- stock transfer records.

MINUTE BOOK

A **minute book** keeps accurate and complete records of all meetings of stockholders and directors. The minute book formally reports actions taken, directives issued, directors elected, officers elected, and other matters.

STOCK CERTIFICATE BOOKS

Capital stock is usually issued by a corporation in the form of a **stock certificate.** A separate series of stock certificates is prepared for each class of stock. A corporation that expects to issue few stock certificates can have them prepared in books. Each certificate is numbered consecutively and attached to a stub from which it is separated at the time of issuance. The certificate indicates the

- name of the corporation,
- name of the stockholder to whom the certificate was issued,
- class of stock,
- number of shares.

Certificates are valid when they are properly signed by corporate officers and have the corporate seal affixed to them.

Figure 20.2 on the next page shows a common stock certificate for The McGraw-Hill Companies, Inc. Certificates for preferred stock are similar to those for common stock and include the details of the preferred stock.

Capital Stock Ledger It is essential for corporations to keep accurate records of the shares of stock issued and the names and addresses of the stockholders. This information is needed to mail dividend checks and official notices about stockholders' meetings and votes.

To keep the required information, corporations set up a **capital stock ledger,** or **stockholders' ledger,** for each class of stock issued. There is a sheet for each stockholder with the following information:

- stockholder's name and address,
- dates of transactions affecting stock holdings,
- certificate numbers,
- number of shares for each transaction.

The balance shows the number of shares held. The ledger sheets can also include a record of dividends. For each class of stock, the stockholders' ledger is a subsidiary to the capital stock

>>11. OBJECTIVE

Describe the capital stock records for a corporation.

LP20

FIGURE 20.2

Stock Certificate

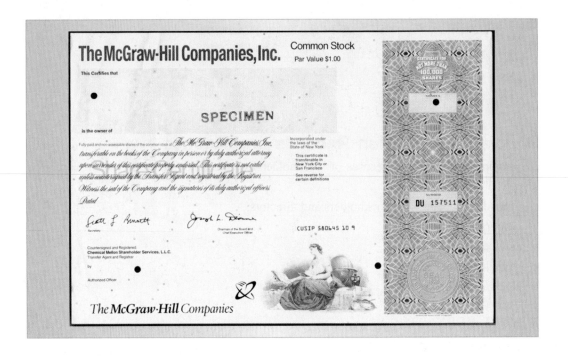

account. The total shares shown in the stockholders' ledger must agree with the number of shares in the capital stock account for that class.

After the corporation issues stock, new stockholders purchase shares from existing stockholders. The process is as follows:

- The buyer pays the seller.
- The seller surrenders the stock certificate to the corporation.
- The corporation issues a new certificate to the buyer.

The **capital stock transfer journal** is a record of stock transfers used for posting to the stockholders' ledger. There is a capital stock transfer journal for each class of stock issued by the corporation.

RECORDS OF STOCK SUBSCRIPTIONS

The corporation tracks stock subscriptions using the subscription book and the subscribers' ledger. The **subscription book**

- is a listing of the stock subscriptions received,
- shows the names and addresses of the subscribers,
- shows the number of shares subscribed,
- contains the amounts and times of payment.

A subscription book can contain the actual stock subscription contracts.

The **subscribers' ledger** contains an account receivable for each stock subscriber. The account is debited for the total subscription and credited when the subscriber makes payments. The subscribers' ledger is a subsidiary ledger. The balances of the individual subscriber accounts must agree with the *Subscriptions Receivable* control account in the general ledger.

SUMMARY OF STOCK CONTROL ACCOUNTS AND SUBSIDIARY LEDGERS

Table 20.4 on page 705 shows the relationship between control accounts and subsidiary ledgers for corporate stock recordkeeping.

Control Account	Subsidiary Ledger
Common Stock	Common Stockholders' Ledger
	Contains an account for each owner of common stock and shows shares bought or transferred and the balance of shares owned
Preferred Stock	Preferred Stockholders' Ledger
	Contains an account for each owner of preferred stock and shows shares bought or transferred and the balance of shares owned
Subscriptions Receivable— Common Stock	Subscribers' Ledger—Common
	Contains the account receivable for each subscriber to common stock
Subscriptions Receivable— Preferred Stock	Subscribers' Ledger—Preferred
	Contains an account receivable for each subscriber to preferred stock

TABLE 20.4

Subsidiary Stock Ledgers

recall

Subsidiary Ledgers
The total of the individual accounts must agree with the control account in the general ledger.

SPECIAL AGENTS

Corporations whose stock is widely held and actively traded do not keep their own stockholder records. Instead, they turn the responsibility over to a transfer agent and a registrar. The **transfer agent** receives the stock certificates surrendered. A bank that serves as a transfer agent is often chosen for its proximity to the stock exchange or market where the corporation's stock is expected to trade. The same bank may also be appointed registrar.

An assignment form on the certificate indicates to whom a new certificate should be issued. The agent

- cancels the old certificates,
- issues the new ones,
- makes the necessary entries in the capital stock ledger,
- prepares lists of stockholders who should receive dividend payments and notices.

The agent might also prepare and mail the dividend checks.

The **registrar** accounts for all the stock issued by the corporation and makes sure that the corporation does not issue more shares than are authorized. The registrar receives from the transfer agent all the canceled certificates and all the new certificates issued. The registrar must countersign the new certificates before they are valid.

Section 3 Self Review

QUESTIONS

1. What are organization costs? How are they accounted for?

2. What are the advantages of issuing no-par-value stock?

3. How do stated value and par value of stock differ?

EXERCISES

4. Which, if any, of the following statements are generally true? The stated value of no-par common stock is

   a. specified in the corporate charter.

   b. shown on the stock certificate.

   c. can be changed by the board of directors.

   d. credited to the **Common Stock** account when issued and any excess of issue price over stated value is credited to **Paid-in Capital in Excess of Stated Value.**

5. Mallard Company receives a subscription to 2,000 shares of its $25 par value common stock for $31 per share. What accounts are debited and credited, and for what amounts? If a balance sheet were prepared on the following day, how would the accounts debited and credited be shown on the balance sheet?

ANALYSIS

6. James McKee was one of the founders of PTM Corporation. Each of the founders, the only three shareholders, owns 10,000 shares of common stock. McKee has had disagreements with the other two owners, who have told McKee that the two of them plan to purchase another 5,000 shares each and to sell 15,000 to a new shareholder. McKee comes to you and asks you whether he should go to his lawyer with the idea of bringing a lawsuit to prevent what they plan to do. Ignoring the legal question of whether he will succeed in his lawsuit, what is the "shareholder right" that McKee is pursuing? Briefly explain that right.

(Answers to Section 3 Self Review are on page 722.)

REVIEW   Chapter Summary

Chapter **20**

In this chapter, you have learned about the basic characteristics of a corporation and the accounting procedures unique to its formation and operation. You have learned about capital stock transactions, dividend declarations, and reporting of stockholders' equity on the balance sheet.

Learning Objectives

1   Explain the characteristics of a corporation.

A corporation is organized under state law to carry on activities permitted by its charter.

- Ownership is indicated by shares of stock.
- Stockholders owning voting stock elect a board of directors.
- The board selects officers to run the business.
- The corporate charter specifies the types and amounts of capital stock authorized.
- The bylaws guide the firm's general operation, which must be consistent with charter provisions.
- The corporation is subject to federal income tax.

2   Describe special "hybrid" organizations that have some characteristics of partnerships and some characteristics of corporations.

A corporation formed as an S corporation is taxed as a partnership. The limited liability partnership and limited liability company avoid federal corporate income tax and also provide limited liability.

3   Describe the different types of stock.

If a corporation issues only one type of stock, it is called *common stock*. Common stockholders vote on corporate matters and receive dividends as declared by the board of directors.

Corporations can issue a second class of stock that carries special preferences, called *preferred stock*. Preferred stockholders are often given priority in the distribution of dividends. Liquidation value is often assigned to preferred stock; this stock class may be convertible to common stock.

4   Compute the number of shares of common stock to be issued on the conversion of convertible preferred stock.

Convertible preferred stock gives its owners the right to convert their shares into common stock after a specified date by using the stated conversion ratio.

5   Compute dividends payable on stock.

The board of directors declares dividends based on corporate earnings. Dividends are first allocated to preferred stockholders, then to common stockholders.

6   Record the issuance of capital stock at par value.

The entire amount of stock issued in return for a cash investment is credited to the appropriate capital stock account. Noncash assets traded for capital stock are recorded at their fair market value.

7   Prepare a balance sheet for a corporation.

The Stockholders' Equity section identifies the classes, values, and number of stock authorized and issued.

8   Record organization costs.

Organization costs are charged to expense when incurred. For income tax purposes, they are capitalized and amortized over a period of not less than 60 months.

9   Record stock issued at a premium and stock with no par value.

A premium on stock is recorded in a *Paid-in Capital in Excess of Par Value* account. Stock without a par value is called *no-par-value stock*. A few states require it to be assigned a stated value, similar to par value for accounting purposes.

10   Record transactions for stock subscriptions.

Stock can be subscribed, then paid for and issued later. It is recorded in a subsidiary ledger with a separate account receivable for each subscriber. Individual accounts receivable are controlled by a *Subscriptions Receivable* account in the general ledger.

11   Describe the capital stock records for a corporation.

Corporate records must include minute books, stockholders' ledgers, stock certificate books, and stock transfer records.

12   Define the accounting terms new to this chapter.

Review and Applications

Glossary

Authorized capital stock (p. 688) The number of shares authorized for issue by the corporate charter

Bylaw (p. 686) The guidelines for conducting a corporation's business affairs

Callable preferred stock (p. 690) Stock that gives the issuing corporation the right to repurchase the preferred shares from the stockholders at a specific price

Capital stock ledger (p. 703) A subsidiary ledger that contains a record of each stockholder's purchases, transfers, and current balance of shares owned; also called stockholders' ledger

Capital stock transfer journal (p. 704) A record of stock transfers used for posting to the stockholders' ledger

Common stock (p. 689) The general class of stock issued when no other class of stock is authorized; each share carries the same rights and privileges as every other share. Even if preferred stock is issued, common stock will also be issued

Convertible preferred stock (p. 689) Preferred stock that conveys the right to convert that stock to common stock after a specified date or during a period of time

Corporate charter (p. 684) A document issued by a state government that establishes a corporation

Cumulative preferred stock (p. 690) Stock that conveys to its owners the right to receive the preference dividend for the current year and any prior years in which the preference dividend was not paid before common stockholders receive any dividends

Dividends (p. 690) Distributions of the profits of a corporation to its shareholders

Limited liability company (LLC) (p. 685) Provides limited liability to the owners, who can elect to have the profits taxed at the LLC level or on their individual tax returns

Limited liability partnership (LLP) (p. 685) A partnership that provides limited liability for all partners

Liquidation value (p. 689) Value of assets to be applied to preferred stock, usually par value or an amount in excess of par value, if the corporation is liquidated

Market value (p. 688) The price per share at which stock is bought and sold

Minute book (p. 703) A book in which accurate and complete records of all meetings of stockholders and directors are kept

Noncumulative preferred stock (p. 690) Stock that conveys to its owners the stated preference dividend for the current year but no rights to dividends for years in which none were declared

Nonparticipating preferred stock (p. 690) Stock that conveys to its owners the right to only the preference dividend amount specified on the stock certificate

No-par-value stock (p. 699) Stock that is not assigned a par value in the corporate charter

Organization costs (p. 697) The costs associated with establishing a corporation

Par value (p. 688) An amount assigned by the corporate charter to each share of stock for accounting purposes

Participating preferred stock (p. 690) Stock that conveys the right not only to the preference dividend amount but also to a share of other dividends paid

Preemptive right (p. 689) A shareholder's right to purchase a proportionate amount of any new stock issued at a later date

Preference dividend (p. 690) A basic or stated dividend rate for preferred stock that must be paid before dividends can be paid on common stock

Preferred stock (p. 689) A class of stock that has special claims on the corporate profits or, in case of liquidation, on corporate assets

Registrar (p. 705) A person or institution in charge of the issuance and transfer of a corporation's stock

Shareholder (p. 684) A person who owns shares of stock in a corporation; also called a stockholder

Stated value (p. 688) The value that can be assigned to no-par-value stock by a board of directors for accounting purposes

Stock certificate (p. 703) The form by which capital stock is issued; the certificate indicates the name of the corporation, the name of the stockholder to whom the certificate was issued, the class of stock, and the number of shares

Stockholders' equity (p. 686) The corporate equivalent of owners' equity; also called shareholders' equity

Stockholders' ledger (p. 703) See Capital stock ledger

Subchapter S corporation (S corporation) (p. 685) An entity formed as a corporation that meets the requirements of Subchapter S of the Internal Revenue Code to be treated essentially as a partnership, so that the corporation pays no income tax

Subscribers' ledger (p. 704) A subsidiary ledger that contains an account receivable for each stock subscriber

Subscription book (p. 704) A list of the stock subscriptions received

Transfer agent (p. 705) A person or institution that handles all stock transfers and transfer records for a corporation

---

Comprehensive **Self Review**

1. What is the "preemptive right" of a shareholder?
2. What is the special benefit of a limited liability partnership?
3. What is callable preferred stock?
4. What is the special right conveyed to holders of convertible preferred stock?
5. What are the duties of the corporation's registrar?
6. What information is found in the subscribers' ledger?
7. What does market value of a stock mean?
8. How are the *Stock Subscribed* accounts reported in the financial statements?

(Answers to Comprehensive Self Review are on page 722.)

 Multiple choice questions are provided on the text Web site at www.mhhe.com/price12e

Quiz20

Discussion **Questions**

1. How does par value differ from stated value?
2. What are some benefits of a Subchapter S corporation?
3. If there is only one class of stock, what is it called?
4. What are the corporation's by-laws?
5. Where is the usual place for organizers of a new corporation to acquire a corporate charter?
6. What is the difference between the *Common Stock Subscribed* account and the *Subscriptions Receivable—Common Stock* account?
7. What is convertible preferred stock?
8. When common stock without a par value or a stated value is issued, what amount is credited to the capital stock account when the stock is issued?
9. What is cumulative preferred stock?
10. What is participating preferred stock?
11. What is the control account for the individual shareholder accounts in the common stockholders' ledger?
12. How are organization costs accounted for?
13. What role does the registrar of a corporation serve?

14. What are organization costs?

15. What is a stock subscription?

16. Describe the flow of authority and responsibility in a corporate entity.

17. Who makes the day-to-day decisions necessary for a corporation to operate?

18. What does the term "restricted agency" mean?

19. What is meant by the "par-value of stock"?

20. What is the role of the transfer agent?

21. What is the purpose of the minute book?

22. How are the members of a corporation's board of directors selected?

23. Selling stock on a subscription basis involves considerable record keeping. Why does a corporation sell its shares in this way?

24. Why would a new corporation issue no-par stock with a stated value, rather than par-value stock?

APPLICATIONS

Exercises

Exercise 20.1

Objective 5

▶ **Computing dividends payable.**

Blackwood Corporation has only one class of stock. There are 40,000 shares outstanding. During 2010, the corporation's net income after taxes was $320,000. The policy of the corporation is to declare dividends equal to 15 percent of its net income. Sam Bright owns 225 shares of the stock. How much will Bright receive as a dividend on his shares?

Exercise 20.2

Objective 5

▶ **Computing dividends payable.**

International Grocer Corporation has outstanding 20,000 shares of noncumulative, 10 percent, $100 par-value preferred stock and 62,500 shares of no-par-value common stock.

1. During 2010, the corporation paid dividends of $180,000. What amount will be paid on each share of preferred stock? What amount will be paid on each share of common stock?

2. During 2011, the corporation paid dividends of $462,500. How much will be paid on each share of preferred stock? How much will be paid on each share of common stock?

Exercise 20.3

Objective 5

▶ **Computing dividends payable.**

Zion Corporation has outstanding 50,000 shares of 15 percent, $80 par-value cumulative preferred stock and 200,000 shares of no-par-value common stock.

1. During 2010, the corporation paid dividends of $700,000. What amount will be paid on each share of preferred stock? What amount will be paid on each share of common stock?

2. During 2010, the corporation distributed dividends of $1,060,000. What amount will be paid on each share of preferred stock? What amount will be paid on each share of common stock?

Exercise 20.4

Objective 4

▶ **Converting preferred stock.**

Salado Corporation has outstanding 150,000 shares of $35 par-value preferred stock, issued at an average price of $42 a share. The preferred stock is convertible into common stock at the rate of two shares of common stock for each share of preferred stock. Melvin Jolly owns 440 shares of the preferred stock. During the current year, he decides to convert 110 shares into common stock. How many shares of common stock will he receive?

Exercise 20.5

Objective 6

▶ **Issuing stock for assets.**

Roy Kline, the owner of a sole proprietorship, is planning to incorporate his business. His capital account has a balance of $270,000 after revaluation of the assets. His cash account totals $33,000.

He will receive 10 percent, $20 par-value preferred stock with a total par value equal to the cash transferred. The balance of his capital is to be exchanged for shares of $40 par-value common stock with a total par value equal to the remaining capital. How many shares of preferred stock should be issued to Kline? How many shares of common stock should be issued to Kline?

Accounting for organization costs.

McDuff Company, a newly organized corporation, received a bill from its lawyers for $6,000 for time spent in organizing the company.

1. How should these costs be treated in the financial reports?
2. How should they be treated for federal income tax purposes?

◀ **Exercise 20.6**
Objective 8

Issuing stock at par value for cash.

On January 2, 2010, Cotton Corporation issued 24,000 shares of $15 par-value common stock and 3,600 shares of 7 percent, $90 par-value preferred stock for cash at par value. Prepare the entry in general journal form to record the issuance of the stock.

◀ **Exercise 20.7**
Objective 6

Issuing par-value stock at premium.

On January 2, 2010, Kettle Corporation issued 1,000 shares of its $10 par-value common stock for cash at $26 a share. Prepare the entry in general journal form to record the issuance of the stock.

◀ **Exercise 20.8**
Objective 9

Issuing no-par stock for cash.

On January 2, 2010, Mitchell Corporation issued 4800 shares of its no-par-value common stock (stated value, $40) for cash at $44 a share. Give the entry in general journal form to record the issuance of the stock.

◀ **Exercise 20.9**
Objective 9

Transactions for stock subscriptions.

On May 1, 2010, Antonelli Corporation received a subscription from Angelina Paz for 600 shares of its $1 par-value common stock at a price of $23 a share.

Paz made a payment of $11.50 per share on the stock at the time of the subscription. Give the entries in general journal form to record receipt of the subscription and the cash payment.

Prepare entries on June 1, 2010, to record payment of the balance of Paz' subscription and issuance of the stock.

◀ **Exercise 20.10**
Objective 10

PROBLEMS

Problem Set A ᴴᴹ™

Computing dividends payable.

Palmer Corporation issued and has outstanding 20,000 shares of $10 par-value common stock and 1,000 shares of $60 par-value 20 percent preferred stock. The board of directors votes to distribute $2,000 as dividends in 2010, $3,000 in 2011, and $53,000 in 2012.

◀ **Problem 20.1A**
Objective 5
e**X**cel

INSTRUCTIONS

Compute the total dividend and the dividend for each share paid to preferred stockholders and common stockholders each year under the following assumed situations.
Case A: The preferred stock is nonparticipating and noncumulative.
Case B: The preferred stock is cumulative and nonparticipating.

Analyze: If a stockholder purchased 250 shares of cumulative preferred stock in 2010, what total dividends should be paid to this stockholder in the fiscal year 2012, assuming Case B?

Computing dividends payable.

This problem consists of two parts.

◀ **Problem 20.2A**
Objective 5
e**X**cel

Part I

A portion of the Stockholders' Equity section of Haley Corporation's balance sheet as of December 31, 2010, appears below. Dividends have not been paid for the years 2008 and 2009. There has been no change in the number of shares of stock issued and outstanding during these years. Assume that the board of directors of Haley Corporation declares a dividend of $12,000 after completing operations for the year 2010.

Stockholders' Equity

Preferred Stock (9% cumulative, $50 par value, 2,000 shares authorized)	
At Par Value (1,500 shares issued)	$ 75,000
Common Stock (no-par value, with stated value of $25, 20,000 shares authorized)	
At Stated Value (14,000 shares issued)	350,000

INSTRUCTIONS

1. Compute the total amount of the dividend to be distributed to preferred stockholders.
2. Compute the amount of the dividend to be paid on each share of preferred stock.
3. Compute the total amount of the dividend available to be distributed to common stockholders.
4. Compute the amount of the dividend to be paid on each share of common stock.
5. Compute the amount of dividends in arrears (if any) that preferred stockholders may expect from future declarations of dividends.

Part II

Use the information given in Part I to solve this part of the problem. Assume that the board of directors of Haley Corporation has declared a dividend of $45,450 instead of $12,000 after operations for 2010 are completed.

INSTRUCTIONS

1. Compute the total amount of the dividend to be distributed to preferred stockholders.
2. Compute the amount of the dividend to be paid on each share of preferred stock.
3. Compute the total amount of the dividend available to be distributed to common stockholders.
4. Compute the amount of the dividend to be paid on each share of common stock.
5. Compute the amount of dividends in arrears (if any) that preferred stockholders may expect from future declarations of dividends.

Analyze: Assume only Part 1 has transpired. If, in 2009, the board of directors declared a dividend of $43,000, what amount would be paid to preferred stockholders?

Problem 20.3A ▶ **Issuing stock for cash and noncash assets at par.**

Objective 6

Jone Nelson and Helen Giddings are equal partners in N&G Appliance Center, which sells appliances and operates an appliance repair service. Nelson and Giddings have decided to incorporate the business. The new corporation will be known as N&G Appliance Center, Inc.

The corporation is authorized to issue 4,000 shares of $100 par-value, 10 percent preferred stock that is noncumulative and nonparticipating, and 100,000 shares of no-par-value common stock with a stated value of $20 per share. It is mutually agreed that the accounting records of N&G Appliance Center will be closed on December 31, 2010, and that certain assets will be revalued. N&G Appliance Center, Inc., will then take over all assets and assume all liabilities of the partnership. In payment for the business, the corporation will issue 500 shares of preferred stock to Nelson and 500 shares of preferred stock to Giddings, plus a sufficient number of shares of common stock to each partner to equal the balance of the partners' capital accounts. After the partners have recorded the revaluation of their assets immediately prior to the dissolution of their partnership and withdrawn the amounts of cash agreed on, the trial balance of N&G Appliance Center as of December 31, 2010, appears below.

INSTRUCTIONS

1. In the corporation's general journal, record a memorandum entry describing the corporation's formation on December 31, 2010.

2. Record general journal entries as of December 31 to show the takeover of the assets and liabilities of the partnership and the issuance of stock in payment to Nelson and Giddings. Use the same account titles that the partnership used for assets and liabilities. Also use two new accounts: *Common Stock* and *Preferred Stock.*

N & G Appliance
Trial Balance
December 31, 2010

ACCOUNT NAME	DEBIT	CREDIT
Cash	12 2 4 0 00	
Accounts Receivable	54 4 0 0 00	
Allowance for Doubtful Accounts		2 7 4 0 00
Merchandise Inventory	450 6 0 0 00	
Parts Inventory	39 2 0 0 00	
Land	80 0 0 0 00	
Building	551 2 8 0 00	
Accumulated Depreciation—Building		73 4 8 0 00
Furniture and Equipment	96 4 0 0 00	
Accumulated Depreciation—Furn. and Equip.		6 9 0 0 00
Accounts Payable		51 0 0 0 00
Jone Nelson, Capital		575 0 0 0 00
Helen Giddings, Capital		575 0 0 0 00
Totals	1,284 1 2 0 00	1,284 1 2 0 00

Analyze: What percentage of authorized common stock has been issued as of January 1, 2011?

Issuing stock at par and no-par value, recording organization costs, and preparing a balance sheet.

◀ **Problem 20.4A**
Objectives 6, 7, 8, 10

Denton Corporation, a new corporation, took over the assets and liabilities of Denton Art on January 2, 2010. The assets and liabilities, after appropriate revaluation by Denton are as follows.

Cash	$47,200
Accounts Receivable	354,800
Allowance for Doubtful Accounts	(9,600)
Merchandise Inventory	660,000
Accounts Payable	(372,000)
Accrued Expenses Payable	(19,200)

The corporation is authorized to issue 600,000 shares of $15 par-value common stock and 400,000 shares of $10 par-value preferred stock. The preferred stock bears a stated yearly dividend rate of $1 per share. The transactions that follow were entered into at the time the corporation was formed.

INSTRUCTIONS

1. Make general journal entries to record the transactions.

2. Prepare the opening balance sheet as of January 2, 2010, for Denton Corporation.

DATE	TRANSACTIONS
Jan. 2	The corporation issued 44,080 shares of common stock to John Denton for his equity in the sole proprietorship business, and the corporation took over Denton's assets and liabilities.
2	Issued 1,000 shares of preferred stock at par to Mildred Denton, John's wife, for cash.
2	Issued 4,000 shares of common stock to James Ready. He paid $60,000 in cash for the stock.
2	Issued 2,000 shares of preferred stock to Aaron Jones. He paid $20,000 in cash for the stock.

Analyze: What is the current ratio for the corporation at January 2, 2010?

Problem 20.5A ▶
Objectives 6, 7, 9, 11

Issuing stock at par and at premium, preparing Stockholders' Equity section of balance sheet, and recording stock subscriptions.

Jaguar Corporation was organized on March 1, 2010, to operate a delivery service. The firm is authorized to issue 75,000 shares of no-par-value common stock with a stated value of $100 per share and 30,000 shares of $100 par-value, 8 percent preferred stock that is nonparticipating and noncumulative. Selected transactions that took place during March 2010 follow.

INSTRUCTIONS

1. Set up the following general ledger accounts.

101 Cash
114 Subscriptions Receivable—Common Stock
115 Subscriptions Receivable—Preferred Stock
301 Common Stock
302 Common Stock Subscribed

305 Paid-in Capital in Excess of Stated Value—Common
311 Preferred Stock
312 Preferred Stock Subscribed
315 Paid-in Capital in Excess of Par Value—Preferred

Record in general journal form the transactions listed below, and post them to the general ledger accounts.

2. Prepare the Stockholders' Equity section of a balance sheet for Jaguar Corporation, as of March 31, 2010.

DATE	TRANSACTIONS
March 1	The corporation received its charter. (Make a memorandum entry.)
1	Issued 400 shares of common stock for cash at $100 per share to Terri Harris.
3	Issued 150 shares of preferred stock for cash at par value to Gloria Amos.
5	Issued 150 shares of common stock for cash at $106 to Carolyn Reed.
5	Received a subscription for 200 shares of common stock at $105 per share from Joan Patterson, payable in two installments due in 10 and 20 days.
14	Received a subscription for 50 shares of preferred stock at $108 per share from Robert Tolliver, payable in two installments due in 15 and 30 days.
20	Received payment of a stock subscription installment due from Joan Patterson (one-half of the purchase price—see March 5 transaction).
29	Received payment of a stock subscription installment due from Robert Tolliver (one-half the purchase price—see March 14 transaction).
30	Received the balance due on the stock subscription of March 5 from Joan Patterson; issued the stock.

Analyze: What percentage of total stockholders' equity is held by common stockholders?

Problem Set B

Computing dividends payable.

Morton Corporation issued and has outstanding 20,000 shares of $5 par-value common stock and 16,000 shares of $60 par-value, 5 percent preferred stock. The board of directors votes to distribute $32,000 as dividends in 2010, $48,000 in 2011, and $240,000 in 2012.

◀   Problem 20.1B
Objective 5

INSTRUCTIONS

Compute the total dividend and the dividend for each share to be paid to preferred stockholders and common stockholders each year under the following assumed situations.

Case A: The preferred stock is nonparticipating and noncumulative.
Case B: The preferred stock is cumulative and nonparticipating.

Analyze: If a stockholder owned 800 shares of preferred stock throughout 2010–2012, what total dividends did he receive for Case B?

Computing dividends payable.

This problem consists of two parts.

◀   Problem 20.2B
Objective 5

Part I

A portion of the Stockholders' Equity section of Clark Corporation's balance sheet as of December 31, 2010, appears below. Dividends have not been paid for the year 2009. There has been no change in the number of shares of stock issued and outstanding during 2009 or 2010. Assume that the board of directors of the corporation declared a dividend of $84,000 after completing operations for the year 2010.

Stockholders' Equity

Preferred Stock (8% cumulative, $100 par value, 20,000 shares authorized)	
At Par Value (12,000 shares issued)	$1,200,000
Common Stock ($25 par value, 70,000 shares authorized)	
At Par Value (60,000 shares issued)	1,500,000

INSTRUCTIONS

1. Compute the total amount of the dividend to be distributed to preferred stockholders.
2. Compute the amount of the dividend to be paid on each share of preferred stock.
3. Compute the total amount of the dividend available to be distributed to common stockholders.
4. Compute the amount of the dividend to be paid on each share of common stock.
5. Compute the amount of dividends in arrears (if any) that preferred stockholders can expect from future declarations of dividends.

Part II

Assume that after operations for 2010 were completed, the board of directors declares a dividend of $480,000 instead of $84,000. Use the information given in Part I to answer questions 1 through 5 above under these new assumptions.

Analyze: In regard to Part I, if dividends of $180,000 were declared in 2011, what per-share amount would be paid to preferred stockholders?

Issuing stock at par for cash and noncash assets.

Laura Cisneros and Kay Osborn are equal partners in Creative Toys Nook. Cisneros and Osborn have decided to form Toy Chest Corporation to take over the operation of Creative Toys Nook on December 31, 2010. The corporation is authorized to issue 8,000 shares of no-par-value common stock with a stated value of $25 per share and 2,000 shares of $50 par-value, 12 percent preferred stock that is noncumulative and nonparticipating. Certain assets are revalued so that the accounts will reflect current values. Cisneros and Osborn will each receive 250 shares of Toy Chest Corporation preferred stock at par value ($50) and sufficient no-par-value shares of common stock at stated value ($25) to cover the partners' adjusted net investment in the partnership.

◀   Problem 20.3B
Objective 6

The trial balance shown below was prepared after the firm's accounting records were closed at the end of its fiscal year on December 31, 2010, and the assets were revalued as agreed on.

INSTRUCTIONS

1. In the corporation's general journal, record a memorandum entry describing its formation on December 31, 2010.

Creative Toys Nook
Adjusted Trial Balance
December 31, 2010

ACCOUNT NAME	DEBIT	CREDIT
Cash	6 9 6 0 00	
Accounts Receivable	26 5 4 0 00	
Allowance for Doubtful Accounts		6 5 0 00
Merchandise Inventory	102 0 0 0 00	
Furniture and Equipment	45 8 0 0 00	
Accumulated Depreciation—Equipment		2 2 0 0 00
Accounts Payable		30 4 5 0 00
Laura Cisneros, Capital		74 0 0 0 00
Kay Osborn, Capital		74 0 0 0 00
Totals	181 3 0 0 00	181 3 0 0 00

2. Make general journal entries as of December 31 to show the takeover of the assets and liabilities of the partnership and the issuance of stock in payment to Laura Cisneros and Kay Osborn. Use the same account names that the partnership used for assets and liabilities. Also use the following new account titles: **Common Stock** and **Preferred Stock.**

Analyze: After the corporation's formation, what is the fundamental accounting equation for Toy Chest Corporation?

Problem 20.4B ▶
Objectives 6, 7, 8, 9

Issuing stock at par for cash and noncash assets, issuing stock at premium, recording organization costs, and preparing corporate balance sheet.

Dallas Travel Agency, a new corporation, took over the assets and liabilities of City Travel Agency, owned by Connie Wilson, on June 5, 2010. The assets and liabilities assumed, after appropriate revaluation by City Travel Agency, are as follows.

Cash	$ 29,200
Accounts Receivable	56,000
Allowance for Doubtful Accounts	(2,000)
Merchandise Inventory	$124,000
Accounts Payable	(10,000)
Accrued Expenses Payable	(11,200)

The corporation is authorized to issue 150,000 shares of no-par-value common stock with a stated value of $10 per share and 10,000 shares of $25 par-value preferred stock. The preferred stock bears a dividend of $2 per share per year. The transactions entered into at the time the corporation was formed follow.

INSTRUCTIONS

1. Prepare the general journal entries to record the transactions.
2. Prepare the opening balance sheet as of January 5, 2010, for Dallas Travel Agency.

DATE	TRANSACTIONS
June 5	The corporation issued to Connie Wilson common stock with a stated value equal to her net equity in the sole proprietorship business, and the corporation took over Wilson's assets and liabilities.
5	Issued 2,000 shares of common stock to Alan Merino for $20,000 cash.
5	Issued 600 shares of preferred stock to Rosa Vasquez. She paid $15,000 in cash for the stock.

Analyze: What is the amount of total stockholders' equity as of June 5, 2010?

Issuing stock at par, issuing stock at a premium, preparing Stockholders' Equity section of balance sheet, and recording stock subscriptions.

◀ **Problem 20.5B**
Objectives 6, 7, 9, 11

Pet Palace Corporation was organized on January 2, 2010, to operate a chain of pet supply stores. The firm is authorized to issue 50,000 shares of $10 par-value common stock and 18,000 shares of $50 par-value, 8 percent preferred stock. The preferred stock is noncumulative and nonparticipating. Selected transactions that took place during January 2010 are given below.

INSTRUCTIONS

1. Set up the following general ledger accounts.

101 Cash
114 Subscriptions Receivable—Common Stock
115 Subscriptions Receivable—Preferred Stock
301 Common Stock
302 Common Stock Subscribed

305 Paid-in Capital in Excess of Par Value—Common
311 Preferred Stock
312 Preferred Stock Subscribed
315 Paid-in Capital in Excess of Par Value—Preferred

Record the transactions listed below in general journal form and post them to the general ledger accounts.

2. Prepare the Stockholders' Equity section of a balance sheet for Pet Palace Corporation as of January 31, 2010.

DATE	TRANSACTIONS
Jan. 2	The corporation received its corporate charter. (Make a memorandum entry.)
3	Issued 3,000 shares of common stock for cash at $10 per share to Alice Young.
3	Issued 1,500 shares of preferred stock for cash at $50 per share to Marcia Greene.
10	Issued 200 shares of common stock for cash at $14 per share to Mark Merki.
12	Received a subscription for 500 shares of common stock at $12 per share from Nora Barnett, payable in two installments due in 5 and 15 days.
14	Received a subscription for 500 shares of preferred stock at $54 per share from Sun Wu, payable in two installments due in 10 and 20 days.
17	Received payment of a stock subscription installment due from Nora Barnett (one-half of purchase price—see January 12 transaction).
24	Received payment of a stock subscription installment due from Sun Wu (one-half of purchase price—see January 14 transaction).
27	Received the balance due from Nora Barnett; issued the stock.

Analyze: What percentage of authorized common stock has been issued at January 27, 2010?

Critical Thinking Problem 20.1

Understanding Stockholders' Equity

Just after its formation on September 1, 2010, the ledger accounts of the Videos Unlimited, Inc., contained the following balances.

Accrued Expenses Payable	$ 20,000
Accounts Payable	160,000
Accounts Receivable	88,000
Allowance for Doubtful Accounts	8,000
Building	400,000
Cash	84,800
Common Stock ($25 par)	505,400
Common Stock Subscribed	132,000
Furniture and Fixtures	100,000
Merchandise Inventory	267,800
Notes Payable—Short Term	100,000
Paid-in Capital in Excess of Par Value—Common	55,200
Paid-in Capital in Excess of Par Value—Preferred	12,000
Preferred Stock (10%, $40 par)	80,000
Preferred Stock Subscribed (10%, $40 par)	40,000
Subscriptions Receivable—Common Stock	132,000
Subscriptions Receivable—Preferred Stock	40,000

The corporation is authorized to issue 100,000 shares of $50 par-value common stock and 20,000 shares of 10 percent, $40 par-value preferred stock (noncumulative and nonparticipating).

INSTRUCTIONS

1. Answer the following questions:
   a. How many shares of common stock are outstanding?
   b. How many shares of common stock are subscribed?
   c. How many shares of preferred stock are outstanding?
   d. How many shares of preferred stock are subscribed?
   e. At what average price has common stock been subscribed or issued?
   f. Assume that no dividends are paid in the first year of the corporation's existence. What are the rights of the preferred stockholders?
   g. Assuming that all of the *Paid-in Capital in Excess of Par Value—Common* was applicable to the shares of common stock that have been subscribed but not yet issued, what was the subscription price per share of the common stock subscribed?
   h. Assuming that the board of directors declared no dividends in 2010, what amount would have to be paid the preferred stockholders in 2011 before any dividend could be paid to the common stockholders?

2. Prepare a classified balance sheet for the corporation just after its formation on September 1, 2010.

Analyze: What is the current ratio for the corporation at September 1, 2010?

Critical Thinking Problem 20.2

Interpreting the Balance Sheet

The Stockholders' Equity section of Foreign Tours Corporation's balance sheet at the close of the current year follows.

Stockholders' Equity

Preferred stock (8%, $75 par value, 30,000 shares authorized)	
At Par Value (40,000 shares issued)	3,000,000
Paid-in Capital in Excess of Par Value	160,000
Common Stock (no-par value, stated value of $5, 1,600,000 shares authorized)	
At Stated Value	4,500,000
Paid-in Capital in Excess of Stated Value	12,600,000
Retained Earnings	5,600,000
Total Stockholders' Equity	$25,860,000

1. What is the amount of the annual dividend on the preferred stock? Per share? In total?
2. How many shares of common stock have been issued?
3. What was the average price paid by the stockholders for the preferred stock?
4. What was the average price paid by the stockholders for the common stock?
5. How many shares of common stock are currently outstanding (held by stockholders)?
6. If total dividends of $1,275,000 were paid to stockholders in the current year, how much was paid to the common stockholders in total? Per share? Assume that no preferred dividends are in arrears.

BUSINESS CONNECTIONS

Forming a Corporation

Managerial FOCUS

1. Ankers and Baker are establishing a new restaurant and discussing whether to organize as a partnership or a corporation. What are some of the most important characteristics of these two types of organizations that they should weigh in making the decision?
2. Ankers and Baker are considering organizing as a Subchapter S corporation. What are the advantages and disadvantages they should consider?
3. Ankers and Baker decide to form a regular corporation for conducting their restaurant business. They are considering whether to issue preferred stock or to borrow funds on a long-term basis. Suggest some factors they should consider. How can they make the preferred stock more attractive to investors?
4. A group of individuals is planning to form a corporation. Explain in general terms the usual steps necessary to do this.
5. Why should the management of a corporation be concerned about the realistic valuation of assets transferred to the firm?

Stock Option

Ethical DILEMMA

Vice president Sally Lee consults the board of directors in regard to the issuance of stock and negotiates initial public offering price per share. As a bonus at the end of each fiscal year she receives stock options. Within weeks of negotiating the highest price possible, Sally sells her stock. Is this an ethical action for Sally?

Common Stock

Refer to the consolidated balance sheets for The Home Depot, Inc., in its *2006 Annual Report* in Appendix A.

1. How many shares of common stock have been authorized as of January 28, 2007? What percentage of authorized shares have been issued as of January 28, 2007?

2. Review the Stockholders' Equity section. What is the par value of the company's common stock? What total amount has been paid for common stock in excess of par value as of January 28, 2007?

Balance Sheet

The information below was compiled from the ConocoPhillips, Inc., balance sheet and footnotes in the *2006 Annual Report*. Use it to answer the following questions.

	December 31	
(in millions except share data)	*2006*	*2005*
Stockholders' Equity		
Preferred Stock, $.01 par value		
500,000,000 shares authorized, none issued	--	--
Class A Common Stock, $.01 par value		
2,500,000,000 shares authorized,		
1,705,502,609 shares issued	$41,943	$26,768

Analyze:

1. What percentage of common stock authorized has been issued at December 31, 2006?

2. What journal entry was made on the books of ConocoPhillips when the company authorized 500,000,000 shares of preferred stock?

3. If all the preferred stock that ConocoPhillips authorized was issued at par, how much capital would be raised?

Analyze Online: Log on to the ConocoPhillips Web site at www.conocophillips.com. Locate the most recent annual report.

4. How many shares of common stock have been issued?

5. Have any shares of preferred stock been issued? If so, how many?

6. What is the current market price for a share of ConocoPhillips stock?

Selective Disclosure

Stock prices hinge on a variety of market factors, including corporate earnings, new product announcements, and revenue projections. Until October 2000, it was common practice for corporations to disclose information selectively to analysts before an announcement was made to the general public. A new SEC ruling prohibits the "selective disclosure" of important information. How do you think this ruling will impact the way that or frequency with which a corporation communicates to the investment community? What types of investors stand to benefit from selective disclosure? How might the ruling affect the rate of increases or decreases in stock prices when, for example, poor earnings are reported by a corporation?

Visual Presentation

As the controller for E-Wise Internet Solutions, Inc., a publicly traded corporation, you have been asked to prepare a presentation for the annual stockholders' meeting to be held on January 31, 2011. Provide visual charts for your audience using the following data:

- Fiscal 2010 quarterly stock prices: at March 31: $53.00; at June 30: $54.67; at August 31: $66.33; at December 31: $52.00

- On August 20, 2010, the company announced plans to release a new plug-n-play e-commerce software bundle. An article appeared in *Fast Company* about the new release. Due to programming delays, the software release will not happen until the first quarter of 2011.

- Quarterly dividends were declared as follows.

2007		2008	
1st Q:	$0.06	1st Q:	$0.07
2nd Q:	$0.06	2nd Q:	$0.08
3rd Q:	$0.06	3rd Q:	$0.10
4th Q:	$0.06	4th Q:	$0.09

Corporation Details

TEAMWORK

Divide into teams of three or four students to decide on a new corporation. Determine a name and a product or service this corporation will provide. Develop a stock certificate for your corporation. How many shares will you ask to be authorized by the state? What will be the par value? Will these shares be preferred, common, or both? How much will you accept as a price per share for the initial public offering (IPO)?

Stock Characteristics

Internet CONNECTION

Go to the Web sites of three corporations. At the corporations' home pages, find the investor's relations (see *Customer Service* and corporate link). What is the par value of the shares of stock? How many shares are authorized, issued, and outstanding? In the last year, what changes have occurred in their stock prices? Is the stock market value at its peak or still rising? How many months is the market value listed for each share? Can you buy stock for the companies from these Web sites?

Answers to Self Reviews

Answers to Section 1 Self Review

1. The primary advantages of the corporate form is that owners generally have no legal liability for the debts of the corporation. Additional benefits are the ease of transferring ownership interests and the fact that the death of a shareholder does not terminate the business.

2. State governments issue a vast majority of corporate charters.

3. The major role of the stockholders is to choose the directors of the company. Stockholders have no inherent right to represent the corporation or take part in its management.

4. **c.** elect the directors of the corporation.

   d. are entitled to a proportionate share of dividends on their classes of stock.

5. **c.** can sell their shares of stock without permission from other stockholders.

6. They have escaped the legal liability associated with a partnership or sole proprietorship. In addition, they can sell the corporation or part of it without any legal problems of continuity of the business. In addition, it is much easier to find persons to purchase an ownership interest (stock) in a corporation than undivided interests in a partnership.

Answers to Section 2 Self Review

1. If things go well, and large dividends are paid, common shares usually benefit from the large distribution while preferred shares do not. Participating preferred stock may be issued which provides that preferred shares participate in the higher dividends.

2. Participating preferred stock shares with common stock a part of increased dividends in excess of the preferred stock's rate of return. The degree of participation depends on the terms of the stock issue.

3. Preferred stock is entitled to a dividend before a dividend is paid on common stock. It may also have certain preferences over distribution of assets in the case of liquidation. In addition, there is a reasonable assurance of a constant and predictable income from dividends.

4. **b.** participating.

5. **a.** Preferred shareholders will receive the entire $48,000 in 2010. There is a carryover of $52,000 that preferred must receive in addition to future preferred dividend requirements before any dividends can be paid to common stockholders.

   b. Common shareholders will receive nothing in 2010.

6. Allocation is $50,000 to preferred and $50,000 to common, computed in following order:

   Step 1: To preferred: All distributions up to amount of preference dividend, $40,000.

   Step 2: To common: All distributions up to rate paid preferred for preference, $40,000.

   Step 3: Balance allocated in proportion to par and/or stated value of shares outstanding:

   To preferred, ($500,000/$1,000,000) × $20,000 = $10,000
   To common, ($500,000/$1,000,000) × $20,000 = $10,000
   Total distributed to preferred stockholders = $40,000 + 10,000 = $50,000.
   Total distributed to common stockholders = $40,000 + 10,000 = $50,000.

Answers to Section 3 Self Review

1. Organization costs are costs in getting the corporation into existence. They include such things as fees charged by the state, legal fees related to the incorporation, and costs of printing stock certificates. Organizations costs are generally charged to expense in the year the corporation commences business.

2. No-par stock makes financing more flexible. State laws prevent or discourage stock from being issued for less than par value. Having no-par stock eliminates this problem.

3. Par value is established in the articles of incorporation. Stated value is set by the directors of the corporation.

4. Statements **c** and **d** are true.

5. *Subscriptions Receivable* is debited for $62,000; *Common Stock Subscribed* is credited for $50,000, and *Paid-in Capital in Excess of Par* (or *Premium on Common Stock*) is credited for $12,000. On the balance sheet, *Subscriptions Receivable* is shown as a current asset, and the other two accounts are shown in the stockholders' equity section.

6. McKee wishes to pursue his "preemptive right." This gives the stockholder the right to purchase a proportionate part of any new shares issued.

Answers to Comprehensive Self Review

1. The preemptive right of the shareholder is to be able to purchase a proportionate part of new shares issued by the corporation.

2. As the name suggests, it frees the partners from some of the liability of a partner. Primarily, it provides relief from liability for actions of other partners, but holds the partner liable for his or her own actions and those employees supervised by that partner.

3. Callable preferred stock is preferred stock that can be called and retired at the option of the corporation within specified terms, including price and time.

4. To convert the preferred shares into common shares under predetermined conditions and exchange rates.

5. The registrar accounts for all stock issued by the corporation, for transfers of shares, for cancellation of shares, and for handling certificates or other records of stock issued.

6. It is a control account for stock subscribed, containing an account receivable from each subscriber. The balance of this account agrees with *Subscriptions Receivable* on the balance sheet.

7. What stock is being sold at in the market. Sometimes market value is defined as what buyers are willing to pay for the shares.

8. As Stockholders' Equity.

Corporate Earnings and Capital Transactions

LEARNING OBJECTIVES

1. Estimate the federal corporate income tax LP21 and prepare related journal entries.
2. Complete a worksheet for a corporation.
3. Record corporate adjusting and closing entries.
4. Prepare an income statement for a corporation.
5. Record the declaration and payment of cash dividends.
6. Record the declaration and issuance of stock dividends.
7. Record stock splits.
8. Record appropriations of retained earnings.
9. Record a corporation's receipt of donated assets.
10. Record treasury stock transactions.
11. Prepare financial statements for a corporation.
12. Define the accounting terms new to this chapter.

NEW TERMS

appropriation of retained earnings
book value (stock)
Common Stock Dividend Distributable account
declaration date
deferred income taxes
donated capital
Extraordinary, Nonrecurring Items
paid-in capital
payment date
record date
retained earnings
statement of retained earnings
statement of stockholders' equity
stock dividend
stock split
stockholders of record
treasury stock

McDonald's www.mcdonalds.com

Nearly 52 million people around the world visit McDonald's every day. With 30,000 restaurants in 100 countries, McDonald's is the world's leading food service retailer. Hungry customers looking for a Big Mac and fries walk away with smiles—and so do McDonald's stockholders.

In 1965, McDonald's went public with the company's first offering on the stock exchange. If an investor purchased a hundred shares of stock in 1965, it would have cost $2,250 or $22.50 per share. Since that time, stockholders have seen 12 stock splits—the 100 shares purchased in 1965 have turned into 74,360 shares today. The $2,250 investment is worth $4.2 million today—not a bad return! Along with the increase in shares, dividends have given stockholders something to smile about, too. Dividends have increased substantially, from $.085 per share in 1991 to $1.50 in 2007.

thinking critically

What financial and nonfinancial factors would be important in deciding whether to purchase stock in a company that is going public?

SECTION OBJECTIVES

>> 1. **Estimate the federal corporate income tax and prepare related journal entries.**

   WHY IT'S IMPORTANT

   Corporations are required to pay federal, state, and local income taxes.

>> 2. **Complete a worksheet for a corporation.**

   WHY IT'S IMPORTANT

   The worksheet is a tool used to prepare financial statements.

>> 3. **Record corporate adjusting and closing entries.**

   WHY IT'S IMPORTANT

   Adjusting and closing entries ensure that revenues are matched with expenses and prepare temporary accounts for the next period.

>> 4. **Prepare an income statement for a corporation.**

   WHY IT'S IMPORTANT

   Corporations must report accurate financial results.

TERMS TO LEARN

deferred income taxes
Extraordinary, Nonrecurring Items

Accounting for Corporate Earnings

Chapter 21 will continue Chapter 20's focus on transactions that are unique to the corporate form. We will look at transactions that affect the statement of retained earnings and the Stockholders' Equity section of the balance sheet.

Corporate Income Tax

One of the disadvantages of the corporate form of business is that corporations must pay income taxes on their profits. Taxable income can be calculated differently for federal, state, and local purposes; however, the procedures to record these taxes are identical. For the sake of simplicity, we will cover federal taxes only and assume that taxable income and financial reporting income are identical. In reality, the two are often different because of special tax provisions.

>>**1. OBJECTIVE**

Estimate the federal corporate income tax and prepare related journal entries.

LP21

FEDERAL INCOME TAX RATES

Periodically, Congress changes corporate income tax rates. As of this writing, the federal rates are:

Taxable Income		Tax Rate
First	$50,000	15 percent
Next	$25,000	25 percent
Next	$25,000	34 percent
Next	$235,000	39 percent
Over	$335,000*	

*See Internal Revenue Service publications for taxable incomes of more than $335,000.

QUARTERLY TAX ESTIMATES

Corporations estimate their income taxes for the year and make estimated tax payments four times during the year. To avoid a penalty, the tax deposits at the end of the year must be equal to or higher than the tax liability for the year. For calendar year corporations, the estimated tax payments are due on April 15, June 15, September 15, and December 15. To record an estimated tax payment, debit *Income Tax Expense* and credit *Cash.*

Outdoor Outfitters, Inc., estimated its tax liability for 2010 to be $24,000. During the year, it made four tax deposits of $6,000 ($24,000 ÷ 4). The journal entry to record the first deposit (April 15) is as follows.

1	2010				1
2	Apr.	15 Income Tax Expense	6 0 0 0 00		2
3		Cash		6 0 0 0 00	3
4		Quarterly income tax deposit			4

At the end of the year, the *Income Tax Expense* account has a balance of $24,000.

YEAR-END ADJUSTMENT OF TAX LIABILITY

At the end of the year, the tentative tax expense for the year is computed. Usually there is a difference between the tentative tax expense and the tax deposits made during the year. An adjustment is recorded to reconcile the difference.

At the end of 2010, Outdoor Outfitters, Inc., computed its tentative tax expense as $26,150. The corporation had underpaid its taxes by $2,150.

Tax liability for the year	$26,150
Quarterly payments	24,000
Additional tax due	$ 2,150

The amount owed is recorded in the *Income Tax Payable* account.

1	2010	Adjusting Entries			1
10	Dec.	31 Income Tax Expense	2 1 5 0 00		10
11		Income Tax Payable		2 1 5 0 00	11
12		Estimate of additional tax due			12

Now suppose that Outdoor Outfitters, Inc., computed its tentative tax expense as $22,600. In this case, the corporation would have overpaid its taxes by $1,400.

Tax liability for the year	$22,600
Quarterly payments	24,000
Overpaid tax	$ (1,400)

The overpayment would be recorded in a receivable account as follows.

1	2010				1
10	Dec.	31 Income Tax Refund Receivable	1 4 0 0 00		10
11		Income Tax Expense		1 4 0 0 00	11
12		Estimate of tax overpayment			12

Note that the adjustment is made at the time the worksheet is completed and the financial statements are prepared. Because the tax return is complex and differences exist between *taxable*

recall

Subchapter S Corporations
Subchapter S corporations do not pay taxes on corporate profits. Instead, corporate income is taxed on the shareholders' individual tax returns.

income and *financial income,* this computation can also be described as an estimate. The tentative tax expense computed at the end of the year usually differs from the actual tax expense shown on the tax return. The difference is recorded in the ***Income Tax Expense*** account.

Suppose that Bruin Corporation made quarterly tax deposits totaling $62,000 in 2010. When the worksheet was prepared, tentative tax expense was computed at $63,200. The following adjustment was made.

1	2010		Adjusting Entries				1
2	Dec.	31	Income Tax Expense	1 20 0 00			2
3			Income Tax Payable		1 20 0 00		3
4			Estimate of additional tax due				4

When the tax return was prepared, the actual tax for the year was $62,800. Bruin Corporation sent a check for $800 to the Internal Revenue Service for the difference between the tax for the year and the tax deposits ($62,800 − $62,000). The entry is recorded as follows.

1	2011						1
2	Mar.	15	Income Tax Payable	1 20 0 00			2
3			Cash		80 0 00		3
4			Income Tax Expense		40 0 00		4
5			Pay balance of federal income tax				5

This entry reduces to zero the ***Income Tax Payable*** account. It records the check sent to the Internal Revenue Service and credits ***Income Tax Expense.*** Notice that the difference between the tentative tax expense and the actual tax expense, $400, is recorded in the year following the tax year. This violates the matching principle. It does not match income tax expense to taxable income. However, these differences are usually minor and do not result in a material misstatement of income.

REPORTING INCOME TAX EXPENSE ON THE INCOME STATEMENT

There are two ways to show income tax expense on the income statement:

1. As a deduction at the bottom of the income statement, after Net Income Before Income Tax. To see this presentation, refer to Figure 21.3 on page 732.

2. As an operating expense, to emphasize that taxes represent a cost of doing business.

> Alcoa Inc. treats income tax expense as a deduction from Income from Continuing Operations Before Income Taxes. For the year ended December 31, 2006, the company reported income tax expense, called "Provision for Income Taxes," of $835 million. The income tax was 24.3 percent of the $3,432 billion Income from Continuing Operations Before Income Taxes.

DEFERRED INCOME TAXES

Usually net income reported on the financial statements does not match taxable income reported on the tax return because tax laws do not always follow generally accepted accounting principles.

■ Income can be included in taxable income this year and appear on the financial statements in later years, or vice versa.

■ Income can be included on the financial statements but never appear in taxable income.

■ Expenses can be included in taxable income this year and appear on the financial statements in later years, or vice versa.

■ Expenses can be included on the financial statements and never be deducted from taxable income.

Accountants use the concept of deferred income taxes to match income tax on the financial statements to the related net income.

Deferred income taxes represent the amount of taxes that will be payable in the future as a result of the difference between taxable income and income for financial statement purposes in the current and past years. Let's use depreciation to illustrate the concept.

Suppose that this year tax depreciation (MACRS) is higher than depreciation on the financial statements (straight-line). In the future, then, tax depreciation should be less than depreciation on the financial statements. As a result, in the future, when taxable income is higher because depreciation is lower, the company will owe more taxes than would be paid on the net income reported for financial accounting purposes. Those future taxes really apply to the income reported on the financial statement in prior years.

Each year the accountant estimates the amount of future taxes that will be paid as a result of the MACRS depreciation taken in this and prior years. An adjustment for the future taxes is made to *Tax Expense* and to the liability account, *Deferred Income Tax Liability.*

Sometimes the cumulative taxable income is higher than that reported on the financial statements. This gives rise to a *deferred tax asset* because some of the taxes that have been paid apply to future financial statement income. Deferred taxes are complex and are not covered in this text. This book assumes that income on the income statement and on the tax return are the same. Therefore, the deferred tax adjustment is not necessary.

Completing the Corporate Worksheet

The worksheet for a corporation and a sole proprietorship are almost identical. The major difference is the income tax adjustment. Figure 21.1 on pages 728 and 729 shows the worksheet for Outdoor Outfitters, Inc., for 2010. This worksheet omits the Adjusted Trial Balance columns. It is common for the experienced accountant to enter the adjusted amounts directly in the Income Statement and Balance Sheet sections. However, when the Adjusted Trial Balance section is omitted, errors in adding and subtracting adjustments are more difficult to detect.

Study the worksheet carefully as you follow the steps to complete the worksheet for Outdoor Outfitters, Inc.

Step 1: *Enter the trial balance in the Trial Balance section.* To simplify the example, control accounts for general expenses and selling expenses are used instead of individual expense accounts. There are a few unfamiliar accounts on the worksheet; they will be explained later.

Step 2: *Enter the adjustments (except the adjustment to income tax expense) in the Adjustments section of the worksheet.*

Step 3: *Extend the balances of all income and expense amounts (except income tax expense) to the Income Statement section of the worksheet.* Total the Debit and Credit columns of the Income Statement section. Write the totals on a separate paper. The difference between the totals represents the income or loss before income taxes. At this point, the Income Statement columns of the worksheet contain the following information.

>>**2. OBJECTIVE**

Complete a worksheet for a corporation.

LP21

	Income Statement	
	Debit	Credit
Sales		1,250,000
Purchases	800,000	
Selling Expenses	200,000	
General and Administrative Expenses	190,000	
Income Summary	200,000	250,000
Totals	1,390,000	1,500,000

The difference between the Credit and Debit column totals is $110,000 ($1,500,000 − $1,390,000). This is income before income tax.

Outdoor Outfitters, Inc.

Worksheet

Year Ended December 31, 2010

	ACCOUNT NAME	TRIAL BALANCE DEBIT	TRIAL BALANCE CREDIT	ADJUSTMENTS DEBIT	ADJUSTMENTS CREDIT
1	Cash	55 3 5 0 00			
2	Accounts Receivable	70 0 0 0 00			
3	Allowance for Doubtful Accounts		2 1 0 0 00		(c) 9 0 0 00
4	Merchandise Inventory	200 0 0 0 00		(b)250 0 0 0 00	(a)200 0 0 0 00
5	Prepaid Insurance	5 0 0 0 00			(d) 2 5 0 0 00
6	Land	70 0 0 0 00			
7	Buildings	120 0 0 0 00			
8	Accumulated Depreciation—Buildings		4 0 0 0 00		(e) 4 0 0 0 00
9	Equipment and Fixtures	72 0 0 0 00			
10	Accumulated Depreciation—Equip. and Fixtures		6 0 0 0 00		(f) 6 0 0 0 00
11	Accounts Payable		39 0 0 0 00		
12	Dividends Payable—Preferred		20 0 0 0 00		
13	Dividends Payable—Common		4 0 0 0 00		
14	Accrued Expenses Payable				(g) 3 5 0 0 00
15	Income Tax Payable				(h) 2 1 5 0 00
16	Preferred Stock—10%, $100 Par		200 0 0 0 00		
17	Paid-in Cap. in Excess of Par—Preferred		12 0 0 0 00		
18	Common Stock, $50 Par		200 0 0 0 00		
19	Paid-in Cap. in Excess of Par—Common		1 6 0 0 00		
20	Retained Earnings		50 7 5 0 00		
21	Sales		1,250 0 0 0 00		
22	Purchases	800 0 0 0 00			
23	Selling Expenses (control)	195 6 0 0 00		(c) 9 0 0 00	
24				(d) 5 0 0 00	
25				(e) 1 0 0 0 00	
26				(f) 2 0 0 0 00	
27	General and Admin. Expenses (control)	177 5 0 0 00		(d) 2 0 0 0 00	
28				(e) 3 0 0 0 00	
29				(f) 4 0 0 0 00	
30				(g) 3 5 0 0 00	
31	Income Tax Expense	24 0 0 0 00		(h) 2 1 5 0 00	
32	Income Summary			(a)200 0 0 0 00	(b)250 0 0 0 00
33	Totals	1,789 4 5 0 00	1,789 4 5 0 00	469 0 5 0 00	469 0 5 0 00
34	Net Income After Income Tax				
35					
36					
37					
38					
39					
40					
41					
42					
43					
44					
45					

FIGURE 21.1 **A Completed, Eight-Column Worksheet**

| INCOME STATEMENT | | BALANCE SHEET | | |
DEBIT	CREDIT	DEBIT	CREDIT	
		55 3 5 0 00		1
		70 0 0 0 00		2
			3 0 0 0 00	3
		250 0 0 0 00		4
		2 5 0 0 00		5
		70 0 0 0 00		6
		120 0 0 0 00		7
			8 0 0 0 00	8
		72 0 0 0 00		9
			12 0 0 0 00	10
			39 0 0 0 00	11
			20 0 0 0 00	12
			4 0 0 0 00	13
			3 5 0 0 00	14
			2 1 5 0 00	15
			200 0 0 0 00	16
			12 0 0 0 00	17
			200 0 0 0 00	18
			1 6 0 0 00	19
			50 7 5 0 00	20
	1,250 0 0 0 00			21
800 0 0 0 00				22
200 0 0 0 00				23
				24
				25
				26
190 0 0 0 00				27
				28
				29
				30
26 1 5 0 00				31
200 0 0 0 00	250 0 0 0 00			32
1,416 1 5 0 00	1,500 0 0 0 00	639 8 5 0 00	556 0 0 0 00	33
83 8 5 0 00			83 8 5 0 00	34
1,500 0 0 0 00	1,500 0 0 0 00	639 8 5 0 00	639 8 5 0 00	35
				36
				37
				38
				39
				40
				41
				42
				43
				44
				45

Step 4: *Compute income tax based on income before tax.* Assume there is no difference between financial and taxable income.

First $50,000 × 15%	$ 7,500
Next $25,000 × 25%	6,250
Next $25,000 × 34%	8,500
Last $10,000 × 39% (rounded)	3,900
Total tax on $110,000	$26,150

Outdoor Outfitters, Inc., made tax deposits of $24,000. The difference between the tax deposits and the total tax is $2,150 ($26,150 − $24,000). An adjustment is made to debit **Income Tax Expense** for $2,150 and to credit **Income Tax Payable** for $2,150.

Step 5: *Total the columns in the Adjustments section.* Extend the balance of **Income Tax Expense** to the Debit column of the Income Statement section of the worksheet.

Step 6: *Total the Debit and Credit columns of the Income Statement section.* The difference between the totals is net income after tax.

Step 7: *Extend the adjusted balances of the asset, liability, and stockholders' equity accounts to the Balance Sheet columns.* Enter net income after income tax to the Credit column of the Balance Sheet section. Complete the worksheet in the usual manner.

>>3. OBJECTIVE

Record corporate adjusting and closing entries.

LP21

Adjusting and Closing Entries

The closing process for a corporation is similar to that of a sole proprietorship. First close revenue to **Income Summary.** Then close expenses to **Income Summary.** Finally close **Income Summary** (net income or net loss) to **Retained Earnings.** The **Retained Earnings** account accumulates the profits and losses of the business.

Figure 21.2 shows the adjusting and closing entries for Outdoor Outfitters, Inc. Compare the journal entries to the worksheet to see how the journal entries are prepared.

>>4. OBJECTIVE

Prepare an income statement for a corporation.

LP21

The Corporate Income Statement

After the worksheet is complete, the financial statements are prepared. The income statement of a sole proprietorship and a corporation are similar. The major difference is income taxes. The corporate income statement contains a deduction for income tax expense.

Figure 21.3 shows the income statement for Outdoor Outfitters, Inc., for 2010. It is prepared from the information on the worksheet in Figure 21.1. Note that income tax expense is deducted from the Net Income Before Income Tax line to arrive at net income after income tax.

VARIATIONS IN INCOME STATEMENT PRESENTATION

Corporations use a variety of formats for the income statement. Some common variations are summarized as follows.

- Some corporations include cost of goods sold with the operating expenses. They do not show gross profit on sales. This text uses the traditional income statement with a separate Gross Profit section.

- Some corporations show income tax expense as an operating expense rather than as a deduction from net income before income tax. This presentation can be used to emphasize that income taxes are a cost of doing business like any other expense.

- If a gain or loss results from a transaction that is highly unusual, is clearly unrelated to routine operations, and is not expected to occur again in the near future, the gain or loss is shown in a separate section called **Extraordinary, Nonrecurring Items.**

Extraordinary items include gains or losses from fires, floods, and other casualties.
Figure 21.4 shows an income statement containing extraordinary items. The tax effect of each extraordinary item is offset against each gain or loss to show the gain or loss "net of taxes."

GENERAL JOURNAL   PAGE _38_

	DATE		DESCRIPTION	POST. REF.	DEBIT	CREDIT	
1	2010						1
2			*Adjusting Entries*				2
3			*(Entry a)*				3
4	Dec.	31	Income Summary		200 000 00		4
5			Merchandise Inventory			200 000 00	5
6							6
7			*(Entry b)*				7
8		31	Merchandise Inventory		250 000 00		8
9			Income Summary			250 000 00	9
10							10
11			*(Entry c)*				11
12		31	Selling Expense (control)		9 00 00		12
13			Allowance for Doubtful Accounts			9 00 00	13
14							14
15			*(Entry d)*				15
16		31	Selling Expenses (control)		5 00 00		16
17			General and Admin. Expenses (control)		2 00 00		17
18			Prepaid Insurance			2 500 00	18
19							19
20			*(Entry e)*				20
21		31	Selling Expenses (control)		1 00 00		21
22			General and Admin. Expenses (control)		3 00 00		22
23			Accumulated Depreciation—Buildings			4 00 00	23
24							24
25			*(Entry f)*				25
26		31	Selling Expenses (control)		2 00 00		26
27			General and Admin. Expenses (control)		4 00 00		27
28			Accum. Depr.—Equip. and Fixtures			6 00 00	28
29							29
30			*(Entry g)*				30
31		31	General and Admin. Expenses (control)		3 500 00		31
32			Accrued Expenses Payable			3 500 00	32
33							33
34			*(Entry h)*				34
35		31	Income Tax Expense		2 150 00		35
36			Income Tax Payable			2 150 00	36
37							37

GENERAL JOURNAL   PAGE _39_

	DATE		DESCRIPTION	POST. REF.	DEBIT	CREDIT	
1	2010						1
2			*Closing Entries*				2
3	Dec.	31	Sales		1,250 000 00		3
4			Income Summary			1,250 000 00	4
5							5
6		31	Income Summary		1,216 150 00		6
7			Purchases			800 000 00	7
8			Selling Expenses (control)			200 000 00	8
9			Gen. and Admin. Expenses (control)			190 000 00	9
10			Income Tax Expense			26 150 00	10
11							11
12		31	Income Summary		83 850 00		12
13			Retained Earnings			83 850 00	13
14			Close Income Summary				14

FIGURE 21.2

Adjusting and Closing Entries

FIGURE 21.3

Corporate Income Statement

Outdoor Outfitters, Inc.
Income Statement
Year Ended December 31, 2010

Sales			1,250 000 00
Cost of Goods Sold			
Inventory, January 1, 2010	200 000 00		
Purchases	800 000 00		
Goods Available for Sale	1,000 000 00		
Less Inventory, December 31, 2010	250 000 00		
Costs of Goods Sold		750 000 00	
Gross Profit on Sales		500 000 00	
Expenses			
Selling Expenses	200 000 00		
General and Administrative Expenses	190 000 00	390 000 00	
Net Income Before Income Tax		110 000 00	
Income Tax Expense		26 150 00	
Net Income After Income Tax		83 850 00	

FIGURE 21.4

Income Statement Showing Extraordinary Items

Bexley Corporation
Partial Income Statement
Year Ended December 31, 2010

Income from Operations			
Before Income Taxes			499 500 00
Income Taxes Applicable to Operating Income			169 830 00
Net Income from Operations, After			
Income Taxes			329 670 00
Extraordinary Gains and Losses			
Add Gain on Condemnation of Land by City	28 200 00		
Less Federal Taxes on Gain	7 800 00	20 400 00	
Deduct Tornado Loss on Building	16 000 00		
Less Federal Tax Reduction	6 240 00	9 760 00	
Excess of Extraordinary Gains over Losses			10 640 00
Net Income for Year			340 310 00

Section 1 Self Review

QUESTIONS

1. Where does the corporate income tax appear in the income statement?

2. At what point in preparing the corporate end-of-year worksheet does the accountant enter the adjustment for income taxes?

3. What is meant by "retained earnings"?

EXERCISES

4. How do the adjusting entries for the beginning and ending inventories for a corporation differ, if at all, from those for a sole proprietorship?

5. Is the taxable income of a large corporation likely to be the same as its income for financial reporting purposes? Explain.

6. A corporation's taxable income for 2010 was $250,000. Using the corporate tax rates on page 724, compute the total federal income tax expense for the year.

ANALYSIS

7. On the worksheet, column totals in the Income Statement section are debit, $192,000, and credit, $242,000.

Assuming income and deductions for tax purposes are the same as those for financial accounting purposes and that the corporation had paid estimated taxes of $8,000, what is the adjusting entry for income taxes based on the income tax rates presented on page 724?

(Answers to Section 1 Self Review are on page 762.)

Section 2

SECTION OBJECTIVES

>> **5.** **Record the declaration and payment of cash dividends.**

WHY IT'S IMPORTANT

Corporate profits are distributed to stockholders through cash dividends.

>> **6.** **Record the declaration and issuance of stock dividends.**

WHY IT'S IMPORTANT

Corporations may declare and issue stock dividends to reward their shareholders.

>> **7.** **Record stock splits.**

WHY IT'S IMPORTANT

Corporations use stock splits to lower market share prices in an effort to attract new investors.

>> **8.** **Record appropriations of retained earnings.**

WHY IT'S IMPORTANT

One way to identify specific future transactions and related cash requirements is by appropriating retained earnings.

TERMS TO LEARN

appropriation of retained earnings
book value (stock)
Common Stock Dividend Distributable account
declaration date
paid-in capital
payment date
record date
retained earnings
stock dividend
stock split
stockholders of record

Accounting for Retained Earnings

The fundamental accounting equation for corporations can be restated as Assets = Liabilities + (Paid-in Capital + Retained Earnings).

Paid-in capital (or contributed capital) represents the amount of capital acquired from capital stock transactions.

Retained earnings represents the cumulative profits and losses of the corporation not distributed as dividends. Dividends reduce retained earnings.

Retained Earnings

There are legal and financial distinctions between paid-in capital and retained earnings. This is why profits and losses are accumulated in retained earnings, separate from the capital paid in by the stockholders.

It is important to remember that retained earnings does not represent a cash fund. Retained earnings are reinvested in inventory, plant and equipment, and various other types of assets. A corporation can have a large cash balance but no retained earnings. Conversely, it can have a large balance in the ***Retained Earnings*** account but no cash.

CASH DIVIDENDS

Stockholders receive a share of the profits of the corporation through cash dividends. Most corporations pay dividends quarterly. In some corporations, the board of directors establishes a policy of making regular cash dividends at the same or an increasing amount. A regular dividend policy tends to make a stock more attractive to investors and may help avoid sharp fluctuations in the stock's market price. Many corporations, however, retain their earnings to finance growth and do not pay cash dividends. This is especially true in the first several years of a corporation's existence.

Dividend Policy Before declaring a dividend, the board of directors considers two issues: legality and financial feasibility.

1. *Legality.* State laws differ, but in general the corporation must have retained earnings in order to declare dividends. These laws are intended to protect the corporation's creditors. The restriction prevents an *impairment of capital.* Capital is impaired when dividends are paid that reduce total stockholders' equity to less than the paid-in capital accounts, which may result from paying excessive dividends.

2. *Financial Feasibility.* The corporation must have the cash to pay the dividend. The board of directors does not declare dividends that lead to a cash shortage or other financial difficulties, even though there may be a large balance in Retained Earnings.

>>**5. OBJECTIVE**

Record the declaration and payment of cash dividends.

LP21

important!

Journal Entries for Dividends

A journal entry is recorded on the date of declaration and the date of payment. A journal entry is not made on the date of record.

Dates Relevant to Dividends Three dates are involved in declaring and paying dividends.

■ The **declaration date** is the date on which the board of directors declares the dividend. The dividend declaration is recorded in the corporation's minute book. Once a dividend is declared, the firm has a liability to the stockholders for the amount of the declared dividend.

■ The **record date** is the date used to determine who will receive the dividend. The capital stock ledger is used to prepare a list of the **stockholders of record,** that is, the stockholders who will receive the declared dividend. This does not require a journal entry.

■ The **payment date** is the date on which the dividend is paid.

Declaration of a Cash Dividend Outdoor Outfitters, Inc.'s board of directors met on November 28, 2010, and declared cash dividends of $5 per share on preferred stock and $4 per share on common stock. The dividends are payable on January 15 to stockholders of record on December 31. On the declaration date, the firm had outstanding 2,000 shares of preferred stock and 4,000 shares of common stock. The dividend declaration is recorded as shown below.

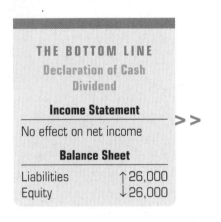

THE BOTTOM LINE

Declaration of Cash Dividend

Income Statement

No effect on net income

Balance Sheet

| Liabilities | ↑ 26,000 |
| Equity | ↓ 26,000 |

1	2010				1
2	Nov. 28	Retained Earnings	10 000 00		2
3		Dividends Payable—Preferred		10 000 00	3
4		Dividend declaration of $5			4
5		per share on 2,000 shares,			5
6		payable Jan. 15 to holders			6
7		of record Dec. 31			7
8					8
9	28	Retained Earnings	16 000 00		9
10		Dividends Payable—Common		16 000 00	10
11		Dividend declaration of $4			11
12		per share on 4,000 shares,			12
13		payable on Jan. 15 to			13
14		holders of record Dec. 31			14

Dividends payable appears on the balance sheet as a current liability. An example is shown in the balance sheet presented later in this chapter (Figure 21.6, page 743).

Payment of a Cash Dividend The capital stock ledger is used to prepare a list of the stockholders and the number of shares owned on the record date. The list is used to determine the dividend due each shareholder. On January 15, 2011, the payment date, the dividend checks are issued to the stockholders on the list. The payment is recorded as follows.

1	2011					1
2	Jan.	15	Dividends Payable—Preferred	10 00 00		2
3			Dividends Payable—Common	16 00 00		3
4			Cash		26 00 00	4
5			Payment of cash dividends			5

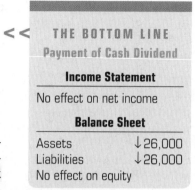
STOCK DIVIDENDS

A corporation may have retained earnings but be short of cash and unable to pay a cash dividend. Or the board of directors may want to transfer part of retained earnings to a paid-in capital account. In these cases, the board of directors may declare a stock dividend. A **stock dividend** is a distribution of the corporation's own stock on a pro rata basis that results in conversion of a portion of the firm's retained earnings to permanent capital.

On November 30, 2010, the board of directors of Outdoor Outfitters, Inc., declared a stock dividend payable the following January 20 to common stockholders of record on December 28. The stock dividend is for one new share of common stock for each 10 shares held. On the declaration date, there were 4,000 shares outstanding, so 400 (4,000 ÷ 10) additional shares will be issued.

When a stock dividend is declared, the total amount charged to the ***Retained Earnings*** account is the estimated market value of the shares to be issued. Assume that each share of Outdoor Outfitters, Inc.'s stock is expected to have a market value of $57. A total of $22,800 (400 shares × $57 market value) is debited to ***Retained Earnings***. The par value of the shares, $20,000 (400 shares × $50 par), is credited to **Common Stock Dividend Distributable,** an equity account used to record par or stated value of shares to be issued as the result of the declaration of a stock dividend. The excess of the market value over the par value, $2,800 ($22,800 − $20,000), is credited to ***Paid-in Capital in Excess of Par Value—Common Stock*** or to ***Paid-in Capital from Common Stock Dividends.*** Let's see how the declaration of a stock dividend is recorded.

>>**6. OBJECTIVE**

Record the declaration and issuance of stock dividends.

LP21

1	2010					1
2	Nov.	30	Retained Earnings	22 80 00		2
3			Common Stock Dividend Distributable		20 00 00	3
4			Paid-in Capital in Excess of Par			4
5			Value—Common Stock		2 80 00	5
6			Declaration of 10% stock dividend,			6
7			distributable on Jan. 20 to holders			7
8			of record on Dec. 28			8

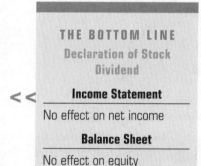
The ***Common Stock Dividend Distributable*** account appears on the balance sheet in the Stockholders' Equity section as a part of paid-in capital. One possible balance sheet presentation follows.

Common Stock ($50 par value, 10,000 shares authorized)	
Issued and outstanding, 4,000 shares	$200,000
Distributable as stock dividend, 400 shares	20,000
Paid-in Capital in Excess of Par	2,800
	$222,800

On December 28, a list is made of the stockholders' names, number of shares owned, and number of new shares to issue. For example, Sandra Key owns 400 shares of common stock. She will receive 40 (400 ÷ 10) new shares as a stock dividend. On January 20, the 400 shares are distributed. This issuance of stock is recorded as follows.

1	2011					1
2	Jan.	20	Common Stock Dividend Distributable	20 00 00		2
3			Common Stock		20 00 00	3
4			Distribution of stock dividend			4

Book value for each share of stock is the total equity applicable to the class of stock divided by the number of shares outstanding. The total book value is the same before and after a stock dividend, but each shareholder owns more shares of stock with a proportionately smaller book value per share.

Before the stock dividend, Key owned 400 shares, or 10 percent (400 ÷ 4,000 shares), of the stock of the corporation. After the stock dividend, Key still owned 10 percent (440 ÷ 4,400 shares) of the corporation's stock.

	Key	Total
Shares before	400	4,000
Stock dividend	40	400
Shares after	440	4,400

In theory, a stock dividend should result in a proportionate reduction in each share's market value. Sometimes the market price declines less than it should in theory because a lower price per share can result in a wider market for the shares and because investors associate stock dividends with successful corporations. Thus, after a stock dividend, the total market value of a stockholder's shares can increase slightly.

>>7. OBJECTIVE

Record stock splits.

LP21

STOCK SPLITS

A **stock split** occurs when a corporation issues two or more shares of new stock to replace each share outstanding without making any changes in the capital accounts. Stock splits are often declared when the stock is relatively difficult to sell because the market price is too high. If par-value stock is split, the corporation's charter is amended to reduce the par value.

Book Corporation is authorized to issue 500,000 shares of no-par-value stock, with a stated value of $75 per share. There are 40,000 shares issued and outstanding. On November 2, the market price of the stock is $300 per share. The board of directors believes that if the price of the stock were lower, the shares would have a wider market. Accordingly, the board declared a 3-for-1 split and reduced the stated value to $25 ($75 ÷ 3) per share. Two additional shares will be issued for each share outstanding. The shares will be issued on November 30 to holders of record on November 15. A stockholder who owned one share of stock with a stated value of $75 before the split will own three shares of stock with a stated value of $25 per share after the split. Stockholders realize no income from the stock split, and the corporation's capital balances are not affected.

Theoretically, the market price will decrease to one-third of the original market value, or to $100 per share ($300 × 1/3). If the price per share does not decrease to its theoretical level, the total market value of a stockholder's shares will be higher.

On the date of declaration of the stock split, a memorandum notation is made in the general journal of Book Corporation.

	2010						
1	2010						1
2	Nov.	2	On this date the board of directors declared a				2
3			3-for-1 stock split and reduced the stated value				3
4			of common stock from $75 to $25 per share.				4
5			Total outstanding shares will be 120,000				5

On November 30, a similar memorandum entry is made in the general journal to note issuance of the new shares.

An entry is made in the **Common Stock** account in the general ledger to indicate that the stated value is now $25 per share, and 120,000 shares are outstanding. The stockholders' records are changed to reflect the number of shares now held by each stockholder.

>>8. OBJECTIVE

Record appropriations of retained earnings.

APPROPRIATIONS OF RETAINED EARNINGS

Most corporations pay out only a portion of retained earnings as dividends. They restrict dividend payments in order to reinvest in plant assets or working capital. Sometimes dividends are restricted by contract, such as the requirements of a bond issue. A footnote to the financial statements can be used to indicate how management's plans or contractual obligations will affect (restrict) the dividends. A more formal way for the board of directors to show an intention to restrict dividends is to make an **appropriation of retained earnings** by resolution. Dividends cannot be declared from appropriated retained earnings.

Outdoor Outfitters, Inc.'s directors foresee the need to build a $200,000 retail center within the next five years. They want to notify the stockholders that the new retail facility will be built and that dividends will be restricted. A resolution is passed at a board meeting on October 5, 2011, to transfer $40,000 from *Retained Earnings* to a *Retained Earnings Appropriated for Retail Center Construction* account. The resolution is recorded in the minutes and the general journal entry is recorded. Similar appropriations and entries are made in each of the next four years.

The balance sheet presentation shows appropriated and unappropriated retained earnings. Assume that *Retained Earnings* had a balance of $134,600 before the first appropriation. The following is the balance sheet presentation immediately after the appropriation. Notice that total retained earnings stays the same, but it now has two parts.

Retained Earnings
   Appropriated
      Appropriated for Retail Center Construction $ 40,000
   Unappropriated   94,600
  Total Retained Earnings $134,600

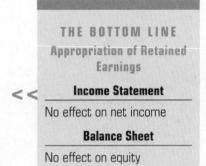

THE BOTTOM LINE
Appropriation of Retained Earnings

Income Statement
No effect on net income

Balance Sheet
No effect on equity

1	2011				1
2	Oct.	5 Retained Earnings	40 000 00		2
3		Retained Earnings Appropriated for			3
4		Retail Center Construction		40 000 00	4
5		Appropriation made by board of			5
6		directors on Oct. 5			6

Remember that retained earnings does not represent cash, nor does appropriating retained earnings provide cash. The appropriation simply restricts the amount of retained earnings available for dividends, thus making it more likely that cash will be available to build the retail center.

Assume that in six years cash was available and the retail center construction project was completed at a cost of $242,000, which is $42,000 more than appropriated. The accounting records reflect an increase to *Building* of $242,000 and a decrease to *Cash* of $242,000. The balance of the *Retained Earnings Appropriated for Retail Center Construction* account has not been affected. When the purpose for which retained earnings was appropriated has been attained, the board can direct that the balance be transferred back to *Retained Earnings,* as follows.

1	2017				1
2	Aug.	7 Retained Earnings Appropriated for			2
3		Retail Center Construction	200 000 00		3
4		Retained Earnings		200 000 00	4

Section 2 Self Review

QUESTIONS

1. How does a "stock split" differ from a "stock dividend," if at all, if the stock has no par value?

2. Explain each of the three dates related to a stock dividend declaration and issue.

3. Does an appropriation of retained earnings include a transfer of cash to a restricted account? Explain.

EXERCISES

4. Which of the following will decrease total stockholders' equity?
   a. stock dividend
   b. stock split
   c. cash dividend
   d. appropriation of retained earnings

5. The balance of an appropriated retained earnings account is reduced
   a. as expenses are accrued.
   b. as payments are made.
   c. when the board of directors passes a resolution to return the amount to unappropriated retained earnings.
   d. when the board declares the appropriation's purpose is completed.

ANALYSIS

6. On April 20, the board of directors of Pohl Corporation declared a 15 percent stock dividend payable on June 1 to stockholders of record on May 15. The market value is expected to be $33 per share. On the declaration date, there are 4,000 shares outstanding. The par value of the shares is $30. What amount is credited to the *Paid-in Capital in Excess of Par Value—Common Stock* account?

(Answers to Section 2 Self Review are on page 762.)

SECTION OBJECTIVES

>> **9. Record a corporation's receipt of donated assets.**

WHY IT'S IMPORTANT

Corporations may receive donated property as an incentive to locate in a community.

>> **10. Record treasury stock transactions.**

WHY IT'S IMPORTANT

The impact of treasury stock purchases must be made clear to statement users.

>> **11. Prepare financial statements for a corporation.**

WHY IT'S IMPORTANT

Shareholders, analysts, and management use financial statements issued by corporations.

TERMS TO LEARN

donated capital

statement of retained earnings

statement of stockholders' equity

treasury stock

Other Capital Transactions and Financial Statements

Many other transactions affect the stockholders' equity. Two types of transactions that occur often are donations of capital and purchase of treasury stock.

Other Capital Transactions

Transactions that affect stockholders' equity include the donation of assets to a corporation and a corporation's purchase of its own stock.

DONATIONS OF CAPITAL

Property can be given to a corporation. This often occurs when a community that wishes to attract new industry gives a corporation land or a building for a plant site. **Donated capital** is capital resulting from the receipt of gifts by a corporation. An asset received as a gift is recorded in the accounting records at the asset's fair market value. The credit is to *Donated Capital,* a paid-in capital account. This account may also be labeled Paid-in Capital from Donations. The following general journal entry indicates how a gift of a plant site valued at $150,000 is recorded.

>> **9. OBJECTIVE**

Record a corporation's receipt of donated assets.

LP21

1	2010				1
2	Jan.	2	Land	150 000 00	2
3			Donated Capital	150 000 00	3
4			Appraised value of plant site donated		4
5			by city		5

On the balance sheet, the *Donated Capital* account is shown as a new category under paid-in capital, following the preferred and common stock accounts.

TREASURY STOCK

Treasury stock is a corporation's own capital stock that has been issued and reacquired. To be considered treasury stock, the stock must have been previously paid for in full and issued to a stockholder. Any class or type of stock can be reacquired as treasury stock. No dividends, voting rights, or liquidation preferences apply to treasury stock.

Stockholders may benefit when the corporation repurchases common stock because there are fewer shares of outstanding stock to share the profits and dividends. If preferred stock is reacquired, the dividends on the stock are no longer payable, thus increasing the dividends available to owners of common stock.

Corporations purchase their own stock for many reasons:

- The corporation has extra cash, and the board of directors thinks that the corporation's own stock is a better investment than other potential investments.
- The corporation wishes to transfer treasury stock to officers and key employees in connection with incentive plans. If unissued shares instead of treasury stock were used, it would be necessary to ask stockholders to give up their preemptive rights. However, preemptive rights do not apply to treasury stock.
- The corporation wants to create a demand for the stock and thus increase its market value.
- In privately held corporations with few owners, the board of directors can vote to purchase the shares of a stockholder who needs cash or wishes to retire.

> In its December 31, 2006, balance sheet, Eastman Kodak Company reported that 391.3 million shares of its common stock had been issued and that 104.0 million of these had been reacquired, leaving 287.3 million shares outstanding (numbers rounded). In other words, the company had reacquired and was holding in the treasury 26.6 percent of the shares previously issued.

Recording the Purchase of Treasury Stock When treasury stock is purchased, the *Treasury Stock* account is debited for the entire amount paid. There is a separate treasury stock account for each class of stock. For example, assume that in 2012, Outdoor Outfitters, Inc., repurchased 400 shares of $50 par preferred stock for $53 per share. The transaction is recorded as follows.

1	2012					1
7	Jan.	10	Treasury Stock—Preferred	21 2 0 0 00		7
8			Cash		21 2 0 0 00	8
9			Purchased 400 shares of treasury stock			9

Appropriation of Retained Earnings for Treasury Stock The purchase of treasury stock reflects a payment to a shareholder and thus reduces capital. Stockholder withdrawals could be disguised as treasury stock purchases. In order to protect creditors, some states require that retained earnings be appropriated in an amount equal to the cost of treasury stock. If a corporation does not have retained earnings with a value higher than the purchase price, it cannot purchase treasury stock. If Outdoor Outfitters, Inc., is required to appropriate retained earnings equal to the cost of treasury stock, the following entry would be made.

1	2012					1
11	Jan.	10	Retained Earnings	21 2 0 0 00		11
12			Retained Earnings Appropriated—			12
13			Treasury Stock		21 2 0 0 00	13
14			To appropriate retained earnings equal			14
15			to purchase price of preferred treasury			15
16			stock			16

On the balance sheet, treasury stock is deducted from the sum of all items in the Stockholders' Equity section. To see how treasury stock and retained earnings appropriated for treasury stock appear on the balance sheet, refer to Figure 21.6 on page 743.

MANAGERIAL IMPLICATIONS   `<<`

CAPITAL TRANSACTIONS

- In order to make prudent decisions, managers need to understand how net income is calculated.

- Managers need to develop a dividend policy that gives appropriate consideration to legal restrictions and to financial feasibility.

- Stock dividends offer management an opportunity to make distributions to shareholders while limiting the distribution of cash.

- Stock dividends provide a means for transforming a part of retained earnings into paid-in capital.

- Both stock dividends and stock splits reduce the price per share of the company's stock, which may make the stock more marketable.

- Prudent managers inform stockholders about restrictions on dividends by appropriating retained earnings.

- Treasury stock purchases can enhance the value of the stock held by other shareholders.

- Treasury stock can be used to offer stock incentives to officers and key employees and to obtain stock for employee stock-purchase plans.

THINKING CRITICALLY

What factors should be considered before a company declares a cash dividend?

Financial Statements for a Corporation

Four financial statements are usually prepared for a corporation:

- income statement,
- statement of retained earnings,
- balance sheet,
- statement of cash flows.

Figure 21.3 on page 732 shows the income statement for 2010 of Outdoor Outfitters, Inc. Let's move ahead a couple of years to 2012 and examine the statement of retained earnings and the balance sheet. These statements will reflect some of the transactions that you have studied in this chapter. The statement of cash flows is explained in Chapter 24.

THE STATEMENT OF RETAINED EARNINGS

The **statement of retained earnings** shows all changes that have occurred in retained earnings during the period. The statement shows the beginning balance, the changes, and the ending balance for the unappropriated and appropriated *Retained Earnings* accounts. Because of the importance of retained earnings to the corporation and the stockholders, a statement of retained earnings should be presented as part of the financial statements.

Figure 21.5 shows the statement of retained earnings of Outdoor Outfitters, Inc. The unappropriated retained earnings are

- increased by net income,
- decreased by dividends and appropriations.

Outdoor Outfitters, Inc., has two appropriation accounts—one for retail center construction and another for treasury stock.

Some corporations combine the statement of retained earnings with the income statement. In the combined statement of income and retained earnings, the beginning balance of *Retained Earnings* is added to the net income after taxes for the period. All other amounts are shown in the same way they are shown on the separate statement of retained earnings.

>>**11. OBJECTIVE**

Prepare financial statements for a corporation.

LP21

Outdoor Outfitters, Inc.
Statement of Retained Earnings
Year Ended December 31, 2012

Unappropriated Retained Earnings			
Balance, January 1, 2012	200 1 4 2 00		
Add: Net Income After Taxes for 2012	169 0 0 0 00	369 1 4 2 00	
Deductions			
Dividends on Preferred Stock	20 0 0 0 00		
Dividends on Common Stock	18 0 0 0 00		
Transfer to Appropriation for Retail Center Construction	60 0 0 0 00		
Transfer to Appropriation for Treasury Stock	21 2 0 0 00	119 2 0 0 00	
Total Unappropriated Retained Earnings, December 31, 2012			249 9 4 2 00
Appropriated Retained Earnings			
Appropriated for Retail Center Construction			
Balance, January 1, 2012	40 0 0 0 00		
Add Appropriation for the Year	40 0 0 0 00		
Balance, December 31, 2012		80 0 0 0 00	
Appropriated for Treasury Stock			
Balance, January 1, 2012	— 0 —		
Add Appropriation for the Year	21 2 0 0 00		
Balance, December 31, 2012		21 2 0 0 00	
Total Appropriated Retained Earnings, December 31, 2012			101 2 0 0 00
Total Retained Earnings, December 31, 2012			351 1 4 2 00

FIGURE 21.5   **Statement of Retained Earnings**

The Securities and Exchange Commission requires publicly held corporations to disclose the reasons for major changes in equity. Corporations find that the most convenient way to make the required disclosures is to prepare a **statement of stockholders' equity** (often referred to as an *analysis of changes in stockholders' equity*). It provides an analysis reconciling the beginning and ending balance of each of the stockholders' equity accounts. There is, however, no specified form for the statement, and various types of schedules are used.

THE CORPORATE BALANCE SHEET

Figure 21.6 shows the balance sheet of Outdoor Outfitters, Inc. Since the statement of retained earnings shows changes in each account, only the ending balances of each appropriated retained earnings account and of the unappropriated retained earnings account are shown on the balance sheet. Note that

- income tax payable and dividends payable appear in the Current Liabilities section,
- treasury stock is subtracted from the Stockholders' Equity section.

Outdoor Outfitters, Inc.
Balance Sheet
December 31, 2012

Assets					
Current Assets					
Cash				190 0 8 4 00	
Accounts Receivable	245 0 0 0 00				
Allowance for Doubtful Accounts	8 6 0 0 00			236 4 0 0 00	
Merchandise Inventory				169 4 5 8 00	
Prepaid Insurance				12 0 0 0 00	
Total Current Assets					607 9 4 2 00
Property, Plant, and Equipment					
Land				70 0 0 0 00	
Buildings	120 0 0 0 00				
Accumulated Depreciation—Buildings	12 0 0 0 00			108 0 0 0 00	
Equipment and Fixtures	72 0 0 0 00				
Less Accumulated Depreciation—Equipment and Fixtures	18 0 0 0 00			54 0 0 0 00	
Total Property, Plant, and Equipment					232 0 0 0 00
Total Assets					839 9 4 2 00
Liabilities and Stockholders' Equity					
Current Liabilities					
Accounts Payable				68 0 0 0 00	
Accrued Expenses Payable				3 2 0 0 00	
Income Tax Payable				2 4 0 0 00	
Total Current Liabilities					73 6 0 0 00
Stockholders' Equity					
Paid-in Capital					
Preferred Stock (10%, $100 par value, 10,000 shares authorized)					
Issued 2,000 shares (of which 400 shares are held as treasury stock)	200 0 0 0 00				
Paid-in Capital in Excess of Par Value—Preferred Stock	12 0 0 0 00			212 0 0 0 00	
Common Stock ($50 par value, 20,000 shares authorized)					
Issued and Outstanding, 4,400 shares	220 0 0 0 00				
Paid-in Capital in Excess of Par Value—Common Stock	4 4 0 0 00			224 4 0 0 00	
Total Paid-in Capital				436 4 0 0 00	
Retained Earnings					
Appropriated					
For Treasury Stock Purchase	21 2 0 0 00				
For Retail Center Construction	80 0 0 0 00				
Total Appropriated				101 2 0 0 00	
Unappropriated				249 9 4 2 00	
Total Retained Earnings				351 1 4 2 00	
Less Treasury Stock, Preferred (400 shares at cost)				21 2 0 0 00	
Total Stockholders' Equity					766 3 4 2 00
Total Liabilities and Stockholders' Equity					839 9 4 2 00

FIGURE 21.6   **An End-of-Year Balance Sheet**

Section 3 Self Review

QUESTIONS

1. How does donated capital arise?

2. Should treasury stock be shown as an asset of the corporation? Explain.

3. Why would a corporation purchase its own stock as treasury stock?

EXERCISES

4. Treasury stock is shown on the balance sheet as:

     a. a deduction from the sum of all other items in the Stockholders' Equity section.

     b. an asset.

     c. an addition to common stock in the Stockholders' Equity section.

     d. an addition to the total of all other Stockholders' Equity accounts.

5. Which of the following would not be found on the statement of retained earnings?

     a. Dividends on preferred stock.

     b. Appropriation for treasury stock.

     c. Appropriation for construction of an office building.

     d. the cash payment made when the corporation completes construction of a building for which an appropriation of retained earnings had been made.

ANALYSIS

6. The balance of the **Retained Earnings** on December 1 is $295,000. During December, dividends of $13,000 on common stock and $10,000 on preferred stock were declared. Neither dividend was paid in December. An **Appropriation for Building Expansion** account with a balance of $100,000 was closed and the balance transferred back to **Retained Earnings.** Net income after taxes is $90,000. What is the balance of unappropriated retained earnings on December 31?

(Answers to Section 3 Self Review are on page 762.)

REVIEW   Chapter Summary

A corporation has two major classifications of corporate capital: paid-in capital from capital stock transactions and retained earnings from its profits and losses. In this chapter, you learned also to account for corporate income taxes and to record capital transactions affecting stockholders' equity: dividends, stock splits, appropriation of retained earnings, and treasury stock.

Learning Objectives

1   **Estimate the federal corporate income tax and prepare related journal entries.**

Debit *Income Tax Expense,* and credit *Cash.* Amounts owed or overpaid are recorded as adjustments.

2   **Complete a worksheet for a corporation.**

Enter the trial balance in the Trial Balance section and the adjustments, except income tax expense, in the Adjustments section. Extend balances of all income and expense amounts except income tax expense to the Income Statement section; total its Debit and Credit columns. The difference is the income or loss before income taxes; compute income tax based on it. After entering the income tax adjustment, total the columns in the Adjustments section. Extend Income Tax Expense to the Debit column of the Income Statement section. Total the Debit and Credit columns of the Income Statement section; the difference is net income after tax. Extend the adjusted balances of the asset, liability, and stockholders' equity accounts to the Balance Sheet columns. Enter net income after income tax to the Credit column of the Balance Sheet section. Complete the worksheet in the usual manner.

3   **Record corporate adjusting and closing entries.**

Close revenues and expenses to the *Income Summary* account; close *Income Summary* to *Retained Earnings.*

4   **Prepare an income statement for a corporation.**

The corporation income statement is similar to that of a sole proprietorship, except for the inclusion of an income tax expense deduction. Extraordinary or Nonrecurring Items are shown in a separate section.

5   **Record the declaration and payment of cash dividends.**

Recording cash dividends involves the following: on the declaration date, debit *Retained Earnings* and credit *Dividends Payable.* No journal entry is made on the record date. On the payment date, record the outgoing cash and the reduction of the *Dividends Payable* liability established on the declaration date.

6   **Record the declaration and issuance of stock dividends.**

Issuance of stock dividends above par value price involves a debit to *Retained Earnings,* a credit to *Common Stock Dividend Distributable,* and a credit to *Paid-in Capital in Excess of Par Value.* Upon distribution, *Common Stock Dividend Distributable* is debited, and *Common Stock* is credited.

7   **Record stock splits.**

A memorandum entry records it on the date of declaration, and another is made on the date of issuance.

8   **Record appropriations of retained earnings.**

Debit *Retained Earnings;* credit the *Appropriated Retained Earnings* account for the appropriation amount.

9   **Record a corporation's receipt of donated assets.**

Property given to a corporation is recorded at fair market value and is credited to *Donated Capital.*

10   **Record treasury stock transactions.**

Treasury stock purchase is recorded as a debit to *Treasury Stock* and a credit to *Cash.*

11   **Prepare financial statements for a corporation.**

The major corporation financial statements discussed in this chapter are the income statement, statement of retained earnings, and balance sheet.

12   **Define the accounting terms new to this chapter.**

Glossary

Appropriation of retained earnings (p. 737) A formal declaration of an intention to restrict dividends

Book value (p. 736) The total equity applicable to a class of stock divided by the number of shares outstanding

Common Stock Dividend Distributable account (p. 735) Equity account used to record par, or stated, value of shares to be issued as the result of the declaration of a stock dividend

Declaration date (p. 734) The date on which the board of directors declares a dividend

Deferred income taxes (p. 727) The amount of taxes that will be payable in the future as a result of the difference between taxable income and income for financial statement purposes in the current year and in past years

Donated capital (p. 739) Capital resulting from the receipt of gifts by a corporation

Extraordinary, Nonrecurring Items (p. 730) Transactions that are highly unusual, clearly unrelated to routine operations, and that do not frequently occur

Paid-in capital (p. 733) Capital acquired from capital stock transactions (also known as contributed capital)

Payment date (p. 734) The date that dividends are paid

Record date (p. 734) The date on which the specific stockholders to receive a dividend are determined

Retained earnings (p. 733) The cumulative profits and losses of the corporation not distributed as dividends

Statement of retained earnings (p. 741) A financial statement that shows all changes that have occurred in retained earnings during the period

Statement of stockholders' equity (p. 742) A financial statement that provides an analysis reconciling the beginning and ending balance of each of the stockholders' equity accounts

Stock dividend (p. 735) Distribution of the corporation's own stock on a pro rata basis that results in conversion of a portion of the firm's retained earnings to permanent capital

Stock split (p. 736) When a corporation issues two or more shares of new stock to replace each share outstanding without making any changes in the capital accounts

Stockholders of record (p. 734) Stockholders in whose name shares are held on date of record and who will receive a declared dividend

Treasury stock (p. 739) A corporation's own capital stock that has been issued and reacquired; the stock must have been previously paid in full and issued to a stockholder

Comprehensive Self Review

1. How is treasury stock shown on the balance sheet?
2. What is the purpose of the statement of retained earnings of a corporation?
3. Does an appropriation of retained earnings assure a cash balance? Explain.
4. What effect does a common stock dividend have on an individual shareholder's share of ownership in a corporation?
5. What is the difference between treasury stock and unissued stock?
6. What is meant by "donated capital"?

(Answers to Comprehensive Self Review are on page 763.)

 Multiple choice questions are provided on the text Web site at www.mhhe.com/price12e

Quiz21

Discussion Questions

1. What causes "deferred income taxes" to arise? How are balances in "deferred income taxes" accounts disposed of?

2. Explain the three dates related to declaration and payment of a cash dividend. On which of these dates must journal entries be made?

3. Compare the effects on stockholders' equity of a cash dividend and a stock dividend.

4. When a stock dividend is declared, what journal entry is made? How is the amount of the dividend determined or measured?

5. How is the *Common Stock Dividend Distributable* account classified in the financial statements?

6. What are "extraordinary gains and losses"?

7. Where are extraordinary gains and losses shown in the income statement?

8. How are income taxes related to "Extraordinary Gains and Losses" shown in the income statement?

9. What effect does a stock split have on retained earnings? Explain.

10. What effect does an appropriation have on total retained earnings?

11. Several years ago a corporation made an appropriation of retained earnings because of a building project. The building project was completed in the current year. What accounting entry will probably be made with respect to the appropriation?

12. As an inducement for Alto Company to locate in Smallville, the local chamber of commerce gave the corporation a tract of land with a fair market value of $250,000. How should the gift be accounted for by Alto?

13. At what amount is treasury stock shown on the balance sheet? How is it classified on the balance sheet?

14. What information is shown on the statement of retained earnings?

15. What is the purpose of the statement of stockholders' equity?

16. What is the major difference between the balance sheet of a partnership and that of a corporation?

17. How is income tax expense classified in the corporation's income statement?

APPLICATIONS

Exercises

Estimating corporation income tax.

After all revenue and expense accounts, other than *Income Tax Expense,* have been extended to the Income Statement section of the worksheet of Mobile Corporation, the net income is determined to be $275,000. Using the tax rates given in this chapter, compute the corporation's federal income taxes payable. (Assume that the firm's taxable income is the same as its income for financial accounting purposes.)

◀ **Exercise 21.1**
Objective 1

Recording journal entries related to taxes.

A corporation has paid estimated income taxes of $40,000 during the year 2010. At the end of the year, the corporation's tax bill is computed to be $41,500. Give the general journal entry to adjust the *Income Tax Expense* account.

◀ **Exercise 21.2**
Objective 1

Exercise 21.3
Objective 3

▶ **Recording closing of Income Summary**

In each of the following situations, what is the amount of profit or loss? In each situation, what account will be debited and credited, and for what amount, in the journal entry to close the *Income Summary* account?

a. The total of the debit column in the Income Statement section of the worksheet was $749,000 and the total of the credit column in that section was $709,000.

b. The total in the debit column of the Income Statement section was $695,000 and the total of the credit column was $731,000.

c. The total of the debit column in the Balance Sheet section was $390,000 and the total of the credit column in that section was $382,825.

Exercise 21.4
Objective 3

▶ **Recording closing of Income Summary.**

After the revenue and expense accounts were closed into *Income Summary* on December 31, 2010, the *Income Summary* account showed a net loss for the year of $49,000. Prepare the general journal entry to close the *Income Summary* account.

Exercise 21.5
Objective 5

▶ **Recording cash dividends.**

On September 15, 2010, the board of directors of Stars Corporation declared a cash dividend of $2 per share on its 150,000 outstanding shares of common stock. The dividend is payable on October 15 to stockholders of record on September 30. Give any general journal entries necessary on September 15, September 30, and October 15, 2010.

Exercise 21.6
Objective 6

▶ **Recording a stock dividend.**

Beta Corporation had outstanding 100,000 shares of $5 par-value common stock on August 13, 2010. On that date, it declared a 10 percent common stock dividend distributable on September 15 to stockholders of record on September 1. The estimated market value of the shares at the time of their issue was $25 per share. Give any general journal entries necessary on August 13, September 1, and September 15, 2010.

Exercise 21.7
Objective 7

▶ **Recording a stock split.**

Lagovista Corporation had outstanding 200,000 shares of no-par-value common stock, with a stated value of $15, on December 1, 2010. The directors voted to split the stock on a 3-for-1 basis, issuing two new shares to stockholders for each share presently owned. The estimated market value of the new shares will be $12. Give any general journal entry required on December 1.

Exercise 21.8
Objective 8

▶ **Recording appropriation of retained earnings.**

On December 31, 2010, the board of directors of Georgia Corporation voted to appropriate $100,000 of retained earnings each year for five years to establish a reserve for contingencies. Give the general journal entry on December 31, 2010, to record the appropriation.

Exercise 21.9
Objective 8

▶ **Closing appropriation of retained earnings.**

Because of fears about the outcome of several lawsuits in progress during the years 2007 through 2009, Titan Corporation had appropriated retained earnings of $178,000, and transferred that amount from the *Retained Earnings* account to *Retained Earnings Appropriated for Contingencies*. In October 2010, the lawsuits were settled, and Titan Corporation paid $150,000 to settle them. The board of directors breathed a sigh of relief and on November 1, 2010, passed a resolution that the appropriation was no longer needed. Prepare the necessary journal entry on November 1 to close the appropriation account.

Exercise 21.10
Objective 9

▶ **Recording receipt of property as gift.**

The city of Orlando contributed to Prairie Corporation a tract of land on which to build a plant. When the contribution was made on May 10, 2010, the land's fair market value was $250,000. Give the general journal entry, if any, necessary to record the receipt of the contribution.

Purchasing treasury stock.

On March 31, 2010, Carolina Corporation had outstanding 200,000 shares of 8 percent preferred stock with a par value of $10. The stock was originally issued for $12.50 per share. On that date, the corporation repurchased 10,000 shares of the preferred stock, paying cash of $12.30 per share for the stock. Give the general journal entry to record repurchase of the treasury stock.

◀ **Exercise 21.11**
Objective 10

Preparing Stockholders' Equity section of balance sheet.

The following are selected accounts from the general ledger of Fred's Web Company on December 31, 2010. Show how the corporation's Stockholders' Equity section would appear on the December 31, 2010, balance sheet.

◀ **Exercise 21.12**
Objective 11

Common Stock, $25 par, authorized 8,000 shares, issued and outstanding 6,000 shares	$150,000
Paid-in Capital in Excess of Par Value—Common	8,000
Retained Earnings (debit balance)	(24,000)

PROBLEMS

Problem Set A

Recording federal income tax transactions and cash dividend transactions.

Selected transactions of Ahmed Corporation during 2010 follow. Record them in the general journal.

Analyze: What annual per share dividend was paid to common stockholders in 2010?

◀ **Problem 21.1A**
Objectives 1, 5

DATE	TRANSACTIONS
Mar. 15	Filed the federal income tax return for 2009. The total tax for the year was $124,000. During 2009, quarterly deposits of estimated tax totaling $122,700 had been made. The additional tax of $1,300 was paid with the return. On December 31, 2009, the accountant had estimated the total tax for 2009 to be $123,600 and had recorded a liability of $900 for federal income tax payable.
Apr. 15	Paid first quarterly installment of $31,000 on 2010 estimated federal income tax.
May 3	Declared dividend of $0.50 per share on the 40,000 shares of common stock outstanding. The dividend is payable on June 2 to stockholders of record as of May 20, 2010.
June 2	Paid dividend declared on May 3.
15	Paid second quarterly installment of $31,000 on 2010 estimated federal income tax.
Sept. 15	Paid third quarterly installment of $31,000 on 2010 estimated federal income tax.
Nov. 2	Declared dividend of $0.50 per share on 40,000 shares of common stock outstanding. The dividend is payable on December 2 to holders of record on November 20.
Dec. 2	Paid dividend declared on November 2.
15	Paid fourth quarterly installment of $31,000 on 2010 estimated income tax.
31	Total income tax for 2010 was $128,940. Record as an adjustment the difference between this amount and the total quarterly deposits.

Problem 21.2A ▶
Objectives 2, 3, 4, 11
eXcel

Completing a corporate worksheet, recording adjusting and closing entries, preparing an income statement and balance sheet.

Bruin Corporation has been authorized to issue 5,000 shares of 12 percent noncumulative, nonparticipating preferred stock with a par value of $100 per share and 200,000 shares of common stock with a par value of $10 per share. As of December 31, 2010, 1,600 shares of preferred stock and 24,000 shares of common stock had been issued. A condensed trial balance as of December 31, 2010, is provided below.

INSTRUCTIONS

1. Enter the December 31, 2010, trial balance on an eight-column worksheet. Provide three lines for the *Selling Expenses* control account and three lines for the *General Expenses* control account. Total and rule the Trial Balance columns.

2. Record the following transactions in general journal form, using page number 6.

   a. Ending merchandise inventory is $105,000. Close the beginning inventory and set up the ending inventory.

   b. Depreciation of buildings is $12,500 ($10,000 is selling expense; $2,500 is general expense).

   c. Depreciation of equipment is $25,000 ($17,000 is selling expense; $8,000 is general expense).

   d. Accrued expenses are $8,000 ($6,000 is selling expense; $2,000 is general expense).

   e. The balance in *Allowance for Doubtful Accounts* is adequate.

   f. The $69,200 balance in *Income Tax Expense* represents the quarterly tax deposits. Adjust the *Income Tax Expense* account using the following procedure.

      (1) Extend the adjusted income and expense items to the Income Statement columns and compute the net income before taxes.

Bruin Corporation
Trial Balance (Condensed)
December 31, 2010

ACCOUNT NAME	DEBIT	CREDIT
Cash	46 5 7 0 00	
Accounts Receivable	149 8 0 0 00	
Allowance for Doubtful Accounts		2 0 0 0 00
Income Tax Refund Receivable		
Inventory	100 0 0 0 00	
Land	100 0 0 0 00	
Buildings	300 0 0 0 00	
Accumulated Depreciation—Buildings		37 5 0 0 00
Equipment	250 0 0 0 00	
Accumulated Depreciation—Equipment		25 0 0 0 00
Accounts Payable		105 2 2 0 00
Dividends Payable—Preferred		19 2 0 0 00
Dividends Payable—Common		21 6 0 0 00
Accrued Expenses Payable		
Income Tax Payable		
Preferred Stock, 12%		160 0 0 0 00
Paid-in Capital in Excess of Par Value—Preferred		16 0 0 0 00
Common Stock		240 0 0 0 00
Retained Earnings		128 0 0 0 00
Sales (Net)		1,100 5 5 0 00
Purchases	600 0 0 0 00	
Selling Expenses Control	162 8 0 0 00	
General Expenses Control	76 7 0 0 00	
Amortization of Organization Costs		
Income Tax Expense	69 2 0 0 00	
Income Summary		
Totals	1,855 0 7 0 00	1,855 0 7 0 00

(2) Assuming that taxable income is the same as net income before income taxes, use the tax rates given in this chapter to compute the federal income tax. Round the computed tax to the nearest whole dollar. Ignore state and local income taxes.

3. Complete the worksheet as shown in the text.

4. Prepare a condensed income statement for the year.

5. Prepare a balance sheet as of December 31, 2010. The balance of *Retained Earnings* on January 1, 2010, was $168,800. All dividends for the year were declared on December 5, 2010, and are payable January 4, 2011.

6. Journalize the adjusting and closing entries on December 31. Explanations are not required.

Analyze: Assume that dividends were declared in equal amounts over the four quarters of 2010. What percentage of Bruin Corporation's annual income before tax was spent on dividends to stockholders?

Recording cash dividends, stock dividends, and appropriation of retained earnings; preparing statement of retained earnings.

◀ **Problem 21.3A**
Objectives 5, 6, 8, 11

The stockholders' equity accounts of Solomon Corporation on January 1, 2010, contained the following balances.

Preferred Stock (10%, $50 par value, 4,000 shares authorized)		
Issued and Outstanding, 1,200 Shares	$60,000	
Paid-in Capital in Excess of Par Value—Preferred	1,200	$ 61,200
Common Stock ($20 par value, 20,000 shares authorized)		
Issued and Outstanding, 10,000 Shares		200,000
Retained Earnings		197,200
Total Stockholders' Equity		$458,400

Transactions affecting stockholders' equity during 2010 follow.

INSTRUCTIONS

1. Set up a ledger account (381) for *Retained Earnings* and record the January 1, 2010, balance.

2. Record the transactions in general journal form and post them to the *Retained Earnings* account only. Use the account titles in the chapter.

3. Prepare a statement of retained earnings for the year 2010.

DATE	TRANSACTIONS
June 15	Declared a semiannual dividend of 5 percent on preferred stock, payable on July 15 to stockholders of record on June 30.
July 15	Paid the dividend on preferred stock.
Dec 15	Declared a semiannual dividend of 5 percent on preferred stock, payable on January 15, 2011, to stockholders of record on December 31, 2010, and a cash dividend of $3 per share on common stock, payable on January 15, 2011, to stockholders of record on December 31, 2010. Make separate entries.
15	Declared a 5 percent common stock dividend to common stockholders of record on December 31, 2010. The new shares are to be issued on January 15, 2011. A market price of $30 per share is expected for the new shares of common stock.
Dec. 31	Created an "appropriation of retained earnings for contingencies" of $50,000 because of the poor economic outlook.
31	The *Income Summary* account contained a debit balance of $15,000. The board had anticipated a net loss for the year and no quarterly deposits of estimated income taxes were made, so income taxes may be ignored.

Analyze: If Solomon Corporation had not declared dividends for common stockholders, what balance would be found in the unappropriated ***Retained Earnings*** account at December 31, 2010?

Problem 21.4A ▶
Objectives 5, 7, 8, 9, 11

Recording cash dividends, stock splits, appropriations of retained earnings, and donated assets; preparing the Stockholders' Equity section of the balance sheet.

The Stockholders' Equity section of the balance sheet of Willy Corporation on January 1, 2010, is shown below; selected transactions for the year follow.

Stockholders' Equity

Preferred Stock (10% cumulative, $10 par value,		
200,000 shares authorized)		
Issued and Outstanding, 8,000 Shares	$ 80,000	
Paid-in Capital in Excess of Par Value	8,000	$ 88,000
Common Stock (no-par value, $50 stated value,		
200,000 shares authorized)		
Issued and Outstanding, 2,000 Shares	100,000	
Paid-in Capital in Excess of Stated Value	4,000	104,000
Total Paid-in Capital		$192,000
Retained Earnings		130,000
Total Stockholders' Equity		$322,000

INSTRUCTIONS

1. Open the stockholders' equity accounts in the general ledger, and enter the beginning balances. In addition to the accounts listed, open the following accounts:

   Donated Capital

   Treasury Stock—Preferred

   Retained Earnings—Appropriated for Treasury Stock

2. Record the transactions in general journal form.

3. Post the transactions to the stockholders' equity accounts.

4. Prepare the Stockholders' Equity section of the balance sheet.

DATE	TRANSACTIONS
Feb. 15	Repurchased 4,000 shares of the outstanding preferred stock for $44,000 in cash. The stock is to be held as treasury stock. State law requires that an amount of retained earnings equal to the cost of treasury stock held must be appropriated. Record the purchase and the appropriation of retained earnings.
Mar. 4	Declared a 2-for-1 stock split of common stock. Each shareholder will own twice as many shares as originally owned. Stated value is reduced to $25 per share. Date of record is March 15. Date of issue of new shares is April 1.
April 1	Issued new shares called for by split.
June 17	Declared semiannual dividend of 5 percent on preferred stock, to be paid on July 12 to holders of record on June 30.
July 12	Paid cash dividend on preferred stock.
Sept. 25	Purchased 500 shares of outstanding preferred stock at $10 per share to be held as treasury stock. Record appropriated retained earnings equal to cost of the treasury stock.

DATE	TRANSACTIONS
Dec. 15	Declared semiannual cash dividend of 5 percent on preferred stock to be paid on January 12 to holders of record on December 30.
15	Declared cash dividend of $1 per share on common stock to be paid on January 12 to holders of record on December 30.
15	Accepted title to a tract of land with a fair market value of $150,000 from the City of Greenville. The tract is to be used as a building site for the corporation's new factory.
31	Had net income after taxes for the year of $70,000. Give the entry to close the **Income Summary** account.

Analyze: If Willy Corporation had not repurchased preferred stock to place in treasury, what total stockholders' equity would be reported on December 31, 2010?

Problem Set B

Recording federal income tax and cash dividend transactions.

◄ **Problem 21.1B**
Objectives 1, 5

Selected transactions of The Ohio Corporation during 2010 are given below. Record them in the general journal.

Analyze: If the dividends declared on October 30 were to be paid on January 15, what balance would be reflected in the **Dividends Payable** account on December 31, 2010?

DATE	TRANSACTIONS
Mar. 15	Filed the federal tax return for 2009. The total tax for the year was $165,000. Estimated tax deposits of $160,000 had been made during 2009, and on December 31, 2009, the accountant had accrued an additional liability of $2,500. Paid the tax due of $5,000.
Apr. 15	Paid first quarterly installment of $42,000 on 2010 estimated federal income tax.
May 30	Declared dividend of $0.50 per share on the 47,000 shares of common stock outstanding. The dividend is payable on June 30 to holders of record on June 15.
June 15	Paid second quarterly installment of $42,000 on 2010 estimated federal income tax.
30	Paid the dividend declared on May 30.
Sept. 15	Paid third quarterly installment of $42,000 on 2010 estimated federal income tax.
Oct. 30	Declared cash dividend of $0.50 per share on the 47,000 shares of common stock outstanding. The dividend is payable on December 1 to holders of record on November 15.
Dec. 1	Paid dividend declared on October 30.
15	Paid fourth quarterly installment of $42,000 on 2010 estimated federal income tax.
31	In completing the worksheet at the end of the year, the accountant determined that the total income tax for 2010 was $169,400. The difference between this amount and the quarterly deposits is to be recorded as an adjustment.

Problem 21.2B ▶
Objectives 2, 3, 4, 11

Completing a corporate worksheet; recording adjusting and closing entries; preparing an income statement and balance sheet.

Atlantic Corporation has been authorized to issue 10,000 shares of 10 percent noncumulative, nonparticipating preferred stock with a par value of $100 per share and 10,000 shares of common stock with a stated value of $100 per share. As of December 31, 2010, 800 shares of preferred stock and 800 shares of common stock have been issued and are outstanding. Dividends are paid quarterly on the preferred stock. A condensed trial balance as of December 31, 2010, is shown below.

INSTRUCTIONS

1. Enter the December 31 trial balance on an eight-column worksheet. Provide four lines for the *Selling Expenses* control account and three lines for the *General Expenses* control account. Total and rule the Trial Balance columns.

2. Enter the necessary adjustments on the worksheet, based on the following data for December 31.

   a. Ending merchandise inventory is $78,000. Close the beginning inventory, and set up the ending inventory.

   b. *Allowance for Doubtful Accounts* should be adjusted to a balance of $1,300 (debit *Selling Expenses*).

   c. Depreciation of buildings is $4,000 ($3,600 is selling expense; $400 is general expense).

   d. Depreciation of equipment is $6,000 ($2,000 is selling expense; $4,000 is general expense).

   e. Accrued expenses are $3,800 ($1,200 is selling expense; $2,600 is general expense).

Atlantic Corporation				
Trial Balance (Condensed)				
December 31, 2010				
ACCOUNT NAME	DEBIT		CREDIT	
Cash	40 0 0 0 00			
Accounts Receivable	52 8 0 0 00			
Allowance for Doubtful Accounts			7 0 0 00	
Merchandise Inventory	74 9 2 0 00			
Land	60 0 0 0 00			
Buildings	88 0 0 0 00			
Accumulated Depreciation—Buildings			8 0 0 0 00	
Equipment	78 0 0 0 00			
Accumulated Depreciation—Equipment			12 0 0 0 00	
Accounts Payable			31 4 5 0 00	
Dividends Payable—Preferred			2 4 0 0 00	
Accrued Expenses Payable				
Income Tax Payable				
Preferred Stock, 10%			80 0 0 0 00	
Paid-in Capital in Excess of Par Value—Preferred			6 0 0 0 00	
Common Stock			80 0 0 0 00	
Retained Earnings			89 1 7 0 00	
Sales (Net)			445 0 0 0 00	
Purchases	220 0 0 0 00			
Selling Expenses Control	85 0 0 0 00			
General Expenses Control	40 0 0 0 00			
Income Tax Expense	16 0 0 0 00			
Income Summary				
Totals	754 7 2 0 00		754 7 2 0 00	

f. The $16,000 balance in *Income Tax Expense* represents the quarterly tax deposits. Adjust the *Income Tax Expense* account using the following procedure.

   (1) Extend the adjusted income and expense items to the Income Statement columns. Using this data, compute the net income before income taxes.

   (2) Assuming that taxable income is the same as net income before income taxes, use the tax rates given in this chapter to compute the federal income tax. Round the computed tax to the nearest whole dollar. Ignore state and local income taxes.

3. Complete the worksheet as shown in the text.

4. Prepare a condensed income statement for the year.

5. Prepare a balance sheet as of December 31, 2010. The balance of *Retained Earnings* on January 1 was $97,170. The only dividends declared during the year were dividends on preferred stock.

6. Journalize the adjusting and closing entries on December 31, 2010. Descriptions are not required.

Analyze: Assume that dividends were declared in equal amounts over the four quarters of fiscal 2010. What percentage of Atlantic Corporation's annual income before tax was spent on dividends to stockholders?

Recording cash dividends, stock dividends, appropriations of retained earnings; preparing statement of retained earnings.

◄ **Problem 21.3B**
   Objectives 5, 6, 8, 11

The stockholders' equity accounts of Toy Hut Corporation on January 1, 2010, contained the following balances.

Preferred Stock (10%, $50 par value,		
2,000 shares authorized)		
Issued and Outstanding, 500 shares		$ 25,000
Common Stock (no-par, $25 stated value,		
8,000 shares authorized)		
Issued and Outstanding, 5,000 shares	$125,000	
Paid-in Capital in Excess of Stated Value	400	125,400
Retained Earnings		43,000
Total Stockholders' Equity		$193,400

The transactions affecting stockholders' equity during 2010 are given below. The worksheet at the end of 2010 showed a net loss of $6,000.

INSTRUCTIONS

1. Set up a ledger account (381) for *Retained Earnings,* and record the January 1, 2010, balance.

2. Record the following transactions in general journal form using page 6. Use the account titles used in the text. No descriptions are required. Post these entries to the *Retained Earnings* account only.

3. Prepare a statement of retained earnings for the year 2010.

DATE	TRANSACTIONS
June 15	Declared a semiannual 5 percent cash dividend on preferred stock and a cash dividend of $1.00 per share on common stock. Both are payable July 15 to stockholders of record on July 1. (Make a compound entry.)
July 15	Paid the cash dividends.
Sept. 15	Declared a 5 percent common stock dividend to be distributed on October 12 to common stockholders of record on October 1. The stock is expected to have a market value of $30 per share when issued.
Oct. 12	Distributed the common stock dividend.
Dec. 15	Declared a semiannual 5 percent cash dividend on preferred stock and a cash dividend of $0.50 per share on common stock. Both dividends are payable January 15 to stockholders of record on December 31. (Make a compound entry.)
15	Directed that retained earnings of $5,000 be appropriated each year for the next four years to purchase a new computer system. Title the account Retained Earnings Appropriated for Equipment Acquisition. Record the appropriation for 2010.
31	Close the debit balance of $6,000 in *Income Summary.*

Analyze: What balances should be reflected in the *Dividends Payable—Preferred* account on December 31, 2010?

Problem 21.4B ▶
Objectives 5, 7, 8, 9, 11

Recording cash dividends, stock splits, appropriation of retained earnings, and donated assets; preparing the Stockholders' Equity section of the balance sheet.

The Stockholders' Equity section of Houston Corporation's balance sheet on January 1, 2010, follows, along with selected transactions for the year.

Stockholders' Equity

Preferred Stock (10%, $50 par value,
   20,000 shares authorized)

Issued and Outstanding, 2,000 Shares	$100,000	
Paid-in Capital in Excess of Par Value	3,500	$ 103,500

Common Stock (no-par value, $25 stated value,
   20,000 shares authorized)

Issued and Outstanding, 3,600 Shares	$ 90,000	
Paid-in Capital in Excess of Stated Value	3,000	93,000
Retained Earnings		165,450
Total Stockholders' Equity		$ 361,950

INSTRUCTIONS

1. Set up general ledger accounts for the stockholders' equity items and enter the given balances. In addition to the accounts listed, open the accounts *Donated Capital, Treasury Stock— Preferred,* and *Retained Earnings Appropriated for Treasury Stock.*

2. Record the transactions listed below in general journal form.

3. Post general journal entries only to the stockholders' equity accounts.

4. Prepare the Stockholders' Equity section of the balance sheet as of December 31, 2010.

DATE	TRANSACTIONS
Feb. 1	Reacquired 100 shares of preferred stock at $55 per share, and set up an appropriation of retained earnings equal to cost of treasury stock purchased, as required by law.
Mar. 1	Declared a 2-for-1 split of common stock and reduced the stated value to $12.50 per share. Date of record is March 20. Date of issue is April 1.
Apr. 1	Issued new shares of common stock called for by split.
June 20	Declared a cash dividend of 5 percent on preferred stock outstanding, payable July 10 to holders of record on July 1.
July 10	Paid cash dividends on preferred stock.
Nov. 10	Purchased 200 shares of the corporation's own preferred stock to be held as treasury stock, paying $53 per share. Appropriated retained earnings equal to cost of the shares.
Dec. 17	Declared the semiannual cash dividends of 5 percent on preferred stock and a $1 per share on common stock. Both are payable to stockholders of record on December 28 and are payable on January 8. Make separate entries.
24	Received land valued at $75,000 as a gift from a neighboring city agreeing to build a new factory.
31	The *Income Summary* account had a credit balance of $45,000 after income tax. Give the entry to close the account.

Analyze: As of December 31, what percent of total authorized preferred stock is held in treasury?

Critical Thinking Problem 21.1

Stockholders' Equity

The Stockholders' Equity section of the balance sheets of Tone Corporation on December 31, 2009, and December 31, 2010, along with other selected account balances on the two dates is provided on page 758. (Certain information is missing from the statements.)

In 2010, the following transactions affecting equity occurred.

a. A stock dividend was declared on common stock and issued in April. No other common stock was issued during the year.

b. A cash dividend of $6 per share was declared and paid on common stock in December.

c. The Treasury Stock—Preferred was purchased at par in January.

d. Additional preferred stock was issued for cash in March.

e. The yearly cash dividend of $4.00 per share was declared and paid on preferred stock outstanding as of December 3, 2010.

INSTRUCTIONS

Answer the following questions about transactions in 2010.

1. How many shares of preferred stock were outstanding at year-end?

2. How many common stock shares were issued as stock dividends?

3. What was the market value per share of common stock at the time the stock dividend was declared?

4. How many shares of preferred stock were purchased as treasury stock?

5. How many shares of preferred stock were issued for cash?
6. What was the sales price per share of the preferred stock issued?
7. What was the total cash dividend on preferred stock?
8. What was the total cash dividend on common stock?
9. What was the corporation's net income or loss after taxes?

	2010	2009
Stockholders' Equity		
Paid-in Capital		
Preferred Stock (8 percent, $50 par, authorized 2,000 shares)		
Issued	$ 80,000	$ 64,000
Paid-in Capital in Excess of Par		
Value—Preferred	600	–0–
Common Stock ($35 par value, 200,000 shares authorized)		
Issued	805,000	700,000
Paid-in Capital in Excess of Par		
Value—Common	15,000	
Total Paid-in Capital	$ 900,600	$ 764,000
Retained Earnings		
Appropriated for Plant Expansion	$ 250,000	$ 250,000
Appropriated for Treasury Stock	40,000	–0–
Unappropriated	640,000	604,000
Total Retained Earnings	$ 930,000	$ 854,000
	$1,830,600	$1,618,000
Less Treasury Stock—Preferred	40,000	–0–
Total Stockholders' Equity	$1,790,600	$1,618,000

Analyze: What percent of net income after taxes went to cash dividends?

Critical Thinking Problem 21.2

Individual Investor

High Tech Inc. has the following stockholders' equity on June 30, 2010.

Common Stock, $15 par (200,000 shares issued)	$3,000,000
Paid-in Capital in Excess of Par	2,000,000
Retained Earnings	4,000,000
Total Stockholders' Equity	$9,000,000

For the past three years, High Tech Inc. has paid dividends of $1.60 per share. On July 1, 2010, the board declared a 20 percent stock dividend instead of the $1.60 cash dividend. Before the end of the year and after the stock dividend distribution, however, the board declared a cash dividend of $1.33 per share.

In June 2010, before the stock dividend was declared, Rosa Dodd purchased 12,000 shares of High Tech Inc. stock for $60 per share. Now she is concerned because she purchased the stock expecting a $1.60 per-share dividend, only to learn that the dividend has been reduced to $1.33 per share.

Answer the following questions concerning this investment.

1. What could have caused High Tech's board of directors to declare a stock dividend rather than a cash dividend in July?

2. How did the book value of Rosa's stock prior to the stock dividend compare with its book value after the stock dividend?

3. Why does the market value of the stock ($60) when Rosa purchased her shares differ from its book value at that time?

4. How does the total amount of cash dividends on Rosa's stock differ between the $1.60 per share on Rosa's original holdings and the $1.33 per share on her holdings after the stock dividend?

5. Assume the market price of the stock fell to $50 after the stock dividend was distributed. Does this drop represent a loss to Rosa?

6. What do you think would have happened to the market price of the stock if the board had not reduced the amount of the cash dividend per share of stock?

BUSINESS CONNECTIONS

Shareholder's Equity

1. Three individuals are planning to form a new business. What are the five major types of entities that they can use to operate their business?

2. Assume that you are the controller of a corporation. Some members of the board of directors have asked you how the firm can have a large balance in the *Retained Earnings* account but no cash with which to pay dividends. Explain.

3. A corporation's balance sheet shows *Retained Earnings Appropriated for Plant Expansion* with a balance of $4,000,000. Does this mean that the corporation has set aside $4,000,000 in cash to expand its plant? Why would management want to establish such an account?

4. O'Neil Corporation's $50 par-value stock has a market price of $250 per share. As a result of the high price per share, finding buyers for stock that existing shareholders wish to sell has become difficult. Suggest a way for management to resolve this problem.

5. Why would the management of a corporation consider using corporate funds to purchase the firms' own outstanding stock?

6. The president of a corporation suggests to the controller that one way to convert retained earnings into permanent capital is to have a stock split. What explanation should the controller give the president?

> Managerial | FOCUS

Corporate Incentives

A small community called Two Trees needs to increase jobs in the community. Two Trees has some public land that could be developed. The city could sell this land to a private individual for $200,000. The city council decided, however, to make arrangements with Wal-Mart to receive the land free if they would build a store in their community. Wal-Mart must first hire from the people that live in Two Trees to receive this free land. Is it ethical for the Two Trees City Council to propose this to Wal-Mart? How would Wal-Mart record this transaction?

> Ethical | DILEMMA

Income Taxes and Dividends

Refer to The Home Depot, Inc., *2006 Annual Report* in Appendix A.

1. Based on the data presented in the consolidated statements of earnings, answer the following.

    a. What approximate income tax rate does the company pay?

    b. Did the company record an accrual for current income taxes payable for the year ended January 28, 2007? If so, on which statement did you locate this information?

> STREETWISE:
> Questions from the
> REAL WORLD

2. Locate the consolidated statements of stockholders' equity and comprehensive income.

   a. What per-share cash dividends were paid to common stockholders in fiscal 2006? In fiscal 2005? In fiscal 2004?

   b. What percent increase did stockholders realize in dividends from 2005 to 2006?

   c. How closely does this percent increase correlate to the percent increase in net earnings before taxes from 2005 to 2006?

Financial Statement ANALYSIS

Statement of Shareholders' Equity

The excerpt on page 761 was taken from McDonald's *2006 Annual Report*.

Analyze:

1. How many shares of common stock were purchased in fiscal 2006 by the company and put into treasury?

2. What percentage of 2006 net income was used to repurchase common stock?

3. What total amount was paid by the company for dividends to common stockholders in 2006?

Analyze Online: Locate the McDonald's Web site (www.mcdonalds.com). Click on *Corporate McDonalds;* within the *Investor* section, review the consolidated statement of shareholders' equity found in the most recent annual report. Answer the following questions.

4. How many shares of common stock are outstanding? By what amount has this figure changed from fiscal 2006?

5. What is the balance of the *Treasury Stock* account?

6. What per-share dividend was paid to common stockholders?

Extending THE THOUGHT

Management Report on Internal Controls

When publicly held corporations release their annual reports, they often include a management report on internal controls. Contents of this report can include the purpose, nature and components of internal controls, the roles of internal audit, the independent auditor, and the audit committee.

Investigate the new federal requirements for reporting on internal control required by Sarbanes-Oxley.

Business COMMUNICATION

Visual Presentation

The board of directors of Midland Medical Group Corporation is engaged in discussions to decide whether the corporation should repurchase shares of its common stock to place in treasury. As the CFO, you have been asked to speak to the group at the next board meeting to offer insight into how the decision will affect the company. The corporation has sufficient cash to repurchase 2,000 shares of its outstanding common stock (15,000 shares) at $33 per share. In your presentation, be sure to cover the following topics: advantages or disadvantages to current common stockholders, impact on the cash flow of the corporation, impact on dividends payment, advantages or disadvantages to the corporation's stock option programs, and impact on the market value of the stock.

TEAMWORK

Dividends to Declare

The board of directors has the responsibility to determine the dollar amount of dividends to be given to investors. As a group of three or four students acting as the board of directors, determine the amount of dividends to declare for your investors given the following information: (1) 100,000 shares outstanding, (2) $249,000 in net income, (3) $1,500,000 proposed future expansion, (4) $900,000 balance in *Retained Earnings.* Should the board approve a dividend in stock, cash, or a combination of both? Justify your answer.

Internet CONNECTION

Earnings and Dividends per Share

From the Web sites of several corporations that pay dividends, find the ratio between the earning per share and the dividends paid per share. How much of the earnings does each corporation return to its stockholders? Does the amount of retained earnings determine the amount of dividends?

From Financial Statement Analysis on previous page.

Consolidated Statement of Shareholders' Equity

In millions except per-share data	Common Stock Issued		Additional Paid-in Capital	Retained Earnings	Accumulated Other Comprehensive Income (Loss)			Common Stock in Treasury		Total Shareholders' Equity
	Shares	Amount			Pensions	Deferred Hedging Adjustment	Foreign Currency Translation	Shares	Amount	
Balance at December 31, 2005	1,660.6	16.6	2,720.2	23,516.0	—	(18.5)	(714.6)	(397.4)	(10,373.6)	15,146.1
Net income				3,544.2						3,544.2
Translation adjustments (including taxes of $95.6)							514.7			514.7
Fair value adjustments—cash flow hedges (including tax benefits of $0.6)						10.7				10.7
Comprehensive income										4,069.0
Adjustment to initially apply SFAS No. 158 (including tax benefits of $39.2)					(89.0)					(89.0)
Common stock cash dividends ($1.00 per share)				(1,216.5)						(1,216.5)
ESOP loan payment			7.3							7.3
Treasury stock purchases								(98.4)	(3,718.9)	(3,718.9)
Share-based compensation			122.5							122.5
Stock option exercises and other (including tax benefits of $125.4)			595.0	1.9				38.9	540.3	1,137.2
Balance at December 31, 2006	1,660.6	$16.6	$3,445.0	$25,845.6	$(89.0)	$(7.8)	$(199.9)	(456.9)	$(13,552.2)	$15,458.3

Answers to **Self Reviews**

Answers to Section 1 Self Review

1. Income tax expense is usually shown as a deduction at the bottom of the income statement, after Net Income Before Tax, but is sometimes shown as an Operating Expense to emphasize that taxes are a cost of doing business.

2. After the balances of income and expense accounts—other than income taxes—have been extended to the Income Statement of the worksheet, the debit column and credit column are totaled. The difference is the income before taxes. The taxes are computed on that income and entered as an adjustment and carried forward to the debit column of the income statement section.

3. Retained earnings represent the cumulative profits and losses of the corporation that have not been distributed as dividends or transferred to Paid-in Capital through cash dividends, stock dividends, or stock splits.

4. These adjustments are the same for sole proprietorships and corporations.

5. No. There are many special rules—for example, depreciation calculations—for tax purposes that are not acceptable under GAAP requirements.

6. $80,750

7. Dr. *Income Tax Refund Receivable* (or a similar account), $500. Credit *Federal Income Tax Expense,* $500. ($8,000 estimate paid, minus $7,500 actual tax for the year.)

Answers to Section 2 Self Review

1. No entry is made in the accounts to record a stock split, except memorandum entries to note the board's action when the split is authorized and again on the date the additional shares are issued. A stock dividend also requires only a memorandum entry if the stock has no par value or stated value assigned.

2. The date of declaration—the date the board of directors formally announces the dividend. The date of record—date on which owners of stock are determined and to whom dividends will be paid. The date of payment is the date on which payment is to be made.

3. No cash is involved in an appropriation of retained earnings. Cash is involved only if a separate fund is established to pay for the object of the appropriation.

4. Of these actions, only a cash dividend (**c**) will result in a decrease in stockholder equity.

5. **c.** A board resolution is necessary to reduce appropriated retained earnings.

6. $1,800 (600 shares × $3)

Answers to Section 3 Self Review

1. Donated capital arises when assets are contributed or donated to the corporation or when the debt of the corporation is forgiven. A common transaction giving rise to donated capital is the gift of land to the corporation as an incentive to locate a new facility on the land. Similarly, cash may be given the corporation to entice it to open a business in a city.

2. The cost of treasury stock should not be shown as an asset on the balance sheet of the issuing corporation. It represents a deduction from the total of the corporation's other stockholders' equity accounts.

3. A common reason is that the corporation's board decides the corporation has excess cash and concludes that its own stock represents the best available investment. Sometimes stock is repurchased to reduce the number of shares outstanding with the expectation of increasing net income per share and/or dividends per share for remaining shareholders.

4. **a.** a deduction from the sum of all other items in the Stockholders' Equity section.

5. **d.** the cash payment made to build a building for which an appropriation of retained earnings had previously been made.

6. $462,000

Answers to Comprehensive Self Review

1. On the balance sheet, treasury stock is deducted from the total of all other stockholders' equity.

2. The statement of retained earnings is to show all changes in retained earnings that have occurred during the period.

3. The appropriation account merely restricts the payment of dividends to the amount of retained earnings in excess of the appropriations. Retained earnings—and the appropriation—have nothing to do with cash.

4. The shareholder's ownership percentage is unaffected by a common stock dividend.

5. Treasury stock is stock that has been issued, paid for, and reacquired. Unissued stock meets none of those requirements for treasury stock.

6. Donated capital represents the value of assets that have been donated to, or contributed to, the corporation. Usually such contributions are to be used for some specified purpose.

Long-Term Bonds

Chapter **22**

LEARNING OBJECTIVES

1. Name and define the various types of bonds. LP22
2. Explain the advantages and disadvantages of using bonds as a method of financing.
3. Record the issuance of bonds.
4. Record the payment of interest on bonds.
5. Record the accrual of interest on bonds.
6. Compute and record the periodic amortization of a bond premium.
7. Compute and record the periodic amortization of a bond discount.
8. Record the transactions of a bond sinking fund investment.
9. Record an increase or decrease in retained earnings appropriated for bond retirement.
10. Record retirement of bonds payable.
11. Define the accounting terms new to this chapter.

NEW TERMS

bond indenture
bond issue costs
bond retirement
bond sinking fund investment
bonds payable
call price
callable bonds
carrying value of bonds
collateral trust bonds
convertible bonds
coupon bonds
debentures

discount on bonds payable
face interest rate
leveraging
market interest rate
mortgage loan
premium on bonds payable
registered bonds
secured bonds
serial bonds
straight-line amortization
trading on the equity

3M www.3m.com

The Minnesota Mining and Manufacturing Co. got its start over 100 years ago in Duluth, Minnesota, and sold mainly sandpaper products. 3M grew into the multibillion dollar company it is today by producing thousands of products to serve markets from health care and highway safety to office products and optical films for LCD displays. In 2006, the company reported net income of $3.85 billion.

In order to diversify and grow, companies often finance expansions as well as research and development efforts using operating cash, long-term bond issues, and additional issues of company stock. As of December 31, 2006, 3M reported approximately $1 billion in long-term debt. Using this type of financing strategy allows 3M to continue to pioneer new technologies and products that help make life easier, safer, and healthier.

thinking critically

What are some other sources of long-term financing that could be used by a firm if selling bonds is not a possibility?

Section 1

SECTION OBJECTIVES

>> 1. **Name and define the various types of bonds.**

   WHY IT'S IMPORTANT

   Corporations frequently issue bonds to raise capital.

>> 2. **Explain the advantages and disadvantages of using bonds as a method of financing.**

   WHY IT'S IMPORTANT

   The use of bonds as a method of financing carries certain financial obligations and tax implications.

TERMS TO LEARN

bond indenture
bonds payable
call price
callable bonds
collateral trust bonds
convertible bonds
coupon bonds
debentures
face interest rate
leveraging
market interest rate
mortgage loan
registered bonds
secured bonds
serial bonds
trading on the equity

Financing Through Bonds

There are many ways for corporations to raise funds. They may sell stock, or they may sign a note payable.

A long-term note may be secured by a mortgage on specific assets such as land, buildings, or equipment. A **mortgage loan** is a long-term debt created when a note is given as part of the purchase price of land or buildings.

Corporations that need long-term funds often obtain those funds by issuing bonds payable. **Bonds payable** are long-term debt instruments that are written promises to repay the principal at a future date. Interest is due at a fixed rate that is payable annually, semiannually, or quarterly over the life of the bond. Bonds are similar to notes payable, but the contract is more formal. Bonds are easily transferred from one owner (or bondholder) to another.

Video22.1

>>1. OBJECTIVE

Name and define the various types of bonds.

LP22

Types of Bonds

Bonds are classified by the following characteristics:

■ Bonds can be secured by collateral, or they can be unsecured.

■ Bonds can be registered or unregistered.

■ Bonds can all mature on the same date, or portions can mature over a period of several years. *Mature* means to fall due or to become payable.

SECURED AND UNSECURED BONDS

Secured bonds have property pledged to secure the claims of the bondholders. **Collateral trust bonds** involve the pledge of securities, such as stocks or bonds of other companies. A bond contract, known as a **bond indenture,** is prepared. A trustee, frequently an investment banker, is named to protect the bondholders' interests. If the bonds are not paid when due, the trustee takes legal steps to sell the pledged property and pay off the bonds.

Bonds are identified according to the nature of the property pledged and the year of maturity. Examples are as follows:

- First Mortgage 9 percent Real Estate Bonds Payable, 2020
- Collateral Trust 10 percent Bonds Payable, 2016

Unsecured bonds backed only by a corporation's general credit are called **debentures.** They involve no pledge of specific property. However, the bondholders do have some protection in case of liquidation. The claims of creditors, including bondholders, rank above those of stockholders. Creditors must be paid in full before stockholders can receive anything.

REGISTERED AND UNREGISTERED BONDS

Registered bonds are bonds issued to a party whose name is listed in the corporation's records. Ownership is transferred by completing an assignment form and having the change of ownership entered in the corporation's records. Interest is paid by check to each registered bondholder. The corporation maintains a detailed subsidiary ledger, similar to the stockholders' ledger, for registered bonds. At all times, the corporation knows who owns the bonds and who is entitled to receive interest payments.

Some bonds do not require that the names of the owners be registered. These bonds are known as **coupon bonds.** The bonds have coupons attached for each interest payment. The coupons are, in effect, checks payable to the bearer. No record of the owner's identity is kept by the corporation. On or after each interest date, the bondholder detaches the coupon from the bond and presents it to a bank for payment. Coupon bonds are often referred to as *bearer bonds* because the bearer is assumed to be the owner. Coupon bonds are rarely issued because the IRS requires corporations to report the name, tax identification number, and interest received by each bondholder. State and local governments continue to issue coupon bonds because the interest is not subject to federal income tax.

SINGLE-MATURITY AND SERIAL-MATURITY BONDS

Most bonds in an issue mature on the same day. However, **serial bonds** are payable over a period of years. For example, a corporation might issue serial bonds totaling $10 million, dated January 1, 2010, with $2,000,000 maturing each year for five years, beginning on January 1, 2020. The corporation might find it easier to retire bonds on a serial basis rather than to have all $10 million due on the same date.

OTHER CHARACTERISTICS OF BONDS PAYABLE

Bonds are issued in various denominations. The denomination specified on the contract is called the *face value.* The typical face value is $1,000 or $10,000.

Convertible bonds give the owner the right to convert the bonds into common stock under specified conditions. For example, an indenture can give the holder of a 20-year, $1,000 bond the right to convert the bond into 50 shares of the corporation's common stock at any time. When the price of the stock reaches $20 or more ($1,000 bond ÷ 50 shares of stock), the bondholder is likely to convert it into stock.

Bonds are frequently callable. **Callable bonds** allow the issuing corporation to require the holders to surrender the bonds for payment before their maturity date. Call provisions are clearly stated on the bond. The **call price** is the amount the corporation must pay for the bond when it is called. Usually the call price is slightly above the face value. If the market interest rate declines below the face interest rate on the bonds, or if the corporation has excess cash, it might call all or part of the bonds and retire them.

Market interest rate refers to the interest rate a corporation is willing to pay and investors are willing to accept at the current time. **Face interest rate** refers to the contractual interest rate specified on the bond. Market interest rate changes constantly. Face interest rate of a bond does not change.

For example, assume that on October 1, 2010, DEL Corporation issues 20-year bonds with a face value of $100,000. The bonds mature on October 1, 2030. Under the terms of the indenture,

ABOUT **ACCOUNTING**
Accounting Textbooks
Benjamin Workman published *The American Accountant,* the earliest known accounting textbook, in 1769.

recall
Face Value
The term "face value" also applies to notes payable and notes receivable. It is sometimes known as "face amount."

DEL can call the bonds at any time after October 1, 2020, at a call price of 103 (103 percent of face value). The bonds are called by DEL on October 1, 2021. Johanson, an owner of bonds with a face value of $30,000, must surrender the bonds and will be paid $30,900 ($30,000 × 1.03).

>>2. OBJECTIVE

Explain the advantages and disadvantages of using bonds as a method of financing.

LP22

Stock versus Bonds as a Financing Method

Corporations raise funds through various combinations of common stock, preferred stock, and bonds. Management considers several factors when deciding whether to issue stock or bonds. Table 22.1 shows some factors to consider when comparing capital stock and bonds.

When deciding whether to issue bonds, a company needs to determine whether the rate of return on the assets acquired with the bond proceeds is higher than the interest rate paid on the bonds. Suppose that a newly formed corporation issued both common stock and bonds payable to provide total capital of $500,000. The owners invest $300,000 for common stock and borrow $200,000 by issuing bonds. The bonds pay 10 percent interest per year. The corporation's income before interest and taxes is $70,000. The corporate income tax rate is 20 percent. Let's compute the rate of profit on the stockholders' investment.

Amount available to stockholders:

Net income before bond interest expense	$70,000
Bond interest expense ($200,000 × 0.10)	(20,000)
Net income before income taxes	$50,000
Income tax expense ($50,000 × 0.20)	(10,000)
Net income after taxes	$40,000

The stockholders invested $300,000 in the business, and the net income is $40,000. The stockholders earned 13.3 percent ($40,000 ÷ $300,000) profit on their equity. Let's see what happens if the owners invest $500,000 in common stock. Since there is no bond payable, there is no interest expense.

Net income before taxes	$70,000
Income tax expense ($70,000 × 0.20)	(14,000)
Net income after income taxes	$56,000

The stockholders invested $500,000, and net income is $56,000. The stockholders earned 11.2 percent ($56,000 ÷ $500,000) on their equity. With financing coming 100 percent from capital stock, the net income available to the stockholders is higher ($56,000 versus $40,000), but the rate of profit on equity is lower (11.2 percent versus 13.3 percent).

TABLE 22.1

Stock and Bonds Compared

Capital Stock	Bonds Payable
Capital stock is permanent capital. There is no debt to be repaid.	Bonds payable are debt. When the bonds fall due, the debt must be repaid.
Because the stock is permanent capital, it is classified as stockholders' equity.	Because the bonds represent debt, they are classified as long-term liabilities.
Dividends are not legally required on common stock. The requirements on preferred stock depend on the contract.	Interest must be paid on the bonds.
Dividends are not deductible for income tax purposes.	Interest is deducted in arriving at the taxable income.
Preference dividends on preferred stock are usually slightly higher than interest rates on bonds because there is more risk associated with preferred stock.	Interest rates on bonds are slightly lower than dividends on preferred stock.

The increase in the rate of profit on stockholders' equity when bonds are used is due to the fact that the company's profits are higher than the face rate of interest (10 percent) on the bonds. Using borrowed funds to earn a profit higher than the interest that must be paid on the borrowing is called **trading on the equity,** or **leveraging.** In lean years, such financing can be dangerous from the stockholders' standpoint. The bond interest expense might leave little or nothing for dividends to the stockholders. Moreover, even when the firm operates at a loss, the interest must be paid in full to the bondholders. In addition, the principal amount of the debt must also be paid when the bonds mature.

For example, if the income before interest and taxes had been only $12,000, the use of bonds payable would result in the corporation having a net loss.

Net income before bond interest expense	$12,000
Bond interest expense ($200,000 × 0.10)	(20,000)
Net loss	($8,000)

Section 1 Self Review

QUESTIONS

1. Why would a corporation issue callable bonds?

2. What is a convertible bond?

3. What is the difference between registered bonds and coupon bonds?

EXERCISES

4. Bonds backed only by the general credit of the corporation are called

   a. secured bonds.

   b. collateral trust bonds.

   c. registered bonds.

   d. debentures.

5. Bonds that are payable over a period of years are called

   a. callable bonds.

   b. serial bonds.

   c. bearer bonds.

   d. coupon bonds.

ANALYSIS

6. A small corporation is considering a bond issue. The amount of stockholders' equity is $250,000. The corporation projects income before bond interest and taxes of $60,000. The corporate income tax rate is 20 percent. If $125,000 of bonds is issued at 10 percent, what is the rate of profit on stockholders' equity?

(Answers to Section 1 Self Review are on page 793.)

Section 2

TERMS TO LEARN

bond issue costs
carrying value of bonds
discount on bonds payable
premium on bonds payable
straight-line amortization

Bond Issue and Interest

Video22.1

The board of directors of Charbo Corporation authorized the issue of 300 registered, unsecured bonds that will mature in 10 years. The face value of each bond is $1,000. The face interest rate is 10 percent. Interest will be paid on April 1 and October 1 of each year. Interest on each bond is $100 per year ($1,000 × 0.10). Because interest is paid semiannually, each interest payment is $50 ($100 ÷ 2). Some of the authorized bonds will be sold immediately. The remainder will be held for future needs.

>>3. OBJECTIVE

Record the issuance of bonds.

LP22

Bonds Issued at Face Value

On April 1, 2010, the issue date, Charbo sells 50 bonds at face value for $50,000 ($1,000 × 50) cash. The journal entry follows.

GENERAL JOURNAL   PAGE _____

	DATE		DESCRIPTION	POST. REF.	DEBIT	CREDIT	
1	2010						1
2	Apr.	1	Cash		50 000 00		2
3			10% Bonds Payable, 2020			50 000 00	3
4			Issued bonds at face value				4
5							5

After the entry is posted, the ledger account for the bonds appears as follows.

ACCOUNT 10% Bonds Payable, 2020								
(Authorized $300,000; Interest April 1, October 1)			ACCOUNT NO. 261					

DATE		DESCRIPTION	POST. REF.	DEBIT	CREDIT	BALANCE DEBIT	BALANCE CREDIT
2010							
Apr.	1		J4		50 000 00		50 000 00

Notice that the amount of bonds authorized is recorded as a memorandum on the ledger account form. On the balance sheet, the bonds payable appear as long-term liabilities. (Bonds that mature within one year from the balance sheet date appear as current liabilities.) There are three ways to report bonds on the balance sheet.

1. Show the face value of the bonds authorized, unissued, and issued.

Long-Term Liabilities
10% Bonds Payable, Due April 1, 2020
Authorized $300,000
Less Unissued   250,000
Issued $ 50,000

2. Show the face value of the bonds authorized as a parenthetical note.

Long-Term Liabilities
10% Bonds Payable, Due April 1, 2020 $50,000
(Bonds with a face value of $300,000 are
authorized, of which $250,000 are unissued.)

3. Show the face value of the bonds issued. Provide details about the bonds in a footnote to the financial statements.

PAYMENT OF INTEREST

On October 1, 2010, the first interest payment is due: 10 percent interest on $50,000 for six months. The interest is $2,500 ($50,000 × 0.10 × 1/2). The journal entry to record the payment is as follows.

	DATE		DESCRIPTION	POST. REF.	DEBIT	CREDIT	
1	2010						1
2	Oct.	1	Bond Interest Expense		2 500 00		2
3			Cash			2 500 00	3
4			Paid semiannual bond				4
5			interest				5
6							6

Corporations with many bondholders open a separate checking account for bond interest payments. A separate account makes it easier to reconcile the bank account and to keep records of interest checks that have not yet been presented for payment.

ACCRUAL OF INTEREST

On December 31, 2010, at the end of the fiscal year, three months (October, November, and December) of bond interest is owed but will not be paid until April 1, 2011. The accrued interest is $1,250 ($50,000 × 0.10 × 3/12). The adjusting entry is as follows.

>>**4. OBJECTIVE**
Record the payment of interest on bonds.

LP22

recall
Interest Formula
I = Prt

>>**5. OBJECTIVE**
Record the accrual of interest on bonds.

1	2010		*Adjusting Entries*				1
26	Dec.	31	Bond Interest Expense		1 2 5 0 00		26
27			*Bond Interest Payable*			1 2 5 0 00	27
28			*Accrued interest for three months*				28
29							29

When the adjusting entry has been posted, the **Bond Interest Expense** account has a balance of $3,750, the correct amount of interest for the nine months the bonds have been outstanding. **Bond Interest Expense** usually appears in the Other Expenses (nonoperating expenses) section of the income statement.

ACCOUNT _Bond Interest Expense_   ACCOUNT NO. _692_

DATE		DESCRIPTION	POST. REF.	DEBIT	CREDIT	BALANCE DEBIT	BALANCE CREDIT
2010							
Oct.	1		J10	2 5 0 0 00		2 5 0 0 00	
Dec.	31	Adjusting	J12	1 2 5 0 00		3 7 5 0 00	

ENTRIES FOR SECOND-YEAR INTEREST

Assuming that the same bonds remain outstanding during all of the second year, 2011, the following entries would be required. Charbo utilizes reversing entries.

- January 1: Reverse the accrued interest payable entry for $1,250 made on December 31:
  Debit **Bond Interest Payable** for $1,250.
      Credit **Bond Interest Expense** for $1,250.
- April 1: Record the payment of interest for six months:
  Debit **Bond Interest Expense** for $2,500.
      Credit **Cash** for $2,500.
- October 1: Record the payment of interest for six months:
  Debit **Bond Interest Expense** for $2,500.
      Credit **Cash** for $2,500.
- December 31: Record accrued interest for three months:
  Debit **Bond Interest Expense** for $1,250.
      Credit **Bond Interest Payable** for $1,250.

After these entries have been posted, the **Bond Interest Expense** account appears as below. Notice that on December 31, 2011, the balance in the **Bond Interest Expense** account is $5,000. This is the annual interest on the bonds ($50,000 × 0.10).

recall

Reversing Entries

The adjusting entry to record accrued interest is reversed on the first day of the following period.

ACCOUNT _Bond Interest Expense_   ACCOUNT NO. _692_

DATE		DESCRIPTION	POST. REF.	DEBIT	CREDIT	BALANCE DEBIT	BALANCE CREDIT
2011							
Jan.	1	Reversing	J1		1 2 5 0 00		1 2 5 0 00
Apr.	1		J4	2 5 0 0 00		1 2 5 0 00	
Oct.	1		J10	2 5 0 0 00		3 7 5 0 00	
Dec.	31	Adjusting	J12	1 2 5 0 00		5 0 0 0 00	

important!

Bond Prices

If the face interest rate on bonds is higher than the market interest rate, the bonds will sell at a premium.

Bonds Issued at a Premium

Two years after the first bonds were sold, Charbo issues another 50 bonds. The market interest rate is about 9.5 percent. The face interest rate on the bonds remains at 10 percent. Bondholders will be attracted by the bond interest rate, which is higher than the market rate. They will be willing to pay more than the face value ($1,000) for each bond in order to earn 10 percent interest.

On April 1, 2012, $50,000 of bonds are sold at 104.8. Bond prices are quoted in terms of percent of face value. Each bond was issued for $1,048 ($1,000 × 1.048), yielding cash of $52,400 ($1,048 × 50). The issue price in excess of face value is $2,400 ($52,400 − $50,000). The excess of the price paid over the face value of a bond is called a **premium on bonds payable.** Investors are willing to pay a premium because the face interest rate is higher than the market interest at the time the bonds are issued. This transaction is recorded in general journal form as follows.

	2012					
1	2012					1
2	Apr.	1	Cash	52 400 00		2
3			10% Bonds payable, 2020		50 000 00	3
4			Premium on Bonds Payable		2 400 00	4
5			Issued bonds at 104.8			5
6						6

AMORTIZATION OF BOND PREMIUM

The issuing corporation writes off, or amortizes, the premium paid by the bond purchasers over the period from the issue date to the maturity date. Amortizing the premium reduces bond interest expense shown on the income statement. In this case, the bonds are 10-year bonds sold two years after their authorization date. That leaves eight years over which to amortize the premium.

There are two ways to compute the amortization: straight-line amortization and effective interest method. The effective interest method is covered in intermediate accounting courses. This text uses the **straight-line amortization** method, which amortizes an equal amount of the premium each interest payment date. The amortization for Charbo is $300 per year ($2,400 ÷ 8 years) or $150 each bond interest payment date.

On October 1, 2012, Charbo records the semiannual interest on the $100,000 of bonds outstanding. The bond interest paid is $5,000 ($100,000 × 0.10 × 6/12). Charbo also records amortization of the premium received on $50,000 of the bonds. The amortization is $150 each payment date. Notice how the amortization of the *Premium on Bonds Payable* reduces the amount of *Bond Interest Expense.*

>>**6. OBJECTIVE**

Compute and record the periodic amortization of a bond premium.

LP22

	2012					
1	2012					1
2	Oct.	1	Bond Interest Expense	5 000 00		2
3			Cash		5 000 00	3
4			Payment of semiannual interest			4
5			on $100,000 of bonds			5
6						6
7		1	Premium on Bonds Payable	1 50 00		7
8			Bond Interest Expense		1 50 00	8
9			Amortization on $50,000 of			9
10			bonds sold at premium			10

ADJUSTING AND REVERSING ENTRIES

On December 31, 2012, an adjusting entry is made for three months of accrued interest on the entire $100,000 of bonds outstanding. The accrued interest is $2,500 ($100,000 × 0.10 × 3/12). An adjustment is also made for the amortization of bond premium at $75 for three months (3/12 × $300 annual amortization). Bond interest expense is $2,425, the interest accrued less the amount of the bond premium ($2,500 − $75). The adjustment is recorded as shown and is reversed on January 1, 2013.

	2012		Adjusting Entries			
1	2012		Adjusting Entries			1
30	Dec.	31	Bond Interest Expense	2 425 00		30
31			Premium on Bonds Payable	75 00		31
32			Bond Interest Payable		2 500 00	32
33			Accrue interest and amortize			33
34			premium for three months			34

important!

Bond Prices

If the face interest rate on bonds is lower than the market interest rate, the bonds will sell at a discount.

Bonds Issued at a Discount

Charbo issues another 50 bonds on April 1, 2013. The market interest rate is 11 percent. The bonds' interest rate remains fixed at 10 percent. Investors will pay less than face value for a bond that pays interest at a lower rate than the market rate. The **discount on bonds payable** is the excess of the face value over the price received for a bond.

Charbo Corporation sells 50 bonds at 97.76. Each bond is issued for $977.60 ($1,000 × 0.9776), yielding cash of $48,880 ($50,000 × 0.9776). The excess of the face value over the issue price is $1,120 ($50,000 − $48,880). The $1,120 is the discount. The entry to record issuance of the bond is shown in general journal form as follows.

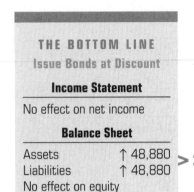

THE BOTTOM LINE

Issue Bonds at Discount

Income Statement

No effect on net income

Balance Sheet

Assets	↑ 48,880
Liabilities	↑ 48,880

No effect on equity

>>

1	2013					1
2	Apr.	1	Cash	48 8 8 0 00		2
3			Discount on Bonds Payable	1 1 2 0 00		3
4			10% Bonds payable, 2020		50 0 0 0 00	4
5			Issued bonds at 97.76			5
6						6

>>7. OBJECTIVE

Compute and record the periodic amortization of a bond discount.

LP22

AMORTIZATION OF BOND DISCOUNT

The issuing corporation amortizes the discount over the period from the issue date to the maturity date. Amortizing the discount increases the bond interest expense shown on the income statement. The bonds are 10-year bonds sold three years after the authorization date. That leaves seven years over which to amortize the discount. On a straight-line basis, the amortization is $160 per year or $80 per interest payment date.

On October 1, 2013, Charbo Corporation records the semiannual interest on the $150,000 of bonds outstanding. The bond interest paid is $7,500 ($150,000 × 0.10 × 6/12). The company records the amortization of the premium for six months ($150). It records the amortization of the discount for six months ($80). The bond interest expense is $7,430, the interest paid ($7,500) less the amortized premium ($150) and plus the amortized discount ($80). Notice how the discount increases the actual cost of borrowing. The journal entry to record the interest payment and the amortization of the premium and the discount follows.

1	2013					1
2	Oct.	1	Bond Interest Expense	7 4 3 0 00		2
3			Premium on Bonds Payable	1 5 0 00		3
4			Discount on Bonds Payable		8 0 00	4
5			Cash		7 5 0 0 00	5
6			Interest payment and amortization			6
7			of premium and discount for			7
8			six months			8

ADJUSTING AND REVERSING ENTRIES

On December 31, 2013, an adjusting entry is made to accrue interest on the bonds for the three-month period. The accrued interest is $3,750 ($150,000 × 0.10 × 3/12). An adjustment is made for the bond discount for three months ($40) and for the bond premium for three months ($75). Bond interest expense is $3,715, the interest accrued plus the discount less the premium ($3,750 + $40 − $75). The adjusting entry is recorded as follows. It is reversed on January 1, 2014.

	2013		Adjusting Entries								
1	2013		Adjusting Entries								1
26	Dec.	31	Bond Interest Expense	3 7 1 5 00				26
27			Premium on Bonds Payable	7 5 00				27
28			Discount on Bonds Payable			4 0 00		28
29			Bond Interest Payable			3 7 5 0 00		29
30			Accrue interest on $150,000 of bonds,					30
31			amortize premium on $50,000 of					31
32			bonds, and amortize discount on					32
33			$50,000 of bonds for three months					33

Balance Sheet Presentation of Bond Premium and Discount

The *Premium on Bonds Payable* account has a normal credit balance. It is shown as an addition to the face value of bonds payable on the balance sheet. The *Discount on Bonds Payable* account has a normal debit balance; it is subtracted from the face value of bonds payable on the balance sheet. When there are both a discount and a premium on a bond issue, the two are combined and shown on the balance sheet as a single figure. For example, on December 31, 2013, Charbo has a net premium on bonds payable of $875 as follows:

Discount	$ 1,120	
Amortization taken	(120)	
Unamortized discount		$1,000
Premium	$ 2,400	
Amortization taken	(525)	
Unamortized premium		(1,875)
Net unamortized premium		$ 875

On December 31, 2013, Charbo reports bonds payable on the balance sheet as follows.

Long-Term Liabilities

10% Bonds Payable, Due April 1, 2020 (authorized $200,000 face value, less $50,000 face value unissued)	$150,000
Net Premium on Bonds Payable	875
Net Liability	$150,875

The book value, or the **carrying value of bonds,** is the balance of the *Bonds Payable* account plus the *Premium on Bonds Payable* account minus the *Discount on Bonds Payable* account.

```
  Bonds payable
+ Premium on bonds
− Discount on bonds
  ─────────────────
  Carrying value or book value
```

recall

Book Value

The term *book value* can apply to assets or liabilities. The book value of property, plant, and equipment is the original cost minus the accumulated depreciation.

Accounting for Bond Issue Costs

Bond issue costs are costs incurred in issuing bonds, including items such as legal and accounting fees and printing costs. Bond issue costs reduce the proceeds of borrowing. Bond issue costs may be handled in two ways:

1. Accounted for as a discount or as a reduction of premium and amortized over the period the bonds are outstanding, or

2. Debited to an expense account in the period they are incurred.

Section 2 Self Review

QUESTIONS

1. How are bond discounts shown on the balance sheet?

2. What is the straight-line method for amortizing bond discount or premium?

3. Why is amortization of a bond premium offset against interest expense?

EXERCISES

4. The entry to record the issuance of bonds includes a
   a. credit to *Bond Interest Payable.*
   b. credit to *Bonds Payable.*
   c. debit to *Bonds Payable.*
   d. debit to *Bond Interest Payable.*

5. If bonds are issued for a price below their face value, the bond discount is
   a. debited to expense on the date the bonds are issued.
   b. amortized over the life of the bond issue.
   c. shown as an addition to bonds payable in the Long-Term Liabilities section of the balance sheet.
   d. shown as a deduction to bonds payable in the Current Liabilities section of the balance sheet.

ANALYSIS

6. Ten-year bonds, dated January 1, 2010, with a face value of $200,000 are issued at 101 on January 1, 2010. How much premium will be amortized on the interest payment date, July 1, 2010?

(Answers to Section 2 Self Review are on page 793.)

Section 3

SECTION OBJECTIVES

>> 8. **Record the transactions of a bond sinking fund investment.**

WHY IT'S IMPORTANT

Companies make plans to ensure that the required funds are available to pay off bonds on their maturity date.

>> 9. **Record an increase or decrease in retained earnings appropriated for bond retirement.**

WHY IT'S IMPORTANT

Retained earnings are often restricted for specific expenditures.

>> 10. **Record retirement of bonds payable.**

WHY IT'S IMPORTANT

Upon retirement of a bond, total long-term debt is adjusted to reflect the payment of the liability.

TERMS TO LEARN

bond retirement
bond sinking fund investment

Bond Retirement

Bond retirement occurs when a bond is paid and the liability is removed from the company's balance sheet. When Charbo's bond issue matures, the corporation has to pay bondholders the face amount of their outstanding bonds, a total of $150,000, in cash.

Accumulating Funds to Retire Bonds

In order to ensure that the cash is available, the corporation established a bond sinking fund investment account. A **bond sinking fund investment** is a fund established to accumulate assets to pay off bonds when they mature. Some bond contracts require bond sinking funds.

BOND SINKING FUND INVESTMENT

Charbo Corporation decides to accumulate $30,000 per year in the bond sinking fund for each of the last five years that the bonds are outstanding. The net earnings of the fund will reduce the amount that the corporation has to add each year. Suppose that the bond sinking fund investment account is started on April 1, 2015, by making a $30,000 cash deposit. The $30,000 is immediately invested. During the year, $1,800 is earned on the sinking fund investments. Expenses of $40 are incurred in operating the bond sinking fund. Net earnings for the year are $1,760. The following year only $28,240 ($30,000 − $1,760) needs to be added to the fund. This procedure is repeated each year, so that at the end of the fifth year the fund will have the $150,000 needed to retire the bonds.

The following journal entries are for the first transfer of cash to the fund, net earnings for the first year, second transfer of cash to the fund, and retirement of the bonds at the end of the fifth year.

>>8. OBJECTIVE
Record the transactions of a bond sinking fund investment.

LP22

1	2015															1
2	Apr.	1	Bond Sinking Fund Investment		30 0 0 0 00									2
3			Cash					30 0 0 0 00		3
4			First annual installment in bond							4
5			sinking fund							5

1	2016															1
2	Apr.	1	Bond Sinking Fund Investment		1 7 6 0 00									2
3			Income from Sinking Fund Investment					1 7 6 0 00		3
4			Net income earned by bond sinking							4
5			fund for year							5

1	2016															1
7	Apr.	1	Bond Sinking Fund Investment		28 2 4 0 00									7
8			Cash					28 2 4 0 00		8
9			Second annual installment in bond							9
10			sinking fund ($30,000 less $1,760							10
11			income earned for year)							11

1	2020															1
2	Apr.	1	10% Bonds Payable, 2020		150 0 0 0 00									2
3			Bond Sinking Fund Investment					150 0 0 0 00		3
4			Retirement of bonds							4

This illustration assumes that an outside trustee managed the sinking fund investment account and made the necessary entries to record the fund transactions. If the corporation handled the bond sinking fund itself, additional entries would be required to show the investment of the fund's cash, the receipt of earnings, and the payment of fund expenses.

Other procedures may be used to finance the sinking fund investment. For example, an assumption may be made about the rate of earnings of the fund. A constant amount would be contributed each period, which when added to the earnings would equal the required balance. If earnings differ from the rate assumed, the contributions would be adjusted.

The bond sinking fund is reported under the heading "Investments" in the Assets section of the balance sheet. Investments are usually shown before property, plant, and equipment.

>>9. OBJECTIVE

Record an increase or decrease in retained earnings appropriated for bond retirement.

RETAINED EARNINGS APPROPRIATED FOR BOND RETIREMENT

To protect bondholders and to restrict dividends, the bond contract might require that retained earnings are appropriated while the bonds are outstanding. Even if the bond contract does not require an appropriation, retained earnings may be appropriated by order of the board of directors.

MANAGERIAL IMPLICATIONS

RAISING CASH

- A critical management task is to ensure that cash is available to the company when it is needed.
- Managers need to know the advantages and disadvantages of raising cash through the sale of bonds and stock.
- Managers need to have a thorough understanding of bond characteristics, including the differences between registered versus bearer bonds and secured versus debenture bonds. They also need to understand convertible bonds and callable bonds.

- Bond sinking fund investments and the appropriation of retained earnings are tools that management can use to ensure that the funds are available to retire the bonds.
- Call provisions and early retirement of bonds allow for flexible financing and can reduce financing costs.

THINKING CRITICALLY

What factors would you consider in choosing between stock financing and bond financing?

Suppose that the board of directors of Charbo Corporation decided to appropriate $30,000 of retained earnings during each of the last five years the bonds are outstanding. When the bonds are retired, the balance in the appropriated retained earnings account is returned to the *Retained Earnings* account. The *Retained Earnings Appropriated for Bond Retirement* account appears on the balance sheet under the heading "Appropriated Retained Earnings." The following entry shows an annual appropriation of retained earnings. Five such entries would be made. The next entry shows the appropriation being returned to retained earnings after the bonds are retired.

2015					
Apr.	1	Retained Earnings	30 0 0 0 00		
		Retained Earnings Appropriated for			
		Bond Retirement		30 0 0 0 00	
		Annual appropriation			
2020					
Apr.	1	Retained Earnings Appropriated for			
		Bond Retirement	150 0 0 0 00		
		Retained Earnings		150 0 0 0 00	
		Close appropriation account			
		upon retirement of bonds			

important!

Bond Retirement
The fact that retained earnings are appropriated for bond retirement does not mean that a bond retirement fund has been established.

Retirement of Bonds

Bonds payable are usually retired at the maturity date, but some or all of the bonds can be retired prior to that date.

>>10. OBJECTIVE
Record retirement of bonds payable.

RETIREMENT ON DUE DATE

If there had been no bond sinking fund, Charbo Corporation would have recorded the retirement on the maturity date by debiting *10% Bonds Payable, 2020,* and crediting *Cash.*

EARLY RETIREMENT

A corporation may retire bonds early because it has surplus cash, or interest rates have decreased or are expected to decrease. The corporation may purchase the bonds on the open market or, if they are callable, it may require the holders to surrender their bonds for cash.

When bonds are retired prior to maturity, the bondholders are paid the agreed-upon price for the bonds plus the accrued interest to the date of purchase. There are two steps to record the retirement of bonds.

Step 1. *Amortize the discount or premium on the bonds up to the date of retirement.*

Step 2. *Remove the book value, and record the gain or loss.*

     a. Remove the book value of the bonds.
     b. Record interest up to the date of retirement.
     c. Record the cash payment for the repurchase price and interest.
     d. Record the gain or loss (book value minus the repurchase price).

Assume that Charbo Corporation decides to retire (call) the April 1, 2013, issue of $50,000 of bonds that were sold at a discount. Remember that these bonds were sold at 97.76 resulting in a debit to *Discount on Bonds Payable* for $1,120 with seven years remaining before the bonds' due date. The amortization of the discount was taken at $160 per year or $80 each time the bond interest was paid. The company has decided to retire these bonds on April 1, 2014.

important!

Gain or Loss
The gain or loss on the retirement of bonds is the book value of the bonds minus the repurchase price.

On December 31, 2013, after adjusting entries, the related account balances of this bond issue are:

Bonds Payable		$50,000
Discount on Bonds Payable	$1,120	
Amortization of Discount on Bonds Payable through December 31, 2013	120	1,000
Net Carrying Value of Bonds		$49,000

Please remember that Charbo has three bond issues and is retiring only those bonds that were issued at a discount. In this early retirement illustration, let's assume that Charbo does not use reversing entries.

On April 1, 2014, the corporation repurchases and retires the $50,000 of bonds. They are purchased at 101.

Step 1. *Amortize the premium or discount on the bonds up to the date of retirement.* Remember that you previously calculated the amount of amortization of the discount would be $80 each interest payment date. Also recall that on December 31 you made an adjusting entry recording the interest expense and amortization of the discount for three months (or one-half an interest payment period).

GENERAL JOURNAL PAGE _____

	DATE		DESCRIPTION	POST. REF.	DEBIT	CREDIT	
1	2014						1
2	Apr.	1	Bond Interest Expense		40 00		2
3			Discount on Bonds Payable			40 00	3
4			Amortization of discount for three months				4
5			on bonds to be retired				5

Step 2. *Remove the book value of the bonds, and record the gain or loss on the repurchase of the bonds.*

   a. Remove the book value of the bonds:

Bonds being retired	$50,000
Discount on retired bonds ($1,000 − $40)	960
Net book value of bonds	$49,040

   b. Record bond interest expense up to the date of bond retirement.

   $50,000 × 0.10 × 3/12 = $1,250

   Recall that you already recorded three months of interest when you made the adjusting entry on December 31, 2013.

   c. Record the cash payment for the repurchase of the bonds.

   $50,000 × 1.01 = $50,500

   d. Record the gain or loss (net book value of bonds minus repurchase price).

   ($50,000 − $960) − $50,500 = $(1,460) loss

GENERAL JOURNAL   PAGE _____

	DATE		DESCRIPTION	POST. REF.	DEBIT	CREDIT	
1	2014						1
2	Apr.	1	Bond Interest Expense		1 2 5 0 00		2
3			Bond Interest Payable		1 2 5 0 00		3
4			Cash			2 5 0 0 00	4
5							5
6	Apr.	1	Bonds Payable		50 0 0 0 00		6
7			Loss on Early Retirement of Bonds		1 4 6 0 00		7
8			Discount on Bonds Payable			9 6 0 00	8
			Cash			50 5 0 0 00	

A significant gain or loss on early retirement of bonds appears on the income statement as an extraordinary gain or loss. If it is immaterial, it may appear in the Other Income or Other Expense section.

Section 3 Self Review

QUESTIONS

1. What is a bond sinking fund investment?

2. Why would a corporation purchase its own bonds and retire them?

3. How is gain or loss on early retirement of bonds shown on the income statement?

EXERCISES

4. The entry to record income earned by a bond sinking fund investment includes a credit to

a. *Bonds Payable.*

b. *Bond Sinking Fund Investment.*

c. *Income from Sinking Fund Investment.*

d. *Interest Income.*

5. The entry to record retirement of a bond includes a debit to

a. *Discount on Bonds Payable.*

b. *Retained Earnings.*

c. *Bonds Payable.*

d. *Retained Earnings Appropriated for Bond Retirement.*

ANALYSIS

6. What is the entry to record $200,000 of bonds that were retired at maturity? Retained earnings were appropriated for $200,000 for bond retirement. There was no bond sinking fund.

(Answers to Section 3 Self Review are on page 794.)

22 Chapter REVIEW   Chapter Summary

Corporations often use bonds to acquire funds. In this chapter, you have reviewed the types of bonds frequently issued by corporations and have learned how to record a variety of bond transactions.

Learning Objectives

1 Name and define the various types of bonds.

- Bonds may be secured by the pledge of specific assets as security, or they may be unsecured.
- Some bonds are registered; owners are listed in corporation records. Other bonds are bearer bonds with interest coupons attached.
- Convertible bonds can be converted into common stock by the bondholder.
- Callable bonds may be recalled before their maturity date.

2 Explain the advantages and disadvantages of using bonds as a method of financing.

- Businesses that choose to raise capital using bonds may deduct bond interest charges when computing taxable income.
- Bonds payable are debts. The face amount of the bond must be repaid at maturity. Interest must also be paid on the bonds.

3 Record the issuance of bonds.

Bonds may be issued at face value, at a premium, or at a discount.

- If the bond's face interest rate exceeds the market interest rate when the bonds are issued, the bonds are issued at a premium.
- If the market interest rate exceeds the face interest rate on the bonds, the bonds are issued at a discount.

4 Record the payment of interest on bonds.

A bond bears interest that is usually payable annually or semiannually at a specified rate. The amount of interest is calculated and recorded as a debit to *Bond Interest Expense* and a credit to *Cash.*

5 Record the accrual of interest on bonds.

When bond interest dates do not coincide with the fiscal year-end, an adjustment is made for accrued bond interest at the end of the year. The adjustment may be reversed at the beginning of the next year.

6 Compute and record the periodic amortization of a bond premium.

The corporation writes off, or amortizes, a bond premium over the period from the issue date through the maturity date. The amortization is treated as a reduction of interest expense for that period.

7 Compute and record the periodic amortization of a bond discount.

A bond discount is amortized over the period that begins on the date the bonds are issued and ends on the date of maturity. The amortization is treated as an increase to interest expense for that period.

8 Record the transactions of a bond sinking fund investment.

A bond sinking fund accumulates cash to pay the bonds at maturity. The cash in the sinking fund is invested, earning interest to reduce the amount that the corporation will have to add in subsequent years. The establishment of the fund is recorded with a debit to *Bond Sinking Fund Investment* and a credit to *Cash.*

9 Record an increase or decrease in retained earnings appropriated for bond retirement.

An appropriation of retained earnings for bond retirement may be established and increased by debits to *Retained Earnings* and credits to *Retained Earnings Appropriated for Bond Retirement.* An appropriation shows that some retained earnings are not available for dividends; they are needed to pay off the bonds.

10 Record retirement of bonds payable.

Bonds are retired at maturity or, under certain circumstances, retired prior to maturity. The difference between the book value and the repurchase price is a gain or loss on retirement of bonds.

11 Define the accounting terms new to this chapter.

Glossary

Bond indenture (p. 766) A bond contract

Bond issue costs (p. 776) Costs incurred in issuing bonds, such as legal and accounting fees and printing costs

Bond retirement (p. 777) When a bond is paid and the liability is removed from the company's balance sheet

Bond sinking fund investment (p. 777) A fund established to accumulate assets to pay off bonds when they mature

Bonds payable (p. 766) Long-term debt instruments that are written promises to repay the principal at a future date; interest is due at a fixed rate payable over the life of the bond

Call price (p. 767) The amount the corporation must pay for the bond when it is called

Callable bonds (p. 767) Bonds that allow the issuing corporation to require the holder to surrender the bonds for payment before their maturity date

Carrying value of bonds (p. 775) The balance of the *Bonds Payable* account plus the *Premium on Bonds Payable* account minus the *Discount on Bonds Payable* account; also called *book value of bonds*

Collateral trust bonds (p. 766) Bonds secured by the pledge of securities, such as stocks or bonds of other companies

Convertible bonds (p. 767) Bonds that give the owner the right to convert the bonds into common stock under specified conditions

Coupon bonds (p. 767) Unregistered bonds that have coupons attached for each interest payment; also called *bearer bonds*

Debentures (p. 767) Unsecured bonds backed only by a corporation's general credit

Discount on bonds payable (p. 774) The excess of the face value over the price received by the corporation for a bond

Face interest rate (p. 767) The contractual interest specified on the bond

Leveraging (p. 769) Using borrowed funds to earn a profit greater than the interest that must be paid on the borrowing

Market interest rate (p. 767) The interest rate a corporation is willing to pay and investors are willing to accept at the current time

Mortgage loan (p. 766) A long-term debt created when a note is given as part of the purchase price for land or buildings

Premium on bonds payable (p. 773) The excess of the price paid over the face value of a bond

Registered bonds (p. 767) Bonds issued to a party whose name is listed in the corporation's records

Secured bonds (p. 766) Bonds for which property is pledged to secure the claims of bondholders

Serial bonds (p. 767) Bonds issued at one time but payable over a period of years

Straight-line amortization (p. 773) Amortizing the premium or discount on bonds payable in equal amounts over the life of the bond

Trading on the equity (p. 769) See Leveraging

Comprehensive Self Review

1. Generally, would an investor want secured bonds or debenture bonds? Why?
2. Name two disadvantages of raising capital through the issue of bonds payable rather than through the issue of preferred stock.
3. What factor or factors would cause bonds to be sold at a premium?

   4. Why does a corporation use an account such as *Appropriation of Retained Earnings* for bond retirement?

   5. What entry, or entries, will be made when bonds are retired at maturity?

(Answers to Comprehensive Self Review are on page 794.)

Multiple choice questions are provided on the text Web site at www.mhhe.com/price12e

Quiz22

Discussion Questions

   1. What is a collateral trust bond?

   2. What is a bond indenture?

   3. How is the *Bonds Payable* account classified on the balance sheet?

   4. Are authorized, unissued bonds shown on the balance sheet? If so, where?

   5. Why might a company use a special bank account for paying bond interest?

   6. In a bond indenture dated January 1, 2010, Blue Corporation authorized the issuance of $500,000 face value, 10 percent, 20-year bonds payable. No bonds were issued until July 1, 2011, when bonds with a face value of $200,000 were issued. At that time, the market rate of interest on similar debt was 9 percent. Would the issue price of the bonds be more than or less than face value? Explain.

   7. Why is a bond premium or discount amortized as part of the adjustment process at the end of the year?

   8. Why is the year-end adjusting entry for amortization of a bond premium or discount reversed at the start of the new year?

   9. How are the legal costs and other costs related to issuing bonds accounted for?

   10. What is a bond sinking fund?

   11. What is the relationship between a bond sinking fund and an appropriation of retained earnings for bond retirement? Explain.

   12. Explain the accounting treatment necessary when bonds are retired before maturity.

APPLICATIONS

Exercises

Exercises 22.1 through 22.3. Alpha Corporation issued $300,000 of its 9 percent bonds payable on April 1, 2010. The bonds were issued at face value. Interest is payable semiannually on October 1 and April 1.

Exercise 22.1
Objective 3
▶ **Issuing bonds.**
Give the general journal entry to record the April 1, 2010, bond issue.

Exercise 22.2
Objective 4
▶ **Paying interest on bonds payable.**
Give the entry in general journal form to record the interest payment by Alpha on October 1, 2010.

Exercise 22.3
Objective 5
▶ **Accruing interest on bonds.**
Give the entry to accrue bond interest on Alpha's bonds payable on December 31, 2010.

Exercises 22.4 through 22.6. Angel Inc. was authorized to issue $1,000,000 of 10 percent bonds. On April 1, 2010, the corporation issued bonds with a face value of $100,000 at a price of 102.2. The bonds mature 10 years from the date of issue. Interest is payable semiannually on October 1 and April 1.

Recording issuance of bonds.

Give the general journal entry to record the April 1, 2010, bond issue.

◀ **Exercise 22.4**
Objective 3

Computing amortization of premium on bonds.

Using the data given above, what amount of premium will be amortized by Angel Inc. on October 1, 2010, using straight-line amortization?

◀ **Exercise 22.5**
Objective 6

Recording adjusting entry for bond interest and premium.

Using the data given above, give the adjusting entry that would be made by Angel Inc. on December 31, 2010, to record accrued interest and to amortize the premium.

◀ **Exercise 22.6**
Objectives 5, 6

Recording transactions of a bond sinking fund investment.

Give the general journal entries to record the following transactions.

◀ **Exercise 22.7**
Objective 8

a. On December 31, 2009, Red Trucking Company established a bond sinking fund investment by depositing $20,000 with the fund trustee.

b. On December 31, 2010, Red Trucking Company recorded $1,800 net income from its bond sinking fund investment for the year.

c. On December 31, 2010, Red Trucking Company made a deposit of $18,200 into the bond sinking fund investment.

Appropriating retained earnings for bond retirement.

Record the appropriation of $75,000 of retained earnings on December 31, 2010, by Jack Inc. to establish an appropriation for bond retirement.

◀ **Exercise 22.8**
Objective 9

Retiring bonds before maturity.

On April 1, 2010, Chuck's Deli issued $60,000 of its 8 percent bonds, maturing 10 years later. Interest is payable semiannually on April 1 and October 1. The issue price was 92.0. Chuck's has decided to retire the bonds on August 1, 2013, three years and four months after the bonds were initially issued. The bonds were repurchased at 97. After recording the accrued interest expense payable through August 1, 2013, the balance in the Discount on Bonds Payable account is $3,200. Give the general journal entry to record the repurchase and retirement of the bonds.

◀ **Exercise 22.9**
Objective 10

PROBLEMS

Problem Set A

Issuing bonds; bond interest transactions.

The board of directors of Misty Services Inc. authorized the issuance of $500,000 face value, 20-year, 9 percent bonds dated March 1, 2010, and maturing on March 1, 2030. Interest is payable semiannually on March 1 and September 1. Misty uses the calendar year as its fiscal year. The bond transactions that occurred in 2010 and 2011 follow.

◀ **Problem 22.1A**
Objectives 3, 4, 5

DATE		TRANSACTIONS FOR 2010
Mar.	1	Issued $200,000 of bonds at face value.
Sept.	1	Paid the semiannual interest on the bonds issued.
Dec.	31	Recorded the adjusting entry for the accrued bond interest.
	31	Closed the **Bond Interest Expense** account to the **Income Summary** account.

DATE		TRANSACTIONS FOR 2011
Jan.	1	Reversed the adjusting entry made on December 31, 2010.
Mar.	1	Issued $200,000 of bonds at face value.
	1	Paid the interest for six months on the bonds previously issued.
Sept.	1	Paid the interest for six months on the outstanding bonds.
Dec.	31	Recorded the adjusting entry for the accrued bond interest.
	31	Closed the **Bond Interest Expense** account to the **Income Summary** account.

INSTRUCTIONS

Record the transactions in general journal form. Use the account names given in the chapter. Round to nearest dollar.

Analyze: Based on the transactions given, what is the balance in the **Bonds Payable** account on December 31, 2010?

Problem 22.2A ▶
Objectives 3, 4, 5, 6

Issuing bonds; recording interest transactions and amortization of premium.

The board of directors of Carolina Motor Shops, Inc., authorized the issuance of $1,000,000 face value, 10-year, 10 percent bonds dated April 1, 2010, and maturing on April 1, 2020. Interest is payable semiannually on April 1 and October 1.

INSTRUCTIONS

1. Record the transactions below in general journal form. Use the account names given in the chapter.
2. Prepare the Long-Term Liabilities section of the corporation's balance sheet on December 31, 2010.

DATE		TRANSACTIONS FOR 2010
Apr.	1	Issued $400,000 face value bonds at 101.2.
Oct.	1	Paid the semiannual interest on the outstanding bonds and amortized the bond premium. (Make two entries. Use the straight-line method to compute the amortization.)
Dec.	31	Recorded the adjusting entry for accrued interest and amortization of the bond premium for three months. (Make one entry.)
	31	Closed the **Bond Interest Expense** account to the **Income Summary** account.

DATE		TRANSACTIONS FOR 2011
Jan.	1	Reversed the adjusting entry made on December 31, 2010.

Analyze: If the reversing entry was not recorded, what entry would be required when the interest expense is paid in April 2011?

Problem 22.3A ▶
Objectives 3, 4, 5, 7

Issuing bonds; bond interest transactions and amortization of discount.

The board of directors of Baylor, LLC, authorized the issuance of $500,000 face value, 20-year, 8 percent bonds, dated March 1, 2010, and maturing on March 1, 2030. Interest is payable semiannually on September 1 and March 1.

INSTRUCTIONS

1. Record the following transactions in general journal form. Use the account names given in the chapter. (Round to nearest dollar.)

2. Prepare the Long-Term Liabilities section of the corporation's balance sheet on December 31, 2010.

DATE		TRANSACTIONS FOR 2010
Apr.	1	Issued bonds with a face value of $200,000 at 95.22 plus accrued interest from March 1. (When bonds are issued between interest payment dates, the accrued interest is paid to the corporation by the purchaser. Credit **Bond Interest Expense.**)
Sept.	1	Paid the semiannual bond interest and amortized the discount for five months. (Make two entries. Use the straight-line method to compute the amortization.)
Dec.	31	Recorded an adjusting entry to accrue the interest and to amortize the discount. (Make one entry.)
	31	Closed the **Bond Interest Expense** account to the **Income Summary** account.

DATE		TRANSACTIONS FOR 2011
Jan.	1	Reversed the adjusting entry made on December 31, 2010.
Mar.	1	Paid the semiannual bond interest and amortized the discount on the outstanding bonds.

Analyze: What is the balance of the *Discount on Bonds Payable* account on December 31, 2010?

Recording bond sinking fund transactions, retained earnings appropriated for bond retirement, and retirement of bonds.

◀ **Problem 22.4A**
Objectives 8, 9, 10

New Computer Technology, Inc., has outstanding $400,000 of its 10 percent bonds payable, dated January 1, 2010, and maturing on January 1, 2030, 20 years later. The corporation is required under the bond contract to transfer $20,000 to a sinking fund each year. The directors have also voted to restrict retained earnings by transferring $20,000 each year on January 1 over the life of the bond issue to a *Retained Earnings Appropriated for Bond Retirement* account.

INSTRUCTIONS

1. Prepare entries in general journal form to record the January 1, 2010, issuance of bonds at face value, the establishment of the *Bond Sinking Fund Investment* account, and the appropriation of retained earnings.

2. Show how the *Bond Sinking Fund Investment* account and the *Retained Earnings Appropriated for Bond Retirement* account would be presented on the balance sheet as of December 31, 2014. (Assume that the ending balance of the *Bond Sinking Fund Investment* was $100,000 and the *Retained Earnings—Unappropriated* account was $310,210.)

3. Assuming that the *Bond Sinking Fund Investment* account had a balance of $400,000 on January 1, 2030, give the entry in general journal form to record the retirement of the bonds and remove the appropriation for retained earnings.

Analyze: What percentage of total retained earnings has been appropriated for bond retirement on December 31, 2014?

Problem 22.5A ▶
Objective 10

Retiring bonds payable prior to maturity.

On May 1, 2010, Big Star Corporation issued $500,000 face value, 9 percent bonds at 98.68. The bonds are dated May 1, 2010, and mature 10 years later. The discount is amortized on each interest payment date. The interest is payable semiannually on May 1 and November 1. On May 1, 2012, after paying the semiannual interest, the corporation purchased the outstanding bonds from the bondholders and retired them. The purchase price was 99.

INSTRUCTION

Give the entry in general journal form to record the repurchase and retirement of the bonds. (Use the *Loss on Early Retirement of Bonds* account.)

Analyze: If Big Star Corporation did not purchase the outstanding bonds, what total bond interest expense would have been incurred over the life of the bond?

Problem Set B

Problem 22.1B ▶
Objectives 3, 4, 5

Issuing bonds; bond interest transactions.

The board of directors of Eastern Products, Inc., authorized the issuance of $1,000,000 face value, 10 percent bonds dated April 1, 2010. The bonds will mature on April 1, 2020. The interest is payable semiannually on April 1 and October 1. The bond transactions that occurred in 2010 and 2011 are shown below.

INSTRUCTIONS

Record the transactions below in general journal form. Use the account names given in the chapter.

DATE		TRANSACTIONS FOR 2010
April	1	Issued $500,000 of bonds at face value.
Oct.	1	Paid the semiannual bond interest on the outstanding bonds.
Dec.	31	Recorded the adjusting entry to accrue the interest on the bonds issued.
	31	Closed the **Bond Interest Expense** account to the **Income Summary** account.

DATE		TRANSACTIONS FOR 2011
Jan.	1	Reversed the adjusting entry of December 31, 2010.
April	1	Paid the semiannual bond interest.
Oct.	1	Paid the semiannual bond interest.
	1	Issued $200,000 of bonds at face value.
Dec.	31	Recorded the adjusting entry to accrue the interest on all bonds issued.
	31	Closed the **Bond Interest Expense** account to the **Income Summary** account.

Analyze: What total bond interest would have been reported on the income statement for the year ended December 31, 2010?

Problem 22.2B ▶
Objectives 3, 4, 5

Issuing bonds; recording interest transactions and amortization of premium.

The board of directors of Roma Company authorized issuance of $1,000,000 of 8 percent bonds. Each bond has a face value of $10,000. The interest is payable semiannually on February 1 and August 1. The bonds are dated February 1, 2010, and mature 10 years later.

INSTRUCTIONS

1. Record the transactions below in general journal form. Use the account names given in the chapter. (Round your numbers to the nearest whole dollar.)

2. Prepare the Long-Term Liabilities section of the corporation's balance sheet on December 31, 2010.

DATE		TRANSACTIONS FOR 2010
Feb.	1	Issued $500,000 of bonds at 103.
Aug.	1	Paid the semiannual interest on the bonds issued and recorded the amortization of the premium.
Dec.	31	Recorded the adjusting entry to accrue interest on the bonds issued and to amortize the premium for five months.
	31	Recorded the closing entry for **Bond Interest Expense.**

DATE		TRANSACTIONS FOR 2011
Jan.	1	Reversed the adjusting entry of December 31, 2010.

Analyze: If the reversing entry had not been recorded in January 2011, how would the payment of bond interest be recorded in February 2011?

Issuing bonds; bond interest transactions and amortization of discount.

◀ **Problem 22.3B**
Objectives 3, 4, 5, 7

The board of directors of CAH Corporation authorized the issuance of $500,000 face value, 9 percent bonds. The bonds mature 10 years from their issue date of March 1, 2010. The interest is payable semiannually on March 1 and September 1. Because the funds were not immediately needed, no bonds were issued until August 1, 2010.

DATE		TRANSACTIONS FOR 2010
August	1	Issued $250,000 of bonds at 94.94 plus accrued interest from March 1. (When bonds are issued between interest payment dates, the accrued interest is paid to the corporation by the purchaser. Credit **Bond Interest Expense.**)
Sept.	1	Paid the semiannual bond interest.
	1	Amortized the discount on the bonds issued.
Dec.	31	Recorded the adjusting entry to accrue the interest on the bonds issued and to amortize the discount for four months. (Make one entry.)
	31	Closed the **Bond Interest Expense** account.

DATE		TRANSACTIONS FOR 2011
Jan.	1	Reversed the adjusting entry of December 31, 2010.
Mar.	1	Paid the semiannual bond interest and amortized the discount on the bonds issued.

INSTRUCTIONS

1. Record the following transactions in general journal form. Use the account names given in the chapter.

2. Prepare the Long-Term Liabilities section of the corporation's balance sheet on December 31, 2010.

Analyze: What is the balance of the **Bond Interest Expense** account at December 31, 2010, prior to closing?

Problem 22.4B ▶ **Recording bond sinking fund transactions, retained earnings appropriated for bond retirement, and retirement of bonds.**

Objectives 8, 9, 10

Mine Research, Inc., has outstanding $200,000 face value, 10 percent bonds payable dated January 1, 2010, and maturing 10 years later. The corporation is required under the bond contract to transfer $18,000 each year to a sinking fund. The directors have also voted to restrict retained earnings by transferring $20,000 each year to a **Retained Earnings Appropriated for Bond Retirement** account.

INSTRUCTIONS

1. Prepare entries in general journal form to record the 2010 transactions.

2. Prepare the partial balance sheet for December 31, 2019, showing the presentation of the **Bond Sinking Fund Investment** and the **Retained Earnings Appropriated for Bond Retirement** (assume **Retained Earnings—Unappropriated** has a balance of $325,000).

3. Prepare the journal entries to retire the bonds and remove the appropriation of retained earnings on January 1, 2020.

DATE		TRANSACTIONS FOR 2010
Jan.	1	Sold the bonds at 100.
	1	Made the annual bond sinking fund investment deposit.
	31	Recorded the annual appropriation of retained earnings.
Dec.	31	The bond sinking fund trustee reported a net income of $1,200 on the sinking fund investments for the year.

On December 31, 2019, the balance in the **Bond Sinking Fund Investment** account is $200,000. The balance in the **Retained Earnings Appropriated for Bond Retirement** account is also $200,000.

Analyze: What percentage of total retained earnings had been allocated for bond retirement at December 31, 2019?

Problem 22.5B ▶ **Retiring bonds payable prior to maturity.**

Objective 10

On April 1, 2010, Big Spring Corporation issued $400,000 face value, 10 percent bonds at 99.16. The bonds were dated April 1, 2010, and will mature in 10 years. The discount is to be amortized on each interest payment date. The interest is payable semiannually on April 1 and October 1. On October 1, 2013, after paying the semiannual bond interest, the corporation decided to retire the bonds. The bondholders were paid 98.5.

INSTRUCTION

Give the entry in general journal form to record the repurchase and retirement of the bonds. (Use the **Gain on Early Retirement of Bonds** account.)

Analyze: If the bond had been retired on the original due date, what credit would have been made to the **Cash** account?

Critical Thinking Problem 22.1

Financing Decision

On December 31, 2010, the equity accounts of Business Solutions, Inc., contained the following balances.

Common stock ($5 par, 100,000 shares authorized)	
50,000 shares issued and outstanding	250,000
Retained earnings	500,000

For the year 2010, the corporation had net income before income taxes of $200,000, income taxes of $70,000, and net income after taxes of $130,000. The corporation's tax rate is 35 percent.

An expansion of the existing plant at a cost of $500,000 is planned. The corporation's president, who owns 60 percent of the corporation's common stock, estimates that the expansion would result in an increased net income of approximately $200,000 before interest and taxes. The financial vice president forecasts that the increase would be only $100,000.

Management is considering two possibilities for financing:

a. Issuance of 20,000 additional shares of common stock for $25 per share

b. Issuance of $500,000 face amount, 10-year, 10 percent bonds payable, secured by a mortgage lien on the plant

Assume that profits from existing operations will remain the same.

INSTRUCTIONS

1. Assume that the president's estimate of net income from the new plant is correct. Prepare a two-column table for each of the proposed financing plans. Show the following items: (a) total net income before interest and tax; (b) total bond interest; (c) total income tax; (d) total income after tax; (e) present income after tax; (f) increase or decrease in total income after bond interest and tax; (g) present earnings per share of common stock (compute earnings per share by dividing the net income after taxes by the number of shares of common stock outstanding); (h) estimated earnings per share of common stock.

2. Construct a similar table, assuming the financial vice president's estimate of earnings is correct.

3. Write a brief comment on the results of your analysis.

Analyze: Assume the company issued 20,000 shares of common stock and net income before taxes was $350,000. Would shareholders have realized an increase or decrease in earnings per share over fiscal 2010?

Critical Thinking Problem 22.2

Early Retirement

On December 31, 2010, Orange Express, Inc., has $1,000,000 of 10 percent, 15-year bonds outstanding. These bonds were issued on January 1, 2004, at par value. Interest rates have dropped to 8 percent, and the president of the company is considering buying back the outstanding 10 percent bonds and issuing new 10-year bonds with an 8 percent interest rate.

1. How much money would Orange Express save in interest payments if new, 8 percent bonds were issued?

2. Under what circumstances would this action be advantageous for Orange Express?

BUSINESS CONNECTIONS

Financing Through Bonds

1. What would cause corporate management to obtain cash by issuing bonds instead of selling stock?

2. Which type of bonds would give management greater flexibility in formulating and controlling a corporation's financial affairs?

3. In what situations would management be wise to issue additional common stock rather than bonds to meet long-term capital needs?

4. Why would management repurchase and retire a corporation's bonds prior to their maturity?

5. Cook Corporation's board of directors is considering authorization of a new bond issue. The controller notes that the bonds are callable at 101.6 at any time beginning five years after the date of the bond contract. What does this mean? What is the advantage of such a provision?

Conflict of Interest

Lawrence Keen is the president of the Safe Water Filter Company. As president, he is in control of the issuance of stocks and bonds. Three years ago when the company needed cash, Lawrence purchased from the company a $100,000, 4 percent, 10-year unsecured bond. The interest rate has begun to increase. Lawrence suggests that the company refinance the bonds to extend the life of the bonds, even though the interest rate has increased to 7 percent. Is this a conflict of interest? Why or why not?

Long-Term Debt

Refer to The Home Depot, Inc., *2006 Annual Report* in Appendix A.

1. Locate the notes to consolidated financial statements. Note 4 presents a detailed list of the company's debt at the end of fiscal 2006 and 2005. What amount of long-term debt is in the form of 4.625 percent Senior Notes?

2. Read Note 4. What was the amount of the discount associated with issuing the 4.625 percent Senior Notes?

Bond Financing Agreements

The following schedule was prepared from data contained in the *2006 Annual Report* for UPS Corporation. The company reported $3,133 million in long-term debt at December 31, 2006.

Note 8: Long-Term Debt and Commitments

In millions	2006	2005
8.38% debentures, due 2020	446	457
8.38% debentures, due 2030	285	293
Special facilities revenue bonds, variable interest rate, due 2029 and 2036	437	397
	$1,168	$1,147

Analyze:

1. What semiannual interest payments would be due to holders of the 8.38 percent debenture bonds, due 2030, each year until maturity?

2. What percentage of total long-term debt do these bonds represent?

Analyze Online: On the UPS Web site (www.ups.com), click on *UPS Corporate,* then go to the *Investor Relations* section and click on the *Annual Report* link.

3. What total long-term debt does the most recent annual report show?

4. What portion of long-term debt is composed of 8.38 percent debentures due in 2030?

Investing in Callable Bonds

Extending THE THOUGHT

Some bonds, especially those issued by utility agencies, can be called under *maintenance and replacement* fund provisions that relate to necessary upgrades of plant and equipment. As a bond investor, you might be quoted a *yield to maturity,* the total return you will receive if you hold a bond until maturity. Yield to maturity includes all interest you will earn plus any gain or loss realized if you bought the bond below or above par. What do you think a *yield to call* is? Explain.

Memo

Business COMMUNICATION

The board of directors of Hashimoto Nurseries, Inc., is currently reviewing the most recent financial statements. As the chief financial officer, you are responsible for ensuring that the board understands the statements. A board member assumes that since a bond sinking fund has been established, there is no need to appropriate retained earnings for bonds payable. Prepare a memo to the board explaining why retained earnings have been appropriated for bond retirement.

Sell Stocks or Bonds

TEAMWORK

Nowhere Man Corporation is a corporate dance studio. It is a popular investment with investors between the ages of 20 and 30. Nowhere Man has a dilemma. It needs money to expand its business to cash in on its popularity. However, management is not sure whether to sell stock in the company or to sell corporate bonds. Nowhere Man has $100,000 in liabilities and 1,000,000 authorized shares of common stock of which 100,000 shares are issued. It has a bid of $1,000,000 to build the additional location. Each group of students represents the board of directors. Discuss whether the company should sell stock or bonds. What price would it need to get for each share? How much should it sell in bonds? What bond characteristics would be the best for the company?

Know Thy Bonds!

Internet CONNECTION

Educating yourself in the various bonds is important before investing in bonds. Use your favorite search engine to find Web sites that have tutorials about bonds. Find the bond in which you are interested. It could be convertible bonds, junk bonds, Treasury notes (STRIPS), or zero coupon bonds. Define your favorite type and find the current market value.

Answers to **Self Reviews**

Answers to Section 1 Self Review

1. In the event of a decrease in the market interest rate, or if the corporation has extra cash, the corporation can redeem the bonds if they are callable.

2. A convertible bond is one that may be converted into common stock, under specified conditions, at the option of the owner.

3. Registered bonds are bonds whose owners are registered in the records of the corporation. Interest is paid each payment date to the registered owner. Coupon bonds are not registered. The corporation does not know the names of owners of the bonds. To collect interest, the bondholder clips a coupon from the bond and presents it to the bank.

4. **d.** debentures.

5. **b.** serial bonds.

6. 15.2% ($38,000 ÷ 250,000)

Answers to Section 2 Self Review

1. Discount on bonds payable is shown on the balance sheet as a deduction from the face value of the bonds.

2. An equal amount of discount or premium is amortized each month from the issue date to the maturity date.

3. Bond premium is a device to adjust the face amount of interest to the market interest rate at the date of issuance. Thus, the premium is directly related to interest expense.

4. **b.** credit to *Bonds Payable.*

5. **b.** amortized over the life of the bond issue.

6. $100 ($2,000/10 yrs. = $200/yr. or $100 per payment date)

Answers to Section 3 Self Review

1. A fund used to accumulate assets to pay off bonds when they mature.

2. Bonds may be retired prior to maturity because management has surplus cash, it wants to save interest costs, or it expects interest costs to decrease.

3. Gain or loss on bond retirement is shown as an extraordinary item if the amount is significant. Otherwise, it is shown as *Other Income* or *Other Expense.*

4. **c.** *Income from Sinking Fund Investment.*

5. **c.** *Bonds Payable.*

6. Debit *Retained Earnings Appropriated for Bond Retirement* for $200,000; credit *Retained Earnings* for $200,000. Debit *Bonds Payable* for $200,000 and credit *Cash* for $200,000.

Answers to Comprehensive Self Review

1. Secured bonds are bonds that have specific assets pledged as security. If the corporation does not pay the principal and interest, the bondholders may take possession of the assets. Debenture bonds have no specific assets pledged to secure payment. So, the secured bond is a more attractive investment.

2. Two disadvantages are (a) interest must be paid and (b) the face amount must be repaid at maturity.

3. Bonds sell at a premium when the face interest rate is greater than the market rate of interest on similar investments on the date of the sale.

4. The appropriation is intended to protect the bondholders. It clearly indicates that dividends are being restricted because of a future need to pay off the bonds.

5. When bonds are retired at maturity, *Bonds Payable* is debited and *Cash* (or *Bond Sinking Fund Investment*) is credited. If the company has *Retained Earnings Appropriated* for the bonds, that account should be closed and returned to *Retained Earnings Unappropriated.*

Mini-Practice Set 3

Corporation Accounting Cycle

The Lincoln Company

This project will give you an opportunity to apply your knowledge of accounting principles and pro-cedures to a corporation. You will handle the accounting work of The Lincoln Company for 2010.

The chart of accounts and account balances of The Lincoln Company on January 1, 2010, are shown on the next page. Lincoln *does not* use reversing entries.

INTRODUCTION

Round all computations to the nearest whole dollar.

INSTRUCTIONS

1. Open the general ledger accounts and enter the balances for January 1, 2010. Obtain the necessary figures from the chart of accounts.

2. Analyze the transactions on the pages that follow, and record them in the general journal. Use 1 as the number of the first journal page.

3. Post the journal entries to the general ledger accounts.

4. Prepare a worksheet for the year ended December 31, 2010.

5. Prepare a summary income statement for the year ended December 31, 2010.

6. Prepare a statement of retained earnings for the year ended December 31, 2010.

7. Prepare a balance sheet as of December 31, 2010.

8. Journalize and post the adjusting entries as of December 31, 2010.

9. Journalize and post the closing entries as of December 31, 2010.

Analyze: Assume that the firm declared and issued a 3:1 stock split of common stock in 2010. What is the effect on total par value?

The Lincoln Company
Chart of Accounts/Account Balances on January 1, 2010

Account Number	Account Name	Debit	Credit
101	Cash	$176,000	
103	Accounts Receivable	170,000	
104	Allowance for Doubtful Accounts		$5,000
105	Subscriptions Receivable—Common Stock		
121	Interest Receivable		
131	Merchandise Inventory	150,000	
141	Land	85,000	
151	Buildings	225,000	
152	Accumulated Depreciation—Buildings		22,500
161	Furniture and Equipment	70,000	
162	Accumulated Depreciation—Furniture and Equipment		14,000
181	Organization Costs	6,000	
202	Accounts Payable		75,000
203	Interest Payable		2,500
205	Estimated Income Taxes Payable		17,000
206	Dividends Payable—Preferred Stock		
207	Dividends Payable—Common Stock		
211	10-year, 10% Bonds Payable		100,000
212	Premium on Bonds Payable		2,625
301	8% Preferred Stock ($100 par, 10,000 shares authorized)		100,000
302	Paid-In Capital in Excess of Par—Preferred Stock		10,000
303	Common Stock ($10 par, 100,000 shares authorized)		200,000
304	Paid in Capital in Excess of Par—Common Stock		25,000
305	Common Stock Subscribed		
306	Common Stock Dividend Distributable		
311	Retained Earnings Appropriated		100,000
312	Retained Earnings Unappropriated		208,375
343	Treasury Stock—Preferred		
399	Income Summary		
401	Sales		
501	Purchases		
601	Operating Expenses		
701	Interest Income		
711	Gain on Early Retirement of Bonds Payable		
751	Interest Expense		
753	Amortization of Organization Costs		
801	Income Tax Expense		
	Totals	$882,000	$882,000

DATE	TRANSACTIONS FOR 2010
Jan. 5	Issued 1,000 shares of 8 percent $100 par preferred stock for $102 per share. (The corporation has been authorized to issue 10,000 shares of preferred stock.)
15	Paid estimated income taxes of $17,000 accrued at the end of 2009.
Apr. 1	Paid semiannual bond interest on the 10-year, 10 percent bonds payable and amortized the premium for the period since December 31, 2009. (The interest and premium were recorded as of December 31, 2009; the entry was not reversed.) The bonds were issued on October 1, 2008, at a price of 103, and they mature on October 1, 2018. Use straight-line amortization.
July 1	The Lincoln Company's board of directors declared a cash dividend of $0.20 per share on the common stock. The dividend is payable on July 26 to stockholders of record as of July 15.
26	Paid the cash dividend on the common stock.
Aug. 12	A purchaser of 600 shares of preferred stock issued on January 5 asked the corporation to repurchase the shares. The corporation repurchased the stock for $103 per share. The stock is to be held by the corporation until it can be resold to another purchaser.
Oct. 1	Paid the semiannual bond interest and recorded amortization of the bond premium.
Dec. 1	Because of its good cash position and current bond prices, The Lincoln Company repurchased and retired $20,000 par value of the 10 percent bonds that it has outstanding. The repurchase price was 98, plus accrued interest.
15	Lincoln's board of directors declared a cash dividend of $8 per share on the outstanding preferred stock. This dividend is payable on January 10 to stockholders of record as of December 31.
15	Lincoln's board of directors also declared a 10 percent stock dividend on the outstanding common stock. The new shares are to be distributed on January 10 to stockholders of record as of December 31. At the time the dividend was declared, the common stock had a fair market value of $15 per share.
30	Received a subscription for 500 shares of The Lincoln Company's common stock at $15 per share from the company's president. Received cash equal to one-half the purchase price on the date of subscription. The balance of the purchase price is to be paid on January 15, 2011. (The subscriber will not be entitled to the stock dividend previously declared on the outstanding shares of common stock.)
Dec. 30	Because the management of Lincoln foresees the need to expand a warehouse the firm owns, the board of directors has restricted future dividend payments. Record the appropriation of $75,000 of retained earnings for plant expansion.

Journalize the following summary transactions using December 31, 2010, as the record date.

	SUMMARY OPERATING TRANSACTIONS FOR 2010
1.	Total sales of merchandise for the year were $2,750,000. All sales were on credit.
2.	Total collections on accounts receivable during the year were $2,675,000.
3.	Total purchases of merchandise for the year were $1,750,000. All purchases were on credit.
4.	Total operating expenses incurred during the year were $650,000. (Debit *Operating Expenses* and credit *Accounts Payable.*)
5.	Total cash payments on accounts payable during the year were $2,415,000.
6.	Total accounts receivable charged off as uncollectible during the year were $10,000. (The Lincoln Company uses the allowance method to record uncollectible accounts.)

Data for Year-End Adjustments

1. The balance of *Allowance for Doubtful Accounts* should be adjusted to equal 3 percent of the balance of *Accounts Receivable.* (Debit *Operating Expenses.*)

2. Depreciation on the buildings should be recorded. (Debit *Operating Expenses.*) The firm uses the straight-line method and an estimated life of 20 years to compute this adjustment.

3. Depreciation on furniture and equipment should be recorded. The firm uses the straight-line method and an estimated life of 10 years to compute this adjustment. (Debit *Operating Expenses.*)

4. Accrued interest on the outstanding bonds payable of The Lincoln Company should be recorded and the premium amortized.

5. The amortization of organization costs for the year should be recorded. The Lincoln Company was formed on January 1, 2008. Organization costs of $10,000 were incurred at the time and are being amortized over a 60-month period.

6. The ending merchandise inventory is $165,000.

Other Data

Estimated federal income taxes are to be recorded using the tax rates given on page 724.

Financial Statement Analysis   Chapter **23**

LEARNING OBJECTIVES

1. Use vertical analysis techniques to analyze a comparative income statement and balance sheet.   LP23

2. Use horizontal analysis techniques to analyze a comparative income statement and balance sheet.

3. Use trend analysis to evaluate financial statements.

4. Interpret the results of the statement analyses by comparison with industry averages.

5. Compute and interpret financial ratios that measure profitability, operating results, and efficiency.

6. Compute and interpret financial ratios that measure financial strength.

7. Compute and interpret financial ratios that measure liquidity.

8. Recognize shortcomings in financial statement analysis.

9. Define the accounting terms new to this chapter.

NEW TERMS

accounts receivable turnover
acid-test ratio
asset turnover
average collection period
common-size statements
comparative statements
current ratio
horizontal analysis
industry averages
leveraged buyout

liquidity
price-earnings ratio
quick assets
ratio analysis
return on common stockholders' equity
total equities
trend analysis
vertical analysis
working capital

The Walt Disney Company   www.disney.com

Disney is more than just a magical home to Mickey and Minnie. Since its founding in 1923, The Walt Disney Company has focused on producing unparalleled entertainment experiences based on the rich legacy of quality creative content and exceptional storytelling. Along with Mickey and Minnie, The Disney Company houses cruise ships, theme parks, resort hotels, television stations, and retail stores.

Disney's Media Networks, Studio Entertainment, Parks and Resorts, and Consumer Products Divisions resulted in a total net income of $4.7 billion in 2007, record earnings for the company. The company's plans for the future focus on maximizing earnings and allocating capital to growth areas in order to increase long-term shareholder value.

thinking critically

What financial ratios are most important to Disney shareholders?

Section 1

SECTION OBJECTIVES

>> 1. Use vertical analysis techniques to analyze a comparative income statement and balance sheet.

WHY IT'S IMPORTANT

Analysis techniques reveal the financial strengths and weaknesses of a business.

TERMS TO LEARN

common-size statements
comparative statements
horizontal analysis
ratio analysis
vertical analysis

Vertical Analysis

Owners, managers, creditors, and other parties use financial statements to gather the information needed to make business decisions.

The Phases of Statement Analysis

The two phases of financial statement analysis are (1) compute differences, percentages, and ratios; and (2) interpret the results.

THE COMPUTATION PHASE

The first step in financial statement analysis is the *computation phase.* Three basic types of calculations are used:

■ **Vertical analysis** is the relationship of each item on a financial statement to some base amount on the statement. On the income statement, each item is expressed as a percentage of net sales. On the balance sheet, each item is expressed as a percentage of total assets or total liabilities and stockholders' equity.

■ **Horizontal analysis** is the percentage change for individual items in the financial statements from year to year.

■ **Ratio analysis** is the relationship between various items in the financial statements. Ratio analysis can involve items on the same statement or items on different statements.

THE INTERPRETATION PHASE

The second step in statement analysis, the *interpretation phase,* is the more difficult and important step. Financial statement interpretation requires an understanding of financial statements and knowledge of the operations of the business and the industry. In the interpretation phase, the analyst develops an understanding of the significance of the percentages and ratios computed. Analysts compare the ratios for the current year to prior years' ratios, budgeted ratios, and industry averages.

>>1. OBJECTIVE
Use vertical analysis techniques to analyze a comparative income statement and balance sheet.

Vertical Analysis of Financial Statements

Let's learn the techniques of vertical analysis of financial statements using comparative financial statements. **Comparative statements** are financial statements presented side by side for two or more years. Figure 23.1 on page 801 shows the comparative income statement of Household Products, Inc., for the years 2009 and 2010.

Household Products, Inc.
Comparative Income Statement (Vertical Analysis)
Years Ended December 31, 2010 and 2009

	Amounts		Percent of Net Sales*	
	2010	2009	2010	2009
Revenue				
Sales	3 1 0 4 4 5 0	2 8 2 5 6 2 5	104.6	104.7
Less Sales Returns and Allowances	1 3 5 4 5 0	1 2 5 6 2 5	4.6	4.7
Net Sales	2 9 6 9 0 0 0	2 7 0 0 0 0 0	100.0	100.0
Cost of Goods Sold				
Merchandise Inventory, January 1	2 2 5 0 0 0	2 1 5 0 0 0	7.6	8.0
Purchases (Net)	1 7 0 6 5 0 0	1 5 6 5 7 2 1	57.5	58.0
Freight In	2 6 0 0 0	1 9 0 0 0	0.9	0.7
Total Merchandise Available for Sale	1 9 5 7 5 0 0	1 7 9 9 7 2 1	65.9	66.7
Less Merchandise Inventory, December 31	2 0 5 0 0 0	2 2 5 0 0 0	6.9	8.3
Cost of Goods Sold	1 7 5 2 5 0 0	1 5 7 4 7 2 1	59.0	58.3
Gross Profit	1 2 1 6 5 0 0	1 1 2 5 2 7 9	41.0	41.7
Operating Expenses				
Selling Expenses	5 2 6 4 2 5	4 9 6 7 5 0	17.7	18.4
General and Administrative Expenses	6 0 5 0 0 0	5 9 9 3 0 0	20.4	22.2
Total Operating Expenses	1 1 3 1 4 2 5	1 0 9 6 0 5 0	38.1	40.6
Net Income from Operations	8 5 0 7 5	2 9 2 2 9	2.9	1.1
Other Income				
Gain on Sale of Equipment	4 0 0 0	1 5 0 0 0	0.1	0.6
Interest Income	1 8 0 0	1 7 0 0	0.1	0.1
Total Other Income	5 8 0 0	1 6 7 0 0	0.2	0.6
Other Expenses				
Bond Interest Expense	9 5 0 0	9 5 0 0	0.3	0.4
Other Interest Expense	2 0 0 0	2 5 0 0	0.1	0.1
Total Other Expenses	1 1 5 0 0	1 2 0 0 0	0.4	0.4
Income Before Income Taxes	7 9 3 7 5	3 3 9 2 9	2.7	1.3
Income Tax Expense	2 3 8 1 2	1 0 1 7 9	0.8	0.4
Net Income After Income Taxes	5 5 5 6 3	2 3 7 5 0	1.9	0.9
*Rounded				

FIGURE 23.1   Comparative Income Statement—Vertical Analysis

VERTICAL ANALYSIS OF THE INCOME STATEMENT

Notice the income statement heading. The third line indicates the periods covered by the statement. The more recent year, 2010, is in the left column. The income statement is in condensed form. In actual practice, separate schedules of the detailed Selling Expenses and General and Administrative Expenses are provided with the financial statements.

Vertical analysis of the income statement expresses each item as a percentage of the *net sales* figure. In each column, the net sales figure is used as the base, or 100 percent. Every amount in the column is expressed as a percentage of net sales. To compute an item's percentage of net sales, divide the amount of that item by the amount of net sales. For example, in 2010 the cost of goods sold is 59.0 percent of net sales.

$$\frac{\text{Cost of goods sold}}{\text{Net sales}} = \frac{\$1,752,500}{\$2,969,000} = 0.5903 = 59.03 \text{ percent}$$
$$\text{(rounded to 59.0 percent)}$$

important!

Rounding

In statement analysis, it is customary to compute percentages to the nearest one-tenth of a percent. This procedure is followed in this chapter.

important!

Percentages

In common-size statements, percentages (of net sales on the income statement and of total assets on the balance sheet) are shown instead of dollar amounts.

In making these types of computations, it is customary to carry the division one place further than needed and then round off. The usual practice is to round percentages to the nearest one-tenth of a percent. The computation in the example is made to the fourth decimal (0.5903). That decimal fraction is converted to a percentage by moving the decimal point two places to the right (59.03 percent). The percentage is then rounded to the nearest one-tenth of a percent; hence, 59.03 is rounded to 59.0.

In Figure 23.1, note that gross sales are more than 100 percent ($3,104,450 ÷ $2,969,000 = 104.6 percent in 2010). That is because of *Sales Returns and Allowances,* which are 4.6 percent of net sales.

The percentages are added and subtracted, giving informative subtotals and totals. Because of rounding, the individual percentages may not add up to 100 percent. In this case, one or more percentages is adjusted slightly until the total equals 100 percent. If the difference is more than a small amount, it is probable that an error has been made, and all the computations should be checked before adjusting any of the amounts.

Financial statements with items expressed as percentages of a base amount are called **common-size statements.** The last two columns in the comparative income statement are referred to as a *comparative common-size statement.*

Percentages obtained by vertical analysis of the income statement are useful when compared with the company's percentages for prior years. It is helpful to make comparisons with several years to detect trends, but even year-to-year comparisons are useful. For example, the comparative income statement of Household Products, Inc., shows gross profit on sales of 41.7 percent in 2009 and 41.0 percent in 2010. A comparison with the industry average might be helpful. For example, suppose that trade association publications reveal that the average gross profit for the industry is 51.7 percent. Household Products, Inc.'s gross profit on sales compares unfavorably to the industry average. This could be attributed to peculiarities of its operations, local competition, or other factors. However, it indicates the need for further examination.

VERTICAL ANALYSIS OF THE BALANCE SHEET

Vertical analysis of the balance sheet expresses each item as either a percentage of total assets or of total liabilities and stockholders' equity.

Figure 23.2 on page 803 shows a comparative balance sheet for Household Products, Inc., with the vertical analysis results. The pair of columns on the right shows each item as a percentage of total assets for each year. The more recent year is on the left. On December 31, 2010, the cash balance was $115,231 and the total assets were $555,711. Thus, the cash balance is 20.7 percent of total assets in 2010.

$$\frac{\text{Cash}}{\text{Total assets}} = \frac{\$115,231}{\$555,711} = 0.2074 = 20.7 \text{ percent}$$

In rounding off, it might be necessary to adjust one or more of the figures to obtain an even 100 percent for each total.

Vertical analysis percentages of the balance sheet are very useful when they are compared with the percentages of the same company for previous years and with those of other companies in the same industry. Changes in the percentages might reveal situations that need investigation. For example, the comparative balance sheet of Household Products, Inc., shows that cash has increased from 15.5 percent of total assets in 2009 to 20.7 percent of total assets in 2010. The accountant may suggest that this increase be studied.

Household Products, Inc.
Comparative Balance Sheet (Vertical Analysis)
December 31, 2010 and 2009

	Amounts on December 31		Percent of Total Assets	
	2010	2009	2010	2009
Assets				
Current Assets				
Cash	115231	80773	20.7	15.5
Accounts Receivable	102000	73500	18.4	14.1
Merchandise Inventory	205000	225000	36.9	43.3
Prepaid Expenses	1200	1500	0.2	0.3
Supplies	500	250	0.1	0.0
Total Current Assets	423931	381023	76.3	73.3
Property, Plant, and Equipment				
Land	80000	80000	14.4	15.4
Building and Store Equipment	71800	77800	12.9	15.0
Less Accumulated Depreciation—Building and Store Equipment	28520	23340	5.1	4.5
Net Book Value—Building and Store Equipment	43280	54460	7.8	10.5
Office Equipment	10500	6000	1.9	1.2
Less Accumulated Depreciation—Office Equipment	2000	1500	0.4	0.3
Net Book Value—Office Equipment	8500	4500	1.5	0.9
Total Property, Plant, and Equipment	131780	138960	23.7	26.7
Total Assets	555711	519983	100.0	100.0
Liabilities and Stockholders' Equity				
Current Liabilities				
Accounts Payable	71000	84500	12.8	16.3
Sales Tax Payable	2900	2500	0.5	0.5
Payroll Taxes Payable	1145	1025	0.2	0.2
Interest Payable	860	215	0.2	0.0
Total Current Liabilities	75905	88240	13.7	17.0
Long-Term Liabilities				
10% Bonds Payable, 2019	100000	100000	18.0	19.2
Premium on Bonds Payable	3500	4000	0.6	0.8
Mortgage Payable	60000	65000	10.8	12.5
Total Long-Term Liabilities	163500	169000	29.4	32.5
Total Liabilities	239405	257240	43.1	49.5
Stockholders' Equity				
Preferred Stock ($100 par, 8%, 500 shares authorized, issued and outstanding)	50000	50000	9.0	9.6
Common Stock ($1 par, 25,000 shares authorized) Issued and outstanding: 7,000 shares in 2009; 8,000 shares in 2010	8000	7000	1.4	1.3
Paid-in Capital—Common Stock	4500	3500	0.8	0.7
Retained Earnings				
Retained Earnings—Unappropriated	253806	202243	45.7	38.9
Total Retained Earnings	253806	202243	45.7	38.9
Total Stockholders' Equity	316306	262743	56.9	50.5
Total Liabilities and Stockholders' Equity	555711	519983	100.0	100.0

FIGURE 23.2 **Comparative Balance Sheet—Vertical Analysis**

Section 1 Self Review

QUESTIONS

1. What is a common-size statement?
2. How does the computation phase of statement analysis differ from the interpretation phase?
3. What item serves as the base for the percentage calculations in a vertical analysis of the income statement?

EXERCISES

4. Which of the following is true of vertical analysis?
   a. Each item on the balance sheet is expressed as a percentage of total liabilities.
   b. Each item in the income statement is divided by net sales.
   c. Each item in the income statement is expressed as a percentage of net income.
   d. The amount of increase or decrease for each item in the income statement is divided by net sales.
5. In a vertical analysis of a balance sheet, each item is expressed as a percentage of
   a. total assets or total liabilities.
   b. total assets or total stockholders' equity.
   c. total assets or total liabilities and stockholders' equity.
   d. total liabilities or total stockholders' equity.

ANALYSIS

6. Net sales for 2009 and 2010 are $1,225,000 and $1,050,000. Net income after income taxes for 2009 and 2010 are $59,000 and $29,000. Compute the percentage of net income after taxes (based on net sales) for 2009 and 2010.

(Answers to Section 1 Self Review are on page 840.)

Horizontal Analysis

In this section, you will learn the second type of basic calculation, horizontal analysis.

Horizontal Analysis of Financial Statements

Financial statements for two or more periods may be evaluated by means of horizontal analysis. Horizontal analysis compares the items on each line to determine the change in dollar amounts. A percentage change can be shown by using the earlier figure as the base.

HORIZONTAL ANALYSIS OF THE INCOME STATEMENT

Let's learn the techniques of horizontal analysis using the comparative income statement. Figure 23.3 on page 806 shows the comparative income statement of Household Products, Inc., for 2009 and 2010.

Each amount for 2010 is compared to the corresponding amount for 2009. The increase or decrease of the change and the percentage of change are shown in the right two columns. Look at the sales figures. The gross sales for 2010 are higher than those for 2009. The increase is $278,825.

Sales for 2010	$3,104,450
Sales for 2009	−2,825,625
Increase	$ 278,825

To find the percentage of increase, divide the increase by the amount for the base year. The base year is always the earlier year. The percentage of increase for gross sales is 9.9 percent.

$$\frac{\text{Increase in sales}}{\text{Sales for base year}} = \frac{\$278,825}{\$2,825,625} = 9.9 \text{ percent}$$

If the amount for the most recent year is less than that for the base year, the percentage decrease is calculated in the same manner. For example, ending merchandise inventory decreased by $20,000 for 2010. Divide the decrease by the base year amount.

$$\frac{\text{Amount of decrease}}{\text{Amount in base year}} = \frac{(\$20,000)}{\$225,000} = (8.9) \text{ percent}$$

>>2. OBJECTIVE

Use horizontal analysis techniques to analyze a comparative income statement and balance sheet.

LP23

Household Products, Inc.
Comparative Income Statement (Horizontal Analysis)
Years Ended December 31, 2010 and 2009

	Amounts		Increase or (Decrease)	
	2010	2009	Amount	Percent*
Revenue				
Sales	3 104 450	2 825 625	278 825	9.9
Less Sales Returns and Allowances	135 450	125 625	9 825	7.8
Net Sales	2 969 000	2 700 000	269 000	10.0
Cost of Goods Sold				
Merchandise Inventory, January 1	225 000	215 000	10 000	4.7
Purchases (Net)	1 706 500	1 565 721	140 779	9.0
Freight In	26 000	19 000	7 000	36.8
Total Merchandise Available for Sale	1 957 500	1 799 721	157 779	8.8
Less Merchandise Inventory, December 31	205 000	225 000	(20 000)	(8.9)
Cost of Goods Sold	1 752 500	1 574 721	177 779	11.3
Gross Profit	1 216 500	1 125 279	91 221	8.1
Operating Expenses				
Selling Expenses	526 425	496 750	29 675	6.0
General and Administrative Expenses	605 000	599 300	5 700	1.0
Total Operating Expenses	1 131 425	1 096 050	35 375	3.2
Net Income from Operations	85 075	29 229	55 846	191.1
Other Income				
Gain on Sale of Equipment	4 000	15 000	(11 000)	(73.3)
Interest Income	1 800	1 700	100	5.9
Total Other Income	5 800	16 700	(10 900)	(65.3)
Other Expenses				
Bond Interest Expense	9 500	9 500	0	0.0
Other Interest Expense	2 000	2 500	(500)	(20.0)
Total Other Expenses	11 500	12 000	(500)	(4.2)
Net Income Before Income Taxes	79 375	33 929	45 446	133.9
Income Tax Expense	23 812	10 179	13 633	133.9
Net Income After Income Taxes	55 563	23 750	31 813	133.9
* Rounded				

FIGURE 23.3   **Comparative Income Statement—Horizontal Analysis**

A decrease can be expressed by using a negative sign before the number, italics, or parentheses.

All the amounts in the right two columns on the comparative statement are computed in the same manner. If the amount of change is zero, there is no percentage of change. When there is no amount for the base period, no percentage change is computed.

Interpretation of the Percentages   The amounts of increase or decrease can be added or subtracted in the column and will give correct subtotals at each point. However, the percentages cannot be added or subtracted. Each percentage relates only to the line on which it appears.

Some important changes shown in the comparative income statement for Household Products, Inc., include the following:

- Gross sales increased 9.9 percent.
- Cost of goods sold increased 11.3 percent.

- Gross profit on sales increased 8.1 percent.
- Total operating expenses increased 3.2 percent.
- Income from operations increased 191.1 percent.
- Income tax expense increased 133.9 percent.
- Net income after income taxes increased 133.9 percent.

Horizontal analysis is especially useful in identifying items that need further investigation. For example, the increase in net sales was 10.0 percent, but the increase in cost of goods sold was 11.3 percent. An alert manager would want to determine the reasons for the increase in cost of goods sold.

Management would also be interested in learning why freight increased 36.8 percent during 2010 while purchases increased only 9.0 percent.

Keep in mind that percentages of increase or decrease can be misleading when small amounts are involved. For example, total other income decreased 65.3 percent. However, in terms of actual dollars, the amount is relatively small, from $16,700 to $5,800. On the other hand, a small percentage change is important for items involving large dollar amounts.

The process of interpretation is easier if some basis of comparison is available, such as a company budget or industry averages. Significant changes need to be investigated in detail and the reasons evaluated.

HORIZONTAL ANALYSIS OF THE BALANCE SHEET

A firm's balance sheets for two or more periods can be presented in comparative form to permit a detailed horizontal analysis. Figure 23.4 on page 808 shows a comparative balance sheet for Household Products, Inc., for December 31 of 2009 and 2010.

The calculations are the same as those for a horizontal analysis of income statements. The amounts are compared line by line. For example, for accounts receivable the difference is an increase of $28,500 ($102,000 − $73,500). The percentage of change is 38.8 percent. It is determined by dividing the amount of the change by the base year (2009) amount: $28,500 ÷ $73,500 = 38.78, or 38.8 percent.

Trend Analysis of Financial Statements

Comparing ratio and percentage relationships of the current year with those of the immediately preceding year is a normal and helpful procedure. However, comparisons between only two years could be misleading and might not be adequate to indicate long-term trends. A better technique is **trend analysis,** which compares selected ratios and percentages over a period of time. Often the time period is five years.

Let's look at one trend. The percentage of gross profit on sales to net sales decreased from 41.7 percent in 2009 to 41.0 percent in 2010 (Figure 23.1). A higher gross profit percentage is desirable, so the decrease is unfavorable. A comparison with the several prior years follows.

	2006	2007	2008	2009	2010
Net sales	2,055,600	2,223,240	2,587,500	2,700,000	2,969,000
Cost of goods sold	1,059,900	1,234,560	1,495,642	1,574,721	1,752,500
Gross profit on sales	995,700	988,680	1,091,858	1,125,279	1,216,500
Percentage of gross profit to net sales	48.4	44.5	42.2	41.7	41.0

In looking at the data over five years, it is clear that the decrease in percentage from 2006 to 2010 is significant. It calls for the attention of management. Management must obtain other facts, talk with employees, and observe other trends before arriving at a solution to the problem.

Household Products, Inc.
Comparative Balance Sheet (Horizontal Analysis)
December 31, 2010 and 2009

	Amounts		Increase or (Decrease)	
	2010	2009	Amount	Percent*
Assets				
Current Assets				
Cash	115231	80773	34458	42.7
Accounts Receivable	102000	73500	28500	38.8
Merchandise Inventory	205000	225000	(20000)	(8.9)
Prepaid Expenses	1200	1500	(300)	(20.0)
Supplies	500	250	250	100.0
Total Current Assets	423931	381023	42908	11.3
Property, Plant, and Equipment				
Land	80000	80000	0	0.0
Building and Store Equipment	71800	77800	(6000)	(7.7)
Less Accumulated Depreciation—Building and Store				22.2
Equipment	28520	23340	5180	(20.5)
Net Book Value—Building and Store Equipment	43280	54460	(11180)	75.0
Office Equipment	10500	6000	4500	33.3
Less Accumulated Depreciation—Office Equipment	2000	1500	500	88.9
Net Book Value—Office Equipment	8500	4500	4000	(5.2)
Total Property, Plant, and Equipment	131780	138960	(7180)	6.9
Total Assets	555711	519983	35728	
Liabilities and Stockholders' Equity				
Current Liabilities				(16.0)
Accounts Payable	71000	84500	(13500)	16.0
Sales Tax Payable	2900	2500	400	11.7
Payroll Taxes Payable	1145	1025	120	300.0
Interest Payable	860	215	645	(14.0)
Total Current Liabilities	75905	88240	(12335)	
Long-Term Liabilities				0.0
10% Bonds Payable, 2019	100000	100000	0	(12.5)
Premium on Bonds Payable	3500	4000	(500)	(7.7)
Mortgage Payable	60000	65000	(5000)	(3.3)
Total Long-Term Liabilities	163500	169000	(5500)	(6.9)
Total Liabilities	239405	257240	(17835)	
Stockholders' Equity				
Preferred Stock ($100 par, 8%, 500 shares				0.0
authorized, issued and outstanding)	50000	50000	0	
Common Stock ($1 par 25,000 shares authorized)				
Issued and outstanding: 7,000 shares in 2009;				14.3
8,000 shares in 2010	8000	7000	1000	28.6
Paid-in Capital—Common Stock	4500	3500	1000	
Retained Earnings				25.5
Retained Earnings—Unappropriated	253806	202243	51563	25.5
Total Retained Earnings	253806	202243	51563	20.4
Total Stockholders' Equity	316306	262743	53563	6.9
Total Liabilities and Stockholders' Equity	555711	519983	35728	
*Rounded				

FIGURE 23.4   Comparative Balance Sheet—Horizontal Analysis

MANAGERIAL IMPLICATIONS   <<

COMPARATIVE STATEMENTS

■ Statement analysis is extremely important to managers in detecting areas of strength and weakness in a business.

■ Comparison of current data with the data of prior years indicates favorable and unfavorable trends.

■ Managers compare percentages from year to year and with industry averages in order to detect variations that require prompt investigation.

■ Management must consider certain factors when using industry averages.

THINKING CRITICALLY

What type of financial statement analysis would you use to assess profitability of a company for the last five years?

Trend analysis makes it possible to ask questions about all aspects of operations of the company. The accountant makes the most valuable contribution to the success of the business when analyzing operating data.

Comparison with Industry Averages

Trade associations survey their members to obtain financial and other data. The financial ratios and percentages that reflect averages for similar companies are called **industry averages.** These data are converted to a uniform presentation, usually in common-size statements arranged by company size (based on sales volume or total assets). Income statement items are expressed as a percentage of net sales and balance sheet items as a percentage of total assets. Common-size statements can be presented for one year or for several years. Individual companies compare their results to industry averages.

Let's look at an example of how the management of Household Products, Inc., might evaluate the corporation in comparison with others in the same industry. Table 23.1 on page 810 shows highly condensed data from its income statement as well as the data provided by the trade association for companies with the same general sales level. Note that income tax expense has been omitted. Because companies included in the trade averages are sole proprietorships, partnerships, and corporations, it is not appropriate to compare net income after income taxes with entities that do not pay taxes.

You can see why the comparison to industry averages would be of interest to management, owners, and others. The operations of Household Products, Inc., are not as efficient or as profitable as those of its competitors. Its rate of gross profit is lower (and on a downward trend) than the industry averages. Its ratio of operating expenses to net sales is higher than that of others in the industry. The end result is that Household Products, Inc.'s ratio of income before income tax to sales is much lower than that of its competitors. Based on this comparison, management needs to immediately determine the causes of its poor results.

In comparing to industry averages, keep in mind the following:

■ Different businesses keep different types of accounts and do not classify items in the same manner.

■ No two businesses are exactly alike. There are differences in the merchandise sold, the type of customers, and the method of financing (owners' equity versus borrowed funds). Some businesses buy fixed assets while others lease all or some of the fixed assets.

■ The industry figures could include data from corporations, partnerships, and sole proprietorships. The different business entities might report salary allowances, benefits for owners, and other items in very different ways.

TABLE 23.1

Comparison of Trade Data

| | Percentage of Net Sales* | | | |
| | Household Products, Inc. | | Industry Average | |
	2010	**2009**	**2010**	**2009**
Revenue				
Sales	104.6	104.7	104.0	103.5
Returns and Allowances	4.6	4.7	4.0	3.5
Net Sales	100.0	100.0	100.0	100.0
Cost of Goods Sold	59.0	58.3	50.5	47.0
Gross Profit on Sales	41.0	41.7	49.5	53.0
Operating Expenses				
Selling Expenses	17.7	18.4	18.2	20.1
General Expenses	20.4	22.2	19.5	22.0
Total Operating Expenses	38.1	40.6*	37.7	42.1
Operating Income	2.9	1.1	11.8	10.9
Other Income and Expenses				
Other Income	0.2	0.6	0.9	1.2
Other Expenses	(0.4)	(0.4)	(0.5)	(0.1)
Net Other Income or (Exp.)	(0.2)	0.2	0.4	1.1
Income Before Income Tax	2.7	1.3	12.2	12.0

*Rounded

Despite these problems, common-size statements provided by trade associations or commercial financial service companies are important to managers in comparing their operations to other firms. They are of special value when comparing data not affected by the factors listed above.

Section 2 Self Review

QUESTIONS

1. Why is comparison with industry averages helpful when analyzing financial statements?

2. In the same industry, when comparing an established company and a newer one, which company would have a higher percentage of property, plant, and equipment to total assets? Why?

3. In horizontal analysis of the balance sheet, how is the percentage of change determined?

EXERCISES

4. If a comparative balance sheet shows the amount and percentage of decrease in merchandise inventory from one year to the next, the firm used

   a. horizontal analysis.

   b. vertical analysis.

   c. common-size analysis.

   d. trend analysis.

5. If current assets are $150,000 and total assets are $500,000, the percentage of current assets to total assets is

   a. 15 percent.

   b. 5 percent.

   c. 30 percent.

   d. 3 percent.

ANALYSIS

6. Total selling expenses for 2009 and 2010 were $715,625 and $814,400, respectively. Net sales for 2009 and 2010 were $3,345,650 and $3,698,425, respectively. For each year, what are total selling expenses as a percentage of net sales? What is the percentage of increase or decrease of total selling expenses?

(Answers to Section 2 Self Review are on page 840.)

Section 3

SECTION OBJECTIVES

>> 5. Compute and interpret financial ratios that measure profitability, operating results, and efficiency.

WHY IT'S IMPORTANT

Various factors, in combination with the measurement of net income, contribute to the overall prosperity of a company.

>> 6. Compute and interpret financial ratios that measure financial strength.

WHY IT'S IMPORTANT

The long-term viability of a business depends on effective use of equity and earnings.

>> 7. Compute and interpret financial ratios that measure liquidity.

WHY IT'S IMPORTANT

To establish financial credibility, a business needs to demonstrate its ability to pay its debts when due.

>> 8. Recognize shortcomings in financial statement analysis.

WHY IT'S IMPORTANT

The analysis of financial statements, without considering different accounting processes or operational procedures, could lead to improper conclusions.

TERMS TO LEARN

accounts receivable turnover
acid-test ratio
asset turnover
average collection period
current ratio
leveraged buyout
liquidity
price-earnings ratio
quick assets
return on common stockholders' equity
total equities
working capital

Ratios

Ratio analysis is used to assess a company's profitability, financial strength, and liquidity. Ratio analysis investigates a relationship between two items either as a ratio (2 to 1 or 2:1) or as a rate (percentage).

Financial ratios have three classifications:

1. Profitability, operating results, and efficiency
2. Financial strength
3. Liquidity

The financial statements of Household Products, Inc., will be used to illustrate ratio analysis. You will need to refer to Figures 23.3 on page 806 and 23.4 on page 808 while studying this section.

Profitability is measured by net income. However, a dollar amount of net income is not a sufficient yardstick. Net income of $150,000 might be excellent for a small firm but unsatisfactory for a large corporation. A number of ratios are used to determine the adequacy of a company's profit.

Profitability Ratios

RATE OF RETURN ON SALES

The rate of return on sales is a measure of managerial efficiency and profitability. It is computed as follows.

$$\frac{\text{Net income}}{\text{Net sales}} = \text{Rate of return on net sales}$$

>> 5. OBJECTIVE
Compute and interpret financial ratios that measure profitability, operating results, and efficiency.

Video23.1

important!

Rate of Return on Sales
The rate of return on sales measures what part of each sales dollar remains as net income. It measures operating efficiency and profitability.

Some companies use income before taxes to calculate the percentage because income taxes depend on factors not related to sales. Household Products, Inc., uses net income after income taxes to calculate the rate.

The rate of return on net sales at Household Products, Inc., was 1.9 percent for 2010 compared to 0.9 percent in 2009 as sales increased significantly in 2010.

2010	2009
$\dfrac{\$55,563}{\$2,969,000} = 1.9\%$	$\dfrac{\$23,750}{\$2,700,000} = 0.9\%$

The higher the rate of return on net sales, the more satisfactory are the business operations. Management should look for and investigate unfavorable trends.

RATE OF RETURN ON COMMON STOCKHOLDERS' EQUITY

Corporations are expected to earn a profit for their shareholders. Preferred shareholders are entitled to the dividends provided for in the preferred stock contract. The remainder of the earnings is available to common shareholders. **Return on common stockholders' equity** is a key measure of how well the corporation is making a profit for its shareholders. It is computed as follows.

$$\frac{\text{Income available to common stockholders}}{\text{Common stockholders' equity}} = \frac{\text{Return on common}}{\text{stockholders' equity}}$$

Step 1. *Compute income available to common stockholders.* Income available to common stockholders is net income after taxes reduced by any preferred dividend requirements. Household Products, Inc., has a $4,000 dividend requirement for preferred stock (500 shares at $100 par value at 8 percent). Subtract $4,000 from net income after taxes to determine the income available for common stockholders.

	2010	2009
Net income after income taxes	$55,563	$23,750
Less dividend requirements on preferred stock	4,000	4,000
Income available to common stockholders	$51,563	$19,750

Step 2. *Compute the common stockholders' equity.* There are many ways to compute common stockholders' equity: end-of-year balance, average of the beginning and ending balances, average based on quarterly balances, or average based on monthly balances. Household Products, Inc., uses the end-of-year balance of total common stockholders' equity.

	2010	2009
Total stockholders' equity	$316,306	$262,743
Less preferred stock equity	50,000	50,000
Common stockholders' equity	$266,306	$212,743

Step 3. *Divide the income available to common stockholders by the common stockholders' equity.*

2010	2009
$\dfrac{\$51,563}{\$266,306} = 19.4\%$	$\dfrac{\$19,750}{\$212,743} = 9.3\%$

The increase in the 2010 rate of return on common stockholders' equity is caused primarily by the increase in net income. As net income increases, you should expect this ratio to improve. As a common stock shareholder, you would want to monitor this ratio yearly.

EARNINGS PER SHARE OF COMMON STOCK

Earnings per share of common stock measures the profit accruing to each share of common stock owned. It is computed as follows.

$$\frac{\text{Income available to common stockholders}}{\begin{array}{c}\text{Average number of shares of common}\\\text{stock outstanding during year}\end{array}} = \text{Earnings per share}$$

Step 1. *Compute income available to common stockholders.* Subtract the dividend requirements on preferred stock from the income after income tax.

	2010	2009
Net income after income taxes	$55,563	$23,750
Less dividend requirements on preferred stock	4,000	4,000
Income available to common stockholders	$51,563	$19,750

Step 2. *Determine the average number of shares of common stock outstanding during the year.* An analysis of the common stock account reveals that 7,000 shares were outstanding throughout 2009 and most of 2010. On October 2, 2010, 1,000 additional shares were issued. *The weighted average number of shares outstanding* for 2010 was 5,250, calculated as follows.

$$7,000 \text{ shares} \times \frac{12 \text{ months}}{12 \text{ months}} = 7,000 \text{ shares}$$

$$1,000 \text{ shares} \times \frac{3 \text{ months}}{12 \text{ months}} = 250 \text{ shares}$$

$$\text{Weighted average number of shares} = 7,250 \text{ shares}$$

Step 3. *Divide the income available to common stockholders by the average number of shares of common stock outstanding.*

2010	2009
$\dfrac{\$51,563}{7,250 \text{ shares}} = \$7.11$	$\dfrac{\$19,750}{7,000 \text{ shares}} = \$2.82$

Earnings per share were $7.11 in 2010 and $2.82 in 2009. The large increase in net income caused earnings per share to increase significantly even though there were more shares of stock outstanding in 2010.

Analysts, stockholders, and creditors watch the earnings per share measurement very closely. Comparing earnings per share for the same company for several years could show a trend. Keep in mind that changes in the number of shares outstanding might distort this measurement.

PRICE-EARNINGS RATIO

The **price-earnings ratio** compares the market value of common stock with the earnings per share of that stock. It is computed as follows.

$$\frac{\text{Market price per share}}{\text{Earnings per share}} = \text{Price-earnings ratio}$$

If a corporation's common stock sells for $144 per share and its earnings are $12 per share, the price-earnings ratio is 12 to 1 ($144 ÷ $12).

The price-earnings ratio is an indicator of the attractiveness of the stock as an investment at its present market value. The amount investors are willing to pay for stock is based on expectations

important!

Price-Earnings Ratio
The price-earnings ratio depends in large part on expectations of future profitability, which cause stock prices to increase or decrease.

for the future. The price-earnings ratio is not computed for privately held companies because there is no readily available market value for the shares.

YIELD ON COMMON STOCK

For a publicly held corporation, the relationship between the dividends received by the stockholders and the market value of each share is important. The yield on common stock is computed as follows.

$$\frac{\text{Dividend per share}}{\text{Market price per share}} = \text{Yield on common stock}$$

For example, if the price of a share of common stock is $60 and the corporation is paying an annual dividend of $6, the yield is 10 percent ($6 ÷ $60).

RATE OF RETURN ON TOTAL ASSETS

The rate of return on total assets measures the rate of return on the assets used by a company. This rate helps the analyst to judge managerial performance, measure the effectiveness of the assets used, and evaluate proposed capital expenditures. The rate is computed as follows.

$$\frac{\text{Income before interest expense and income taxes}}{\text{Total assets}} = \frac{\text{Rate of return on}}{\text{total assets}}$$

Income before interest and taxes is used to measure how effectively management utilized the assets, regardless of how the assets were financed. If nonoperating revenue amounts (such as dividend and interest income) are large, they should not be included in income. This ensures that only income from normal business operations is considered. For Household Products, Inc., income is computed by adding interest expense to income before income taxes.

	2010	**2009**
Income before income taxes	$79,375	$33,929
Interest expense	11,500	12,000
Income before interest and taxes	$90,875	$45,929

Analysts might average the assets at the beginning and end of the year, average the assets monthly, use the beginning assets, or use the ending assets. Household Products, Inc., uses year-end total assets.

The rate of return on total assets for Household Products, Inc., is as follows.

2010	**2009**
$\dfrac{\$90,875}{\$555,711} = 16.4\%$	$\dfrac{\$45,929}{\$519,983} = 8.8\%$

The results are meaningful only if compared with rates of prior years and with the industry average.

ASSET TURNOVER

The ratio of net sales to total assets measures the effective use of assets in making sales. This ratio is usually called **asset turnover.** It is computed as follows.

$$\frac{\text{Net sales}}{\text{Total assets}} = \text{Asset turnover}$$

Assets that are not used in producing sales, primarily investments, are excluded. Assets may be measured as end-of-year totals, average of beginning and ending totals, or average of monthly totals. Household Products, Inc., uses net sales and total assets at the end of the year.

important!

Asset Turnover

A low asset turnover compared to the industry average shows that the business uses more assets to generate the same sales volume as its competitors.

$$\frac{\$2,969,000}{\$555,711} = 5.3 \text{ to } 1 \qquad \frac{\$2,700,000}{\$519,983} = 5.2 \text{ to } 1$$

The higher the asset turnover, the more effectively the assets of the company are being used. The trend of this ratio is important because it indicates whether asset growth is accompanied by corresponding sales growth. If sales increase proportionately more than total assets, the ratio increases, which is a favorable indicator.

Financial Strength Ratios

NUMBER OF TIMES BOND INTEREST EARNED

A corporation's bondholders and stockholders want to know if net income is sufficient to cover the required bond interest payments. Times bond interest earned measures this. It is computed as follows.

$$\frac{\text{Income before bond interest and income taxes}}{\text{Bond interest cash requirement}} = \text{Times bond interest earned}$$

Step 1. *Compute the income before bond interest and income taxes.* To compute the income amount, add the bond interest expense to income before income taxes. For Household Products, Inc., bond interest expense was $9,500 in 2009 and $9,500 in 2010 (interest paid on the bonds minus the amortization of bond premium). Household Products, Inc., uses the straight-line method to amortize the premium on bonds payable. The amount is computed as follows.

	2010	2009
Income before income tax	$79,375	$33,929
Add bond interest expense	9,500	9,500
Available for bond interest	$88,875	$43,429

Step 2. *Compute the cash required to pay bond interest.* The cash interest for bonds outstanding at the end of each year is computed as follows.

2010: $100,000 × 0.10 = $10,000

2009: $100,000 × 0.10 = $10,000

Step 3. *Compute the ratio.*

$$\frac{\$88,875}{\$10,000} = 8.9 \text{ times} \qquad \frac{\$43,429}{\$10,000} = 4.3 \text{ times}$$

Household Products, Inc.'s income easily covers required bond payments.

RATIO OF STOCKHOLDERS' EQUITY TO TOTAL EQUITIES

The sum of a corporation's liabilities and stockholders' equity is referred to as its **total equities.** The ratio of stockholders' equity to total equities measures the portion of total capital provided by the stockholders. It indicates the protection afforded creditors against possible losses. The more capital provided by the stockholders, the greater the protection to creditors. The ratio of stockholders' equity to total equities is computed as follows.

$$\frac{\text{Stockholders' equity}}{\text{Total equities}} = \text{Ratio of stockholders' equities to total equities}$$

>>6. OBJECTIVE
Compute and interpret financial ratios that measure financial strength.

LP23

recall

Bond Premium
The excess of the price paid over the face value of a bond is known as bond premium.

Financial Statement Analysis

The ratios for Household Products, Inc., follow.

2010	2009
$\dfrac{\$316{,}306}{\$555{,}711} = 0.57 \text{ to } 1$	$\dfrac{\$262{,}743}{\$519{,}983} = 0.51 \text{ to } 1$

In 2010, the stockholders of Household Products, Inc., provided 57 cents of each dollar of total equities compared to 51 cents in 2009. This ratio varies widely from industry to industry. A comparison with the industry average is important in determining a desirable ratio for a particular business.

RATIO OF STOCKHOLDERS' EQUITY TO TOTAL LIABILITIES

The ratio of stockholders' equity to total liabilities is known as the *ratio of owned capital to borrowed capital.* It is computed as follows.

$$\frac{\text{Stockholders' equity}}{\text{Total liabilities}} = \text{Ratio of stockholders' equity to total liabilities}$$

The ratios for Household Products, Inc., follow.

2010	2009
$\dfrac{\$316{,}306}{\$239{,}405} = 1.32 \text{ to } 1$	$\dfrac{\$262{,}743}{\$257{,}240} = 1.02 \text{ to } 1$

This ratio reveals a significant improvement in 2010. In 2009, stockholders provided slightly more than $1 of equity for each dollar of liability. In 2010, they provided $1.32 of equity for each dollar of debt.

In a **leveraged buyout,** the purchasers of a business buy the stock, having the corporation agree to pay the sellers. The result is that the debt created by the purchase is a debt of the corporation. In many cases, the debt, usually with a high interest rate, makes up a large part of the total equities of the corporation. In the mid-1980s to early 1990s, many corporations went bankrupt because they could not meet the interest and principal payments on the debts. The balance sheets of these corporations would reflect a very low ratio of stockholders' equity to total liabilities.

BOOK VALUE PER SHARE OF STOCK

Book value per share measures the financial strength underlying each share of stock. It is frequently reported in financial publications. It represents the amount that each share would receive in case of liquidation if the assets were sold for book value.

When there is one class of stock outstanding, the book value of each share is total stockholders' equity divided by the number of shares outstanding. If more than one class of stock is outstanding, the rights of the various classes of stock are considered. The book value of preferred stock is computed first. Then the remaining balance of stockholders' equity is divided by the number of common shares. Special treatment is given to dividends in arrears on cumulative preferred stock. In case of liquidation, the owner of a share of preferred stock will receive its par value.

$$\frac{\text{Common stockholders' equity}}{\text{Number of common shares}} = \text{Book value per share of common stock}$$

Follow these steps to compute the book value per share of stock for Household Products, Inc.

Step 1. *Compute the claims of preferred stockholders.* There are no cumulative dividends or special liquidation provisions for the preferred stock of Household Products, Inc. Therefore, the book value is the same as the par value, $100 per share. There were 500 shares of preferred stock outstanding during 2009 and 2010, so the claims of the preferred stockholders for both years are $50,000 (500 shares at $100 par value).

Step 2. *Deduct the claims of preferred stockholders from total stockholders' equity to compute the claims of common stockholders.* The common stockholders are entitled to the difference between the total stockholders' equity and the portion assigned to the preferred stock.

	2010	2009
Stockholders' equity	$316,306	$262,743
Less preferred stock equity	50,000	50,000
To common stockholders	$266,306	$212,743

Step 3. *Divide the total claims of common stockholders by the number of shares of common stock outstanding.* Household Products, Inc., had 8,000 shares of common stock outstanding on December 31, 2010, and 7,000 shares outstanding on December 31, 2009. The book value of each share is computed as follows.

2010	2009
$$\frac{\$266,306}{8,000 \text{ shares}} = \$33.29$$	$$\frac{\$212,743}{7,000 \text{ shares}} = \$30.39$$

The book value of Household Products, Inc.'s common stock increased from $30.39 to $33.29 per share.

Liquidity Ratios

WORKING CAPITAL

Liquidity measures the ability of a business to pay its debts when due. Many businesses fail because they cannot pay their debts, even though they are profitable and have long-term financial strength. **Working capital** is a measure of the ability of a company to meet its current obligations. It represents the margin of security afforded short-term creditors. Working capital, sometimes called *net working capital*, is computed as follows.

$$\text{Current assets} - \text{Current liabilities} = \text{Working capital}$$

In 2010, Household Products, Inc.'s working capital increased by $55,243. This is a significant change that needs to be investigated.

	2010	2009	Increase or (Decrease)
Current assets	$423,931	$381,023	$42,908
Current liabilities	75,905	88,240	(12,335)
Working capital	$348,026	$292,783	$55,243

> In the FedEx Corporation *2007 10K,* net working capital for the period ended May 31, 2007, was computed by subtracting current liabilities of $5.4 billion from current assets of $6.6 billion.

CURRENT RATIO

Working capital is a very important measure of liquidity. The current ratio is another way to evaluate liquidity. The **current ratio** measures the ability of a business to pay its current debts using current assets. The current ratio is computed as follows.

$$\frac{\text{Current assets}}{\text{Current liabilities}} = \text{Current ratio}$$

>>7. OBJECTIVE

Compute and interpret financial ratios that measure liquidity.

LP23

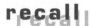

recall

Current Assets

Assets are considered current if they will be converted to cash or used within one year.

In 2010, Household Products, Inc., had $5.59 of current assets for each dollar of current liabilities.

2010	2009
$\dfrac{\$423,931}{\$75,905} = 5.59{:}1$	$\dfrac{\$381,023}{\$88,240} = 4.32{:}1$

The current ratio varies widely among industries and even from company to company within an industry. A popular guideline is that a current ratio of at least 2 to 1 is desirable in retail and manufacturing businesses. This guideline is not applicable, however, to all businesses.

From the viewpoint of a short-term creditor, the higher the current ratio, the greater the amount of protection afforded. However, the current ratio can be too high. A very high current ratio indicates that excess current assets are on hand and are not earning income. A high current ratio could be caused by large sums of money tied up in accounts receivable that might be uncollectible. A high current ratio could also be caused by obsolete inventory or an inventory level higher than required to conduct normal operations.

ACID-TEST RATIO

Although the current ratio measures a company's ability to cover current liabilities using current assets, it is not a measure of immediate liquidity. A considerable period of time might be necessary to sell the inventory and convert it into cash in the normal course of business. The **acid-test ratio** measures immediate liquidity. This ratio uses **quick assets,** which are cash, receivables, and marketable securities.

$$\frac{\text{Cash + Receivables + Marketable securities}}{\text{Current liabilities}} = \text{Acid-test ratio}$$

Household Products, Inc.'s acid-test ratios follow.

2010	2009
$\dfrac{\$115,231 + \$102,000}{\$75,905} = 2.86{:}1$	$\dfrac{\$80,773 + \$73,500}{\$88,240} = 1.75{:}1$

The acid-test ratio shows that in 2010, Household Products, Inc., had $2.86 of quick assets for each dollar of current liabilities. In 2009, the acid-test ratio was 1.75. This dramatic increase should be investigated.

Acid-test ratios vary widely from industry to industry. A general guideline is that the acid-test ratio should be at least 1 to 1. The due dates of current liabilities, composition of quick assets, and various operating factors are considered when evaluating the adequacy of the ratio. Comparisons with the industry average and with the company's ratio in prior years can be helpful.

INVENTORY TURNOVER

It is important that a business sell its inventory rapidly so that excess working capital is not tied up in merchandise. Inventory turnover measures the number of times the inventory is replaced during the period. The higher the turnover, the shorter the time between the purchase and sale of the inventory. Inventory turnover is computed as follows.

$$\frac{\text{Cost of goods sold}}{\text{Average inventory}} = \text{Inventory turnover}$$

Ideally, average inventory is computed using month-end balances. However, these amounts are not available to analysts outside the business. Therefore, year-end balances are often used, but they might not be typical of the inventory levels during the year. Inventory is often at its lowest level at year-end.

To compute the inventory turnover for Household Products, Inc., follow these steps.

Step 1. *Compute the average inventory.*

	2010	**2009**
Inventory, Jan. 1	$225,000	$215,000
Inventory, Dec. 31	205,000	225,000
Totals	$430,000	$440,000
	÷ 2	÷ 2
Average inventory	$215,000	$220,000

Step 2. *Divide the cost of goods sold by the average inventory.*

2010

$$\frac{\$1,752,500}{\$215,000} = 8.15 \text{ times}$$

2009

$$\frac{\$1,574,721}{\$220,000} = 7.16 \text{ times}$$

The inventory turnover ratio varies widely by industry. Inventory turnover for a bakery is almost daily. A vendor of construction equipment might turn inventory just twice a year. A business must compare its inventory turnover with prior years and with the industry average.

ACCOUNTS RECEIVABLE TURNOVER

A company should collect accounts and notes receivable promptly. This minimizes the amount of working capital tied up in receivables and reduces the likelihood that accounts will become uncollectible. The **accounts receivable turnover** is a measure of the reasonableness of the accounts outstanding. This measurement uses net credit sales, which includes notes receivable from sales transactions. The accounts receivable turnover is computed as follows.

$$\frac{\text{Net credit sales}}{\text{Average receivables}} = \text{Accounts receivable turnover}$$

It is desirable to use monthly balances to compute the average receivables. However, since these amounts are not available to analysts outside the business, year-end balances are often used. Outside analysts normally use net sales since they cannot determine net credit sales. For Household Products, Inc., accounts receivable on January 1, 2009, were $71,500. Net credit sales were $2,700,000 in 2010 and $2,500,000 in 2009.

Step 1. *Compute average accounts receivable.*

	2010	**2009**
Accounts receivable, Jan. 1	$ 73,500	$ 71,500
Accounts receivable, Dec. 31	102,000	73,500
Totals	$175,500	$145,000
	÷ 2	÷ 2
Average accounts receivable	$ 87,750	$ 72,500

Step 2. *Divide net credit sales by average accounts receivable.*

2010

$$\frac{\$2,700,000}{\$87,750} = 30.8 \text{ times}$$

2009

$$\frac{\$2,500,000}{\$72,500} = 34.5 \text{ times}$$

The accounts receivable turnover can be used to determine the **average collection period** of accounts receivable, or *number of days' sales in receivables*. The average collection period is computed as follows.

$$\frac{365 \text{ days}}{\text{Accounts receivable turnover}}$$

2010

$$\frac{365}{30.8} = 11.9 \text{ days}$$

2009

$$\frac{365}{34.5} = 10.6 \text{ days}$$

MANAGERIAL IMPLICATIONS   <<

INTERPRETING FINANCIAL STATEMENTS

■ It is important that managers understand the relationships among the items on the financial statements. Understanding these relationships will help management run the business effectively.

■ Managers use statement analysis to identify areas of operations that are weak and need attention.

■ It is essential that management know how to compute and interpret financial ratios. For example, a low inventory turnover compared with the industry average might reflect obsolete goods, excess merchandise, poor purchasing procedures, or other operating inefficiencies.

■ Effective managers recognize the key role the accountant plays in financial statement analysis and interpretation. Accountants understand what each line on the financial statements represents and can assist management in analyzing and understanding accounting reports.

THINKING CRITICALLY
Which ratios will best measure the company's ability to meet current obligations?

Household Products, Inc., collected accounts receivable in 2010 in about 12 days and about 11 days in 2009. As a general rule, the average collection period should not exceed the net credit period plus one-third. The credit terms for customers of Household Products, Inc., are net 15 days. The collection period should be 20 days or less [15 + (1/3 × 15)]. For both years, the collection period for Household Products, Inc., is much less than the guideline.

OTHER RATIOS

The number of ratios that could be developed from financial statements is almost limitless. Analysts use their preferred ratios. Financial writers use many more ratios than those presented in this chapter. Depending on the industry, some ratios are more important than others. The ratios in this chapter are those most often used by accountants.

SOME PRECAUTIONARY NOTES ON STATEMENT ANALYSIS

>>**8. OBJECTIVE**

Recognize shortcomings in financial statement analysis.

Video23.1

recall

Cost Basis Principle
Accounts reflect historical costs, not current market values. This must be considered when analyzing financial statements. Book value rarely reflects fair market value.

There are limits to the benefits of financial statement analysis. Financial statements use book values. Book value depends on accounting procedures and policies. Different accounting policies and procedures make it difficult to compare financial results across companies. One firm, for example, might record a purchase as an asset and another firm could record it as an expense. Businesses also have many choices regarding depreciation methods, useful lives, and salvage value.

Another limitation of financial statement analysis is that financial statements are prepared assuming that the dollar is a stable monetary unit; this is far from correct. The amounts reported do not necessarily represent dollars with today's purchasing power.

Finally, it is difficult to compare financial results of businesses that use different financing methods, classify expenses differently, have different policies for paying owner-employees, and operate as different types of business entities. Financial statement analysis is useful only if these limitations are clearly understood.

Summary of Ratios

This chapter examined many ratios that are commonly used by analysts to evaluate a business. A summary of the ratios is shown in Table 23.2.

TABLE 23.2   Summary of Ratios Used in Statement Analysis

Ratio	Equation	Performance Measured
Ratios That Measure Profitability, Operating Results, and Efficiency		
Rate of return on net sales	$\dfrac{\text{Net income after taxes}}{\text{Net sales}}$	Percentage of each sales dollar that reflects net income
Rate of return on common stockholders' equity	$\dfrac{\text{Net income after taxes} - \text{Preferred dividend requirements}}{\text{Common stockholders' equity}}$	Rate of return on book value of common stock
Earnings per share of common stock	$\dfrac{\text{Net income after taxes} - \text{Preferred dividend requirements}}{\text{Average number of shares of common stock outstanding during year}}$	Income accruing on each share of common stock
Price-earnings ratio	$\dfrac{\text{Market price per share of common stock}}{\text{Earnings per share of common stock}}$	Value of a share of common stock compared with income accruing to that share
Yield on common stock	$\dfrac{\text{Cash dividend per share of common stock}}{\text{Market value per share of common stock}}$	Cash income (dividend) from a share of common stock as a percentage of the market value of the share
Rate of return on total assets	$\dfrac{\text{Income before interest expense and income taxes}}{\text{Total assets}}$	Effectiveness of management in utilizing assets, regardless of how they were financed
Asset turnover	$\dfrac{\text{Net sales}}{\text{Total assets}}$	Effectiveness of management in using assets to generate sales
Ratios That Measure Financial Strength		
Number of times bond interest earned	$\dfrac{\text{Income before bond interest and income taxes}}{\text{Bond interest cash requirement}}$	Security afforded bondholders
Ratio of stockholders' equity to total equities	$\dfrac{\text{Stockholders' equity}}{\text{Total equities}}$	Portion of assets provided by stockholders and therefore security afforded creditors
Ratio of stockholders' equity to total liabilities	$\dfrac{\text{Stockholders' equity}}{\text{Total liabilities}}$	Owners' capital compared with liabilities; measures security afforded creditors
Book value per share of common stock	$\dfrac{\text{Total stockholders' equity} - \text{Equity of preferred stock}}{\text{Number of common shares outstanding}}$	Amount owner of each share would receive if assets were sold for their book value and the corporation was liquidated

TABLE 23.2 [continued] **Summary of Ratios Used in Statement Analysis**

Ratios That Measure Liquidity		
Working capital	Current assets − Current liabilities	Dollar amount of security provided short-term creditors
Current ratio	$\dfrac{\text{Current assets}}{\text{Current liabilities}}$	Ability of business to pay current debts using current assets
Acid-test ratio	$\dfrac{\text{Cash + receivables + marketable securities}}{\text{Current liabilities}}$	Immediate liquidity or short-run debt-paying ability
Inventory turnover	$\dfrac{\text{Cost of goods sold}}{\text{Average merchandise inventory}}$	Effectiveness of control of inventory for sales volume
Accounts receivable turnover	$\dfrac{\text{Net credit sales}}{\text{Average receivables}}$	Efficiency with which sales on account are collected
Average collection period	$\dfrac{\text{365 days}}{\text{Accounts receivable turnover}}$	Average number of days required to collect sales on account

Section 3 Self Review

QUESTIONS

1. Name three measurements often used in evaluating profitability.

2. What does book value per share measure?

3. Why is it useful to know the inventory turnover for a company?

EXERCISES

4. The price-earnings ratio for common stock is computed using
   a. par value.
   b. market value.
   c. book value.
   d. stated value.

5. The average collection period is determined by dividing
   a. 365 days by the accounts receivable turnover.
   b. net credit sales by 365 days.
   c. net credit sales by average receivables.
   d. beginning accounts receivable by ending accountings receivable.

ANALYSIS

6. A corporation's stock is selling at $36 per share, and its earnings are $6 per share. The corporation is paying an annual dividend of $3.00. What is the price-earnings ratio? What is the yield on common stock?

(Answers to Section 3 Self Review are on page 841.)

REVIEW   Chapter Summary

Financial statement analysis involves computation and interpretation. Computation includes the calculation of percentages and ratios. Interpretation means comparing one set of figures with another (prior statements, budgets, or industrial averages) and determining the financial implications of those comparisons. The comparative statement is a convenient form for the presentation of figures for analysis and appraisal.

Learning Objectives

1 Use vertical analysis techniques to analyze a comparative income statement and balance sheet.

Vertical analysis expresses each item as a percentage of a base amount on the statement.

■ Net sales are the base for all income statement items. To compute an item's percentage of net sales, divide the amount of that item by the amount of net sales.

Example: $\dfrac{\text{Total operating expenses}}{\text{Net sales}}$

■ Total assets (or total liabilities plus owner's equity) are the base for vertical analysis items on a balance sheet. Each figure is expressed as a percentage of the base.

Example: $\dfrac{\text{Cash}}{\text{Total assets}}$

It is customary to carry the percentage computed to one decimal place further than needed and then to round it off. The usual practice is to round percentages to the nearest one-tenth of a percent.

2 Use horizontal analysis techniques to analyze a comparative income statement and balance sheet.

Horizontal analysis compares items from one year to the next. The amount of change and the percentage change is computed.

■ Changes to items such as gross sales, cost of goods sold, operating expenses, and net income can be studied on the income statement.

Example: $\dfrac{\text{Increase in total operating expenses}}{\text{Total operating expenses for base year}}$

■ A firm's balance sheets for two or more periods can be presented in comparative form to permit a comparison of items from year to year.

Example: $\dfrac{\text{Increase in cash}}{\text{Cash in base year}}$

3 Use trend analysis to evaluate financial statements.

Comparing ratio and percentage relationships of the current year with only those of the previous year can be misleading and are not adequate to indicate long-term trends.

Using data from five or more years, trend analysis compares selected ratios and percentages to analyze operations.

Trend analysis often omits income tax expense because the companies' forms of business could be different (that is, sole proprietorships, partnerships, corporations).

4 Interpret the results of the statement analyses by comparison with industry averages.

Companies often compare financial statements with industry averages to determine how the company's operations stack up against other businesses in the industry. In order to make these comparisons, similar classification structures must be in place.

Varied operational procedures and accounting treatments can create inconsistency in data presentation:

■ Different businesses keep different types of accounts and do not classify items in a consistent manner.

■ No two businesses are exactly alike in terms of merchandise, customers, financing, asset acquisition, and other areas.

■ Industry averages might include data from sole proprietorships, partnerships, and corporations. This creates inconsistency in presentation of financial information.

5 Compute and interpret financial ratios that measure profitability, operating results, and efficiency.

Net income and other factors are used to evaluate profitability, operating results, and business efficiencies. Analysts review the sales of the company in

Learning Objectives (continued)

relation to net income, the nature of operations, how assets are used to earn income for the business, and how successful the company has been in rewarding its stockholders.

Measures of profitability, operating results, and efficiency include

- rate of return on net sales,
- rate of return on common stockholders' equity,
- earnings per share of common stock,
- price-earnings ratio,
- yield on common stock,
- rate of return on total assets,
- asset turnover.

6   **Compute and interpret financial ratios that measure financial strength.**

The ability to satisfy long-term debt obligations and to deliver adequate dividend returns to stockholders offers key indications of a company's overall financial strength. Comparison of a company's long-term liabilities to the book value of its property, plant, and equipment can reveal the level of security afforded to long-term creditors. In addition, measurements of book value indicate the financial strength underlying each share of stock.

Measures of financial strength include

- number of times bond interest earned,
- ratio of stockholders' equity to total equities,
- ratio of stockholders' equity to total liabilities,
- book value per share of common stock.

7   **Compute and interpret financial ratios that measure liquidity.**

A company's ability to pay its currently maturing debts is of critical importance to short-term creditors, long-term creditors, and stockholders. Current assets such as cash, inventories, and accounts receivable are measured against items such as current liabilities and credit sales to establish the liquidity of the business.

Measures of liquidity include

- working capital,
- current ratio,
- acid-test ratio,
- inventory turnover,
- accounts receivable turnover,
- days' sales in receivables.

8   **Recognize shortcomings in financial statement analysis.**

The benefits of analysis are limited by a number of significant issues:

- Different companies use different accounting methods. No two companies are exactly the same: there are different mixes of products sold, different organizational structures, and different types of entities.
- Financial statements reflect historical costs, rather than current market values.
- Financial statements are prepared assuming that the dollar is a stable monetary unit.

9   **Define the accounting terms new to this chapter.**

Glossary

Accounts receivable turnover (p. 819) A measure of the speed with which sales on account are collected; the ratio of net credit sales to average receivables

Acid-test ratio (p. 818) A measure of immediate liquidity; the ratio of quick assets to current liabilities

Asset turnover (p. 814) A measure of the effective use of assets in making sales; the ratio of net sales to total assets

Average collection period (p. 819) The ratio of 365 days to the accounts receivable turnover; also called the *number of days' sales in receivables*

Common-size statements (p. 802) Financial statements with items expressed as percentages of a base amount

Comparative statements (p. 800) Financial statements presented side by side for two or more years

Current ratio (p. 817) A measure of the ability of a business to pay its current debts using current assets; the ratio of current assets to current liabilities

Horizontal analysis (p. 800) Computing the percentage change for individual items in the financial statements from year to year

Industry averages (p. 809) Financial ratios and percentages reflecting averages for similar companies

Leveraged buyout (p. 816) Purchasing a business by acquiring the stock and obligating the business to pay the debt incurred

Liquidity (p. 817) The ability of a business to pay its debts when due

Price-earnings ratio (p. 813) The ratio of the current market value of common stock to earnings per share of that stock

Quick assets (p. 818) Cash, receivables, and marketable securities

Ratio analysis (p. 800) Computing the relationship between various items in the financial statements

Return on common stockholders' equity (p. 812) A measure of how well the corporation is making a profit for its shareholders; the ratio of net income available for common stockholders to common stockholders' equity

Total equities (p. 815) The sum of a corporation's liabilities and stockholders' equity

Trend analysis (p. 807) Comparing selected ratios and percentages over a period of time

Vertical analysis (p. 800) Computing the relationship between each item on a financial statement to some base amount on the statement

Working capital (p. 817) The measure of the ability of a company to meet its current obligations; the excess of current assets over current liabilities

Comprehensive **Self Review**

1. What is the difference between vertical analysis and horizontal analysis?
2. Name several factors that may cause misleading results when comparing percentage figures of a specific company to industry averages.
3. In general, would it be preferable in a retail store to have a higher or lower inventory turnover? Explain.
4. What does the current ratio tell you?
5. Explain how to compute book value per share of common stock.

(Answers to Comprehensive Self Review are on page 841.)

 Multiple choice questions are provided on the text Web site at www.mhhe.com/price12e

Quiz23

Discussion **Questions**

1. What is meant by vertical analysis of the income statement?
2. Why would a short-term creditor be interested in the analysis of a company's income statement?
3. If a company's net sales and its cost of goods sold both increase by 12 percent from 2009 to 2010, would gross profit on sales also increase by 12 percent?
4. What are common-size statements?
5. In a vertical analysis of the statement of retained earnings, what is the base for comparing each item on the statement?
6. Which is more important: a larger change in percentage or a large change in dollar amount?
7. What does the rate of net income on stockholders' equity tell stockholders?
8. What is the procedure for measuring earnings per share of common stock.
9. How does the acid-test ratio differ from the current ratio?
10. How is inventory turnover computed?
11. What does the accounts receivable turnover measure?
12. As a rule of thumb, what is the minimum desired current ratio?

APPLICATIONS

Exercises

Use the comparative income statement and the comparative balance sheet for Columbus, Inc., to solve Exercises 23.1 through 23.12.

Columbus, Inc.
Comparative Income Statement
Years Ended December 31, 2010 and 2009

	Amounts	
	2010	2009
Sales	1 4 5 0 0 0 0	1 2 5 0 0 0 0
Less Sales Returns and Allowances	9 0 0 0 0	5 0 0 0 0
Net Sales	1 3 6 0 0 0 0	1 2 0 0 0 0 0
Cost of Goods Sold	7 9 5 0 0 0	7 1 5 0 0 0
Gross Profit on Sales	5 6 5 0 0 0	4 8 5 0 0 0
Selling Expenses	1 5 5 5 0 0	1 3 0 0 0 0
General Expenses	1 9 0 0 0 0	1 8 0 0 0 0
Total Expenses	3 4 5 5 0 0	3 1 0 0 0 0
Net Income Before Income Taxes	2 1 9 5 0 0	1 7 5 0 0 0
Income Tax Expense	6 5 8 5 0	5 2 5 0 0
Net Income After Income Taxes	1 5 3 6 5 0	1 2 2 5 0 0

Exercise 23.1
Objective 1
▶ **Vertical analysis of income statement.**

Using the comparative income statement, prepare a vertical analysis of all items from sales through gross profit on sales for the years 2009 and 2010.

Exercise 23.2
Objective 1
▶ **Vertical analysis of balance sheet.**

Prepare a vertical analysis of all asset items on the comparative balance sheet for the years 2010 and 2009.

Exercise 23.3
Objective 2
▶ **Horizontal analysis of income statement.**

Using the comparative income statement, prepare a horizontal analysis of all items on the income statement for 2010 and 2009.

Exercise 23.4
Objective 2
▶ **Horizontal analysis of balance sheet.**

Prepare a horizontal analysis of all items on the comparative balance sheet for the years 2010 and 2009.

Exercise 23.5
Objective 1
▶ **Rate of return on sales.**

Calculate the rate of net income on sales for 2010 and 2009.

Exercise 23.6
Objective 1
▶ **Rate of return on stockholders' equity.**

Compute the rate of net income on stockholders' equity for 2010 and 2009. Retained earnings on January 1, 2009, was $191,525.

Exercise 23.7
Objective 1
▶ **Rate of return on assets.**

Compute the rate of net income before income taxes on total assets for 2010 and 2009. Base your calculation on total ending assets each year.

Exercise 23.8
Objective 1
▶ **Earnings per share.**

Calculate the earnings per share of common stock for 2010 and 2009.

Columbus, Inc.
Comparative Balance Sheet
December 31, 2010 and 2009

	2010	2009
Assets		
Current Assets		
Cash	161 0 0 0	100 0 0 0
Accounts Receivable (Net)	194 0 0 0	160 0 0 0
Inventory	124 0 0 0	90 0 0 0
Total Current Assets	479 0 0 0	350 0 0 0
Property, Plant, and Equipment		
Buildings (Net)	190 0 0 0	200 0 0 0
Equipment (Net)	85 0 0 0	90 0 0 0
Land	70 0 0 0	70 0 0 0
Total Property, Plant, and Equipment	345 0 0 0	360 0 0 0
Total Assets	824 0 0 0	710 0 0 0
Liabilities and Stockholders' Equity		
Current Liabilities		
Accounts Payable	169 8 5 0	200 0 0 0
Other Current Liabilities	22 5 0 0	32 0 0 0
Total Current Liabilities	192 3 5 0	232 0 0 0
Long-Term Liabilities		
Bonds Payable	100 0 0 0	100 0 0 0
Total Long-Term Liabilities	100 0 0 0	100 0 0 0
Total Liabilities	292 3 5 0	332 0 0 0
Stockholders' Equity		
Common Stock ($1 par)	200 0 0 0	200 0 0 0
Retained Earnings	331 6 5 0	178 0 0 0
Total Stockholders' Equity	531 6 5 0	378 0 0 0
Total Liabilities and Stockholders' Equity	824 0 0 0	710 0 0 0

Price-earnings ratio.

Calculate the price-earnings ratio for 2010 and 2009. The common stock selling price at year-end 2010 was $1.50 and for 2009 was $1.10.

◀ **Exercise 23.9**
Objective 5

Current ratio.

Calculate the current ratio for 2010 and 2009.

◀ **Exercise 23.10**
Objective 7

Inventory turnover.

Using the data for 2010 and 2009, calculate the inventory turnover for each year. The beginning inventory for year 2009 was $88,000.

◀ **Exercise 23.11**
Objective 3

Accounts receivable turnover.

Compute the accounts receivable turnover on December 31, 2010, for Columbus, Inc. Assume that all sales were credit sales.

◀ **Exercise 23.12**
Objective 3

PROBLEMS

Problem Set A H·M™

Problem 23.1A ▶
Objectives 1, 2

eXcel

Horizontal and vertical analysis of income statement and balance sheet.

The Printer Company sells computer parts through a retail store that it operates. The firm's comparative income statement and balance sheet for the years 2010 and 2009 are shown below and on page 829.

The Printer Company
Comparative Income Statement
Years Ended December 31, 2010 and 2009

	Amounts	
	2010	2009
Revenue		
Sales	8 9 5 0 0 0	7 0 5 4 5 0
Less Sales Returns and Allowances	1 2 5 0 0	1 1 6 5 0
Net Sales	8 8 2 5 0 0	6 9 3 8 0 0
Cost of Goods Sold		
Merchandise Inventory, January 1	8 2 5 0 0	8 0 0 0 0
Net Purchases	3 0 6 0 0 0	2 6 2 0 0 0
Total Merchandise Available for Sale	3 8 8 5 0 0	3 4 2 0 0 0
Less Merchandise Inventory, December 31	8 5 0 0 0	8 2 5 0 0
Cost of Goods Sold	3 0 3 5 0 0	2 5 9 5 0 0
Gross Profit on Sales	5 7 9 0 0 0	4 3 4 3 0 0
Operating Expenses		
Selling Expenses		
Sales Salaries Expenses	8 7 0 0 0	7 9 0 0 0
Payroll Tax Expense—Selling	8 7 0 0	7 9 0 0
Other Selling Expenses	2 5 8 0 0	1 5 2 0 0
Total Selling Expenses	1 2 1 5 0 0	1 0 2 1 0 0
General and Administrative Expenses		
Officers Salaries Expense	1 3 0 0 0 0	1 1 0 0 0 0
Payroll Tax Expense—Administrative	1 3 0 0 0	1 1 0 0 0
Depreciation Expense	8 2 5 0	8 2 5 0
Other General and Administrative Expenses	9 4 5 0	7 0 0 0
Total General and Administrative Expenses	1 6 0 7 0 0	1 3 6 2 5 0
Total Operating Expenses	2 8 2 2 0 0	2 3 8 3 5 0
Net Income Before Income Taxes	2 9 6 8 0 0	1 9 5 9 5 0
Income Tax Expense	8 9 0 4 0	5 8 7 8 5
Net Income After Income Taxes	2 0 7 7 6 0	1 3 7 1 6 5

The Printer Company
Comparative Balance Sheet
December 31, 2010 and 2009

	Amounts	
	2010	2009
Assets		
Current Assets		
Cash	88375	47256
Accounts Receivable	60000	37500
Merchandise Inventory	85000	82500
Prepaid Expenses	9500	5000
Supplies	1000	434
Total Current Assets	243875	172690
Property, Plant, and Equipment		
Land	75000	75000
Building and Equipment	82500	82500
Less Accumulated Depreciation	(33000)	(24750)
Net Book Value—Building and Equipment	49500	57750
Total Property, Plant, and Equipment	124500	132750
Total Assets	368375	305440
Liabilities and Stockholders' Equity		
Current Liabilities		
Accounts Payable	22600	55542
Sales Tax Payable	1000	3000
Payroll Taxes Payable	1142	1025
Income Taxes Payable	1000	5000
Total Current Liabilities	25742	64567
Long-Term Liabilities		
Mortgage Payable	39000	45000
Total Long-Term Liabilities	39000	45000
Total Liabilities	64742	109567
Stockholders' Equity		
Common Stock ($1 par, 10,000 shares authorized; 10,000 shares issued and outstanding)	10000	10000
Paid-in Capital—Common Stock	10000	10000
Retained Earnings	283633	175873
Total Stockholders' Equity	303633	195873
Total Liabilities and Stockholders' Equity	368375	305440

INSTRUCTIONS

1. Prepare both a horizontal and a vertical analysis of the statements. Carry all calculations to two decimal places, and then round to one decimal place. (Leave all vertical analysis percentages unadjusted in this problem.)

2. Make written comments about any of the results that seem worthy of investigation.

Analyze: Based on your analysis, which expense category experienced the greatest percentage change?

Problem 23.2A ▶

Objectives 5, 6, 7

CONTINUING >>>

Problem

Computing financial ratios.

Part I Using the financial statements for The Printer Company from Problem 23.1A, calculate the following financial ratios for 2009 and 2010. Comment on any ratio that merits additional consideration.

1. Current ratio
2. Acid-test ratio
3. Inventory turnover
4. Return on sales
5. Earnings per share of common stock
6. Book value per share of common stock
7. Return on total assets
8. Ratio of stockholders' equity to total equities
9. Rate of return on stockholders' equity
10. Asset turnover

Assume all sales are credit sales.

Part II Selected ratios for other common-size companies in the same industry as The Printer Company follow. Using this data and the ratios you computed in Part I, write brief comments on areas you feel are strengths, weaknesses, or require further observation for The Printer Company.

1. Rate of return on stockholders' equity, 45.0 percent
2. Stockholders' equity to total equities, 0.6 to 1 (or 60%)
3. Asset turnover, 2.5 to 1
4. Merchandise inventory turnover, 4.5 times

Analyze: The Printer Company experienced a 51.5 percent increase in net income after taxes from 2009 to 2010. What return on sales can be anticipated if net sales increase by 5 percent in 2011?

Problem 23.3A ▶

Objectives 5, 6, 7

eXcel

Compute and interpret ratios.

On the following page, you will find the condensed financial statements for Five Inc. and Six Inc. for 2010.

INSTRUCTIONS

1. Compute the following ratios for each company.
   a. Rate of return on net sales
   b. Rate of return on total assets at year-end.
   c. Rate of return on stockholders' equity at year-end.
   d. Earnings per share of common stock.
   e. Ratio of stockholders' equity to total equities.
   f. Current ratio.
   g. Asset turnover.
   h. Book value per share of common stock.
2. Comment on any similarities or differences in the two companies' ratios. When possible, comment on the cause for these differences.
3. From the investor's point of view, is one company more at risk than the other?
4. Would you grant a five-year loan to either company? Explain.

Income Statements
Year Ended December 31, 2010

	Five Inc.	Six Inc.
Sales (Net)	7 9 5 0 0 0	6 5 0 0 0 0
Cost of Goods Sold	5 0 5 0 0 0	3 5 0 0 0 0
Gross Profit	2 9 0 0 0 0	3 0 0 0 0 0
Operating Expenses	1 6 9 5 0 0	1 2 5 0 0 0
Net Income from Operations	1 2 0 5 0 0	1 7 5 0 0 0
Interest Expense	1 0 0 0 0	0
Net Income Before Income Tax	1 1 0 5 0 0	1 7 5 0 0 0
Income Tax Expense	2 7 6 2 5	4 3 7 5 0
Net Income After Income Tax	8 2 8 7 5	1 3 1 2 5 0

Balance Sheets
December 31, 2010

	Five Inc.	Six Inc.
Assets		
Current Assets	1 2 5 0 0 0	1 0 4 9 0 0
Property, Plant, and Equipment (Net)	2 2 5 0 0 0	1 9 6 0 0 0
Total Assets	3 5 0 0 0 0	3 0 0 9 0 0
Liabilities and Stockholders' Equity		
Liabilities		
Current Liabilities	9 8 5 0 0	7 9 8 0 0
Long-Term Liabilities (Bonds Payable)	1 0 0 0 0 0	0
Total Liabilities	1 9 8 5 0 0	7 9 8 0 0
Stockholders' Equity		
Common Stock ($10 Par Value)	2 0 0 0 0	2 0 0 0 0
Retained Earnings	1 3 1 5 0 0	2 0 1 1 0 0
Total Stockholders' Equity	1 5 1 5 0 0	2 2 1 1 0 0
Total Liabilities and Stockholders' Equity	3 5 0 0 0 0	3 0 0 9 0 0

Analyze: Assume that Six Inc. believes that it can cut the cost of goods sold by 5 percent in 2011 while keeping net sales and operating expenses at 2010 levels. If the company met this goal, discuss the potential implications to the rate of return on sales and earnings per share. Assume a tax rate of 25 percent.

Problem Set B

Problem 23.1B ▶
Objectives 1, 2

Horizontal and vertical analysis of income statement and balance sheet.

On Sales, Inc., sells old books. The firm's comparative income statement and balance sheet for the years 2009 and 2010 follow.

On Sales, Inc.
Comparative Income Statement
For Years Ended December 31, 2010 and 2009

	Amounts	
	2010	2009
Revenue		
Sales	5 9 5 5 0 0	4 0 5 5 0 0
Less Sales Returns and Allowances	3 5 0 0	1 2 5 0
Net Sales	5 9 2 0 0 0	4 0 4 2 5 0
Cost of Goods Sold		
Merchandise Inventory, January 1	3 6 0 0 0	4 0 0 0 0
Net Purchases	2 7 5 0 0 0	1 6 2 0 0 0
Total Merchandise Available for Sale	3 1 1 0 0 0	2 0 2 0 0 0
Less Merchandise Inventory, December 31	3 5 0 0 0	3 6 0 0 0
Cost of Goods Sold	2 7 6 0 0 0	1 6 6 0 0 0
Gross Profit on Sales	3 1 6 0 0 0	2 3 8 2 5 0
Operating Expenses		
Selling Expenses		
Sales Salaries Expenses	8 7 0 0 0	8 0 0 0 0
Payroll Tax Expense—Selling	8 7 0 0	8 0 0 0
Other Selling Expenses	2 5 8 0 0	1 5 2 0 0
Total Selling Expenses	1 2 1 5 0 0	1 0 3 2 0 0
General and Administrative Expenses		
Officers Salaries Expense	7 5 0 0 0	5 0 0 0 0
Payroll Tax Expense—Administrative	7 5 0 0	5 0 0 0
Depreciation Expense	7 0 0 0	7 0 0 0
Other General and Administrative Expenses	4 5 0 0	2 0 0 0
Total General and Administrative Expenses	9 4 0 0 0	6 4 0 0 0
Total Operating Expenses	2 1 5 5 0 0	1 6 7 2 0 0
Net Income Before Income Taxes	1 0 0 5 0 0	7 1 0 5 0
Income Tax Expense	2 5 1 2 5	1 7 7 6 2
Net Income After Income Taxes	7 5 3 7 5	5 3 2 8 8

On Sales, Inc.
Comparative Balance Sheet
December 31, 2010 and 2009

	Amounts	
	2010	2009
Assets		
Current Assets		
Cash	8 8 3 7 5	3 0 1 1 7
Accounts Receivable	4 0 0 0 0	2 0 0 0 0
Merchandise Inventory	3 5 0 0 0	3 6 0 0 0
Prepaid Expenses	1 5 0 0	5 0 0
Supplies	5 0 0	4 3 4
Total Current Assets	1 6 5 3 7 5	8 7 0 5 1
Property, Plant, and Equipment		
Land	4 0 0 0 0	4 0 0 0 0
Building and Store Equipment	8 2 5 0 0	8 2 5 0 0
Less Accumulated Depreciation	(1 4 0 0 0)	(7 0 0 0)
Net Book Value—Building and Store Equipment	6 8 5 0 0	7 5 5 0 0
Total Property, Plant, and Equipment	1 0 8 5 0 0	1 1 5 5 0 0
Total Assets	2 7 3 8 7 5	2 0 2 5 5 1
Liabilities and Stockholders' Equity		
Current Liabilities		
Accounts Payable	4 0 8 8 7	4 5 0 0 0
Sales Tax Payable	2 0 0 0	2 5 0 0
Payroll Taxes Payable	1 2 0 0	1 0 0 0
Interest Payable	2 1 2 5	7 6 3
Total Current Liabilities	4 6 2 1 2	4 9 2 6 3
Long-Term Liabilities		
Mortgage Payable	7 4 0 0 0	7 5 0 0 0
Total Long-Term Liabilities	7 4 0 0 0	7 5 0 0 0
Total Liabilities	1 2 0 2 1 2	1 2 4 2 6 3
Stockholders' Equity		
Common Stock ($1 par, 20,000 shares authorized;		
20,000 shares issued and outstanding)	2 0 0 0 0	2 0 0 0 0
Paid-in Capital—Common Stock	5 0 0 0	5 0 0 0
Retained Earnings	1 2 8 6 6 3	5 3 2 8 8
Total Stockholders' Equity	1 5 3 6 6 3	7 8 2 8 8
Total Liabilities and Stockholders' Equity	2 7 3 8 7 5	2 0 2 5 5 1

INSTRUCTIONS

1. Prepare both a horizontal and a vertical analysis of the two statements. Carry all calculations to two decimal places, and then round to one place. (Leave all vertical analysis percentages unadjusted in this problem.)

2. Make written comments about any of the results that seem worthy of investigation.

Analyze: If On Sales experiences the same growth in net sales in 2011 as was reported in 2010, what net sales can be projected?

Problem 23.2B ▶

Objectives 1, 2, 3

Problem

Computing financial ratios.

Using the data from Problem 23.1B, On Sales, Inc., calculate the following financial ratios. Comment on any ratio that merits further consideration. Inventory on December 31, 2008, was $40,000.

Part I

1. Current ratio
2. Acid-test ratio
3. Inventory turnover
4. Return on sales
5. Earnings per share of common stock
6. Book value per share of common stock
7. Return on total assets
8. Ratio of stockholders' equity to total equities
9. Ratio of stockholders' equity to total liabilities
10. Rate of return on ending stockholders' equity
11. The dividend yield per share of common stock. Assume a dividend of $1.00 per share was paid in 2010 and $0.50 per share was paid in 2009. The market value per share of common stock in 2010 was $2.50 and in 2009 was $1.50.

Part II

Selected industry ratios are given below. Compare the ratios of On Sales, Inc., with these ratios.

1. Rate of return on sales, 10 percent
2. Return on total assets, 25 percent
3. Merchandise inventory turnover, 6 times
4. Current ratio, 2.5 to 1

Analyze: Based on the analysis you have performed, do you see a trend that could affect the company's stock in the next fiscal year?

Compute and interpret various ratios.

Condensed financial statements for ABC Corp. and XYZ Corp. for 2010 follow.

◄ **Problem 23.3B**
Objectives 1, 2, 3

Income Statements
Year Ended December 31, 2010

	ABC Corp.	XYZ Corp.
Sales (Net)	2 500 000	2 350 000
Costs of Goods Sold	1 475 000	1 222 000
Gross Profit on Sales	1 025 000	1 128 000
Operating Expenses	776 400	859 550
Net Income from Operations	248 600	268 450
Interest Expense	25 000	25 000
Net Income Before Income Tax	223 600	243 450
Income Tax Expense	76 024	82 773
Net Income After Income Tax	147 576	160 677

INSTRUCTIONS

1. Compute the following ratios for each company.

   a. Rate of return on net sales

   b. Rate of return on total assets at end of year

   c. Rate of return on stockholders' equity at end of year

   d. Earnings per share of common stock

   e. Ratio of stockholders' equity to total equities

   f. Current ratio

   g. Asset turnover

   h. Book value per share of common stock

2. Comment on the similarities and differences in the ratios computed for the two companies, pointing out the major factor that causes differences.

3. In which corporation would stock ownership be riskier? Explain.

Balance Sheets
December 31, 2010

	ABC Corp.	XYZ Corp.
Assets		
Current Assets	558 630	526 600
Property, Plant, and Equipment (Net)	817 000	750 000
Total Assets	1 375 630	1 276 600
Liabilities and Stockholders' Equity		
Liabilities		
Current Liabilities	315 000	205 500
Long-Term Liabilities (Bonds Payable)	250 000	150 000
Total Liabilities	565 000	355 500
Stockholders' Equity		
Common Stock ($10 Par Value)	500 000	500 000
Retained Earnings	310 630	421 100
Total Stockholders' Equity	810 630	921 100
Total Liabilities and Stockholders' Equity	1 375 630	1 276 600

4. Would you consider the extension of short-term credit to ABC Corp. or XYZ Corp. riskier? Explain.

Analyze: What percentage of net sales was expended for operating expenses by ABC Corp.? By XYZ Corp.?

Critical Thinking Problem 23.1

Company Improvements

Produce Sales Company's condensed income statement and balance sheet for the years 2010 and 2009 follow.

INSTRUCTIONS

Using the following additional information, fill in the missing values.

1. Accounts Receivable increased 20 percent from 2009 to 2010.

2. There were no new purchases of land, property, or equipment in 2010.

3. Accounts Payable increased 10 percent from 2009 to 2010.

4. No new shares of common stock were issued in 2010.

5. The company paid out cash dividends of $50,000 in 2010.

6. The inventory turnover ratio for 2010 was 6 times.

7. The asset turnover ratio in 2010 was 2.4 times and in 2009 was 2.3 times.

8. The earnings per share in 2010 was $29.25 and in 2009 was $19.425.

9. The income tax rate in both years was 25 percent.

Analyze: Assume that the management of Produce Sales Company had been given a directive by the board of directors to improve the company's current ratio in 2010. Did the company improve its standing in this regard from 2009?

Produce Sales Company Condensed Comparative Income Statement For Years Ending December 31, 2010 and 2009		
	Amounts	
	2010	**2009**
Sales	?	?
Less:Cost of Goods Sold	?	500,000
Gross Profit	?	?
Operating Expenses		
Selling Expenses	405,000	292,000
General and Administrative Expenses	345,000	240,000
Total Operating Expenses	750,000	532,000
Net Income Before Income Tax	?	?
Income Tax Expense	?	?
Net Income After Income Tax	?	?

Produce Sales Company
Comparative Balance Sheet
December 31, 2010 and 2009

	Amounts	
	2010	2009
Assets		
Current Assets		
Cash	175,000	90,000
Accounts Receivable	?	100,000
Merchandise Inventory	110,000	75,000
Total Current Assets	?	265,000
Property, Plant, and Equipment		
Land	60,000	?
Property, Plant, and Equipment	200,000	?
Less Accumulated Depreciation	(40,000)	?
Total Property, Plant, and Equipment	?	240,000
Total Assets	?	505,000
Liabilities and Stockholders' Equity		
Current Liabilities		
Accounts Payable	121,000	?
Accrued Expenses	?	?
Total Current Liabilities	158,750	135,000
Stockholders' Equity		
Common Stock ($10 par, 10,000 shares authorized)	50,000	?
Paid in Capital in Excess of Par—Common Stock	100,000	?
Retained Earnings	?	220,000
Total Stockholders' Equity	?	?
Total Liabilities and Stockholders' Equity	?	?

Critical Thinking Problem 23.2

Filling in the Blanks

Rick Hunter, the accountant for Hunter Incorporated, was asked to make a presentation to the board of directors concerning the corporation's year-end financial position. While flying to the meeting on Saturday morning, Hunter checked the papers in his briefcase and realized he had left the income statement on his desk back at the office. Since he knew there would not be enough time for anyone to get to the office and fax him a copy of the statement, he examined the rest of the material in his briefcase to see what information was available.

A review of the statement of retained earnings revealed that net income after income taxes for the year was $96,800. From some notes he had made for the presentation, he knew that the corporation's gross profit on sales was 40 percent and net income as a percentage of net sales was 8 percent. The income tax rate for the corporation is 28 percent, and Hunter also remembered that the selling and administrative expenses were the same amount. With this information, he was able to reconstruct the income statement for the corporation before the plane reached its destination.

INSTRUCTIONS

Using the same information given above, prepare an income statement for Hunter Incorporated for the current year. To get started, first list the major headings for a condensed income statement. Then, starting with the net income figure, work to fill in the dollar amounts based on the percentage relationships given.

BUSINESS CONNECTIONS

Statement Analysis

Managerial FOCUS

1. Suppose that a vertical analysis of the income statement shows an item to be 18 percent of net sales. How would this information be used in order to make it meaningful? With what would it be compared?

2. In 2010, the cost of goods sold was 66 percent of net sales. For 2009, the same item was 63 percent, and for 2008 it was 60 percent. What recommendations would you make about items or activities that should be investigated further?

3. In deciding whether an increase in accounts receivable during the current year is desirable or undesirable, what factors should management consider?

4. Management is concerned that over a three-year period a company's balance sheets show that the total stockholders' equity has changed from 56 percent to 51 percent to 43 percent of total equities. What factors might explain this trend?

5. A company's income statements reveal that its net income after taxes has been 4.3 percent of net sales for each of the past three years. During that time, the industry average has been about 7 percent. What types of questions would management want answered in seeking an explanation for this difference?

6. A company's net sales increased by 35 percent from one year to the next year. During that period, selling expenses increased by 41 percent. Is this desirable? Explain.

Timing of Adjusting Entry

Ethical DILEMMA

The timing of adjusting entries can alter the analysis of a company. As the full-charge bookkeeper, it is your job to ensure that the adjusting entries are entered on a timely basis. You have noticed that the adjusting entry to transfer the current year's portion from mortgage payable—long term to mortgage payable—current has not been entered. You mention it to your controller and are told not to record this adjusting entry. The company is applying for a loan from the bank and the controller found out that the loan officer looks only at the current assets and current liabilities. You are further told that if anyone questions the lack of the adjusting entry to apologize for the error and record it immediately. Is this ethical for you and the company's controller? Provide justification for your decision.

Analysis

Refer to the *2006 Annual Report* for The Home Depot, Inc., in Appendix A.

STREETWISE: Questions from the REAL WORLD

1. Locate the consolidated statements of earnings. Using vertical analysis, what is the cost of goods sold expressed as a percentage of net sales for the year ended January 28, 2007? If the industry average for this percentage is 70 percent, is The Home Depot, Inc., performing better than the industry average or worse? Why?

2. Locate the consolidated balance sheets. Using horizontal analysis, by what dollar amount and percentage have total assets increased from fiscal 2005 to 2006?

Performance Analysis

The following excerpt was taken from the Safeway Inc. *2006 Annual Report*.

Three-Year Summary Financial Information			
(Dollars in millions, except per-share amounts)	52 Weeks 2006	52 Weeks 2005	52 Weeks 2004
Results of Operations			
Sales and Other Revenue	$40,185.0	$38,416.0	$35,822.9
Gross Profit	$11,581.0	$11,112.9	$10,595.3
Operating Profit	1,599.8	1,214.7	1,172.8
Net Income (loss)	$ 870.6	$ (561.1)	$ (560.2)

Analyze:

1. Compute the increase in sales for each fiscal year. Compute the increase in gross profit for each fiscal year.

2. Based on your computations, describe any figure that appears to be out of line or inconsistent with other amounts. Explain.

3. What further investigation do you think is required to understand the situation?

Analyze Online: Locate the Safeway Inc. Web site (www.safeway.com). Access company financials using the *Investors* link.

4. Click on the *News Releases* link and select one of the financial press releases posted. Describe the type of financial information reported in the press release. What percentage increases or decreases were reported? Describe how these computations were made.

5. What reasons were given for the increased or decreased figures cited?

Capital Structure

The methods in which a company's capital is obtained from various sources are very important in analyzing the soundness of the company's financial position. Explain the differences between equity capital and debt capital. From a company's point of view, describe the risks associated with each type of capital.

Investigating the Numbers

The balance sheet of Crandall Gifts Company revealed a 25 percent increase in accounts receivable from fiscal 2009 to 2010. Net sales remained constant. As the senior accountant for the company, you are responsible for explaining this increase to upper management. Your accounting clerk will help you investigate the figure. Draft a memo to your accounting clerk with directions about the types of investigations you would like the clerk to perform. What supporting documents or schedules should be examined? What might be the cause of such an increase?

Vertical Analysis

Vertical analysis of comparative financial statements can indicate the success or failure of a business. As a loan officer for a bank, you must choose the company that will receive a $50,000 loan. Perform a vertical analysis of each company listed on the next page to help make the decision. In groups of two, decide who should receive the loan. Explain why you consider your company better able to repay the loan. Defend your decision to the class.

	Javier's Junk Store	Ling's Little Loot
Cash	$ 30,000	$ 30,000
Accounts Receivable	2,000	3,500
Total Current Assets	40,000	50,000
Total Assets	100,000	100,000
Current Liabilities	20,000	50,000
Total Liabilities	50,000	70,000
Common Stock	20,000	20,000
Retained Earnings	30,000	10,000
Total Stockholders' Equity	50,000	30,000
Net Sales	10,000	7,000
Cost of Sales	7,000	3,500
Operating Expenses	2,000	1,500
Net Income	1,000	2,000

Internet | CONNECTION

Trend Analysis

A wise decision is to investigate the company in which you plan to invest time or money. Go to the Web site of a company you have an interest in investing in or accepting employment from. Look for the trend analysis over 5 to 10 years. Is the trend declining, increasing, or remaining constant? What does this trend tell you about any investment or employment in this company? Would your investment be safe over the next five years? Do you see an opportunity for advancement if you accepted employment with this company?

Answers to **Self Reviews**

Answers to Section 1 Self Review

1. It is a financial statement with items expressed as a percentage of a base rather than in dollar amounts.
2. The computation phase involves simple mathematical computations. The interpretation phase considers what caused relationships or changes and what can be done to improve the relationships or changes.
3. Vertical analysis of the income statement is based on net sales.
4. **b.** Each item in the income statement is divided by net sales.
5. **c.** total assets or total liabilities and stockholders' equity.
6. In 2009, the percentage of net income after taxes was 4.8 percent. In 2010, the percentage was 2.8 percent.

Answers to Section 2 Self Review

1. Such comparisons point out areas in which the business is performing either better or worse than average. The areas showing poorer performance can be investigated to determine the reason and then to address it.
2. The newer company would probably have a higher ratio because its book value is likely to be higher (less depreciation that has been charged off), and its assets are likely to be newer, which means they were acquired at higher price levels than those acquired in earlier years by the older company.
3. It is determined by first subtracting an amount from the base year amount and then dividing the difference by the base year amount.

4. **a.** horizontal analysis.
5. **c.** 30 percent.
6. ■ 2009: 21.4 percent
   ■ 2010: 22.0 percent
   ■ $98,775 increase; 13.8 percent

Answers to Section 3 Self Review

1. Rate of return on net sales, rate of return on total assets, and earnings per share of common stock are all common measures of profitability.
2. Measures the amount each common stockholder would receive if assets were sold for their book value and the corporation liquidated.
3. If inventory turnover is too low, compared to industry standards, it suggests that the amounts tied up in the inventory are excessive for the sales volume being generated.
4. **b.** market value
5. **a.** 365 days by the accounts receivable turnover
6. The price-earnings ratio is $36/$6 or 6.0. The yield on common stock is $3/$36 or 8.3 percent.

Answers to Comprehensive Self Review

1. Vertical analysis refers to a comparison of items on an individual financial statement, using one number as the base. The income statement uses net sales as 100 percent while the balance sheet uses total assets or total liabilities and stockholders' equity as 100 percent. Each item on the statement is compared to the base. Horizontal analysis refers to a comparison of data for the current period with data of a prior period for the financial statement.
2. Different accounting methods, different types of entities, different ages of assets, and different financing methods can impair comparability.
3. A higher inventory turnover number would probably indicate that assets are being used more effectively in generating sales in a retail business.
4. It tells you the general ability of the business to pay its debts on time. It is computed by dividing current assets by current liabilities.
5. The value is determined by dividing the common stockholders' equity (total stockholders' equity minus the book value of preferred stock) by the number of shares of common stock outstanding.

The Statement of Cash Flows

LEARNING OBJECTIVES

1. Distinguish between operating, investing, and financing activities.   LP24
2. Compute cash flows from operating activities.
3. Compute cash flows from investing activities.
4. Compute cash flows from financing activities.
5. Prepare a statement of cash flows.
6. Define the accounting terms new to this chapter.

NEW TERMS

cash equivalents
direct method
financing activities
indirect method
investing activities
operating activities

operating assets and liabilities
schedule of operating expenses
statement of cash flows

Apple Inc.   www.apple.com

Apple Inc. is committed to bringing the best personal computing, portable digital music, and mobile communication experience to consumers through its innovative hardware, software, peripherals, services, and Internet offerings. The company's unique approach to design coupled with hip advertising campaigns have generated a distinctive identity and significant brand loyalty for the Apple line of products. As of 2007, Apple had sold over 110 million iPods, making it the best-selling digital audio player in history.

As the company evolves from a computer company to a consumer electronics company, executives review Apple's financial capabilities for growth. The consolidated statement of cash flows for 2007 reported nearly $5.5 billion in cash flow provided by operating activities. In its *2007 Annual Report*, the company discussed its strategy to expand its distribution network to effectively reach more of its targeted customers

thinking critically

How does the cash flow statement complement the income statement and the balance sheet?

Section 1

SECTION OBJECTIVE

>> 1. Distinguish between operating, investing, and financing activities.

WHY IT'S IMPORTANT

When forecasting the cash needs of a business, accountants need to understand how cash and cash equivalents are generated as well as how the business uses its cash.

TERMS TO LEARN

cash equivalents
financing activities
investing activities
operating activities
statement of cash flows

Video24.1

Sources and Uses of Cash

Corporations issue four financial statements: income statement, balance sheet, statement of retained earnings or stockholders' equity, and statement of cash flows.

The Importance of a Statement of Cash Flows

The **statement of cash flows** provides information about the cash receipts and cash payments of a business. Creditors, including bondholders, noteholders, and suppliers of goods and services, review the statement of cash flows to determine how the firm will pay interest and principal on debts. Investors examine the statement of cash flows to determine if the corporation will have the cash to pay dividends. Management is also interested in cash flows. The firm needs cash to pay employees, suppliers, and to meet other obligations. Analyzing past cash flows is helpful because they indicate the sources and uses of cash in the future.

The Meaning of Cash

On the statement of cash flows, the term *cash* includes cash and cash equivalents. As you know, cash consists of coin, currency, and bank accounts. **Cash equivalents** are easily convertible into known amounts of cash. They include certificates of deposit (CDs), U.S. Treasury bills, and money market funds. A short-term investment is a cash equivalent if it matures within three months from the date the business acquired it. Suppose a certificate of deposit acquired by a corporation on September 1, 2009, matures on March 1, 2010. The CD is not classified as a cash equivalent on the December 31, 2009, balance sheet because the maturity date is more than three months from the date the certificate was acquired.

>>1. OBJECTIVE

Distinguish between operating, investing, and financing activities.

LP24

Sources and Uses of Cash

Cash inflows are called *sources of cash*. *Cash outflows* are called *uses of cash*. Sources and uses of cash are classified under three headings on the statement of cash flows.

■ **Cash Flows from Operating Activities. Operating activities** are routine business operations. Cash inflows from operating activities include the sale of merchandise or services for cash, collection of accounts receivable created by the sale of merchandise or services, and miscellaneous sources, such as interest income. Cash outflows from operations commonly result from paying operating expenses when they are incurred, paying accounts payable for merchandise purchased on account, and paying accounts payable for operating expenses incurred but not immediately paid.

■ **Cash Flows from Investing Activities. Investing activities** involve the acquisition (cash outflow) or disposal (cash inflow) of long-term assets, including land, buildings, equipment, and investments in bonds and other securities.

844

	Sources of Cash	**Uses of Cash**
Operating Activities	Sale of merchandise Sale of services Interest income Dividend income Miscellaneous income	Pay for merchandise Pay taxes Pay salaries and wages Pay interest expense Pay for other expenses
Investing Activities	Sale of land, buildings, or equipment Principal payments collected on receivable for long-term assets Sale of investment in bonds or other securities	Pay for purchase of land buildings, or equipment Pay for the purchase of investments in bonds or other securities
Financing Activities	Issuance of common stock Issuance of preferred stock Issuance of bonds payable Borrowing through signing a note payable Resale of treasury stock	Pay cash dividends on common stock Pay cash dividends on preferred stock Repay bond indebtedness Repay notes payable or other borrowing Purchase treasury stock

TABLE 24.1

Sources and Uses of Cash in a Corporation

■ **Cash Flows from Financing Activities. Financing activities** involve transactions that provide cash to the business to carry on its activities. Cash inflows from financing activities include issuing bonds and capital stock for cash, borrowing cash by signing notes payable, and reselling treasury stock. Cash outflows from financing activities include paying notes or bonds payable, purchasing treasury stock, and paying cash dividends.

Table 24.1 summarizes sources (inflows) and uses (outflows) of cash.

Section **1** Self Review

QUESTIONS

1. What are cash equivalents?

2. What are investing activities?

3. Is short-term borrowing by signing a note payable a financing or investing activity? Explain.

EXERCISES

4. Investing activities include

   a. purchases of merchandise for cash.

   b. purchases of plant and equipment for cash.

   c. purchases of prepaid expense items such as supplies and insurance for cash.

   d. issuance of common stock.

5. An example of a financing activity is the

   a. sale of merchandise for cash.

   b. issuance of stock for cash.

   c. sale of used equipment for cash.

   d. collection of debts acquired from the sale of long-term assets.

ANALYSIS

6. Indicate whether each account or transaction is a source of cash or use of cash.

   a. issuance of preferred stock

   b. interest expense

   c. taxes expense

   d. interest income

   e. resale of treasury stock

(Answers to Section 1 Self Review are on page 875.)

SECTION OBJECTIVE	TERMS TO LEARN
>> 2. **Compute cash flows from operating activities.**	operating assets and liabilities
WHY IT'S IMPORTANT	schedule of operating expenses
The income statement reports net income on an accrual basis. It does not report actual cash flows. To identify cash flows from operating activities, the financial statement reader needs to review the statement of cash flows.	

Cash Flows from Operating Activities

To prepare the statement of cash flows, you need the income statement, schedule of operating expenses, the statement of retained earnings, and a comparative balance sheet. The **schedule of operating expenses** is a supplemental schedule showing the selling and general and administrative expenses in greater detail.

Let's use the financial statements for Household Products, Inc., to explain the statement of cash flows. These statements appear in Figures 24.1 through 24.4.

FIGURE 24.1

Income Statement

Household Products, Inc. Income Statement Year Ended December 31, 2010			
Revenue			
Sales		3 1 0 4 4 5 0	
Less Sales Returns and Allowances		1 3 5 4 5 0	
Net Sales			2 9 6 9 0 0 0
Cost of Goods Sold			
Merchandise Inventory, January 1		2 2 5 0 0 0	
Purchases (Net)		1 7 0 6 5 0 0	
Freight In		2 6 0 0 0	
Total Merchandise Available for Sale		1 9 5 7 5 0 0	
Less Merchandise Inventory, December 31		2 0 5 0 0 0	
Cost of Goods Sold			1 7 5 2 5 0 0
Gross Profit			1 2 1 6 5 0 0
Operating Expenses			
Selling Expenses		5 2 6 4 2 5	
General and Administrative Expenses		6 0 5 0 0 0	
Total Operating Expenses			1 1 3 1 4 2 5
Net Income from Operations			8 5 0 7 5
Other Income			
Gain on Sale of Equipment		4 0 0 0	
Interest Income		1 8 0 0	
Total Other Income			5 8 0 0
Other Expenses			
Bond Interest Expense		9 5 0 0	
Other Interest Expense		2 0 0 0	
Total Other Expenses			1 1 5 0 0
Net Income Before Income Taxes			7 9 3 7 5
Income Tax Expense			2 3 8 1 2
Net Income After Income Taxes			5 5 5 6 3

FIGURE 24.2

Schedule of Operating Expenses

Household Products, Inc.
Schedule of Operating Expenses
Year Ended December 31, 2010

Selling Expenses		
Advertising	22 800 00	
Depreciation	7 180 00	
Employee Fringe Benefits	30 000 00	
Freight Out and Deliveries	16 000 00	
Insurance	3 000 00	
Miscellaneous	2 070 00	
Other Taxes	3 000 00	
Payroll Taxes—Sales Staff	30 000 00	
Rent	12 000 00	
Repairs and Maintenance	5 000 00	
Sales Commissions	164 500 00	
Sales Salaries	175 000 00	
Sales Supplies	22 500 00	
Travel and Entertainment	26 875 00	
Utilities	6 500 00	
Total Selling Expenses		526 425 00
General and Administrative Expenses		
Officers' Salaries	350 000 00	
Office Employees' Salaries	150 000 00	
Payroll Taxes—Administrative Staff	35 000 00	
Office Supplies	6 500 00	
Postage, Copying, and Miscellaneous	7 000 00	
Uncollectible Accounts Expense	16 500 00	
Rent or Lease Expense	8 750 00	
Depreciation	5 000 00	
Other Taxes	16 500 00	
Utilities	14 250 00	
Total General and Administrative Expenses		605 000 00
Total Operating Expenses		1 131 425 00

Household Products, Inc.
Comparative Statement of Retained Earnings
Years Ended December 31, 2010 and 2009

	Amounts		Increase or Decrease
	2010	2009	
Balance, January 1	202 243	164 993	37 250
Additions			
Net Income After Taxes	55 563	41 250	14 313
Total	257 806	206 243	51 563
Deductions			
Dividends, Preferred	4 000	4 000	0
Total Deductions	4 000	4 000	0
Balance, December 31	253 806	202 243	51 563

FIGURE 24.3   **Comparative Statement of Retained Earnings**

Household Products, Inc.
Comparative Balance Sheet
December 31, 2010 and 2009

	Amounts 2010	Amounts 2009	Increase or (Decrease) Amount
Assets			
Current Assets			
Cash	1 1 5 2 3 1	8 0 7 7 3	3 4 4 5 8
Accounts Receivable	1 0 2 0 0 0	7 3 5 0 0	2 8 5 0 0
Merchandise Inventory	2 0 5 0 0 0	2 2 5 0 0 0	(2 0 0 0 0)
Prepaid Expenses	1 2 0 0	1 5 0 0	(3 0 0)
Supplies	5 0 0	2 5 0	2 5 0
Total Current Assets	4 2 3 9 3 1	3 8 1 0 2 3	4 2 9 0 8
Property, Plant, and Equipment			
Land	8 0 0 0 0	8 0 0 0 0	0
Building and Store Equipment	7 1 8 0 0	7 7 8 0 0	(6 0 0 0)
Less Accumulated Depreciation—Building and Store Equipment	2 8 5 2 0	2 3 3 4 0	5 1 8 0
Net Book Value—Building and Store Equipment	4 3 2 8 0	5 4 4 6 0	(1 1 1 8 0)
Office Equipment	1 0 5 0 0	6 0 0 0	4 5 0 0
Less Accumulated Depreciation—Office Equipment	2 0 0 0	1 5 0 0	5 0 0
Net Book Value—Office Equipment	8 5 0 0	4 5 0 0	4 0 0 0
Total Property, Plant, and Equipment	1 3 1 7 8 0	1 3 8 9 6 0	(7 1 8 0)
Total Assets	5 5 5 7 1 1	5 1 9 9 8 3	3 5 7 2 8
Liabilities and Stockholders' Equity			
Current Liabilities			
Accounts Payable	7 1 0 0 0	8 4 5 0 0	(1 3 5 0 0)
Sales Tax Payable	2 9 0 0	2 5 0 0	4 0 0
Payroll Taxes Payable	1 1 4 5	1 0 2 5	1 2 0
Interest Payable	8 6 0	2 1 5	6 4 5
Total Current Liabilities	7 5 9 0 5	8 8 2 4 0	(1 2 3 3 5)
Long-Term Liabilities			
10% Bonds Payable, 2019	1 0 0 0 0 0	1 0 0 0 0 0	0
Premium on Bonds Payable	3 5 0 0	4 0 0 0	(5 0 0)
Mortgage Payable	6 0 0 0 0	6 5 0 0 0	(5 0 0 0)
Total Long-Term Liabilities	1 6 3 5 0 0	1 6 9 0 0 0	(5 5 0 0)
Total Liabilities	2 3 9 4 0 5	2 5 7 2 4 0	(1 7 8 3 5)
Stockholders' Equity			
Preferred Stock ($100 par, 8%, 500 shares authorized, issued and outstanding)	5 0 0 0 0	5 0 0 0 0	0
Common Stock ($1 par, 25,000 shares authorized			
Issued and outstanding: 7,000 shares in 2009; 8,000 shares in 2010)	8 0 0 0	7 0 0 0	1 0 0 0
Paid-in Capital—Common Stock	4 5 0 0	3 5 0 0	1 0 0 0
Retained Earnings			
Retained Earnings—Unappropriated	2 5 3 8 0 6	2 0 2 2 4 3	5 1 5 6 3
Total Retained Earnings	2 5 3 8 0 6	2 0 2 2 4 3	5 1 5 6 3
Total Stockholders' Equity	3 1 6 3 0 6	2 6 2 7 4 3	5 3 5 6 3
Total Liabilities and Stockholders' Equity	5 5 5 7 1 1	5 1 9 9 8 3	3 5 7 2 8

FIGURE 24.4 **Comparative Balance Sheet**

Statement of Cash Flows

The statement of cash flows reconciles the beginning and ending cash balances. It ties together the income statement and the changes in the noncash items on the balance sheet and on the statement of retained earnings.

Figure 24.4 shows the comparative balance sheet for Household Products, Inc. There are no cash equivalents on the balance sheet. In 2010, the beginning cash balance was $80,773; the ending cash balance was $115,231. Cash increased by $34,458. The statement of cash flows shows the factors that caused the increase in cash.

There are two ways to prepare the statement of cash flows: the direct method and the indirect method. Household Products, Inc., uses the indirect method. The direct method will be described later in this chapter. The indirect method treats net income as the primary source of cash from operating activities and adjusts net income for changes in noncash items.

The accrual basis of accounting is used when recording transactions and preparing the balance sheet and the income statement. Net income shown on the income statement includes both cash and noncash transactions. On the statement of cash flows, net income is adjusted for the noncash items.

Figure 24.5 on page 850 shows the statement of cash flows for Household Products, Inc. Let's examine it and learn how to prepare the statement of cash flows. Throughout this chapter, you will need to refer to the financial statements and reports for Household Products, Inc.

Cash Flows from Operating Activities

The first section of the statement of cash flows shows net cash provided by operating activities. For Household Products, Inc., $37,958 was provided by operating activities. Since cash flows from operating activities are closely related to net income, the starting point for the analysis of the cash flows from operating activities is the net income after income taxes, taken from the income statement in Figure 24.1. The Cash Flows from Operating Activities section of the cash flows statement explains why the net cash flows from operations ($37,958) differs from the net income after taxes ($55,563). There were several income and expense items reported on the income statement that did not involve cash inflows or outflows during that period. Lets analyze those items.

EXPENSE AND INCOME ITEMS INVOLVING LONG-TERM ASSETS AND LIABILITIES

Some items on the income statement result from adjustments related to long-term assets or long-term liabilities. They do not involve cash inflows or outflows in the current year. These adjustments are added to or subtracted from net income.

Depreciation Expense The acquisition of property, plant, and equipment is reported in the Cash Flows from Investing Activities section of the statement of cash flows in the year acquired. Depreciation, depletion, and amortization of assets do not involve a cash outlay in the year the expense is recorded. Instead, these expenses represent a reduction in the net asset value. Figure 24.2 shows depreciation expense of $7,680 (sum of $7,180 recorded as selling expenses and $500 recorded as general and administrative expenses). The depreciation expense was recorded as follows.

1	2010					1
2	Dec.	31	Depreciation Expense (Selling)	7 1 8 0 00		2
3			Depreciation Expense (General)	5 0 0 00		3
4			Accumulated Depreciation		7 6 8 0 00	4

Note that the depreciation expense did not involve a cash outflow. Net income was reduced by a noncash expense. To obtain cash flows from operating activities, the depreciation expense is added back to net income.

FIGURE 24.5

Statement of Cash Flows

Household Products, Inc. Statement of Cash Flows Year Ended December 31, 2010			
Cash Flows from Operating Activities			
Net income after taxes (per income statement)			5 5 5 6 3
Adjustments to reconcile net income to net cash			
provided by operating activities			
Depreciation Expense	7 6 8 0		
Amortization of premium on bonds payable	(5 0 0)		
Gain on sale of equipment	(4 0 0 0)		
Changes in noncash current assets and current			
liabilities			
Increase in Accounts Receivable	(2 8 5 0 0)		
Decrease in Merchandise Inventory	2 0 0 0 0		
Decrease in Prepaid Expenses	3 0 0		
Increase in Supplies	(2 5 0)		
Decrease in Accounts Payable	(1 3 5 0 0)		
Increase in Sales Tax Payable	4 0 0		
Increase in Payroll Taxes Payable	1 2 0		
Increase in Interest Payable	6 4 5		
Total Adjustments		(1 7 6 0 5)	
Net Cash Provided by Operating Activities			3 7 9 5 8
Cash Flows from Investing Activities			
Proceeds from sale of equipment	8 0 0 0		
Purchase of Office Equipment	(4 5 0 0)		
Net Cash Provided by Investing Activities			3 5 0 0
Cash Flows from Financing Activities			
Payment of Mortgage Payable principal	(5 0 0 0)		
Proceeds from issue of Common Stock	2 0 0 0		
Payment of dividends on Preferred Stock	(4 0 0 0)		
Net Cash used in Financing Activities		(7 0 0 0)	
Net Increase in Cash and Cash Equivalents			3 4 4 5 8
Cash and Cash Equivalents, January 1, 2010			8 0 7 7 3
Cash and Cash Equivalents, December 31, 2010			1 1 5 2 3 1

Note: During the year, payments for income taxes were $23,813 and payments for interest expense were $11,355.

important!

Bond Interest Expense

The bond interest expense on the income statement is less than the actual cash outflow; therefore, on the statement of cash flows, the difference is subtracted from net income.

Amortization of Premium on Bonds Payable The income statement shows bond interest expense of $9,500. This is not the actual cash outflow for interest. It reflects the cash paid minus $500 of bond premium amortization. The bond interest expense was recorded as follows.

11		Bond Interest Expense	9 5 0 0 0 0		11
12		Premium on Bonds Payable	5 0 0 0 0		12
13		Cash		1 0 0 0 0 0 0	13

The amount of bond interest expense reported on the income statement understates the actual cash outflow by $500. To obtain cash flows from operating activities, the amortization of the bond premium is deducted from net income.

Gain or Loss on Sale of Equipment The income statement shows a gain of $4,000 on the sale of equipment. The equipment was sold for $8,000 cash. Thus, the proceeds from the sale of the equipment was shown as a cash inflow from investing activities. At the time of sale, the following entry was made.

21	Cash	8 000 00			21
22	Accumulated Depreciation—Equipment	2 000 00			22
23	Equipment		6 000 00		23
24	Gain on Sale of Equipment		4 000 00		24

The sale of the equipment is not a part of the routine operating activities of the business. The gain of $4,000 is a part of the $8,000 in cash received from the asset sale. As we see, the entire $8,000 was included in cash inflows from investing activities. It is therefore necessary to remove (deduct) the $4,000 of gain on sale of equipment from the net income figure in arriving at the net cash inflow provided by operations. A loss on sale of long-term assets would be added to net income.

INCOME AND EXPENSE ITEMS INVOLVING CHANGES IN CURRENT ASSETS AND CURRENT LIABILITIES

Current assets and current liabilities are often referred to as **operating assets and liabilities.** Usually, changes in current assets and current liabilities are related to routine business operations and are reflected in net income. Assume that all the changes in the current assets and current liabilities of Household Products, Inc., resulted from routine operating activities.

Increases in Current Assets Current assets include accounts receivable, merchandise inventory, and prepaid expenses. Increases in current assets are deducted from net income to arrive at cash flows from operating activities. Look at the following examples. The comparative balance sheet for Household Products, Inc., Figure 24.4, shows that several current assets increased during the year.

Increase in Accounts Receivable Figure 24.4 shows that *Accounts Receivable* increased by $28,500. This means that more sales on account were recorded than collected. The sales were included in net income, but the cash has not been received. To obtain cash flows from operating activities, the increase in accounts receivable is subtracted from net income.

> The Hasbro, Inc., consolidated statements of cash flows for the fiscal year ended December 31, 2003, reported net cash provided by operating activities of $454.2 million. Depreciation of plant and equipment, increases in accounts receivable, increases in inventories, and increases in prepaid expenses were considered when reconciling net income to net cash provided by operating activities on the statement of cash flows. These transactions affected net income, but they did not affect cash flows.

Increase in Supplies Figure 24.4 shows that *Supplies* increased by $250. This means that more supplies were paid for than were used. Net income does not reflect all cash paid for supplies. To obtain cash flows from operating activities, the increase in supplies is subtracted from net income.

Decreases in Current Assets Decreases in noncash current assets are added to net income to arrive at cash flows from operating activities. The following example will illustrate why this rule applies.

Decrease in Prepaid Expenses Figure 24.4 shows that *Prepaid Expenses* decreased by $300. This means that more was charged to expenses than was paid for prepaid expenses in arriving at net income for the year. In other words, net income reflects the use of prepaid expenses. To obtain cash flows from operating activities, the decrease in prepaid expenses is added to net income.

Decrease in Merchandise Inventory Figure 24.4 shows that *Merchandise Inventory* decreased by $20,000. This means that more inventory was sold than was purchased. The sale of the inventory was reflected in net income as cost of goods sold, but cash was not paid to replace the inventory. Net income reflects higher costs than actual cash outflows. To obtain cash flows from operating activities, a decrease in inventory is added to net income.

Increases in Current Liabilities Current liabilities include accounts payable, sales tax payable, payroll taxes payable, and interest payable. Increases in current liabilities are added to net income to obtain the cash flows from operating activities. Look over the following situations.

Increase in Sales Tax Payable Figure 24.4 shows that *Sales Tax Payable* increased by $400. This means that more sales tax was owed than was paid during the year. To obtain cash flows from operating activities, the increase in sales tax payable is added to net income.

Increase in Payroll Taxes Payable Figure 24.4 shows that *Payroll Taxes Payable* increased by $120. This means that more payroll taxes were owed than were paid. To obtain cash flow from operating activities, the increase in payroll taxes payable is added to net income.

Increase in Interest Payable Figure 24.4 shows that *Interest Payable* increased by $645. This means that more interest was recorded as expense than was paid in cash. To obtain cash flows from operating activities, the increase in interest payable is added to net income.

Decreases in Current Liabilities Decreases in current liabilities are subtracted from net income. An illustration using *Accounts Payable* will show why this rule exists.

Decrease in Accounts Payable Figure 24.4 shows that *Accounts Payable* decreased $13,500. This means more cash was paid on account than purchases were recorded on account. The cash was paid out but was not reflected in net income. To obtain cash flows from operating activities, the decrease in accounts payable is subtracted from net income.

Summary of Effects of Changes in Current Assets and Current Liabilities Let's summarize how net income is adjusted for changes in current assets and current liabilities when computing cash flows from operating activities.

	Add to Net Income	Deduct from Net Income
Increase in current asset		X
Decrease in current asset	X	
Increase in current liability	X	
Decrease in current liability		X

Figure 24.5 shows all items considered when computing net cash provided by operating activities. During the year, operating activities for Household Products, Inc., provided $37,958 of cash.

EFFECT OF NET LOSS ON CASH FLOWS FROM OPERATIONS

If the income statement reflects a net loss, the first line of the statement of cash flows is the net loss. All adjustments for changes in current assets and current liabilities are made to the net loss figure.

Section 2 Self Review

QUESTIONS

1. The income statement shows a loss of $20,000 on the sale of a building. How is the loss handled when computing net cash provided by operating activities?

2. The income statement shows depreciation expense of $12,500. How is the expense handled when computing net cash provided by operating activities?

3. During the year, the notes payable account increased from $45,000 to $50,000. How, if at all, is this reflected when computing net income from operations?

EXERCISES

4. The net cash provided by operating activities is affected by
   a. the issue of bonds payable for cash.
   b. a purchase of land for cash.
   c. the sale of stock for cash.
   d. a change in merchandise inventory.

5. To determine the net cash provided by operating activities, an increase in prepaid assets should be
   a. added to net cash flow.
   b. deducted from net income.
   c. added to net income.
   d. not included in the calculation.

ANALYSIS

6. The net loss for the year was $15,000. Depreciation expense was $4,000. *Merchandise Inventory* decreased by $3,000. *Accounts Receivable* decreased by $5,000. *Accounts Payable* decreased by $2,500. *Income Tax Payable* decreased by $5,000. Calculate the net cash provided or used by operating activities for the year.

(Answers to Section 2 Self Review are on page 875.)

Cash Flows from Investing and Financing Activities

Investing and financing activities can produce both cash outflows and cash inflows.

Cash Flows from Investing Activities

Investing activities are transactions involving the acquisition or disposal of assets that are not consumed in routine operations within one year.

CASH OUTFLOWS FROM INVESTING ACTIVITIES

The most common cash outflows from investing activities are cash payments for purchases of property, plant, and equipment and for purchases of the stocks and bonds of other corporations.

Figure 24.4 shows that the *Office Equipment* account increased by $4,500 during 2010. The increase resulted from the purchase of office equipment for $4,500 in cash. This is a cash outflow from investing activities. It is reported on the statement of cash flows in Figure 24.5.

>>3. OBJECTIVE

Compute cash flows from investing activities.

LP24

CASH INFLOWS FROM INVESTING ACTIVITIES

Most cash inflows from investing activities reflect the sale of land, buildings, equipment, or investments in securities of other corporations. Payments of principal received on mortgages or notes held by the company in connection with the sale of plant and equipment are classified as cash inflows from investing activities.

In 2010, Household Products, Inc., had one cash inflow from investing activities. The corporation sold store equipment for $8,000 in cash.

Sales price (cash inflow)		$8,000
Asset cost	$6,000	
Accumulated depreciation	(2,000)	(4,000)
Gain on sale		$4,000

The statement of cash flows shows the $8,000 received from the sale of the store equipment as a cash inflow from investing activities. Recall that the gain was subtracted from net income in the Cash Flows from Operating Activities section.

At this point, it is possible to reconcile the changes in the long-term asset accounts. The net change of $6,000 (decrease) in the **Building and Store Equipment** account is reconciled as follows.

Building and store equipment, Dec. 31, 2009	$77,800
Add: Purchases during 2010	–0–
Less: Cost of equipment sold during 2010	6,000
Building and store equipment, Dec. 31, 2010	$71,800

The increase in accumulated depreciation can be reconciled to the depreciation expense for the year as follows.

Accumulated Depreciation

	Building & Store Equip.		Office Equip.		Total
2010	$28,520	+	$2,000	=	$30,520
2009	(23,340)	+	(1,500)	=	(24,840)
Increase	$ 5,180	+	$ 500	=	$ 5,680
Accumulated depreciation on equipment sold					2,000
Depreciation expense for 2010					$ 7,680

The Cash Flows from Investing Activities section of the statement of cash flows for Household Products, Inc., shows that $3,500 cash was provided by investing activities during 2010.

Cash Flows from Financing Activities

Financing activities include debt and equity transactions.

CASH INFLOWS FROM FINANCING ACTIVITIES

Cash inflows from financing activities include amounts received from the original issue of preferred stock or common stock, the resale of treasury stock, and the issue of bonds and notes payable.

Proceeds of Cash Investments by Stockholders Figure 24.4 shows that the **Common Stock** account increased by $1,000 and the **Paid-in Capital—Common Stock** account increased by $1,000. During 2010, Household Products, Inc., issued 1,000 shares of common stock for $2.00 per share. This resulted in a cash inflow of $2,000 (1,000 × $2.00) as reported on the statement of cash flows.

Proceeds of Short-Term and Long-Term Borrowing Figure 24.4 shows that Household Products, Inc., did not seek additional cash from short-term or long-term note payable during 2010. If the company had obtained cash from borrowing, it would have been reported in the financing activities section of the cash flow statement as noted in Table 24.1.

During 2010, bond premium of $500 was amortized. Remember that the amortized premium was included in the Cash Flows from Operating Activities section. The change of $500 in **Premium on Bonds Payable** is reconciled as follows.

Premium on bonds payable, Dec. 31, 2009	$4,000
Add: Premium on bonds sold in 2010	0
Less: Premium amortized in 2010	(500)
Premium on bonds payable, Dec. 31, 2010	$3,500

important!

Investing Activities
Investing activities are transactions that involve the acquisition or disposal of assets that will not be used up or consumed in routine operations in a short time.

ABOUT
ACCOUNTING

Managing Cash
Large companies actively manage their own corporate cash. Smaller businesses often place their cash in money market funds or "sweep accounts" by their banker, due to the limited time and resources available for cash management.

>>4. OBJECTIVE
Compute cash flows from financing activities.

LP24

recall

Treasury Stock
Treasury stock is a corporation's own capital stock that has been issued, fully paid for, and reacquired by the corporation.

recall

Bonds Issued at a Premium
On the day that bonds are issued, if the market rate of interest is lower than the face rate of interest, the bonds will sell at a premium.

CASH OUTFLOWS FROM FINANCING ACTIVITIES

Cash outflows from financing activities result from the repayment of debt obligations such as bonds payable, notes payable, and mortgages; the purchase of treasury stock; and the retirement of preferred stock. The payment of cash dividends is classified as a cash outflow from financing activities. Interest expense, however, is classified as an outflow of cash from operating activities.

Payment of Mortgage Payable Figure 24.4 shows a decrease of $5,000 in the *Mortgage Payable* account during 2010. This decrease is a result of $5,000 of principal payments. These payments are shown on the statement of cash flows as a cash outflow from financing activities.

During 2010, Household Products, Inc., did not acquire cash through short-term borrowing, nor did it repay any short-term loans. However, if it had, these short-term transactions might not appear on the balance sheet. For example, the corporation could have borrowed $10,000 by signing a three-month note payable on March 1, 2010, and repaid the note on June 1, 2010. The note would not appear on the December 31, 2010, balance sheet. However, the note would represent both an inflow and an outflow of cash. The note would be reported in the Cash Flows from Financing Activities section of the statement of cash flows.

Payment of Cash Dividends Figure 24.3 indicates that during the year Household Products, Inc., paid cash dividends of $4,000 on preferred stock. This amount is included as a part of cash flows from financing activities.

The statement of cash flows shows that in 2010 cash of $7,000 was used by the financing activities of Household Products, Inc.

>>5. OBJECTIVE

Prepare a statement of cash flows.

LP24

Preparing a Statement of Cash Flows

The cash flows from the three types of business activities—operating, investing, and financing—are combined to arrive at the net change in cash and cash equivalents for the year. The net change is then combined with the beginning balance of cash and cash equivalents to reconcile to the ending balance of cash and cash equivalents. Figure 24.5 shows that the net change in the cash and cash equivalents was an increase of $34,458. The cash balance was $80,773 on January 1, 2010, and $115,231 on December 31, 2010. These are the same amounts reported on the comparative balance sheet in Figure 24.4.

DIRECT AND INDIRECT METHODS OF PREPARING THE STATEMENT OF CASH FLOWS

There are two methods of preparing the statement of cash flows: the indirect and direct methods. Figure 24.5 was prepared using the **indirect method.** Under this method, in the Cash Flows from Operating Activities section, net income is treated as the primary source of cash and is adjusted for changes in current assets and liabilities associated with net income, non-cash transactions, and other items. Most corporations use the indirect method.

The Financial Accounting Standards Board allows the indirect or direct method. Under the **direct method,** all revenue and expenses reported on the income statement appear in the operating section of the statement of cash flows and show the cash received or paid out for each type of transaction. Under the direct method, a corporation reports cash flows from operating activities in two major classes: gross cash receipts and gross cash payments. The FASB suggests the following classifications for reporting cash inflows and outflows:

- cash collected from customers
- interest and dividends received
- cash paid to employees and other suppliers of goods or services, including suppliers of insurance and advertising
- interest paid
- income taxes paid

Corporations that use the direct method are encouraged to provide additional meaningful information about operating cash receipts and cash payments if feasible. The direct method is not commonly used because many businesses do not have easy access to the records of cash payments for each type of expenditure.

MANAGERIAL IMPLICATIONS <<

CASH FLOW

- Management needs to ensure that cash is available to meet operating expenses and to pay debts promptly.
- Management analyzes the statement of cash flows to evaluate the operations of the company, plan future operations, forecast cash needs, arrange proper financing, and plan dividend payments.
- Management uses the statement of cash flows to determine how well the company will be able to meet its maturing obligations.
- Management analyzes past cash flows in order to make plans that will keep the company solvent and profitable.

THINKING CRITICALLY

If the only financial statement available to you is the cash flow statement, could you evaluate the business as a potential investment?

inte rnal **CONTROL**

When the statement of cash flows is based on the direct method, it must be accompanied by a reconciliation of net income to the net cash provided by operating activities. This reconciliation shows the same information as the Cash Flows from Operating Activities section of the statement of cash flows prepared using the indirect method. The additional work is another reason that many corporations avoid the direct method of preparing the statement of cash flows. Intermediate accounting textbooks provide detailed information about the direct method.

DISCLOSURES REQUIRED IN THE STATEMENT OF CASH FLOWS

Various disclosures are added to the statement of cash flows. If the indirect method of presentation is used, the amount of interest and income taxes paid during the period are reported in notes accompanying the statement. The note at the bottom of Figure 24.5 shows that cash payments were $23,813 for income taxes and $11,355 for interest.

In order to provide complete information to statement readers, information about noncash investing and financing activities are disclosed on the statement of cash flows. Examples of financing and investing activities not affecting cash flows include issuing bonds payable for land or converting bonds payable into common stock.

important!

Disclosures
If the indirect method is used, the interest and income taxes paid during the period are separately disclosed.

Amazon.com reported net income during 2006 of approximately $190 million. During the same period, cash provided by operating activities was $702 million and the balance sheet reported cash and cash equivalents of over $1.0 billion. Net sales during the same period were approximately $10.7 billion, an increase of $2.2 billion over 2005.

Section **3** Self Review

QUESTIONS

1. During the year, equipment was sold for $80,000, and a $6,000 gain was recorded. How is this transaction reported on the statement of cash flows?

2. During the year, a corporation issued $100,000 of bonds payable in return for land with a fair market value of $100,000. How is this reported on the statement of cash flows?

3. On the statement of cash flows, how is the payment of a cash dividend reported?

EXERCISES

4. Most corporations prepare the statement of cash flows using the
   a. indirect method.
   b. accrual method.
   c. direct method.
   d. equivalent method.

5. The purchase of equipment for cash is shown on the statement of cash flows as a(n)
   a. decrease in Cash Flows from Financing Activities.
   b. decrease in Cash Flows from Investing Activities.
   c. increase in Cash Flows from Financing Activities.
   d. increase in Cash Flows from Investing Activities.

ANALYSIS

6. A truck that originally cost $40,000 was sold for $12,000 cash. Accumulated depreciation up to the date of the sale was $32,000. A $4,000 gain was reported on the income statement. What is the effect on the statement of cash flows?

(Answers to Section 3 Self Review are on page 875.)

REVIEW   Chapter Summary

In previous chapters, you learned about the three major financial statements prepared for corporations—the income statement, the balance sheet, and the statement of retained earnings. In addition, some corporations prepare a statement of stockholders' equity. The annually published financial statements should also include a statement of cash flows showing the sources and uses of cash.

Learning Objectives

1 Distinguish between operating, investing, and financing activities.

The corporation's activities are divided into three categories on the statement of cash flows: operating, investing, and financing. Cash inflows and outflows from transactions for each type of activity are shown, along with the net cash inflow or outflow.

- Cash flows from operating activities involve routine business operations: selling merchandise for cash, collecting accounts receivable, paying expenses when incurred, and paying accounts payable.

- Investing activities are transactions that involve the acquisition of assets or disposal of assets such as land, equipment, or buildings.

- Financing activities involve transactions such as issuing stocks or bonds, paying a note or bond payable, or paying cash dividends.

2 Compute cash flows from operating activities.

The first section of the statement of cash flows involves operating activities—buying, selling, and administrative activities. This section begins with the net income amount from the income statement.

- To arrive at the net cash flow provided by operating activities, the net income amount is adjusted for noncash items used to calculate net income.

- The most common items added to net income are (1) depreciation, (2) losses on sales of assets, (3) amortization of bond discount, (4) decreases in current assets, and (5) increases in current liabilities.

- The most common items deducted from net income are (1) gains on sales of assets, (2) amortization of bond premium, (3) increases in current assets, and (4) decreases in current liabilities.

3 Compute cash flows from investing activities.

The second section of the statement discloses investing activities.

- Cash inflows from investing often result from cash sales of property, plant, and equipment and cash sales of the stocks and bonds of other corporations held as investments.

- Cash outflows come from cash purchases of plant and equipment and cash purchases of the stocks and bonds of other corporations.

4 Compute cash flows from financing activities.

The third section of the statement concerns financing activities. These activities may reflect transactions between a corporation and its stockholders.

- Cash inflows often result from the issuing of common or preferred stock or selling treasury stock.

- Typical cash outflows are dividend payments and the purchase of treasury stock.

- Cash inflows result from issuing bonds payable for cash and from borrowing money by issuing or discounting notes payable. Cash outflows result when notes payable or bonds payable are repaid. However, interest paid on debt is seen as resulting from an operating activity.

5 Prepare a statement of cash flows.

There are two statement preparation methods—direct and indirect.

- Most corporations use the indirect method because the statement is easier to prepare when this method is used.

- The Financial Accounting Standards Board allows either method.

- Some major transactions that do not involve cash should be disclosed in notes to the statement of cash flows.

6 Define the accounting terms new to this chapter.

Glossary

Cash equivalents (p. 844) Assets that are easily convertible into known amounts of cash

Direct method (p. 856) A means of reporting sources and uses of cash under which all revenue and expenses reported on the income statement appear in the operating section of the statement of cash flows and show the cash received or paid out for each type of transaction

Financing activities (p. 845) Transactions with those who provide cash to the business to carry on its activities

Indirect method (p. 856) A means of reporting cash generated from operating activities by treating net income as the primary source of cash in the operating section of the statement of cash flows and adjusting that amount for changes in current assets and liabilities associated with net income, noncash transactions, and other items

Investing activities (p. 844) Transactions that involve the acquisition or disposal of long-term assets

Operating activities (p. 844) Routine business transactions—selling goods or services and incurring expenses

Operating assets and liabilities (p. 851) Current assets and current liabilities

Schedule of operating expenses (p. 846) A schedule that supplements the income statement, showing the selling and general and administrative expenses in greater detail

Statement of cash flows (p. 844) A financial statement that provides information about the cash receipts and cash payments of a business

Comprehensive **Self Review**

1. What are the three types of activities for which cash flows must be shown in a statement of cash flows?

2. What are some financing activities?

3. During the year, accounts payable increased from $35,000 to $50,000. How, if at all, would this change be reflected in computing net income from operations?

4. Where on the statement of cash flows should a payment of interest expense be shown?

5. Where on the statement of cash flows should a loss on the sale of equipment be shown?

(Answers to Comprehensive Self Review are on page 875.)

 Multiple choice questions are provided on the text Web site at www.mhhe.com/price12e

Quiz24

Discussion Questions

1. What is the purpose of the statement of cash flows?

2. Where is information obtained for preparing the statement of cash flows?

3. Give two examples of cash inflows from investing activities.

4. Give two examples of cash outflows from investing activities.

5. Give two examples of cash outflows from financing activities.

6. Give two examples of cash inflows from financing activities.

7. What are cash and cash equivalents?

8. Is an investment in a corporate bond maturing 180 days after the purchase date a cash equivalent? Explain.

9. A corporation's income statement shows a gain of $8,000 on the sale of plant and equipment. In computing the net cash provided by operating activities, how would this $8,000 be treated?

10. A corporation's income statement shows bond interest expense of $16,500. Amortization of the discount on the bonds during the year was $1,500. What is the amount of cash outflow for bond interest expense?

11. Explain the difference between the direct method and the indirect method of preparing the statement of cash flows.

12. On January 1, 2010, the balance of the **Accounts Payable** account was $31,000. On December 31, 2010, the balance was $41,000. How, if at all, would this change be reflected in the statement of cash flows?

13. On January 1, 2010, the balance of the **Accrued Income Taxes Payable** account was $6,000. On December 31, 2010, the balance was $7,500. How, if at all, would this change be reflected in the statement of cash flows?

14. Why are cash equivalents included on the statement of cash flows?

15. Why must noncash investing and financing activities be disclosed on the statement of cash flows?

16. Identify in which of the three types of activities on the statement of cash flows the following transactions appear. Indicate whether each is a cash inflow or outflow.

    a. Cash dividends paid.

    b. Cash interest payment received.

    c. Cash on notes receivable collected.

    d. Cash interest paid.

    e. Cash received from customers.

    f. Cash proceeds from issuing stock.

APPLICATIONS

Exercises

Effects of transactions on cash flows.

What effect would each of the following transactions have on the statement of cash flows?

◀ **Exercise 24.1**
Objective 1

1. The sum of $3,000 in cash was received from the sale of used office equipment that originally cost $15,000. Depreciation of $12,500 had been taken on the asset up to the date of the sale. The resulting $500 gain was shown on the income statement.

2. The sum of $87,000 in cash was received from the sale of investments in the stock of another corporation. The stock had a book value of $90,000. The $3,000 loss on the sale was shown on the income statement.

Cash flows from operating activities.

The following data are summarized from the income statement of Fiber, Inc., for the year ended December 31, 2010. Using these data and ignoring changes in current assets and current liabilities, prepare a schedule of cash flows from operating activities for the year. (Use Figure 24.5 as a model for this schedule.)

◀ **Exercise 24.2**
Objective 2

Fiber, Inc.		
Income Statement		
Year Ended December 31, 2010		
Sales		520 5 0 0 00
Cost of Goods Sold		246 5 0 0 00
Gross Profit on Sales		274 0 0 0 00

(continued)

(continued from previous page)

Operating Expenses			
Depreciation	20 0 0 0 00		
Other Selling Expenses	145 6 0 0 00		
Other Administrative Expenses	82 5 0 0 00	248 1 0 0 00	
Net Income from Operations		25 9 0 0 00	
Bond Interest Expense			
Cash Interest	16 0 0 0 00		
Amortization of Discount on Bonds Payable	2 0 0 0 00	18 0 0 0 00	
Net Income for Year		7 9 0 0 00	

Exercise 24.3
Objective 2

▶ **Cash flows from operating activities.**

The current assets and current liabilities of Miami Company on December 31, 2010 and 2009, are as follows. The corporation's net income for 2010 was $50,000. Included in its expenses was depreciation of $15,000. Prepare a schedule of the cash flows from operating activities for 2010. (Use Figure 24.5 as a model for this schedule.)

	Dec. 31, 2010	Dec. 31, 2009
Cash	$ 76,500	$60,000
Accounts Receivable	100,000	85,000
Prepaid Expenses	12,000	14,500
Merchandise Inventory	69,000	68,000
Accounts Payable	72,000	78,000
Notes Payable (Borrowing)	25,000	15,000

Exercise 24.4
Objective 2

▶ **Cash flows from operating activities.**

The income statement of Stonebrook, Inc., showed net income of $60,000 for 2010. The firm's beginning inventory was $40,000, and its ending inventory was $44,000. Accounts payable were $34,000 on January 1 and $30,500 on December 31. Compute the net cash provided by the firm's operating activities during the year.

Exercise 24.5
Objective 2

▶ **Cash flows from operating activities.**

The following information is taken from the income statement of HAMCO Inc. for 2010.

Sales		$850,000
Cost of Goods Sold		550,000
Gross Profit on Sales		$300,000
Operating Expenses		
Depreciation	$ 15,000	
Other Operating Expenses	170,000	185,000
Net Income from Operations		$115,000

Additional information relating to account balances at the beginning and end of the year appears below.

	Jan. 1, 2010	Dec. 31, 2010
Accounts Receivable	$46,000	$41,000
Merchandise Inventory	65,000	68,000
Accrued Liabilities	3,000	1,500
Accounts Payable	28,000	20,000

Determine the cash flows from operations for 2010.

Cash flows from investing activities.

The following transactions occurred at Lookout Corporation in 2010. Use this information to compute the company's net cash flow from investing activities.

1. The company issued 10,000 shares of its own $5 par-value common stock for land with a fair market value of $50,000.

2. The company gave its president a loan of $75,000 and obtained a 10 percent note receivable, dated December 22, 2010, and maturing two years later.

3. The company sold a used truck for $8,000 in cash. The original cost of the truck was $24,000. Depreciation of $14,000 had been deducted.

◀ **Exercise 24.6**
Objective 3

Cash flows from investing activities.

The following transactions occurred at Craft Company in 2010. Use this information to compute the company's net cash flow from investing activities.

1. The company purchased a new building for $300,000. A down payment of $50,000 was made. The balance is due in four equal annual installments (plus interest) beginning July 1, 2011.

2. The company bought 1,000 shares of its own common stock for $20,000.

3. The company purchased as an investment $50,000 par value of Ridge Way Company's 10 percent bonds, maturing in five years. The purchase price was $49,000.

◀ **Exercise 24.7**
Objective 3

Cash flows from financing activities.

The following transactions occurred at the Indiana Company in 2010. Use this information to compute the company's net cash flow from financing activities for the year.

1. Holders of $100,000 par-value 7 percent bonds surrendered the bonds for redemption and were paid $106,000 in cash. The unamortized discount on these bonds as of the date of redemption was $1,000.

2. Cash interest of $32,700 was paid on bonds during the year. The bond discount amortized was $300.

3. Cash dividends of $40,000 were paid on common stock during the year.

◀ **Exercise 24.8**
Objective 4

Cash flows from financing activities.

The following transactions occurred at Peter Company in 2010. Use this information to compute the company's net cash flow from financing activities for the year.

1. The company reacquired as treasury stock 10,000 shares of its outstanding common stock, paying a total of $50,000 for the shares.

2. On November 30, the company borrowed $50,000 from the bank, signing a 90-day, 10 percent note payable.

◀ **Exercise 24.9**
Objective 4 ·

PROBLEMS

Problem Set A

Prepare a statement of cash flows.

A comparative balance sheet for Ebeth, Inc., on December 31, 2010 and 2009, follows. Additional information about the firm's financial activities during 2010 is also given below.

◀ Problem 24.1A
Objectives 1, 2, 3, 4, 5
e**X**cel

INSTRUCTIONS

Prepare a statement of cash flows for 2010. Additional information for 2010 follows.

a. Had a $20,000 net income.

b. Recorded $7,000 in depreciation.

c. Issued bonds payable with a par value of $20,000 at par and received cash.

d. Received $10,000 in cash for the issue of an additional 1,000 shares of $10 par value common stock.

e. Purchased equipment for $25,000 in cash.

Ebeth, Inc.
Comparative Balance Sheet
December 31, 2010 and 2009

Assets	2010	2009
Cash	4 8 9 0 0	3 9 5 0 0
Accounts Receivable (Net)	8 2 6 0 0	7 9 6 0 0
Merchandise Inventory	4 5 6 0 0	4 3 0 0 0
Property, Plant, and Equipment	2 1 5 0 0 0	1 9 0 0 0 0
Less: Accumulated Depreciation	(2 6 0 0 0)	(1 9 0 0 0)
Total Assets	3 6 6 1 0 0	3 3 3 1 0 0
Liabilities and Stockholders' Equity		
Liabilities		
Accounts Payable	4 5 0 0 0	6 2 0 0 0
Bonds Payable	1 2 0 0 0 0	1 0 0 0 0 0
Total Liabilities	1 6 5 0 0 0	1 6 2 0 0 0
Stockholders' Equity		
Common Stock, ($1 par, 50,000 shares authorized, 5,000 shares issued in 2009 and 6,000 shares issued in 2010)	6 0 0 0 0	5 0 0 0 0
Retained Earnings	1 4 1 1 0 0	1 2 1 1 0 0
Total Stockholders' Equity	2 0 1 1 0 0	1 7 1 1 0 0
Total Liabilities and Stockholders' Equity	3 6 6 1 0 0	3 3 3 1 0 0

Analyze: Explain why an increase in accounts payable is considered an adjustment to cash flows from operating activities.

Problem 24.2A
Objectives 1, 2, 3, 4, 5

▶ **Prepare a statement of cash flows.**

Postclosing trial balance data and other financial data for The Candy Company as of December 31, 2010 and 2009, follow.

INSTRUCTIONS

Prepare a statement of cash flows for 2010. Additional information for 2010 follows.

a. Sold common stock for $10,000 in cash.

b. Had net income of $60,000 after income taxes.

c. Sold bonds payable for $40,000 cash at par value.

d. Completed a major addition to the building for $60,000 in cash.

e. Bought additional land for $25,000 in cash.

f. Paid common stock dividends of $15,000 in cash.

g. Amortized intangible assets for $600.

h. The short-term note payable resulted from operating activities not borrowing or financing activities.

The Candy Company
Postclosing Trial Balance
December 31, 2010 and 2009

Account Name	2010 Debit	2010 Credit	2009 Debit	2009 Credit
Cash	7 6 4 0 0 0 0		7 2 0 0 0 0 0	
Accounts Receivable (Net)	9 0 5 0 0 0 0		8 5 5 0 0 0 0	
Merchandise Inventory	6 2 2 5 0 0 0		6 5 4 5 0 0 0	
Prepaid Expenses	2 5 0 0 0 0		2 0 0 0 0 0	
Land	5 5 0 0 0 0 0		3 0 0 0 0 0 0	
Plant and Equipment	1 6 5 0 0 0 0 0		1 0 5 0 0 0 0 0	
Accumulated Depreciation—Plant and Equipment		1 6 5 0 0 0 0		1 0 5 0 0 0 0
Intangible Assets	4 4 0 0 0 0		5 0 0 0 0 0	
Notes Payable—Short Term		5 0 0 0 0 0		8 0 0 0 0 0
Accounts Payable		2 4 7 5 0 0 0		2 9 7 5 0 0 0
Payroll Taxes Payable		2 5 0 0 0 0		2 4 0 0 0 0
Income Taxes Payable		1 0 0 0 0 0		2 0 0 0 0 0
Mortgage Payable, 2020		1 2 4 0 0 0 0 0		1 2 5 0 0 0 0 0
7% Bonds Payable, 2015		4 0 0 0 0 0 0		0
Common Stock $1 par		5 0 0 0 0 0 0		4 0 0 0 0 0 0
Retained Earnings		1 9 2 3 0 0 0 0		1 4 7 3 0 0 0 0
Totals	4 5 6 0 5 0 0 0	4 5 6 0 5 0 0 0	3 6 4 9 5 0 0 0	3 6 4 9 5 0 0 0

Analyze: Were activities related to operations, investing, or financing responsible for the largest net inflow of cash?

Preparing a statement of cash flows.

The condensed income statement and comparative balance sheet of Jackson Corporation as of December 31, 2010 and 2009, are provided below. Other financial data is also given.

◀ **Problem 24.3A**
Objectives 1, 2, 3, 4, 5

e**X**cel

INSTRUCTIONS

Prepare a statement of cash flows for Jackson Corporation for 2010. Additional information for 2010 that is pertinent to its preparation follows.

a. No items of property, plant, and equipment were disposed of during the year.

b. Paid cash for the additions to property, plant, and equipment during the year.

c. Paid $10,000 dividends on the common stock in cash during the year.

d. Issued common stock at par value for cash.

e. Paid cash to retire the long-term note payable.

Jackson Corporation
Condensed Income Statement
Year Ended December 31, 2010

Revenues		6 7 5 5 0 0
Costs and Expenses		
Cost of Goods Sold	4 2 9 0 0 0	
Salaries Expense	1 2 5 0 0 0	
Depreciation Expense	1 5 0 0 0	
Advertising Expense	1 4 9 0 0	
Utilities Expense	1 8 0 0 0	
Total Costs and Expenses		6 0 1 9 0 0
Net Income Before Income Taxes		7 3 6 0 0
Income Taxes Expense		1 8 4 0 0
Net Income After Income Taxes		5 5 2 0 0

Jackson Corporation
Comparative Balance Sheet
December 31, 2010 and 2009

Assets	2010	2009
Cash	8 1 0 0 0	7 0 0 0 0
Accounts Receivable (Net)	5 5 6 5 0	5 2 0 0 0
Merchandise Inventory	4 9 0 0 0	5 4 0 0 0
Prepaid Advertising	8 0 0 0	1 0 0 0 0
Property, Plant, and Equipment	1 2 0 0 0 0	1 0 0 0 0 0
Less: Accumulated Depreciation	(2 5 0 0 0)	(1 0 0 0 0)
Total Assets	2 8 8 6 5 0	2 7 6 0 0 0
Liabilities and Stockholders' Equity		
Liabilities		
Accounts Payable	5 0 4 5 0	7 9 0 0 0
Salaries Payable	4 5 0 0	3 5 0 0
Unearned Revenues	4 0 0 0	5 0 0 0
Income Taxes Payable	6 0 0 0	5 0 0 0
Note Payable—2012	0	3 0 0 0 0
Total Liabilities	6 4 9 5 0	1 2 2 5 0 0
Stockholders' Equity		
Common Stock ($2 par)	7 5 0 0 0	5 0 0 0 0
Retained Earnings	1 4 8 7 0 0	1 0 3 5 0 0
Total Stockholders' Equity	2 2 3 7 0 0	1 5 3 5 0 0
Total Liabilities and Stockholders' Equity	2 8 8 6 5 0	2 7 6 0 0 0

Analyze: If Jackson Corporation had written off an uncollectible account receivable of $5,000 during this fiscal period, what adjustment, if any, would be required on the statement of cash flows?

Problem 24.4A ▶

Objectives 1, 2, 3, 4, 5

e**X**cel

Prepare a statement of cash flows.

The comparative balance sheet for Short Company as of December 31, 2010 and 2009, is shown below, followed by the condensed income statement. Other financial data for 2010 is also given.

INSTRUCTIONS

Prepare a statement of cash flows for 2010. Additional information for 2010 follows.

a. Acquired land at a cost of $60,000; paid one-half of the purchase price in cash and issued common stock for the balance.

b. Sold used equipment for $20,000 in cash. The original cost was $40,000; depreciation of $10,000 had been taken. The remaining change in the *Property, Plant, and Equipment* account represents a purchase of equipment for cash. Total depreciation expense for the year was $9,000.

c. Issued bonds payable at par value for cash.

d. Sold bond investments costing $20,000 at no gain or loss during the year.

e. Paid $20,000 cash dividends on the common stock.

Analyze: By what percentage did *Cash* increase from January 1 to December 31?

Short Company
Comparative Balance Sheet
December 31, 2010 and 2009

Assets	2010	2009
Cash	1 1 6 8 7 5	5 3 2 5 0
Accounts Receivable (Net)	8 6 0 0 0	6 7 2 5 0
Merchandise Inventory	8 2 6 5 0	7 4 0 0 0
Prepaid Rent	5 5 0 0	4 5 0 0
Land	8 5 0 0 0	2 5 0 0 0
Property, Plant, and Equipment	1 8 9 0 0 0	2 1 9 0 0 0
Less: Accumulated Depreciation—PPE	(2 0 9 0 0)	(2 1 9 0 0)
Investment in TVA Bonds	3 0 0 0 0	5 0 0 0 0
Total Assets	5 7 4 1 2 5	4 7 1 1 0 0
Liabilities and Stockholders' Equity		
Liabilities		
Accounts Payable	6 6 3 0 0	8 6 6 0 0
Income Taxes Payable	9 2 5 0	9 5 0 0
Bonds Payable	1 4 0 0 0 0	1 0 0 0 0 0
Total Liabilities	2 1 5 5 5 0	1 9 6 1 0 0
Stockholders' Equity		
Common Stock	1 0 5 0 0 0	7 5 0 0 0
Retained Earnings	2 5 3 5 7 5	2 0 0 0 0 0
Total Stockholders' Equity	3 5 8 5 7 5	2 7 5 0 0 0
Total Liabilities and Stockholders' Equity	5 7 4 1 2 5	4 7 1 1 0 0

Short Company
Condensed Income Statement
Year Ended December 31, 2010

Revenues		8 0 9 0 0 0
Costs and Expenses		
Cost of Goods Sold	4 7 5 7 5 0	
Depreciation Expense	9 0 0 0	
Selling and Administrative Expenses	1 9 7 6 5 0	
Interest Expense	1 8 5 0 0	
Loss on Sale of Equipment	1 0 0 0 0	
Income Taxes Expense	2 4 5 2 5	
Total Costs and Expenses		7 3 5 4 2 5
Net Income After Income Taxes		7 3 5 7 5

Problem Set B

Prepare a statement of cash flows.

A comparative balance sheet for Trucking Corporation as of December 31, 2010 and 2009, is given below.

◄ **Problem 24.1B**
Objectives 1, 2, 3, 4, 5

INSTRUCTIONS

Use this data to prepare a statement of cash flows for 2010. Additional information for 2010 follows.

Trucking Corporation
Comparative Balance Sheet
December 31, 2010 and 2009

Assets	2010	2009
Cash	4 3 6 0 0	4 4 9 0 0
Accounts Receivable (Net)	8 4 0 0 0	6 0 8 2 5
Merchandise Inventory	4 5 0 0 0	3 5 0 0 0
Property, Plant, and Equipment	1 3 5 0 0 0	1 5 0 0 0 0
Less: Accumulated Depreciation	(4 8 0 0 0)	(4 5 0 0 0)
Total Assets	2 5 9 6 0 0	2 4 5 7 2 5
Liabilities and Stockholders' Equity		
Liabilities		
Accounts Payable	4 9 6 0 0	4 5 7 2 5
Total Liabilities	4 9 6 0 0	4 5 7 2 5
Stockholders' Equity		
Common Stock, ($1 par, 50,000 shares authorized:		
50,000 shares issued in 2009 and 75,000 shares issued in 2010)	7 5 0 0 0	5 0 0 0 0
Retained Earnings	1 3 5 0 0 0	1 5 0 0 0 0
Total Stockholders' Equity	2 1 0 0 0 0	2 0 0 0 0 0
Total Liabilities and Stockholders' Equity	2 5 9 6 0 0	2 4 5 7 2 5

a. Sold used machinery for $23,000 cash. The original cost was $30,000, and the accumulated depreciation was $9,000; included the gain of $2,000 in net income.

b. Paid $15,000 cash for new store equipment.

c. Had a net loss of $5,000.

d. Paid cash dividends of $10,000.

e. Recorded $12,000 in depreciation.

Analyze: List the transactions that required the greatest outlay of cash during fiscal 2010.

Problem 24.2B ▶ **Prepare a statement of cash flows.**

Objectives 1, 2, 3, 4, 5   Postclosing trial balance data and other financial data for Strings, Inc., as of December 31, 2010 and 2009, follow.

INSTRUCTIONS

Prepare a statement of cash flows for 2010. Additional information for 2010 follows.

a. Sold an unused lot for $30,000 in cash; it originally cost $10,000.

b. Constructed a new building for $150,000, of which $25,000 was paid in cash and $125,000 is a long-term mortgage payable.

c. Issued $25,000 of 10 percent bonds payable, maturing in 2015, for cash at par.

d. Sold common stock at par $25,000 in cash.

e. Had net income of $60,000 after income taxes.

f. Paid common stock dividends of $15,000 in cash.

g. Amortized organization costs of $1,000.

h. The short-term note payable resulted from operating activities not financing.

Analyze: Did operating, investing, or financing activities generate the greatest net inflow of cash?

Strings, Inc.
Postclosing Trial Balance
December 31, 2010 and 2009

Account Name	2010 Debit	2010 Credit	2009 Debit	2009 Credit
Cash	9 7 1 0 0		5 4 0 0 0	
Accounts Receivable (Net)	6 9 1 0 0		4 5 0 0 0	
Merchandise Inventory	6 8 4 0 0		5 5 0 0 0	
Prepaid Expenses	2 5 0 0		1 0 0 0	
Land	3 9 0 0 0		4 9 0 0 0	
Plant and Equipment	2 7 5 0 0 0		1 2 5 0 0 0	
Accumulated Depreciation—Plant and Equipment		2 4 7 5 0		1 0 0 0 0
Organization Costs	4 0 0 0		5 0 0 0	
Notes Payable—Short Term				5 0 0 0
Accounts Payable		3 1 7 5 0		3 9 5 0 0
Payroll Taxes Payable		2 6 0 0		2 5 0 0
Income Taxes Payable		1 0 0 0		2 0 0 0
Mortgage Payable, 2017		2 0 0 0 0 0		7 5 0 0 0
7% Bonds Payable, 2015		2 5 0 0 0		0
Common Stock, $1 par		7 5 0 0 0		5 0 0 0 0
Retained Earnings		1 9 5 0 0 0		1 5 0 0 0 0
Totals	5 5 5 1 0 0	5 5 5 1 0 0	3 3 4 0 0 0	3 3 4 0 0 0

Prepare a statement of cash flows.

Gulf Corporation's comparative balance sheet as of December 31, 2010 and 2009, and 2010 condensed income statement appear below.

◀ **Problem 24.3B**
Objectives 1, 2, 3, 4, 5

INSTRUCTIONS

Prepare a statement of cash flows for 2010. Additional information for 2010 follows.

a. Depreciation totaling $9,000 is included in expenses.

b. Sold land for $35,000 in cash; the land, which is included in plant and equipment, had a cost of $35,000.

c. Acquired a building with a fair market value of $100,000 by issuing common stock.

d. Purchased equipment for $25,000 in cash.

e. Paid dividends of $50,000.

Gulf Corporation
Comparative Balance Sheet
December 31, 2010 and 2009

Assets	2010	2009
Cash	1 0 9 2 0 0	9 0 0 0 0
Accounts Receivable (Net)	6 5 6 5 0	7 0 0 0 0
Merchandise Inventory	5 0 0 0 0	6 4 0 0 0
Prepaid Advertising	8 0 0 0	1 0 0 0 0
Property, Plant, and Equipment	2 9 0 0 0 0	2 0 0 0 0 0
Less: Accumulated Depreciation	(1 9 0 0 0)	(1 0 0 0 0)
Total Assets	5 0 3 8 5 0	4 2 4 0 0 0

(continued)

(continued)

Liabilities and Stockholders' Equity		
Liabilities		
Accounts Payable	6 4 5 0 0	9 5 0 0 0
Income Taxes Payable	6 0 0 0	2 5 0 0 0
Notes Payable—2012	2 5 0 0 0	4 0 0 0 0
Total Liabilities	9 5 5 0 0	1 6 0 0 0 0
Stockholders' Equity		
Common Stock ($1 par)	2 0 0 0 0 0	1 0 0 0 0 0
Retained Earnings	2 0 8 3 5 0	1 6 4 0 0 0
Total Stockholders' Equity	4 0 8 3 5 0	2 6 4 0 0 0
Total Liabilities and Stockholders' Equity	5 0 3 8 5 0	4 2 4 0 0 0

Gulf Corporation
Condensed Income Statement
Year Ended December 31, 2010

Revenues		7 7 5 0 0 0
Costs and Expenses		
Cost of Goods Sold	3 8 5 0 0 0	
Expenses	2 9 5 6 5 0	
Net Income		9 4 3 5 0

Analyze: If the company had purchased equipment on credit instead of using cash, what would the cash balance have been at year-end?

Problem 24.4B ▶ **Prepare a statement of cash flows.**

Objectives 1, 2, 3, 4, 5

The comparative balance sheet for Beach Products, Inc., as of December 31, 2010 and 2009, is shown below, followed by the condensed income statement and other financial data for 2010.

INSTRUCTIONS

Prepare a statement of cash flows for 2010.

a. Sold used equipment for $27,000 in cash that originally cost $32,000; accumulated depreciation was $8,000. The remainder of the change in *Equipment* represents equipment purchased for cash.

b. Issued short-term notes payable with a par value of $20,000. Retired bonds payable at maturity.

c. Paid cash dividends of $30,000.

d. Issued common stock at par value for cash.

Beach Products, Inc.
Comparative Balance Sheet
December 31, 2010 and 2009

Assets	2010	2009
Cash	1 1 8 4 1 0	1 0 1 5 0
Accounts Receivable (Net)	8 8 6 5 0	6 6 2 5 0
Merchandise Inventory	8 9 0 0 0	7 5 0 0 0
Prepaid Advertising	5 5 0 0	3 5 0 0
Land	7 5 0 0 0	7 5 0 0 0
Property, Plant, and Equipment	2 0 7 0 0 0	2 1 9 0 0 0
Less: Accumulated Depreciation—Property, Plant, and Equipment	(3 4 6 0 0)	(2 1 9 0 0)
Total Assets	5 4 8 9 6 0	4 2 7 0 0 0

Liabilities and Stockholders' Equity		
Liabilities		
Accounts Payable	6 1 3 0 0	6 8 5 0 0
Notes Payable—Short Term	2 0 0 0 0	0
Income Taxes Payable	1 0 2 5 0	8 5 0 0
Bonds Payable	0	5 0 0 0 0
Total Liabilities	9 1 5 5 0	1 2 7 0 0 0
Stockholders' Equity		
Common Stock	1 5 0 0 0 0	1 0 0 0 0 0
Retained Earnings	3 0 7 4 1 0	2 0 0 0 0 0
Total Stockholders' Equity	4 5 7 4 1 0	3 0 0 0 0 0
Total Liabilities and Stockholders' Equity	5 4 8 9 6 0	4 2 7 0 0 0

Beach Products, Inc.
Condensed Income Statement
Year Ended December 31, 2010

Revenues (including gain on sale of equipment)	9 2 5 6 0 0
Costs and Expenses	
Cost of Goods Sold	5 0 1 6 0 0
Depreciation Expense	2 0 7 0 0
Selling and Administrative Expenses	1 9 5 0 0 0
Interest Expense	1 2 0 0 0
Income Taxes Expense	5 8 8 9 0
Total Costs and Expenses	7 8 8 1 9 0
Net Income After Income Taxes	1 3 7 4 1 0

Analyze: Was the amount of net cash provided by operating activities sufficient to cover the cash that the company required for financing activities? Explain.

Critical Thinking Problem 24.1

Adjustments

Malibu Company was formed and began business on January 1, 2010, when R. B. Street transferred merchandise inventory with a value of $65,000, cash of $50,000, accounts receivable of $50,000, and accounts payable of $20,000 to the corporation in exchange for common stock with a par value of $5 per share. The company's common stock was recorded at par.

Malibu Company's statement of cash flows for 2010 is shown below and on the next page.

Malibu Company
Statement of Cash Flows
Year Ended December 31, 2010

Cash Flow from Operations		
Net Income		7 0 0 0 0
Adjustments		
Depreciation of building	5 0 0 0	
Depreciation of equipment	5 0 0 0	
Increase in accounts receivable	(1 6 0 0 0)	

Increase in inventory	(5 0 0 0)	
Increase in prepaid insurance	(8 0 0)	
Increase in accounts payable	2 7 0 0 0	
Increase in income tax payable	2 5 0 0	1 7 7 0 0
Net cash flow provided by operations		8 7 7 0 0
Cash Flow from Investing Activities		
Purchase of land	(3 0 0 0 0)	
Purchase of building	(2 5 0 0 0)	
Purchase of equipment	(5 0 0 0 0)	
Net cash used in investing activities		(1 0 5 0 0 0)
Cash Flow from Financing Activities		
Issuance of common stock at $5/share	5 0 0 0	
Borrowing at bank by issuance of note payable	5 0 0 0 0	
Net cash provided by financing activities		5 5 0 0 0
Net increase in cash balance		3 7 7 0 0
Cash balance, January 1, 2010		5 0 0 0 0
Cash balance, December 31, 2010		8 7 7 0 0

Note: A building was acquired at a cost of $250,000. Cash of $25,000 was paid, and a mortgage of $225,000 was given for the balance.

INSTRUCTIONS

Based on the data supplied, prepare the December 31, 2010, balance sheet for the corporation.

Analyze: Describe four adjusting entries that were made by Malibu Company in fiscal 2010.

Critical Thinking Problem 24.2

Transactions

Sandy Fields, the bookkeeper for River Valley Company, asks for your help in identifying whether the following transactions should be reported on the corporation's statement of cash flows. Prepare a list for Fields indicating whether or not each transaction should be reported on the statement. If the transaction should appear on the statement, indicate whether it should be classified as a financing activity, an investing activity, or an operating activity. If the transaction should not be part of the statement of cash flows, explain why not.

1. Prepaid three months of rent on warehouse storage facilities at the end of the year.
2. Paid suppliers amounts due on accounts payable.
3. Issued preferred stock for cash.
4. Collected an accounts receivable from a customer.
5. Paid cash dividends on common stock.
6. Purchased common stock of Google as investment for cash.
7. Borrowed cash, signing a short-term note that was repaid before the end of the year.
8. Paid federal income taxes due.
9. Issued long-term bonds for cash.
10. Used proceeds from bond issue to purchase new equipment for plant.

11. Received principal payments on note receivable held in connection with sale of building last year.

12. Distributed a stock dividend on common stock.

BUSINESS CONNECTIONS

Using All Statements

1. How can the statement of cash flows help management arrange for proper financing?

2. A corporation's income statement shows a net income of $10,000 after income taxes for the year. Its statement of cash flows shows that its cash balance increased by $150,000: net cash outflow from operating activities, $100,000; net cash inflow from financing activities, $50,000; and net cash inflow from investing activities, $200,000. The president of the corporation has commented, "Even though the company's profit is small, it is clear, based on our positive cash flow, that we are doing quite well." Do you agree with this comment? Why or why not?

3. A member of a corporation's board of directors commented that because the statement of cash flows and the income statement are so similar, there is no need to prepare the income statement. Respond.

4. Assume that you are an accountant preparing the statement of cash flows for the year. Should the cash proceeds of $100,000 from a short-term note payable discounted in May of this year be included in the statement? The note was repaid in October. Would it be preferable to simply ignore both the loan and the repayment because it might confuse management to show both? Explain.

5. A potential customer has applied for an open-account credit line with a manufacturing firm. Explain how the potential customer's statement of cash flows would help to evaluate its short-term debt-paying ability.

Delay Payment of Bonds

Aileen Corporation has a cash flow problem. They have bonds due before the end of the fiscal year. They will need to sell more bonds to pay the bonds due. Ida, the controller, understands that many investors consider the cash flow statement to be the key statement that indicates the company's future value. She has decided to delay the payment of the bonds until after the end of the fiscal year. This will show a higher balance in cash since the bonds will not be paid. There will be no indication in the financial statements that she has defaulted on the bonds. It is Ida's plan to issue additional bonds after the close of the fiscal year to pay off the current bonds. However, she will need to record the interest paid in the current fiscal year. Are Ida's actions acceptable accounting practices?

Sources of Cash

Refer to the *2006 Annual Report* for The Home Depot, Inc., in Appendix A.

1. Locate the consolidated statements of cash flows. For the year ended January 28, 2007, what net cash was (1) provided by operations? (2) used in investing activities? (3) provided by financing activities?

2. Is the most significant source of cash generated from the company's operating, investing, or financing activities?

Statement of Cash Flows

The excerpt on page 874 was taken from the Pier 1 Imports, Inc., *2007 Annual Report*.

Pier 1 imports

Consolidated Statement of Cash Flows (in thousands)			
	Year Ended		
	2007	2006	2005
Cash Flow from Operating Activities			
Net Income	($227,645)	($ 39,804)	$ 60,457
Adjustment to reconcile net cash provided by operating activities:			
Depreciation and amortization	63,496	78,781	75,624
Deferred taxes	24,576	(14,496)	2,035
Other noncash Items	73,870	(54,256)	(87,994)
Change in cash from:			
Inventories	9,757	882	(6,860)
Accounts receivable and other current assets	(14,428)	(22,778)	(11,302)
Accounts payable and accrued expenses	(6,983)	403	7,456
Other, net	(27,548)	(13,029)	11,714
Net cash provided by operating activities	(104,905)	(64,297)	51,130
Net cash used in financing activities	(12,962)	118,043	(80,668)
Change in cash and cash equivalents	(86,037)	64,134	(36,020)
Cash and cash equivalents, beginning of year	253,215	189,081	225,101
Cash and cash equivalents, end of year	$167,178	$ 253,215	$ 189,081

Analyze:

1. Compute the net cash provided by investing activities for the year ended 2006.

2. On the statement of cash flows for the year ended 2008, what figure will be used for Cash and Cash Equivalents at Beginning of Year?

3. What total adjustments were made to net income to determine net cash provided by operating activities for each year presented above?

Analyze Online: Locate the Pier 1 Imports' Web site (www.pier1.com). Click on the *About Us* link. Use the *Investing* link to find the company's most recent annual report and consolidated statement of cash flows.

4. What net change occurred in cash and cash equivalents?

5. What activities generate the largest cash inflows for Pier 1 Imports?

Improving Cash Flow

Extending THE THOUGHT

Proper management of cash is imperative for a successful operation. Describe practices that would help an organization improve its cash flow. Consider credit policies, collections, pricing, and accounting processes.

Memo

Business COMMUNICATION

Prepare a memo to Al Lee, your new staff accountant, describing the four financial statements that should be prepared at year-end. Use all the new terms in this chapter.

Cash Flow Information

TEAMWORK

As a team of four students, obtain the cash flow statements from two companies. Each group of two students should explain their company's cash flow statements to the other two students. The explanation should include the following: (1) Has cash increased or decreased? (2) What is the main source of cash? (3) What are the principle uses of cash? (4) Is the company's business expanding or contracting? (5) Has more common stock been sold? (6) Is the company paying down debt or getting further into debt? (7) Has treasury stock been purchased?

Different Business, Different Cash Flow?

Go to the Web site for Federated Stores (federated-fds.com), IBM (ibm.com), and Microsoft (Microsoft.com). Compare the cash flow from operating, investing, and financing of the three companies for three years. Is there a difference in the cash flow for the type of business (compare Microsoft to Federated)? Does a company that has been in business for a long time like IBM have a higher cash balance than Microsoft?

Answers to **Self Reviews**

Answers to Section 1 Self Review

1. Short-term liquid investments that are easily convertible into cash.
2. Transactions that involve the acquisition or disposal of long-term assets.
3. This transaction is one of financing the business, not an investing activity.
4. **b.** purchases of plant and equipment for cash.
5. **b.** issuance of stock for cash.
6. **(a)** source, **(b)** use, **(c)** use, **(d)** source, **(e)** source

Answers to Section 2 Self Review

1. The loss does not relate to operating activities and must be added back to net income.
2. Depreciation expense does not reflect a cash outlay, so it must be added back to net income.
3. An increase in notes payable does not affect cash flow from operations, unless the notes were credited when merchandise inventory or other operating assets were purchased.
4. **d.** a change in merchandise inventory.
5. **b.** deducted from net income.
6. $10,500 used

Answers to Section 3 Self Review

1. $80,000—included as inflow from investing activities. $6,000 gain—deducted from net income.
2. Disclosed in footnotes to the statement.
3. As cash used in financing activities.
4. **a.** indirect method.
5. **b.** decrease in Cash Flows from Investing Activities.
6. $4,000 gain—subtracted from net income. $12,000—included as cash inflow from investing activities.

Answers to Comprehensive Self Review

1. Operating, investing, and financing activities are shown in a statement of cash flows.
2. Financing activities are transactions that provide or use cash through selling stock, issuing bonds, or paying cash dividends.
3. The increase in accounts payable must be added to net income to arrive at cash flow from operations.
4. In a note to the statement of cash flows.
5. In the operating activities section as an addition to net income.

Mini-Practice Set 4

Financial Analysis and Decision Making

Panama

This project will give you an opportunity to evaluate financial statements and to make decisions based on the information presented in the financial statements of Panama Merchandise, Inc.

INTRODUCTION

Panama Merchandise, Inc., sells a variety of consumer products. The firm is organized as a corporation. The fiscal year-end is the same as the calendar year-end, December 31.

The *Study Guide & Working Papers, Chapters 14–24,* contain the following financial statements for Panama Merchandise, Inc.

- Comparative Income Statement (Years Ended December 31, 2010 and 2009)
- Comparative Balance Sheet (December 31, 2010 and 2009)

INSTRUCTIONS

The instructions for completing Mini-Practice Set 4 are in the *Study Guide & Working Papers, Chapters 14–24.*

Analyze: Assume that the firm declared and distributed a 5 percent common stock dividend in 2010. What is the effect on earnings per share in 2010? Assume that market value is equal to par value and all other information is the same.

Departmentalized Profit and Cost Centers

LEARNING OBJECTIVES

LP25

1. Explain profit centers and cost centers.
2. Prepare the Gross Profit section of a departmental income statement.
3. Explain and identify direct and indirect departmental expenses.
4. Choose the basis for allocation of indirect expenses and compute the amounts to be allocated to each department.
5. Prepare a departmental income statement showing the contribution margin and operating income for each department.
6. Use a departmental income statement in making decisions such as whether a department should be closed.
7. Define the accounting terms new to this chapter.

NEW TERMS

break-even point
contribution margin
cost center
departmental income statement
direct expenses

indirect expenses
managerial accounting
profit center
responsibility accounting
semidirect expenses
transfer price

 www.mattel.com

Mattel has done well pursuing its vision of "The World's Premier Toy Brands—Today and Tomorrow." The company began with a single brand—Barbie—who was introduced to the world in 1959 as a teenage fashion model. As she approaches her 50th birthday, she has reason to celebrate. Barbie is the best-selling girl's toy in the world with annual sales topping $3 million.

How is Mattel building on the success of the Barbie brand? By weaving education and entertainment through books, dolls, and accessories and making every girl want the American Girl experience. The American Girl Places in New York and Los Angeles and the Bistros in Atlanta and Dallas thrill young girls with live entertainment, fine dining, and, of course, shopping.

thinking critically

What types of financial and nonfinancial data do you think Mattel considered in the creation of the American Girl brand?

Section **1**

SECTION OBJECTIVES

>> 1. **Explain profit centers and cost centers.**

WHY IT'S IMPORTANT
Different business segments contribute to a firm's financial success in varying degrees.

>> 2. **Prepare the Gross Profit section of a departmental income statement.**

WHY IT'S IMPORTANT
Operating results are evaluated for each segment of the business.

>> 3. **Explain and identify direct and indirect departmental expenses.**

WHY IT'S IMPORTANT
Some operating expenses relate directly to a specific department; others benefit all company operations.

>> 4. **Choose the basis for allocation of indirect expenses and compute the amounts to be allocated to each department.**

WHY IT'S IMPORTANT
Indirect and semidirect expenses benefit all company operations and are assigned using a logical method.

TERMS TO LEARN

cost center
direct expenses
indirect expenses
managerial accounting
profit center
responsibility accounting
semidirect expenses
transfer price

Profit and Cost Centers and Departmental Accounting

In previous chapters, you have studied financial statements that report the results of transactions that happened in the past. This chapter shows how management can use financial data for forward-looking analysis and decision making, not just historical reporting.

Video25.1

Managerial Accounting

Managerial accounting is the branch of accounting that provides financial information about business segments, activities, or products. Managerial accounting supplies information about the profit made on an order or the profitability of a specific department. Management uses this information to make decisions such as when to replace a machine, whether to discontinue a product, or to determine the selling price for a new product.

> In 1998, Ford Motor Company adopted Statement of Financial Accounting Standards No. 131, Disclosures about Segments of an Enterprise and Related Information. In accordance with this standard, Ford publishes information on revenues, net income, and assets for two primary segments: Automotive and Financial Services.

Profit Centers and Cost Centers

Managerial accounting is concerned with segments of a business. The segments are often called *centers*. Accounting information is accumulated and analyzed separately for each center. There are two types of centers: cost centers and profit centers. A **cost center** is a business segment that incurs costs but does not produce revenue. A **profit center** is a business segment that produces revenue.

> Beginning with the second quarter of 2006, Ford Motor Company changed the reporting of its Automotive sector to show five primary segments: (1) Ford North America, (2) Ford South America, (3) Ford Europe, (4) PAG, and (5) Ford Asia Pacific and Africa/Mazda. Segment selection is based upon the organizational structure that Ford uses to evaluate performance and make decisions on resource allocation, as well as availability and materiality of separate financial results consistent with that structure.

Cost centers do not directly earn revenue. Cost centers often provide services to other segments of the business. The emphasis in accounting for cost centers is on cost control. Typical cost centers include the accounting department, information systems department, maintenance department, storeroom, research laboratory, and purchasing department.

Profit centers are revenue-producing segments that sell products or services to customers outside the business. For example, a clothing store might have separate profit centers for the coat, dress, suit, and shoe departments. Sales and costs are accumulated for each department. A "profit" is computed for the department.

Sometimes it is convenient to think of a segment of a company as a profit center even though it does not sell products or services to outside customers. For example, the segment of an oil company that produces crude oil from the ground can be treated as a profit center even though the oil it produces is transferred to the company's refinery. The revenue from the segment's activities is the **transfer price** of its product—the price at which the segment's goods are transferred to another segment of the company.

Responsibility Accounting

Responsibility accounting allows management to evaluate the performance of each segment of the business and assign responsibility for its financial results. Internal accounting reports provide detailed data for each cost and profit center so that management can determine how efficiently the individual segments are functioning.

Departmentalized Operations

When a business has more than one type of sales or service activity, it is important to know what each activity is contributing to the income or loss of the business. Let's learn how accountants gather revenue and expenses for the different activities by studying the system used by Third Avenue, a business that sells men's clothing and shoes. Income taxes will be ignored in the following illustration.

GROSS PROFIT SECTION OF A DEPARTMENTAL INCOME STATEMENT

To calculate gross profit by department, Third Avenue gathers data by department for each transaction.

Departmental Accounts in the General Ledger Businesses that prepare departmental financial statements maintain general ledger accounts for sales, purchases, merchandise inventory, and some operating expenses. For example, Third Avenue has two sales departments, clothing and shoes. The sales accounts are *Sales—Clothing* and *Sales—Shoes.*

>>1. OBJECTIVE

Explain profit centers and cost centers.

LP25

important!

Responsibility Accounting
Responsibility accounting provides information that helps in evaluating each segment of a business and assigning responsibility for results.

>>2. OBJECTIVE

Prepare the Gross Profit section of a departmental income statement.

LP25

SALES JOURNAL　　　　　PAGE ___1___

DATE	SALES SLIP NO.	CUSTOMER'S NAME	POST. REF.	ACCOUNTS RECEIVABLE DEBIT	SALES TAX PAYABLE CREDIT	SALES— CLOTHING CREDIT	SALES— SHOES CREDIT
2010							
Jan. 2	1005	Sullivan Morgan	✓	212 00	12 00	200 00	
3	1006	Rob Cortez	✓	477 00	27 00	300 00	150 00
3	1007	Billy Williams	✓	190 80	10 80	115 00	65 00
31		Totals		9 540 00	540 00	6 200 00	2 800 00
				(111)	(231)	(401)	(402)

FIGURE 25.1　**Departmental Sales Journal**

important!

Sales Journal

When the sales account is departmentalized, the sales journal records transactions by department.

Recording Sales and Purchases by Departments Figure 25.1 shows the sales journal for Third Avenue. Notice that there are two sales columns, one for clothing and one for shoes. Sales are recorded in the usual manner except that the sales amounts are divided between the sales columns. For example, Rob Cortez purchased $300 of clothing and $150 of shoes. These amounts are reported in separate columns. The sales tax rate is 6 percent.

> The six Sara Lee Corporation business segments are North American Retail Meats, North American Retail Bakery, Food Service, International Beverage, International Bakery, and Household and Body Care. In fiscal 2007, the North American Retail Meats segment accounted for more than 21 percent of all sales.

recall

Posting

Postings are made daily from the sales journal to the individual accounts receivable subsidiary ledger accounts.

The departmental sales journal is posted in the usual manner. Transactions are posted daily in the accounts receivable subsidiary ledger. The sales journal column totals are posted to the general ledger at month-end. Similarly, the voucher register and the sales returns and allowances journal have separate columns for the two departments.

Merchandise Inventories Merchandise inventory is counted by department so that the departmental cost of goods sold can be computed.

A Sample Gross Profit Section Figure 25.2 shows the Gross Profit section of the departmental income statement for Third Avenue.

OPERATING EXPENSES SECTION OF A DEPARTMENTAL INCOME STATEMENT

>>3. OBJECTIVE

Explain and identify direct and indirect departmental expenses.

There are two types of operating expenses: direct expenses and indirect (or semidirect) expenses.

Direct Expenses **Direct expenses** are identified directly with a department and are recorded by department. At Third Avenue, sales clerks work in only one department, so it is easy to record salary expenses. Advertising costs, store supplies, cash short or over, and delivery expenses are also recorded by department.

Figure 25.3 shows the direct expenses for Third Avenue.

Indirect and Semidirect Expenses Not all operating costs are direct expenses. **Semidirect expenses** cannot be directly assigned to a department, but they are closely related to departmental activities. Semidirect expenses are allocated among the departments at the end of the accounting period. Semidirect expenses include depreciation on store equipment and the cost of insurance for equipment and inventory.

FIGURE 25.2   **Departmental Income Statement (Partial)**

Third Avenue
Income Statement (Partial)
Year Ended December 31, 2010

	Clothing	Shoes	Total
Operating Revenue			
Sales	5 4 3 7 5 0	1 8 1 2 5 0	7 2 5 0 0 0
Less Sales Returns and Allowances	4 1 2 5	1 3 7 5	5 5 0 0
Net Sales	5 3 9 6 2 5	1 7 9 8 7 5	7 1 9 5 0 0
Cost of Goods Sold			
Merchandise Inventory, January 1, 2010	3 5 0 0 0	1 5 0 0 0	5 0 0 0 0
Purchases	2 2 5 0 0 0	4 8 0 0 0	2 7 3 0 0 0
Freight In	4 2 0 0	5 0 0	4 7 0 0
Delivered Cost of Purchases	2 2 9 2 0 0	4 8 5 0 0	2 7 7 7 0 0
Less: Purchases Returns and Allowances	3 5 0 0	3 5 0	3 8 5 0
Purchases Discounts	4 0 0 0	4 0 0	4 4 0 0
Total Deductions	7 5 0 0	7 5 0	8 2 5 0
Net Delivered Cost of Purchases	2 2 1 7 0 0	4 7 7 5 0	2 6 9 4 5 0
Total Merchandise Available for Sale	2 5 6 7 0 0	6 2 7 5 0	3 1 9 4 5 0
Less Merchandise Inventory, December 31, 2010	3 6 0 0 0	9 5 0 0	4 5 5 0 0
Cost of Goods Sold	2 2 0 7 0 0	5 3 2 5 0	2 7 3 9 5 0
Gross Profit	3 1 8 9 2 5	1 2 6 6 2 5	4 4 5 5 5 0

Third Avenue
Schedule of Direct Departmental Expenses
Year Ended December 31, 2010

	Clothing	Shoes	Total
Sales Salaries Expense	1 0 2 5 0 0	4 2 5 0 0	1 4 5 0 0 0
Advertising Expense	1 8 0 0 0	1 0 0 0 0	2 8 0 0 0
Store Supplies Expense	5 0 0	1 5 0	6 5 0
Cash Short or Over	6 5	2 5	9 0
Delivery Expense	5 0 0	2 5 0	7 5 0
Total Direct Expenses	1 2 1 5 6 5	5 2 9 2 5	1 7 4 4 9 0

FIGURE 25.3

Schedule of Direct Departmental Expenses

Indirect expenses are operating expenses that cannot be readily identified and are not closely related to activity within a department. At the end of the accounting period, indirect expenses are allocated to the departments. Examples of indirect expenses are postage and stationery.

The accountant for Third Avenue treats semidirect and indirect expenses as indirect expenses. The indirect expenses for Third Avenue follow.

Indirect Expenses

Insurance expense	$ 25,000
Rent expense	36,000

>>**4. OBJECTIVE**

Choose the basis for allocation of indirect expenses and compute the amounts to be allocated to each department.

TABLE 25.1

Allocation of Insurance Expense

Utilities expense	11,000
Office salaries expense	50,000
Other office expenses	1,800
Uncollectible accounts expense	2,000
Depreciation expense—furniture and fixtures	1,000
Depreciation expense—office equipment	500
Total indirect expenses	$127,300

Allocating Semidirect and Indirect Expense Items After the worksheet has been completed, the accountant allocates indirect expenses to the departments. The accountant tries to find some logical relationship between the departments and each type of expense. Let's see how the accountant allocates the indirect costs for Third Avenue. The allocated costs appear in Figure 25.4, the departmental income statement for Third Avenue, which appears on page 886 of this chapter. Notice that the allocated expenses are rounded to the nearest dollar.

Insurance Expense Insurance premiums total $25,000. They are allocated based on the cost of the furniture, fixtures, and inventory used in the department's operations. As of December 31, Third Avenue's total of these items was $42,000 in the clothing department and $18,000 in the shoes department. The accountant allocates $17,500 of insurance expense to the clothing department and $7,500 to the shoes department as shown in Table 25.1.

Asset Item	Clothing Department	Shoes Department	Percent	Total Insurance Expense	Amount Allocated to Each Department
Merchandise inventory	$35,000	$15,000			
Furniture and fixtures	7,000	3,000			
Total clothing	$42,000	$18,000	70 ×	$25,000 =	$17,500
Total shoes	18,000		30 ×	25,000 =	7,500
Combined Totals	$60,000		100		$25,000

Rent Expense Rent expense was $36,000. It is allocated based on square footage. The accountant allocates $28,800 to the clothing department and $7,200 to the shoes department.

Department	Basis: Square Feet	Percent	Rent Expense	Allocation
Clothing	2,400	80 ×	$36,000 =	$28,800
Shoes	600	20 ×	36,000 =	7,200
Total	3,000	100		$36,000

Utilities Expense Utilities expense was $11,000. It is allocated based on square footage. The accountant allocates $8,800 ($11,000 × 0.80) to the clothing department and $2,200 ($11,000 × 0.20) to the shoes department.

Office Salaries Expense Office salaries expense was $50,000. It is allocated based on total sales for each department. The accountant allocates $37,500 to the clothing department and $12,500 to the shoes department as shown.

Department	Basis: Total Sales	Percent		Office Salaries Expense		Allocation
Clothing	$543,750	75	×	$50,000	=	$37,500
Shoes	181,250	25	×	50,000	=	12,500
Total	$725,000	100				$50,000

Other Office Expenses Other office expenses, including postage and stationery, totaled $1,800. They are allocated based on total sales for each department. The accountant allocates $1,350 ($1,800 × 0.75) to the clothing department and $450 ($1,800 × 0.25) to the shoes department.

Uncollectible Accounts Expense As a result of the aging of the accounts receivable balance on December 31, an adjustment of $2,000 was recorded as an expense for uncollectible accounts. The uncollectible accounts expense is allocated on the basis of credit sales, preferably on net credit sales. Sometimes it takes too much time to distinguish between returns from cash and credit sales, so gross sales on account are used to make the allocation. The accountant for Third Avenue uses gross credit sales. Based on the following calculations, the accountant allocates uncollectible accounts expenses of $1,500 to the clothing department and $500 to the shoes department.

Department	Basis: Credit Sales	Percent		Uncollectible Accounts Expense		Allocation
Clothing	$300,000	75	×	$2,000	=	$1,500
Shoes	100,000	25	×	2,000	=	500
Total	$400,000	100				$2,000

important!

Uncollectible Accounts Expense
If feasible, the expense for uncollectible accounts is allocated based on net credit sales.

Depreciation Expense—Furniture and Fixtures The assets used to compute depreciation for furniture and fixtures are identified with specific departments. Depreciation is computed at 10 percent per year. Third Avenue uses $7,000 of furniture and fixtures in the clothing department and $3,000 in the shoes department. The accountant allocates $700 ($7,000 × 0.10) of depreciation to the clothing department and $300 ($3,000 × 0.10) to the shoes department.

Depreciation Expense—Office Equipment Depreciation on the office equipment was $500. It is allocated according to total sales by department—the same basis used to allocate office salaries. The accountant allocates $375 ($500 × 0.75) to the clothing department and $125 ($500 × 0.25) to the shoes department.

Nondepartmentalized Expenses Revenue and expenses that do not apply to operations are not allocated to the departments. Generally, all items that appear in the Other Income and Other Expenses section of the income statement are treated as nondepartmental items. For example, interest income and interest expense are not allocated to departments because they relate to the financing of the business, rather than to its operating activities.

Other income and expense accounts that are not allocated to the departments at Third Avenue are *Miscellaneous Income* for $775 and *Interest Expense* for $750.

Section 1 Self Review

QUESTIONS

1. What distinguishes a profit center from a cost center?

2. Why do managers like responsibility accounting?

3. What is a logical basis for allocating tangible property tax expense to departments?

EXERCISES

4. If a segment of a business is considered a profit center,

   a. no expenses can be allocated to the segment.

   b. it incurs costs but does not have revenues.

   c. both revenue and costs are accumulated for the segment.

   d. it must sell products or services to customers outside the business.

5. In a store with several sales departments, departmentalized accounts are used for

   a. sales and other income items only.

   b. purchases and expense items only.

   c. sales, purchases, and merchandise inventory.

   d. sales only.

ANALYSIS

6. Department A had total sales of $200,000, and Department B had total sales of $50,000. Office salaries expense of $30,000 is allocated on the basis of total sales. How much would be allocated to Department B?

(Answers to Section 1 Self Review are on page 899.)

SECTION OBJECTIVES

>> **5.** **Prepare a departmental income statement showing the contribution margin and operating income for each department.**

WHY IT'S IMPORTANT

Individual departments need to cover their direct expenses and contribute toward increasing the income of the business.

>> **6.** **Use a departmental income statement in making decisions such as whether a department should be closed.**

WHY IT'S IMPORTANT

The viability of business segments can be evaluated based on departmental income statements.

TERMS TO LEARN

break-even point
contribution margin
departmental income statement

Departmental Income Statements

The balance sheet is prepared in the same manner whether or not a business has departmentalized operations. The income statement for a departmentalized firm, however, is expanded to highlight the individual departments' financial information.

Preparing the Departmental Income Statement

A **departmental income statement** shows each department's contribution margin and net income from operations after all expenses are allocated. Figure 25.4 on page 886 shows the departmental income statement for Third Avenue. Notice the amount labeled "Contribution Margin." It appears between "Total Direct Expenses" and "Indirect Expenses." **Contribution margin** is gross profit on sales minus direct expenses. It is the amount that the department has earned beyond its direct costs. The contribution margin is available to cover the semidirect and indirect expenses of running the business. A department that has a positive contribution margin is contributing toward increasing the net income (or decreasing the net loss) of the business.

DEPARTMENTAL INCOME

Income from operations by department is used to make many business decisions. However, there are limitations to using departmental operating income. For example, it is difficult to determine each department's fair share of semidirect and indirect expenses. Another limitation is that if a particular department were eliminated, many of the indirect expenses allocated to it would not be eliminated. They would have to be absorbed by the remaining departments. When making decisions knowledgeable managers rely more on contribution margin per department than on income from operations.

CONTRIBUTION MARGIN

Departments with a positive contribution margin help to pay the semidirect and indirect costs of the business. As already mentioned, many of the indirect costs allocated to an eliminated department may have to be absorbed by the remaining departments. Departments with a negative contribution margin reduce the net income (or increase the net loss) of the business as a whole. The business would be more profitable if the department with the negative contribution margin was eliminated.

>>**5. OBJECTIVE**

Prepare a departmental income statement showing the contribution margin and operating income for each department.

LP25

>>**6. OBJECTIVE**

Use a departmental income statement in making decisions such as whether a department should be closed.

LP25

Third Avenue

Income Statement (Partial)

Year Ended December 31, 2010

	Clothing	Shoes	Total
Operating Revenue			
Sales	5 4 3 7 5 0	1 8 1 2 5 0	7 2 5 0 0 0
Less Sales Returns and Allowances	4 1 2 5	1 3 7 5	5 5 0 0
Net Sales	5 3 9 6 2 5	1 7 9 8 7 5	7 1 9 5 0 0
Cost of Goods Sold			
Merchandise Inventory, January 1, 2010	3 5 0 0 0	1 5 0 0 0	5 0 0 0 0
Purchases	2 2 5 0 0 0	4 8 0 0 0	2 7 3 0 0 0
Freight In	4 2 0 0	5 0 0	4 7 0 0
Delivered Cost of Purchases	2 2 9 2 0 0	4 8 5 0 0	2 7 7 7 0 0
Less: Purchases Returns and Allowances	3 5 0 0	3 5 0	3 8 5 0
Purchases Discounts	4 0 0 0	4 0 0	4 4 0 0
Total Deductions	7 5 0 0	7 5 0	8 2 5 0
Net Delivered Cost of Purchases	2 2 1 7 0 0	4 7 7 5 0	2 6 9 4 5 0
Total Merchandise Available for Sale	2 5 6 7 0 0	6 2 7 5 0	3 1 9 4 5 0
Less Merchandise Inventory, December 31, 2010	3 6 0 0 0	9 5 0 0	4 5 5 0 0
Cost of Goods Sold	2 2 0 7 0 0	5 3 2 5 0	2 7 3 9 5 0
Gross Profit	3 1 8 9 2 5	1 2 6 6 2 5	4 4 5 5 5 0
Operating Expenses			
Direct Expenses			
Sales Salaries Expense	1 0 2 5 0 0	4 2 5 0 0	1 4 5 0 0 0
Advertising Expense	1 8 0 0 0	1 0 0 0 0	2 8 0 0 0
Store Supplies Expense	5 0 0	1 5 0	6 5 0
Cash Short or Over	6 5	2 5	9 0
Delivery Expense	5 0 0	2 5 0	7 5 0
Total Direct Expenses	1 2 1 5 6 5	5 2 9 2 5	1 7 4 4 9 0
Contribution Margin	1 9 7 3 6 0	7 3 7 0 0	2 7 1 0 6 0
Indirect Expenses			
Insurance Expense	1 7 5 0 0	7 5 0 0	2 5 0 0 0
Rent Expense	2 8 8 0 0	7 2 0 0	3 6 0 0 0
Utilities Expense	8 8 0 0	2 2 0 0	1 1 0 0 0
Office Salaries Expense	3 7 5 0 0	1 2 5 0 0	5 0 0 0 0
Other Office Expenses	1 3 5 0	4 5 0	1 8 0 0
Uncollectible Accounts Expense	1 5 0 0	5 0 0	2 0 0 0
Depreciation Expense—Furniture and Fixtures	7 0 0	3 0 0	1 0 0 0
Depreciation Expense—Office Equipment	3 7 5	1 2 5	5 0 0
Total Indirect Expenses	9 6 5 2 5	3 0 7 7 5	1 2 7 3 0 0
Net Income from Operations	1 0 0 8 3 5	4 2 9 2 5	1 4 3 7 6 0
Other Income			
Miscellaneous Income			7 7 5
Other Expenses			
Interest Expense			7 5 0
Net Other Expenses/Income			2 5
Net Income before Income Taxes			1 4 3 7 8 5

FIGURE 25.4   **Departmental Income Statement**

As can readily be seen, the concept of contribution margin is important to business owners and managers because it provides them with valuable assistance in making decisions. Unfortunately, contribution margin figures are not provided in traditional financial reports.

BREAK-EVEN POINT

A business is said to "break even" when total revenues equal total expenses. Obviously, businesses exist to make a profit, not just break even, but it is very important for management to know the **break-even point** (BEP). While this chapter focuses just on operating expenses, you will learn more about fixed and variable expenses in a later chapter. Simply put, a fixed expense is one that does not change with the volume of unit sales of the business. Other expenses would be variable or semi-variable. The break-even point is when the contribution margin equals fixed expenses.

A simple example will illustrate. Let's say a business has fixed monthly expenses of $1,000 for rent, $500 for utilities, and $3,000 for salaries. The average selling price of the business's product is $29 and the average variable costs of obtaining the product is $9, making the contribution margin equal to $20 ($29 − $9). Dividing the fixed monthly expenses of $4,500 ($1,000 + $500 + $3,000) by the contribution margin of $20 gives you a break-even point of 225 units. In other words, the business must sell 225 units to break even for the month.

MANAGERIAL IMPLICATIONS   <<

DEPARTMENTAL INCOME STATEMENTS

- Departmentalized income statements illustrate which departments are most profitable and which are losing money or have low profit margins. Once alerted, department managers can take steps to improve the profit picture.
- Profitable departments may be expanded. Less profitable departments may undergo policy changes or may be closed.
- Departmentalized income statements help managers evaluate and control the operations of each unit.
- The contribution margin is very important in making managerial decisions. The contribution margin is gross profit minus direct expenses. It indicates how much each department contributes toward the indirect expenses and income for the business.
- Decisions to retain, eliminate, expand, or contract a segment of the business are based on the analysis of the contribution margin of the department or product.
- Departmental income is, at best, an estimate. It should be used with great care when making decisions.
- Managers need to consider that many of the indirect expenses would not be eliminated by the decision to do away with a department.

THINKING CRITICALLY

Should a business base a manager's bonus on gross profit, contribution margin, or net income from operations of a department?

Section 2 Self Review

QUESTIONS

1. Define contribution margin.

2. What is the difference between direct departmental expenses and indirect expenses?

3. How does the accountant choose a basis for allocating indirect expenses to sales departments?

EXERCISES

4. A department probably would be considered for elimination if it had a

   a. positive contribution margin and income from operations.

   b. positive contribution margin and no income tax expense.

   c. positive contribution margin and a loss from operations.

   d. negative contribution margin and a loss from operations.

5. Dept. A had gross profit of $30,000, total direct expenses of $15,000, and total indirect expenses of $6,000. What is its contribution margin?

   a. $14,000

   b. $15,000

   c. $6,000

   d. $9,000

ANALYSIS

6. A department had a contribution margin of $18,000 and a loss from operations of $5,000. If the department is eliminated, the indirect expenses allocated to it will still be incurred. If the department is eliminated, how will net income for the business be affected?

(Answers to Section 2 Self Review are on page 899.)

REVIEW   Chapter Summary

The basic financial statements summarize the financial operations and position of the business as a whole, but they do not provide all of the accounting information necessary in running a business. Additional information needed about individual segments and activities of the business is provided by managerial accounting. In this chapter, you have learned how departmental financial reports are prepared and how they contribute to business decision making.

Learning Objectives

1 Explain profit centers and cost centers.

Managerial accounting provides information about the operating centers of a business.

- Some operating centers are called *profit centers* because they generate both revenues and expenses.
- Other operating centers are called *cost centers* because they incur expenses in providing services but do not produce revenues.

Many retail stores refer to profit and cost centers as departments.

- Separate accounts for sales, inventory, and other elements of the cost of goods sold are established because separate information is needed for each department.
- Departmental accounts can be established in the ledger with a column for each department.
- The sales journal, voucher register, and other records of original entry gather transaction data by department.

2 Prepare the Gross Profit section of a departmental income statement.

To determine departmental gross profit, the following figures for each department must be determined:

- gross sales
- sales returns and allowances
- sales discounts
- purchases
- purchases returns and allowances
- beginning and ending inventories

3 Explain and identify direct and indirect departmental expenses.

Operating expenses that can be identified directly with a specific department are considered direct expenses.

Other expenses must be allocated to departments on some predetermined basis at the end of the accounting period.

- Expenses that are allocated on a logical basis closely related to use are sometimes referred to as *semidirect expenses.*
- Expenses that must be allocated on a more arbitrary basis are called *indirect expenses.*
- Many accountants refer to both types as indirect expenses.

4 Choose the basis for allocation of indirect expenses and compute the amounts to be allocated to each department.

When selecting the basis for making the allocation of expenses, the accountant chooses a basis that

- relates the department and the expense in a logical manner,
- can be measured for each department.

5 Prepare a departmental income statement showing the contribution margin and operating income for each department.

The departmental income statement shows the contribution margin of each department as well as a final net income figure after allocation of all expenses.

6 Use a departmental income statement in making decisions such as whether a department should be closed.

The departmental income statement helps managers assess the profitability of a department. Departments with low profit margins or other operational weaknesses can be identified.

7 Define the accounting terms new to this chapter.

Glossary

Break-even point (BEP) (p. 887) The sales volume when total revenue equals total expenses

Contribution margin (p. 885) Gross profit on sales minus direct expenses

Cost center (p. 879) A business segment that incurs costs but does not produce revenue

Departmental income statement (p. 885) Income statement that shows each department's contribution margin and net income from operations after all expenses are allocated

Direct expenses (p. 880) Operating expenses that are identified directly with a department and are recorded by department

Indirect expenses (p. 881) Operating expenses that cannot be readily identified and are not closely related to activity within a department

Managerial accounting (p. 878) The branch of accounting that provides financial information about business segments, activities, or products

Profit center (p. 879) A business segment that produces revenue

Responsibility accounting (p. 879) The process that allows management to evaluate the performance of each segment of the business and assign responsibility for its financial results

Semidirect expenses (p. 880) Operating expenses that cannot be directly assigned to a department but are closely related to departmental activities

Transfer price (p. 879) The price at which one segment's goods are transferred to another segment of the company

---

Comprehensive **Self Review**

1. What are the logical profit centers in a retail store?
2. How can a nonselling business segment be called a profit center?
3. Compare the recording process for direct and indirect expenses.
4. Why are indirect expenses allocated to departments?
5. Give the steps in determining a department's contribution margin.

(Answers to Comprehensive Self Review are on page 899.)

 Multiple choice questions are provided on the text Web site at www.mhhe.com/price12e Quiz25

Discussion Questions

1. How does managerial accounting differ from financial accounting?
2. Why does managerial accounting focus on the future?
3. Briefly define responsibility accounting?
4. Is departmental accounting a form of responsibility accounting? Explain.
5. Why would a retail operation departmentalize its records?
6. How is contribution margin computed?
7. How does a departmentalized income statement differ from one that is not departmentalized?
8. Explain the difference between semidirect and indirect expenses.
9. Suggest a logical basis for allocating these indirect expenses: housekeeping services; office equipment repairs; general institutional advertising.
10. Why is interest expense not allocated to departments?

APPLICATIONS

Exercises HM™

Information for Exercises 25.1 through 25.3
Selected financial data, as of December 31, 2010, for Best for Less, a discount retail store, follows. Round all calculations off to the nearest dollar.

Credit sales

    Women's clothing, $472,500

    Men's clothing, $157,500

Total sales

    Women's clothing, $675,000

    Men's clothing, $225,000

Sales returns and allowances

    Women's clothing

        Credit sales, $4,500

        Cash sales, $500

    Men's clothing

        Credit sales, $2,500

        Cash sales, $500

Book value of inventory and equipment

    Women's clothing, $160,000

    Men's clothing, $40,000

Computing the amount of indirect expense to be allocated to a department.

◀ **Exercise 25.1**
Objective 4

Best for Less insurance expense for the year totaled $10,000 and is to be allocated on the basis of the book value of the inventory and equipment in each department. Compute the amount to be allocated to each department.

Computing the amount of indirect expense to be allocated to a department.

◀ **Exercise 25.2**
Objective 4

The total office expense for the year at Best for Less was $60,000. Compute the amount to be allocated to each department using total sales as the basis for the allocation.

Computing the amount of indirect expense to be allocated to a department.

◀ **Exercise 25.3**
Objective 4

The uncollectible accounts expense at Best for Less is estimated to be 1/2 of 1 percent of net credit sales. Compute the amount to be allocated to each department.

Preparing a departmental income statement showing contribution margin and net income for each department.

◀ **Exercise 25.4**
Objective 5

Data related to the income and expenses of Jackson Company for the year ending December 31, 2010, follow.

Allocated indirect expenses

    Kitchen department $75,900

    Bath department   36,400

Interest income   300

Gross profit

    Kitchen department $285,500

    Bath department   194,500

Direct expenses

    Kitchen department   134,600

    Bath department   95,400

Prepare a partial departmental income statement showing the contribution margin and net income of each department.

Exercise 25.5

Objective 6

▶ **Using departmental income statements in making decisions.**

Data from the departmental income statement of Clear Water Inc. for the year ended December 31, 2010, is given below. Assuming that a department's direct expenses can be eliminated if it is closed, what factors should management consider when deciding whether to close Department 1?

Clear Water Inc. Income Statement (Partial) For Year Ended December 31, 2010			
	Department 1	Department 2	Total
Net Sales	3 0 0 0 0 0	6 0 0 0 0 0	9 0 0 0 0 0
Cost of Goods Sold	2 1 0 0 0 0	3 6 0 0 0 0	5 7 0 0 0 0
Gross Profit on Sales	9 0 0 0 0	2 4 0 0 0 0	3 3 0 0 0 0
Direct Expenses	5 0 0 0 0	1 0 5 0 0 0	1 5 5 0 0 0
Contribution Margin	4 0 0 0 0	1 3 5 0 0 0	1 7 5 0 0 0
Indirect Expenses	4 5 0 0 0	8 0 0 0 0	1 2 5 0 0 0
Net Income (Loss)	(5 0 0 0)	5 5 0 0 0	5 0 0 0 0

Exercise 25.6

Objective 5

▶ **Preparing a departmental income statement showing contribution margin and net income of departments.**

Using the data given in Exercise 25.5, prepare an income statement for the company if Department 1 is closed.

Exercise 25.7

Objective 6

▶ **Using a departmental income statement in making decisions.**

Using the data given in Exercise 25.5, would you recommend closing Department 1? Why or why not?

Exercise 25.8

Objective 6

▶ **Calculating the break-even point.**

The Easter Company sells a product for $35. It costs $9 to obtain the product. The company has a total of $7,800 of fixed expenses. What is the break-even point?

PROBLEMS

Problem Set A

Problem 25.1A

Objectives 4, 5

eXcel

▶ **Allocating indirect expenses to departments and preparing a departmental income statement.**

Selected information from the adjusted trial balance of Shoe Fair as of December 31, 2010, follows.

	Department A	Department B	Total
Merchandise Inventory, January 1	$ 35,000	$ 15,000	$ 50,000
Merchandise Inventory, December 31	31,000	11,000	42,000
Sales	430,800	287,200	718,000
Sales Returns and Allowances	4,200	2,800	7,000
Purchases	195,600	115,000	310,600
Freight In	4,500	500	5,000

(continued)

(continued)

	Department A	Department B	Total
Purchases Returns and Allowances	1,500	500	2,000
Sales Salaries Expense	90,000	45,000	135,000
Advertising Expense	15,000	5,000	20,000
Store Supplies Expense	600	200	800
Cash Short or Over	40	80	120
Insurance Expense			15,000
Rent Expense			36,000
Utilities Expense			3,600
Office Salaries Expense			40,000
Other Office Expense			1,400
Uncollectible Accounts Expense			5,000
Depreciation Expense—Furniture and Fixtures			6,000
Depreciation Expense—Office Equipment			500
Interest Income			425
Interest Expense			450

INSTRUCTIONS

Prepare a departmental income statement for the year ended December 31, 2010. The bases for allocating indirect expenses are given below. (**Note:** Because allocations are not precise, round each allocated amount to the nearest whole percent and dollar.) Show all allocations in a neat and orderly form.

1. *Insurance Expense:* in proportion to the total of the furniture and fixtures (the gross assets before depreciation) and the ending inventory in the departments. These totals are as follows.

Department A	$130,000
Department B	70,000
Total	$200,000

2. *Rent Expense* and *Utilities Expense:* on the basis of floor space occupied, as follows.

Department A	4,500 square feet
Department B	1,500 square feet
Total	6,000 square feet

3. *Office Salaries Expense, Other Office Expenses,* and *Depreciation Expense—Office Equipment:* on the basis of the gross sales in each department.

4. *Uncollectible Accounts Expense:* on the basis of net sales in each department.

5. *Depreciation Expense—Furniture and Fixtures:* in proportion to cost of furniture and fixtures in each department. These costs are as follows. (Round to nearest dollar.)

Department A	$40,000
Department B	20,000
Total	$60,000

Analyze: Which department reports the highest return on net sales?

Preparing a departmental income statement and using the statement in making a business decision.

◄ **Problem 25.2A**
Objectives 5, 6

The Yard Shop sells plants, fertilizers, and other garden products. The store has three departments: plants, chemicals, and tools. Certain information about the revenues and expenses of the departments for the year ended December 31, 2010, is given below. Indirect expenses have been allocated on bases similar to those discussed and illustrated in the text.

	Plants	Chemicals	Tools
Allocated indirect expenses	$ 9,600	$ 5,400	$ 5,000
Beginning merchandise inventory	2,600	2,600	2,900
Direct expenses	30,000	17,500	15,500
Ending merchandise inventory	2,500	2,400	2,000
Purchases	50,000	47,000	36,000
Purchases returns and allowances	500	400	300
Sales	126,750	75,500	50,400
Sales returns and allowances	1,750	500	400

INSTRUCTIONS

1. Prepare a departmental income statement showing the contribution margin and the net profit for each department.

2. Based solely on accounting information, would you recommend that any departments be closed? Explain.

3. What information, other than accounting data, would you suggest the owners consider in deciding whether to close any departments?

Analyze: If the indirect expenses had been allocated on the basis of net sales, what conclusions would you draw about the viability of each department? Explain.

Problem Set B

Problem 25.1B
Objectives 4, 5

▶ **Allocating indirect expenses and preparing a departmental income statement.**

Selected information from the adjusted trial balance of Athletic House as of December 31, 2010, is shown below.

	Equipment	Clothes	Total
Merchandise Inventory, January 1	$ 30,000	$ 20,500	$ 50,500
Merchandise Inventory, December 31	28,750	24,000	52,750
Sales	315,000	199,800	514,800
Sales Returns and Allowances	3,500	2,800	6,300
Purchases	122,550	90,000	212,550
Freight In	4,550	900	5,450
Purchases Returns and Allowances	2,500	1,500	4,000
Sales Salaries Expense	87,000	55,000	142,000
Advertising Expense	10,000	5,000	15,000
Store Supplies Expense	500	300	800
Cash Short or Over	35	20	55
Insurance Expense			15,000
Rent Expense			24,000
Utilities Expense			5,000
Office Salaries Expense			55,000
Other Office Expense			1,600
Uncollectible Accounts Expense			2,500
Depreciation Expense—Furniture and Fixtures			4,200
Depreciation Expense—Office Equipment			300
Interest Income			205

INSTRUCTIONS

Prepare a departmental income statement for the year ended December 31, 2010. The bases for allocating indirect expenses are given below. (**Note:** Because allocations are not precise, round each allocated amount to the nearest whole percent and dollar.) Show all allocations in a neat and orderly form.

1. *Insurance Expense:* in proportion to the total of the furniture and fixtures (the gross assets before depreciation) and the ending inventory in the departments. These totals are as follows.

Equipment	$ 84,000
Clothes	36,000
Total	$120,000

2. *Rent Expense* and *Utilities Expense:* on the basis of floor space occupied, as follows.

Equipment	2,520 square feet
Clothes	1,680 square feet
Total	4,200 square feet

3. *Office Salaries Expense, Other Office Expenses,* and *Depreciation Expense—Office Equipment:* on the basis of the gross sales in each department.

4. *Uncollectible Accounts Expense:* on the basis of net sales in each department.

5. *Depreciation Expense—Furniture and Fixtures:* in proportion to cost of furniture and fixtures in each department. These costs are as follows.

Equipment	$4,800
Clothes	3,200
Total	$8,000

Analyze: To what degree does Clothes contribute to the overall net income of the business? Express your answer as a percentage.

Preparing a departmental income statement and using the statement in making a business decision.

◄ **Problem 25.2B**
Objective 5, 6

It's All Paper has three departments: printing, supplies, and cards. Certain information about the revenues and expenses of the departments for the year ending December 31, 2010, is given below. Indirect expenses have been allocated on bases similar to those discussed and illustrated in the text.

	Printing	Supplies	Cards	Total
Allocated Indirect Expenses	$ 2,300	$ 1,100	$ 600	$ 4,000
Beginning Merchandise Inventory	5,000	4,200	1,800	11,000
Direct Expenses	15,000	8,000	6,000	29,000
Ending Merchandise Inventory	4,500	2,900	1,000	8,400
Purchases	29,800	34,000	17,300	81,100
Purchases Returns and Allowances	500	300	300	1,100
Sales	76,900	44,250	30,200	151,350
Sales Returns and Allowances	900	250	200	1,350

INSTRUCTIONS

1. Prepare a departmental income statement showing the contribution margin and the net profit for each department.

2. Based solely on accounting information, would you recommend that any departments be closed? Explain.

3. What information, other than accounting data, would you suggest the owners consider in deciding whether to close any departments?

Analyze: What increase in net sales would be required to ensure that the Supplies Department would be able to cover its indirect expenses? Assume that all other figures remained steady.

Critical Thinking Problem 25.1

Departmental Closure

Mountain Gifts has three sales departments: wood crafts, clothing items, and paper goods. The store's condensed income statement for the year ended December 31, 2010, is shown below.

	Wood Crafts	Clothing Items	Paper Goods
Mountain Gifts			
Condensed Income Statement			
Year Ended December 31, 2010			
Sales	70 0 0 0	50 0 0 0	20 0 0 0
Cost of Goods Sold	22 0 0 0	29 5 0 0	12 0 0 0
Gross Profit	48 0 0 0	20 5 0 0	8 0 0 0
Operating Expenses			
Direct Expenses	18 5 0 0	11 0 0 0	8 0 0 0
Indirect Expenses	9 0 0 0	8 0 0 0	5 0 0 0
Total Operating Expenses	27 5 0 0	19 0 0 0	13 0 0 0
Net Profit	20 5 0 0	1 5 0 0	(5 0 0 0)

The proprietor asked the auditor if the Clothing Items and/or Paper Goods departments should be closed. In the opinion of both the owner and the auditor, if the Clothing Items department is closed, the total indirect expenses could possibly be reduced to $16,000. If only the Paper Goods department is closed, the indirect expenses could possibly to be reduced to a total of $19,000. In the opinion of the owner, if the Paper Goods department is closed, a loss of $7,000 in sales could be lost from the Wood Crafts department. This loss in sales would reduce the Wood Crafts Cost of Goods Sold by $3,000. She also thinks that closing the Paper Goods department would have no effect on sales of the Clothing Items department.

INSTRUCTIONS

1. Based on the preceding information, what would the estimated total profit or loss be if the Paper Goods department were closed?
2. What would the estimated total profit or loss be if the Clothing Items department were closed?
3. What advice would you give the proprietor?

Analyze: What is the current contribution margin for each department?

Critical Thinking Problem 25.2

Indirect Costs

At the last staff meeting of the Aqua Shop, the question of how expenses are allocated to each department was raised. Since year-end bonuses are awarded to the managers on the basis of departmental net income from operations, the discussion was lively.

Bill Sharp, manager of the repair department, said that each department should be charged only with the expenses directly related to the department. He indicated that while managers can influence the sales and direct expenses in their departments, they have little control over many of the indirect expenses such as depreciation, office salaries, and taxes.

Beth Brandon, manager of the new boat sales department, argued that all expenses—direct and indirect—should be allocated. "After all," she said, "all the revenue is allocated to each department, so why not allocate all the expenses? The store could not operate if it did not incur the indirect expenses." She also stated that many of the indirect expenses, such as insurance and cleaning services, could be allocated on a meaningful basis.

INSTRUCTIONS

Evaluate these comments.

BUSINESS CONNECTIONS

Departmental Accounting

Managerial | FOCUS

1. Is the identification of purchases returns and allowances by department valuable to managerial control? Explain.

2. If one department consistently has a comparatively large amount of cash short in its operations, what management action might be appropriate?

3. Why is it better for managers to use contribution margin analysis rather than net income analysis when deciding whether to retain, expand, or contract operations?

4. How does a firm's accountant determine the reasonable basis to be used in allocating a specific indirect expense? Should management be concerned about the basis used?

5. The management of a store with three sales departments plans to install a bonus system for department managers. Do you think the bonus system should be based on each department's contribution margin or on the department's net income after allocating all administrative expenses? Explain.

Assigning Indirect Costs

Ethical | DILEMMA

Allocation of indirect costs to various departments can alter the departmental profit. Jacobs Company manufactures plates for drum brakes. To make the brake plate, three departments are required: stamping, plating, and packaging. At Jacobs, each department manager is eligible for a bonus based on departmental profit. You are the manager of the stamping department. Top management has given you the responsibility of assigning the indirect costs to each department. Stamping has higher material costs whereas plating has higher labor costs. You decide that it would be best to have the indirect costs evenly distributed to each department. Is this a correct decision? Should you have the authority to make this decision?

Segments

STREETWISE:
Questions from the
REAL WORLD

Refer to the *2006 Annual Report* for The Home Depot, Inc., in Appendix A.

1. Review the Letter To Shareholders, Associates, Customers, Suppliers, and Communities. What are the challenges that The Home Depot, Inc., is facing? What are the five priorities The Home Depot, Inc., is focusing on?

2. Review the Letter To Shareholders, Associates, Customers, Suppliers, and Communities. What foreign company did The Home Depot, Inc., acquire, and why did they acquire it?

**Financial Statement
ANALYSIS**

Segment Reporting

The following excerpt was taken from the *2006 Annual Report* for Alcoa Inc., the world's leading producer of primary aluminum, fabricated aluminum, and alumina.

Segment Information (in millions)	Alumina	Primary Metals	Flat-Rolled Products	Extruded and End Products	Engineered Solutions	Packaging & Consumer	Total
2006							
Total sales	$4,929	$12,379	$8,543	$4,518	$5,456	$3,235	$39,060
After-tax operating income	$1,050	$ 1,760	$ 255	$ 60	$ 331	$ 95	$ 3,551

Analyze:

1. List Alcoa's six operating segments.
2. Which segment yields the highest after tax operating income?
3. Which segment yields the highest rate of return on total sales?

Analyze Online: Find the *Investor Information* section on the Alcoa Web site (www.alcoa.com). Click on the *Financial Data* link, and review the information presented for *Segment and Geographic Information.*

4. Describe the operations of the segment labeled *Other.*
5. Describe the items that have been excluded from segment profit computations.

Extending THE THOUGHT

Intersegment Transactions

Some corporations are organized into functional segments such as merchandising, manufacturing, and distribution divisions. Imagine that the merchandising division of a company has requested to use personnel and office supplies from the distribution division for a one-time promotion. The merchandising operation needs two clerical workers for three days and approximately $3,000 in office supplies to complete the project. The CFO decides that since the resources all come from the same corporation, he will not charge the merchandising operation for the use of the distribution division's time and supplies. Do you agree with his decision? Why or why not?

Business COMMUNICATION

Accounting for Segments

As the controller of Crown City Fashions, you have decided it would be advantageous to track financial performance for each of the company's departments: Sports Wear, Men's Wear, Kid's & Teen's Wear, and Women's Wear. Currently, the accounting records are not structured for recording department-specific transactions. Create a checklist of the types of changes that you will need to make to the general ledger in order to record transactions on a divisional basis. What types of changes will be required when preparing financial reports at month-end or year-end?

TEAMWORK

Direct and Indirect Costs

Select a food product your group can produce. For example, tortilla chips, ice cream, cookies, or pretzels. List the steps to produce this product. Determine the direct and indirect materials and labor needed in its production. Present your findings to the class. How are the costs similar and dissimilar?

Internet CONNECTION

Two Departments—One Report?

Ford Motor Company (www.fordmotorcompany.com) and General Motors (www.gm.com) have two departments: Automobile Sales and Financing. Go to each company's financial statements on its Web site (investors, annual report). Both companies provide a consolidated statement of income.

One company separates Automobile Sales and Financing only on sales. Which company provides net income (before income taxes) by department and which one combines both departments? Why do you think the companies differ in their presentation of income information?

Answers to **Self Reviews**

Answers to Section 1 Self Review

1. A cost center incurs expenses but does not have revenues; a profit center does produce revenues.
2. It provides information for evaluating segment performance and assigning responsibility for financial results.
3. The total value of insured assets in each department.
4. **c.** both revenue and costs are accumulated for the segment.
5. **c.** sales, purchases, and merchandise inventory.
6. $6,000

Answers to Section 2 Self Review

1. Gross profit on sales minus direct expenses.
2. Direct expenses relate to a specific department. Indirect expenses must be allocated on a logical basis.
3. The accountant seeks a basis that seems to be correlated with the amount of expense and that can be measured for each department.
4. **d.** negative contribution margin and a loss from operations.
5. **b.** $15,000
6. Net income would be $18,000 lower.

Answers to Comprehensive Self Review

1. Departments that sell similar items to customers outside the business.
2. Some cost centers render services or make products that are transferred to other centers in the same company. In such cases, a hypothetical revenue, or transfer price, is attributed to the goods or services transferred. This price permits measuring a "profit" for the center.
3. Direct expenses are usually charged when incurred. Indirect expenses are allocated at the end of the fiscal period.
4. Indirect expenses are allocated to departments to attempt to measure the profitability of each department.
5. Subtract the department's direct expenses from its gross profit.

Accounting for Manufacturing Activities

Chapter 26

LP26

LEARNING OBJECTIVES

1. Prepare a statement of cost of goods manufactured.
2. Explain the basic components of manufacturing cost.
3. Prepare an income statement for a manufacturing business.
4. Prepare a balance sheet for a manufacturing business.
5. Prepare a worksheet for a manufacturing business.
6. Record the end-of-period adjusting entries for a manufacturing business.
7. Record closing entries for a manufacturing business.
8. Record reversing entries for a manufacturing business.
9. Define the accounting terms new to this chapter.

NEW TERMS

direct labor
direct materials
finished goods inventory
indirect labor
indirect materials and supplies
manufacturing overhead
Manufacturing Summary account
raw materials
statement of cost of goods manufactured
work in process

 TOYOTA   www.toyota.com

Fifty years ago, Toyota Motor Sales (TMS), U.S.A., Inc., began marketing cars and trucks in the United States. By the end of 1958, it had sold just 287 sedans and one Land Cruiser. The company has certainly come a long way. With sales of over 2.5 million cars and trucks in 2006, the Toyota, Scion, and Lexus lineups feature 27 models offered by more than 1,400 dealers across the nation. After overtaking Ford and Chrysler, Toyota is poised to gain the position as the number 1 automaker in the world—a position General Motors has held for 76 years.

Toyota currently produces 19, vehicles in North America; including the Avalon, Camry, Camry Hybrid, Corolla, Matrix, Sienna, Solara, Sequoia, Tacoma, and the Tundra. By 2010, Toyota will have the annual capacity to build approximately 2.2 million cars and trucks, 1.45 million engines, and 600,000 automatic transmissions. Toyota's annual purchasing of parts, materials, goods, and services from North American suppliers totals more than $28.5 billion.

thinking critically

What are some of the costs that might contribute to the over $28 billion Toyota pays to North American suppliers?

SECTION OBJECTIVES

>> 1. **Prepare a statement of cost of goods manufactured.**

WHY IT'S IMPORTANT

Manufacturing businesses carefully track production costs to maximize profits.

>> 2. **Explain the basic components of manufacturing cost.**

WHY IT'S IMPORTANT

Manufacturing costs consist of many elements such as labor, materials, and manufacturing overhead.

>> 3. **Prepare an income statement for a manufacturing business.**

WHY IT'S IMPORTANT

The income statement for a manufacturing business differs slightly from the merchandising income statement.

>> 4. **Prepare a balance sheet for a manufacturing business.**

WHY IT'S IMPORTANT

The balance sheet for a manufacturer shows inventory accounts for raw material, work in process, and finished goods.

TERMS TO LEARN

direct labor

direct materials

finished goods inventory

indirect labor

indirect materials and supplies

manufacturing overhead

raw materials

statement of cost of goods manufactured

work in process

Accounting for Manufacturing Costs

Merchandising businesses purchase merchandise to be resold in the same condition and form but at a profit. Manufacturing businesses purchase and convert raw materials into finished goods to be sold at a profit.

Cost of Goods Manufactured

The difference between merchandising and manufacturing businesses is reflected in the income statements of the two types of businesses. You can see the similarities and differences by examining the partial income statements that follow for Boat Merchandising Company and Trailer Manufacturing Company. Note that the major difference is that a manufacturing business uses "Cost of Goods Manufactured" instead of "Purchases."

Boat Merchandising Company
Partial Income Statement
Year Ended December 31, 2010

Revenue			
Sales (Net)			6 9 0 0 0 0 0
Cost of Goods Sold			
Merchandise Inventory, Jan. 1	3 0 0 0 0 0		
Purchases (Net)	3 2 7 5 0 6 0 0		
Goods Available for Sale	3 5 7 5 0 6 0 0		
Less Merchandise Inventory, Dec. 31	2 9 0 0 0 0 0		
Cost of Goods Sold		3 2 8 5 0 6 0 0	
Gross Profit on Sales		3 6 1 4 9 4 0 0	

Trailer Manufacturing Company			
Partial Income Statement			
Year Ended December 31, 2010			
Revenue			
Sales (Net)			6 9 0 0 0 0 0 0
Cost of Goods Sold			
Finished Goods Inventory, Jan. 1	3 0 0 0 0 0 0		
Cost of Goods Manufactured	3 2 7 5 0 6 0 0		
Total Goods Available for Sale	3 5 7 5 0 6 0 0		
Less Finished Goods Inventory, Dec. 31	2 9 0 0 0 0 0		
Cost of Goods Sold		3 2 8 5 0 6 0 0	
Gross Profit on Sales		3 6 1 4 9 4 0 0	

>>1. OBJECTIVE

Prepare a statement of cost of goods manufactured.

LP26

Let's look more closely at the components that make up the cost of goods manufactured in the financial statements of a manufacturing concern. We will examine the accounts and financial statements of Trailer Manufacturing Company, a producer of trailers. Its manufacturing process involves the acquisition and use of raw materials such as steel, lumber, rivets, screws, nails, and paint. These materials are cut, shaped, assembled, painted, and polished in the factory and emerge as finished products ready for sale.

Statement of Cost of Goods Manufactured

The **statement of cost of goods manufactured** shows details of the cost of goods completed for a manufacturing business. This statement supports the Cost of Goods Sold figure shown on the income statement. Figure 26.1 on page 904 shows the statement of cost of goods manufactured for Trailer Manufacturing Company.

COMPONENTS OF MANUFACTURING COSTS

The components of manufacturing cost are the raw materials used **(1)**, the direct labor **(2)**, and the manufacturing overhead **(3)**. The numbers in parentheses refer to amounts in Figure 26.1.

Raw Materials A major component of manufacturing cost is **raw materials**—the materials placed into production. Let's examine how data about the cost of raw materials appears on the statement of cost of goods manufactured. The beginning inventory of raw materials, $25,000, is added to net purchases of raw materials, $165,000. Net purchases is materials purchases minus purchases discounts ($168,000 − $3,000). The result is total materials available, $190,000. The ending raw materials inventory, $24,000, is subtracted to determine the raw materials used, $166,000.

In this section, all references to materials (raw materials, materials purchases, and materials available) relate to direct materials. **Direct materials** are all items that go into a product and become part of it. For example, the direct materials in a trailer include the metal, rivets, screws, and paint.

Indirect materials and supplies are used in manufacturing a product but do not become part of the product. Indirect materials appear in the Manufacturing Overhead section of the statement. Indirect materials include sandpaper, steel wool, cleaning materials, and lubricants. Some businesses treat insignificant direct materials, such as glue, as indirect materials.

Direct Labor **Direct labor** costs are the costs of the personnel who work directly on the product being manufactured. Direct labor includes workers who cut and shape the metals, assemble the pieces into trailers, and finish or paint them. On the statement of cost of goods manufactured, direct labor is $98,500. This amount is obtained from the *Direct Labor* account.

Indirect labor costs are the costs of personnel who support production but are not directly involved in the manufacture of a product, such as supervisory, repair and maintenance, and janitorial staff. Supervisors are included in indirect labor because although they ensure that the work is done properly, they do not work directly on the product. Indirect labor is included in the Manufacturing Overhead section of the statement.

>>2. OBJECTIVE

Explain the basic components of manufacturing cost.

ABOUT
ACCOUNTING

Benchmarking
Benchmarking involves evaluating another company's business processes and adopting them to incorporate best practices to improve performance, search for innovative ideas, and gain a competitive advantage. The goal of benchmarking is to learn from others, adapt, implement, and improve.

Trailer Manufacturing Company
Statement of Cost of Goods Manufactured
Year Ended December 31, 2010

Work in Process Inventory, Jan. 1				(5) 1 6 0 0 0 0 0
Raw Materials				
Raw Materials Inventory, Jan. 1			2 5 0 0 0 0 0	
Materials Purchases	1 6 8 0 0 0 0 0			
Less Purchases Discounts	3 0 0 0 0 0			
Net Purchases			1 6 5 0 0 0 0 0	
Total Materials Available			1 9 0 0 0 0 0 0	
Less Raw Materials Inventory, Dec. 31			2 4 0 0 0 0 0	
Raw Materials Used			(1) 1 6 6 0 0 0 0 0	
Direct Labor			(2) 9 8 5 0 0 0 0	
Manufacturing Overhead				
Indirect Labor	4 5 0 0 0 0			
Payroll Taxes—Factory	9 8 0 6 0 0			
Utilities—Factory	9 0 0 0 0 0			
Repairs and Maintenance—Factory	5 0 0 0 0 0			
Indirect Materials and Supplies	7 2 0 0 0 0			
Depreciation—Factory Building	7 5 0 0 0 0			
Depreciation—Factory Equipment	5 0 0 0 0 0			
Insurance—Factory	3 5 0 0 0 0			
Property Taxes—Factory	7 5 0 0 0 0			
Total Manufacturing Overhead			(3) 5 9 0 0 6 0 0	
Total Manufacturing Cost				(4) 3 2 3 5 0 6 0 0
Total Work in Process for Year				3 3 9 5 0 6 0 0
Less Work in Process Inventory, Dec. 31				(6) 1 2 0 0 0 0 0
Cost of Goods Manufactured				(7) 3 2 7 5 0 6 0 0

FIGURE 26.1   Statement of Cost of Goods Manufactured

Manufacturing Overhead   **Manufacturing overhead**   includes all manufacturing costs that are not classified as direct materials or direct labor. In addition to indirect materials and supplies and indirect labor, manufacturing overhead includes utilities, depreciation, repair and maintenance, insurance, and property taxes for factory buildings and equipment. Manufacturing overhead also includes payroll taxes on factory wages.

> The Boeing Company, the United States' second-largest defense contractor, is the world's premier manufacturer of commercial aircraft. A 2003 Malcolm Baldrige National Quality Award recipient, Boeing is producing the Boeing 787 Dreamliner aircraft to compete with Europe's Airbus. Another innovation for many air passengers is the Connexion by Boeing[SM] that features areas in the aircraft that function like an office for business travelers. Only by controlling costs can a larger manufacturer, like Boeing, begin new business ventures.

WORK IN PROCESS

On the statement of cost of goods manufactured, the total manufacturing cost (4) includes all raw materials used, all direct labor costs incurred, and all manufacturing overhead applicable to the current production period. However, it does not represent the total cost of goods manufactured because some products that were finished this period were started in the previous period. **Work in process** refers to partially completed units in the production process. At the end of each period, an estimate is made of the costs of raw materials, direct labor, and manufacturing overhead for the work in process. For Trailer Manufacturing Company, the beginning inventory of work in process was $16,000 **(5),** and the ending inventory of work in process was $12,000 **(6).** The numbers in parentheses refer to amounts in Figure 26.1.

On the statement of cost of goods manufactured, the beginning work in process is added to total manufacturing cost. The result is total work in process for the year. The ending work in process is subtracted from the total work in process for the year to arrive at the cost of goods manufactured **(7).**

Income Statement for a Manufacturing Concern

Notice that the cost of goods manufactured from Figure 26.1 is used to calculate the cost of goods sold in the income statement. The income statement for Trailer Manufacturing Company appears in Figure 26.2 below.

The cost of goods sold can differ from the cost of goods manufactured because of changes in the level of **finished goods inventory.** Some finished goods that are sold in the current period were made in previous periods. Some products made during the current period will be sold in later periods. In order to prepare the income statement, a count is made of the finished goods inventory at the end of each period.

In Figure 26.2, the beginning finished goods inventory, $30,000, is added to the cost of goods manufactured, $327,506. The result is the total finished goods available for sale, $357,506. The ending finished goods inventory, $29,000, is subtracted, and the difference represents the cost of goods sold, $328,506.

Balance Sheet for a Manufacturing Concern

Figure 26.3 on page 906 shows the balance sheet for a manufacturing business. Notice that it includes three inventory categories: raw materials, work in process, and finished goods.

>>**3. OBJECTIVE**
Prepare an income statement for a manufacturing business.

important!

Income Statement
In the income statement of a manufacturing company, the line item "Cost of Goods Manufactured" replaces "Purchases."

>>**4. OBJECTIVE**
Prepare a balance sheet for a manufacturing business.

LP26

important!

Cost of Goods Sold
The cost of goods sold may differ from the cost of goods manufactured because of beginning and ending inventories of finished goods.

Trailer Manufacturing Company		
Income Statement		
Year Ended December 31, 2010		
Revenue		
Sales		6 9 5 0 0 0 0 0
Less Sales Returns and Allowances		5 0 0 0 0 0
Net Sales		6 9 0 0 0 0 0 0
Cost of Goods Sold		
Finished Goods Inventory, Jan. 1	3 0 0 0 0 0 0	
Cost of Goods Manufactured	3 2 7 5 0 6 0 0	
Total Goods Available for Sale	3 5 7 5 0 6 0 0	
Less Finished Goods Inventory, Dec. 31	2 9 0 0 0 0 0	
Cost of Goods Sold		3 2 8 5 0 6 0 0
Gross Profit on Sales		3 6 1 4 9 4 0 0
Operating Expenses		
Selling Expenses (Control)	1 0 0 0 0 0 0 0	
Administrative Expenses (Control)	9 2 8 8 0 0 0	
Total Operating Expenses		1 9 2 8 8 0 0 0
Net Income Before Income Taxes		1 6 8 6 1 4 0 0
Income Tax Expense		4 2 1 5 4 0 0
Net Income After Income Taxes		1 2 6 4 6 0 0 0

FIGURE 26.2

Income Statement for a Manufacturing Concern

Trailer Manufacturing Company
Balance Sheet
Year Ended December 31, 2010

Assets				
Current Assets				
Cash				4 0 0 0 0 0 0
Accounts Receivable		6 5 5 0 0 0 0		
Less Allowance for Doubtful Accounts		1 8 8 0 0 0	6 3 6 2 0 0 0	
Inventories				
Raw Materials		2 4 0 0 0 0 0		
Work in Process		1 2 0 0 0 0 0		
Finished Goods		2 9 0 0 0 0 0	6 5 0 0 0 0 0	
Prepaid Expenses				
Prepaid Insurance		2 0 0 0 0 0		
Supplies on Hand		8 0 0 0 0	2 8 0 0 0 0	
Total Current Assets			1 7 1 4 2 0 0 0	
Property, Plant, and Equipment				
Land		5 0 0 0 0 0 0		
Factory Building	1 5 0 0 0 0 0 0			
Accumulated Depreciation—Factory Building	2 2 5 0 0 0 0	1 2 7 5 0 0 0 0		
Factory Equipment	1 0 0 0 0 0 0 0			
Accumulated Depreciation—Factory Equipment	2 5 0 0 0 0 0	7 5 0 0 0 0 0		
Office Equipment	1 0 0 0 0 0 0			
Accumulated Depreciation—Office Equipment	6 0 0 0 0 0	4 0 0 0 0 0		
Total Property, Plant, and Equipment			2 5 6 5 0 0 0 0	
Total Assets			4 2 7 9 2 0 0 0	
Liabilities and Stockholders' Equity				
Current Liabilities				
Accounts Payable			3 0 0 0 0 0 0	
Salaries and Wages Payable			4 0 0 0 0 0	
Income Tax Payable			2 1 5 4 0 0	
Social Security Tax Payable			2 4 8 0 0	
Medicare Tax Payable			5 8 0 0	
Total Liabilities			3 6 4 6 0 0 0	
Stockholders' Equity				
Common Stock $1 par value (200,000 shares authorized, 100,000 issued and outstanding)	1 0 0 0 0 0 0 0			
Paid-in Capital in Excess of Par Value	5 0 0 0 0 0 0			
Total Paid-in Capital		1 5 0 0 0 0 0 0		
Retained Earnings		2 4 1 4 6 0 0 0		
Total Stockholders' Equity			3 9 1 4 6 0 0 0	
Total Liabilities and Stockholders' Equity			4 2 7 9 2 0 0 0	

FIGURE 26.3   **Balance Sheet for a Manufacturing Concern**

Manufacturing businesses balance the costs of production with quality and speed to market. Quincy Compressors, an EnPro Industries company, makes and sells highest-quality air compressors and vacuum pumps. This balancing act (of high quality and costs of production) has been recognized recently with Quincy Compressor manufacturing facilities being recognized as one of the winners of the 2007 Progressive Manufacturing Award.

IMPORTANCE OF INVENTORY IN MANUFACTURING BUSINESS

*inte*rnal CONTROL

Managing Inventory Chapter 17 discussed the importance of the valuation of inventory. Many businesses actually count the number of each type of goods on hand, then multiply the number of units obtained during the count by the appropriate cost per unit. This is referred to as the process of taking a *physical inventory.* It is generally performed only at the end of a period.

Managers of manufacturing businesses, however, frequently need reliable information about inventory more frequently, sometimes on a daily basis. The procedure used to obtain this information is known as keeping a *perpetual inventory.* Additions to and deletions from all inventory accounts, such as finished goods, work in process, and materials, are recorded as they occur. Although this requires additional bookkeeping, many managers justify this cost because it enables them to aggressively control costs. Perpetual inventory records are customarily verified by taking a physical count at least once a year.

Section 1 Self Review

QUESTIONS

1. What are direct materials?
2. What does work in process represent?
3. How does the cost of goods manufactured relate to the income statement?

EXERCISES

4. The components of total manufacturing cost are
   a. raw materials used, direct labor, and manufacturing overhead.
   b. selling expenses, administrative expenses, and manufacturing overhead.
   c. manufacturing overhead and administrative expenses.
   d. cost of goods manufactured, cost of goods sold, and work in process.

5. Indirect labor for a manufacturing business includes the wages of
   a. employees who assemble the product.
   b. factory repair and maintenance employees.
   c. employees who finish and paint the product.
   d. employees who sell the product.

ANALYSIS

6. What is the cost of goods manufactured if beginning work in process was $45,000, ending work in process was $35,000, raw materials used were $30,000, direct labor was $40,000, and manufacturing overhead was $20,000?

(Answers to Section 1 Self Review are on page 928.)

>> 5. **Prepare a worksheet for a manufacturing business.**

WHY IT'S IMPORTANT

There are accounts on the worksheet that are specific to manufacturing businesses.

>> 6. **Record the end-of-period adjusting entries for a manufacturing business.**

WHY IT'S IMPORTANT

Adjusting entries are made in the same way for merchandising and manufacturing businesses.

>> 7. **Record closing entries for a manufacturing business.**

WHY IT'S IMPORTANT

All manufacturing and operating costs are closed at the end of the period.

>> 8. **Record reversing entries for a manufacturing business.**

WHY IT'S IMPORTANT

Reversing entries save time and help to reduce errors.

Manufacturing Summary account

Completing the Accounting Cycle

The worksheet for a manufacturing business has a section to facilitate the preparation of the statement of cost of goods manufactured. Refer to Figure 26.4 on pages 910–911 as we complete the worksheet for Trailer Manufacturing Company.

The Worksheet and Financial Statements

>>**5. OBJECTIVE**

Prepare a worksheet for a manufacturing business.

LP26

After all transactions have been journalized and posted, the worksheet is completed. The first step is to enter the trial balance.

ENTERING THE TRIAL BALANCE ON THE WORKSHEET

Notice that there are several accounts unique to manufacturing businesses. There are three inventory accounts: *Raw Materials Inventory, Work in Process Inventory,* and *Finished Goods Inventory.* There is a *Direct Labor* account as well as various manufacturing overhead accounts that appear on the statement of cost of goods manufactured.

The **Manufacturing Summary account** is similar to the *Income Summary* account. All of the accounts that appear on the statement of cost of goods manufactured are closed to *Manufacturing Summary.* Then the balance of *Manufacturing Summary,* which represents the cost of goods manufactured, is closed to *Income Summary.*

ENTERING ADJUSTING ENTRIES ON THE WORKSHEET

Notice that there are some adjustments that pertain to manufacturing operations only. Carefully trace each adjustment. For the sake of simplicity, selling and administrative expenses are recorded in the control accounts.

ENDING INVENTORIES

Six adjustments are made for inventory. *Raw Materials Inventory* (**a**) and (**b**), *Work in Process Inventory* (**c**) and (**d**), and *Finished Goods Inventory* (**e**) and (**f**). The inventory accounts are credited for beginning inventory amounts and debited for the ending inventory amounts. For *Raw Materials Inventory* and *Work in Process Inventory*, the adjustment is made to *Manufacturing Summary*. For *Finished Goods Inventory*, the adjustment is made to *Income Summary*.

UNCOLLECTIBLE ACCOUNTS

Entry (**g**) is made to record the uncollectible accounts expense, which is estimated to be 0.2 percent of net sales, or $1,380 (0.002 × $690,000).

EXPIRED INSURANCE

Entry (**h**) records insurance expired during the year. Expired insurance includes $3,500 on assets related to manufacturing (equipment, buildings, and inventories) and $500 on office equipment.

SUPPLIES ON HAND

Entry (**i**) records the adjustment for supplies on hand. At Trailer Manufacturing Company, when manufacturing supplies are purchased they are debited to the *Indirect Materials and Supplies* account, a manufacturing overhead expense account. Manufacturing companies follow this procedure because most of the supplies are consumed in a short time. Supplies used in selling and in administrative activities are debited to the *Selling Expenses Control* and *Administrative Expenses Control* accounts.

At the end of December, there was $800 of factory supplies on hand. Adjustment (**i**) debits the asset account *Supplies on Hand* for $800 and credits the overhead account *Indirect Materials and Supplies* for $800. The cost of the sales and office supplies on hand is deemed immaterial.

important!

Manufacturing Summary
All items that appear on the statement of cost of goods manufactured are transferred to the *Manufacturing Summary* account.

DEPRECIATION

Entry (**j**) records the adjustment for depreciation on assets for the year: $7,500 on the factory building, $5,000 on the factory equipment, and $1,000 on the office equipment.

ACCRUED SALARIES AND WAGES

On December 31, accrued wages are $3,500 for direct labor and $500 for indirect labor. These accruals are recorded by entry (**k**).

PAYROLL TAXES ON ACCRUED PAYROLL

Entry (**l**) records payroll taxes on the $4,000 accrued wages of factory workers at the end of the year. All of the workers have earned the maximum amount subject to federal and state unemployment taxes. Therefore, the accrual is for $248 (0.062 × $4,000) of social security tax and $58 (0.0145 × $4,000) of Medicare tax.

INCOME TAX PAYABLE

The federal income tax is estimated to be 25 percent of the taxable income. Based on the worksheet, the estimated taxable income is $168,614, and the estimated income tax (rounded to nearest dollar) for the year is $42,154 ($168,614 × 0.25). During the year, $40,000 of estimated tax payments were made. As a result, $2,154 ($42,154 − $40,000) of additional taxes are accrued on December 31. The accrual is recorded on the worksheet as entry (**m**).

recall

Accruals
Adjustments are made for items that relate to the current period but that have not been paid for and do not yet appear in the accounts.

FIGURE 26.4 Worksheet for a Manufacturing Concern

Trailer Manufacturing Company
Worksheet
Year Ended December 31, 2010

#	ACCOUNT NAME	TRIAL BALANCE DEBIT	TRIAL BALANCE CREDIT	ADJUSTMENTS DEBIT	ADJUSTMENTS CREDIT	ADJUSTED TRIAL BALANCE DEBIT	ADJUSTED TRIAL BALANCE CREDIT
1	Cash	4 0 0 0 0 0 0				4 0 0 0 0 0 0	
2	Accounts Receivable	6 5 5 0 0 0 0				6 5 5 0 0 0 0	
3	Allowance for Doubtful Accounts		5 0 0 0 0		(g) 1 3 8 0 0 0		1 8 8 0 0 0
4	Raw Materials Inventory	2 5 0 0 0 0 0		(b)2 4 0 0 0 0 0	(a)2 5 0 0 0 0 0	2 4 0 0 0 0 0	
5	Work in Process Inventory	1 6 0 0 0 0 0		(d)1 2 0 0 0 0 0	(c)1 6 0 0 0 0 0	1 2 0 0 0 0 0	
6	Finished Goods Inventory	3 0 0 0 0 0 0		(f)2 9 0 0 0 0 0	(e)3 0 0 0 0 0 0	2 9 0 0 0 0 0	
7	Prepaid Insurance	6 0 0 0 0 0			(h) 4 0 0 0 0 0	2 0 0 0 0 0	
8	Supplies on Hand			(i) 8 0 0 0 0		8 0 0 0 0	
9	Land	5 0 0 0 0 0 0				5 0 0 0 0 0 0	
10	Factory Building	15 0 0 0 0 0 0				15 0 0 0 0 0 0	
11	Accum. Depr.—Building		1 5 0 0 0 0 0		(j) 7 5 0 0 0 0		2 2 5 0 0 0 0
12	Factory Equipment	10 0 0 0 0 0 0				10 0 0 0 0 0 0	
13	Accum. Depr.—Factory Equipment		2 0 0 0 0 0 0		(j) 5 0 0 0 0 0		2 5 0 0 0 0 0
14	Office Equipment	1 0 0 0 0 0 0				1 0 0 0 0 0 0	
15	Accum. Depr.—Office Equipment		5 0 0 0 0 0		(j) 1 0 0 0 0 0		6 0 0 0 0 0
16	Accounts Payable		3 0 0 0 0 0 0				3 0 0 0 0 0 0
17	Salaries and Wages Payable				(k) 4 0 0 0 0 0		4 0 0 0 0 0
18	Income Tax Payable				(m) 2 1 5 4 0 0		2 1 5 4 0 0
19	Social Security Tax Payable				(l) 2 4 8 0 0		2 4 8 0 0
20	Medicare Tax Payable				(l) 5 8 0 0		5 8 0 0
21	Common Stock, $1 par		10 0 0 0 0 0 0				10 0 0 0 0 0 0
22	Paid-in Cap. in Exc. of par Value		5 0 0 0 0 0 0				5 0 0 0 0 0 0
23	Retained Earnings		11 5 0 0 0 0 0				11 5 0 0 0 0 0
24	Sales		69 5 0 0 0 0 0				69 5 0 0 0 0 0
25	Sales Returns and Allowances	5 0 0 0 0 0				5 0 0 0 0 0	
26	Materials Purchases	16 8 0 0 0 0 0				16 8 0 0 0 0 0	
27	Purchases Discounts		3 0 0 0 0 0				3 0 0 0 0 0
28	Direct Labor	9 5 0 0 0 0 0		(k) 3 5 0 0 0 0		9 8 5 0 0 0 0	
29	Indirect Labor	4 0 0 0 0 0		(k) 5 0 0 0 0		4 5 0 0 0 0	
30	Payroll Taxes—Factory	9 5 0 0 0 0		(l) 3 0 6 0 0		9 8 0 6 0 0	
31	Utilities—Factory	9 0 0 0 0 0				9 0 0 0 0 0	
32	Repairs & Maintenance—Factory	5 0 0 0 0 0				5 0 0 0 0 0	
33	Indirect Materials and Supplies	8 0 0 0 0 0			(i) 8 0 0 0 0	7 2 0 0 0 0	
34	Depreciation—Factory Building			(j) 7 5 0 0 0 0		7 5 0 0 0 0	
35	Depreciation—Factory Equipment			(j) 5 0 0 0 0 0		5 0 0 0 0 0	
36	Insurance—Factory			(h) 3 5 0 0 0 0		3 5 0 0 0 0	
37	Property Taxes—Factory	7 5 0 0 0 0				7 5 0 0 0 0	
38	Selling Expense (Control)	10 0 0 0 0 0 0				10 0 0 0 0 0 0	
39	Administrative Expense (Control)	9 0 0 0 0 0 0		(g) 1 3 8 0 0 0		9 2 8 8 0 0 0	
40				(h) 5 0 0 0 0			
41				(j) 1 0 0 0 0 0			
42	Income Tax Expense	4 0 0 0 0 0 0		(m) 2 1 5 4 0 0		4 2 1 5 4 0 0	
43	Manufacturing Summary			(a)2 5 0 0 0 0 0	(b)2 4 0 0 0 0 0	2 5 0 0 0 0 0	2 4 0 0 0 0 0
44				(c)1 6 0 0 0 0 0	(d)1 2 0 0 0 0 0	1 6 0 0 0 0 0	1 2 0 0 0 0 0
45	Income Summary			(e)3 0 0 0 0 0 0	(f)2 9 0 0 0 0 0	3 0 0 0 0 0 0	2 9 0 0 0 0 0
46		1033 5 0 0 0 0	1033 5 0 0 0 0	162 1 4 0 0 0	162 1 4 0 0 0	1119 8 4 0 0 0	1119 8 4 0 0 0
47	Cost of Goods Manufactured						
48							
49	Net Income						
50	Totals						

FIGURE 26.4 (concluded) Worksheet for a Manufacturing Concern

COST OF GOODS MANUFACTURED		INCOME STATEMENT		BALANCE SHEET		
DEBIT	CREDIT	DEBIT	CREDIT	DEBIT	CREDIT	
				4000000		1
				6550000		2
					188000	3
				2400000		4
				1200000		5
				2900000		6
				200000		7
				80000		8
				5000000		9
				15000000		10
					2250000	11
				10000000		12
					2500000	13
				1000000		14
					600000	15
					3000000	16
					400000	17
					215400	18
					24800	19
					5800	20
					10000000	21
					5000000	22
					11500000	23
			69500000			24
		500000				25
16800000						26
	300000					27
9850000						28
450000						29
980600						30
900000						31
500000						32
720000						33
750000						34
500000						35
350000						36
750000						37
		10000000				38
		9288000				39
						40
						41
		4215400				42
2500000	2400000					43
1600000	1200000					44
		3000000	2900000			45
36650600	3900000					46
	32750600	32750600				47
36650600	36650600	59754000	72400000	48330000	35684000	48
		12646000			12646000	49
		72400000	72400000	48330000	48330000	50

PREPARING THE ADJUSTED TRIAL BALANCE ON THE WORKSHEET

Note that for the inventory accounts both the debit and credit amounts are entered in the *Manufacturing Summary* and *Income Summary* accounts because these amounts appear on the cost of goods manufactured statement and on the income statement.

Some accountants omit the Adjusted Trial Balance columns to reduce the number of columns in the worksheet. If these columns are omitted, the adjusted balances are extended to the appropriate statement columns.

COMPLETING THE FINANCIAL STATEMENT COLUMNS

Accounts that appear on the statement of cost of goods manufactured are extended to Cost of Goods Manufactured columns. Accounts that appear on the income statement are transferred to the Income Statement columns. Accounts that appear on the balance sheet are extended to the Balance Sheet columns.

In the Cost of Goods Manufactured section, total debits are $366,506 and total credits are $39,000. The difference is $327,506, which is the cost of goods manufactured. The $327,506 is entered in the Credit column of the Cost of Goods Manufactured section and the Debit column of the Income Statement section.

PREPARING THE FINANCIAL STATEMENTS

The financial statements and the statement of cost of goods manufactured are prepared from the worksheet.

Completing the Accounting Cycle

Once the financial statements have been prepared, the accountant completes the steps in the accounting cycle: adjusting entries, closing entries, postclosing trial balance, and interpretation of the financial information.

>>6. OBJECTIVE

Record the end-of-period adjusting entries for a manufacturing business.

LP26

RECORDING AND POSTING ADJUSTING ENTRIES

Figure 26.5 shows how the adjustments recorded on the worksheet are journalized. For the sake of brevity, journal entry explanations have been omitted.

FIGURE 26.5

Adjusting Entries

	GENERAL JOURNAL				PAGE _____	
	DATE	DESCRIPTION	POST. REF.	DEBIT	CREDIT	
1	2010	*Adjusting Entries*				1
2		(Adjustment a)				2
3	Dec. 31	Manufacturing Summary		25 0 0 0 00		3
4		Raw Materials Inventory			25 0 0 0 00	4
5						5
6		(Adjustment b)				6
7		31 Raw Materials Inventory		24 0 0 0 00		7
8		Manufacturing Summary			24 0 0 0 00	8
9						9
10		(Adjustment c)				10
11		31 Manufacturing Summary		16 0 0 0 00		11
12		Work in Process Inventory			16 0 0 0 00	12
13						13
14		(Adjustment d)				14
15		31 Work in Process Inventory		12 0 0 0 00		15
16		Manufacturing Summary			12 0 0 0 00	16
17						17

18	2010	(Adjustment e)						18
19	Dec.	31	Income Summary	30 0 0 0	00			19
20			Finished Goods Inventory			30 0 0 0	00	20
21								21
22			(Adjustment f)					22
23		31	Finished Goods Inventory	29 0 0 0	00			23
24			Income Summary			29 0 0 0	00	24
25								25
26			(Adjustment g)					26
27		31	Uncollectible Accounts Expense	1 3 8 0	00			27
28			Allowance for Doubtful Accounts			1 3 8 0	00	28
29								29
30			(Adjustment h)					30
31		31	Insurance—Factory	3 5 0 0	00			31
32			Administrative Expense (Control)	5 0 0	00			32
33			Prepaid Insurance			4 0 0 0	00	33
34								34
35			(Adjustment i)					35
36		31	Supplies on Hand	8 0 0	00			36
37			Indirect Materials and Supplies			8 0 0	00	37
38								38
1			(Adjustment j)					1
2		31	Depreciation—Factory Building	7 5 0 0	00			2
3			Depreciation—Factory Equipment	5 0 0 0	00			3
4			Administrative Expense (Control)	1 0 0 0	00			4
5			Accumulated Depr.—Factory Building			7 5 0 0	00	5
6			Accumulated Depr.—Factory Equipment			5 0 0 0	00	6
7			Accumulated Depr.—Office Equipment			1 0 0 0	00	7
8								8
9			(Adjustment k)					9
10		31	Direct Labor	3 5 0 0	00			10
11			Indirect Labor	5 0 0	00			11
12			Salaries and Wages Payable			4 0 0 0	00	12
13								13
14			(Adjustment l)					14
15		31	Payroll Taxes—Factory	3 0 6	00			15
16			Social Security Tax Payable			2 4 8	00	16
17			Medicare Tax Payable			5 8	00	17
18								18
19			(Adjustment m)					19
20		31	Income Tax Expense	2 1 5 4	00			20
21			Income Tax Payable			2 1 5 4	00	21

FIGURE 26.5 (concluded)

Adjusting Entries

RECORDING CLOSING ENTRIES

The closing entries of a manufacturing business are done in three steps.

Closing Accounts to Manufacturing Summary Refer to the Cost of Goods Manufactured section of the worksheet (Figure 26.4). From the Credit column, close the *Purchases Discounts* account to *Manufacturing Summary*.

>>**7. OBJECTIVE**

Record closing entries for a manufacturing business.

LP26

1			Closing Entries					1
2	2010							2
3	Dec.	31	Purchases Discounts	3 0 0 0	00			3
4			Manufacturing Summary			3 0 0 0	00	4
5								5

MANAGERIAL IMPLICATIONS   <<

MANUFACTURING COSTS

- Managers of manufacturing concerns must have reliable accounting data in order to plan and control operations.
- In manufacturing businesses, managers need timely information to control the costs incurred in the production of goods.
- The cost of goods manufactured statement provides detailed information about the individual cost elements and the total cost of manufacturing. Managers use this information to evaluate past performance and to guide future operations.
- The worksheet is an efficient way to summarize and classify information so that financial statements can be prepared easily and quickly.
- Reversing entries save time and help to prevent errors in the new period.

THINKING CRITICALLY
Why does a manufacturing business have multiple inventory accounts?

From the Debit column, close the manufacturing costs to *Manufacturing Summary*. After these entries have been posted, the balance in the *Manufacturing Summary* account is a debit of $327,506.

5	Dec.	31	Manufacturing Summary	325 506 00		5
6			Materials Purchases		168 000 00	6
7			Direct Labor		98 500 00	7
8			Indirect Labor		4 500 00	8
9			Payroll Taxes—Factory		9 806 00	9
10			Utilities—Factory		9 000 00	10
11			Repairs and Maintenance—Factory		5 000 00	11
12			Indirect Materials and Supplies		7 200 00	12
13			Depreciation—Factory Building		7 500 00	13
14			Depreciation—Factory Equipment		5 000 00	14
15			Insurance—Factory		3 500 00	15
16			Property Taxes—Factory		7 500 00	16
17						17

ACCOUNT _Manufacturing Summary_   ACCOUNT NO. _398_

DATE		DESCRIPTION	POST. REF.	DEBIT	CREDIT	BALANCE DEBIT	BALANCE CREDIT
2010							
Dec.	31	Adj. a		25 000 00		25 000 00	
	31	Adj. b			24 000 00	1 000 00	
	31	Adj. c		16 000 00		17 000 00	
	31	Adj. d			12 000 00	5 000 00	
	31	Closing			3 000 00	2 000 00	
	31	Closing		325 506 00		327 506 00	

Closing Revenue and Expense Accounts into Income Summary The entries to close the revenue and expense accounts into *Income Summary* are almost identical to those for a merchandising concern. An additional account, *Manufacturing Summary,* is closed into *Income Summary.*

17	Dec.	31	Sales	695 00 0 00		17
18			Income Summary		695 00 0 00	18
19						19
20		31	Income Summary	567 54 0 00		20
21			Sales Returns and Allowances		5 00 0 00	21
22			Selling Expense (Control)		100 00 0 00	22
23			Administrative Expense (Control)		92 88 0 00	23
24			Income Tax Expense		42 15 4 00	24
25			Manufacturing Summary		327 50 6 00	25

Closing Income Summary At this point, all revenue and expense accounts are closed. The balance in the *Income Summary* account, $126,460, represents the net income after income taxes.

ACCOUNT _Income Summary_   ACCOUNT NO. _399_

DATE		DESCRIPTION	POST. REF.	DEBIT	CREDIT	BALANCE	
						DEBIT	CREDIT
2010							
Dec.	31	Adj. e		30 0 0 0 00		30 0 0 0 00	
	31	Adj. f			29 0 0 0 00	1 0 0 0 00	
	31	Closing			695 0 0 0 00		694 0 0 0 00
	31	Closing		567 5 4 0 00			126 4 6 0 00

The balance of the *Income Summary* account is closed to *Retained Earnings.*

27	Dec.	31	Income Summary	126 46 0 00		27
28			Retained Earnings		126 46 0 00	28

PREPARING THE POSTCLOSING TRIAL BALANCE

After adjusting and closing entries have been posted to the ledger accounts, a postclosing trial balance is prepared to prove that the adjusting and closing entries were posted correctly. The ledger account balances should match those listed in the Balance Sheet section of the worksheet.

RECORDING THE REVERSING ENTRIES

Reversing entries may be made for adjustments for accruals. Reversing entries are also made for expenditures initially debited to expense accounts and then adjusted at the end of the year. Remember that reversing entries are optional, not required by GAAP.

>>8. OBJECTIVE
Record reversing entries for a manufacturing business.

LP26

Section **2** Self Review

QUESTIONS

1. What is the difference between the worksheet for a manufacturing and a merchandising business?

2. What are the column headings on the worksheet of a manufacturing business?

3. To what account is the *Manufacturing Summary* account closed?

EXERCISES

4. On the completed worksheet of a manufacturing business, the accounts related to materials purchases, direct labor, and factory overhead appear in the

   a. Income Statement section.

   b. Cost of Goods Sold section.

   c. Cost of Goods Manufactured section.

   d. Balance Sheet section.

5. On the completed worksheet of a manufacturing business, the accounts related to raw materials inventory, work in process inventory, and finished goods inventory appear in the

   a. Cost of Goods Manufactured section.

   b. Balance Sheet section.

   c. Cost of Goods Sold section.

   d. Income Statement section.

ANALYSIS

6. What is the journal entry to adjust for accrued wages of $2,000 for direct labor and $500 for indirect labor?

(Answers to Section 2 Self Review are on page 928.)

26 Chapter REVIEW Chapter Summary

A manufacturing company purchases raw materials that it converts into finished goods to be sold at a profit. You have learned the differences in the preparation of financial statements for a manufacturer and a merchandiser. A different set of accounts is required to classify the costs associated with manufacturing processes.

Learning Objectives

1 Prepare a statement of cost of goods manufactured.

A statement of cost of goods manufactured is prepared to show the results of the manufacturing activities and to support the income statement.

2 Explain the basic components of manufacturing cost.

Manufacturing costs are recorded in three categories:

- Raw materials are those materials placed into production and used to create finished goods. Raw materials include direct materials and indirect materials.
- Direct labor costs are costs of personnel who work directly on the product as it is manufactured.
- Manufacturing overhead includes costs of manufacturing operations that are not classified as direct labor or direct materials. Examples are insurance, property taxes, and utilities.

3 Prepare an income statement for a manufacturing business.

One major difference distinguishes the format of an income statement of a manufacturing business from that of a merchandising company.

The cost of goods manufactured is included on the income statement as part of Cost of Goods Sold, corresponding to the merchandise purchases on the income statement of a merchandising business.

4 Prepare a balance sheet for a manufacturing business.

The balance sheet of a manufacturing business is similar to that of a merchandising business. The only new accounts required are inventory accounts for raw materials, work in process, and finished goods. The *Finished Goods Inventory* account corresponds to the *Merchandise Inventory* account of a merchandising business.

5 Prepare a worksheet for a manufacturing business.

The worksheet for a manufacturing business is similar to one for a merchandising firm, but it has an added pair of columns in which to record the figures from the cost of goods manufactured statement.

- The worksheet gives the data used for the statement of cost of goods manufactured, the income statement, and the balance sheet.
- To prepare a statement of retained earnings, accountants analyze the *Retained Earnings* account in the general ledger for the details.

6 Record the end-of-period adjusting entries for a manufacturing business.

Adjustments for inventories, expired insurance, and accruals or deferrals are entered on the worksheet and then recorded and posted in the accounting records.

7 Record closing entries for a manufacturing business.

All accounts relating to the cost of goods manufactured are closed to *Manufacturing Summary*.

- The *Manufacturing Summary* account final balance—the cost of goods manufactured—is closed to the *Income Summary* account.
- All items in the Income Statement section of the worksheet are closed to *Income Summary*.
- The final closing entry transfers net income after income taxes to the *Retained Earnings* account.

8 Record reversing entries for a manufacturing business.

After the accounting records are adjusted and closed, a postclosing trial balance is prepared. At each new period, certain adjusting entries are reversed if the business uses reversing entries.

9 Define the accounting terms new to this chapter.

Glossary

Direct labor (p. 903) The costs attributable to personnel who work directly on the product being manufactured

Direct materials (p. 903) All items that go into a product and become a part of it

Finished goods inventory (p. 905) The cost of completed products ready for sale; corresponds to the *Merchandise Inventory* account of a merchandising business

Indirect labor (p. 903) Costs attributable to personnel who support production but are not directly involved in the manufacture of a product; for example, supervisory, repair and maintenance, and janitorial staff

Indirect materials and supplies (p. 903) Materials used in manufacturing a product that do not become a part of the product

Manufacturing overhead (p. 904) All manufacturing costs that are not classified as direct materials or direct labor

Manufacturing Summary account (p. 908) The account to which all items on the statement of cost of goods manufactured are closed; similar to the *Income Summary* account

Raw materials (p. 903) The materials placed into production

Statement of cost of goods manufactured (p. 903) A financial report showing details of the cost of goods completed for a manufacturing business

Work in process (p. 905) Partially completed units in the production process

Comprehensive **Self Review**

1. What are indirect materials?
2. What is direct labor cost?
3. Explain how the following items are handled on the worksheet:
   a. beginning and ending inventories of raw materials
   b. beginning and ending inventories of work in process
   c. beginning and ending inventories of finished goods
4. Does the *Manufacturing Summary* account have a balance during the fiscal period? Explain.
5. What entries are reversed at the beginning of the accounting period?

(Answers to Comprehensive Self Review are on page 929.)

 Multiple choice questions are provided on the text Web site at www.mhhe.com/price12e

Quiz26

Discussion **Questions**

1. How do the accounting problems of a manufacturing business differ from those of a merchandising business?
2. What procedure is used on the statement of cost of goods manufactured to arrive at the cost of raw materials used?
3. What is indirect labor?
4. It is possible that one company might consider an item, such as glue, as one of its direct materials, while another company with identical manufacturing processes might classify the item as one of its indirect materials. Why?
5. How would the wages of the employee who issues materials from the factory storeroom be classified?
6. What is manufacturing overhead?

7. Why does the figure for total manufacturing cost not equal the cost of goods manufactured?

8. Name the three inventory accounts found in the chart of accounts of a manufacturing business and explain each one.

9. How is the work in process inventory determined?

10. Give some examples of manufacturing overhead items.

11. What is the relationship between the cost of goods manufactured and the income statement?

12. What is the source of the information for preparing the journal entry to close manufacturing cost accounts to the *Manufacturing Summary* account?

13. Are the financial statements prepared after the closing entries have been posted? Explain.

14. Is the statement of cost of goods manufactured prepared before or after the income statement? Explain.

15. Describe the flow of costs through the inventory accounts of a merchandising firm.

16. Give three examples not given in the chapter of indirect labor for a manufacturing firm.

17. How is the cost of goods sold determined for a manufacturing business?

18. Explain how a manufacturing business records reversing entries and why the reversing entries are made.

APPLICATIONS

Exercises

Exercise 26.1
Objective 1

▶ **Cost of goods manufactured statement (partial).**

The following selected items appeared in the adjusted trial balance columns of the worksheet for Perez Company on December 31, 2010. From this information, prepare the section of the statement of cost of goods manufactured relating to the cost of raw materials used.

	Dr.	Cr.
Finished Goods Inventory	$ 58,000	$60,000
Work in Process Inventory	70,000	80,000
Raw Materials Inventory	45,000	39,000
Materials Purchases	700,000	
Purchases Returns and Allowances		6,500
Freight In (on Materials Purchases)	18,000	

Exercise 26.2
Objective 6

▶ **Adjusting entries.**

Using the data given in Exercise 26.1, prepare the general journal entry to record adjustments for inventory accounts.

Exercise 26.3
Objective 2

▶ **Components of manufacturing cost.**

RSB Company's beginning raw materials inventory was $100,000. Its net purchases for the period were $750,000, and its ending raw materials inventory was $125,000. What was its cost of raw materials used?

Components of manufacturing cost.

Kym Company's total manufacturing cost for the year was $1,900,000. Its manufacturing overhead was $250,000, and its cost of raw materials used was $800,000. What was its direct labor cost for the year?

◀ **Exercise 26.4**
Objective 2

Components of manufacturing cost.

Which of the following items would not appear on the statement of cost of goods manufactured?

1. Insurance on office building
2. Depreciation of factory equipment
3. Direct labor

◀ **Exercise 26.5**
Objective 2

Components of manufacturing cost.

Which of the following items would appear on the statement of cost of goods manufactured?

1. Work in process inventory
2. Finished goods inventory
3. Raw materials inventory

◀ **Exercise 26.6**
Objective 2

Components of manufacturing cost.

Which of the following items would not be included in the Manufacturing Overhead section of the statement of cost of goods manufactured?

1. Payroll taxes on wages of plant security guards
2. Insurance costs for factory
3. Freight in charges on purchases of raw materials

◀ **Exercise 26.7**
Objective 2

Components of manufacturing cost.

Which of the following items would be included in the Manufacturing Overhead section of the statement of cost of goods manufactured?

1. Direct labor
2. Raw materials used
3. Indirect materials and supplies
4. Repairs to factory building
5. Depreciation of factory equipment
6. Office supplies expense
7. Advertising expense

◀ **Exercise 26.8**
Objective 2

Worksheet for a manufacturing business.

Which of the following account balances would not be extended to the Cost of Goods Manufactured section of the worksheet?

1. Insurance on finished goods
2. Payroll taxes on outside sales salaries
3. Salary of factory shift supervisor
4. Insurance on raw materials in factory storeroom
5. Salary of accounts receivable clerk
6. Utilities for factory
7. Payroll taxes on factory wages
8. Insurance on factory equipment
9. Freight out
10. Salary of factory material handler

◀ **Exercise 26.9**
Objective 5

Exercise 26.10
Objectives 6, 7, 8

Adjusting, closing, and reversing entries.

Information about certain account balances in the trial balance of Utah Corporation on December 31, 2010, follows.

a. Balance in *Raw Materials Inventory* account that reflects the beginning balance, December 31, $42,000; physical count on December 31 that reflects the ending balance, $40,000

b. Balance in *Prepaid Insurance* account, $15,000; insurance expired, $12,000

c. Balance in *Direct Labor* account, $90,000; accrued direct labor, $6,000

d. Balance in *Factory Supplies on Hand* account, $7,500; physical count shows supplies on hand, $500

Record the following in the general journal.

1. Adjusting entries required
2. Closing entries required
3. Reversing entries on January 1, 2011

PROBLEMS

Problem Set A

Problem 26.1A
Objectives 1, 3

Preparing a statement of cost of goods manufactured and an income statement.

Black Manufacturing Company makes water heaters. Selected account balances on December 31, 2010, the end of its fiscal year, are given below. Data about the beginning and ending inventories are also given.

INSTRUCTIONS

1. Prepare a statement of cost of goods manufactured for 2010.
2. Prepare an income statement for 2010.

Accounts	Balances	(cont.) Accounts	Balances
Sales	$900,000	Property Taxes—Factory	5,000
Sales Returns and Allowances	5,500	Sales Salaries Expense	110,000
Materials Purchases	189,000	Payroll Taxes Expense—Selling	11,000
Direct Labor	135,000	Delivery Expense	7,000
Indirect Labor	35,000	Advertising Expense	5,000
Payroll Taxes—Factory	17,000	Miscellaneous Selling Expenses	20,000
Utilities—Factory	15,000	Officers' Salaries Expense	125,000
Repairs and Maintenance—Factory	6,500	Office Salaries Expense	30,000
Indirect Materials and Supplies	6,000	Payroll Taxes Expense—Administrative	15,500
Depreciation—Factory Building	5,000	Other Administrative Expenses	5,000
Depreciation—Factory Equipment	4,500	Income Tax Expense	33,000
Insurance—Factory	8,000		

Inventory Data	Jan. 1, 2010	Dec. 31, 2010
Finished Goods Inventory	$30,000	$25,000
Work in Process Inventory	41,000	37,000
Raw Materials Inventory	21,000	22,000

Analyze: For every dollar earned in net sales, what portion was spent on manufacturing costs?

Preparing a statement of cost of goods manufactured, an income statement, a statement of retained earnings, and a balance sheet; completing the worksheet; recording adjusting, closing, and reversing entries.

◀ **Problem 26.2A**
Objectives 1, 3, 4,
eX**cel**   **5, 6, 7, 8**

Bay Corp. manufactures parts for DVD players. The Trial Balance section of its worksheet and other year-end data follow.

INSTRUCTIONS

1. Prepare a 12-column manufacturing worksheet for the year ended December 31, 2010. Enter the trial balance in the first two columns.

2. Using the data given, enter the adjustments. Then complete the worksheet. Label all inventory adjustments as (a).

3. Prepare a statement of cost of goods manufactured.

4. Prepare an income statement.

5. Prepare a statement of retained earnings. Additional data needed is as follows.

   a. Balance of **Retained Earnings** on January 1 was $348,500.

   b. Dividends declared and paid on common stock during the year amounted to $100,000.

   c. There were no changes in any other stockholders' equity accounts.

6. Prepare a balance sheet as of December 31, 2010. There are 100,000 shares of $1 par common stock outstanding, out of the 100,000 shares authorized.

7. Record the adjusting entries shown on the worksheet in general journal form. For each journal entry, use the letter that identifies the adjustment on the worksheet. Make a separate entry for each inventory adjustment. Do not give explanations.

8. Prepare the closing entries for all accounts involved in the cost of goods manufactured.

9. Prepare the closing entries for all revenue and expense accounts and the **Manufacturing Summary** account.

10. Prepare the closing entry to close the **Income Summary** account.

11. Journalize the reversing entries. Date the entries January 1, 2011.

Bay Corp.
Trial Balance
December 31, 2010

ACCOUNT NAME	DEBIT	CREDIT
Cash	5 0 0 0 0 0 0	
Accounts Receivable	7 5 0 0 0 0 0	
Allowance for Doubtful Accounts		2 0 0 0 0 0
Raw Materials Inventory	2 5 0 0 0 0 0	
Work in Process Inventory	4 0 0 0 0 0 0	
Finished Goods Inventory	4 2 0 0 0 0 0	
Prepaid Insurance	6 0 0 0 0 0	
Factory Supplies	4 0 0 0 0 0	
Land	5 0 0 0 0 0 0	
Factory Building	2 0 0 0 0 0 0 0	
Accumulated Depreciation—Factory Building		2 0 0 0 0 0 0

Account	Debit	Credit
Factory Machines	1,000,000.00	
Accumulated Depreciation—Factory Machines		200,000.00
Office Furniture and Equipment	200,000.00	
Accumulated Depreciation—Office Furniture and Equipment		40,000.00
Accounts Payable		760,000.00
Salaries and Wages Payable		
Income Tax Payable		
Social Security Tax Payable		
Medicare Tax Payable		
Employee Income Tax Payable		
Common Stock		1,000,000.00
Retained Earnings		2,485,000.00
Sales		9,955,000.00
Sales Returns and Allowances	55,000.00	
Materials Purchases	2,520,000.00	
Purchases Returns and Allowances		20,000.00
Freight In	100,000.00	
Direct Labor	1,810,000.00	
Indirect Labor	200,000.00	
Payroll Taxes Expenses—Factory	206,000.00	
Utilities—Factory	80,000.00	
Repairs and Maintenance—Factory	24,000.00	
Indirect Materials and Supplies	20,000.00	
Depreciation—Factory Building		
Depreciation—Factory Machines		
Insurance—Factory		
Property Taxes—Factory	60,000.00	
Sales Salaries Expense	850,000.00	
Payroll Taxes Expense—Sales	85,000.00	
Delivery Expense	50,000.00	
Advertising Expense	50,000.00	
Uncollectible Accounts Expense		
Miscellaneous Selling Expense	65,000.00	
Officers' Salaries Expense	1,450,000.00	
Office Salaries Expense	400,000.00	
Payroll Taxes Expense—Administrative	185,000.00	
Depreciation Expense—Office Furniture and Equipment		
Other Administrative Expenses	50,000.00	
Income Tax Expense	300,000.00	
Totals	14,680,000.00	14,680,000.00

YEAR-END DATA

a. Physical inventories taken on December 31, 2010, show $21,000 of raw materials on hand and $35,000 of finished goods on hand. The work in process inventory is estimated to be $38,000 on the same date.

b. It is estimated that 3 percent of the outstanding accounts receivable might not be collectible.

c. Of the prepaid insurance, $5,000 covering the factory building and equipment has expired.

d. A physical inventory discloses $3,500 of factory supplies on hand at the end of the period.

e. Depreciation expense for the year is as follows: $10,000 on the factory building, $10,000 on the factory machines, and $2,000 on the office furniture. (Make a compound entry.)

f. Payroll accruals at the end of the period include $1,800 of direct labor and $200 of indirect labor.

g. Payroll taxes on accrued wages are social security, 6.2 percent, and Medicare tax, 1.45 percent.

h. The income tax rate is 25 percent. (Round to nearest dollar).

Analyze: Assume that the industry standard for direct labor costs is 20 percent of cost of goods manufactured. How is Bay Corp. performing as compared to this industry standard? Explain.

Problem Set B

Preparing a statement of cost of goods manufactured and an income statement.

◀ **Problem 26.1B**
Objectives 1, 3

Jordan Manufacturing Company makes camping equipment. Selected account balances (listed alphabetically) for this firm on December 31, 2010, the end of its fiscal year, are given below. Data about the beginning and ending inventories is also shown.

INSTRUCTIONS

1. Prepare a statement of cost of goods manufactured for 2010.
2. Prepare an income statement for 2010.

Accounts	Balances
Depreciation—Factory Assets	$ 9,000
Depreciation Expense—Office Assets	3,000
Direct Labor	175,000
Freight In	12,000
Income Tax Expense	18,270
Indirect Labor	19,000
Indirect Materials and Supplies	7,000
Insurance—Factory	12,000
Materials Purchases	325,000
Office Salaries Expense	25,000
Officers' Salaries Expense	125,000
Other Administrative Expenses	1,800
Other Selling Expenses	12,000
Payroll Taxes Expense—Administrative	15,000
Payroll Taxes Expense—Factory	19,400
Payroll Taxes Expense—Sales Salaries	9,000
Property Taxes—Office	2,000
Property Taxes—Factory	5,000
Purchases Returns and Allowances	4,000
Repairs and Maintenance—Factory	3,000
Repairs and Maintenance—Office	1,000
Sales	995,000
Sales Returns and Allowances	5,000
Sales Salaries Expense	90,000

Inventory Data	Jan. 1, 2010	Dec. 31, 2010
Finished Goods Inventory	$30,000	$32,000
Work in Process Inventory	28,000	25,000
Raw Materials Inventory	35,000	34,000

Analyze: What percentage of cost of goods manufactured did the company spend on raw materials? On direct labor costs? On overhead costs?

Problem 26.2B ▶
Objectives 1, 3, 4, 5, 6, 7, 8

Preparing a statement of cost of goods manufactured, an income statement, a statement of retained earnings, and a balance sheet; completing the worksheet; recording adjusting, closing, and reversing entries.

Square Company makes shipping containers. The Trial Balance section of its worksheet and other year-end data follow.

INSTRUCTIONS

1. Prepare a 12-column manufacturing worksheet for the fiscal year ended December 31, 2010. Enter the trial balance in the first two columns.
2. Using the data given, enter the adjustments and complete the worksheet. Label all inventory adjustments as (a).
3. Prepare a statement of cost of goods manufactured.
4. Prepare an income statement.
5. Prepare a statement of retained earnings. Additional data follows:
   a. Balance of *Retained Earnings,* January 1, was $185,000.
   b. Dividends declared and paid on common stock were $10,000.
6. Prepare a balance sheet as of December 31, 2010.
7. Record the adjusting entries shown on the worksheet in general journal form. For each journal entry, use the letter that identifies the adjustment on the worksheet. Make a separate entry for each inventory adjustment. Do not give explanations.
8. Prepare the closing entries for all accounts involved in the cost of goods manufactured.
9. Prepare the closing entries for all revenue and expense accounts and the *Manufacturing Summary* account.
10. Prepare the closing entry to close the *Income Summary* account.
11. Journalize the reversing entries. Date the entries January 1, 2011.

YEAR-END DATA

a. Ending inventories: finished goods, $25,000; work in process, $36,000; and raw materials, $21,000.
b. Estimated uncollectible accounts: increase *Allowance for Uncollectible Accounts* to 3 percent of *Accounts Receivable.*
c. Expired insurance, $2,000; debit the *Insurance—Factory* account for the amount of the necessary adjustment.
d. Factory supplies on hand, $1,000.
e. Depreciation for the year: on factory building, $15,000; on factory machinery, $5,000; and on office equipment, $2,000.
f. Accrued factory wages: direct labor, $1,800; indirect labor, $200.
g. Accrued payroll taxes: social security, $124; Medicare tax, $29.
h. Total income tax expense for the year, $17,962.

Analyze: Assume that the industry standard for direct labor costs in its manufacturing industry is 31 percent of costs of goods manufactured. How does this company compare to others in regard to this standard? Explain.

Square Company
Trial Balance
December 31, 2010

ACCOUNT NAME	DEBIT	CREDIT
Cash	4 0 0 0 0 0	
Accounts Receivable	8 0 0 0 0 0	
Allowance for Doubtful Accounts		2 0 0 0 0
Raw Materials Inventory	2 0 0 0 0 0	
Work in Process Inventory	3 8 0 0 0 0	
Finished Goods Inventory	2 6 0 0 0 0	
Prepaid Insurance	2 4 0 0 0	
Factory Supplies	4 0 0 0 0	
Land	5 0 0 0 0 0	
Factory Building	1 5 0 0 0 0 0	
Accumulated Depreciation—Factory Building		6 0 0 0 0 0
Factory Machines	5 0 0 0 0 0	
Accumulated Depreciation—Factory Machines		2 0 0 0 0 0
Office Furniture and Equipment	2 0 0 0 0 0	
Accumulated Depreciation—Office Furniture and Equipment		8 0 0 0 0
Accounts Payable		7 8 0 0 0 0
Salaries and Wages Payable		
Income Tax Payable		
Social Security Tax Payable		
Medicare Tax Payable		
Employee Income Tax Payable		
Common Stock		5 0 0 0 0 0
Retained Earnings		1 7 5 0 0 0 0
Sales		9 4 6 5 0 0 0 0
Sales Returns and Allowances	6 5 0 0 0 0	
Materials Purchases	2 7 5 0 0 0 0	
Purchases Returns and Allowances		5 0 0 0 0
Freight In	9 0 0 0 0 0	
Direct Labor	1 4 5 0 0 0 0 0	
Indirect Labor	2 5 0 0 0 0 0	
Payroll Taxes—Factory	1 8 0 0 0 0 0	
Utilities—Factory	2 4 0 0 0 0	
Repairs and Maintenance—Factory	5 0 0 0 0	
Indirect Materials and Supplies	4 0 0 0 0	
Depreciation—Factory Building		
Depreciation—Factory Machines		
Insurance—Factory		
Property Taxes—Factory	6 0 0 0 0 0	
Sales Salaries Expense	9 5 0 0 0 0	
Payroll Taxes Expense—Sales	9 5 0 0 0	
Delivery Expense	7 5 0 0 0	
Advertising Expense	2 0 0 0 0 0	
Uncollectible Accounts Expense		
Miscellaneous Selling Expense	6 5 0 0 0	
Officers' Salaries Expense	1 5 0 0 0 0 0	
Office Salaries Expense	4 0 0 0 0 0	
Payroll Taxes Expense—Administrative	1 9 0 0 0 0	
Depreciation Expense—Office Furniture and Equipment		
Other Administrative Expenses	1 1 0 0 0 0	
Income Tax Expense	1 6 0 0 0 0	
Manufacturing Summary		
Income Summary		
Totals	1 3 4 4 5 0 0 0 0	1 3 4 4 5 0 0 0 0

Critical Thinking Problem 26.1

Inventories

Certain information about the statement of cost of goods manufactured and the income statement for the year ended December 31, 2010, for SPC Products, a sole proprietorship, is given below.

Beginning inventory of finished goods, 105 percent of ending inventory	
Work in process inventory, January 1, 95 percent of ending inventory	
Net income	$130,000
Raw materials inventory, January 1	$25,000
Direct labor costs	$90,000
Manufacturing overhead, 120 percent of direct labor costs	
Work in process inventory, December 31	$20,000
Finished goods inventory, December 31	$38,000
Raw materials inventory, December 31	$27,000
Net purchases of raw material	$179,000

INSTRUCTIONS

Prepare a statement of cost of goods manufactured and an income statement for the year.

Analyze: Did total inventories for SPC Products increase or decrease during the year? By what amount?

Critical Thinking Problem 26.2

Incomplete Records

In January 2010, Charlotte Ann started NeckWarmers, a business manufacturing ladies' scarves. Ann was so busy with the manufacturing side of the business that she did not take time to set up detailed accounting records; the business checkbook was her only record of accounting transactions. When cash came in, she deposited the receipts in the bank, and when invoices were due, she wrote checks to pay them. Now it is the end of the year and Ann would like to know how the business did during its first year of operation.

Ann asks for your help in summarizing the first year's operations. A review of the checkbook yields the following information.

- Raw materials purchases paid for totaled $70,000.
- Wages paid to employees totaled $45,000, with payroll taxes relating to their wages of $4,500.
- Factory supplies cost $2,000.
- Utility bills paid totaled $2,200.
- Repairs to factory equipment were $500.
- Rent of $12,000 was paid on the factory building.

Discussions with Ann disclose that $2,000 of raw materials have been received and used in the manufacturing process but have not yet been paid because the invoice for the purchase is not due until next year. Ann has determined depreciation on the factory equipment for the year to be $900. An inventory taken on the last day of the year showed $3,500 of raw materials on hand, $4,500 of scarves partially completed, and $3,500 of finished scarves waiting to be sold.

INSTRUCTIONS

Prepare a statement of cost of goods manufactured for 2010 for NeckWarmers.

BUSINESS CONNECTIONS

Manufacturing Concerns

1. Why do managers need special manufacturing records and a separate statement reporting the costs involved in producing goods?

2. How can an inventory be taken if work in process items are in varying stages of completion at the end of the accounting period?

3. Why might management want to separate direct and indirect labor costs?

4. Why should the statement of cost of goods manufactured not be used alone to measure efficiency and control costs?

5. In this chapter, we said that the value of sales supplies and office supplies on hand at period-end is considered too small to justify an adjusting entry. If this omission were questioned, (arguing that the accounting records should show everything), what would you say?

Hiding Returns

Frederick is the manager of a company that produces toasters. He has instructed his production department to replace a steel handle shaft with a plastic shaft. This will save the company $1 per toaster. Since making this change, the toasters are being returned in great quantities because of handle breakage. Frederick tries to hide his poor decision. He instructs the accountant to ignore the returned items and put them back into inventory so they can be resold. Manufacturing was told to install new plastic handles and place the toasters into finished goods. What effect does Frederick's action have on the Cost of Goods Sold section? Is it ethical? What could be the eventual result of his actions?

Purchases

Refer to the *2006 Annual Report* for The Home Depot, Inc., in Appendix A.

1. What types of manufactured products does The Home Depot, Inc., purchase? What factors do you think the company weighs when purchasing items for resale in The Home Depot stores?

2. Where does the Home Depot, Inc., buy their manufactured products from?

Manufacturing Inventories

The following excerpt was taken from the Cisco Systems, Inc., *2007 Annual Report.*

Note 5: Current Assets and Liabilities (in millions)	2007	2006
Inventories		
Raw materials	$ 173	$ 131
Work in process	45	377
Finished goods	858	659
Service-related spares	211	170
Demonstration systems	35	34
	$1,322	$1,371

Analyze:

1. What five categories does the company use to identify its inventories?

2. Which category accounts for the largest percentage of the total inventory amount in 2007?

3. How might this financial information be used by Cisco Systems, Inc., managers?

Analyze Online: Locate the company's Web site (www.cisco.com). Find the most recent annual report within the *Investors* section of the site.

4. Review the Notes to Consolidated Financial Statements related to the company's inventories. What is the value of the ending inventory?

5. How is the total inventory categorized? What notable changes, if any, can you identify to the amounts of each inventory?

Manufacturing Costs and Profits

Ben & Jerry's Homemade Ice Cream merged with Unilever Corporation in 2000, but operates independently from Unilever's other ice cream producing businesses. In 1999, Ben & Jerry's manufacturing and packaging divisions introduced unbleached containers for ice cream. Using unbleached paper reduces the reliance on chlorine in the production process and thereby reduces the amount of dioxin, a carcinogen, in the environment. The company incurred increased manufacturing costs due to the pursuit of this environmental-friendly packaging option. Why do you think Ben & Jerry's management chose to incur additional manufacturing costs? What impact do you think the decision had on the company's profitability? Do you agree with the decision? Why or why not?

Letter

You have been hired as a consultant to Kevin O'Brien, a local businessman interested in purchasing the Glaze Ceramics Manufacturing Company. O'Brien has been the owner of a retail ceramics company for 12 years. He is not familiar, therefore, with manufacturing accounting practices or financial statements. Prepare a letter to O'Brien outlining the major differences between the financial statements for a merchandising business and those of a manufacturing concern. Include any other information that you feel would benefit O'Brien as he evaluates the accounting records of the manufacturing company. Remember that O'Brien will need your help in understanding terms that are unique to a manufacturing business.

Cost Flowchart

The costs for items manufactured are collected in work in process and then sent to finished goods when the items are complete. When the items are sold, the costs are taken out of finished goods and put into cost of goods sold. As a group, select a product to be manufactured, such as a skateboard. Determine the direct costs to make this product. Assume the indirect costs are equal to the direct labor costs. Show the class how the costs for your product will move from work in process to finished goods to cost of goods sold.

Certified Management Accountant

Since 1972, the Institute of Management Accountants has been issuing certification for the certified management accountant (CMA). Go to the IMA Web site at www.imanet.org. What are the four parts of the CMA exam to become certified?

Answers to **Self Reviews**

Answers to Section 1 Self Review

1. Materials that go into a product and become a part of it.

2. Items that have been started into production but are not yet completed.

3. It becomes a part of the Total Goods Available for Sale in the income statement; it replaces Purchases.

4   **a.** raw materials used, direct labor, and manufacturing overhead.

5. **b.** factory repair and maintenance employees.

6. $100,000

Answers to Section 2 Self Review

1. The major way in which a manufacturing worksheet differs is in the addition of the Cost of Goods Manufactured columns.

2. Trial Balance, Adjustments, Adjusted Trial Balance, Cost of Goods Manufactured, Income Statement, and Balance Sheet.

3. The *Manufacturing Summary* account is closed into the *Income Summary* account.

4. **c.** Cost of Goods Manufactured section.

5. **b.** Balance Sheet section.

6.

Direct Labor	2,000	
Indirect Labor	500	
Salaries and Wages Payable		2,500

Answers to Comprehensive Self Review

1. Materials used in the manufacturing process that do not become part of the finished product.

2. The cost of those employees who are working directly on the product being manufactured.

3. The balances of the beginning inventories of raw materials and work in process are entered in the Adjustments columns as credits to the two inventory accounts and debits to the *Manufacturing Summary* account. The ending inventories of raw materials and work in process are entered in the Adjustments columns as debits to the inventory accounts and credits to the *Manufacturing Summary* account. The beginning inventory of finished goods is credited to *Finished Goods Inventory* and debited to *Income Summary*. The ending inventory of finished goods is debited to *Finished Goods Inventory* and credited to *Income Summary*.

4. No, the account is used only during the closing process.

5. The adjusting entries for accrued expenses and accrued income.

Job Order Cost Accounting   Chapter 27

Spring Air   www.springair.com   The Spring Air Company manufactures premium bedding products sold to consumers through leading retailers. It is the fourth largest bedding manufacturer in the world.

Following a merger with Consolidated Bedding, Inc., the company found itself in need of a new system to assist with resource planning. After an extensive review of a number of programs, Spring Air decided to use a program developed by Microsoft. By using this new system to improve its manufacturing processes, Spring Air anticipates cost savings on raw materials. It will be able to go to a single-point ordering and pricing system nationally, instead of requiring each plant to buy individually at different prices. Furthermore, the manufacturing process will be streamlined by automating processes such as production scheduling that previously were done manually. Delivery costs will be lower as well because the company will be able to determine the most efficient routes and plant origination sites.

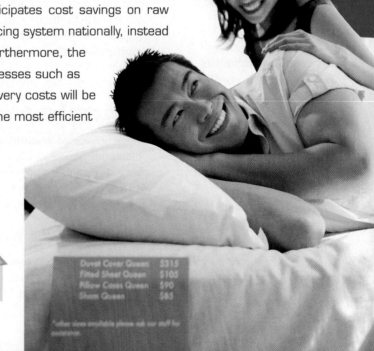

thinking critically

What types of raw materials inventories do you think Spring Air holds?

Cost Accounting

The statement of cost of goods manufactured provides information on manufacturing costs. However, it cannot be used to determine the cost of each unit produced and does not help in controlling costs during the accounting period. In this and subsequent chapters, you will learn how to calculate the cost of producing items and track manufacturing costs.

>> **1. OBJECTIVE**

Explain how a job order cost accounting system operates.

LP27

Video27.1

important!

Job Order Cost Accounting

Under a job order cost accounting system, unit costs are determined for products manufactured for each job order.

important!

Process Cost Accounting

Under the process cost system, the unit cost of a product is computed by adding the unit costs from each producing department.

Types of Cost Accounting Systems

There are two principal cost accounting systems:

- job order cost accounting system
- process cost accounting system

This chapter covers the job order cost accounting system. Chapter 28 introduces process cost accounting.

Standard cost accounting is described in Chapter 29. Standard cost accounting may be used with either the job order cost system or the process cost system.

JOB ORDER COST ACCOUNTING

The job order cost accounting system is used by businesses that produce special orders or produce more than one product in batches. Businesses that use job order cost accounting systems include custom drapery manufacturers, machine tool plants, and furniture manufacturers.

Under the **job order cost accounting** system, each "batch" of goods is produced under a **production order,** which is also known as a **job order.** Unit costs are determined for each production order. To calculate the cost per unit, divide the manufacturing costs for each order by the number of units produced.

PROCESS COST ACCOUNTING

The **process cost accounting** system is used when standard products are manufactured using a continuous process. Businesses that use process cost accounting systems include cement plants, flour mills, and manufacturers of cake mixes.

Under the process cost accounting system, the cost of a unit of product is the sum of the unit costs in each department through which the product passes while it is being manufactured.

STANDARD COST ACCOUNTING

Standard costs are a measure of what costs should be in an efficient operation. Managers can compare actual costs with standard costs to determine manufacturing efficiency. Standard cost accounting systems can be used with a job order cost accounting system or a process cost accounting system.

Cost Flows in a Job Order Cost System

Mobile Manufacturing Inc. makes several types of work tables. Customers order various tables in different quantities. Mobile does not have a continuous manufacturing process; it produces the tables in batches. The business uses the job order cost system, which is designed to facilitate recording costs related to the following four manufacturing operations:

- Procurement (Purchasing)—obtaining materials, labor, and services necessary for the manufacturing process,
- Production—using materials, labor, and services on the factory floor,
- Warehousing—handling and storing finished goods,
- Selling—removing finished goods from the storeroom to fill orders.

Figure 27.1 summarizes the flow of costs through a job order cost accounting system.

To understand how *Raw Materials Inventory, Work in Process Inventory,* and *Finished Goods Inventory* fit into the flow of costs shown in Figure 27.1, you need to comprehend the perpetual inventory system.

THE PERPETUAL INVENTORY SYSTEM

The **perpetual inventory system** tracks the inventories on hand at all times. The following are typical procedures for the three types of inventory.

Raw Materials Inventory Throughout the accounting period, raw materials and manufacturing supplies are recorded in the *Raw Materials Inventory* account. Purchases of raw materials and manufacturing supplies increase the *Raw Materials Inventory* account. The costs of materials used in production reduce the *Raw Materials Inventory* account. Direct materials used in production increase the *Work in Process Inventory* account. The costs of indirect materials and supplies used in production increase the *Manufacturing Overhead* account.

FIGURE 27.1

Flow of Costs through Four Phases of Manufacturing

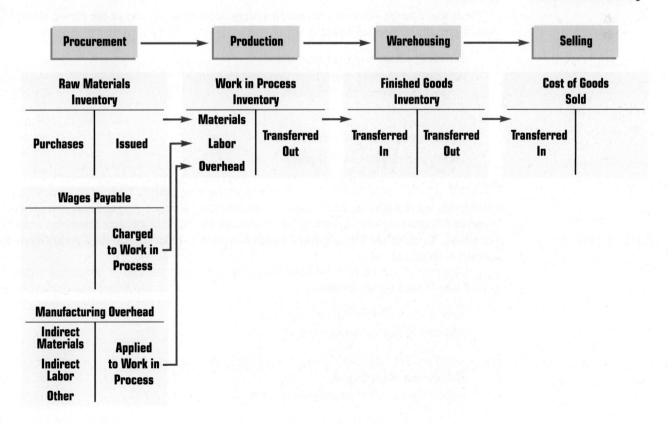

At the end of the accounting period, the balance of the ***Raw Materials Inventory*** account reflects the cost of materials and supplies on hand.

Beginning inventory of raw materials	xxx
Add purchases during period	xxx
Total available for use	xxx
Deduct materials used during year	xxx
Ending inventory of raw materials	xxx

At least once a year, a physical inventory count is taken to check the accuracy of the recorded inventory. In the event of a difference, the ***Raw Materials Inventory*** account is adjusted to agree with the physical inventory count.

> Manufacturers constantly look for productivity improvement ideas. Avery Dennison has adopted the Six Sigma continuous productivity improvement model. By training thousands of its employees in Six Sigma ideas, virtually every facet of Avery Dennison's business is impacted by continuous productivity improvement. These concepts have enabled the company to improve productivity and enhance customer satisfaction at the same time.

Work in Process Inventory Throughout the accounting period, transactions involving production are recorded in the ***Work in Process Inventory*** account. All manufacturing costs placed into production during the accounting period are recorded in ***Work in Process Inventory***. ***Work in Process Inventory*** is increased when direct materials are issued for production and for direct labor and manufacturing overhead charged into production. As production is completed, the manufacturing costs reduce ***Work in Process Inventory*** and increase ***Finished Goods Inventory***. See Figure 27.1 for the flow of costs into and out of ***Work in Process Inventory***.

The balance in the ***Work in Process Inventory*** account at the end of the period reflects the cost of partially completed units.

Beginning inventory of work in process	xxx
Add direct materials, direct labor, and manufacturing overhead charged to production	xxx
	xxx
Deduct cost of goods completed	xxx
Ending inventory of work in process	xxx

Finished Goods Inventory Throughout the accounting period, transactions involving finished goods are recorded in the ***Finished Goods Inventory*** account. As goods are completed, the ***Finished Goods Inventory*** account is increased and the ***Work in Process Inventory*** account is decreased. As goods are sold, ***Finished Goods Inventory*** is reduced, and the ***Cost of Goods Sold*** account is increased.

The balance of the ***Finished Goods Inventory*** account at the end of the period equals the cost of the finished goods on hand.

Beginning inventory of finished goods	xxx
Add cost of goods manufactured	xxx
	xxx
Deduct cost of goods sold	xxx
Ending inventory of finished goods	xxx

At least once a year, a physical inventory count of all invertories is taken to check the accuracy of the recorded inventory.

JUST-IN-TIME INVENTORY SYSTEMS

Some manufacturing companies attempt to eliminate raw materials inventory by using the **just-in-time system,** in which raw materials are ordered so they arrive just in time to be placed into production. When the goods arrive, they are moved immediately to the factory floor and the **Work in Process Inventory** account is increased. No entry is made in the **Raw Materials Inventory** account; in fact, there might not be a **Raw Materials Inventory** account.

The advantages of a just-in-time system are that it reduces the amount of working capital tied up in inventory, the space necessary for inventory storage, and the costs associated with storeroom personnel, insurance, and recordkeeping.

Just-in-time systems are risky unless the source of supply is highly dependable. Late deliveries or damaged materials could cause an interruption in supply that could halt manufacturing operations.

Section 1 Self Review

QUESTIONS

1. What is a standard cost?

2. Why are physical inventory counts made when a perpetual inventory system is used?

3. What is a job order cost accounting system?

EXERCISES

4. Job order cost accounting is appropriate

    a. only when a company orders materials just-in-time to be placed into production.

    b. when there are continuous operations on standard types of products.

    c. when a company produces more than one product in batches rather than on a continuous basis.

    d. only for goods produced on special order.

5. A standard cost system can be used

    a. in place of the job order cost system.

    b. only with the process cost system.

    c. only with the job order cost system.

    d. with either the job order cost system or the process cost system.

ANALYSIS

6. The beginning balance of **Work in Process Inventory** was $100,000. During the year, direct materials of $50,000, direct labor of $35,000, and manufacturing overhead of $17,500 were charged to production. The ending inventory of work in process is $50,000. What is the cost of goods completed?

(Answers to Section 1 Self Review are on page 955.)

SECTION OBJECTIVES

>> 2. **Journalize the purchase and issuance of direct and indirect materials.**

WHY IT'S IMPORTANT

Raw materials must be accounted for.

>> 3. **Maintain perpetual inventory records.**

WHY IT'S IMPORTANT

Physical counts are compared to inventory records.

>> 4. **Record labor costs incurred and charge labor into production.**

WHY IT'S IMPORTANT

Labor costs are often substantial.

>> 5. **Compute overhead rates and apply overhead to jobs.**

WHY IT'S IMPORTANT

Businesses apply overhead to specific production jobs.

>> 6. **Compute overapplied or underapplied overhead and report it in the financial statements.**

WHY IT'S IMPORTANT

Financial statements reflect a period's costs.

TERMS TO LEARN

finished goods subsidiary ledger

manufacturing overhead ledger

materials requisition

overapplied overhead

overhead application rate

raw materials ledger card

raw materials subsidiary ledger

time ticket

underapplied overhead

work in process subsidiary ledger

Job Order Cost Accounting System

Examples of companies that use the job order cost accounting system are toy manufacturers, automobile manufacturers, and computer manufacturers.

A Job Order Cost Accounting System

Video27.1

The job order cost accounting system has procedures to record the costs incurred, the costs of items placed into production, and the transfer of products to finished goods.

PERPETUAL INVENTORY ACCOUNTS

The job order cost system uses three inventory accounts—*Raw Materials Inventory, Work in Process Inventory,* and *Finished Goods Inventory.* Each inventory account has a related subsidiary account. The **raw materials subsidiary ledger** contains a record for each of the different types of raw materials and manufacturing supplies used by the firm.

The **work in process subsidiary ledger** includes a job order cost sheet for each job in production. The **finished goods subsidiary ledger** contains a record for each of the different types of finished products.

ACCOUNTING FOR MATERIALS

The *Raw Materials Inventory* account reflects all of the transactions related to raw materials and supplies.

Purchases of Materials

Purchases of raw materials and supplies are debited to the *Raw Materials Inventory* account. When a company uses a voucher register system, a special column is typically set up for Raw Materials Debit. All material purchases would be debited to that column. For simplicity, the raw material purchases are shown below as they would be entered in a general journal.

1	2010			1
2	Jun. 30	Raw Materials Inventory	15 00 00	2
3		Accounts Payable	15 00 00	3
4		Cost of materials and supplies		4
5		purchased during June		5

Raw Materials Ledger

For internal control purposes, all purchases are made using prenumbered purchase orders. When the materials and supplies are received, they are checked and counted or weighed. They are sent to the storeroom with a report showing what was received. Before the invoice is approved for payment, a copy of the receiving report is compared with the supplier's invoice and with the purchase order. Prices and quantities are entered in each item's **raw materials ledger card.**

Figure 27.2 shows a raw materials ledger card. This card is for BRC02, a brace. The card shows no balance for material BRC02 at the beginning of the month. On June 4, 200 braces were purchased on Purchase Order PO-3 for $1 each. After this transaction, the 200 units are reflected in the Balance section of the ledger card.

Materials Requisition

Materials or supplies are issued by the storeroom only upon presentation of a materials requisition signed by an authorized employee. The **materials requisition** describes the item and quantity needed and shows the job or purpose. Jobs are identified by a job order number, which is assigned when production on the job begins. The raw materials ledger clerk prices the items listed on the materials requisition. The storeroom clerk uses the materials requisition to record materials issued on the individual raw materials ledger cards.

Figure 27.3 illustrates a requisition for Mobile Manufacturing Inc. issuing 100 units of material BRC02 on June 8.

Now look at the second entry on the raw materials ledger card in Figure 27.2. This entry on Requisition R-24 shows the issuance of 100 braces. The braces cost $1 each. After this transaction, 100 units are on hand at a cost of $1 per brace.

At the end of the month, the raw materials ledger clerk at Mobile Manufacturing Inc. summarized all issued material requisitions. The summary classified the direct materials costs by

important!

Perpetual Inventory System
When a cost accounting system is used, perpetual inventory records are kept for raw materials, work in process, and finished goods.

*inte*rnal **CONTROL**

>>2. OBJECTIVE
Journalize the purchase and issuance of direct and indirect materials.

>>3. OBJECTIVE
Maintain perpetual inventory records.

LP27

RAW MATERIALS LEDGER CARD
(FIFO Cost Method)

ITEM: Brace   NUMBER: BRC02

DATE	REF.	RECEIVED UNITS	RECEIVED PRICE	RECEIVED AMOUNT	ISSUED UNITS	ISSUED PRICE	ISSUED AMOUNT	BALANCE UNITS	BALANCE PRICE	BALANCE AMOUNT
2010	Bal									0
Jun. 4	PO-3	200	1 00	200 00				200	1 00	200 00
8	R-24				100	1 00	100 00	100	1 00	100 00
12	PO-14	150	1 10	165 00				100	1 00	
								150	1 10	265 00
17	R-51				100	1 00		100	1 10	110 00
					50	1 10	155 00			
24	PO-32	100	1 15	115 00				100	1 10	
								100	1 15	225 00
29	R-90				100	1 10	110 00	100	1 15	115 00

*inte*rnal **CONTROL**

FIGURE 27.2

Raw Materials Ledger Card

FIGURE 27.3

Materials Requisition Form

recall

Subsidiary Records
The job order cost sheet is a subsidiary record showing all manufacturing costs charged to a specific job. The subsidiary record supports the **Work in Process Inventory** account.

MATERIALS REQUISITION				No. R-24

Charged to Account No. _122_

Job No. _J-5_   Date: _June 8, 2010_

Quantity	Description	Unit Cost	Total Cost
100	Braces BRC02	1 00	100 00

Authorized by:	Issued by:	Received by:
J. Sinclair	E. Layden	T. Santos

jobs and listed the supplies and indirect materials issued. The summary is the basis for entries on the job order cost sheets and for a journal entry to record materials issued. The journal entry has a debit to **Work in Process Inventory** for $28,000 of direct materials placed into production, a debit to **Manufacturing Overhead** for $2,000 of indirect materials and supplies issued, and a credit to **Raw Materials Inventory** for the $30,000. The journal entry to record materials and supplies issued is as follows.

recall

Methods determining costs of inventory:
- First in, first out (FIFO)
- Last in, first out (LIFO)
- Average cost of similar items during a specified period (average cost)

	2010					
1						1
2	Jun.	30	Work in Process Inventory	28 00 00		2
3			Manufacturing Overhead	2 00 00		3
4			Raw Materials Inventory		30 00 00	4
5			Cost of materials and supplies			5
6			issued during month			6
7						7
8						8

Cost Basis In Chapter 17, you learned that there are different methods for determining the cost of inventory including FIFO, LIFO, and average cost methods. In conformity with the consistency principle, each business chooses a cost method and follows it. Mobile Manufacturing Inc. uses the FIFO method. Figure 27.2 shows how the FIFO method is applied to purchases and requisitions of BRC02 braces. The entry on June 12 reflects the purchase of an additional 150 units at a cost of $1.10 per unit. After this transaction, there are 250 units on hand. The units are identified with specific purchases. There are 100 units from the purchase of June 4, at a cost of $1.00 per unit, and 150 units from the purchase of June 12, at a cost of $1.10 per unit. The entry on June 17 reflects the issuance of 150 units. Under the FIFO method, the units issued are assumed to be:

100 units from the purchase of June 4	
100 units × $1.00 per unit	$100.00
50 units from purchase of June 12	
50 units × $1.10 per unit	55.00
Total 150 units	$155.00

It is assumed that all units purchased on the June 4 order were issued. The 100 units on hand come from the June 12 purchase. The balance of BRC02 after the June 17 issuance is 100 units at $110 (100 × $1.10).

ACCOUNTING FOR LABOR

Factory labor costs are identified as direct labor, which is recorded in **Work in Process Inventory,** or as indirect labor, which is recorded in **Manufacturing Overhead.** The factory labor costs incurred during June follow.

Payroll Period	Direct Labor	Indirect Labor	Total
June 8	$ 3,000	$ 800	$ 3,800
15	2,000	300	2,300
22	2,500	200	2,700
29	2,500	200	2,700
Totals	$10,000	$1,500	$11,500

The entry to record the payroll data in general journal form follows.

	2010					
14	Jun.	30	Work in Process Inv. (Direct Labor)	10 000 00		14
15			Manufacturing Overhead (Indirect Labor)	1 500 00		15
16			Social Security Tax Payable		7 13 00	16
17			Medicare Tax Payable		1 66 75	17
18			Employee Income Tax Payable		1 200 00	18
19			Salaries and Wages Payable		9 420 25	19
20			Total labor costs for June			20
21						21

Employees record the time they enter and leave the plant. Workers complete a separate **time ticket** for each job indicating the job performed and the starting and stopping time. If the worker is idle for part of the day, an "idle time" time ticket is prepared so that the cost of idle time can be charged appropriately.

Usually, idle time is charged to manufacturing overhead. If, however, the idle time is due solely to the specifications or peculiarities of a particular job, the idle time costs are charged to that job. Figure 27.4 shows a manual time ticket.

A cost clerk computes the total time shown on the time ticket and applies the worker's rate to obtain the cost of the labor. Labor time tickets are sorted by job and summarized at the end of each payroll period for entry on individual job order cost sheets. The total charged to all the cost sheets must agree with the direct labor debited to **Work in Process Inventory.**

Many factories use automated systems for recording the time spent by an employee on each task. Each employee has an identification card. When starting and completing work on a specific

>>4. OBJECTIVE
Record labor costs incurred and charge labor into production.

important!

Work in Process Inventory
The balance in the **Work in Process Inventory** account at the end of the period reflects the cost of work still incomplete at that time.

LABOR TIME TICKET

Name _John Bennett_   Date: _June 8,_ 20 _10_

Description of work
  Assembling tables

Time started _8:00_
Time stopped _10:20_
Hours worked _2 1/3_
Rate of pay _$12.00_
Total charge _$28.00_

Charge Job No. _J-5_

Approved by: _J. Sinclair_

FIGURE 27.4

Labor Time Ticket

job, the employee inserts the identification card into a register or scanner. The time spent on the job is recorded electronically.

>>5. OBJECTIVE

Compute overhead rates and apply overhead to jobs.

LP27

ACCOUNTING FOR MANUFACTURING OVERHEAD

Manufacturing overhead includes all manufacturing costs except direct materials and direct labor. Common overhead items are indirect labor, indirect materials, depreciation of factory buildings and equipment, insurance, utilities, property taxes, repairs and maintenance, and payroll taxes on factory labor. There are different ways to enter overhead costs in the accounting records. Mobile Manufacturing Inc. uses an account called *Manufacturing Overhead.* A subsidiary ledger, the **manufacturing overhead ledger,** contains a record for each overhead item. The overhead costs incurred are debited to the control account, and the details are posted to the appropriate subsidiary ledger accounts.

We have already seen that Mobile incurred indirect materials costs (supplies) of $2,000 and indirect labor costs of $1,500. These amounts were debited to *Manufacturing Overhead* (see entries on pages 938 and 939). In addition to indirect materials and indirect labor, the company incurred overhead costs of $3,500. The entry to record these additional overhead costs in general journal form follows.

9	Jun.	30	Manufacturing Overhead	3 5 0 0 00	
10			Accounts Payable and other accounts		3 5 0 0 00
11			Overhead costs for June		
12					
13					
14					

Basing Overhead Application on Direct Labor Costs Several methods are used to apply overhead to specific jobs, including those based on direct labor costs or direct labor hours. Mobile Manufacturing Inc.'s accountant estimates overhead and direct labor costs for the coming year. Estimated total overhead is divided by estimated total direct labor costs. The result is a predetermined **overhead application rate.** Using summaries of labor time tickets, direct labor is recorded for each job. At the same time, the direct labor costs are multiplied by the overhead rate. The result is the amount of overhead to record for each job.

Mobile Manufacturing Inc. calculated an overhead rate of 75 percent of direct labor costs as follows.

$$\frac{\text{Estimated overhead costs}}{\text{Estimated direct labor costs}} = \frac{\$ \ 90,000}{\$120,000} = 75 \text{ percent}$$

In June, direct labor costs charged to jobs totaled $10,000. The overhead applied to jobs was $7,500 ($10,000 × 0.75). This is recorded in general journal form as follows.

15	Jun.	30	Work in Process Inventory	7 5 0 0 00	
16			Manufacturing Overhead Applied		7 5 0 0 00
17			Overhead applied to jobs in June at		
18			75% of direct labor costs		
19					
20					
21					

>>6. OBJECTIVE

Compute overapplied or underapplied overhead and report it in the financial statements.

Overapplied or Underapplied Overhead During the year, the actual overhead incurred is debited to *Manufacturing Overhead.* When overhead is applied to jobs, the credit is to *Manufacturing Overhead Applied.* At the end of each month, the two accounts are compared.

LP27

- If the total debits in *Manufacturing Overhead* are higher than the total credits in *Manufacturing Overhead Applied,* there is **underapplied overhead.**
- If the total debits in *Manufacturing Overhead* are less than the total credits in *Manufacturing Overhead Applied,* there is **overapplied overhead.**

In June, overhead was overapplied by $500.

Manufacturing Overhead (debits)		
Indirect materials and supplies	$ 2,000	
Indirect labor	1,500	
Other overhead costs	3,500	
Total charged to manufacturing overhead		$7,000
Manufacturing Overhead Applied (credits)		7,500
Overapplied overhead in June		$ 500

During the year, underapplied or overapplied overhead occurs, in part, because the application rate is an average based on estimates for the year, and fluctuations happen from month to month.

At the end of the year, the *Manufacturing Overhead Applied* account is closed into the *Manufacturing Overhead* account. The balance in the *Manufacturing Overhead* account represents the underapplied or overapplied overhead for the year, which is closed to the *Cost of Goods Sold* account. The overapplied or underapplied amount appears as an adjustment to the Cost of Goods Sold amount on the income statement.

Video27.1

Section 2 Self Review

QUESTIONS

1. What entry is made for indirect materials issued from the storeroom?

2. When direct materials are issued from the storeroom, are any entries made in the subsidiary records?

3. What is underapplied overhead?

EXERCISES

4. The entry to record the application of overhead to jobs consists of a

   a. debit to **Manufacturing Overhead** and a credit to **Manufacturing Overhead Applied.**

   b. debit to **Manufacturing Overhead Applied** and a credit to **Manufacturing Overhead.**

   c. debit to **Work in Process Inventory** and a credit to **Manufacturing Overhead Applied.**

   d. debit to **Manufacturing Overhead Applied** and a credit to **Work in Process Inventory.**

5. At the end of the year, any underapplied overhead is shown as an adjustment to

   a. **Manufacturing Overhead Applied.**

   b. **Manufacturing Overhead.**

   c. **Raw Materials Inventory.**

   d. **Cost of Goods Sold.**

ANALYSIS

6. A firm applies overhead based on direct labor hours. The firm estimates direct labor hours of 5,000 and overhead costs of $20,000. What is the overhead application rate?

(Answers to Section 2 Self Review are on page 955.)

Section 3

SECTION OBJECTIVES	TERMS TO LEARN
>> 7. Maintain job order cost sheets. WHY IT'S IMPORTANT The job order cost sheet shows all manufacturing costs for a specific job.	job order cost sheet
>> 8. Record the cost of jobs completed and the cost of goods sold under a perpetual inventory system. WHY IT'S IMPORTANT Manufacturing records need to reflect all the costs of a manufactured product.	

Accounting for Job Orders

Each new job started in production is assigned a number for identification and reference. A job order cost sheet is also set up at this time.

>>7. OBJECTIVE

Maintain job order cost sheets.

LP27

The Job Order Cost Sheet

A **job order cost sheet** is a record of all manufacturing costs charged to a specific job. It is set up when a job starts production. The cost sheets for all jobs currently in production constitute the subsidiary ledger for the *Work in Process Inventory* account.

Figure 27.5 shows the job order cost sheet for job J-8. The job was started and completed during the month of June. The information at the top of the sheet shows the job number and the product being manufactured, the start and completion dates, and the number of units ordered and produced.

- Direct materials used are entered weekly in the Materials section from summaries of materials requisitions.
- Direct labor costs are entered weekly in the Labor section from summaries of the labor time tickets.

JOB ORDER COST SHEET

For Stock __X__
Customer's Name _____
Address _____
Item _____ *Stang Tables* _____

Job No. __J-8__   Date *June 15, 2010*
Started _*June 3, 2010*_
Completed _*June 15, 2010*_
Quantity __25__ (ordered)   __25__ (completed)

MATERIALS		LABOR		OVERHEAD APPLIED				SUMMARY		
Date	Amount	Date	Amount	Date	Rate	Amount		Item	Amount	
June 8	150 00	June 8	150 50	June 8	75%	112	88	Materials	250	00
15	100 00	15	75 00	15	75%	56	25	Labor	225	50
								Overhead	169	13
								Total	644	63
								Unit Cost	25	785
								Comments:		
Totals	250 00		225 50			169	13			

FIGURE 27.5

Job Order Cost Sheet

942

■ Overhead is computed using the predetermined overhead application rate (75 percent of direct labor costs). Overhead is entered in the Overhead Applied section.

■ When the job has been completed, the costs are totaled in the Summary section. The unit cost is determined by dividing the total cost by the number of units produced.

ACCOUNTING FOR WORK COMPLETED

As each job is completed, the units are transferred to finished goods. The job order cost sheet contains the quantity, unit cost, and total cost needed to post to the inventory card in the finished goods subsidiary ledger. The finished goods ledger card is similar to the raw materials ledger card shown in Figure 27.2.

At the end of the month, a summary of completed jobs is prepared and an entry is made to transfer the total cost from the *Work in Process Inventory* account to the *Finished Goods Inventory* account.

>>**8. OBJECTIVE**

Record the cost of jobs completed and the cost of goods sold under a perpetual inventory system.

LP27

1	2010				1
2	Jun.	30	Finished Goods Inventory	30 50 0 00		2
3			Work in Process Inventory		30 50 0 00	3
4			Cost of jobs completed during June			4
5						5

ACCOUNTING FOR COST OF GOODS SOLD

As goods are sold, sales invoices are prepared for the customers. The cost of each order is entered on the office copy of the invoice; the cost information comes from the finished goods ledger card. Entries are made on the finished goods ledger card to record the quantities and costs of units sold. At month-end, the total cost of goods sold is determined from a summary of the information entered on the invoice copies.

6	Jun.	30	Cost of Goods Sold	40 00 0 00		6
7			Finished Goods Inventory		40 00 0 00	7
8			Cost of goods sold during June			8

10	Jun.	30	Accounts Receivable	70 00 0 00		10
11			Sales		70 00 0 00	11
12			Sales for June			12
13						13

MANAGERIAL IMPLICATIONS   <<

JOB ORDER COST SYSTEM

■ The job order cost system keeps managers informed of the cost of manufacturing specific orders or batches of goods. It permits the computation of the cost per unit of product.

■ The use of an overhead application rate helps to develop a consistent unit cost from month to month because the effects of unusual expenses or variations in monthly volume of output are averaged over the entire year.

■ Unit costs help management to evaluate and maintain efficiency.

■ Perpetual inventory procedures are useful tools for inventory control because they help keep management informed about inventory balances.

THINKING CRITICALLY

When is it appropriate to use a job order cost accounting system?

On the June income statement, the *Cost of Goods Sold* account and adjustment for underapplied or overapplied overhead appear as follows.

Sales		$70,000
Cost of Goods Sold (per ledger account)	$40,000	
Subtract Overapplied Manufacturing Overhead	500	
Cost of Goods Sold (adjusted)		39,500
Gross Profit on Sales		$30,500

Instead of showing overapplied or underapplied overhead on the income statement, the accountant might prefer to show actual manufacturing costs on the statement of cost of goods manufactured.

Summary of Cost Flow Through Inventory Accounts

The flow of costs during June is illustrated in the following three perpetual inventory accounts and the *Cost of Goods Sold* account. Mobile Manufacturing Inc. had inventories of raw materials and finished goods on June 1 but no beginning inventory of work in process.

ACCOUNT Raw Materials Inventory   ACCOUNT NO. 121

DATE	DESCRIPTION	POST. REF.	DEBIT	CREDIT	BALANCE DEBIT	BALANCE CREDIT
2010						
Jun. 1	Balance	✓			22 500 00	
30		J1	15 000 00		37 500 00	
30		J1		30 000 00	7 500 00	

ACCOUNT Work in Process Inventory   ACCOUNT NO. 122

DATE	DESCRIPTION	POST. REF.	DEBIT	CREDIT	BALANCE DEBIT	BALANCE CREDIT
2010						
Jun. 30	Materials	J1	28 000 00		28 000 00	
30	Labor	J1	10 000 00		38 000 00	
30	Overhead					
	Applied	J1	7 500 00		45 500 00	
30	To Finished					
	Goods	J1		30 500 00	15 000 00	

ACCOUNT Finished Goods Inventory   ACCOUNT NO. 126

DATE	DESCRIPTION	POST. REF.	DEBIT	CREDIT	BALANCE DEBIT	BALANCE CREDIT
2010						
Jun. 1	Balance	✓			20 000 00	
30		J1	30 500 00		50 500 00	
30		J1		40 000 00	10 500 00	

ACCOUNT Cost of Goods Sold   ACCOUNT NO. 560

DATE	DESCRIPTION	POST. REF.	DEBIT	CREDIT	BALANCE DEBIT	BALANCE CREDIT
2010						
Jun. 30		J1	40 000 00		40 000 00	

Section 3 Self Review

QUESTIONS

1. What is an overhead application rate?

2. How are job order cost sheets used?

3. Under the perpetual inventory system, what journal entries are made for sales and cost of goods sold?

EXERCISES

4. The entry to transfer work in process to finished goods is a

   a. debit to *Finished Goods Inventory* and a credit to *Work in Process Inventory*.

   b. debit to *Cost of Goods Sold* and a credit to *Finished Goods Inventory*.

   c. debit to *Finished Goods Inventory* and a credit to *Cost of Goods Sold*.

   d. debit to *Work in Process Inventory* and a credit to *Finished Goods Inventory*.

5. The entry to record cost of goods sold at the end of the month is a

   a. debit to *Finished Goods Inventory* and a credit to *Cost of Goods Sold*.

   b. debit to *Cost of Goods Sold* and a credit to *Finished Goods Inventory*.

   c. debit to *Work in Process Inventory* and a credit to *Finished Goods Inventory*.

   d. debit to *Finished Goods Inventory* and a credit to *Work in Process Inventory*.

ANALYSIS

6. During the year, sales were $350,000. The unadjusted balance of *Cost of Goods Sold* was $220,000. Overapplied manufacturing overhead was $5,000. What is the gross profit on sales?

(Answers to Section 3 Self Review are on page 955.)

Manufacturing companies use accounting systems that best supply detailed information about the costs of production. The job order cost system, as you learned in this chapter, provides records of costs identified to specific job orders.

Learning Objectives

Review and Applications

1 Explain how a job order cost accounting system operates.

Under the job order cost accounting system, each batch of goods is produced under a production order called a job order. The job order cost system requires that inventory accounts and related subsidiary ledgers are set up for *Raw Materials, Work in Process,* and *Finished Goods.*

- The raw materials ledger is a subsidiary ledger to the *Raw Materials Inventory* account and contains a ledger card for each material.
- A job cost sheet is a subsidiary ledger for *Work in Process Inventory* in the general ledger.
- The finished goods ledger is a subsidiary ledger to the *Finished Goods Inventory* account and has a record for each type of item.

2 Journalize the purchase and issuance of direct and indirect materials.

The account, *Raw Materials Inventory,* reflects all transactions related to materials and supplies.

- Purchases of raw materials are debited to the *Raw Materials Inventory* account.
- Raw materials are issued by a written requisition that shows the number of the job involved; that job is charged with the proper cost. A requisition for indirect materials or supplies is charged to the proper overhead account.

3 Maintain perpetual inventory records.

Materials or supplies are issued by the storeroom only upon presentation of a materials requisition describing the item and quantity needed and the job or purpose for which it is needed.

- Costs of materials placed into production are debited to *Work in Process Inventory.*
- Costs of indirect materials and supplies used are debited to *Manufacturing Overhead.*
- The total of indirect and direct materials is credited to *Raw Materials Inventory.*

4 Record labor costs incurred and charge labor into production.

Factory labor costs are identified as either direct labor or indirect labor. Time tickets are used for charging direct labor to specific jobs.

5 Compute overhead rates and apply overhead to jobs.

Manufacturing overhead is assigned to jobs based on a rate that is commonly related to direct labor costs or to direct labor hours.

6 Compute overapplied or underapplied overhead and report it in the financial statements.

To apply overhead to jobs, debit *Work in Process Inventory* and credit *Manufacturing Overhead Applied.* Compute the overapplied or underapplied overhead by comparing total credits recorded in *Manufacturing Overhead Applied* with total debits recorded in *Manufacturing Overhead* for the month.

- Underapplied or overapplied overhead is carried forward from month to month.
- Net underapplied or overapplied overhead is closed out each year, usually as an adjustment to *Cost of Goods Sold* on the income statement.

7 Maintain job order cost sheets.

The job order cost sheet shows all manufacturing costs for a specific job.

8 Record the cost of jobs completed and the cost of goods sold under a perpetual inventory system.

As a job is done, the cost sheet gives data needed for transferring costs from *Work in Process Inventory* to *Finished Goods Inventory.*

- Record an order's cost on the sales invoice office copy.
- Summarize the cost of goods sold each month from the invoices.
- Record the transfer entry in the general journal.

9 Define the accounting terms new to this chapter.

Glossary

Finished goods subsidiary ledger (p. 936) A ledger containing a record for each of the different types of finished products

Job order (p. 932) A specific order for a specific batch of manufactured items

Job order cost accounting (p. 932) A cost accounting system that determines the unit cost of manufactured items for each separate production order

Job order cost sheet (942) A record of all manufacturing costs charged to a specific job

Just-in-time system (p. 935) An inventory system in which raw materials are ordered so they arrive just in time to be placed into production

Manufacturing overhead ledger (p. 940) A subsidiary ledger that contains a record for each overhead item

Materials requisition (p. 937) A form that describes the item and quantity needed and shows the job or purpose

Overapplied overhead (p. 941) The result of applied overhead exceeding the actual overhead costs

Overhead application rate (p. 940) The rate at which the estimated cost of overhead is charged to each job

Perpetual inventory system (p. 933) An inventory system that tracks the inventories on hand at all times

Process cost accounting (p. 932) A cost accounting system whereby unit costs of manufactured items are determined by totaling unit costs in each production department

Production order (p. 932) See Job order

Raw materials ledger card (p. 937) A record showing details of receipts and issues for a type of raw material

Raw materials subsidiary ledger (p. 936) A ledger containing the raw materials ledger cards

Standard costs (p. 932) A measure of what costs should be in an efficient operation

Time ticket (p. 939) Form used to record hours worked and jobs performed

Underapplied overhead (p. 941) The result of actual overhead costs exceeding applied overhead

Work in process subsidiary ledger (p. 936) A ledger containing the job order cost sheets

Comprehensive **Self Review**

1. How is a cost accounting system used?
2. What is a process cost accounting system?
3. Why is a perpetual inventory system used with a job order cost accounting system?
4. What would you find on a raw materials ledger card?
5. How is underapplied or overapplied manufacturing overhead disposed of at the end of the year?

(Answers to Comprehensive Self Review are on page 956.)

 Multiple choice questions are provided on the text Web site at www.mhhe.com/price12e

Quiz27

Discussion **Questions**

1. What is a perpetual inventory?
2. What information does a job order cost sheet contain?
3. When direct materials are issued from the storeroom, what entries are made in the subsidiary records?

4. What is a materials requisition?

5. What does the *Raw Materials Inventory* account show?

6. What entry is made for indirect materials issued from the storeroom?

7. What is idle time? How is the cost of idle time usually accounted for?

8. Name the sources of postings to the job order cost sheet.

9. What account is debited and what account is credited when manufacturing overhead is applied?

10. Name five common manufacturing overhead costs.

11. Why is an overhead application rate used?

12. What account is debited and what account is credited when completed goods are transferred from the factory floor to the finished goods storeroom?

13. What is a time ticket? What is its relationship to an order cost sheet?

14. Name three types of businesses that would use a job order cost accounting system.

15. Discuss how costs flow through the *Raw Materials Inventory, Work in Process Inventory,* and *Finished Goods Inventory* accounts to cost of goods sold.

16. Describe a just-in-time inventory system, including its advantages and disadvantages, if any.

APPLICATIONS

Exercises HM™

The following data is for Exercises 27.1 through 27.4.
During July 2010, CHA, Inc., purchased and issued the following materials and supplies. Use July 31 as the date for all entries.

Purchases		Issues from Storeroom	
Materials	$60,000	Direct materials	$50,000
Manufacturing supplies	5,000	Manufacturing supplies	4,000

Exercise 27.1
Objective 2

▶ **Journalizing purchase of materials.**

Give the entry in general journal form to record the cost of the materials purchased.

Exercise 27.2
Objective 2

▶ **Journalizing purchase of indirect materials.**

Give the entry in general journal form to record the cost of the manufacturing supplies purchased.

Exercise 27.3
Objective 2

▶ **Journalizing the assignment of indirect materials into production.**

Give the entry in general journal form to record the issuance of the manufacturing supplies into production.

Exercise 27.4
Objective 2

▶ **Journalizing the assignment of direct materials into production.**

Give the entry in general journal form to record the issuance of the direct materials into production.

Exercise 27.5
Objective 4

▶ **Recording labor costs incurred.**

A payroll summary prepared at Eli Manufacturing Company showed the following figures for January 2010.

Direct labor costs incurred	$50,000.00
Indirect labor costs incurred	5,000.00
Social security tax withheld	3,410.00
Medicare tax withheld	797.50
Income tax withheld	11,000.00

Give the January 31 entry in general journal form to record the labor costs incurred.

Computing overhead rate.

◀ **Exercise 27.6**
Objective 5

Porch Screen Inc. estimates the following manufacturing overhead costs for 2010.

Estimated direct labor hours	50,000 hours
Estimated direct labor costs	$750,000
Estimated overhead costs	$150,000

What is the overhead application rate based on direct labor costs?

Applying manufacturing overhead.

◀ **Exercise 27.7**
Objective 5

Ebeth Company's direct labor costs were $100,000 for May 2010. Assuming that the company applies overhead at the rate of 60 percent of direct labor costs, give the general journal entry for May summarizing the overhead applied for the month.

Applying overhead and cost of job.

◀ **Exercise 27.8**
Objective 5

During 2010, Royal Manufacturing Company began and completed Job 1203. Costs entered on the job cost sheet for this job were $40,000 for materials and $8,000 for direct labor.

1. Assuming that overhead is applied at 60 percent of direct labor costs, compute the amount of overhead that should be applied to this job.
2. Compute the total cost of Job 1203.

Computing overapplied or underapplied overhead.

◀ **Exercise 27.9**
Objective 6

For the year 2010, Frost Inc. had actual overhead costs of $90,000, and its applied overhead was $87,000.

1. Did the firm have overapplied or underapplied overhead for the year?
2. What was the amount of overapplied or underapplied overhead?

Recording cost of goods completed and cost of goods sold.

◀ **Exercise 27.10**
Objective 8

The records of Pacific Inc. for 2010 show that it completed goods costing $150,000 and that it sold goods costing $199,000 for the year. Give the entries in general journal form on December 31, 2010, to record the cost of goods completed and the cost of goods sold for the year.

PROBLEMS

Problem Set A ▉▉™

Recording purchase and issuance of direct and indirect materials, recording labor costs, applying overhead, computing overapplied or underapplied overhead, recording cost of jobs completed and cost of goods sold.

◀ **Problem 27.1A**
**Objectives 2, 4, 5
6, 8**

e**X**cel QB

In March 2010, Texas Trailers Co. had the following cost data.

COST DATA

a. Raw materials costing $76,000 were purchased.

b. Raw materials costing $68,000 were used: direct materials, $65,000; indirect materials $3,000.

c. Factory wages of $50,000 were incurred: direct labor $48,000; indirect labor $2,000. Social security tax deductions were $3,100, Medicare tax deductions were $725, federal income tax deductions were $6,500.

d. Other overhead costs of $32,000 were incurred. (Credit *Accounts Payable.*)

e. Estimated manufacturing overhead costs were applied to jobs in production at the rate of 75 percent of direct labor costs.

f. Finished goods costing $100,000 were transferred from production to the warehouse.

g. The cost of goods sold was $70,000.

h. Sales on account for the month were $175,000.

INSTRUCTIONS

1. Prepare general journal entries to record each item of cost data given. Use the account titles listed in your textbook.

2. Compute the amount of overapplied or underapplied overhead for the month.

3. Prepare a partial income statement for March. Adjust the *Cost of Goods Sold* for any overapplied or underapplied overhead.

Analyze: Based on the partial income statement you have prepared, what portion of each sales dollar is realized as gross profit?

Problem 27.2A ▶

Objectives 5, 6, 7, 8

e**X**cel

Maintaining job order cost sheets, applying overhead to jobs, computing overapplied or underapplied overhead, recording cost of jobs completed and cost of goods sold.

The Cherry Company builds kitchen cabinets. On January 1, 2010, one job (D42) was in progress. The order is from Dallas Apartment Corporation and was begun on December 21, 2009. Costs accumulated to date on that job are materials, $2,000; labor, $1,000; and overhead, $500. During January, the following costs were incurred in production work on Job D42 and on Jobs J01 and J02, which were started on January 5, 2010.

	Materials	Labor	Overhead	Quantity
Job D42	$ 500	$ 500	$ 250	5
Job J01	4,000	2,000	1,000	8
Job J02	4,000	3,000	1,500	5

Job J01 is being manufactured for Luxery Cabinets, and Job J02 is for stock.

Manufacturing overhead is applied at the rate of 50 percent of direct labor costs. During January, actual manufacturing overhead costs of $3,000 were incurred. Job D42 was completed on January 19 and was delivered to the customer. The sales price was $9,000.

INSTRUCTIONS

1. Prepare job order cost sheets for the three jobs. Enter the beginning balances applicable to Job D42.

2. Post the costs of the materials and labor for January to the job order cost sheets.

3. Enter the overhead amounts that should be applied to the three jobs worked on during the month on the job cost sheets.

4. Give the entry in general journal form to transfer the cost of the job completed from work in process to finished goods.

5. Compute the amount of underapplied or overapplied overhead for January. Give the entry in general journal form to transfer your result to Cost of Goods Sold.

Analyze: If The Cherry Company sold the five cabinets referenced in Job D42 to Dallas Apartment Corporation for a new total invoice price of $10,000, what gross profit amount was realized on the job? Assume that no overapplication or underapplication of overhead occurred on this job.

Problem Set B

◀ Problem 27.1B
Objectives 2, 4, 5
6, 8

Recording purchase and issuance of direct and indirect materials, recording labor costs, applying overhead, computing overapplied or underapplied overhead, recording cost of jobs completed and cost of goods sold.

In April 2010, Metal Company had the following cost data.

COST DATA

a. Raw materials costing $92,000 were purchased.

b. Raw materials costing $87,000 were used: direct materials, $81,000; indirect materials, $6,000.

c. Factory wages of $70,000 were incurred: direct labor, $65,000; indirect labor, $5,000. Social security tax deductions were $4,340, Medicare tax deductions were $1,015, and income tax deductions were $7,000.

d. Other overhead costs amounting to $34,000 were incurred. (Credit *Accounts Payable.*)

e. Estimated manufacturing overhead costs were applied to jobs in production at the rate of 70 percent of direct labor costs.

f. Finished goods costing $150,000 were transferred to the warehouse.

g. Goods costing $125,000 were sold and billed to customers for $250,000.

INSTRUCTIONS

1. Prepare general journal entries to record each item of cost data given. Use the account titles in the textbook.

2. Compute the amount of overapplied or underapplied overhead for the month.

3. Prepare a partial income statement for the month of April. Adjust the cost of goods sold for any overapplied or underapplied overhead.

Analyze: What percentage of raw materials purchased during the month of April was used?

◀ Problem 27.2B
Objectives 5, 6, 7, 8

Maintaining job order cost sheets, applying overhead to jobs, computing overapplied or underapplied overhead, recording cost of jobs completed and cost of goods sold.

ABE's Cabinet Company builds kitchen cabinets. On November 1, 2010, two jobs, Job 045 and Job 048, were in progress. The order is from Clift Apartments and was begun on October 5, 2010. The accumulated costs for each job are detailed as follows.

	Job 045	Job 048
Materials	$20,000	$12,000
Labor	15,000	6,000
Overhead	7,500	3,000

During November, Job N01 was begun. Following are the November costs incurred for each of the three jobs.

	Materials	Labor	Overhead
Job 045	$3,000	$3,000	$1,500
Job 048	4,000	4,000	2,000
Job N01	6,000	2,000	1,000

Manufacturing overhead is applied at the rate of 50 percent of direct labor costs. During November, actual manufacturing overhead costs of $4,400 were incurred. Job 045 was completed on November 20 and was delivered to the customer. The sales price was $85,000.

INSTRUCTIONS

1. Prepare job order cost sheets for the three jobs. Enter the beginning balances applicable to Jobs 045 and 048.

2. Post the costs of the materials and labor for November to the job order cost sheets.

3. Post the overhead amounts that should be applied to the three jobs worked on during the month on the job cost sheets.

4. Give the entry in general journal form to transfer the cost of the job completed from work in process to finished goods.

5. Compute the amount of underapplied or overapplied overhead for November.

Analyze: What adjusted cost of goods sold should be reported for November manufacturing activities?

Critical Thinking Problem 27.1

Reaching Goals

Joseph Manufacturing Company manufactures one product that has several model styles. All materials are added at the beginning of production. Manufacturing overhead is applied as a percentage of direct labor cost. On January 1, 2010, one job, DE31, was in process, with the following accumulated costs:

Materials	$ 8,000
Direct labor	3,500
Manufacturing overhead	1,050
Total	$12,550

The beginning finished goods inventory for Joseph Manufacturing Company on January 1, 2010, was $19,500.

The following additional data is given for the month of January.

Total labor costs incurred	$24,000
Total cost of completed Job DE31	19,050
Total materials costs incurred	21,000

In addition, Job JA01 was begun and completed during the month. Its costs included materials of $8,500 and labor of $5,000. Job JA02 was begun during the month and was in process at the end of the month. During the month, sales were $70,000, and the gross profit rate was 40 percent.

INSTRUCTIONS

1. For Jobs DE31, JA01, and JA02, calculate the cost of materials, labor, and overhead for the month of January to find the total cost of each job.

2. Prepare a schedule of cost of goods sold for the month of January.

Analyze: On January 1, 2010, Joseph Manufacturing Company established a goal to hold raw materials costs at or below 48 percent of total job costs. Based on your computations, has the company attained this goal? Explain.

Critical Thinking Problem 27.2

Gross Profit

The job order cost sheets for Containers Inc., show the following information about special orders for June and July of the current year.

	Manufacturing Costs		
Job Number	June	July	Status of Job
JU–688	$10,000		Sold, 7/3
JU–689	4,500		Completed, 6/27
JU–690	2,150	$3,850	Completed, 7/8
JU–691	500	3,500	Sold, 7/10
JU–692	300	3,200	Sold, 7/16
JL–701		4,800	Sold, 7/22
JL–702		7,000	Completed, 7/20
JL–703		6,000	In process, 7/31
JL–704		1,900	In process, 7/31

The company prices its jobs to make a 50 percent gross profit on sales. Operating expenses for July totaled $8,300, and the company's income tax rate is 25 percent of net income before income taxes.

INSTRUCTIONS

1. From this data, compute the following:
   a. Work in Process Inventory, July 1
   b. Finished Goods Inventory, July 1
   c. Cost of Goods Sold for July
   d. Work in Process Inventory, July 31
   e. Finished Goods Inventory, July 31
   f. Sales for July
2. Prepare a condensed income statement for Containers Inc., for the month of July.

BUSINESS CONNECTIONS

Cost Accounting Controls

Managerial | FOCUS

1. The president of a fairly large manufacturing company suggests that it would be more efficient to discontinue the job of storeroom clerk and to let factory workers enter the storeroom and select their own materials. Comment on this suggestion.

2. Assume that you are an accountant for a manufacturing firm. At the end of one year, there is a large overapplied overhead amount. How would you explain to management why this balance might exist?

3. Why should management insist that a physical inventory be taken once a year even though perpetual inventory records are kept?

4. From an administrative standpoint, why is direct labor cost a simple basis to use for the application of manufacturing overhead?

5. In general, would managers prefer to see overapplied or underapplied overhead? Why?

Travel Costs

The costs for a supervisor are included in indirect costs. The supervisor's travel is included in the indirect costs. Rachael is a supervisor for a sewing department at a clothing construction company. As a supervisor, she makes $90,000 per year. Lately, Rachael has been traveling to conferences and recruiting employees. She has completed her own travel reports with copies of her receipts, not originals. Terry, Rachael's administrative assistant, noticed that Rachael has submitted a travel report for days she was in the office. Terry then reviews all of Rachael's travel reports. Terry's investigation revealed that Rachael had been in the office on at least half of the dates listed on the travel reports. What should Terry do? What effect does Rachael's fraud have on the company?

Sales

Refer to the *2006 Annual Report* for The Home Depot, Inc., in Appendix A.

1. Under the Table Of Contents, locate Part 1, Item 1. Under the *Products* section is a table showing the percentage of Net Sales for each product group. List each product group and the percentage of net sales for 2006.

2. Locate the section "Management's Discussion and Analysis of Financial Condition and Results of Operations." Review the discussion of *Results of Operations, Fiscal 2006 compared to 2005,* under the "Gross Profit" heading. As a percentage of Net Sales, did gross profit increase or decrease for 2006? What about 2005? Why?

Inventories

The following excerpt was taken from the *2006 Annual Report* for Alcoa.

Approximately 44 percent of total inventories on December 31, 2006, were valued on a LIFO basis. If valued on an average cost basis, total inventories would have been $1,077 and $836 higher at the end of 2006 and 2005, respectively.

Inventories:
(in millions)

December 31	2006	2005
Finished goods	$ 1,137	$ 918
Work in process	1,157	907
Bauxite and alumina	535	486
Purchased raw materials	729	667
Operating supplies	247	213
	$ 3,805	$3,191

Analyze:

1. In 2006, if the average cost basis had been used to value total inventories, what would the value have been?

2. Using the LIFO basis of inventory valuation in 2006, what percentage of total inventories was composed of finished goods?

3. By what amount did total inventories increase from 2005 to 2006?

Analyze Online: Locate the *About Alcoa* section within the Alcoa Web site (www.alcoa.com).

4. Describe the premises of the "Alcoa Business System."

Cost Accounting Systems

Accounting processes and systems vary from company to company. A ship builder will employ a different costing system than a furniture builder. If you were asked to design an accounting structure and costing system for a manufacturing company, what steps would you take? How would you familiarize yourself with the processes and costs involved?

Job Order Records

Job order cost accounting systems require specific forms and ledgers used to record job-specific costs. List the ledgers, cards, sheets, or requisitions necessary to record costs using a job order cost system and create blank samples for each.

Job Cost Card Design

Keeping track of materials that are provided by each vendor and the employees working on each job is an important process to maintain the high quality of your product. Job cost cards can accumulate this information if properly designed. In a group, design a job cost card for a selected product making sure to include an area to collect the information needed to monitor materials and labor. Share your job cost card design with the class.

Just in Time

Do a search for articles on just-in-time manufacturing. Be sure to include the word "manufacturing" to find the most relevant information. What is the definition of just in time? Notice all the articles that include JIT.

Answers to **Self Reviews**

Answers to Section 1 Self Review

1. A measure of what the cost should be in an efficient operation.
2. To check the accuracy of the recorded inventory.
3. A system in which the unit costs of production are determined for each separate production order.
4. **c.** when a company produces more than one product in batches rather than on a continuous basis.
5. **d.** with either the job order cost system or the process cost system.
6. $152,500

Answers to Section 2 Self Review

1. Indirect materials issued are entered on the raw materials inventory cards. Periodically, based on the summary of materials requisitions, the cost of indirect materials will be charged to the *Manufacturing Overhead* account and credited to the *Raw Materials Inventory* account.
2. Direct materials issued from the storeroom are entered on the raw materials ledger card for the material. Also, a posting will be made from the summary of materials requisitions to the Materials section of the job order cost sheet.
3. When the actual costs of overhead were more than the amount of overhead charged into production.
4. **c.** debit to *Work in Process Inventory* and a credit to *Manufacturing Overhead Applied.*
5. **d.** *Cost of Goods Sold.*
6. $4.00 per hour ($20,000 ÷ 5,000 hours)

Answers to Section 3 Self Review

1. A predetermined rate to assign overhead to each job, usually based on direct labor hours or direct labor cost.
2. The totals on the job order cost sheet are used as the basis of entries on the finished goods ledger sheet and to make the journal entry to transfer cost of completed jobs from *Work in Process* to *Finished Goods.*
3. Sales are recorded by debiting *Accounts Receivable* and crediting *Sales.* The cost of goods sold is recorded by debiting *Cost of Goods Sold* and crediting *Finished Goods Inventory.*

4. **a.** debit to *Finished Goods Inventory* and a credit to *Work in Process Inventory.*

5. **b.** debit to *Cost of Goods Sold* and a credit to *Finished Goods Inventory.*

6. $135,000

Answers to Comprehensive Self Review

1. To determine the cost of each manufactured unit and help managers watch cost behavior and control costs.

2. One in which the total cost of a unit of product is found by adding the unit costs in each department through which the product passes during the manufacturing process.

3. Because the firm must always know the costs of the inventory being used at each stage of production.

4. The quantities and costs of items purchased, issued, and balance on hand.

5. It is closed. It is usually closed into Cost of Goods Sold.

Process Cost Accounting

ConocoPhillips   www.conoco.com | ConocoPhillips is a global, integrated petroleum company with operations on nearly every continent on our planet. Recent activities reported in the company's annual report included:

- Acquiring Burlington Resources, making ConocoPhillips one of the largest natural gas producers in North America.
- Starting operation of a liquefied natural gas project in Australia that can accommodate future expansion.
- Expanding our European and Atlantic refining presence through the purchase of a large refinery and associated assets in Wilhelmshaven, Germany.
- Restoring our U.S. refineries to normal operations following significant damage and disruptions caused by the 2005 Gulf Coast hurricanes.
- Completing major refining and transportation modifications in the United States to process and distribute ultraclean-burning highway diesel fuel and gasoline,

Headquartered in Houston, Texas, ConocoPhillips operates in more than 40 countries and had net income of $15.6 billion in 2006.

thinking critically

How do you think ConocoPhillips estimates ending work in process inventory in its petroleum plants?

SECTION OBJECTIVES

>> 1. **Compute equivalent units of production with no beginning work in process inventory.**

WHY IT'S IMPORTANT

Manufacturers estimate units completed based on labor, materials, and overhead costs.

>> 2. **Prepare a cost of production report with no beginning work in process inventory.**

WHY IT'S IMPORTANT

Tracking production costs can help identify manufacturing inefficiencies or cost overruns.

>> 3. **Compute the unit cost of manufacturing under the process cost accounting system.**

WHY IT'S IMPORTANT

Unit costs help management set prices.

>> 4. **Record costs incurred and the flow of costs as products move through the manufacturing process and are sold.**

WHY IT'S IMPORTANT

Cumulative product costs are tracked and categorized at every point in the manufacturing process.

TERMS TO LEARN

cost of production report
equivalent production
process cost accounting
system

Process Cost Accounting System

A process cost accounting system is used in operations when a single product is manufactured and production is continuous. Examples of companies that use process cost accounting systems include oil refineries, cement producers, and paint manufacturers.

The Process Cost Accounting System

In a **process cost accounting system,** costs are accumulated for each process or department and then transferred on to the next process or department. The flow of costs is similar to that shown in Figure 27.1. There are *Raw Materials Inventory* and *Finished Goods Inventory* accounts. However, job order cost sheets are not needed because products are not made in batches or by order; instead they are produced continuously. There is a separate *Work in Process* account for each department. Materials, labor, and overhead costs are identified with each department and charged to the departmental *Work in Process* accounts. At the end of the month, each departmental *Work in Process* account reflects the materials, labor, and overhead costs incurred by the department.

The process cost accounting system is like an average cost system. Total manufacturing costs are divided by the number of units worked on to obtain a cost per unit of product. As products are physically transferred from one department to the next, the related costs are also transferred.

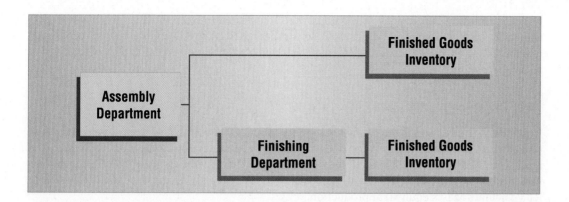

FIGURE 28.1

Flow of Goods in a Factory
Operation

Nash Manufacturing Company has two production departments: assembly and finishing. All products begin in the assembly department. Trays that are to be sold in an unpainted state are moved directly to the finished goods store-room and are recorded in the *Finished Goods Inventory* account. Other trays are moved to the finishing department. This flow of goods is shown in Figure 28.1.

ANALYZING PROCESS COST DATA

Let's study the process cost accounting system used by Nash Manufacturing Company. All transactions involving materials, labor, and overhead are recorded by department. The service department costs are allocated as overhead to the departments that benefit from the services. For each department, there is a record of products started, completed, and in process. The stage of completion of the ending work in process is estimated. Table 28.1 summarizes the production data for May.

In the assembly department, 6,000 units were started in production, 5,000 were transferred to the finishing department, and 500 were transferred to finished goods for sale as unpainted trays. At the end of the month, there were 500 trays in process in the assembly department. For the trays in process, all the required materials were issued, and 70 percent of the labor and overhead was added.

recall

Work in Process
Work in process refers to products that have started but have not completed the production process.

TABLE 28.1

Departmental Cost Data
for May 2010

important!

Unit Cost
Under the process cost system, unit costs are calculated by dividing all departmental manufacturing costs by the production for the period.

	Assembly Department	Finishing Department
Costs		
Materials	$24,000.00	$ 5,000.00
Labor	25,000.00	16,000.00
Manufacturing overhead	12,400.00	7,800.00
Total costs	$61,400.00	$28,800.00
Quantities		
Started in production	6,000	0
Transferred in from prior department	0	5,000
Transferred out to next department	5,000	0
Transferred out to finished goods	500	4,200
Work in process—ending	500	800
Stages of Completion—Ending Work in Process		
Materials	100%	90%
Labor	70%	50%
Manufacturing overhead	70%	50%

In the finishing department, 5,000 units were transferred in from the assembly department, and 4,200 were completed and transferred to finished goods. There were 800 trays in process at month-end, to which 90 percent of the materials and 50 percent of the labor and overhead was added.

DETERMINING EQUIVALENT PRODUCTION

Equivalent production is the estimated number of units that could have been started and completed with the same effort and costs incurred in the department during the month. Thus, if two units were started during the period and only one-half of the materials were added to each, one unit could have been started and completed using those materials. Using the data in Table 28.1, let's calculate May's equivalent production.

Calculating Equivalent Units for Assembly Department Separate equivalent unit computations are made for the materials, labor, and overhead. Table 28.2 shows how to compute the equivalent units of production for the assembly department. For materials, the equivalent units of production are 6,000 units (5,500 + 500). All the materials were issued for the 5,500 units transferred out and for the 500 trays in process.

For labor and manufacturing overhead, the equivalent units of production are 5,850 (5,500 + 350). All the labor and overhead were applied to the units transferred out. Of the 500 trays in ending work in process, 70 percent of the labor and overhead was applied. This is the equivalent of 350 (500 × 0.7) completed units.

>>**1. OBJECTIVE**

Compute equivalent units of production with no beginning work in process inventory.

important!

Equivalent Production

In computing equivalent production, accountants frequently consider labor and overhead to be at the same stage of production.

TABLE 28.2

Computation of Equivalent Production, Assembly Department

Materials		
Units transferred out		
To next department: 100% × 5,000 units	5,000	
To finished goods: 100% × 500 units	500	
Total transferred out		5,500
Work in process: 100% × 500 units		500
Equivalent units of production for materials		6,000
Labor and Manufacturing Overhead		
Units transferred out		
To next department: 100% × 5,000 units	5,000	
To finished goods: 100% × 500 units	500	
Total transferred out		5,500
Work in process: 70% × 500 units		350
Equivalent units of production for labor and overhead		5,850

Video28.1

recall

Manufacturing Overhead

Manufacturing overhead is all of the manufacturing costs not classified as direct materials or direct labor. Manufacturing overhead includes utilities, depreciation, maintenance, taxes, and insurance for the factory building and payroll taxes for factory wages.

Calculating Equivalent Units for Finishing Department Table 28.3 shows the equivalent units of production for the finishing department. For materials, the equivalent units are 4,920 (4,200 + 720). All the materials were issued for the 4,200 units transferred out. For the 800 trays in process, 90 percent of the materials were issued. The ending work in process for materials is 720 (800 × 0.9) equivalent units.

For labor and manufacturing overhead, the equivalent units of production are 4,600 (4,200 + 400). All the labor and overhead were applied to the units transferred out. Of the 800 trays in ending work in process, 50 percent of the labor and overhead was applied. This is the equivalent of 400 (800 × 0.5) completed units.

TABLE 28.3

Computation of Equivalent Production, Finishing Department

Materials

Units transferred out		
To finished goods: 100% × 4,200 units	4,200	
Total transferred out		4,200
Work in process: 90% × 800 units		720
Equivalent units of production for materials		4,920

Labor and Manufacturing Overhead

Units transferred out		
To finished goods: 100% × 4,200 units	4,200	
Total transferred out		4,200
Work in process: 50% × 800 units		400
Equivalent units of production for labor and overhead		4,600

LP28

PREPARING THE COST OF PRODUCTION REPORT

The **cost of production report** summarizes all costs charged to each department and shows the costs assigned to the goods transferred out of the department and to the goods still in process. It has separate sections to summarize quantities and costs. Each section has two parts that reconcile the total *to be accounted for* with the total *accounted for.*

Calculating Costs for the Assembly Department Table 28.4 on page 962 shows the cost of production report for the assembly department. The Quantity Schedule shows the units to be accounted for (a) and explains what happened to these units (b). The first part of the Cost Schedule (c) shows the total and unit cost of each element and the cumulative cost total. The unit cost is the total cost divided by the equivalent units. The unit cost for the assembly department totals $10.39.

The second part of the Cost Schedule (d) shows the cost of units completed and transferred out, $57,145. It lists the cost of the ending work in process by element, which is computed by multiplying the equivalent units by the cost per unit. For example, the ending work in process for materials is $2,000 (500 equivalent units × $4). The total work in process is the sum of the three elements plus an adjustment for rounding, $4,255. Note that the costs to account for (cumulative cost total) equal the total costs accounted for.

It is customary to round unit costs to the nearest cent. Often an adjustment is required due to rounding. The accountant for Nash Manufacturing Company adjusts the ending work in process inventory to ensure that the cumulative cost total equals the total costs accounted for. In subsequent periods, the rounding adjustment is added to or subtracted from manufacturing overhead in work in process.

Calculating Costs for the Finishing Department Table 28.5 on page 963 shows the cost of production report for the finishing department. In the Quantity Schedule (a), the quantity to be accounted for consists of units transferred in from the assembly department. These units are accounted for (b) as transferred to finished goods or still in process.

In the Cost Schedule (c), there is a new item. The cost of units transferred in from the assembly department is $51,950 for 5,000 units. Costs in the finishing department are listed next, in total and per unit. The total department costs are $28,800 and the cumulative cost total is $80,750 ($51,950 + $28,800). The unit cost from the assembly department was $10.39. The unit cost for the finishing department is $6.20. The cumulative unit cost is $16.59 ($10.39 + $6.20).

>>**2. OBJECTIVE**

Prepare a cost of production report with no beginning work in process inventory.

>>**3. OBJECTIVE**

Compute the unit cost of manufacturing under the process cost accounting system.

important!

Costs Accounted For
The total costs accounted for must equal the cumulative cost total for the department.

important!

Work in Process
If there is no beginning inventory of work in process, the total cost to be accounted for is the total of (1) costs transferred in from the prior department and (2) costs incurred in the current department.

TABLE 28.4 Cost of Production Report, May 2010, Assembly Department

Quantity Schedule		Units		
(a) Quantity to be accounted for				
Started in production		6,000		
Total to be accounted for		6,000		
(b) Quantity accounted for				
Transferred out to next department		5,000		
Transferred out to finished goods		500		
Work in process—ending		500		
Total accounted for		6,000		

Cost Schedule	Total Cost		E.P. Units*		Unit Cost
(c) Costs to be accounted for					
Costs in current department					
Materials	$24,000.00	÷	6,000	=	$ 4.00
Labor	25,000.00	÷	5,850	=	4.27
Manufacturing overhead	12,400.00	÷	5,850	=	2.12
Cumulative cost total	$61,400.00				$10.39
(d) Costs accounted for					
Transferred out to next department	$51,950.00	=	5,000	×	$10.39
Transferred out to finished goods	$ 5,195.00	=	500	×	10.39
Total costs transferred out	$57,145.00				
Work in process—ending					
Materials	$ 2,000.00	=	500	×	4.00
Labor	1,494.50	=	350	×	4.27
Manufacturing overhead	742.00	=	350	×	2.12
Rounding adjustment	18.50				
Total work in process—ending	$ 4,255.00				
Total costs accounted for	$61,400.00				

*Equivalent Production Units or Equivalent Units of Production

The second part of the Cost Schedule (d) shows the cost of units completed and transferred out, $69,678 (4,200 units × $16.59). In addition, it lists the cost of the ending work in process by element, which is computed by multiplying the equivalent units by the cost per unit. For example, the ending work in process for labor is $1,392 (400 × $3.48). The total work in process is $11,072. It includes the costs from the prior department ($8,312) and the sum of the three cost elements minus the rounding adjustment. Note that the costs to be accounted for equal the total costs accounted for.

>>4. OBJECTIVE

Record costs incurred and the flow of costs as products move through the manufacturing process and are sold. LP28

RECORDING COST FLOWS

The flow of costs in the accounting records follows the flow of production. Let's look at the journal entries that summarize May's operations.

TABLE 28.5   Cost of Production Report, May 2010, Finishing Department

Quantity Schedule			Units		
(a) Quantity to be accounted for					
Transferred in from prior department			5,000		
Total to be accounted for			5,000		
(b) Quantity accounted for					
Transferred out to finished goods			4,200		
Work in process—ending			800		
Total accounted for			5,000		

Cost Schedule	Total Cost		E.P. Units*		Unit Cost
(c) Costs to be accounted for					
Costs in prior department	$51,950.00	÷	5,000	=	$ 10.39
Costs in current department					
Materials	$ 5,000.00	÷	4,920	=	$ 1.02
Labor	16,000.00	÷	4,600	=	3.48
Manufacturing overhead	7,800.00	÷	4,600	=	1.70
Total current department costs	$28,800.00				$ 6.20
Cumulative cost total	$80,750.00				$ 16.59
(d) Costs accounted for					
Transferred out to finished goods	$69,678.00	=	4,200	×	$ 16.59
Work in process—ending					
Costs in prior department	8,312.00	=	800	×	10.39
Cost in current department					
Materials	734.40	=	720	×	1.02
Labor	1,392.00	=	400	×	3.48
Manufacturing overhead	680.00	=	400	×	1.70
Rounding adjustment	−46.40				
Total work in process	$11,072.00				
Total costs accounted for	$80,750.00				

*Equivalent Production Units or Equivalent Units of Production

Charging Costs to Work in Process Departmental *Work in Process* accounts are debited for direct materials issued to production as follows.

	2010						
2	May	31	Work in Process—Assembly Department	24 000 00			2
3			Work in Process—Finishing Department	5 000 00			3
4			Raw Materials Inventory		29 000 00		4
5			Allocation of materials to production				5

Departmental *Work in Process* accounts are debited for direct labor; various liability accounts are credited.

	2010						1
2	May	31	Work in Process—Assembly Department	25 000 00			2
3			Work in Process—Finishing Department	16 000 00			3
4			Social Security Tax Payable		2 542 00		4
5			Medicare Tax Payable		594 50		5
6			Employee Income Tax Payable		6 150 00		6
7			Salaries and Wages Payable		31 713 50		7
8			Salaries and wages for May				8

When manufacturing overhead costs are incurred, they are debited to the *Manufacturing Overhead* control account. At the same time, they are entered in manufacturing overhead subsidiary ledger sheets for each department. At the end of the month, the overhead costs of all service departments are allocated to the producing departments. After this allocation, the total of the overhead ledger sheets for the departments equal the total manufacturing overhead costs incurred during the month. This total also equals the balance in the *Manufacturing Overhead* control account. The *Manufacturing Overhead* control account is closed into the departmental *Work in Process* accounts.

Manufacturing overhead for May was $20,200—$12,400 for the assembly department and $7,800 for the finishing department. The following entry charges the overhead to production.

	2010						1
2	May	31	Work in Process—Assembly Department	12 400 00			2
3			Work in Process—Finishing Department	7 800 00			3
4			Manufacturing Overhead		20 200 00		4
5			Charge overhead to work in process				5

Recording Transfers of Products out of Departments The cost of production reports show the cost of goods transferred from the assembly department to the finishing department and to finished goods inventory, Table 28.4, and from the finishing department to finished goods inventory, Table 28.5. Based on these reports, a journal entry is made to transfer the costs.

	2010						1
2	May	31	Work in Process—Finishing Department	51 950 00			2
3			Finished Goods Inventory	5 195 00			3
4			Work in Process—Assembly Department		57 145 00		4
5			Cost of goods transferred out of				5
6			assembly department in May				6
7							7
8		31	Finished Goods Inventory	69 678 00			8
9			Work in Process—Finishing Department		69 678 00		9
10			Cost of goods completed in May				10

After the above entries are posted, the departmental *Work in Process* accounts appear as follows. Note that ending balances agree with the amounts shown on the departmental cost of production reports.

ACCOUNT Work in Process—Assembly Department   ACCOUNT NO. _122_

DATE		DESCRIPTION	POST. REF.	DEBIT	CREDIT	BALANCE DEBIT	BALANCE CREDIT
2010							
May	31	Materials	J1	24 000 00		24 000 00	
	31	Labor	J1	25 000 00		49 000 00	
	31	Overhead	J1	12 400 00		61 400 00	
	31	Transferred Out	J1		57 145 00	4 255 00	

ACCOUNT Work in Process—Finishing Department   ACCOUNT NO. _123_

DATE		DESCRIPTION	POST. REF.	DEBIT	CREDIT	BALANCE DEBIT	BALANCE CREDIT
2010							
May	31	Materials	J1	5 000 00		5 000 00	
	31	Labor	J1	16 000 00		21 000 00	
	31	Overhead	J1	7 800 00		28 800 00	
	31	Prior Dept.	J1	51 950 00		80 750 00	
	31	Transferred Out	J1		69 678 00	11 072 00	

> H-B Instrument Company has embraced a total quality management (TQM) philosophy, applicable from raw materials to customer service. Production is completely automated for statistical process control and accounting is fully integrated into an ISO 9001 system.

Recording Sale of Finished Goods The final step is to record the sale of finished goods. Assume that May sales were $125,000 and the cost of the goods sold was $66,360. Note that it takes two journal entries, one to record the sales and another to record the cost of goods sold.

				DEBIT	CREDIT	
1	2010					1
2	May	31	Accounts Receivable	125 000 00		2
3			Sales		125 000 00	3
4			Record sales on credit for May			4
5						5
6		31	Cost of Goods Sold	66 360 00		6
7			Finished Goods		66 360 00	7
8			Cost of goods sold in May			8

After the sales and cost of goods sold are posted, the *Finished Goods Inventory* and *Cost of Goods Sold* ledger accounts appear as follows.

ACCOUNT _Finished Goods Inventory_   ACCOUNT NO. _126_

DATE	DESCRIPTION	POST. REF.	DEBIT	CREDIT	BALANCE DEBIT	BALANCE CREDIT
2010						
May 31		J1	5 1 9 5 00		5 1 9 5 00	
31		J1	69 6 7 8 00		74 8 7 3 00	
31		J1		66 3 6 0 00	8 5 1 3 00	

ACCOUNT _Cost of Goods Sold_   ACCOUNT NO. _560_

DATE	DESCRIPTION	POST. REF.	DEBIT	CREDIT	BALANCE DEBIT	BALANCE CREDIT
2010						
May 31		J1	66 3 6 0 00		66 3 6 0 00	

Section 1   Self Review

QUESTIONS

1. What information appears in the Quantity Schedule section of the cost of production report?

2. What journal entry is made to record the transfer of goods from the final producing department to the finished goods inventory?

3. Some of the units processed in a department are sold without further processing. Others are transferred to a second department for further processing. How will this reflect on the cost of production report?

EXERCISES

4. Goods are transferred from the cleaning department to the mixing department. The costs transferred in April totaled $85,000. The journal entry to record the transfer is to

   a. debit *Work in Process—Mixing* for $85,000 and credit *Work in Process—Cleaning* for $85,000.

   b. debit *Work in Process—Cleaning* for $85,000 and credit *Work in Process—Mixing* for $85,000.

   c. debit *Cost of Goods Sold* for $85,000 and credit *Work in Process—Mixing* for $85,000.

   d. debit *Cost of Goods Sold* for $85,000 and credit *Work in Process—Cleaning* for $85,000.

5. Materials issued to production are recorded by

   a. debiting the departmental *Work in Process* account and crediting *Raw Materials Inventory.*

   b. debiting *Raw Materials Inventory* and crediting the departmental *Finished Goods* account.

   c. debiting *Raw Materials Inventory* and crediting the departmental *Work in Process* account.

   d. debiting the departmental *Finished Goods* account and crediting *Raw Materials Inventory.*

ANALYSIS

6. Compute the equivalent units of production for the finishing department assuming materials, labor, and manufacturing overhead are at the same stage of completion. The 300 units in ending work in process are 60 percent complete. There were 2,000 units transferred out.

(Answers to Section 1 Self Review are on page 983.)

SECTION OBJECTIVE		TERMS TO LEARN
>> 5. Compute equivalent production and prepare a cost of production report with a beginning work in process inventory.		average method of process costing
WHY IT'S IMPORTANT		
Inventories that are carried from one period to the next need to be included in cost of production computations.		

Work in Process Inventory

In May there was no beginning work in process for Nash Manufacturing Company.

The Beginning Work in Process Inventory

Table 28.6 on the next page shows the production and cost data for June. It includes beginning work in process by department and by cost element. Notice that manufacturing overhead in beginning work in process is adjusted for rounding. For the assembly department at the end of May, manufacturing overhead in ending work in process was $742.00, and the rounding adjustment was $18.50 (see Table 28.4). In June, the beginning work in process for manufacturing overhead was $760.50 ($742.00 + $18.50).

DETERMINING EQUIVALENT PRODUCTION

Table 28.7 on page 969 summarizes the equivalent units of production for June.

PREPARING THE COST OF PRODUCTION REPORT

Table 28.8 on page 970 shows the June cost of production report for both departments. Nash Manufacturing Company uses the **average method of process costing,** which combines the cost of beginning inventory for each cost element with the costs of the current period.

Quantity Schedule The Quantity Schedule section combines the beginning inventory of work in process plus the units started in production or received from the prior department during the period. The result is the total to be accounted for (a). These units are either transferred out or remain in process at the end of the period (b).

Cost Schedule In the Cost Schedule for the assembly department, there are costs for the beginning work in process (c), (d), and (e). To determine the unit costs, the accountant adds the beginning inventory and the current period costs (f), (g), and (h) and divides the result by the equivalent units.

	Materials	Labor	Overhead
Beginning	$ 2,000.00	$ 1,494.50	$ 760.50
Current	19,000.00	25,500.00	12,500.00
Total	$21,000.00	$26,994.50	$13,260.50
Equivalent units	6,500	6,320	6,320
Cost per unit	$ 3.23	$ 4.27	$ 2.10

>> **5. OBJECTIVE**

Compute equivalent production and prepare a cost of production report with a beginning work in process inventory.

LP28

TABLE 28.6

Departmental Production and Cost
Data for June 2010

	Assembly Department	Finishing Department
Costs		
Work in process—beginning		
Costs in prior department		$ 8,312.00
Costs in current department		
Materials	$ 2,000.00	734.40
Labor	1,494.50	1,392.00
Manufacturing overhead*	760.50	633.60
Costs transferred in from prior department		52,800.00
Current department costs		
Materials	19,000.00	7,900.00
Labor	25,500.00	17,000.00
Manufacturing overhead	12,500.00	8,600.00
Total costs	$61,255.00	$97,372.00
Quantities		
Work in process—beginning	500	800
Started in production	6,000	
Transferred in from prior department		5,500
Transferred out to next department	5,500	
Transferred out to finished goods	400	5,900
Work in process—ending	600	400
Stage of completion—Ending Work in Process		
Materials	100%	80%
Labor	70%	50%
Manufacturing overhead	70%	50%
*Rounding adjustment included in overhead.		

The total unit cost for the assembly department is $9.60.

The total cost transferred out is the quantity transferred to the finishing department (i) and to finished goods inventory (j) multiplied by the total unit cost. The ending work in process inventory (k) is the equivalent production units for each cost element multiplied by the unit cost. There is a rounding adjustment of $1.60.

Assembly Department—Ending Work in Process:

	Materials	Labor	Overhead
Equivalent units	600	420	420
Unit cost	× $3.23	× $4.27	× $2.10
Total	$1,938.00	$1,793.40	$882.00

For the finishing department, there are two costs from the prior department: the prior department costs ($8,312) and the cost transferred in ($52,800). The total cost ($61,112) is divided by the total units (6,300) to get an average unit cost of $9.70.

TABLE 28.7

Computation of Equivalent Units of Production for June 2010

Assembly Department

Materials

Units transferred out		
To next department	5,500	
To finished goods	400	5,900
Work in process—ending: 100% × 600 units		600
Equivalent units for materials		6,500

Labor and manufacturing overhead

Units transferred out		
To next department	5,500	
To finished goods	400	5,900
Work in process—ending: 70% × 600 units		420
Equivalent units for labor and overhead		6,320

Finishing Department

Prior department costs: 100% × 6,300 units		6,300

Materials

Units transferred out	5,900	
Work in process—80% × 400 units	320	
Equivalent units for materials		6,220

Labor and overhead

Units transferred out	5,900	
Work in process—50% × 400 units	200	
Equivalent units for labor and overhead		6,100

Department unit costs are computed in the same manner as they were for the assembly department.

	Materials	Labor	Overhead
Beginning	$ 734.40	$ 1,392.00	$ 633.60
Current	7,900.00	17,000.00	8,600.00
Total	$8,634.40	$18,392.00	$9,233.60
Equivalent units	6,220	6,100	6,100
Cost per unit	$ 1.39	$ 3.02	$ 1.51

The unit cost for the current department is $5.92. The total unit cost for the finishing department is $15.62. The total cost transferred out is the quantity transferred to finished goods (j) multiplied by the total unit cost. The ending work in process inventory (k) is the equivalent production units for units transferred in and for each cost element multiplied by the unit cost. There is a $16.80 rounding adjustment.

Finishing Department—Ending Work in Process:

	Transferred In	Materials	Labor	Overhead
Equivalent units	400	320	200	200
Unit cost	× $9.70	× $1.39	× $3.02	× $1.51
Total	$3,880.00	$444.80	$604.00	$302.00

TABLE 28.8   **Cost of Production Report, June 2010**

	Assembly Department		Finishing Department	
Quantity Schedule	**Units**			**Units**
(a) Quantity to be accounted for				
Work in process—beginning	500			800
Started in production	6,000			–0–
Transferred in from prior department	–0–			5,500
Total to be accounted for	6,500			6,300
(b) Quantity accounted for				
Transferred out to next department	5,500			
Transferred out to finished goods	400			5,900
Work in process—ending	600			400
Total accounted for	6,500			6,300
Cost Schedule	**Total Cost**	**Unit Cost**	**Total Cost**	**Unit Cost**
Costs to be accounted for				
Costs in prior department				
Work in process—beginning			$ 8,312.00	
Transfers in—current month			52,800.00	
Total prior department cost			$ 61,112.00	$ 9.70
Costs in current department				
Work in process—beginning				
(c) Materials	$ 2,000.00		$ 734.40	
(d) Labor	1,494.50		1,392.00	
(e) Manufacturing overhead*	760.50		633.60	
Current period costs				
(f) Materials	19,000.00	$3.23	7,900.00	$ 1.39
(g) Labor	25,500.00	4.27	17,000.00	3.02
(h) Manufacturing overhead	12,500.00	2.10	8,600.00	1.51
Total current department cost	$61,255.00	$9.60	$ 36,260.00	$ 5.92
Cumulative total cost	$61,255.00	$9.60	$ 97,372.00	$ 15.62
Costs accounted for				
(i) Transferred out to next department	$52,800.00	$9.60	–0–	
(j) Transferred out to finished goods	3,840.00	9.60	92,158.00	$ 15.62
Total costs transferred out	$56,640.00		$ 92,158.00	
(k) Work in process—ending				
Costs in prior department				
Transferred in			$ 3,880.00	9.70
Costs in current department				
Materials	$ 1,938.00	3.23	444.80	1.39
Labor	1,793.40	4.27	604.00	3.02
Manufacturing overhead	882.00	2.10	302.00	1.51
Rounding adjustment	1.60		(16.80)	
Total work in process	$ 4,615.00		$ 5,214.00	
Total costs accounted for	$61,255.00		$ 97,372.00	

*Rounding adjustment included in overhead.

RECORDING COST FLOWS

Entries to summarize the June costs and transfers, and the departmental *Work in Process* accounts after the entries are posted, appear as follows. The June beginning balances of the *Work in Process* accounts are the same as the ending balances for May. Balances in the accounts at the end of June correspond to the amounts on the June cost of production report. The two entries to record the sale of finished goods are not shown but would be recorded as described in Section 1 of this chapter.

1	2010					1
2	Jun.	30	Work in Process—Assembly Department	19 000 00		2
3			Work in Process—Finishing Department	7 900 00		3
4			Raw Materials Inventory		26 900 00	4
5			Charge materials to production			5
6						6
7		30	Work in Process—Assembly Department	25 500 00		7
8			Work in Process—Finishing Department	17 000 00		8
9			Social Security Tax Payable		2 635 00	9
10			Medicare Tax Payable		616 25	10
11			Employee Income Tax Payable		6 375 00	11
12			Salaries and Wages Payable		32 873 75	12
13			Salaries and wages for month			13
14						14
15		30	Work in Process—Assembly Department	12 500 00		15
16			Work in Process—Finishing Department	8 600 00		16
17			Manufacturing Overhead		21 100 00	17
18			Charge overhead to work in process			18
19						19
20		30	Work in Process—Finishing Department	52 800 00		20
21			Finished Goods Inventory	3 840 00		21
22			Work in Process—Assembly Department		56 640 00	22
23			Cost of goods transferred out of			23
24			assembly department in June			24
25						25
26		30	Finished Goods Inventory	92 158 00		26
27			Work in Process—Finishing Department		92 158 00	27
28			Cost of goods completed in June			28
29			and transferred out			29

ACCOUNT _Work in Process—Assembly Department_   ACCOUNT NO. __122__

DATE		DESCRIPTION	POST. REF.	DEBIT	CREDIT	BALANCE	
						DEBIT	CREDIT
2010							
Jun.	1	Balance				4 2 5 5 00	
	30	Materials	J1	19 0 0 0 00		23 2 5 5 00	
	30	Labor	J1	25 5 0 0 00		48 7 5 5 00	
	30	Overhead	J1	12 5 0 0 00		61 2 5 5 00	
	30	Trans. Out	J1		56 6 4 0 00	4 6 1 5 00	

ACCOUNT _Work in Process—Finishing Department_   ACCOUNT NO. __123__

DATE		DESCRIPTION	POST. REF.	DEBIT	CREDIT	BALANCE	
						DEBIT	CREDIT
2010							
Jun.	1	Balance				11 0 7 2 00	
	30	Materials	J1	7 9 0 0 00		18 9 7 2 00	
	30	Labor	J1	17 0 0 0 00		35 9 7 2 00	
	30	Overhead	J1	8 6 0 0 00		44 5 7 2 00	
	30	Prior Dept.	J1	52 8 0 0 00		97 3 7 2 00	
	30	Trans. Out	J1		92 1 5 8 00	5 2 1 4 00	

Section 2 Self Review

QUESTIONS

1. What is the difference between cost of production reports with and without beginning work in process inventory?

2. How is the unit cost of labor calculated when there is beginning work in process inventory?

3. In the cost of production report, how are the costs transferred in from a prior department handled?

EXERCISES

4. The source of the cost data in a cost of production report is

    a. job order costs sheets.

    b. _Work in Process_ accounts.

    c. _Raw Materials_ accounts.

    d. prior period income statement.

5. March sales are $100,000 and cost of goods sold is $60,000. What is the entry to _Finished Goods Inventory?_

    a. $60,000 debit

    b. $40,000 credit

    c. $40,000 debit

    d. $60,000 credit

ANALYSIS

6. Compute the unit cost for materials when beginning work in process is $965, current period costs are $12,835, and equivalent units for the department are 4,000.

(Answers to Section 2 Self Review are on page 983.)

REVIEW   Chapter Summary   Chapter 28

The process cost accounting system is commonly used when only one product is manufactured in a department and production is on a continuous basis rather than in batches or by specific job. In this chapter, you have reviewed the procedures for process cost accounting systems and how they differ from a job order cost accounting system.

Learning Objectives

1   **Compute equivalent units of production with no beginning work in process inventory.**

The equivalent production unit technique is used to convert ending work in process to equivalent finished production. Separate computations must be made for the three elements of production (materials, labor, and overhead) whenever the states of completion of the three elements in the work in process inventory are different.

2   **Prepare a cost of production report with no beginning work in process inventory.**

The cost of production report summarizes all costs charged to each department during the month and shows how these costs are assigned to the goods transferred out of the department and those still in process.

- The equivalent production unit technique is used to convert ending work in process to equivalent finished production.
- Then the costs for each equivalent unit of materials, labor, and overhead are computed.
- The value of goods transferred out of the department, as well as of work in process inventories, is determined on the basis of the equivalent units of production for each cost element.
- The costs of the goods transferred from one department to another are charged to the receiving department and removed from the *Work in Process* account of the first department.

3   **Compute the unit cost of manufacturing under the process cost accounting system.**

The unit cost to manufacture a product is computed by dividing the total cost of each production element by the appropriate equivalent production units.

4   **Record costs incurred and the flow of costs as products move through the manufacturing process and are sold.**

- A work in process inventory account is set up for each producing department.
- Direct materials costs and direct labor costs are charged to the departmental *Work in Process* accounts.
- Overhead costs incurred are charged to the *Manufacturing Overhead* control account.
- Each producing and service department has a cost sheet in the subsidiary ledger.
- At the end of each month, the costs of the service departments are allocated to the producing departments.

5   **Compute equivalent production and prepare a cost of production report with a beginning work in process inventory.**

If there is a beginning work in process inventory, the same basic process cost accounting procedures are followed to prepare a cost of production report.

- Under the average cost system, the cost of each element in the beginning work in process is added to the cost of that element during the month.
- Equivalent units of production are computed for each element just as when there was no beginning inventory of work in process.
- The total cost of an element divided by the equivalent units of production for the element yields the unit cost for the element.
- Cost of product transferred out of the department and cost of ending work in process are then computed in the usual manner.

6   **Define the accounting terms new to this chapter.**

Glossary

Average method of process costing (p. 967) A method of costing that combines the cost of beginning inventory for each cost element with the costs during the current period

Cost of production report (p. 961) Summarizes all costs charged to each department and shows the costs assigned to the goods transferred out of the department and to the goods still in process

Equivalent production (p. 960) The estimated number of units that could have been started and completed with the same effort and costs incurred in the department during the same time period

Process cost accounting system (p. 958) A method of accounting in which costs are accumulated for each process or department and then transferred on to the next process or department

Comprehensive **Self Review**

1. Why can a process cost accounting system be referred to as an average cost system?
2. What is the source of the information in the Costs to Be Accounted For section of a cost of production report?
3. A company uses the process cost accounting system. It has two service departments. How will the costs of the service departments enter into the cost of an equivalent unit for the producing departments?
4. What is the purpose of the cost of production report?
5. Explain the flow of costs in the accounting records.

(Answers to Comprehensive Self Review are on page 983.)

 Multiple choice questions are provided on the text Web site at www.mhhe.com/price12e

Quiz28

Discussion Questions

1. Why are job order cost sheets not used in the process cost accounting system?
2. What are equivalent units of production?
3. In a cost of production report, what items are found in the Costs to Be Accounted For section?
4. How is the ending work in process inventory computed in a process cost accounting system?
5. Will the same equivalent units always be used for materials, labor, and overhead? Explain.
6. Will the amount shown as a department's ending inventory of work in process on the cost of production report agree with the work in process for the department in the general ledger after adjusting and closing entries have been posted? Explain.
7. Why is it not necessary to use an overhead application rate when the process cost accounting system is employed?
8. Why might the process cost accounting system be unsatisfactory when several different products are being manufactured in the same department?
9. How does accounting for the raw materials inventory and the finished goods inventory differ under the process cost accounting system and the job order cost accounting system?
10. Explain what is meant by "the average method" of accounting for beginning work in process inventories in a process cost system.
11. Explain how to compute the equivalent production for labor when there is a beginning work in process inventory for the period, assuming that the average cost method is used.

APPLICATIONS

Exercises

Data for Exercises 28.1 through 28.3.
Information about production in the fabricating department of the P&P Company for August 2010 follows:

Beginning inventory	–0–
Transferred in from prior department	12,000 units
Transferred out to next department	9,000 units
Ending inventory, work in process	3,000 units

Stage of completion of ending work in process

Prior department costs	100%
Materials	90%
Labor and overhead	60%

Computing equivalent production for prior department costs with no beginning inventory.

Compute the equivalent units of production for the prior department costs for the month of August for P&P Company.

◄ Exercise 28.1
Objective 1

Computing equivalent production for materials with no beginning inventory.

Compute the equivalent units of production for materials for the month of August for P&P Company.

◄ Exercise 28.2
Objective 1

Computing equivalent production for labor and overhead with no beginning inventory.

Compute the equivalent units of production for labor and overhead for the month of August for P&P Company.

◄ Exercise 28.3
Objective 1

Computing equivalent production for materials and unit cost of materials with no beginning work in process.

On May 1, 2010, the assembly department of AMY Corporation had no beginning work in process. During the month, production was started on 5,000 units. The total cost of materials was $25,500. All materials were placed in production at the start of the manufacturing process in the department. During the month, 4,800 units were transferred to the next department, and 200 units were still in process at the end of the month.

1. What is the cost per equivalent unit for materials?
2. What is the cost of materials in the goods transferred to the next department?
3. What is the cost of materials in the ending work in process inventory?

◄ Exercise 28.4
Objectives 1, 3

Data for Exercises 28.5 and 28.6.
The cutting department is the first department of the Sneaker Manufacturing Company. On March 1, 2010, the beginning inventory in this department consisted of 600 units. Costs for the beginning work in process were as follows:

Materials (100% complete)	$6,000
Labor (70% complete)	4,000
Overhead (70% complete)	3,000

During March 2010, 2,400 units were started into production with the following costs:

Materials	$25,900
Labor	16,000
Overhead	15,000

The number of units completed and sent to the finishing department was 2,500. The ending inventory of 500 units were 100 percent complete in regard to materials, 80 percent complete with regard to labor and overhead.

Computing equivalent production for materials and cost per equivalent unit with beginning work in process.

1. Compute the March equivalent production for materials for Sneaker Manufacturing Company.
2. Compute the cost per equivalent unit for materials for March.
3. Compute the cost of materials in the work transferred out of the department during the month.
4. Compute the month-end cost of materials in the ending work in process.

◄ Exercise 28.5
Objectives 3, 5

Exercise 28.6 ▶ **Computing equivalent production for overhead and cost per equivalent unit with beginning work in process.**

Objectives 3, 5

1. Compute the equivalent production for overhead for March.
2. Compute the cost per equivalent unit for overhead for March.
3. Compute the cost of overhead in the goods transferred out.
4. Compute the cost of overhead in the ending work in process inventory.

Data for Exercises 28.7 through 28.9.

At Lookout Corporation, production is started in the fab department. The work is then transferred to the finishing department where goods are completed and then transferred to the finished goods storeroom. Data about the company's costs during September 2010 follows.

Material costs placed into production	
Fab department	$41,000.00
Finishing department	6,000.00
Direct labor costs	
Fab department	18,000.00
Finishing department	10,800.00
Taxes withheld from employees' earnings	
Social security tax withheld	1,785.60
Medicare tax withheld	417.60
Federal income tax withheld	4,320.00
Overhead costs	
Fab department	12,000.00
Finishing department	14,500.00

During the month, products costing $59,000 were transferred from the fab department to the finishing department; goods costing $75,000 were transferred from the finishing department to finished goods inventory; and goods that cost $60,000 were sold on account for $100,000.

Exercise 28.7 ▶ **Recording costs incurred in production.**

Objective 4

Give the journal entries on September 30 to summarize the following.

1. Materials placed into production
2. Labor costs charged into production
3. Overhead costs charged into production

Exercise 28.8 ▶ **Recording transfer of product between departments and from work in process to finished goods.**

Objective 4

Give the general journal entries on September 30 to record the following.

1. Transfer of product from the fab department to the finishing department
2. Transfer of finished goods from the finishing department to finished goods inventory

Exercise 28.9 ▶ **Recording cost of goods completed.**

Objective 4

Give general journal entries to record the following events during September.

1. Sale of goods
2. Cost of goods sold

PROBLEMS

Problem Set A HM™

Computing equivalent production with no beginning work in process.

◀ Problem 28.1A
eXcel Objective 1

Green Products, Inc., manufactures a single type of garden cart. The monthly production report for December 2010 follows.

Green Products, Inc. Monthly Production Report for December 2010			
	Molding Department	**Assembly Department**	**Completion Department**
Quantities			
Started in production—current month	2,200	–0–	–0–
Transferred in from prior department	–0–	1,900	1,700
Transferred out to next department	1,900	1,700	–0–
Transferred out to finished goods	–0–	–0–	1,400
Work in process—ending	300	200	300
Stage of Completion— Ending Work in Process			
Materials	100%	100%	90%
Labor	90	70	90
Overhead	90	70	90

INSTRUCTIONS

Prepare the equivalent production computations for each department.

Analyze: Which department's ending work in process inventory is at the lowest stage of completion in regard to labor and overhead in the month of December?

Computing equivalent production, preparing a cost of production report, computing unit costs, and recording flow of cost through manufacturing process and sale.

◀ Problem 28.2A
Objectives 1, 2, 3, 4
eXcel

Rahc Games Inc. has two producing departments—fabricating and assembly. The following data is from the firm's records for the month of June 2010. There were no beginning inventories.

INSTRUCTIONS

1. In general journal form, record the flow of costs that follow. Date all entries June 30, 2010.
   a. The issuance of materials to each department
   b. The monthly payroll withholdings for the producing departments: social security, $3,086.11; Medicare, $721.75; federal income tax, $7,500
   c. The distribution of manufacturing overhead to each department

	Fabricating Department	Assembly Department
Costs		
Materials	$ 45,000.00	$ 7,380.00
Labor	34,986.00	14,790.00
Manufacturing overhead	16,513.00	7,830.00
Total costs	$ 96,499.00	$30,000.00
Quantities		
Started in production	5,000	–0–
Transferred in from prior department	–0–	4,500
Transferred out to next department	4,500	–0–
Transferred out to finished goods	–0–	4,200
Work in process—ending	500	300
Stage of Completion—Ending Work in Process		
Materials	100%	100%
Labor	80	50
Manufacturing overhead	80	50

2. Prepare equivalent production computations for each department.

3. Prepare a cost of production report for each department.

4. Record the following in general journal form.

    a. The transfer of goods from the fabricating department to the assembly department

    b. The transfer of completed goods from the assembly department to the finished goods storeroom

    c. Sales on credit for $150,000; these goods cost $76,500 to manufacture

Analyze: What was the balance of the *Work in Process* account for the fabricating department on June 30?

Problem 28.3A ▶ **Computing equivalent production and preparing a cost of production report with a beginning work in process.**

Objective 5

Jasper Corporation adds all materials at the beginning of production. On August 1, 2010, 1,000 gallons of its product were in production in the first department. During the month of August, 11,000 gallons were put into production. On August 31, 1,500 gallons were still in production. The ending inventory is estimated to be 50 percent complete as to labor and overhead. Cost data for the month follows.

	Materials	Labor	Overhead
Beginning inventory of work in process	$ 7,960	$ 5,300	$ 2,750
Added during August	$35,000	14,950	8,500

INSTRUCTIONS

Prepare a cost of production report for the month of August, assuming that the average cost method is used.

Analyze: How many gallons of product will be held as beginning inventory of work in process on September 1 for the first department? What is the total cost for this quantity of product?

Problem Set B

Computing equivalent production with no beginning work in process.

◀ **Problem 28.1B**
Objective 1

The Hat Company manufactures plastic safety hats. The monthly production report for March 2010 follows.

The Hat Company Monthly Production Report for March 2010			
	Molding Department	Assembly Department	Finishing Department
Quantities			
Started in production—current month	4,000	–0–	–0–
Transferred in from prior department	–0–	3,700	3,500
Transferred out to next department	3,700	3,500	–0–
Transferred out to finished goods	–0–	–0–	3,300
Work in process—ending	300	200	200
Stage of Completion— Ending Work in Process			
Materials	100%	100%	100%
Labor	90	80	50
Overhead	90	80	50

INSTRUCTIONS

Prepare the equivalent production computations for each department.

Analyze: What portion of materials was added in March in the assembly department's ending work in process inventory?

Computing equivalent production, preparing a cost of production report, computing unit costs, and recording flow of costs through manufacturing process and sale.

◀ **Problem 28.2B**
Objectives 1, 2, 3, 4

Box Makers Inc. has two producing departments—fabricating and assembly. The data at the top of page 980 is from the firm's records for the month of May 2010. There were no beginning inventories.

INSTRUCTIONS

1. In general journal form, record the flow of costs that follow. Date all entries May 31, 2010.
   a. The issuance of materials to each department
   b. The producing department's monthly payroll taxes withheld: social security, $3,077.68; Medicare, $719.78; federal income tax, $7,500.00
   c. The distribution of manufacturing overhead to each department
2. Prepare equivalent production computations for each department.
3. Prepare a cost of production report for each department.
4. Record the following in general journal form.
   a. The transfer of goods from fabricating to assembly
   b. The transfer of completed goods from the assembly department to the finished goods storeroom
   c. Sales on credit for $230,000; cost of goods sold, $115,000

Analyze: What is the balance of the *Work in Process* account for the fabricating department on May 31?

	Fabricating Department	Assembly Department
Costs		
Materials	$ 51,920.00	$ 7,980.00
Labor	34,880.00	14,760.00
Manufacturing overhead	17,222.00	10,455.00
Total costs	$104,022.00	$ 33,195.00
Quantities		
Started in production	22,000	0
Transferred in from prior department	0	21,000
Transferred out to next department	21,000	0
Transferred out to finished goods		20,000
Work in process—ending	1,000	1,000
Stage of completion—Ending Work in Process		
Materials	100%	100%
Labor	80%	50%
Manufacturing overhead	80%	50%

Problem 28.3B ▶
Objective 5

Computing equivalent production and preparing a cost of production report when there is beginning work in process.

NC Chemical Company manufactures a pharmaceutical chemical. All materials are put into process at the beginning of production. On April 1, 2010, 2,000 pounds of the product were in process in the first department. During the month of April, 48,000 pounds were put into production. On April 30, 3,000 pounds were still in production. The ending inventory is estimated to be complete as to materials and 60 percent complete as to labor and overhead. Cost data for the month is as follows.

	Materials	Labor	Overhead
Beginning inventory of work in process	$ 6,500	$ 5,300	$ 2,580
Added during April	45,000	23,980	14,500

INSTRUCTIONS

Compute equivalent production, and prepare a cost of production report for the month of April, assuming that the average cost method is used.

Analyze: What total production cost is attributable to products transferred from the first department to the next department?

Critical Thinking Problem 28.1

Tebow Manufacturing, Inc.

Selected data about the operations of the mixing department, the first department of Tebow Manufacturing, Inc., for July 2010 follows.

At the beginning of the month, there were 1,000 units in process with total costs of $16,400. Included in the total was $6,460 of material costs. The labor and overhead costs in the beginning work in process were equal.

During the month, 45,000 units were transferred to the next department at a per unit cost of $5.01. Included in this amount was a per unit cost of $2.22 for labor. The overhead per unit cost was 50 percent of the labor per unit cost. Materials added to production this month were $72,500.

At the end of the month, the 2,000 units in process were 100 percent complete with material costs and 50 percent complete with labor and overhead costs.

INSTRUCTIONS

1. Compute the equivalent units of production for the month.
2. Prepare a cost of production report for the department for the month.

Analyze: What percentage of total current department costs is attributable to materials costs in the mixing department?

Critical Thinking Problem 28.2

Cost Flows

The Sweet Company makes candy. The continuous production operation starts in the mixing department where the chocolate, sugar, water, and other ingredients are blended. It then moves to the second department (cooking) where the ingredient mix is heated and poured into molds. Finally, in the last department (cooling and packaging), the product is packed 24 boxes to a container. The containers are sealed, ready for shipping to supermarkets around the country. Prepare a diagram to show the flow of costs through The Sweet Company's perpetual inventory accounts. Indicate with arrows the direction of the cost flow through the accounts.

BUSINESS CONNECTIONS

Accurate Cost Accounting

1. The directors of the firm where you work have asked you to explain whether the job order cost accounting system or the process cost accounting system provides the more accurate costs for each unit of product. What will you tell them?
2. What are the benefits of perpetual inventories to management?
3. How would managers use the cost of labor for each equivalent unit to help control costs?
4. Why would a comparison of the cost per equivalent unit of each cost element (materials, labor, and overhead) for the current month with that of the preceding month be useful to management?
5. A manager in the company where you work asks why it is necessary to convert production to equivalent units when determining the cost of each unit of product produced under the process cost accounting system. Explain.

Percentage Complete

The percentage complete for the beginning and ending inventory is an important figure to determine the cost of the work in process inventory and the finished goods inventory. If the ending finished goods inventory is overstated so is the net income. Virginia works for The Paint Palace. She knew that the beginning inventory is last month's ending inventory. She has decided to help the business by overstating the ending inventory percentage complete. Has Virginia violated any ethical area of accounting?

Accounting Processes

Refer to the *2006 Annual Report* for The Home Depot, Inc., in Appendix A.

1. The Home Depot, Inc., purchases wood products such as plywood, pressed wallboard, and solid wood doors for resale in its stores. Do you think manufacturers of wood products use process or job order costing systems? Explain your answer.
2. Locate the section "Management's Discussion and Analysis of Financial Condition and Results of Operations," *Results of Operations,* Fiscal 2006 Compared to Fiscal 2005. Read the discussion under Net Sales. What was the primary factor that caused a decrease in retail comparable store sales for fiscal 2006?

Manufacturing Operations and the Environment

The following excerpts were taken from the *Kodak 2005 Health, Safety, Environment and Responsible Growth Annual Report*. In just three years, Kodak significantly surpassed a goal for a 50 percent reduction in safety incidents in five years. The reduction reached 67 percent in 2005.

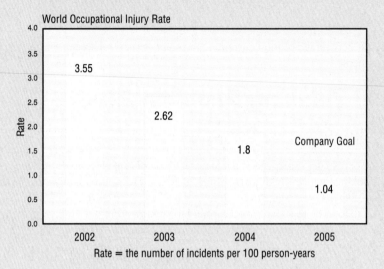

World Occupational Injury Rate

Rate = the number of incidents per 100 person-years

Analyze:

1. By what percentage has the worldwide occupational injury rate declined from 2002 to 2005?
2. Reducing safety incidents impacts manufacturing costs for a business such as Kodak. Describe how you think a goal such as reducing safety incidents might impact total manufacturing costs.

Analyze Online: Locate Kodak's current year *Health, Safety, and Environment Annual Report* on the company's Web site (www.kodak.com).

3. What amount of savings has Kodak realized annually as a result of its improved safety record?
4. What results were realized in the company's film safety program over the past five years?

Manufacturing Standards

Extending THE THOUGHT

Corporations that compete in manufacturing environments are often faced with balancing the need to manufacture products quickly with the desire to produce quality goods. If manufacturing managers are held accountable for manufacturing costs, inventory levels, and labor variances, what types of quality standards should also be considered?

Sharing Financial Data

Business COMMUNICATION

Assume that you are the purchasing officer for Blazing Trails, Inc., a manufacturer of mountain bikes. You are responsible for buying all materials such as bike frames, gear systems, seats, and pedals that are used in the assembly of mountain bikes. In the past, you have not been given the cost of production reports generated by the accounting department. You would like to be included on the distribution list for these monthly reports. In a memo to the accounting manager, Stan Foreman, explain why you would like to receive these reports and why you think this information will benefit you in your job.

Process or Job Costing

TEAMWORK

The manufacturing of concrete includes three processes: (1) crushing the gravel with water, (2) burning the wet gravel in a rotary kiln, and (3) grinding the mix while adding gypsum. Discuss why the process costing approach would be the best approach. Could the job cost approach be used?

Inventory Associations

Internet CONNECTION

The Internet has a great deal of help with inventory for businesses. Enter as a search phrase "inventory management." List the various organizations that can provide assistance for a business.

Answers to **Self Reviews**

Answers to Section 1 Self Review

1. The first part shows the units to be accounted for. The second part shows what happened to the units.

2. Debit **Finished Goods Inventory** and credit the **Work in Process** account of the final department.

3. The Costs Accounted For section of the cost of production report will require two lines for products transferred out of the department. One line will be Transferred Out to Next Department and the second will be Transferred Out to Finished Goods. The total of the two amounts would equal Total Costs Transferred Out.

4. **a.** debit **Work in Process—Mixing** for $85,000 and credit **Work in Process—Cleaning** for $85,000.

5. **a.** debiting the departmental **Work in Process** account and crediting **Raw Materials Inventory.**

6. 2,180 (2,000 + (300 × 0.60))

Answers to Section 2 Self Review

1. When there is a beginning work in process inventory, both the quantities and the costs for the inventory must be accounted for. The costs per equivalent unit must consider the beginning inventory of each element as well as the costs added during the current period.

2. The amount of labor cost in the beginning work in process inventory must be added to the labor costs incurred during the current period. The total is divided by the equivalent units of production to arrive at the labor cost per unit.

3. They must be treated as a "cost to be accounted for" in the department to which the product is transferred.

4. **b. Work in Process** accounts.

5. **d.** $60,000 credit (The debit is to **Cost of Goods Sold** for $60,000.)

6. $3.45

Answers to Comprehensive Self Review

1. All costs for each manufacturing element (materials, labor, and overhead) incurred during the month are added together and divided by the equivalent units of production for that element during the month. Costs incurred for each element are, in a sense, averaged.

2. The current month's costs to be accounted for in the cost of production report are taken from the departmental **Work in Process** accounts. The details of beginning inventory of work in process can be determined from the cost of production report of the prior month.

3. At the end of the month, the costs of service departments are allocated to the overhead of the producing departments.

4. It summarizes all costs charged to each department during the month and shows how these costs are assigned to the goods transferred out of the department and those still in process.

5. Direct costs are charged to the departmental **Work in Process** accounts. Overhead costs are charged to the **Manufacturing Overhead** control account, and then allocated to departmental overhead sheets for each department. At the end of the month, the costs of the service departments are allocated to the producing department. Finally, the **Manufacturing Overhead** control account is closed into the departmental **Work in Process** accounts.

Controlling Manufacturing Costs: Standard Costs

LEARNING OBJECTIVES

1. Explain how fixed, variable, and semivariable costs change as the level of manufacturing activity changes.   LP29

2. Use the high-low point method to determine the fixed and variable components of a semi-variable cost.

3. Prepare a fixed budget for manufacturing costs.

4. Develop a flexible budget for manufacturing costs.

5. Develop standard costs per unit of product.

6. Compute the standard costs of products manufactured during the period and determine cost variances between actual costs and standard costs.

7. Compute the amounts and analyze the nature of variances from standard for raw materials, labor, and manufacturing overhead.

8. Define the accounting terms new to this chapter.

NEW TERMS

budget
budget performance report
cost variance
fixed budget
fixed costs
flexible budget
high-low point method
labor efficiency variance
labor rate variance
labor time variance

manufacturing cost budget
materials price variance
materials quantity variance
materials usage variance
relevant range of activity
semivariable costs
standard cost card
variable costs
variance analysis

Harley-Davidson   www.harleydavidson.com | For the past 20 years, Harley-Davidson has consistently out-paced its record performance. Much of the company's success can be attributed to its commitment to operational excellence. The company has been able to narrow the gap between supply and demand, and through capacity expansion it has been able to improve product availability and reduce costs.

In the over 100 years since the original Harley-Davidson Motor company occupied a 10 × 50 shed in Milwaukee, the company expanded its operations considerably and currently operates three manufacturing plants employing 4,700 people. In 2006, Harley shipped its 5 millionth motorcycle and the company's net income passed the $1 billion dollar mark.

The Harley-Davidson Vehicle Operations in York, Pennsylvania, is the company's largest facility, employing half the company's production workers and covering 1.5 million square feet.

thinking critically

How do you think Harley-Davidson accountants budget for the changing levels of production at the three plants the company operates?

Section 1

SECTION OBJECTIVES

>> 1. **Explain how fixed, variable, and semivariable costs change as the level of manufacturing activity changes.**

WHY IT'S IMPORTANT

Planning for varying levels of activity helps managers anticipate costs.

>> 2. **Use the high-low point method to determine the fixed and variable components of a semivariable cost.**

WHY IT'S IMPORTANT

To measure efficiency it is necessary to separate costs into their components.

>> 3. **Prepare a fixed budget for manufacturing costs.**

WHY IT'S IMPORTANT

Accountants must estimate costs for an expected level of activity.

>> 4. **Develop a flexible budget for manufacturing costs.**

WHY IT'S IMPORTANT

Production levels can fluctuate.

TERMS TO LEARN

budget
budget performance report
fixed budget
fixed costs
flexible budget
high-low point method
manufacturing cost budget
relevant range of activity
semivariable costs
variable costs

Cost Behavior and the Budget

To control costs and make effective decisions, managers need information on the *variability of costs*—how costs change as the volume of output changes. In this chapter, you will learn how cost variability is measured. You will also learn how to use cost behavior to develop budgets and standard costs.

>>1. OBJECTIVE

Explain how fixed, variable, and semivariable costs change as the level of manufacturing activity changes.

LP29

Cost Behavior

Manufacturing costs can be classified as variable, fixed, and semivariable. It is essential to understand these terms in order to analyze costs.

VARIABLE COSTS

Variable costs are costs that vary *in total* in direct proportion to changes in the level of activity. Direct materials and direct labor are examples of variable costs. If direct materials cost $5 for one unit, then the materials cost for 1,000 units is $5,000 (1,000 × $5) and for 5,000 units is $25,000 (5,000 × $5). If direct labor cost is $5 per unit of product, the total labor cost for manufacturing 1,000 units is $5,000 (1,000 × $5) and for 4,000 units is $20,000 (4,000 units × $5).

Note that the term *variable* refers to the *total* cost. The cost *per unit* of material or labor does not change as output changes, but the total cost of material or labor changes.

FIXED COSTS

Fixed costs are costs that do not change *in total* as the level of activity changes. For example, the salary of the production vice president does not vary from month to month based on the number of units produced.

Note that although fixed costs do not change in total as the level of activity changes, the cost per unit does change. For example, if factory supervisory salaries are $10,000 for the month, the cost per unit is $5.00 if 2,000 units are produced ($10,000 ÷ 2,000) and $4.00 if 2,500 units are produced ($10,000 ÷ 2,500).

SEMIVARIABLE COSTS

Semivariable costs, also called *mixed costs,* are costs that vary with, but not in direct proportion to, the volume of activity. A semivariable cost contains a fixed element that does not change because of changes in the level of activity. It also contains a variable component that does vary with changes in activity.

Utilities are an example of a semivariable cost. Lighting, heating, and cooling are necessary to operate the factory regardless of how many units are produced. The fixed portion of these costs ensures basic service. However, the electricity used to operate machines will vary in proportion to the level of production.

To prepare budgets, measure efficiency, develop expected costs, and analyze the differences between actual costs and expected costs, it is necessary to separate semivariable costs into their fixed and variable components. The **high-low point method** is a simple method to determine the fixed and variable components of a semivariable cost.

Let's examine how Noah Production Company uses the high-low point method. Noah uses the job order cost system.

1. Determine the production and cost data for the months of highest and lowest production during the past year. The data for Noah Production Company follows. The month of July had the highest production level. January had the lowest production level.

Month	Direct Labor Hours	Utilities Cost
January	1,600	$1,900
February	2,160	2,360
March	2,600	2,750
April	2,800	3,000
May	2,950	3,050
June	2,700	3,000
July	3,200	3,500
August	2,040	2,240
September	2,120	2,320
October	2,200	2,400
November	2,060	2,260
December	1,750	1,950

2. Compute the difference in direct labor hours in the months of highest and lowest production. Also compute the difference in utilities costs.

Month	Direct Labor Hours	Utilities Cost
July	3,200	$3,500
January	1,600	1,900
Difference	1,600	$1,600

>>**2. OBJECTIVE**

Use the high-low point method to determine the fixed and variable components of a semivariable cost.

LP29

important!

Fixed Costs

As the volume of output increases, the fixed cost per unit of output decreases.

3. Compute the variable cost per direct labor hour by dividing the difference in utilities costs by the difference in direct labor hours. The variable cost per direct labor hour is $1 ($1,600 ÷ 1,600 hours).

4. Compute the fixed cost for a month by deducting the variable cost from the total cost for that month. The variable cost is the cost per direct labor hour, computed in step 3, multiplied by the number of hours of direct labor worked during the month selected. For example, using the month of July, the total variable costs are $3,200 (3,200 hours × $1 per hour).

Total cost	$3,500
Less variable costs	3,200
Fixed costs	$ 300

The major advantage of using the high-low point method is its simplicity. The results could be misleading, however, if the highest and lowest months are not representative of the other months. For this reason, some accountants also compute fixed costs using the second highest and second lowest months. They compare the results of the two calculations to ensure that they are consistent. If the results are not similar, the accountant might need to use other methods to separate fixed and variable costs; these methods are covered in cost accounting textbooks.

>>3. OBJECTIVE

Prepare a fixed budget for manufacturing costs.

LP29

Preparation of the Fixed Budget

A **budget** is an operating plan expressed in monetary units. Well-run companies prepare detailed budgets for each year and for each month within the year. The **manufacturing cost budget** is a budget for each manufacturing cost for the budget period.

The management of Noah Production Company plans to produce various products during August. The budgets for direct materials and direct labor are relatively easy to compute. The unit costs of materials and unit costs of labor are multiplied by the number of units to be produced.

For example, suppose that 500 toy cars are to be produced and each car requires $1.50 of direct materials. The budgeted direct material cost for toy cars is $750.00 (500 × $1.50).

Computations are also made for all other products to be manufactured. The expected materials costs for each product are added to arrive at the materials budget for the period. Similar computations are made for direct labor costs.

The budget for manufacturing overhead costs is more complex. It is necessary to identify the cost behavior of each manufacturing overhead item as fixed, variable, or semivariable. The accountant for Noah Production Company used the high-low point method to determine the cost behavior of each item as shown below.

	Fixed Costs per Month	Variable Costs per Direct Labor Hour
Supervision and clerical wages	$6,000	$ –0–
Other indirect labor		2.00
Payroll taxes and fringe benefits	600	1.50
Manufacturing supplies	200	0.50
Depreciation	1,500	
Utilities	300	1.00
Insurance and taxes	400	–0–
Total	$9,000	$5.00

Figure 29.1 shows the budget of manufacturing costs for Noah Production Company for August. It is called a **fixed budget** since it shows only one level of activity—1,000 direct labor hours. Management expects that $30,000 of direct materials will be used and that 1,000 direct labor hours will be worked at $15 per hour.

FIGURE 29.1

Fixed Budget of Manufacturing Costs

Noah Production Company
Budget of Manufacturing Costs
Month Ended August 31, 2010

Direct materials		30 000 00
Direct labor		15 000 00
Manufacturing overhead		
Supervision and clerical wages	6 000 00	
Other indirect labor (1,000 × $2)	2 000 00	
Payroll taxes and fringe benefits		
[$600 + (1,000 × $1.50)]	2 100 00	
Manufacturing supplies		
[$200 + (1,000 × $0.50)]	700 00	
Depreciation	1 500 00	
Utilities [$300 + (1,000 × $1.00)]	1 300 00	
Insurance and taxes	400 00	
Total manufacturing overhead		14 000 00
Total manufacturing cost		59 000 00

Fixed overhead costs include supervision and clerical wages, depreciation, and insurance and taxes. There is one budgeted variable overhead cost—other indirect labor. It is calculated by multiplying the budgeted direct labor hours by the variable cost per hour (1,000 hours × $2).

There are three semivariable overhead costs: payroll taxes and fringe benefits, manufacturing supplies, and utilities. The budgeted overhead for utilities includes $300 as a fixed cost and $1,000 as a variable cost. The budgeted variable cost for utilities is 1,000 direct labor hours multiplied by the variable cost per hour of $1.00 (1,000 × $1.00). The budgeted amounts for payroll taxes and fringe benefits and manufacturing supplies are calculated in a similar manner.

Budgets serve many purposes. One key purpose is to provide a basis for measuring performance. Management needs to know how well manufacturing costs are being controlled. As soon as actual manufacturing costs have been accumulated and reported for the month, the accountant prepares a **budget performance report,** which compares actual costs and budgeted costs. Figure 29.2 shows the budget performance report for Noah Production Company for August.

Noah Production Company
Budget of Manufacturing Costs
Month of August 2010

	Budget	Actual	(Over) Under
Direct materials	3 0 0 0 0	2 9 0 0 0	1 0 0 0
Direct labor	1 5 0 0 0	1 4 5 0 0	5 0 0
Manufacturing overhead			
Supervision and clerical wages	6 0 0 0	5 0 0 0	1 0 0 0
Other indirect labor	2 0 0 0	2 1 5 0	(1 5 0)
Payroll taxes and fringe benefits	2 1 0 0	2 2 0 0	(1 0 0)
Manufacturing supplies	7 0 0	3 5 0	3 5 0
Depreciation	1 5 0 0	1 6 0 0	(1 0 0)
Utilities	1 3 0 0	5 5 0	7 5 0
Insurance and taxes	4 0 0	5 0 0	(1 0 0)
Total manufacturing overhead	1 4 0 0 0	1 2 3 5 0	1 6 5 0
Total manufacturing cost	5 9 0 0 0	5 5 8 5 0	3 1 5 0

FIGURE 29.2   **Budget Performance Report**

The budget performance report shows that there are numerous differences between the budgeted amounts and the actual costs incurred. In some cases, actual costs exceeded the amounts budgeted, while in others the actual costs were less than budgeted costs. Management needs to determine why costs were over or under budget.

One of the first considerations is to determine how many hours were worked during the month. Was the actual number more or less than the hours budgeted? If the actual hours worked is close to the hours budgeted, then the fixed budget is a meaningful way to evaluate manufacturing performance. However, if the number of hours worked is materially more or less than the budgeted hours, the fixed budget is not the best tool to use to measure efficiency and cost control.

The fixed budget is based on 1,000 direct labor hours. Direct labor was budgeted at $15,000. Suppose that in August only 960 direct labor hours were worked. When management compares the actual labor costs of $14,500 to the budgeted labor costs of $15,000, the difference appears favorable. The company was under budget by $500. Actually, the difference is not favorable. Direct labor should have been $14,400 (960 hours × $15). At the level of 960 direct labor hours, the company spent $100 more than it should have ($14,500 − $14,400).

In order to provide management with a more useful tool for estimating and controlling manufacturing overhead costs, companies often prepare a budget that takes into account different levels of activity.

<table>
<tr><td>

>>4. OBJECTIVE

Develop a flexible budget for manufacturing costs.

LP29
</td><td>

Preparation of the Flexible Budget

A **flexible budget** shows the budgeted costs at various levels of activity. Flexible budgets are particularly useful when the level of activity fluctuates from month to month. The flexible budget usually shows fixed and variable costs separately. The different levels of activity are called the **relevant range of activity.** For example, separate budgets might be prepared for the expected activity level as well as levels of 90 percent, 95 percent, 105 percent, and 110 percent of the expected activity level.

Figure 29.3 shows the flexible budget for Noah Production Company for August. It has columns for the expected level of activity (1,000 direct labor hours), for 95 percent of expected activity (950 direct labor hours), and for 105 percent of expected activity (1,050 direct labor hours).
</td></tr>
</table>

Noah Production Company
Budget of Manufacturing Costs
Month of August 2010

	Activity Level		
Number of direct labor hours	950	1 000	1 050
Percent of expected activity	95	100	105
Variable costs			
Other indirect labor	1 900	2 000	2 100
Payroll taxes and fringe benefits	1 425	1 500	1 575
Manufacturing supplies	475	500	525
Utilities	950	1 000	1 050
Total variable costs	4 750	5 000	5 250
Fixed costs			
Supervision and clerical wages	6 000	6 000	6 000
Payroll taxes and fringe benefits	600	600	600
Manufacturing supplies	200	200	200
Depreciation	1 500	1 500	1 500
Utilities	300	300	300
Insurance and taxes	400	400	400
Total fixed costs	9 000	9 000	9 000
Total manufacturing overhead	13 750	14 000	14 250

FIGURE 29.3   **Flexible Budget of Manufacturing Costs**

FIGURE 29.4   **Budget Performance Report for August**

Noah Production Company
Manufacturing Overhead Budget Performance Report
Month Ended August 31, 2010

	Budget for 960 hours	Actual	(Over) Under
Supervision and clerical wages	6 0 0 0	6 1 0 0	(1 0 0)
Other indirect labor (960 × $2)	1 9 2 0	2 0 0 0	(8 0)
Payroll taxes and fringe benefits [$600 + (960 × $1.50)]	2 0 4 0	1 8 5 0	1 9 0
Manufacturing supplies [$200 + (960 × $0.50)]	6 8 0	6 0 0	8 0
Depreciation	1 5 0 0	1 4 5 0	5 0
Utilities [$300 + (960 × $1.00)]	1 2 6 0	1 1 0 0	1 6 0
Insurance and taxes	4 0 0	4 5 0	(5 0)
Total manufacturing overhead	1 3 8 0 0	1 3 5 5 0	2 5 0

A flexible budget prepared for several activity levels is helpful for planning purposes. In addition, it allows management to see whether manufacturing overhead costs are being controlled. For example, management can compare overhead expenses at an actual activity level of 960 hours with the flexible budget for 950 hours. This will provide a reasonable indication of how well costs are being controlled. For a more precise measure of efficiency and cost control, however, a flexible budget can be prepared for the actual activity level.

Figure 29.4 shows a flexible overhead budget for an actual activity of 960 hours in August. Note that the various actual costs are both over and under the budgeted costs, although no single amount is significant.

important!

Budget Performance Report
Efficiency and cost control can be evaluated by comparing actual overhead costs with the budget for the actual level of operations.

Section 1 Self Review

QUESTIONS

1. Why is it important to analyze semivariable costs to determine the fixed and variable components?

2. How does an increase in the level of activity affect (a) fixed costs per unit of activity, (b) total variable costs for the period, and (c) variable cost per unit?

3. What is a fixed budget?

EXERCISES

4. The salary of the factory supervisor is an example of a

a. mixed cost.
b. semivariable cost.
c. variable cost.
d. fixed cost.

5. A flexible budget contains
a. fixed costs only.
b. variable costs only.
c. semivariable costs only.
d. fixed, variable, and semivariable costs.

ANALYSIS

6. The budget performance report shows the following budgeted and actual amounts. What is the total actual amount over budget or under budget?

	Budget	Actual
Wages	$5,000	$5,500
Payroll taxes	500	400
Supplies	800	600
Repairs	200	500

(Answers to Section 1 Self Review are on page 1011.)

Section 2

Standard Costs as a Control Tool

Recall that standard costs reflect what costs *should be* per unit manufactured under normal, efficient operating conditions. If standard costs are used to measure the efficiency and effectiveness of operations, the standards should be achievable. If they are set artificially high and cannot be attained, workers might become discouraged and demoralized, and they could make little or no attempt to achieve the standards.

There are two ways to handle standard costs. Some companies actually enter standard costs in the accounts. This procedure is discussed in cost accounting textbooks. Other companies record actual costs in the accounting system but compare these actual costs with standards in order to measure efficiency and to control manufacturing costs. This is the method used by Noah Production Company.

Developing Standard Costs

Video29.1

To develop the standard cost of a specific unit of product, standards are set for each cost element, including materials, labor, and overhead.

DEVELOPING RAW MATERIALS STANDARDS

The *standard quantity* is the number of units of each type of raw material required to manufacture one unit of finished product. Engineers usually determine the standard quantity, although it is sometimes based on past experience in manufacturing the product. The *standard cost* is the cost of each unit of raw material required to make the product. The purchasing department determines standard cost. The *raw material standard* is the standard quantity of each raw material multiplied by its standard cost.

DEVELOPING DIRECT LABOR STANDARDS

The standard quantity is the number of hours of each type of labor needed to manufacture one unit of finished product. Industrial engineers usually determine the standard quantity by making time and motion studies. Sometimes the standard quantity is based on past experience in making the product. The standard cost is the cost of each type of labor used to make the product. The human resources department and union contracts provide wage rate information used in setting the standard cost. The *direct labor standard* is the standard quantity of each type of labor multiplied by its standard cost.

DEVELOPING MANUFACTURING OVERHEAD STANDARDS

The *standard overhead cost* per unit of product is usually based on the overhead application rate used to assign overhead costs to products. The overhead application rate can be based on direct labor cost, direct labor hours, or some other measure.

If the overhead application rate is based on direct labor hours, the standard overhead cost per unit is the standard labor *hours* for each finished unit multiplied by the overhead application rate. If the overhead application rate is based on direct labor costs, the standard overhead cost per unit is the standard labor *cost* for each finished unit multiplied by the overhead application rate.

Noah Production Company uses a job order cost accounting system. Prior to the start of each year, the accountant prepares a manufacturing overhead budget for the year. This year's budget is based on a projection that 20,000 direct labor hours will be worked during the year.

Budgeted manufacturing overhead	
Fixed manufacturing overhead	$ 108,000
Variable manufacturing overhead, 20,000 hours × $5.00 per hour	100,000
Total budgeted manufacturing overhead	$ 208,000

Noah's manufacturing overhead application rate is based on direct labor hours. Using the budgeted manufacturing costs of $208,000 and the expectation that 20,000 direct labor hours will be used, the overhead application rate is computed as $10.40 per direct labor hour.

$$\frac{\text{Estimated overhead costs}}{\text{Estimated direct labor hours}} = \frac{\$208,000}{20,000} = \$10.40 \text{ per hour}$$

Using Standard Costs

Most well-managed manufacturing companies use standard costs to evaluate efficiency.

PREPARING A STANDARD COST CARD

Standard costs are measured on a per-unit basis. A standard cost card helps facilitate the comparison of actual costs to standard costs. The **standard cost card** shows the per-unit standard costs for materials, labor, and overhead.

Figure 29.5 shows the standard cost card for product BA 25, a toy car. Each toy car requires $1.65 in direct materials and one-tenth hour of direct labor. Manufacturing overhead rate is applied at $1.04 per toy car (1/10 hour × $10.40).

COMPARING ACTUAL AND STANDARD COSTS

The following is from the job order cost sheet for Job Order A16, for the manufacture of 1,000 decorated cars.

Job A16
Product: Toy Car BA 25
Number of units manufactured: 1,000

>>5. OBJECTIVE
Develop standard costs per unit of product.

LP29

>>6. OBJECTIVE
Compute the standard costs of products manufactured during the period and determine cost variances between actual costs and standard costs.

Manufacturing costs:
  Materials:

Base material, 990 pounds @ $1.52 per pound	$1,504.80
Finishing material, 3,060 ounces @ $.045 per ounce	137.70
Total materials	$1,642.50
Direct labor: 110 hours @ $15.20 per hour	1,672.00
Manufacturing overhead: 110 hours @ $10.40 per hour	1,144.00
Total manufacturing costs	$4,458.50

Using the standard cost card and the job order cost sheet, the accountant can compare the actual costs to the standard costs for Job A16. The **cost variance** is the difference between the total standard cost and the total actual cost. The cost variance is $268.50; the actual cost is $268.50 more than the standard cost.

Standard cost of 1,000 units: 1,000 units × $4.19 per unit	$4,190.00
Manufacturing costs charged to job	4,458.50
Unfavorable variance	$ (268.50)

Since the actual cost is more than the standard cost of the job, the variance is unfavorable. When the actual cost is less than the standard cost, the variance is favorable.

FIGURE 29.5

Standard Cost Card

STANDARD COST CARD

Item: Toy Car—Product BA 25

<u>Materials</u>

Base material: 1 pound @ $1.50/lb.	$1.50
Finishing material: 3 ounces @ 0.05/oz.	0.15
Total materials	$1.65

<u>Labor</u>

1/10 hour @ $15/hour	$1.50

<u>Manufacturing Overhead</u>

1/10 hour @ $10.40/hr.	$1.04

<u>Total Standard Cost per Unit</u>	$4.19

>>7. OBJECTIVE

Compute the amounts and analyze the nature of variances from standard for raw materials, labor, and manufacturing overhead.

Video29.1

ANALYZING VARIANCES BETWEEN STANDARD AND ACTUAL COSTS

The total variance helps measure how well costs were controlled. It is also useful to compute the variances between actual and standard cost for each cost element—materials, labor, and overhead.

Analyzing Materials Variances The following is a summary of the materials costs for Job A16. The left side shows the standard costs and the right side shows the actual costs.

	Standard			Actual			Favorable (Unfavor.) Variance
	Quantity	Unit Cost	Total Cost	Quantity	Unit Cost	Total Cost	
Base material	1,000	$1.50	$1,500.00	990	$1.52	$1,504.80	$(4.80)
Finishing material	3,000	0.05	150.00	3,060	0.045	137.70	12.30
Totals			$1,650.00			$1,642.50	$ 7.50

Variance analysis explains the difference between standard cost and actual cost. The **materials quantity variance** (also called **materials usage variance**) is the cost of the actual quantity of raw materials used on a job minus the standard cost of the raw materials allowable for the units produced. The **materials price variance** is the actual cost of the raw materials used on a job minus the standard cost of the material used.

Determining Materials Quantity Variance The materials quantity variance is the difference between the actual quantity used and the standard quantity allowed multiplied by the standard cost of the material. The following are the quantity variances for the materials used on Job A16.

Base Material

Standard quantity (1,000 units × 1 lb./unit)	1,000 pounds
Actual quantity	990 pounds
Base material under standard	10 pounds
Times standard price per pound	$ 1.50
Favorable quantity variance	$15.00

Because the actual quantity of base material used was less than the standard quantity allowed for the job, the quantity variance for base material is favorable.

Finishing Material

Actual quantity	3,060 ounces
Standard quantity (1,000 units × 3 oz./unit)	3,000 ounces
Excess finishing material used	60 ounces
Times standard price per ounce	$ 0.05
Unfavorable quantity variance	$(3.00)

Because the actual quantity of finishing material exceeded the standard quantity allowed for the job, the quantity variance for finishing material is unfavorable.

The materials quantity variance measures how well the production manager and factory employees are controlling material waste. Unfavorable quantity variances often result because of defective materials or inexperienced workers.

Determining Materials Price Variance The materials price variance is the difference between the actual price and the standard cost multiplied by the actual quantity used. The following are the price variances for the materials used on Job A16.

Base Material

Actual price per pound	$ 1.52
Standard price per pound	1.50
Excess of actual over standard price	$ 0.02
Times actual number of pounds consumed	990
Unfavorable materials price variance	$(19.80)

Since the actual price for the base material was more than the standard price, the price variance for base materials is unfavorable.

Finishing Material

Actual price per ounce	$ 0.045
Standard price per ounce	0.050
Excess of standard over actual price	$ 0.005
Times actual number of ounces consumed	3,060
Favorable materials price variance	$ 15.30

Because the actual price of finishing material was *less than* the standard price, the price variance is *favorable*.

The purchasing department is usually responsible for the price variance. There is little that the manufacturing department can do to control the prices paid for raw materials.

Summary of Materials Variance Analysis The materials variances for Job A16 are summarized as follows.

	Favorable or (Unfavorable) Variance	
Base material		
Quantity variance	$ 15.00	
Price variance	(19.80)	$ (4.80)
Finishing material		
Quantity variance	$ (3.00)	
Price variance	15.30	12.30
Total material variance		$ 7.50

Analyzing Labor Variance   The total labor variance for Job A16 is $172.00 (unfavorable), calculated as follows.

Actual labor costs, 110 hours × $15.20 per hour	$1,672.00
Standard labor costs, 1,000 units × 1/10 hour per unit × $15 per hour	1,500.00
Unfavorable labor variance	$ (172.00)

The total labor variance is divided into the labor time (or efficiency) variance and the labor rate variance.

Determining Labor Time Variance The **labor time variance** (or **labor efficiency variance**) is the difference between the actual hours worked and the standard labor hours allowed for the job multiplied by the standard cost per hour.

Actual hours worked	110
Standard hours allowed (1,000 units × 1/10 hour per unit)	100
Excess of actual over standard hours	10
Times standard rate per hour	$ 15.00
Unfavorable labor time variance	$(150.00)

Because more hours were worked than the numbers of hours allowed by the standard, the labor time variance is unfavorable.

The production manager is usually responsible for the labor time variances. Part of the time variance might be attributed to the human resources department, which hires factory employees.

Determining Labor Rate Variance The **labor rate variance** is the difference between the actual labor rate per hour and the standard labor rate per hour multiplied by the actual number of hours worked on the job.

Actual rate per hour	$ 15.20
Standard rate per hour	15.00
Excess of actual over standard rate	$ 0.20
Times actual number of hours worked	110
Unfavorable labor rate variance	$(22.00)

MANAGERIAL IMPLICATIONS <<

COST BEHAVIOR

- Management needs to understand cost behavior in order to make decisions and to plan for the future.
- Budgets help in planning and controlling manufacturing costs. Fixed budgets are useful, but flexible budgets allow management to evaluate cost containment for the level of production activity.
- Standard costs reflect what costs should be when based on efficient, yet attainable, operating conditions.
- Management analyzes the difference between actual and standard costs to determine what factors caused the variances.
  - The materials price variance is the responsibility of the purchasing department.
  - The materials quantity variance is the responsibility of factory management.
  - The labor rate variance is the responsibility of the human resources department.
  - The labor time variance is the responsibility of factory management.

THINKING CRITICALLY
What can factory management do to minimize the labor time variance?

Usually the human resources department is responsible for the labor rate variance. However, operating decisions also affect the labor rate variance, including whether to work overtime at one and one-half the normal rate or how to assign workers to jobs. In addition, labor market conditions and wage scales set in union contracts may make it difficult to hire workers at the standard rates.

Summary of Direct Labor Variance Analysis   The total direct labor variance is summarized as follows.

Labor time variance, unfavorable	$(150.00)
Labor rate variance, unfavorable	(22.00)
Total labor variance, unfavorable	$(172.00)

Analyzing Manufacturing Overhead Variance Recall that under the cost system described for Noah Production Company, manufacturing overhead is applied to jobs on the basis of a predetermined manufacturing overhead rate. As illustrated in this chapter, manufacturing overhead is applied at $10.40 per direct labor hour (based on a standard of 20,000 direct labor hours for the year). This $10.40 rate includes $5.40 for fixed manufacturing overhead and $5.00 for variable manufacturing overhead.

The calculation of the manufacturing overhead variance is beyond the scope of this text and is included in most cost accounting courses. However, for illustrative purposes, a brief discussion and monthly summary of overhead variances follows.

In computing the variance analysis for manufacturing overhead, the accountant will calculate two primary variances: (1) flexible budget or controllable variance (difference between the actual overhead costs incurred and the flexible budgeted amount for overhead applied based on standard hours for units produced); and (2) production volume or uncontrollable variance (difference between the flexible budgeted amount for overhead applied based on standard hours for units produced and the total standard overhead costs). A cost accounting course will teach you how to calculate all the variances related to manufacturing overhead.

Analysis of Monthly Overhead Variances Because of the nature (fixed and variable components) of overhead, businesses are unable to determine the actual overhead costs related to individual jobs. Usually overhead is analyzed based on the total actual overhead and the total standard overhead for the products manufactured during a period of time.

ABOUT ACCOUNTING

Injuries
Musculoskeletal disorders such as carpal tunnel syndrome are common problems in the manufacturing industry. Companies that emphasize employee involvement, such as Honda, Timken, and Goodyear, tackle these problems through worker participation programs.

The following is a summary of the production and cost data in August for Noah Production Company. The company had a $104 unfavorable total overhead variance.

Total standard hours for goods manufactured	100
Total actual hours required for work completed	110
Manufacturing overhead applied to products	
100 hours × $10.40 per hour	$1,040
Actual manufacturing overhead costs incurred:	
Fixed costs (110 hours × $5.00)	$550
Variable costs (110 hours × $5.40)	594
Total	1,144
Total overhead variance, unfavorable	$ (104)

The variance is unfavorable because actual costs were greater than allowed costs for the quantity produced. A common cause for such a variance is a production level that is different from the level used to calculate the predetermined overhead application rate.

Section 2 Self Review

QUESTIONS

1. What information appears on the standard cost card?

2. How is the materials quantity variance computed?

3. How is the labor rate variance computed?

EXERCISES

4. Which variance is controllable by the production manager?

   a. materials price variance.

   b. labor rate variance.

   c. labor time variance.

   d. standard variance.

5. The price variance is the difference between the actual price and the standard price multiplied by

   a. actual quantity.

   b. standard quantity.

   c. difference between the actual quantity and the standard quantity.

   d. unused capacity.

ANALYSIS

6. Determine the total standard cost per unit from the following data. Budgeted production is 5,000 units. Standard materials are 5 yards at $6 per yard. Standard labor is two hours at $10 per hour. Manufacturing overhead is $100,000 based on production of 5,000 units of finished goods.

(Answers to Section 2 Self Review are on page 1011.)

REVIEW   Chapter Summary

To control costs and make effective business decisions, management also needs information based on the variability of manufacturing costs. In this chapter, you have learned how cost variability is measured and how budgets are developed and evaluated for manufacturing entities.

Learning Objectives

1 **Explain how fixed, variable, and semivariable costs change as the level of manufacturing activity changes.**

Accountants must understand cost variability—how costs behave as the volume of manufacturing activity increases or decreases.

- Total variable costs vary in direct proportion to activity level. The per-unit variable cost remains constant.

- Fixed costs remain relatively constant within the range of activity level at which the factory is likely to operate.

- Semivariable costs vary to some extent with changes in the volume of activity, but not in direct proportion. An element of these costs is fixed, while another element is variable.

2 **Use the high-low point method to determine the fixed and variable components of a semivariable cost.**

The high-low method compares the activity and the cost of the highest month of activity in a year with the activity and cost of the lowest month of activity. The difference in cost is divided by the difference in activity to measure the variable cost per unit of activity.

3 **Prepare a fixed budget for manufacturing costs.**

A budget is important for planning manufacturing activities and for controlling costs. A fixed budget shows the anticipated costs for a period—a month, a quarter, or a year—for one level of production.

- At the end of the period, actual results are compared with the budget and differences are noted and investigated.

- If the production volume is significantly different from the volume assumed in preparing the budget, the budgeted figures for variable and semivariable costs will not be meaningful.

4 **Develop a flexible budget for manufacturing costs.**

Flexible budgets show what the budgeted costs should be at several levels within the relevant range of activity. Actual results can then be compared with more meaningful budgeted amounts.

5 **Develop standard costs per unit of product.**

Standard costs help businesses control and evaluate manufacturing efficiency. Costs of efficient, yet attainable, levels of performance are set for each element of materials, labor, and overhead. A standard cost card for each product details cost.

6 **Compute the standard costs of products manufactured during the period and determine cost variances between actual costs and standard costs.**

The difference between the total standard cost and the total actual cost is called the cost variance. At the end of the period, actual costs related to the product are compared with the standard costs allowed for each unit. Variances between standard costs and actual costs are analyzed.

7 **Compute the amounts and analyze the nature of variances from standard for raw materials, labor, and manufacturing overhead.**

- The total variance between the actual cost and standard cost of material is separated into two components: a materials quantity variance and a materials price variance.

- Similarly, the total labor cost variance is separated into two components: a labor time variance and a labor rate variance.

- Manufacturing overhead variances cannot be easily computed on a per-job or per-unit basis, especially under the job order cost accounting system. Instead, manufacturing overhead is applied to jobs using a predetermined rate often based on direct labor hours.

8 **Define the accounting terms new to this chapter.**

Glossary

Budget (p. 988) An operating plan expressed in monetary units

Budget performance report (p. 989) A comparison of actual costs and budgeted costs

Cost variance (p. 994) The difference between the total standard cost and the total actual cost

Fixed budget (p. 988) A budget representing only one level of activity

Fixed costs (p. 986) Costs that do not change in total as the level of activity changes

Flexible budget (p. 990) A budget that shows the budgeted costs at various levels of activity

High-low point method (p. 987) A method to determine the fixed and variable components of a semivariable cost

Labor efficiency variance (p. 996) See Labor time variance

Labor rate variance (p. 996) The difference between the actual labor rate per hour and the standard labor rate per hour multiplied by the actual number of hours worked on the job

Labor time variance (p. 996) The difference between the actual hours worked and the standard labor hours allowed for the job multiplied by the standard cost per hour

Manufacturing cost budget (p. 988) A budget made for each manufacturing cost

Materials price variance (p. 995) The difference between the actual price and the standard cost for materials multiplied by the actual quantity of materials used

Materials quantity variance (p. 995) The difference between the actual quantity used and the quantity of materials allowed multiplied by the standard cost of the materials

Materials usage variance (p. 995) See Materials quantity variance

Relevant range of activity (p. 990) The different levels of activity at which a factory is expected to operate

Semivariable costs (p. 987) Costs that vary with, but not in direct proportion to, the volume of activity

Standard cost card (p. 993) A form that shows the per unit standard costs for materials, labor, and overhead

Variable costs (p. 986) Costs that vary in total in direct proportion to changes in the level of activity

Variance analysis (p. 995) Explains the difference between standard cost and actual cost

Comprehensive **Self Review**

1. What is the primary characteristic of a fixed cost?
2. What does the following statement mean? A variable cost remains fixed per unit.
3. Is there a weakness in using a fixed budget as a cost control tool?
4. What is a flexible budget?
5. When will a job be charged more overhead than the standard allowed for the units produced?

(Answers to Comprehensive Self Review are on page 1011.)

 Multiple choice questions are provided on the text Web site at www.mhhe.com/price12e Quiz29

Discussion **Questions**

1. Define the term *fixed cost.*
2. Explain how variable costs per unit change as the level of activity changes.
3. What are semivariable costs?

4. Briefly explain the high-low point method for analyzing semivariable costs.

5. What is the relevant range of activity as used in budgeting?

6. What is a budget?

7. What is included in a budget performance report?

8. What is a flexible budget?

9. What is the advantage of using a flexible budget?

10. What are standard costs?

11. How are standards set for materials?

12. Who provides information about wage rates in setting labor standards?

13. Explain how to compute the quantity variance for materials.

14. What does the price variance for materials show?

15. What two variances make up the total labor variance?

16. Which manager would more likely be responsible for materials quantity variances?

17. What are the possible causes of materials variances?

18. What are the possible causes of labor variances?

19. What are the possible causes of overhead variances?

APPLICATIONS

Exercises

Using the high-low point method.

Abel Company's records show the following data for the four quarters of 2010.

◀ **Exercise 29.1**
Objective 2

Quarter	Direct Labor Hours	Utilities Cost
First	10,000	$2,500
Second	12,000	3,200
Third	15,000	3,500
Fourth	11,000	3,000

Compute the fixed and variable elements of utilities cost, using the high-low point method.

Developing a flexible budget for overhead.

In Boat Corporation's factory, fixed indirect labor costs are $6,000 per month. Variable indirect labor costs are $1.25 per direct labor hour. The budget for the month of May 2010 calls for employment of 15,000 direct labor hours. Compute the flexible budget amounts for indirect labor costs at the following levels of activity: 100 percent of budget, 95 percent of budget, and 105 percent of budget.

◀ **Exercise 29.2**
Objective 4

Developing standard costs per unit of product.

In preparing the standard cost for each unit of P10, the company's only product, the accountant for Gortor Manufacturing, Ltd., has developed the following data for the year 2010.

◀ **Exercise 29.3**
Objective 5

Total budgeted production, 20,000 units

Raw material:

Two units of raw material are required for each unit of finished goods. The cost of each unit of raw material is $10.

Labor:

Two hours of direct labor are required for each unit of finished goods. The labor rate per hour is $15.00.

Manufacturing overhead:

Overhead is 20 percent of direct labor.

Compute the standard cost per unit of product, showing the standard cost of materials, labor, and overhead.

Data for Exercises 29.4 through 29.11. Please round your answers to nearest dollar.
The standard cost card for a unit of product at the Liquid Corporation shows the following standard cost information.

Materials: 3 gallons at $2 per gallon	$ 6
Labor: 1 hour at $15 per hour	15
Overhead: 60% of direct labor	9
Total	$30

During the month of September 2010, Job S-31 was completed. It was the only job worked on during September. Five thousand units were produced from the job. The actual costs were as shown below.

Materials: 15,100 gallons at $2.05 per gallon	$ 30,955
Labor: 4,950 hours at $15.10 per hour	74,745
Overhead applied: 60% of direct labor	44,847
Total	$150,547

Exercise 29.4
Objective 6
▶ **Computing total variance between standard costs and actual costs.**
Calculate the total variance between the actual cost and the standard cost in September.

Exercise 29.5
Objective 7
▶ **Computing total variance for materials.**
Calculate the total variance for materials in September.

Exercise 29.6
Objective 7
▶ **Computing quantity variance for materials.**
Calculate the quantity variance for materials in September.

Exercise 29.7
Objective 7
▶ **Computing price variance for materials.**
Calculate the price variance for materials in September.

Exercise 29.8
Objective 7
▶ **Computing total variance for labor.**
Calculate the total variance for labor in September.

Exercise 29.9
Objective 7
▶ **Computing quantity variance for labor.**
Calculate the quantity variance for labor in September.

Exercise 29.10
Objective 7
▶ **Computing rate variance for labor.**
Calculate the rate variance for labor in September.

Exercise 29.11
Objective 7
▶ **Computing total overhead variance.**
Calculate the total variance for overhead in September.

PROBLEMS

Problem Set A HM™

Analyzing semivariable costs using the high-low point method.

The accountant of Valley Manufacturing Company has compiled the following information about the direct labor hours and the indirect labor costs for each month of 2010.

◀ **Problem 29.1A**
Objective 2

INSTRUCTIONS

1. Compute the monthly fixed costs and the variable costs per hour, using the high-low point method.
2. Compute the estimated total indirect labor cost if 2,400 hours of direct labor are employed during a month.

Month	Direct Labor Hours	Indirect Labor Costs
January	1,700	$6,250
February	1,400	5,925
March	2,050	6,295
April	2,100	6,395
May	2,600	6,850
June	2,900	7,800
July	2,750	7,250
August	2,500	6,900
September	2,360	6,345
October	2,700	7,300
November	2,600	6,690
December	1,900	5,990

Analyze: What percentage of total costs for June is attributable to variable costs?

Preparing a flexible overhead budget and an overhead performance report.

The accountant for Bibee Products, Inc., has analyzed the manufacturing overhead costs for the company's assembly department. The fixed and variable costs follow.

◀ **Problem 29.2A**
Objective 3

e**X**cel

	Variable Cost Element per Hour	Monthly Fixed Cost Element
Indirect labor	$1.00	$1,800
Payroll taxes	0.25	100
Indirect materials	0.15	100
Utilities	0.40	200
Depreciation	—	1,200
Taxes and insurance	—	500
Maintenance	0.25	200

INSTRUCTIONS

1. Prepare a flexible budget for the department for the month of May 2010, assuming that the expected production is for 2,500 direct labor hours. Show costs for production levels of 90 percent and 110 percent of the expected production level of 2,500 hours.

2. Assume that during the month of May, actual production was 1,900 hours. Actual costs for the month were as follows.

Indirect labor	$3,650
Payroll taxes	375
Indirect materials	400
Utilities	1,000
Depreciation	1,200
Taxes and insurance	475
Maintenance	650

Prepare a departmental monthly overhead performance report comparing actual costs with the budget allowance for the total number of hours worked. Round amounts to nearest dollar.

Analyze: If Bibee Products, Inc., operates at the expected production level of 2,500 direct labor hours, what total manufacturing overhead cost is projected per direct labor hour?

Problem 29.3A ▶ **Analyzing materials variances.**

Objective 7

Cal Chemical Company manufactures a product called Licon, which requires three raw materials. Production is in batches of 1,000 gallons of finished product. The firm uses standard costs as a control device. Its standard costs for materials for each batch of Licon have been established as follows.

Material	Quantity	Standard Cost per Gallon	Standard Cost per Batch
Starter	700 gal.	$ 0.40	$ 280.00
Acid	250 gal.	1.20	300.00
Activator	50 gal.	12.00	600.00
Total standard cost		$13.60	$1,180.00

The output is packaged in 50-gallon drums. During the month of June 2010, 200 drums of Licon were produced. There was no beginning or ending inventory of work in process. The materials actually used during June are listed below.

Material	Quantity	Cost per Gallon
Starter	7,050 gal.	$ 0.38
Acid	2,550 gal.	1.22
Activator	490 gal.	12.20

INSTRUCTIONS

1. Compute the total variance between the actual cost of the materials used during June and the standard cost of the materials. Also compute the total variance for each type of material.

2. Analyze the variances for each type of material for the month.

Analyze: Which raw materials were obtained at a price that was lower than standard cost?

Analyzing material and labor variances.

Evad Manufacturing Company makes a product that is processed through two departments: cutting and final. All materials are added in the first department. During the month of March 2010, the company made 5,000 units of the product. Standard costs and actual costs for materials and labor are given below.

◄ **Problem 29.4A**

Objective 7

e**X**cel

STANDARD COSTS

Raw materials

Framing: 10 square feet at $0.25 per square foot	$ 2.50
Filler: 15 pounds at $0.05 per pound	0.75
Standard materials cost per unit	$ 3.25

Direct labor

Cutting dept.: 1 hour at $14.00 per hour	$14.00
Final dept.: 1/2 hour at $15.00 per hour	7.50
Standard direct labor cost per unit	$21.50

ACTUAL COSTS

Raw materials

Framing: 49,650 square feet at $0.255 per square foot	$ 12,660.75
Filler: 75,100 pounds at $0.045 per pound	3,379.50
Total actual materials cost	$ 16,040.25

Direct labor

Cutting dept.: 4,980 hours at $14.05 per hour	$ 69,969.00
Final dept.: 2,550 hours at $14.98 per hour	38,199.00
Total actual direct labor cost	$108,168.00

INSTRUCTIONS

1. Prepare a comparison of the actual cost of materials with the standard cost of materials for the 5,000 units of product. Then prepare an analysis of the materials variances.

2. Prepare a comparison of the actual cost of labor with the standard cost of labor for the 5,000 units of product. Then prepare an analysis of the labor variances.

Analyze: What total variance in labor was reported by the final department?

Problem Set B

Analyzing semivariable costs using the high-low point method.

The accountant of FMU Manufacturing Company has compiled the following information (see top next page) about the direct labor hours and utility costs for each month of 2010.

◄ **Problem 29.1B**

Objective 2

INSTRUCTIONS

1. Compute the monthly fixed costs (rounded to nearest whole dollar) and the variable costs per hour (rounded to nearest whole cent) using the high-low point method.

2. Compute the estimated total indirect labor cost if 3,600 hours of direct labor are employed during the month.

Analyze: What approximate percentage of total costs is attributable to fixed costs?

Month	Direct Labor Hours	Utility Costs
January	3,295	$2,540
February	3,350	2,650
March	3,280	2,630
April	3,745	2,885
May	4,300	3,200
June	4,190	3,185
July	4,312	3,250
August	3,810	2,975
September	3,679	2,895
October	3,542	2,895
November	3,250	2,840
December	3,212	2,425

Problem 29.2B
Objective 3

Preparing a flexible overhead budget and an overhead performance report.

Atlanta Manufacturing Company makes a single product that requires one hour of labor for each unit. The budgeted output for 2010 is 35,000 units. Fixed and variable overhead cost data are as follows.

	Variable Element per Hour	Yearly Fixed Cost Element
Indirect labor	$0.75	$20,000
Payroll taxes	0.25	1,500
Indirect materials	0.25	1,800
Utilities	0.35	2,400
Depreciation	—	18,000
Taxes and insurance	—	4,800
Maintenance	0.30	2,400

INSTRUCTIONS

1. Prepare a flexible budget for Atlanta for the year 2010. The flexible budget should show costs for production levels of 90 percent, 100 percent, and 110 percent of the expected production level of 36,000 units (36,000 hours).

2. Assume that during the year 2010, actual production was 35,000 hours. Actual costs for the year were as follows.

Indirect labor	$45,950
Payroll taxes	10,200
Indirect materials	10,900
Utilities	15,000
Depreciation	18,000
Taxes and insurance	4,900
Maintenance	12,550

Prepare a yearly overhead performance report comparing actual costs with the budget allowance for the number of hours worked.

Analyze: If Atlanta Manufacturing Company operates at the expected production level of 36,000 direct labor hours, what total manufacturing overhead cost can be projected per direct labor hour? (Round to nearest cent.)

Analyzing materials variances.

◀ **Problem 29.3B**
Objective 7

Synthetic Manufacturing Co. manufactures the product Syntex, which requires three raw materials. Production is in batches of 2,500 pounds of materials. Any waste is thrown away. The firm uses standard costs as a control device. Its standard costs for materials are as follows.

Material	Quantity	Standard Cost per Pound	Standard Cost per Batch
Plastic base	2,200 lb.	$0.65	$1,430
Tint	100 lb.	0.22	22
Hardener	200 lb.	0.65	130
Totals	2,500 lb.		$1,582

During the month of July 2010, 25,000 pounds of Syntex were produced. There was no beginning or ending inventory of work in process. The materials actually used during July are listed below.

Material	Quantity	Total Cost
Plastic base	22,100 lb.	$14,144
Tint	1,150 lb.	230
Hardener	2,050 lb.	1,353

INSTRUCTIONS

1. Compute the total variance between the actual cost of the materials used during July and the standard cost of the materials. Also compute the total variance for each type of material.

2. Analyze the variances for each type of material for the month.

Analyze: Which raw materials were obtained at lower-than-standard unit costs?

Analyzing material and labor variances.

◀ **Problem 29.4B**
Objective 7

Leather Products Company makes one product that is processed through two departments: cutting and accessory. All materials are added in the first department. During the month of January 2010, 5,000 units of the product were made. Standard costs and actual costs for materials and labor are given as follows.

STANDARD COSTS
Raw materials
    Raw material, 5 sections at $2.00 per unit $10.00
    Accessory sets: 2 sets at $0.50 per unit   1.00
    Standard materials cost per unit $11.00

Direct labor
    Cutting dept.: 1/10 hour at $14.00 per hour $ 1.40
    Accessory dept.: 1/4 hour at $12.00 per hour   3.00
    Standard direct labor cost per unit $ 4.40

ACTUAL COSTS
Raw materials

Raw material: 25,650 sections at $2.04 per unit	$ 52,326.00
Accessory sets: 10,050 sets at $0.52 per unit	5,226.00
Total actual materials cost	$ 57,552.00

Direct labor

Cutting dept.: 498 hours at $13.95 per hour	$ 6,947.10
Accessory dept.: 1,280 hours at $12.20 per hour	15,616.00
Total actual direct labor cost	$ 22,563.10

INSTRUCTIONS

1. Prepare a comparison of the actual cost of materials with the standard cost of materials for the 5,000 units of product. Then prepare an analysis of the materials variances.

2. Prepare a comparison of the actual cost of labor with the standard cost of labor for the 5,000 units of product. Then prepare an analysis of the labor variances.

Analyze: Is the greatest portion of the total accessory set materials variance attributable to quantity or to price?

Critical Thinking Problem 29.1

Costs Incurred

Dos Company manufactures one product. Standard costs for each unit of the product follow.

Materials, 5 gallons @ $1.25	$ 6.25
Direct labor, 1 hour @ $15	15.00
Manufacturing overhead, 0.5 hour @ $15	7.50
Total standard costs per unit	$28.75

During the month of April 2010, 2,000 units of product were manufactured. At the end of the month, the following data was available.

a. The total materials variance was $364 unfavorable.

b. The materials quantity variance was $62.50 unfavorable.

c. The labor rate variance was $199 unfavorable.

d. Actual hours worked amounted to 1,990.

INSTRUCTIONS

Answer the following questions. Show all computations.

1. What was the actual total materials cost?
2. How many units of raw material were used?
3. What was the amount of materials price variance?
4. What was the actual labor rate per hour?
5. What was the actual labor cost for the month?
6. What was the amount of labor time variance?

Analyze: What was the cost incurred per gallon of raw materials? (Round to nearest cent.)

Critical Thinking Problem 29.2

Recreating Data

Bball Industries, a manufacturer of sports shoes, uses a standard cost system. When Frankie Coleman, the cost accountant for the company, started to analyze the labor variances for May, he discovered that some of the data had inadvertently been destroyed.

From a review of the data available, Frankie learns that the total labor cost variance for May was $255 unfavorable and that the standard labor rate was $15 per hour. A cost-of-living adjustment in the workers' hourly rate caused an unfavorable labor price variance of $0.10 per hour. Total standard labor hours for May's output of shoes was 5,000 hours.

Determine the actual number of labor hours worked in May. (*Hint:* First compute the actual labor rate per hour. Then set up an equation representing the computation of the total labor variance of $255.)

BUSINESS CONNECTIONS

Controlling Costs

1. How would the distinction between fixed and variable costs help management in forecasting cash needs for the business?

2. Explain how a flexible budget can be used by management to help control costs.

3. Briefly explain to management the reasons why variances between actual and standard costs of materials might exist.

4. The accountant for JRH Corporation has noticed that historically, when there have been favorable labor rate variances, there have been unfavorable labor time variances. What factors could explain this phenomenon?

5. In a large company, the overall wage structure is determined by the personnel department. However, the manager of each producing department has limited control over the rates paid to individual workers. Who would be responsible for labor rate variances?

6. Explain how determination of standard costs enables managers to pinpoint responsibility for inefficient performance.

Evaluating Standards

The budget uses standards that are developed by management. These standards determine if a product is being produced according to the business plan. If the product is using more materials than planned, it will cause net income to decrease from the planned income. If labor hours being used are more but the budgeted rate is less than planned, the net income could increase from the planned income. Shelly is an accountant who determines the standards to be used for materials and labor. Shelly feels she understands the payroll rates much better than the payroll department. She has set a labor rate less than what has been suggested by the payroll department. Her attitude is that the skill of the worker should be less and she is trying to force management to see her point of view. At the end of the month, the total labor costs have a favorable variance. The labor rate is the reason for the variance. Is Shelly unethical in her actions? What could happen because of her actions?

Budget and Actual

Refer to the "Results of Operations" discussion in the *2006 Annual Report* for the Home Depot, Inc., in Appendix A.

1. As the company's accountants prepare budgets for the year ended January 30, 2007, what factors might be considered when forecasting net sales? (*Hint:* What factors affected sales in the year ended January 30, 2006?)

2. What was the change in the company's combined federal and state effective income tax rate? What caused the change?

Market Demand Projections

Paccar Inc. is a global technology company that manufactures Class 4 through 8 trucks under the Kenworth, Peterbilt, and DAF nameplates. The company's *2006 Annual Report* included the following information, taken from the Management's Discussion and Analysis of Financial Condition and Results of Operations.

(In Millions, Except Truck Unit and Per Share Amounts)	2006	2005
Net sales and revenues	$15,503.3	$13,298.4
Net income (loss)	$ 1,846.6	$ 1,516.8
Manufacturing gross margin	14.7%	14.5%

Truck segment gross margin as a percentage of net sales and revenues improved to 14.7 percent in 2006 from 14.5 percent in 2005 as a result of improved operating efficiencies and strong demand for the Company's products. Higher material costs from suppliers, including the impacts of higher crude oil, copper, steel, aluminum and other commodities, have generally been reflected in higher costs and sales prices for new trucks.

Analyze:

1. What factors were responsible for the improvement in gross margin from 2005 to 2006?
2. What factors partially offset the improvements in gross margin?
3. By what percentage has manufacturing gross margin improved from 2005 to 2006? What is the manufacturing gross profit amount for 2006?

Analyze Online: Locate the most recent annual report on the Paccar Web site (www.paccar.com).

4. What manufacturing gross margin was reported? Is this figure an improvement over the 2006 gross margin?
5. What reasons are offered for increases or decreases in the manufacturing gross margin?

Standard Costing and Service Firms

Standard costing and variance analysis techniques are most often associated with manufacturing businesses. The owner of a small graphic design company believes that standard costs should be established for the services her firm provides. Do you agree with this statement? Why or why not? How do you think such standards might be established?

Speech Preparation

You have been asked to speak at the Manufacturing Professionals monthly meeting on the topic "Establishing and Utilizing Standard Costs." In your company, Illuminations Lighting Manufacturing, standard costs were recently established for the production of one of your company's products, the Retro Desk Lamp, #335998. You worked with production managers, engineers, and purchasing officers to establish standard costs for materials, labor, and overhead. Prepare notes for a 10-minute speech describing how standard costs are developed and companies might use these standard costs as a control tool.

Standard Costs Development

Your company makes crayons. Determine the materials and labor you would need to make a box of 10 crayons. Next, determine the amount of materials per box and the labor hours per box. Next determine the cost per ounce of each material and the cost per hour for each worker. These are your standards. Your company has an order from Vans Supermarkets for 10,000 boxes. Using the standards you have developed, calculate the standard cost for materials and labor. Compare your group standards to the other groups. What are the differences? Can you see how different groups can develop standards differently?

International Organization of Standards

Go to the International Organization of Standardization Web site at (www.iso.ch). Go to the site map and identify what is the purpose of an international standard. Who benefits from the standards developed?

Answers to **Self Reviews**

Answers to Section 1 Self Review

1. To control costs and measure efficiency it is necessary to be able to measure what costs should be at any level of activity. This requires an analysis of fixed and variable costs.

2. (a) Decrease, (b) increase, (c) no change.

3. A budget showing expected costs at only one level of production activity.

4. **d.** fixed cost.

5. **d.** fixed, variable, and semivariable costs.

6. $500 over

Answers to Section 2 Self Review

1. The per unit standard costs of materials, labor, and overhead.

2. (1) Compute the difference between the actual number of units of a material used and the standard quantity of that material allowed for the job and (2) multiply the difference in quantity by the standard cost per unit.

3. By multiplying the difference between (1) the standard rate per hour and (2) the actual rate per hour by (3) the actual number of hours worked.

4. **c.** labor time variance.

5. **a.** actual quantity.

6. $65 (materials $25; labor $20; overhead $20)

Answers to Comprehensive Self-Review

1. It remains constant in total during the period and does not change merely because the level of activity changes.

2. A variable cost is one whose total varies in direct proportion to the level of activity, yet the cost per unit of activity remains the same within the usual range of activity level.

3. Yes, if the level of production activity is substantially different from the level anticipated in the fixed budget, the actual and budgeted costs will not be related to comparable bases.

4. A flexible budget is a budget showing expected costs at more than one level of activity.

5. When actual hours worked exceed the standard hours allowed (assuming that the overhead application rate is based on direct labor hours) and the business is allocating overhead on each job.

Cost-Revenue Analysis for Decision Making

Chapter **30**

LEARNING OBJECTIVES

LP30

1. Explain the basic steps in the decision-making process.
2. Prepare income statements using the absorption costing and direct costing methods.
3. Using the contribution approach, analyze the profits of segments of a business.
4. Determine relevant cost and revenue data for decision-making purposes.
5. Apply an appropriate decision process in three situations:
   a. Pricing products in special cases
   b. Deciding whether to purchase new equipment
   c. Deciding whether to make or to buy a part
6. Define the accounting terms new to this chapter.

NEW TERMS

absorption costing
capacity
common costs
contribution margin
controllable fixed costs
differential cost
direct costing
manufacturing margin
marginal income
opportunity cost
sunk cost
variable costing

Bristol-Myers Squibb www.bristolmyers.com

Bristol-Myers Squibb is a global producer and distributor of a variety of pharmaceuticals and related health care products. Recently the company decided to close a plant that made heart disease and diabetes medicine in western Puerto Rico, eliminating about 400 jobs. The plant, which was in operation for 36 years, produced Pravachol for heart disease and Glucophage for diabetes. The introduction of generic versions of the two drugs was one of the contributing factors to the closing.

The company recently remodeled its plant in the northern city of Manati, investing $220 million in two years. Boris Jaskille, executive director of Puerto Rico's Industrial Development Company, said Bristol-Myers ". . . envisions that Manati will be the center of production for biological medications on a global level."

thinking critically

What do you think are the critical questions a company like Bristol-Myers Squibb asks before making a decision to close a plant?

SECTION OBJECTIVES	TERMS TO LEARN
>> 1. **Explain the basic steps in the decision-making process.** WHY IT'S IMPORTANT Decisions require data about feasible alternatives.	absorption costing common costs contribution margin controllable fixed costs differential cost direct costing manufacturing margin marginal income opportunity cost sunk cost variable costing
>> 2. **Prepare income statements using the absorption costing and direct costing methods.** WHY IT'S IMPORTANT How costs are treated must be considered when decisions are made.	
>> 3. **Using the contribution approach, analyze the profits of segments of a business.** WHY IT'S IMPORTANT A business needs to assess the performance of its segments.	
>> 4. **Determine relevant cost and revenue data for decision-making purposes.** WHY IT'S IMPORTANT Decision makers need to identify relevant from nonrelevant data.	

The Decision Process

Video30.1

Accountants play a key role in a company's decision-making processes. They gather, analyze, and present large amounts of financial information to decision makers.

>>**1. OBJECTIVE**

Explain the basic steps in the decision-making process.

LP30

Exploring the Decision Process

The decision-making process involves the following six steps.

Step 1. *Define the problem.*
Step 2. *Identify workable alternatives.*
Step 3. *Determine relevant cost and revenue data.*
Step 4. *Evaluate the cost and revenue data.*
Step 5. *Consider appropriate nonfinancial factors.*
Step 6. *Make a decision.*

DIRECT COSTING VERSUS ABSORPTION COSTING

Recall that some costs are *fixed;* they do not vary in total during a period, even though the volume of goods manufactured or sold might be higher or lower than anticipated. Examples of fixed costs are depreciation of equipment, rent on the building, and salaries and related expenses for employees. *Variable costs* vary in total directly with the volume of manufacturing or sales activity. Variable costs include sales commissions, delivery expenses, and the loss from uncollectible accounts. *Semivariable costs* have characteristics of both fixed and variable costs. Utilities expense is an example of a semivariable cost.

Under **absorption costing,** all manufacturing costs, including fixed costs, are included in the cost of goods manufactured. The value of the ending inventory includes fixed costs. Under **direct costing,** which is also known as **variable costing,** only variable costs are included in the cost of goods manufactured. Fixed manufacturing costs are written off as expenses in the period in which they are incurred. Accountants who support direct costing contend that fixed costs are not dependent on the quantity of goods produced, so they should not be allocated to specific units manufactured. They believe that fixed costs relate to the capacity to produce goods, not to the actual goods produced.

Direct costing is widely used when making business decisions; however, **direct costing is not acceptable for GAAP financial reporting purposes.**

Absorption Costing
Let's use Brown Manufacturing Corporation to illustrate the difference between absorption and direct costing. The manufacturing costs are separated into fixed and variable elements as follows.

Beginning inventory of finished goods	–0–
Units produced (no work in process inventories)	10,000
Units sold	9,000
Units in ending inventory of finished goods	1,000
Sales price for each unit	$50
Variable manufacturing costs per unit—materials, labor, and variable manufacturing overhead	$15
Variable selling and administrative expenses per unit sold	$5
Fixed manufacturing costs	$70,000
Fixed selling and administrative expenses	$100,000

Figure 30.1 is a condensed income statement using absorption costing. It includes the cost of goods manufactured.

Direct Costing
Figure 30.2 on page 1016 is a condensed income statement using direct costing. Note these differences in direct costing:

- Only variable manufacturing costs are included in the cost of goods manufactured and in the finished goods inventory.
- The **manufacturing margin** is sales minus the variable cost of goods sold.
- The **marginal income** on sales is the manufacturing margin minus variable operating expenses.

>>2. OBJECTIVE
Prepare income statements using the absorption costing and direct costing methods.

LP30

ABOUT
ACCOUNTING

Problem Solving
General problem-solving skills might not be sufficient to meet the demands of a global economy. Accountants must develop a quick sense of assessing relevant costs in decision making.

Brown Manufacturing Corporation Partial Income Statement Year Ended December 31, 2010	
Sales (9,000 units @ $50)	4 5 0 0 0 0 0
Cost of goods sold	
Variable manufacturing costs (10,000 units @ $15)	1 5 0 0 0 0 0
Fixed manufacturing costs	7 0 0 0 0 0
Total cost of goods manufacturing	
($220,000/10,000 units = $22 per unit)	2 2 0 0 0 0 0
Less finished goods ending inventory (1,000 units @ $22)	2 2 0 0 0 0
Cost of goods sold	1 9 8 0 0 0 0
Gross profit on sales	2 5 2 0 0 0 0
Selling and administrative expenses	
Variable expenses (9,000 units @ $5)	4 5 0 0 0 0
Fixed expenses	1 0 0 0 0 0 0
Total selling and administrative expenses	1 4 5 0 0 0 0
Net income before taxes	1 0 7 0 0 0 0

FIGURE 30.1

Income Statement Using Absorption Costing

FIGURE 30.2

Income Statement Using Direct Costing

Brown Manufacturing Corporation Income Statement Year Ended December 31, 2010			
Sales (9,000 units @ $50)			450 0 0 0 00
Cost of Goods Sold			
Variable manufacturing costs			
(10,000 units @ $15)	150 0 0 0 00		
Less finished goods inventory			
(1,000 units @ $15)	15 0 0 0 00		
Cost of goods sold			135 0 0 0 00
Manufacturing margin			315 0 0 0 00
Variable selling and administrative expenses			
(9,000 units @ $5)			45 0 0 0 00
Marginal income on sales			270 0 0 0 00
Fixed costs and expenses			
Fixed manufacturing costs	70 0 0 0 00		
Fixed selling and administrative expenses	100 0 0 0 00		170 0 0 0 00
Net income before taxes			100 0 0 0 00

important!

Direct Costing

Under direct costing, all fixed manufacturing overhead costs are expensed in the period in which they are incurred.

- The net income is the marginal income on sales minus fixed manufacturing costs and fixed selling and administrative expenses.
- If there is a change in the inventory level, income under absorption costing will be different from income under direct costing.

The statement in Figure 30.2 illustrates only one of several different arrangements that might be used.

When absorption costing is used, a portion of the fixed manufacturing overhead is included in finished goods inventory and is not expensed in the current period. Under absorption costing, if the number of units in ending inventory increases, the amount of fixed overhead in finished goods inventory increases and the amount of fixed overhead expensed in the current period decreases. In contrast, under direct costing all fixed overhead is expensed in the current period. Under direct costing, an increase in finished goods inventory does not affect the amount of fixed costs expensed.

When finished goods inventory increases, net income under absorption costing is higher than that under direct costing. This is the case in Figures 30.1 and 30.2. Finished goods inventory increased by 1,000 units and net income under absorption costing is $7,000 higher than net income under direct costing. When the finished goods inventory level decreases, net income under absorption costing is less than net income under direct costing.

>>3. OBJECTIVE

Using the contribution approach, analyze the profits of segments of a business.

LP30

THE CONCEPT OF CONTRIBUTION MARGIN

Contribution margin is revenues minus variable costs. Most decisions concerning segments of a business, such as branch stores, divisions, and products, also involve an analysis of the contribution margin because it avoids arbitrary allocations of common costs. **Common costs** are costs not directly traceable to a specific segment of a business. The profitability of a segment is judged by its contribution margin; that is, the amount contributed towards covering the common costs of the business and producing a profit.

Under the contribution margin approach, the contribution margin is calculated for the business segment. Then the controllable fixed costs of the segment are deducted to determine the segment's contribution to the overall profit of the business. **Controllable fixed costs** are costs that the segment manager can control. Common costs are not allocated to specific segments when computing the contribution margin. They are deducted from the total of all segment contributions to determine the company's profit.

The contribution margin approach allows managers to make sound decisions about adding, keeping, or eliminating a segment of the business. If a segment produces a positive contribution margin, it is helping to cover total fixed costs and to provide a profit for the business. Management would consider eliminating any segment with a negative contribution margin. Plans for adding a new segment would include a contribution margin analysis. Management would favorably consider segments with a projected positive contribution margin.

THE CONCEPT OF RELEVANT COSTS

A **sunk cost** is a cost that has already been incurred. When making decisions, sunk costs are irrelevant. Relevant costs are future or expected costs that will change as a result of a decision. For example, when deciding whether to replace a machine, the cost of the existing machine is irrelevant. The cost of the new machine is relevant. When deciding whether to close a warehouse, a relevant cost is the salaries of the warehouse personnel. The nonrefundable prepaid rent on the warehouse is irrelevant since it has been paid and cannot be recovered.

THE CONCEPT OF DIFFERENTIAL COSTS

Decision making involves comparing two or more alternatives. A **differential cost** is the difference in cost between one alternative and another. For example, the difference in cost between using a hand-operated press and an automated press is a *differential cost*. While the term *incremental cost* is often used interchangeably with differential cost, incremental cost actually means only an *increase* in cost from one alternative to another. For example, if it costs $40,000 to produce 20 units and $45,000 to produce 30 units, the incremental cost of producing the additional 10 units is $5,000 ($45,000 − $40,000).

THE CONCEPT OF OPPORTUNITY COST

Opportunity cost is the potential earnings or benefits that are given up because a certain course of action is taken. For example, assume management is deciding between purchasing equipment or investing in securities. The opportunity cost of the decision to purchase the equipment is the amount of interest or dividends that would be received on the securities if the securities had been purchased instead of the equipment.

>>**4. OBJECTIVE**

Determine relevant cost and revenue data for decision-making purposes.

LP30

Section **1** Self Review

QUESTIONS

1. What is the primary difference between absorption costing and direct costing?

2. When the finished goods inventory decreases, is net income higher under absorption costing or direct costing?

3. What is a differential cost?

EXERCISES

4. When direct costing is used, cost of goods sold reflects

   a. variable manufacturing costs and variable selling and administrative expenses.

   b. variable manufacturing costs only.

   c. all manufacturing costs.

   d. both variable and fixed manufacturing costs.

5. The potential earnings or benefits given up as a result of a certain course of action is a(n)

   a. opportunity cost.

   b. incremental cost.

   c. sunk cost.

   d. differential cost.

ANALYSIS

6. Compute the contribution margin for the following case. Sales are $500,000. Variable manufacturing costs are $150,000. Finished goods inventory is $65,000. Variable selling and administrative expenses are $50,000.

(Answers to Section 1 Self Review are on page 1033.)

Cost-Revenue Analysis

Video30.1

In many different situations, managers analyze costs and revenues in order to make decisions. Three common cost-revenue analysis situations will be discussed in this section: (1) product pricing in special situations, (2) purchasing new equipment, and (3) making or buying a part.

> Newspaper Association of America (www.naa.org) provides comprehensive data covering critical financial areas for newspapers. Most industry trade organizations report similar data useful for management decision making.

>> **5. OBJECTIVE**

a. Apply an appropriate decision process in pricing products in special cases.

LP30

Product Pricing in Special Situations

Direct costing is often useful in setting prices and considering offers to buy products in special circumstances. For example, Brown Manufacturing Corporation received an offer from an overseas customer to purchase 1,000 units at $25 per unit. The units would incur the usual manufacturing and selling and administrative costs. In addition, there would be a shipping cost of $1 per unit. The company has adequate manufacturing capacity to take the special order without endangering its regular production or its ability to take care of existing customers. **Capacity** in this sense refers to a facility's power to produce or use.

> In the semiconductor industry, improving cost effectiveness and productivity have always been high priorities. They have become more critical with increasing competition. Simulation software, the Y4 (Yield FOREcaster), helps manufacturers predict defect-related yield loss and manufacturing costs in a multiproduct fabrication line. For example, the software predicts the failure rates when foreign particles are introduced during wafer processing.

Management reviewed the information shown in Figure 30.1 on page 1015 and found the computed following average unit cost under absorption costing.

Manufacturing costs ($220,000 ÷ 10,000 units)	$22.00
Selling and administrative expenses ($145,000 ÷ 9,000 units)	16.11
Total average cost per unit	$38.11

Management also reviewed the information shown in Figure 30.2 to determine the costs under direct costing. The additional shipping expense of $1 per unit was also considered.

Variable manufacturing costs	$15
Variable selling and administrative expenses	5
Variable costs per unit	$20
Additional shipping cost	1
Total variable cost per unit	$21

The difference between the costs ($38.11 and $21.00) is due to fixed costs, and in this situation the fixed costs are irrelevant. The fixed costs will be incurred whether or not the order is accepted. The incremental cost of making the additional 1,000 units is $21 per unit. Based on this analysis, the company would make a profit of $4 ($25 − $21) per unit if the order were accepted.

Management needs to consider carefully all relevant factors when analyzing special pricing situations. For example, management would not accept the special order if the company did not have sufficient capacity or if the special order jeopardized sales to existing customers. Also, management would need to ensure that the company does not violate federal laws that prohibit price differentials.

Purchasing New Equipment

The management of JACE Industries, Inc., is considering the purchase of a new machine that will improve worker productivity. The machine costs $50,000 and has an estimated useful life of 10 years, with no anticipated salvage value. Table 30.1 shows the relevant data for the two alternatives.

Table 30.2 (on page 1020) shows the analysis. The left two columns reflect the net income under each alternative. The differential cost data is in the right column. This analysis indicates that if JACE Industries, Inc., were to purchase the machine, its net income would increase by $5,000 each year. Before making the final decision, however, management needs to consider employee morale and the quality of the product that the new machine will make.

Making or Buying a Part

JACE Industries, Inc., purchases a part for $15 per unit. The company uses 24,000 of these parts each year. Management has determined that the part could be made in the company's molding department.

>>**5. OBJECTIVE**

b. Apply an appropriate decision process in deciding whether to purchase new equipment.

LP30

>>**5. OBJECTIVE**

c. Apply an appropriate decision process in deciding whether to make or to buy a part.

TABLE 30.1

Cost and Revenue Data Needed for an Analysis of the Effects of Purchasing a New Machine

	If Machine Is Not Purchased	If Machine Is Purchased
Annual sales (units)	10,000	10,000
Sales price (per unit)	$ 45	$ 45
Cost of machine		$50,000
Other cost data		
Materials (per unit)	$ 15	$ 15
Labor (per unit)	10	9
Variable overhead (per unit)	3	3
Fixed overhead (per year)	$19,000	$24,000*

*Includes $5,000 per year for additional depreciation for new machine.

TABLE 30.2

Analysis of the Effects of Purchasing a New Machine (based on annual income)

	If Machine Is Not Purchased	If Machine Is Purchased	Differential If Purchased
Annual sales	$450,000	$450,000	
Variable costs			
Materials	$150,000	$150,000	
Labor	100,000	90,000	$ (10,000)
Manufacturing overhead	30,000	30,000	
Total variable costs	$280,000	$270,000	
Contribution margin	$170,000	$180,000	10,000
Fixed costs	19,000	24,000	5,000
Net income	$151,000	$156,000	$ 5,000

The molding department has a capacity of 20,000 direct labor hours per year. For several years, it has operated at 15,000 direct labor hours per year. For the molding department, the direct labor costs are $16 per hour and variable manufacturing overhead costs are $8 per hour. Annual fixed costs for the department total $75,000. The estimated cost of materials is $7 for each part. Four parts can be produced per hour.

Table 30.3 shows the analysis of the data. If JACE Industries, Inc., decides to manufacture the part, it will realize a savings of $2 per part, which is a $48,000 savings per year.

Notice that the fixed manufacturing overhead costs are not considered because they remain the same whether the part is purchased or made.

Every day managers must consider decisions similar to those covered in this chapter. Accountants who understand cost-revenue analysis can assist management to consider the appropriate factors to enable them to reach logical decisions that will increase the company's profitability.

In addition to the factors covered in this chapter, accountants also consider the impact of income taxes and the timing of cash receipts and expenditures. These elements have significant impact on the company's profitability.

Cost to purchase part		$ 15.00
Cost to manufacture part		
Variable costs only		
Materials	$7.00	
Labor (1/4 hour @ $16 per hour)	4.00	
Manufacturing overhead (1/4 hour @ $8 per hour)	2.00	13.00
Differential cost (savings per unit if part is manufactured)		$ 2.00
Number of parts per year		24,000
Total annual savings		$48,000

TABLE 30.3

Analysis of the Effects of Making or Buying a Part

MANAGERIAL IMPLICATIONS   <<

USING COST REVENUE ANALYSIS TO MAKE DECISIONS

- Accountants gather and analyze data so that managers have the necessary information to make effective decisions between alternative courses of action.
- When making decisions managers are concerned about future costs and revenues.
- Managers use cost-revenue analysis to evaluate the financial effects of decisions before they are made.
- It is critical that managers understand cost analysis and related concepts including sunk costs, relevant costs, differential costs, opportunity costs, and contribution margin.
- Managers focus on the differential revenues and differential costs for each course of action.
- Usually, sunk costs are irrelevant in making decisions.

THINKING CRITICALLY

Why should sunk costs be ignored when making decisions?

Section **2** Self Review

QUESTIONS

1. How is direct costing helpful in special pricing situations?

2. What is the contribution margin approach to decision analysis?

3. Are fixed costs relevant when making a pricing decision for a special order if there is sufficient manufacturing capacity available?

EXERCISES

4. Contribution margin is calculated by deducting

a. variable costs and controllable fixed costs from revenue.

b. variable costs from revenue.

c. controllable fixed costs from revenue.

d. variable costs and common costs from revenue.

5. In deciding whether to purchase a new machine, which of the following is not relevant?

a. depreciation

b. labor cost savings

c. savings in materials used

d. cost of the old machine

ANALYSIS

6. Carlos Corporation is considering the purchase of a new machine at a cost of $15,000 to replace its current, fully depreciated machine. The new machine would have a life of five years and would produce 5,000 units per year (the current output). Direct labor costs would be reduced by $1.00 per unit. Variable overhead costs would be reduced by 50 cents per unit. Fixed costs, other than depreciation, would increase by $2,000 per year. Assuming all 5,000 units are sold, what is the amount of increase or decrease in net income per year if the machine is purchased?

(Answers to Section 2 Self Review are on page 1034.)

30 Chapter REVIEW Chapter Summary

To make decisions, management constantly requires financial data, which must be gathered and analyzed by the accountant. In this chapter, you have learned how to evaluate data when cost and revenue considerations are involved.

Learning Objectives

1 Explain the basic steps in the decision-making process.

Managers use financial information not only to help identify a problem but also to help reach decisions for solving the problem. The decision-making process involves the following steps:

- Define the problem.
- Identify workable alternatives.
- Determine relevant cost and revenue data.
- Evaluate the cost and revenue data.
- Consider appropriate nonfinancial factors.
- Make a decision.

2 Prepare income statements using the absorption costing and direct costing methods.

- In direct costing, only the variable manufacturing costs are considered as part of the cost of goods manufactured. The cost of goods sold, based solely on variable costs, is subtracted from net sales to arrive at the manufacturing margin.
- Variable selling and administrative expenses are deducted from the manufacturing margin to obtain the marginal income on sales.
- Fixed manufacturing costs and fixed operating expenses are subtracted from the marginal income on sales to obtain the net income for the period.

3 Using the contribution approach, analyze the profits of segments of a business.

The contribution margin measures the excess of revenues over variable costs. If a segment produces a contribution margin, it is helping to meet company-wide common expenses.

4 Determine relevant cost and revenue data for decision-making purposes.

- Relevant costs for making decisions are usually future costs.
- Sunk costs are historical costs and are therefore generally not relevant to business decisions.
- Determining differential costs—the differences in cost between various alternatives—is important in decision making.
- Often the contribution approach is used in evaluating the data that results from the analysis.

5 Apply an appropriate decision process in three situations:

a. Pricing products in special cases

Direct costing is often useful in setting prices, especially when special offers from potential customers to buy the company's product are being considered.

b. Deciding whether to purchase new equipment

Accountants gather relevant data to compare the proposed purchase of a new machine versus continuing to use the old machine, estimating net income under each alternative and calculating the difference.

c. Deciding whether to make or to buy a part

When comparing alternatives to make or buy a part, data can be analyzed on the basis of unit cost or annual total costs. Fixed manufacturing costs are not considered when making this analysis, since these costs remain the same whether the part is made or bought.

6 Define the accounting terms new to this chapter.

Glossary

Absorption costing (p. 1015) The accounting procedure whereby all manufacturing costs, including fixed costs, are included in the cost of goods manufactured

Capacity (p. 1018) A facility's ability to produce or use

Common costs (p. 1016) Costs not directly traceable to a specific segment of a business

Contribution margin (p. 1016) Revenues minus variable costs

Controllable fixed costs (p. 1016) Costs that the segment manager can control

Differential cost (p. 1017) The difference in cost between one alternative and another

Direct costing (p. 1015) The accounting procedure whereby only variable costs are included in the cost of goods manufactured, and fixed manufacturing costs are written off as expenses in the period in which they are incurred

Manufacturing margin (p. 1015) Sales minus the variable cost of goods sold

Marginal income (p. 1015) The manufacturing margin minus variable operating expenses

Opportunity cost (p. 1017) Potential earnings or benefits that are given up because a certain course of action is taken

Sunk cost (p. 1017) A cost that has been incurred and will not change as a result of a decision

Variable costing (p. 1015) See Direct costing

Comprehensive **Self Review**

1. What are relevant costs?
2. Why are sunk costs ignored in most managerial decisions?
3. Should management automatically reject an offer by a potential customer to purchase some of the company's product at a price that is less than the company's total cost to manufacture the product? Explain.
4. Give some reasons why a company might decide to purchase a part from an outside supplier that is used in its finished product rather than manufacture the part.
5. Briefly define incremental costs.

(Answers to Comprehensive Self Review are on page 1034.)

Multiple choice questions are provided on the text Web site at www.mhhe.com/price12e Quiz30

Discussion Questions

1. Which of the following items are subtracted from net sales to arrive at contribution margin?
   a. fixed administrative expenses
   b. variable administrative expenses
   c. fixed manufacturing costs
   d. variable manufacturing costs
   e. fixed selling expenses
   f. variable selling expenses

2. Briefly describe absorption costing.
3. What is the fundamental difference between direct costing and absorption costing?
4. Is absorption costing or direct costing more useful in making decisions? Why?
5. What is the manufacturing margin?
6. Explain the meaning of marginal income on sales.
7. What is a differential cost?
8. Explain opportunity costs.
9. What are sunk costs?
10. Suggest some nonmeasurable data that might be considered in deciding to replace existing equipment with new equipment.
11. Why might management be reluctant to accept a special order for its products at less than the normal price even though such an order would be legal and profitable?
12. Suppose that a company is considering the purchase of new equipment. The old equipment will be sold when the new equipment is acquired. How should the proceeds from the sale of the old equipment be considered in the analysis of the effects of the purchase?

13. Why do the analyses presented in this chapter focus on future costs rather than on past costs? Does this mean that historical costs are useless? Explain.

14. Why might employee morale be a factor in deciding whether to replace existing equipment with new equipment?

APPLICATIONS

Exercises

Data for Exercises 30.1 and 30.2.
Moc Corporation has divided all of its costs and expenses into fixed and variable components. Data for the company's first year of operations follows. Ignore income taxes.

Beginning inventory of finished goods	0
Units produced (no work in process)	12,000
Units sold	10,000
Units in ending inventory of finished goods	2,000
Sales price	$145 per unit
Variable manufacturing costs	$55 for each unit manufactured
Variable selling and administrative expenses	$25 per unit sold
Fixed manufacturing costs for year	$150,000
Fixed selling and administrative expenses for year	$100,000

Exercise 30.1
Objective 2

▶ **Using the absorption method.**

Using the absorption method, calculate the following:

1. Cost of goods manufactured for the year.
2. The value of the ending inventory of finished goods.
3. The cost of goods sold for the year.
4. Net income for the year.

Exercise 30.2
Objective 2

▶ **Using direct costing.**

Using the direct costing method, calculate the following:

1. Ending inventory of finished goods.
2. The manufacturing margin for the year.
3. Net income for the year.

Exercise 30.3
Objective 4

▶ **Identifying relevant costs.**

Travis Company is considering replacing its existing telephone system with new equipment. The existing system has a book value of $240,000 and a remaining useful life of three years. The new telephone system would cost $300,000 and have a useful life of five years with an estimated salvage value of $30,000. The annual production of 10,000 units would not change. It would, however, reduce direct labor costs by $5 per unit. Other fixed costs would increase by $40,000 per year. Of the information just given, which items are relevant to the decision to replace the equipment?

Exercise 30.4
Objectives 4, 5a

▶ **Determining relevant costs and making a pricing decision.**

Georgia Industries has an opportunity to export 1,000 units of its product to a foreign country. The current selling price is $135, but the special order will be sold at a unit price of $99. This special order will not affect its current sales, all of which are domestic. Freight and shipping costs of $15 per unit would be incurred on the foreign order. Current variable manufacturing costs are $45 per unit manufactured, and variable selling and administrative costs are $24 per unit sold. Included in variable selling expenses is a sales commission of $3 per unit, which would not apply to the foreign order. Fixed manufacturing costs are $175,000 per year and fixed selling and administrative expenses are $160,000 per year. The company now manufactures and sells 6,000 units per year. What is the effect on profits if the special order is taken? Show all calculations.

Selecting relevant data, determining contribution margin of segment, and making a pricing decision.

◀ **Exercise 30.5**
Objectives 3, 4, 5a

The standard cost sheet for the leading product made by TLC Corporation shows the following data.

Direct materials	$60
Direct labor (2 hours at $15/hour)	30
Manufacturing overhead	
Variable costs (2 hours at $15/hour)	30
Fixed costs (2 hours at $12/hour)	24
Total standard cost	$144

The product normally sells for $299. The company is presently operating at only slightly over 70 percent of capacity.

1. A chain of discount stores has offered to purchase 3,000 units of the product for $219 per unit. Shipping costs would be $3 per unit. Special packaging would be needed and would cost an additional $2 per unit. There would be no other variable selling or administrative expenses. Should the order be accepted? (Show all calculations.)

2. Ignoring all factors except those given, what is the least amount that TLC Corporation could profitably accept for a special order of 3,000 units?

Selecting relevant data and deciding whether to purchase equipment.

◀ **Exercise 30.6**
Objectives 4, 5b

BIG Company is considering the purchase of a new factory machine at a cost of $150,000. The machine would perform a function that is now being performed by hand. The new machine would have a life of 10 years, would produce 12,000 units a year (the current output), and have no salvage value. Direct labor costs would be reduced by $1.00 per unit, and variable overhead costs would also be reduced by $1.00 per unit. Fixed costs other than depreciation would increase by $2,000 per year. Should the machine be purchased? What is the impact of the decision on net income?

Data for Exercises 30.7 and 30.8.

Bay Corporation is manufacturing a part that is used in its finished product. The costs for each unit of the part follow.

Direct materials		$17
Direct labor		18
Manufacturing overhead		
Variable costs	$8	
Fixed costs	2	10
Total cost		$45

The fixed overhead is based on $200,000 of fixed costs to manufacture 100,000 parts per year. If the part is not manufactured, fixed costs will be reduced by approximately $100,000 per year.

Selecting relevant data, determining contribution margin of a segment, and deciding whether to make or to buy a part.

◀ **Exercise 30.7**
Objectives 3, 4, 5c

Instead of making the part, Bay has an opportunity to purchase the part from an outside company for $42 per unit. Should the company accept the offer, or should it continue to manufacture the part?

Exercise 30.8
Objectives 3, 4, 5c

▶ **Selecting relevant data, determining contribution margin of a segment, and deciding whether to make or buy a part.**

What is the most that Bay should pay to an outside vendor to buy the part?

PROBLEMS

Problem Set A

Problem 30.1A ▶
Objective 2 e**X**cel

Preparing income statements based on absorption costing and direct costing.

The following data pertains to the operations of Alpha Corporation for the year ended December 31, 2010. It manufactures computer keyboards.

DATA FOR 2010	
Sales	2,500 units @ $119/unit
Variable manufacturing costs	2,500 units @ $44/unit
Variable selling and administrative expenses	$5/unit
Fixed manufacturing costs	$50,000
Fixed selling and administrative expenses	$25,000
Finished goods inventory, January 1, 2010	200 units
Finished goods inventory, December 31, 2010	200 units

INSTRUCTIONS

1. Prepare an income statement for the year using the absorption costing approach. Assume that the 200 units in the beginning inventory of finished goods had a cost of $46 per unit.

2. Prepare an income statement for the year using the direct costing approach. Assume that the 200 units in the beginning inventory of finished goods cost $46 per unit.

3. Explain the reason for the difference between the net income or loss computed under the two methods.

Analyze: Assume that Alpha Corporation's manufacturing managers believe that only those costs that contribute directly to product production should be assigned to cost of goods manufactured. Which costing method would these managers prefer?

Problem 30.2A ▶
Objectives 2, 3, 4, 5a

e**X**cel

Preparing an income statement based on direct costing, choosing relevant data, determining contribution margin of a segment, and making a pricing decision.

Tech Inc. began operations in 2010 to manufacture a single product. There are no ending work in process inventories. Relevant data for the year follow.

OPERATING DATA FOR 2010	
Quantities	
Beginning inventories, finished goods	–0–
Units produced during the year	5,400
Units sold during the year	5,000
Costs	
Direct materials ($24 per unit)	$129,600
Direct labor ($22 per unit)	118,800
Variable factory overhead ($10 per unit)	54,000
Fixed factory overhead	56,000

Variable selling and administrative expenses ($9 per unit)	45,000
Fixed selling and administrative expenses	75,000
Selling price for each unit	105

INSTRUCTIONS

1. Prepare an income statement for 2010, using direct costing.

2. Assume that the company has an opportunity to sell 400 units of the product in a foreign country for $75 per unit. No fixed or variable selling and administrative expenses would be incurred in connection with these units except shipping costs of $8 per unit and miscellaneous administrative expenses of $2 per unit. The company has idle capacity, and the order would not affect present markets. Would it be profitable for the company to accept the order? Show all computations.

Analyze: What percentage of the foreign sales order would be realized as marginal income?

Choosing relevant data, determining contribution margin of a segment, and deciding whether to purchase equipment.

◀ **Problem 30.3A**
Objectives 3, 4, 5b

Raider Company makes a single product that it sells to retail stores. The firm's finishing department uses hand labor to perform its work on all products. A proposal has been made by the company's vice president to acquire machinery that will perform most of the functions of this department. The finishing department has consistently produced 40,000 units a year, and that is the estimated production for the foreseeable future. A summary of the manufacturing costs of the department follows.

Direct materials	$100,000
Direct labor	750,000
Manufacturing overhead	
Variable costs	150,000
Fixed costs	100,000

The machinery being considered will cost $750,000 and have an estimated useful life of five years, with no salvage value. The machinery will cause the following changes in costs.

a. Direct labor will decrease by $8 per unit.

b. Direct materials will not change.

c. Variable manufacturing overhead will decrease by $1.25 per unit.

d. Fixed manufacturing overhead will increase by $40,000 per year.

INSTRUCTIONS

1. Prepare an analysis showing the effect on net income of purchasing the equipment.

2. What other factors should be considered in making the decision?

Analyze: Assume that the use of the new machinery will increase the number of imperfect products produced by 3 percent of total production. These imperfect products must be reprocessed at a cost of $10 per unit, increasing variable manufacturing costs. What net annual increase or decrease in costs can be projected?

Choosing relevant data and deciding whether to make or buy a part.

◀ **Problem 30.4A**
Objectives 4, 5c

Chicago Equipment Corporation is currently manufacturing a part that goes into its main product. Each year 5,000 of these parts are used. Cost data for the past year that relates to the 5,000 parts is given below. Fixed costs are allocated on the basis of direct labor hours. An outside company has offered to supply the part for $48 per unit, plus a shipping charge of $5 per unit. The plant now used by Chicago to manufacture the part would not be used to capacity within the foreseeable future if the part is purchased outside.

Direct materials	$150,000
Direct labor	100,000

Variable overhead costs	10,000
Fixed overhead costs	25,000

INSTRUCTIONS

1. Prepare an analysis comparing the unit cost of manufacturing the part with the unit cost of purchasing it.

2. What other factors are important in making the decision to accept or reject the offer?

Analyze: What is the highest cost that Chicago should consider to pay for the part in an outside purchase?

Problem Set B

Problem 30.1B ▶

Objective 2

Preparing income statements based on absorption costing and direct costing.

The following data pertains to the operations of BX Industries for the year ended December 31, 2010. The firm makes kitchen appliances.

DATA FOR 2010	
Sales	5,000 units @ $69/unit
Variable manufacturing costs	5,000 units @ $35/unit
Variable selling and administrative costs	$3/unit
Fixed manufacturing costs	$50,000
Fixed selling and administrative expenses	$24,000
Finished goods inventory, January 1, 2010	300 units
Finished goods inventory, December 31, 2010	300 units

INSTRUCTIONS

1. Prepare an income statement for the year using the absorption costing approach. Assume that the 300 units in the beginning inventory of finished goods had a cost of $42 per unit.

2. Prepare an income statement for the year using the direct costing approach. Assume that the 300 units in the beginning inventory of finished goods cost $40 per unit.

3. Explain the reason for the difference between the net income or loss computed by the two different methods.

Analyze: Under the absorption costing method, what percentage of cost of goods sold is attributable to fixed manufacturing costs?

Problem 30.2B ▶

Objectives 2, 3, 4, 5a

Preparing an income statement based on direct costing, choosing relevant data, determining contribution margin of a segment, and making a pricing decision.

Pitt Corporation began operations in 2010 to manufacture a single product. Relevant data for the year follow. There are no work in process inventories.

OPERATING DATA FOR 2010 Quantities	
Beginning inventories, finished goods	–0–
Units produced during the year	5,000
Units sold during the year	4,800
Costs	
Direct materials ($26 per unit)	$130,000
Direct labor ($24 per unit)	120,000
Variable factory overhead ($10 per unit)	50,000
Fixed factory overhead	125,000
Variable selling and administrative expenses ($7 per unit)	33,600

Fixed selling and administrative expenses	75,000
Selling price for each unit	125

INSTRUCTIONS

1. Prepare an income statement for 2010 using direct costing.

2. Assume that the company has an opportunity to sell 1,000 units of the product in a foreign country for $79 per unit. No fixed or variable selling and administrative expenses would be incurred in connection with these units except a $7 shipping and handling cost per unit. The company has idle capacity, and the order would not affect present markets. Would it be profitable for the company to accept the order? Show all computations.

Analyze: If Pitt Corporation had used the absorption costing method, would the value of ending inventories be higher or lower than that reflected in the statement you prepared? Explain.

Choosing relevant data, determining contribution margin of a segment, and deciding whether to purchase equipment.

◀ **Problem 30.3B**
Objectives 3, 4, 5b

Exterior Manufacturing makes doors, which it sells to home builders. The firm's finishing department is not mechanized. Employees use hand tools to finish the product. The factory superintendent has proposed that the firm acquire an electric-powered machine to perform some of the finishing functions. Presently, 5,000 units per year are manufactured and sold. A summary of the manufacturing costs of the finishing department follows.

Direct materials	$60,000
Direct labor	70,000
Manufacturing overhead	
Variable costs	10,000
Fixed costs	15,000

The machine being considered will cost $50,000 and have a useful life of five years, with no salvage value. The machine will cause the following changes in costs.

a. Direct labor will decrease by $10,000.

b. Indirect materials will decrease by $1 per unit.

c. No change in direct materials.

d. Fixed manufacturing overhead will decrease by $10,000 per year before considering depreciation on the new machine.

INSTRUCTIONS

1. Prepare an analysis showing the effect on net income of purchasing the equipment.

2. What other factors should be considered in making the decision?

Analyze: What direct labor costs are incurred per unit for the current manual process?

Choosing relevant data and deciding whether to make or buy a part.

◀ **Problem 30.4B**
Objectives 4, 5c

Cal Computer Company is currently manufacturing a part that goes into its main product. Each year, 2,000 of these parts are used. Cost data for the past year that relate to the 2,000 parts are given below. Fixed costs are allocated on the basis of direct labor hours. An outside company has offered to supply the part at $85 per unit, plus a shipping charge of $5 per unit. The plant capacity now used by Cal to manufacture the part would not be used in the foreseeable future if the part is purchased outside.

Variable costs	
Direct materials	$100,000
Direct labor	50,000
Variable overhead	24,000
Fixed overhead costs	50,000

INSTRUCTIONS

1. Prepare an analysis comparing the unit cost of manufacturing the part with the unit cost of purchasing it.

2. What other factors are important in making the decision to accept or reject the offer?

Analyze: If Cal Computer could negotiate a $1 reduction in shipping charge per unit for the outside supplier, what is the per unit difference between the cost to make and the cost to purchase?

Critical Thinking Problem 30.1

New Line of Business

Shine Industries distributes beauty and barber supplies to retail stores, beauty shops, and barber shops. Early in 2010, officers of the company decided to develop and market a line of shampoos and hair conditioners under their own private brand. They contracted with another company to manufacture and package the products. After the end of the first year, however, officers of Shine Industries became quite concerned over the profitability of the new line. An analysis of operations is shown below.

	Fixed Cost per Month	Percent of Selling Price per Unit
Average cost of products		40
Average cost of containers and packaging		10
Average freight in		2
Average delivery costs		3
Sales commissions		15
Advertising expenses		
Variable		9
Fixed	$500	
Warehousing costs		
Variable		2
Fixed	$300	
Other costs		
Variable		10
Fixed	$450	

An analysis of the fourth quarter 2010 showed sales of $15,000 for the quarter. Several officers in the company have suggested that the line of products should be discontinued.

INSTRUCTIONS

1. Based on the information above, what is the amount of income or loss for the fourth quarter?

2. Based on the information above only, should the venture be discontinued? The fixed costs are allocated costs and will not be eliminated by discontinuing the venture.

3. What questions, other than those related to the information given above, should be asked by the officers to arrive at a decision on whether or not to discontinue the product line?

4. What sales volume would be necessary to pay all variable costs and cover the allocated fixed costs?

Analyze: Assume that the sales staff has been asked to forfeit half of its sales commissions for the fourth quarter of 2010. What effect do you think this measure would have on the company's income for the period?

Critical Thinking Problem 30.2

Making Decisions

The cost accountant for Bruin Manufacturing, Inc., has prepared the analysis given below of the profitability of each of the firm's three products. All fixed costs are allocated costs and are not related to specific products.

	Item 101	Item 102	Item 103	Total
Sales	$60,000.00	$64,000.00	$87,500.00	$211,500.00
Cost of goods sold	28,400.00	32,800.00	65,500.00	126,700.00
Gross profit	$31,600.00	$31,200.00	$22,000.00	$ 84,800.00
Operating expenses	12,200.00	11,000.00	25,000.00	48,200.00
Net income (loss)	$19,400.00	$20,200.00	$ (3,000.00)	$ 36,600.00
Units sold	1,200	1,600	2,500	
Sales price per unit	$50	$40	$35	
Variable cost of goods sold per unit	$22	$18	$23	
Variable operating expenses per unit	$6	$5	$7	

Management has been considering several options concerning the company's product mix to reduce or eliminate the loss on Item 103. The company's president has asked you to prepare an analysis of the effects on the company's net income before taxes for each of the following proposals. Consider each proposal independently; no changes would occur in the other products.

PROPOSALS

1. Discontinue Item 103.

2. Increase the sales price of Item 103 to $40. Marketing analysis indicates that the increase in price will cause a decrease in sales of Item 103 to 1,000 units.

3. Discontinue Item 103 and use the resulting plant capacity to produce a new product, Item 104. The department's marketing studies estimate that 1,500 units could be sold at $35 each. The variable costs and expenses per unit of Item 104 are estimated to be $11 per unit manufacturing cost and $8 per unit for operating expenses.

BUSINESS CONNECTIONS

Decision Making

Managerial | FOCUS

1. The vice president of the manufacturing company for which you are the accountant has suggested to the president that all prices should be established on the basis of direct costing. Respond to this suggestion.

2. Assume that the company where you are employed has a substantial amount of unused plant capacity. A foreign company has offered to purchase a large quantity of your company's product, but at a price of 12 percent less than the product's normal selling price. What types of information are needed to arrive at a decision about whether to accept the order?

3. Suppose that your company is considering the purchase of a new machine for use in its production process. The cost of the machine is $295,000. If the purchase is made, an old machine currently in use will be scrapped. It has no net salvage value because its removal cost is equal to its gross salvage amount. The old machine has a book value of $150,000, and

management is reluctant to take the loss that would result if this machine is scrapped. Discuss the types of information that management would need to make a decision about purchasing the new asset. Give special attention to the problem of the old asset's book value.

4. Suppose that your company has been manufacturing a part used in its finished product. The total manufacturing cost of the part is $35. An outside supplier has offered to provide the part for $32. Describe the measurable data that management would need in making a decision about whether to accept the supplier's offer.

Ethical DILEMMA

Eliminating a Region

Brad's company, an eastern-based firm, is going through tough times. Downsizing is the only way to keep the company from going bankrupt. Brad has been given the assignment to eliminate an unprofitable region. His analysis has shown that the southwest region has a positive contribution margin but a net loss due to fixed costs. The western region has a positive contribution margin and a net loss. The eastern region has a positive contribution margin and a net income. The northeastern region has a positive contribution margin but a net loss. Brad further discovers that the net losses of the western and southwestern regions are due to fixed costs. Further investigation finds that the fixed costs can be separated by region costs and corporate costs. In Brad's investigation, the eastern region, though having all the costs of a corporate office, has lower fixed costs, making it a profitable region. Brad finds that Joe Black, the manager of the eastern region, has decided to allocate all the corporate office expenses to the other three divisions to make his region appear more profitable. More analysis indicates that if the corporate offices are allocated evenly to all four regions, the eastern region would have a net loss and the other regions would have a slight net income. What should Brad do? Should Joe have the ability to allocate costs to other regions?

STREETWISE:
Questions from the REAL WORLD

Cost and Revenue Decisions

Refer to the *2006 Annual Report* for The Home Depot, Inc., in Appendix A.

1. Locate "Management's Discussion and Analysis of Results of Operations and Financial Condition." Review the section *Results of Operations,* under Fiscal 2006 Compared to Fiscal 2005. During 2006, management believes the same store sales were reduced 2.8 percent due in part to "cannibalization"—locating new stores near existing stores. Based on this information, what cost- or revenue-based decisions are implied?

2. Review the section "Our Associates" of The Home Depot, Inc. Why does The Home Depot, Inc., invest in their associates? What cost and revenue comparisons do you think management made when arriving at this decision?

Financial Statement ANALYSIS

Product Mix and Cost-Revenue Analysis

Following are excerpts from the Mattel, Inc., *2006 Annual Report.*

Management's Discussion and Analysis of Financial Condition and Results of Operations

	For the Years	
Millions of Dollars	**2006**	**2005**
Net sales	$5,650.2	$5,179.0
Gross profit	$2,611.8	$2,372.9
Other selling and administrative expenses	$1,232.0	$1,079.3
Income from continuing operations before income taxes	$ 684	$ 652

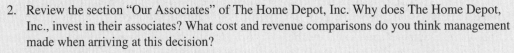

The increase in gross profit was driven by price increases and supply chain savings, which were partially offset by higher external cost pressures and unfavorable product mix, including higher royalty costs for licensed products.

The increase in other selling and administrative expenses in 2006 is primarily attributable to an $86.3 million increase in incentive compensation accruals, an increase of $27.3 million in stock-based compensation, including a pre-tax charge of $19.3 million for prior period unintentional stock option accounting errors . . . , costs associated with the third American Girl Place retail store, and additional selling and administrative expenses for Radica (acquired in October 2006), partially offset by savings related to the 2006 streamlining of the Mattel Brands organization.

Analyze:

1. Compute gross profit as a percentage of net sales for both 2006 and 2005.

2. How did Mattel's sales mix in 2006 impact its gross profit margin?

3. What nonfinancial factors might be considered in the American Girl Place retail store?

Analyze Online: Go to the *Company* section of the Mattel, Inc., Web site (www.mattel.com) and find the *Investors* section. Locate the most recent annual report and answer the following questions related to *Management's Discussion and Analysis of Financial Condition and Results of Operations.*

4. What product-related decisions has the company considered in the fiscal year?

5. What nonfinancial factors might have impacted those decisions?

Labor and Manufacturing

Manufacturing businesses must be sensitive to market trends and product demand as they establish production levels. The manager of a steel manufacturing plant hires and fires employees frequently as a result of production activity and fluctuating product demand. Do you agree or disagree with this practice? Explain. How do you think this practice affects employee morale or productivity?

Costing Methods

Assume that your company has issued a directive that manufacturing managers must assume responsibility for control of both variable and direct costs. Absorption costing has been adopted toward that end. Prepare a memo to your new CEO describing why this choice has been made and how this method will help managers identify cost concerns.

Choosing a Machine

Knowing the right questions to be asked and information to be obtained is important in making the correct decision. Your company has just decided to purchase a new machine. This machine will double production, decrease the material waste, and increase profits by 20 percent. However, it is double the size of the old one and takes twice as many workers to run. Your group has been given the task to decide to purchase this machine or stay with the current old machine. What questions would you need to ask to make your decision?

IRS Tax Topics

It is in the best interest of the Internal Revenue Service for companies to succeed. More taxes are paid if more companies make a higher profit. Go to the IRS Web site at IRS.gov. At the IRS home page, notice there is a search area where you can find topics located within the Web site. Enter variable and fixed costs in the search area. What do you find? Are there more than tax topics on the IRS Web site?

Extending THE THOUGHT

Business COMMUNICATION

TEAMWORK

Internet CONNECTION

Answers to **Self Reviews**

Answers to Section 1 Self Review

1. Under absorption costing, all manufacturing costs, including fixed costs, are included in the cost of goods manufactured and in the ending inventory. Under direct costing, all fixed overhead is charged off as a current expense of the period when it is incurred.

2. Direct costing

3. The difference in cost between one alternative and another.

4. **b.** variable manufacturing costs only.

5. **a.** opportunity cost.

6. $300,000 ($500,000 − $150,000 − $50,000)

Answers to Section 2 Self Review

1. It helps to determine if the company should seize the opportunity to acquire additional business at special prices that can contribute new sources of income and better utilize resources.

2. The contribution approach to analysis compares the impact of the proposed action on incremental revenues and incremental costs.

3. No, fixed costs are not relevant.

4. **b.** variable costs from revenue.

5. **d.** cost of the old machine

6. $2,500 increase ($7,500 savings − $5,000 increased fixed costs)

Answers to Comprehensive Self Review

1. Future or expected costs that will be incurred as a result of a specific decision.

2. Because they have already been incurred and will not change as a result of the decision being considered.

3. Acceptance of an order for less than total cost may be considered if the company has idle capacity, the price exceeds variable costs, the pricing would be legal, and the special order would not interfere with existing business.

4. It may be cheaper to purchase a part than to manufacture it; purchase may be necessary in order to assure supply; there may be a need to purchase one part in order to get favorable terms on other parts or supplies, and it may simplify the hiring of personnel or the handling of raw materials.

5. Incremental costs are the increases in total costs from one alternative to another.

Appendix A

 # Excerpts from The Home Depot, Inc., 2006 Annual Report

DEAR SHAREHOLDERS, ASSOCIATES, CUSTOMERS, SUPPLIERS AND COMMUNITIES:

From the beginning, outstanding customer service has been the cornerstone of our company. Our customers have high expectations of us because our associates set them. This expectation of outstanding customer service is what sets us apart as a retailer. The most critical job for those of us leading this company is to sustain a culture that never falls short of those customer expectations. Our "values wheel" summarizes that culture:

As you'll read in the attached financial report, 2006 was a challenging year for us. We experienced a tough housing market, particularly in the second half of the year. We addressed this challenge by accelerating investment in our retail business and intensifying our focus on customer service and satisfaction.

Going forward, we expect 2007 to be a challenging year as the housing environment remains soft. We will continue to make the necessary investments in our retail business so that we will emerge even stronger when the industry recovers. We are focused on five priorities around which our leadership team, our associates and our investments are aligned.

Associate engagement: Deliver differentiated customer service and the know-how our customers have come to expect from The Home Depot.

Product excitement: Drive value, price leadership and innovation through merchandising.

Product availability: Improve in-stock positions so customers can find and buy exactly what they need.

Shopping environment: Ensure that our stores are safe, clean and uncluttered.

Own the Pro: Be the number one destination for professional contractors, whose business today makes up roughly 30 percent of our retail sales.

2006 was a milestone year for our Supply segment. We completed the acquisition of Hughes Supply and successfully integrated it into our HD Supply business. We are now the second largest commercial distribution business in the United States. As we announced in February 2007, we are exploring strategic alternatives for HD Supply, including a possible sale of the business.

In 2006, we made a significant acquisition in China, a country with one of the largest and fastest growing home improvement markets in the world. The company we acquired, The Home Way, has stores that look very similar to ours in North America for a very good reason: We trained its founding management team in the mid 1990s.

Our goal is to provide the best customer experience in home improvement retail, the best place to work for our associates and the best place to invest. The five priorities described above are clearly aligned with the first two goals, and we will use a disciplined capital allocation approach to drive toward the third goal.

The most important barometer of the health of our company is the health of our culture. I hope that you shop our stores and experience our customer-focused culture firsthand.

Frank

Francis S. Blake
Chairman & Chief Executive Officer
March 29, 2007

Item 7. Management's Discussion and Analysis of Financial Condition and Results of Operations.

Executive Summary and Selected Consolidated Statements of Earnings Data

For fiscal year ended January 28, 2007 ("fiscal 2006"), we reported Net Earnings of $5.8 billion and Diluted Earnings per Share of $2.79 compared to Net Earnings of $5.8 billion and Diluted Earnings per Share of $2.72 for fiscal year ended January 29, 2006 ("fiscal 2005"). Net Sales increased 11.4% to $90.8 billion for fiscal 2006 from $81.5 billion for fiscal 2005. Our gross profit margin was 32.8% and our operating margin was 10.7% for fiscal 2006.

In the face of a slowdown in the housing market, our retail comparable store sales declined 2.8% in fiscal 2006 driven by a decline in comparable store customer transactions. This was partially offset by an increase in our average ticket of 1.6% in fiscal 2006 to $58.90, including increases in 8 of 10 selling departments.

We grew our numerous installation and home maintenance programs serving our do-it-for-me customers through our stores. Our retail services revenue increased 8.3% to $3.8 billion for fiscal 2006. We experienced sustained growth in categories such as countertops, exterior patios, solar, windows and HVAC.

We continued to introduce innovative and distinctive merchandise that reflects emerging consumer trends, supported by continued investments in store modernization and technology. We invested $3.5 billion in capital expenditures during fiscal 2006 primarily for new store construction, store modernization and technology. We began an accelerated store reinvestment program whereby we increased our investment in existing stores by $350 million more than our plan in the second half of fiscal 2006 to enhance the customer experience. This investment included capital and expense dollars to reset 100 merchandise bays in 540 stores, incorporate a richer staffing model and support our "Orange Juiced" program, a customer service incentive program for our store associates.

We added 125 new stores in fiscal 2006, including 12 stores through our acquisition of The Home Way, a Chinese home improvement retailer, and 10 relocations, bringing our total store count at the end of fiscal 2006 to 2,147. As of the end of fiscal 2006, 228, or approximately 11%, of our stores were located in Canada, Mexico or China compared to 191, or approximately 9%, at the end of fiscal 2005.

We have expanded our business by capturing a growing share of the professional residential, commercial and heavy construction markets through the growth of HD Supply. HD Supply experienced 162% Net Sales growth in fiscal 2006 and accounted for approximately 13% of our total Net Sales in fiscal 2006. We completed 12 acquisitions in fiscal 2006 that were integrated into HD Supply, including Hughes Supply, Inc., a leading distributor of construction and repair products. Organic Net Sales growth for the HD Supply segment was 5.6% in fiscal 2006.

In February 2007, we announced our decision to evaluate strategic alternatives for HD Supply. In order to maximize the value of HD Supply, we would need to further integrate it with our Retail business. We are currently evaluating whether this integration or other strategic alternatives, such as a sale or initial public offering of the business, would create the most shareholder value.

We generated $7.7 billion of cash flow from operations in fiscal 2006. We used this cash flow, along with the net proceeds of additional borrowings of $7.6 billion, to fund $8.1 billion of share repurchases and dividends, $4.3 billion in acquisitions and $3.5 billion in capital expenditures. At the end of fiscal 2006, our long-term debt-to-equity ratio was 47%. Our return on invested capital (computed on beginning long-term debt and equity for the trailing four quarters) was 20.5% at the end of fiscal 2006 compared to 22.4% for fiscal 2005.

We believe the selected sales data, the percentage relationship between Net Sales and major categories in the Consolidated Statements of Earnings and the percentage change in the dollar amounts of each of the items presented as follows is important in evaluating the performance of our business operations.

	% of Net Sales			% Increase (Decrease) In Dollar Amounts	
	Fiscal Year[1]				
	2006	2005	2004	2006 vs. 2005	2005 vs. 2004
NET SALES	100.0%	100.0%	100.0%	11.4%	11.5%
Gross Profit	32.8	33.5	33.4	9.0	11.8
Operating Expenses:					
Selling, General and Administrative	20.2	20.2	20.9	11.3	8.1
Depreciation and Amortization	1.9	1.8	1.7	19.7	17.9
Total Operating Expenses	22.1	22.0	22.6	12.0	8.8
OPERATING INCOME	10.7	11.5	10.8	3.3	18.1
Interest Income (Expense):					
Interest and Investment Income	—	0.1	0.1	(56.5)	10.7
Interest Expense	(0.4)	(0.2)	(0.1)	174.1	104.3
Interest, net	(0.4)	(0.1)	—	350.6	478.6
EARNINGS BEFORE PROVISION FOR INCOME TAXES	10.3	11.4	10.8	0.3	17.3
Provision for Income Taxes	4.0	4.2	4.0	3.0	18.3
NET EARNINGS	6.3%	7.2%	6.8%	(1.3)%	16.7%
SELECTED SALES DATA[2]					
Number of Retail Customer Transactions (millions)	1,330	1,330	1,295	0.0%	2.7%
Average Ticket	$ 58.90	$ 57.98	$ 54.89	1.6	5.6
Weighted Average Weekly Sales per Operating Store (000s)	$ 723	$ 763	$ 766	(5.2)	(0.4)
Weighted Average Sales per Square Foot	$357.83	$377.01	$375.26	(5.1)	0.5
Retail Comparable Store Sales (Decrease) Increase (%)[3]	(2.8)%	3.1%	5.1%	N/A	N/A

(1) Fiscal years 2006, 2005 and 2004 refer to the fiscal years ended January 28, 2007, January 29, 2006 and January 30, 2005, respectively. Fiscal years 2006, 2005 and 2004 include 52 weeks.

(2) Includes Retail segment only.

(3) Includes Net Sales at locations open greater than 12 months, including relocated and remodeled stores. Retail stores become comparable on the Monday following their 365th day of operation. Retail comparable store sales is intended only as supplemental information and is not a substitute for Net Sales or Net Earnings presented in accordance with generally accepted accounting principles.

Results of Operations

For an understanding of the significant factors that influenced our performance during the past three fiscal years, the following discussion should be read in conjunction with the Consolidated Financial Statements and the Notes to Consolidated Financial Statements presented in this report.

We operate in two reportable business segments: Retail and HD Supply. The Retail segment is principally engaged in the operation of retail stores located in the United States, Canada, Mexico and our recently acquired stores in China. The HD Supply segment distributes products and sells installation services to business-to-business customers, including home builders, professional contractors, municipalities and maintenance professionals. We identify segments based on how management makes operating decisions, assesses performance and allocates resources. The first quarter of fiscal 2006 was the first period in which we began to report our results of operations in two segments. This change was a result of the purchase of Hughes Supply, which significantly increased the size of HD Supply and resulted in changes in our internal reporting and management structure.

The Retail segment includes The Home Depot stores, EXPO Design Center stores ("EXPO") and other retail formats. The Retail segment also includes our retail services business and our catalog and on-line sales businesses.

The HD Supply segment consists of four major platforms: 1) infrastructure, including waterworks and utilities; 2) construction, including construction supply, lumber and building materials, electrical, plumbing/HVAC and interiors; 3) maintenance, including facilities maintenance and industrial PVF; and 4) repair and remodel.

Fiscal 2006 Compared to Fiscal 2005

Net Sales

Total Net Sales for fiscal 2006 increased 11.4%, or $9.3 billion, to $90.8 billion from $81.5 billion for fiscal 2005. Of the $9.3 billion increase, $7.3 billion, net of intercompany sales, came from our HD Supply segment and $2.0 billion came from our Retail segment.

Net Sales for our Retail segment were $79.0 billion for fiscal 2006, a 2.6% increase over fiscal 2005. Fiscal 2006 Retail segment Net Sales growth was primarily driven by sales from new stores. Retail comparable store sales decreased 2.8% for fiscal 2006 compared to an increase of 3.1% for fiscal 2005. The decline in retail comparable store sales was driven by a 4.6% decline in comparable store customer transactions offset in part by a 1.6% increase in average ticket. Our average ticket increased to $58.90 for fiscal 2006 and increased in 8 of 10 selling departments. The decrease in retail comparable store sales for fiscal 2006 was due to the significant slowdown in the U.S. retail home improvement market as well as difficult year-over-year comparisons due to sales arising from hurricane activity in fiscal 2005. Both Canada and Mexico, however, experienced positive retail comparable store sales for fiscal 2006. Additionally, our retail comparable store sales results reflect in part the impact of cannibalization. In order to meet our customer service objectives, we strategically open stores near market areas served by existing stores ("cannibalize") to enhance service levels, gain incremental sales and increase market penetration. Our new stores cannibalized approximately 13.5% of our existing stores during fiscal 2006, which had a negative impact to retail comparable store sales of approximately 1.9%.

Despite the difficult U.S. retail home improvement market, we continued to expand our retail services revenue, which increased 8.3% to $3.8 billion for fiscal 2006 from $3.5 billion for fiscal 2005. The growth in retail services revenue was driven by strength in a number of areas including countertops, exterior patios, solar, windows and HVAC. Our retail services programs focus primarily on providing products and services to our do-it-for-me customers. Our services revenue is expected to benefit from the growing percentage of aging "baby-boomers" as they rely more heavily on installation services.

Net Sales for our HD Supply segment for fiscal 2006 were $12.1 billion, an increase of 162% over fiscal 2005. The increase was primarily a result of recent acquisitions. Organic Net Sales growth for the HD Supply segment was 5.6% in fiscal 2006, which includes the impact of commodity price inflation and market share gains.

We believe that our sales performance has been, and could continue to be, negatively impacted by the level of competition that we encounter in various markets. Due to the highly-fragmented U.S. home improvement and professional supply industry, in which we estimate our market share is approximately 10%, measuring the impact on our sales by our competitors is difficult.

Gross Profit

Total Gross Profit increased 9.0% to $29.8 billion for fiscal 2006 from $27.3 billion for fiscal 2005. Gross Profit as a percent of Net Sales decreased 73 basis points to 32.8% for fiscal 2006 compared to 33.5% for fiscal 2005. The decline in total Gross Profit as a percent of Net Sales was primarily due to a higher penetration of the lower margin HD Supply segment. In fiscal 2006, 65 basis points of the total Gross Profit decline was a result of a higher penetration of HD Supply businesses as well as a drop in HD Supply's Gross Profit rate due to a change in the mix of businesses owned.

Operating Expenses

Operating Expenses increased 12.0% to $20.1 billion for fiscal 2006 from $18.0 billion for fiscal 2005. Operating Expenses as a percent of Net Sales were 22.1% for fiscal 2006 compared to 22.0% for fiscal 2005.

Selling, General and Administrative Expenses ("SG&A") increased 11.3% to $18.3 billion for fiscal 2006 from $16.5 billion for fiscal 2005. As a percent of Net Sales, SG&A was 20.2% for fiscal 2006 and fiscal 2005. The increase in SG&A during fiscal 2006 was due to added associate labor hours on the floor of our stores, increased spending on store maintenance programs and the expansion of merchandise display resets. This increase was partially offset by reduced self-insurance costs as we continue to realize benefits from safety programs and other initiatives. Fiscal 2006 SG&A also reflects benefits from our private label credit card, which carries a lower discount rate than other forms of credit, like bank cards. Through our private label credit card we offer no interest/no payment programs. The cost of deferred interest associated with these programs is included in Cost of Sales. We believe these programs deliver long-term benefits, including higher average ticket and customer loyalty. For fiscal 2006, the penetration of our private label credit sales was 28.0% compared to 25.6% for fiscal 2005.

Also impacting our SG&A in fiscal 2006 is expense associated with executive severance of $129 million and the adoption of Statement of Financial Accounting Standards ("SFAS") No. 123(R), "Share-Based Payment" ("SFAS 123(R)"), whereby we recorded approximately $40 million of stock compensation expense related to the continued vesting of options granted prior to fiscal 2003. Partially offsetting the increase in SG&A was $91 million of impairment charges and expense related to lease obligations associated with the closing of 20 EXPO stores in fiscal 2005.

Depreciation and Amortization increased 19.7% to $1.8 billion for fiscal 2006 from $1.5 billion for fiscal 2005. Depreciation and Amortization as a percent of Net Sales was 1.9% for fiscal 2006 and 1.8% for fiscal 2005. The increase as a percent of Net Sales was primarily due to the amortization of intangible assets acquired as part of our recent acquisitions and the depreciation of our investments in store modernization and technology.

Interest, net

In fiscal 2006, we recognized $365 million of net Interest Expense compared to $81 million in fiscal 2005. Net Interest Expense as a percent of Net Sales was 0.4% for fiscal 2006 compared to 0.1% for fiscal 2005. The increase was primarily due to additional interest incurred related to the March 2006 issuance of $1.0 billion of 5.20% Senior Notes and $3.0 billion of 5.40% Senior Notes and the December 2006 issuance of $750 million of floating rate Senior Notes, $1.25 billion of 5.25% Senior Notes and $3.0 billion of 5.875% Senior Notes.

Provision for Income Taxes

Our combined federal, state and foreign effective income tax rate increased to 38.1% for fiscal 2006 from 37.1% for fiscal 2005. The increase in our effective income tax rate for fiscal 2006 was primarily due to the impact of a retroactive tax assessment from the Canadian province of Quebec. During the second quarter of fiscal 2006, the Quebec National Assembly passed legislation that retroactively changed certain tax laws that subjected us to additional tax and interest. As a result, we received an assessment from Quebec for $57 million in retroactive tax and $12 million in related interest for the 2002 through 2005 taxable years.

Diluted Earnings per Share

Diluted Earnings per Share were $2.79 for fiscal 2006 and $2.72 for fiscal 2005. Diluted Earnings per Share were favorably impacted in both fiscal 2006 and fiscal 2005 by the repurchase of shares of our common stock under our $17.5 billion repurchase authorization. Since the inception of the program in 2002, we have repurchased 451 million shares of our common stock for a total of $16.4 billion, including $5 billion through accelerated share repurchases in fiscal 2006. As of January 28, 2007, we had $1.1 billion remaining under our authorized share repurchase program.

Fiscal 2005 Compared to Fiscal Year Ended January 30, 2005 ("fiscal 2004")

Net Sales

Net Sales for fiscal 2005 increased 11.5% to $81.5 billion from $73.1 billion for fiscal 2004. Fiscal 2005 Net Sales growth was driven by an increase in retail comparable store sales of 3.1%, sales from new stores opened during fiscal 2005 and fiscal 2004 and sales from our newly acquired businesses within HD Supply.

The increase in retail comparable store sales in fiscal 2005 reflects a number of factors. Our average ticket, which increased 5.6% to $57.98, increased in all selling departments and our retail comparable store sales growth in fiscal 2005 was positive in 9 of 10 selling departments. Building materials had the strongest retail comparable store sales increase through sales growth of gypsum, roofing, concrete and insulation, due in part to the impact of one of the most destructive hurricane seasons in modern U.S. history. We experienced strong retail comparable store sales growth in kitchen and bath driven by continued growth in appliances and kitchen installations. We also experienced strong retail comparable store sales in our Pro categories, including plumbing, electrical and hardware in fiscal 2005. The impact of cannibalization partially offset our fiscal 2005 retail comparable store sales growth. As of the end of fiscal 2005, certain new stores cannibalized approximately 20% of our existing stores and we estimate that store cannibalization reduced fiscal 2005 retail comparable store sales by approximately 1.8%.

The growth in Net Sales for fiscal 2005 also reflects growth in services revenue, which increased 16.6% to $3.5 billion for fiscal 2005 from $3.0 billion for fiscal 2004. The growth in services revenue was driven by strength in a number of areas including countertops, roofing, kitchens, windows and HVAC.

Gross Profit

Gross Profit increased 11.8% to $27.3 billion for fiscal 2005 from $24.4 billion for fiscal 2004. Gross Profit as a percent of Net Sales increased 10 basis points to 33.5% for fiscal 2005, the highest annual rate in our Company's history. Our gross profit margin was impacted by a number of factors during the year including a change in the mix of merchandise sold, markdowns taken in connection with our decision to close 20 EXPO stores, the increasing penetration of our HD Supply business and the cost of our deferred interest programs. For fiscal 2005, the penetration of our private label credit sales was 25.6% compared to 24.1% for fiscal 2004.

Operating Expenses

Operating Expenses increased 8.8% to $18.0 billion for fiscal 2005 from $16.5 billion for fiscal 2004. Operating Expenses as a percent of Net Sales were 22.0% for fiscal 2005 compared to 22.6% for fiscal 2004.

SG&A increased 8.1% to $16.5 billion for fiscal 2005 from $15.3 billion for fiscal 2004. As a percent of Net Sales, SG&A was 20.2% for fiscal 2005 compared to 20.9% for fiscal 2004. The reduction of SG&A as a percent of Net Sales for fiscal 2005 was primarily a result of continued focus on cost take-out initiatives and driving productivity gains throughout the Company. We also continue to see benefits from our private label credit card, which carries a lower discount rate than other forms of credit, like bank cards. In fiscal 2005, we recorded $52 million of income related to gift card breakage as a reduction of SG&A. Fiscal 2005 was the first year in which we recognized gift card breakage, and therefore, the amount recognized in fiscal 2005 includes the breakage income related to gift cards sold since the inception of our gift card program. Finally, for fiscal 2005, we recorded $91 million of impairment charges and expense related to lease obligations in connection with our decision to close 20 EXPO stores.

Depreciation and Amortization increased 17.9% to $1.5 billion for fiscal 2005 from $1.2 billion for fiscal 2004. Depreciation and Amortization as a percent of Net Sales was 1.8% for fiscal 2005 and 1.7% for fiscal 2004. The increase as a percent of Net Sales was primarily due to our investments in store modernization and technology.

Interest, net

In fiscal 2005, we recognized $81 million of net Interest Expense compared to $14 million in fiscal 2004. Net Interest Expense as a percent of Net Sales was 0.1% for fiscal 2005 and less than 0.1% for fiscal 2004. Interest Expense increased to $143 million for fiscal 2005 from $70 million for fiscal 2004 primarily due to additional interest incurred related to the August 2005 $1.0 billion issuance of 4.625% Senior Notes and the September 2004 $1.0 billion issuance of 3.75% Senior Notes. Interest and Investment Income increased 10.7% to $62 million for fiscal 2005 from $56 million for fiscal 2004 due primarily to a higher interest rate environment.

Provision for Income Taxes

Our combined federal and state effective income tax rate increased to 37.1% for fiscal 2005 from 36.8% for fiscal 2004. The majority of the increase in our effective income tax rate was due to an increase in the state effective tax rate in fiscal 2005.

Diluted Earnings per Share

Diluted Earnings per Share were $2.72 and $2.26 for fiscal 2005 and fiscal 2004, respectively. Diluted Earnings per Share were favorably impacted in both fiscal 2005 and fiscal 2004 as a result of the repurchase of shares of our common stock.

Liquidity and Capital Resources

Cash flow generated from operations provides a significant source of liquidity. For fiscal 2006, Net Cash Provided by Operating Activities was $7.7 billion as compared to $6.6 billion for fiscal 2005. The increase was primarily a result of more productive working capital in fiscal 2006.

Net Cash Used in Investing Activities increased to $7.6 billion for fiscal 2006 from $4.6 billion for fiscal 2005. This increase was primarily the result of an increase in Payments for Businesses Acquired of $1.7 billion as well as a decrease in net Proceeds from Sales and Maturities of Investments of $1.7 billion, partially offset by a $339 million decrease in Capital Expenditures. We paid $4.3 billion to complete 15 acquisitions in fiscal 2006, including Hughes Supply. Our fiscal 2006 acquisitions resulted in increases in Receivables, Merchandise Inventories, Goodwill, Other Assets and Accounts Payable in the Consolidated Balance Sheet as of January 28, 2007. See Note 11 to our "Notes to Consolidated Financial Statements" included in Item 8 of this report for further discussion.

Additionally in fiscal 2006, we spent $3.5 billion on Capital Expenditures, allocated as follows: 64% for new stores, 11% for store modernization, 6% for technology and 19% for other initiatives. In fiscal 2006, we added 125 new stores, including 12 stores in China through our acquisition of The Home Way, and 10 relocations.

Net Cash Used in Financing Activities for fiscal 2006 was $203 million compared with $1.7 billion for fiscal 2005. The decrease in Net Cash Used in Financing Activities was primarily due to net proceeds of $7.6 billion from the issuance of additional long-term debt, partially offset by a net increase of $4.2 billion in Repurchases of Common Stock and Cash Dividends Paid to Stockholders.

In February 2006, May 2006 and August 2006, our Board of Directors authorized an additional $1.0 billion, $2.0 billion and $3.5 billion, respectively, in our share repurchase program, bringing the total authorization by our Board of Directors since inception of the program in 2002 to $17.5 billion as of January 28, 2007. Pursuant to this authorization, we have repurchased approximately 451 million shares of our common stock for a total of $16.4 billion as of January 28, 2007. During fiscal 2006, we repurchased approximately 174 million shares of our common stock for $6.7 billion and during fiscal 2005 we repurchased approximately 76 million shares of our common stock for $3.0 billion. As of January 28, 2007, approximately $1.1 billion remained under our share repurchase program. During fiscal 2006, we also increased dividends paid by 62.8% to $1.4 billion from $857 million in fiscal 2005.

We have a commercial paper program that allows for borrowings up to $2.5 billion. In connection with the program, we have a back-up credit facility with a consortium of banks for borrowings up to $2.0 billion. As of January 28, 2007, there were no borrowings outstanding under the commercial paper program or the credit facility. The credit facility, which expires in December 2010, contains various restrictions, none of which is expected to impact our liquidity or capital resources.

We use capital and operating leases to finance a portion of our real estate, including our stores, distribution centers, HD Supply locations and store support centers. The net present value of capital lease obligations is reflected in our Consolidated Balance Sheets in Long-Term Debt. In accordance with generally accepted accounting principles, the operating leases are not reflected in our Consolidated Balance Sheets. As of the end of fiscal 2006, our long-term debt-to-equity ratio was 46.5% compared to 9.9% at the end of fiscal 2005. This increase reflects the net increase in Long-Term Debt as a result of the issuance of Senior Notes in March and December of fiscal 2006.

As of January 28, 2007, we had $614 million in Cash and Short-Term Investments. We believe that our current cash position and cash flow generated from operations should be sufficient to enable us to complete our capital expenditure programs and any required long-term debt payments through the next several fiscal years. In addition, we have funds available from the $2.5 billion commercial paper program and the ability to obtain alternative sources of financing for other requirements.

In March 2006, we entered into a forward starting interest rate swap agreement with a notional amount of $2.0 billion, accounted for as a cash flow hedge, to hedge interest rate fluctuations in anticipation of the issuance of the 5.40% Senior Notes due March 1, 2016. Upon issuance of the hedged debt, we settled our forward starting interest rate swap agreement and recorded a $12 million decrease, net of income taxes, to Accumulated Other Comprehensive Income, which will be amortized to interest expense over the life of the related debt.

In May 2006, we entered into a $2 billion accelerated share repurchase agreement with a financial institution pursuant to which we repurchased approximately 53 million shares of our common stock. Under the agreement, the financial institution purchased an equivalent number of shares of our common stock in the open market. The shares repurchased by us were subject to a future purchase price adjustment based upon the weighted average price of our common stock over an agreed period, subject to a specified collar. In August 2006, we settled the accelerated share repurchase. We elected settlement in cash and received $61 million from the financial institution, which was recorded as an offset to our cost of treasury stock.

In October 2006, we entered into a forward starting interest rate swap agreement with a notional amount of $1.0 billion, accounted for as a cash flow hedge, to hedge interest rate fluctuations in anticipation of the issuance of the 5.875% Senior Notes due December 16, 2036. Upon issuance of the hedged debt in December 2006, we settled our forward starting interest rate swap agreement and recorded an $11 million decrease, net of income taxes, to Accumulated Other Comprehensive Income, which will be amortized to interest expense over the life of the related debt.

In December 2006, we entered into a $3 billion accelerated share repurchase agreement with a financial institution pursuant to which we repurchased approximately 75 million shares of our common stock. Under the agreement, the financial institution purchased an equivalent number of shares of our common stock in the open market. The shares repurchased by us were subject to a future purchase price adjustment based upon the weighted average price of our common stock over an agreed period. In March 2007, we settled the accelerated share repurchase. We elected settlement in cash and received $36 million from the financial institution, which was recorded as an offset to our cost of treasury stock in fiscal 2007.

The following table summarizes our significant contractual obligations and commercial commitments as of January 28, 2007 (amounts in millions):

Contractual Obligations[1]	Payments Due by Fiscal Year				
	Total	2007	2008-2009	2010-2011	Thereafter
Total Debt[2]	$19,358	$ 607	$3,224	$2,946	$12,581
Capital Lease Obligations[3]	1,323	78	157	160	928
Operating Leases	9,131	917	1,580	1,213	5,421
Subtotal	$29,812	$1,602	$4,961	$4,319	$18,930

Commercial Commitments[4]	Amount of Commitment Expiration per Fiscal Year				
	Total	2007	2008-2009	2010-2011	Thereafter
Letters of Credit	$ 1,238	$1,230	$ 8	$ —	$ —
Purchase Obligations[5]	2,741	1,379	1,336	22	4
Guarantees	72	72	—	—	—
Subtotal	4,051	2,681	1,344	22	4
Total	$33,863	$4,283	$6,305	$4,341	$18,934

(1) *Contractual obligations include Long-Term Debt comprised primarily of $11 billion of Senior Notes further discussed in "Quantitative and Qualitative Disclosures about Market Risk" and future minimum lease payments under capital and operating leases used in the normal course of business.*

(2) *Excludes present value of capital lease obligations of $419 million. Includes $8.0 billion of interest payments and $69 million of unamortized discount.*

(3) *Includes $904 million of imputed interest.*

(4) *Commercial commitments include letters of credit from certain business transactions, purchase obligations and commitments to purchase store assets. We issue letters of credit for insurance programs, purchases of import merchandise inventories and construction contracts. Our purchase obligations consist of commitments for both merchandise and services.*

(5) *Purchase obligations include all legally binding contracts such as firm commitments for inventory purchases, utility purchases, capital expenditures, software acquisition and license commitments and legally binding service contracts. Purchase orders that are not binding agreements are excluded from the table above. Additionally, we have included a commitment to purchase the underlying asset under an off-balance sheet lease related to certain stores for $282 million during 2008.*

Quantitative and Qualitative Disclosures about Market Risk

Our exposure to market risk results primarily from fluctuations in interest rates. Although we have international operating entities, our exposure to foreign currency rate fluctuations is not significant to our financial condition and results of operations. Our primary objective for entering into derivative instruments is to manage our exposure to interest rates, as well as to maintain an appropriate mix of fixed and variable rate debt.

As of January 28, 2007 we had, net of discounts, $10.9 billion of Senior Notes outstanding. The market values of the publicly traded Senior Notes as of January 28, 2007, were approximately $10.9 billion.

Impact of Inflation, Deflation and Changing Prices

We have experienced inflation and deflation related to our purchase of certain commodity products.

Item 8. Financial Statements and Supplementary Data.

Management's Responsibility for Financial Statements

The financial statements presented in this Annual Report have been prepared with integrity and objectivity and are the responsibility of the management of The Home Depot, Inc. These financial statements have been prepared in conformity with U.S. generally accepted accounting principles and properly reflect certain estimates and judgments based upon the best available information.

The financial statements of the Company have been audited by KPMG LLP, an independent registered public accounting firm. Their accompanying report is based upon an audit conducted in accordance with the standards of the Public Company Accounting Oversight Board (United States).

The Audit Committee of the Board of Directors, consisting solely of outside directors, meets five times a year with the independent registered public accounting firm, the internal auditors and representatives of management to discuss auditing and financial reporting matters. In addition, a telephonic meeting is held prior to each quarterly earnings release. The Audit Committee retains the independent registered public accounting firm and regularly reviews the internal accounting controls, the activities of the independent registered public accounting firm and internal auditors and the financial condition of the Company. Both the Company's independent registered pubic accounting firm and the internal auditors have free access to the Audit Committee.

Management's Report on Internal Control over Financial Reporting

Our management is responsible for establishing and maintaining adequate internal control over financial reporting, as such term is defined in Rule 13a-15(f) promulgated under the Securities Exchange Act of 1934, as amended. Under the supervision and with the participation of our management, including our principal executive officer and principal financial officer, we conducted an evaluation of the effectiveness of our internal control over financial reporting based on the framework in *Internal Control – Integrated Framework* issued by the Committee of Sponsoring Organizations of the Treadway Commission (COSO). Based on our evaluation, our management concluded that our internal control over financial reporting was effective as of January 28, 2007 in providing reasonable assurance regarding reliability of financial reporting and the preparation of financial statements for external purposes in accordance with generally accepted accounting principles. Our management's assessment of the effectiveness of our internal control over financial reporting as of January 28, 2007 has been audited by KPMG LLP, an independent registered public accounting firm, as stated in its report which is included herein.

/s/ FRANCIS S. BLAKE   /s/ CAROL B. TOMÉ

Francis S. Blake   **Carol B. Tomé**
Chairman &   **Chief Financial Officer &**
Chief Executive Officer   **Executive Vice President –**
                                        Corporate Services

Report of Independent Registered Public Accounting Firm

The Board of Directors and Stockholders
The Home Depot, Inc.:

We have audited management's assessment, included in the accompanying Management's Report on Internal Control Over Financial Reporting, that The Home Depot, Inc. and subsidiaries maintained effective internal control over financial reporting as of January 28, 2007, based on criteria established in *Internal Control – Integrated Framework* issued by the Committee of Sponsoring Organizations of the Treadway Commission (COSO). The Company's management is responsible for maintaining effective internal control over financial reporting and for its assessment of the effectiveness of internal control over financial reporting. Our responsibility is to express an opinion on management's assessment and an opinion on the effectiveness of the Company's internal control over financial reporting based on our audit.

We conducted our audit in accordance with the standards of the Public Company Accounting Oversight Board (United States). Those standards require that we plan and perform the audit to obtain reasonable assurance about whether effective internal control over financial reporting was maintained in all material respects. Our audit included obtaining an understanding of internal control over financial reporting, evaluating management's assessment, testing and evaluating the design and operating effectiveness of internal control, and performing such other procedures as we considered necessary in the circumstances. We believe that our audit provides a reasonable basis for our opinion.

A company's internal control over financial reporting is a process designed to provide reasonable assurance regarding the reliability of financial reporting and the preparation of financial statements for external purposes in accordance with generally accepted accounting principles. A company's internal control over financial reporting includes those policies and procedures that (1) pertain to the maintenance of records that, in reasonable detail, accurately and fairly reflect the transactions and dispositions of the assets of the company; (2) provide reasonable assurance that transactions are recorded as necessary to permit preparation of financial statements in accordance with generally accepted accounting principles, and that receipts and expenditures of the company are being made only in accordance with authorizations of management and directors of the company; and (3) provide reasonable assurance regarding prevention or timely detection of unauthorized acquisition, use, or disposition of the company's assets that could have a material effect on the financial statements.

Because of its inherent limitations, internal control over financial reporting may not prevent or detect misstatements. Also, projections of any evaluation of effectiveness to future periods are subject to the risk that controls may become inadequate because of changes in conditions, or that the degree of compliance with the policies or procedures may deteriorate.

In our opinion, management's assessment that The Home Depot, Inc. and subsidiaries maintained effective internal control over financial reporting as of January 28, 2007, is fairly stated, in all material respects, based on criteria established in *Internal Control – Integrated Framework* issued by the Committee of Sponsoring Organizations of the Treadway Commission (COSO). Also, in our opinion, The Home Depot, Inc. and subsidiaries maintained, in all material respects, effective internal control over financial reporting as of January 28, 2007, based on criteria established in *Internal Control – Integrated Framework* issued by the Committee of Sponsoring Organizations of the Treadway Commission (COSO).

We also have audited, in accordance with the standards of the Public Company Accounting Oversight Board (United States), the Consolidated Balance Sheets of The Home Depot, Inc. and subsidiaries as of January 28, 2007 and January 29, 2006, and the related Consolidated Statements of Earnings, Stockholders' Equity and Comprehensive Income, and Cash Flows for each of the fiscal years in the three-year period ended January 28, 2007, and our report dated March 21, 2007 expressed an unqualified opinion on those consolidated financial statements. Our report refers to the Company's adoption of Securities and Exchange Commission Staff Accounting Bulletin No. 108, *Considering the Effects of Prior Year Misstatements when Quantifying Misstatements in the Current Year Financial Statements*, effective January 30, 2006, the beginning of the fiscal year ended January 28, 2007.

/s/ KPMG LLP

Atlanta, Georgia
March 21, 2007

Report of Independent Registered Public Accounting Firm

The Board of Directors and Stockholders
The Home Depot, Inc.:

We have audited the accompanying Consolidated Balance Sheets of The Home Depot, Inc. and subsidiaries as of January 28, 2007 and January 29, 2006, and the related Consolidated Statements of Earnings, Stockholders' Equity and Comprehensive Income, and Cash Flows for each of the fiscal years in the three-year period ended January 28, 2007. These Consolidated Financial Statements are the responsibility of the Company's management. Our responsibility is to express an opinion on these Consolidated Financial Statements based on our audits.

We conducted our audits in accordance with the standards of the Public Company Accounting Oversight Board (United States). Those standards require that we plan and perform the audit to obtain reasonable assurance about whether the financial statements are free of material misstatement. An audit includes examining, on a test basis, evidence supporting the amounts and disclosures in the financial statements. An audit also includes assessing the accounting principles used and significant estimates made by management, as well as evaluating the overall financial statement presentation. We believe that our audits provide a reasonable basis for our opinion.

In our opinion, the Consolidated Financial Statements referred to above present fairly, in all material respects, the financial position of The Home Depot, Inc. and subsidiaries as of January 28, 2007 and January 29, 2006, and the results of their operations and their cash flows for each of the fiscal years in the three-year period ended January 28, 2007, in conformity with U.S. generally accepted accounting principles.

As discussed in Note 2 to the consolidated financial statements, effective January 30, 2006, the beginning of the fiscal year ended January 28, 2007, the Company adopted Securities and Exchange Commission Staff Accounting Bulletin No. 108, *Considering the Effects of Prior Year Misstatements when Quantifying Misstatements in the Current Year Financial Statements*.

We also have audited, in accordance with the standards of the Public Company Accounting Oversight Board (United States), the effectiveness of The Home Depot, Inc.'s internal control over financial reporting as of January 28, 2007, based on criteria established in *Internal Control – Integrated Framework* issued by the Committee of Sponsoring Organizations of the Treadway Commission (COSO), and our report dated March 21, 2007 expressed an unqualified opinion on management's assessment of, and the effective operation of, internal control over financial reporting.

/s/ KPMG LLP

Atlanta, Georgia
March 21, 2007

THE HOME DEPOT, INC. AND SUBSIDIARIES
CONSOLIDATED STATEMENTS OF EARNINGS

	Fiscal Year Ended[1]		
amounts in millions, except per share data	January 28, 2007	January 29, 2006	January 30, 2005
NET SALES	**$90,837**	$81,511	$73,094
Cost of Sales	**61,054**	54,191	48,664
GROSS PROFIT	**29,783**	27,320	24,430
Operating Expenses:			
Selling, General and Administrative	**18,348**	16,485	15,256
Depreciation and Amortization	**1,762**	1,472	1,248
Total Operating Expenses	**20,110**	17,957	16,504
OPERATING INCOME	**9,673**	9,363	7,926
Interest Income (Expense):			
Interest and Investment Income	**27**	62	56
Interest Expense	**(392)**	(143)	(70)
Interest, net	**(365)**	(81)	(14)
EARNINGS BEFORE PROVISION FOR INCOME TAXES	**9,308**	9,282	7,912
Provision for Income Taxes	**3,547**	3,444	2,911
NET EARNINGS	**$ 5,761**	$ 5,838	$ 5,001
Weighted Average Common Shares	**2,054**	2,138	2,207
BASIC EARNINGS PER SHARE	**$ 2.80**	$ 2.73	$ 2.27
Diluted Weighted Average Common Shares	**2,062**	2,147	2,216
DILUTED EARNINGS PER SHARE	**$ 2.79**	$ 2.72	$ 2.26

(1) *Fiscal years ended January 28, 2007, January 29, 2006 and January 30, 2005 include 52 weeks.*

See accompanying Notes to Consolidated Financial Statements.

THE HOME DEPOT, INC. AND SUBSIDIARIES
CONSOLIDATED BALANCE SHEETS

amounts in millions, except per share data	January 28, 2007	January 29, 2006
ASSETS		
Current Assets:		
Cash and Cash Equivalents	$ 600	$ 793
Short-Term Investments	14	14
Receivables, net	3,223	2,396
Merchandise Inventories	12,822	11,401
Other Current Assets	1,341	665
Total Current Assets	18,000	15,269
Property and Equipment, at cost:		
Land	8,355	7,924
Buildings	15,215	14,056
Furniture, Fixtures and Equipment	7,799	7,073
Leasehold Improvements	1,391	1,207
Construction in Progress	1,123	843
Capital Leases	475	427
	34,358	31,530
Less Accumulated Depreciation and Amortization	7,753	6,629
Net Property and Equipment	26,605	24,901
Notes Receivable	343	348
Goodwill	6,314	3,286
Other Assets	1,001	601
Total Assets	**$52,263**	**$44,405**
LIABILITIES AND STOCKHOLDERS' EQUITY		
Current Liabilities:		
Short-Term Debt	$ —	$ 900
Accounts Payable	7,356	6,032
Accrued Salaries and Related Expenses	1,295	1,068
Sales Taxes Payable	475	488
Deferred Revenue	1,634	1,757
Income Taxes Payable	217	388
Current Installments of Long-Term Debt	18	513
Other Accrued Expenses	1,936	1,560
Total Current Liabilities	12,931	12,706
Long-Term Debt, excluding current installments	11,643	2,672
Other Long-Term Liabilities	1,243	1,172
Deferred Income Taxes	1,416	946
STOCKHOLDERS' EQUITY		
Common Stock, par value $0.05; authorized: 10,000 shares; issued 2,421 shares at January 28, 2007 and 2,401 shares at January 29, 2006; outstanding 1,970 shares at January 28, 2007 and 2,124 shares at January 29, 2006	121	120
Paid-In Capital	7,930	7,149
Retained Earnings	33,052	28,943
Accumulated Other Comprehensive Income	310	409
Treasury Stock, at cost, 451 shares at January 28, 2007 and 277 shares at January 29, 2006	(16,383)	(9,712)
Total Stockholders' Equity	25,030	26,909
Total Liabilities and Stockholders' Equity	**$52,263**	**$44,405**

See accompanying Notes to Consolidated Financial Statements.

THE HOME DEPOT, INC. AND SUBSIDIARIES
CONSOLIDATED STATEMENTS OF STOCKHOLDERS' EQUITY AND COMPREHENSIVE INCOME

amounts in millions, except per share data	Common Stock Shares	Common Stock Amount	Paid-In Capital	Retained Earnings	Accumulated Other Comprehensive Income (Loss)	Treasury Stock Shares	Treasury Stock Amount	Stockholders' Equity	Total Comprehensive Income
BALANCE, FEBRUARY 1, 2004	**2,373**	**$119**	**$6,108**	**$19,680**	**$ 90**	**(116)**	**$ (3,590)**	**$22,407**	
Net Earnings	—	—	—	5,001	—	—	—	5,001	$5,001
Shares Issued Under Employee Stock Plans	12	—	286	—	—	—	—	286	
Tax Effect of Sale of Option Shares by Employees	—	—	26	—	—	—	—	26	
Translation Adjustments	—	—	—	—	137	—	—	137	137
Stock Options, Awards and Amortization of Restricted Stock	—	—	122	—	—	—	—	122	
Repurchase of Common Stock	—	—	—	—	—	(84)	(3,102)	(3,102)	
Cash Dividends ($0.325 per share)	—	—	—	(719)	—	—	—	(719)	
Comprehensive Income									$5,138
BALANCE, JANUARY 30, 2005	**2,385**	**$119**	**$6,542**	**$23,962**	**$227**	**(200)**	**$ (6,692)**	**$24,158**	
Net Earnings	—	—	—	5,838	—	—	—	5,838	$5,838
Shares Issued Under Employee Stock Plans	16	1	409	—	—	—	—	410	
Tax Effect of Sale of Option Shares by Employees	—	—	24	—	—	—	—	24	
Translation Adjustments	—	—	—	—	182	—	—	182	182
Stock Options, Awards and Amortization of Restricted Stock	—	—	174	—	—	—	—	174	
Repurchase of Common Stock	—	—	—	—	—	(77)	(3,020)	(3,020)	
Cash Dividends ($0.40 per share)	—	—	—	(857)	—	—	—	(857)	
Comprehensive Income									$6,020
BALANCE, JANUARY 29, 2006	**2,401**	**$120**	**$7,149**	**$28,943**	**$409**	**(277)**	**$ (9,712)**	**$26,909**	
Cumulative Effect of Adjustments Resulting from the Adoption of SAB 108, net of tax	—	—	201	(257)	—	—	—	(56)	
ADJUSTED BALANCE, JANUARY 29, 2006	**2,401**	**$120**	**$7,350**	**$28,686**	**$409**	**(277)**	**$ (9,712)**	**$26,853**	
Net Earnings	—	—	—	5,761	—	—	—	5,761	$5,761
Shares Issued Under Employee Stock Plans	20	1	351	—	—	—	—	352	
Tax Effect of Sale of Option Shares by Employees	—	—	18	—	—	—	—	18	
Translation Adjustments	—	—	—	—	(77)	—	—	(77)	(77)
Interest Rate Hedges	—	—	—	—	(22)	—	—	(22)	(22)
Stock Options, Awards and Amortization of Restricted Stock	—	—	296	—	—	—	—	296	
Repurchase of Common Stock	—	—	—	—	—	(174)	(6,671)	(6,671)	
Cash Dividends ($0.675 per share)	—	—	—	(1,395)	—	—	—	(1,395)	
Other	—	—	(85)	—	—	—	—	(85)	
Comprehensive Income									$5,662
BALANCE, JANUARY 28, 2007	**2,421**	**$121**	**$7,930**	**$33,052**	**$310**	**(451)**	**$(16,383)**	**$25,030**	

See accompanying Notes to Consolidated Financial Statements.

THE HOME DEPOT, INC. AND SUBSIDIARIES
CONSOLIDATED STATEMENTS OF CASH FLOWS

	Fiscal Year Ended[1]		
amounts in millions	January 28, 2007	January 29, 2006	January 30, 2005
CASH FLOWS FROM OPERATING ACTIVITIES:			
Net Earnings	$ 5,761	$ 5,838	$ 5,001
Reconciliation of Net Earnings to Net Cash Provided by Operating Activities:			
Depreciation and Amortization	1,886	1,579	1,319
Impairment Related to Disposition of EXPO Real Estate	—	78	—
Stock-Based Compensation Expense	297	175	125
Changes in Assets and Liabilities, net of the effects of acquisitions:			
Decrease (Increase) in Receivables, net	96	(358)	(266)
Increase in Merchandise Inventories	(563)	(971)	(849)
(Increase) Decrease in Other Current Assets	(225)	16	29
Increase in Accounts Payable and Accrued Liabilities	531	148	645
(Decrease) Increase in Deferred Revenue	(123)	209	263
(Decrease) Increase in Income Taxes Payable	(172)	175	2
Increase (Decrease) in Deferred Income Taxes	46	(609)	319
(Decrease) Increase in Other Long-Term Liabilities	(51)	151	119
Other	178	189	(75)
Net Cash Provided by Operating Activities	7,661	6,620	6,632
CASH FLOWS FROM INVESTING ACTIVITIES:			
Capital Expenditures, net of $49, $51 and $38 of non-cash capital expenditures in fiscal 2006, 2005 and 2004, respectively	(3,542)	(3,881)	(3,948)
Payments for Businesses Acquired, net	(4,268)	(2,546)	(727)
Proceeds from Sales of Property and Equipment	138	164	96
Purchases of Investments	(5,409)	(18,230)	(25,890)
Proceeds from Sales and Maturities of Investments	5,434	19,907	25,990
Net Cash Used in Investing Activities	(7,647)	(4,586)	(4,479)
CASH FLOWS FROM FINANCING ACTIVITIES:			
(Repayments of) Proceeds from Short-Term Borrowings, net	(900)	900	—
Proceeds from Long-Term Borrowings, net of discount	8,935	995	995
Repayments of Long-Term Debt	(509)	(24)	(510)
Repurchases of Common Stock	(6,684)	(3,040)	(3,106)
Proceeds from Sale of Common Stock	381	414	285
Cash Dividends Paid to Stockholders	(1,395)	(857)	(719)
Other Financing Activities	(31)	(136)	272
Net Cash Used in Financing Activities	(203)	(1,748)	(2,783)
(Decrease) Increase in Cash and Cash Equivalents	(189)	286	(630)
Effect of Exchange Rate Changes on Cash and Cash Equivalents	(4)	1	33
Cash and Cash Equivalents at Beginning of Year	793	506	1,103
Cash and Cash Equivalents at End of Year	$ 600	$ 793	$ 506
SUPPLEMENTAL DISCLOSURE OF CASH PAYMENTS MADE FOR:			
Interest, net of interest capitalized	$ 270	$ 114	$ 78
Income Taxes	$ 3,963	$ 3,860	$ 2,793

(1) Fiscal years ended January 28, 2007, January 29, 2006 and January 30, 2005 include 52 weeks.

See accompanying Notes to Consolidated Financial Statements.

NOTES TO CONSOLIDATED FINANCIAL STATEMENTS

1.   SUMMARY OF SIGNIFICANT ACCOUNTING POLICIES

Business, Consolidation and Presentation

The Home Depot, Inc. and its subsidiaries (the "Company") operate The Home Depot stores, which are full-service, warehouse-style stores averaging approximately 105,000 square feet in size. The stores stock approximately 35,000 to 45,000 different kinds of building materials, home improvement supplies and lawn and garden products that are sold to do-it-yourself customers, do-it-for-me customers, home improvement contractors, tradespeople and building maintenance professionals. In addition, the Company operates EXPO Design Center stores ("EXPO"), which offer products and services primarily related to design and renovation projects, and The Home Depot Landscape Supply stores, which service landscape professionals and garden enthusiasts with lawn, landscape and garden products. At the end of fiscal 2006, the Company was operating 2,147 stores in total, which included 1,872 The Home Depot stores, 34 EXPO Design Center stores, 11 The Home Depot Landscape Supply stores and two The Home Depot Floor Stores in the United States, including the territories of Puerto Rico and the Virgin Islands ("U.S."), 155 The Home Depot stores in Canada, 61 The Home Depot stores in Mexico and 12 The Home Depot stores in China.

Additionally, HD Supply, through the Company's wholly-owned subsidiaries, distributes products and sells installation services primarily to business-to-business customers, including home builders, professional contractors, municipalities and maintenance professionals. HD Supply consists of four major platforms: 1) infrastructure, including waterworks and utilities; 2) construction, including construction supply, lumber and building materials, electrical, plumbing/HVAC and interiors; 3) maintenance, including facilities maintenance and industrial PVF; and 4) repair and remodel.

The Company operates its business in two reportable segments, Retail and HD Supply. See Note 12 for further information on the Company's segments. The Consolidated Financial Statements include the accounts of the Company and its wholly-owned subsidiaries. All significant intercompany transactions have been eliminated in consolidation.

Fiscal Year

The Company's fiscal year is a 52- or 53-week period ending on the Sunday nearest to January 31. Fiscal years ended January 28, 2007 ("fiscal 2006"), January 29, 2006 ("fiscal 2005") and January 30, 2005 ("fiscal 2004") include 52 weeks.

Use of Estimates

Management of the Company has made a number of estimates and assumptions relating to the reporting of assets and liabilities, the disclosure of contingent assets and liabilities, and reported amounts of revenues and expenses in preparing these financial statements in conformity with generally accepted accounting principles. Actual results could differ from these estimates.

Fair Value of Financial Instruments

The carrying amounts of Cash and Cash Equivalents, Receivables, Short-Term Debt and Accounts Payable approximate fair value due to the short-term maturities of these financial instruments. The fair value of the Company's investments is discussed under the caption "Short-Term Investments" in this Note 1. The fair value of the Company's Long-Term Debt is discussed in Note 4.

Cash Equivalents

The Company considers all highly liquid investments purchased with maturities of three months or less to be cash equivalents. The Company's Cash Equivalents are carried at fair market value and consist primarily of high-grade commercial paper, money market funds, U.S. government agency securities and tax-exempt notes and bonds.

Short-Term Investments

Short-Term Investments are recorded at fair value based on current market rates and are classified as available-for-sale. Changes in the fair value are included in Accumulated Other Comprehensive Income (Loss), net of applicable taxes, in the accompanying Consolidated Financial Statements. The Company periodically invests in auction rate securities, which are debt instruments with long-term scheduled maturities and periodic interest rate reset dates. The interest rates on these securities are typically reset to market prevailing rates every 35 days or less, and in all cases every 90 days or less. Due to the liquidity provided by the interest rate reset mechanism and the short-term nature of the Company's investment in these securities, they have been classified as current assets in the accompanying Consolidated Balance Sheets.

Accounts Receivable

The Company has an agreement with a third-party service provider who directly extends credit to customers and manages the Company's private label credit card program. In addition, certain subsidiaries of the Company extend credit directly to customers in the ordinary course of business. The receivables due from customers were $1.8 billion and $865 million as of January 28, 2007 and January 29, 2006, respectively. The Company's valuation reserve related to accounts receivable was not material to the Consolidated Financial Statements of the Company as of the end of fiscal 2006 and fiscal 2005.

Merchandise Inventories

The majority of the Company's Merchandise Inventories are stated at the lower of cost (first-in, first-out) or market, as determined by the retail inventory method. As the inventory retail value is adjusted regularly to reflect market conditions, the inventory valued using the retail method approximates the lower of cost or market. Certain subsidiaries, including retail operations in Mexico and China, and distribution centers record Merchandise Inventories at the lower of cost (first-in, first-out) or market, as determined by the cost method. These Merchandise Inventories represent approximately 20% of the total Merchandise Inventories balance. The Company evaluates the inventory valued using the cost method at the end of each quarter to ensure that it is carried at the lower of cost or market. The valuation allowance for Merchandise Inventories valued under the cost method was not material to the Consolidated Financial Statements of the Company as of the end of fiscal 2006 and fiscal 2005.

Independent physical inventory counts or cycle counts are taken on a regular basis in each store, distribution center and HD Supply location to ensure that amounts reflected in the accompanying Consolidated Financial Statements for Merchandise Inventories are properly stated. During the period between physical inventory counts in stores, the Company accrues for estimated losses related to shrink on a store-by-store basis based on historical shrink results and current trends in the business. Shrink (or in the case of excess inventory, "swell") is the difference between the recorded amount of inventory and the physical inventory. Shrink may occur due to theft, loss, inaccurate records for the receipt of inventory or deterioration of goods, among other things.

Income Taxes

The Company provides for federal, state and foreign income taxes currently payable, as well as for those deferred due to timing differences between reporting income and expenses for financial statement purposes versus tax purposes. Federal, state and foreign tax benefits are recorded as a reduction of income taxes. Deferred tax assets and liabilities are recognized for the future tax consequences attributable to temporary differences between the financial statement carrying amounts of existing assets and liabilities and their respective tax bases. Deferred tax assets and liabilities are measured using enacted income tax rates expected to apply to taxable income in the years in which those temporary differences are expected to be recovered or settled. The effect of a change in income tax rates is recognized as income or expense in the period that includes the enactment date.

The Company and its eligible subsidiaries file a consolidated U.S. federal income tax return. Non-U.S. subsidiaries and certain U.S. subsidiaries, which are consolidated for financial reporting purposes, are not eligible to be included in the Company's consolidated U.S. federal income tax return. Separate provisions for income taxes have been determined for these entities. The Company intends to reinvest the unremitted earnings of its non-U.S. subsidiaries and postpone their remittance indefinitely. Accordingly, no provision for U.S. income taxes for non-U.S. subsidiaries was recorded in the accompanying Consolidated Statements of Earnings.

Depreciation and Amortization

The Company's Buildings, Furniture, Fixtures and Equipment are depreciated using the straight-line method over the estimated useful lives of the assets. Leasehold Improvements are amortized using the straight-line method over the original term of the lease or the useful life of the improvement, whichever is shorter. The Company's Property and Equipment is depreciated using the following estimated useful lives:

	Life
Buildings	10-45 years
Furniture, Fixtures and Equipment	3-20 years
Leasehold Improvements	5-45 years

Capitalized Software Costs

The Company capitalizes certain costs related to the acquisition and development of software and amortizes these costs using the straight-line method over the estimated useful life of the software, which is three to six years. These costs are included in Furniture, Fixtures and Equipment in the accompanying Consolidated Balance Sheets. Certain development costs not meeting the criteria for capitalization are expensed as incurred.

Revenues

The Company recognizes revenue, net of estimated returns, at the time the customer takes possession of merchandise or receives services. The liability for sales returns is estimated based on historical return levels. When the Company receives payment from customers before the customer has taken possession of the merchandise or the service has been performed, the amount received is recorded as Deferred Revenue in the accompanying Consolidated Balance Sheets until the sale or service is complete. The Company also records Deferred Revenue for the sale of gift cards and recognizes this revenue upon the redemption of gift cards in Net Sales. Gift card breakage income is recognized based upon historical redemption patterns and represents the balance of gift cards for which the Company believes the likelihood of redemption by the customer is remote. During fiscal 2006 and fiscal 2005, the Company recognized $33 million and $52 million, respectively, of gift card breakage income. Fiscal

2005 was the first year in which the Company recognized gift card breakage income, and therefore, the amount recognized includes the gift card breakage income related to gift cards sold since the inception of the gift card program. This income is recorded as other income and is included in the accompanying Consolidated Statements of Earnings as a reduction in Selling, General and Administrative Expenses ("SG&A").

Services Revenue

Net Sales include services revenue generated through a variety of installation, home maintenance and professional service programs. In these programs, the customer selects and purchases material for a project and the Company provides or arranges professional installation. These programs are offered through the Company's stores and certain HD Supply locations. Under certain programs, when the Company provides or arranges the installation of a project and the subcontractor provides material as part of the installation, both the material and labor are included in services revenue. The Company recognizes this revenue when the service for the customer is complete.

All payments received prior to the completion of services are recorded in Deferred Revenue in the accompanying Consolidated Balance Sheets. Retail services revenue was $3.8 billion, $3.5 billion and $3.0 billion for fiscal 2006, 2005 and 2004, respectively.

Self-Insurance

The Company is self-insured for certain losses related to general liability, product liability, automobile, workers' compensation and medical claims. The expected ultimate cost for claims incurred as of the balance sheet date is not discounted and is recognized as a liability. The expected ultimate cost of claims is estimated based upon analysis of historical data and actuarial estimates.

Prepaid Advertising

Television and radio advertising production costs along with media placement costs are expensed when the advertisement first appears. Included in Other Current Assets in the accompanying Consolidated Balance Sheets are $44 million and $42 million, respectively, at the end of fiscal 2006 and 2005 relating to prepayments of production costs for print and broadcast advertising.

Vendor Allowances

Vendor allowances primarily consist of volume rebates that are earned as a result of attaining certain purchase levels and advertising co-op allowances for the promotion of vendors' products that are typically based on guaranteed minimum amounts with additional amounts being earned for attaining certain purchase levels. These vendor allowances are accrued as earned, with those allowances received as a result of attaining certain purchase levels accrued over the incentive period based on estimates of purchases.

Volume rebates and advertising co-op allowances earned are initially recorded as a reduction in Merchandise Inventories and a subsequent reduction in Cost of Sales when the related product is sold. Certain advertising co-op allowances that are reimbursements of specific, incremental and identifiable costs incurred to promote vendors' products are recorded as an offset against advertising expense. In fiscal 2006, 2005 and 2004, net advertising expense was $1.1 billion, $1.1 billion and $1.0 billion, respectively, which was recorded in SG&A.

Cost of Sales

Cost of Sales includes the actual cost of merchandise sold and services performed, the cost of transportation of merchandise from vendors to the Company's stores, locations or customers, the operating cost of the Company's distribution centers and the cost of deferred interest programs offered through the Company's private label credit card program.

The cost of handling and shipping merchandise from the Company's stores, locations or distribution centers to the customer is classified as SG&A. The cost of shipping and handling, including internal costs and payments to third parties, classified as SG&A was $741 million, $563 million and $499 million in fiscal 2006, 2005 and 2004, respectively.

Goodwill and Other Intangible Assets

Goodwill represents the excess of purchase price over the fair value of net assets acquired. The Company does not amortize goodwill, but does assess the recoverability of goodwill in the third quarter of each fiscal year by determining whether the fair value of each reporting unit supports its carrying value. The fair values of the Company's identified reporting units were estimated using the expected present value of discounted cash flows.

The Company amortizes the cost of other intangible assets over their estimated useful lives, which range from 1 to 14 years, unless such lives are deemed indefinite. Intangible assets with indefinite lives are tested in the third quarter of each fiscal year for impairment. The Company recorded no impairment charges for fiscal 2006, 2005 or 2004.

Impairment of Long-Lived Assets

The Company evaluates the carrying value of long-lived assets when management makes the decision to relocate or close a store or other location, or when circumstances indicate the carrying amount of an asset may not be recoverable. Losses related to the impairment of long-lived assets are recognized to the extent the sum of undiscounted estimated future cash flows expected to result from the use of the asset are less than the asset's carrying value. If the carrying value is greater than the future cash flows, a provision is made to write down the related assets to the estimated net recoverable value. Impairment losses were recorded as a component of SG&A in the accompanying Consolidated Statements of Earnings. When a location closes, the Company also recognizes in SG&A the net present value of future lease obligations, less estimated sublease income.

In fiscal 2005, the Company recorded $91 million in SG&A related to asset impairment charges and on-going lease obligations associated with the closing of 20 of its EXPO stores. Additionally, the Company recorded $29 million of expense in Cost of Sales in fiscal 2005 related to inventory markdowns in these stores. The Company also recorded impairments on other closings and relocations in the ordinary course of business, which were not material to the Consolidated Financial Statements of the Company in fiscal 2006, 2005 and 2004.

Stock-Based Compensation

Effective February 3, 2003, the Company adopted the fair value method of recording stock-based compensation expense in accordance with Statement of Financial Accounting Standards ("SFAS") No. 123, "Accounting for Stock-Based Compensation" ("SFAS 123"). The Company selected the prospective method of adoption as described in SFAS No. 148, "Accounting for Stock-Based Compensation – Transition and Disclosure," and accordingly, stock-based compensation expense was recognized for stock options granted, modified or settled and expense related to the Employee Stock Purchase Plan ("ESPP") after the beginning of fiscal 2003. Effective January 30, 2006, the Company adopted the fair value recognition provisions of SFAS No. 123(R), "Share-Based Payment" ("SFAS 123(R)"), using the modified prospective transition method. Under the modified prospective transition method, the Company began expensing unvested options granted prior to fiscal 2003 in addition to continuing to recognize stock-based compensation expense for all share-based payments awarded since the adoption of SFAS 123 in fiscal 2003. During fiscal 2006, the Company recognized additional stock compensation expense of approximately $40 million as a result of the adoption of SFAS 123(R). As the majority of stock options granted prior to 2003 are now fully vested, the Company does not expect SFAS 123(R) to have a material impact on its consolidated financial condition or results of operations subsequent to fiscal 2006. Results of prior periods have not been restated.

The per share weighted average fair value of stock options granted during fiscal 2006, 2005 and 2004 was $11.88, $12.83 and $13.57, respectively. The fair value of these options was determined at the date of grant using the Black-Scholes option-pricing model with the following assumptions:

	Fiscal Year Ended		
	January 28, 2007	January 29, 2006	January 30, 2005
Risk-free interest rate	4.7%	4.3%	2.6%
Assumed volatility	28.5%	33.7%	41.3%
Assumed dividend yield	1.5%	1.1%	0.8%
Assumed lives of option	5 years	5 years	5 years

The following table illustrates the effect on Net Earnings and Earnings per Share as if the Company had applied the fair value recognition provisions of SFAS 123(R) to all stock-based compensation in each period (amounts in millions, except per share data):

	Fiscal Year Ended		
	January 28, 2007	January 29, 2006	January 30, 2005
Net Earnings, as reported	$5,761	$5,838	$5,001
Add: Stock-based compensation expense included in reported Net Earnings, net of related tax effects	186	110	79
Deduct: Total stock-based compensation expense determined under fair value based method for all awards, net of related tax effects	(186)	(197)	(237)
Pro forma net earnings	$5,761	$5,751	$4,843
Earnings per Share:			
Basic – as reported	$ 2.80	$ 2.73	$ 2.27
Basic – pro forma	$ 2.80	$ 2.69	$ 2.19
Diluted – as reported	$ 2.79	$ 2.72	$ 2.26
Diluted – pro forma	$ 2.79	$ 2.68	$ 2.19

Derivatives

The Company uses derivative financial instruments from time to time in the management of its interest rate exposure on long-term debt. The Company accounts for its derivative financial instruments in accordance with SFAS No. 133, "Accounting for Derivative Instruments and Hedging Activities." There were no derivative instruments outstanding as of January 28, 2007.

Comprehensive Income

Comprehensive Income includes Net Earnings adjusted for certain revenues, expenses, gains and losses that are excluded from Net Earnings under generally accepted accounting principles. Adjustments to Net Earnings are primarily for foreign currency translation adjustments and interest rate hedges.

Foreign Currency Translation

Assets and Liabilities denominated in a foreign currency are translated into U.S. dollars at the current rate of exchange on the last day of the reporting period. Revenues and Expenses are generally translated at a daily exchange rate and equity transactions are translated using the actual rate on the day of the transaction.

Reclassifications

Certain amounts in prior fiscal years have been reclassified to conform with the presentation adopted in the current fiscal year.

2. STAFF ACCOUNTING BULLETIN NO. 108

In September 2006, the Securities and Exchange Commission ("SEC") issued Staff Accounting Bulletin No. 108, "Considering the Effects of Prior Year Misstatements when Quantifying Misstatements in Current Year Financial Statements" ("SAB 108"). SAB 108 addresses the process of quantifying prior year financial statement misstatements and their impact on current year financial statements. The provisions of SAB 108 allow companies to report the cumulative effect of correcting immaterial prior year misstatements, based on the Company's historical method for evaluating misstatements, by adjusting the opening balance of retained earnings in the current year financial statements rather than amending previously filed reports. SAB 108 is effective for fiscal years ending after November 15, 2006, and therefore was effective for The Home Depot in fiscal 2006. In accordance with SAB 108, the Company has adjusted beginning Retained Earnings for fiscal 2006 in the accompanying Consolidated Financial Statements for the items described below. The Company does not consider these adjustments to have a material impact on the Company's consolidated financial statements in any of the prior years affected.

Historical Stock Option Practices

During fiscal 2006, the Company requested that its Board of Directors review its historical stock option granting practices. A subcommittee of the Audit Committee undertook the review with the assistance of independent outside counsel, and it has completed its review. The principal findings of the review are as follows:

- All options granted in the period from 2002 through the present had an exercise price based on the market price of the Company's stock on the date the grant was approved by the Board of Directors or an officer acting pursuant to delegated authority. During this period, the stock administration department corrected administrative errors retroactively and without separate approvals. The administrative errors included inadvertent omissions of grantees from lists that were approved previously and miscalculations of the number of options granted to particular employees on approved lists.

- All options granted from December 1, 2000 through the end of 2001 had an exercise price based on the market price of the Company's stock on the date of a meeting of the Board of Directors or some other date selected without the benefit of hindsight. The February 2001 annual grant was not finally allocated to recipients until several weeks after the grant was approved. During this period, the stock administration department also corrected administrative errors retroactively and without separate approvals as in the period 2002 to the present.

- For annual option grants and certain quarterly option grants from 1981 through November 2000, the stated grant date was routinely earlier than the actual date on which the grants were approved by a committee of the Board of Directors. In almost every instance, the stock price on the apparent approval date was higher than the price on the stated grant date. The backdating occurred for grants at all levels of the Company. Management personnel, who have since left the Company, generally followed a practice of reviewing closing prices for a prior period and selecting a date with a low stock price to increase the value of the options to employees on lists of grantees subsequently approved by a committee of the Board of Directors.

• The annual option grants in 1994 through 2000, as well as many quarterly grants during this period, were not finally allocated among the recipients until several weeks after the stated grant date. Because of the absence of records prior to 1994, it is unclear whether allocations also postdated the selected grant dates from 1981 through 1993. Moreover, for many of these annual and quarterly grants from 1981 through December 2000, there is insufficient documentation to determine with certainty when the grants were actually authorized by a committee of the Board of Directors. Finally, the Company's stock administration department also retroactively added employees to lists of approved grantees, or changed the number of options granted to specific employees, without authorization of the Board of Directors or a board committee, to correct administrative errors.

• Numerous option grants to rank-and-file employees were made pursuant to delegations of authority that may not have been effective under Delaware law.

• In numerous instances, and primarily prior to 2003, beneficiaries of grants who were required to report them to the SEC failed to do so in a timely manner or at all.

• The subcommittee concluded that there was no intentional wrongdoing by any current member of the Company's management team or its Board of Directors.

The Company believes that because of these errors, it had unrecorded expense over the affected period (1981 through 2005) of $227 million in the aggregate, including related tax items. In accordance with the provisions of SAB 108, the Company decreased beginning Retained Earnings for fiscal 2006 by $227 million within the accompanying Consolidated Financial Statements.

As previously disclosed, the staff of the SEC has begun an informal inquiry into the Company's stock option practices, and the U.S. Attorney for the Southern District of New York has also requested information on the subject. The Company is continuing to cooperate with these agencies. While the Company cannot predict the outcome of these matters, it does not believe that they will have a material adverse impact on its consolidated financial condition or results of operations.

The Company does not believe that the effect of the stock option adjustment was material, either quantitatively or qualitatively, in any of the years covered by the review of these items. In reaching that determination, the following quantitative measures were considered (dollars in millions):

Fiscal Year	Net After-tax Effect of Adjustment	Reported Net Earnings	Percent of Reported Net Earnings
2005	$ 11	$ 5,838	0.19%
2004	18	5,001	0.36
2003	18	4,304	0.42
2002	21	3,664	0.57
1981-2001	159	14,531	1.09
Total	$227	$33,338	0.68%

Vendor Credits

The Company records credits against vendor invoices for various issues related to the receipt of goods. The Company previously identified that it was not recording an allowance for subsequent reversals of these credits based on historical experience. Beginning Retained Earnings for fiscal 2006 has been decreased by $30 million in the accompanying Consolidated Financial Statements to reflect the appropriate adjustments to Merchandise Inventories and Accounts Payable, net of tax.

Impact of Adjustments

The impact of each of the items noted above, net of tax, on fiscal 2006 beginning balances are presented below (amounts in millions):

	Cumulative Effect as of January 30, 2006		
	Stock Option Practices	Vendor Credits	Total
Merchandise Inventories	$ —	$ 9	$ 9
Accounts Payable	—	(59)	(59)
Deferred Income Taxes	11	20	31
Other Accrued Expenses	(37)	—	(37)
Paid-In Capital	(201)	—	(201)
Retained Earnings	227	30	257
Total	$ —	$ —	$ —

3. INTANGIBLE ASSETS

The Company's intangible assets at the end of fiscal 2006 and fiscal 2005, which are included in Other Assets in the accompanying Consolidated Balance Sheets, consisted of the following (amounts in millions):

	January 28, 2007	January 29, 2006
Customer relationships	$ 756	$283
Trademarks and franchises	106	92
Other	67	58
Less accumulated amortization	(151)	(35)
Total	$ 778	$398

Amortization expense related to intangible assets was $117 million, $29 million and $4 million for fiscal 2006, 2005 and 2004, respectively. Estimated future amortization expense for intangible assets recorded as of January 28, 2007 is $107 million, $105 million, $99 million, $94 million and $82 million for fiscal 2007 through fiscal 2011, respectively.

4. DEBT

The Company has a commercial paper program that allows for borrowings up to $2.5 billion. All of the Company's short-term borrowings in fiscal 2006 and 2005 were made under this commercial paper program. In connection with the commercial paper program, the Company has a back-up credit facility with a consortium of banks for borrowings up to $2.0 billion. The credit facility, which expires in December 2010, contains various restrictions, none of which is expected to materially impact the Company's liquidity or capital resources.

Short-Term Debt under the commercial paper program was as follows (dollars in millions):

	January 28, 2007	January 29, 2006
Balance outstanding at fiscal year-end	$ —	$900
Maximum amount outstanding at any month-end	**$1,470**	$900
Average daily short-term borrowings	**$ 300**	$ 22
Weighted average interest rate	**5.1%**	4.3%

The Company's Long-Term Debt at the end of fiscal 2006 and fiscal 2005 consisted of the following (amounts in millions):

	January 28, 2007	January 29, 2006
5.375% Senior Notes; due April 1, 2006; interest payable semi-annually on April 1 and October 1	$ —	$ 500
3.75% Senior Notes; due September 15, 2009; interest payable semi-annually on March 15 and September 15	**997**	996
Floating Rate Senior Notes; due December 16, 2009; interest payable on March 16, June 16, September 16 and December 16	**750**	—
4.625% Senior Notes; due August 15, 2010; interest payable semi-annually on February 15 and August 15	**997**	996
5.20% Senior Notes; due March 1, 2011; interest payable semi-annually on March 1 and September 1	**1,000**	—
5.25% Senior Notes; due December 16, 2013; interest payable semi-annually on June 16 and December 16	**1,243**	—
5.40% Senior Notes; due March 1, 2016; interest payable semi-annually on March 1 and September 1	**2,986**	—
5.875% Senior Notes; due December 16, 2036; interest payable semi-annually on June 16 and December 16	**2,958**	—
Capital Lease Obligations; payable in varying installments through January 31, 2055	**419**	381
Other	**311**	312
Total Long-Term Debt	**11,661**	3,185
Less current installments	**18**	513
Long-Term Debt, excluding current installments	**$11,643**	$2,672

In December 2006, the Company issued $750 million of floating rate Senior Notes due December 16, 2009 at par value, $1.25 billion of 5.25% Senior Notes due December 16, 2013 at a discount of $7 million and $3.0 billion of 5.875% Senior Notes due December 16, 2036 at a discount of $42 million, together the "December 2006 Issuance." The net proceeds of the December 2006 Issuance were used to fund, in part, the Company's common stock repurchases, to repay outstanding commercial paper and for general corporate purposes. The $49 million discount and $37 million of issuance costs associated with the December 2006 Issuance are being amortized to interest expense over the term of the related Senior Notes.

Additionally in October 2006, the Company entered into a forward starting interest rate swap agreement with a notional amount of $1.0 billion, accounted for as a cash flow hedge, to hedge interest rate fluctuations in anticipation of the issuance of the 5.875% Senior Notes due December 16, 2036. Upon issuance of the hedged debt in December 2006, the Company settled its forward starting interest rate swap agreements and recorded an $11 million decrease, net of income taxes, to Accumulated

Other Comprehensive Income, which will be amortized to interest expense over the life of the related debt.

In March 2006, the Company issued $1.0 billion of 5.20% Senior Notes due March 1, 2011 at a discount of $1 million and $3.0 billion of 5.40% Senior Notes due March 1, 2016 at a discount of $15 million, together the "March 2006 Issuance." The net proceeds of the March 2006 Issuance were used to pay for the acquisition price of Hughes Supply, Inc. and for the repayment of the Company's 5.375% Senior Notes due April 2006 in the aggregate principal amount of $500 million. The $16 million discount and $19 million of issuance costs associated with the March 2006 Issuance are being amortized to interest expense over the term of the related Senior Notes.

Additionally in March 2006, the Company entered into a forward starting interest rate swap agreement with a notional amount of $2.0 billion, accounted for as a cash flow hedge, to hedge interest rate fluctuations in anticipation of the issuance of the 5.40% Senior Notes due March 1, 2016. Upon issuance of the hedged debt, the Company settled its forward starting interest rate swap agreements and recorded a $12 million decrease, net of income taxes, to Accumulated Other Comprehensive Income, which will be amortized to interest expense over the life of the related debt.

In August 2005, the Company issued $1.0 billion of 4.625% Notes due August 15, 2010 ("August 2005 Issuance") at a discount of $5 million. The net proceeds of $995 million were used to pay for a portion of the acquisition price of National Waterworks, Inc. The $5 million discount and $7 million of issuance costs associated with the August 2005 Issuance are being amortized to interest expense over the term of the related Senior Notes.

The Company also had $1.0 billion of 3.75% Senior Notes due September 15, 2009 outstanding as of January 28, 2007, collectively referred to with the December 2006 Issuance, March 2006 Issuance and August 2005 Issuance as "Senior Notes." The Senior Notes may be redeemed by the Company at any time, in whole or in part, at a redemption price plus accrued interest up to the redemption date. The redemption price is equal to the greater of (1) 100% of the principal amount of the Senior Notes to be redeemed, or (2) the sum of the present values of the remaining scheduled payments of principal and interest to maturity. Additionally, if a Change in Control Triggering Event occurs, as defined by the terms of the December 2006 Issuance, holders of the December 2006 Issuance have the right to require the Company to redeem those notes at 101% of the aggregate principal amount of the notes plus accrued interest up to the redemption date.

The Company is generally not limited under the indenture governing the Senior Notes in its ability to incur additional indebtedness or required to maintain financial ratios or specified levels of net worth or liquidity. However, the indenture governing the Senior Notes contains various restrictive covenants, none of which is expected to impact the Company's liquidity or capital resources.

Interest Expense in the accompanying Consolidated Statements of Earnings is net of interest capitalized of $47 million, $51 million and $40 million in fiscal 2006, 2005 and 2004, respectively. Maturities of Long-Term Debt are $18 million for fiscal 2007, $301 million for fiscal 2008, $1.8 billion for fiscal 2009, $1.0 billion for fiscal 2010, $1.0 billion for fiscal 2011 and $7.5 billion thereafter.

As of January 28, 2007, the market value of the Senior Notes was approximately $10.9 billion. The estimated fair value of all other long-term borrowings, excluding capital lease obligations, was approximately $316 million compared to the carrying value of $311 million. These fair values were estimated using a discounted cash flow analysis based on the Company's incremental borrowing rate for similar liabilities.

5. INCOME TAXES

The components of Earnings before Provision for Income Taxes for fiscal 2006, 2005 and 2004 were as follows (amounts in millions):

	Fiscal Year Ended		
	January 28, 2007	January 29, 2006	January 30, 2005
United States	$8,709	$8,736	$7,508
Foreign	599	546	404
Total	$9,308	$9,282	$7,912

The Provision for Income Taxes consisted of the following (amounts in millions):

	Fiscal Year Ended		
	January 28, 2007	January 29, 2006	January 30, 2005
Current:			
Federal	$2,831	$3,394	$2,153
State	409	507	279
Foreign	329	156	139
	3,569	4,057	2,571
Deferred:			
Federal	(9)	(527)	304
State	(9)	(111)	52
Foreign	(4)	25	(16)
	(22)	(613)	340
Total	$3,547	$3,444	$2,911

The Company's combined federal, state and foreign effective tax rates for fiscal 2006, 2005 and 2004, net of offsets generated by federal, state and foreign tax benefits, were approximately 38.1%, 37.1% and 36.8%, respectively.

The reconciliation of the Provision for Income Taxes at the federal statutory rate of 35% to the actual tax expense for the applicable fiscal years was as follows (amounts in millions):

	Fiscal Year Ended		
	January 28, 2007	January 29, 2006	January 30, 2005
Income taxes at federal statutory rate	$3,258	$3,249	$2,769
State income taxes, net of federal income tax benefit	261	279	215
Foreign rate differences	5	(10)	(17)
Change in valuation allowance	—	(23)	(31)
Other, net	23	(51)	(25)
Total	$3,547	$3,444	$2,911

The tax effects of temporary differences that give rise to significant portions of the deferred tax assets and deferred tax liabilities as of January 28, 2007 and January 29, 2006, were as follows (amounts in millions):

	January 28, 2007	January 29, 2006
Current:		
Deferred Tax Assets:		
Accrued self-insurance liabilities	$ 94	$ 143
Other accrued liabilities	603	278
Other	—	28
Current Deferred Tax Assets	697	449
Deferred Tax Liabilities:		
Accelerated inventory deduction	(137)	(271)
Other	(29)	(17)
Current Deferred Tax Liabilities	(166)	(288)
Current Deferred Tax Assets, net	531	161
Noncurrent:		
Deferred Tax Assets:		
Accrued self-insurance liabilities	325	354
Other accrued liabilities	—	35
Net operating losses	66	63
Noncurrent Deferred Tax Assets	391	452
Deferred Tax Liabilities:		
Property and equipment	(1,365)	(1,160)
Goodwill and other intangibles	(361)	(209)
Other	(74)	—
Noncurrent Deferred Tax Liabilities	(1,800)	(1,369)
Noncurrent Deferred Tax Liabilities, net	(1,409)	(917)
Net Deferred Tax Liabilities	$ (878)	$ (756)

Current deferred tax assets and current deferred tax liabilities are netted by tax jurisdiction and noncurrent deferred tax assets and noncurrent deferred tax liabilities are netted by tax jurisdiction, and are included in the accompanying Consolidated Balance Sheets as follows (amounts in millions):

	January 28, 2007	January 29, 2006
Other Current Assets	$ 561	$ 221
Other Assets	7	29
Other Accrued Expenses	(30)	(60)
Deferred Income Taxes	(1,416)	(946)
Net Deferred Tax Liabilities	$ (878)	$(756)

The Company believes that the realization of the deferred tax assets is more likely than not, based upon the expectation that it will generate the necessary taxable income in future periods and, accordingly, no valuation reserves have been provided. As a result of acquisitions that were accounted for under the purchase method of accounting, deferred tax liabilities of $118 million were recorded in fiscal 2006 representing the difference between the book value and the tax basis of acquired assets.

At January 28, 2007, the Company had state and foreign net operating loss carry-forwards to reduce future taxable income, which will expire at various dates from 2010 to 2026. Management has concluded that it is more likely than not that these tax benefits related to the net operating losses will be realized and hence no valuation allowance has been provided. The Company has not provided for U.S. deferred income taxes on $1.2 billion of undistributed earnings of international subsidiaries because of its intention to indefinitely reinvest these earnings outside the U.S. The determination of the amount of the unrecognized deferred U.S. income tax liability related to the undistributed earnings is not practicable; however, unrecognized foreign income tax credits would be available to reduce a portion of this liability.

The Company's income tax returns are routinely under audit by domestic and foreign tax authorities. These audits include questions regarding its tax filing positions, including the timing and amount of deductions and the allocation of income among various tax jurisdictions. In 2005, the IRS completed its examination of the Company's U.S. federal income tax returns through fiscal 2002. Certain issues relating to the examinations of fiscal 2001 and 2002 are under appeal, the outcome of which is not expected to have a material impact on the Company's financial statements. During 2006, the IRS initiated an audit of the Company's fiscal 2003 and 2004 income tax returns. This audit will likely not be completely settled until after fiscal 2007. At this time, the Company does not expect the results of the audit to have a material impact on the Company's financial statements.

During the second quarter of fiscal 2006, the Quebec National Assembly passed legislation that retroactively changed certain tax laws that subjected the Company to additional tax and interest. As a result, the Company received an assessment from Quebec for $57 million in retroactive tax and $12 million in related interest for the 2002 through 2005 taxable years. This retroactive tax is included in the Company's current year foreign tax expense.

In July 2006, the Financial Accounting Standards Board ("FASB") issued FASB Interpretation No. 48, "Accounting for Uncertainty in Income Taxes – an Interpretation of FASB Statement No. 109" ("FIN 48"). FIN 48 clarifies the accounting for uncertainty in income tax reporting by prescribing a recognition threshold and measurement attribute for the financial statement recognition and measurement of a tax position taken or expected to be taken in a tax return. FIN 48 requires that companies recognize tax benefits in their financial statements for a tax position only if that position is more likely than not of being sustained on audit, based on the technical merits of the position. Additionally, FIN 48 provides guidance on de-recognition, classification, interest and penalties, accounting in interim periods, disclosure and transition. FIN 48 becomes effective for fiscal years beginning after December 15, 2006, and will therefore be effective for The Home Depot in fiscal 2007. The cumulative impact of adopting FIN 48 in fiscal 2007 is not expected to have a material impact on the financial condition of the Company.

6. EMPLOYEE STOCK PLANS

The Home Depot, Inc. 2005 Omnibus Stock Incentive Plan ("2005 Plan") and The Home Depot, Inc. 1997 Omnibus Stock Incentive Plan ("1997 Plan") (collectively the "Plans") provide that incentive, non-qualified stock options, stock appreciation rights, restricted shares, performance shares, performance units and deferred shares may be issued to selected associates, officers and directors of the Company. Under the 2005 Plan, the maximum number of shares of the Company's common stock authorized for issuance is 255 million shares, with any award other than a stock option reducing the number of shares available for issuance by 2.11 shares. As of January 28, 2007, there were 236 million shares available for future grant under the 2005 Plan. No additional equity awards may be issued from the 1997 Plan after the adoption of the 2005 Plan on May 26, 2005.

Under the Plans, as of January 28, 2007, the Company had granted incentive and non-qualified stock options for 184 million shares, net of cancellations (of which 120 million have been exercised). Under the terms of the Plans, incentive stock options and non-qualified stock options are to be priced at or above the fair market value of the Company's stock on the date of the grant. Typically, incentive stock options and non-qualified stock options vest at the rate of 25% per year commencing on the first anniversary date of the grant and expire on the tenth anniversary date of the grant. The Company recognized $148 million, $117 million and $71 million of stock-based compensation expense in fiscal 2006, 2005 and 2004, respectively, related to stock options.

Under the Plans, as of January 28, 2007, the Company had issued 12 million shares of restricted stock, net of cancellations (the restrictions on 2 million shares have lapsed). Generally, the restrictions on the restricted stock lapse according to one of the following schedules: (1) the restrictions on 100% of the restricted stock lapse at 3, 4 or 5 years, (2) the restrictions on 25% of the restricted stock lapse upon the third and sixth year anniversaries of the date of issuance with the remaining 50% of the restricted stock lapsing upon the associate's attainment of age 62, or (3) the restrictions on 25% of the restricted stock lapse upon the third and sixth year anniversaries of the date of issuance with the remaining 50% of the restricted stock lapsing upon the earlier of the associate's attainment of age 60 or the tenth anniversary date. Additionally, certain awards may become non-forfeitable upon the attainment of age 60, provided the associate has had five years of continuous service. The fair value of the restricted stock is expensed over the period during which the restrictions lapse. The Company recorded stock-based compensation expense related to restricted stock of $95 million, $32 million and $22 million in fiscal 2006, 2005 and 2004, respectively.

In fiscal 2006, 2005 and 2004, there were 417,000, 461,000 and 461,000 deferred shares, respectively, granted under the Plans. Each deferred share entitles the associate to one share of common stock to be received up to five years after the vesting date of the deferred share, subject to certain deferral rights of the associate. The Company recorded stock-based compensation expense related to deferred shares of $37 million, $10 million and $14 million in fiscal 2006, 2005 and 2004, respectively.

As of January 28, 2007, there were 2.5 million non-qualified stock options outstanding under non-qualified stock option plans that are not part of the Plans.

The Company maintains two ESPPs (U.S. and non-U.S. plans). The plan for U.S. associates is a tax-qualified plan under Section 423 of the Internal Revenue Code. The non-U.S. plan is not a Section 423 plan. The ESPPs allow associates to purchase up to 152 million shares of common stock, of which 120 million shares have been purchased from inception of the plans. The purchase price of shares under the ESPPs is equal to 85% of the stock's fair market value on the last day of the purchase period. During fiscal 2006, there were 3 million shares purchased under the ESPPs at an average price of $32.06. Under the outstanding ESPPs as of January 28, 2007, employees have contributed $10 million to purchase shares at 85% of the stock's fair market value on the last day (June 30, 2007) of the purchase period. The Company had 32 million shares available for issuance under the ESPPs at January 28, 2007. The Company recognized $17 million, $16 million and $15 million of stock-based compensation in fiscal 2006, 2005 and 2004, respectively, related to the ESPPs.

In total, the Company recorded stock-based compensation expense, including the expense of stock options, ESPPs, restricted stock and deferred stock units, of $297 million, $175 million and $125 million, in fiscal 2006, 2005 and 2004, respectively.

The following table summarizes stock options outstanding at January 28, 2007, January 29, 2006 and January 30, 2005, and changes during the fiscal years ended on these dates (shares in thousands):

	Number of Shares	Weighted Average Option Price
Outstanding at February 1, 2004	87,779	$35.40
Granted	16,713	36.46
Exercised	(7,825)	25.94
Canceled	(10,273)	38.27
Outstanding at January 30, 2005	86,394	$36.12
Granted	17,721	37.96
Exercised	(11,457)	28.83
Canceled	(8,626)	38.65
Outstanding at January 29, 2006	84,032	$37.24
Granted	257	39.53
Exercised	(10,045)	28.69
Canceled	(8,103)	40.12
Outstanding at January 28, 2007	66,141	$38.20

The total intrinsic value of stock options exercised during fiscal 2006 was $120 million.

As of January 28, 2007, there were approximately 66 million stock options outstanding with a weighted average remaining life of 5.6 years and an intrinsic value of $248 million. As of January 28, 2007, there were approximately 47 million options exercisable with a weighted average option price of $39.20 and an intrinsic value of $162 million. As of January 28, 2007, there were approximately 63 million shares vested or expected to ultimately vest.

The following table summarizes restricted stock outstanding at January 28, 2007 (shares in thousands):

	Number of Shares	Weighted Average Grant Date Fair Value
Outstanding at January 29, 2006	5,308	$35.76
Granted	7,575	41.37
Restrictions lapsed	(1,202)	38.03
Canceled	(1,551)	39.00
Outstanding at January 28, 2007	10,130	$39.20

7.   LEASES

The Company leases certain retail locations, office space, warehouse and distribution space, equipment and vehicles. While most of the leases are operating leases, certain locations and equipment are leased under capital leases. As leases expire, it can be expected that, in the normal course of business, certain leases will be renewed or replaced.

Certain lease agreements include escalating rents over the lease terms. The Company expenses rent on a straight-line basis over the life of the lease which commences on the date the Company has the right to control the property. The cumulative expense recognized on a straight-line basis in excess of the cumulative payments is included in Other Accrued Expenses and Other Long-Term Liabilities in the accompanying Consolidated Balance Sheets.

The Company has a lease agreement under which the Company leases certain assets totaling $282 million. This lease was originally created under a structured financing arrangement and involves two special purpose entities. The Company financed a portion of its new stores opened in fiscal years 1997 through 2003 under this lease agreement. Under this agreement, the lessor purchased the properties, paid for the construction costs and subsequently leased the facilities to the Company. The Company records the rental payments under the terms of the operating lease agreements as SG&A in the accompanying Consolidated Statements of Earnings.

The $282 million lease agreement expires in fiscal 2008 with no renewal option. The lease provides for a substantial residual value guarantee limited to 79% of the initial book value of the assets and includes a purchase option at the original cost of each property. During fiscal 2005, the Company committed to exercise its option to purchase the assets under this lease for $282 million at the end of the lease term in fiscal 2008.

In the first quarter of fiscal 2004, the Company adopted the revised version of FASB Interpretation No. 46, "Consolidation of Variable Interest Entities" ("FIN 46"). FIN 46 requires consolidation of a variable interest entity if a company's variable interest absorbs a majority of the entity's expected losses or receives a majority of the entity's expected residual returns, or both.

In accordance with FIN 46, the Company was required to consolidate one of the two aforementioned special purpose entities that, before the effective date of FIN 46, met the requirements for non-consolidation. The second special purpose entity that owns the assets leased by the Company totaling $282 million is not owned by or affiliated with the Company, its management or its officers. Pursuant to FIN 46, the Company was not deemed to have a variable interest, and therefore was not required to consolidate this entity.

FIN 46 requires the Company to measure the assets and liabilities at their carrying amounts, which amounts would have been recorded if FIN 46 had been effective at the inception of the transaction. Accordingly, during the first quarter of fiscal 2004, the Company recorded Long-Term Debt of $282 million and Long-Term Notes Receivable of $282 million on the Consolidated Balance Sheets. The Company continues to record the rental payments under the operating lease agreements as SG&A in the Consolidated Statements of Earnings. The adoption of FIN 46 had no economic impact on the Company.

Total rent expense, net of minor sublease income for fiscal 2006, 2005 and 2004 was $958 million, $782 million and $684 million, respectively. Certain store leases also provide for contingent rent payments based on percentages of sales in excess of specified minimums. Contingent rent expense for fiscal 2006, 2005 and 2004 was approximately $9 million, $9 million and $11 million, respectively. Real estate taxes, insurance, maintenance and operating expenses applicable to the leased property are obligations of the Company under the lease agreements.

The approximate future minimum lease payments under capital and all other leases at January 28, 2007 were as follows (in millions):

Fiscal Year	Capital Leases	Operating Leases
2007	$ 78	$ 917
2008	79	846
2009	78	734
2010	80	647
2011	80	566
Thereafter through 2097	928	5,421
	1,323	$9,131
Less imputed interest	904	
Net present value of capital lease obligations	419	
Less current installments	13	
Long-term capital lease obligations, excluding current installments	$ 406	

Short-term and long-term obligations for capital leases are included in the accompanying Consolidated Balance Sheets in Current Installments of Long-Term Debt and Long-Term Debt, respectively. The assets under capital leases recorded in Property and Equipment, net of amortization, totaled $340 million and $304 million at January 28, 2007 and January 29, 2006, respectively.

8. EMPLOYEE BENEFIT PLANS

The Company maintains active defined contribution retirement plans for its employees ("the Benefit Plans"). All associates satisfying certain service requirements are eligible to participate in the Benefit Plans. The Company makes cash contributions each payroll period up to specified percentages of associates' contributions as approved by the Board of Directors.

The Company also maintains a restoration plan to provide certain associates deferred compensation that they would have received under the Benefit Plans as a matching contribution if not for the maximum compensation limits under the Internal Revenue Code. The Company funds the restoration plan through contributions made to a grantor trust, which are then used to purchase shares of the Company's common stock in the open market.

The Company's contributions to the Benefit Plans and the restoration plan were $159 million, $132 million and $114 million for fiscal 2006, 2005 and 2004, respectively. At January 28, 2007, the Benefit Plans and the restoration plan held a total of 26 million shares of the Company's common stock in trust for plan participants.

9. BASIC AND DILUTED WEIGHTED AVERAGE COMMON SHARES

The reconciliation of basic to diluted weighted average common shares for fiscal 2006, 2005 and 2004 was as follows (amounts in millions):

	Fiscal Year Ended		
	January 28, 2007	January 29, 2006	January 30, 2005
Weighted average common shares	**2,054**	2,138	2,207
Effect of potentially dilutive securities:			
Stock Plans	**8**	9	9
Diluted weighted average common shares	**2,062**	2,147	2,216

Stock plans include shares granted under the Company's employee stock plans as described in Note 6 to the Consolidated Financial Statements. Options to purchase 45.4 million, 55.1 million and 49.1 million shares of common stock at January 28, 2007, January 29, 2006 and January 30, 2005, respectively, were excluded from the computation of Diluted Earnings per Share because their effect would have been anti-dilutive.

10. COMMITMENTS AND CONTINGENCIES

At January 28, 2007, the Company was contingently liable for approximately $1.2 billion under outstanding letters of credit issued for certain business transactions, including insurance programs, trade and construction contracts. The Company's letters of credit are primarily performance-based and are not based on changes in variable components, a liability or an equity security of the other party.

The Company is involved in litigation arising from the normal course of business and in certain securities and derivative litigation matters. In management's opinion, this litigation is not expected to have a material adverse effect on the Company's consolidated financial condition or results of operations.

11. ACQUISITIONS

The following acquisitions completed by the Company were all accounted for under the purchase method of accounting and, accordingly, their results of operations have been consolidated in the Company's financial statements since the date of acquisition. Pro forma results of operations for fiscal 2006, 2005 and 2004 would not be materially different as a result of these acquisitions and therefore are not presented.

During fiscal 2006, the Company made the following acquisitions under its HD Supply segment:

- Burrus Contractors Supply
- Cox Lumber Company
- CTF Supply
- Edson Electric Supply
- Forest Products Supply
- Grafton Utility Supply
- Heartland Waterworks Supply
- Hughes Supply
- Rice Planter Carpets
- Sioux Pipe
- Texas Contractors Supply
- Western Fasteners

Additionally, during fiscal 2006, the Company acquired Home Decorators Collection, The Home Way and Jubilee Home Solutions under its Retail segment.

The aggregate purchase price for acquisitions in fiscal 2006, 2005 and 2004 was $4.5 billion, $2.6 billion and $729 million, respectively, including $3.5 billion for Hughes Supply in fiscal 2006. The Company recorded Goodwill related to the HD Supply segment of $2.8 billion, $1.8 billion and $391 million for fiscal 2006, 2005 and 2004, respectively, and Goodwill related to the Retail segment of $229 million, $111 million and $163 million for fiscal 2006, 2005 and 2004, respectively, in the accompanying Consolidated Balance Sheets. Of the Goodwill recorded in fiscal 2006, approximately $500 million will be deductible for income taxes.

The following table summarizes the estimated fair values of the assets acquired and liabilities assumed at the dates of acquisition for all acquisitions made during fiscal 2006, and is subject to the final fair value determination of certain assets and liabilities (amounts in millions):

Cash	$ 224
Receivables	948
Inventories	874
Property and Equipment	231
Intangible Assets[1]	547
Goodwill	3,007
Other Assets	187
Total assets acquired	6,018
Current Liabilities	1,321
Other Liabilities	193
Total liabilities assumed	1,514
Net assets acquired	$4,504

(1) *Primarily customer relationships and tradenames which are included in Other Assets in the accompanying Consolidated Balance Sheets and are being amortized over a weighted average useful life of 10 years.*

12. SEGMENT INFORMATION

The Company operates in two reportable business segments: Retail and HD Supply. The Retail segment is principally engaged in the operation of retail stores located in the United States, Canada, Mexico and the Company's recently acquired stores in China. The HD Supply segment distributes products and sells installation services to business-to-business customers, including home builders, professional contractors, municipalities and maintenance professionals. The Company identifies segments based on how management makes operating decisions, assesses performance and allocates resources. The first quarter of fiscal 2006 was the first period in which the Company began to report its results of operations in two segments. This change was a result of the purchase of Hughes Supply, which significantly increased the size of HD Supply and resulted in changes in the Company's internal reporting and management structure.

The Retail segment includes The Home Depot stores, EXPO Design Center stores and other retail formats. The Retail segment also includes our retail services business and our catalog and on-line sales businesses.

The HD Supply segment consists of four major platforms: 1) infrastructure, including waterworks and utilities; 2) construction, including construction supply, lumber and building materials, electrical, plumbing/HVAC and interiors; 3) maintenance, including facilities maintenance and industrial PVF; and 4) repair and remodel.

The Company measures the profit of its segments as Operating Income, which is defined as earnings before net interest expense and provision for income taxes. The amounts under the caption Eliminations/Other in the following tables are unallocated corporate overhead, invested cash and short-term investments and intersegment eliminations. Additionally, Operating Income under Eliminations/Other for the fiscal year ended January 28, 2007 includes $129 million of cost associated with executive severance and separation agreements. The following tables present financial information by segment for the fiscal years ended January 28, 2007, January 29, 2006 and January 30, 2005, respectively (amounts in millions):

| | Fiscal Year Ended January 28, 2007 | | | |
	Retail	HD Supply	Eliminations/ Other	Consolidated
Net Sales	$79,027	$12,070	$(260)	$90,837
Operating Income	$ 9,024	$ 800	$(151)	$ 9,673
Interest, net				(365)
Earnings Before Provision for Income Taxes				$ 9,308
Depreciation and Amortization	$ 1,682	$ 194	$ 10	$ 1,886
Total Assets	$42,094	$10,021	$ 148	$52,263
Capital Expenditures	$ 3,321	$ 221	$ —	$ 3,542
Payments for Businesses Acquired, net	$ 305	$ 3,963	$ —	$ 4,268

| | Fiscal Year Ended January 29, 2006 | | | |
	Retail	HD Supply	Eliminations/ Other	Consolidated
Net Sales	$77,022	$ 4,614	$(125)	$81,511
Operating Income	$ 9,058	$ 319	$ (14)	$ 9,363
Interest, net				(81)
Earnings Before Provision for Income Taxes				$ 9,282
Depreciation and Amortization	$ 1,510	$ 63	$ 6	$ 1,579
Total Assets	$39,827	$ 4,517	$ 61	$44,405
Capital Expenditures	$ 3,777	$ 104	$ —	$ 3,881
Payments for Businesses Acquired, net	$ 190	$ 2,356	$ —	$ 2,546

| | Fiscal Year Ended January 30, 2005 | | | |
	Retail	HD Supply	Eliminations/ Other	Consolidated
Net Sales	$71,101	$ 2,040	$ (47)	$73,094
Operating Income	$ 7,812	$ 122	$ (8)	$ 7,926
Interest, net				(14)
Earnings Before Provision for Income Taxes				$ 7,912
Depreciation and Amortization	$ 1,296	$ 20	$ 3	$ 1,319
Total Assets	$36,902	$ 1,406	$ 712	$39,020
Capital Expenditures	$ 3,905	$ 43	$ —	$ 3,948
Payments for Businesses Acquired, net	$ 202	$ 525	$ —	$ 727

Net Sales for the Company outside of the United States were $6.4 billion, $5.3 billion and $4.2 billion during fiscal 2006, 2005 and 2004, respectively. Long-lived assets outside of the United States totaled $2.5 billion and $2.2 billion as of January 28, 2007 and January 29, 2006, respectively.

13. QUARTERLY FINANCIAL DATA (UNAUDITED)

The following is a summary of the quarterly consolidated results of operations for the fiscal years ended January 28, 2007 and January 29, 2006 (dollars in millions, except per share data):

	Net Sales	Gross Profit	Net Earnings	Basic Earnings per Share	Diluted Earnings per Share
Fiscal Year Ended January 28, 2007:					
First Quarter	$21,461	$ 7,228	$1,484	$0.70	$0.70
Second Quarter	26,026	8,380	1,862	0.90	0.90
Third Quarter	23,085	7,537	1,490	0.73	0.73
Fourth Quarter	20,265	6,638	925	0.46	0.46
Fiscal Year	$90,837	$29,783	$5,761	$2.80	$2.79
Fiscal Year Ended January 29, 2006:					
First Quarter	$18,973	$ 6,355	$1,247	$0.58	$0.57
Second Quarter	22,305	7,409	1,768	0.83	0.82
Third Quarter	20,744	6,963	1,538	0.72	0.72
Fourth Quarter	19,489	6,593	1,285	0.61	0.60
Fiscal Year	$81,511	$27,320	$5,838	$2.73	$2.72

Note: The quarterly data may not sum to fiscal year totals due to rounding.

Corporate and Shareholder Information

STORE SUPPORT CENTER
The Home Depot, Inc.
2455 Paces Ferry Road, NW
Atlanta, GA 30339-4024
Telephone: (770) 433-8211

THE HOME DEPOT WEB SITE
www.homedepot.com

TRANSFER AGENT AND REGISTRAR
Computershare Trust Company, N.A.
P.O. Box 43078
Providence, RI 02940-3078
Telephone: (800) 577-0177
Internet address: www.computershare.com/investor

**INDEPENDENT REGISTERED PUBLIC
ACCOUNTING FIRM**
KPMG LLP
Suite 2000
303 Peachtree Street, NE
Atlanta, GA 30308

STOCK EXCHANGE LISTING
New York Stock Exchange
Trading symbol - HD

ANNUAL MEETING
The Annual Meeting of Shareholders will be held at
9 a.m., Eastern Time, May 24, 2007, at Cobb Galleria
Centre in Atlanta, Georgia.

NUMBER OF SHAREHOLDERS
As of March 26, 2007, there were approximately
180,000 shareholders of record and approximately
1,700,000 individual shareholders holding stock
under nominee security position listings.

DIVIDENDS DECLARED PER COMMON SHARE

	First Quarter	Second Quarter	Third Quarter	Fourth Quarter
Fiscal 2006	**$0.150**	**$0.150**	**$0.225**	**$0.225**
Fiscal 2005	$0.100	$0.100	$0.100	$0.150

**DIRECT STOCK PURCHASE/DIVIDEND
REINVESTMENT PLAN**
New investors may make an initial investment,
and shareholders of record may acquire additional
shares, of our common stock through our direct
stock purchase and dividend reinvestment plan.
Subject to certain requirements, initial cash
investments, cash dividends and/or additional
optional cash purchases may be invested through
this plan.

To obtain enrollment materials, including the
prospectus, access The Home Depot web site,
or call (877) HD-SHARE or (877) 437-4273.
For all other communications regarding these
services, contact Computershare.

**FINANCIAL AND OTHER COMPANY
INFORMATION**
Our Annual Report on Form 10-K for the fiscal year
ended January 28, 2007 is available on our web site
at www.homedepot.com under the Investor Relations
section. In addition, financial reports, filings with the
Securities and Exchange Commission, news releases
and other information are available on The Home
Depot web site.

The Home Depot, Inc. has included as exhibits
to its Annual Report on Form 10-K for the fiscal
year ended January 28, 2007 certifications of
The Home Depot's Chief Executive Officer and
Chief Financial Officer. The Home Depot's
Chief Executive Officer has also submitted to the
New York Stock Exchange (NYSE) a certificate
certifying that he is not aware of any violations
by The Home Depot of the NYSE corporate
governance listing standards.

QUARTERLY STOCK PRICE RANGE

	First Quarter	Second Quarter	Third Quarter	Fourth Quarter
Fiscal 2006				
High	**$43.95**	**$41.61**	**$38.24**	**$41.84**
Low	**$38.50**	**$32.85**	**$33.07**	**$35.77**
Fiscal 2005				
High	$42.99	$43.98	$43.39	$43.27
Low	$34.56	$35.54	$37.14	$39.65

This paper contains fiber from well-managed,
independently certified forests and contains 10%
post consumer recycled fiber.

Concept and Design: Sagepath (www.sagepath.com)
Photography: Ambrosi, Craig Bromley, Doug Coulter
Printer: Cenveo

Appendix B

Combined Journal

Most small businesses have just a few employees and can devote only a limited amount of time to the preparation of accounting records. To serve the needs of these businesses, accountants have developed certain types of record systems that have special time-saving and labor-saving features but still produce all the necessary financial information for management. One example of such a system is the combined journal discussed in this appendix.

Small firms play an important role in our economy today. In fact, almost one-half of the businesses in the United States are classified as small entities. Despite their limited size, these businesses need good accounting systems that can produce accurate and timely information.

Systems Involving the Combined Journal

The **combined journal,** also called the *combination journal*, provides the cornerstone for a simple yet effective accounting system in many small firms. As its name indicates, this journal combines features of the general journal and the special journals in a single record.

If a small business has enough transactions to make the general journal difficult to use but too few transactions to make it worthwhile to set up special journals, the combined journal offers a solution. It has many of the advantages of special journals but provides the simplicity of a single journal. Like the special journals, the combined journal contains separate money columns for the accounts used most often to record a firm's transactions. This speeds up the initial entry of transactions and permits summary postings at the end of the month. Most transactions can be recorded on a single line, and the need to write account names is minimized.

Other Accounts columns allow the recording of transactions that do not fit into any of the special columns. These columns are also used for entries that would normally appear in the general journal, such as adjusting and closing entries.

Some small firms just use a combined journal and a general ledger in their accounting systems. Others need one or more subsidiary ledgers in addition to the general ledger.

DESIGNING A COMBINED JOURNAL

To function effectively, a combined journal must be designed to meet the specific needs of a firm. For a new business, the accountant first studies the proposed operations and develops an appropriate chart of accounts. Then the accountant decides which accounts are likely to be used often enough in recording daily transactions to justify special columns in the combined journal.

Consider the combined journal on the next page which belongs to the Quality Lawn Care and Landscaping Services, a small business that provides lawn and landscaping services. In designing this journal before the firm opened, the accountant established a Cash section with Debit and Credit columns because it was known that the business would constantly be receiving cash from customers and paying out cash for expenses and other obligations. Debit and Credit columns were also set up in Accounts Receivable and Accounts Payable sections because the firm planned to offer credit to qualified customers and would make credit purchases of supplies and other items.

After further analysis it was realized that the business would have numerous entries for the sale of services, the payment of employee salaries, and the purchase of supplies. Therefore, columns were established for recording credits to *Sales*, debits to *Salaries Expense*, and debits to *Supplies*. Finally, a column was set up for an Other Accounts section to take care of transactions that cannot be entered in the special columns.

COMBINED JOURNAL

	DATE	CK. NO.	DESCRIPTION	POST. REF.	CASH DEBIT	CASH CREDIT	ACCOUNTS RECEIVABLE DEBIT	ACCOUNTS RECEIVABLE CREDIT
1	2010							
2	Jan. 3	711	Rent for month			1 0 5 0 00		
3	5		Treschell Seymore	✓			2 5 0 00	
4	6		C & M Garden Supply	✓				
5	7		Cash sales		2 3 0 0 00			
6	7	712	Payroll			7 8 0 00		
7	10		Annie McGowan	✓	1 5 0 00			1 5 0 00
8	12		The Greenery	✓				
9	13		Allen Clark	✓	4 4 0 00			4 4 0 00
10	14		Cash sales		2 7 7 0 00			
11	14	713	Payroll			7 8 0 00		
12	17		Jessica Savage	✓			1 7 5 00	
13	18		Lawn and Garden Supply	✓				
14	19	714	Telephone service			2 0 1 00		
15	20		Ned Jones	✓	1 2 5 00			1 2 5 00
16	20		Starlene Neal	✓			1 1 0 00	
17	21		Cash sales		2 5 4 0 00			
18	21	715	Payroll	✓		7 8 0 00		
19	24		Lawn and Garden Supply	✓				
20	25		Jeraldine Wells	✓			2 2 5 00	
21	26	716	Ace Garden Supply			4 6 0 00		
22	28		Cash sales		2 2 0 0 00			
23	28	717	Payroll			7 8 0 00		
24	30		Note issued for purchase					
25			of landscape equipment					
26	31		Juanda Fischer	✓			9 8 00	
27	31		Totals		10 5 2 5 00	4 8 3 1 00	8 5 8 00	7 1 5 00
28					(101)	(101)	(111)	(111)

FIGURE B.1 Combined Journal

RECORDING TRANSACTIONS IN THE COMBINED JOURNAL

The combined journal shown in Figure B.1 contains the January 2010 transactions of Quality Lawn Care and Landscaping Services. Notice that most of these transactions require only a single line and involve the use of just the special columns. The entries for major types of transactions are explained in the following paragraphs.

Payment of Expenses   During January, Quality Lawn Care and Landscaping Services issued checks to pay three kinds of expenses: rent, telephone service, and employee salaries. Notice how the payment of the monthly rent on January 3 was recorded in the combined journal. Since there is no special column for rent expense, the debit part of this entry appears in the Other Accounts section. The offsetting credit appears in the Cash Credit column. The payment of the monthly telephone bill on January 19 was recorded in a similar manner. However, when employee salaries were paid on January 7, 14, 21, and 28, both parts of the entries could be made in special columns. Because the firm has a weekly payroll period, a separate column in the combined journal was set up for debits to Salaries Expense.

PAGE ___1___

ACCOUNTS PAYABLE DEBIT	ACCOUNTS PAYABLE CREDIT	SALES CREDIT	SUPPLIES DEBIT	SALARIES EXPENSE DEBIT	ACCOUNT TITLE	POST REF.	DEBIT	CREDIT	
									1
					Rent Expense	511	1 0 5 0 00		2
		2 5 0 00							3
	4 5 0 00		4 5 0 00						4
		2 3 0 0 00							5
				7 8 0 00					6
									7
	2 2 5 00		2 2 5 00						8
									9
		2 7 7 0 00							10
				7 8 0 00					11
		1 7 5 00							12
	1 2 0 0 00				Equipment	131	1 2 0 0 00		13
					Telephone Exp.	514	2 0 1 00		14
									15
		1 1 0 00							16
		2 5 4 0 00							17
				7 8 0 00					18
	2 9 0 00		2 9 0 00						19
		2 2 5 00							20
4 6 0 00									21
		2 2 0 0 00							22
				7 8 0 00					23
					Equipment	131	8 5 0 0 00		24
					Notes Payable	201		8 5 0 0 00	25
		9 8 00							26
4 6 0 00	2 1 6 5 00	10 6 6 8 00	9 6 5 00	3 1 2 0 00			10 9 5 1 00	8 5 0 0 00	27
(202)	(202)	(401)	(121)	(517)			(X)	(X)	28

Sales on Credit
On January 5, 17, 20, 25, and 31, Quality Lawn Care and Landscaping Services sold services on credit. The necessary entries were made in two special columns of the combined journal—the Accounts Receivable Debit column and the Sales Credit column.

Cash Sales
Entries for the firm's weekly cash sales were recorded on January 7, 14, 21, and 28. Again, special columns were used—the Cash Debit column and the Sales Credit column.

Cash Received on Account
When Quality Lawn Care and Landscaping Services collected cash on account from credit customers on January 10, 13, and 20, the transactions were entered in the Cash Debit column and the Accounts Receivable Credit column.

Purchases of Supplies on Credit
Because the firm's combined journal includes a Supplies Debit column and an Accounts Payable Credit column, all purchases of supplies on credit can be recorded in special columns. Refer to the entries made on January 6, 12, and 24.

Purchases of Equipment on Credit   On January 18, Quality Lawn Care and Landscaping Services bought some store equipment on credit. Since there is no special column for equipment, the debit part of the entry was made in the Other Accounts section. The offsetting credit appears in the Accounts Payable Credit column.

Payments on Account   Any payments made on account to creditors are recorded in two special columns—Accounts Payable Debit and Cash Credit, as shown in the entry of January 26.

Issuance of a Promissory Note   On January 30, the business purchased new cleaning equipment and issued a promissory note to the seller. Notice that both the debit to Equipment and the credit to Notes Payable had to be recorded in the Other Accounts section.

POSTING FROM THE COMBINED JOURNAL

One of the advantages of the combined journal is that it simplifies the posting process. All amounts in the special columns can be posted to the general ledger on a summary basis at the end of the month. Only the figures that appear in the Other Accounts section require individual postings to the general ledger during the month. Of course, if the firm has subsidiary ledgers, individual postings must also be made to these ledgers.

Daily Postings   The procedures followed at Quality Lawn Care and Landscaping Services will illustrate the techniques used to post from the combined journal. Each day any entries appearing in the Other Accounts section are posted to the proper accounts in the general ledger. For example, refer to the combined journal shown on pages B-2 and B-3. The five amounts listed in the Other Accounts Debit and Credit columns were posted individually during the month. The account numbers recorded in the Posting Reference column of the Other Accounts section show that the postings have been made.

Because Quality Lawn Care and Landscaping Services has subsidiary ledgers for accounts receivable and accounts payable, individual postings were also made on a daily basis to these ledgers. As each amount was posted, a check mark was placed in the Posting Reference column of the combined journal.

End-of-Month Postings   At the end of the month, the combined journal is totaled, proved, and ruled. Then the totals of the special columns are posted to the general ledger. Proving the combined journal involves a comparison of the column totals to make sure that the debits and credits are equal. The following procedure is used:

Proof of Combined Journal	
	Debits
Cash Debit Column	10,525
Accounts Receivable Debit Column	858
Accounts Payable Debit Column	460
Supplies Debit Column	965
Salaries Expense Debit Column	3,120
Other Accounts Debit Column	10,951
	26,879
	Credits
Cash Credit Column	4,831
Accounts Receivable Credit Column	715
Accounts Payable Credit Column	2,165
Sales Credit Column	10,668
Other Accounts Credit Column	8,500
	26,879

After the combined journal is proved, all column totals except those in the Other Accounts section are posted to the appropriate general ledger accounts. As each total is posted, the account number is entered beneath the column in the journal. Notice that an X is used to indicate that the column totals in the Other Accounts section are not posted, since the individual amounts were posted on a daily basis.

TYPICAL USES OF THE COMBINED JOURNAL

The combined journal is used most often in small professional offices and small service businesses. It is less suitable for merchandising businesses but is sometimes used in firms of this type if they are very small and have only a limited number of transactions.

Professional Offices   The combined journal can be ideal to record the transactions that occur in a professional office, such as the office of a doctor, lawyer, accountant, or architect. However, special journals are more efficient if transactions become very numerous or are too varied.

Service Businesses   The use of the combined journal to record the transactions of Quality Lawn Care and Landscaping Services has already been illustrated. The combined journal may be advantageous for a small service business, provided that the volume of transactions does not become excessive and the nature of the transactions does not become too complex.

Merchandising Businesses   The combined journal can be used by a merchandising business, but only if the firm is quite small and has a limited number and variety of transactions involving few accounts. However, even for a small merchandising business, the use of special journals might prove more advantageous.

Disadvantages of the Combined Journal

If the variety of transactions is so great that many different accounts are required, the combined journal will not work well. Either the business will have to set up so many columns that the journal will become unwieldy, or it will be necessary to record so many transactions in the Other Accounts columns that little efficiency will result. As a general rule, if the transactions of a business are numerous enough to merit the use of special journals, any attempt to substitute the combined journal is a mistake. Remember that each special journal can be designed for maximum efficiency in recording transactions.

Glossary

Absorption costing The accounting procedure whereby all manufacturing costs, including fixed costs, are included in the cost of goods manufactured

Accelerated method of depreciation A method of depreciating asset cost that allocates greater amounts of depreciation to an asset's early years of useful life

Account balance The difference between the amounts recorded on the two sides of an account

Account form balance sheet A balance sheet that lists assets on the left and liabilities and owner's equity on the right (*see also* Report form balance sheet)

Accounting The process by which financial information about a business is recorded, classified, summarized, interpreted, and communicated to owners, managers, and other interested parties

Accounting cycle A series of steps performed during each accounting period to classify, record, and summarize data for a business and to produce needed financial information

Accounting system A process designed to accumulate, classify, and summarize financial data

Accounts Written records of the assets, liabilities, and owner's equity of a business

Accounts payable Amounts a business must pay in the future

Accounts payable ledger A subsidiary ledger that contains a separate account for each creditor

Accounts receivable Claims for future collection from customers

Accounts receivable ledger A subsidiary ledger that contains credit customer accounts

Accounts receivable turnover A measure of the speed with which sales on account are collected; the ratio of net credit sales to average receivables

Accrual basis A system of accounting by which all revenues and expenses are matched and reported on financial statements for the applicable period, regardless of when the cash related to the transaction is received or paid

Accrued expenses Expense items that relate to the current period but have not yet been paid and do not yet appear in the accounting records

Accrued income Income that has been earned but not yet received and recorded

Acid-test ratio A measure of immediate liquidity; the ratio of quick assets to current liabilities

Adjusting entries Journal entries made to update accounts for items that were not recorded during the accounting period

Adjustments *See* Adjusting entries

Aging the accounts receivable Classifying accounts receivable balances according to how long they have been outstanding

Allowance method A method of recording uncollectible accounts that estimates losses from uncollectible accounts and charges them to expense in the period when the sales are recorded

Amortization The process of periodically transferring the acquisition cost of an intangible asset to an expense account

Appropriation of retained earnings A formal declaration of an intention to restrict dividends

Articles of partnership *See* Partnership agreement

Asset turnover A measure of the effective use of assets in making sales; the ratio of net sales to total assets

Assets Property owned by a business

Audit trail A chain of references that makes it possible to trace information, locate errors, and prevent fraud

Auditing The review of financial statements to assess their fairness and adherence to generally accepted accounting principles

Auditor's report An independent accountant's review of a firm's financial statements

Authorized capital stock The number of shares authorized for issue by the corporate charter

Average collection period The ratio of 365 days to the accounts receivable turnover; also called the number of days' sales in receivables

Average cost method A method of inventory costing using the average cost of units of an item available for sale during the period to arrive at cost of the ending inventory

Average method of process costing A method of costing that combines the cost of beginning inventory for each cost element with the costs during the current period

Balance ledger form A ledger account form that shows the balance of the account after each entry is posted

Balance sheet A formal report of a business's financial condition on a certain date; reports the assets, liabilities, and owner's equity of the business

Bank draft A check written by a bank that orders another bank to pay the stated amount to a specific party

Bank reconciliation statement A statement that accounts for all differences between the balance on the bank statement and the book balance of cash

Banker's year A 360-day period used to calculate interest on a note

Bill of lading A business document that lists goods accepted for transportation

Blank endorsement A signature of the payee written on the back of the check that transfers ownership of the check without specifying to whom or for what purpose

Bond indenture A bond contract

Bond issue costs Costs incurred in issuing bonds, such as legal and accounting fees and printing costs

Bond retirement When a bond is paid and the liability is removed from the company's balance sheet

Bond sinking fund investment A fund established to accumulate assets to pay off bonds when they mature

Bonding The process by which employees are investigated by an insurance company that will insure the business against losses through employee theft or mishandling of funds

Bonds payable Long-term debt instruments that are written promises to repay the principal at a future date; interest is due at a fixed rate payable over the life of the bond

Book value That portion of an asset's original cost that has not yet been depreciated

Book value per share The total equity applicable to a class of stock divided by the number of shares outstanding

Brand name *See* Trade name

Break even A point at which revenue equals expenses

Budget An operating plan expressed in monetary units

Budget performance report A comparison of actual costs and budgeted costs

Business transaction A financial event that changes the resources of a firm

Bylaws The guidelines for conducting a corporation's business affairs

Call price The amount the corporation must pay for the bond when it is called

Callable bonds Bonds that allow the issuing corporation to require the holder to surrender the bonds for payment before their maturity date

Callable preferred stock Stock that gives the issuing corporation the right to repurchase the preferred shares from the stockholders at a specific price

Canceled check A check paid by the bank on which it was drawn

Capacity A facility's ability to produce or use

Capital Financial investment in a business; equity

Capital stock ledger A subsidiary ledger that contains a record of each stockholder's purchases, transfers, and current balance of shares owned; also called stockholders' ledger

Capital stock transfer journal A record of stock transfers used for posting to the stockholders' ledger

Capitalized costs All costs recorded as part of an asset's costs

Carrying value of bonds The balance of the *Bonds Payable* account plus the *Premium on Bonds Payable* account minus the *Discount on Bonds Payable* account; also called book value of bonds

Cash In accounting, currency, coins, checks, money orders, and funds on deposit in a bank

Cash discount A discount offered by suppliers for payment received within a specified period of time

Cash equivalents Assets that are easily convertible into known amounts of cash

Cash payments journal A special journal used to record transactions involving the payment of cash

Cash receipts journal A special journal used to record and post transactions involving the receipt of cash

Cash register proof A verification that the amount of currency and coins in a cash register agrees with the amount shown on the cash register audit tape

Cash Short or Over account An account used to record any discrepancies between the amount of currency and coins in the cash register and the amount shown on the audit tape

Cashier's check A draft on the issuing bank's own funds

Certified public accountant (CPA) An independent accountant who provides accounting services to the public for a fee

Charge-account sales Sales made through the use of open-account credit or one of various types of credit cards

Chart of accounts A list of the accounts used by a business to record its financial transactions

Check A written order signed by an authorized person instructing a bank to pay a specific sum of money to a designated person or business

Chronological order Organized in the order in which the events occur

Classification A means of identifying each account as an asset, liability, or owner's equity

Classified financial statement A format by which revenues and expenses on the income statement, and assets and liabilities on the balance sheet, are divided into groups of similar accounts and a subtotal is given for each group

Closing entries Journal entries that transfer the results of operations (net income or net loss) to owner's equity and reduce the revenue, expense, and drawing account balances to zero

Collateral trust bonds Bonds secured by the pledge of securities, such as stocks or bonds of other companies

Combined journal A journal that combines features of the general journal and the special journals in a single record

Commercial draft A note issued by one party that orders another party to pay a specified sum on a specified date

Commission basis A method of paying employees according to a percentage of net sales

Common costs Costs not directly traceable to a specific segment of a business

Common-size statements Financial statements with items expressed as percentages of a base amount

Common stock The general class of stock issued when no other class of stock is authorized; each share carries the same rights and privileges as every other share. Even if preferred stock is issued, common stock will also be issued

Common Stock Dividend Distributable account Equity account used to record par, or stated, value of shares to be issued as the result of the declaration of a stock dividend

Comparative statements Financial statements presented side by side for two or more years

Compensation record *See* Individual earnings record

Compound entry A journal entry with more than one debit or credit

Conceptual framework A basic framework developed by the FASB to provide conceptual guidelines for financial statements. The most important features are statements of qualitative features of statements, basic assumptions underlying statements, basic accounting principles, and modifying constraints

Conservatism The concept that revenue and assets should be understated rather than overstated if GAAP allows alternatives. Similarly, expenses and liabilities should be overstated rather than understated

Contingent liability An item that can become a liability if certain things happen

Contra account An account with a normal balance that is opposite that of a related account

Contra asset account An asset account with a credit balance, which is contrary to the normal balance of an asset account

Contra revenue account An account with a debit balance, which is contrary to the normal balance for a revenue account

Contribution margin Gross profit on sales minus direct expenses; revenues minus variable costs

Control account An account that links a subsidiary ledger and the general ledger since its balance summarizes the balances of the accounts in the subsidiary ledger

Controllable fixed costs Costs that the segment manager can control

Convertible bonds Bonds that give the owner the right to convert the bonds into common stock under specified conditions

Convertible preferred stock Preferred stock that conveys the right to convert that stock to common stock after a specified date or during a period of time

Copyright An intangible asset; an exclusive right granted by the federal government to produce, publish, and sell a literary or artistic work for a period equal to the creator's life plus 70 years

Corporate charter A document issued by a state government that establishes a corporation

Corporation A publicly or privately owned business entity that is separate from its owners and has a legal right to own property and do business in its own name; stockholders are not responsible for the debts or taxes of the business

Correcting entry A journal entry made to correct an erroneous entry

Cost basis principle The principle that requires assets to be recorded at their cost at the time they are acquired

Cost-benefit test If accounting concepts suggest a particular accounting treatment for an item but it appears that the theoretically correct treatment would require an unreasonable amount of work, the accountant may analyze the benefits and costs of the preferred treatment to see if the benefit gained from its adoption is justified by the cost

Cost center A business segment that incurs costs but does not produce revenue

Cost of goods sold The actual cost to the business of the merchandise sold to customers

Cost of production report Summarizes all costs charged to each department and shows the costs assigned to the goods transferred out of the department and to the goods still in process

Cost variance The difference between the total standard cost and the total actual cost

Coupon bonds Unregistered bonds that have coupons attached for each interest payment; also called bearer bonds

Credit An entry on the right side of an account

Credit memorandum (accounts receivable) A note verifying that a customer's account is being reduced by the amount of a sales return or sales allowance plus any sales tax that may have been involved

Credit memorandum (banking) A form that explains any addition, other than a deposit, to a checking account

Creditor One to whom money is owed

Cumulative preferred stock Stock that conveys to its owners the right to receive the preference dividend for the current year and any prior years in which the preference dividend was not paid before common stockholders receive any dividends.

Current assets Assets consisting of cash, items that normally will be converted into cash within one year, or items that will be used up within one year

Current liabilities Debts that must be paid within one year

Current ratio A relationship between current assets and current liabilities that provides a measure of a firm's ability to pay its current debts (current ratio = current assets ÷ current liabilities)

Debentures Unsecured bonds backed only by a corporation's general credit

Debit An entry on the left side of an account

Debit memorandum A form that explains any deduction, other than a check, from a checking account

Declaration date The date on which the board of directors declares a dividend

Declining-balance method An accelerated method of depreciation in which an asset's book value at the beginning of a year is multiplied by a percentage to determine depreciation for the year and any prior years in which the preference dividend was not paid before common stockholders receive any dividends

Deferred expenses *See* Prepaid expenses

Deferred income *See* Unearned income

Deferred income taxes The amount of taxes that will be payable in the future as a result of the difference between taxable income and income for financial statement purposes in the current year and in past years

Departmental income statement Income statement that shows each department's contribution margin and net income from operations after all expenses are allocated

Depletion Allocating the cost of a natural resource to expense over the period in which the resource produces revenue

Deposit in transit A deposit that is recorded in the cash receipts journal but that reaches the bank too late to be shown on the monthly bank statement

Deposit slip A form prepared to record the deposit of cash or checks to a bank account

Depreciation Allocation of the cost of a long-term asset to operations during its expected useful life

Differential cost The difference in cost between one alternative and another

Direct charge-off method A method of recording uncollectible account losses as they occur

Direct costing The accounting procedure whereby only variable costs are included in the cost of goods manufactured, and fixed manufacturing costs are written off as expenses in the period in which they are incurred

Direct expenses Operating expenses that are identified directly with a department and are recorded by department

Direct labor The costs attributable to personnel who work directly on the product being manufactured

Direct materials All items that go into a product and become a part of it

Direct method A means of reporting sources and uses of cash under which all revenue and expenses reported on the income statement appear in the operating section of the statement of cash flows and show the cash received or paid out for each type of transaction

Discount on bonds payable The excess of the face value over the price received by the corporation for a bond

Discounting Deducting the interest from the principal on a note payable or receivable in advance

Discussion memorandum An explanation of a topic under consideration by the Financial Accounting Standards Board

Dishonored check A check returned to the depositor unpaid because of insufficient funds in the drawer's account; also called an NSF check

Dissolution The legal termination of a partnership

Distributive share The amount of net income or net loss allocated to each partner

Dividends Distributions of the profits of a corporation to its shareholders

Donated capital Capital resulting from the receipt of gifts by a corporation

Double-declining-balance method A method of depreciation that uses a rate equal to twice the straight-line rate and applies that rate to the book value of the asset at the beginning of the year

Double-entry system An accounting system that involves recording the effects of each transaction as debits and credits

Draft A written order that requires one party (a person or business) to pay a stated sum of money to another party

Drawee The bank on which a check is written

Drawer The person or firm issuing a check

Drawing account A special type of owner's equity account set up to record the owner's withdrawal of cash from the business

Economic entity A business or organization whose major purpose is to produce a profit for its owners

Employee A person who is hired by and works under the control and direction of the employer

Employee's Withholding Allowance Certificate, Form W-4 A form used to claim exemption (withholding) allowances

Employer's Annual Federal Unemployment Tax Return, Form 940 or 940-EZ Preprinted government form used by the employer to report unemployment taxes for the calendar year

Employer's Quarterly Federal Tax Return, Form 941 Preprinted government form used by the employer to report payroll tax information relating to social security, Medicare, and employee income tax withholding to the Internal Revenue Service

Endorsement A written authorization that transfers ownership of a check

Entity Anything having its own separate identity, such as an individual, a town, a university, or a business

Equity An owner's financial interest in a business

Equivalent production The estimated number of units that could have been started and completed with the same effort and costs incurred in the department during the same time period

Exempt employees Salaried employees who hold supervisory or managerial positions who are not subject to the maximum hour and overtime pay provisions of the Wage and Hour Law

Expense An outflow of cash, use of other assets, or incurring of a liability

Experience rating system A system that rewards an employer for maintaining steady employment conditions by reducing the firm's state unemployment tax rate

Exposure draft A proposed solution to a problem being considered by the Financial Accounting Standards Board

Extraordinary, nonrecurring items Transactions that are highly unusual, clearly unrelated to routine operations, and that do not frequently occur

Face interest rate The contractual interest specified on the bond

Face value An amount of money indicated to be paid, exclusive of interest or discounts

Fair market value The current worth of an asset or the price the asset would bring if sold on the open market

Federal unemployment taxes (FUTA) Taxes levied by the federal government against employers to benefit unemployed workers

Financial statements Periodic reports of a firm's financial position or operating results

Financing activities Transactions with those who provide cash to the business to carry on its activities

Finished goods inventory The cost of completed products ready for sale; corresponds to the Merchandise Inventory account of a merchandising business

Finished goods subsidiary ledger A ledger containing a record for each of the different types of finished products

First in, first out (FIFO) method A method of inventory costing that assumes the oldest merchandise is sold first

Fixed budget A budget representing only one level of activity

Fixed costs Costs that do not change in total as the level of activity changes

Flexible budget A budget that shows the budgeted costs at various levels of activity

Footing A small pencil figure written at the base of an amount column showing the sum of the entries in the column

Franchise An intangible asset; a right to exclusive dealership granted by a governmental unit or a business entity

Freight In account An account showing transportation charges for items purchased

Full disclosure principle The requirement that all information that might affect the user's interpretation of the profitability and financial position of a business be disclosed in the financial statements or in footnotes to the statements

Full endorsement A signature transferring a check to a specific person, firm, or bank

Fundamental accounting equation The relationship between assets and liabilities plus owner's equity

Gain The disposition of an asset for more than its book value

General journal A financial record for entering all types of business transactions; a record of original entry

General ledger A permanent, classified record of all accounts used in a firm's operation; a record of final entry

General partner A member of a partnership who has unlimited liability

Generally accepted accounting principles (GAAP) Accounting standards developed and applied by professional accountants

Going concern assumption The assumption that a firm will continue to operate indefinitely

Goodwill An intangible asset; the value of a business in excess of the value of its identifiable assets

Governmental accounting Accounting work performed for a federal, state, or local governmental unit

Gross profit The difference between net sales and the cost of goods sold

Gross profit method A method of estimating inventory cost based on the assumption that the rate of gross profit on sales and the ratio of cost of goods sold to net sales are relatively constant from period to period

Gross profit percentage The amount of gross profit from each dollar of sales (gross profit percentage = gross profit ÷ net sales)

High-low point method A method to determine the fixed and variable components of a semivariable cost

Historical cost basis principle *See* Cost basis principle

Horizontal analysis Computing the percentage change for individual items in the financial statements from year to year

Hourly rate basis A method of paying employees according to a stated rate per hour

Impairment A situation that occurs when the asset is determined to have a market value or a value in use less than its book value

Income statement A formal report of business operations covering a specific period of time; also called a profit and loss statement or a statement of income and expenses

Income Summary account A special owner's equity account that is used only in the closing process to summarize the results of operations

Income tax method A method of recording the trade-in of an asset for income tax purposes. It does not permit a gain or loss to be recognized on the transaction.

Independent contractor One who is paid by a company to carry out a specific task or job but is not under the direct supervision or control of the company

Indirect expenses Operating expenses that cannot be readily identified and are not closely related to activity within a department

Indirect labor Costs attributable to personnel who support production but are not directly involved in the manufacture of a product; for example, supervisory, repair and maintenance, and janitorial staff

Indirect materials and supplies Materials used in manufacturing a product that do not become a part of the product

Indirect method A means of reporting cash generated from operating activities by treating net income as the primary source of cash in the operating section of the statement of cash flows and adjusting that amount for changes in current assets and liabilities associated with net income, noncash transactions, and other items

Individual earnings record An employee record that contains information needed to compute earnings and complete tax reports

Industry averages Financial ratios and percentages reflecting averages for similar companies

Industry practice constraint In a few limited cases unusual operating characteristics of an industry, usually based on risk, for which special accounting principles and procedures have been developed. These may not conform completely with GAAP for other industries

Intangible assets Assets that lack a physical substance, such as goodwill, patents, copyrights, and computer software, although software has, in a sense, a physical attribute

Interest The fee charged for the use of money

International accounting The study of accounting principles used by different countries

Interpret To understand and explain the meaning and importance of something (such as financial statements)

Inventory sheet A form used to list the volume and type of goods a firm has in stock

Inventory turnover The number of times inventory is purchased and sold during the accounting period (inventory turnover cost of goods sold average inventory)

Investing activities Transactions that involve the acquisition or disposal of long-term assets

Invoice A customer billing for merchandise bought on credit

Job order A specific order for a specific batch of manufactured items

Job order cost accounting A cost accounting system that determines the unit cost of manufactured items for each separate production order

Job order cost sheet A record of all manufacturing costs charged to a specific job

Journal The record of original entry

Journalizing Recording transactions in a journal

Just-in-time system An inventory system in which raw materials are ordered so they arrive just in time to be placed into production

Labor efficiency variance *See* Labor time variance

Labor rate variance The difference between the actual labor rate per hour and the standard labor rate per hour multiplied by the actual number of hours worked on the job

Labor time variance The difference between the actual hours worked and the standard labor hours allowed for the job multiplied by the standard cost per hour

Last in, first out (LIFO) method A method of inventory costing that assumes that the most recently purchased merchandise is sold first

Ledger The record of final entry

Leveraged buyout Purchasing a business by acquiring the stock and obligating the business to pay the debt incurred

Leveraging Using borrowed funds to earn a profit greater than the interest that must be paid on the borrowing

Liabilities Debts or obligations of a business

Limited liability company (LLC) Provides limited liability to the owners, who can elect to have the profits taxed at the LLC level or on their individual tax returns

Limited liability partnership (LLP) A partnership that provides some limited liability for all partners

Limited partner A member of a partnership whose liability is limited to his or her investment in the partnership

Limited partnership A partnership having one or more limited partners

Liquidation Termination of a business by distributing all assets and discontinuing the business

Liquidation value Value of assets to be applied to preferred stock, usually par value or an amount in excess of par value, if the corporation is liquidated

Liquidity The ease with which an item can be converted into cash; the ability of a business to pay its debts when due

List price An established retail price

Long-term liabilities Debts of a business that are due more than one year in the future

Loss The disposition of an asset for less than its book value

Lower of cost or market rule The principle by which inventory is reported at either its original cost or its replacement cost, whichever is lower

Management advisory services Services designed to help clients improve their information systems or their business performance

Managerial accounting Accounting work carried on by an accountant employed by a single business in industry; the branch of accounting that provides financial information about business segments, activities, or products

Manufacturing business A business that sells goods that it has produced

Manufacturing cost budget A budget made for each manufacturing cost

Manufacturing margin Sales minus the variable cost of goods sold

Manufacturing overhead All manufacturing costs that are not classified as direct materials or direct labor

Manufacturing overhead ledger A subsidiary ledger that contains a record for each overhead item

Manufacturing Summary* account** The account to which all items on the statement of cost of goods manufactured are closed; similar to the ***Income Summary account

Marginal income The manufacturing margin minus variable operating expenses

Markdown Price reduction below the original markon

Market interest rate The interest rate a corporation is willing to pay and investors are willing to accept at the current time

Market price The price the business would pay to buy an item of inventory through usual channels in usual quantities

Market value The price per share at which stock is bought and sold

Markon The difference between the cost and the initial retail price of merchandise

Markup A price increase above the original markon

Matching principle The concept that revenue and the costs incurred in earning the revenue should be matched in the appropriate accounting periods

Materiality constraint The significance of an item in relation to a particular situation or set of facts

Materials price variance The difference between the actual price and the standard cost for materials multiplied by the actual quantity of materials used

Materials quantity variance The difference between the actual quantity used and the quantity of materials allowed multiplied by the standard cost of the materials

Materials requisition A form that describes the item and quantity needed and shows the job or purpose

Materials usage variance *See* Materials quantity variance

Maturity value The total amount (principal plus interest) that must be paid when a note comes due

Medicare tax A tax levied on employees and employers to provide medical care for the employee and the employee's spouse after each has reached age 65

Memorandum entry An informational entry in the general journal

Merchandise inventory The stock of goods a merchandising business keeps on hand

Merchandising business A business that sells goods purchased for resale

Merit rating system *See* Experience rating system

Minute book A book in which accurate and complete records of all meetings of stockholders and directors are kept

Monetary unit assumption It is assumed that only those items and events that can be measured in monetary terms are included in the financial statements. An inherent part of this assumption is that the monetary unit is stable

Mortgage loan A long-term debt created when a note is given as part of the purchase price for land or buildings

Multiple-step income statement A type of income statement on which several subtotals are computed before the net income is calculated

Mutual agency The characteristic of a partnership by which each partner is empowered to act as an agent for the partnership, binding the firm by his or her acts

Negotiable A financial instrument whose ownership can be transferred to another person or business

Negotiable instrument A financial document containing a promise or order to pay that meets all requirements of the Uniform Commercial Code in order to be transferable to another party

Net book value The cost of an asset minus its accumulated depreciation, depletion, or amortization, also known as book value

Net income The result of an excess of revenue over expenses

Net income line The worksheet line immediately following the column totals on which net income (or net loss) is recorded in two places: the Income Statement section and the Balance Sheet section

Net loss The result of an excess of expenses over revenue

Net price The list price less all trade discounts

Net sales The difference between the balance in the Sales account and the balance in the ***Sales Returns and Allowances*** account

Net salvage value The salvage value of an asset less any costs to remove or sell the asset

Neutrality concept The concept that information in financial statements cannot be selected or presented in a way to favor one set of interested parties over another

Noncumulative preferred stock Stock that conveys to its owners the stated preference dividend for the current year but no rights to dividends for years in which none were declared

Nonparticipating preferred stock Stock that conveys to its owners the right to only the preference dividend amount specified on the stock certificate

No-par-value stock Stock that is not assigned a par value in the corporate charter

Normal balance The increase side of an account

Note payable A liability representing a written promise by the maker of the note (the debtor) to pay another party (the creditor) a specified amount at a specified future date

Note receivable An asset representing a written promise by another party (the debtor) to pay the note holder (the creditor) a specified amount at a specified future date

Objectivity assumption The idea that financial reports are unbiased and fair to all parties

On account An arrangement to allow payment at a later date; also called a charge account or open-account credit

Open-account credit A system that allows the sale of services or goods with the understanding that payment will be made at a later date

Operating activities Routine business transactions—selling goods or services and incurring expenses

Operating assets and liabilities Current assets and current liabilities

Opportunity cost Potential earnings or benefits that are given up because a certain course of action is taken

Organization costs The costs associated with establishing a corporation; an intangible asset account

Outstanding checks Checks that have been recorded in the cash payments journal but have not yet been paid by the bank

Overapplied overhead The result of applied overhead exceeding the actual overhead costs

Overhead application rate The rate at which the estimated cost of overhead is charged to each job

Owner's equity The financial interest of the owner of a business; also called proprietorship or net worth

Paid-in capital Capital acquired from capital stock transactions

Par value An amount assigned by the corporate charter to each share of stock for accounting purposes

Participating preferred stock Stock that conveys the right not only to the preference dividend amount but also to a share of other dividends paid

Partnership A business entity owned by two or more persons who carry on a business for profit and who are legally responsible for the debts and taxes of the business

Partnership agreement A legal contract forming a partnership and specifying certain details of operation

Patent An intangible asset; an exclusive right given by the U.S. Patent Office to manufacture and sell an invention for a period of 17 years from the date the patent is granted

Payee The person or firm to whom a check is payable

Payment date The date that dividends are paid

Payroll register A record of payroll information for each employee for the pay period

Periodic inventory Inventory based on a periodic count of goods on hand

Periodicity of income assumption The concept that income should be reported in certain time periods

Permanent account An account that is kept open from one accounting period to the next

Perpetual inventory Inventory based on a running total of number of units

Perpetual inventory system An inventory system that tracks the inventories on hand at all times

Petty cash analysis sheet A form used to record transactions involving petty cash

Petty cash fund A special-purpose fund used to handle payments involving small amounts of money

Petty cash voucher A form used to record the payments made from a petty cash fund

Physical inventory An actual count of the number of units of each type of good on hand

Piece-rate basis A method of paying employees according to the number of units produced

Plant and equipment Property that will be used in the business for longer than one year

Postclosing trial balance A statement that is prepared to prove the equality of total debits and credits after the closing process is completed

Postdated check A check dated some time in the future

Posting Transferring data from a journal to a ledger

Preemptive right A shareholder's right to purchase a proportionate amount of any new stock issued at a later date

Preference dividend A basic or stated dividend rate for preferred stock that must be paid before dividends can be paid on common stock

Preferred stock A class of stock that has special claims on the corporate profits or, in case of liquidation, on corporate assets

Premium on bonds payable The excess of the price paid over the face value of a bond

Prepaid expenses Expense items acquired, recorded, and paid for in advance of their use

Price-earnings ratio The ratio of the current market value of common stock to earnings per share of that stock

Principal The amount shown on the face of a note

Private sector The business sector, which is represented in developing accounting principles by the Financial Accounting Standards Board (FASB)

Process cost accounting A cost accounting system whereby unit costs of manufactured items are determined by totaling unit costs in each production department

Process cost accounting system A method of accounting in which costs are accumulated for each process or department and then transferred on to the next process or department

Production order *See* Job order

Profit center A business segment that produces revenue

Promissory note A written promise to pay a specified amount of money on a specific date

Property, plant, and equipment Long-term assets that are used in the operation of a business and that are subject to depreciation (except for land, which is not depreciated)

Public accountants Members of firms that perform accounting services for other companies

Public sector The government sector, which is represented in developing accounting principles by the Securities and Exchange Commission (SEC)

Purchase allowance A price reduction from the amount originally billed

Purchase invoice A bill received for goods purchased

Purchase order An order to the supplier of goods specifying items needed, quantity, price, and credit terms

Purchase requisition A list sent to the purchasing department showing the items to be ordered

Purchase return Return of unsatisfactory goods

***Purchases* account** An account used to record cost of goods bought for resale during a period

Purchases discount A cash discount offered to customers for payment within a specified period

Purchases journal A special journal used to record the purchase of goods on credit

Qualitative characteristics Traits necessary for credible financial statements: usefulness, relevance, reliability, verifiability, neutrality, understandability, timeliness, comparability, and completeness

Quick assets Cash, receivables, and marketable securities

Ratio analysis Computing the relationship between various items in the financial statements

Raw materials The materials placed into production

Raw materials ledger card A record showing details of receipts and issues for a type of raw material

Raw materials subsidiary ledger A ledger containing the raw materials ledger cards

Real property Assets such as land, land improvements, buildings, and other structures attached to the land

Realization principle The concept that revenue occurs when goods or services, merchandise, or other assets are exchanged for cash or claims to cash

Receiving report A form showing quantity and condition of goods received

Recognition The determination of the period in which to record a business transaction

Record date The date on which the specific stockholders to receive a dividend are determined

Recoverability test Test for possible impairment that compares the asset's net book value with the estimated net cash flows from future use of the asset

Registered bonds Bonds issued to a party whose name is listed in the corporation's records

Registrar A person or institution in charge of the issuance and transfer of a corporation's stock

Reinstate To put back or restore an accounts receivable amount that was previously written off

Relevant range of activity The different levels of activity at which a factory is expected to operate

Replacement cost *See* Market price

Report form balance sheet A balance sheet that lists the asset accounts first, followed by liabilities and owner's equity

Residual value The estimate of the amount that could be obtained from the sale or disposition of an asset at the end of its useful life; also called salvage or scrap value

Responsibility accounting The process that allows management to evaluate the performance of each segment of the business and assign responsibility for its financial results

Restrictive endorsement A signature that transfers a check to a specific party for a stated purpose

Retail business A business that sells directly to individual consumers

Retail method A method of estimating inventory cost by applying the ratio of cost to selling price in the current accounting period to the retail price of the inventory

Retained earnings The cumulative profits and losses of the corporation not distributed as dividends

Return on common stockholders' equity A measure of how well the corporation is making a profit for its shareholders; the ratio of net income available for common stockholders to common stockholders' equity

Revenue An inflow of money or other assets that results from the sales of goods or services or from the use of money or property; also called income

Revenue recognition principle Revenue is recognized when it has been earned and realized

Reversing entries Journal entries made to reverse the effect of certain adjusting entries involving accrued income or accrued expenses to avoid problems in recording future payments or receipts of cash in a new accounting period

Salary basis A method of paying employees according to an agreed-upon amount for each week or month

Sales allowance A reduction in the price originally charged to customers for goods or services

Sales discount A cash discount offered by the supplier to customers for payment within a specified period

Sales invoice A supplier's billing document

Sales journal A special journal used to record sales of merchandise on credit

Sales return A firm's acceptance of a return of goods from a customer

Salvage value An estimate of the amount that could be received by selling or disposing of an asset at the end of its useful life

Schedule of accounts payable A list of all balances owed to creditors

Schedule of accounts receivable A listing of all balances of the accounts in the accounts receivable subsidiary ledger

Schedule of operating expenses A schedule that supplements the income statement, showing the selling and general and administrative expenses in greater detail

Scrap value *See* Residual value

Secured bonds Bonds for which property is pledged to secure the claims of bondholders

Semidirect expenses Operating expenses that cannot be directly assigned to a department but are closely related to departmental activities

Semivariable costs Costs that vary with, but not in direct proportion to, the volume of activity

Separate economic entity assumption The concept that a business is separate from its owners; the concept of keeping a firm's financial records separate from the owner's personal financial records

Serial bonds Bonds issued at one time but payable over a period of years

Service business A business that sells services

Service charge A fee charged by a bank to cover the costs of maintaining accounts and providing services

Shareholder A person who owns shares of stock in a corporation; also called a stockholder

Sight draft A commercial draft that is payable on presentation

Single-step income statement A type of income statement where only one computation is needed to determine the net income (total revenue − total expenses = net income)

Slide An accounting error involving a misplaced decimal point

Social entity A nonprofit organization, such as a city, public school, or public hospital

Social Security Act A federal act providing certain benefits for employees and their families; officially the Federal Insurance Contributions Act

Social security tax (FICA) A tax imposed by the Federal Insurance Contributions Act and collected on employee earnings to provide retirement and disability benefits

Sole proprietorship A business entity owned by one person who is legally responsible for the debts and taxes of the business

Special journal A journal used to record only one type of transaction

Specific identification method A method of inventory costing based on the actual cost of each item of merchandise

Standard cost card A form that shows the per-unit standard costs for materials, labor, and overhead

Standard costs A measure of what costs should be in an efficient operation

State unemployment taxes (SUTA) Taxes levied by a state government against employers to benefit unemployed workers

Stated value The value that can be assigned to no-par-value stock by a board of directors for accounting purposes

Statement of account A form sent to a firm's customers showing transactions during the month and the balance owed

Statement of cash flows A financial statement that provides information about the cash receipts and cash payments of a business

Statement of cost of goods manufactured A financial report showing details of the cost of goods completed for a manufacturing business

Statement of owner's equity A formal report of changes that occurred in the owner's financial interest during a reporting period

Statement of partners' equities A financial statement prepared to summarize the changes in the partners' capital accounts during an accounting period

Statement of retained earnings A financial statement that shows all changes that have occurred in retained earnings during the period

Statement of stockholders' equity A financial statement that provides an analysis reconciling the beginning and ending balance of each of the stockholders' equity accounts

Statements of Financial Accounting Standards Accounting principles established by the Financial Accounting Standards Board

Stock Certificates that represent ownership of a corporation

Stock certificate The form by which capital stock is issued; the certificate indicates the name of the corporation, the name of the stockholder to whom the certificate was issued, the class of stock, and the number of shares

Stock dividend Distribution of the corporation's own stock on a pro rata basis that results in conversion of a portion of the firm's retained earnings to permanent capital

Stock split When a corporation issues two or more shares of new stock to replace each share outstanding without making any changes in the capital accounts

Stockholders The owners of a corporation; also called shareholders

Stockholders of record Stockholders in whose name shares are held on date of record and who will receive a declared dividend

Stockholders' equity The corporate equivalent of owners' equity; also called shareholders' equity

Stockholders' ledger See Capital stock ledger

Straight-line amortization Amortizing the premium or discount on bonds payable in equal amounts each month over the life of the bond

Straight-line depreciation Allocation of an asset's cost in equal amounts to each accounting period of the asset's useful life

Subchapter S corporation (S corporation) An entity formed as a corporation that meets the requirements of Subchapter S of the Internal Revenue Code to be treated essentially as a partnership, so that the corporation pays no income tax

Subscribers' ledger A subsidiary ledger that contains an account receivable for each stock subscriber

Subscription book A list of the stock subscriptions received

Subsidiary ledger A ledger dedicated to accounts of a single type and showing details to support a general ledger account

Sum-of-the-years'-digits method A method of depreciating asset costs by allocating as expense each year a fractional part of the asset's depreciable cost, based on the sum of the digits of the number of years in the asset's useful life

Sunk cost A cost that has been incurred and will not change as a result of a decision

T account A type of account, resembling a T, used to analyze the effects of a business transaction

Tangible personal property Assets such as machinery, equipment, furniture, and fixtures that can be removed and used elsewhere

Tax accounting A service that involves tax compliance and tax planning

Tax-exempt wages Earnings in excess of the base amount set by the Social Security Act

Temporary account An account whose balance is transferred to another account at the end of an accounting period

Time and a half Rate of pay for an employee's work in excess of 40 hours a week

Time draft A commercial draft that is payable during a specified period of time

Time ticket Form used to record hours worked and jobs performed

Total equities The sum of a corporation's liabilities and stockholders' equity

Trade acceptance A form of commercial time draft used in transactions involving the sale of goods

Trade discount A reduction from list price

Trade name An intangible asset; an exclusive business name registered with the U.S. Patent Office; also called brand name

Trademark An intangible asset; an exclusive business symbol registered with the U.S. Patent Office

Trading on the equity See Leveraging

Transfer agent A person or institution that handles all stock transfers and transfer records for a corporation

Transfer price The price at which one segment's goods are transferred to another segment of the company

Transmittal of Wage and Tax Statements, Form W-3 Preprinted government form submitted with Forms W-2 to the Social Security Administration

Transparency Information provided in the financial statements and notes accompanying them should provide a clear and accurate picture of the financial affairs of the company

Transportation In account See Freight In account

Transposition An accounting error involving misplaced digits in a number

Treasury stock A corporation's own capital stock that has been issued and reacquired; the stock must have been previously paid in full and issued to a stockholder

Trend analysis Comparing selected ratios and percentages over a period of time

Trial balance A statement to test the accuracy of total debits and credits after transactions have been recorded

Underapplied overhead The result of actual overhead costs exceeding applied overhead

Unearned income Income received before it is earned

Unemployment insurance program A program that provides unemployment compensation through a tax levied on employers

Units-of-output method See Units-of-production method

Units-of-production method A method of depreciating asset cost at the same rate for each unit produced during each period

Unlimited liability The implication that a creditor can look to all partners' personal assets as well as the assets of the partnership for payment of the firm's debts

Updated account balances The amounts entered in the Adjusted Trial Balance section of the worksheet

Valuation account An account, such as *Allowance for Doubtful Accounts,* whose balance is revalued or reappraised in light of reasonable expectations

Variable costing *See* Direct costing

Variable costs Costs that vary in total in direct proportion to changes in the level of activity

Variance analysis Explains the difference between standard cost and actual cost

Vertical analysis Computing the relationship between each item on a financial statement to some base amount on the statement

Wage and Tax Statement, Form W-2 Preprinted government form that contains information about an employee's earnings and tax withholdings for the year

Wage-bracket table method A simple method to determine the amount of federal income tax to be withheld using a table provided by the government

Weighted average method *See* Average cost method

Wholesale business A business that manufactures or distributes goods to retail businesses or large consumers such as hotels and hospitals

Withdrawals Funds taken from the business by the owner for personal use

Withholding statement *See* Wage and Tax Statement, Form W-2

Workers' compensation insurance Insurance that protects employees against losses from job-related injuries or illnesses, or compensates their families if death occurs in the course of the employment

Work in process Partially completed units in the production process

Work in process subsidiary ledger A ledger containing the job order cost sheets

Working capital The measure of the ability of a company to meet its current obligations; the excess of current assets over current liabilities

Worksheet A form used to gather all data needed at the end of an accounting period to prepare financial statements

Credits

Index

Key terms and page numbers where defined are in **bold.**

SAMPLE GENERAL LEDGER ACCOUNTS

Account Name	Classification	Permanent or Temporary	Normal Balance
INCOME STATEMENT			
Fees Income	Revenue	Temporary	Credit
Sales	Revenue	Temporary	Credit
Sales Discounts	Contra Revenue	Temporary	Debit
Sales Returns and Allowances	Contra Revenue	Temporary	Debit
Purchases	Cost of Goods Sold	Temporary	Debit
Freight In	Cost of Goods Sold	Temporary	Debit
Purchases Discounts	Contra Cost of Goods Sold	Temporary	Credit
Purchases Returns and Allowances	Contra Cost of Goods Sold	Temporary	Credit
Direct Labor	Cost of Goods Manufactured	Temporary	Debit
Indirect Labor	Cost of Goods Manufactured	Temporary	Debit
Indirect Materials and Supplies	Cost of Goods Manufactured	Temporary	Debit
Payroll Taxes—Factory	Cost of Goods Manufactured	Temporary	Debit
Repairs and Maintenance—Factory	Cost of Goods Manufactured	Temporary	Debit
Depreciation—Factory	Cost of Goods Manufactured	Temporary	Debit
Insurance—Factory	Cost of Goods Manufactured	Temporary	Debit
Property Taxes—Factory	Cost of Goods Manufactured	Temporary	Debit
Advertising Expense	Operating Expense	Temporary	Debit
Amortization Expense	Operating Expense	Temporary	Debit
Bank Fees Expense	Operating Expense	Temporary	Debit
Cash Short or Over	Operating Expense	Temporary	Debit
Delivery Expense	Operating Expense	Temporary	Debit
Depreciation Expense	Operating Expense	Temporary	Debit
Insurance Expense	Operating Expense	Temporary	Debit
Payroll Taxes Expense	Operating Expense	Temporary	Debit
Property Tax Expense	Operating Expense	Temporary	Debit
Rent Expense	Operating Expense	Temporary	Debit
Research and Development Expense	Operating Expense	Temporary	Debit
Salaries Expense	Operating Expense	Temporary	Debit
Supplies Expense	Operating Expense	Temporary	Debit
Telephone Expense	Operating Expense	Temporary	Debit
Uncollectible Accounts Expense	Operating Expense	Temporary	Debit
Utilities Expense	Operating Expense	Temporary	Debit
Workers' Compensation Insurance Expense	Operating Expense	Temporary	Debit
Gain/Loss on Sale of Assets	Other Income/Expense	Temporary	—
Interest Income/Expense	Other Income/Expense	Temporary	—
Miscellaneous Income/Expense	Other Income/Expense	Temporary	—
Income Tax Expense	Other Expense	Temporary	Debit
STATEMENT OF OWNER'S EQUITY			
*(Owner's Name), Capital	Owner's Equity	Permanent	Credit
(Owner's Name), Drawing	Owner's Equity	Temporary	Debit
STATEMENT OF PARTNERS' EQUITY			
*(Partner's Name), Capital	Partners' Equity	Permanent	Credit
(Partner's Name), Drawing	Partners' Equity	Temporary	Debit
STATEMENT OF RETAINED EARNINGS			
*Retained Earnings—Appropriated	Stockholders' Equity	Permanent	Credit
*Retained Earnings	Stockholders' Equity	Permanent	Credit

*Account also appears on the balance sheet.